Handbook of Research on Digital Libraries:
Design, Development, and Impact

Yin-Leng Theng
Nanyang Technological University, Singapore

Schubert Foo
Nanyang Technological University, Singapore

Dion Goh
Nanyang Technological University, Singapore

Jin-Cheon Na
Nanyang Technological University, Singapore

**INFORMATION SCIENCE REFERENCE**

Hershey · New York

Director of Editorial Content:	Kristin Klinger
Director of Production:	Jennifer Neidig
Managing Editor:	Jamie Snavely
Assistant Managing Editor:	Carole Coulson
Typesetter:	Chris Hrobak
Copy Editors:	Ashlee Kunkel and Laura Kochanowski
Cover Design:	Lisa Tosheff
Printed at:	Yurchak Printing Inc.

Published in the United States of America by
Information Science Reference (an imprint of IGI Global)
701 E. Chocolate Avenue, Suite 200
Hershey PA 17033
Tel: 717-533-8845
Fax: 717-533-8661
E-mail: cust@igi-global.com
Web site: http://www.igi-global.com

and in the United Kingdom by
Information Science Reference (an imprint of IGI Global)
3 Henrietta Street
Covent Garden
London WC2E 8LU
Tel: 44 20 7240 0856
Fax: 44 20 7379 0609
Web site: http://www.eurospanbookstore.com

Library of Congress Cataloging-in-Publication Data

Handbook of research on digital libraries : design, development, and impact / Yin-Leng Theng ... [et al.], editors.
    p. cm.
  Includes bibliographical references and index.
  Summary: "This book is an in-depth collection aimed at developers and scholars of research articles from the expanding field of digital libraries"--Provided by publisher.
  ISBN 978-1-59904-879-6 -- ISBN 978-1-59904-880-2 (ebook)
  1. Digital libraries. I. Theng, Yin-Leng, 1961-
  ZA4080.H36 2009
  025.00285--dc22
                    2008028570

British Cataloguing in Publication Data
A Cataloguing in Publication record for this book is available from the British Library.

All work contributed to this book set is original material. The views expressed in this book are those of the authors, but not necessarily of the publisher.

List of Reviewers

Alan O. Allwardt, *USGS Pacific Science Center, USA*
Ali Shiri, *University of Alberta, Canada*
Alicia Sellés Carot, *Masmedios Ltd, Spain*
Alton Y.K. Chua, *Nanyang Technological University, Singapore*
Ana Kovačević, *University of Belgrade, Serbia*
Andreas Rauber, *Vienna University of Technology, Austria*
Ann O'Brien, *Loughborough University, UK*
Antonio Amescua-Seco, *Carlos III University of Madrid, Spain*
Barbara M. Wildemuth, *University of North Carolina at Chapel Hill, USA*
Björn Ortelbach, *Henkel KgaA, Germany*
Carmen Galvez, *University of Granada, Spain*
Cecilia Ferreyra, *International Potato Center, Peru*
Chao-chen Chen, *National Taiwan Normal University, Taiwan*
Chei Sian Lee, *Nanyang Technological University, Singapore*
Chew-Hung Chang, *Nanyang Technological University, Singapore*
Christoph Becker, *Vienna University of Technology, Austria*
Christopher C. Yang, *Drexel University, USA*
Christopher S.G. Khoo, *Nanyang Technological University, Singapore*
Christos Papatheodorou, *Ionian University, Greece*
Cláudio de Souza Baptista, *University of Campina Grande, Brazil*
David A. Garza-Salazar, *Tecnológico de Monterrey, Mexico*
David Bainbridge, *University of Waikato, New Zealand*
David M. Nichols, *University of Waikato, New Zealand*
Dhavalkumar Thakker, *Nottingham Trent University, UK*
Diljit Singh, *University of Malaya, Malaysia*
Dion Hoe-Lian Goh, *Nanyang Technological University, Singapore*
Donatella Castelli, *Istituto di Scienza e Tecnologie dell'Informazione "A. Faedo," Italy*
Edward A. Fox, *Virginia Tech, USA*
Emanuele Panizzi, *University of Rome "La Sapienza," Italy*
Esther O. A. Fatuyi, *Elsie Whitlow Stokes Community Freedom Public Charter School, USA*
F.J. Zarazaga-Soria, *University of Zaragoza, Spain*
Faisal Ahmad, *University of Colorado at Boulder, USA*
Fernanda C. A. Campos, *Universidade Federal de Juiz de Fora, Brazil*
Fernando Ferri, *Istituto di Ricerca sulla Popolazione e le Politiche Sociali Consiglio Nazionale delle Ricerche, Italy*
Frances L. Lightsom, *U.S. Geological Survey USGS Woods Hole Science Center, USA*
Fu Lee Wang, *City University of Hong Kong, Hong Kong*

Oscar Cantán, *University of San Jorge, Spain*

Pasquale Lops, *University of Bari, Italy*

Pasquale Pagano, *Istituto di Scienza e Tecnologie dell'Informazione "A. Faedo," Italy*

Patrizia Grifoni, *Istituto di Ricerca sulla Popolazione e le Politiche Sociali Consiglio Nazionale delle Ricerche, Italy*

Paul Horng-Jyh Wu, *Nanyang Technological University, Singapore*

Payam M. Barnaghi, *University of Nottingham, Malaysia*

Pedro Rafael Muro-Medrano, *University of Zaragoza, Spain*

Peter Shelton, *International Food Policy Research Institute, USA*

Piedad Garrido Picazo, *University of Zaragoza, Spain*

Pierpaolo Basile, *University of Bari, Italy*

Regina M. M. Braga Villela, Universidade Federal de Juiz de Fora, Brazil

Robert Neumayer, *Vienna University of Technology, Austria*

Ruben Béjar, *University of Zaragoza, Spain*

Sanghee Oh, *University of North Carolina at Chapel Hill, USA*

Sarah-Jane Saravani, *Waikato Institute of Technology, New Zealand*

Schubert Foo, *Nanyang Technological University, Singapore*

Seungwon Yang, *Virginia Tech, USA*

Shiyan Ou, *University of Wolverhampton, UK*

Shun-hong Sie, *Fu-Jen Catholic University, Taiwan*

Simon Ruszala, *Aston University, UK*

Sofia Stamou, *Patras University, Greece*

Soh Whee Kheng, *Nanyang Technological University, Singapore*

Spyros Veronikis, *Ionian University, Greece*

Stefano Paolozzi, *Istituto di Ricerca sulla Popolazione e le Politiche Sociali Consiglio Nazionale delle Ricerche, Italy*

Stephan Strodl, *Vienna University of Technology, Austria*

Stephen Kimani, *Institute of Computer Science and Information Technology JKUAT, Kenya*

Svenja Hagenhoff, *Georg-August-Universität Göttingen, Germany*

Taha Osman, *Nottingham Trent University, UK*

Tamara Sumner, *University of Colorado at Boulder, USA*

Thomas Lidy, *Vienna University of Technology, Austria*

Thomas Mandl, *University of Hildesheim, Germany*

Tiziana Catarci, *University of Rome "La Sapienza," Italy*

Tun Thura Thet, *Nanyang Technological University, Singapore*

Ulrich Schiel, *University of Campina Grande, Brazil*

Vladan Devedžić, *University of Belgrade, Serbia*

Wan Ab. Kadir Wan Dollah, *MARA University of Technology, Malaysia*

Warwick Clegg, *Victoria University of Wellington, New Zealand*

Wei Wang, *University of Nottingham, Malaysia*

Wolfgang Ratzek, *Stuttgart Media University, Germany*

Wooil Kim, *University of Texas at Dallas, USA*

Yin-Leng Theng, *Nanyang Technological University, Singapore*

Yongqing Ma, *Victoria University of Wellington, New Zealand*

List of Contributors

Table of Contents

Section I
Design and Development

Leonardo Candela, Istituto di Scienza e Tecnologie dell'Informazione "A. Faedo"
(ISTI-CNR), Italy
Donatella Castelli, Istituto di Scienza e Tecnologie dell'Informazione "A. Faedo"
(ISTI-CNR), Italy
Pasquale Pagano, Istituto di Scienza e Tecnologie dell'Informazione "A. Faedo"
(ISTI-CNR), Italy
Manuele Simi, Istituto di Scienza e Tecnologie dell'Informazione "A. Faedo" (ISTI-CNR),
Italy

Mohammed Nasser Al-Suqri, Sultan Qaboos University, Oman
Esther O.A. Fatuyi, Elsie Whitlow Stokes Community Freedom Public School, USA

Sarah-Jane Saravani, Waikato Institute of Technology, New Zealand

Jian-hua Yeh, Aletheia University, Taiwan
Shun-hong Sie, National Taiwan Normal University, Taiwan
Chao-chen Chen, National Taiwan Normal University, Taiwan

Section II
Information Processing and Content Management

Section III
Users, Interactions, and Experiences

Section IV
Case Studies and Applications

Section V
Digital Library Education and Future Trends

Detailed Table of Contents

Section I
Design and Development

Chapter I
Leonardo Candela, Istituto di Scienza e Tecnologie dell'Informazione "A. Faedo"
(ISTI-CNR), Italy
Donatella Castelli, Istituto di Scienza e Tecnologie dell'Informazione "A. Faedo"
(ISTI-CNR), Italy
Pasquale Pagano, Istituto di Scienza e Tecnologie dell'Informazione "A. Faedo"
(ISTI-CNR), Italy
Manuele Simi, Istituto di Scienza e Tecnologie dell'Informazione "A. Faedo" (ISTI-CNR),
Italy

This chapter describes OpenDLib, a Digital Library Service system developed at ISTI-CNR to support the creation and management of digital libraries. It addresses the characteristics of the contents that can be managed by the system, a corresponding set of supporting functions, system architecture paradigm and technologies utilised in the development of the system.

Chapter II
Mohammed Nasser Al-Suqri, Sultan Qaboos University, Oman
Esther O.A. Fatuyi, Elsie Whitlow Stokes Community Freedom Public School, USA

This chapter examines how appropriate technologies and software must be ensured to enable digital library systems to provide accurate, secure, and timely information over a sustainable future. Specifically, it addresses issues protection of the information infrastructure and access control; identification and authentication; standards and policies; and ethical considerations.

This chapter describes a case study undertaken by the Waikato Institute of Technology, New Zealand on OS-LOR, an open source learning object repository of digital resources that are contributed by various education communities. The key success hinges on the ability to develop a metadata application profile that is reducible and extensible to ensure searchability, durability, and ultimate value of the repository.

This chapter outlines a digital system architecture designed to support flexible content management and development of user services. A data model and storage with high portability and use of stackable service features are proposed as part of the requirements of the X-System, which is a general digital library platform that is capable of handling large-scale digital contents with flexible, extensible management features.

This chapter presents the services and functionality that a personal digital library system should provide, including a reference architecture to support such a design. A current system, PDLib, is used to demonstrate such a personal digital library that can be used to manage personal collections and its potential to become a commodity and means of social interaction.

This chapter does a comparative evaluation of the basic characteristics and system features of five well-known and extensively used open source digital library software, namely, DSpace, Fedora, Greenstone, Keystone, and EPrints. The findings are summarized in a score table along with cases where each system is considered as most suitable are proposed.

This chapter provides a definitive and coherent account of the Greenstone open source digital library project developed at University of Waikato by its developers. In addition to its production system that is widely adopted globally, it also serves as a framework for digital library research. It outlines a strategy for reconciling this conflict of these two different dimensions of the project in the future.

Chapter VIII

Yin-Leng Theng, Nanyang Technological University, Singapore
Nyein Chan Lwin Lwin, Nanyang Technological University, Singapore
Jin-Cheon Na, Nanyang Technological University, Singapore
Schubert Foo, Nanyang Technological University, Singapore
Dion Hoe-Lian Goh, Nanyang Technological University, Singapore

This chapter addresses the issues of resource discovery and the importance of using knowledge organization tools to build digital libraries. A prototype Taxonomy Generation Tool, utilizing a hierarchical classification of contents by subjects, was designed and built to categorize contents in the Greenstone Digital Library software. The taxonomy template supports controlled vocabulary terms and allows users to select the labels for the taxonomy structure.

Chapter IX

Schubert Foo, Nanyang Technological University, Singapore
Yin-Leng Theng, Nanyang Technological University, Singapore
Dion Hoe-Lian Goh, Nanyang Technological University, Singapore
Jin-Cheon Na, Nanyang Technological University, Singapore

This chapter demonstrates how digital archives, and in particular, its derivative in the form of virtual exhibitions can be developed using the multimedia digital contents of the archives. It presents a number of concepts and design considerations and illustrates this with a proposed generic system architecture that encapsulates the important issues of metadata, system architecture design, and developmental techniques for creating effective and usable virtual exhibitions.

Section II
Information Processing and Content Management

Chapter X

Carmen Galvez, University of Granada, Spain

This chapter introduces the standardization methods of terms using the two basic approaches, computational and linguistic techniques, and justifies the application of processes based on Finite-State Transducers (FST). Standardization of terms is the procedure of matching and grouping together variants of the same term that are semantically equivalent.

This chapter presents a hierarchical summarization approach that generates a summary for a document based on the hierarchical structure and salient features of the document. User evaluations conducted by the authors indicate that the hierarchical summarization outperforms traditional summarization.

This chapter describes the various Metadata standards for digital document description in the context of bibliographic databases. It also examines metadata interoperability and mapping issues among the various standards.

This chapter firstly introduces various approaches towards ontology development, ontology population from heterogeneous data sources, semantic association discovery, semantic association ranking and presentation, and social network analysis. Then the authors present their approach for an ontology-based information search and retrieval.

This chapter presents an effective and efficient approach for managing image databases which allow user-centred navigation and visualisation of complete image collections. Image thumbnails are projected onto a spherical surface so that images that are visually similar are located close to each other in the visualisation space. Images are placed on regular grid structure to avoid overlapping and occlusion effect while large databases are handled through a clustering technique paired with a hierarchical tree structure which allows for intuitive real-time browsing experience.

This chapter introduces a machine learning-based approach which builds user profiles for intelligent document filtering in digital libraries. This study exploits knowledge stored in machine-readable dictionaries to obtain accurate user profiles that describe user interests by referring to concepts in those dictionaries.

Chapter XVI

This chapter provides the literature review of various text summarization and evaluation techniques, and discusses the application of text summarization in digital libraries. This chapter helps the reader to obtain a clear overview of the text summarization field and facilitate the application of text summarization in digital libraries.

This chapter describes a number of advances in formulating spoken document retrieval for the National Gallery of the Spoken Word (NGSW) and the U.S.-based Collaborative Digitization Program (CDP). Their experimental online system called "SpeechFind" is presented, which allows for audio retrieval from the NGSW and CDP corpus.

Chapter XVIII

This chapter introduces a personalized ranking function that encapsulates the user interests in the process of ordering retrieved results so as to meet the user needs. The ranking function relies on a lexical ontology that encodes a number of concepts and their inter-relations, and determines the semantics of both the query keywords and the query matching pages. Based on the correlation between the query and document semantics, it decides upon the ordering of search results so that these are personalized.

Chapter XIX

This chapter introduces basic guidelines for developing and maintaining digital cultural collections in order to be interoperable and easily retrievable from users. The requirements of cultural material are discussed and it is shown how in combination with the adequate metadata schema policy, a digital cultural collection can cover the various needs for learning and retrieving information.

This chapter describes a digital library for the e-learning domain which main service is a search engine that retrieves information by tracing the domain vocabulary met on ontology. The digital library extends Web portal's functionalities, providing technical information and communication and collaboration spaces, and hosts a wide variety of information. It provides services for cataloging, storing, searching, and retrieving information, based on ontology-based semantic queries.

Modern information and communication technologies (ICT) introduce new publication forms and services in the area of scholarly communication, which seem to enable a faster and more cost efficient distribution of research results. This chapter presents a classification scheme which aims to allow describing new forms of scholarly communication in a standardized way.

This chapter describes multimodality as a means of augmenting information retrieval activities in multimedia digital libraries. Multimodal interaction systems combine visual information with voice, gestures, and other modalities to provide flexible and powerful dialogue approaches. The authors propose a new approach to match a multimodal sentence expressed by the user with a template stored in a knowledge base to interpret the multimodal sentence and define the multimodal templates similarity.

This chapter explores text mining techniques for matching abbreviated journal titles from citations with journals in existing digital libraries. The main problem is that for one journal there is often a number of different abbreviated forms in the citation report, hence the matching depends on the detection of duplicate records. The author uses character-based and token-based metrics together with a generated thesaurus for detecting duplicate records.

    Jin-Cheon Na, Nanyang Technological University, Singapore
    Tun Thura Thet, Nanyang Technological University, Singapore
    Dion Hoe-Lian Goh, Nanyang Technological University, Singapore
    Yin-Leng Theng, Nanyang Technological University, Singapore
    Schubert Foo, Nanyang Technological University, Singapore
    Paul Horng-Jyh Wu, Nanyang Technological University, Singapore

This chapter introduces word segmentation methods for Indo-China languages. It describes six different word segmentation methods developed for the Thai, Vietnamese, and Myanmar languages, and compare different approaches in terms of their algorithms and results achieved. It provides underlying views about how word segmentation can be employed in Indo-China languages to support search functionality in digital libraries.

    Dion Hoe-Lian Goh, Nanyang Technological University, Singapore
    Khasfariyati Razikin, Nanyang Technological University, Singapore
    Alton Y. K. Chua, Nanyang Technological University, Singapore
    Chei Sian Lee, Nanyang Technological University, Singapore
    Schubert Foo, Nanyang Technological University, Singapore
    Jin-Cheon Na, Nanyang Technological University, Singapore
    Yin-Leng Theng, Nanyang Technological University, Singapore

This chapter explores the effectiveness of social tags as resource descriptors. Social tags are freely selected terms by users to resources, and shared among other users. Two text categorization experiments via Support Vector Machines (SVM) were done for this research. The first study concentrated on the use of terms as its features, while the second used both terms and its tags as part of its feature set.

    Taha Osman, Nottingham Trent University, UK
    Dhavalkumar Thakker, Nottingham Trent University, UK
    Gerald Schaefer, Aston University, UK

This chapter presents an ontology-based semantic annotation scheme for image retrieval in digital libraries. The authors show that the employment of a semantic framework for image annotation provides more accurate retrieval results than general search techniques typically relying on statistical analysis of keyword recurrences in image annotations.

Section III
Users, Interactions, and Experiences

    Ali Shiri, University of Alberta, Canada

Drawing on earlier information retrieval visual interfaces that have made use of thesauri, this chapter explores metadata-enhanced visual interfaces. The chapter describes a study to explore the design of visual interfaces for digital libraries design ideas and discusses implications for digital library interface design in terms of metadata-based information search and retrieval features for visualization.

This chapter gives a critical review of common usability evaluation methods and describes empirical user studies employing a combination of usability methods to understand user interaction issues.

This chapter describes a questionnaire-based study covering a wide range of issues pertinent to the design of user interfaces for DLs, including: user characteristics/profiles, current experience in DL usage, functional requirements, nonfunctional requirements, and contextual requirements.

This chapter examines the services that can be accessed by means of portable devices and analyzes the main sociotechnical issues that arise and influence user interaction. Factors that affect acceptance of these devices are discussed, and future trends are presented to outline the research landscape in the future.

This chapter introduces the Consultative Group on International Agricultural Research (CGIAR) Virtual Library as a tool linking researchers and agricultural research results. The CGIAR is a strategic alliance of countries, international and regional organizations, and private foundations supporting 15 international agricultural Centers that work in partnerships with national agricultural research institutions and societies. The chapter explains their work, and discusses implications to the design of virtual libraries.

This chapter reviews alternative ways to access digital audio collections, and describes two applications—Play-SOM and PocketSOM—for accessing audio files that are based on the Self-Organising Map, an unsupervised neural network model. Alternative interfaces to large audio collections for both desktop computers and mobile devices are discussed, and presents a practical approach to pressing issues in accessing digital collections.

This chapter reviews the patent and trade secret issues in digital libraries, especially patentable parameter setting components implemented as computer-related inventions in digital libraries, restricted within the current standard of the U.S. laws and cases in transnational transaction and licensing of intellectual properties regarding digital libraries. The chapter then discusses the directions for embedding and protecting numerical parametric information as trade secret in the patentable parameter setting components performing retrieval operations of digital libraries and the future of intellectual property protection in multimedia digital libraries.

This chapter describes personalization strategies adopted in digital libraries as a means to improve the usability of digital library services, and the modeling of these strategies based on users' interests, search histories, and documents accessed during the search process. Typical approaches and systems for individualizing the results of information retrieval systems are also presented.

This chapter presents a study based on an online survey in a university environment aimed to investigate the extent to which digital resources are utilized and to identify the critical factors for the effective use of digital resources. The study reveals that the usage of digital resources is significant in higher education and the utilization of digital resources is very much dependent on users and purposes. The awareness and the quality of information are critical for the use of digital resources. The findings of this study shed light on the use of digital resources and help libraries better understand users' perceptions and experiences of using digital resources services in university libraries.

Following the ever-growing sizes of image databases, effective methods for visualising such databases and navigating through them are much sought after. These methods should provide an "overview" of a complete database together with the possibility to zoom into certain areas during a specific search. It is crucial that the user interacts in an intuitive way with such a system in order to effectively arrive at images of interest. In this chapter, several techniques are presented that allow for effective browsing and navigation of large image databases.

Section IV
Case Studies and Applications

Chapter XXXVII

    Cláudio de Souza Baptista, University of Campina Grande, Brazil
    Ulrich Schiel, University of Campina Grande, Brazil

This chapter presents a multimedia digital library that copes with the storage and retrieval of resources of different media such as video, audio, maps, images, and text documents. The main improvement with regard to textual digital libraries is the possibility of retrieving documents in different media combining metadata and content analysis. We discuss the problems and solutions associated each media.

Chapter XXXVIII

    Nuria Lloret Romero, Polytechnic University of Valencia, Spain
    Margarita Cabrera Méndez, Polytechnic University of Valencia, Spain
    Alicia Sellés Carot, Masmedios Ltd., Spain
    Lilia Fernandez Aquino, Masmedios Ltd., Spain

The Biblioteca Valenciana was created to meet, conserve, and provide access to the Valencian bibliographic inheritance and all the printed, sound, and visual production, about the Comunidad Valenciana. To support this work, the Biblioteca Valenciana has embarked on the design and implementation of a digital library project, the Biblioteca Valenciana Digital (BIVALDI). This chapter describes this endeavour, as well as discusses the unique challenges associated with the project.

Chapter XXXIX

    Rubén Béjar, University of Zaragoza, Spain
    J. Nogueras-Iso, University of Zaragoza, Spain
    Miguel Ángel Latre, University of Zaragoza, Spain
    Pedro Rafael Muro-Medrano, University of Zaragoza, Spain
    F. J. Zarazaga-Soria, University of Zaragoza, Spain

This chapter introduces Spatial Data Infrastructures (SDI) and establishes their strong conceptual and technical relationships with geographic digital libraries (geolibraries). The authors describe the origin of SDIs, and highlight their role as geographic resources providers. The chapter also discusses the key differences between SDIs and geolibraries, in order to provide a broader view of these infrastructures.

Challenges remain in serving users of Digital Libraries (DL) and Geographic Information (GI) services. This is due to the proliferation of different representation formats, proprietary standards, protocols, and platforms in which information is published. In this chapter, we share some of the lessons learned during architectural design and standardization activities carried out in the GI domain.

This chapter introduces Digital Libraries as a means of cultural heritage access and diffusion. It argues that Digital Libraries, combined with superimposed information techniques, offer a potentially more substantive approach to understanding the historical documentation analysis problem. The chapter also discusses how techniques such as agents, information management, and information visualization can be incorporated to implement a versatile digital library that meets the cultural heritage information needs of users need.

Rapid development in information and communication technologies have significantly influenced both the way libraries provide information services to their users and the way they choose to access information. Digital reference services are thus gaining popularity especially in academic and public libraries. This chapter discusses how such services can play a vital role in terms of providing personalized assistance to library users in accessing resources to meet their information needs.

This chapter describes the design and implementation of three related digital libraries developed by the U.S. Geological Survey for topical and georeferenced information for coastal and marine science: the Marine Realms Information Bank (MRIB) and its two offshoots, the Monterey Bay Science Digital Library and Coastal Change Hazards Digital Library. The chapter also discusses important challenges facing digital library developers.

Digital preservation is one of the most pressing challenges not only within the digital library community, but also in other areas such as archives and data centres. This chapter introduces the concepts and challenges in the field of digital preservation. We provide an overview of the projects and initiatives worldwide dealing with this challenge, and present preservation planning as a key concept at the heart of preservation endeavours.

Compressed domain techniques are becoming increasingly important in processing or retrieving image without prior decompression. In this chapter, we show that such midstream content access is possible, and present a compressed domain retrieval methods based on a visual pattern compression algorithm. Experiments conducted on a medium sized image database demonstrate the effectiveness and efficiency of the presented approach.

This chapter provides an overview of the increasingly important domain of Music Information Retrieval, which investigates efficient and intelligent methods to analyze, recognize, retrieve, and organize music. The chapter describes the background and problems that are addressed by research, and introduces methods for the extraction of semantic descriptors from music. Next, music retrieval, music classification, and music library visualization systems are described.

This chapter describes the cooperation of academic libraries and the consortium of digital libraries of Finnish universities of applied sciences. It argues that it is necessary to adopt networking and cooperative strategies among libraries to provide electronic services of users. The findings of this chapter are useful to administrators of educational institutions aiming to plan a networked strategy and improve the cost-efficient cooperation of otherwise independent organizations.

This chapter establishes the incorporation of Knowledge Management techniques as a means to improve actual software process asset libraries. It presents how Knowledge Management contributes to the creation of a new generation of process libraries as repositories of knowledge as well as the mechanisms to allow the acquisition, storage, collaboration, sharing, and distribution of knowledge related to the software development processes.

Chapter XLIX

Educators and learners have long relied on libraries as their main sources of learning resources and libraries have in turn provided the infrastructure that promotes the creation, assimilation, and leverage of knowledge. However, with the growth of e-learning in recent years, libraries are facing new challenges to the way they develop, manage, and deliver their services and resources to their users. This chapter discusses how libraries can meet these challenges by providing electronic or partially electronic services.

This chapter aims to discuss the development of digital libraries in Pakistan. It gives an account of the digital transformation taking place in the country and reviews a few digital library initiatives. It discusses a number of issues associated with the development of digital libraries with specific reference to Pakistan. The major issues appear are as follows: misconception about digital libraries; lack of technological applications; lack of human resources with needed skills; copyright and publishing; cultural divide; digital divide; and insufficient financial support. The authors believe that understanding the underlying issues will not only accelerate the development of DL in Pakistan, but also in other developing countries with more or less common environment.

Section V
Digital Library Education and Future Trends

This chapter presents the effort of developing a digital library (DL) curriculum by an interdisciplinary group from Virginia Tech and the University of North Carolina at Chapel Hill. It describes the foundations of the curriculum building, the DL curriculum framework, the DL educational module template, a list of draft modules that are currently developed and evaluated by multiple experts in the area, and more details about the resources used in the draft modules and DL-related workshop topics mapped to the DL curriculum framework.

This chapter presents the role of technology in digital library education. It investigates how elements of computer science and library science can be merged to produce an appropriate "computational sense" for future digital librarians. The discussion in this chapter aims to inform the development of digital library software tools—particularly those used in educational contexts.

This chapter presents an overview of how national libraries of 14 countries in Asia-Pacific region are involving in the digital library initiatives. Most libraries participate in the collaborative efforts to build the digital libraries with the support from their government. With the understanding of the current situation in Asia Pacific, the reader can understand the readiness of national libraries aiming for globalization.

Foreword

THE DESIGN, CONTENT, AND USE OF DIGITAL LIBRARIES

Digital libraries are meant to provide intellectual access to distributed stores of information by creating information environments which advance access beyond electronic access to raw data—the bits—to the fuller knowledge and meaning contained in digital collections. Electronic access is increasing at a rapid pace through global efforts to increase network connectivity and bandwidth, new information management tools, and importantly, interoperability across systems and information content. The quantity of online digital information is increasing ten-fold each year in a relatively uncontrolled, open environment. This pace of information creation far surpasses that of the development of technologies to use the material effectively. The number of people accessing digital collections though the WWW also shows explosive rates of growth. Finally, internationalization is making a "global information environment" a reality. (Griffin, 1998)

As this statement by Griffin suggests, one of the seminal developments in the field of information management at the end of the last century and the early part of this century has been the rapid growth of digital library initiatives. Griffin also hints at the key areas of development for digital libraries: network connectivity and interoperability (design), knowledge and meaning (content), intellectual access (use). Ten years on from Griffin's 1998 observations, we now have before us the *Handbook of Research on Digital Libraries: Design, Development and Impact.* In this collection, Professor Foo and his colleagues address these same issues in considerable detail: design, content, use. The issues remain, but the solutions have advanced considerably in the past decade as digital "libraries" have come to encompass not only libraries, but also institutional digital repositories, certain kinds of portals and Web sites and digital archives.

The term "digital library" probably was coined in the 1980s during discussions among a number of U.S. agencies that culminated in the Digital Libraries Initiative (DLI) in 1993 (Griffin, 1998). The impact of the DLI began in earnest with the establishment of six DLI projects (http://www.cise.nsf.gov/iis/dli_home.html).

From the beginning, DLI was regarded as a community-based process which, although this may have been downplayed in recent years, is resuming significance in current developments. The community basis of early digital library initiatives was evident in the breadth of interest and involvement of researchers across many disciplines; this extended quite rapidly to absorb researchers and practitioners from many disciplines far beyond the hard sciences and information science into the human and social sciences. This much is evident in the many digital library projects currently established or under development, covering such topics as ancient Near Eastern materials, medicine, children's literature, Greek and Latin classics, and much more.

In all such projects, whether community-based or otherwise, digital library *design* remains a significant concern, and we are still seeking improvements on a number of fronts, some of which are becoming critical.

This is especially true of system architecture, which must become increasingly sophisticated in order to deal adequately not only with the more complex content of digital libraries, but also with the greater expectations of users in terms of flexible content management. Another important design consideration involves metadata and metadata applications that can be developed and fine-tuned in terms of "searchability" and long-term sustainability. And a third, perhaps most critical, issue is that of privacy and security in digital library applications. Interestingly, as these words are being written, Victoria University of Wellington has just hosted the International Conference on Managing Identity in New Zealand: User-centric Identity in the 21st Century (http://www.identityconference.victoria.ac.nz/). As the Conference publicity indicates, "…the representation of personal identity in digital environments takes place on a different footing compared to identification processes in the physical world." As a consequence, we now face new challenges on several fronts—social, technical, legal, political, and economic—to ensure secure identity management in an online environment. It is within this framework that we must consider ways of ensuring secure and accurate information access and transfer within digital libraries through the use of appropriate technologies.

From design, we move to digital library *content*, and especially how this content can be processed and managed; again, there are several areas of critical importance. One of these may be broadly termed semantics and ontology: how terms can be understood and standardized both to aid effective searching to improve text summarization, which in turn leads to better search results. Also within the broad ambit of semantics are metadata standards, and how these can be used to improve document description. A second major issue in terms of content processing and management relates to use and usability. In order to improve processing and management with a view to the use of digital library content, we face the enduring issue of user-friendly interfaces—what the technology can do must match what the users want it to do. Here, the concern is how we can use the technology, particularly machine learning, to build user profiles in terms of their interests, thereby improving search and retrieval functions in digital libraries. Through better understanding of user needs and interests, it is possible, for example, to employ ranking functions when ordering retrieved results in a manner most suited to individual requirements.

This focus on understanding the use of digital resources leads seamlessly into the third area of concern, the *use and users* of digital libraries. How usable are digital libraries, and how can usability be evaluated? What are the critical factors behind effective use of digital library content? What interfaces are available, and how appropriate are they for the intended users? How effective is the visualisation feature of digital library collections, and how navigable is the visual content of digital collections from the user perspective? These are enduring use and user questions from the predigital era now translated into a digital environment, with the advantage of better technological support for possible answers.

Design, content, and use—these three areas of principal concern in the digital library environment are also addressed by the editors of the *Handbook of Research on Digital Libraries: Design, Development and Impact,* which should come as no surprise to anyone who knows this team. The collection of papers in the *Handbook* will go some way towards improving our understanding of how current research is addressing these three areas of principal concern, and where this research may be taking us in the immediate future.

What must be addressed next by researchers is the community-based nature of digital libraries and how this community basis can and must inform future digital library developments. Understanding the community or communities of users, or perhaps the communities of practice, implies a more realistic awareness of not only ICT availability in much of the world, but also the digital literacy of such communities where the enabling ICTs are embedded in regional or national information infrastructures.

In the early 1980s, I participated in a Unesco-sponsored conference on the topic of documentation for development (as in "Third World" development), at which a sadly misguided participant stated adamantly that "even the smallest information centre in the most underdeveloped part of the world has a desktop computer." It was not true then, and it certainly is not true now, but a similar misconception is still with us:

One of the great boons of the Web is the online availability of the treasures of the world's libraries and museums. Great paintings, personal letters, dairies of the famous and infamous, ancient papyri, important national documents—all are there for any student with a computer and Internet access. (Anderson & Maxwell, 2004, p. 1)

The operative phrase in this statement is "any student with a computer and Internet access," with the unstated assumption is that this applies to most students. However, the reality is different: in the USA alone, it was estimated in 2004 that

- 33% of urban residents do not use the Internet
- 34% of suburban residents do not use the Internet
- 48% of rural residents do not use the Internet (Stefl-Mabry & Lynch, 2006, p. 66).

The residents are reported as not *using* the Internet; in how many developing countries would the more appropriate comment be "unable to use because access does not exist" or "unable to use through lack of digital literacy"? For most of Africa, for vast swathes of Asia and Oceania, for much of the Middle East, for significant parts of Latin America, this would be the reality.

Since digital libraries depend ultimately on the ability to access and to understand their content, it is incumbent upon researchers to tackle this double-edged sword of access and understanding with the same vigour with which they have tackled the issues of design, content, and use. There is perhaps less we can do as researchers in relation to regional and national information infrastructures, except to lobby for greater commitment and investment and to make our expertise available for development, than in relation to understanding through digital literacy. Indeed, as we broaden our horizons from literacy to information literacy—and now to digital literacy—there is much that is already being done, as can be seen in Rivoltella's edited collection, *Literacy: Tools and Methodologies for Information Society*. As long as the digital divide, digital illiteracy, and digital exclusion are with us, digital libraries will be that much less effective than their potential warrants. "Digital exclusion [...] is to remain incapable of thinking, or creating and organizing new more just and dynamic forms of production and distribution of symbolic and material wealth" (Fantin & Girardello, 2008, p. 312).

With this situation as an underlying imperative, the editors and authors who have contributed to the *Handbook of Research on Digital Libraries: Design, Development and Impact* deserve particular commendation for the manner in which they have delved with insight and scholarly rigour into the areas underpinning forward motion in digital library development and use. In 58 chapters, this collection addresses a range of issues under the broad rubric of design-content-use that will inform our thinking on future digital library development for some time. And in the final section, there are several chapters that serve as links between the specific technical issues addressed in earlier sections and possible future developments—food for thought indeed.

Professor G E Gorman FCLIP FRSA AALIA
Professor of Information Management
Victoria University of Wellington
New Zealand

REFERENCES

Anderson, C.G., & Maxwell, D.C. (2004) *Starting a digitization centre*. Chandos Information Professional Series. Oxford: Chandos Publishing.

Fantin, M., & Girardello, G. (2008). Digital literacy and cultural mediations to the digital divide. In P.C. Rivoltella (Ed.), *Digital Literacy: Tools and Methodologies for Information Society* (pp. 310–340). Hershey, PA: IGI Publishing.

Griffin, S.M. (1998). NSF/DARPA/NASA Digital libraries initiative: A program manager's perspective. *D-Lib Magazine (July/August)*. Retrieved August 30, 2008, from http://www.dlib.org/dlib/july98/07griffin.html

Rivoltella, P.C. (Ed.). (2008). *Digital literacy: Tools and methodologies for information society*. Hershey, PA: IGI Publishing.

Stefl-Mabry, J., & Lynch, B.L. (2006). *Knowledge communities: Bringing the village into the classroom*. Lanham, MD: Scarecrow Press.

Preface

The history of digital libraries is rich and varied because the "digital library" concept is not so much a new idea as an evolving conception of contributions from many disciplines. Digital libraries are interactive systems with organised collections of information. As digital libraries become more complex, the number of facilities provided by them will increase, and the difficulty of learning to use these facilities will also increase correspondingly. Like the Web, digital libraries also provide nonlinear information spaces in which chunks of information are interconnected via links. However, they are different in character from the Web in several important aspects: a digital library represents a collection for a specific purpose, and has search strategies that are clearly defined and more powerful.

In recent years, there has been an emergence of subject-based digital libraries on the Web. Many people have contributed to the idea, and everyone seems to have something different in mind. The metaphor of the traditional library is both empowering and constraining: (i) *empowering*, because digital libraries automate and extend opportunities offered by traditional libraries, as well as harnessing opportunities not possible on the anarchic Web; and (ii) *constraining*, because the metaphor evokes certain legacy impressions, many originating in arbitrary physical constraints.

The design of interactive systems, including digital libraries, is often inspired by what technology makes possible. In user-centered design, design emphasizes users, their tasks, and needs. Because digital libraries mean different things to different people, the design of digital libraries is, therefore, dependent of the perceptions of the purpose/functionality of digital libraries.

It is now more than ten years since the first digital library conference on "Theory and Practice of Digital Libraries" was held in 1994 that predicted the beginning of an electronic period, but warned that we needed to construct a social environment for the information highway. Digital libraries have matured from seemingly static to more dynamic and interactive repositories of user-contributed resources with diverse applications. They are part of the global infrastructure being envisioned to interconnect many computer networks and various forms of information technologies around the world, a partial fulfillment of Bush's 1945 dream "memex" of a personal microfiche-based system to tackle the problem of information overload. Digital libraries, more organized and structured than the Web, are an overwhelming example of a shared world-wide collection of information.

In such an emerging and ever-evolving field, educators, researchers, and professionals need access to seminal works as well as the most current information about concepts, issues, trends, and technologies, and hence, the motivation of this handbook.

This handbook aims to provide comprehensive coverage and definitions of the most important issues, concepts, trends, and technologies relating to digital library technology and applications. This important new publication will be distributed worldwide among academic and professional institutions and will be instrumental in providing researchers, scholars, students, and professionals with access to the latest knowledge relating to digital libraries. The authors of the chapters in this handbook are representatives from scholars and practitioners with well-established research portfolios and expertise in digital libraries throughout the world.

The Handbook is divided into 5 sections with 58 chapters: (I) Design and Development; (II) Information Processing and Content Management; (III) Users, Interactions, and Experiences; (IV) Case Studies and Applications; and (V) Digital Library Education and Future Trends. In addition, the Handbook also compiles a compendium of terms, definitions, and explanations of concepts, processes, and acronyms.

In Section I: Design and Development, the focus is to highlight a range of design and development techniques, challenges, and solutions in creating usable and effective digital library systems. Drawing from the experiences of the various authors of these 9 chapters, readers are introduced to a series of digital library projects, case studies and evaluative studies that addresse a wide facet of design and development issues that include data modeling, application profiling, system architecture design, use of technologies, metadata, security, and privacy.

In Section II: Information Processing and Content Management, the focus is on information processing and content management. In these 17 chapters, the readers will encounter details in techniques and issues related to information processing and content management for developing and organizing various digital libraries. In the information processing related chapters, the following techniques are discussed: text summarization, user-centred navigation for browsing large image databases, ontology-based information retrieval, personalization, audio-based information retrieval, ranked query algorithm for personalization, multimodal user interface for multimedia digital libraries, and word segmentation in Indo-China languages. In the content management related chapters, the following techniques and issues are discussed: standardization of terms, metadata interoperability, guidelines for developing digital cultural collection, a classification scheme for new forms of scholarly communication, duplicate journal title detection in references, and the effectiveness of social tagging for resource discovery.

In Section III: Users, Interactions, and Experiences, the focus is on the applicability, use, and impact on the targeted users of the digital library systems. The 10 chapters cover the importance of these various forms of digital libraries, and their roles, key success factors, problems, issues, and contribution to the society at large are important aspects that are typically expounded in this section. Usability evaluation techniques employed are also discussed in the development of large digital library systems, addressing users, requirements, and context of use.

In Section IV: Case Studies and Applications, the focus is on designing and implementing digital libraries, as well as important applications of digital libraries. The 14 chapters cover diverse, but important, areas such as multimedia digital libraries, geospatial digital libraries, music as well as image information access, and digital preservation. Other chapters discuss national digital library projects, as well as the challenges associated with implementing large-scale digital libraries. Delivering effective electronic services in various domains for digital library users are also covered in this section.

In Section V: Digital Library Education and Future Trends, the focus is on digital library education and future trends. In these 8 chapters, the readers will encounter details in current status and issues related to digital library education and future trends for digital libraries. In the digital library education related chapters, the following topics are discussed: a digital library curriculum and its framework, trends in digital library education, the LIS (Library and Information Science) educational and training programs in Europe, and the role of technology in digital library education. In the future trends related chapters, the following issues are discussed: the core role of libraries as centers of knowledge using historical perspectives, the new role of digital libraries for a new breed of consumers, the future of learning with digital libraries, and an overview of national libraries in Asia Pacific region, and their readiness for globalization.

Yin-Leng Theng, Schubert Foo, Dion Goh, and Jin-Cheon Na
Division of Information Studies
Wee Kim Wee School of Communication and Information
Nanyang Technological University
Singapore
June 2008

Acknowledgment

The editors would like to thank all authors who have submitted chapter proposals, and reviewers for their excellent contributions and insights, without which this book would not have been possible. Not forgetting our editorial representatives, particularly Kristin Roth and Rebecca Beistline, who demonstrated patience and extreme cooperation in the development and production of this handbook; and Lia Maisarah Umar, Eunice Chua, and Dawn Tan provided valuable administrative support throughout the process. Special thanks go to Gary Gorman who, despite his busy commitments, wrote the foreword and gave us a comprehensive overview of the design, content, and use of digital libraries. We are also grateful to IGI Global for the opportunity to publish this handbook, which we hope will be the first of many more books to come in the future.

Section I
Design and Development

Chapter I
OpenDLib:
A Digital Library Service System

Leonardo Candela
Istituto di Scienza e Tecnologie dell'Informazione "A. Faedo" (ISTI-CNR), Italy

Donatella Castelli
Istituto di Scienza e Tecnologie dell'Informazione "A. Faedo" (ISTI-CNR), Italy

Pasquale Pagano
Istituto di Scienza e Tecnologie dell'Informazione "A. Faedo" (ISTI-CNR), Italy

Manuele Simi
Istituto di Scienza e Tecnologie dell'Informazione "A. Faedo" (ISTI-CNR), Italy

ABSTRACT

This chapter introduces OpenDLib, a digital library service system developed at ISTI-CNR for easing the creation and management of digital libraries. It discusses the motivations underlying the development of such a system and describes it by presenting (i) the characteristics of the huge kind of content it is capable of managing, (ii) the set of functions it natively provides its digital libraries with, (iii) the powerful and flexibility of its component-oriented architectural paradigm as a key feature for addressing different application scenarios, and (iv) the technologies the system development relies on. The authors hope that understanding the OpenDLib foundational principles will not only inform stakeholders and decision makers of the features implemented by this existing system, but also assist researchers and application developers in the understanding of the issues, and their possible solutions, that arises when building digital library systems aimed at serving such a broad class of application scenarios.

INTRODUCTION

Digital libraries (DLs) are complex systems whose lifetime span approximately crosses the last 15 years. Along this period, a lot of focused and from-scratch developed systems have been realized to serve the needs of specific communities. These systems are tightly bound to the characteristics of the single scenario they have been conceived for and the results are hard to maintain along time. In addition to them, a few general-purpose digital library systems, that is, software systems designed to be easily used for realizing digital libraries suitable for certain application contexts, have been conceived. Such second class of systems systematizes the techniques and the software needed to implement digital libraries with certain characteristics, resulting in a product that communities can use to build their digital libraries.

OpenDLib is an example of such a second class of digital library systems with an architecture explicitly designed to support plug-and-play expansions. The design and development of OpenDLib was initiated in 2000 as a response to a pressing request for software that could enable different user communities to create their own DLs. We decided to design general purpose software that could be customized to meet the needs of the different application scenarios. At that time we called this software a digital library service system to stress that it is a system that manages digital library services and makes them publicly available (Castelli & Pagano, 2003). The role of OpenDLib is analogous to the role of a database management system for a database, that is, it supports the creation and maintenance of distributed DLs. A DL can be created by instantiating OpenDLib appropriately and then either loading or harvesting the content to be managed. Our initial aim was to design a software tool that could provide a number of core DL functions on general content and that could easily be expandable. A DL is a very expensive resource, therefore it must be maintained over time even when new

technologies that enable new functions are developed or when new kinds of usages are proposed. To satisfy this dynamic scenario, the DL must grow over time along several dimensions, for example, services, metadata formats supported, hosting servers, user communities, and so forth. OpenDLib was designed to support this powerful notion of evolution.

BACKGROUND AND REQUIREMENTS FOR A DIGITAL LIBRARY SYSTEM

The systems developed in the digital library area until now were mainly dedicated to support digital repositories for satisfying the needs of single institutions. Among such systems, usually called "digital repository systems," Fedora (Lagoze, Payette, Shin, & Wilper, 2005), DSpace (Tansley, Bass, & Smith, 2003), and EPrints (Millington & Nixon, 2007) represent the most popular and adopted ones.

Fedora is a repository system specifically designed for storing and managing complex objects. It is implemented as a set of Web services that provide full programmatic management of digital objects as well and search and access to multiple representations of such objects (Payette & Thornton, 2002). Fedora is particularly well suited to work in a broad Web service framework and act as the foundation layer for a variety of multitiered systems, service-oriented architectures, and end-user applications.

DSpace is an open source digital repository software system for research institutions (Tansley, Bass, Stuve, Branschofsky, Chudnov, McClellan, et al., 2003). It enables organizations to capture and describe digital material using a submission workflow module, or a variety of programmatic ingest options, to distribute an organization's digital assets over the Web through a search and retrieval system and to preserve digital assets over the long term.

EPrints, now in its third version, is among the first free repository software for building OAI-compliant repositories and probably one of the most diffused (in December 2007, there existed 240 known archives running this software). This new version is a major leap forward in functionality, aiming at simplifying the tasks of the various players (e.g., depositors, researchers, and managers) involved in running and maintaining a repository.

Digital repository systems, however, only provide core functionalities, such as search, retrieval, and access to information objects, which are not able to meet application specific requirements as those digital libraries are usually requested to satisfy. For example, during its lifetime a DL may have to support additional functionalities for satisfy the needs of new organizations that join the DL, offering their specific information content and their computers to host the system; or it may have to manage policies that regulate the access to content and services. OpenDLib (Castelli & Pagano, 2002, 2003; OpenDLib) has been conceived to meet these specific DL requirements.

OPENDLIB FEATURES

OpenDLib was created as a software toolkit for setting up digital libraries capable of satisfying multifaceted needs expressed by heterogeneous user communities. Because of this goal, it must be capable of supporting a powerful and flexible content model, a set of functions for appropriately dealing with such potentially rich content, and an architectural paradigm making it capable to be exploited in application scenarios having different deployment requirements.

As regards the content, OpenDLib can handle a wide variety of information object types. This capability originates from the fact that it exploits a powerful and flexible **document model** named DoMDL (Candela, Castelli, Pagano, & Simi, 2005).

DoMDL has been designed to represent structured, multilingual, and multimedia objects in a way that can be customized according to which content has to be handled. For example, it can be used to describe a lecture as the composition of the teacher's presentation together with the slides and the summary of the talk transcript. Moreover, the object may be disseminated as the MPEG3 format of the video or the SMIL object synchronizing its parts.

In order to represent objects with completely different structures, DoMDL distinguishes four main aspects of document modelling and, using terms and definitions very similar to those coined in the IFLA FRBR model (IFLA, 1998), it represents these aspects through the following entities: *document, edition, view,* and *manifestation*. The document entity, representing the object as a distinct intellectual creation, captures the more general aspect of it. The edition entity models an instance of the document entity along the time dimension. The preliminary version of a paper and the version published in the proceedings are examples of successive editions of the same object. The view is the way through which an edition is perceived. A view excludes physical aspects that are not related to how a document is to be perceived. For example, the original edition of the proceedings of a workshop might be disseminated under two different views: (*a*) a "structured textual view" containing a "preface" created by the conference chairs and the list of thematic sessions containing the accepted papers; and (*b*) a "presentation view" containing the list of the slides used in the presentations. The manifestation models the physical formats by which an object is disseminated, for example, the MPEG file containing the video recording of a lecture given at a certain summer school, or the AVI file of the same video. These entities are semantically connected by means of a set of possibly multiple relationships, that is, there may be multiple editions of the same document, multiple views of the same edition, and multiple manifestations of the same view.

Each of the entities of the model has a set of attributes that specify the rights on the modelled document aspects. This enables, for example, to model possibly different rights on different editions, different access policies on different views or on different parts of the same view, and so on.

The information objects of an OpenDLib digital library are organized into a set of *virtual collections*, each characterized by its own access policy. Authorized people can define new collections dynamically, that is, by specifying membership criteria. In the same digital library, for example, it is possible to maintain a collection of grey literature accessible to all users and a collection of historical images accessible only to a specific group of researchers. Each collection is automatically updated whenever a new object matching the membership criteria is published in the digital library.

From the functional point of view, the basic release of OpenDLib provides services to support the submission, description, indexing, search, browsing, retrieval, access, preservation, and visualization of information objects. These objects can be submitted as files in a chosen format or as URLs to objects stored elsewhere. They can be described using one or more metadata formats. The OpenDLib search service offers different search options, such as free text or fielded (where fields can be selected from a variety of known metadata formats) or single or cross-language, with or without relevance feedback. Information objects retrieved can be navigated over all their editions, versions, structures, metadata, and formats. All the above services can be customized according to several dimensions, such as, for example, metadata formats, controlled vocabularies, and browseable fields.

OpenDLib is also equipped with other digital library specific services, such as the ones providing the enforcement of access policies on information objects and the management of "user-shelves" able to maintain information objects versions,

result-sets, session results, and other information. In addition, a number of administration functions are also given to support the preservation of objects, objects reviewing process, and handling of users and user group profiles.

From the architectural point of view, OpenDLib adopts a **component-based approach**. This application development approach is the most suitable to realize the OpenDLib goal because: (*i*) the system is assembled from discrete executable components which are developed and deployed somewhat independently of one another, potentially by different players; and (*ii*) the system may be upgraded with smaller increments, that is, by upgrading only some of the constituent components. In particular, this aspect is one of the key points in reaching interoperability, as upgrading the appropriate constituents of a system makes it able to interact with other systems. Furthermore, (*iii*) components may be shared by systems; this creates opportunities for reuse that heavily contributes to lowering the development and maintenance costs and the time to market. And (*iv*) though not strictly related to their being component-based, component-based systems tend to be distributed. OpenDLib implements this approach by realizing a **service-oriented architecture** so it consists of an open federation of services that can be distributed and replicated on different hosting servers. By exploiting this feature, OpenDLib supports three kinds of dynamic expansions: (i) new classes of services can easily be added to the federation; (ii) new instances of a replicated or distributed service can be deployed on either an existing or a new hosting server; and (iii) the configurations of the services can be modified so that they can handle new object types, new metadata formats, and support new usages. Thus the architectural configuration, chosen when the digital library is set up, can be changed later to satisfy new emerging needs. For instance, a replication of an index instance can be created to reduce workloads when the number of search requests exceeds an established threshold, whereas an index instance, able to serve queries in a language not previously supported, can be added to satisfy the needs of a new community of users. All the above dynamic updates in the configuration of the federation can be done on the fly, that is, without switching off the digital library.

This architectural design provides a great flexibility in the management of the digital library, so that it can be managed and hosted either by a single organization or by a multitude of organizations. For example, an organization can decide to maintain an instance of the repository service, in order to have local control over its own documents, but to share all the other services with other institutions.

The OpenDLib architecture has been designed to be highly interoperable with other digital libraries. In particular, an OpenDLib library can act both as an OAI-PMH data provider and as an OAI-PMH service provider (Lagoze & Van de Sompel, 2001). This implies that the metadata maintained by an OpenDLib digital library can be open to other digital libraries and, vice-versa, the OpenDLib services can access the metadata published by any other OAI-PMH compliant digital library.

From an implementation point of view, OpenDLib is an hyper text transfer protocol (HTTP) (Web) server-based software system, requiring only open source technologies and running on several of the major operating systems, such as Solaris, Linux, SCO, Digital Unix, Unix V, and AIX.

OpenDLib is distributed as an Apache server module that contains all the modules belonging to the OpenDLib kernel. At activation time, it loads the set of self-installing modules representing DL Web services in accordance with the configuration instructions. DL service modules are either function libraries or object libraries used to define a class and its methods.

The system adopts XML as a standard for internal (service to service) and external exchange of messages. An HTTP-based communication protocol, named OpenDLib protocol (OLP), has been designed in order to regulate the communication among the services. The OLP messages can be sent as REST or simple object access protocol (SOAP) requests while a set of APIs have been defined to facilitate its exploitation in other existing systems.

CONCLUSION

OpenDLib is now an operational system that has been used for building a number of DLs. Each of these DLs has its own specific distributed architectural configuration that reflects the needs of the application scenario where it operates. Thanks to its expandability, OpenDLib proved to support the creation of very different DLs by dynamically and progressively aggregating resources provided by many disperse organizations.

Recently OpenDLib has been extended. Its new version, OpenDLibG (Candela, Castelli, Pagano, & Simi, 2006) makes it able to exploit the storage and processing capabilities offered by a grid infrastructure. Thanks to this extension an OpenDLib digital library is now able to handle a much wider class of information objects, namely objects requiring huge storage capabilities like raw data and particular types of images, videos, and 3D objects. Further, it is also able to process on-demand such data to generate new information as the result of computational intensive elaborations that OpenDLib automatically distributes to exploit the available computational resources. This extension has confirmed the goodness of the system, its openness, and the power and flexibility of the DoMDL.

REFERENCES

Candela, L., Castelli, D., Pagano, P., & Simi, M. (2005). From heterogeneous information spaces to virtual documents. In E. A. Fox, E. J. Neuhold, P. Premsmit, & V. Wuwongse (Eds.), *Digital Libraries. Implementing Strategies and Sharing Experiences: 8th International Conference on Asian Digital Libraries, ICADL 2005* (LNCS, pp. 11-22). Berlin: Springer-Verlag.

Candela, L., Castelli, D., Pagano, P., & Simi, M. (2006). OpenDLibG: Extending OpenDLib by exploiting a gLite grid infrastructure. In *Proceeding of the 10th European Conference on Research and Advanced Technology for Digital Libraries, ECDL 2006* (LNCS, pp.) Berlin: Springer-Verlag.

Castelli, D., & Pagano, P. (2002). OpenDLib: A digital library service system. In M. Agosti & C. Thanos (Eds.), *Research and Advanced Technology for Digital Libraries: Sixth European Conference ECDL 2002* (LNCS, pp. 292-308). Berlin: Springer-Verlag.

Castelli, D., & Pagano, P. (2003). *A system for building expandable digital libraries.* Paper presented at the ACM/IEEE 2003 Joint Conference on Digital Libraries JCDL 2003 (pp. 335-345). Berlin: Springer-Verlag.

EPrints for digital repositories. Retrieved December 2007, from http://www.eprints.org

IFLA study group on the functional requirements for bibliographic records. (1998). *Functional requirements for bibliographic records: Final report.* Muenche: Saur, K.G. Retrieved August 11, 2008, from http://www.ifla.org/VII/s13/frbr/frbr.htm

Lagoze, C., Payette, S., Shin, E., & Wilper, C. (2005). Fedora: An architecture for complex objects and their relationships. *International Journal on Digital Libraries, 6,* 124-138.

Lagoze, C., & Van de Sompel, H. (2001). The open archives initiative: Building a low-barrier interoperability framework. In *Proceedings of the 1st ACM/IEEE-CS Joint Conference on Digital Libraries (JCDL '01),* Roanoke, VA. New York: ACM.

Lynch, C. A. (2003). Institutional repositories: Essential infrastructure for scholarship in the digital age. *ARL, 226,* 1-7.

Millington, P., & Nixon, W. J. (2007). EPrints 3 pre-launch briefing. *Ariadne, 50.*

OpenDLib. *A digital library service system.* Retrieved December 2007, from http://www.opendlib.com

Payette, S., & Thornton, S. (2002). The Mellon Fedora project: Digital library architecture meets XML and Web services. In M. Agosti & C. Thanos (Eds.), *Research and Advanced Technology for Digital Libraries: Sixth European Conference ECDL 2002* (LNCS, pp. 406-421). Berlin: Springer-Verlag.

Tansley, R., Bass, M., & Smith, M. (2003, August 17-22). DSpace as an open archival information system: Current status and future directions. In *Proceedings of the 7th European Conference Research and Advanced Technology for Digital Libraries, ECDL 2003,* Trondheim, Norway (pp. 446-460). Springer-Verlag.

Tansley, R., Bass, M., Stuve, D., Branschofsky, M., Chudnov, D., McClellan, G., et al. (2003). The DSpace institutional digital repository system: Current functionality. In *Proceedings of the Third ACM/IEEE-CS Joint Conference on Digital Libraries* (pp. 87-97). IEEE Computer Society.

KEY TERMS

Digital Library Service System: A digital library system based on a service-oriented architecture providing the functionality required by a digital library in terms of distributed services.

Digital Library System: A software system that is based on a (potentially distributed) architecture and provides all functionality that is required by a particular digital library. Users interact with a digital library through the corresponding digital library system.

Document Model: The abstract representation of the physical or semantic structure of a given set of documents.

Grid Computing: Computing model that provides the ability to perform higher throughput computing by taking advantage of many networked computers to model a virtual computer architecture that is able to distribute process execution across a parallel infrastructure.

Grid Infrastructure: The underlying basic framework for grid computing.

Institutional Repository: A set of services that a research institution offers to the members of its community for the management and dissemination of digital materials created by the institution and its community members. It is most essentially an organizational commitment to the stewardship of these digital materials, including long-term preservation where appropriate, as well as organization and access or distribution (Lynch, 2003).

Service Oriented Architecture: A style of information systems architecture that enables the creation of applications that are built by combining loosely couplet and interoperable services.

8

Chapter II
Information Security and Privacy in Digital Libraries

Mohammed Nasser Al-Suqri
Sultan Qaboos University, Oman

Esther O.A. Fatuyi
Elsie Whitlow Stokes Community Freedom Public School, USA

ABSTRACT

Deliberate exploitation of natural resources and excessive use of environmentally abhorrent materials have resulted in environmental disruptions threatening the life support systems. A human centric approach of development has already damaged nature to a large extent. This has attracted the attention of environmental specialists and policy makers. It has also led to discussions at various national and international conventions. The objective of protecting natural resources cannot be achieved without the involvement of professionals from multidisciplinary areas. This chapter recommends a model for the creation of knowledge-based systems for natural resources management. Further, it describes making use of unique capabilities of remote sensing satellites for conserving natural resources and managing natural disasters. It is exclusively for the people who are not familiar with the technology and who are given the task of framing policies.

ABSTRACT

Digital libraries became evident about a decade ago. They have created many opportunities as well as challenges. One of the biggest challenges for digital libraries is to select appropriate technologies and software so they can continue to progress in providing accurate, secure, and timely information to its users. The purpose of this chapter is to provide a closer look at the challenges that digital libraries face in the new Digital Age. It addresses the following issues: protecting the information infrastructure; identification and authentication in security and privacy; standards and policies; access and control of digital information; ethical decision making in design, implementation, and evaluation of digital libraries; and privacy, anonymity, and identity. The chapter concludes with future trends of security and privacy in digital libraries.

INTRODUCTION

The future has always been regarded with fascination. For some people it is because of the perceived benefits that will be realized; for others because it will bring change and create problems that will need to be resolved. One thing that everyone agrees with, however, is that the future inevitably brings with it change, and life will, in some ways, be different. Today we live in a world economy and one in which great distances can be traveled much more quickly than 100 years ago. In like manner, the transmission of information has moved beyond print and now includes digital text and images. Libraries, as traditional providers of information and knowledge, are undergoing particularly challenging situations in transitioning from ownership of materials to accessing knowledge and information from networked, electronic sources, from providing users with the information that they are looking for to teaching users how to find the information for themselves, and from moving from an environment that has changed slowly over the past 150 years to one in which change is necessary, constant, and revolutionary.

While it can be said that all libraries are in some degree alike, they are also different in rather critical ways. Technology should be viewed as a tool and a means for accomplishing a task. The definition of the task to be performed must be identified by librarians taking a careful and ongoing assessment of users. The details of how information delivery takes place will vary from environment to environment, but change will take place depending upon how libraries create (or react to) changes in their clientele, the work that is performed, and the availability and cost of technology. In fact, the big challenge for libraries is to use the evolution of the new technologies to their benefit, so these libraries can continue as information providers.

Digital libraries became evident about a decade ago. They have created many opportunities as well as challenges. One of the biggest challenges for digital libraries is to select appropriate technologies and software so they can continue to progress in providing accurate, secure, and timely information to its users.

Digital libraries, according to the **Digital Library Federation**, are "organizations that provide the resources, including the specialized staff, to select, structure, offer intellectual access to, interpret, distribute, preserve the integrity of, and ensure the persistence over time of collections of digital works, so that they are readily and commercially available for use by a defined community or set of communities." Likewise, Ershova and Hohlov (2001) define it as "a distributed information systems ensuring reliable storage and effective use of heterogeneous collections of electronic documents -text, graphics, audio, video, and so forth. - via global data transfer networks in a way convenient for the end user." In other words, digital libraries are organizations that would have all the information resources in the digital form.

BACKGROUND: INFORMATION OF DIGITAL LIBRARIES

Emerging digital culture has paved the way to the creation of digital libraries, which have made it easier for users to access information through digital systems and networks. With the global increase in the quantity of information and the digital devices that store it comes an increase in the issues of security and privacy for library users and digital materials. Users of such digital devices would need to understand the capacity of each device and the restrictions associated with the information being disseminated. The cost of updating current technologies and the security of information has become a vital concern for digital librarians. Also of equal concern is the environmental impact of the security and privacy of information available to its originators and its users in digital libraries.

The digital library is a hybrid library designed to perform and serve the same primary functions and tasks as those of a traditional library. What makes it different, though, is that it uses data stored on computerized devices instead of books and research paraphernalia. As the debate over their validity continues, digital libraries still provide services in the method used by traditional libraries but with a greater focus on technical issues. In today's globalize world, data are transmitted across the planet through a network system known as the Internet. This technology has enhanced the chance of educating people since the Internet makes access to information easier and more prevalent. While providing universal learning within the globe, this technology is required to keep digital information preserved and available for the next generations.

The primary functions performed by libraries are developing and producing information records in print and nonprint, managing the information records, and distributing the information for future generations' access. This arduous role of libraries as a mechanism that facilitates information access and freedom has been widely discussed by many researchers (Borgman, 2000; Hamilton & Pors, 2003; Sturges, 2001). The constant evolution of technology and the interface between the user and the information changes the librarian's professional environment. Fifty years ago, a librarian would help patrons find a book through a card catalogue, but today, digital librarians use

a computer to assist more patrons to find books, audiovisual media, and online resources simultaneously. For instance, Google search engine, a product of digital libraries which emanated from Stanford University, has left paper-based libraries behind with its tremendous capacity of 250 million searches per day (see http://computer.howstuffworks.com/search-engine1.htm).

Digital libraries are more interested in the preservation of data in a more durable format and in the provision of access to vast information while keeping pace with the changing technologies. Such libraries are able to address the issues of compatibility between old and new technologies while transferring information and providing access to the end user. There is, however, a need for digital libraries to focus on ensuring the **protection** of the information infrastructure and the privacy of end users. According to Sturges, Davies, Dearnley, Iliffe, Oppenheim, and Hardy (2003), library users believe "that libraries will have policies on privacy and data protection in force" (p. 49).

PROTECTING THE INFORMATION INFRASTRUCTURE

Standards for the protection of information in any format and especially in digital forms are very important for several reasons. As the information explosion is recorded around the globe, and as technology changes and improvements in the storage of information are made, earlier information records stored in print need to be saved to the newer technologies and transferred yet to another as many technologies become obsolete. Similarly, there is a need for the ease of information transfer from one record to another.

The privacy of end users will be more easily addressed as long as set standards of digital laws are met. There is a need for the filtration of information in digital forms by set standards to assist in creating contents that could shape and guard the dissemination of such information to end users. Digital information users have access to a wide range of information and sources through agencies and agents to facilitate the selection of quality and relevant information.

This concept allows end users to access digital information that is subject to the standards of a particular source. It also ensures strict adherence to the rules and regulations that could protect the users' security and privacy. These sets of standards are increasing and adjusting to the proliferations of information on the Web and the demands of usage. Digital information professionals are enjoined to identify and authenticate the security and privacy of their patrons.

IDENTIFICATION AND AUTHENTICATION IN SECURITY AND PRIVACY

The fundamental roles of information professionals have changed due to the information explosion, different forms of recording information, different processes of information, different procedures for dissemination of information, and the increase in the number of users. Governments in every country know how important it is to protect its citizens' privacy in the online world, and have policies to properly enlighten them on their rights for being accurately informed on protection of personal information submitted to Web sites. Digital libraries are also aware that they should respect the privacy of their patron.

The Internet and its enabling technology are constantly charging; in similar vein, the standards for privacy are also on the increase. Privacy laws are effectively in place to aid digital libraries to ensure that users' personal information are protected with security safeguards appropriate to the sensitivity of the information. Identification and authentication of digital library users can assist in the protection of privacy and reduction in authorized disclosures of private and sensi-

tive information. Digital libraries' identification and authentication of users involves continued verification of their claims or their statements of identity.

The information age is considerably changing the ways and circumstances by which consumers are identified and authenticated. The use of password and identification cards is becoming critical in prevention of identity theft, and other frauds. E-mail-based identification and authentication (EBIA) is emerging and provides purposeful security. Garfinkel (2003), while discussing the advantages, weaknesses of EBIA, and how it could evolve into a security system with stronger features posit, "this technique uses an e-mail address as a universal identifier and the ability to receive e-mail at that address as a kind of authenticator" (p. 22).

The digital information professional is a key player in the digital library environment for the identification and authentication of quality and relevant information. The public must have access to the digital information professional for inquiries and assistance in retrieving the needed information in a digital format. As technology changes and the need for information grows, the environment will change to help the professionals assist in identifying the information needs of users and in retrieving and disseminating the requested information. The entire identified procedures will need to be followed and authenticated with standardized policies beneficial to the information profession.

STANDARDS AND POLICIES IN DIGITAL LIBRARIES

Information is a main component of a government. As digital information becomes more popular, and as competition over the velocity of information dissemination sometimes overshadows integrity, the regulations and policies that govern the circulation of information have also become more complex.

Hence, an information professional's role is to provide accurate information in a timely manner and ensure that the integrity of that information is not compromised. **Copyright laws**, such as the American Copyright Revision Act of 1976 and the Software Copyright Act of 1980, are in place to protect software.

As extensive databases and storage systems are being developed to preserve digital information, standards and policies should be enforced to protect the security and privacy of users. The Digital Revolution has made information more accessible; it has also affected society's morals by altering the perception of standards and policies of retrieving information or downloading media from the Internet. It is sometimes perceived the same as borrowing electronic devices from a friend.

Information seekers are often found to put laws and moral implications aside when they "choose" to pirate or rectify information for their own illicit purposes based on their own "ethical" standards. For instance, 1997 records confirm instances of commercial software being copied not only by customers but the programmers themselves. According to Seadle (2004), even "a reasonable fair use in ethical terms could still be an infringement in strict legal judgment" (p. 109). Hence, there is a need to have an enforcement mechanism in place, instead of the current trends where peer pressure ethical judgments are enabling or discouraging intellectual property infringements. That is why the guidelines set by law need to be enforced on how digital criminal behavior shall be dealt with. Many governments have created protection stipulations in the form of copyrights, but such stipulations protect only an intellectual thought, leaving information in physical and digital forms as victims of chance.

The information superhighway, epitomized by the World Wide Web and digital libraries, is constantly faced with security issues, such as identity theft, data corruption, illegal downloads, and piracy. These moral issues could be seen as the result of easy access to vast information, which opens easy opportunities for slack security, which consequently invokes a possibility of wrong-doing. The Information Age is generating more reasons for security-consciousness with the Internet and digital libraries. This is essential for the **access** and **control** of digital information in order to prevent all from being lost to our own plunders as we raid the information superhighway.

ACCESS AND CONTROL OF DIGITAL INFORMATION

The more information pumped into a society the more complex are the regulations needed. Today, the information superhighway is where all the information is collected and kept in databases, retrieval systems, and digital libraries for the use of patrons. Access is given to the content of such materials based on the users' skills and knowledge (Borgman, 2000). Control is given to creators, and government is given ownership as a means to initiate statutes, laws, and guidelines on the use and distribution of the information. Many nations have taken to using agencies to regulate information for national defense and broadcasting reasons. Access to information gets affected by how organizations control it. Content of information determines where and what agency will oversee its access. Governments help protect all matters of national or global interest from finances to homeland defense. Global and national agencies and commissions assist in keeping information flowing through a society. These same agencies help to protect digital information, its content, its access, its design, and its implementation, while simultaneously regulating its ethical usage. The digital library as an agency has a key role to play in ensuring access to digital information as well as controlling it. Today, the digital library is a central hub to the world of digital information and institutional study. Digital libraries are now enjoined to provide access and control to the information from the stacks of old by compiling them into digital format for preservation. Since the act of preservation has always been a primary function of libraries, they are now concerned about future preservation of materials in the digital paradigm, a function that is "slowly shifting to the publishers" (Urs, 2004, p. 206).

ETHICAL DECISION-MAKING IN DESIGN, IMPLEMENTATION AND EVALUATION OF DIGITAL LIBRARIES

Information ethics in digital libraries is extremely vital. Digital librarians have the responsibility to keep information confidential and to use it only in a professional way. Digital information professionals have the responsibility to abide by the four principles of information ethics as described by Severson (1997). While designing, implementing, and evaluating the usage of digital information, digital library professionals should consider customer protection as a top priority ethical obligation.

In the Information Age, security and privacy are the main issues. Digital librarians need to protect patrons' research interests because people took the time to log, record, report, research, and create the information from day to day in libraries or in business settings. Hence, having regulations for digital information implementation and evaluation is a practical tool in information ethics. This is necessary to safeguard the interest of all those who are affected by the copyright or illegal distribution of digital information. The digital librarian's professional ethics should regard personal intellect in nonprint materials, artworks, music, and other creative ideas as personal property. As such, digital information professionals should make efforts to preserve the privacy of these valuable resources and safeguard them.

PRIVACY, ANONYMITY, AND IDENTITY

Digital information professionals have higher skills of retrieving information than other people. Hence, there is a need to be extra sensitive in terms of anonymity and identity on how information being provided is going to be used. Sometimes digital libraries may be unable to stop an executive from using information incorrectly, but they should not stand on the excuse that "they were following orders." They should voice their objection if information is to be used unethically. For instance, digital libraries should be cautious with the privacy and identity of patients while disseminating information on medical issues. The wavelet technology discovered at Stanford by Wang, Li, and Wielderhold (1997, 2001) is an "image processing technology," a project undertaken in order to avoid violations of security and privacy of medical images. The researchers use the electronic medical records such as x-rays as domain, and the technology provides the image filtering services within the broader context of security mediator architecture.

Severson (1997) aptly describes how the moral character of humans dictates how we make decisions based upon the usage and organization of information. The privacy concern of digital libraries is to prevent patrons' information from being disseminated among other users and organizations in an unethical manner. Digital librarians cannot give out information to parties not associated with the patron, and must not violate the patron's privacy. Furthermore, in a university setting, digital information professionals should prevent the sharing of student information and should uphold their rights to privacy.

There is a need for digital libraries to apply the four models of information ethics: principles of respect for user's intellectual property, privacy, fair representation, and principles of nonmaleficence to daily information dissemination to users (Severson, 1997). For instance, the **American**

Library Association (ALA)'s Code of Ethics states that "[they] protect each library user's right to privacy and confidentiality with respect to information sought or received and resources consulted, borrowed, acquired or transmitted" (ALA, 1995).

FUTURE TRENDS OF SECURITY AND PRIVACY IN DIGITAL LIBRARIES

It is currently complex to predict the future trends of digital libraries in terms of security and privacy of originators and users of information because of various requirements involved. According to Pope (1998), future digital libraries "need flexibility and continued expandability as more resources—in both numbers and types-are added" (p. 150). Future security of digital libraries should focus more on privacy, anonymity, and authorization. It should guarantee the integrity of its information contents, and it should enforce the confidentiality of library users. Digital libraries should also protect the intellectual property rights of the originators of digital materials in any language and culture. The quality of services in digital libraries is equally vital for future viability.

The future trends of digital libraries call for efficiency of use. Facilitating factors for enhancing future usage consists of simple user interfaces with visual formats. Digital libraries should also customize their information and collaborate with other international digital libraries to promote universal access to information with multilingual and multicultural interaction, using multichannel access ("Brainstorming report," 2001; Greenstein, 2002; Shiri, 2003). Finally, the future of digital libraries lies in global cooperation to give synergy to further research into problems such as digital evaluation and preservation, which will be needed for the continuous sustenance of this noble venture.

REFERENCES

American Library Association (ALA). (1995). *Code of ethics of the American Library Association.* Retrieved September 26, 2006, from http//www.ala.org/alaorg/oif/ethics.html

Borgman, C. L. (2000). *From Gutenberg to the global information infrastructure: Access to information in the networked world.* Cambridge, MA: MIT Press.

Brainstorming report. (2001, June, 13-15). *Digital libraries: Future directions for a European research program.* San Cassiano, Venice, Italy: Alta Badia-Italy.

Digital Library Federation. *What is digital library?* Retrieved April 12, 2007, from www.clir.org/diglib

Ershova, T. V., & Hohlov, Y. E. (2001). Integration of Russian electronic information resources of social value on the basis of DL concept. *Russian Digital Libraries Journal, 4*(1), 32-41.

Garfinkel, S. L. (2003). Understanding privacy-email-based identification and authentication: An alternative to PKI. *IEEE Security & Privacy, 1*(6), 20-26.

Greenstein, D. (2002). *Next-generation digital libraries.* Retrieved September 26, 2006, from http://www.vala.org.au/vala2002/2002pdf/01Grnstn.pdf

Hamilton, S., & Pors, N. O. (2003). Freedom of access to information and freedom of expression: The Internet as a tool for global social inclusion. *Library Management, 24*(8/9), 407-416.

Pope, N. L. (1998). Digital libraries: Future potentials and challenges. *Digital Libraries, 63-16*(3/4), 147-155.

Seadle, M. (2004). Copyright in a networked world: Ethics and infringement. *Library HiTech, 22*(1), 106-110.

Severson, W. (1997). *The principles of information ethics*. Amonk, N.Y: M.E. Sharpe.

Shiri, A. (2003). Digital library research: Current developments and trends. *Library Review, 52*(5), 198-202.

Sturges, P. (2001). The library and freedom of information: Agent or icon? *Alexandria, 13*(1), 3-16.

Sturges, P., Davies, E., Dearnley, J., Iliffe, U., Oppenheim, C., & Hardy, R. (2003).

User privacy in the digital library environment: An investigation of policies and preparedness. *Library Management, 24*(1/2), 44-50.

Urs, S. R. (2004). Copyright, academic research libraries: Balancing the rights of stakeholders in the digital age. *Program: Electronic Library and Information Systems, 38*(3), 201-207.

Wang, J. Z., Li, J., & Wiederhold, G. (1997). *TID - Trusted image dissemination: Image filtering for secure distribution of medical information*. Retrieved October, 12, 2007, from http://infolab.stanford.edu/pub/gio/TIHI/TID.html

Wang, J. Z., Li, J., & Wiederhold, G. (2001). SIMPLIcity: Semantics-sensitive integrated matching for picture libraries. *IEEE Transactions on Pattern Analysis and Machine Intelligence, 23*(9), 947-963.

KEY TERMS

Access and Control: A custodial contract governing the relationship of digital library materials and users; it provides strategies and procedures for usage of digitalized materials.

Information Ethics: Exploration and evaluation of the development of moral values in the travel of information from production to the ultimate consumption.

Privacy: A conformance to authorizations in regards to dissemination of individual or corporate private information.

Security: This refers to a conformance to proper authorizations for data movement/release out of digital libraries for patrons.

Chapter III
Digital Learning Objects and Metadata

Sarah-Jane Saravani
Waikato Institute of Technology, New Zealand

ABSTRACT

This chapter describes a learning object repository case study undertaken at the Waikato Institute of Technology, Hamilton, New Zealand, during 2005 to 2006. The project, known as the open source learning object repository (OSLOR), involved establishing a functional learning object repository, using open source software, able to be populated with digital resources from across the various education communities. Input from librarians was deemed a critical success factor; high quality metadata determine the searchability, durability, and ultimate value of the repository. The metadata application profile developed was specific to a learning object repository but was also designed to be both reducible and extensible. It was also interoperable to ensure future viability. Close consultation with the National Library of New Zealand was an additional prerequisite. The author hopes the decisions underpinning the application profile design will inform others involved in describing digital resources for a specific community.

BACKGROUND

The Centre for Learning Technologies at the Waikato Institute of Technology, Hamilton, New Zealand, successfully attracted external government funding 2005/06 to lead a multiinstitutional project, including five Institutes of Technology and Polytechnics (ITPs) and one private training establishment, to establish a learning object repository suitable for deployment across the primary to tertiary education sectors in New Zealand. Such a repository would be capable of creating communities of practice around the submission and reuse of digital learning objects related to curriculum areas.

The open source repository software EPrints (EPrints, 2007) was chosen for deployment. EPrints had good potential for integration with the learning management system in operation, Moodle (Moodle, 2007), and had the capacity to support the translation of the interface into multiple languages, in this case the Pasifika languages of Maori, Tongan, and Samoan. The open source learning management system Moodle, already in widespread use across the secondary and tertiary education sectors in New Zealand, was utilised for front-end access to the open source learning object repository (OSLOR). The library was approached to provide a metadata application profile suited to the specific requirements of the repository, resources, and the environment.

DEVELOPMENT OF LEARNING OBJECT REPOSITORIES

The exponential growth of repositories for the controlled storage of digitally-created resources has resulted from the need to link communities of practice or interest with resources within a contextual dimension. The increasing use of information technologies to create new learning resources, to manage existing learning resources, and to aggregate learning content from a wide variety of academic and publishing sources has completely altered expectations for teaching and learning. Around the world, academic institutions, professional associations, and corporations are striving to make better use of networks and databases to efficiently and effectively achieve learning and professional development goals. One of the ways they have chosen to pursue these goals is to make learning resources readily accessible to educators and learners through learning object repositories (CANARIE, 2002, p. 5).

The fundamental purpose of learning object repositories is to support teaching and learning through the storage, retrieval capabilities, and maintenance of learning objects. Object repositories are seen as key enablers for bringing increased value to learning resources by providing opportunities for reuse, repurposing, or reengineering to suit a variety of purposes and end user needs. Creating learning resources in object formats is

seen as a way to bring about increased flexibility, customisation, ease of update, searchability, and manageability to rich stores of content and learning resources that are available from publishers or that have been created by faculty members or teachers (CANARIE, 2002, p. 5).

A distinguishing feature of repositories is their architecture, including a tailored user interface, and the manner of incorporating structure and organisation around the information that is contained to facilitate the location and use or reuse of such material. From research undertaken for the Australian Flexible Learning Network, Higgs, Meredith, and Hand (2003, p. 60) suggest that in order to provide access to learning objects, a repository must include a series of functionalities that include searching, quality control, maintaining, gathering from other repositories, and publishing (i.e., providing metadata to other repositories).

Early repository development concentrated on building intrainstitutional models, a "silo" trend that quickly extended into collaborative, international projects designed to allow aggregated collections with multisearching capabilities. The initial intraorganisational repositories were regarded as useful in promoting sharing and reuse within the organisation. At the same time, far-sighted educationalists warned of their limited potential that ran the risk of becoming closed systems (Downes, 2001). Network initiatives were made possible through the application of interoperable metadata that permitted cross-repository searching.

The online repositories or collections of learning objects that support higher education needs is a targeted growth area currently showing almost limitless potential. A quick scan of the repository environment reveals a few well-established players:

- ARIADNE Foundation runs a network of knowledge pool systems and has contributed to the development of several standards (including learning object metadata and the simple query interface) (http://www. ariadne-eu.org/)

- Australian Flexible Learning Framework - The Vocational Education and Training (VET) Learning Object Repository Project (http://lorn.flexiblelearning.net.au/Home. aspx)
- Campus Alberta Repository of Educational Objects (Careo) (http://www.careo.org/)
- Commonwealth of Learning Learning Object Repository (http://www.collor.org/col/)
- EduSource Canada - Canadian network of learning object repositories (http://www. edusource.ca/english/objects_eng.html)
- Gateway to Educational Materials (GEM) Project (http://www.thegateway.org/)
- Joint Information Systems Committee (JISC) provides assistance to a number of educational repositories (http://www.jisc. ac.uk/search.aspx?keywords=repository& filter=s)
- Multimedia Educational Resource for On-line Learning and Teaching (MERLOT) (www.merlot.org)
- TLT Group (www.tltgroup.org/OpenSource/Base.htm)
- XanEdu (www.xanedu.com)

Developments are indicating the growth of distributed systems, networks of interoperable repositories that facilitate the access, sharing, and transfer of learning objects based on compatible standards. Such systems allow for the possibility of connecting a number of individual repositories in such a way that the learning object metadata are contained in a number of connected servers or Web sites. Distributed learning object repositories typically employ a peer-to-peer architecture which permits a variety of repositories to be searched from a single portal.

THE CONCEPT OF LEARNING OBJECTS

The concept of learning objects, which has been the subject of ongoing debate (Busetti, Dettori, Forcheri, Ierardi, 2007; Churchill, 2007; Metros, 2005; Metros & Bennett, 2002; University of Milwaukee, 2007; Wiley, 2000), indicates an element of educational content that will be shareable, dynamic, and reusable. The development and use of such material has the capability to create communities committed to the reduction of costs and the improvement of quality of content presented to learners.

A fundamental issue addressed early in the project was levels of granularity: Was a learning object a single piece of digital material, a combination of materials, and did it include a learning sequence with assessment? A learning object can be as small as a paragraph or as large as a complete online course and come in the form of HTML/text files, simulations, JAVA, Flash, and QuickTime movies. They are of inconsistent size, language, complexity, and format (Nash, 2005, p. 220).

The project determined that the characteristics of a learning object were, primarily, a learning activity with strong internal cohesion and, secondly, evidence of operation as an independent entity with weak coupling (Clayton, 2006). This allowed such resources, once stored in a manner that ensured their sustainability and searchability, to be retrieved, repurposed according to requirements, and resubmitted to the repository. The requirement for prerequisites to be associated with the learning object and the ability to establish relationships between newly-created, granular learning objects and existing information is also regarded as essential by Dahn (2006) if the learning object is to have any value in the learning process. Deployment across multiple settings and inclusive of both teachers and students was an additional characterising factor. In this manner, learning objects were deemed nonstatic, able to be shared freely across communities of practice in both predicted and nonpredicted ways. It was anticipated that benefits of increasing availability of information and lowered access barriers would result from such a participatory and self-regulatory approach to managing information. Critical to the use and reuse of learning objects was the requirement to describe them in a manner that would allow discovery and access within an educational context. Specht and Kravcik (2006) have advocated the need to contextualise data to allow appropriate use for adaptive learning on demand and personalised learning experiences. Context rather than content allows flexible access to learning objects. For the purposes of the OSLOR metadata profile developed, learning objects were defined as a set of digital, specifiable files and file types, available via the Internet, and associated with a unique identifier.

METADATA AND ITS RELATION TO LEARNING OBJECTS

The purpose of metadata in their practical application to learning objects is to facilitate the storage, maintenance, access, and reuse of these digital resources in a manner suited to purpose. A metadata profile for learning resources is a multipart referencing that specifies substructures and data elements. The acknowledgement and potential integration of standards and guidelines is an underlying factor in the consideration of metadata application. Duval, Hodgins, Sutton, and Weibel (2002) have defined an application profile as "an assemblage of metadata elements selected from one or more metadata schemas and combined in a compound schema."

The basic functions of a digital repository are to accept, store, maintain, preserve, and ensure access; in other words, to undertake that the contained resources continue to serve their purpose and to be accessible (Ally, Cleveland-Innes, Boskic, & Larwill, 2006). Additionally, during the process of establishing the open source learning object repository, requirements were addressed to ensure that determined levels of quality would be implemented at critical stages, that accepted standards would guide procedures, and that, where extensibility and interoperability between systems or repositories were likely, such fundamental drivers would be incorporated into the architecture of the repository.

The creation of metadata is a commitment to quality and preservation. The elements chosen for a particular purpose should not be adapted to any other purpose as this decreases potential interoperability. It was acknowledged that different collections have different metadata requirements, and learning objects, by the very lack of agreement over their definition, possess a range of features that could test the chosen schema to their limits.

The library was invited onto the project because of its acknowledged expertise in indexing, classification, and ability to provide ongoing access to categories of resources. Members started with a number of requirements which were seen as necessary for developing a profile for resource discovery. These included the need for the profile to be able to interoperate with similar profiles or standards, to offer improved searchability for users of the repository, to be cost effective, easy to use, extensible, able to accommodate automation of field entry, and devolve as much tagging as possible, and able to draw on the expertise of a number of contributors. It should include both free text input and the use of controlled vocabularies and thesauri.

A wide range of metadata standards and initiatives relating to digital preservation are now in existence and their number is growing steadily. ISO/IEC JTC1 SC32 WG2 (2007) is the multination working group that develops international standards for metadata and related technologies and their Web site contains one of the more comprehensive listings of standards under review, development, and final release. The OS-LOR project expanded this preliminary work into detailed study of the following metadata schemas and profiles: Dublin Core Metadata Element Set Version 1.1 (DC) (Dublin Core metadata initiative, 2007), Dublin Core-Education Application Profile (DC-Ed) (Dublin Core metadata initiative, 2006), IEEE Learning Object Metadata v1.0 (IEEE LOM) (IEEE Learning Technology Standards Committee, 1999), UK Learning Object Metadata Core Draft 0.2 (UK LOM) (Metadata for Education Group, 2004), Education Network Australia Metadata Standard v1.1 (EdNA) (Education Network Australia, 2007), VETADATA v1.01 (Australian Flexible Learning Framework, 2007), CanCore (CanCore Learning Resource Metadata Initiative, 2007), Te Kete Ipurangi (TKI) metadata set (Te Kete Ipurangi, 2007), and SCORM v1.2 (Advanced distributed learning, 2007).

The creation of a metadata application profile suited for purpose from the above mentioned metadata standards or profiles was to allow digital resources destined for the repository to be described, located, and maintained properly. The profile was designed specifically to deal with learning objects, but extensibility was built in to allow for developments to the repository. EPrints is a repository software very suited to the ingress of research outputs, an area of relevance to the Waikato Institute of Technology, and it may also be developed into a full institutional repository at a later stage. The profile, therefore, needed sufficient flexibility to cope with a variety of potential resource submissions without the unwanted scenario of major changes to elements or qualifiers or, worse still, retrospective changes to data already housed on the EPrints server. One of the prerequisites for the library team was to ensure relevancy to the New Zealand education environment. It was anticipated that such a profile would serve the institution's requirements for digital resource submission into the repository. It was also hoped that it might serve as a model for the rest of the Institutes of Technology and Polytechnics (ITP) sector.

DETERMINING ELEMENTS FOR INCLUSION

Metadata standards have been in existence for a number of years and include the machine-readable cataloging (MARC) record, developed by the Library of Congress in the 1960s (The Library of Congress, 2007). For the purposes of the OSLOR project, we discounted MARC and concentrated instead on two more recent standards which have arisen as a result of the exponential growth of, and accessibility to, resources via the Internet. The Dublin Core Metadata Element Set, ISO 15836:2003, was developed in 1995 (ISO TC 46/SC 4 N515, 2003). The scheme comprises a simple set of 15 descriptive data elements intended to be generally applicable to all types of resources. The IEEE LOM standard 1484.12.1, developed in 2002 and comprising around 70 elements, is intended to enable the management, location, and evaluation of learning materials.

The UK LOM Core is one of many application profiles of the IEEE LOM standard, and it narrows down the metadata standard for use in a particular area, that is, UK education. The ability to map across standards has attracted much attention to ensure that interoperability remains at the heart of any endeavours in providing descriptive resource data. An example of the DCMI interoperability is IEEE 1484.12.1 - 2002 Standard for LOM conceptual data model, which includes a mapping from the IEEE LOM to unqualified Dublin Core.

LOM is the standard required for sharable content object reference model (SCORM) standard. SCORM is an evolving standard that packages resources in a repository in such a way that they can be combined and reused in a range of learning management systems. It continues to evolve to meet learning demands. Baker (2006) analyses the significant progress SCORM has made in providing a framework for interoperability of learning content among LMS brands but offers the reservation of its not addressing the issues of creating and using rich learning experiences. For the purposes of the OSLOR project SCORM was identified as suitable to the requirements of the project and employed for this purpose. The application profile created contained the mandatory LOM elements that comprise SCORM.

Mapping between various metadata schemas is important for searching. Various mapping combinations were undertaken to ensure a profile sufficiently robust to accomodate interoperability. It needed to be fit for both immediate, particular purposes and also for any future requirements.

In the end, the metadata profile compiled for the OSLOR included elements from three education-related schemas:

- EdNA metadata standard elements to describe the intended audience
- DC-Ed elements to describe the object
- UK LOM elements to describe educational and technical attributes

EdNA metadata was identified as suitable for inclusion as a consequence of close similarities between the resources developed by the Education Network Australia and those applicable to the New Zealand curriculum. Education Network Australia (**EdNA**) is Australia's leading online resource collection and collaborative network for the education and training community. Its sectors include early childhood, school, vocational education and training, adult, and community and higher education. These were the sectors the OSLOR project had identified as target audiences with the expectation that the functioning repository would be populated with objects relevant to the New Zealand education environment, possibly Australasian. Recommendations were offered which included use of New Zealand standard classification of education (NZSCED), developed by the New Zealand Ministry of Education, also the Australian Schools Catalogue Information Service (SCIS), and, specifically, EdNA online categories, such as, Edna-audience, Edna-curriculum, Edna-sector, and Edna-user level.

Dublin Core-Education application profile (DC-Ed AP) was used as a base for all considerations relating to resource description. The DC-Ed AP defines metadata elements for employment in describing properties of resources related to their use in teaching and learning. It also suggests vocabularies in association with these elements. Three areas of purpose underpin use of DC-Ed: creating a description of an educational resource; repurposing a general resource as an educational resource; and determining the quality of an educational resource description (Dublin Core Metadata Initiative, 2007). The grouping of elements within the OSLOR AP highlighted the strength of DC-Ed within the description and contribution categories; UK LOM accounted for the other categories, with EdNA being incorporated with the contextualisation category.

SUBMISSION RESPONSIBILITY

The application of metadata to learning objects was regarded as an interdisciplinary, cross-functional undertaking. At the heart of its activity lies the requirement, not to describe a digital resource submitted by its creator to the repository, but rather to describe that resource in a manner likely to enhance successful searching by its intended user. This moved the emphasis traditionally found in the learning paradigm and involved a crossing of boundaries between diverse subject disciplines, different instructional levels, and a broader spectrum of specialists associated with learning. It also demanded a limited degree of contextuality being assigned to ingested resources to ensure the potential for repurposing was not unduly constrained.

The library team agreed that a multilayer arrangement of contribution would be most effective in developing a seamless and sustainable infrastructure: collaboration between the three layers of creator (resource creator and submitter),

Table 1. OSLOR application profile categories including metadata element sets

Description Category – An account of the intellectual content of the resource	Instantiation Category – Information identifying one or more instances of the resource	Contribution Category – Information about contributions to the resource	Contextualisation Category – Information concerning the environment in which the resource is intended to be used	Access Category – Conditions of use of the resources	Record Category – Description of the record itself
Identifier Title Description Subject Type Relation Classification. Purpose Relation General. Aggregation Level	Language Format Technical. Format Life Cycle. Version Life Cycle. Status Technical. Size	Creator Publisher Date Approver Contributor Annotation. Entity Annotation. Date	Audience Context. Typical Age Range Learning Resource Type Instructional Method Technical. Duration Educational. Description Annotation. Description	Rights Technical. Location Technical. Other Platform Require-ments	Meta-metadata. Identifier. Catalog Meta-metadata. Identifier. Entry Meta-metadata. Metadata Schema Meta-metadata. Contribute. Role Meta-metadata. Contribute. Entity Meta-metadata. Contribute. Date

instructional design/technical staff (technical expertise), and editorial staff (library cataloguer). An additional contributor at a later stage in the process—an annotator—was included to ensure that after resources had been accessed and used there was the requirement to comment upon their usefulness. The purpose of this was to build up a context around resources in the repository of value to the community using it. This layered approach was designed to ensure that each role built upon the other and that the required elements at each level of input were completed by those with the most detailed knowledge to assist data quality (Table 2).

Research has shown that creators prefer fewer rather than more required fields for inputting, that is, between four to eight; beyond this number they begin to question the benefits of submission (Carr & Harnad, 2005; Greenberg, Pattuelli, Parsia, & Davenport Robertson, 2002). Maintaining the number of required fields at an acceptable level while, at the same time, ensuring quality data are captured at a point of submission proved a fine balancing act.

The creator was asked to provide a description of the resource and its purpose. As mandatory elements, this included title, description, creator, rights, date, relation, audience, purpose, and typical age range. After completing the submission form, the resource and accompanying metadata moved to a "holding" area for further metadata input.

The next contributor — technical — added details such as format, size, location, and other platform requirements. Lastly, the editor (cata-

Table 2. Number of metadata elements to be contributed at each input layer

Elements	Layer 1: Creator	Layer 2: Technical Staff	Layer 3: Editorial Staff	Layer 4: Annotator
Mandatory	10	4	3	
Optional	10	3	1	3

loguer) added identifier (1), catalogue (2), entry, metadata schema, and completed a final check for accuracy and the learning object resource was ready to appear publicly in the repository.

The integration of encoding schemes was recommended for those elements that allowed this structured concept. Both free-text language (DC-ED. Description), entered by the resource creator, and controlled vocabulary schemes (DC-ED. Subject, LOM.Classification.Purpose) entered by both creator and editor, were accommodated within the profile. The reasons behind this decision were the requirement for flexibility and applicability on the one hand, and taxonomic consistency or standardisation of terminology on the other.

The benefits of this common approach are the collaborative use of technology within the learning environment, the pooling of disparate expertise into an identifiable outcome, development of semantic consistency, and the extending of existing workflows and systems into a new architectural environment. Disadvantages include a need to attain a coherent approach and an acknowledgement of interdependence, a required common understanding of processes, potential quality assurance difficulties, including those of intellectual property management, and determination of initial and ongoing cost-effectiveness.

ADVANTAGES OF ADOPTING APPLICATION PROFILES

Clifford Lynch (1997) provides the commonly-accepted definition of an application profile — "customizations of [a] standard to meet the needs of particular communities of implementers with common applications requirements." The crucial element here is the word customisation. Throughout the 1990s, efforts to develop digital repositories and make their contents available for sharing produced disappointing results. This arose from the inflexible use of particular meta-data schemas which had the result of erecting the very barriers that they were intended to overcome. Flexibility across metadata schemas came to be recognised as critical to successful exposure of repository contents.

Heery and Patel (2000) proposed the ground-breaking development of the application profile concept, with their requirement to break down the perceived boundaries of established metadata schemas, and to recognise that implementers both needed and demanded more flexibility to achieve their aims (Hillmann & Phipps, 2007). Their definition remains the standard for all subsequent work in the field: "Application profiles consist of data elements drawn from one or more namespace schemas combined together by implementers and optimised for a particular local application. Application profiles are useful as they allow the implementer to declare how they are using standard schemas" (Heery & Patel, 2000). The ability to "mix and match" elements from one or more different element sets, while ensuring that any new elements introduced required their own namespace schema, provided the flexibility to tailor descriptive requirements for particular communities.

The librarians working on the learning object repository were allocated the responsibility of determining specific, local requirements and examining existing schemas for suitability. They then constructed an application profile fit for purpose that would also enable the sharing of resources submitted to the repository.

CONCLUSION

The purpose of the OSLOR project was to design and implement a learning object repository using the EPrints repository software application that would fulfil the purpose of efficient, flexible, and sustainable management of digital learning resources within a multilingual environment. Library contribution was sought at the outset of the project and resulted in the creation of a metadata application profile based upon recognised standards and suited for the purpose of managing shared, reusable educational resources.

REFERENCES

Advanced distributed learning. (2007). *SCORM® version 1.2*. Retrieved November 15, 2007, from http://www.adlnet.gov/scorm/history/Scorm12/index.aspx

Ally, M., Clevelend-Innes, M., Boskic, N., & Larwill, S. (2006). Learners' use of learning objects. *Journal of Distance Education, 21*(2), 44-57. Retrieved November 16, 2007, from Academic Research Library database (Document ID: 1255253871).

Australian flexible learning framework. (2007). *Metadata (for Vetadata profile and guides)*. Retrieved November 15, 2007, from http://e-standards.flexiblelearning.net.au/vetadata/index.htm

Baker, K. D. (2006). Learning objects and process interoperability. *International Journal on ELearning, 5*(1), 167-172. Retrieved November 16, 2007, from Academic Research Library database (Document ID: 986673161).

Busetti, E., Dettori, G., Forcheri, P., & Ierardi, M. G. (2007). A pedagogical approach to the design of learning objects for complex domains. *International Journal of Distance Education Technologies, 5*(2), 1-10, 13-17. Retrieved November 16, 2007, from ABI/Inform Global database (Document ID: 1205735741).

CANARIE, & Industry Canada. (2002). *A report on learning object repositories: Review and recommendations for a Pan-Canadian approach to repository implementation in Canada*. Ottawa: Author. Retrieved November 19, 2007, from http://www.canarie.ca/funding/elearning/lor.pdf

CanCore Learning Resource Metadata Initiative. (2007). *CanCore guidelines for the "access for all" digital resource description metadata elements*. Retrieved November 15, 2007, from http://www.cancore.ca/guidelines/drd/

Carr, L., & Harnad, S. (2005). *Keystroke economy: A study of the time and effort involved in self-archiving*. Retrieved March 14, 2006, from http://eprints.ecs.soton.ac.uk/10688/01/KeystrokeCosting-publicdraft1.pdf

Churchill, D. (2007). Towards a useful classification of learning objects. *Educational Technology, Research and Development, 55*(5), 479-497. Retrieved November 16, 2007, from Academic Library database (Document ID: 1361006251).

Clayton, J. F. (2006). Learning objects: Seeking simple solutions. In J. Clayton & B. Gower (Eds.), *Final report: E-learning collaborative development find: Open source learning object repository* (pp. 121-126). Hamilton: Tertiary Education Commission.

Dahn, I. (2006). A metadata profile to establish the context of small learning objects: The slicing book approach. *International Journal on ELearning, 5*(1), 59-66. Retrieved November 16, 2007, from Academic Research library database (Document ID: 986673111).

Downes, S. (2001). Learning objects: Resources for distance education worldwide. *The International Review of Research in Open and Distance Learning, 2*(1). Retrieved November 21, 2007, from http://www.irrodl.org/index.php/irrodl/article/view/32/378

Dublin core metadata initiative. (2007a). *Dublin core education application profile (working draft of v0.4)*. Retrieved November 18, 2007, from http://docs.google.com/View?docid=dn8z3gs_38cgwkvv

Dublin core metadata initiative. (2007b). *Dublin core metadata element set, version 1.1*. Retrieved

November 15, 2007, from http://dublincore.org/documents/dces/

Dublin core metadata initiative. Education working group. (2006). *Education application profile.* Retrieved November 15, 2007, from http://projects.ischool.washington.edu/sasutton/dcmi/DC-EdAP-7-18-06.html

Duval, E., Hodgins, W., Sutton, S. A., & Weibel, S. L. (2002). Metadata principles and practicalities. *D-Lib Magazine, 8*(4). Retrieved November 21, 2007, from http://www.dlib.org/dlib/april02/weibel/04weibel.html

Education network Australia. (2007). *EdNA metadata standard v1.1.* Retrieved November 15, 2007, from http://www.edna.edu.au/edna/go/resources/metadata/edna_metadata_profile

Eprints. (2007). *EPrints for digital repositories.* Retrieved November 15, 2007, from http://www.eprints.org/

Greenberg, J., Pattuelli, C., Parsia, B., & Davenport Robertson, W. (2002). Author-generated Dublin Core metadata for web resources: A baseline study in an organization. *Journal of Digital Information, 2*(2), Article 78. Retrieved March 28, 2006, from http://jodi.ecs.soton.ac.uk/Articles/v02/i02/Greenberg/

Heery, R., & Patel, M. (2000). Application profiles: Mixing and matching metadata schemas. *Ariadne, 25.* Retrieved November 21, 2007, from http://www.ariadne.ac.uk/issue25/app-profiles/

Higgs, P. E., Meredith, S., & Hand, T. (2003). Technology for sharing: Researching learning objects and digital rights management. Final report. *Flexible learning leader 2002 report.* Retrieved November 23, 2007, from http://leaders.flexiblelearning.net.au/fl_leaders/fl02/finalreport/final_hand_higgs_meredith.pdf

Hillmann, D. I., & Phipps, J. (2007). Application profiles: Exposing and enforcing metadata quality. In *Proceedings of the International Conference on Dublin Core and Metadata Applications 2007.* Retrieved November 24, 2007, from http://www.dcmipubs.org/ojs/index.php/pubs/article/viewFile/41/20

IEEE Learning Technology Standards Committee. (1999). IEEE 1484 learning objects metadata (IEEE LOM) mappings to Dublin Core. *Learning object metadata: Draft document v3.6.* Retrieved November 15, 2007, from http://www.ischool.washington.edu/sasutton/IEEE1484.html

International Organization for Standardization/International Electrotechnical Commission Joint Technical Committee. (2007). *Metadata standards.* Retrieved November 15, 2007, from http://metadata-stds.org/

ISO TC 46/SC 4 N515. (2003). *Information and documentation – the Dublin Core metadata element set.* Retrieved November 18, 2007, from http://www.niso.org/international/SC4/n515.pdf

Library of Congress. (2007). *MARC standards.* Retrieved November 18, 2007, from http://www.loc.gov/marc/

Lynch, C. A. (1997, April). The Z39.50 information retrieval standard. Part I: A strategic view of its past, present and future. *D-Lib Magazine.* Retrieved November 21, 2007, from http://www.dlib.org/dlib/april97/04lynch.html

Metadata for education group. (2004). *UK learning object metadata core (draft 0.2).* Retrieved November 15, 2007, from http://www.cetis.ac.uk/profiles/uklomcore/uklomcore_v0p2_may04.doc

Metros, S. E. (2005). Learning objects: A rose by any other name... *EDUCAUSE Review, 40*(4), 12-13. Retrieved November 15, 2007, from http://www.educause.edu/apps/er/erm05/erm05410.asp?bhcp=1

Metros, S. E., & Bennett, K. (2002). Learning objects in higher education. *EDUCAUSE Research Bulletin, 2002*(19), 1-10. Retrieved November 15, 2007, from http://www.educause.edu/ir/library/pdf/ERB0219.pdf

Moodle. (2007). *Moodle: A free, open source course management system for online learning.* Retrieved November 15, 2007, from http://moodle. org/

Nash, S. S. (2005). Learning objects, learning object repositories and learning theory: Preliminary best practices for online courses. *Interdisciplinary Journal of Knowledge and Learning Objects, 2005*(1), 217-228. Retrieved November 22, 2007, from http://ijklo.org/Volume1/v1p217-228Nash.pdf

New Zealand. Ministry of Education. Te Kete Ipurangi. (2007). *The metadata record.* Retrieved November 15, 2007, from http://www.tki.org. nz/e/tki/help/metadata.php

Specht, M., & Kravcik, M. (2006). Authoring of learning objects in context. *International Journal of ELearning, 5*(1), 25-33. Retrieved November 16, 2007, from Academic Research Library database (Document ID: 986665391).

University of Milwaukee, Center for International Education. (2007). *What are learning objects?* Retrieved November 15, 2007, from http://www. uwm.edu/Dept/CIE/AOP/LO_what.html

Wiley, D. A. (2000). Connecting learning objects to instructional design theory: A definition, a metaphor, and a taxonomy. *The instructional use of learning objects (section 1).* Retrieved November 15, 2007, from http://reusability.org/ read/chapters/wiley.doc

KEY TERMS

Application Profile: Metadata elements drawn from one or more existing namespaces, combined together and optimised for a particular application or purpose.

Learning Objects: Self-contained, reusable small units of learning that can be aggregated and tagged with metadata.

Learning Object Repository: A site intended to develop, establish, maintain, and refine integrated sets of reusable learning objects to support and sustain educational networks.

Metadata: Information about data or a data source. It is associated with objects or systems for the purposes of description, administration, legal requirements, technical functionality, usage, and preservation. Metadata terms include elements, element refinements, encoding schemes, and vocabulary terms.

Namespace Schema: A schema in which namespaces are declared using a family of reserved attributes, for example, an extensible markup language (XML) namespace is a collection of names, identified by a URI reference, which are used in XML documents as element types and attribute names. The namespace declaration is considered to apply to the element where it is specified and to all elements within the content of that element, unless overridden by another namespace declaration.

Open Source: Source code is available to the general public for use and/or modification from its original design free of charge.

XML Namespace: A simple method for qualifying element and attribute names used in XML documents by associating them with a collection of names identified by URI references.

Chapter IV
Extensible Digital Library Service Platform

Jian-hua Yeh
Aletheia University, Taiwan

Shun-hong Sie
National Taiwan Normal University, Taiwan

Chao-chen Chen
National Taiwan Normal University, Taiwan

ABSTRACT

In this chapter, we describe X-system, a general digital library platform which is capable of handling large-scale digital contents with flexible, extensible management features. The development of X-system achieves several important goals of modern digital library systems, including a fully functional system, neutral and portable architecture, stackable modules, data exchange, and universal access. The model and architecture are discussed in this chapter. Moreover, several extension case studies of X-system are demonstrated to show the extensibility of our system. In addition, to act as a basic digital archive/library system, the X-system has been adopted as various different usages, including e-learning platform, knowledge management platform, and library circulation system.

INTRODUCTION

Advances in computer network and storage technologies have inspired the design of digital libraries in recent years. The emergence of digital libraries has introduced a number of important issues (Chen, Chen, Chen, & Hsiang, 2002; Chen, & Chen, 2001; Dempsey & Heery, 1997). One issue that has not attracted much attention but is essential to digital library development is the flexible design of digital library systems. After the construction of a digital library, it is natural for the digital library to push the content circulation and application as much as possible in order to show its maximum effect. Based on this point of view, it is important to design a suitable architecture to support flexible contents management and fast service development. For the flexible contents management aspect, it is known that if a closed data storage system is adopted, the circulation of digital library contents decreases. So the data model and storage with high portability is necessary for easy data access and manipulation. For the fast service development aspect, it is more competitive for a system architecture with stackable service features to develop digital library services according to different information needs. If a digital library system meets the requirements of both flexible contents management and fast service development, it is more likely to create many kinds of information service based on it. The evolving trend of digital library technologies contains several issues: (1) from closed system to open system; (2) from table-based schema to extensible markup language (XML)-based data model; (3) from modular or object-oriented design to component-based design; and (4) from single purpose (digital archive) only to multipurpose scenario. In this chapter, we introduce X-system (Yeh & Chen, 2003), a general digital library platform which is capable of handling large-scale digital contents with flexible, extensible management features.

DESIGN ISSUES OF DIGIAL LIBRARY SYSTEMS

As mentioned earlier, the most important features of a modern digital library system are flexibility and generality. Since 2003, the year of X-system's announcement, several extensions and applications have been developed and deployed. The aim of our research is to create a powerful digital library system which meets the following important design issues:

1. **Fully functional digital library system:** The design of X-system aims at handling multiple metadata formats which meet the needs of various digital content applications. For example, digital archive systems, knowledge management systems, and e-learning systems all require various kinds of metadata coexisting in a repository system. So the ability of handling various metadata formats becomes a fundamental requirement of digital library systems. This is also one of the basic features of function design in X-system.

2. **Platform neutral, fully portable system architecture:** The development of X-system is totally based on platform-independent technologies, including Java programming language, Java application servers, XML data presentation, XSL/XPath (Clark & DeRose, 1999) data transformation, and so on. Also we use a Java-based, native XML database server as the metadata storage, which means the whole system is fully portable. Currently the X-system has many deployment experiences, including Windows-based systems, Linux-based systems, and Solaris-based systems. Any platform which supports Java virtual machine will run our system.

3. **Stackable information service modules:** In addition to the modular and object-oriented design concepts, the X-system introduces the layered function design concept, which makes system services stackable. Any newly extended service (we call them "upper-layer services") may use basic services ("lower-layer services") provided by the base system, and the extended services will also be used by future extended services. The layered architecture makes X-system more extensible than many current digital library systems, and there will be several extension

case studies of X-system demonstrated in the latter section.

4. **Portable data exchange:** The XML data flow between service modules is a basic design of the X-system. In the layered architecture of X-System, each kind of data flows between system services is XML-encapsulated, and the data rendering to end users is also XML-based, with XSL transformation as the way of HTML rendering. This feature makes data exchange very easy to be customized to meet the user needs. Also the extension of any X-System service is easy since the XML-based data semantics is all a service programmer should know.

5. **Universal data access:** X-system is a Web-based digital library system, so the data accessibility is a major concern of the system design. We introduce the handle system, which behaves similar to CNRI handle system (Sun, 1998), as the universal way of resource access. Any resource registered in X-system will be able to be accessible globally through the build-in handle system. Since the handle system is able to register original and alternative resources, the accessibility of multiple versions of resource instances is thus increased in X-system.

The above issues are core design principles of X-system. Most of the XML-based digital libraries today are either using relational database solutions (such as Oracle, DB2, or SQL server) with XML middleware or just connect native XML storage as the second or third tier (VUDL, MC). These digital library systems with native XML database as their backend storage is only the first step of modern XML-based service design; only XML data exchange is focused, but not fast system service development. In the MyCoRe project (MyCoRe), a three-tier architecture is designed and made it easy to customize the middle tier services, but the middle tier is still not in a stackable style. That is, a newly designed service in the middle tier will follow the traditional modular- or object-oriented design. This design style is still not as fast as X-system in new service development since function call or class inheritance should be taken care of during the programming phase. In X-system, the native XML storage acts as backend storage and the XML data exchange is the standard way for passing data between system services in the middle-tier. Besides, we found that it is hard to find a digital library system with stackable services currently. In the next section, the data model and system architecture of X-system are depicted.

THE X-SYSTEM: DATA MODEL AND SERVICE ARCHITECTURE

The Data Model

The data model designed in X-system defines major data entities of the system, including document schema, metadata documents, user domains (or called "organizations"), user groups (or called "projects"), document collections, users, and universal identifiers (or called "handles"). These data entities are treated as basic data units in the whole system, as described below:

1. **Metadata documents:** The metadata documents stored in X-system are created according to the specification of document schema. In our system, all the metadata documents and other digital objects are regarded as important intellectual properties, so the metadata structure defined in X-system consists of several aspects of attributes, including subject description, rights description, and administrative information:

   a. **Subject description:** The subject description in X-system is called subject or object metadata. The subject metadata contains semantic interpretation of the target object, such as background information, subject keywords, creator information, and so forth. Any attribute that is a subjective explanation can be treated as subject metadata. The object metadata represents format description of digital objects, such as file format, digital scale, color information, and so forth. The subject description provides most of the inner features of the target entities.

b. **Rights description:** The rights description in X-system is called digital rights metadata. The digital rights metadata describes the rights management information of the target object. Digital rights management (DRM) is getting more and more attention in recent years, and embedding rights management information in media files is also an emerging trend of many digital technologies, such as computer media player, cell phones software, and so forth. In X-system, it is allowed to use any custom designed rights management metadata format as rights description, but use of international standard is recommended

(e.g., XrML, ODRL, or other standards). The digital rights metadata in X-system is not only able to provide digital rights information of target object, but also capable of interchanging with other systems for interoperability.

c. Administrative information: The administrative information in X-system is called administrative metadata. The administrative metadata, like its name, is designed to record information for administration. This part of metadata aims at representing administrative information of target objects such as data maintenance history, record creation time, language of description, and other related remarks.

In Figure 1, three aspects of metadata form a complete metadata document. The X-system supports a definition of each aspect by assigning different XML schema, so a single metadata document will consist of three XML substructures. Since the metadata document is a big XML structure, it is easy to manage these documents in the backend storage of X-system, which is a native XML database in our design.

Figure 1. The structure of metadata documents in X-system, (a) a single document (b) hierarchical relationship of documents is supported

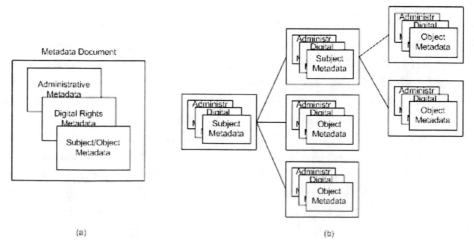

2. **Document schema:** As mentioned earlier, all metadata documents stored in X-system is XML-based with user-defined document formats. These formats are called document schema which are different from XML schema since the metadata document that exists in X-system consists of three major parts (i.e., subject/object metadata, digital rights metadata, and administrative metadata), so the document schema here is a combination of three XML schema but not a single one. However, the settings of each part are followed by the standard W3C specification. Other X-system specific configurations are recorded outside the document schema, such as index assignment, presentation setting, access point (for query action) management, and so forth.

3. **User domains, user group, and individual users:** The X-system is originally designed for maintenance across multiple user domains and groups. With this prerequisite, the system must support different organizations to operate their digital content separately and will not interfere with each other. Currently, the X-system organizes domains ("organizations"), groups ("projects"), and individual users ("users") in a hierarchical manner, as depicted in Figure 2. Please note that a user is able to join one or more different projects in X-system since this relationship is quite natural in the real-world scenario.

4. Document collections: The document collection design in X-system is just like the shopping cart in an online store. Each collection belongs to a single user which is able to collect multiple metadata documents at a time. Figure 3 shows the relationship between collection and metadata documents in the X-system. A user-specific document collection shows the interests of a user on the contents of the system. Any user is able to use the "add to my collection" function to group contents, which makes a customized

Figure 2. Hierarchical relationships of user domains (organization), user groups (projects), and individual users

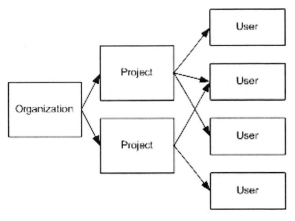

Figure 3. Document collection structure

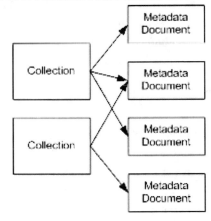

category (other than system category) on user's interests.

5. **Universal identifiers:** The digital library contents are mostly archive metadata and digital materials (most of the digital materials are in binary form). Since there will be a large amount of metadata and digital files, it is important to develop an appropriate identification scheme which guarantees the local and global uniqueness of digital contents. In X-system, each of the digital contents is made up to be identifiable by a system-wide identifier called "handle."

Figure 4. The service architecture of X-system

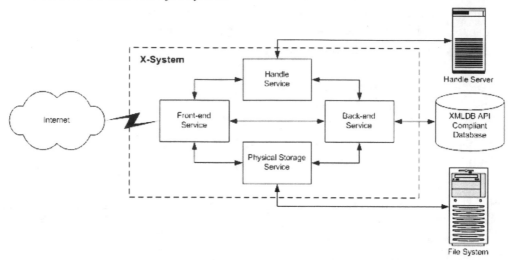

A handle is a representative of one or more copies of identical digital contents, including metadata documents and digital objects. In X-system, any service related to digital content uses handle as identification.

Service Architecture

The service architecture of the X-system is shown in Figure 4.

In Figure 4, the service architecture of X-system contains front-end service manager, backend service manager, physical storage service manager, and handle service manager. These services provide main functions of X-system, as discussed below:

1. **Front-end service manager:** The front-end service manager acts as a single service entry for all add-on modules to access X-system functions; the front-end service manager is also called a front-end proxy. The design of the front-end proxy is to provide a single, integrated service interface for other modules or parties; it thus increases the extensibility, scalability, and availability of the X-system. The module structure of front-end proxy consists of several core levels, which clas-

sifies the service level and functionality. The core levels also create the modular design rules: The higher core level functions ("upper-layer services") must be formed by the lower core level functions ("lower-layer services"); if a function cannot be formed from the lower level functions, then it should stay in the lower level, or it should be the most generic function. Currently, the front-end proxy in X-system contains two core levels called core level 0 and core level 1 functions, as shown in Figure 5.

2. **Backend service manager:** The backend service manager is the communication gateway of front-end service manager and underlying database systems. The core level functions in the front-end service manager

Figure 5. Core level functions of X-system

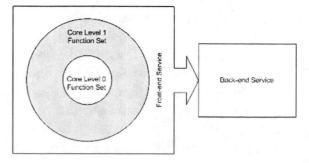

have corresponding service functions in backend service manager. The functions in the front-end service manager only perform logical data manipulations, which are called object level manipulations. But the service functions in backend service manager will interact with database system directly. This version of backend service manager in X-system communicates with native XML databases, which is compatible with XML: DB application programming interface (API) 1.0 (Staken, 2001). There are two reasons of this design: open standard compatibility and native XML processing. The XML DB API supports various XML processing standards, such as XPath (Clark & DeRose, 1999), XQL/XQuery (Boag et al., 2003), XUpdate (IMS, 2003), which are all W3C standards.

3. **Physical storage service manager:** Unlike the backend service manager, which focuses on metadata management, the physical storage service manager provides functions for physical digital material management. In X-system, the physical storage is organized by a set of mount points in file systems, that is, the management of physical digital materials is file-based. The advantage of this design is simplicity and flexibility. The digital content imported into X-system will be no longer needed to change the physical form they stored, and the mount point can be changed easily when necessary. Another advantage of this design is that it is easy to integrate other applications such as video-on-demand server for streaming media. Currently the physical digital material is saved by classifying the multipurpose Internet mail extensions (MIME) (Freed, 1996) type.

4. **Handle service manager:** As described in the data model section, there is an identification scheme in the X-system, which makes digital contents uniquely identifiable. In this system, we introduce a handle ser-

vice manager to support digital content identification which covered both metadata documents and physical digital objects. The handle service manager operates similar to the CNRI handle system (Sun, 1998), which is able to translate a unique identifier (handle) into one or more copies of digital contents. For the handle service manager, we are planning to collaborate with the CNRI handle system in the future version of the system.

The operations of the X-system can be categorized into three major parts: basic configuration, metadata operation, and digital object maintenance. Most of the basic configuration operations can be accessed by system administrator only; these functions are related to user/group/domain management, schema setting. The metadata and digital object operations can be accessed by staff with data maintenance privilege; theses functions are related to metadata editing, metadata upload and download, digital objects upload and download, and auxiliary information maintenance (such as authority files and enumeration setting). Any user without any privilege will be granted to browse and search contents only. Figure 6 shows some of the operation screenshots in X-system, including basic configuration: 6(a) schema setting; 6(b) metadata editing; 6(c) archive content presentation; and 6(d) both metadata and image file are displayed.

EXTENSIONS AND APPLICATIONS

X-Learning: E-learning Content Management System

Nowadays, most electronic learning systems do not integrate with digital archive systems. Therefore, an institution usually has to hold one digital archive contents management system and one electronic learning contents management system

Figure 6. X-system in operation: (a) user group setup page (b) schema setup page (c) metadata editing page (d) presentation page

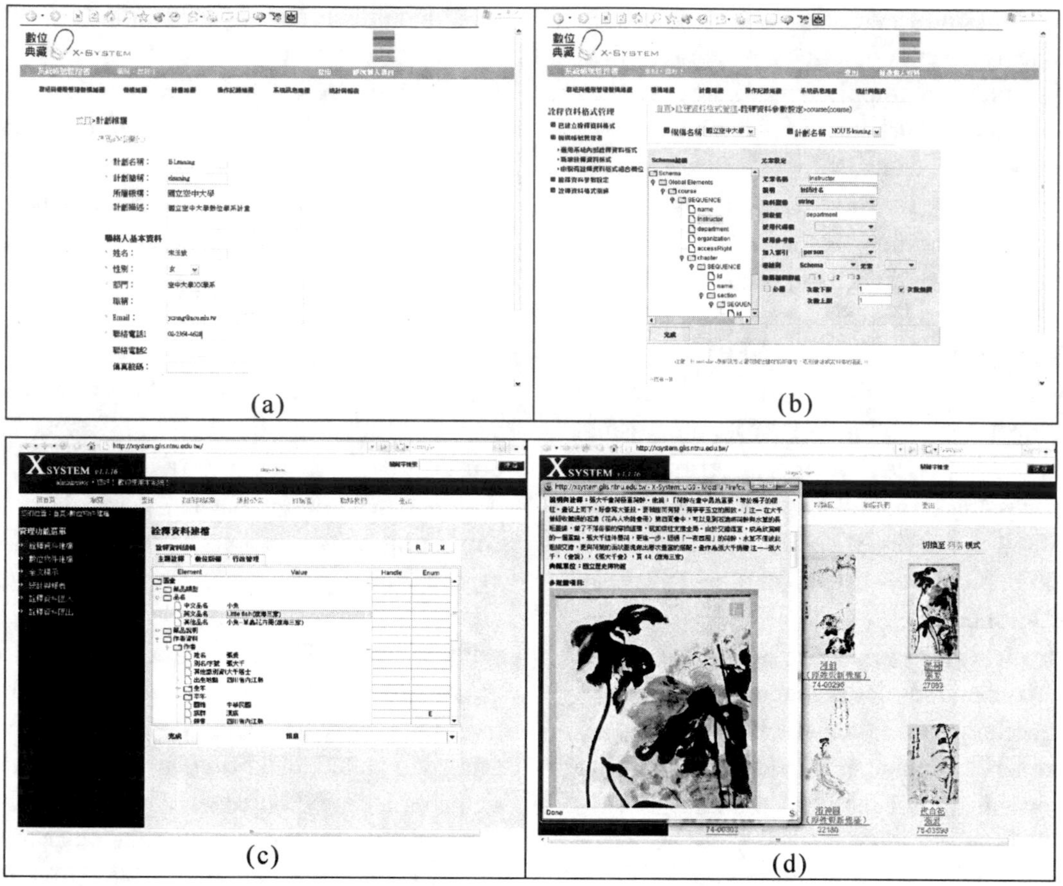

(a)

(b)

(c)

(d)

independently. Therefore, teachers or learners are not able to use the digital archive contents in electronic learning system seamlessly. According to the concept of collaborative online learning and information services (COLIS) project, planned by Department of Education, Science and Training, learning functions should be integrated to digital library system. The COLIS system modules include: learning content management, content management, learning management, library e-services/e-reserve/e-journal, digital rights management, directory services, and registries (McLean, 2001). We thought to create a platform which can convert the metadata of digital archive contents into learning object metadata (LOM), and an authoring tool that can aggregate the assets to courses by teacher is very important after a large number of digital contents was produced by digital projects. This is the key motivation for us to develop the X-learning platform. The X-learning platform is capable of integrating the digital archive contents and e-learning objects.

Figure 7 shows that there are two major set of functions of X-learning: metadata processing service module and content aggregation support. The major function of X-learning (Chen, Yeh, & Sie, 2006) is to provide support for all e-learning related services (Macromedia, 2001; MASIE, 2002; McLean, 2001, 2002), including course and material management, course presentation, and so on. For the transformation from digital archive content to e-learning content, the X-learning provides necessary functions, including schema mapping rule setup, sharable content object reference model (SCORM)-compatible (ADL, 2001; IMS, 2001, 2003) content packaging service, IEEE LOM (IEEE, 2002) transformation, and so on. X-learning is designed to act as a SCORM-compatible learning content management system (LCMS), which is capable of packaging and previewing e-learning packages. The packaging and previewing of e-learning packages are supported in content aggregation authoring services of X-learning. Figure 8 shows a schema mapping configuration page for content metadata

transformation in X-learning. The right part of Figure 8 also shows a content packaging interface for e-learning content aggregation.

X-Ontology: Government Ontology Management System

The number of Web sites of the Taiwan government has grown fast in recent years, which has made Taiwan a popular e-government country. Due to the quantity and the diversity involved in e-government presentations and operations, traditional approaches to Web sites informa-

Figure 7. The service architecture of X-learning over X-system

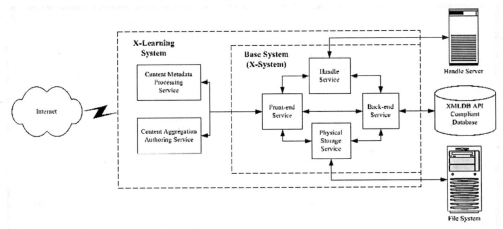

Figure 8. The screenshots of X-learning (left part: schema mapping rule setup; right part: content packaging/manifestation utility)

tion management have been found to be rather inefficient in time and cost. Consequently, the necessity naturally arises regarding the trend to establish government knowledge management system, so as to speed up information lookups, sharing, and linkups. Moreover, a knowledge management system would in turn enhance e-government effectiveness as it helps to store and transmit information, be it explicit or implicit in nature. The first thing of knowledge management system is building up the government ontology and thesaurus. Upon the completion of the ontology and thesaurus needed, semantic searching can begin to function properly, that in turn would kick into place mechanisms required for effective information management.

Figure 9 shows that there are two major set of functions of X-ontology: maintenance service module and ontology presentation support. The major component in X-ontology (Chen, Yeh, & Sie, 2005) is the ontology hierarchy maintenance service. The X-ontology provides a tree-based hierarchy maintenance interface for user to manipulate a concept hierarchy at a time. In addition, associations between hierarchies (ontologies) can also be maintained in this interface. Figure 5 shows the tree-based hierarchy maintenance applet. The upper-right part of the applet shows

the basic information form of the selected concept along with associations with other concepts (intrahierarchy or interhierarchy is possible). The lower-right part of the applet maintains the additional information, which comes from the thesaurus existed in the system.

The ontology presentation service in X-Ontology is quite straight-forward, that is, the information contained in the concept is presented. Figure 10 shows a tree-based Web page for ontology presentation in X-ontology. The user can interactively traverse the hierarchy, check the thesaurus information, and jump to other concept through the association created by ontology maintenance interface.

X-Library: Library Automation System

As the number of digital library system grows, it is more important for a traditional library automation system to be able to handle pure digital contents. The X-library system evolved from X-system to define a library automation system over the base digital archive system. Besides the migration of a library automation system on X-system, it is possible to extend the linking possibilities between digital contents and physical library materials in

Figure 9. The service architecture of X-ontology over X-system

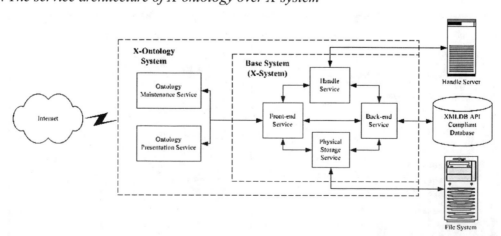

Figure 10. The screenshots of X-ontology (left part: ontology editing tool; right part: ontology navigation/presentation)

order to provide more consolidated information to library users.

Figure 11 shows that there are two major set of functions of X-library: reader service module and cataloguing/circulation support. The X-library provides users with a simple interface to look up bibliographic records, reserve books, organize personal favorites using a shopping cart function, and so on.

The library cataloguing and circulation process supported by X-library includes various features based on the underlying X-system. Except for the bibliographic records maintenance supported by the base system, X-library has developed library-specific functions that are comparative to a traditional library automation system. In reader service module, a user of X-library is not only able to browse and search library catalogue but also able to make reservations on books interested. Another service module of X-library operated by library staff contains cataloguing and circulation functions; these functions are similar to a traditional library automation system. Figure 12 shows the operation screenshots of the X-library system.

Figure 11. The service architecture of X-library over X-system

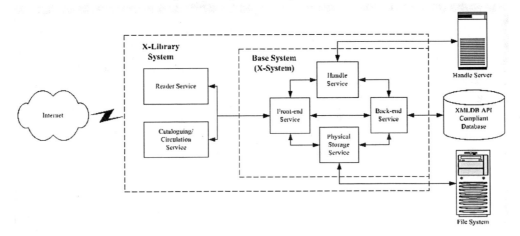

Figure 12. The screenshots of X-library (left part: reservation management; right part: bibliographic/MARC records maintenance)

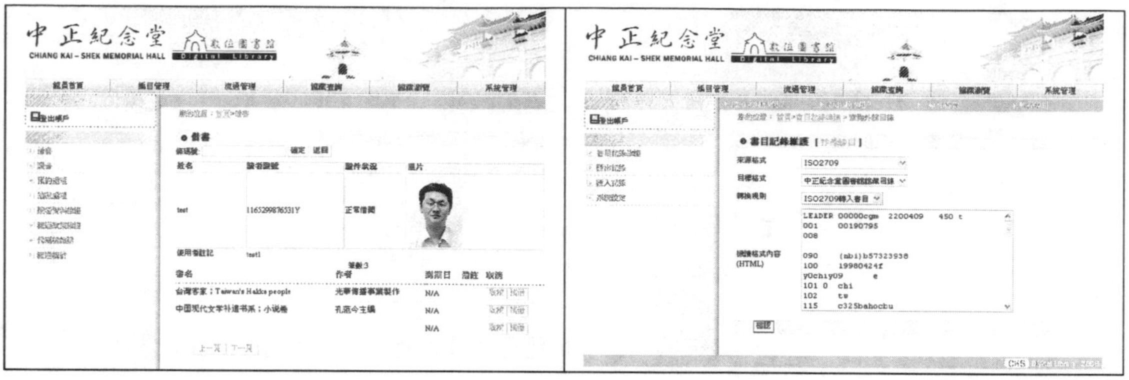

CONCLUSION

The Semantic Web environment development, which heavily focused on XML-related technologies and standards (e.g., XML, RDF, Web ontology language [OWL], etc.), has grown fast in recent years. Since the XML-based digital library systems are close to these standards, it is natural that these systems have to be compatible with the Semantic Web environment in the future to maximize its effectiveness. Some of the possible developments include Web services support, ontology reasoning/knowledge discovery support, personal agent support, and knowledge interchange support.

More extensions of X-system are still under development and the application domains of X-system are still increasing. The next steps of our system aim at integrating popular access protocols such as OAI (Carl & Herbert, 2001), Z39.50 (Lynch, 1991), DOI (IDF, 2002), and so forth. Although Z39.50 protocol has been integrated in the X-library system, we are planning to implement it as an access protocol support by the base X-system. Some ongoing extensions of X-system include media asset management (MAM), e-publishing, and virtual reality (VR) presentation integration. We are looking forward to the integration of multidiscipline domains and to make X-system a more general and useful digital library system.

REFERENCES

ADL. (2001). *Sharable content object reference model (SCORM) version 1.2.*

Boag, S. et al (2003). *XQuery 1.0: An XML query language (working draft).* Retrieved August 12, 2008, from http://www.w3.org/TR/2003/WD-xquery-20030822/

Carl, L., & Herbert, V. S. (2001). The open archives initiative: Building a low-barrier interoperability framework. In *Proceedings of the 1st ACM/IEEE-CS Joint Conference on Digital Libraries*, Virginia.

Chen, C. C, Chen, H. H., & Chen, K. H. (2001). The design of metadata interchange for Chinese information and implementation of metadata management system. *Bulletin of the American Society for Information Science and Technology, 27*(5), 21-27.

Chen, C. C., Chen, H. H., Chen, K. H., & Hsiang, J. (2002). The design of metadata for the digital museum initiative in Taiwan. *Online Information Review, 26*(5), 295-306.

Chen, C. C., Yeh, J. H., & Sie, S. H. (2005). Government ontology and thesaurus construction: A Taiwan experience. In *Proceedings of the 8th International Conference of Asian Digital Libraries (ICADL2005)*, Bankok, Tailand.

Chen, C. C., Yeh, J. H., & Sie, S. H. (2006). A research project to convert traditional Chinese calligraphic paintings to SCORM-compatible e-learning materials. In *Proceedings of the 9th International Conference of Asian Digital Libraries (ICADL2006)*, Kyoto, Japan.

Clark, J., & DeRose, S. (1999). *XPath: XML path language (Version 1.0)*. Retrieved August 12, 2008, from http://www.w3.org/TR/1999/REC-xpath-19991116

Dempsey, L., & Heery, R. (1997). Metadata: An overview of current resource description practice. *Peer review draft of deliverable for Work Package 3 of Telematics for research project DESIRE*. Retrieved August 12, 2008, from http://www.ukoln.ac.uk/metadata/DESIRE/overview/

Freed, N. (1996). RFC 2046, MIME part two: Media types. *IETF*. Retrieved August 12, 2008, from http://www.ietf.org/rfc/rfc2046.txt

IEEE. (2002). Draft standard for learning object metadata. *IEEE 1484.12.1-2002*. Retrieved August 12, 2008, from http://ltsc.ieee.org/doc/wg12/LOM_1484_12_1_v1_Final_Draft.pdf

IMS Global Learning Consortium, Inc. (2001). *IMS digital repositories white paper version 1.6*. Retrieved August 12, 2008, from http://www.imsproject.org/imsdr_whitepaper_v1p6.pdf

IMS Global Learning Consortium, Inc. (2003). *IMS digital repositories interoperability: Core functions information model version 1.0 final specification*. Retrieved August 12, 2008, from http://www.imsglobal.org/digitalrepositories/index.cfm

The International DOI Foundation (IDF). (2002). *DOI introductory overview*. Retrieved August 12, 2008, from http://www.doi.org/overview/sys_overview_021601.html

Laux, A., & Martin, L. (2000). *XUpdate - XML update language, XML:DB initiative*. Retrieved August 12, 2008, from http://www.xmldb.org/xupdate/xupdate-wd.html

Lynch, C. A. (1991). The Z39.50 information retrieval protocol: An overview and status report. *ACM SIGCOMM Computer Communication Review, 21*(1), 58-70.

Macromedia, Inc. (2001). *Getting started with eLearning standards*. Retrieved August 12, 2008, form http://download.macromedia.com/pub/solutions/downloads /elearning/standards.pdf

The MASIE Center e-Learning Consortium. (2002). *Making sense of learning specifications & standards: A decision maker's guide to their adoption*. Retrieved August 12, 2008, from http://www.masie.com/standards/S3_Guide.pdf

McLean, N. (2001). *Collaborative online learning and information services (COLIS) consortium*. Retrieved August 12, 2008, from http://www.colis.mq.edu. au/goals/synopsis.htm

McLean, N. (2002). *Libraries and e-learning: Organizational and technical interoperability*. Retrieved August 12, 2008, from http://www.colis.mq.edu.au/ news_archives/demo/docs/lib_e_learning.pdf

MuseiCapitolini.Net (MC). Retrieved August 12, 2008, from http://museicapitolini.net/hyperrecord/index.xml

MyCoRe open source project (MyCoRe). Retrieved August 12, 2008, from http://www.mycore.de/

Staken, K. (2001). *XMLDB: Application programming interface for XML databases, XML: DB initiative*. Retrieved August 12, 2008, from http://www.xmldb.org/xapi /xapi-draft.html

Sun, S. (1998). Internationalization of the handle system: A persistent global name service. In

Proceeding of the 12th International Unicode Conference. Retrieved August 12, 2008, from http://www.cnri.reston.va.us/unicode-paper.ps

Villanova University Digital Library (VUDL). Retrieved August 12, 2008, from http://digital.library.villanova.edu/

Yeh, J. H., & Chen, C. C. (2003). *The x-system: Design and implementation of a digital archive system* (Tech. Rep.) Retrieved August 12, 2008, from http://mars.csie.ntu.edu.tw/~jhyeh/xsys.pdf

KEY TERMS

Handle System: General purpose distributed information system that provides efficient, extensible, and secure identifier and resolution services for use on networks such as the Internet.

Ontology: A specification of a conceptualization. Ontology can be said to study conceptions of reality.

XML:DB API: A standard application programming interface (API) for native XML databases.

XPath: A W3C standard language for finding information in an XML document. XPath is used to navigate through elements and attributes in an XML document.

XQuery: Powerful and convenient language designed for processing and querying XML data.

XSL: A language for expressing style sheets which describes how to display an XML document of a given type.

XUpdate: XML update language, a project under development by XML:DB for definition of a language for updating information in an XML document.

Chapter V
Personal Digital Libraries

Juan C. Lavariega
Tecnológico de Monterrey, Mexico

Lorena G. Gomez
Tecnológico de Monterrey, Mexico

Martha Sordia-Salinas
Tecnológico de Monterrey, Mexico

David A. Garza-Salazar
Tecnológico de Monterrey, Mexico

ABSTRACT

This chapter presents the services and functionality that a personal digital library (PDL) system should provide. The chapter includes a reference architecture for supporting the characteristics and functionality of the personal digital library. In particular, a currently available project called PDLib is used as an example of this type of system. The authors address some of the particular problems that personal libraries impose with respect to the overall administration of personal collections of digital documents and how personal libraries may become a commodity and a way of social interaction. The chapter objective is to increase the research interests on personalized digital libraries and their usability in our daily live.

INTRODUCTION

As digital and information technology advances, the effects of the adoption of such advances to our daily life are more evident. Today we, as users of information technology goods, produce a large amount of digital documents such as e-mail messages, office paperwork, personal documents, school homework, and even still-images, audio, and video. These myriad of digital documents usually reside in our personal computers or workstations, and some of them are placed on public places (i.e., our personal Web page and/or a Web sharing repository) where others can access our digital content. We are not only producers, but also consumers of digital documents; more and more frequently we get our daily news from the Web or via an e-mail service subscription. Also, while doing research in our area of interest, we consult the digital content available through the digital library services that our local library provides.

The personal computer is the place where we collect our personal digital archives and we have been using hierarchical folders to classify this information; with the increase in volume data the search utilities provided by operating systems are inadequate to ease the finding of documents, e-mail messages, or multimedia files because they do not analyze content. In the last couple of years, the search engine industry has introduced desktop search engines, tools that try to index the data in the file and gather as much metadata available (Cole, 2005) to provide a better search experience.

We organize all of those documents into collections, which will form in a way our personal library. Each user decides the contents of each collection following the user's own classification schema. Creating, organizing, sharing, searching, and retrieving documents from our personal collections are the intentions of personal digital libraries. A personal digital library (PDL) includes traditional digital library services for individual users.

In this chapter, we present and discuss the services, functionality, and characteristics of personal digital libraries in the context of our own development project called PDLib (Alvarez, Garza-Salazar, Lavariega, & Gómez-Martínez, 2005). PDLib is a universally available personal digital library. It is "universally available" in the sense that it allows the user to access personal digital library from most computing devices connected to the Internet, including mobile phones and PDAs, therefore granting access "from any place at anytime." We also discuss how social interac-

tions happen at different levels in the context of PDLib.

BACKGROUND

Digital library research has produced specialized, cohesive repositories, typically delivered via a Web interface and targeted to support both academic and industry organizations. A requirement to bridge organizational boundaries has been issued as the interoperability challenge (OAI, 2006), which calls digital library systems to take measures to share data with other digital repositories. Traditional digital library systems are seen as large data repositories that provide services to multiple users. Many of these systems are supported by distributed architectures for scalability purposes (Janssen, 2004; Smith, Barton, Bass, Branschofsky, McClellan, Tansley, et al., 2003; Witten, Boddie, Bainbridge, & McNab, 2000; Witten, Moffat, & Bell, 1999).

We propose a different perspective of the digital library, that is, a PDL universally available. The objective of personal digital libraries is to take the concepts of traditional (or collective) digital libraries to the user level and provide tools to promote the social interaction. Our PDL's concept proposes the notion of providing one repository for each user, enabling users to interact with each other with regards to both personal and shared data objects. We also emphasize on universal access, that is, users should be able to access their own personal libraries wherever they are.

Personal digital libraries provide traditional digital library services such as document submission, full-text and metadata indexing, and document search and retrieval, augmented with innovative services for the moment-to-moment information management needs of the individual user. These innovations include provisions to customize the classification of documents, interact with other digital libraries (whether personal or collective), and support user-to-user exchange of generic digital content.

The creation of the personal digital library implies the submission of digital documents and their placement on the personal digital library under user-defined classification schemas. The documents of a personal digital library must be accessible via a mechanism capable of providing meaningful answers to users' queries. In a personal digital library system, search and retrieval mechanisms must adapt to the personalized classification schema defined by the users of the system. The effectiveness of the document retrieval process from personal digital libraries must be assured with the provision of an intuitive classification schema and the indexing of documents. A personal digital library must provide each user with mechanisms to restrict unauthorized access to their personal digital library and with administrative tools to manage digital library content.

Since PDLs extend the traditional library services for the mobile environment in order to realize the abstraction of personal libraries, we must cope with the technological challenges imposed by the implementation of digital library services (Adam, Holowczak, Halem, & Yesha, 1996; Bhargava & Annamalai 1995; Garza-Salazar & Lavariega, 2003), the mobile environment (Barbara 1999; Madria, Mohania, Bhowmick, & Bhargava, 2002; Pitoura & Samaras, 1998), and the specific requirements of personal digital libraries. In the next sections we present the services, characteristics, architecture, and relevant problems presented in personal digital libraries.

PERSONAL LIBRARY SERVICES

Traditional digital library systems grant to a group of users access to a digital library. Personal digital library systems provide a digital library to each user with supporting functionality found in traditional digital libraries plus services that allow users to form their own collections, share documents with other users, and have universal access to the library contents.

Traditional digital libraries provide services such as digital document creation, efficient storage, classification and indexing, capabilities to search, filter, and summarize big volumes of data, images, and information, use of interfaces suitable for the presentation of results, distribution of the library content to the end user, and administration and access control. Also in traditional DL systems there are at least three types of users:

- **Administrators:** This group of users is the technical people who create users accounts and access rights to the collections in the DL. Administrators are responsible of the normal operation of the DL system.
- **Contributors:** This group represents people authorized to submit documents in the digital collections. They are authors, curators, or information science experts.
- **Common users:** This group represents the information consumers. People that browse in the DL collection or search for specific works based on some metadata such as author, topic, publication date, and so forth. Searches may be also set as a combination of metadata elements and document content.

In traditional DL a user may play more than one role simultaneously, but it is not a requirement. In contrast, in a personal digital library, a user necessarily plays the three roles simultaneously. The user needs to define who is granted access in the user's personal collection (or collections); also, users are responsible for placing content in the user's personal collections and set a classification criterion for the submitted documents. And of course the user can search for information inside the user's own collection or in the collections of other users who have authorized others to browse and search in their collections.

Another notable difference between traditional and personal digital libraries is the notion in normal DL that users "go" to someplace to search and browse in well-formed collections (i.e., collection which content has been validate and approved by a collegiate body). On the contrary, in personal DL, personal collections "travel" or move with the user, and collections' content is defined by the user. In personal digital libraries there exists the notion of universal available collections due to the "traveling" of user's collections. This notion is mainly realized by providing access to collections through any personal device (i.e., laptops, PDAs, and cellular phones). Dealing with mobile devices of limited capabilities presents interesting challenges for a personal digital library (Barbara, 1999) such as limited display space, and connection availability.

In order to support our vision and illustrate the functionality and capabilities of the PDL concept, we developed PDLib. PDLib is a personal library system that allows the user to shape and access the user's digital library from anyplace at anytime using nearly any computing device (i.e., universal access). To realize universally available digital libraries, the following requirements were defined for the PDLib system. The following functional requirements define the personal digital library services available in PDLib:

- **Flexible collection and metadata management:** Collections must be provided as a mechanism for document classification. Users should be provided with the ability to define the metadata set that will be used to describe the contents of each collection. These interactions will allow the user to customize a personal library as desired.
- **Digital document submission:** The user should be able to add any digital document to a personal digital library. Submission from several device types should be supported. The personal digital library must be able to accommodate several document formats for the same document. Additionally, the user must be able to (a) select or create the collection that will contain the document and (b) provide metadata information for

the document according to the collection's metadata set.

- **Search and retrieval:** Search and retrieval mechanisms must adapt to the personalized classification schema defined by the users of the system.
- **Universal access:** In order to provide universal access to the documents and services of the personal digital library, several client application types suitable for mobile and fixed hosts of mobile environments must be considered. Clients with diverse capabilities may be supported.
- **Administration and access control:** The owner of a personal digital library always has unrestricted access to the owner's personal digital library content. In addition, the owner has the capability to grant other users with access to the owner's individual personal digital library.
- **Interoperability:** Interoperability with other personal library users and with other digital library systems using well-known interoperability protocols must be provided. Interoperability happens in PDLib with other systems by using the open archive initiative protocol OAI-PHM (OAI, 2006). However, users should be allowed to define their own document descriptors. It is also desirable to support direct interaction with digital content providers such as Web search engine, as well as to store the results from the Web search into a personal collection.
- **Data model:** Personal digital libraries must provide a simple and flexible data model where each user's library is composed of collections. Collections contain, in turn, other collections and/or documents. Users can interact with personal digital libraries by creating and deleting collections and submitting, moving, copying, or downloading documents. In addition, users can define the metadata set that will be used to describe the contents of each collection. These interac-

tions allow the user to customize a personal library as desired

ARCHITECTURE OF PERSONAL DIGITAL LIBRARY

An overview of the PDLib system is shown in Figure 1. The PDLib software architecture consists of three layers:

1. **The client tier** includes the variety of devices with which a user can interact with PDLib. Clients can be classified depending of their mobility and client-side architecture into: mobile thin client, mobile thick clients, fixed thin clients, and fixed thin clients. In thin clients, the application is delivered on a browser or microbrowser, while in thick clients both code and data may reside in the client device. Mobile thick clients are especially important to achieve off-line operations possible, therefore mobile applications should be based in this type of

clients. Web applications typically focus on fixed thin clients.

2. **The server tier** includes the server system infrastructure that provides services to clients: (a) data server, (b) mobile connection middleware (MCM), and the (c) Web front-end. These components are addressed in a further section within this chapter.

3. **The interoperability tier** which allows the connection to other (PDLib) data servers and/or to OAI-PMH (OAI, 2006) compliant digital library systems.

The devices of the client tier communicate with the server tier to access PDLib digital library services. The access type of the client tier with the server tier varies according to the client device's capabilities: *middleware access* supports mobile devices, especially those with limited computing resources; *Web access* provides hypertext transfer protocol (HTTP) access to any device that includes a Web browser (WML/hypertext markup language [HTML]); and *direct access* for applications with very particular require-

Figure 1. PDLib system overview

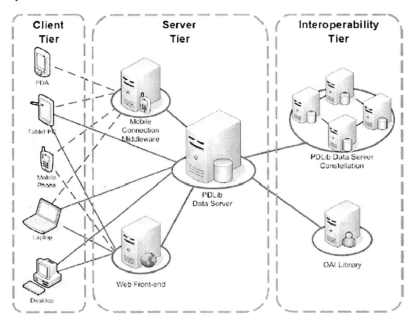

Figure 2. PDLib architecture

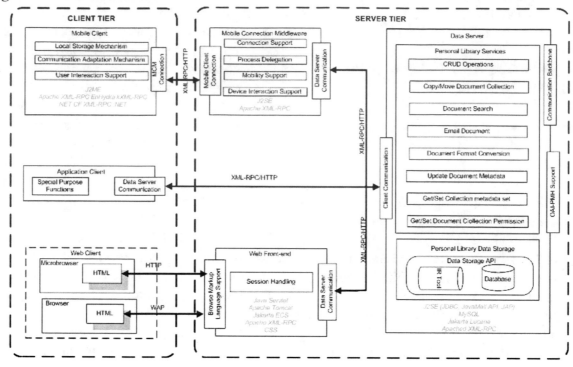

ments can access the data server directly. PDLib architecture (Figure 2) is supported in two main components: 1) mobile connection middleware and 2) data server.

Mobile Connection Middleware

One of the main problems to solve in order to provide the data server services is the fact that the data server has been designed to be used by a wide range of devices and not just mobile devices. However, there is a clear difference in computing resources between mobile and fixed devices. This computing resource disparity makes it difficult to adapt the data server to the capabilities of mobile devices and signals the need of a middleware component to mediate the interaction of the mobile device and the data server. We call this middleware the mobile connection middleware (MCM), which provides the following functionality:

- **Connection support:** It is required by mobile clients in order to perform adaptation to the high bandwidth variability of the mobile environment and to cope with the frequent disconnections of mobile devices.

- **Process delegation:** Execute functions that would demand an excessive (or unavailable) amount of computing resources to the mobile device.

- **Mobility support:** Operations such as prefetching can be performed to speed up the retrieval of documents from the data server and store them in cache servers that are closer to the user. When the user changes location, it would be necessary to support migration of the information between different instances of the MCM.

- **Device interaction support:** Performs adaptation of content according to the characteristics of the device on which it is desired to show the information.

Data Server

The data server provides the services of a personal digital library, stores, indexes, and classifies digital documents. It supports interoperability with other digital libraries and helps users to organize their collections. The data server provides the following:

- **Personal library services:** The data server offers creation, retrieval, update, and deletion operations over the library objects stored in the personal data storage (collections, documents and metadata). The data server also provides services to copy and move documents or collections search for documents in a personal library, and send documents to the personal library of other users.
- **Data model:** The digital library data model in PDLib establishes that a library contains one or more collections. A collection contains documents or more collections and is associated with a metadata set. The metadata set is composed by one or more metadata definitions. The fields that compose document metadata are determined by the metadata set of the collection. The metadata set of a collection defaults to the metadata set of the parent collection and can be redefined by the user on a per collection basis. Both collections and documents have an associated permission. Permissions are particularized in the following access rights: (a) personal, where access is restricted to library owner; and (b) incoming, where other users are allowed to create documents and collections. This access right applies only to collections.
- **Information retrieval:** One of the most interesting challenges in personal systems such as PDLib is the retrieval of information based on metadata, where the metadata set for describing documents within the library

may be quite different. Some work has been initiated (Saavedra, 2007), considering that different representations and labels may exist for a single concept.

- **Personal data storage:** It stores the data of the personal digital libraries. A text search engine is used to index the content of the personal digital libraries. A database is used to store the objects of the personal digital libraries. The use of a text search engine and a database in the data server permit to combined text-based queries and SQL queries, supporting the hierarchical classification of personal library content.
- **OAI-MHP support:** The data server exposes the metadata of the personal digital library documents via the OAI-MHP. In addition, the data server harvests metadata of other OAI-MHP compliant library systems to provide users with a subset of the personal digital library services to interact with other (OAIMHP compliant) library systems.

PDLib services allow users to collaborate by sharing documents and collections of documents of different types. Documents and collections are indexed and stored for further user navigation and accessing. Collections act as a collaborative memory. The main services that we provide as a means of collaboration are:

- **Public/Private access control:** Any collection or document can be made public or private by the owner. When a user has at least one public element as part of the user's library, then any user can browse and retrieve such public collections and documents.
- **Document sharing:** When a PDLib user wants to share a private copy of a document with another user, there are two services available for this purpose. 1) If the target user has a PDLib repository, the "send to PDLib user" service places the document into the target user's special collection named

"unfilled documents." This is a very fast and efficient way of sharing the information since no actual network bandwidth is used for this purpose. 2) For non-PDLib users, the send library content via e-mail service is available.

- **RSS support:** RSS (RSS, 2006) is supported for collections and queries. At the collection level, any user with an aggregator can subscribe to any user's PDLib public collection. Any time that the PDLib user adds a new document to the user's collection, the feed is updated. PDLib supports the retrieval, storage. and indexing of syndicated information from any RSS source and allows users to have collections of feeds as part of their own personal space.

- **Collection creation from external search engines results:** Search engines offer an excellent list of initial resources (documents including Web pages) while looking for a unknown topic. Usually results from Web search engines are relevant to user interest in the first few hits. Those results may be consulted immediately, but a very useful service should be to store them for further reference in a collection instead of click and saving bookmarks one by one. PDLib offers the service for creation of collections based on results of external Web search engines such as Google or Yahoo!.

- **Mobility support:** In order to enhance the possibilities for social interactions, personal digital libraries services have to be available wherever the user needs it. The mobile environment challenges are addressed by the PDLib's mobile clients. Our current PDLib's mobile client implementation supports two platforms, one based on CLDC/MIDP J2ME and other based on .Net technology

CONCLUSION

This chapter presented an overview of the PDLib system and the services it provides. PDLib services not only facilitate the management of user's personal documents, but also help users to increase interactions among colleagues and friends. In this way, a personal digital library system can be seen as an approach for supporting social computing. The current version of PDLib supports all the functionality described here.

Digital libraries are systems that have much to offer to social computing (Schuler, 1994). Even though the focus of both areas may seem to be initially quite different, on one hand, social computing is working with system informality and spontaneous communication to enable people collaboration and interconnection, and on the other hand, the digital library community has focused its efforts towards classification services and content structuring within centralized documents repositories. However, personal digital libraries support perfectly the management of personal information and the notion of collaborative/cooperative work by sharing collections of documents among individuals, making available to groups interesting findings, and consulting several sources of information from a single entry point.

As future areas of research and development we envision the incorporation of off-line operations and a synchronization mechanism from personal digital libraries mobile clients. Creation of ad hoc networks for the sharing of documents in small groups is also an area of opportunity for enhancing the user experience.

Currently we are developing a voice-processing capability that makes it possible to capture voice conversations, to convert them to text, and to store them into the system. Another development in progress is the creation of a peer-to-peer network of PDLib library servers. There are other issues such as scalability of the collections, consistency of information, and optimal document management that need to be addressed not only in PDLib, but also in personal information systems.

REFERENCES

Adam, N. R, Holowczak, R., Halem, R., & Yesha, Y. (1996). Digital library task force. *IEEE Computer, 29*(8).

Alvarez, F., Garza-Salazar, D., Lavariega, J., & Gómez-Martínez, L. (2005, July). *PDLib: Personal digital libraries with universal access.* Paper presented at the Joint International Conference on Digital Libraries, Denver, CO.

Barbara, D. (1999). Mobile computing and databases: A survey. *Knowledge and Data Engineering, 11*(1), 108-117.

Bhargava, B. K., & Annamalai, M. (1995). Communication costs in digital library databases. *Database and Expert Systems Applications*, 1-13.

Cole, B. (2005, March). Search engines tackle the desktop. *IEEE Computer, 38*(3), 14-17.

Garza-Salazar, D., & Lavariega, J. (2003). Information retrieval and administration of distributed documents in Internet: The Phronesis digital library project. *Knowledge based information retrieval and filtering from Internet* (pp. 53-73). Kluwer Academic Publishers.

Janssen, W. C. (2004). Collaborative extensions for the uplib system. In *Proceedings of the 4th Joint Conference on Digital Libraries* (pp. 239-240). ACM Press.

Madria, S., Mohania, M., Bhowmick, S., & Bhargava, B. (2002). Mobile data and transaction management. *Information Sciences—Informatics and Computer Science: An International Journal, 141*(3-4), 279-309.

OAI. (2006). *The open archive initiative.* Retrieved December 2006, from www.openarchives.org

Pitoura, E., & Samaras, G. (1998). *Data management for mobile computing.* Kluwer Academic Publishers.

RSS. (2006). RSS 2.0 specification. *RSS advisory board.* Retrieved December 2006, from www.rssboard.org/rss-specification

Saavedra, A. (2007). *Context based search in personal digital libraries.* Unpublished mater's thesis, Tecnologico de Monterrey.

Schuler, D. (1994). Social computing. *Communications of the ACM, 37*(1), 28-29.

Smith, M., Barton, M., Bass, M., Branschofsky, M., McClellan, D., Tansley, R., et al. (2003). Dspace: An open source dynamic digital repository. *D-Lib Magazine, 9*(1).

Witten, I. H., Boddie, S. J., Bainbridge, D., & McNab, R. J. (2000). Greenstone: A comprehensive open-source digital library software system. In *Proceedings of the 5th Conference on Digital Libraries* (pp. 113-121). ACM Press.

Witten, I. H., Moffat, A., & Bell, T. C. (1999). *Managing gigabytes: Compressing and indexing documents and images.* Morgan Kaufmann.

KEY TERMS

Digital Document: Any document in a digital format. A digital document can be text, image, video, or any combination of these formats.

Middleware: Any software component that mediates between an application server and a set of mobile clients.

PDLib: The personal digital library project developed at Monterrey Tech. Information and product available at http://copernico.mty.itesm.mx/pdlib.

Personal Collection: A set of digital documents that belongs to a specific user.

Social Computing: The ways of using computer applications to enhance and influence forms of social relations. The term "social computing" also refers to the social and ethical implications that software professionals have in an increasing "computerized" society

Thick Client: Software product that request information to a central information server. Thick clients have both application code and data residing on the client device (e.g., desktop, laptop, PDA, or cell phone)

Thin Client: Software product that request information to a central information server. In thin clients, the application is delivered on a browser (for large or middle size devices) or microbrowser (for a more restrictive device such as a PDA). Thick and thin clients can coexist in a single device.

Chapter VI
Comparing Open Source Digital Library Software

George Pyrounakis
University of Athens, Greece

Mara Nikolaidou
Harokopio University of Athens, Greece

ABSTRACT

In the last years, a great number of digital library and digital repository systems have been developed by individual organizations, mostly universities, and given to the public as open-source software. The advantage of having many choices becomes a great headache when selecting a digital library (DL) system for a specific organization. To make the decision easier, five well-known and extensively used systems that are publicly available using an open source license are compared, namely DSpace, Fedora, Greenstone, Keystone, and EPrints. Each of them have been thoroughly studied based on basic characteristics and system features emphasizing multiple and heterogeneous digital collection support. Results are summarized in a score table. Cases for which each of these systems is considered as the most suitable are proposed.

INTRODUCTION

In the last years, a great number of digital library and digital repository systems have been developed by individual organizations, mostly universities, and given to the public as open-source software. The advantage of having many choices becomes a great headache when selecting a digital library (DL) system for a specific organization. To make the decision easier, we compared five such systems that are publicly available using an open source license, are compliant with open archives initiative protocol for metadata harvesting (OAI-PMH) (Lagoze & Sompel, 2001), and already have a number of installations worldwide. Using these basic restrictions, we selected for comparison the following five broadly used DL systems:

- DSpace (DSpace Federation), developed by the MIT libraries and Hewlett-Packard Labs (BSD open source license)
- Fedora (Fedora Project), jointly developed by Cornell University and the University of Virginia Library (educational community license)
- Greenstone (Greenstone digital library software), produced by the University of Waikato (GNU general public license)
- Keystone (Keystone DLS), developed by Index Data (GNU general public license)
- EPrints (EPrints for digital repositories), developed by the University of Southampton

Each of these systems has been thoroughly studied based on basic characteristics and system features described in the following sections. The latest versions of those systems were examined. When writing this chapter, the versions provided were: DSpace 1.4, Fedora 2.2, Greenstone 3, Keystone 1.5, and EPrints 3. The DL systems are compared based on stated characteristics and the level of support on each of them. In the following section, the characteristics needed by a modern DL system are discussed. In the third section the five DL systems are compared based on each of the DL characteristics and the results are summarized in a score table. Finally, in the fourth section, the results of this comparison are commented on and cases for which each of these systems is suitable are proposed.

DL SYSTEMS CHARACTERISTICS

The basic characteristics and features that are expected from modern integrated DL software are:

1. **Object model:** The internal structure of the digital object (Kahn & Wilensky, 2005) (entity that integrates metadata and digital content) in the DL system. Existence of unique identifiers for the digital object and every part of it is also important to ensure preservation and easy access.

2. **Collections and relations support:** Collection description metadata, definition of subcollections, and templates that describe the format of the digital objects or the presentation of the collection. It is the definition of relations between objects of the same or different types.

3. **Metadata and digital content storage:** The storage capabilities are stated, along with the preservation issues. It is important for the DL system to ensure standards as well as user-defined metadata sets and multiple formats of digital content.

4. **Search and browse:** The mechanisms used for indexing and searching the metadata. It is important for the DL system to support indexing not only for a restricted metadata set, but also for selected metadata fields.

5. **Object management:** Methods and user interfaces provided from the DL system to manipulate (i.e., insert, update, and delete) metadata and digital content.

6. **User interfaces:** Provided user interfaces for end-user access on the DL, its collections, and the digital objects.

7. **Access control:** Support for users and groups and authentication and authorization methods. It provides a level of restriction for access and update (e.g., DL, collection, digital object, and content).

8. **Multiple languages support:** Multiple languages should be supported in the user interface, in the metadata fields, and in the digital content. The character encoding is of great importance in order for the DL systems to be fully multilingual.

9. **Interoperability features:** Standards that the DL systems support in order to ensure interoperability with other systems. Export of the digital objects in open standard formats is also important.

10. **Level of customization:** Customization of the DL system in the collection level, the format of the digital objects, and the services provided. The quality and methods provided by the application programming interfaces (APIs) of the DL systems are also included.

DL SYSTEMS COMPARISON

In the following, the five open access DL systems are compared based on the characteristics identified in the previous section. The level of support of each characteristic and specific considerations for each DL system are discussed.

Object Model

DSpace: The basic entity in DSpace is *item*, which contains both metadata and digital content. Qualified Dublin Core (DC) (DCMI metadata terms) metadata fields are stored in the item, while other metadata sets and digital content are defined as bitstreams and categorized as bundles of the item. The internal structure of an item is expressed by structural metadata, which define the relationships between the constituent parts of an item. DSpace uses globally unique identifiers for items based on the CNRI handle system (The handle system). Persistent identifiers are also used for the bitstreams of every item.

Fedora: The basic entity in Fedora is *digital object*. The internal structure of a digital object is determined from the Fedora Object XML (FOXML), which is based on metadata encoding and transmission standard (METS) (Library of Congress). A digital object contains metadata and digital content (both treated as datastreams). A digital object also contains links to the behaviors defined for it. A unique persistent identifier is used for every digital object. Datastreams are also uniquely identified by a combination of the object persistent identifier and the datastream identifier.

Greenstone: Basic entity in Greenstone is *document,* which is expressed in XML format. Documents are linked with one or more resources that represent the digital content of the object. Each document contains a unique document identifier but there is no support for persistent identifiers of the resources.

Keystone: Basic entity in Keystone is *document*. The internal structure of each document is defined in a user-defined XML schema corresponding to a specific document type. The directory structure of the documents represents the object's structure. A persistent identifier is not used to uniquely identify documents.

EPrints: Basic entity in EPrints is the *data object*, which is a record containing metadata. One or more documents (files) can be linked with the data object. Each data object has a unique identifier.

Collections and Relations Support

DSpace: Dspace supports collections of items and communities that hold one or more collections. An item belongs to one or more collections, but has only one owner collection. It is feasible to define default values for the metadata fields in a collection. The descriptive metadata defined for a collection are the title and description. There is no support of relations between different items.

Fedora: Fedora supports collections using RELS-EXT datastream that contains a basic relationship ontology. In this datastream, the relationships between digital objects (like isMemberOfCollection or isPartOf) are expressed as resource description framework (RDF) (W3C). Fedora does not provide a mechanism to manipulate these relations.

Greenstone: A collection in Greenstone defines a set of characteristics that describe its functionality. These characteristics are indexing, searching and browsing capabilities, file formats, conversion plugins, and entry points for the digital content import. There are also some characteristics for the presentation of the collection. The representation of hierarchical structure in text documents is supported for chapters, sections, and paragraphs. The definition of specific sections in text document is implemented through special XML tags. XLinks in a document can be used to relate it with other documents or resources.

Keystone: Collections in Keystone are not defined as entities but they are imposed by the directory structure of the documents. The document XML schema specifies common behavior (i.e., elements are viewable, repeatable, mandatory, multilingual, and use a restricted vocabulary) for the documents of the specific type. There is no definition of relations between documents, except using URLs in specific metadata fields.

EPrints: There is no consideration of collections in EPrints. Data objects are grouped depending on specific fields (e.g., subject, year, title, etc.). There is no definition of relations between documents, except using URLs in specific metadata fields.

Metadata and Digital Content Storage

DSpace: DSpace stores qualified DC metadata in a relational database (PostgreSQL [PostgreSQL] or Oracle [Oracle database]). Other metadata sets and digital content are represented as bitstreams and are stored on filesystem. Each bitstream is associated with a specific bistream format. A support level is defined for every bistream format, indicating the level of preservation for the specified file format.

Fedora: Metadata and digital content are both considered datastreams of the digital object. Datastreams can be stored (a) internally on the digital object XML file, (b) on filesystem as managed content, or (c) on an external source. One or more metadata sets can be concurrently used, while different file formats can be stored as separate datastreams in a digital object. Basic technical metadata are stored for each datastream, such as multipurpose Internet mail extensions (MIME) type, file size, and checksums, ensuring content preservation. Fedora supports versioning of specified datastreams, allowing user to access older datastream instances.

Greenstone: Both documents and resources are stored on filesystem. Metadata are user-defined and are stored in documents using an internal XML format.

Keystone: Each object in Keystone contains its metadata in an XML document. The metadata are not restricted to a specific metadata standard but are stated in a user-defined XML schema denoting each document type. Digital content is stored in the directory structure that contains the XML documents.

EPrints: Metadata fields in EPrints are user-defined. The data object, containing metadata, is stored in a MySQL database (MySQL database) and the documents (digital content) are stored on filesystem.

Search and Browse

DSpace: DSpace provides indexing for the basic metadata set (qualified DC) by default, using the relational database. Indexing of other defined metadata sets is also provided using Lucene API

(Apache Lucene). Lucene supports fielded search, stemming, and stop words removal. Searching can be constrained in a collection or community. Also, browsing is offered by default on title, author, and date fields.

Fedora: Default indexing is provided for the DC metadata set and digital object's system metadata (i.e., persistent identifier, creation/modification date, label, content model). Indexing and searching is managed from a relational database (e.g., MySQL, Oracle, or PostgreSQL). Searching is available in all indexed fields using constraints on a combination of fields. A generic search (gSearch) is also provided using Lucene or Zebra (Zebra index data) search engines. In addition, relationships between digital objects are indexed and are searchable using the Fedora resource index. Browsing mechanism is not provided.

Greenstone: Indexing is offered for the text documents and specific metadata fields. Searching capabilities is provided for defined sections within a document (e.g., title, chapter, or paragraph) or in a whole document. Stemming and case sensitive searching is also available. Managing gigabytes (MG) (Managing gigabytes) open-source applications are used to support indexing and searching. Browsing catalogs can be defined for specific fields using hierarchical structure.

Keystone: Indexing is supported on specified document types for the whole metadata set. Free text searching is offered. A browsing mechanism is not provided.

EPrints: Indexing is supported for every metadata field using the MySQL database. Full text indexing is supported for selected fields. Combined fielded search and free text search are provided to the end user. Browsing is provided using specified fields (e.g., title, author, or subject).

Object Management

DSpace: Items in DSpace are created using the Web submission user interface or the batch item importer, which ingests XML metadata documents and the constituent content files. In both cases a workflow process may initiate depending on the collection configuration. The workflow can be configured to contain from one to three steps where different users or groups may intervene to the item submission. Collections and communities are created using the Web user interface.

Fedora: Creation of digital objects is feasible using the administrator client or the batch import utility (XML files in METS or FOXML format). Metadata addition or editing is provided through a text editor in the administrator client. The same client is used for addition and removal of digital content (as datastreams).

Greenstone: New collections and the contained documents are built using the Greenstone librarian interface or the command line building program.

Keystone: The content management system of Keystone provides the Web interface for editing documents. It allows specified users to manage the content of documents as well as the files structure.

EPrints: A default Web user interface is provided for the creation and editing of objects. Authority records can be used to help the completion of specific fields (e.g., authors, title, etc.). Objects can also be imported from text files using multiple formats (METS, DC, MODS [Library of Congress 2], BibTeX [BibTeX], EndNote [EndNote]).

User Interfaces

DSpace: A default Web user interface is provided in order for the end user to browse a collection, view the qualified DC metadata of an item, and navigate to its bistreams. Navigation into an item is supported through the structural metadata that may determine the ordering of complex content (like book pages or Web pages). A searching interface is provided by default that allows the user to search using keywords.

Fedora: The Web interface of Fedora provides a search environment to the end user, where the end user may execute simple keyword or field search queries. The default view of digital objects is restricted to the presentation of the system metadata and the datastreams. Behavior digital objects define the presentation or manipulation methods of datastreams. A developer may build specific Web services and attach them on digital objects as behaviors. A DC metadata viewing page and an image manipulation applet are provided as default behaviors.

Greenstone: The default Web user interface provides browsing and searching into collections, navigating into hierarchical objects (like books) using a table of contents. Presentation of documents or search results may differ depending on specified XSLTs.

Keystone: Presentation of a document is controlled by an XSLT style sheet that reflects the associated document type. The main Web user interface is based on a portal-like environment. In this environment a user may browse the documents' directory structure and search in the digital library.

EPrints: The Web user interface provides browsing by selected metadata fields (usually subject, title or date). Browsing can be hierarchical for subject fields. A searching environment allows user to restrict the search query using multiple fields and selecting values from lists.

Access Control

DSpace: It supports users (e-people) and groups that hold different rights. Authentication is provided through user passwords, X509 certificates, or lightweight directory access protocol (LDAP). Access control rights are kept for each item and define the actions that a user is able to perform. These actions are: read/write the bitstreams of an item, add/remove the bundles of an item, read/write an item, and add/remove an item in a collection. Rights are based in a default-deny policy.

Fedora: It supports users and groups authorized for accessing specific digital objects using XACML policies. Authentication is provided through LDAP or for specific Internet protocol (IP) addresses.

Greenstone: A user in Greenstone belongs to one of two predefined user groups, that is, an administrator or a collection builder. The first user group has the right to create and delete users, while the second builds and updates collections. End users have access to all the collections and the documents.

Keystone: A simple access control is supported where you can define administrators and simple users that have access rights on specific parts of the documents structure.

EPrints: Registered users in EPrints are able to create and edit objects. Users are logged in using their username and password pair.

Multiple Languages Support

All the DL systems use Unicode character encoding so the support of different languages can be supported. Every system can use multiple languages in the metadata fields and digital content. Keystone and EPrints provide an XML attribute on metadata fields to define the language used for the field value. Greenstone provides ready to use multilingual interfaces already translated in many languages.

Interoperability Features

All the DL systems support OAI-PMH in order to share the metadata of the DL with other repositories. Greenstone and Keystone also support Z39.50 protocol (Z390.50 maintenance agency page) for answering queries on specific metadata sets. Fedora and DSpace are able to export digital objects as METS XML files. Both systems also use persistence URIs to access the digital content providing a unified access mechanism to external services. DSpace also supports OpenURL protocol (NISO) providing links for every item page. EPrints exports data objects in METS and MPEG-21 digital item declaration language (DIDL) format (Bormans & Hill, 2002).

Level of Customization

DSpace: Although DSpace has a flexible object model, it is not so open in constructing very different objects with independent metadata sets because of its database-oriented architecture. The user interface is fixed and provides only minor

presentation interventions. Another disadvantage is the full support of only specific file formats as digital content.

Fedora: In Fedora, every digital object can follow a different content model that describes its format. It is also possible to provide multiple behaviors in it that determine the access and manipulation methods of the digital object. These two characteristics result in a fully customizable DL. The user interface, although by default is poor, is fully customizable based on two APIs (i.e., access API and management API).

Greenstone: It provides customization for the presentation of a collection based on XSLTs and agents that control specific actions of the DL. Greenstone architecture provides (i) a back end that contains the collections and the documents as well as services to manage them and (ii) a Web-based front end that is responsible for the presentation of collections, documents, and their searching environment.

Keystone: Document's structure is based on a customized document type, which is formed by an XML schema. In addition, the presentation of a document is dependent on the XSLTs associated with the document type. The separation of

Table 1.

Characteristics	DSpace	Fedora	Greenstone	Keystone	EPrints
Object model	4	5	3	3	2
Collection support and relations	4	4	5	2	1
Metadata and digital content storage	4	5	3	3	3
Search and browse	4	3	4	2	4
Object management	4	2	2	3	4
User interfaces	4	2	4	4	4
Access control	5	4	2	2	2
Multiple languages support	3	3	4	4	4
Interoperability features	5	5	4	4	5
Level of customization	3	5	4	5	3

document storage and presentation layer, as well as the typing of documents, provides a fully customizable DL architecture.

EPrints: The data objects in EPrints contain user-defined metadata. Plugins can be written in order to export the data objects in different text formats. A core API in Perl is provided for developers who prefer to access basic DL functionality.

Based on the aforementioned analysis, the five DL systems were graded for each of the characteristics, the minimum score is 1 and the maximum is 5.

CONCLUSION AND SUGGESTIONS

It is difficult to propose one specific DL system as the most suitable for all cases. Each system has its advantages and drawbacks, as stated in the aforementioned comparison, categorized by basic DL system characteristics and features. That comparison can only be used as a guideline by an organization in order to decide if one of these DL systems is suitable to host its digital collections. Usually the needs for each organization vary depending on the number of collections, the types of objects, the nature of the material, the frequency of update, the distribution of content, and the time limits for the development of a DL. In the next paragraphs, guidelines for the selection of a DL system are provided depending on different organization needs.

1. Consider a case where an institution or university needs a digital repository for research papers and dissertations produced by students and staff. In that case, the most appropriate DL system is DSpace, since it by default represents communities (e.g., university departments) and collections (e.g., papers and dissertations), while workflow management support is important for item submission by individuals.

2. Consider a case where an organization needs one digital collection to publish its digital content in a simple form and in strict time limits. In addition, the organization prefers to integrate the Web interfaces of the DL with a portal-like Web site. In that case, the most appropriate DL systems are Keystone or EPrints, since they separate the concerns of presentation and storage, are not bound to specific metadata standards, and provide simple Web interfaces for the submission and presentation of documents and metadata.

3. Consider a case where an organization is responsible for digitizing collections from libraries, archives, and museums and hosting them in a single DL system. The organization has human resources and the amount of time in order to customize the DL system and develop extra modules. The highest priority needs are the support of preservation issues, the use of multiple metadata standards, and the different formats of digital content. In that case, the most suitable DL system is Fedora, since it provides a very customizable modular architecture. Although it does not provide easy-to-use Web interfaces or built-in functionality, it is the best choice for the case where many collections and different material must be hosted.

4. Consider a case where an organization wants to electronically publish books in an easy-to-use customizable DL system. In that case, the most appropriate DL system is Greenstone, since it is easy to represent books in a hierarchical manner, using table of contents, while the full text of chapters can be searchable.

REFERENCES

Apache Lucene. Retrieved August 14, 2008, from http://lucene.apache.org/

BibTeX. Retrieved August 14, 2008, from http://www.bibtex.org/

Bormans, J., & Hill, K. (2002). *MPEG-21 overview v.5.* Retrieved August 14, 2008, from http://www.chiariglione.org/mpeg/standards/mpeg-21/mpeg-21.htm

DCMI metadata terms. *Dublin Core metadata initiative.* Retrieved August 14, 2008, from http://www.dublincore.org/documents/dcmi-terms/

DSpace Federation. Retrieved August 14, 2008, from http://www.dspace.org/

EndNote. Retrieved August 14, 2008, from http://www.endnote.com/

EPrints for digital repositories. Retrieved August 14, 2008, from http://www.eprints.org/

Fedora Project. Retrieved August 14, 2008, from http://www.fedora.info/

Greenstone digital library software. Retrieved August 14, 2008, from http://www.greenstone.org/

The handle system. *Corporation for National Research Initiatives.* Retrieved August 14, 2008, from http://www.handle.net/

Kahn, R., & Wilensky, R. (1995). A framework for distributed digital object services. In *Corporation of National Research Initiative - Reston USA.* Retrieved August 14, 2008, from http://www.cnri.reston.va.us/k-w.html

Keystone DLS. Retrieved August 14, 2008, from http://www.indexdata.dk/keystone/

Lagoze C. and H. Van de Sompel, 2001.The Open Archives Initiative: Building a low-barrier interoperability framework. In *Proceedings of the Joint Conference on Digital Libraries* (JCDL '01).

Library of Congress. *METS: An overview & tutorial.* Retrieved August 14, 2008, from http://www.loc.gov/standards/mets/METSOverview.v2.html

Library of Congress 2. *Metadata object description schema (MODS).* Retrieved August 14, 2008, from http://www.loc.gov/standards/mods/

Managing gigabytes (MG). *New Zealand Digital Library.* Retrieved August 14, 2008, from http://www.nzdl.org/html/mg.html

MySQL database. Retrieved August 14, 2008, from http://www.mysql.com/

NISO. *The OpenURL framework for context-sensitive services standard.* Retrieved August 14, 2008, from http://www.niso.org/standards/standard_detail.cfm?std_id=783

Oracle database. Retrieved August 14, 2008, from http://www.oracle.com/database/index.html

PostgreSQL. Retrieved August 14, 2008, from http://www.postgresql.org/

W3C. *Resource description framework (RDF).* Retrieved August 14, 2008, from http://www.w3.org/RDF/

Z39.50 maintenance agency page. Retrieved August 14, 2008, from http://www.loc.gov/z3950/agency/

Zebra index data. Retrieved August 14, 2008, from http://www.indexdata.dk/zebra/

KEY TERMS

DSpace: Open source DL platform developed by the MIT libraries and Hewlett-Packard Labs (BSD open source license).

Fedora: Open source DL platform jointly developed by Cornell University and the University of Virginia Library (educational community license).

EPrints: Open source DL platform developed by the University of Southampton.

Greenstone: Open source DL platform produced by the University of Waikato (GNU general public license).

Interoperability Features: Standards that the DL systems support in order to ensure interoperability with other systems.

Keystone: Open source DL platform developed by Index Data (GNU general public license).

Level of Customization: Customization of the DL system in collection level, the format of the digital objects, and the services provided.

Object Management: Methods and user interfaces provided from the DL system to manipulate metadata and digital content.

Object Model: The internal structure of the digital object (i.e., entity that integrates metadata and digital content) in the DL system.

Open Source DL: A digital library software platform based on open source technology.

Chapter VII
The Greenstone Digital Library Software

Ian H. Witten
University of Waikato, New Zealand

David Bainbridge
University of Waikato, New Zealand

ABSTRACT

This chapter describes the evolution of the Greenstone digital library project through its first 10 years of development. It provides an overview of the software, which includes both production and research versions, as well as a chronological account of notable events that occurred in this period. The chapter also focuses on the tension that occurs between trying to support two versions of the software, and our strategy for resolving this conflict, that is, of reconciling production values with a research framework.

INTRODUCTION

At the time of writing (December 2007) Greenstone—a versatile open source multilingual digital library environment with over a decade of pedigree—has a user base hailing from over 70 countries, is downloaded 4,500 times a month, runs on all popular operating systems (even the iPod!), and has a Web interface in over 50 languages. It is also a successful framework for research, as evidenced through the group's pub-

lication record.[1] How did this software project and the research team behind it reach this point? Team members often give anecdotal stories at conferences and workshops about life behind the scenes; this chapter provides a more definitive and coherent account of the project.

This chapter is divided into three parts. First we present an overview of the software in its current form. It comes in two flavors: a production system and a research framework. Next we give a chronological account of its development from the very beginning, including origins, early adopters, and our approach to the key issues of sustainability, support, and interoperability. The existence of two flavors creates a tension—the versions compete for the resources that we can commit to their development—and the chapter culminates in a discussion of our strategy for reconciling this conflict.

Production Version

The production version of Greenstone provides the ability to create collections of digital content, display the content in a Web browser (either over the intranet or standalone from CDROM or similar), and access and search the collections that have been built. Its development was informed by the experience of non-governmental organizations (NGOs) such as Human Info and United Nations agencies such as UNESCO and Food and Agriculture Organization (FAO) in facilitating the dissemination of humanitarian information, particularly in developing countries. Through UNESCO sponsorship the software is fully documented—right down to configuration options embedded in scripts—in all six official UNESCO languages of English, French, Spanish, Russian, Chinese, and Arabic. The Web interface has been translated into over 50 other languages through the efforts of a large cohort of volunteers.

Countless digital libraries have been built with Greenstone. They range from historic newspapers to books on humanitarian aid, from eclectic multimedia content on pop-artists to curated first editions of works by Chopin, and from scientific institutional repositories to personal collections of photos and other documents. All kinds of topics are covered: the black abolitionist movement, bridge construction, flora and fauna, the history of the Indian working class, medical artwork, and shipping statistics are just a random selection.

Greenstone accommodates a wide variety of data types. Document formats include HTML, PDF, OpenOffice, Word, PowerPoint, and Excel. Metadata formats include MARC, Refer, Dublin Core, learning object metadata (LOM), and BibTeX. Greenstone also accepts a wide variety of image, audio, and video formats. Full-text indexing of all document text and metadata is the standard and supplied by default. Greenstone supports numerous interoperability standards, including open archives initiative protocol for metadata harvesting (OAI-PMH), Z39.50, and metadata encoding and transmission standard (METS). Collections can be exported to Fedora, DSpace, and MARC. See our Web site www.greenstone.org for more details.

End users experience Greenstone through a Web interface such as the one shown in Figure 1,

Figure 1. Screenshots of Greenstone's Web-based readers' interface: (a) the collection interface; (b) reading a document

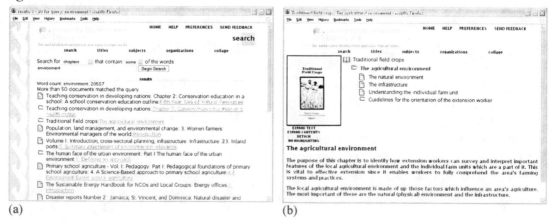

(a)　　　　　　　　　　　　(b)

taken from the Human Info NGO's *Humanity Development Library*. Documents in this collection can be searched by chapter title, as well as the standard full text search by chapter or book. Alternatively, users might choose to browse alphabetically by title or hierarchically by subject or organization. In Figure 1(a) the user has searched within chapters for the word "environment" and a ranked listed of matches has been displayed. In Figure 1(b) they are viewing the document that results from selecting the second matching item, that is, Chapter 3 of *Teaching Conservation in Developing Nations*. Greenstone collections are designed individually, depending on the document formats and metadata available and the facilities that the designer wants to offer the user. Figure 1 shows a representative example, but other collections often look completely different.

Figure 2 shows the Greenstone librarian interface (GLI), an interactive application for creating and maintaining collections such as the Humanity Development Library. Through a system of tabbed panels accessed along the top of the interface, the digital librarian decides what files to include in the collection, what metadata to assign manually (in addition to that automatically extracted by Greenstone from the source files), the

collection's searching and browsing capabilities, and the crafting of presentation details. Although collections are designed individually, the design of an existing collection can be copied and populated with new material.

Research Framework

As the development of Greenstone matured, our research group became concerned that while its growing adoption in developing countries provided strong motivation and a great deal of personal satisfaction, it was beginning to stymie innovation within the software. There is a disincentive to introduce new research-led concepts into a maturing code base because they are less reliable, difficult to test on multiple platforms, and often entail substantial upheavals of the code. Regression testing is difficult to apply to digital library systems in a comprehensive manner. Given the wide gamut of people and platforms using the production system, seemingly modest changes sometimes introduced bugs that affected users in unforeseen ways. Our desire to support the developing world led to unusual challenges; for example, Greenstone collections could be viewed—and searched—on any Windows

Figure 2. Screenshot of the Greenstone librarian interface

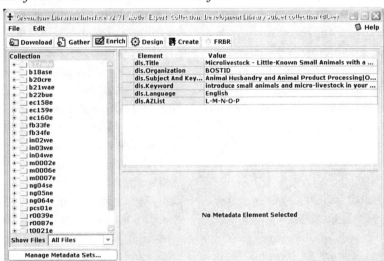

platform from 3.1 upwards. Even Microsoft no longer supports prior versions of their operating system! Moreover, the fact that the interface and documentation have been translated into many languages has a conservative, even stultifying, influence on new developments.

Our solution was to formulate a redesign of the software with the express intention that it constitutes a new research framework, based on the experiences we had learned thus far. In order to take advantage of new developments in software technology we decided to start the implementation afresh. Java was chosen as the primary programming language to minimize cross-platform dependencies. Our goals included extensive backwards compatibility, different levels of customization, software modularity, dynamic services, distributed architecture, future compatibility, integrated documentation, self-describing modules, and integration into the computing environment. The resulting software was named Greenstone 3 to differentiate it from the production version, retrospectively dubbed Greenstone 2 (to coincide with the version numbering we had already been using).

In essence, Greenstone 3 is based upon a distributed network of modules and uses simple object access protocol (SOAP) to stream extensible markup language (XML) messages between them, with the option of customization of messages at any point through the use of XSL transforms. Dynamically loadable services (preferably Webservice based) are layered on top of this communication channel. A "describe-yourself" call is a mandatory fixture that allows service discovery in a heterogeneous world of communicating applications; it also assists future compatibility. METS is used to represent ingested documents. For more details, refer to work by Buchanan, Bainbridge, Don, and Witten (2005).

Using this framework we have investigated dynamic text mining (Witten, Don, Dewsnip, & Tablan, 2004), query visualization (Rüger, 2005), alerting services (Buchanan & Hinze, 2005),

spatial searching (Jones, Jones, Barr, & Keegan, 2004), and ontologies (Buchanan, 2006), amonge other things. Figure 2 is actually a snapshot of the research framework version of the Greenstone librarian interface (coincidentally demonstrating backwards compatibility). The functionality invoked by the rightmost tab (labeled FRBR for functional requirements for bibliographic records) is not a feature of the production version. However, it was easy to introduce this functionality in the research framework and launch the graphical interface with a tab that invokes it.

We have also been exploring the role of AJAX in supporting wider integration tasks based around a digital library infrastructure. This tests our ability to provide future compatibility, for AJAX has arisen subsequent to the inception of Greenstone 3. Koru (Milne, Witten, & Nichols, 2007) is a new search interface to digital library content that offers effective domain-independent knowledge-based information retrieval. It exhibits an understanding of the topics involved in both queries and documents, allowing them to be matched more accurately and evolving queries automatically and interactively. Flax (Wu & Witten, 2006) melds language learning with digital libraries to automate the production and delivery of practice exercises for overseas students who are learning English. Leveraging off digital library software allows teachers and students to capitalize on top-quality prose and multimedia resources already present in the world's libraries. This yields an unprecedented supply of linguistic material for students to practice on. Realistic 3D books (Liesaputra, Witten, & Bainbridg, in press) interact with a digital library at a subdocument level (i.e., chapters, page-level, and illustrations) to provide an enhanced reading experience.

Although versions of Greenstone 3 have been released, continual demands from users for further development of Greenstone 2 have drawn more heavily on our time than we had envisaged when we embarked upon the reimplementation. We return to this point and the tension it creates at the end of the chapter.

HISTORY AND BACKGROUND

The New Zealand digital library project grew out of research on text compression (Bell, Cleary, & Witten, 1990) and, later, index compression (Witten, Moffat, & Bell, 1994). Around this time we heard of digital libraries, and pointed out the potential advantages of compression at the first-ever digital library conference (Bell, Moffat, & Witten, 1994). The New Zealand digital library project was established in 1995, beginning with a collection of 50,000 computer science technical reports downloaded from the Internet (Witten, Cunningham, Vallabh, & Bell, 1995). At the time several research groups in computer science departments were collecting technical reports and making them available on the Web; our main contribution was the use of full-text indexing for effective search. We were assisted by equipment funding from the New Zealand Lotteries Board and operating funding from the New Zealand Foundation for Research, Science and Technology (1996-1998 and 2002-2011).

Earlier Adopters

In 1997, we began to work with Human Info NGO to help them produce fully-searchable CD-ROM collections of humanitarian information. This necessitated making our server (and in particular, the full-text search engine it used), which had been developed under Linux, run on Windows machines, including the early Windows 3.1 and 3.11, because, although by then obsolete, they were prevalent in developing countries. This was demanding but largely uninteresting technically; we had to develop expertise in long-forgotten software systems, and it was hard to find suitable compilers (eventually we obtained a "second-hand" one from a software auction).

The first publicly available CD-ROM, the *Humanity Development Library 1.3*, was issued in April 1998. A French collection, UNESCO's *Sahel point Doc*, appeared a year later; all the documents, along with the entire interface, help text, and full-text search mechanism, were in French. The first multilingual collection came 6 months later with a Spanish/English *Biblioteca Virtual de Desastres/Virtual Disaster Collection*. Since then about 40 CD-ROM collections have been published. They are produced by Human Info in Romania. We wrote the software and were heavily involved in preparing the first few CD-ROMs, and then transferred the technology to them so that they could proceed independently. At this point we realized that we did not aspire to be a digital library site ourselves, but rather to develop software that others could use for their own digital libraries.

Towards the end of 1997 we adopted the term *Greenstone* because we decided that "New Zealand Digital Library Software" was not only clumsy but could impede international acceptance and therefore sought a new name. "Greenstone" turned out to be an inspired choice because it is snappy, memorable, and unnationalistic but with strong national connotations within New Zealand: a form of nephrite jade, greenstone is a hallowed substance for Māori, valued more highly than gold. Moreover, it is easy to spell and pronounce. Our earlier *Weka* (think *mecca*) machine learning workbench, an acronym that in Māori spells the name of a flightless native bird, suffers from being mispronounced *weaka* by some. And the term Greenstone is not overly common; today we are the number one Google hit for it.

The decision to issue the software as an open source, and to use the GNU general public licence, was made around the same time. We did not discuss this with University of Waikato authorities—New Zealand universities are obsessed with commercialization and we would have been forced into an endless round of deliberations on commercial licensing—but simply began to release under GPL. Early releases were posted on our Web site *greenstone.org* (which was registered on August 13, 1998), but in November 2000, we moved to the SourceForge site for distribution (partly due to the per-megabyte charging scheme that our university levied for both outgoing and incoming Web traffic). Our employers were not particularly happy when our licensing *fait accompli* became apparent years later, but have grown to accept (and perhaps even appreciate) the status quo because of our evident international success.

An early in-house project utilizing Greenstone was the Niupepa collection of Māori-language newspapers. We began the work of OCRing 20,000 page images in 1998, and made an initial demonstration collection. In 2000-2001 we received (retrospective!) funding from the Ministry of Education to continue the work. Virtually the entire Niupepa was available online early in 2001, but the collection was not officially launched until March 2002 at the annual general meeting of Te Rūnanga o Ngā Kura Kaupapa Māori (the controlling body of Māori medium/theology schools). Niupepa is still the largest collection of online Māori-language documents, and is extensively used. Apperley, Keegan, Cunningham, and Witten (2002) give a comprehensive description of how it was developed. On November 13, 2000, in a moving ceremony, the Māori people presented our project with a ceremonial *toki* (adze) as a gift in recognition of our contributions to indigenous language preservation (see Figure 3).

In 1999, the BBC in London were concerned about the threat of Y2K bugs on their database of one million lengthy metadata records for radio and television programs. They decided to augment their heavy-duty mainframe database with a fully-searchable Greenstone system that could run on ordinary desktop machines. A Greenstone collection was duly built and delivered (within 2 days of receiving the full dataset). We tried to get them to the point where they could maintain it themselves, but they were not interested; instead we updated it for them regularly (incidentally providing us with a useful small source of revenue). They eventually moved to different technology in early 2006, with the aim of making the metadata (and ultimately the program content) publicly available online in a way that resembles what Amazon does for books, something that we think requires a tailor-made portal rather than a general-purpose digital library system.

Sustainability

We became acquainted with UNESCO through Human Info's long-term relationship with them. Although they supported Human Info's goal of producing humanitarian CD-ROMs and distributing them in developing countries, UNESCO were really interested in *sustainable* development, which requires empowering people in those countries to produce and distribute their own digital library collections—following that

Figure 3. The Greenstone toki

This *toki* (adze) was a gift from the Māori people in recognition of our project's contributions to indigenous language preservation, and resides in the project laboratory at the University of Waikato. In Māori culture there are several kinds of *toki*, with different purposes. This one is a ceremonial adze, *toki pou t angata*, a symbol of chieftainship. The *rau* (blade) is sharp, hard, and made of *pounamu* or greenstone, hence the Greenstone software, at the cutting edge of digital library technology. There are three figures carved into the *toki*. The forward-looking one looks out to where the *rau* is pointing to ensure that the *toki* is appropriately targeted. The backward-looking one at the top is a sentinel that guards where the *rau* cannot see. There is a third head at the bottom of the handle which makes sure that the chief's decisions—to which the *toki* lends authority—are properly grounded in reality. The name of this *taonga*, or art-treasure, is *Toki P ou H inengaro*, which translates roughly as "the adze that shapes the excellence of thought."

old Chinese proverb about giving a man fish vs. teaching him to fish.[2] We had by then transferred our collection-building technology to Human Info, and tried—though without success—to transfer it to the BBC, but this was a completely different proposition, that is, to put the power to *build* collections into the hands of those other than IT specialists, typically librarians.

We began by packaging up our PERL scripts and documenting them so that others could use them, and slowly, painfully, came to terms with the fact that operating at this level is anathema for librarians. In 2001, we produced a Web-based system called the "Collector" that was announced in a paper whose title proudly proclaimed "Power to the people: end-user building of digital library collections" (Witten, Bainbridge, & Boddie, 2001). However, this was never a great success: Web-based submission to repository systems (including Greenstone collections) is commonplace today, but we were trying to allow users to design and configure digital library collections over the Web as well as populate them. The next year we began a Java development that became known as the Greenstone librarian interface (Bainbridge et al., 2003), which grew over the years into a comprehensive system for designing and building collections and includes its own metadata editor.

From the outset, UNESCO's goal was to produce CD-ROMs containing the entire Greenstone software (not just individual collections plus the run-time system, as in Human Info's products) so that it could be used by people in developing countries who did not have ready access to the Internet.[3] There were the tangible outcomes of a series of small contracts with UNESCO. We feel that the CD-ROMs are more of symbolic than actual significance because in practice they rapidly became outdated by frequent new releases of the software appearing on the Internet. They have been produced every year from 2002 onwards. The CD-ROMs contain all the auxiliary software needed to run Greenstone as well, which are not included in the Internet distributions because they can be obtained from other sources (links are provided).

When we and others started to give workshops, tutorials, and courses on Greenstone we naturally benefited from the expertise built up of producing self-contained CD-ROMs. We further extended the resources included and adopted a policy of putting all instructional material (i.e., PowerPoint slides, exercises, and sample files for projects) on a workshop CD-ROM, and began to include this auxiliary material on the UNESCO distributions also. This almost led to their downfall, for the company producing the CD-ROMs began to question the provenance of some of the sample files they contained, and ultimately demanded explicit proof of permission to reproduce all the information and software. Although everything was, in principle, open source, some of the external software projects used in Greenstone did not always provide meticulous licensing details, and at such short notice so much had to be stripped out that the 2006 CD-ROM distribution was seriously emasculated. Over the next year licenses were clarified and clearer copyright statements collated. Alternatives were utilized when copyright holders did not reply to our enquiries or no longer seemed to exist (a research project, for instance, that had reached its end of its funding and members had moved on to other work).

Support

Good documentation was (rightly!) seen by UNESCO as crucial. They were keen to make the Greenstone technology available in all six official UNESCO languages; we began with English Spanish, French, and added Russian and Arabic and Chinese only recently. We already had versions of the interface in these (and many other) languages, but UNESCO wanted *everything* to be translated; not just the documentation, which was extensive (four substantial manuals) but all the installation instructions, README files, example collections, and so forth. We might have demurred had we realized the extent to which such a massive translation effort would threaten to hobble the potential for future development, and have since suffered mightily in getting everything—including last-minute interface tweaks—translated for each upcoming UNESCO CD-ROM release. The cumbersome process of maintaining up-to-date translations in the face of continual evolution of the software—which is, of course, to be expected in open source systems—led us to devise a scheme for maintaining all language fragments in a version control system so that the system could tell what needed updating. This resulted in the Greenstone translator's interface, a Web portal where officially registered translators can examine the status of the language interface for which they are responsible, and update it (Bainbridge et al., 2003). Today the interface has been translated into 48 languages (with a further 11 in progress), 36 of which have an active designated volunteer maintainer.

Most people are surprised by the small size of the Greenstone team. Historically, for most of the duration of the project we have employed 1-2 programmers, although recently the number has crept up to 3-4. Several faculty involved in aspects of digital library research are associated with the project, but only two (the present authors) have viewed the Greenstone software as their main interest, partly because although the work is ground-breaking the research outputs are of questionable value in the university evaluation and promotion process. Graduate students rarely contribute to the code base directly because of concerns about retaining the production-level code quality and programming conventions painstakingly acquired over many years, although several students work in areas cognate to digital libraries. Our external users tend to be librarians rather than software specialists and we have received few major contributions or bug fixes from them. To summarize, the Greenstone digital library software has been created by a couple of skilled people working over a 10-year period, and along the way there have

been several changes of personnel. It is amazing what excellent programmers can do.

With UNESCO's encouragement (and occasional sponsorship), we have worked to enable developing countries to take advantage of digital library technology by running hands-on workshops. This has enabled team members to travel to many interesting places. In what other area, for example, might a computer science professor get the opportunity to spend a week giving a course at the UN International Criminal Tribunal for Rwanda in Arusha, Tanzania, at the foot of Mount Kilimanjaro, or in Havana, Cuba, Windhoek, Namibia, or Kathmandu, Nepal? Recognizing that devolution is essential for sustainability and we are now attempting to distribute this effort by establishing regional Greenstone Support Groups; the first, for South Asia, was launched in April 2006.

Greenstone won the 2004 IFIP Namur award, which recognizes recipients for raising awareness internationally of the social implications of information and communication technologies; and was a finalist for the 2006 Stockholm Challenge, the world's leading ICT prize for entrepreneurs who use ICT to improve living conditions and increase economic growth. Our project received the Vannevar Bush award for the best paper at the ACM Digital Libraries Conference in 1999, the Literati Club Highly Commended Award in 2003, and the best international paper award at the Joint Conference on Digital Libraries in 2004.

Greenstone is promoted by UNESCO (Paris) under its Information for All program. It is distributed with the FAO's (Rome) *Information Management Resource Kit* (2005), along with tutorial information on its use. It forms the basis of the Institute for Information Technology in Education's course on Digital Libraries in Education (2006). An extensive early description appears in Witten and Bainbridge's (2003) book *How to Build a Digital Library*. In 2002-2003, our principal developer at that time left the project to form DL Consulting, an enterprise that specializes in building and customizing Greenstone collections and has won several awards as the region's fastest-growing exporter and ICT company.

Interoperability

Many early digital library projects focused on interoperability. Although this is clearly a very important issue, we felt that this attention was premature; we well remember a digital library conference where interest was so strong that there were two panel discussions on interoperability, the only catch being that they were parallel sessions, which permitted no interoperability. We adopted the informal motto "first operability, then interoperability," and focused on other issues such as ingesting documents and metadata in a very wide variety of formats. More recently we have added many interoperability features, which, as we had expected, were not hard to retrofit: communication with Z39.50, SRW, OAI-PMH, DSpace, and METS are just a few examples (Bainbridge, Ke, & Witten, 2006).

RECONCILING RESEARCH AND PRODUCTION

Greenstone 3 was originally envisaged purely as a research framework; backwards compatibility would be possible but required IT skills. We have achieved this aim. It is now much easier for external projects to build upon the digital library core and a selection of examples such as alerting services and language learning were mentioned above. By and large these projects work by developing new or enhanced functionality that augments the document searching, browsing, and access already provided. Some projects, notably ones that utilize AJAX, develop Web-browser embedded interfaces that issue requests to the (potentially distributed) digital library infrastructure and manipulate the XML messages that are returned. Other projects develop standalone applications (in whatever language and toolkit suits their needs) that integrate with the infrastructure, potentially at a deeper level if required. In applications that run locally with respect to the digital library core, the communication can be bypassed in favor of direct procedure calls through the API.

We have found that maintaining two independent versions of Greenstone—in particular, ensuring backwards compatibility when new and enhanced features are still being added to Greenstone 2—is beyond our resources. Consequently we have committed to a new vision, that is, to develop Greenstone 3 to the point that, by default, its installation and operation is, to the user, indistinguishable from Greenstone 2. We have invested significant resources over the last year to achieve this goal, and the first release of Greenstone 3 encapsulating this new vision was made available in November 2007. This was only 1 month before the completion of this chapter, so it is too early for any substantial remarks about how successful (or not) this has been. However, here is a summary of the key points included in the work undertaken.

We have ported the InstallShield procedure utilized by Greenstone 2 to produce a comparable cross-platform installation wizard which contrasts markedly with the former Greenstone 3 command-line repository checkout and compile experience. Multilingual translations have been migrated to Greenstone 3 in a semiautomated fashion and enhancements made to the default services so the readers' interface (experienced through a Web browser) could be matched, step for step, with what users already experience in Greenstone 2. Previously, although Greenstone 3's default functionality matched Greenstone 2, the interaction steps were not the same; these enhancements corrected this and other minor differences. We have also developed automated regression tests to help minimize the work of checking for undesired side effects of recently committed changes. Workshop and tutorial material have also been checked to ensure they work with Greenstone 3 just as they did for Greenstone 2.

In terms of ingesting documents into a digital library collection, we utilized Greenstone 2's already rich exporting ability (originally designed to facilitate interoperability) to output to the registered METS profile utilized by Greenstone 3. Viewed in a particular way, this can be seen as interoperating between two distinct digital library systems, only here they happened to be produced by the same team. Greenstone 2's collection building code was upgraded to natively parse Greenstone 3 configuration files and included in the shipped code. This tied things up nicely from a software point of view, and allowed the graphical librarian interface to operate equally well within Greenstone 2 and 3.

Notwithstanding Greenstone 3's aim of supplanting its predecessor, overall this pattern of gradually moving the two code bases closer together seems to be working well. To take a different example, originally the 3D realistic books were planned for the research framework alone. However, we quickly realized that by introducing an extra optional CGI parameter to Greenstone 2 that made it generate XML compliant with the Greenstone 3 syntax, this work could be "back ported" to all existing Greenstone 2 collections. Doing this took less than a day!

Looking to the future, our longer term goals are to broaden the realms in which digital libraries are utilized. This can be seen in the existing examples, cited above, that employ Greenstone 3. Multimedia is also being brought under the spotlight through a 4-year grant from the New Zealand Foundation for Research, Science and Technology that will see Greenstone harness content-based analysis for images, audio, video, and so forth with particular specializations to newspapers, music, and maps. We foresee an extension mechanism as the key to managing this ever widening and diversifying spectrum of research-inspired functionality. Hence, we have begun work on an administration tool that facilitates general maintenance of an installation along with the ability to download and incorporate particular extensions.

CONCLUSION

We believe that digital libraries are a key aspect of civil society, particularly in developing countries. Their importance grows with every passing day. People are beginning to recognize the dangers of relying on one or two giant universal search engines for access to our society's treasure-house of information, which constitutes our entire literary, scientific, and cultural heritage. What the world needs, we believe, are focused collections of information, created and curated by people with an intellectual stake in their contents. We mean digital libraries, built by librarians!

We are proud and very pleased that the Greenstone digital library software is playing a part in this international endeavor. Year by year its technical strength grows and its rate of adoption increases. Yet this success comes at a high price, for we are essentially a research group, yet feel obliged to provide support for the growing user base of our production system. This chapter has given an account of the Greenstone software and its development, and conveyed our approach to the difficult problem of reconciling production values of stability and reliability with a vigorous research framework of innovation.

REFERENCES

Apperley, M., Keegan, T. T., Cunningham, S. J., & Witten, I. H. (2002). Delivering the Maori-language newspapers on the Internet. In J. Curnow, N. Hopa, & J. McRae (Eds.), *Rere atu, taku manu! Discovering history, language and politics in the Maori-language newspapers* (pp. 211-232). Auckland University Press.

Bainbridge, D., Edgar, K. D., McPherson, J. R., & Witten, I. H. (2003). Managing change in a digital library system with many interface languages. In *Proceedings of the European Conference on Digital Libraries ECDL2003*, Trondheim, Norway.

Bainbridge, D., Ke, K.-Y. J., & Witten, I. H. (2006). Document level interoperability for collection creators. In *Proceedings of the Joint Conference on Digital Libraries*, Chapel Hill, NC (pp. 105-106).

Bainbridge, D., Thompson, J., & Witten, I. H. (2003). Assembling and enriching digital library collections. In *Proceedings of the Joint Conference on Digital Libraries*, Houston.

Bell, T. C., Cleary, J. G., & Witten, I. H. (1990). *Text compression*. Englewood Cliffs, NJ: Prentice Hall.

Bell, T. C., Moffat, A., & Witten, I. H. (1994, June). Compressing the digital library. In *Proceedings of the Digital Libraries '94*, College Station, TX (pp. 41-46).

Buchanan, G. (2006). FRBR: Enriching and integrating digital libraries. In *Proceedings of the Joint Conference on Digital Libraries*, Chapel Hill (pp. 260-269).

Buchanan, G., Bainbridge, D., Don, K. J., & Witten, I. H. (2005). A new framework for building digital library collections. In *Proceedings of the Joint Conference on Digital Libraries*, Denver (pp. 23-31).

Buchanan, G., & Hinze, A. (2005). A generic alerting service for digital libraries. In *Proceedings of the Joint Conference on Digital Libraries*, Denver (pp. 131-140).

Jones, S., Jones, M., Barr, M., & Keegan, T. K. (2004). Searching and browsing in a digital library of historical maps and newspapers. *Journal of Digital Information, 6*(2), 12-19.

Liesaputra, V., Witten, I. H., & Bainbridg, D. (in press). Creating and reading realistic books. *IEEE Computer Magazine*.

Milne, D. N., Witten, I. H., & Nichols, D. N. (2007). A knowledge-based search engine powered by Wikipedia. In *Proceedings of the ACM Conference on Information and Knowledge Management*, Lisbon, Portugal (pp. 445-454).

Rüger, S. (2006). *Putting the user in the loop: Visual resource discovery*. Paper presented at the Workshop on Adaptive Multimedia Retrieval (AMR, Glasgow, July 2005) (LNCS 3877, pp. 1-18).

Witten, I. H., & Bainbridge, D. (2003). *How to build a digital library*. San Francisco: Morgan Kaufmann.

Witten, I. H., Bainbridge, D., & Boddie, S. J. (2001). Power to the people: End-user building of digital library collections. In *Proceedings of the Joint Conference on Digital Libraries*, Roanoke, VA.

Witten, I. H., Cunningham, S. J., Vallabh, M., & Bell, T. C. (1995, June). A New Zealand digital library for computer science research. In *Proceedings of the Digital Libraries '95*, Austin (pp. 25-30).

Witten, I. H., Don, K. J., Dewsnip, M., & Tablan, V. (2004). Text mining in a digital library. *International Journal of Digital Libraries, 4*(1), 56-59.

Witten, I. H., Moffat, A., & Bell, T. C. (1994). *Managing gigabytes: Compressing and indexing documents and images*. New York: Van Nostrand Reinhold.

Wu, S., & Witten, I. H. (2006). Towards a digital library for language learning. In *Proceedings of the European Conference on Digital Libraries*, Alicante, Spain.

KEY TERMS

Greenstone: The name given to our open source digital library software that encapsulates over a decade of research led by the digital library group at the University of Waikato, New Zealand. Greenstone 2 is a production version of the software, originally developed for the United Nations to deliver digital library collections on humanitarian aid. Greenstone 3, originally designed as a purely research framework, has recently been reengineered so it can additionally serve as a replacement for the production version.

Greenstone Librarian Interface (GLI): The graphical tool that librarians, archivists, and other digital collection managers interact with to develop their Greenstone digital library collections. Works with both Greenstone 2 and 3.

ENDNOTES

[1]	In fact, the group has had papers accepted at all the main digital library conferences since their inception

[2]	In New Zealand, by the way, they say "give a man a fish and he'll eat for a day; teach a man to fish and he'll sit in a boat and drink beer for the rest of his life."

[3]	Incidentally, UNESCO refused to use our *toki* logo on the CD-ROMs because they feel that in some developing countries axes are irrevocably linked to genocide. Our protests that this object is clearly ceremonial fell on deaf ears. Dealing with international agencies is sometimes very frustrating.

Chapter VIII
Design and Development
of a Taxonomy Generator:
A Case Example for Greenstone

Yin-Leng Theng
Nanyang Technological University, Singapore

Nyein Chan Lwin Lwin
Nanyang Technological University, Singapore

Jin-Cheon Na
Nanyang Technological University, Singapore

Schubert Foo
Nanyang Technological University, Singapore

Dion Hoe-Lian Goh
Nanyang Technological University, Singapore

ABSTRACT

This chapter addresses the issues of resource discovery in digital libraries (DLs) and the importance of knowledge organization tools in building DLs. Using the Greenstone digital library (GSDL) software as a case example, we describe a taxonomy generation tool (TGT) prototype, a hierarchical classification of contents module, designed and built to categorize contents within DLs. TGT was developed as a desktop application using Microsoft .NET Framework 2.0 in Visual C# language and object-oriented programming. In TGT, Z39.19 was implemented providing standard guidelines to construct, format, and manage monolingual controlled vocabularies, usage of broader terms, narrower terms and related terms as well as their semantic relationships, and the simple knowledge organization system (SKOS) for vocabulary specification. The XML schema definition was designed to validate against rules developed for the XML taxonomy template, hence, resulting in the generated taxonomy template supporting controlled vocabulary terms as well as allowing users to select the labels for the taxonomy structure. A pilot user study was then conducted to evaluate the usability and usefulness of TGT and the taxonomy template. In this study, we observed four subjects using TGT, followed by a focus group for comments. Initial feedback was positive, indicating the importance of having a taxonomy structure in GSDL. Recommendations for future work include content classification and metadata technologies in TGT.

INTRODUCTION

One of the important contributions of the Web technology to modern information technology development has been the evolution of digital libraries (DLs) that provide virtual accessibility of information resources to users at anytime, from any place where Internet access is available. DLs can be considered as the continuation of the traditional library work in digital form with the support of Internet access. DLs basically involve both primary data and manually created metadata sets. The effort in constructing a DL from scratch is huge since it actually requires an attractive and user-friendly interface with effective content management and powerful search and browsing capabilities.

A solution to this problem was implemented by creating software applications that would help to automate the DL building processes with enhanced facilities to multilingual information retrieval systems, support for interoperability protocols, and effective metadata management for diverse media formats (Witten, McNab, Boddie, & Bainbridge, 2000). During the last decade, several DL building tools have emerged aiming to provide management and distribution processes of DL collections. Some DL software packages may be subject-oriented, institution-oriented, mission-oriented, or used for digital object management. Currently, DSpace, Fedora, EPrint, and Greenstone are the most popular open-source DL software packages available that aim to empower users with capabilities to

design, build, and manage digital collections. For example, DSpace offers a platform for digital preservation for an institutional repository system while Fedora provides a service for managing digital objects. EPrint allows open access to digital contents, primarily for institutional repositories and scientific journals. Greenstone is particularly aimed at providing users with easily automated DL building processes.

Despite success in open-source software making DLs more accessible to many users, content management and metadata tagging remain important research challenges in DLs, and, in general, Web portals and Internet resources in facilitating efficient search and discovery of relevant information resources (Yan, 2004). In this chapter, we describe the design and development of a taxonomy generator supporting tagging and classification of digital resources in DLs, focusing on enhancing open-source DL software to provide more efficient search and discovery of information sources.

As a case illustration, we have selected Greenstone (http://www.zdl.org) to implement a taxonomy structure for better resource discovery of the digital collections. In subsequent sections, we give a brief overview of Greenstone, explain the design rationale of the taxonomy generator tool (TGT), and discuss the implementation and initial feedback of TGT. Finally, the chapter concludes with design challenges faced and lessons learned.

OVERVIEW OF GREENSTONE

Greenstone is a software suite designed to build and distribute DL collections for publishing on the Internet or on CD-ROM. It is an open-source application developed under the terms of the general public license (GNU) and is particularly easy to install and use (Witten, 2003). In cooperation with UNESCO and Human Info, Greenstone has helped to support user testing, internationalization, and mount courses (Witten & Bainbridge, 2005). Aligning with the goal of UNESCO for the preservation and distribution of educational, scientific, and cultural information of developing countries, Greenstone came in as an important tool in this context. The core facilities aiming to provide in Greenstone were for designing and construction of the document collections, distributing them on the Web and/or CD-ROM, as well as to providing customizable structure on available metadata, easy-to-use collection-building interface, multilingual support, and multiplatform operation (Witten & Bainbridge, 2005). Although initially focused on helping developing countries, its user base has expanded to 70 countries and the reader's interface has been translated into 45 languages to-date, with increasing volume of download hits from a steady 4,500 times per month to 6,500 over the last 2 years (Witten & Bainbridge, 2007). Greenstone's popularity comes from a simple, user-friendly interface providing:

- **Essential and efficient basic features:** Greenstone is platform independent and multilingual with the capability to handle different types of digital formats from text, image, to video files. End users can access Greenstone through two interfaces, firstly, the *reader interface,* where end users access the digital collections generally through a standard Web browsers, and secondly, the *greenstone's librarian interface* (GLI), where end users can manage the digital

resources in five basic activities to gather, enrich, design, create, and format. Tagging the documents, four prespecified metadata sets including Dublin Core (DC) are currently provided with the software and new metadata sets can be created within the librarian interface using Greenstone editor for metadata set (GEMS) (Witten & Bainbridge, 2007). Various search indexes and browsing structures can be configured for each specific collection. Greenstone allows full-text as well as fielded *searching* across the collections of different index levels and results are usually ranked by relevancy or sorted by a metadata element (Witten et al., 2003). *Browsing* facility is through the metadata value tagged to each document. Greenstone offers different types of browsing structures (i.e., list, hierarchy, date, etc.) where end users could define for each collection. Unlike other DL building software, Greenstone provides a customizable user interface feature using *format string* and *macro* files. Macros are written especially for Greenstone and are loaded at run-time to generate Web pages dynamically (Bainbridge, McKay, & Witten, 2004). Supporting *interoperability* across different collections and metadata standards, it serves to be compatible with open archives protocol for metadata harvesting (OAI-PMH), Z39.50, and SRW for harvesting and exported to and from metadata encoding and transmission standard (METS) and DSpace collections (Witten & Bainbridge, 2007). For *security and administration* purposes, Greenstone provides an access control mechanism with a password protection scheme for documents/collections for different levels of end users. At the point of writing, Greenstone is in its Version 3 with an improved, flexible, and extensible design structure. It is now written in Java language and structured as a set of independent modules communicating using extensible markup language (XML).

- **Content management:** The survey carried out by Goh, Chua, Khoo, Khoo, Mak, and Ng (2006) shows that Greenstone was able to meet most of the important demands in DLs because of its strong support for end-user functionality, and hence achieving high scores for content management and acquisition compared to other DL building tools such as Fedora, EPrint, and CDSware. The GUI-enabled librarian interface manages the documents in an easy and simplified manner, even for end users without a library science background. Before a collection goes online, it undergoes two processes (Witten & Bainbridge, 2003):

  o *Importing* (import.pl) is a facility to create new collections, add more contents, or delete the collection. Each document and its associated metadata are converted to the XML-compliant Greenstone archive format at this stage of importing. Greenstone allows more than one metadata sets associated to the document collections. Existing metadata sets such as DC are readily available in the system as well as new sets can be created according to user needs (Bainbridge et al., 2004). Metadata in documents and metadata sets are stored as XML files. For each document to be persistent across the collection, an *object identifier or OID* is calculated and stored as an attribute in the document's archive file. In order to support extensibility, the task of format conversion and metadata extraction is processed by software modules called *plug-ins* where each input document is passed through until a suitable plug-in is found. For example, HTML pages are converted to the Greenstone archive format with the extracted metadata such as title, document name, source, and so forth until the HTML plug-in is found. Plug-ins for each specific collection were identified in the collection configuration file (Bainbridge et al., 2004).

  o The *building* (buildcol.pl) process handles all the indexes and data structures necessary to make the collection work. Greenstone offers three levels of index for each document, that is, document level, section level, and paragraph level, with each described inside the document itself. The building process also compresses the text of the documents for better disk utilization and faster retrieval of the contents. Indexing and compressing techniques are handled by managing gigabytes (MG), which is the core engine in Greenstone that makes use of the GNU database manager program (GDBM) for storing and retrieving the objects by unique keys. To facilitate browsing for available metadata, modules called *classifiers* are used to create various types of browsers, such as scrollable lists, alphabetic selectors, dates, and arbitrary hierarchies (Bainbridge et al., 2004). Based on classifier types listed in the collection configuration file, the building process initializes each by obtaining the metadata value on which the document is to be classified. With advanced skills on programming, both plug-ins and classifiers can be written to customize functions for new document, metadata formats, and new browsing and document access facilities. Once the building process is finished successfully, the collection is ready to go online and be accessible to the users.

- **Browsing:** What make DLs superior over physical libraries are its better resource discovery capabilities. Greenstone has implemented a browsing system consisting of classifiers, that is, structures constructed through available metadata in documents. The possible structures in a collection address various levels, for example, section level or document level. During collection building time, documents are grouped into classes according to their metadata while browsing structures are prebuilt and available upon request (McKay, Shukla, Hunt, & Cunningham, 2004). Greenstone supports different kinds of classifiers:

o *List classifier* is the simplest form which presents the sorted documents in a single list structure.

o *Alphabetic classifier* is slightly different than the list structure in which documents are organized into A to Z indexes displayed on top of the alphabetically sorted list.

o *Hierarchical classifier* is more complex than list classifiers with each having an arbitrary number of levels to narrow down the hierarchy, which is specified during metadata tagging (Bainbridge et al., 2004).

o *Date classifier* is like the alphabetic classifier, categorizing the documents by date metadata instead of the A to Z list used (Bainbridge et al., 2004).

o *Phind classifier* creates the classifier not based on metadata values but on a word or the phrases in the documents during collection building time (McKay et al., 2004).

OUR PROPOSAL

Need for Better Classification of Resources in Greenstone

On the whole, Greenstone provides a new way of collecting and representing the digital contents on the Internet in the form of fully-searchable,

metadata-driven DLs, catered with simple, customizable browsing structures for users from novices to experts.

Although the classifier system automates the browsing system, there are weaknesses in the design of the system. McKay et al. (2004) point out two weaknesses to the current classifier system. The first weakness is that because of the ability to switch between searching and browsing, Greenstone treats search and browse features as two standalone systems, displaying search results in a list structure without ranking and sorting facility. Most browsing classifiers built from metadata are not able to search. The second weakness is due to the rigidity of the classifier system in terms of using only static, prebuilt browsing structures presenting a collection in a predetermined format only.

With powerful indexing mechanisms like MG, it offers full-text search to all contents available in the collection. However, in the current classification system of GSDL, the categorization of resources according to subjects is still not supported yet, although the powerful indexing and rich metadata support is already present.

Although Greenstone provides the facilities in multilingual, metadata, and customizable content classifiers for browsing the collection, the current support for browsing lacks a normalized structure for hierarchically organizing the terms. McKay et al. (2004) discuss the current browsing structure of Greenstone and highlight the importance of term suggestion, vocabulary control, and the role of thesaurus in searching and browsing of digital contents. The browsing system in Greenstone is entirely based on the metadata tagged to each document and limits the way it is structured. Additionally, the controlled vocabulary tool for multiple subject access is not managed in the current scenario of Greenstone browsing system. Controlled vocabulary is important to provide the consistent usage of the terminology in the digital resources for better management of indexing and searching capability. Hence, controlled vocabulary tools such as a taxonomy or thesaurus for richer terms and vocabulary organization are important to incorporate in constructing large knowledge repository using GSDL.

Aim and Objectives

Therefore, in this chapter, we describe our research aimed at designing and implementing a taxonomy structure in GSDL to achieve the following objectives:

- To develop a *set of guidelines* for implementing a taxonomy template for GSDL.
- To produce a *taxonomy schema* with the support of controlled vocabulary, semantic relationships, and multiple language support for GSDL.
- To build a *software tool* that would automate the generation of a taxonomy template to be integrated with GSDL.

DESIGN AND DEVELOPMENT

Due to space constraints, we are not able to discuss in detail the steps taken in constructing the taxonomy structure. In summary, five separate processes were involved in designing and developing the taxonomy structure for GSDL:

- **Step 1:** Incorporates controlled vocabularies for taxonomy adapting Z39.19 to determine the terms to be employed in the taxonomy template.
- **Step 2:** Determines the taxonomy scheme to represent various terms suggested in Step 1.
- **Step 3:** Sets the rules to validate against the taxonomy template using the XML schema definition language considered for its powerful support for complex terms.
- **Step 4:** Implements the tool to generate the taxonomy template.

Figure 1. Implementation processes for TGT

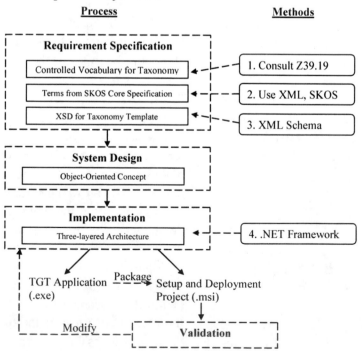

- **Step 5:** Integrates the taxonomy template with GSDL.

Figure 1 shows the overview processes of TGT conceptually grouped onto the software development lifecycle (SDLC) phases.

The TGT prototype was developed using the Visual C#.NET 2.0 and XML technologies and we describe briefly these six areas:

1. **Development platform:** Visual C#.NET is the object-oriented programming language and provides easy setup and installation mechanisms. We used a three-layered architecture to implement this prototype, that is, "forms" for the presentation layer, codes (C# language) for the application logic layer, and XML for the data storage layer. The resultant XML template records each term and their relationships inside the taxonomy hierarchy. There are two solution files included in the project: one for the taxonomy generation application and another one for the setup and deployment project which generates the Windows Installer to distribute the application. The setup project would produce the installer "taxonomy generation tool.msi" file, which contains the application, any dependency files, and application-related information. However, one needs to make assure the prerequisites (e.g., .NET Framework 2.0 to be installed) are well-placed before the installation is made. Otherwise, the process would fail

and be back in its preinstallation state.

2. **System requirements:** For optimum application performance of TGT, the machine that the TGT application will be resided in is recommended to have the following system requirements (see Table 1):

3. **Application package:** To install the TGT prototype into the hard drive, the Windows installer file "Taxonomy Generation Tool.msi" has to run. The package will load the step-by-step installation wizard and install the necessary files to the designated location (the default location is 'C:\Program Files\Taxonomy Generation Tool\Taxonomy Generation Tool'). Once the installation is finished, the application will be accessible from Start Menu or from Desktop Shortcut. From the Start Menu, users are allowed to do two operations: load TGT or read User Guide for assistance in operating TGT.

4. **System design:** Two main functions for this prototype have been developed, namely, creating the new taxonomy template and updating the existing taxonomy template. The help facility includes "User Guidance" and "About" information. Figure 2 shows the overview process flow diagram of TGT.

5. **User interface and features:** The user interface and layout settings are designed as closely related to the existing editor in Greenstone package. The control settings and operation allows multiple language inputs as the term properties are structured to conform to Greenstone editor for metadata set (GEMS). To support the multilingual service, Greenstone uses one XML file named 'languages.xml' stored in the folder 'C:\Program Files\Greenstone\gli\classes\xml' which contains 139 languages from various countries. Language names and their associated codes, stored in the 'languages.xml' file, are retrieved by calling the private method `private void prepareComboItems()` in code behind and populated

Table 1. Recommended system requirements

Operating Systems	Windows XP and later versions
Memory	256 MB RAM or higher
Hard Disk	60 GB with minimum 30 MB of free space
Processor	1.8 GHz or faster
Software Requirement	.NET framework 2.0

Figure 2. Process flow diagram of TGT

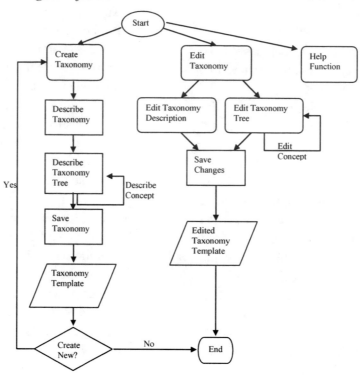

Figure 3. 'Languages.xml' from Greenstone digital library

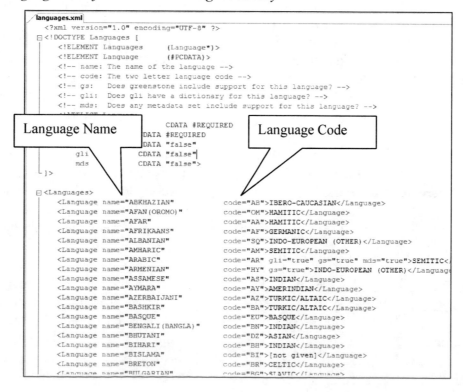

inside the Combo box whose selected value will be stored in taxonomy template as 'xml: lang' attribute value. The language name and their associated language code used in 'languages.xml' file are presented in Figure 3.

Each concept in the taxonomy is seen as an object and stored in memory. An application session-based model is used for temporarily storing the various concept objects in memory using hash table object class 'ApplicationSession.cs' (see Figure 4).

The user interface and features are designed to be understandable for users from novices to experts. The simple tab-based incorporation to describe the concepts and their related properties, guiding users step-by-step and with descriptive labels, aims to provide no barriers for users in operating the features provided by the system.

The taxonomy scheme can be created by using a "*New*" menu item or by simply using the shortcut by pressing Ctrl+N. The "*Close*" item in the File menu (Figure 5) will unload the active form opened inside the multiple document interface (MDI) while "*Exit*" menu (Alt+F4) will quit the application without saving anything. Creating the new taxonomy scheme can be logically divided into three parts: describing the taxonomy, describing the concept, and managing the taxonomy tree.

a. **Describing the taxonomy:** Information related to the taxonomy such as name, objective, and scope is recorded before the taxonomy tree is constructed (see Figures 6 and 7).

b. **Describing the concept:** For each label in the taxonomy tree, the associated properties are recorded before it is saved to the taxonomy tree (see Figure 8). The prototype allows for the creation of alternate labels (see Figure 9) and related labels (see Figure 10).

c. **Managing the taxonomy tree:** After the concepts have been described for the taxonomy tree, they are allowed to remove, edit, or save the tree (see Figure 11).

Figure 4. Sample code for ApplicationSession.cs class

```
public class ApplicationSession : Hashtable
  {
      private static ApplicationSession instance = new ApplicationSession();

      private ApplicationSession()
      {
      }

      public static ApplicationSession getInstance()
      {
        return instance;
      }

      public override void Add(object key, object value)
      {
        if (this.Contains(key) == true)
        {
          this.Remove(key);
        }
        base.Add(key, value);
      }
  }
```

Figure 5. File menu

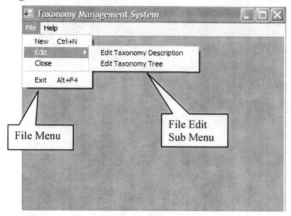

Figure 8. Label description tab

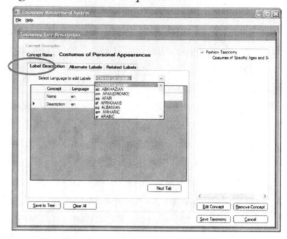

Figure 6. Taxonomy description form

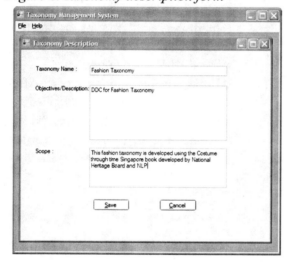

Figure 9. Alternate labels tab

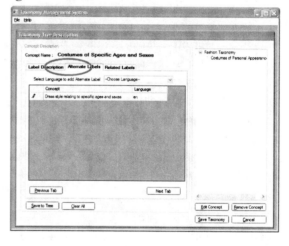

Figure 7. Taxonomy tree description form

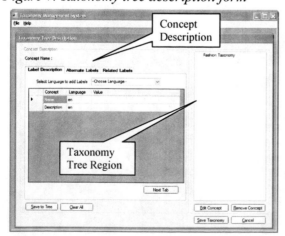

Figure 10. Related labels tab

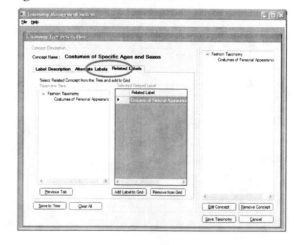

Figure 11. Four control buttons for taxonomy tree

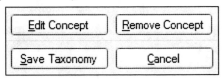

Figure 12. Hierarchical tree for fashion taxonomy and its associated nodeID

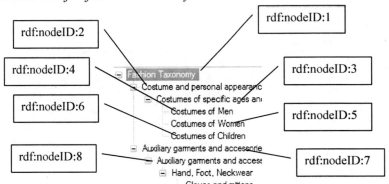

Figure 13. Taxonomy template generated for fashion taxonomy for NodeIDs 1-4

6. **XML output generated by TGT:** Once the user saves the taxonomy after defining the concepts and their descriptions, a taxonomy template is generated by TGT. The tool was validated by inputting several taxonomy structures, one of which is the sample taxonomy data using the Dewey decimal classification (DDC) of fashion taxonomy. Figure 12, for example, shows the DDC for the fashion taxonomy. Internally, TGT sets each label in the hierarchy a unique id with tag name 'rdf:nodeID'. Figure 13 shows the XML template generated for the hierarchical representation of the fashion taxonomy.

Table 2. Focus group discussion guide

Dur:	Section	Sub-Section/Activities

5mins	1.Introduction	1.1 Greeting
		1.2 Purpose of the focus group
		  • Opportunity to provide input about a new software tool for GSDL Software, to assist in generating Taxonomy.
		1.3 Ground rules
		  • Role of moderator, Confidentiality of comments, Individual opinions, Speak one at a time and as clearly as possible
		1.4 Brief get acquainted period
		  • Subjects' names, positions, institution, Digital Library building experience

10mins	2.Brief on Objectives of the study	2.1 The areas to be covered in the study 2.2 About taxonomies, thesauri 2.3 Content management
10mins	3.Demo section	3.1 Give demo presentation & a walkthrough on TGT
15mins	4.Hands-on trial	4.1 Subject try out the tool
10mins	5.Initial Evaluation	5.1 Subjects were asked what they like/dislike about the tool and the idea of using XML template as the output. 5.2 Would it somehow have possibility to improve the resource discovery of Greenstone?
15mins	6.General Usability	6.1 How user-friendly is this tool? 6.2 Likes and dislikes regarding ease of use 6.3 Suggestions to improve the tool based on their experience

20mins	7.Feature Evaluation	7.1 What are the standard features – those they would definitely use?
		7.2 Are there features they would not use or not require in their own situations?
		7.3 Are there any features that would be useful provided they were changed in some manner?
		7.4 Are there any features that would be good in adding as future improvement?
		7.5 Specific features
		  • Concept Description Tab
		  • Taxonomy Tree
		  • Help capability
		  • Screen layouts

10mins	8.Consolidation section	Summary of the discussion and comments made by each subjects
5mins	9.Closing	Any additional comments?

Initial Feedback

In gathering initial feedback on the TGT prototype, we carried out a focus group session with a discussion guide drawn up as shown in Table 2. The objectives of the focus group session were:

- To identify the most important features for users;
- To brainstorm the potential add-on features necessary to fine-tune the tool; and
- To assess and measure the usability and usefulness of the tool.

Positive Feedback

Four subjects (postgraduate and PhD students) at a local university were recruited based on their familiarity with GSDL and the taxonomy concept. Each subject represented various levels of knowledge in understanding and utilizing GSDL and taxonomy.

All the subjects commented that the tool was user-friendly and easy to understand and use. As for using XML template as the output, the subjects thought its flexibility made it easy for them to define their own concepts and make them compatible with Greenstone.

They agreed that TGT followed a good user interface design guideline which could lead the users through a simple and straightforward layout. They seemed to be satisfied with the descriptive labels on top of each frame as it suggested time-saving in capturing the functions and eliminated human errors.

Through the demo section and hands-on experience, the subjects found the core facility useful in allowing for the creation of the taxonomy structure, which includes defining concepts and saving to the tree.

Recommendations

The following recommendations were highlighted by the subjects:

- For better user interface design layout of TGT, intuitive graphics and icons that match the features provided in the system were suggested.
- Subjects pointed out that flexibility in relocating the concept of the taxonomy was important. Each node in the taxonomy structure should then be allowed to move up and down the hierarchy whenever necessary.
- Subjects showed their satisfaction in using the Help facility in TGT, and commented on the need for a table-of-contents-like hyperlink that goes deeper in the help contents for better "findability" of search item.
- Since TGT followed the design structured in GEMS, the languages selected for the preferred terms and alternate terms should be expressed as the short form in the datagrid. For example, the label description in English means to use the code "en" for the language selected. However, users viewed it as not descriptive and the selected language should be displayed as it is, rather than displaying the code name.
- Subjects recommended that for future extension, the interface itself should be allowed to be express in multiple languages, just like Greenstone does. The labels and help facility could be translated into multiple languages that Greenstone supported.
- Subjects pointed out that in order to improve efficiency in defining related labels for the concept, a subject thesaurus tool can be incorporated for better suggestion of associated terms. This facility could lead to future enhancement of this research work.

CONCLUSION AND RECOMMENDATIONS FOR FURTHER WORK

As browsing and searching are the core functionality for DLs, content management and metadata tagging remain important issues for managing digital repositories and emergent technologies, such as Semantic Web and ontology (Zeng, 2005; Zeng & Chan, 2004). This chapter proposes TGT, a taxonomy generator tool with a hierarchical classification of contents module, designed and built to categorize contents in GSDL. TGT, built upon a common framework for taxonomy construction, is customizable to other DL building environments.

A pilot user study was conducted to evaluate the usability and usefulness of TGT and the taxonomy template. Initial feedback was positive, indicating the importance of having a taxonomy structure in GSDL. Recommendations for future work include content classification and metadata technologies in TGT — a way of addressing data management of resources in Greenstone, focusing specifically on incorporating taxonomy in GSDL and

ACKNOWLEDGMENT

The authors are grateful to David Bainbridge for his inputs on design and implementation of the taxonomy generator, and the subjects for their feedback on the usefulness and usability of the generator.

REFERENCES

Bainbridge, D., McKay, D., & Witten, I. H. (2004). *Greenstone developer's guide.* Retrieved May 24, 2007, from http://www.greenstone.org/manuals/gsdl2/en/html/Develop_en_index.html

Goh, D. H.-L., Chua, A., Khoo, D. A., Khoo, E. B.-H., Mak, E. B.-T., & Ng, M. W.-M (2006). A checklist for evaluating open source digital library software. *Online Information Review, 30*(4), 360-379.

Greenstone. (2007). Retrieved May 11, 2007, from http://www.greenstone.org/

McKay, D., Shukla, P., Hunt, R., & Cunningham, S. J. (2004). Enhanced browsing in digital libraries: Three new approaches to browsing in Greenstone. *International Journal on Digital Libraries, 4*(4), 283-297.

Witten, I. H. (2003). *How to build a digital library.* Morgan Kaufmann.

Witten, I. H., & Bainbridge, D. (2005). Creating digital library collections with Greenstone. *Library Hi Tech., 23*(4), 541-560.

Witten, I. H., McNab, R. J., Boddie, S. J., & Bainbridge, D. (2000). Greenstone: A comprehensive open-source digital library software system. In *Proceedings of the Fifth ACM Conference on Digital Libraries DL '00.* ACM Press.

Yan, H. (2004). Digital content management: The search for a content management system. *Library Hi Tech., 22*(4), 355-365.

Zeng, M. L. (2005). *Construction of controlled vocabularies: A primer.* Retrieved May 25, 2007, from http://www.slis.kent.edu/~mzeng/Z3919/index.htm

Zeng, M. L., & Chan, L. M. (2004). Trends and issues in establishing interoperability among knowledge organization systems. *Journal of the American Society for Information Science and Technology, 55*(5), 377-95.

KEY TERMS

Digital Libraries: They mean different things to different people. The design of digital libraries is, therefore, dependent of the perceptions of the purpose/functionality of digital libraries. To the library science community, the roles of traditional libraries are to: (a) provide access to information in any format that has been evaluated, organized, archived, and preserved; (b) have information professionals that make judgments and interpret users' needs; and (c) provide services and resources to people (e.g., students, faculty, others, etc.). To the computer science community, digital libraries may refer to a distributed text-based information system, a collection of distributed information services, a distributed space of interlinked information system, or a networked multimedia information system.

DSpace: It is jointly implemented by Massachusetts Institute of Technology (MIT) and Hewlett-Packard (HP) laboratories and was released in November 2002. DSpace (see http://www.dspace.org) aims to provide a digital institutional repository system to capture, store, index, preserve, and redistribute an organization's research data.

Fedora: It was originally implemented as a DARPA and NSF funded research project at Cornell University and later funded by the Andrew W. Mellon foundation. Fedora (http://www.fedora-commons.org) offers a service-oriented architecture by providing a powerful digital object model which supports multiple views for digital objects.

Greenstone: Greenstone (http://www.greenstone.org) is produced under the New Zealand Digital Library Project, a research project for text compression at University of Waikato. It focuses on personalization and construction of the digital collection from end-user perspectives.

Metadata: A set of attributes that describes the content, quality, condition, and other characteristics of a resource.

Taxonomy: According to the definition by ANSI/NISO (2005), taxonomy is a collection of controlled vocabulary terms organized into a hierarchical structure with each term having one or more parent/child (broader/narrower) relationships to others. It gives a high level view of contents systematically and provides users a roadmap for discovering knowledge available. Taxonomies can appear as lists, trees, hierarchies, polyhierarchies, matrices, facets, or system maps.

Usability: ISO 9241-11 defines usability as "the extent to which a product can be used by specified users to achieve specified goals with effectiveness, efficiency and satisfaction in a specified context of use." Usability of hypertext/Web is commonly measured using established usability dimensions covering categories of usability defects such as screen design, terminology and system information, system capabilities and user control, navigation, and completing tasks.

Usefulness: This is debatable. Some make the distinction between usability and usefulness. Although it is impossible to quantify the usefulness of a system, attempts have been made to measure its attainment in reference to system specifications and the extent of coverage of end users' tasks supported by the system, but not on end user performance testing.

Chapter IX
From Digital Archives to Virtual Exhibitions

Schubert Foo
Nanyang Technological University, Singapore

Yin-Leng Theng
Nanyang Technological University, Singapore

Dion Hoe-Lian Goh
Nanyang Technological University, Singapore

Jin-Cheon Na
Nanyang Technological University, Singapore

ABSTRACT

Digital archives typically act as stand-alone digital libraries to support search and discovery by users to access its rich set of digitized materials. Additionally, content stored in these archives have been utilized and combined to create different thematic online virtual exhibitions (VEs). Such exhibitions are important complimentary counterparts to physical exhibitions, especially in the context of cultural institutions such as museums, archives, and libraries. Well constructed VEs can offer alternative experiences to the "real thing" and open up other opportunities that include education and learning, more content beyond physical exhibits, support for active participation and contribution by visitors through forums and uploads, online shopping, and others. This chapter outlines a number of concepts and design considerations for the development of VEs from digital archives. When supported by the right tools and approaches, creation of VEs can be highly effective and efficient with minimal technological knowledge. By considering the important issues of metadata, system architecture design, and development techniques, it becomes possible to generate a series of VEs to meet the needs of different user groups and at the same time cater to the constraints of the client computers, thereby providing the users the best possible experience in engaging with the VEs.

INTRODUCTION

The Digital Library Federation defines digital libraries (DLs) as "organisations that provide the resources, including the specialised staff, to select, structure, offer intellectual access to, interpret, distribute, preserve the integrity of, and ensure the persistence over time of collections of digital works so that they are readily available for use by a defined community or set of communities" (www.diglib.org/about/dldefinition.htm). One of the most important areas of application of digital libraries is in education. Examples of early educational digital libraries that arose out from the U.S.-led DL initiatives are the Alexandria Digital Library which is a distributed digital library with collections of georeferenced materials (www.alexandria.ucsb.edu/), the National Science Digital Library which is an online library for education and research in science, technology, engineering, and mathematics (http://nsdl.org/), and the Digital Library of Information Science and Technology which is an open source searchable archive about information literacy (http://dlist.sir.arizona.edu/; Farmer, 2007). Another important educational digital library development is JSTOR and the like. JSTOR, originally conceived as a project at The Andrew W. Mellon Foundation, is a nonprofit organization with a dual mission to create and maintain a trusted archive of important scholarly journals, and to provide access to these journals as widely as possible. High-resolution scanned images of back journal issues and pages can retrieved for a very large set of titles across many disciplines. It has become a standard offering at most U.S. universities and colleges as well as a growing number of higher education institutions beyond U.S. (Spinella, 2007). In these digital libraries, content can already exist, or more generally, they would be sourced and populated over time.

Across the world, nonprofit cultural heritage organizations that encompass museums, archives, and national libraries, would generally already have accumulated a rich amount of content in the form of artifacts and documents in different forms, medium, and formats that have been acquired, preserved, and conserved for a long time. Many of these would now be increasingly digitized, described, and stored in digital archives. They are subsequently made available directly to the public through the use of digital library technologies, either as stand-alone documents that can be searched and retrieved, or packaged or curated through other means such as virtual online exhibitions.

Beyond the heritage dimension, we also witness the creation of digital archives and digital preservation initiatives in the area of newspapers and other born-digital documents. In the U.S., KODAK Digital Archive Services preserve 75 years of Pittsburgh Steelers history (Reuters, 2007) and a 19th century newspaper digital archive is also been developed by Thomson Gale (http://gale.cengage.com/usnewspapers/index.htm; Bruns, 2007). Similarly, in the UK, 19th century British Library newspaper and old books are being digitized and preserved (Ashling, 2008) by British Library. Additionally, the Library will build a secure national digital archive of 300 terabytes to store all publications born digitally like CD-ROMS and electronic journals. Alongside this development, the National Archives have been tasked with securing Whitehall's digital legacy by preserving government information that is born digital (Griffin, 2007). Other parts of the world like Australia and Singapore are also embarking upon such initiatives.

These trends are in line with that predicted for a 10 year period commencing in 2006 by the Association of College & Research Libraries (ACRL) Research Committee on 10 assumptions about the future that would have a significant impact on libraries (Mullins, Allen, & Hufford, 2007). At the top of the list of assumptions is that there will be an increased emphasis on digitizing collections, preserving digital archives, and improving methods of data storage and retrieval. Others assumptions suggest that users and consumers expect high quality facilities and services, and free public access to information stemming from public funds.

The aforementioned examples have a common thread among them in that all have potential in education even though they are not originally conceived as an educational service, but as repositories of information that are made accessible to users for knowledge and information discovery. In the context of this chapter, we will focus on digital archives and how these contents can be packaged and developed into virtual exhibitions which have an educational aspect beyond the exhibits.

VIRTUAL EXHIBITION DEFINITION AND CASE FOR SUPPORT FOR DEVELOPMENT

A virtual exhibition (VE) was earlier defined as an online Web-based hyper-textual dynamic collection devoted to a specific theme, topic, concept, or idea (Silver, 1997). Most virtual exhibitions are attributed to museums and archives to make visible their collections to end users, generally the public or specialized user groups (e.g., Hunt, Lundberg, & Zuckerman, 2005). Original artifacts are digitally captured and rendered into 2D or 3D objects which are packaged together and linked by hyperlinks to allow nonlinearity or multiple-linearity by users (exhibition visitors). Virtual exhibitions are viewed as dynamic entities as they often undergo ongoing change in terms of design, activity, and content, including encouraging users to contribute towards its collective memory, thereby adding to its dynamism.

Many early virtual exhibitions are undertaken as distinct projects and packaged as standalone exhibits with little regard on the reusability of objects, and the adoption of standards to support interoperability, extensible, and scalable system architectures to support growth and pervasiveness of exhibitions.

Some examples of early VEs include *Building a National Collection: 150 Years of Print Collecting at the Smithsonian* by the National Museum of American History (americanhistory.si.edu/prints/index.htm), *American History Documents* (www.indiana.edu/~liblilly/history/history.html), *Birds: A Virtual Exhibition* by Canadian Heritage Information Network (www.virtualmuseum.ca/Exhibitions/Birds/Birds/), *Colours of the Wind* by the National Archives of Singapore (www.a2o.com.sg/a2o/public/html/online_exhibit/misas/exhibit/index2.html; Leong, Chennupati & Foo, 2002, 2003), and others.

Over the last decade, improvements to these areas have been seen and virtual exhibitions have reached a stage of sophistication, although a number of fundamental challenges remain. While the basic tenets of virtual exhibition have not changed, an updated definition of virtual exhibition is proposed (Foo, in press):

A virtual exhibition (VE) is a Web-based hypermedia collection of captured or rendered multidimensional information objects, possibly stored in distributed networks, designed around a specific theme, topic concept or idea, and harnessed with state-of-art technology and architecture to deliver a user-centered and engaging experience of discovery, learning, contributing and being entertained through its nature of its dynamic product and service offerings.

The case for investing in the design and development of VE has been well documented in literature (e.g., Chennupati, 2007; Lester, 2006). First and foremost is the recognition that hosting VEs provides a gateway to showcase an institution's collections that are not bound by time (temporal), distance (spatial), and space (spatial) constraints, unlike physical exhibitions. This addresses the important issue to make valuable artifacts available to the masses while playing the role of custodianship of national and international treasures.

Users are unlikely to pay visits to these institutions unless they are aware of their collections and holdings. One way round this is to create VEs that are coupled with educational functionality to promote the institution as a center for learning, and to further encourage users to physically access the brick-and-mortar building, or virtually access and retrieve digitized information objects. Such an approach helps to demonstrate institutional relevance and societal value through a strong public profile. In turn, high usage figures can be used to help secure adequate funding and resources for survival, sustainability, and growth of the institution into the future. In view of this, user outreach through VEs is seen to be an important strategic activity that needs to be properly planned and executed. Other forms of more traditional outreach activities like publications, Web sites, tours, talks, demonstrations, and other activities can be undertaken alongside VEs to create the impact and yield the desired outcomes.

Online strategies (VEs and Web sites) have particular advantages: it is relatively easy to add new products and services or revamp existing ones in the form of adding new materials; updating and reusing existing materials; adding new learning and edutainment components; online shopping; online forums; and users' contributions, to name just a few.

VEs, through digitization and rendering, also have the distinct advantage to create and use electronic surrogates of original fragile or sensitive records, or priceless artifacts which might otherwise be damaged in physical consultation. Established institutions such as Smithsonian Institute (www.si.edu), Auckland Art Museum (www.ackland.org/index.php), and most national heritage boards and museums around the world have a permanent and rich set of VEs hosted on their servers. Collectively, they are able to display and make available a significant amount of "treasures" held by the institution which is by far much than what physical exhibitions can display and achieve at any one time. This means

of extending outreach has significant long term returns of investment once these VEs are curated and implemented for public access and use.

While VEs have been critiqued in the past for its inability to provide the experience of the "real thing," VEs can allow users to understand, discover, learn, and do far more than physical exhibitions. By adopting a carefully researched user-centered design, VEs through hyper-linking support both linear and nonlinear discovery and learning pathways, creating learning opportunities that are difficult to replicate in physical exhibitions.

The ability to engage in multiple forms of media (e.g., text, image, audio, sound, video, augmented reality, and virtual reality components) on one page, having the ability to reverse, revisit, translate, and read text tailored for different user groups, proficiencies, and requirements, and immersion in well crafted theme-games and so forth, collectively help to establish a deeper sense of understanding, awareness, and learning of contents than physical exhibits. VEs are therefore no longer viewed as passing fads but an important logical companion and extension to physical exhibitions.

While the discussion of VEs has so far being related to nonprofit institutions such as museums and archives, it should be borne in mind that the ideas put forth subsequently are equally applicable to profit organizations for the marketing of its products and services. While some functionality and features are no longer slanted towards the social responsibility aspects in such organizations, these VEs still rely on similar characteristics such as the ability to deliver attractive, interesting, engaging, and intriguing "exhibits" through user-friendly interfaces to encourage users (buyers) to visit and access the site, and ultimately become customers of the organization. These sites typically have the common features of hyper-animated graphics, brief exhibitions, and high interactivity zones to showcase products and services, online areas for mailing list sign-ups, and online stores to order and make purchases. However, it should be made aware that these VEs are often characterized with biased education in an attempt to gain competitive advantage over other competitors' VE sites, which one should really expect in today's competitive landscape. In contrast, VEs developed by nonprofit organizations and government agencies are almost always constructed with different objectives in mind: archival, preservation, discovery, education, and others. They are deemed more authoritative, and contain better researched and trusted resources, and higher educational value.

Nonetheless, a similar set of user-centered design paradigms, use of technological tools, well designed system architectures to high level of automation with minimal human intervention, and effort to create new versions of VEs are equally applicable for all forms of organizations. At a higher abstract level, we may consider VEs as digital libraries that contain a set of information objects that can be accessed individually, or packaged together by applications supported by the DLs.

The aim of this chapter is to treat VEs from this generic angle to examine a number of issues in the design and delivery of virtual exhibitions. This includes addressing the stakeholders of VEs, the important role of metadata, and approaches to system architectural design and development.

STAKEHOLDERS OF VIRTUAL EXHIBITIONS

Virtual exhibitions are extraordinary difficult to design and develop. One main reason is the number of stakeholders involved in the process. Patel, White, Mourkoussis, Walczak, Wojciechowski, and Chmielewski (2005) suggest that there are actually six groups of stakeholders involved in the process of creating and using the VE, with each group playing different roles:

1. *Curator,* who is knowledgeable of the information objections and primarily responsible for artifact selection (i.e., identifying and selecting the artifacts for the VE).
2. *Photographer,* who is responsible for digital acquisition to create the information objects to be stored in the digital repository.
3. *Cataloguer,* who is responsible for data management to describe, catalogue, and group individual objects together.
4. *Modeler,* who is responsible for model refinement to create and describe object interpretations and/or refinements.
5. *Curator exhibition* designer, who is responsible for exhibition building.
6. *End users,* who are the consumers of the final VE.

The first five categories of stakeholders are typically part of the VE team, each with a different set of knowledge, expertise, and skill and differing metadata requirements. VE teams can be large and can comprise professional writers, artists, archivists, graphic designers, multimedia technicians, technical specialists, and curators. External advisory and editorial committees may also be roped in the VE design and construction to create a more balanced and effective exhibition.

End users, on the other hand, can evolve from a myriad of different user groups: children and adults, students and teachers, academics and researchers, novice and expert users, tourists and casual Internet surfers, and the general public and professional users (i.e., archivists, librarians and information professionals). The important aspect to note in this multiplicity of stakeholders is that it translates into a varying and large set of differing user requirements and expectations throughout the process of designing, developing, and using the exhibition.

A "one size fits all" paradigm is almost certain to fail to meet these expectations. VEs need to be carefully curated and designed to ensure the potential for success. Typically, this encompasses a need for good metadata design and management, novel and effective ways to generate different versions of VEs at least, or acceptable costs and high productivity in order to satisfy the needs of different user groups. With this, we can expect to find the requirement to tailor varying levels of content generation and online media types to cater to the needs of these different types of users. Contents would typically include multimedia elements, 2D, 3D, augmented reality (AR), and virtual reality (VR) (Gotz & Mayer-Patel, 2005; Lim & Foo, 2003).

METADATA REQUIREMENTS

Metadata has always been an extremely crucial aspect for describing and managing artifacts in the collection. When these are digitally acquired and transformed into information objects, a new set of corresponding metadata becomes necessary. When new applications such as VEs are developed, more metadata are required to describe and manage the exhibition, page contents, access information, and so on. The different stakeholder groups in the previous section provide an idea of the wide ranging metadata requirements needed by various constituents of the cultural heritage industry.

Active researches done on metadata and continuing developments of standards such as SPECTRUM, EAD, Dublin Core, and other metadata schemes attest to the importance of having relevant metadata to support a variety of needs. Metadata can typically be classified as descriptive metadata, technical metadata, presentation metadata, preservation metadata, administrative metadata, and resource discovery metadata. It should be noted that while Dublin Core is an important, well-established metadata standard for descriptive and resource discovery across domains and used by all almost all systems, it

does not specifically deal with museum, archive, and education requirements that have their own set of detailed metadata elements.

This overwhelming amount of metadata has prompted the proposal for having a system for authoring, maintaining, and managing metadata to support the development of the augmented representation of cultural objects (ARCO) system for museums to create, manipulate, manage, and present small to medium artifacts in VEs for both internally within museums and externally on the Web (Patel et. al., 2005). They envisaged the creation of digital artifacts providing opportunities to develop virtual learning environments (VLEs) which in turn entail creating new additional metadata such as those defined by ADL sharable content object reference model (SCORM) or IEEE learning object metadata (LOM) standards to support e-learning. Furthermore, they envisage commercial exploitation by institutions in the form of virtual loans for VEs (through information objects) that requires the support of a digital rights management system (DRMS). All this translates into more and more need for metadata.

Two issues are particularly important for metadata in the context of VEs. First is the highly recommended use of standards to support interoperability. When this becomes not possible for whatever reasons, the exchange of metadata information across systems becomes more costly due to the need for validation, optimization, and mapping. In terms of metadata definition and storage, extensible markup language (XML) has turned out to be the de-facto emerging preferred means to manage information objects and VEs. VE exhibition pages contain a series of exhibition objects that can be neatly encapsulated in a XML-based conceptual hypermedia document model. Such a document typical includes different types of information, such as text, data, graphics, images, hyperlinks, and other elements. Likewise, the information object's metadata can be neatly based on the XML structure. Effectively, an XML-based solution exhibits the advantages such as platform independence, clear structuring and encapsulation, modularity, and so on.

The second issue pertains to the need to create a range of representations for one same original artifact. As an example, an image can be captured at different resolutions and sizes. They can be used as thumbnails, medium resolution for browsing, and very high resolution for zooming and detailed analysis. These different versions of content basically share the same metadata except for those entities that are distinct and different.

Figure 1 shows an example of a photograph metadata set in XML format (Lim & Foo, 2003). In this example, the accession ID is used to uniquely identify a photograph artifact while the location element is used to define the repository directory where all the images are stored. As indicated previously, the image element can be defined more than once to cater to the different available

versions of the same original photograph. These versions may contain resized, enhanced, or digitally-manipulated variations (e.g., colour, addition of borders) of the original photograph.

The same approach can be adopted for textual artifact metadata to incorporate the standard DC elements plus text specific elements. For example, the "content_version" element can be used the support layering of information through different descriptive layers of a textual artifact. These text descriptions can range from summarized abstract information to detailed information, or specially text written for children or adults, and so on. Likewise, we can adopt the same approach for different audio, video, and other artifacts to cater for different network conditions, resolutions, and the like. In doing so, we have one associated metadata record across different content versions that can be drawn by the VE to create a series of VEs for different users.

Figure 1. Example of photograph metadata document type definition (Lim & Foo, 2003)

```
<?xml version = "1.0" encoding = "UTF-8">
<!DOCTYPE photo [
<!ELEMENT photo ( title*, creator*, subject*, description*, contributor*, date*, t ype*, format, accession_id, source*,
    language*, relation*, coverage*, copyright*, identifier*, location, image+)>
    <!ELEMENT title (#PCDATA)>
    <!ELEMENT creator (#PCDATA)>
    <!ELEMENT subject (#PCDATA)>
    <!ELEMENT description (#PCDATA)>
    <!ELEMENT contributor (#PCDATA)>
    <!ELEMENT date (#PCDATA)>
    <!ELEMENT type (#PCDATA)>          Standard Dublin Core 15 metadata
    <!ELEMENT format (#PCDATA)>        elements
    <!ELEMENT accession_id (#PCDATA)>
    <!ELEMENT source (#PCDATA)>
    <!ELEMENT language (#PCDATA)>
    <!ELEMENT relation (#PCDATA)>
    <!ELEMENT coverage (#PCDATA)>
    <!ELEMENT copyright (#PCDATA)>
    <!ELEMENT identifier (#PCDATA)>
    <!ELEMENT location (#PCDATA)>
    <!ELEMENT image (img_id, i mg_height?, img_width?, i mg_file_size?, img_description?, reproduction_date?,
    photoCD?, photoCD_imgno?)
        <!ELEMENT img_no (#PCDATA)>
        <!ELEMENT photo_size (#PCDATA)>
<!ELEMENT img_height (#PCDATA)>        Additional metadata
        <!ELEMENT img_width (#PCDATA)>        for photograph artifact
        <!ELEMENT img_file_size (#PCDATA)>
        <!ELEMENT img_description (#PCDATA)>
        <!ELEMENT reproduction_date (#PCDATA)>
        <!ELEMENT photoCD (#PCDATA)>
        <!ELEMENT photoCD_imgno(#PCDATA)>
]       >
```

CREATION OF MULTIPLE VERSIONS OF VES EFFECTIVELY AND EFFICIENTLY

By using this approach of layering metadata and use of style sheets, Lim and Foo (2003) developed a VE authoring system to interface with the National Archives of Singapore digital archive to support the creation of VEs. The XML-based digital archive provides different artifact types that form the contents in the exhibition through the reference and reuse model. This means that only one copy of information object resides in the repository which is in turn referenced and used by more than one VE as necessary. Information objects and exhibitions are endowed with rich metadata that include the Dublin Core elements and other new attributes to support enhanced search support for field and free text searches. An authoring tool using a grid-layout approach is used to define and layout the exhibition contents. XML's cascading style sheet and extended style sheets are then selected from a range of predefined templates and applied to the XML documents to yield the final VE in hypertext markup language (HTML) format. By adopting the notion of information layering in the descriptors or different editions of the information objects, and the application of different style sheets, it becomes possible to create multiple versions of the same exhibition that varies in content, layout, and interface to create different versions of VEs for different user groups. The use of style sheets is particularly useful as it allows content and structure to be separated cleanly so that the information can be rendered to yield different look-and-feel interface versions of VEs, thereby enhancing the productivity of creating VEs and updating existing VEs. A second version of this system was subsequently developed (Yang, Chennupati & Foo, 2007) to enhance the authoring aspect by supporting a WYSIWYG interface for VE content layout and addition of different information objects types.

A similar approach was also adopted by Cruz-Lara, Chen, and Hong (2002) in the development of a distributed content management framework for digital museums based on XML and XSL techniques. Using this framework, they developed a Lanyu Digital Museum for the Lanyu Island and its Yami inhabitants, and a Lanyu Virtual Exhibition Hall. In a related article by Hong, Chen, and Hung (2004), they propose an intelligent styling system to help museums efficiently and effectively produce and publish attractive VEs through the use of loosely coupled fine-grained style modules (FGSM) to present specific content fragments coupled with a hypermedia authoring system.

GENERIC SYSTEM ARCHITECTURE FOR DEVELOPING VIRTUAL EXHIBITIONS

At the formative stages of VE development, we witness the emergence of different stand-alone proprietary systems as one would expect. Over a period of time, there is a growing emergence of acceptance of standards and techniques, notably in the areas of metadata definition for VE artifacts, XML for storing metadata and exhibition data, utilization of style templates for generating versions of VEs, and inclusion of e-learning functionality in VEs.

Examples of different system architectures have been report in literature. These include the virtual exhibition system (VES) by Lim and Foo (2003), virtual archive exhibition system (VAES) by Yang et al. (2007), and the Lanyu Digital Museum architecture and proposed framework for an integrated digital museum system by Hong, Chen, Hung, and Hsiang (2005). The salient features and approaches of these systems have also been described previously.

Although these and other current VE applications have adopted different system architecture for their systems, they tend to share a number of basic components to support VE functionality. Figure 2 attempts to encapsulate a generic system

Figure 2. Generic system architecture for VE development

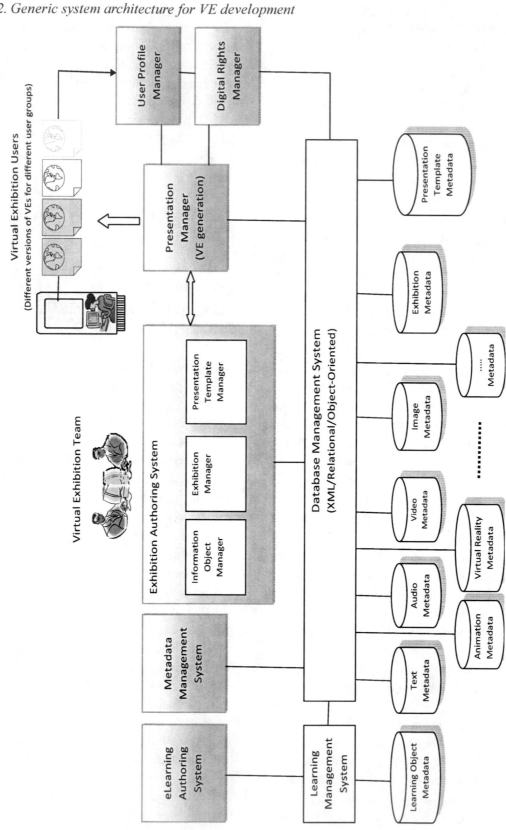

architecture that can be used as a useful platform for the development of VE systems in future. The architecture aims to support effectiveness and efficiency in generating, maintaining, and managing VEs. It attempts to provide VE exhibition teams with useful tool sets to generate different versions of the same VEs for end users' consumption, taking into account users' needs and system constraints of the client's setup in accessing the exhibition.

The primitive data level contains all the information objects that can be used for VEs: text, image, audio, video, 3D graphics, interactive media, and so on. These information objects can be different versions of digitized artifacts or born digital objects. When e-learning is considered, this can also include questions for quizzes for assessment, and other learning activities. These primitive learning and information objects can be combined to form larger learning entities through the learning management system (LMS) or e-learning authoring system (which can either be stand-alone or an integral part of the LMS) to generate stand-alone learning objects which in turn can be aggregated to form larger learning modules. These variations of learning content can be incorporated into VEs as necessary.

Each primitive information object is defined by a set of appropriate metadata which is created, updated, and maintained through a database management system (DMS). If necessary, a metadata management system (MMS) can be used to provide an interface to the DMS to support various metadata operations. This system is not confined to managing primitive information objects; it can also be used to manage metadata for the exhibition, presentation templates, and other metadata which the system uses.

The exhibition authoring system forms the crux of VEs authoring. The VE exhibition team uses the system to define the exhibition framework, select information objects (including learning objects if these are present in the VE) for page contents, and create the layout and look-and-feel

of the exhibition pages. This functionality can be integrated as one system, or split into different modules for exhibition page definition, page element selection, and presentation definition. This latter approach attempts to clearly separate data from structure and layout. Using an information object manager, exhibition pages can incorporate background music or a background image, use a specific layer of information, and select different layout settings and font settings during the authoring stage.

As mentioned previously, different presentations are usually achieved through different presentation or style templates selected during this authoring stage. These templates can be predefined for selection, or created and managed by a more sophisticated presentation template manager. The exhibition manager defines and manages the whole exhibition and combines these various pages together to form the exhibition whose metadata can be stored in the exhibition repository for future reference, editing, or updates. The internally generated VE definition can be stored in a suitable data exchange format that is used by the presentation manager, whose role is to render and generate the VE into its final form for use by users.

Depending on the way the exhibition authoring system is designed, all the necessary information can be made available for the presentation manager to complete the work so that VEs can be generated off-line. Alternatively, VEs can be generated on-the-fly to take into account client system characteristics and end-users characteristics or preferences. As such, the presentation manager may be interfaced with a user profile manager to manage these aspects of system and user requirements.

System requirements would typically consider client computer processing capability, network bandwidth, and so on, in order for the content to be adapted as necessary. For example, different resolution image, sound, and video may be used as necessary to attain an acceptable quality of service for the VEs with different constraints; and resource intensive 3D graphics may be eliminated if they cannot be adequately by the client computer. User characteristics would typically consider age, literacy level, motive for using VE, kind of experience desired, and so on in order for the VE to be adapted as necessary. As such, the user profile manager may require some form of interaction and inputs from the user to complete the information necessary for the VEs to be generated.

Another component that might be interfaced to the presentation manager might be a digital rights manager to support a digital rights management system in the case where VEs are loaned out to other institutions and where constraints are placed on the information objects' use. Such a system may allow other VEs from other institutions to have access to the primitive information objects as content for these VEs. Such an attempt to either provide free or fee-paying access can help promote reusability and sharing, and potentially enhance the quality of the final VEs.

Through the presentation manager and these other interfaces, a stand-alone or many different versions of the same exhibition may be generated at one pass. Ultimately, the aim is to generate different versions of VEs to meet the needs of different user groups, and to user technology to support VE authoring efficiently and effectively, thereby minimizing human effort and intervention.

In terms of implementation, a number of common data types, standards, and techniques have been utilized in most systems for VEs as shown in Table 1. The table also shows the desirable contents, characteristics, and features that have been suggested in literature for successful VEs.

CONCLUSION

Digital archives, as a stand-alone digital library, can be endowed with added functionality to create applications such as virtual exhibitions that will

Table 1. Data types, desirable content and features of VEs

Information Objects
Text: ASCII, Unicode
Image: GIF, JPEG, PNG, SVG, BMP, TIFF
Audio: MP3, MP4, MIDI, SND, WMA, WAV
Video: MPEG, AVI, MOV, WMD, QT
Interactive Media: Java applets, Flash, Shockwave, X3D, VRML
Metadata: Dublin Core, SPECTRUM
Learning Object Metadata: LOM, SCORM
Style/Presentation Templates: XSL
Database Management System: XML database
Metadata/Internal document representation: XML, XDE
Across server access and information exchange: SOAP (Simple Object Access Protocol)

VE Contents
Comprehensive and well organized contents
Contextual information to ensure understandability by Web visitors
Online courses (eLearning)
Educative interactional games
Engaging multimedia
Frequently asked questions
Guest book
User forums (for ideas, comments, critiques, suggestions)
User resource contributions (e.g., users' own photographs, stories, oral history)
Online shopping (e.g., souvenirs)
Downloadable content (e.g., wallpaper, screen-savers, free content)
Educational resource center for teacher classroom teaching
List of useful resources for further research
Help (e.g., How to Navigate, Technical support)

Features
Different versions for different user groups
High aesthetics and appealing
User-centered styles and interactivity
Good navigation design (including possible automatic navigation)
Good browsing and searching capability
Use of standards to support interoperability
Metadata details upon users request (for research)

not only enhance the value of digital objects in the archives being used by users through browsing or searching, but allow well designed virtual exhibitions to be curated, designed, and developed to support discovery, learning, and other opportunities beyond what physical exhibitions and stand-alone digital objects can offer.

This chapter has presented the case for VEs, surfaced the myriad of stakeholders of VEs, and demonstrated the need for good metadata. Using a generic system architecture, the various components and approaches widely adopted in VE system design and development are highlighted.

A list of desirable VE contents and features are also articulated to aid future VE development. The continuing developments of Web 2.0 and Library 2.0 work, VE researches, wireless, and other technological advances are likely to change the form and capability of future VEs, and perhaps change how users would view and use such applications in future.

We believe that virtual exhibitions can, and are expected to, survive and grow as they stand to yield a rich set of both tangible and intangible for institutions that fully embrace the idea of both the physical and virtual operating environment in this Internet age. The key is to keep close watch on the trends which at this time of writing seems to rage on social networking sites (such as Friendster, Facebook, MySpace, Flickr, and many others), where developers have embraced Web 2.0 technology offerings to allow users to create ownership, have their personal "voice/face" in these applications, and have ability to contribute, discuss, and engage other users in the community virtually. By endowing virtual exhibitions with such attributes, and making the contents searchable in such social spaces, can help to land users on board to use, learn, and contribute to these exhibitions (that contain trusted authoritative contents) and the physical institutions.

REFERENCES

Ashling, J. (2008). Preserving 19th century British Library newspaper. *Information Today, 25*(1), 28.

Bruns, C. W. (2007). 19th century U.S. newspaper archive. *Choice: Current Reviews for Academic Libraries, 45*(2), 256-258.

Chennupati, K. R. (2007, December) Case for virtual Salar Jung Museum. *Deccan Chronicle, 5,* 9. Retrieved February 20, 2008, from http://deccan.com/cultureplus/cultureplus.asp

Cruz-Lara, S., Chen, B. H., & Hong, J. S. (2002, November 14-15). Distributed content management framework for digital museum exhibitions. In *Proceedings of EUROPIX Scholars Network Conference*, Tampere, Finland. Retrieved February 20, 2008, from http://www.acten.org/cgi-bin/WebGUI/www/index.pl/sc_announcements

Farmer, L. (2007). Digital library of information science and technology. *Reference Reviews, 21*(2), 11.

Foo, S. (in press). Online virtual exhibitions: Concepts and design considerations. *DESIDOC (Defence Scientific Information & Documentation Centre) Bulletin of Information Technology.*

Gotz, D., & Mayer-Patel, K. (2005). A framework for scalable delivery of digitized spaces. *International Journal on Digital Libraries, 5*(3), 205-218.

Griffin, D. (2007). National archives takes charge of securing Whitehall's digital legacy. *Information World Review, 238,* 6.

Hong, J. S., Chen, B. H., & Hung, S. H. (2004). Toward intelligent styling for digital museum exhibitions: Modularization framework for aesthetic hypermedia presentations. *International Journal on Digital Libraries, 4,* 64-68.

Hong, J. S., Chen, B. H., Hung, S. H., & Hsiang, J. (2005). Toward an integrated digital museum system: The Chi Nan experiences. *International Journal on Digital Libraries, 5*(3), 231-251.

Hunt, L., Lundberg, M., & Zuckerman, B. (2005). InscriptiFact: A virtual archive of ancient inscriptions from the Near East. *International Journal of Digital Libraries, 5,* 153-166.

Lester, P. (2006). Is the virtual exhibition the natural successor to the physical? *Journal of the Society of Archivists, 27*(1), 5-101.

Lim, J. C., & Foo, S. (2003). Creating virtual exhibitions from an XML-based digital archive. *Journal of Information Science, 29*(3), 143-158.

Mullins, J. L., Allen, F. R., & Hufford, J. R. (2007). Top ten assumptions for the future of academic libraries and librarians: A report from the ACRL research committee. *C&RL News, 68*(4). Retrieved February 20, 2008, from http://www.ala.org/ala/acrl/acrlpubs/crlnews/backissues2007/april07/tenassumptions.cfm.

Patel, M., White, M., Mourkoussis, N., Walczak, K., Wojciechowski, R., & Chmielewski, J. (2005). Metadata requirements for digital museums environment. *International Journal of Digital Libraries, 5,* 179-192.

Reuters. (2007, November 29). *KODAK digital archive services preserves 75 years of Pittsburgh Steelers history.* Retrieved February 20, 2008, from http://www.reuters.com/article/pressRelease/idUS46928+29-Nov-2007+BW20071129

Silver, D. (1997). Interfacing American culture: The perils and potentials of virtual exhibitions. *American Quarterly, 49*(4), 825-850.

Spinella, M. P. (2007). JSTOR: Past, present, and future. *Journal of Library Administration, 46*(2), 55-78.

Yang, R., Chennupati, K. R., & Foo, S. (2007, August 27-31,). Virtual archival exhibition system: An authoring tool for developing web-based virtual exhibitions. In *Proceedings of the International Conference on Dublin Core and Metadata Applications (DC-2007),* Singapore (pp. 96-105).

KEY TERMS

Digital Archives: An information retrieval system that stores digitized primary sources of information and is accessible by computers for browsing, search, and retrieval. The digital content, generally grouped by provenance and original order, may be stored locally, or accessed remotely via computer networks. The content is usually unique and one-of-a-kind and cannot be found or consulted at any other location except at the archive that holds them.

Metadata: Metadata is data about data, or information about information. Metadata are documentation about documents and objects; they describe resources, indicate where they are located, and outline what is required in order to use them successfully. Metadata are data associated with objects which relieves their potential users of having to have full advanced knowledge of their existence or characteristics. Metadata are data that describe attributes of a resource, characterize its relationships, support its discovery and effective use, and exists in an electronic environment.

System Architecture: The design and representation of a system in which there is a mapping of functionality onto hardware and software components, a mapping of software architecture onto the hardware architecture, and the human interaction with these components to form a software or information retrieval system.

Virtual Exhibitions: A Web-based hypermedia collection of captured or rendered multi-dimensional information objects, possibly stored in distributed networks, designed around a specific theme, topic concept or idea, and harnessed with state-of-art technology and architecture to deliver a user-centered and engaging experience of discovery, learning, contributing, and being entertained through its nature of its dynamic product and service offerings.

Section II
Information Processing and Content Management

Chapter X
Standardization of Terms Applying Finite-State Transducers (FST)

Carmen Galvez
University of Granada, Spain

ABSTRACT

This chapter presents the different standardization methods of terms at the two basic approaches of nonlinguistic and linguistic techniques, and sets out to justify the application of processes based on finite-state transducers (FST). Standardization of terms is the procedure of matching and grouping together variants of the same term that are semantically equivalent. A term variant is a text occurrence that is conceptually related to an original term and can be used to search for information in a text database. The uniterm and multiterm variants can be considered equivalent units for the purposes of automatic indexing. This chapter describes the computational and linguistic base of the finite-state approach, with emphasis on the influence of the formal language theory in the standardization process of uniterms and multiterms. The lemmatization and the use of syntactic pattern-matching, through equivalence relations represented in FSTs, are emerging methods for the standardization of terms.

INTRODUCTION

The purpose of a information retrieval system (IRS) consists of retrieving, from amongst a collection of documents, those that respond to an informational need, and to reorganize these documents according to a factor of relevance.

This process normally involves *statistical methods* in charge of selecting the most appropriate terms for representing documental contents, and an *inverse index file* that accesses the documents containing these terms (Salton & McGill, 1983). The relationship of pertinence between queries and documents is established by the number of terms they have in common. For this reason the queries and documents are represented as sets of characteristics or indexing terms, which can be derived directly or indirectly from the text using either a thesaurus or a manual or automatic indexing procedure. In many IRS, the documents are indexed by uniterms. However, these may result ambiguous, and therefore unable to discriminate only the pertinent information. One solution to this problem is to work with multiword terms (or *phrases*) often obtained through statistical methods. The traditional IRS approach is based on this type of automatic indexing technique for representing documentary contents (Croft, Turtle, & Lewis, 1991; Frakes, 1992; Salton, 1989).

Matching query terms to documents involves a number of advanced retrieval techniques, and one problem that has not yet been solved is the inadequate representation of the two (Strzalkowski, Lin, Wang, & Pérez-Carballo, 1999). At the root of this problem is the great variability of the lexical, syntactic, and morphological features of a term, variants that cannot be recognized by simple *string-matching algorithms* without some sort of *natural language processing* (NLP) (Hull, 1996). It is generally agreed that NLP techniques could improve IRS yields; yet it is still not clear exactly how we might incorporate the advancements of computational linguistics into retrieval systems. The grouping of morphological variants would increase the average recall, while the identification and grouping of syntactic variants is determinant in increasing the accuracy of retrieval. One study about the problems involved in using linguistic variants in IRS is detailed by Sparck Jones and Tait (1984).

The term standardization is the process of matching and grouping together variants of the same term that are semantically equivalent. A variant is defined as a text occurrence that is conceptually related to an original term and can be used to search for information in text databases (Jacquemin & Tzoukermann, 1999; Sparck Jones & Tait, 1984; Tzoukermann, Klavans, &

Jacquemin, 1997). This is done by means of computational procedures known as *standardization or conflation algorithms*, whose primary goal is the normalization of uniterms and multiterms (Galvez, Moya-Anegón, & Solana, 2005). In order to avoid the loss of relevant documents, an IRS recognizes and groups variants by means of so-called conflation algorithms. The process of standardization may involve linguistic techniques such as the segmentation of words and the elimination of affixes, or lexical searches through thesauri. The latter is concerned with the recognition of semantic variants, and remains beyond the scope of the present study.

This chapter focuses on the initial stage of automatic indexing in natural language, that is, on the process of algorithmically examining the indexing terms to generate and control the units that will then be incorporated as potential entries to the search file. The recognition and grouping of lexical and syntactic variants can thus be considered a process of normalization; when a term does not appear in a normalized form, it is replaced with the canonical form. Along these lines, we will review the most relevant techniques for grouping variants, departing from the premise that conflation techniques featuring linguistic devices can be considered normalization techniques, their function being to regulate linguistic variants.

THE PROBLEM OF TERM VARIANTS

During the first stage of automatic indexing in natural language we encounter a tremendous number of variants gathered up by the indexing terms. The variants are considered semantically similar units that can be treated as equivalents in IRS. To arrive at these equivalencies, standardization methods of variants are used, grouping the terms that refer to equivalent concepts. The variants can be used to extract information in the textual databases (Jacquemin & Tzoukermann,

1999). Arampatzis, Tsoris, Koster, and Van der Weide (1998) identify three main types of variations: *(a)* morphological variation linked to the internal structure of words, by virtue of which a term can appear in different forms (e.g., *"connect," "connected," "connecting,"* and *"connection"* are reduced to *"connect."* which is considered to be identical for all these morphologically and conceptually related terms); (b) lexico-semantic variation linked to the semantic proximity of the words, so that different terms can represent the same meaning, and multiple meanings can be represented by the same term (e.g., *"anoxaemia," "anoxemia,"* and *"breathing problems"* are reduced to *"breathing disorders"*); and (c) syntactic variation linked to the structure of the multiword terms, where altenative syntactic structures are reduced to a canonical syntactic structure (e.g., constructions that are structurally distinct but semantically equivalent, such as *"consideration of these domain properties"* and *"considering certain domain properties"* are conflated to the single structure *"considering domain properties"*).

In most cases, the variants are considered semantically similar units that can be treated as equivalents in IRS (Hull, 1996). To arrive at these equivalencies, standardization methods of variants are used, grouping the terms that refer to equivalent concepts. Standardization methods are applied when the terms are morphologically similar. But when the similarity is semantic, lexical search methods are used. To reduce semantic variation, most systems resort to lexical lookup to relate two words that are completely different in form (Paice, 1996). The problems involved in fusing the lexico-semantic variants remain beyond the scope of the present review.

AN APPROACH TO STANDARDIZATION METHODS OF TERMS

Term standardization methods have essentially been developed for English because it is the pre-

dominant language in IR experiments. However, with a view to the reduction of uniterm variants, English features a relatively weak morphology and therefore linguistic techniques are not necessarily the most suitable ones. To the contrary, because English relies largely on the combination of terms, the linguisitc techniques would indeed be more effective in merging multiterm variants. The procedures for the reduction of variants of single-word terms can be classified as: (1) *nonlinguistic techniques*, which are stemming methods consisting mainly of suffix stripping, stem-suffix segmentation rules, similarity measures, and clustering techniques; and (2) *linguistic techniques*, which are lemmatization methods consisting of morphological analysis. That is, term standardization based on the regular relations (RR), or equivalence relations, between inflectional forms and canonical forms, represented in *finite-state transducers* (FSTs).

On the other hand, the multiterms that represent concepts are included among what are known as *complex descriptors*. Fagan (1989) suggests two types of relationships: *syntactic* and *semantic*. First, the syntactic relationships depend on the grammatical structure of these same terms and are represented in phrases. The syntactic relationships are of a *syntagmatic* type, allowing the reduction of terms used in document representation, and their contribution in the IRS is to increase average precision. Second, the semantic relationships depend on the inherent meaning of the terms involved and are represented in the classes of a thesaurus. The semantic relationships are of a *paradigmatic* type, allowing us to broaden the terms used in the representation of the documents, and their purpose in the retrieval systems is to increase average recall. Multiword terms are considered to be more specific indicators of document content than are single words, and for this reason many methods have been developed for their identification. Basically there are two approaches: (1) *nonlinguistic techniques*, which are statistical methods based on the computation of similarity coefficients, association measures, and clustering techniques by means of word and n-gram cooccurrence; and (2) *linguistic techniques,* which are syntactic methods based on syntactic pattern-matching according to local grammars (LG) represented in *finite-state automata* (FSA) (a LG consists of rigorous and explicit specifications of particular structures) and pattern standardization through equivalence relations, established between syntactic structure variants and canonical syntactic structures, represented in FSTs.

The application of standardization techniques to single-word terms is a way of considering the different lexical variants as equivalent units for retrieval purposes. One of the most widely used nonlinguistic techniques is that of stemming algorithms, through which the inflectional and derivational variants are reduced to one canonical form. Stemming or suffix stripping uses a list of frequent suffixes to conflate words to their *stem* or base form. Two well known stemming algorithms for English are the Lovins stemmer (1968) and the Porter stemmer (1980). Another means of dealing with language variability through linguistic methods is the fusion of lexical variants into *lemmas,* defined as a set of terms with the same stem and, optionally, belonging to the same syntactic category. The process of lemmatization, or morphological analysis of the variants and their reduction to controlled forms, relies on lexical information stored in electronic dictionaries or lexicons. One such example is the morphological analyzer developed by Karttunen (1983).

In addition to these approaches, it is possible to group multiword terms within a context, assigning specific indicators of relationship geared to connect different identifiers, so that *noun phrases* (NPs) can be built (Salton & McGill, 1983). NPs are made up of two or more consecutive units, and the relationships between or among these units are interpreted and codified as endocentric constructions, or *modifier-head-structures* (Harris, 1951). When we deal with single-word

terms, the content identifiers are known as indexing terms, keywords or descriptors, and they are represented by uniterms. Uniterms may on occasion be combined or coordinated in the actual formulation of the search. When multiword terms or NPs are used for indexing purposes, they can include *articles, nouns, adjectives,* or different indicators of relationship, all parts of a process known as *precoordination* (Salton & McGill, 1983). In indexing multiword terms, most extraction systems employ *part-of-speech* (POS) taggers, which reflect the syntactic role of a word in a sentence, then gather together the words that are components of that NP (Brill, 1992; Church, 1988; Tolle & Chen, 2000; Voutilainen, 1997).

When standardization algorithms are applied to multiword terms, the different variants are grouped according to two general approaches: term cooccurrence and matching syntactic patterns. The systems that use cooccurrence techniques make term associations through different coefficients of similarity. The systems that match syntactic patterns carry out a surface linguistic analysis of certain segments or textual fragments. In addition to the surface analysis and the analysis of fragments from the corpus, many systems effectuate a POS category disambiguation process (Kupiec, 1992). The syntactic variants identified through these methods can be grouped, finally, in canonical syntactic structures (Schwarz, 1990; Sheridan & Smeaton, 1992; Smadja, 1993; Strzalkowski, 1996).

The recognition and standardization of linguistic structures in IRS is an area pertaining to NLP. Within the NLP understanding of the mathematical modelling of language, there are two clearly distinguished conceptions: *symbolic models* and *probabilistic* or *stochastic models.* These models can be traced back to the contribution of Kleene (1956) regarding finite-state mechanisms and to the work by Shannon and Weaver (1949) on the application of the probabilistic processes to finite automatas. Chomsky was the first to consider automatas as mechanisms characterizing the structures of language through grammars, thereby setting the foundations for the *theory of formal languages* (Chomsky, 1957). Finite-state mechanisms are efficient for many aspects of NLP, including morphology (Koskenniemi, 1983) and parsing (Abney, 1991; Roche, 1996).

STANDARDIZATION OF TERMS THROUGH FINITE-STATE TECHNIQUES

Formal language theory focuses on languages that can be described in very precise terms, such as programming languages. Natural languages are not formal, as no well-defined boundary exists between correct sentences or those that are incorrect. Notwithstanding, formal definitions approximating natural language phenomena can be encoded into computer programs and be used for the automated processing of natural language. Likewise, formal descriptions can be utilized by linguists to express theories about specific aspects of natural languages, including morphological analysis. The most important application of the formal language theory to linguistics came from Chomsky (1957). His basic hypothesis was that the different types of formal languages were capable of modeling natural language syntax. This theoretical foundation beneath formal languages and grammars has a direct relation with the theory of machines or *automata*, abstract devices able to receive and transmit information. A finite automata accepts a string or a sentence if it can trace a path from the initial state to the final state by jumping along the stepping stones of *labeled transitions*. A finite automata is thus defined as a network of states and transitions, or edges, in which each transition has a label (ROCHE, 1996). Formally, a FSA is a 5-tuple:

$$FSA = <\Sigma, Q, q_0, F, \delta>$$

where

Σ *is the input alphabet*
Q *is a finite set of states*
q_0 *is the initial state, $q_0 \in Q$*
F *is the final state, $F \subseteq Q$*
δ *is a function of transition, $\delta: Q \times \Sigma \rightarrow Q$*

To determine whether a string or sequence belongs to the regular language accepted by the FSA, the automata reads the string from left to right, comparing each one of the symbols of the sequence with the symbols tagging the transitions. If the transition is tagged with the same symbol as the input chain, the automata moves on to the following state, until the sequence is recognized in its entirety by reaching the final state.

Otherwise, a FST is just like a FSA, except that the transitions have both an *input* label and an *output* label. A FST transforms one string into another string if there is a path through the FST that allows it to trace the first string using *input* labels and, simultaneously, the second string using *output* labels. The transition function is tagged with a pair of symbols, which proceed respectively from an input alphabet and an output alphabet. This mechanism can be represented in the form of *finite-state graphs* or transition diagrams, or else as a *matrix* or *transition table*. The transducers can be characterized as directed graphs, whose vertices denote states, while the transitions form the edges, or arcs, with arrows pointing from the initial state to the final state (Figure 1). The FST accepts input strings and associates them with output strings. Formally, a FST is referred to as a 6-tuple (Roche & Schabes, 1995) expressed as shown below:

$$FST = <\Sigma_1, \Sigma_2, Q, q_0, F, E>$$

where

Σ_1 *is the input alphabet*
Σ_2 *is the output alphabet*

Q is a finite set of states
q_0 *is the initial state,* $q_0 \in Q$
F is the final state, $F \subseteq Q$
E is a number of transition relations, $E \subseteq Q$
$x \, \Sigma_1 \, x \, \Sigma_2$

One application of FST is to establish a relation between input strings and output strings, that is, between term variants and standardized forms. The objective of this chapter is to defend the application of finite-state techniques for the standardization and grouping of the different variants into an equivalence class that would be configured as the standard form.

STANDARDIZATION OF UNITERM VARIANTS

The standardization techniques based on morphological analysis were first presented in a lexical analyzer developed by a group of computational linguists at Xerox, the *Multi-Lingual Theory and Technology Group* (MLTT). The Xerox analyzer is based on the model of two-level morphological analysis proposed by Koskenniemi (1983). The premise behind this model is that all lexical units can be represented as a correspondence between a *lexical form* (or canonical form) and *surface form* (or inflected form). Further computational development of the Koskenniemi model led to the lexical analyzer by Karttunen known as PC-KIMMO (Karttunen, 1983), the more direct forerunner of the Xerox morphological analyzer.

An alternative lexical analyzer based on finite mechanisms is the one proposed by Silberztein (1993), which works without morphological rules. Its technology has been described by Roche and Schabes (1997). A FST associates sets of suffixes to the corresponding inflectional information. In order to produce the inflected forms, one needs to be able to delete characters from the lemma. For this purpose, a delete character operator (*L*) is used, which does not require morphological rules or the help of a finite-state calculus (Silberztein, 1993, 2000). The application developed by Silberztein consists of a dictionary, known as DELAS, of canonical forms with syntactic codes that indicate the POS category of each entry. Each code is linked to a graphic FST made up of an initial node and a final node that describes the path the morphological analyzer should trace. For instance, all the nouns associated with the same inflectional information are associated with the same inflectional FST.

Once the FSTs are compiled, they are projected upon the dictionary of canonical forms, automatically producing the expanded dictionary of inflected forms (known as DELAF) that contains the canonical forms along with inflected forms, POS categories, and inflectional information. With the application of the dictionaries on the lexical units of a corpus, we finally effect two transformations: lemmatization of the inflected forms and POS tagging (Figure 2).

STANDARDIZATION OF MULTITERM VARIANTS

Multiword terms, or NPs, are considered to be more specific indicators of document content than are single words. The identification of phrases using statistical techniques is based on the cooccurrence of the terms, on the application of similarity coefficients and clustering techniques. To identify these, the text must be preprocessed to obtain a phrasal lexicon, defined as a list of NP

Figure 1. Finite-state transducers (FST)

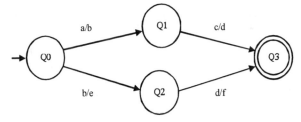

Figure 2. The FST N01 associates the sets of suffixes of the DELAS entries to the corresponding inflectional codes (s, singular, and p, plural). In order to obtain the inflected forms from the lemmas in the DELAF entries, the last letter 'f' of the lemma should be eliminated using the delete operator L (Left)

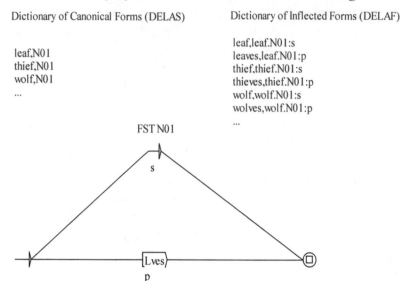

Dictionary of Canonical Forms (DELAS)

Dictionary of Inflected Forms (DELAF)

leaf,N01
thief,N01
wolf,N01
...

leaf,leaf.N01:s
leaves,leaf.N01:p
thief,thief.N01:s
thieves,thief.N01:p
wolf,wolf.N01:s
wolves,wolf.N01:p
...

FST N01

appearing with certain frequency (Fagan, 1989). The subsequent indexing of the documents is based on the identification of the phrases using the lexicon. Salton and McGill (1983) demonstrate that the statistical procedures suffer from certain weaknesses: (1) the selected phrases are very often improperly structured from a syntactic standpoint; and (2) the lack of control in the selection of the phrases may lead to errors that reduce the efficiency of the IRS.

To reduce these problems, we need NLP linguistic methods that can identify the syntactic structures of these constructions and establish some sort of control in the selection of multiword terms. The application of NLP to texts involves a sequence of analytical tasks performed in the separate modules that constitute the linguistic architecture of the system. Among available tools for NP extraction are: the category tagger based on Brill's (1992) rules; the *Xerox morphological analyzer* (Karttunen, Kaplan, & Zaenen, 1992); disambiguation devices of POS categories based on stochastic methods, such as the *hidden Markov*

model (HMM) (Cutting, Kupiec, Pedersen, & Sibun, 1992; Kupiec, 1992, 1993); the *NPtool phrase analyzer* (Voutilainen, 1997); or the *AZ noun phraser* (Tolle & Chen, 2000), which combines *tokenizing* with POS tagging (Brill, 1993).

Whether general linguistic resources or specific tools are used, recognizing the variants of phrases continues to be a problem. Ideally, programs would be able to reduce all the variants to normalized forms, where each phrase would be assigned a clearly defined role reflecting the complexity of the syntactic structure. This network of nodes and transitions tagged with POS categories—such as *N* (noun), *AT* (article), *ORD* (ordinal), *CARD* (cardinal), and *DEM* (demonstratives pronouns)—determines sequences in the input, and supplies some form of linguistic information as the output. An entry stream is recognized and transformed into a normalized stream if a path is produced from one node, considered the initial state, to another node, constituting the final state.

To recognize multiword terms through a FST, their structures must be described using regular expressions (RE), defined as a metalanguage for the identification of syntactic patterns. Through this technique, we use the specification of RE to determine the language formed by syntactic patterns. The association of each possible RE with the FSA is represented graphically, with the graphic editor *FSGraph* (Silberztein, 1993, 2000). In order that the FSTs themselves recognize the syntactic patterns, a previous morphological analysis will be needed, giving POS tags to the lexical units. A path between two FST nodes takes place only if the input chain string belongs to the category with which the transition is tagged. In order to use this formalism of the IRS as a means of controlling NP structures, we propose the transformation of the canonical syntactic forms into identifiers of enumerated NP which will be implemented as groupers of structures (Figure 3).

The similar structures can then be transferred to a FST, where the syntactic patterns will be recognized and be standardized into hand-made standardized structures. Thus, we considered that a FST is a method for reducing syntactic structures, comprising two automata that work in a parallel manner. One automata identifies the surface strings, and the other establishes an equivalence relation between the different syntactic structures and an unified structure, or standardized NP:

$N = NP01$
$DEM\ N = NP01$
$AT\ CARD\ N = NP01$
$AT\ ORD\ N = NP01$

FUTURE TRENDS AND CONCLUSION

In IRS, the textual documents are habitually transformed into document representatives by means of linguistic structures configured as indexing terms, classified essentially as single-word terms or uniterms, and multiword terms or multiterms. The single-word terms have morphological variants that refer to the same meaning, and their grouping would improve average recall. Although uniterms may be ambiguous, they usually have relatively few variants, and from a computational treatment, they are easier to formalize. In contrast, multiterms are much more specific, but the grouping of their variants is plagued by difficulties in their identification, because IRS tend to work under the assumption that similar

Figure 3. Relation between variants of syntactic patterns and normalized NP

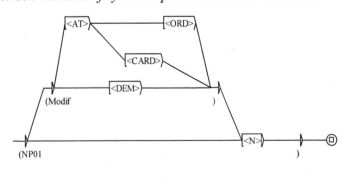

Regular Relation

<N> <DEM><N> <AT><CARD><N> <AT><ORD><N>   =>   (NP01   )

syntactic structures have similar meanings, and should be treated as equivalents, and this is very difficult to regulate in view of the variability of syntactic structures.

There are morphological, lexical, and syntactic variants that cannot be recognized other than through standardization processes of terms. The standardization methods most widely evaluated on retrieval performance involve stemming, segmentation rules, assessing similarity measures of pairs of terms, and clustering techniques. In the linguistic framework, term standardization methods could be considered *equivalence techniques*, employed to regulate linguistic variants and optimize retrieval performance. The application of NLP tools in IR involves morphological analysis, POS taggers, disambiguation processes, lemmatization, and shallow parsing for syntactic pattern-matching. Again we must insist on the influence of language on the results of term standardization. The complexity of terms varies along with the inflectional structure of a language. One interesting study about the morphological phenomena in IRS can be found detailed by Pirkola (2001). Roughly speaking, *synthetic languages*, including French, Spanish, Italian, and the other Romance languages, require term inflection to indicate term function in the sentence. Yet *analytic languages* such as English and German rely on the placement or the combination of terms to indicate their function in the sentence. The synthetic languages have many morphologic variants of single-word terms, whereas the analytic languages have many syntactic variants of multiword terms. Further study should help clarify the positive and negative end effects of these factors on retrieval effectiveness.

To conclude, data quality and standardization are complex concepts governed by multiple dimensions on many variables. Now-a-days, electronic data are at the core of all kinds of treatments; the standardization of terms based on finite-state techniques would adapt well to many other specific applications, such as digital information extraction, bibliometrics, and bioinformatics. The development of finite-state methods may also, however, afford advantages that have not yet been properly explored and evaluated, and their alternative or complementary use might enhance the management of term variants in retrieval performance.

REFERENCES

Abney, S. (1991). Parsing by chunks. In R. Berwick, S. Abney, & C. Tenny (Eds.), *Principle-based parsing*. Dordrecht: Kluwer Academic Publishers.

Arampatzis, A. T., Tsoris, T., Koster, C. H. A., & Van der Weide, P. (1998). Phrase-based information retrieval. *Information Processing & Management, 34*(6), 693-707.

Brill, E. (1992). *A simple rule based part-of-speech tagger*. Paper presented at the Third Conference on Applied Natural Language Proceedings (pp. 152-155). ACM Press.

Chomsky, N. (1957). *Syntactic structures*. The Hague: Mouton.

Church, K. (1988). A stochastic parts program and noun phrase parser for unrestricted text. In *Proceedings of the Second Conference on Applied Natural Language Processing* (pp. 136-143). Austin, TX: ACL.

Croft, W. B., Turtle, H. R., & Lewis, D. D. (1991). The use of phrases and structured queries in information retrieval. In *Proceedings of the SIGIR 1991*.

Cutting, D., Kupiec, J., Pedersen, J., & Sibun, P. (1992). *A practical part-of-speech tagger*. Paper presented at the Third Conference on Applied Natural Language Processing (pp. 133-140). ACM Press.

Fagan, J. L. (1989). The effectiveness of a non-syntactic approach to automatic phrase indexing for document retrieval. *Journal of the American Society for Information Science, 40*(2), 115-132.

Frakes, W. B. (1992), Stemming algorithms. In W. B. Frakes & R. Baeza-Yates (Eds.), *Information retrieval: Data structures and algorithms* (pp.131-161). Englewood Cliffs, NJ: Prentice-Hall.

Galvez, C., Moya-Anegón, F., & Solana, V. H. (2005). Term conflation methods in information retrieval: Non-linguistic and linguistic approaches. *Journal of Documentation, 61*(4), 520-547.

Harris, Z. S. (1951). *Methods in structural linguistics.* Chicago: University of Chicago Press.

Hull, D. A. (1996). Stemming algorithms: A case study for detailed evaluation. *Journal of the American Society for Information Science, 47*(1), 70-84.

Karttunen, L. (1983). KIMMO: A general morphological processor. *Texas Linguistics Forum, 22*, 217-228.

Karttunen, L., Kaplan, R. M., & Zaenen, A. (1992). Two-level morphology with composition. In *Proceedings of the 15th International Conference on Computational Linguistics (COLING'92)* (pp. 141-148). ACM Press.

Koskenniemi, K. (1983). *Two-level morphology: A general computational model for word-form recognition and production.* Helsinki: Department of General Linguistics, University of Helsinki.

Kupiec, J. (1992). Robust part-of-speech tagging using a Hidden Markov model. *Computer Speech and Language, 6*, 225-242.

Kupiec, J. (1993). Murax: A robust linguistic approach for question answer using an on-line encyclopedia. In R. Korfhage, E. Rasmussen, & P. Willett (Eds.), *Proceedings of the 16th Annual International ACM SIGIR Conference on Research and Development in Information Retrieval* (pp. 160-169). ACM Press.

Lovins, J. B. (1968). Development of a stemming algorithm. *Mechanical Translation and Computational Linguistics, 11*, 22-31.

Paice, C. D. (1996). A method for evaluation of stemming algorithms based on error counting. *Journal of the American Society for Information Science, 47*(8), 632-649.

Pirkola, A. (2001). Morphological typology of languages for IR. *Journal of Documentation, 57*(3), 330-348.

Porter, M. F. (1980). An algorithm for suffix stripping. *Program, 14*, 130-137.

Roche, E. (1996). Finite-state transducers: Parsing free and frozen sentences. In *Proceedings of the ECAI 96 Workshop Extended Finite State Models of Language* (pp. 52-57). Budapest, Hungary: ECAI.

Roche, E., & Schabes, Y. (1995). Deterministic part-of-speech tagging with finite state transducers. *Computational Linguistics, 21*(2), 227-253.

Roche, E., & Schabes, Y. (1997). *Finite state language processing.* Cambridge, MA: MIT Press.

Salton, G. (1989). *Automatic text processing: The transformation, analysis and retrieval of information by computer.* Reading, MA: Addison-Wesley.

Salton, G., & McGill, M. J. (1983). *Introduction to modern information retrieval.* New York: McGraw-Hill.

Schwarz, C. (1990). Automatic syntactic analysis of free text. *Journal of the American Society for Information Science, 41*(6), 408-417.

Sheridan, P., & Smeaton, A. F. (1992). The application of morpho-syntactic language processing to effective phrase matching. *Information Processing & Management, 28*(3), 349-369.

Silberztein, M. (1993). *Dictionnaires électroniques et analyse automatique de textes: Le systčme INTEX.* Paris: Masson.

Silberztein, M. (2000). INTEX: An FST toolbox. *Theoretical Computer Science, 231*(1), 33-46.

Smadja, F. (1993). Retrieving collocations from text: XTRACT. *Computational Linguistics, 19*(1), 143-177.

Sparck Jones, K., & Tait, J. I. (1984). Automatic search term variant generation. *Journal of Documentation, 40*(1), 50-66.

Strzalkowski, T. (1996). Natural language information retrieval. *Information Processing & Management, 31*(3), 397-417.

Strzalkowski, T., Lin, F., Wang, J., & Pérez-Carballo, J. (1999). Evaluating natural language processing techniques in information retrieval: A TREC perspective. In T. Strzalkowski (Ed.), *Natural language information retrieval* (pp. 113-145). Dordrecht: Kluwer Academic Publishers.

Tolle, K. M. & Chen, H. (2000). Comparing noun phrasing techniques for use with medical digital library tools. *Journal of the American Society for Information Science, 51*(4), 352-370.

Tzoukermann, E., Klavans, J. L., & Jacquemin, C. (1997). Effective use of natural language processing techniques for automatic conflation of multi-word terms: The role of derivational morphology, part of speech tagging, and shallow parsing. In *Proceedings 20th Annual International ACM SIGIR Conference on Research and Development in Information Retrieval (SIGIR'97),* Philadelphia (pp. 148-155).

Voutilainen, A. (1997). *A short introduction to NPtool.* Retrieved August 16, 2008, from http://www.lingsoft.fi/doc/nptool/intro/

KEY TERMS

Finite-State Automata (FSA): A finite-state machine, or finite-state automata, is a mathematical model defined as a finite set of states and a set of transitions from state to state that occur on input symbols chosen from an alphabet.

Lemmatization: Algorithms for reducing a family of words to the same lemma, defined as the combination of the stem and its part-of-speech (POS) tag. This process involves linguistic techniques, such as morphological analysis through regular relations compiled in finite-state transducers.

N-Gram: A *n-gram* is a substring of a word, where *n* is the number of characters in the substring, typical values for n being bigrams (*n=2*) or trigrams (*n=3*).

Noun Phrase (NP): In grammatical theory, a noun phrase is a phrase whose head is a noun, accompanied by a set of modifiers, such as articles, demostratives, quantifiers, numeral, or adjectives.

Stemming: Algorithms for reducing a family of words to a common root, or stem, defined as the base form of a word from which inflected forms are derived. Stemming algorithms eliminate all affixes and give good results for the conflation and normalization of uniterm variants. Within this group, the most effective are the longest match algorithms.

Term Conflation: The process of matching and grouping together variants of the same term that are equivalent. A variant is defined as a text occurrence that is conceptually related to an original term and can be used to search for information in text databases. This is done by means of computational procedures known as conflation algorithms, whose primary goal is the standardization of uniterms and multiterms.

Chapter XI
Extracting the Essence:
Automatic Text Summarization

Fu Lee Wang
City University of Hong Kong, Hong Kong

Christopher C. Yang
Drexel University, USA

ABSTRACT

As more information becomes available online, information-overloading results. This problem can be resolved through the application of automatic summarization. Traditional summarization models consider a document as a sequence of sentences. Actually, a large document has a well-defined hierarchical structure. Human abstractors use the hierarchical structure of the document to extract topic sentences. They start searching for topic sentences from the top level of the document structure downwards. Similarly, hierarchical summarization generates a summary for a document based on the hierarchical structure and salient features of the document. User evaluations that have been conducted indicate that hierarchical summarization outperforms traditional summarization.

INTRODUCTION

The explosion in the amount of information available online has resulted in a well-recognized problem of information overloading. This problem can be eased through the application of automatic summarization. Automatic summarization extracts the most important information from the source document and presents the information to the users in a condensed form. By reading these summaries, users can understand the information that is contained in the source documents in a short time, and make decisions quickly.

Human professionals produce high quality summaries; however, it is too time-consuming and labor-intensive. Automatic summarization is capable of generating summaries for a large volume of information efficiently. In recent years, there has been an increasing need for automatic summarization due to the information explosion.

Moreover, automatic summarization is indispensable in digital libraries. This chapter will review techniques in automatic summarization. We will also introduce hierarchical summarization, which is a new summarization technique (Yang & Wang, 2003a, 2003b).

The traditional summarization models consider the source document as a sequence of sentences and ignore the hierarchical structure of the document. Similar to the abstracting process of human professionals, hierarchical summarization generates a summary by exploring the hierarchical structure and salient features of the document (Yang & Wang, 2003a). Experimental results have indicated that hierarchical summarization is promising and outperforms traditional summarization techniques that do not consider the hierarchical structure of documents.

BACKGROUND

In general, automatic summarization is represented by a three-stage framework, that is, representation of source document, extraction of information, and generation of summary (Sparck-Jones, 1999). Most of the current research work focuses on the second stage. Traditionally, the summarization system calculates the significance of sentences to the document based on the salient features of the document (Edmundson, 1969; Luhn, 1958). The most significant sentences are then extracted and concatenated as a summary. The compression ratio of the summary can be adjusted to specify the amount of information to be extracted. A lot of extraction features have been proposed.

The extraction approaches are usually classified into three major groups according to the level of processing in the linguistic space (Mani & Maybury, 1999). The surface-level approaches use salient features of a document to extract the important information. The entity-level approaches build an internal representation for text units and their relationships, and use graph theories to determine the significance of units. The discourse-level approaches model the global structure of the text, and the text units are extracted based on the structure. Generally, the deeper approaches are more promising to give more informative summaries. However, the surface-level approaches are proved to be robust and reliable (Goldstein, Kantrowitz, Mittal, & Carbonell 1999). They are still widely adopted at present.

The summarization systems can be evaluated either by intrinsic or extrinsic evaluation (Sparck-Jones & Galliers, 1996). The intrinsic evaluation judges the quality of the summarization by direct analysis of the summary (Kupiec, Pedersen, & Chen, 1995). The extrinsic evaluation judges the quality of the summarization based on how it affects the completion of some other tasks (Morris, Kasper, & Adams, 1992). A number of general-purpose summarization systems have been developed. Experiments have been conducted on these systems. All the systems identify an upper bound for the precision of the summarization system, the performance of the system grows fast with addition of extraction features, and they reach their upper bound after three or four extraction features (Kupiec et al., 1995).

AUTOMATIC SUMMARIZATION

Related research has shown that human abstractors use readymade text passages from a source document for summarization (Endres-Niggemeyer, 2002). Eighty percent of the sentences in the man-made abstracts are closely matched with sentences in the source documents (Kupiec et al., 1995). As a result, selection of representative sentences is considered as a good approximation of summarization (Aminin & Gallinari, 2002). The existing automatic text summarization is mainly the selection of sentences from the source document based on their significances in the document using statistical techniques and linguistic analyses (Aminin & Gallinari, 2002; Luhn, 1958). The statistical approach of selection of sentences is conducted based on the salient features of the document. The thematic, location, heading, and cue features are the most widely used extraction features.

- The thematic feature is first identified by Luhn (1958). Edmundson (1969) proposes to assign each term a thematic score based on its term frequency. The thematic score of a sentence is calculated as the sum of thematic score of its constituent terms. In information retrieval, absolute term frequency by itself is considered as less useful than term frequency normalized to the document length and term frequency in the collection. As a result, the *term frequency, inverse document frequency* (TFIDF) method is proposed to calculate the thematic score of keywords (Salton & Buckley, 1988). Most recent summarization systems use TFIDF score to compute the thematic scores.

- The location feature is proposed based on the hypotheses that representative sentences tend to occur at the beginning or in the end of documents or paragraphs. Edmundson (1969) proposes to assign positive scores to sentences according to their position in the document. There are several functions proposed to calculate the location score of sentences; they commonly assign the sentences at the beginning or ending of documents with relatively higher location scores. Alternatively, the preference of sentence locations can be stored in a list, and the sentences will be selected based on their ordering in the list (Lin & Hovy, 1997).

- The heading feature is proposed based on the hypothesis that the author conceives the heading as circumscribing the subject matter of the document. When the author partitions the document into major sections, the author summarizes it by choosing the appropriate heading (Baxendale, 1958). The heading feature is very similar to the thematic feature. A heading glossary is a list consisting of all the terms in headings and subheadings. Positive scores are assigned to the heading glossary, where the heading terms will be assigned a score relatively prime to the subheading terms. The heading score of a sentence is calculated by the sum of heading score of its constituent terms.

- The cue approach, proposed by Edmundson (1969), is based on the hypothesis that the probable relevance of a sentence is affected by the presence of pragmatic words such as "significant," "impossible," and "hardly." A cue dictionary is preconstructed to identify the cue phrases, which comprise of three subdictionaries: (i) bonus words that are positively relevant; (ii) stigma words that are negatively relevant; and (iii) null words that are irrelevant. The cue score of sentence is computed as the sum of the cue scores of constituent terms.

Most of the existing summarization systems choose a hybrid combination of different extraction features. The systems calculate the significance score of a sentence for each feature separately. The sentence score is calculated based on a weighted sum of feature scores (Edmundson, 1969; Lam-Adesina & Jones, 2001). The sentences with a significance score higher than a threshold value are selected. However, it has been proved that the weighting of extraction features does not have any substantial effect on average precision of summarization (Lam-Adesina & Jones, 2001).

HIERARCHICAL SUMMARIZATION

A large document has a hierarchical structure with multiple levels, chapters, sections, subsections, paragraphs, and sentences. At the lower abstraction level, more specific information can be obtained. Related studies of human abstraction have shown that the human abstractors extract the topic sentences according to the document structure from top level to low level until they have extracted sufficient information (Endres-Niggemeyer, Maier, & Sigel, 1995).

Advanced summarization techniques take document structure into consideration to compute the probability that a sentence should be included in the summary, but most traditional summarizations consider the source document as a sequence of sentences and ignore its structure. By contrast, hierarchical summarization generates a summary based on the hierarchical structure (Yang & Wang, 2003a). Hierarchical summarization was proposed to simulate the abstracting process of human professionals. Experimental results have shown that hierarchical summarization is a promising summarization technique.

Hierarchical summarization partitions the original document into range-blocks according to its document structure. The document is then transformed into a hierarchical tree structure, where each range-block is represented by a node. The important information is captured from the source document by exploring the hierarchical structure and the salient features of the document. The system calculates the number of sentences to be extracted according to the compression ratio. The number of sentences is assigned to the root of the tree as the quota of sentences. The system calculates the significance score of each node by summing up the sentence scores of all sentences under the nodes. The quota of sentences is allocated to child-nodes by propagation, that is, the quota of a parent node is shared by its child-nodes directly proportional to their significance scores. The quota is then iteratively allocated to child-nodes of child-nodes until the quota allocated is less than a threshold value and the node can be transformed to some key sentences by traditional summarization methods.

In hierarchical summarization, the traditional features are adopted and the hierarchical structure is also considered (Yang & Wang 2003a, 2003b). However, the traditional features cannot fully utilize the hierarchical structure. The features are modified to integrate with the hierarchical structure.

- Among the thematic features, the TFIDF score is the most widely used approach; however, it does not take into account the document structure in the traditional summarization. Most researchers assume that the score of a term remains the same over the entire document. However, Hearst (1993) claims that a term should carry different scores at different locations of a full-length document. For example, a term is considered more important in a range-block than other range-blocks if the term appears in the range-block more frequently than others. In hierarchical summarization, the TFIDF of a term in a range-block is defined as proportional to the term frequency within a range-block and inversely proportional to the frequency of the range-block containing the term.

- Traditional summarizations assume that the location score of a sentence is static, however, the hierarchical summarization calculates the location score based on which document level we are looking at. For example, if we consider the first and second sentences on the same paragraph at the paragraph level, the first sentence is more important to the paragraph, however, the difference is insignificant if we are looking at the whole document. In hierarchical summarization, the location score for a range-block is calculated by traditional methods, and the sentence quota is adjusted accordingly.

- At a different abstraction level, some headings should be hidden and some are emphasized. For example, only the document heading is considered if we look at the document level. However, if we look at the chapter level, we consider the document heading and chapter heading, and we consider the chapter heading as more important since the main concept of this chapter is represented by the chapter heading. Therefore, the significance of the heading is inversely proportional to its distance from the sentence. Propagation of fractal value (Koike, 1995) is a promising approach to calculate the heading score for a sentence.

- When human abstractors extract the sentences, they pay more attention to the range-block when heading contains some bonus words such as "conclusion," since they consider it as a more important part and more sentences are extracted. The cue feature of a heading sentence is classified as a rhetorical feature (Teufel & Moens, 1998). Hierarchical summarization considers the cue feature not only at sentence level. Given a document tree, it examines the heading of each range-block and adjusts their quota accordingly. This procedure can be repeated iteratively until sentence level.

To illustrate the feasibility of the model, experiments of hierarchical summarization have been conducted (Yang & Wang, 2003a, 2003b). The hierarchical summarization model achieves 85.05% precision on average and up to a maximum of 91.25% precision, while the traditional summarization without considering the hierarchical structure of documents achieves 67.00% precision on average and up to a maximum of 77.50% precision. This demonstrates that the hierarchical summarization has outperformed the traditional summarization without considering the hierarchical structure of documents.

RECENT DEVELOPMENT IN AUTOMATIC SUMMARIZATION

The automatic summarization at the discourse level is one of the new research directions in recent years. The discourse structure of a text document is the explicit and implicit relationship between sentences, groups of sentences, and elements within a sentence (Kintsch & van Dijk, 1983; Rumelhart, 1975). Discourse-level summarization approaches model the global structure of the text, and its relation to communicative goals. Some researches focus on utilization of discourse structure in automatic summarization. For instance, Teufel and Moens (1998) present a summarization technique based on rhetorical structure. The text units can be extracted according to their rhetorical role. In general, the summarization techniques at discourse level can produce a summary with better quality (Teufel & Moens, 1998). However, the discourse-level approaches require an in-depth knowledge of linguistics, therefore they are difficult to be implemented. Moreover, the time complexity for analysis of discourse structure for a text is high. They have been tested only in small-scale experiment.

Traditional summarization techniques generate a covering summary, which extracts all the important information from the source document. The information retrieval technique has been combined with the statistical learning algorithms and user customization. User directed summarization is another trend in automatic summarization (Gong & Liu, 2001; Sanderson, 1998). A user can specify the information needed to be summarized by giving a query. The summarization system extracts specific information from the source document based on the query, and generates a summary to answer the query. This approach allows the user to control the contents of the summary.

Access to the Internet through mobile phones and other handheld devices has been growing significantly in recent years. The convenience of handheld devices allows information access without geographical limitations. However, these devices have their shortcomings that restrict their capability and limit the wireless access to information. Automatic summarization of documents can partially solve the problem (Yang & Wang, 2003b). It provides an ideal tool for visualizing documents on handheld devices. In particular, summarization of a Web page on a mobile device has been well studied (White, Jose, & Ruthven, 2001, Buyukkokten, Kaljuvee, Garcia-Molina, Paepcke, & Winograd, 2002).

Recently, the research of automatic summarization has also been extended to summarization of multimedia documents, that is, summarization of spoken document (Zechner & Waibel, 2000), video (Vasconcelos & Lippman, 1998), figures (Futrelle, 1999), and so forth. Techniques have been developed to extract the key features of multimedia documents, and their summaries can be generated by extracting the key features.

CONCLUSION AND FUTURE TRENDS

The hierarchical summarization generates the summary of a document by a recursive algorithm based on the document structure. Thematic features, location features, heading features, and cue features are adopted. An experimental result has shown that the hierarchical summarization can produce summary with good quality. The hierarchical summarization is developed based on the statistical analysis and the hierarchical structure of documents. It requires no special domain knowledge, and is easy to be implemented. On the other hand, the time complexity for hierarchical summarization is low. Hence, it can be utilized for summarization for large documents (Yang & Wang, in press). The hierarchical summarization is a promising technique in automatic summarization.

Automatic summarization provides useful tools to support fast decision making. Research of automatic summarization has been extended to multidocument summarization. In information retrieval, most systems return a set of related documents in response to a query. The multidocument summarization provides an overview of a topic based on a set of topic-related documents. We can understand a topic by reading the topic summary. The research of automatic summarization for multiple documents is very important.

There may be a large number of documents related to a topic. It is extremely difficult to summarize a large set of documents without a proper organization of documents. Techniques have been developed to group documents into document sets before summarization (Nobata, Sekine, Uchimoto, & Isahara, 2003). Related studies have shown that the hierarchical summarization of multiple documents organized in a hierarchical structure significantly outperforms other multidocument summarization systems without using the hierarchical structure (Wang & Yang, 2006; Yang & Wang, 20036). A large set of documents can be organized in a hierarchical structure by different classifications. Future research will focus on the design of algorithms that discover the document structure from a large set of related documents and organize the set of documents in a hierarchical structure to give an effective information organization.

REFERENCES

Aminin, M., & Gallinari, P. (2002). The use of unlabeled data to improve supervised learning for text summarization. In *Proceedings of the 25th Annual International ACM SIGIR Conference* (pp. 105-112). ACM.

Baxendale, P. B. (1958). Machine-made index for technical literature: An experiment. *IBM Journal of Research and Development, 2*(4), 354-361.

Buyukkokten, O., Kaljuvee, O., Garcia-Molina, H., Paepcke, A., & Winograd, T. (2002). Efficient Web browsing on handheld devices using page and form summarization. *ACM Transactions on Information Systems, 20*(1), 82-115.

Edmundson, H. P. (1969). New methods in automatic extraction. *Journal of the ACM, 16*(2), 264-285.

Endres-Niggemeyer, B. (2002). SimSum: An empirically founded simulation of summarizing. *Information Processing & Management, 36*(4), 659-682.

Endres-Niggemeyer, B., Maier, E., & Sigel, A. (1995). How to implement a naturalistic model of abstracting: Four core working steps of an expert abstractor. *Information Processing & Management, 31*(5), 631-674.

Futrelle, R. (1999). Summarization of diagram in document. In I. Mani & M. Maybury (Eds.), *Advance in automatic summarization* (pp. 403-421). Cambridge, MA: MIT Press.

Goldstein, J., Kantrowitz, M., Mittal, V., & Carbonell J. (1999). Summarizing text documents: Sentence selection and evaluation metrics. In *Proceedings of the 22nd Annual International ACM SIGIR Conference* (pp.121-128). ACM.

Gong, Y., & Liu, X. (2001). Generic text summarization using relevance measure and latent semantic analysis. In *Proceedings of the 24th Annual International ACM SIGIR Conference* (pp. 19-25). ACM.

Hearst, M. A. (1993). Subtopic structuring for full-length document access. In *Proceedings of the 16th Annual International ACM SIGIR Conference* (pp. 56-68). ACM.

Kintsch, W., & van Dijk, T. A. (1983). *Strategies of discourse comprehension*. New York: Academic Press.

Koike, H. (1995). Fractal views: A fractal-based method for controlling information display. *ACM Transaction on Information Systems, 13*(3), 305-323.

Kupiec, J., Pedersen J., & Chen, F. (1995). A trainable document summarizer. In *Proceedings of the 18th Annual International ACM SIGIR Conference* (pp. 68-73). ACM.

Lam-Adesina, M., & Jones, G. J. F. (2001). Applying summarization techniques for term selection in relevance feedback. In *Proceeding of the 24th Annual International ACM SIGIR Conference* (pp. 1-9). ACM.

Lin, C. Y., & Hovy, E. H. (1997). Identifying topics by position. In *Proceedings of the Applied Natural Language Processing Conference* (pp. 283-290). San Francisco: Morgan Kaufmann.

Luhn, H. P. (1958). The automatic creation of literature abstracts. *IBM Journal of Research and Development, 2*(2), 159-165.

Mani, I., & Maybury, M. (1999). *Advances in automatic text summarization*. Cambridge, MA: MIT Press.

Morris, G., Kasper, G. M., & Adams, D. A. (1992). The effect and limitation of automated text condensing on reading comprehension performance. *Information System Research, 3*(1), 17-35.

Nobata, C., Sekine, S., Uchimoto, K., & Isahara, H. (2003). *A summarization system with categorization of document sets*. Paper presented at the Third NTCIR Workshop.

Rumelhart, D. E. (1975). Notes on a schema for stories. In D. G. Bobrown & A. M. Collins (Eds.), *Representation and understanding: Studies in cognitive science* (pp. 211-236). New York: Academic Press.

Salton, G., & Buckley, C. (1988). Term-weighting approaches in automatic text retrieval. *Information Processing and Management, 24*(5), 513-523.

Sanderson, M. (1998). Accurate user directed summarization from existing tools. In *Proceedings of the 7th International Conference on Information and Knowledge Management (CIKM 98)* (pp. 45-51).

Sparck-Jones, K. (1999). Automatic summarising: Factors and directions. In I. Mani & M. Maybury (Eds.), *Advances in automatic text summarization*. Cambridge, MA: MIT Press.

Sparck-Jones, K., & Galliers, J. (1996). *Evaluating natural language processing systems: An analysis and review*. Springer-Verlag.

Teufel, S., & Moens, M. (1998). Sentence extraction and rhetorical classification for flexible abstracts. In *Proceedings of the AAAI Spring Symposium on Intelligent Text Summarization* (pp. 89-97), Menlo Park, CA: AAAI.

Vasconcelos, N., & Lippman, A. (1998, October). *Bayesian modeling of video editing and structure: Semantic features for video summarization and browsing*. Paper presented at the IEEE ICIP (Vol. 3, pp.153-157).

Wang, F. L., & Yang, C. C. (2006). Impact of document structure on hierarchical summarization. In *Proceedings of 9th International Conference on Asian Digital Libraries* (pp. 459-469). Springer.

White, R., Jose, J. M., & Ruthven, I. (2001). Query-based Web page summarization: A task-oriented evaluation. In *Proceedings of the 24th Annual International ACM SIGIR Conference on Research and Development in Information Retrieval (SIGIR'2001)*, New Orleans (pp. 412-413).

Yang, C. C., & Wang, F. L. (in press). Hierarchical summarization of large documents. *Journal of the American Society for Information Science and Technology*.

Yang, C. C., & Wang, F. L. (2003a). Fractal summarization: Summarization based on fractal theory. In *Proceedings of the 26th Annual International ACM SIGIR Conference* (pp. 392-392). ACM.

Yang, C. C., & Wang, F. L. (2003b). Fractal summarization for mobile devices to access large documents on the Web. In *Proceedings of the 12th International World Wide Web Conference* (p. 215-224). ACM.

Zechner, K., & Waibel, A. (2000, May). Minimizing word error rate in textual summaries of spoken language. In *Proceedings of NAACL-ANLP-2000*, Seattle (pp. 186-193).

KEY TERMS

Automatic Summarization: A technique where a computer program summarizes a text. The existing automatic text summarization is mainly the selection of sentences from the source document based on their significance to the document using statistical techniques and linguistic analyses.

Cue Feature: An extraction feature which calculates the significance of a sentence based on the presence of some pragmatic words.

Extraction Feature: Most summarization models use salient features of a document to extract the important information content. There are many features identified as key features, including thematic feature, location feature, background feature, cue feature, and so forth.

Extrinsic Evaluation: Summarization evaluation methods which judge the quality of the summaries based on how they affect the completion of some other tasks.

Heading Feature: An extraction feature which calculates the significance of a sentence based on the presence of heading or subheading words in the sentence.

Hierarchical Summarization: A document exhibits a well-defined hierarchical structure. Hierarchical summarization extracts the important information from the source document by exploring the hierarchical structure and salient features of the document.

Intrinsic Evaluation: Summarization evaluation methods which judge the quality of summaries by direct analyses in terms of some set of norms.

Location Feature: An extraction feature which calculates the significance of a sentence based on the position of the sentence within the document.

Thematic Feature: An extraction feature which calculates the significance of a term to a document based on the properties of the terms.

Chapter XII
Metadata Interoperability

K. S. Chudamani
JRDTML, IISc, Bangalore-12, India

H. C. Nagarathna
JRDTML, IISc, Bangalore-12, India

ABSTRACT

Metadata is data about data. Metadata originated in the context of digital information in databases. This chapter looks at the various standards available for digital document description in the context of bibliographic databases. It also describes the variety of metadata associated with such systems. Some of the metadata standards examined are MARC21, Dublin Core (DC), and Libsys. The second part examines metadata interoperability and mapping among these standards.

INTRODUCTION

The first use of "**metadata**" originated in contexts related to digital information (chiefly with regard to databases). Since then, the general understanding of the term has broadened to include any kind of standardized descriptive information about resources, including nondigital ones. For example, library catalogues, abstracting and indexing services, archival finding aids, and museum documentation might all be seen as stored and retrieved based on metadata. The advantages of this are two fold. Firstly, it allows librarians, archivists, and museum documentation specialists to cooperate usefully across professional bound-

aries. Secondly, it enables the cultural heritage professions to communicate more effectively with those domains that also have an interest in metadata (e.g., software developers, publishers, the recording industry, television companies, the producers of digital educational content, and those concerned with geographical and satellite-based information). Therefore, metadata is critical to physical and intellectual accessibility and utility of digital document. In this sense, to quote Gilliland Swetland (2000),[5] "Metadata provides us with the Rosetta stone that will make possible to decode information objects and their transformation into knowledge in the cultural heritage information systems of the twenty first century." According to

Day, metadata is defined literally as "data about data." The term is normally understood to mean structured data about resources that can be used to help support a wide range of operations. These might include, for example, resource description and discovery, and the management of information resources and their long-term preservation.

Interoperable systems allow the exchange of information and sharing of resources. They focus on the storage of data in a **standard format**. The role of metadata in facilitating interoperability can be seen in number of contexts, such as:

1. e-governance;
2. electronic record management;
3. educational technology; and
4. library management systems.

Information about a resource needs to be embedded in the database. The catalogue record used for library management is the basis for identifying individual items and their management. Machine readable cataloguing **(MARC21)** covers all kinds of library materials and is used in automated library management systems in the Western libraries. Although most library management systems can import and export data in MARC21 (http://www.loc.gov/marc/bibliographic/ebcdmain.html) format, they usually have their own internal metadata standards. The availability of MARC records stimulated the development of searchable electronic catalogues. The user benefited from wider access to searchable catalogues, and later to a union catalogue, which allowed them to search several library catalogues at once.

Structured information is used to describe, explain, and locate resources. According to Harrasowitz's home page on e-journal resource guide,[5] "metadata functionality goes beyond the cataloguing functions of description and access to include content rating for filtering out sensitive or objectionable materials, the linking of physically separate information objects, and description of intellectual property rights of electronic publications."

Metadata used with one application can be used for several different purposes. Metadata in a library catalogue can be used to provide a variety of search options for the retrieval of items. Now-a-days, its main focus is on information retrieval and improving retrieval on the Internet. The Dublin Core (http://www.dublincore.org/) is currently based on a set of 15 data elements and can be used as a markup language in hypertext markup language (HTML), extensible markup language (XML), or RDF.

Metadata is required to allow users to search on a number of fields, such as author, title, and description. These facilities are useful not only for end users but also to the editorial team in order to collate statistics needed to generate reports. Storing metadata in a certain format and then converting it into HTML <META> tags using programs or scripts is meant to make the metadata conversion into other formats (such as XHTML) by altering the script.

Metadata is key in making resources accessible in the future. There are three main types of metadata:[4]

1. **Descriptive metadata:** These metadata describe a resource for purposes such as discovery and identification. They can include elements such as title, abstract, author, and keywords
2. **Structural metadata:** This type of metadata indicate how compound objects are put together, for example, how pages are ordered to form chapters
3. **Administrative metadata:** The administrative metadata gather information to help manage a resource, such as when and how it was created, file type, and other technical information. It also collects copyright information, such as who can accesses it. There are several subsets of cataloguers who make decisions about whether a catalogue record should be created for a whole set of volumes or for each particular volume in the

set. So the metadata creator makes similar decisions.

In the context of bibliographic information systems, a book has as its metadata the author, title, place publisher, subject code, subject heading, and so forth. In the case of serials, it is the title, publisher, ISSN, and so forth. In the case of a bank account it is the name, address, signature, and so forth.

The purpose of metadata is five-fold as pointed out by Haynes (2004): information retrieval, management of information services, documenting ownership and authenticity, and interoperability. Information retrieval is a dynamic process which involves the user, the system, and the librarian. The system here mainly refers to the computers, but can also be the manual catalogue. To obtain proper retrieval of relevant documents, the metadata recorded are most important and should be the ones satisfying the users. Metadata also help in management of various information services like **OPAC**, SDI, and so forth. It is a vehicle for documenting ownership and authenticity of the information. The last but not the least important is the interoperability of information across continents.

The different types of metadata pertain to administrative, descriptive, preservative, technical, and use. Administrative metadata pertain to acquisition, vendor, location, and so forth. Descriptive metadata refer to the author, title, content, and so forth. Preservation metadata refer to the best way of preserving documents, like air conditioning and so forth. Technical metadata, especially in the case of digital documents, refer to hardware, software, and so forth. Use-related metadata provide information for tracing the user.

The representation of the metadata description can be done using standard generalized markup language (SGML), XML, and so forth.

Metadata Standards

Some of the metadata standards available are Marc, Marc21, Doublin Core, UKmarc (now transformed to Marc21), and so forth. Marc21 is the latest standard metadata available in the context of libraries. The first level metadata elements of Marc21 are: http://www.loc.gov/marc/bibliographic/ecbdhome.html)

- Leader and directory
- Control fields 001-008
- Number and code fields 01X-04X
- Classification and call number fields 05X-08X
- Main entry fields 1XX
- Title and Title related fields 20X-24X
- Edition, Imprint, and so forth fields 250-270
- Physical description etc fields 3XX
- Series statement fields 4XX
- Note Fields: Part 1 50X-53X
- Note Fields Part 2 53X-58X
- Subject access fields 6XX
- Added entry fields 70X-75X
- Linking entry fields 76X-78X
- Series added entry fields 80X-830
- Holdings, location, alternate graphs and so forth fields 841-88X
- and so forth

The **Dublin Core** metadata elements are (http://www.dublincore.org)

- Title
- Creator
- Subject
- Description (i.e., table of content, abstract)
- Publisher
- Contributor
- Date

- Type nature of content
- Format: physical or digital
- Identifier URL and so forth
- Source journal article collection, and so forth
- Language
- Relation is version, has revision
- Coverage extent or scope of content
- Rights, copyright date, and so forth

It can be noticed here that there is very limited scope for content management. Hierarchies cannot be incorporated, association relations cannot be specified directly, and so on. Though MARC21 has a provision for incorporating the facet structure in content designation, it does not provide the mechanism to build content. The digital environment provides the necessary mechanism for content augmentation based on a classification scheme. Now, let us examine content management in the digital environment, based on an example. However, it is essential to understand metadata interoperability before examining a practical application. The next section describes metadata interoperability.

METADATA INTEROPERABILITY

Interoperability, as defined by IEEE (1990), is the ability of two or more systems or components to exchange information and to use the information that has been exchanged.

In the specific context of a digital library, Arms (2000) defines interoperability as the "task of building coherent services for the users when the individual components are technically different and managed by different organization," and he perceives it as a fundamental challenge to all aspects of digital libraries wherein the problem is of getting a wide variety of computing system to work together.

Borgman (2000) identifies three main aspects relating to interoperability:

1. Getting systems to work with one another in real time;
2. Enabling software to work as different systems (portability); and
3. Enabling data to be exchanged among different systems

Arms (2000) discusses the challenges in achieving interoperability in various areas that affect the implementation of digital library:

Common user interfaces;
Uniform naming and identification systems;
Standard format for information resources;
Standards metadata format;
Standard network protocols;
Standard information retrieval protocols;
Standard measures for authentication, security;
and so on.

Mechanisms of Interoperability

One can follow a variety of steps to achieve interoperability:

1. Following a common standard such as MARC21.
2. Creating as map between metadata to a commonly accepted standard such as Dublin Core, MARC21, and so forth.
3. Converting each metadata set into another as and when needed.
4. Converting to web_opac, which can be searchable.

MARC21 was developed by the Library of Congress in USA. It has been adopted by most libraries in the USA and UK. In spite of this, as far as data entry is concerned, there is sufficient variation among the two countries based on individual cataloguing practice. This leads to various approaches of information seeking by the cataloguer without affecting the user, as the user display is uniquely defined by AACR2.

As already pointed out, Dublin Core has 15 elements into which all bibliographic description can be loaded. This has been visualized by the computer community to simplify data mapping. If a metadata map between Dublin Core and MARC21 is carried out, almost all library records of the USA in particular become accessible in a simplified format. Other libraries can also carryout similar mapping. Then, Dublin Core becomes the standard metadata for exchange. For this purpose, many metadata elements need to be aggregated.

The third possibility is that every time metadata is converted to another format by using a metadata mapping program. This can lead to metadata harvesting. However, in the long run, this leads to proliferation of metadata without a uniform structure and may lead to chaos in information management. Hence, it is preferable to have one or two major valid metadata standards based on which subsets are derived.

The last mechanism leads to searching through web_opac for records which are based on the international standard bibliographic description structure (which has been accepted for the presentation of the data). However, this is an arduous task as each record is searched completely with reference to a query, with a large number of homonyms being retrieved after the search. Hence, it is preferable to have metadata mapping to increase efficiency in retrieval. The next section deals with metadata mapping.

Metadata Mapping

Mapping metadata involves the creation of a table of equivalent elements among a set of metadata used by different agencies. Here a demonstration of the mapping between CONSER, MARC21, Dublin Core, and Libsys. Some descriptions about MARC21 and Dublin Core have been provided in the earlier sections. In this section, descriptions about LIBSYS and CONSER have been provided before presenting the mapping.

Libsys

According to www.libsys.co.in/home.html:

'LibSys for library automation' is the prime mission of New Delhi based software company - Info-Tek Consultants Pvt. Ltd., engaged in providing software solutions for General Insurance and ERP/CRM since 1984. Its continued growth for the last 12 years has made LibSys a defacto standard for libraries in India. Its acceptance in global market further strengthens its popularity across the country as the most field proven library system in a wide spectrum of libraries with unmatchable depth in functionality and features.

CONSER is:

- A cooperative online serials cataloging program
- A source of high quality bibliographic records for serials
- A source of high quality documentation and training materials for the cataloging of serials and the input of serial records
- A group of serial experts who work together in an atmosphere of collegiality and trust
- A promulgator of standards related to serials
- A voice for serials in the library community
- A component of the Program for Cooperative Cataloging

CONSER began in the early 1970s as a project to convert manual serial cataloging into machine-readable records. It has evolved into an ongoing program to create and maintain high quality bibliographic records for serials. In keeping with its evolution, the name changed in 1986 from the Conversion of Serials (CONSER) Project to the Cooperative Online Serials (CONSER) Program. In October 1997, CONSER became a bibliographic component of the Program for Cooperative Cataloging.

Table 1.

Dublin Core	Libsys	CONSER	MARC21
Title	Title	Title (245)	245 : Title
Publishers	Pub	Pub (260)	260 : Pub
Combined with Pub	Place	Combined with pub	Combined with pub
Country	Country	Country (combined with pub)	257can be used
Location/URL	Manual: Yes	Yes (Electronic) (856)	856 (Electronic location)
	Frequency	Frequency (310)	310
	Starting Date: Manual	Yes (Electronic) (362)	362 (Starting electronic pub)
Language	Language	Language (Lang)	041
	Alphe code	Not available	030
Control Number	Control Number	Control Number (010)	010
ISSN	ISSN	ISSN (022)	022
Description	Available in separate file	Available in separate file	841
Subject	Subject	Subject	650
	Supplement recorded as an issue	NA	050
Note	Yes	Yes (500)	500

Serials catalogers will soon be in position to utilize all the computer file-based bibliographic record elements. CONSER has taken a major step in developing policies for these new elements with the publication.

Given in Table 1 is a mapping of journal description interoperable metadata between DC, Libsys, CONSER, and MARC21

Metadata Interoperability for Books

A detailed metadata mapping for books in DC, MARC21, Libsys, and UNIMARC has been provided in an article by Chudamani and Nagarathna from the Planner 2006 workshop. Here a section of the mapping for two metadata elements, namely author and title, is provided.

Further, an experiment was conducted at JRDTML to import e-book metadata into Libsys. A description of the process involved is provided here. The original record was received in MARC

format, as shown below. Some records were received in Excel format also.

**4500001000900000005001700009006001900
026007001500045008004100060906004500010
192500440014695502380019001000170042 80
200028004450400018004730420008004910 5
000220049908200150052124501170053626 00
043006533000045006964900054007415040 0
510079565000380084665000370088470000 2
600921700001600947830004800963856011 70
1011-13084766-20060728205444.0-m   d   -cr
cn ---aucaa-030206s2003   flua   sb   001 0 eng
-   a7bcbccorignewd1eocipf20gy-gencatlg-0
aacquireb2 shelf copiesxpolicy default- apc22
2003-02-06 RUSH to ASCDcjf05 2003-02-11
to subj.djf02 2003-02-11 to slejf12 2003-02-11
to Deweyaaa07 2003-02-12aps09 2003-04-15
1 copy rec'd., to CIP ver.fpv10 2003-04-24
CIP ver to BCCDacopy 2 added jf16 to BCCD
05-15-03- a 2002041783- a0849316847 (alk.**

Table 2. Mapping from Dublin Core to UNIMARC, MARC21, and LIBSYS for title and author

Dublin Core	UNIMARC	MARC21	LIBSYS
Title	200 $a Title Proper 200 $e Other Title Information (for subtitle) 517 $a Other Variant Titles (for other titles)	245 title proper statement 210 abbreviated title 222 key title 240 uniform title 242 collective uniform title 246 varying form of title 247 former title	Title, Sub title, Alternate title, Uniform title
Creator	700 $a Personal Name - Primary Intellectual Responsibility, or if more than one: 701 $a Personal Name - Alternative Intellectual Responsibility 710 $a Corporate Body Name - Primary Intellectual Responsibility, or: 711 $a Corporate Body Name - Alternative Intellectual Responsibility 200 $f First Statement of Responsibility	100 main entry personal name 110 main entry corporate name 111 main entry meeting name 130 main entry uniform title	Main entry Corporate body., and so forth Personal author title

paper)- aDLCcDLCdDLC- apcc-00aTG300b. B752 2003-00a624/.2221-00aBridge engineering h[electronic resource] :bconstruction and maintenance /cedited by Wai-Fah Chen, Lian Duan.- aBoca Raton, Fla. :bCRC Press,cc2003.- a1 v. (various pagings) :bill. ;c27 cm.-1 aPrinciples and applications in engineering series- aIncludes bibliographical references and index.- 0aBridgesxDesign and construction.- 0aBridgesxMaintenance and repair.-1 aChen, Wai-Fah,d1936--1 aDuan, Lian.- 0aPrinciples and applications in engineering.-403CRCnet-BASEuhttp://www.engnetbase.com/ejournals/books/book_km.asp?id=4505zClick here for the electronic version-

Using Marcedit software the MARC21 data were converted to Dublin Core format. As a next

Figure 1.

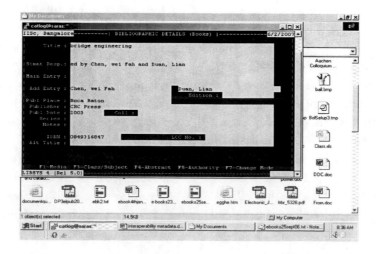

Figure 2.

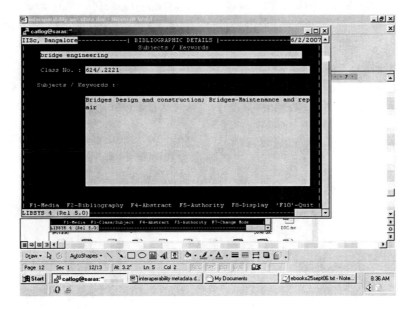

step, the records were converted to text format, and after manually editing records, they were loaded to Libsys. The sample record from Libsys is shown in Figures 1 and 2.

Advantages of Metadata Interoperability

Metadata is an essential component of large or small Web sites, document collections (e.g., library catalogues), product catalogues, and so forth. The metadata have a component for content management. Usually, codes like class number and keywords are provided in the metadata. But the main problem relates to the incorporation of new subjects both in the classification scheme and subject headings. This is particularly so when either the classification scheme is not updated as fast as the subjects develop, and in turn, keywords are not updated in the subject headings lists. In order to overcome this problem a new approach to data modeling and content management can be visualized. The database can become OAI-PMH compliant, enabling global data harvesting. Then, international data exchange is possible.

CONCLUSION

Interoperability can import required catalogue records. Good selection procedures, quality control, and a common data standard help in managing data across the world. Harvesting metadata through cooperation between communities is vital in the digital environment. Therefore, universal models for metadata exchange should be encouraged for further developments in metadata interoperability.

REFERENCES

Anderson, B., & Hawkins, L. (1996). Development of CONSER cataloging policies for remote access computer file serials. *The Public-Access Computer Systems Review, 7*(1), 6-25.

Arms, W. Y. (2000). *Digital libraries.* Cambridge, MA: MIT Press.

Borgamon, C. L. (2000). *From Gutenberg to the global infrastructure: Access to information in the networked world.* Cambridge: MIT Press.

Chudamani, K. S. (2005). Metadata and content management. *Srels Journal of Information Management, 2*, 205-209.

Chudamani, K. S., & Nagarathna, H. C. (2006). *Interoperability between Dublin Core, UNI-MARC, MARC21, with AACR2R as the standards frameworks for cataloging in the digital environment.* Paper presented at Planner INFLIBNET, Silchar, India.

Haynes, D. (2004). *Metadata for information management and retrieval.* London: Facet Publishing.

IEEE. (1990). *Glossary.* Retrieved August 17, 2008, from http://www.sei.cmu.edu/str/indexes/glossary/interoperability.html

http://www.harrassowitz.de/top_resources/ejres-guidestandards.html

www.libsys.co.in/home.html

Chapter XIII
Semantic Association Analysis in Ontology–Based Information Retrieval

Payam M. Barnaghi
University of Nottingham, Malaysia

Wei Wang
University of Nottingham, Malaysia

Jayan C. Kurian
University of Nottingham, Malaysia

ABSTRACT

The Semantic Web is an extension to the current Web in which information is provided in machine-processable format. It allows interoperable data representation and expression of meaningful relationships between the information resources. In other words, it is envisaged with the supremacy of deduction capabilities on the Web, that being one of the limitations of the current Web. In a Semantic Web framework, an ontology provides a knowledge sharing structure. The research on Semantic Web in the past few years has offered an opportunity for conventional information search and retrieval systems to migrate from keyword to semantics-based methods. The fundamental difference is that the Semantic Web is not a Web of interlinked documents; rather, it is a Web of relations between resources denoting real world objects, together with well-defined metadata attached to those resources. In this chapter, we first investigate various approaches towards ontology development, ontology population from heterogeneous data sources, semantic association discovery, semantic association ranking and presentation, and social network analysis, and then we present our methodology for an ontology-based information search and retrieval. In particular, we are interested in developing efficient algorithms to resolve the semantic association discovery and analysis issues.

INTRODUCTION

The current Web provides a universal platform to explore and contribute to the global information network. Undoubtedly, the Web has emerged as the world's major information resource with immediate accessibility in a world-wide scale. Currently, in most of the cases, in order to transform available information into meaningful knowledge, machines have to depend on the human inference ability (Craven, DiPasquo, Freitag, McCallum, Mitchell, Nigam, et al., 2000). Contemporary popular online search engines and information retrieval systems index and search the Web documents based on analysis of the document link structures and keywords. The keywords are often extracted from the documents according to the frequency of occurrence and considered as standalone entities without application contexts and other semantic relationships. This superficial understanding of content prevents retrieving implicitly-related information in most of the cases. It also in some cases returns irrelevant results to the user. In the context of multimedia Web, the current search systems are even more limited. Most of the multimedia search on the current Web relies on text explanations extracted from accompanying pages or tags provided by content authors. There are commercially successful Web sites for multimedia publishing, sharing, and retrieval on the Web such as MySpace[1], YouTube[2], and Flickr[3]. These Web sites have demonstrated a great achievement in acquiring millions of users to form communities and contribute to content generation; they also provide interfaces to search and view the published contents, but the search functions regularly rely on conventional methods and keyword matching mechanisms. As overwhelming information is published on the Web, new information search and retrieval methods are needed in order to enable users to find more relevant information based not only on keywords, but also context and preferences of each individual user. This has lead to the

introduction of a new era for Web information search and retrieval, namely, community-based and semantic-enhanced search.

The emergent **Semantic Web** technologies provide the possibility to realize the vision of meaningful relations and structured data on the Web. As an extension to the current Web, the Semantic Web technologies enable computers and people to work in cooperation (Berners-Lee, Hendler, & Lassila, 2001). The Semantic Web focuses on publishing and retrieving machine-processable Web contents (Dayal, Kuno, & Wilkinson, 2003). In the Semantic Web framework, flexible and interoperable structures such as Web ontology language (OWL)[4] and resource description framework (RDF)[5] are used to represent resources. The relationships between entities in a particular domain can be explicitly expressed using an ontology (Chandrasekaran, Josephson, & Benjamins, 1999). To describe multimedia data and documents on the Semantic Web, the ontology concepts are required to be mapped to the metadata description structure, which is usually referred to as semantic annotation. The semantic-enhanced search focuses on utilizing the structured description and knowledge description ontologies to enhance the results of information search and retrieval process on the Web. The better the relationships are processed and analyzed, the more relevant context results are obtained to be shown to users.

A significant feature in the information search and retrieval systems developed based on Semantic Web technologies is the analysis of meaningful relationships between Web resources to provide enhanced search results. In order to do so, a semantic query framework is required to support this process. There are various semantic query languages such as SPARQL (2007), RQL (Karvounarakis, Alexaki, Christophides, Plexousakis, & Scholl, 2002), and SeRQL (Broekstra, Kampman, & Harmelen, 2002) that are able to query the Semantic Web data (i.e., RDF or OWL data) based on ontological concepts. However, these languages do not adequately provide a query mechanism to discover the complex and implicit relationships between the resources. Such complex relationships are called semantic associations (Aleman-Meza, Halaschek-Wiener, Sahoo, Sheth, & Arpinar, 2005; Sheth, Aleman-Meza, Arpinar, Bertram, Warke, Ramakrishnan, et al., 2005). The process of discovering semantic associations is also referred to as semantic analytics. This can be viewed as a special class of search applications which facilitates obtaining decidable knowledge from massive interconnected data resources. This process assists information analysis and provides new and unexpected insights to information search and retrieval (Aleman-Meza, Halaschek, Arpinar, & Sheth, 2003).

RELATED WORK

The successful development of the Semantic Web applications depends on availability and adoption of ontologies and semantic data (Guha, 2003; Kiryakov, Popov, Terziev, Manov, & Ognyanoff, 2005; Shadbolt, Hall, & Berners-Lee, 2006). In the last few years different thesauruses, ontologies, and metadata structures have been introduced, such as friend of a friend (FOAF[6]) ontology, the GENE ontology[7], NCI meta thesaurus (Golbeck, Fragoso, Hartel, Hendler, Oberthaler, & Parsia, 2003), and Cyc ontology[8]. A number of works have been carried out to apply ontology-based information search and retrieval in various domains (e.g., Swoogle ontology search engine [Ding, 2004], TAP generic semantic search framework [Guha, 2003], semantic annotation in KIM (Kiryakov et al., 2005), semantics-enhanced multimedia presentation generation [Falkovych, Werner, & Nack, 2004; Rutledge, Alberink, Brussee, Pokraev, van Dieten, & Veenstra, 2003], and the semantic-based multimedia search engine Squiggle]Celino, Valle, Cerzza, & Turati, 2006]). The following section reviews two representative domain independent semantic search infrastructures, that is, TAP

(Guha, 2003) and KIM (Kiryakov et al., 2005). The next section describes related work to semantic association analysis, and then discusses the community-based approach to discover and analyze semantic associations.

Semantic-Enhanced Search

TAP is an infrastructure for sites to publish structured data, and for applications to consume this data. The main ontology in TAP is a broad knowledge base containing concepts such as people (e.g., musicians, athletes), organizations, places, and products, and a set of properties. TAP improves search results by utilizing semantic-enhanced and context-based approaches. It provides a simple mechanism to help the semantic search module to interpret the denotation of a query. This is important because one needs to deal with concepts ambiguity in the real world based on semantics rather than focusing only on the syntax. It also enhances the search results by considering search context and exploring closely related resources within a specified context.

KIM introduces a holistic architecture of semantic annotation, indexing, and retrieval of documents. Its aim is to provide fully automatic annotation methods using information extraction methods. The annotation framework is built upon a semantic repository which consists of two major components: a light-weight upper level ontology and a broadly-populated knowledge base. The ontology includes generic classes representing real world entities across various domains, such as people, location, organization, as well as their attributes and relationships. The advantage of using light-weight ontology is that it is easier to understand, build, verify, maintain, and get consensus upon. The entity annotation for an object in KIM includes both a reference to its most specific entity type in the ontology, and a reference to its entity description in the knowledge base. KIM improves search precision and recall by indexing and searching documents using the semantic annotation. Compared to traditional information search and retrieval approaches, semantic search and ontology-based information retrieval methods demonstrate several salient advantages, such as being able to incorporate query denotation, context-based exploration, enhanced data integration, query expansion, and consequently better recall and precision.

Semantic Association Analysis

The conventional- and semantic-supported search approaches typically respond to user queries by returning a collection of links to various resources. Users have to verify each document to find out the information they need; in most cases the answer is a combination of information from different resources. Relations are at the heart of Semantic Web (Anyanwu, Maduko, & Sheth, 2005). Focusing on Semantic Web technologies, the emphasis of search will shift from searching for documents to finding facts and practical knowledge. Relation searching is a special class of search methods which is concerned with representing, discovering, and interpreting complex relationships or connections between resources. As the development of semantic-enhanced and community-based Web search continues, more ontologies are developed and used across the domains. This also leads to deployment and support of more semantic data in different systems and applications. One can expect that connections between entities on Semantic Web will become more complex and obscure. However, in some applications it is extremely important to have the ability to discover those distant and obscure connections between resources (Sheth et al., 2005). There are some existing work which have demonstrated utilizing semantic association analysis in different applications, for example, detection of conflict of interest (COI) (Aleman-Meza et al., 2005), detection of insider threat (Sheth et al., 2005), terrorism identification and flight security (Aleman-Meza et al., 2005; Sheth et al., 2005), and so forth. The

semantic association discovery and analysis also plays a significant role in business intelligence, antimoney laundry, gene relationship discovery, medicine, and geographical systems.

Sheth et al. (2005) discuss an algorithm developed to process different kinds of semantic associations using graph traversal algorithms at the ontology level. The relationships between two entities in the results of a semantic query could be established through one or more semantic associations. In this case the semantic associations could be represented by a graph which shows the connection between entities. It is also important to process and prioritize the semantic association based on user preferences and the context of search. There are also ranking algorithms proposed based on different metrics to grade the semantic association (Anyanwu et al., 2005; Barnaghi & Kareem, 2007).

Baziz, Boughanem, Pasi, and Prade (2006) compare the classical keyword-based approach with the concept-based approach for information retrieval, and propose a fuzzy approach for query evaluation. The target documents and user queries are conceptually represented by means of weighted structures, and they are associated to an ontology. The documents and queries are compared with the fuzzy model based on the computation of degree of inclusion of features. The method holds its importance since the documents are retrieved based on conceptually-related documents, even if it does not contain weighted query keywords explicitly.

There are also ongoing researches to incorporate community interests and similarities amongst different groups and individuals to provide enhanced search results. The next section discusses the main issues of a community-based approach for a Web search.

Social Network Analysis

A social network indicates the ways in which nodes (e.g., individual or organization) are connected through various relationships to each other. The social network analysis, in this context, is a way of processing and interpreting the nodes and relationships to realize mutual interests and connection between different groups and individuals in a community. Several studies have been carried out—mostly focusing on graph theory and statistical methods—to analyze relationships and connections in a social network. The Semantic Web technologies support social network analysis by providing explicit representation of the social network information (Ding, 2004). In recent years some social network studies have been conducted to adapt Semantic Web technologies in the social network research (Ding, 2004; Ding, Zhou, Finin, & Joshi, 2005; Matsuo, Hamasaki, Nakamura, Nishimura, Hasida, Takeda, et al., 2006; Mika, 2005). Flink (Mika, 2005) is one of the early works in this area that employs Semantic Web technologies for reasoning personal information extracted from heterogeneous sources, including Web pages, e-mails, publication archives, and FOAF profiles. It presents the professional work and social connectivity of researchers in the Semantic Web area. In a similar context, Ding et al. (2005) performed a network study based on the "*foaf:knows*" relation in a dataset constructed from online FOAF documents using Swoogle and other tools. The study primarily concentrates on basic graph features of the extracted social network. The authors state that the social network could be an implicit trust network to support applications such as knowledge outsourcing and online communities.

Matsuo et al. (2006) utilize extraction, analysis, and integration of multiple social networks from communities with similar characteristics. The work indicates the efficiency and significance of the research for locating experts and authorities, calculating trustworthiness of a person, detecting relevance and relations among people (e.g., COI detection), promoting communication, information exchange and discussion, ontology extraction by identifying communities, and so on.

In recent years, the Semantic Web community has been very active in promoting different applications of the proposed technologies in various application domains. The above discussed work outlines examples of several ongoing researches on semantic-enhanced and ontology-based information search and retrieval. They demonstrate the significance of semantic association analysis in different applications.

PROCESSES AND COMPONENTS OF SEMANTIC ANALYTICS

The semantic association analysis consists of several key processes and components. We discuss ontology development, data set construction, semantic association discovery, semantic association ranking, results presentation, and performance evaluation in the following sections, respectively. However, there are also other important issues such as entity disambiguation, data set maintenance, and so forth. As our focus is to describe semantic association identification and interpretation, we will not discuss these issues in this chapter.

Ontology Development

The creation of an **ontology** has been made easier because of the availability of some open source ontology creation tools like protégé,[9] ontology libraries such as DAML[10] and SchemaWeb,[11] and search engines (e.g., Swoogle[12]). For example, if one wants to create an ontology about countries, the creator does not need to create it from scratch, instead, the creator may find an existing ontology (or one in a similar context) through browsing the ontology library or using the ontology search engines. Further more, existing authoritative ontologies or vocabularies such as FOAF and Dublin Core[13] also contribute to the ontology engineering process. The adoption of existing vocabularies also promotes reuse and interoperability of an ontology.

Data Set Construction

The data set, in some papers referred to as test bed (Aleman-Meza, Halaschek, Sheth, Arpinar, & Sannapareddy, 2004) or knowledge base (Guha, 2003), (Kiryakov et al., 2005), is in fact a collection of instances for a created ontology, or in Semantic Web jargon, the population of an ontology. The semantic association discovery is performed upon the test bed. The data usually come from different sources and are connected through relations defined in the ontology. Existing data sets for semantic analytics applications have some characteristics as summarized by Aleman-Meza et al. (2006). The data should be selected from highly reliable Web sites which provide data in structured, semistructured, or parse-able unstructured form, or with database backend. Structured data are preferred (i.e., RDF or OWL). Semistructured or parse-able unstructured data (i.e., XML) can be transformed to structured data using xPath or XSLT. Data with rich metadata and relations are preferred. For example, for a "computer scientist" class, the source also provides "address" and "country" attributes as well as some relations with other classes, such as "research area," "publication," and "organization." The data set should have rich relations and a large amount of instances which are highly connected.

Semantic Association Discovery Algorithms

Semantic association discovery can be seen as a special class of semantic search aiming to find out complex relationships between entities. The problem can be generalized as enumerating all possible paths between any two nodes in a semantic graph. The search is performed using ontologies and semantic data sets. The structure of the ontology constrains the possible paths that one can take from one node to another. Typically, the structure of the ontology or relation between

classes is simple; however, the relations between instances in the knowledge base (i.e., instances) might be very complicated depending on the connectedness of the graph.

RDF and OWL, which, in most cases, are the data model of the aforementioned data sets, have been visualized as a model of directed labeled graph and the problem of finding the semantic associations has been generalized as finding all paths between any given two entities in the graph (Aleman-Meza et al., 2004). A method for finding path associations using a recursive depth-first search is described by Sheth et al. (2005). The search is performed on the ontology, which can be viewed as a schema of the RDF instance data, to prune the search at the data level. The reason is that the number of entities in the schema is much less than in RDF data, thus the complexity of algorithm is reduced to a greater extent. The result of a search is a set of possible paths between C1 and C2 (both C1 and C2 are classes in an ontology) at the schema level and it is used to guide the search for paths between two entities e1 and e2 (e1 and e2 have "*rdf:type*" C1 and C2, respectively) at the data level. The search for join association is more complicated and is based on the path association algorithm. First it tries to find all paths between two classes and every other class at the schema level; the result is two sets of path. Then it compares every path in one path set and the other path set. If there is an intersection (e.g., joined node), then these two paths end at the same node in the schema. Finally, the result is used to perform a search at the data level.

Semantic Association Ranking

A ranking mechanism is an important part of a search engine. A good ranking algorithm reflects the cognitive thought of human beings towards the ranking of real world objects according to their perceived importance. The PageRank algorithm (Anyanwub & Sheth, 2003) contributes to Google's success and it is one of the most important reasons that most people prefer to use it. Most of the current search engines rank documents based on vector space model and citation analysis (The PageRank algorithm can be seen as a variation of the citation-based approach) (Brin & Page, 1998). In semantic association analysis, an important task is incorporating the most meaningful associations out of all detected relations. However, new ranking algorithms need to be developed in order to utilize the advantages of Semantic Web technologies. SemRank (Anyanwu et al., 2005) describes a ranking algorithm which uses semantic and statistical metrics. The semantic metrics consists of context, subsumption, and trust. The value of trust is assigned according to the trustworthiness of source that made a statement. The statistical metrics includes rarity, popularity, and link length. The weight of a semantic association is the accumulated value of six factors. In a similar work, we have developed a relation robustness evaluation algorithm for semantic associations which computes the weight of an entity in the knowledge base with the queried entity using context, association length, and popularity metrics (Barnaghi & Kareem, 2007). It is worthwhile to note that the objects are being ranked in this algorithm rather than the semantic associations.

Results Presentation

The presentation of the results is not the focus of this chapter, but for the sake of unification we briefly describe it here. In an existing work, the discovered semantic associations are presented as a list of property sequence with ranked value or as a 3D graph representation (Baclawski & Niu, 2005). The identified semantic associations could be presented to users in a meaningful way, which is able to help users understand the meaning of entities. We have implemented an automated hypermedia presentation generation engine, called MANA, to construct hypermedia presentations based on documents relating to

entities in semantic associations (Deligiannidis, Sheth, & Aleman-Meza, 2006).

The entities are hyperlinked to those documents which are able to provide external explanations that help users to explore relevant information regarding a submitted query. Figure 1 shows different components and layers in an ontology-based information search, retrieval, and presentation.

SEMANTIC SEARCH ARCHITECTURE

We have built a test bed upon which our semantic association discovery and ranking algorithms are evaluated. The system uses a domain ontology and semantic annotated resources in fine arts domain. When applied to fine arts (in particular, painting), analytical modules of the MANA are typically able to extract the name of an artwork, its creator, details on its features (i.e., style, period, materials), its image file, and possibly some information about other related documents. Paintings, as well as other objects, are associated with other

Figure 1. Different components in a semantic-enhanced information search and retrieval system

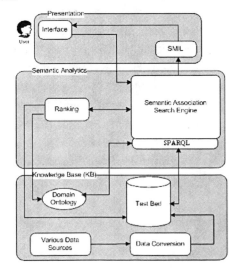

artworks in terms of creator, style, material, and so forth. Examples of information "triples" (in free-text form, to avoid syntax issues) are listed in the following:

"Painter X Paints Painting Y".
"Painting Y's style is cubism".
"Painting Y is a contemporary artwork".
"Contemporary artworks have specific features".
"The features of contemporary art are described in Z".

The logical reasoning could be outlined based on stated triples. For example:

X painted Y, Y's style is cubism, Z describes cubism [implies that] "X's work style is described in Z".

Other spatial and temporal similarities between entities could also be considered in a semantic association discovery. For example, two painters living in the same period of time and same geographical location would be related based on some queries and contexts. The domain ontology's hierarchical structure is shown in Figure 2.

The system uses an inference engine which is responsible for discovering the relationships between entities, and calculating and assigning weights to selected objects based on the proposed ranking mechanism. The details of the ranking mechanism are described by Barnaghi and Kareem (2007). The work introduces a knowledge-driven methodology which provides a multicriteria search method based on different attributes and ranking metrics. Figure 3 illustrates the results of a query (e.g., Cubism) and the associated ranking weights for the results obtained from the semantic association analysis.

CONCLUSION

This chapter describes research and issues in the semantic analytics area and, in particular, discovery and interpretation of complex relations between entities in a knowledge base. In the Semantic Web, semantic analytics demonstrate significant importance in various application domains by enabling search mechanism to discover and process meaningful relations between infor-

Figure 2. The domain ontology concepts

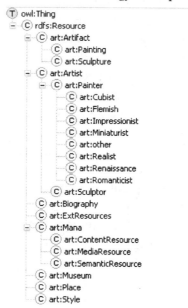

Figure 3. Semantic search and ranking

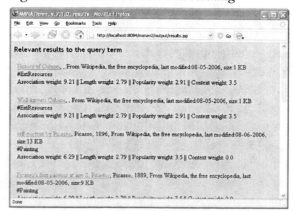

mation resources. In this chapter, we introduced the problem of semantic association identification, and we described the enhanced search methods based on semantic and community-based approaches. A prototype of semantic association-based information search and retrieval is also described through the chapter.

Future work focuses on automated semantic annotation and constructing a social network and community information for academic publication archives.

REFERENCES

Aleman-Meza, B., Halaschek, C., Arpinar, I. B., & Sheth, A. (2003). *Context-aware semantic association ranking* (Tech. Rep. 03-010). University of Georgia, LSDIS Lab, Computer Science.

Aleman-Meza, B., Halaschek-Wiener, C., Sahoo, S. S., Sheth, A., & Arpinar, I. B. (2005). *Template based semantic similarity for security applications* (Tech. Rep.). University of Georgia, LSDIS Lab, Computer Science Department.

Aleman-Meza, B., Halaschek, C., Sheth, A., Arpinar, I. B., & Sannapareddy, G. (2004). SWETO: Large-scale Semantic Web test-bed. In *Proceedings of the 16th International Conference on Software Engineering & Knowledge Engineering Workshop on Ontology in Action, Knowledge Systems Inst.* (pp. 490-493).

Anyanwu, K., Maduko, A., & Sheth, A. (2005). SemRank: Ranking complex relationship search results on the Semantic Web. In *Proceedings of the WWW 2005 Conference.*

Anyanwu, K., & Sheth, A. P. (2003). ρ-Queries: Enabling querying for semantic associations on the Semantic Web. In *Proceedings of the 12th International World Wide Web Conference.*

Baclawski, K., & Niu, T. (2005). *Ontologies for bioinformatics.* MIT Press.

Barnaghi, P. M., & Kareem, S. A. (2006). A flexible architecture for semantic annotation and automated multimedia presentation generation, In *Proceedings of the 1st International Workshop on Semantic-enhanced Multimedia Presentation Systems.*

Barnaghi, P. M., & Kareem, S. A. (2007). Relation robustness evaluation for the Semantic associations. *The Electronic Journal of Knowledge Management, 5*(3), 265-272.

Baziz, M., Boughanem, M., Pasi, P., & Prade, H. (2006). A fuzzy logic approach to information retrieval using an ontology-based representation of documents. *Fuzzy logic and the Semantic Web.* Elsevier.

Berners-Lee., T., Hendler, J., & Lassila, O. (2001). The Semantic Web. *Scientific American, 284*(5), 35-35.

Brin, S., & Page, L. (1998). The anatomy of a large-scale hypertextual Web search engine. In *Proceedings of the WWW 1998 Conference* (pp 107-117).

Broekstra, J., Kampman, A., & Harmelen, F. V. (2002). Sesame: An architecture for storing and querying RDF and RDF schema. In *Proceedings of the 1st International Semantic Web Conference* (LNCS 2342, pp. 54-68). Springer-Verlag.

Celino, I., Valle, E. D., Cerzza, D., & Turati, A. (2006). Squiggle: A semantic search engine for indexing and retrieval of multimedia content. In *Proceedings of the 1st International Workshop on Semantic-Enhanced Multimedia Presentation Systems.*

Chandrasekaran, B., Josephson, J. R., & Benjamins, V. R. (1999). What are ontologies, and why do we need them? *IEEE Intelligent Systems,* 20-26.

Craven, M., DiPasquo, D., Freitag, D., McCallum, A., Mitchell, T., Nigam, K., et al. (2000). Learning to construct knowledge bases from the World Wide Web. *Artificial Intelligence,* 69-113.

Dayal, U., Kuno, H., & Wilkinson, K. (2003). Making the Semantic Web real. *IEEE Data Engineering Bulletin, 26*(4), 4.

Deligiannidis, L., Sheth, A. P., & Aleman-Meza, B. (2006). Semantic analytics visualization. In *Proceedings of the Intelligence and Security Informatics, ISI-2006* (pp. 48-59).

Ding, L., Finin, T., & Joshi, A. (2004). Analyzing social networks on the Semantic Web. *IEEE Intelligent Systems, 8*(6).

Ding, L., Finin, T., Joshi, A., Pan, R., Cost, R. S., Peng, Y., et al. (2004). Swoogle: A search and metadata engine for the Semantic Web. In *Proceedings the 13th ACM international Conference on Information and Knowledge Management* (pp. 652-659).

Ding, L., Zhou, L., Finin, T., & Joshi, A. (2005). How the Semantic Web is being used: An analysis of FOAF documents. In *Proceedings of the 38th International Conference on System Sciences* (pp. 113.3).

Falkovych, K., Werner, & Nack, F. (2004). Semantic-based support for the semi-automatic construction of multimedia presentations. In *Proceedings of the Interaction Design and the Semantic Web Workshop, the 13th World Wide Web Conference.*

Guha, R., & McCool, R., (2003). TAP: A Semantic Web test-bed. *Journal of Web Semantics, 1*(1), 81-88.

Guha, R., McCool, R., & Miller, E. (2003). Semantic search. In *Proceedings of the WWW 2003 Conference.*

Golbeck, J., Fragoso, G., Hartel, F., Hendler, J., Oberthaler, J., & Parsia, B. (2003). The National Cancer Institute's thésaurus and ontology. *Journal of Web Semantics, 1*(1).

Karvounarakis, G., Alexaki, S., Christophides, V., Plexousakis, D., & Scholl, M. (2002). RQL: A declarative query language for RDF. In *Proceedings of the 11th World Wide Web Conference* (pp. 592-603).

Kiryakov, A., Popov, B., Terziev, I., Manov, D., & Ognyanoff, D. (2005). Semantic annotation, indexing, and retrieval. *Elsevier's Journal of Web Semantics, 2*(1).

Matsuo, Y., Hamasaki, M., Nakamura, Y., Nishimura, T., Hasida, K., Takeda, H., et al. (2006). *Spinning multiple social networks for Semantic Web.* American Association for Artificial Intelligence.

Mika, P. (2005). Flink: Semantic Web technology for the extraction and analysis of social networks. *Journal of Web Semantics Science, 3*(2-3), 211-223.

Rutledge, L., Alberink, M., Brussee, R., Pokraev, S., van Dieten, W., & Veenstra, M. (2003). Finding the story: Broader applicability of semantics and discourse for hypermedia generation. In *Proceedings of the 14th ACM Conference on Hypertext and Hypermedia* (pp. 67-76).

Shadbolt, N., Hall, W., & Berners-Lee, T. (2006). The Semantic Web revisited. *IEEE Intelligent Systems.*

Sheth, A., Aleman-Meza, B., Arpinar, I. B., Bertram, C., Warke, Y., Ramakrishnan, C., et al. (2005). Semantic association identification and knowledge discovery for national security applications. *Journal of Database Management on Database Technology, 16*(1), 33-53.

SPARQL Query Language for RDF (2007, November 12). *W3C proposed recommendation.* Retrieved August 17, 2008, from http://www.w3.org/TR/rdf-sparql-query/

KEY TERMS

Information Search and Retrieval: Finding out queried information and its descriptive details.

Ontology: Object description and relationship between objects in a domain.

Semantic Association Analysis: Discovering complex and meaningful relationship between objects.

Semantic Web: A Web of relations between resources together with well-defined metadata attached to those resources.

ENDNOTES

1. http://www.myspace.com
2. http://www.youtube.com/
3. http://www.flickr.com/
4. http://www.w3.org/TR/owl-features/
5. www.w3.org/RDF/
6. http://xmlns.com/foaf/0.1/
7. http://www.geneontology.org/
8. http://www.opencyc.org/
9. http://protege.stanford.edu
10. http://www.daml.org/ontologies
11. http://www.schemaWeb.info
12. http://swoogle.umbc.edu
13. http://dublincore.org

Chapter XIV
Effective and Efficient Browsing of Large Image Databases

Gerald Schaefer
Aston University, UK

ABSTRACT

As image databases are growing, efficient and effective methods for managing such large collections are highly sought after. Content-based approaches have shown large potential in this area as they do not require textual annotation of images. However, while for image databases the query-by-example concept is at the moment the most commonly adopted retrieval method, it is only of limited practical use. Techniques which allow human-centred navigation and visualization of complete image collections therefore provide an interesting alternative. In this chapter we present an effective and efficient approach for user-centred navigation of large image databases. Image thumbnails are projected onto a spherical surface so that images that are visually similar are located close to each other in the visualization space. To avoid overlapping and occlusion effects images are placed on a regular grid structure while large databases are handled through a clustering technique paired with a hierarchical tree structure which allows for intuitive real-time browsing experience.

INTRODUCTION

With sizes of image databases ever growing, these collections need to be managed not only for professional but also increasingly for private use. Clearly one of the decisive parts of this is the ability to effectively retrieve those images a user is looking for. As the traditional approach of annotating images with a textual description

and/or keywords is only feasible for smaller image collections, it is an automatic, content-based image retrieval (CBIR) approach that is required to query larger datasets (Smeulders, Worring, Santini, Gupta, & Jain, 2000). Unfortunately the current state-of-the-art of computer vision is still far from being able to correctly interpret captured scenes and "see" the objects they contain. Nevertheless, much research has focussed on content-based techniques for retrieving images, much of which employs low level visual features such as color or texture to judge the similarity between images (Smeulders et al., 2000).

The most common form of image retrieval systems is based on the query-by-example concept (Jain, 1996) where the user provides an image and the system retrieves those images that are deemed to be most similar to the query. As this approach requires an actual image as input, it is only of limited practical use for various applications. An alternative is to employ the query-by-navigation paradigm where the user has the ability to visualize and browse interactively an entire image collection via a graphical user interface and, through a series of operations, zoom in on those images that are of interest. Various authors have recently introduced such intuitive navigation interfaces (Ruszala & Schaefer, 2004). The basic idea behind most of these is to place thumbnails of visually similar images, as established by the calculation of image similarity metrics based on features derived from image content, also close to each other on the visualization screen, a principle that has been shown to decrease the time it takes to localize images (Rodden, Basalaj, Sinclair, & Wood, 1999). One of the first approaches was the application of multidimensional scaling (MDS) (Kruskal & Wish, 1978) to project images being represented by high dimensional feature vectors to a 2-dimensional visualization plane (Rubner, Guibas, & Tomasi, 1997). In the PicSOM system (Laaksonen, Koskela, Laakkso, & Oja, 2000), tree-structured self organizing maps are employed to provide both image browsing and retrieval capabilities. Krishnamachari and Abdel-Mottaleb (1999) employ a hierarchical tree to cluster images of similar concepts, while image database navigation on a hue sphere is proposed by Schaefer and Ruszala (2005). The application of virtual reality ideas and equipment to provide the user with an interactive browsing experience was introduced by Nakazato and Huang (2001).

While the application of techniques such as MDS provides an intuitive and powerful tool for browsing image collections, it is only of limited use for medium-sized and large image collections. For such databases it provides a relatively poor representation as many images are occluded, either fully or partially, by other images with similar feature vectors. In addition, empty spaces are common in areas where no images fall, creating an unbalanced representation on screen. Furthermore, some techniques (e.g., MDS) are computationally expensive and hence not suitable for real-time browsing environments.

In this chapter we present an image database navigation method that addresses these issues. Based on a spherical visualization space (Schaefer & Ruszala, 2005), a navigation interface for image collections is created. Yet in contrast to the previous approaches, this is being done in a hierarchical manner which can cope also with large image datasets and has the advantage that all levels of the hierarchy can be precomputed, thus allowing real-time browsing of the image database. In addition, images are laid out on a regular grid structure which avoids any unwanted overlapping effect between images. Furthermore, the visualization space is better utilized by branching out images into otherwise unoccupied parts of the screen. The proposed method hence provides an effective, intuitive, and efficient interface for image database navigation, as is demonstrated on a medium-sized image collection.

HUE SPHERE

While MDS browsing typically employs a 2-dimensional plane as navigation and visualization space, Schaefer and Ruszala (2005) introduced the application of a spherical browsing interface. The reasoning behind this is twofold. On one hand, the concept of a globe will almost certainly be familiar to the average user as it is a direct analogy of the Earth globe. It therefore provides a very intuitive interface to the user who will have experience on how to navigate and find something on its surface. On the other hand, a sphere as navigation space evolves naturally from the features that are employed in this approach. For each image the average (or median) hue and brightness are calculated and serve as visual descriptors. As hues of 0 and 360 are identical, hue describes an angular attribute which goes from red to yellow to green to blue back to red. All colors with high brightness values are similar, that is, close to white, while all colors with low brightness values are similarly close to black. Black and white as achromatic colors do not have a hue quality, and hence, these two points describe the poles of the sphere.

Hue and value pairs are converted to latitude and longitude values and image thumbnails are placed at the calculated coordinates. The whole image database is then displayed in a global view. Navigation is achieved through three kinds of operations: rotation which focuses on images with a different hue; tilt which allows one to see brighter or darker images; and a zoom operation which brings up previously hidden images.

GRID LAYOUT

In an MDS visualization, the image thumbnails are placed so as to minimize the distortions in terms of distances in the projected space while in hue sphere browsing their coordinates are given directly by the hue-value features calculated. In both methods, out of necessity, images will partially overlap with each other. However, this overlapping will have a negative impact on the browsing experience (Rodden et al., 1999). An approach to minimize these effects has been proposed by Moghaddam, Tian, Lesh, Shen, and Huang (2004), where images are slightly moved as a result of a local optimization problem; yet this method provides only a partial solution to the problem. Rodden et al. (1999) carried out a user study which compared image visualization models

where images overlap with each other, as is the case in a typical MDS layout with those where images are placed on a regular lattice without any overlapping. The results demonstrated that users largely prefer the latter as overlap adds to confusion between images; hence, a visualization that avoids overlapping will lead to faster retrieval times.

In our approach we adopt these findings and constrain images to be placed on a regular grid structure where images do not overlap each other (Schaefer & Ruszala, 2006). That is, we carry out the initial hue sphere calculations but then map each image to its closest grid cell. The size of the grid structure is typically dependent upon monitor size and resolution but can also be changed by the user. In our experiments we usually use grid sizes of either 24x30 or 27x35. Clearly, and in particular for larger image sets, this will mean that more than one image can be mapped to a particular cell. Later, we will describe how we are handling this case in an efficient and intuitive way through the employment of a hierarchical structure.

Filling Empty Cells

While snapping images to a grid lattice prevents any overlapping effects, in essence it provides a "quantized" form of a hue sphere display. Thus, it still suffers from the relatively unbalanced view that is usually generated where certain areas of the visualization space are not filled, which is in particular often the case for smaller image collections. To address this problem and to provide a more uniformly inhabited browsing screen, local search strategies are employed which move images across grid boundaries to previously unoccupied cells. First the positions of all empty cells are retrieved. For each of these cells the 4-neighborhood is then inspected. If 3 or 4 of the neighbors are occupied, a relative percentage of those images closest to the borders is moved across the border to fill the previously empty cell.

Performing this operation will usually fill some, but not all, of the empty cells. However, repeating the process based on the newly generated layout will in turn fill more cells. Hence the process is repeated a few (usually 3 or 4) times. Not all empty cells will have been assigned after that, but then this is not desired as it would mean images being positioned too far from their original coordinates, which in turn would distort the overall premise that images that are visually close should remain close on the browsing display.

HIERARCHICAL BROWSING

As mentioned above, classical MDS displays will provide only limited usability when being applied to large but also to even medium-sized databases of a few thousand images. The reason for this is that due to the limited space on the visualization plane images not only overlap each other partially but many images do not appear at all due to occlusion; hence, only a partial view of the database is provided (Schaefer & Ruszala, 2006). Zooming in provides only a partial solution, in particular if there are many images with similar image features. Furthermore, a zooming operation usually reapplies MDS on the selected images which, although it tends to spread the images more evenly, also constitutes a serious computational overhead. Zoom operations are also employed in hue sphere navigation, although here no additional calculations are necessary. Here however, images in the zoomed part are not spread out and hence images that were occluded before are still likely to be so after zooming in.

In our approach we employ a hierarchical tree structure to address both the navigation through large image collections and to eliminate the need for further computations. Hierarchical browsing environments such as the one described by Krishnamachari and Abdel-Mottaleb (1999) have been shown to provide an effective and efficient way of moving through large image datasets. In our approach we make direct use of the grid mapping introduced above to build a hierarchical tree based on clustering images. The resolution of the grid layout (e.g., 24x30 cells) directly determines the maximal number of clusters present at a given level (which will only be met if all cells are filled). The grid cells—after applying the filling strategy explained earlier—also determine which images fall into which clusters. What remains to be performed is the selection of a representative image to be displayed on the visualization grid. To do this we simply select the centroid image c, that is, the image for which the cumulative distance to all other images in the cluster $D_i = \sum_{j=1}^{N} d(I_i, I_j)$ where i is the ith of N images in the cluster and $d(.,.)$ denotes the distance between two images, is minimal, that is, $D_c < D_i, \forall i \neq c$. Note that we always keep both the original and the derived coordinates for each image.

This procedure is adopted at the each level of the tree hierarchy, that is, first at the root node (the initial global display) and then for each nonempty cell again in a recursive manner, where the images of each child node are again mapped to a grid structure, until the complete tree is derived.

The resulting interface provides an intuitive way of browsing to the user who can, starting from the initial display, successively select a representative image to refine the search. That image cluster—plus, if wanted, the eight neighboring clusters—is then expanded in the next level of the display where the user can again select an image group to navigate further into the image collection. Even based on a small grid of 24x30 cells and a fairly conservative estimate of 50% of cells being filled on average, this approach requires—on average—only three levels of the hierarchy to provide access to each of more than 370 million images (i.e., $720^3 = 3.73 * 10^8$), which will suffice for even the largest image databases.

The grid-tree structure also provides another advantage. As the structure is fixed it can be precomputed in completeness off-line, together with all possible grid view configurations the user can encounter, which in turn provides the user with the possibility of real-time browsing of a large image collection.

Image Spreading in Tree Cells

In the tree nodes of the cells it will commonly occur that only a few images occur, most of which will be visually fairly similar. To avoid them from being mapped to the same cell and, hence, triggering another tree level, a spreading algorithm is applied which displays them on the same screen once only a certain percentage of cells are filled for a cluster (we currently set this threshold to 25%).

The algorithm is based on the "place," "bump," and "double-bump" principle and is similar to the one employed by Rodden et al. (1999). When a cluster is encountered, a spiral scan is initiated that searches for and fills empty cells close by, until all images are distributed. If an empty cell is encountered on the first ring around the cell, the next image of the cluster is assigned to that cell ("place"). When an empty cell in the second ring is found it is first established which of the cells of the first ring is closest to the direct path to the identified empty cell. The image from the identified cell is then moved to the empty cell

whereas the next image from the cluster is placed in the cell from the first ring ("bump"). The same principle is applied to empty cells identified in the third ring with images from the first and second ring being moved ("double bump").

EXPERIMENTAL RESULTS

We tested the presented approach on a medium-size image database of about 4,500 images, that is, on the MPEG-7 common color dataset (Moving Picture Experts Group, 1999).

Figure 1 shows the global grid hue sphere view of the MPEG-7 database. As seen, in contrast to the standard MDS layout where many images overlap each other, the grid structure greatly contributes to the clarity of the visualization. Figure 2 displays the result of some user interaction where the user first rotated the sphere to focus on images with a different hue followed by a tilt operation to bring up resulting darker images (left of Figure 2) and then performed a zoom operation to display those images covered by a certain part of the tree (right of Figure 2). As with the MDS displays, previous navigation levels are also displayed and the spreading algorithm has been applied to the images in the tree node.

Figure 1. Global grid hue sphere view of the MPEG-7 dataset

Figure 2. Hue sphere view after rotation and tilt operations (left) and a further zoom operation (right)

CONCLUSION

In this chapter we presented an effective and efficient approach to interactive image database browsing which allows the visualization of complete image collections and subsequent intuitive navigation through the dataset. An initial global display of the image set is produced based on the application of a hue sphere visualization paradigm. Crucially, images are placed on a regular grid structure to avoid overlapping and occlusion of images. Based on a hierarchical tree structure, previously hidden images are brought up through a zoom operation that expands a selected tree node. As the entire tree structure can be computed off-line, the resulting browsing interface is suitable for real-time navigation of large image datasets.

REFERENCES

Jain, R. (1996). Infoscopes: Multimedia information systems. In B. Furht (Ed.), *Multimedia systems and techniques* (pp. 217-253). Kluwer.

Krishnamachari, S., & Abdel-Mottaleb, M. (1999). Image browsing using hierarchical clustering. In *Proceedings of the 4th IEEE Symposium on Computers and Communications* (pp. 301-307).

Kruskal, J. B., & Wish, M. (1978). *Multidimensional scaling.* Sage Publications.

Laaksonen, J., Koskela, M., Laakkso, P., & Oja, E. (2000). PicSOM: Content-based image retrieval with self organising maps. *Pattern Recognition Letters, 21,* 1197-1207.

Moghaddam, B., Tian, Q., Lesh, N., Shen, C., & Huang, T. S. (2004). Visualization and user-modeling for browsing personal photo libraries. *International Journal of Computer Vision, 56*(1-2), 109-130.

Moving Picture Experts Group. (1999). *Description of core experiments for MPEG-7 color/texture descriptors* (Tech. Rep. ISO/IEC JTC1/SC29/WG11/ N2929). Author.

Nakazato, M., & Huang, T. S. (2001). *3D MARS: Immersive virtual reality for content-based image retrieval.* Paper presented at the IEEE International Conference on Multimedia and Expo.

Rodden, K., Basalaj, D., Sinclair, W., & Wood, K. (1999). Evaluating a visualisation of image similarity as a tool for image browsing. In *Proceedings of the IEEE Symposium on Information Visualization* (pp. 36-43).

Rubner, Y., Guibas, L., & Tomasi, C. (1997). The earth mover's distance, multi-dimensional scaling, and color-based image retrieval. In *Pro-*

ceedings of the Image Understanding Workshop (pp. 661-668).

Ruszala, S. D., & Schaefer, G. (2004). Visualisation models for image databases: A comparison of six approaches. In *Proceedings of the Irish Machine Vision and Image Processing Conference* (pp. 186-191).

Schaefer, G., & Ruszala, S. (2005). Image database navigation: A globe-al approach. In *Proceedings of the International Symposium on Visual Computing* (LNCS 3804, pp. 279-286). Springer.

Schaefer, G., & Ruszala, S. (2006). Hierarchical image database navigation on a hue sphere. In *Proceedings of the International Symposium on Visual Computing* (LNCS 4292, pp. 814-823). Springer.

Smeulders, A. W. M., Worring, M., Santini, S., Gupta, G., & Jain, R. (2000). Content-based image retrieval at the end of the early years. *IEEE Transactions on Pattern Analysis and Machine Intelligence, 22*(12), 1249-1380.

KEY TERMS

Content-Based Image Retrieval (CBIR): Retrieval of images based not on keywords or annotations but on features extracted directly from the image data.

Hue: The attribute of a visual sensation according to which an area appears to be similar to red, green, yellow, blue, or a combination of two of them.

Image Database Navigation: The browsing of a complete image collection based, for example, on CBIR concepts.

Image Similarity Metric: Quantitative measure whereby the features of two images are compared in order to provide a judgement related to the visual similarity of the images.

Query-by-Example Retrieval: Retrieval paradigm in which a query is provided by the user and the system retrieves instances similar to the query.

Chapter XV
User Profiles for Personalizing Digital Libraries

Giovanni Semeraro
University of Bari, Italy

Pierpaolo Basile
University of Bari, Italy

Marco de Gemmis
University of Bari, Italy

Pasquale Lops
University of Bari, Italy

ABSTRACT

Exploring digital collections to find information relevant to a user's interests is a challenging task. Information preferences vary greatly across users; therefore, filtering systems must be highly personalized to serve the individual interests of the user. Algorithms designed to solve this problem base their relevance computations on user profiles in which representations of the users' interests are maintained. The main focus of this chapter is the adoption of machine learning to build user profiles that capture user interests from documents. Profiles are used for intelligent document filtering in digital libraries. This work suggests the exploiting of knowledge stored in machine-readable dictionaries to obtain accurate user profiles that describe user interests by referring to concepts in those dictionaries. The main aim of the proposed approach is to show a real-world scenario in which the combination of machine learning techniques and linguistic knowledge is helpful to achieve intelligent document filtering.

INTRODUCTION

Personalization has become an important topic for digital libraries to take a more active role in dynamically tailoring their information and service offers to individuals in order to better meet their needs (Callan & Smeaton, 2003). Most of the work on *personalized information access* focuses on the use of machine learning algorithms for the automated induction of a structured model of a user's interests, referred to as user profile, from labeled text documents (Mladenic, 1999). Keyword-based user profiles suffer from problems of polysemy and synonymy. The result is that, due to synonymy, relevant information can be missed if the profile does not contain the exact keywords occurring in the documents and, due to polysemy, wrong documents could be deemed as relevant.

This work explores a possible solution for this kind of issue: the adoption of semantic user profiles that capture key concepts representing users' interests from relevant documents. Semantic profiles will contain references to concepts defined in lexicons like WordNet (Miller, 1995) or ontologies. The solution is implemented in the item recommender (ITR) system which induces semantic user profiles from documents represented by using WordNet (Degemmis, Lops, & Semeraro, 2007). An example of intelligent personalized recommendation service based on ITR will be shown.

RELATED WORK

Our research was mainly inspired by the following works.

Syskill & Webert (Pazzani & Billsus, 1997) is an agent that learns a user profile to identify interesting Web pages. The learning process is performed by first converting a hypertext markup language (HTML) source into positive and negative examples, represented as keyword vectors, and then using learning algorithms like Bayesian classifiers, a nearest neighbor algorithm, and a decision tree learner.

Personal WebWatcher (Mladenic, 1999) is a Web browsing recommendation service that generates a user profile based on the content analysis of the requested pages. Learning is done by a naïve Bayes classifier where documents are represented as weighted keyword vectors, and classes are "interesting" and "not interesting."

Mooney and Roy (2000) adopt a text categorization method in their Libra system that performs content-based book recommendations by exploiting product descriptions obtained from the Web pages of the Amazon online digital store. Also in this case, documents are represented by using keywords, and a naïve Bayes text classifier is adopted.

The main limitation of these approaches is that they represent items by using keywords. The objective of our research is to create accurate semantic user profiles. Among the state-of-the-art systems that produce semantic user profiles, SiteIF (Magnini & Strapparava, 2001) is a personal agent for a multilingual news Web site that exploits a sense-based representation to build a user profile as a semantic network, whose nodes represent senses of the words in documents requested by the user.

The role of linguistic ontologies in knowledge-retrieval systems is explored in OntoSeek (Guarino, Masolo, & Vetere, 1999), a system designed for content-based information retrieval from online yellow pages and product catalogs. OntoSeek combines an ontology-driven content-matching mechanism based on WordNet with a moderately expressive representation formalism. The approach has shown that structured content representations coupled with linguistic ontologies can increase both recall and precision of content-based retrieval.

We adopted a content-based method able to learn user profiles from documents represented by using senses of words obtained by a word sense disambiguation strategy that exploits the WordNet IS-A hierarchy.

WORDNET-BASED DOCUMENT INDEXING

Text categorization (Sebastiani, 2002) is commonly described as follows: given a set of classes $C=\{c_1,....,c_n\}$ and a set of training documents labeled with the class the document belongs to, the problem consists of building a classifier able to assign to a new document the proper class. We consider the problem of learning user profiles as a binary classification task; each document has to be classified as interesting or not according to the user preferences. The set of classes is restricted to c_+, the positive class (user likes), and c_-, the negative one (user dislikes).

We propose a strategy to learn *semantic* sense-based profiles that consists of two steps. This section describes the first one, that is, a document indexing method that exploits word senses in WordNet to represent documents. In the second step, described in the next section, a naïve Bayes approach learns semantic user profiles as binary text classifiers from disambiguated documents.

In the classic bag-of-words (BOW) model, each feature used to represent a document corresponds to a single word found in the document.

We propose a document representation strategy that takes into account the senses of words found in the training documents. Here, *word sense* is used as a synonym of *word meaning*. The problem is that, while words occur in a document, meanings do not, since they are often hidden in the context. Therefore, a procedure is needed for assigning senses to words. The task of word sense disambiguation (WSD) consists of determining which sense of an ambiguous word is invoked in a particular use of the word (Manning & Schütze, 1999). As for sense repository, we adopted WordNet, a lexical database for English designed to establish connections between four types of parts of speech (POS): *noun, verb, adjective*, and *adverb*. The basic building block for WordNet is the *synset* (SYNonym SET), which represents a specific meaning or sense of a word. Synsets are structures containing sets of words with synonymous meanings and are connected through a series of relations. The *hyponymy* relation (IS-A) serves to organize the lexicon into a hierarchical structure. There are separate hierarchies for nouns, verbs, adjectives, and adverbs. We addressed the WSD problem by proposing an algorithm based on semantic similarity between synsets (Semeraro, Degemmis, Lops, & Basile, 2007). The WSD procedure is fundamental to obtain a synset-based vector space representation that we called bag-of-synsets (BOS). In this model a synset vector, rather than a word vector, corresponds to a document. Another key feature of the approach is that each document is represented by a set of slots. Each slot is a textual field corresponding to a specific feature of the document, in an attempt to take into account also the structure of documents. For example, in a paper recommendation scenario, each document could be represented by slots title, authors, and abstract.

The text in each slot is represented in the BOS model by counting separately the occurrences of a synset in the slots in which it appears. More formally, assume that we have a collection of N documents structured in M slots. Let m be the index of the slot, for $n = 1, 2, ...,N$ the n-th document is reduced to M bags of synsets, one for each slot. Each bag of synsets d_n^m is defined as follows:

$$d_n^m = \left\langle t_{n1}^m, t_{n2}^m, ..., t_{nD_{nm}}^m \right\rangle \quad m=1,...M \quad n=1,...N$$

where t_{nk}^m is the k-th synset in the slot s_m of the document d_n and D_{nm} is the total number of synsets appearing in the m-th slot of document d_n. For all n, k, and $m, t_{nk}^m \in V_m$ where V_m is the vocabulary for the slot s_m (the set of all different synsets found in slot s_m). Document d_n is finally represented in the vector space by M synset-frequency vectors. Each synset-frequency vector f_n^m is defined as follows:

$$f_n^m = \left\langle w_{n1}^m, w_{n2}^m, ..., w_{nD_{nm}}^m \right\rangle \qquad m = 1, ... M \quad n = 1, ... N$$

where w_{nk}^m is the weight of synset t_{nk}^m and can be computed in different ways: It can be simply the number of times the synset appears in the slot s_m or a more complex *tf-idf* score.

LEARNING BAYESIAN USER PROFILES: THE ITEM RECOMMENDER SYSTEM

ITR is a system able to recommend items by learning from their textual descriptions and ratings given by users. The system implements the naïve Bayes classifier, an increasingly popular algorithm in text classification applications (Mitchell, 1997). The system is able to classify documents as interesting or uninteresting for a particular user by exploiting a probabilistic model, learned from training examples. ITR represents

documents by using synsets corresponding to concepts identified from words in the original text through an automated word sense disambiguation (WSD) procedure, as stated in the previous section. The final outcome of the learning process is a probabilistic model used to classify a new document as interesting or uninteresting. The model is used as a personal profile including those concepts (synsets) that turn out to be most indicative of the user's preferences, according to the value of the parameters of the model. Figure 1 shows the ITR conceptual architecture.

The document collection (including training documents) is processed by the content analyzer, a NLP tool that performs the following operations:

- Tokenization
- Part-of-speech (POS) tagging
- Stop words elimination

Figure 1. ITR conceptual achitecture

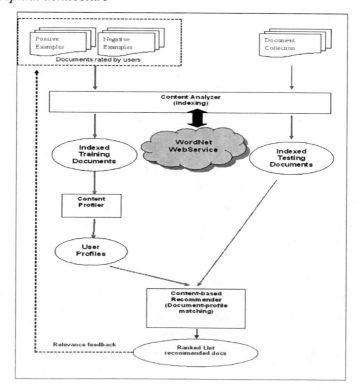

- Word sense disambiguation by using Word-Net
- Token count and corresponding tf-idf computation

The content profiler component implements the learning algorithm which induces user profiles as naïve Bayes classifiers. Details about the algorithm adopted in the content profiler follow.

The algorithm adopted in the ITR system (Degemmis et al., 2007) induces a probabilistic model by estimating the a-posteriori probability, $P(c_j|d_i)$, of document d_i belonging to class c_j as follows:

$$P(c_j \mid d_i) = \frac{P(c_j) \prod_{t_k \in d_i} P(t_k \mid c_j)^{N(t_k, d_i)}}{P(d_i)} \qquad (1)$$

where $N(t_k, d_i)$ is the number of times token (synset) t_k occurs in document d_i. Since, for any given document, $P(d_i)$ is a constant with respect to c_j, this factor can be ignored in calculating Equation (1), because all we need is to find the hypothesis with the highest posterior probability—*maximum a posteriori hypothesis*—rather than a probability estimate. In ITR, each document is encoded as a vector of BOS in the synset-based representation described in the previous section. Therefore, Equation (1) becomes

$$P(c_j \mid d_i) = P(c_j) \prod_{m=1}^{|S|} \prod_{k=1}^{|b_{im}|} P(t_k \mid c_j, s_m)^{n_{kim}} \qquad (2)$$

where $S = \{s_1, s_2, \ldots, s_{|S|}\}$ is the set of slots, b_{im} is the BOS in the slot s_m of d_i, and n_{kim} is the number of occurrences of token t_k in b_{im}. When training is performed on BOS-represented documents, tokens are synsets, and the induced model relies on synset frequencies. To calculate Equation (2), the system has to estimate $P(c_j)$ and $P(t_k|c_j, s_m)$ in the training phase. The documents used to train the system are labeled with a discrete rating, from 1 to MAX, provided by a user according to the user's degree of interest in the item. Following the idea proposed by Mooney and Roy (2000), each training document d_i is labeled with two scores, that is, a "user-likes" score ω_i^+ and a "user-dislikes" score ω_i^-, obtained from the original rating r_i:

$$\omega_i^+ = \frac{r_i - 1}{MAX - 1} \qquad \omega_i^- = 1 - \omega_i^+ \qquad (3)$$

The scores in Equation (3) are exploited for weighting the occurrences of tokens in the documents and to estimate their probabilities from the training set TR. The prior probabilities of the classes are computed according to the following equation:

$$\hat{P}(c_j) = \frac{\sum_{i=1}^{|TR|} \omega_i^j + 1}{|TR| + 2} \qquad (4)$$

Witten-Bell smoothing (1991) is adopted to estimate $P(t_k|c_j, s_m)$ by taking into account that documents are structured into slots and that token occurrences are weighted using scores in

Equation 5.

$$\hat{P}(t_k \mid c_j, s_m) = \begin{cases} \dfrac{N(t_k, c_j, s_m)}{|V_{cj}| + \sum_i N(t_i, c_j, s_m)} & \text{if } N(t_k, c_j, s_m) \neq 0 \\[3ex] \dfrac{|V_{cj}|}{|V_{cj}| + \sum_i N(t_i, c_j, s_m)} \cdot \dfrac{1}{|V| - |V_{cj}|} & \text{if } N(t_k, c_j, s_m) = 0 \end{cases}$$

Equation (3) (see Equation 5.) where $N(t_k, c_j, s_m)$ is the number of weighted occurrences of the token t_k in the training data for class c_j in the slot s_m, V_{cj} is the vocabulary for the class c_j, and V is the vocabulary for all classes. $N(t_k, c_j, s_m)$ is computed as follows:

$$N(t_k, c_j, s_m) = \sum_{i=1}^{|TR|} \omega_i^j n_{kim} \qquad (6)$$

In Equation (6), n_{kim} is the count of occurrences of the token t_k in the slot s_m of the document d_i. The sum of all $N(t_k, c_j, s_m)$ in the denominator of Equation (5) denotes the total weighted length of the slot s_m in the class c_j. In other words, $\hat{P}(t_k | c_j, s_m)$ is estimated as a ratio between the weighted occurrences of token t_k in slot s_m of class c_j and the total weighted length of the slot. The final outcome of the learning process is a probabilistic model used to classify a new document in the class c_+ or c_-. This model is the semantic user profile, which includes those tokens that turn out to be most indicative of the user preferences according to the value of the conditional probabilities in Equation (5).

The content-based recommender performs the matching between profiles and testing documents and assigns a score representing the degree of interest of the user on those documents by using the Bayes classification formula (Equation 2).

As a proof of concepts, we integrated the ITR functionalities to develop a service for supporting users to plan the participation to a scientific congress.

AN INTELLIGENT SERVICE FOR DIGITAL LIBRARIES

The conference participant advisor service is based on ITR and provides personalized support for conference participation planning. The semantic user profile of each participant registered to the service is exploited to suggest the most interesting talks to be attended at the conference by producing a one-to-one personalized conference program.

The prototype has been realized for the International Semantic Web Conference 2004, by adding to the conference homepage (a copy of the official Web site) a login/registration form to access the service (Figure 2).

The user registers by providing an e-mail address and can browse the whole document repository or search for papers presented during

Figure 2. ISWC 2004 home page

Figure 3. The user selects the most appropriate sense for the keyword "categorization"

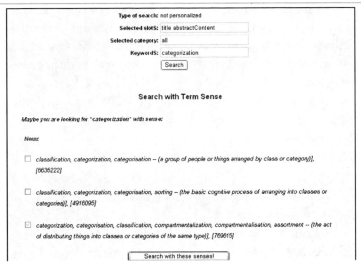

2002 and 2003 ISWC events, in order to provide ratings. The search engine used to select the training examples relies on the BOS model in order to allow users to perform a *semantic* search and to reduce the overload in providing the system with appropriate training examples. Let us suppose that the user now submits the query "categorization" to the paper retrieval system. The search engine analyzes the query and shows the sense inventory corresponding to the keyword. Among all the possible senses listed, the user can choose one or more of them according to the user's wishes. In the proposed scenario, the user is interested in papers about "text categorization," which is the task of assigning documents to a list of predefined categories. Therefore, the most appropriate sense for the query is the third one in the sense inventory (Figure 3).

Each retrieved paper can be rated on a discrete rating scale, as shown in Figure 4.

Figure 4. A paper retrieved by the semantic search provided by ITR and the interface for rating it

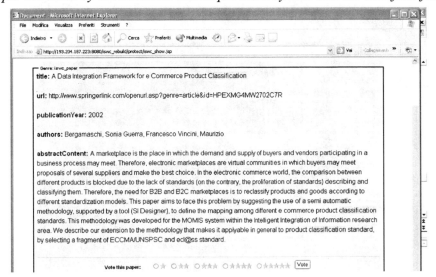

Notice that the word matching against the query, highlighted by the search engine, is different from the one in the query issued by the user. This is due to the fact that the two words are in the same synset, thus the system was able to realize a *semantic* matching by exploiting the synonymy relation in WordNet. This semantic search allows for a more accurate selection of training examples; the document retrieved in the aforementioned example would not have been retrieved by using a traditional keyword search.

Given a sufficient number of ratings (at present the minimum number of training documents is set to 20), the system learns the semantic profile of the participant. In the profile, concepts representing the participant's research interests are stored. ISWC 2004 accepted papers are classified using the learned profile to obtain a personalized list of recommended papers and talks, which is sent by e-mail to the participant. Recommended talks are highlighted in the personalized electronic program (Figure 5).

An experimental evaluation of semantic profiles was carried out on ISWC papers in order to estimate if the BOS version of ITR improves the performance with respect to the BOW one.

Experiments were carried out on a collection of 100 papers rated by 11 real users. Classification effectiveness was evaluated in terms of precision and recall (Sebastiani, 2002). We obtained an improvement both in precision (+1%) and recall (+2%) of the BOS-generated profiles with respect to the BOW-generated ones (Degemmis, Lops, & Basile, 2006).

CONCLUSION AND FUTURE TRENDS

We presented the ITR system exploiting a Bayesian learning method to induce semantic user profiles from documents represented using WordNet synsets. Our hypothesis is that replacing words with synsets in the indexing phase produces a more accurate document representation to infer more accurate profiles. This is confirmed by the experiments carried out to evaluate the effectiveness of the conference participant advisor service and can be explained by the fact that synset-based classification allows one to select documents with a high degree of semantic coherence, not guaranteed by word-based classification. As a future work, we

Figure 5. The personalized program sent to the user

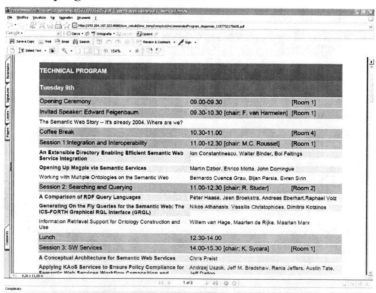

plan to also exploit domain ontologies to realize a more powerful document indexing.

REFERENCES

Callan, J., & Smeaton, A. (2003). *Personalization and recommender systems in digital libraries* (Tech. Rep.). NSF-EU DELOS Working Group.

Degemmis, M., Lops, P., & Basile, P. (2006). An intelligent personalized service for conference prticipants. In F. Esposito, Z. W. Ras, D. Malerba, & G. Semeraro (Eds.), *Foundations of Intelligent Systems: Proceedings of ISMIS 2006, 16th International. Symposium on Methodologies for Intelligent Systems* (LNAI 4203, pp. 707-712). Berlin: Springer.

Degemmis, M., Lops, P., & Semeraro, G. (2007). A content-collaborative recommender that exploits WordNet-based user profiles for neighborhood formation. *User Modeling and User-Adapted Interaction: The Journal of Personalization Research, 17*(3), 217-255.

Guarino, N., Masolo, C., & Vetere, G. (1999). OntoSeek: Content-based access to the Web. *IEEE Intelligent Systems, 14*(3), 70-80.

Magnini, B., & Strapparava C. (2001). Improving user modelling with content-based techniques. In M. Bauer, P. J. Gmytrasiewicz, & J. Vassileva (Eds.), *Proceedings of 8th International Conference on User Modeling 2001* (LNCS 2109, pp. 74-83). Berlin: Springer.

Manning, C., & Schütze, H. (1999). Word sense disambiguation. *Foundations of statistical natural language processing* (pp. 229-264). Cambridge: The MIT Press.

Miller, G. A. (1995). WordNet: A lexical database for English. *Communications of the ACM, 38*(11), 39-41.

Mitchell, T. (1997). *Machine learning.* New York: McGraw-Hill.

Mladenic, D. (1999). Text-learning and related intelligent agents: A survey. *IEEE Intelligent Systems, 14*(4), 44-54.

Mooney, R. J., & Roy, L. (2000). Content-based book recommending using learning for text categorization. In P. J. Nürnberg, D. L. Hicks, & R. Furuta (Eds.), *Proceedings of the 5th ACM Conference on Digital Libraries* (pp. 195-204). New York: ACM.

Pazzani, M., & Billsus, D. (1997). Learning and revising user profiles: The identification of interesting Web sites. *Machine Learning, 27*(3), 313-331.

Sebastiani, F. (2002). Machine learning in automated text categorization. *ACM Computing Surveys, 34*(1), 1-47.

Semeraro, G., Degemmis, M., Lops, P., & Basile P. (2007). Combining learning and word sense disambiguation for intelligent user profiling. In M. Veloso (Ed.), *Proceedings of the Twentieth International Joint Conference on Artificial Intelligence IJCAI-07* (pp. 2856-2861). San Francisco: Morgan Kaufmann.

Witten, I., & Bell, T. (1991). The zero-frequency problem: Estimating the probabilities of novel events in adaptive text compression. *IEEE Transactions on Information Theory, 37*(4), 1085-1094.

KEY TERMS

NLP (Natural Language Processing): A subfield of artificial intelligence and linguistics that studies the problems of automated generation and understanding of natural human languages. It converts samples of human language into more formal representations that are easier for computer programs to manipulate.

Personalization: The process of tailoring products or services to users based on their user profiles.

Recommender System: A system that guides users in a personalized way to interesting or useful objects in a large space of possible options.

Synset: A group of data elements that are considered semantically equivalent for the purposes of information retrieval.

User Profile: A structured representation of interests (and *dis*interests) of a user or group of users.

WordNet: A semantic lexicon for the English language. It groups English words into sets of synonyms called synsets. It provides short, general definitions, and records the various semantic relations between these synonym sets.

Word Sense Disambiguation: The problem of determining in which sense a word having a number of distinct senses is used in a given sentence.

Chapter XVI
Automatic Text Summarization in Digital Libraries

Shiyan Ou
University of Wolverhampton, UK

Christopher S. G. Khoo
Nanyang Technological University, Singapore

Dion Hoe-Lian Goh
Nanyang Technological University, Singapore

ABSTRACT

This chapter describes various text summarization techniques and evaluation techniques that have been proposed in literature and discusses the application of text summarization in digital libraries. First, it introduces the history of automatic text summarization and various types of summaries. Next, it reviews various approaches which have been used for single-document and multidocument summarization. Then, it describes the major evaluation approaches for assessing the generated summaries. Finally, it outlines the principal trends of the area of automatic text summarization. This chapter aims to help the reader to obtain a clear overview of the text summarization field and facilitate the application of text summarization in digital libraries.

INTRODUCTION

With the rapid growth of the World Wide Web, more and more information is available and accessible online and information overload becomes a big problem for users. Automatic text summa-rization has attracted attention both in research communities and commercial organizations as a solution for reducing information overload and helping users to scan a large number of documents to identify documents of interest. Text summa-rization is regarded as "the process of distilling the most important information from a source to produce an abridged version for a particular user and task" (Mani & Maybury, 1999, p. ix). It is an important function that should be available in large digital library systems, information retrieval systems, and Web search engines, where the retrieval of too many documents and the resulting information overload is a major problem for users.

In addition to facilitating the user's searching and browsing, text summarization can do much more in digital libraries. Rather than serving as information providers, digital libraries are becoming knowledge repositories which strive to add value to the collections that they create and maintain. Text summarization is expected to be most helpful in this aspect since it could perform knowledge integration and support knowledge discovery and knowledge acquisition, especially in a multidocument environment.

BACKGROUND AND TYPES OF SUMMARIES

Research in automatic text summarization has had a history of almost 50 years since the earliest attempt by Luhn (1958). However, there was little work and slow progress in the first 30 years. In the 1990s, as a result of information explosion in the World Wide Web, automatic text summarization became crucial to reduce information overload and this brought about its renaissance. It could be used for different purposes and different users and, thus, various types of summaries have been constructed.

Depending on the summarization method, a summary can be an *extract* (produced by sentence extraction) or an *abstract* (produced by an abstraction process). Using Mani's (2001a, p. 6) definition:

- An extract is a summary consisting entirely of material copied from the input; and

- An abstract is a summary at least some of whose material is not present in the input.

Since extracts are much easier to be constructed automatically than abstracts which require more complex techniques such as rephrasing and paraphrasing, extracts are generally used in current digital library systems.

With reference to the content and intended use, a summary can be *indicative, informative,* or *evaluative* (Borko & Bernier, 1975):

- An indicative summary provides an indication of what the original document is about. It can help users to determine whether the original document is worth reading or not, but users have to consult the original for details.
- An informative summary reflects the content of the original document and represents the content in a concise way. It can be used as a substitute for the original document so that users do not need to read the original.
- An evaluative or critical summary not only contains the main topics of the original document but also provides the abstractor's comments on the document content.

Indicative summaries are more generally used in current digital library systems to help users identify documents of interest. On the other hand, informative summaries are more often used for news articles to inform users about news events, for example, Columbia's Newsblaster[1].

Depending on the purpose and intended users, a summary can be *generic* or *user-focused* (Mani, 2001):

- *A* generic summary covers all major themes or aspects of the original document to serve a broad readership community rather than a particular group.
- A user-focused (or topic-focused, query-oriented) summary favors specific themes

or aspects of the original document, which are relevant to a user query, to cater to special needs or interests of an individual or a particular group.

With the need for providing personalized services in digital libraries, user-focused summaries are becoming important to tailor content to users' intents and queries, though generic summaries are still dominant in current digital library systems.

Depending on the number of documents being encapsulated, a summary can be *single-document* or *multidocument* (Hahn & Mani, 2000):

- *A* single-document summary is a shorter representation of one document.
- A multidocument summary is a shorter representation of a set of documents.

Single-document summaries are generally used in current digital library systems, for example, ACM digital library. Multidocument summaries are still seldom employed in real-world digital library systems, but will inevitably grow in importance as the technology matures and system developers seek to make the digital library systems more useful to users.

In the subsequent sections, the state-of-the-art in the area of single-document and multidocument summarization is reviewed, and the major evaluation techniques for the generated summaries are also surveyed.

SINGLE-DOCUMENT SUMMARIZATION

Most digital library systems attempt to address the problem of information overload by ranking documents retrieved by their likelihood of relevance, and displaying titles and snippets to give users some indication of the document content. For example, the ACM digital library returns a list of ranked document "snippets" to a search query (see Figure 1). This "snippet" kind of summary could be constructed automatically using various methods, for example, extracting the first few lines of the document text (e.g., Alta Vista), extracting the text fragments which have the highest keyword similarity to the query (e.g., Google), and extracting those fragments which have the strongest correlation both to the query and the document semantics (Zotos, Tzekou, Tsatsaronis, Kozanidis, Stamou, & Varlamis, 2007).

Figure 1. A list of document snippets returned by the ACM digital library

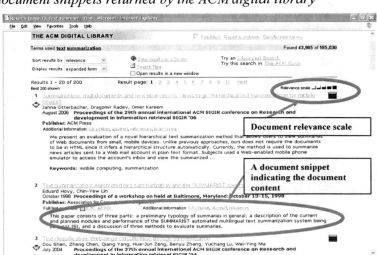

Approaches for single-document summarization can be divided broadly into *extractive* and *abstractive* categories. Extractive approaches extract salient text passages (typically sentences) from the original document using various criteria and assemble them to form an extract. Sentence extraction can be divided into three types, that is, *statistics-based, cohesion-based,* and *discourse-based*, which represent increasing understanding of text and increasing complexity in text processing.

The statistics-based approaches are domain independent and do not attempt to understand the meaning and structure of the text. They make use of statistical and linguistic features to measure the significance of sentences, thereby extracting the highest ranked sentences. The features used in most summarization systems include frequent keywords, title keywords, cue phrases, and sentence position (Luhn, 1958; Edmundson, 1969; Paice, 1990). To combine these features for identifying the most significant sentences, supervised machine learning techniques are often used, such as support vector machines (Hirao, Isozaki, Maeda, & Matsumoto, 2002), Bayes (Aone et al., 1999; Kupiec, Pedersen, & Chen, 1995), decision tree (Lin, 1999), and gene expression program (Xie, Li, Di Eugenio, Nelson, Xiao, & Tirpak, 2004). However, this is a difficult and time-consuming task to prepare labeled training data for supervised learning. Thus semi-supervised (Massih-Reza & Gallinari, 2001) and unsupervised (Mihalcea, 2004) learning techniques are used instead if labeled corpora are not available.

Using the statistics-based approaches, a collection of sentences is extracted separately and thus often lack context. This sometimes results in unintelligible and even misleading extracts, due to lack of cohesion and coherence as well as the presence of "dangling anaphors." To solve the above problems, the cohesion-based approaches are developed, which use cohesive links, such as lexical chains (Barzilay & Elhadad, 1998), coreferences (Azzam, Humphreys, & Gaizauskas, 1999),

and word cooccurrence (Salton, Singhal, Mitra, & Buckley, 1997) to extract related sentences or paragraphs instead of separate sentences for producing more readable and coherent summaries.

Although cohesion-based approaches can create fluent summaries, the resulting summaries still lack coherence because they do not convey a full understanding of the text. The construction of highly coherent summaries depends on an analysis of discourse structure. This focuses on linguistic processing of text to derive a discourse representation of the text used for determining important text units in a text. Well-known discourse models that have been used for text summarization include rhetorical structure theory (Mann & Thompson, 1988), rhetorically defined annotation scheme (Teufel & Moens, 2002), and text component identification model (Myaeng & Jang, 1999).

In contrast to extractive approaches, abstractive approaches create grammatical and coherent new texts to paraphrase and replace salient information extracted from the source document. Real abstractive approaches that completely imitate human abstracting behavior are difficult to achieve with current natural language processing techniques. Current abstractive approaches are in reality hybrid approaches involving both extraction and abstraction. They are of three types of approaches: *sentence compression, knowledge representation,* and *concept generalization.*

Sentence compression is a simple version of abstraction. It extracts important sentences and drops unimportant constituents (mostly determiners, auxiliaries, or other low-content modifiers) from the extracted sentences based on the parse tree of each sentence and arranges the remaining words in the original order to form a short sentence (Angheluta, Mitra, Jing, & Moens, 2004).

Knowledge representation involves a detailed semantic analysis of the source document and construction of a knowledge representation of the meaning of the document. A set of domain-specific templates, frames, or scripts is usually predefined using domain knowledge to support extraction of the information relevant to each slot of the template and filling it. When document analysis is complete, the instantiated slots are used as the material to generate a fluent summary using natural language generation techniques. Such a kind of summarization system include FRUMP (DeJong, 1982) and SISCOR (Jacobs & Rau, 1990), both of which were used for news articles.

Concept generalization or concept fusion involves extracting important concepts and generalizing them to capture the main content of a document. Generalization is the process of replacing a collection of concepts with a higher-level unifying concept (Lin, 1995), which can be performed at the semantic level or syntactic level. Lin (1995) and Hovy and Lin (1999) generalize concepts based on semantic relations among concepts such as instance, subclass, and part-of. Such generalization requires a thesaurus, ontology, or knowledge base to provide an appropriate concept hierarchy for a specific domain. In contrast, the syntactic-level generalization is easy to realize but not very accurate, since it identifies similar concepts only according to their syntactic structures rather than their meanings (Ibekwe-SanJuan & SanJuan, 2004; Ou, Khoo, & Goh, 2005).

For a computer program, extractive approaches are easier to implement than abstractive approaches since the program does not need to create new texts. Among the extractive approaches, the statistics-based type is the lowest-cost solution according to its speed, scalability, and robustness, and thus most real-world summarization systems are implemented with this type of approach, for example, MS-AutoSummarizer (MS Word'97). Compared to extractive approaches, abstractive approaches are knowledge-intensive, domain-dependent, and expensive, but produce better summaries for a specific domain. They often require a sizable and complex domain-specific knowledge base as well as involve natural language generation techniques, and thus they become complex to implement and lack portability to other domains

and text corpora. The strengths of text abstraction are in the conciseness and readability of the resulting abstracts.

MULTIDOCUMENT SUMMARIZATION

A weakness of single-document summaries is that the documents retrieved by a query are related, often contain overlapping information, and share the same background. Thus their extracts are likely to be fairly similar to each other and do not highlight unique information in individual documents. It is also hard to obtain an overview of the content of a document set from the separate extracts. Furthermore, browsing so many similar extracts is tedious and time-consuming. Users have patience to scan only a small number of document titles and abstracts, in the range of 10 to 30 (Jansen, Spink, & Saracevic, 2000). Thus a multidocument summary would be very useful in such a situation. A good example of multidocument summarization can be found in PERSIVAL,[2] a patient care digital library (Mckeown, McKeown, Chang, Cimino, Feiner, Friedman, Gravano, et al., 2001). It retrieves a set of medical articles matching the input patient record and produces a summary for the highest ranked 10 articles that contain the most relevant information for the patient (see Figure 2).

Multidocument summarization condenses a set of related documents, instead of a single document, into one summary. It can be seen as an extension of single-document summarization, but is also much more. Multidocument summarization performs knowledge synthesis and knowledge discovery by combining and integrating information extracted from different documents, and thus can be used for knowledge acquisition. A multidocument summary has several features different from a single-document summary. It provides a domain overview of a document set and indicates common information across many documents, unique information in each document, and relationships

Figure 2. A multidocument summary provided by the PERSIVAL digital library

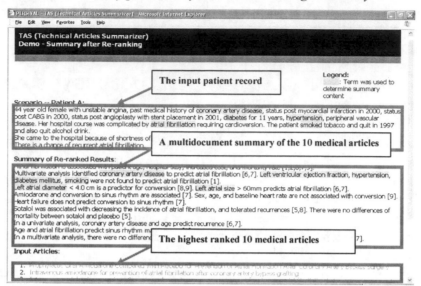

between pieces of information in different documents. If presented in a graphical way, it can also support browsing and information visualization, and allow users to zoom in for more details on aspects of interest. Multidocument summaries are useful in large digital library systems, especially in academic and research institutions. It can be used to identify similarities and differences between different research studies, and identify research gaps for future work.

All the approaches used in single-document summarization are applicable in a multidocument environment. A simple transformation from single-document summarization to multidocument summarization is to extract important sentences from each document to create summaries for individual documents and concatenating these single-document summaries to form a multidocument summary, for example, GE multidocument summarizer (Stein, Strzalkowski, & Wise, 2000). However, if there are too many documents in a collection, simply concatenating the summaries of individual documents will result in a very long multidocument summary which contains redundant information and lacks cohesion and

coherence. Thus, in multidocument summarization, important sentences are usually extracted across different documents at the same time instead of from individual documents separately. Furthermore, some revisions have to be done to reduce redundancy as well as to ensure cohesion and coherence. For example, to reduce redundant sentences, the MEAD summarizer (Radev, Jing, & Budzikowska, 2000) clustered similar documents and the XDoxX summarizer (Hardy, Shimizu, Strzalkowski, Ting, Wise, & Zhang, 2002) clustered similar sentences, and they then extracted representative sentences from each cluster as the components of the summary. In addition, the maximal marginal relevance (MMR) metric was used in some work to minimize redundancy and maximize the diversity among the sentences extracted from different documents (Carbonell & Goldstein, 1998). However, multidocument summarization has more challenges than single-document summarization in the issues of compression rate, redundancy, cohesion, coherence, temporal dimension, and so forth (Goldstein, Mittal, Carbonell, & Kantrowitz, 2000). Thus, the traditional statistics-based sentence extraction approaches do not always work well in a multidocument environment.

In a set of documents, many of them are likely to contain similar information and only differ in certain parts. An ideal multidocument summary should contain similar information repeated in many documents, plus important unique information present in some individual documents (Goldstein et al., 2000). Thus multidocument summarization should mainly focus on the similarities and differences across documents. Shallow and deep approaches have been used to compare pieces of information extracted from different documents and synthesize them together. Shallow approaches extract text passages based on statistical and linguistic features, and remove repeated information by vocabulary comparison (Mani & Bloedorn, 1999). Deep approaches extract text passages based on statistical and linguistic features or predefined templates, and synthesize them using concept generalization (Lin, 1995; Ou, Khoo, & Goh, 2008), summary operators (McKeown & Radev, 1995), and cross-document rhetorical relations (Afantenos, Doura, Kapellou, & Karkaletsis, 2004; Zhang, Blair-Goldensohn, & Radev, 2002). The deep approaches are more promising for constructing multidocument summaries, since they involve information synthesis and some inferencing to produce a coherent and concise summary.

Presenting a multidocument summary in fluent text and in a form that is useful to users is an important issue. In the sentence-extraction approaches, the most important sentences are extracted from original documents and arranged in a particular order that will hopefully make sense to users. Most systems arrange sentences in the same order as in the original document text or in chronological order. Some systems organize the sentences in other formats to facilitate users' reading and understanding. For example, Farzindar and Lapalme (2004) present the extracted sentences in a tabular format that is divided by such themes as "decision data," "introduction,"

"context," "juridical analysis," and "conclusion" found in the legal text. Although the sentence-based scheme is extensively used to present a summary, a few studies also present concepts or terms as complements to the sentences in the summary. Aone et al. (1999) present a summary in multiple dimensions through a graphical user interface. A list of keywords (i.e., person names, entity names, place names, and others) is presented in the left window for quick and easy browsing, whereas the full text is presented in the right window where the important sentences are identified and highlighted. Ando, Boguraev, Byrd, and Neff (2000) identified multiple topics in a set of documents and present the summary by listing several terms and two sentences that were most closely related to each topic.

SUMMARIZATION EVALUATION

Evaluation has long been of interest to the community of automatic text summarization, with extensive work carried out as early as the 1960s (Edmunson, 1969). Approaches for evaluating text summarization can be divided broadly into two types (Jones & Galliers, 1996): *intrinsic evaluation* and *extrinsic evaluation*. In intrinsic evaluation, the quality of summaries is judged directly according to some criteria (e.g., conciseness, readability, and understandability), or comparing them to "ideal" summaries. In extrinsic evaluation, the quality of summaries is judged indirectly depending on how well the summaries can help users complete some tasks, such as finding documents relevant to the user's need and answering some questions related to the original documents.

In some studies, intrinsic evaluations were performed by direct human judgment on the grammaticality, cohesion, coherence, organization, and coverage of stipulated "key/essential ideas" of summaries (Brandow, Mitze, & Rau, 1995). Often, a machine-generated summary was also compared against an "ideal" summary (Edmunson, 1969). Precision, recall, and F-measure are used to measure the degree of match between the machine-generated summary and the "ideal" summary. The main problem of usin an "ideal" summary as reference is that there is no single correct summary. There could be a number of ways for humans to create abstracts for a given document.

Although most intrinsic evaluations still depend on manual judgments, some automatic evaluation methods or tools have been developed to facilitate the judging process. To automatically measure the coherence of summaries, Foltz, Kintsch, and Lndauer (1998) propose the use of latent semantic analysis, whereas Lapata and Barzilay (2005) propose a syntactic model which abstracts local coherence as the distribution of entities among sentences and a semantic model which quantifies local coherence as the degree of connectivity across sentences. In Document Understanding Conferences (DUC)[3] 2001 and 2002, human assessors used an evaluation program SEE[4] to assess both the content and the quality of the summaries manually. SEE decomposes a machine-generated summary and a human-generated reference summary into a list of units (often sentences) and displays them in separate windows. Human assessors then identify the matches between summary pairs by examining unit by unit and computing the overlap as precision and recall scores. For DUC 2004, an automatic evaluation package, ROUGE[5], was used to measure the similarity between a machine-generated summary and a reference summary by automatically counting the number of overlapping units between them. Since ROUGE measures consider both word-level and sentence-level overlap, it is expected to be more accurate than the traditional precision, recall, and F-measure which only consider sentence-level overlap. However, ROUGE focuses more on the overlap of units (e.g., n-gram, word sequences, and word pairs) in form and does not consider the meaningful relations among them, such as inclusion, synonymy, and entailment.

Compared to intrinsic evaluation, extrinsic evaluation is more attractive because it is based on objective evaluation measures. Tasks designed and used in extrinsic evaluation fall under two main types: *relevance assessment task* and *reading comprehension task* (i.e., question-answering task). In relevance assessment tasks, human subjects are presented with a document (full text or summary) and a topic, and are asked to determine the relevance of the document to the topic. Time and accuracy (often precision and recall) are used to evaluate the performance of a summarization system. The real-world activity represented by this task is that of a human, conducting full-text search using an information retrieval system, who must determine quickly and accurately the relevance of a retrieved document. Most researchers performed their relevance assessment evaluations by imitating this real-world activity (e.g., Mani & Bloedorn, 1999; Tomros & Sanderson, 1998). In reading comprehension tasks, human subjects are asked to answer multiple-choice questions using full-text sources or summaries. Thus a human's comprehension based on the summary can be compared with that based on the source. For example, Morris, Kasper, and Adams (1992) carried out four multichoice graduate management admission test (GMAT) reading comprehension exercises under four conditions of full-text sources, extracts, abstracts, and no text (depending on guess) to compare their impacts on the completion of the question-answering task.

The largest extrinsic evaluation carried out to date is the TIPSTER text summarization evaluation (SUMMAC). It is the first large-scale evaluation effort of summarization systems and differs from earlier extrinsic evaluations in task details and methodology. Although the SUMMAC evaluation also included an intrinsic acceptability test, its main focus was on an extrinsic evaluation based on the tasks which modeled real-world activities typically carried out by information analysts in the U.S. Government. In the SUMMAC evaluation, three main tasks were performed: ad hoc task, categorization task, and question-answering task (Mani, Firmin, House, Chrzanowski, Klein, Hirschman, et al., 1998).

Mani (2001b) points out that the choice of an intrinsic or extrinsic evaluation method depends on the goals of the developers and the users of the summarization system. In general, at the early development stages of the system, an intrinsic evaluation is recommended focusing on evaluating the summarization components. As the system becomes more developed, an extrinsic evaluation is more suitable, focusing on the test of the whole system involving "real" users. In previous studies, intrinsic evaluations were used extensively (e.g., Edumunson 1969; Kupiec et al., 1995; Paice, 1990; Salton et al., 1997).

In comparison to single-document summaries, multidocument summaries are more difficult to evaluate. Currently, there is no widely accepted procedure or methodology for evaluating multidocument summaries (Schlesinger, Conroy, Okurowski, & O'Leary, 2003). Most of the tasks used in extrinsic evaluation were designed for evaluating single-document summaries. Moreover, it is more difficult to obtain uniform reference summaries, since humans differ greatly from each other in summarizing multiple documents (Schlesinger et al., 2003).

FUTURE TRENDS

Single-document summarization has been employed in most digital library systems for helping users to identify documents of interest. With the growth of similar information across different information sources, single-document summarization cannot remove redundant information from a variety of related documents and thus often result in a set of similar summaries for individual documents. In recent years, more attention has been paid to multidocument summarization in digital library systems (e.g., PERSIVAL digital library [Mckeown et al., 2001]). Initially, multi-

document summarization focused on the most important topics that are often repeated in many documents of a document set to create generic summaries. Recently, there is a trend towards developing advanced multidocument summaries that go beyond the classical, generic summaries to user-focused summaries, answer-focused summaries, and update summaries.

User-focused Summaries

In the real world, different users have different information needs to the same search query and even the same user may have different information needs at different points in time for the same topic. Based on this fact, some intelligent search systems (e.g., MyYahoo and Google Web History) return personalized results to users according to their behavior models and profiles. This idea leads to the development of user-focused summarization systems, for example, WebInEssence (Radev, Fan, & Zhang, 2001), which select documents based on users' personal profiles and produce user-focused summaries with the selected documents. A user-focused summary focuses on the content that matches the user's specific requirement and discards others to reduce information overload. Since DUC 2005, user-focused summaries have been extensively evaluated. These summaries were produced based on the predefined context that was modeled as a set of open-ended questions. The ability to generate user-focused summaries is an important step towards a personalized digital library environment.

Answer-Focused Summaries

In DUC 2003 and 2004, a task was designed to produce a summary of a document set which aimed to answer a given question like *"Who is X?"* (X is a person name).This indicates a recent trend towards answer-focused summaries which are related to but still different from user-focused summaries. User-focused summaries aim to provide an indication of the main content of a document or a set of documents according to a specific user' preference and help the user to locate documents of interest quickly. However, users often want to express their information needs in the form of natural language questions, for example, *"What is text summarization?"* instead of several key words, and require specific answers to a question rather than whole documents. Many questions cannot be answered in one or two words but require a number of relevant facts which may be distributed across multiple documents returned by a search engine. The answer is thus a multidocument summary of these facts extracted from different documents. Some answer-focused summarization systems have been developed in previous studies. Mori, Nozawa, and Asada (2005) calculated sentence importance with the scores from a question answering system and then integrated the calculation to a generic multidocument summarization system for answering multiple questions. Wu, Radev, and Fan (2004) identified question types and integrated them into a proximity-based extraction summarization system for question answering, and they furthermore propose a set of criteria and performance metrics for evaluating answer-focused summarization systems.

Update Summaries

In DUC 2007, an update task was defined to produce short multidocument summaries of news articles under the assumption that the user has already read a set of earlier articles and is only interested in new information which has not been covered before. An update summary is used to inform the reader of new information about a particular topic. It can be traced back to the temporal summaries produced by Alan, Gupta, and Khandelwal (2001) and Jatowt and Ishizuka (2004). Since the Web sites of news are built dynamically to show different information content evolving over time in the same URL, it is expected that update summaries will be very useful in a digital library of Web news to provide a trace of a news event.

REFERENCES

Afantenos, S., Doura, I., Kapellou, E., & Karkaletsis, V. (2004). Exploiting cross-document relations for multi-document evolving summarization. In G. A. Vouros & T. Panayiotopoulos (Eds.), *Proceedings of the 3rd Helenic Conference on Artificial Intelligence* (LNCS 3025, pp. 410-419). Berlin: Springer-Verlag.

Allan, J., Gupta, R., & Khandelwal, V. (2001). Temporal summaries of new topics. In *Proceedings of the 24th Annual International ACM SIGIR Conference on Research and Development in Information Retrieval* (pp.10-18). New York: ACM.

Ando, R., Boguraev, B., Byrd, R., & Neff, M. (2000). Multi-document summarization by visualizing topic content. In *Proceedings of ANLP/ NAACL 2000 Workshop on Automatic Summarization* (pp.79-98). Morristown, NJ: ACL.

Angheluta, R., Mitra, R., Jing, X., & Moens, M. (2004). K.U.Leuven summarization system at DUC 2004. In *Proceedings of the Document Understanding Conference 2004*. Retrieved April 4, 2007, from http://www-nlpir.nist.gov/projects/duc/pubs.html.

Aone, C., Okurowski, M. E., & Gorlinsky, J. (1998). Trainable, scalable summarization using robust NLP and machine learning. In *Proceedings of the 17th International Conference on Computational Linguistics and 36th Annual Meeting of Association for Computational Linguistics* (Vol. 1, pp. 62-66). Morristown, NJ: ACL.

Azzam, S., Humphreys, K., & Gaizauskas, R. (1999). Using coreference chains for text summarization. In *Proceedings of the ACL-99 Workshop on Conference and its Applications* (pp. 77-84). Morristown, NJ: ACL.

Barzilay, R., & Elhadad, M. (1998). Using lexical chains for text summarization. In *Proceedings of the ACL-97/EACL-97 Workshop on Intelligent Scalable Text Summarization* (pp. 10-17). Morristown, NJ: ACL.

Borko, H., & Bernier, L. (1975). *Abstracting concepts and methods*. San Diego: Academic Press.

Brandow, R., Mitze, K., & Rau, L. F. (1995). Automatic condensation of electronic publications by sentence selection. *Information Processing and Management, 31*(5), 675-685.

Carbonell, J. G., & Goldstein, J. (1998). The use of MMR, diversity-based reranking for reordering documents and producing summaries. In *Proceedings of the 21st Annual International ACM SIGIR Conference on Research and Development in Information Retrieval* (pp. 335-336). New York: ACM.

DeJong, G. (1982). An overview of the FRUMP system. In W. G. Lehnert & M. H. Ringle (Eds.), *Strategies for natural language processing* (pp. 149-176). Hillsdale, NJ: Lawrence Erlbaum Associates.

Edmundson, H. P. (1969). New methods in automatic extracting. *Journal of the ACM, 16*(2), 264-285.

Farzindar, A., & Lapalme, G. (2004). LetSum, an automatic legal text summarizing system. In T. F. Gordon (Ed.), *Volume 120 of Frontiers in Artificial Intelligence and Applications: Proceedings of the 17th Annual Conference on Legal Knowledge and Information Systems* (pp. 11-18). Amsterdam: IOS Press.

Foltz, P., Kintsch W., & Landauer, K. (1998). Textual coherence using latent semantic analysis. *Discourse Processes, 25*(2&3), 285-307.

Goldstein, J., Mittal, V., Carbonell, J., & Kantrowitz, M. (2000). Multi-document summarization by sentence extraction. In *Proceedings*

of ANLP/NAACL 2000 Workshop on Automatic Summarization (Vol. 4, pp. 40-48). Morristown, NJ: ACL.

Hahn, U., & Mani, I. (2000). The challenges of automatic summarization. *IEEE Computer, 33*(11), 29-36.

Hardy, H., Shimizu, N., Strzalkowski, T., Ting, L., Wise, G., & Zhang, X. (2002). Cross-document summarization by concept classification. In *Proceedings of the 25th Annual International ACM SIGIR Conference on Research and Development in Information Retrieval* (pp. 121-128). New York: ACM.

Hirao, T., Isozaki, H., Maeda, E., & Matsumoto, Y. (2002). Extracting important sentences with support vector machines. In *Proceedings of the 19th International Conference on Computational Linguistics* (pp. 1-7). Morristown, NJ: ACL.

Hovy, E. H., & Lin, C. (1999). Automated text summarization in SUMMARIST. In I. Mani & M. T. Maybury (Eds.), *Advances in automatic text summarization* (pp. 81-94). Cambridge, MA: MIT Press.

Ibekwe-SanJuan, F., & SanJuan, E. (2004). Mining for knowledge chunks in a terminology network. In I. C. McIlwaine (Ed.), *Volume 9 of Advances in Knowledge Organization: Proceedings of the 8th International Society for Knowledge Organization Conference* (pp. 41-46). Verkehrs-Nr: Ergon-Verlag.

Jacobs, P., & Rau, L. (1990). SCISOR: Extracting information from on-line news source. *Communications of the ACM, 33*(11), 88-97.

Jansen, B., Spink, A., & Saracevic, T. (2000). Real life, real users and real needs: A study and analysis of user queries on the Web. *Information Processing and Management, 36*(2), 207-227.

Jatowt, A., & Ishizuka, M. (2004). Change summarization in Web collections. In *Proceedings of the 5th International Conference on Web Informa-*

tion Systems Engineering (pp. 303-312). Berlin: Springer-Verlag.

Jones, K. S., & Galliers, J. R. (1996). Evaluating natural language processing systems: An analysis and review. In J. G. Carbonell & J. Siekmann (Eds.), *Volume 1083 of lecturer notes in artificial intelligence*. Berlin: Springer-Verlag.

Kupiec, J., Pedersen, J., & Chen, F. (1995). A trainable document summarizer. In *Proceedings of the 18th Annual International ACM SIGIR Conference on Research and Development in Information Retrieval* (pp. 68-73). New York: ACM.

Lapata, M., & Barzilay, R. (2005). Automatic evaluation of text coherence: Models and representations. In L. P. Kaelbling & A. Saffiotti (Eds.), *Proceedings of the 19th International Joint Conference on Artificial Intelligence* (pp. 1085-1090). San Francisco: Morgan Kaufmann Publishers Inc.

Lin, C. (1995). Topic identification by concept generalization. In *Proceedings of the 33rd Annual Meeting of the Association for Computation Linguistics* (pp. 308-310). Morristown, NJ: ACL.

Lin, C. (1999). Training a selection function for extraction. In *Proceedings of the 8th International Conference on Information and Knowledge Management* (pp. 55-62). New York: ACM.

Luhn, H. (1958). The automatic creation of literature abstracts. *IBM Journal of Research and Development, 2*(2), 159-165.

Mani, I. (2001a). *Automatic summarization.* Amsterdam: John Benjamins Publishing Company.

Mani, I. (2001b). Summarization evaluation: An overview. In *Proceedings of the 2nd NTCIR Workshop on Research in Chinese and Japanese Text Retrieval and Text Summarization.* Tokyo: National Institute of Informatics.

Mani, I., & Bloedorn, E. (1999). Summarizing similarities and differences among related documents. *Information Retrieval, 1*(1-2), 35-67.

Mani, I., Firmin, T., House, D., Chrzanowski, M., Klein, G., Hirschman, L., et al. (1998). *The TIPSTER SUMMAC text summarization evaluation: Final report* (MITRE Tech. Rep. MTR 98W0000138). McLean, VA: MITRE Corporation.

Mani, I., & Maybury, M. T. (1999). Introduction. In I. Mani & M. T. Maybury (Eds.), *Advances in automatic text summarization* (p. ix). Cambridge, MA: MIT Press.

Mann, W., & Thompson, S. (1988). Rhetorical structure theory: Toward a functional theory of text organization. *Text, 8*(3), 243-281.

Massih-Reza, A., & Gallinari, P. (2001). Learning for text summarization using labeled and unlabeled sentences. In *Proceedings of the 2001 International Conference on Artificial Neural Networks* (pp. 1177-1184). Berlin: Springer-Verlag.

McKeown, R., Chang, S., Cimino, J., Feiner, K., Friedman, C., Gravano, L., et al. (2001). PERSIVAL, a system for personalized search and summarization over multimedia healthcare information. In *Proceedings of the 1st ACM/IEEE-CS Joint Conference on Digital Libraries* (pp. 331-340). New York: ACM.

McKeown, K., & Radev, D. (1995). Generating summaries of multiple news articles. In *Proceedings of the 18th Annual International ACM SIGIR Conference on Research and Development in Information Retrieval* (pp. 74-82). New York: ACM.

Mihalcea, R. (2004). Graph-based ranking algorithms for sentence extraction, applied to text summarization. In *Proceedings of the 42nd Annual Meeting of Association for Computational Linguistics.* Morristown, NJ: ACL.

Mori, T., Nozawa, M., & Asada, Y. (2005). Multi-answer-focused multi-document summarization using a question-answering engine. *ACM Transactions on Asian Language, 4*(3), 305-320.

Morris, A., Kasper, G., & Adams, D. (1992). The effects and limitations of automatic text condensing on reading comprehension performance. *Information Systems Research, 3*(1), 17-35.

Myaeng, S., & Jang, D. (1999). Development and evaluation of statistically based document summarization system. In I. Mani & M. T. Maybury (Eds.), *Advances in automatic text summarization* (pp. 61-70). Cambridge, MA: MIT Press.

Ou, S., Khoo, S., & Goh, D. (2008). Design and development of a concept-based multi-document summarization systems for research abstracts. *Journal of Information Science, 24*(3), 308-326.

Ou, S., Khoo, S., & Goh, D. (2005). Constructing a taxonomy to support multi-document summarization of dissertation abstracts. *Journal of Zhejiang University SCIENCE, 6A*(11), 1258-1267.

Ou, S., Khoo, S., & Goh, D. (2007). Automatic multi-document summarization of research abstracts: Design and user evaluation. *Journal of the American Society for Information Science and Technology, 58*(10), 1-17.

Paice, C. (1990). Constructing literature abstracts by computer: Techniques and prospects. *Information Processing and Management, 26*(1), 171-186.

Radev, D., Fan, W., & Zhang, Z. (2001). WebInEssence: A personalized Web-based multi-document summarization and recommendation system. In *Proceedings of the Automatic Summarization Workshop of the 2nd Meeting of the North American Chapter of the Association for Computational Linguistics*. Morristown, NJ: ACL.

Radev, D., Jing, H., & Budzikowska, M. (2000). Centroid-based summarization of multiple documents: Sentence extraction, utility-based evaluation and user studies. In *Proceedings of the ANLP/NAACL 2000 Workshop on Automatic Summarization* (pp. 21-30). Morristown, NJ: ACL.

Salton, G., Singhal, A., Mitra, M., & Buckley, C. (1997). Automatic text structuring and summarization. *Information Processing and Management, 33*(2), 193-207.

Schlesinger, J., Conroy, J., Okurowski, M., & O'Leary, D. (2003). Machine and human performance for single and multidocument summarization. *IEEE Intelligent Systems, 18*(1), 46-54.

Stein, G., Strzalkowski, T., & Wise, G. (2000). Interactive, text-based summarization of multiple documents. *Computational Intelligence, 16*(4), 606-613.

Teufel, S., & Moens, M. (2002). Summarizing scientific articles: Experiments with relevance and rhetorical status. *Computational Linguistics, 28*(4), 409-445.

Tombros, A., & Sanderson, M. (1998). Advantage of query biased summaries in information retrieval. In *Proceedings of the 21st ACM SIGIR Conference on Research and Development in Information Retrieval* (pp. 2-10). New York: ACM.

Wu, H., Radev, D., & Fan, W. (2004). Towards answer-focused summarization using search engines. In M. T. Maybury (Ed.), *New directions in question answering* (pp. 227-236). Menlo Park: AAAI.

Xie, Z., Li, X., Di Eugenio, B., Nelson, P., Xiao, W., & Tirpak, T. (2004). Using gene expression programming to construct sentence ranking functions for text summarization. In *Proceedings of the 20th International Conference on Computational Linguistics* (pp. 1381-1384). Morristown, NJ: ACL.

Zhang, Z., Blair-Goldensohn, S., & Radev, D. (2002). Towards CST-enhanced summarization. In *Proceedings of the 18th National Conference on Artificial Intelligence* (pp. 439-445). Menlo Park, CA: AAAI.

Zotos, N., Tzekou, P., Tsatsaronis G., Kozanidis, L., Stamou, S., & Varlamis, I. (2007). To click or not to click? The role of contextualized and user-centric Web snippets. In *Proceedings of the SIGIR 2007 Workshop on Focused Retrieval* (pp. 57-64). Dunedin: University of Otago.

KEY TERMS

Abstraction: A kind of summarization approach, with rephrasing or paraphrasing the main content of a document to form a summary.

Extraction: A kind of summarization approach that extracts important pieces of information (typically sentences) from the input to form a summary.

Extrinsic Evaluation: An evaluation which assesses the quality of summaries indirectly through user performance of some tasks using the summaries.

Intrinsic Evaluation: An evaluation which assesses the quality of summaries through direct human judgment of some criteria (e.g., grammaticality, conciseness, and readability) or comparing of "ideal" summaries.

Multidocument Summarization: The process of representing the main content of a set of related documents on a topic, instead of only one document.

Single-document Summarization: The process of representing the main content of one document.

Summary: A brief representation of the main content of a source (or sources).

Text Summarization: The process of distilling the most important information from a source (or sources) to produce an abridged version for a particular user and task.

ENDNOTES

[1]   The Newsblaster summarization system is accessible for educational or non-commercial research purposes at http://www1.cs.columbia.edu/nlp/newsblaster/.

[2]   The PERSIVAL Digital Library is at http://persival.cs.columbia.edu.

[3]   Conference series focusing on summarization and the large-scale evaluation of summarization systems, which is run by the National Institute of Standards and Technology and started in 2001 in the United States, see http://duc.nist.gov/.

[4]   Summary Evaluation Environment, see at http://www.isi.edu/~cyl/SEE/

[5]   Recall-Oriented Understudy for Gisting Evaluation, see at http:// www.isi.edu/~cyl/ROUGE/

Chapter XVII
Speechfind:
Advances in Rich Content Based Spoken Document Retrieval

Wooil Kim
Center for Robust Speech Systems (CRSS), Erik Jonsson School of Engineering and Computer Science, University of Texas at Dallas, USA

John H. L. Hansen
Center for Robust Speech Systems (CRSS), Erik Jonsson School of Engineering and Computer Science, University of Texas at Dallas, USA

ABSTRACT

This chapter addresses a number of advances in formulating spoken document retrieval for the National Gallery of the Spoken Word (NGSW) and the U.S.-based Collaborative Digitization Program (CDP). After presenting an overview of the audio stream content of the NGSW and CDP audio corpus, an overall system diagram is presented with a discussion of critical tasks associated with effective audio information retrieval that include advanced audio segmentation, speech recognition model adaptation for acoustic background noise and speaker variability, and information retrieval using natural language processing for text query requests that include document and query expansion. Our experimental online system entitled "SpeechFind" is presented which allows for audio retrieval from the NGSW and CDP corpus. Finally, a number of research challenges as well as new directions are discussed in order to address the overall task of robust phrase searching in unrestricted audio corpora.

INTRODUCTION

The focus of chapter is to provide an overview of the SpeechFind online spoken document retrieval system, including its subtasks, corpus enrollment, and online search and retrieval engines (Hansen, Huang, Zhou, Seadle, Deller, Gurijala, et al., 2005, http://speechfind.utdallas.edu). SpeechFind is serving as the platform for several programs across the United States for audio indexing and retrieval, including the National Gallery of the Spoken Word (NGSW, http://www.ngsw.org) and the Collaborative Digitization Program (CDP, http://cdpheritage.org). The field of spoken document retrieval requires an interdisciplinary effort, with researchers from electrical engineering (speech recognition), computer science (natural language processing), historians, library archivists, and so forth. As such, we provide a summary of acronyms and definition of terms at the end of this chapter to assist those interested in spoken document retrieval for audio archives.

The problem of reliable speech recognition for spoken document/information retrieval is a challenging problem when data are recorded across different media, equipment, and time periods. NGSW is the first large-scale repository of its kind, consisting of speeches, news broadcasts, and recordings that are of significant historical content. The U.S. National Science Foundation recently established an initiative to provide better transition of library services to digital format. As part of this Phase-II Digital Libraries Initiative, researchers from Michigan State University (MSU) and University of Texas at Dallas (UTD, formerly at Univ. of Colorado at Boulder) have teamed to establish a fully searchable, online WWW database of spoken word collections that span the 20th century. The database draws primarily from holdings of MSU's Vincent Voice Library (VVL) that includes +60,000 hours of recordings.

In the field of robust speech recognition, there are a variety challenging problems that persist, such as reliable speech recognition across wireless communications channels, recognition of speech across changing speaker conditions (e.g. emotion and stress [Bou-Ghazale & Hansen, 2000; Hansen, 1996; Sarikaya & Hansen, 2000] and accent [Angkititrakul & Hansen, 2006; Arslan & Hansen, 1997]), or recognition of speech from unknown or changing acoustic environments.

The ability to achieve effective performance in changing speaker conditions for large vocabulary continuous speech recognition (LVCSR) remains a challenge, as demonstrated in recent DARPA evaluations focused on broadcast news (BN) vs. previous results from the Wall Street Journal (WSJ) corpus.

One natural solution to audio stream search is to perform forced transcription for the entire dataset, and simply search the synchronized text stream. While this may be a manageable task for BN (consisting of about 100 hours), the initial offering for NGSW will be 5000 hours (with a potential of +60,000 total hours), and it will simply not be possible to achieve accurate forced transcription since text data will generally not be available. Other studies have also considered Web-based spoken document retrieval (SDR) (Fujii & Itou, 2003; Hansen, Zhou, Akbacak, Sarikaya, & Pellom, 2000; Zhou & Hansen, 2002). Transcript generation of broadcast news can also be conducted in an effort to obtain near real-time close-captioning (Saraclar, Riley, Bocchieri, & Goffin, 2002). Instead of generating exact transcripts, some studies have considered summarization and topic indexing (Hori & Furui, 2000; Maskey & Hirschberg, 2003; Neukirchen, Willett, & Rigoll, 1999), or more specifically, topic detection and tracking (Walls, Jin, Sista, & Schwartz, 1999), and others have considered lattice-based search (Saraclar & Sproat, 2004). Some of these ideas are related to speaker clustering (Moh, Nguyen, & Junqua, 2003; Mori & Nakagawa, 2001), which is needed to improve acoustic model adaptation for BN transcription generation. Language model adaptation (Langzhou, Gauvain, Lamel, & Adda, 2003) and multiple/alternative language modeling (Kurimo, Zhou, Huang, & Hansen, 2004) have also been considered for SDR. Finally, cross and multilingual-based studies have also been performed for SDR (Akbacak & Hansen, 2006; Navratil, 2001; Wang, Meng, Schone, Chen, & Lo, 2001).

In this chapter, we introduce SpeechFind (http://speechfind.utdallas.edu), an experimental online spoken document retrieval system for the NGSW. In the following section we discuss the structure of the audio materials contained in the VVL, including time periods, recording conditions, audio format, and acoustic conditions. In addition, CDP (http://cdpheritage.org) is also addressed. The third sectdion presents an overview of the SpeechFind system including transcript generation and text-based search. Next, the fourth section addresses transcript generation based on (i) unsupervised segmentation, (ii) model adaptation, (iii) LVCSR, and (iv) text-based information retrieval. Finally, the last section summarizes the main contributions and areas for future research.

NGSW AUDIO CORPUS AND CDP PROGRAM

While automatic speech recognition (ASR) technology has advanced significantly, the ability to perform ASR for spoken document retrieval presents some unique challenges. These challenges include: (i) a diverse range of audio recording conditions, (ii) the ability to search output text materials with variable levels of recognition (i.e., word-error-rate [WER]) performance, and (iii) decisions on what material/content should be extracted for transcript knowledge to be used for SDR (e.g., text content, speaker identification or tracking, environmental sniffing [Akbacak & Hansen 2003, 2007], etc.). Audio streams from NGSW encompass one of the widest ranges of audio materials available today. Figure 1 presents an overview of the types of audio files and recording structure seen in the audio. The types of audio include monologues, two-way conversations, speeches, interviews/debates, radio/TV news broadcasts, field news broadcasts, recording media/transmission, meetings/hearings, and historical recordings.

So, the audio content includes a diverse range of audio formats, recording media, and diverse time periods including names, places, topics, and choice of vocabulary. The following issues arise for transcript generation for SDR: Do we transcribe commercials? Do we transcribe background acoustic noise/events? Do we identify speakers with the text? What if there are old recordings and only some of the speakers are known? Do we identify where the speakers are speaking from (i.e., the environment/location)? How do we deal with errors in ASR (i.e., "dirty transcripts")? Since automatic transcription for such a diverse range of audio materials will lead to significant variability in WER, SDR employing text-based search of such transcripts will be an important research issue to consider. For our initial system, we focus on transcript generation of speech from individual speakers, and disable transcription production for music/commercials.

To illustrate the range of NGSW recording conditions, three example spectrograms are shown

Figure 1. Structure of (i) NGSW Audio Recordings – speakers, microphone(s), recording media, and (ii) segmentation and classification, speech recognition and transcript generation

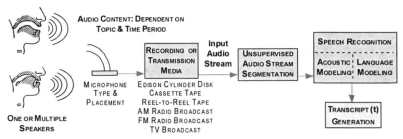

Figure 2. Example Audio Stream (8kHz) spectrograms from NGSW: (A) Thomas Edison, recorded in 1908, (B) Thomas Watson, recorded in 1926, and (C) Pres. William J. Clinton, recorded in 1999

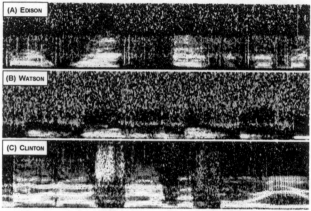

in Figure 2. The recordings are: (a)Thomas Edison, "my work as an electrician" (talking about contributions of 19th century scientists; original Edison cylinder disk recording, 1908), (b) Thomas Watson, "as Bell was about to speak into the new instrument," (talking about the first telephone message from A.G. Bell on March 10, 1876; recorded in 1926), and (c) President Bill Clinton, "tonight I stand before you," (State of the Union Address on economic expansion, Jan. 19, 1999). This example indicates the wide range of distortions present in the speech corpus. Some of these include: severe bandwidth restrictions (e.g., Edison style cylinder disks); poor audio from scratchy, used, or aging recording media; differences in microphone type and placement; reverberation for speeches from public figures; recordings from telephone, radio, or TV broadcasts; background noise including audience and multiple speakers or interviewers; as well as a wide range of speaking styles and accents.

The CDP is a cooperative program providing oversight to more than 40 libraries and archives interested in establishing or maintaining audio collections. Their efforts include best practices for digital audio archives in terms of digitization, recording, maintaining, and planning for future holdings. Our efforts here have concentrated on establishing a collaborative arrangement whereby we provide seamless automatic transcription support to improve online search capabilities. It has also been a major point to educate the library and information services sectors on what they can expect from automatic transcription support, and that while in some cases the resulting transcripts can be used by users for reviewing audio content, in other examples the transcripts contain such a high level or word errors that they are useful only for audio search and indexing, since WERs can range from 5-70%, though WERs as high as 30-35% can still achieve reasonable search performance (Abberley, Kirby, Renals, & Robinson, 1999).

SPEECHFIND SYSTEM OVERVIEW

Here, we present an overview of the SpeechFind system (see Figure 3) and describe several key modules. The system is constructed in two phases: (i) enrollment and (ii) query and retrieval. In the enrollment phase, large audio sets are submitted for audio segmentation and transcription generation and metadata construction (EAD: extended archive descriptor). Once this phase is completed, the audio material is now available through the online audio search engine (i.e., "query and retrieval" phase). The system includes the following

Figure 3. Overview of SpeechFind system architecture (http://SpeechFind.utdallas.edu)

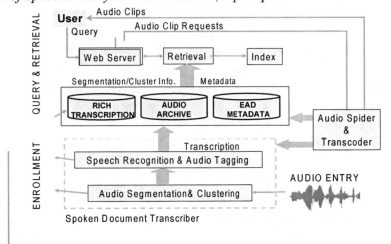

modules: an audio spider and transcoder, spoken documents transcriber, "rich" transcription database, and an online public accessible search engine. As shown in the figure, the audio spider and transcoder are responsible for automatically fetching available audio archives from a range of available servers and transcoding the heterogeneous incoming audio files into uniform 16kHz, 16bit linear PCM raw audio data (note: in general, the transcoding process is done off-line prior to being available for user retrieval). In addition, for those audio documents with metadata labels, this module also parses the metadata and extracts relevant information into a "rich" transcript database for guiding information retrieval.

The spoken document transcriber includes two components, namely the audio segmenter and transcriber. The audio segmenter partitions audio data into manageable small segments by detecting speaker, channel, and environmental change points. The transcriber decodes every speech segment into text. If human transcripts are available for any of the audio documents, the segmenter is still applied to detect speaker, channel, and environmental changes in a guided manner, with the decoder being reduced to a forced aligner for each speech segment to tag timing information for spoken words. Figure 4(i) shows that for the proposed SpeechFind system, transcript generation is first performed which requires reliable acoustic and language models appropriate for the type of audio stream and time period. After transcript generation, Figure 4(ii) shows that three associated files are linked together, namely (i) the audio stream in (_.wav) format, (ii) the transcript (_.trs) file with time indexed locations into the audio file, and (iii) extended archive descriptor (_.ead) file that contains metadata information. The EAD file has an agreed upon format and structure from a consortium of participating libraries (i.e., VVL, U. S. National Archives, and U. S. Library of

Figure 4. (i) Automatic Transcript Generation (SDR), (ii) Statistical Information Retrieval (SIR)

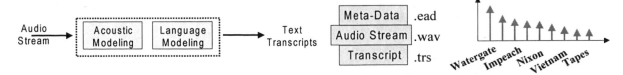

Congress). Each audio stream has a reverse index word histogram (with all stop words – "the, a, or, ..." set aside) that is employed with the natural language processing text search engine. These integrated files form the statistical information retrieval (SIR) engine.

The online search engine is responsible for information retrieval tasks, including a Web-based user interface as the front-end, and search and index engines at the back-end. The Web-based search engine responds to a user query by launching back-end retrieval commands, formatting the output with relevant transcribed documents that are ranked by relevance scores and associated with timing information, and providing the user with Web-based page links to access the corresponding audio clips. It should be noted that the local system does not store the entire audio archive collection, due to both copyright and disk space issues. Several hundred hours of audio have been digitized by MSU, and a portion is accessible via SpeechFind (see Figure 5).

SPEECHFIND: TRANSCRIBING AND SEARCH OF AUDIO ARCHIVES

As Figure 3 illustrates, the enrollment phase for an audio stream first requires audio segmentation and clustering (Sec. 4.1). Having segmented

the stream, speech recognition is performed for transcript generation (Sec. 4.2). In Sec. 4.3, we consider advances also in acoustic model adaptation to improve transcripts for non-native and native speakers. Finally, Sec. 4.4 considers the text based information retrieval (IR) search framework.

Spoken Archives Segmentation

The goal of audio segmentation and classification is to partition and label an audio stream into speech, music, commercials, environmental background noise, or other acoustic conditions. This preliminary stage is necessary for effective LVCSR, audio content analysis and understanding, audio information retrieval, audio transcription, audio clustering, and other audio recognition and indexing applications. Audio archive segmentation obtains manageable audio blocks for subsequent speech decoding, as well as allowing for location analysis of speaker(s), channel, and environmental change points to help track audio segments of interest.

The goals of effective audio/speaker segmentation (Adami, Kajarekar, & Hermansky, 2002; Lu & Zhang, 2002) are different than those for ASR, and therefore features, processing methods, and modeling concepts successful for ASR may not necessarily be appropriate for segmentation.

Figure 5. (i) Sample Web Page & (ii) Output web page format. (http://SpeechFind.utdallas.edu)

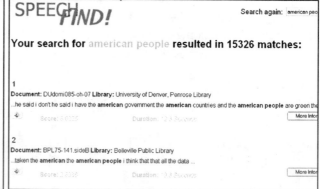

Features used for speech recognition attempt to minimize the differences across speakers and acoustic environments (i.e., speaker variance), and maximize the differences across phoneme space (i.e., phoneme variance). However, in speaker segmentation for audio streams, we want to maximize speaker traits to produce segments that contain a single acoustic event or speaker, and therefore traditional Mel frequency cepstral coefficients (MFCCs) may not be as effective for speaker segmentation. In this section, we consider segmentation for several features (e.g., PMVDR [Yapanel & Hansen, 2003], SZCR, and FBLC), and performance of the composite segmentation scheme (CompSeg) for NGSW audio data. We consider three features and compare them to traditional MFCCs (Huang & Hansen, 2006).

PMVDR: A high order minimum variance distortionless response (MVDR) provides better upper envelope representations of the short-term speech spectrum than MFCCs (Dharanipragada & Rao, 2001). A perceptual-based MVDR feature was proposed by Yapanel and Hansen (2003), which we consider for segmentation here (i.e., PMVDRs), that does not require an explicit filterbank analysis of the speech signal. We also apply a detailed Bark frequency warping for better results.

SZCR: A high zero crossing rate ratio (ZCR) has previously been proposed for speaker classifi-cation (Lu, Zhang, & Jiang, 2002). We propose that a smoothed ZCR can be effective for segmentation (Huang & Hansen, 2006), which is computed using five sets of ZCR evenly spaced across an analysis window with no intermediate overlap; SZCR is the mean of the five sets for this frame.

FBLC: Although, it has been suggested that direct warping of the FFT power spectrum without filterbank processing can preserve most information in the short-term speech spectrum (Yapanel & Hansen, 2003), we find that filterbank processing is more sensitive than other features in detecting speaker change. As such, the FBLC are the 20 Mel frequency filterbank log energy coefficients.

Table 1 shows that PMVDR can outperform MFCC on all levels (Huang & Hansen, 2006) using Hub4 '96 training data and Hub4 '97 evaluation data obtained from the U. S. DARPA Broadcast News corpus. FBLCs have a very small average mismatch, implying they are sensitive to changes between speakers and environments. Because PMVDR does not apply filterbank processing, we combine PMVDR and FBLC together. Also, the SZCR encodes information directly from the waveform that we combine as well. The CompSeg (Huang & Hansen, 2006) algorithm combines PMVDR, SZCR, and FBLC features, applies the T2-Mean measure (Zhou & Hansen, 2005) for segments of less than 5 secs, and provides a

Table 1. SDR Segmentation Feature Performance. Note: '(x.x%)' represents the relative improvement in FA: false alarm rate, MIS: miss detection rate, MMatch: average mismatch (msec), and FES: fused error score

Feature	FA: False Alarm	MIS: Miss Rate	MMatch: mismatch in (msec)	FES: fused error score
MFCC	29.6%	25.0%	298.47	237.58
FBLC	29.8% (-0.7%)	25.3% (-1.2%)	266.80 (10.6%)	214.51 (9.7%)
MPVDR	25.9% (12.5%)	24.9% (0.4%)	284.29 (4.8%)	215.21 (9.4%)
Combine 45-D	23.8% (19.6%)	24.3% (2.8%)	265.06 (11.2%)	191.99 (19.2%)

Figure 6. Block Diagram of CompSeg Segmentation Algorithm

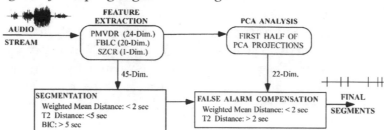

novel false alarm compensation post-processing routine (Huang & Hansen, 2006) (see Figure 6). The improvement using these advances vs. a baseline system employing MFCCs and traditional BIC (Chen & Gopalakrishnan, 1998) is shown in Table 2(i). We also evaluate the CompSeg with a portion of the NGSW corpus (http://www.ngsw.org), using audio material from the 1960s. From Table 2(ii), we see that CompSeg effectively detects not only speaker changes, but also music and long silence (>2s) segments. The fused error score (FES) is a proposed measure discussed by Huang and Hansen (2006), which, like the WER for automatic speech recognition, attempts to incorporate the false alarm, miss rate, and mismatch boundary into a single measure. The proposed CompSeg scheme outperforms the baseline approach by 30.5%.

Spoken Archives Transcription

For SpeechFind, all speech segments are decoded with a large vocabulary recognizer. We currently employ the CMU Sphinx3 for this task. Using the Sphinx system, we employed acoustic models that contain 5270 GMMs, each of which has 32 mixture Gaussians. Acoustic models are built using a subset of the 200 hours of broadcast news released by LDC in 1997 and 1998. The language model is composed of 64 K unigrams, 4.7 M bigrams, and 15 M trigrams. The average decoding speed is about 6.2x real time on a P4-1.7GHz Linux machine. In establishing the baseline experiments, no model adaptation schemes were applied at this stage, and first pass decoding output is used as the automatic transcriptions, though a second pass

Table 2. SDR Segmentation performance using CompSeg with improved features, audio clustering and false alarm compensation with (i) DARPA Hub4-97 Broadcast News data (relative improvements listed in %), and (ii) sample 1960's NGSW audio materials

(i)

Algorithm	FA: False Alarm	MIS: Miss Rate	MMatch: mismatch in (msec)	FES: fused error score
Baseline	26.7%	26.9%	293.02	235.82
CompSeg	21.1% (21.0%)	20.6% (23.4%)	262.99 (10.2%)	163.84 (30.5%)

(ii)

NGSW 1960's Data	Speaker Change	Speaker MMatch	Music & Sil Change	Music & Sil MMatch	False Alarm
	100%	129msec	26.9%	118msec	5.6%

Table 3. Description & Evaluation performance of a sample portion of the NGSW audio corpus (29,628 words, 3.8hrs)

Decade	# of Doc	Audio Length (Min)	# Words	OOV(%)	Avg. SNR (dB)	Avg. WER (%)
1950	4	52	6241	1.42	26.63	38.6
1960	2	17	2142	1.52	21.34	36.7
1970	2	35	4434	0.81	20.87	25.6
1980	3	27	3330	0.63	17.97	60.1
1990	4	47	5951	1.28	14.79	48.0
2000	3	50	7530	0.78	26.81	59.1

rescoring using a more complex language model could produce better text results.

To evaluate recognition performance, 3.8 hours of sample audio data from the past 6 decades in NGSW is used as the test data. Table 3 provides a summary of the audio statistics along with WER averaged for each decade. Here we note that average WER does not increase as we move back in time, though the out-of-vocabulary (OOV) rate does. Instead, the first three decades achieve better recognition accuracy, and the lowest WER is observed for corpora from the 1970s. This can be attributed to the lower average SNR for the recordings used from the 1980s and 1990s. For example, three long audio recordings of the 1990s that contain 2,681 words have an average SNR near 12 dB, which produce WERs above 75%, while other recordings with a higher average SNR of 21 dB achieve WERs less than 25%. The average SNR of recordings from the 2000s is relatively high, while the audio files are from news conferences regarding the hand counting of votes for the U.S. President in Florida. As a result, this portion becomes transcribed primarily as noise by the recognizer and as much as 35% of the overall WER is from deletions. This performance is sufficient for effective spoken document retrieval; however, it is clear that all possible methods for achieving robust speech recognition will need to be brought to bear to further reduce the WER as the diversity of the audio materials continue to expand.

Model Adaptation for Automatic Transcription

From Sec. 4.2, it is clear that advances in acoustic model adaptation would improve speech recognition performance. Currently, the most commonly-used speaker adaptation algorithms include transformation-based techniques, the most common being maximum likelihood linear regression (MLLR) (Leggetter & Woodland, 1995) achieved with affine transformations, and Bayesian learning that include maximum a posterior (MAP) (Gauvain & Lee, 1994), which combines adaptation data with some a priori knowledge concerning the model parameters. In addition, there are also several extensions to MAP and MLLR that have been extensively investigated in recent years that include regression-based model prediction (RMP) (Ahadi & Woodland, 1997), structural MAP (Shinoda & Lee, 1997), block-diagonal MLLR (Neumeyer, Sankar, & Digalakis, 1995), MAP linear regression (MAPLR) (Chesta, Siohan, & Lee, 1999; Chou, 1999), structural MA-PLR (Siohan, Myrvoll, & Lee, 2002), and others (Woodland [1999] details more comparisons). For relatively small amounts of adaptation data, transformation-based schemes have demonstrated superior performance over MAP due to its global adaptation via transformation sharing. On the other hand, MAP adaptation is more desirable for its asymptotic convergence to maximum likelihood estimation when the amount of adaptation data continues to increase (Gauvain & Lee, 1994). However, both MLLR and MAP have not been able to show comparable improvements when only limited amounts of adaptation data are available (e.g., 5 seconds of adaptation data).

Here, we consider a novel approach based on primary eignendirections called EigMap (EM) (Zhou & Hansen, 2005). The basic idea of EigMap is to maintain the between-class variances (i.e., the discrimination power) of the baseline Gaussian means along the first primary eigendirections in the test speaker's eigenspace. In EigMap, the baseline model is not only adapted through the transformation, but also compressed with reduced Gaussian dimensions of model mean, which further suggests that faster recognition speed can also be achieved using the adapted model due to reduced Gaussian computations. We point out that a number of extensions to this EigMap model adaptation scheme have also been considered (Zhou & Hansen, 2005). One such extension is structured maximum likelihood eigenspace mapping (SMLEM), which extends the core EigMap algorithm by imposing a further shift in the model space to maximize the adaptation data likelihood. To account for the adaptation data likelihood, the EigMap formulation can be extended by adding a linear bias in the test speaker's eigenspace. The linear bias is derived in a manner that maximizes the adaptation data likelihood. Since only the Gaussian means are adapted, we ignore other model parameters in the auxiliary function using the EM algorithm. Further details concerning this extension are discussed by Zhou and Hansen (2005). An example of improved transcript generation using EigMap and SMLEM of the baseline (with no adaptation) and with block-diagonal MLLR are shown in Table 4.

IR Over Automatic Transcripts & IR Advances

The current SpeechFind retrieval engine is a modified version of managing gigabytes (MG)

Table 4. WER (%) of non-nativespeakers (WSJ Spoke3) with approximately 4.5 seconds of unsupervised adaptation data

	Baseline (%)	BD-MLLR (%)	EigMap (%)	SMLEM (%)
Avg. Across Speakers	20.7	17.4	16.9	16.2
Relative Improvement	---	15.9%	18.4%	21.7%

(Witten, Moffat, & Bell, 1999). Here, the *tfidf* weighting scheme is replaced with Okapi weighting (Robertson & Walker, 1999), and several query and document expansion technologies are incorporated. To ensure sufficient documents from the perspective of IR, the transcript from each recognition segment is treated as a single document. In our case, many historical spoken documents are typically longer than 30 minutes, so the use of small segments as a search unit allows for a more specific user search. The SpeechFind Web interface provides the user access to the detected speech segments and automatic transcripts, and allows the user to preview/listen to any parts of the entire audio file containing the original detected segments.

An inherent difference exists between transcribed spoken documents and typical text documents. Automatic transcriptions essentially decode acoustic recordings using the most probable in-vocabulary word sequences. On the other hand, text documents and queries written by humans tend to use a simplified notation. For example, "1960" could be widely used in human-written documents to indicate the year 1960, but it is usually not included in either the dictionary or language models in most state-of-the-art speech recognizers. Hence the audio phrase will appear as "nineteen sixty" in automatic spoken document transcripts. To address this issue, the spoken transcripts and queries are normalized in the SpeechFind system to bridge this gap. Through a predefined dictionary of mappings between "spoken words" and "simplified human notations," the automatic transcripts are filtered, which, for example, replace "N. B. C." with "NBC." Using an inverse of a similar dictionary, the queries are filtered as well (e.g., we change the query word "1st" to "first").

Query expansion (QE) is an application that could be used to address the problem of missing query terms directly, or missing term relations indirectly (Robertson & Sparck Jones, 1997). The idea behind document expansion (DE) (Singhal & Pereira, 1999) is that given a document, first identify other parallel documents related to those in hand and bring "signal" words from the related documents into the present document. To expand spoken documents, we first run automatic transcription of the speech document as a query on a parallel collection, and then the query documents are expanded using parallel blind relevance feedback (PBRF). The effect of document expansion largely depends on the selection of the parallel text collection, which should be related to the spoken corpus.

SUMMARY AND DISCUSSION

In this chapter, we have addressed a number of advances in establishing spoken document retrieval for a new National Gallery of the Spoken Word. We first discussed an overview of the audio stream content of the NGSW with sample audio files. Next, we presented the SpeechFind system, an experimental online spoken document retrieval system for an historical archive with 60,000 hours of audio recordings from the last century. We introduced the SDR system architecture, and focused on audio data transcription and information retrieval components. We considered a segmentation method and several features as alternatives to traditional MFCCs. Next, we considered transcript generation for a portion of the NGSW corpus, and novel model adaptation using structure maximum likelihood

eigenspace mapping. Information retrieval over automatic transcripts was considered by combining DE and QE using RF and PBRF.

We note that recent advances in the following areas of (i) speaker accent/dialect (Angkititrakul & Hansen, 2006, 2007; Huang & Hansen, 2007), (ii) speaker stress/emotion (Varadarajan & Hansen, 2006), and (iii) environment/noise analysis (Akbacak & Hansen, 2007) offer some challenges as SDR technologies move to the general population. Some of these include: (i) How do speech researchers deal with "dirty transcripts" which have word errors when users (e.g., both librarians and general users) expect perfect transcription support? (ii) How do we interpret the text and intent of the transcribed message and enrich the search capabilities? (i.e., transcripts have word errors, users do not say their names, and topics are sometimes assumed or known by those discussing/talking) (iii) How do we assign "labels" when we do not know "groundtruth" for the audio materials? (i.e., for audio streams, we may not know the identity of the subject, we may not know the true accent/dialect of the subject speaking, we may not know how angry or the stress level of a subject, etc.). Since many of these issues require that the audio signal be tagged with labels which will have absolute certainty, it is important to emphasize how this knowledge is presented and incorporated by the user in the search process. Further progress in SDR could benefit from improving IR performance. In our task, reliable document categorization could be achieved with the help of metadata associated with some spoken documents (i.e., so called EAD extended archive descriptor, files used in library archive services, etc.), which narrows a search and hence improves the retrieval precision.

REFERENCES

Abberley, D., Kirby, D., Renals, S., & Robinson, T. (1999). The THISL broadcast new retrieval system. In *Proceedings of the ESCA ETRW Workshop Accessing Information in Spoken Audio* (pp.14-19).

Adami, A., Kajarekar, S., & Hermansky, H. (2002). *A new speaker change detection method for two-speaker segmentation.* Paper presented at ICASSP-02.

Ahadi, S. M., & Woodland, P. C. (1997). Combined Bayesian and predictive techniques for rapid speaker adaptation of continuous density hidden Markov models. *Computer Speech and Language, 11*, 187-206.

Akbacak, M., & Hansen, J. H. L. (2003). Environmental sniffing: Noise knowledge estimation for robust speech systems. In *Proceedings of the IEEE ICASSP-2003: Inter. Conf. Acoust. Speech & Signal*, Hong Kong (Vol. 2, pp. 113-116).

Akbacak, M., & Hansen, J. H. L. (2006). A robust fusion method for multilingual spoken document retrieval systems employing tiered resources. In *Proceedings of the ISCA INTERSPEECH-2006/ICSLP-2006*, Pittsburgh (pp. 1177-1180).

Akbacak, M., & Hansen, J. H. L. (2007). Environmental sniffing: Noise knowledge estimation for robust speech systems. *IEEE Transactions on Audio, Speech and Language Processing, 15*(2), 465-477.

Angkititrakul, P., & Hansen, J. H. L. (2006). Advances in phone-based modeling for automatic accent classification. *IEEE Trans. Audio, Speech & Language Proc., 14*(2), 634-646.

Angkititrakul, P., & Hansen, J. H. L. (2007). Discriminative in-set/out-of-set speaker recognition. *IEEE Transactions on Audio, Speech and Language Processing, 15*(2), 498-508.

Arslan, L. M., & Hansen, J. H. L. (1997). A study of temporal features and frequency characteristics in American English foreign accent. *The Journal of the Acoustical Society of America, 102*(1), 28-40.

Bou-Ghazale, S. E., & Hansen, J. H. L. (2000). A comparative study of traditional and newly proposed features for recognition of speech under stress. *IEEE Transactions on Speech & Audio Processing, 8*(4), 429-442.

Chen, S., & Gopalakrishnan, P. (1998). Speaker, environment and channel change detection and clustering via the Bayesian information criterion. In *Proceedings of the Broadcast News Trans. & Under. Workshop.*

Chesta, C., Siohan, O., & Lee, C. H. (1999). Maximum a posterior linear regression for hidden Markov model adaptation. In *Proceedings of Eurospeech-99*, Budapest (pp. 203-206).

Chou, W. (1999). Maximum a posterior linear regression with elliptically symmetric matrix priors. In *Proceedings of Eurospeech* (pp. 1-4).

Dharanipragada, S., & Rao, B. (2001). *MVDR-based feature extraction for robust speech recognition.* Paper presented at ICASSP-01, Utah.

Fujii, A., & Itou, K. (2003). Building a test collection for speech-driven Web retrieval. In *Proceedings of Eurospeech-2003*, Geneva (pp. 1153-1156).

Gauvain, J.-L., & Lee, C.-H. (1994). Maximum a posteriori estimation for multivariate Gaussian mixture observations of Markov chains. *IEEE Trans. on Speech and Audio Proc., 2*, 291-298.

Hansen, J. H. L. (1996). Analysis and compensation of speech under stress and noise for environmental robustness in speech recognition. *Speech Communications, Special Issue on Speech Under Stress, 20*(2), 151-170.

Hansen, J. H. L., Huang, R., Zhou, B., Seadle, M., Deller, J. R., Jr., Gurijala, A. R., et al. (2005). SpeechFind: Advances in spoken document retrieval for a national gallery of the spoken word. *IEEE Trans. on Speech and Audio Proc., 13*(5), 712-730.

Hansen, J. H. L., Zhou, B., Akbacak, M., Sarikaya, R., & Pellom, B. (2000). Audio stream phrase recognition for a national gallery of the spoken word: 'One small step'. In *Proceedings of the ICSLP-2000: Inter. Conf. Spoken Lang. Proc.*, Beijing (Vol. 3, pp. 1089-1092).

Hori, C., & Furui, S. (2000). Automatic speech summarization based on word significance and linguistic likelihood. In *Proceedings of the IEEE ICASSP-00: Inter. Conf. Acoust. Speech, Sig. Proc.* (Vol. 3, pp. 1579-1582).

Huang, R., & Hansen, J. H. L. (2006). Advances in unsupervised audio classification and segmentation for the broadcast news and NGSW corpora. *IEEE Trans. Audio, Speech and Language Processing, 14*(3), 907-919.

Huang, R., & Hansen, J. H. L. (2007). Dialect/accent classification using unrestricted audio. *IEEE Trans. on Audio, Speech and Language Processing, 15*(2), 453-464.

Kurimo, M., Zhou, B., Huang, R., & Hansen, J. H. L. (2004). *Language modeling structures in audio transcription for retrieval of historical speeches.* Paper presented at the EUSIPCO-2004, 12th European Signal Processing Conference, Vienna, Austria (Paper 1530).

Langzhou, C., Gauvain, J.-L., Lamel, L., & Adda, G. (2003). Unsupervised language model adaptation for broadcast news. In *Proceedings of the IEEE ICASSP-03: Inter. Conf. Acoust. Speech, Sig. Proc.* (Vol. 1, pp. 220-223).

Leggetter, C., & Woodland, P. (1995). Maximum likelihood linear regression for speaker adaptation of continuous density hidden Markov models. *Computer Speech and Language, 9,* 171-185.

Lu, L., & Zhang, H. (2002). *Speaker change detection and tracking in real-time news broadcasting analysis.* France: ACM Multimedia.

Lu, L., Zhang, H., & Jiang, H. (2002). Content analysis for audio classification and segmenta-

tion. *IEEE Trans. Speech & Audio Proc., 10*(7), 504-516.

Maskey, S. R., & Hirschberg, J. (2003). Automatic summarization of broadcast news using structural features. In Proceedings of *Eurospeech-2003,* Geneva (pp. 1173-1176).

Moh, Y., Nguyen, P., & Junqua, J.-C. (2003). Towards domain independent speaker clustering. In *Proceedings of the IEEE ICASSP-03: Inter. Conf. Acoust. Speech, Sig. Proc.* (Vol. 2, pp. 85-88).

Mori, K., & Nakagawa, S. (2001). Speaker change detection and speaker clustering using VQ distortion for broadcast news speech recognition. In *Proceedings of the IEEE ICASSP-01: Inter. Conf. Acoust. Speech, Sig. Proc.* (Vol. 1, pp. 413-416).

Navratil, J. (2001). Spoken language recognition-a step toward multilinguality in speech processing. *IEEE Transactions on Speech & Audio Processing, 9,* 678-685.

Neukirchen, C., Willett, D., & Rigoll, G. (1999). Experiments in topic indexing of broadcast news using neural networks. In Proceedings of the *IEEE ICASSP-99: Inter. Conf. Acoust. Speech, Sig. Proc.* (Vol. 2, pp. 1093-1096).

Neumeyer, L. R., Sankar, A., & Digalakis, V. V. (1995). A comparative study of speaker adaptation techniques. In *Proceedings of Eurospeech-95* (pp. 1127-1130).

Robertson, S. E., & Sparck Jones, K. (1997). *Simple, proven approaches to text retrieval* (Tech. Rep.). Cambridge University.

Robertson, S. E., & Walker, S. (1999). Okapi/Keenbow at TREC-8). In *Proceedings of TREC-8.*

Sarikaya, R., & Hansen, J. H. L. (2000). High resolution speech feature parameterization for monophone based stressed speech recognition. *IEEE Signal Processing Letters, 7*(7), 182-185.

Saraclar, M., Riley, M., Bocchieri, E., & Goffin, V. (2002). Towards automatic closed captioning:

Low latency real time broadcast news transcription. In *Proceedings of the ICSLP-2002: Inter. Conf. Spoken Lang.*, Denver (pp. 1741-1744).

Saraclar, M., & Sproat, R. (2004). Lattice-based search for spoken utterance retrieval. In *Proceedings of the HLT-NAACL 2004*, Boston (pp. 129-136).

Shinoda, K., & Lee, C. H. (1997). Structural MAP speaker adaptation using hierarchical priors. In *Proceedings of the IEEE Workshop on Automatic Speech Recognition and Understanding*, Santa Barbara, CA (pp. 381-388).

Singhal, A., & Pereira, F. (1999). *Document expansion for speech retrieval.* Paper presented at the 22nd ACM SIGIR Conference, Berkeley, CA.

Siohan, O., Myrvoll, T. A., & Lee, C. H. (2002). Structural maximum a posteriori linear regression for fast HMM adaptation. *Computer Speech and Language, 16*(1), 5-24.

Varadarajan, V. S., & Hansen, J. H. L. (2006). Analysis of Lombard effect under different types and levels of background noise with application to in-set speaker ID systems. In *Proceedings of the ISCA INTERSPEECH-2006/ICSLP-2006*, Pittsburgh (pp. 937-940).

Walls, F., Jin, H., Sista, S., & Schwartz, R. (1999). Probabilistic models for topic detection and tracking. In *Proceedings of the IEEE ICASSP-99: Inter. Conf. Acoust. Speech, Sig. Proc.* (Vol. 1, pp. 521-524).

Wang, H.-M., Meng, H., Schone, P., Chen, B., & Lo, W.-K. (2001). Multi-scale-audio indexing for translingual spoken document retrieval. In *Proceedings of the IEEE ICASSP-01: Inter. Conf. Acoust. Speech, Sig. Proc.* (Vol. 1, pp. 605-608).

Witten, I. H., Moffat, A., & Bell, T. C. (1999). *Managing gigabytes: Compressing and indexing documents and images.* Morgan Kaufmann.

Woodland, P. C. (1999). Speaker adaptation: Techniques and challenges. In Proceedings of the *IEEE Workshop on Automatic Speech Recognition & Understanding*, Keystone, CO (pp. 85-90).

Yapanel, U., & Hansen, J. H. L. (2003). A new perspective on feature extraction for robust in-vehicle speech recognition. In *Proceedings of Eurospeech-03*, Geneva (pp. 1281-1284).

Zhou, B., & Hansen, J. H. L. (2002). SPEECH-FIND: An experimental on-line spoken document retrieval system for historical audio archives. In *Proceedings of the ICSLP-2002: International Conferference on Spoken Language Processing*, Denver (Vol. 3, pp. 1969-1972).

Zhou, B., & Hansen, J. H. L. (2005a). Efficient audio stream segmentation via the T2 statistic based Bayesian information criterion. *IEEE Trans. Speech & Audio Proc., 13*(4), 467-474.

Zhou, B., & Hansen, J. H. L. (2005b). Rapid discriminative acoustic modeling based on Eigenspace mapping for fast speaker adaptation. *IEEE Trans. Speech & Audio Proc., 13*(4), 554-564.

WEB SITES

http://speechfind.utdallas.edu

http://www.ngsw.org

http://cdpheritage.org

KEY TERMS

ASR: Automatic Speech Recognition

Broadcast News (BN): An audio corpus consisting of recordings from TV and radio broadcasts used for developing/performance assessment of speech recognition systems

Collaborative Digitization Program (CDP): A consortium of libraries, universities, and archives working together to establish best practices for transitioning materials (e.g., audio, image, etc.) to digital format.

LVCSR: Large Vocabulary Continuous Speech Recognition

Mel Frequency Cepstral Coefficients (MFCC): A standard set of features used to parameterize speech for acoustic models in speech recognition

Managing Gigabytes (MG): One of the two general purpose-based systems available for text search and indexing. See the textbook by Witten, Moffat, and Bell (1999) for extended discussion.

NGSW: The National Gallery of the Spoken Word – National Science Foundation (NSF in USA) supported Digital Libraries Initiative consortium of Universities to establish the first nationally recognized, fully searchable online audio archive.

Out-of-Vocabulary (OOV): In speech recognition, the available vocabulary must first be defined. OOV refers to vocabulary contained in the input audio signal, which is not part of the available vocabulary lexicon, and therefore will always be miss-recognized using automatic speech recognition.

SDR: Spoken Document Retrieval

Word Error Rate (WER): A performance measure for speech recognition that includes substitution errors (i.e., miss-recognition of one word for another), deletion errors (i.e., words missed by the recognition system), and insertions (i.e., words introduced into the text output by the recognition system).

Chapter XVIII
Using Topic–Specific Ranks to Personalize Web Search

Sofia Stamou
Patras University, Greece

ABSTRACT

This chapter introduces a personalized ranking function as a means of offering Web information seekers with search results that satisfy their particular interests. It argues that users' preferences can be accurately identified based on the semantic analysis of their previous searches and that learnt user preferences can be fruitfully employed for personalizing search results. In this respect, we introduce a ranking formula that encapsulates the user's interests in the process of ordering retrieved results so as to meet the user's needs. For carrying out our study we relied on a lexical ontology that encodes a number of concepts and their interrelations and which helps us determine the semantics of both the query keywords and the query matching pages. Based on the correlation between the query and document semantics, our model decides upon the ordering of search results so that these are personalized.

INTRODUCTION

The most convenient way for finding information on the Web is go to a search engine, type one or more search keywords that describe the user's information need, and receive in response a ranked list of URLs pointing to query relevant pages. Despite the success of the Web searching paradigm, users are becoming more and more eager to receive qualitative search results. One way to satisfy the above users' need is to tailor search results so as to meet specific user interests and search intentions; a task widely known as search personalization. Tailoring the search results to particular user preferences has attracted a substantial amount of interest and works in the last few years, but still remains a challenge. The most important issue that Web personalization systems have to confront is to learn the user's interests based on very little data (typically the user's search keywords and less often the user's previous searches) and based on this knowledge to customize the ordering of search results in a way that interesting pages show up first in the list of retrieved data. In this chapter, we propose a technique that tries to automatically identify users' interests based on the semantic analysis of their previous searches and we introduce a personalized ranking function that explores the similarity between the identified user interests and the retrieved pages' content in order to rerank results in way that satisfies the user interests. Our work aims at introducing some theoretical aspects on Web search personalization and we defer experimental evaluation for a future study. The rest of the chapter is organized as follows. We begin with an overview of related works on Web search personalization and personalized ranking. In the following section, we present our approach on how we can leverage a lexical ontology for identifying the users' interests though the semantic analysis of their search requests. We then discuss how we can encapsulate the identified users' interests in the process of ordering search results and we outline a ranking function that combines the users' preferences and the pages' relevance to the query keywords in order to prioritize among a set of query relevant pages the ones that are highly probable of satisfying the users' needs. Finally, we conclude the chapter with some discussion on our approach and we outline our plans for future work.

BACKGROUND

There has been previous work in personalizing Web search. One approach to personalization is to have users explicitly describe their general search interests, which are stored as personal profiles (Pazzani, Muramatsu, & Billsus, 1996). Personal profiles, specified explicitly by the users have also been used to personalize rankings, such as the PageRank algorithm (Aktas, Nacar, & Menczer, 2004; Jeh & Widom, 2003). There also exist many works on the automatic learning of a

user's preference based on the analysis of the user's past clickthrough history (Chen & Sycara, 2004; Pretschner & Gauch, 1999, Sugiyama, Hatano, & Yoshikawa, 2004). Pretschner and Gauch (1999) for instance, describe how a user's preference is identified based on the five most frequent topics in the user's log data.

On the other hand, Chen and Sycara (2004) generate multiple TF-IDF vectors, each representing the user's interests in one area. Sugiyama et al. (2004) employ collaborative filtering techniques for learning the user's preference from both the pages the user visited and those visited by users with similar interests. Likewise, Teevan, Dumais, and Horvitz (2005) employ rich models of user interests, built from both search-related information and information about the documents a user has read, created, and/or e-mailed.

A promising approach to personalizing search is to develop algorithms that infer intentions implicitly rather than requiring that the users' intentions be explicitly specified. For an overview of such approaches, we refer the reader to the work of Kelly and Teevan (2003). A multitude of implicit user activities have been proposed as sources of information for enhanced Web search, including the user's query (Shen & Zhai, 2003; Speretta & Gauch, 2004) and browsing history (Sugiyama et al., 2004). Sun, Zeng, Liu, Lu, and Chen (2005) explore the correlation between users, their queries, and search results clicked to model the users' preferences. A lot of research in metasearch (e.g., Powel, French, Callan, & Connell, 2000; Yu, Meng, Wu, & Liu, 2001) investigate mapping user queries to a set of categories or collections. However, the above techniques return the same results for a given query, regardless of who submitted the query. Our approach is different from the above in that we try to map user queries to particular topics based on the user's preferences for those topics.

Besides statistical approaches that analyze the user's clickthrough history and past queries for learning the user's search profile, researchers have also explored the role of semantics in the personalization process. In this direction, there exist several works that utilize ontologies (either lexical or topical) for processing users' past search data and identifying their search preferences. Dai and Mobasher (2002) propose the exploitation of ontologies in order to identify the user interests, which they subsequently transform into domain-level aggregate profiles through the representation of every page as a set of related ontology objects. Oberle, Berendt, Hotho, and Gonzalez (2003) propose a framework based on a Semantic Web site that employs Web mining techniques on the site's underlying RDF ontology in order to semantically analyze Web logs based on the ontology's concepts. Moreover, Kearney and Anand (2005) use an ontology to estimate the impact that every ontology concept has on the users' navigational behavior, and based on these estimations, they define the similarity between the different users and the user preferences in order to build personalized recommendations for Web information seekers. In a recent work (i.e., Tzekou, Stamou, Kozanidis, & Zotos, 2007), we have introduced a novel recommendation mechanism that relies on a topical ontology for offering Web users with customized site views.

Finally, researchers have proposed methods to personalize Web search by modifying PageRank to account for user personal preferences. Richardson and Domingos (2002) tailor the PageRank vectors based on query terms but not by individual users. Haveliwala (2002) introduces the topic-sensitive PageRank scheme, which personalizes PageRank values by giving different weights to pages, one for each topic listed in the open directory. Recently, Qui and Cho (2006) proposed a formal framework for learning the user's interest and used that knowledge for further improvement of the search quality of the topic-sensitive PageRank.

SEARCH PERSONALIZATION

In this chapter, we introduce a formal framework to investigate the problem of identifying a user's search interests through the semantic analysis of the user's previous searches. The proposed model explores a topical ontology for disambiguating user-issued queries as well as for identifying the user's hidden search interests. Throughout the user's search preferences detection process, there is no burden put on the user as no feedback (neither implicit nor explicit) is asked from the user. Additionally, we equip our proposed model with a ranking function which measures the pages' relevance to the query semantics and orders them in way that reflects the correlation between the users' interests and the page's contents. Based on a combined analysis of the users' interests and the pages' relevance values, our model personalizes retrieved results by prioritizing among a set of query-relevant pages those whose contents match the respective users' preferences.

Motivation

The main intuition for building our model is that every search query communicates implicit information about the topic preferences of the user. Based on this assumption, the problem of identifying a user's search interests translates into finding the topics of the queries issued to a search engine by that user. For the effective query topic detection, we build upon previous work (i.e., Stamou, Ntoulas, & Christodoulakis, 2007), where we showed the contribution of a topical ontology for annotating Web pages with suitable topical categories. Here, we expand our work and propose a model that automatically identifies the user's preferences through the analysis of the user's past searches. In particular, we investigate the correlation between the semantics of the user's queries and the semantics of the Web pages that the user has visited in response to each of those queries in order to build that user's profile.

User Interests Detection

Considering the multitude of topics that are discussed over the Web, it is reasonable to assume that a Web user is primarily interested in a small subset of topics in the user's Web transactions. Moreover, assuming that a Web user has a particular interest in mind every time the user searches for information on the Web, we might conclude that every query issued by the user communicates implicit information about a given interest at the time of query submission. Based on these assumptions, we try to learn the user's search preferences based on the semantic analysis of the user's past queries. The main challenges that we have to deal with summarize to the following: first, we need to associate every query previously issued by the user with a particular interest, and second, we need to identify among a set of interests that might be associated with the same query across its submissions a single user preference. In the end, we need to combine the different user interests, each corresponding to a number of past search queries, into a rich user profile that reflects the user's general search preferences.

For the first challenge, we leverage the Word-Net lexical ontology (Fellbaum, 1998) in order to analyze a user's past clickthrough data and disambiguate the intention associated with each of the user's past queries. Having deciphered the user's preferences that are latent behind the user's previous queries, we try to deal with the second challenge, that is, how to select among a set of possibly distinct interests that characterize the same query across its different submissions a single general preference that characterizes the user's intentions. Finally, we show how we can combine the interests learned from each of the user's queries in order to build a user profile that corresponds to the user's search preferences.

For disambiguating the intention of every query previously issued by the user, our method operates upon the semantics of the pages that the user has visited in response to that query. More specifically, we collect for every query that the user has issued the number of pages that the user has visited and we also record the amount of time the user spent on those pages. Assuming that the time the user devotes on reading a page is analogous to the page's size (i.e., amount of content), we firstly normalize the time interval the user spent on every page by that page's size. Thereafter, we process the contents of all the pages visited by the user for a single query for more that 30 seconds in order to derive information about their semantic content. Processing the visited pages accounts to hypertext markup language (HTML) parsing in order to remove markup, tokenization, POS-tagging, and lemmatization. Thereafter, we rely on the pages' nouns and we map them to their corresponding WordNet nodes in order to identify, for every noun inside a page, a suitable concept for representing its meaning. In case a term extracted from a visited page matches several WordNet nodes (i.e., it's a polysemous term), we rely on the Resnik (1995) similarity metric in order to annotate every term with a concept that is most likely to express that term's semantics.

Having annotated every noun inside a query-visited page with an appropriate concept, the next step is to identify the topical categories to which these concepts correspond. In other words, we need to group the pages' concepts into topical clusters that represent the pages' semantic content. Topical clustering is enabled though the exploitation of a topical ontology that we have built in the course of an earlier study (Stamou et al., 2007) and which contains a number of topics borrowed from the open directory taxonomy enriched with their corresponding WordNet lexical hierarchies. In brief, our approach works as follows: given the topical ontology and a set of concepts that have been assigned to the pages' nouns, we compute the likelihood that every concept represents (i.e., semantically relates to) each of the ontology's topics. For our computations, we rely on the distance that the noun-matching concepts have to each of the ontology's topical concepts (i.e., top level categories) so that the closest a noun-matching concept is to a topical node the greatest the probability that it belongs to that topic. Based on the above, we estimate the probability with which each of the ontology's topics is expressive of the query matching pages' terms as a function that averages the concept-topic probabilities over the pages' terms. At the end of this process, we represent every page that the user has visited for a single query as a set of topics weighted by their probability of being expressive of the pages' concepts. Based on the above information, we rely on the topical category that exhibits the greatest probability for representing the visited pages' semantics as the category that describes the query intention.

After annotating every query in the user's search logs with a suitable topical category, the next step is to identify a single topic for representing a query that has been issued multiple times by the user, but every time with a different interest in mind. In particular, we need to ensure that each query corresponds to a single topic and as such we need to eliminate multiple query topic annotations. In this direction, we first identify the query keywords that have been associated with multiple ontology topics and we employ our topical ontology in order to explore any underlying correlation between these topics. In other words, we try to identify whether there is a semantic correlation between the different ontology topics computed by our method for describing the query intention. In doing so, we essentially try to capture whether there is a single search interest latent behind a particular query or whether the query intended the retrieval of different information sources in terms of semantic content. For estimating the correlation between the different query matching topics, we basically rely on the semantic relations that connect the query matching topics in the ontology and upon their identification we compute their semantic distance as the number of nodes that need to be traversed in the ontology graph in order to reach from one topical node to

the other. Query-matching topics that do correlate in the ontology graph are deemed as semantically similar and as such we employ their most specific common subsumer as a more general topic that can successfully represent the query intention. On the other hand, in case the query matching topics exhibit no semantic correlation with each other in the ontology graph, we retain all identified topics for describing that query's intention. At the end of this process, we end up with the most suitable topical categories for representing each of the user's past queries.

We now turn our attention on how we can combine the topics associated with the user's previous searchers in order to build that user's profile. Recall that every query previously issued by the user is represented as a set of topics weighted by their probability of expressing the query intention. To build the user profile we concatenate the queries annotated with the same topical category into a single user interest and we sum the query-topic probabilities in order to derive the degree of the user preference in each the underlying topics. Having computed the user interest in each of the topics expressed by the user's past queries, we model the user's profile as a set of weighted topics, each one representing the user's preferences. We finally sort the topics identified for building the user's profile in terms of interest and we store them locally in order to utilize them in the user's future searches. In the following section, we present a ranking formula that takes the identified user interests into account while ordering search results. Before that, let us outline some practical issues pertaining to our user profiling method so that it can be fruitfully employed by others. Our method is completely automated in the sense that it does not ask for the user involvement in the profiling process. The only prerequisites for our model is a Web transactions recording module that collects information about the user's Web searches and clickthrough data, and a topical ontology that helps us disambiguate the query intentions and utilize them for estimating the general user interests. However, our method is not bound to a particular ontology or query sense detection model and it can be fruitfully employed for any ontology or word sense disambiguation technique that one would like to use.

Topic-Specific Rankings

Having introduced our approach to the automatic identification of the users' search preferences, we now suggest the utilization of a topic-specific ranking function for ordering retrieved results in response to a query in a way that the most important pages in a topic show up first. The baseline ranking function upon which our model operates for personalizing search results can be any of those that have been proposed in the literature. In the course of this study, we employ the traditional query-page relevance metric as the core ranking formula and we further extend it by encapsulating the identified user interests in the results' ordering process. In other words, our proposed personalized ranking considers not only the correlation between the query and each of the retrieved documents but it also considers the correlation between the identified user interests and the semantics of the returned pages, in order to determine the ordering of search results.

More specifically, given that our model represents the user interests as a set of topics, weighted by their degree of preference, we first need to model Web pages in an analogous manner. That is, we need to represent pages as a set of weighted topics, and based on this representation, to estimate the likelihood that each of the pages' topics will satisfy the user's search interests. For modeling documents as a set of weighted topics, we proceed as before and rely on WordNet for disambiguating the pages' terms. Thereafter, we turn to our topical ontology for computing a set of topical categories that are likely to describe the pages' contents. Having modeled user interests and pages' contents as a set of weighted topics,

the next step is to combine this data into a single function for ordering search results.

As said before, our ranking function operates upon the traditional IR query page similarity values in order to determine a baseline ordering for the query-marching pages, that is, the pages that contain the query keywords. Query-page similarity is essentially based on the vector space model and estimates the degree to which each of the query matching pages relates to the given query. In particular, we represent every page p that contains the query keywords as a vector $p = <w_{p1}, w_{p2}, ..., w_{pm}>$ and we also represent every query q containing m keywords as a vector $q = <w_{q1}, w_{q2}, ..., w_{qm}>$. We then estimate the query-page similarity as

$$sim(p, q) = \sum_{k=1}^{m} w_{pk} \times w_{qk}$$

Based on the above similarity measure we measure the degree to which each of the query matching documents relates to the query. Based on the above, we determine a baseline ordering for the query matching pages in the search results. Our next step is to personalize this ordering so that the query-relevant pages that match the user's interests show up first in the list of search results. For personalizing the delivered rankings, we first measure the degree to which each of the returned pages matches the user's interests. To enable that, we compute the similarity between the topics identified for representing the user's interests and the topics detected for representing the pages' semantic content.

Topical similarity values are computed in the ontology's graph and they essentially rely on the amount of information that the examined topical concepts share in common. Specifically, consider that the user is interested in topics T_a, T_b and T_c with preferences P_a for the topic T_a, P_b for the topic T_b and P_c for topic T_c. Assume also that a query matching page contains concepts that belong to topics T_a and T_b. To estimate the probability that the pages matches the user's profile we compute the paired similarity values between the concepts representing topics T_a, T_b, and T_c in the ontology graph. Similarity is defined as the number of concepts that two topical concepts share in common (Resnik, 1995) and is formally given by:

$$sim(c_i, c_j) = -\log(mscs(c_i, c_j))$$

Where c_i and c_j are the concepts representing a pair of topics and *mscs* is the most specific common subsumer of c_i and c_j in the ontology graph. The measure of the most specific common subsumer (*mscs*) depends on (i) the length of the shortest path from the root to the most specific common subsumer of c_i and c_j and (ii) the density of concepts on this path. Based on the above formula we compute paired similarity values between the topics used to represent the user's interests and the topics that correspond to the pages' concepts. We then rely on the average similarity values between the page and the user's interesting topics in order to derive the probability that a user interested in topic T_k will prefer page p discussing topic T_i as:

$$P(p, u) = \sum sim(T_i, T_k)$$

Where P(p,u) denotes the estimated user preference for page p and *sim* (T_i, T_k) denotes the average similarity values between the topic T_i discussed in p and the topic T_k identified as interesting to the user.

Having computed the degree to which each of the retrieved pages relates to the query and having also estimated the degree of the user's preference in each of the returned pages, we put those measures together to determine the ordering of the retrieved pages in the search results so that these are tailored to the user's interests. Formally, our personalized ranking function determines the ordering of search results as the sum of the pages' relevance to the query keywords and the

pages' preference by the user issuing the query, given by:

$$Rank(p) = sim(p, q) + P(p, u)$$

Based on the above, we can estimate the ranking of every page returned in response to some query and ensure that the ordering of search results will reflect not only their similarity to the query keywords but also their closeness to the query intention. Note that in case the topic discussed in a returned page is of no interest to the user (i.e., P(p.u)=0) then the ordering of that page will solely rely on its relevance to the query.

Based on the process described above, our ranking algorithm prioritizes among a set of query relevant pages the ones that are most likely to be preferred by the user, thus it personalizes search results. Finally, note that our ranking function is not bound to a particular baseline ranking scheme and as such it can be fruitfully combined with any other ranking formula that one would like to use. One such option is to employ the PageRank function that considers the pages' popularity in conjunction to the pages' query relatedness in order to derive a baseline ranking for the retrieved results, and based on the delivered ordering, to apply our personalization approach in order to refine the ordering of search results in a personalized manner.

FUTURE TRENDS AND CONCLUSION

In this chapter, we investigated the search personalization problem and we have presented a novel framework which automatically learns the users' search interests based on the analysis of their past clickthrough data. In particular, we investigated how a topical ontology serves towards annotating the user-issued queries with a suitable topic. The topics assigned to the user-issued queries represent the search interests of the respective users. Moreover, we have proposed a ranking framework that takes the identified user interests into account in order to sort search results in a way that reflects the probability that the user will prefer each of the pages retrieved in response to a query.

In the future we plan, on the one hand, to extensively evaluate the performance of our method in personalizing Web search by comparing it to the performance of other rankings schemes, such as the topic-sensitive PageRank (Haveliwala, 2002) or the personalized topic-sensitive PageRank scheme (Qui & Cho, 2006). On the other hand, we plan to expand our framework to take rich models of user interests into account, such as users' activity while visiting a page, e-mail, bookmarks information, and so forth.

REFERENCES

Aktas, M., Nacar, N., & Menczer, F. (2004). Personalizing PageRank based on domain profiles. In *Proceedings of the KDD Workshop on Web Mining and Web Usage* (pp. 83-90).

Chen, L., & Sycara, K. (2004). Webmate: A personal agent for browsing and searching. In *Proceedings of the 2nd International Conference on Autonomous Agents & Multiagent Systems* (pp. 132-139).

Dai, H., & Mobasher, B. (2002). Using ontologies to discover domain-level Web usage profiles. In *Proceedings of the 2nd Workshop on Semantic Web Mining*, Finland.

Fellbaum, C. (1998). *WordNet: An electronic lexical database*. MIT Press.

Haveliwala, T. (2002). Topic sensitive PageRank. In *Proceedings of the 11th International World Wide Web Conference* (pp. 517-526).

Jeh, G., & Widom, J. (2003). Scaling personalized Web search. In *Proceedings of the 12th International World Wide Web Conference* (pp. 271-279).

Kearney, P., & Anand, S.S. (2005). Employing a domain ontology to gain insight into user behavior. In *Proceedings of the 3rd Workshop on Intelligent Techniques for Web Personalization*, Scotland.

Kelly, D., & Teevan, J. (2003). Implicit feedback for inferring user preference: A bibliography. *SIGIR Forum, 32*(2), 18-28.

Oberle, D., Berendt, B., Hotho, A., & Gonzalez, J. (2003). Conceptual user tracking. In *Proceedings of the 1st Atlantic Web Intelligence Conference*.

Page, L., Brin, S., Motwani, R., & Winograd, T. (1998). *The PageRank citation ranking: Bringing order to the Web* (Tech. Rep.). Stanford University Database Group. Retrieved August 26, 2008, from http://dbpubs.stanford.edu:8090/pub/1999-66.

Pazzani, M., Muramatsu, J., & Billsus, D. (1996). Syskill & Webert: Identifying interesting Web sites. In *Proceedings of the 13th National Conference on Artificial Intelligence*, Portland (pp. 54-61).

Powel, A. L., French, J. C., Callan, J. P., & Connell, M. (2002). The impact of database selection on distributed searching. In *Proceedings of the SIGIR Conference*.

Pretschner, A., & Gauch, S. (1999). Ontology-based personalized search. In *Proceedings of the 11th IEEE International Conference on Tools with Artificial Intelligence* (pp. 391-398).

Qui, F., & Cho, J. (2006). Automatic identification of user interest for personalized search. In *Proceedings of the 15th International World Wide Web Conference* (pp. 727-236).

Resnik, P. (1995). Disambiguating noun groupings with respect to WordNet senses. In *Proceedings of the 3rd Workshop on Very Large Corpora*. MIT Press.

Richardson, M., & Domingos, R. (2002). The intelligent surfer: Probabilistic combination of link and content information in PageRank. *Advances in Neural Information Processing Systems, 14.* MIT Press.

Shen, X., & Zhai, C. X. (2003). Exploiting query history for document ranking in interactive information retrieval. In *Proceedings of the SIGIR Conference* (pp. 377-378).

Speretta, M., & Gauch, S. (2004). Personalizing search based in user search history. In *Proceedings of the CIKM Conference.*

Stamou, S., Ntoulas, A., & Christodoulakis, D. (2007). TODE: An ontology based model for the dynamic population of Web directories. *Data management with ontologies: Implementations, findings and frameworks.* Hershey, PA: IGI Global, Inc.

Sugiyama, K., Hatano, K., & Yoshikawa, M. (2004). Adaptive Web search based on user profile constructed without any effort from users. In *Proceedings of the 13th International World Wide Web Conference* (pp. 675-684).

Sun, J., Zeng, H., Liu, H., Lu, Y., & Chen, Z. (2005). CubeSVD: A novel approach to personalized Web search. In *Proceedings of the 14th International World Wide Web Conference* (pp. 382-390).

Teevan, J., Dumais, S., & Horvitz, E. (2005). Personalizing search via automated analysis of interests and activities. In *Proceedings of the 28th International Conference on Research and Development in Information Retrieval* (pp. 449-456).

Tzekou, P., Stamou, S., Kozanidis, L., & Zotos, N. (2007, December 16-19). Effective site customization based on Web semantics and usage mining. In *Proceedings of the 3rd International IEEE SITIS Conference: Information Management and Retrieval Technologies Track*, Shanghai, China.

Yu, C., Meng, W., Wu, W., & Liu, K. (2001). Efficient and effective metasearch for text databases incorporating linkages among documents. In *Proceedings of the ACM SIGMOD Conference.*

KEY TERMS

Collaborative Filtering: The method of making automatic predictions (filtering) about the interests of a user by collecting taste information from many users (collaborating). The underlying assumption of collaborative filtering approach is that those who agreed in the past tend to agree again in the future.

Open Directory: The Open Directory Project (ODP) is a multilingual open content directory of World Wide Web links that is constructed and maintained by a community of volunteer editors.

PageRank: A link analysis algorithm which assigns a numerical weighting to each element of a hyperlinked set of documents, such as the World Wide Web, with the purpose of "measuring" its relative importance within the set. The algorithm may be applied to any collection of entities with reciprocal quotations and references. The numerical weight that it assigns to any given element E is also called the *PageRank of E* and denoted by $PR(E)$.

Search Engine: A search engine is an information retrieval system designed to help find information stored on a computer system, such as on the World Wide Web, inside a corporate or proprietary network, or in a personal computer.

Search Personalization: Search results customization for specific interests is widely known as *personalized search*. Personalized search has a significant potential in providing users with information that greatly satisfies their particular search intentions.

Topical Ontology: In both computer science and information science, an ontology is a data model that represents a set of concepts within a domain and the relationships between those concepts. It is used to reason about the objects within that domain.

WordNet: WordNet is a semantic lexicon for the English language. It groups English words into sets of synonyms called *synsets*, provides short, general definitions, and records the various semantic relations between these synonym sets. The purpose is twofold: to produce a combination of dictionary and thesaurus that is more intuitively usable, and to support automatic text analysis and artificial intelligence applications.

Chapter XIX
Guidelines for Developing Digital Cultural Collections

Irene Lourdi
National & Kapodistrian University of Athens, Greece

Mara Nikolaidou
Harokopio University of Athens, Greece

ABSTRACT

This chapter presents basic guidelines for maintaining digital cultural collections in order for them to be interoperable and easily retrievable from users. The requirements of cultural material are discussed and it is shown how in combination with the adequate metadata schema policy a digital cultural collection can cover the various needs for learning and retrieving information. The authors emphasize the fact that various metadata schemas are used for describing cultural collections and that this leads to problems for interoperability. It is analyzed that while designing a digital collection, the internal structure of material must be followed and the metadata model must cover specific needs; furthermore, a data preservation policy is a considerable issue in the digital era.

INTRODUCTION

Cultural heritage, especially in the digital era, is the cornerstone of the unique identity of a society or a nation; cultural heritage sources enable people to anchor themselves in a historical period, create a reference framework for their way of living, and provide a value base for their lives. Thus, cultural heritage can be perceived as a multidimensional and multiform representation of a nation or a society over time and place. In view of cultural material importance, the last few years many digitization projects related to cultural collections have taken place, trying to expose their material to a wider audience through the Web. Most of these digitization efforts are following guidelines published by international organizations and are based on general practices and experiences gained from similar projects.

In the following, guidelines are discussed considering the requirements and issues concerning the planning and organizing of a digital cultural collection in order to be functional for all user categories and easily retrievable through the Web. The focused issues are: i) material organization and management policy, ii) metadata standards, and iii) data preservation practices. There is a great need for cultural institutions (e.g., library, museum, or archives) to offer wide and easy access to qualitative cultural data demands to approach all the issues above from an integrated aspect without concerning institutional or national boundaries. Proposals need to satisfy various and sometimes different information seeking behaviours by always keeping the authenticity and integrity of cultural material.

MATERIAL ORGANIZATION AND MANAGEMENT POLICY

Cultural heritage institutions should adjust their digital collection planning according to user needs and the nature of material. In most cases, cultural collections contain heterogeneous material with unique characteristics, like written texts, photographs, physical objects, sound recordings, maps, or even born-digital material. Consequently, it is justifiable to have collections and subcollections with complex structure and rich semantics.

Since cultural objects are heterogeneous, they should be grouped according to criteria either, facilitating users with easy access or expressing internal standards following the holding institution (owner of the collection). As such, criteria can be, for instance, the topic coverage, the specific usage or purpose that each resource has in the context of the collection, the provenance, the type of material, or the geographic region and historical period the object covers. It is useful to create subcollections (if they do not preexist), since it is easier to represent composite structures and accredit rich semantics to any level. By defining specific groups of objects, the whole collection and subcollections can easily be manipulated as separate objects with their characteristics and metadata elements; like all the other digital items, the attributes inherited from the collection to subcollections are identified and the overall collection can be effectively navigated by users (Lourdi, 2005).

In case a cultural heritage collection consists of composite objects like texts with photographs or traditional dressings, it is a good practice to separate them into their parts and represent their structure. Composite objects must be decomposed into their disparate parts since it is possible to characterize them individually with the appropriate metadata elements, as it is proposed above.

Besides material organization, another crucial issue for a cultural collection is the management policy, and more specifically the administration policy. In a digitization project, it is important to preserve the holding institution policy concerning the access restrictions and material protection rules. For instance, whether it is about unique and rare material with copyright issues or the purposes of the institution is not to provide the material freely to audience, digital collection plan shall respect these matters and shall not give full access to a collection and its contents.

The most prevailing factor for a digitization project is material preservation. Most cultural heritage institutions consider digitization as the best solution for preserving rare and vulnerable material in the future. So for administration purposes, a digital collection shall follow the most accepted digitization practices and shall preserve all the information related with digitization process and devices.

The main requirements for the cultural information management and dissemination process can be summarized by the following: a) the material should preserve its unique characteristics; b) the semantic context of the collection and of its objects should be expressed clearly; and c) cultural data should be retrievable at any structural information level. It is obvious that for manipulating and representing cultural information objects, which are characterized by complexity and intense heterogeneity, rich and flexible metadata models are required, capable of encapsulating and manipulating contextual information.

METADATA MODEL/STANDARDS

In the current digital environment, users are called to find information among various resources without easily being able to criticize and define whether it is of their interest. For this reason the basic parameter in a digitization project is to characterize meaningfully the material with the metadata model. For this purpose, many metadata standards have been developed either by international committees or by local projects describing cultural heritage collections and providing semantically-rich information to users.

Metadata Model Requirements

The metadata model for a cultural collection ought to contain features that will provide users with effective services to access and retrieve data about the objects either by browsing the collections or by searching those using keywords. Metadata authoring practices must be compliant with community accepted standard schema(s).

The metadata model needs to be focused both on collection entity and item level. Collection-level description allows users to search for information across all kinds of memory institutions and domains, enabling them to identify appropriate collections to visit or item-level searching. High-level collection description is important in order to help the navigation, discovery, and selection of cultural content (Dempsey, 1999). The collection-level description simplifies the retrieval of information because the user can decide whether the collection is of interest without getting into details about the objects and also contributes to

better administration of large collections. Thus, it is required to offer a detailed collection- and subcollection-level description with the appropriate metadata elements, after specifying the structure of the collection.

Librarians' understanding of the descriptive and analytical needs of three-dimensional objects has to be expanded. The descriptive metadata needs not only to support the subject coverage of the items but also to:

a. Express the relationships between digital objects. It is necessary to represent all kinds of relations that exist inside and outside the collection throughout structural levels, in order to provide the users with all the information that is hidden in the collection. For example, the relation between a photograph referenced on a text page and the actual photograph belonging in the photographs subcollection—probably in another format- - should be identified (e.g., "has format" or "is converted to" or "is the same with").

b. Contain elements concerning the digitization process and the digital surrogates of the items (technical metadata). This is considered important mainly for preservation reasons and for protecting digital sources from future risks (e.g., data transfer, operational system changes, physical destructions, etc.) (Patel et al., 2005).

c. Inform about the copyrights and material usage restrictions (administrative metadata). This is a strong necessity in order to keep all the valuable information for the preservation, authenticity, and retrieval of information.

In general, the main metadata principles for a cultural collection are: a) to be appropriate for the described material, users, and future uses; b) to support interoperability, standard, and controlled vocabulary employed to reflect content and a clear statement of conditions/terms of use; c) support the long term management of objects in the collection (distinctions: administrative, technical, and preservation metadata) (NISO, 2004); and d) metadata records should be considered as objects themselves and so they should have the qualities of good objects and should be authoritative and verifiable.

Metadata Standards/Interoperability Matters

Information retrieval from heterogeneous resources is quite difficult since each memory institution (i.e., museum, library, and archives) follows different material administration and metadata generation policies. Due to the diversity of museum, archives, and library management perspectives, it is impossible to create a single metadata schema meeting almost all the communities' needs (Gill, 2004). Therefore, a plethora of general standards and local community-specific metadata models have evolved for the documentation of cultural collections. Parallel technologies for description have been developed, meaning that they employ different data structures, data content rules, and (to some extent) data formats to encode their collections. It is not possible to describe all the existing metadata standards for cultural heritage collections but a general statement about them is documented in the next paragraphs and emphasis is given in matters of interoperability.

The existing metadata standards for cultural collections and items can be separated in two categories: according to the coverage domain and according to the description level. For instance, concerning the domain, there are metadata standards that are used by libraries (e.g., MARC and MODS), others by museum collections (e.g., CDWA, VRA, SPECTRUM), and those by archives (e.g., EAD). Besides them, there also exist some metadata standards for general use like Dublin Core and RSLP. On the other hand, concerning the description level, some of the above standards cover item-level description while others cover collection-level description ("Dublin Core collection description application profile"; RSLP).

At this point, no one can claim which metadata schema is the most appropriate to apply. Nevertheless, the best practice for designing a "good" metadata model for a cultural collection is to be compatible with general practices and protocols that contribute to the effective resource discovery and to the maintenance of a high level of consistency. A source that can be used as reference are the "descriptive metadata guidelines" for RLG cultural materials, which negotiate the different practices in the communities by establishing a guide to description that can be applied in any case (RLG, 2005). So, the metadata schema for a cultural collection needs to include all kinds of data: descriptive (describe the resources intellectual content), structural (document the structure of the objects and the relationships between them), and administrative (provide information about the digitization process and the collection preservation).

The above aspects are based on the expectation to assure the greatest interoperability with other projects and applications and to be able to exchange and transfer data from other systems. Let us not forget current user needs for access to all available information across the board of digital libraries and virtual museums address information professionals to give priority to the task of creating the highest feasible level of interoperability among metadata models. Maintaining interoperable collection-level and object-level metadata enhance the facility to aggregate and disaggregate content from multiple heterogeneous resources, without thinking of the type of holding institutions. For this reason, in recent years, numerous projects have been undertaken in the information community to achieve interoperability among different metadata schemas. Some of the mechanisms that have addressed metadata interoperability are the following: crosswalks/ mappings, application profiles/modification, metadata framework/container, and protocols.

Many papers have been written about the challenging issues of creating crosswalks between standards but they are still considered to be a widely applied solution. There have been a substantial number of crosswalks like: MARC21 to Dublin Core, VRA to Dublin Core, EAD to ISAD, and so forth. The concept of *application profiles* is based on the idea that in the heterogeneous information environment each community has different characteristics; consequently, metadata standards are necessarily localized and optimized for specific requirements. So to cover various user needs, it is often required to mix elements from separate metadata schemas and to customize them according to local requirements. *A metadata framework* is used as a container within which fields from multiple metadata schemas can be accommodated. For instance resource description framework (RDF) and metadata encoding and transmission standard (METS) are considered to be examples At last, *protocols* for data share between various digital services ensure the data communication and transfer among digital library services. The most public protocol for metadata share is the OAI-PMH that supports standardized exchange of metadata, describing items in diffused collections.

In general, for covering the needs of a cultural collection with heterogeneous material and composite structure, there are two prevailing aspects:

- To design a metadata model that will be based on a widely accepted standard (a core schema like DC) and further extend it to cover other required aspects, such as: i) the technique of digitization and the technical requirements; ii) meta-metadata information because of the heterogeneous material; and iii) the educational character and the purpose of every resource. change it according to project needs (either by extending it with additional local elements or with elements from other metadata standards).

- To combine or apply different metadata standards in order to cover all the formats and types of physical and digital objects (e.g., text, sound, image, etc.) and create afterwards mappings between these standards or mappings from these standards to only one schema for reasons of interoperability, persistency, and querying processes (Cornell University, 2001).

Since memory institutions handle all types of material, the need for information integration is quite apparent. The goals of cultural heritage communities to provide wide usefulness, portability (across networks, systems, organizations), and longevity of digital cultural resources are encapsulated by having interoperability between the metadata standards and models they use (Gill et al., 2002).

DATA PRESERVATION POLICY

Each organization dealing with digitization projects should also implement preservation standards widely used from the international cultural community. The fact that information is increasingly stored in digital form makes data preservation policy a considerable issue for a cultural digital collection to manage. A preservation metadata set is intended to include the elements that are believed to facilitate digital information resources persistency. It is meant to be not only a data input model, but also a data output model. It indicates the information we want our metadata system to preserve (i.e., what data should be entered, how it should be entered, by whom, and at what time) and also the information we want to take from the system for a digital resource. In other words, preservation metadata is the structured information that describes, explains, locates, or otherwise makes it easier to retrieve, use, or manage an information resource.

So a digital project needs to design and clarify the preservation metadata set that is preferred to be kept for digital objects. The model needs to contain information about the digital object *provenance* (Who has had custody/ownership of the digital object?), *authenticity, any preservation activity* (What has been done to preserve the digital object?), *technical environment,* and *rights management.* There are some quite remarkable efforts that deal with this matter, such as OAIS reference model, PREMIS, CEDARS guide, and many others.

CONCLUSION

Crucial factors in designing an effective and flexible digital cultural collection are interoperability, verification, documentation, reusability, persistence, and so forth. Except from the selection of digital repository system, focus should be given to the issues of composite collection/objects description, metadata definition, and project purposes, but there are not strict rules to follow. In order to manage and expose the wealth of composite cultural heritage collections, a functional metadata policy covering collection-level and item-level descriptions as well as facilitating effective access to digital content should be defined. This policy, in most cases, results in the integration of more the one metadata schemes. Furthermore, there are metadata interoperability issues since a variety of metadata standards are used to describe heterogeneous material collections. The basic purpose is to create a cultural digital collection that will serve not only local needs but will be reusable in new and innovative contexts.

The most important indicators for an effective planning of a cultural digital collection are whether: a) users can easily find the information they need (information retrieval); b) the digital collection administrator is able to preserve and locate digital data and manage big collections without much effort (functionality); c) digital planning respects the institution's management policy and priorities; d) there is respect for the intellectual property rights; and e) digital information resources fit into a larger context of significant related national and international digital library initiatives (i.e., ability to contribute metadata to more inclusive search engines) and be exchangeable across platforms.

REFERENCES

Categories for the Description of Works of Art (CDWA). Retrieved August 20, 2008, from http://www.getty.edu/research/institute/standards/cdwa/

Cornell University. (2001). Mixing and mapping metadata to provide integrated access to digital Library collections. In *Proceedings of the International Conference on Dublin Core and Metadata Applications (DC-2001),* Japan. Retrieved August 20, 2008, from http://www.nii.ac.jp/dc2001/proceedings/product/paper-23.pdf

Dempsey, L. (1999). Scientific, industrial, and cultural heritage: A shared approach. *Ariadne, 22.* Retrieved August 20, 2008, from http://www.ariadne.ac.uk/issue22/

Dublin Core collection description application profile. Retrieved August 20, 2008, from http://www.ukoln.ac.uk/metadata/dcmi/collection-application-profile/2003-08-25/

Dublin Core Metadata Initiative (DCMI). Retrieved August 20, 2008, from http://dublincore.org/

Encoded archival description (EAD). Retrieved August 20, 2008, from http://www.loc.gov/ead/

Gill, T. (2004, May 3). Building semantic bridges between museums, libraries and archives: The CIDOC conceptual reference model. *First Monday, 9*(5). Retrieved August 20, 2008, from http://www.firstmonday.org/

Gill, T. et al. (2002, January). Re-inventing the wheel? Standards, interoperability and digital cultural content. *D-Lib Magazine, 8*(1). Retrieved August 20, 2008, from http://www.dlib.org/dlib/january02/01contents.html

Joint Information Systems Committee (JISC). *Cedars project.* Retrieved August 20, 2008, from http://www.leeds.ac.uk/cedars/indexold.htm

Library of Congress. (2004). *Metadata encoding and transmission standard (METS).* Retrieved August 20, 2008, from http://www.loc.gov/standards/mets/

Library of Congress. (2005). *Machine readable cataloging 21 (MARC 21).* Retrieved August 20, 2008, from http://www.loc.gov/marc/

Library of Congress. (2006). *Metadata object description schema (MODS).* Retrieved August 20, 2008, from http://www.loc.gov/standards/mods/

Lourdi, E., Nikolaidou, M., & Papatheodorou, C. (2004, December 27-29). Implementing digital folklore collections. In *Proceedings of ISCA Third International Conference on Computer Science, Software Engineering, Information Technology, e-Business, and Applications (CSITeA-04)*, Cairo, Egypt.

MDA. *SPECTRUM units of information.* Retrieved August 20, 2008, from http://www.mda.org.uk/spectrum.htm/

NSO. (2004). *Understanding metadata.* NISO Press.

Patel, M., et al. (2005, May). Metadata requirements for digital museum environments. *International Journal on Digital Libraries, 5*(3), 179-192. Retrieved August 20, 2008, from http://www.springerlink.com

Research Libraries Group. (2005). Descriptive metadata guidelines for RLG cultural materials. *RLG.* Retrieved August 20, 2008, from http://www.rlg.org/en/pdfs/RLG_desc_metadata.pdf

Research Support Libraries Program (RSLP). *Collection description schema.* Retrieved August 20, 2008, from http://www.ukoln.ac.uk/metadata/rslp/

RLG and the library consortium OCLC. (2005). *Preservation metadata maintenance activity.* Retrieved August 20, 2008, from http://www.loc.gov/standards/premis/

The open archives initiative protocol for metadata harvesting. Retrieved August 20, 2008, from http://www.openarchives.org/

VRA core categories (2002, February 20). Retrieved August 20, 2008, from http://www.vraweb.org/vracore3.htm

W3C. *Resource description framework (RDF).* Retrieved August 20, 2008, from http://www.w3.org/RDF/

KEY TERMS

Application Profiles: They usually consist of multiple metadata elements drawn from one or more metadata schemas, combined into a compound schema, and optimized for a particular requirement.

Crosswalks: It is used to translate elements in one metadata schema into those in another metadata schema. It is one of the most commonly used methods to implement interoperability between metadata schemas. The mechanism is usually a table that represents the semantic mapping of data elements in one metadata schema (source) to those in another metadata schema (target) based on the similarity of meaning of the elements.

Digital Cultural Collection: It is a digital collection which contains digitized or born-digital cultural material.

Interoperability: The ability of two or more systems or components to exchange information and to use the exchanged information without special effort on either system.

Metadata: Metadata are data about data, that is, where that data are located and what they is used for. A good analogy is that of a library catalogue card which contains data about the nature and location of a book.

Metadata Container: It is the unit for aggregating the typed metadata sets, which are known as *packages*. A container may be either transient or persistent. In its transient form, it exists as a transport object between and among repositories, clients, and agents. In its persistent form, it exists as a first-class object in the information infrastructure. That is, it is stored on one or more servers and is accessible from these servers using a globally accessible identifier (URI). We note that a container may also be wrapped within another object (i.e., one that is a wrapper for both data and metadata). In this case the "wrapper" object will have a URI rather than the metadata container itself.

Chapter XX
Digital Libraries and Ontology

Neide Santos
Universidade do Estado do Rio de Janeiro, Brazil

Fernanda C. A. Campos
Universidade Federal de Juiz de Fora, Brazil

Regina M. M. Braga Villela
Universidade Federal de Juiz de Fora, Brazil

ABSTRACT

Nowadays, social, economical, cultural, and technological changes deeply stress the professional profiles. As a consequence, everyone needs to be continually improving his/her professional skills by means of different kinds of continuing learning or lifelong learning. This changeable context also stresses the teachers' job. Networking technologies can be useful in helping teachers to improve their skills anywhere (i.e., home, office, or school). However, the Web had grown up as a business space and has become an important repository of all kinds of information. As a result, searching information is a hard and slow process. Tools for data retrieval work at the syntactic level, disregarding the semantic aspects. Solutions show up to Web Semantic technologies. Our contribution is to develop a digital library for the e-learning specific domain using ontology-based semantic querying.

INTRODUCTION

Technological changes are deeply stressing professional profiles and people need to continually improve their professional skills using different kinds of lifelong learning. Networking technologies became widely adopted to promote lifelong learning. However, searching information on the Web is a hard process. Current search engines were developed to work as productivity tools, helping users to retrieve data by means of information retrieval at the syntactic level, disregarding the semantics aspect. Words have different meanings depending on the context. The Web, on the other hand, is organized as an information network without any hierarchy or navigational contexts. Users often feel lost and cognitively overloaded, and they not always find the information they are searching for. Solutions point to the Semantic Web (Bernes-Lee, Handler, & Lassila, 2001) and a *key point is the notion of ontology (Guarino, 1998).*

Aiming to help lifelong learning initiatives and improve information search at the Web, we are developing a digital library for the e-learning domain which main service is a search engine that retrieves information by tracing the domain vocabulary met on ontology (Santos, Campos, & Braga, 2005). Our digital library extends the Web portal's functionalities, providing technical information and communication and collaboration spaces, and hosts a wide variety of information (e.g., technical papers, Web sites of systems and tools, Web sites of Brazilian and international experience on e-learning, and some e-learning software artifacts to be used to create tailored e-learning applications). It provides services for cataloging, storing, searching, and retrieving information based on ontology-based semantic queries. The next sections argue domain ontology and e-learning ontology, describe the digital library, and offer the conclusions and future works.

Domain Ontology and e-learning Ontology

Ontology, in philosophy, refers to a conception of what can exist or "be" in the world. The artificial intelligence community has appropriated the term to mean the construction of *knowledge models* (Gruber, 1993), which specify concepts or objects, their attributes, and interrelationships. A knowledge model is a specification of a domain, or problem solving behavior, which abstracts from implementation-specific considerations and focuses instead on the concepts, relations, and reasoning steps in order to solve the problem (Shum, Motta, & Domingue, 2000).

Ontology specifies a shared understanding of a domain of interest and contains a set of concepts, together with its definitions and interrelationships, and possibly encodes a logical layer for inference and reasoning. The role of ontology is to reflect a community's consensus on a useful way to conceptualize a particular domain. Building ontology implies acquiring the domain knowledge and collecting appropriate information resources that will define, with consensus and consistency, the terms used formally to describe the domain of study.

Ontology is beginning to be used in the context of digital libraries for many different purposes. It can assist the extraction of concepts from unstructured textual documents (Embley, Campbell, Smith, & Liddle, 1998) by serving as a source of knowledge about the particular topic. In addition, it can also assist in managing documents descriptions in large digital libraries (Weinstein & Alloway, 1997).

The understanding about digital library is quite different according to its specific users. A digital library is a Web-based electronic storage and access environment for information stored in the digital format either locally in a library, in a group of networked libraries, or at a remote location (Cleveland, 1998). It also means an integrated set of services for capturing, cataloging, storing, searching, protecting, and retrieving information. It comprises digital collections, services, and infrastructure to support lifelong learning, research, scholarly communication, and preservation.

For many people the Web is not a digital library, because digital libraries are libraries with the same purposes, functions, and goals as traditional libraries, that is, collection development and management, subject analysis, index creation, provision of access, reference work, and preservation. Due to its inherent complexity, the current tendency in building digital libraries is to move forward in small, manageable, evolutionary steps, rather than in a rapid revolutionary manner. We are following this tendency.

Building ontology means different things to different practitioners. The distinction of how one carries out describing something reflects a progression in ontology: from simple lexicons or controlled vocabularies to categorically organized thesauri; to hierarchies called taxonomies where terms are given distinguishing properties; to full-blown ontologies where these properties can define new concepts and where concepts have named relationships with other concepts.

Ontology is composed of taxonomy and a set of inference rules (Berners-Lee et al., 2001). Taxonomy describes classes of objects and the relationships among them. If it is properly described, it preserves the specific meaning of terms and current expressions in knowledge domains. Taxonomy is not enough to put semantic on the Web because taxonomy information is expressed under stanched and self-constrained categories, subcategories, classes, and subclasses, in our ontology domains, subdomains, sectors, subsectors, functionalities, and subfuncitonalities. It restrains relationship of information not explicitly related. Our work assumes Berners-Lee vision of Web ontology, that is, we have built taxonomy and some inference rules about the domain. Our search engine works by sweeping the ontological terms and their relationships. We also adopted the notion of domain ontology (Guarino, 1998), that is, to organize the common vocabulary related to a generic domain (e.g., medicine or automobiles). One way to express a domain ontology is the employment of a feature model (Cohen, 1994) that specifies the domain vocabulary and shapes a semantic net of terms. The model captures the domain general features and allows the insertion of new terms as domains grow up.

Ontology development is necessarily an iterative process. The first steps to build an ontology imply delimitating the ontology scope, and acquiring and validating the domain knowledge. We must:

- Determine the domain and scope of the ontology,
- Enumerate important terms in the ontology,
- Define the classes and the class hierarchy and the properties of classes (i.e., slots and the facets of the slots), and
- Create instances.

In a pragmatic point of view, ontology is a set of concepts, properties, and restrictions. Properties of each concept describe features and attributes of the concept (slots, sometimes called roles or properties). Concepts are the focus of most ontologies, because they describe the classes in the domain (Noy & McGuinness, 2001). A class can have subclasses that represent concepts that are more specific than the super class. Slots describe properties of classes and instances. From this point of view, developing ontology includes:

- Defining classes in the ontology,
- Arranging the classes in a taxonomic (subclass–super class) hierarchy,
- Defining slots and describing allowed values for these slots, and,
- Filling in the values for slots for instances.

We start to specify the e-learning ontology, studying the related concepts and the domain. We have organized the domain vocabulary based on available works (e.g., Paulsen, 2002; The Learning Technology Standards Committee, 2001; the e-learning Cybrary, www1.). Our ontology embodies the main technical features of the e-learning domain as showed in Table 1, which presents the main subdomains, sectors, and subsectors.

The ontology was expressed using the ontology editor Protégé 2000 (www.protégé.stanford.edu). Protégé 2000 is a free, open source ontology editor and knowledge-base framework based on Java, and is extensible and provides a foundation for customized knowledge-based applications.

The digital library users can search information using any ontological term, and, based on one or more ontological terms, the search engine may expand the search using other related terms. In the particular case of our ontology, some inference rules were defined and expressed by a set of propositions. Table 2 details some of these rules to facilitate their comprehension.

In order to discover new ontological relationships, we defined a complementary set of rules

Table 1. E-learning technology subdomains, sectors, and subsectors

SUBDOMAINS	
Web-based Instruction (WBI)	Computer-Supported Cooperative Learning (CSCL)
SECTORS E SUBSECTORS	

Integrated and Distributed Learning Environments (IDLE)
    Course management systems
    Courses authoring systems
    Virtual classroom
    Online learning systems
    Distance courses
    Online didactic material
    Web-based contents
Educational Web sites
Educational Portals
<u>Digital libraries</u>
Virtual Universities
	CSCL Environments
	    Forums-based systems
	    MOO-based systems
	    Solving problems environments
	    Project-based learning environment
	    Text discussion-based environments
	    Coauthoring environments
	    Concepts learning-based environments
	CSCL Tools
	    Synchronous tools
	    Asynchronous tools
	Virtual Learning Communities
	    Chat-based communities
	    Virtual worlds communities

Table 2. E-learning ontology: Inference rules

RULES
All subdomains belong to a domain
All domains have at least a subdomain
All sectors belong to a subdomain All sectors may or not have a subsector
All sectors have at least a functionality
All functionalities may or not have a subfunctionality

to support the discovery process of new relationships into the same ontology or into a related ontology:

- **Synonym (A, B) → Synonym (B, A):** If term A has term B as synonym then term B has term A as synonym;
- **Hyponym (A, B) ^ Hyponym (B, C) → Hyponym (A, C):** If term A has term B as hyponym (more specialized term) and B has term C as hyponym then term A has term C as hyponym.

Representing the ontological terms of a domain demands one to specify a model for the domain that gathers together terms and functionality commonly used by the community. The features

model and the analysis of the different kinds of e-learning applications allow one to identify the common functionalities and to start the process of modeling the ontology. Table 1 presents a partial representation of the ontology subdomains, sectors, and subsectors. Each term of the sectors and subsectors were described and related to others related terms. The main functionalities, subfunctionalities, and specific functionalities of e-learning systems were also described. For example, the subsector virtual classroom, was defined as a "multi user environments in where online resources are used to facilitate the learning process among students, between students and instructors, and between a class and wider academic and non-academic community." It also can be defined as "a teaching and learning environment located within a Web based-instruction system."

A virtual classroom subsector encompasses many functionalities, subfunctionalities, and specific functionalities, converted in computational tools that support the work of its three kinds of users: the administrator, the instructor (or teacher or tutor), and the student.

Administrator tools congregate, for example, the functionality management system tools that in turn include one or more specific functionalities. These specific functionalities are known by terms such as authorization tools, security access, remote access tools, crash recovery tools, and so forth. Other functionality tools are course management tools, which include a set of tools or software facilities, defined by terms such as student support tools, instructor support tools, online registration, guest account creation, system installing tools, course fault retrieval tools, and resource monitoring.

Instructor tools include a set of functionality able to provide support to:

- Course development by means of many software functionality, designed by terms such as syllabus facilities, course materials editing tools, multimedia features, automated glossary tool, automated index tool, importing/exporting capabilities, links to supplemental resources capabilities, presenting information tools, and previewing courses resources.

- Students assessing by means of tools designed by terms such as assessing tools, self-evaluation, peer review, instruments of assessment, with specific functionalities, such as online testing, essays, *portfolios,* reports, tutorial, and automated grading tools.

Virtual classroom systems also offer a set of student tools, such as productivity tools that gather together many software functionalities, designed by terms as bookmarks, calendar, progress review, orientation/help, search tool for course content, student involvement tools, self-assessment, student community building, student portfolios, help online, online testing, file download, and file upload.

Digital library on E-learning Domain

Our digital library is a Web-based electronic storage and access environment for information stored in the digital format. It comprises digital collections, services, and infrastructure to support lifelong learning, research, scholarly communication, and preservation.

For many people, the Web is not a digital library, because digital libraries are libraries with the same purposes, functions, and goals as traditional libraries, that is, collection development and management, subject analysis, index creation, provision of access, reference work, and preservation. Due to its inherent complexity, the current tendency in building digital libraries is to move forward in small, manageable, evolutionary steps, rather than in a rapid revolutionary manner. We are following this tendency.

The key point to the successful use of our digital library is its search engine. Traditionally, available approaches are based on the use of keywords and often work by searching information at the syntactic level, returning to the user a large amount of unwished results. It happens because it is lacking descriptive information about information (metadata). In addition, it is also lacking the semantic about different vocabularies used to describe similar information into a same context. These issues decrease the quality and accuracy of many available search engines.

Digital libraries commonly use more sophisticated approaches. DLNET (Pushpagiri & Rahman, 2002), a digital library for lifelong learning on engineering and technology domains, for example, adopts other two approaches: an advanced search and a taxonomy-based browse search. A three-level taxonomy has been designed to subclassify the engineering field into two subgroups. Our approach is a bit different since it provides ontological search to guide semantic querying, by using domain ontology built from the features model basis. It is potentially more precise because the search goes deeper, searching information in a more detailed level of specificity. In order to provide the ontological search, each searchable information (i.e., documents, binary code, URLs, etc.) must be classified according to the domain terms. This classification is done by the digital library administrator, together with a domain engineer. Currently, it is a manual process but it will be improved soon with a semiautomatic mechanism based on agents. Successful matches require correctness in this classification of the information at the moment of its storage into the library database and it must follow closely the ontology terms.

We use a hypertree as a supporting tool for information organization and visualization. The hyperbolic representation system (Lamping, Rao, & Pirolli, 1995) has been used to create a site map that allows the user to identify rapidly searched information. Figure 1 shows a partial view of the ontological search graphical interface of our digital library for the sector of integrated and distributed learning environments (IDLE).

The library has three kinds of users to portray different information meanings and points of view:

- **Library administrators:** They insert and classify information according to ontology terms.
- **Domain experts:** They examine and classify information. They evaluate the relationship between stored information and user needs. They also evaluate the coherence between the information classification and the ontology terms. These users have access to an online Web feature that allows them to assign values to the presence of the semantic relationship of information and the domain vocabulary.
- **Library end users:** They utilize the search engine to find information that fulfills their needs. They use the ontology to select the terms related to their search, according to the interest features.

Word sense disambiguation in semantic analysis involves picking the correct set of senses in order to maximize the global needs. At this time,

this disambiguation is manual in our approach, that is, the disambiguation process is done by the domain engineer. It is so crucial for the approach success that we ask the expert users to explicit the straight of the relationship between the information to be inserted into the library and the ontology terms. It is a value that the experts and other library users assign to their classification of the information regarding the ontology terms. When experts and users classify information, they assign the relationship level of the information with ontology terms, following the ontology organization, that is.: subdomain, sector, subsector, functionalities, subfunctionalities, and specific functionalities. There are five relationship levels: tightly related (score 4), partially related (3), related (2), loosely related (1), and not related (score 0).

At the digital library, users can query using keywords or can use the ontological search:

- **Keyword search**: It aims to identify the ontology terms related to the words typed by users at the search engines interface. The engine searches the term, looking at the synonym database, and if it does not find any similarity, it searches for synonyms, hypernyms, hyponyms, and/or use rules described on Table 2 in the same ontology and also in related ontologies. In this manner, the search universe will be enlarged, but the search is more precise because it will involve different vocabulary for the same domain.
- **Ontological search**: The digital library presents a graphical interface with the ontological terms (Figure 1). The users browse for information, through the different hierarchical levels of the ontology, choosing at each level the interested terms. They must select one or more subdomain, one or more sectors, and one or more subsectors (see Table 2). They also can search terms for e-learning functionalities. The search engine shows first all functionalities and later all functionalities related to the chosen

Figure 1. The Ontological search graphical interface sector integrated and distributed learning environments (IDLE)

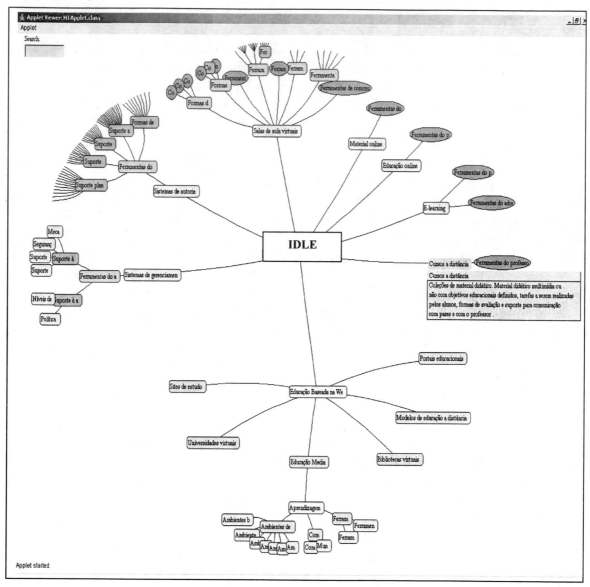

functionalities. At the end of this process, the search engine presents the list of matches related to the terms as information links.

The semantic issue also involves different vocabularies describing similar information in similar domains or contexts. This is a complex semantic problem that the digital library tries to solve using a set of complementary rules, to link *inter* and *intra* domains terms, providing the necessary mapping among terms of the same domain and of different domains. In addition, it updates domain information, reinforcing the straightness or weakness of terms' relationship.

The library currently works with three kinds of relationships: synonym (same semantic terms), hypernym (more generic terms), and hyponym (more specific terms). These relationships are being improved using other types of relationships, like meronyms. In this sense, some domain rules described in Table 2 will be deprecated. In this way, the user's search can be rewritten with the same semantic, replacing the searched term by related terms in the same ontology or in different ontologies using proposed mapping. A query using unknown terms in a specific ontology can be translated into terms of related ontologies, resulting in more satisfactory matches for users. The mapping between ontologies works under a set of rules and an inference machine.

CONCLUSION

The Web is a useful repository of e-learning resources, but finding information in its databases is still a hard task, since it was conceived as a networked and not as a hierarchical model of information. Its approach to information retrieval basically considers the syntactic aspects involved in the searches, often neglecting the semantic aspects. The solution is the development of more effective search engines than those available nowadays.

On the other hand, the speed of knowledge production changes marketplaces and stresses professional skills. The teacher's job is being stressed by the increasing use of information and communications technologies, labeled under the broad term "e-learning." Our contribution to help Brazilian teachers to update their professional background was to develop a digital library on e-learning domain, with a search engine based on ontology.

At the moment, the prototype is available at www.npqs.ufjf.br/bv. The challenge now is to populate the digital library with information. The authors of the chapter started this process, including some e-learning information. The expectation, moreover, is that our information providers continually insert massive information following the ontology terms and experts validate provider's

classification in order to deliver the digital library to its end users, that is, the teachers, soon.

Digital libraries follow the standard interface of Web pages, with common icons and highlighted links. Even so, future works intend to test system interface usability, by means of laboratory tests. In the computational point-of-view, over time, we expect to improve the search engine accuracy by forming a knowledge base that will compare and accumulate the needs fulfillment of end users and the provided information, making the searches progressively more accurate.

REFERENCES

Berners-Lee, T., Handler, J., & Lassila, O. (2001, May). *The Semantic Web. Scientific American*, 35-43.

Cleveland, G. (1998). *Digital libraries: Definitions, issues and challenges*. Retrieved August 21, 2008, from http://www.ifla.org/VI/5/op/ud-top8/udtop8.htm

Cohen, S. (1994, November). *Feature-oriented domain analysis: Domain modeling* (tutorial notes). Paper presented at the 3rd International Conference on Software Reuse, Rio de Janeiro.

Embley, D. W., Campbell, D. M., Smith, R. D., & Liddle, S. W. (1998). Ontology-based extraction and structuring of information from data-rich unstructured documents. In *Proceedings of the CIKM'98: Conference on Information and Knowledge Management*, Bethesda (pp. 52-59). New York: ACM Press.

Gruber, T. R. (1993). A translation approach to portable ontology specifications. *Knowledge Acquisition, 5*(2), 199-220.

Guarino, N. (1998, June). Formal ontology in information systems. *In Proceedings of FOIS'98*, Trento, Italy (pp. 3-15). Amsterdam: IOS Press.

Lamping, J., Rao, R., & Pirolli, P. (1995). A focus+context technique based on hyperbolic geometry for visualizing large hierarchies. In *Proceedings of the ACM Conference on Human Factors in Computing Systems*, New York (pp. 401-408).

Noy, N., & McGuinness, D. (2001). *Ontology development 101: A guide to creating your first ontology*. Retrieved August 21, 2008, from http://protege.stanford.edu/publications/ontology_development/ontology101-noy-mcguinness.html

Paulsen, M. F. (2002, July). *Online education systems: Discussion and definition of terms*. Retrieved August 21, 2008, from http://home.nettskolen.com/~mortenantos

Pushpagiri, V. P., & Rahman, S. (2002). DLNET: A digital library architecture for lifelong learning. In P. Kommers, V. Petrushin, Kinshuk, & I. Galeev (Eds.), *Proceedings of the 2nd IEEE International Conference on Advanced Learning Technologies,* Kazan, Russia (pp. 155-160).

Santos, N, Campos, F. C. A, & Braga-Villela, R. M. (2005, October). A digital library for lifelong education on e-learning domain. In *Proceedings of the World Conference on E-learning in Corporate, Government, Healthcare, & Higher Education (E-Learn 2005)*, Vancouver (Vol. 4, pp. 3121-3128).

Shum, S. B., Motta, E., & Domingue, J. (2000, August/September). ScholOnto: An ontology-based digital library server for research documents and discourse. *International Journal on Digital Libraries, 3*(3), 237-248.

The Learning Technology Standards Committee of the IEEE Computer Society. (2001). Retrieved August 21, 2008, from http://jtc1sc36.org/doc/36N0175.pdf at July 4th 2005)

Weinstein, P., & Alloway, G. (1997, July). Seed ontologies: Growing digital libraries as distributed, intelligent systems. In *Proceedings of the Second ACM Digital Library Conference*, Philadelphia (pp. 83-91). ACM Press.www.1. e-Learning Cybrary: http://www.co-i-l.com/elearning/about/

KEY TERMS

Digital Library: A collection of texts, images, and so forth encoded so as to be stored, retrieved, and read by the computer. It comprises digital collections, services, and infrastructure to support lifelong learning, research, scholarly communication, and preservation.

Domain Ontology: Domain ontology, or domain-specific ontology, models a specific domain, or part of the world. It represents the particular meanings of terms as they apply to that domain.

E-learning: Any technologically mediated learning using computers, whether from a distance or in face-to-face classroom setting (computer-assisted learning). It can cover a wide set of applications and processes such as Web-based learning, computer-based learning, virtual classrooms, and digital collaboration.

Lifelong Learning: A continuum of the learning process that takes place at all levels, that is, formal, nonformal, and informal, utilizing various modalities such as distance learning and conventional learning. Also known as continuing education

Ontology: A data model that represents a domain and is used to reason about the objects in that domain and the relations between them.

Ontological Search: A new type of search engine that understands semantics and the meaning of whole phrases, rather than just looking for individual words or groups of words

Search Engine: Software that enables users to search the Internet using keywords.

Semantics: Refers to the aspects of meaning that are expressed in a language, code, or other form of representation. Semantics is contrasted with two other aspects of meaningful expression, namely, *syntax,* which is the construction of complex signs from simpler signs, and *pragmatics,* which is the practical use of signs by agents or communities of interpretation in particular circumstances and context.

Semantic Web: An extension of the current Web that will allow a user to find, share, and combine information more easily. It relies on machine-readable information and metadata expressed in resource description framework (RDF). RDF is a family of World Wide Web Consortium (W3C) specifications originally designed as a metadata model using XML but which has come to be used as a general method of modeling knowledge through a variety of syntax formats (XML and non-XML).

Chapter XXI
A Classification Scheme for Innovative Types in Scholarly Communication

Svenja Hagenhoff
University of Goettingen, Germany

Björn Ortelbach
University of Goettingen, Germany

Lutz Seidenfaden
University of Goettingen, Germany

ABSTRACT

Information and communication technologies seem to bring new dynamics to the established, but partly deadlocked, system of scholarly communication. Technologies are the basis for new publication forms and services which seem to enable a faster and more cost-efficient distribution of research results. Up to now new forms of scholarly communication have been described in the literature only in the form of single and often anecdotic reports. Despite the large number of papers in that area, no classification scheme for new forms of scholarly communication can be found. Therefore, this chapter aims at presenting such a classification scheme. It allows the description of new forms of scholarly communication in a standardized way. A structured comparison of new activities is possible. For this purpose, original publication media on the one hand and complementary services on the other are differentiated. With the help of morphological boxes, characteristics of both kinds of new means of scholarly communication are presented.

INTRODUCTION

The number of scientific journals and, subsequently, the number of published articles grew at an enormous rate over the last century (Henderson, 2002). In the second half of the 20th century the system seemed to abut against its boundaries, because, in comparison to research budgets, library budgets did not grow fast enough to cover the entire academic output produced (ARL, 2004). Price increases well above the inflation rate were set by commercial publishers whose disproportionately high market power—especially for journals in the science-technical-medicine-sector in the last 30 years—has worsened the situation even further ("serial crisis"). New information and communication technologies (ICT) seem to bring new dynamics and radical changes to the long established but partly deadlocked system of scholarly communication. The new technologies are the basis for innovative publication forms and services in the area of scholarly communication, which seem to facilitate a faster and more cost-efficient distribution of research results.

In this changed context, the role of libraries will change. It has to evolve from being a collector and provider of physical media to being a service provider and consultant for scholars in the area of scholarly communication. To fulfill this role, it is essential that the libraries themselves gain a deeper understanding of the emerging development in electronic scholarly communication. Furthermore, discussions and further research work should be based on a precise and systematic description of reality.

Up to now new forms of scholarly communication have been described in the literature mainly in the form of single and often anecdotic reports. Despite a large number of papers in that area, no classification scheme for new forms of scholarly communication is available from the literature. Therefore, this chapter aims at presenting such a classification scheme. It allows the description of new forms of scholarly communication in a standardized way and facilitates a structured comparison of new activities.

BACKGROUND

Functions of Scholarly Communication

Scholarly communication is an important part of the research process. For systematic and efficient scientific progress to take place, research results have to be published and made accessible to other researchers who need to incorporate them in their own research (Figure 1).

Scientific publications are the formal means of communication between scientists. In general, a scientific publication fulfils four main functions that are valuable for the scholarly communication (Kircz & Roosendaal, 1996):

- The registration function that relates research results to a particular scientist who claims priority for them,
- The certification function that concerns the validation of research,
- The awareness function that leads to disclosure and search needs, and
- The archiving function that concerns the storage and accessibility of research results.

Every kind of scholarly publishing must fulfill these abstract functions in some way or another (Geurts & Roosendaal, 2001).

Classic Rolls in Scholarly Communication

Figure 2 provides an overview of the interaction among players and their position in the scholarly communication value chain that prevails in the traditional model.

Figure 1. The system of scholarly communication

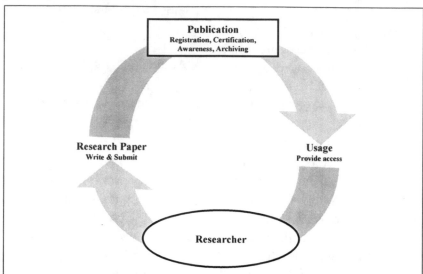

Figure 2. Interaction of players in the traditional model of scholarly communication

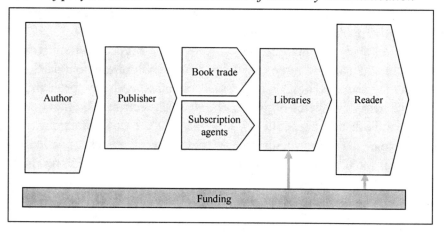

In traditional scholarly communication, an author submits a manuscript to a publisher. The publisher's task (Morris, 1999) is to evaluate and select manuscripts for publication, to transform the manuscript into a publishable form, and to publish it as a print medium. The publisher's main customers are research and university libraries. Typically, they acquire their material by means of intermediaries, such as the book trade industry or subscription agents. Libraries provide the acquired material to their users, mainly scholars. The scholarly communication system is mainly financed by public funds that are allocated to libraries, which then distribute them to the system in the course of their acquisition process.

In the recent past, tremendous changes of the traditional system have taken place. The following section analyzes these changes and the challenges they imply for the players.

Drivers for Change in the Scholarly Communication System

The key driver of the change process is the progress of new ICT. Traditional print media are substituted by electronic networks (Willinsky, 2006). Firstly, traditional communication structures were transferred from paper to electronic; printed books and journals are now substituted by e-books and e-journals. Secondly, the digital technology enables genuinely innovative forms of communication, such as databases and repositories, as well as search and usage tools (The British Library Board, 1998).

Further, the cooccurrence of the serials crisis (Machlup, 1977; Woodward & Pilling, 1993) on the one hand and the opportunities of electronic publishing as facilitator on the other hand created the open access movement, which demands free access to all scientific results (Bailey 2005a; BOAI, 2001; Crow, 2002; Lagoze & van de Sompel, 2001). The growing support of this paradigm can also be seen as a driver of the change process in scholarly communication.

In this environment, libraries have to ask themselves what their future role should be. Their traditional task of selecting, providing, and archiving physical media is loosing importance. Digital content, for example, e-journals, is frequently provided by the suppliers, that is, the publishers. The role of libraries is reduced to that of a license party. But a fundamental new task is emerging, that is, future libraries will become service providers and consultants for scholars in the area of electronic scholarly communication. For example, they collect and assemble various digital material and tools for a specific discipline in a virtual specialized library.

To be prepared for these new tasks, it is essential that the libraries themselves gain a deeper understanding of emerging tools and services in the area of electronic scholarly communication.

BLUEPRINT OF A CLASSIFICATION SCHEME

In recent years a large variety of new forms of scholarly communication has emerged. Although there is a large set of sources describing these new forms, these descriptions are typically limited to anecdotic evidence. However, up to now no classification of new communication forms is available from the literature. Therefore, this chapter aims at developing a classification that reflects the outlined evolution.

Basically two basic types of scholarly communication means can be differentiated (see Figure 1): original publishing media and complementary services. The former provide a basis to publish results of research and thereby fulfill all four functions of scholarly communication (see above). The latter are services based on publishing media which enhance the communication process by providing additional functionality, for example, special certification services or enhanced search mechanisms. They intensify one or more of the scholarly communication functions.

Starting with these two main types, a set of criteria and characteristics were identified to further classify the main type. The results of these analyses are shown in Tables 1 and 2 as morphological boxes (read row by row).

The most basic classification is made according to the output medium. *Paper*-based and *electronic* media are to be distinguished. Electronic media can be further differentiated into *off-line* and *online* media. Quality assurance plays an important role in scholarly communication because its standard determines the reputation of a medium. Thus, the review process can be seen as another criterion to distinguish means of scholarly communication. Review processes take place at many different levels, but to keep the classification as generic as possible it will suffice to differentiate between media *with (formal) peer review* and media *without (formal) peer review.* Complementary services may support media of different kinds and therefore comprise reviewed as well as nonreviewed material (e.g., preprints).

Communication media usually consist of bundles of independently fragmented content. Therefore, media that bundle *topic-specific* content (of one or more scientific disciplines) and media that bundle *institution-specific* content (e.g., from a university's departments) are to be differentiated. Complementary services may offer across-the-board bundling, that is, their content is restricted neither to specific topics nor to institutions.

It is obvious that access to scholarly information is a central issue in scholarly communication (Willinsky, 2006). For this reason, it seems sensible to further distinguish means of scholarly communication according to the kind of access they offer: *free of charge for users* or *user charges.* If the users are charged, a further distinction can be observed based upon the type of charges. The first type is to charge users *per item* (i.e., pay per use or pay per submission) while the second type is a *flat fee.*

The funding of scholarly communication has been a major point in recent discussions. In general, scholarly communication is publicly funded. However, differences exist in the way the funding money is distributed between the actors. Therefore, the question arises how a service provider can cover its cost for running the service (e.g., scientific journal or abstract & indexing-service). The mode of distributing the revenue generated provides another distinction of the means of scholarly communication. In addition to the traditional ways of funding, for example, through subscription fees or charging authors for the publishing of their works, a service may also be completely *funded by public funds.* Although *other revenue sources* (e.g., through advertising) are imaginable, they have not yet gained importance in scholarly communication. The revenue models mentioned above do not mark alternative concepts because they may appear in combination (already now in some scientific disciplines authors are charged publishing fees per page while there are also subscription fees to be paid by the user).

In addition to the classification according to revenue models, the means of scholarly communication may be divided into *for-profit* and *not-for-profit* services. The former are run with the intention of generating revenue while the latter have nonmonetary objectives (e.g., fostering scientific development). This criterion has gained importance in recent discussions as one of the main topics discussed has been the question whether it is socially acceptable for commercial publishers as a third party to generate revenue from publicly funded scholarly communication.

As mentioned above, the means of publication cover all four functions of scholarly communication. Complementary services are based upon means of publication, but they do not cover all functions (if they would cover the registration function, they would be means of publication rather than complementary services); but they support certain functions. Therefore, it seems reasonable to use the *functions of scholarly communication* as a criterion for the classification of complementary services. However, it should be kept in mind that not all functions are equally important. As an example, the registration function is the publication of a contribution and its linkage to an author and, therefore, a prerequisite for other functions. "The act of discovery is incomplete without [...] publication that enables the world's peer group to validate by acceptance and valuate by use" (de Solla Price [1986] as cited in Schauder, 1994). Therefore, only the *certification, awareness,* and *archiving* functions are used to classify complementary services.

To conclude this section, the criteria are consolidated in morphological boxes whereas publication media (Table 1) and complementary services (Table 2) are distinguished.

Table 1. Classification of original publication media

Criterion	Characteristics				
Output medium	Paper		Electronic offline		Electronic online
Review	Without peer review			With peer review	
Type of content aggregation	Discipline-specific			Institutional-specific	
Type of access	User will be charged			Free of charge for users	
Revenue/funding model	Payment for usage		Payment for publishing		Directly supported by public funds	Other revenue sources
	Per item	Flat fee (sub-scription)	Per item	Flat fee		
Aims of operator	commercial			Non-commercial	

Table 2. Classification of complementary services

Criterion	Characteristics		
Supported scholarly communication function	Certification	Awareness	Archiving
Output medium	Paper	Electronic offline	Electronic online
Review	Without peer review	with peer review	mixed
Type of content aggregation	Discipline-specific	Institutional-specific	Spanning
Type of access	User will be charged		Free of charge for users
Revenue/funding model	Payment for usage	Directly supported by public funds	Other revenue sources
	Per item / Flat fee		
Aims of operator	Commercial		Non-commercial

It should be noted that interdependencies among criteria may occur. In certain cases a specific characteristic of one criterion can only occur in conjunction with a specific characteristic of another criterion.

Now, the classification scheme developed above is applied to several scholarly communication forms to denote the heterogeneity of today's scholarly communication. The four cases detailed below represent innovative services that have attracted a lot of attention in recent discussions.

BioMed Central (BMC) (Poynder, 2005; Velterop, 2002) is the first global commercial open access publisher whose journals primarily cover medicine and science topics. These peer-reviewed journals are available online free of charge for the reader, but authors are charged a fee upon acceptance of their manuscript for publication.

Research Papers in Economics (RePEc) (Karlsson, 1999) is a collection of discussion papers and articles in economics. The aim of the services is twofold: firstly, it pursues the bibliographic aim to develop a complete description of economic research through the collection of relevant literature, and secondly, to provide users free access to that material.

Scopus is a commercial database run by the publisher Elsevier that comprises a comprehensive collection of abstracts, references, and keywords of scholarly literature (de Groot & Knapp, 2004). The aim of the service is to ease the search and retrieval of relevant literature primarily in the sciences and medicine. Users are charged a subscription fee to access the database.

Google Scholar is a specific search engine provided by the for-profit organization Google. The service supports the awareness function by searching the Web for all scientific material.

Papers published in reviewed journals as well as discussion papers are found. Both the well known Google page rank approach and citation analyses are used for ranking the search results. Google scholar is financed by advertisement; therefore, the users do not have to pay anything.

Table 3. Biomed Central classification (original publication media)

Criterion	Characteristics				
Output medium	Paper		Electronic offline		Electronic online
Review	Without peer review			With peer review	
Type of content aggregation	Discipline-specific			Institutional-specific	
Type of access	User will be charged			Free of charge for users	
Revenue/funding model	Payment for usage		Payment for publishing	Directly supported by public funds	Other revenue sources
	Per item	Flat fee (subscription)	Per item	Flat fee		
Aims of operator	Commercial			Non-commercial	

Table 4. RePEc classification of original publication media (original publication media)

Criterion	Characteristics				
Output medium	Paper		Electronic offline		Electronic online
Review	Without peer review			With peer review	
Type of content aggregation	Discipline-specific			Institutional-specific	
Type of access	User will be charged			Free of charge for users	
Revenue/funding model	Payment for usage		Payment for publishing	Directly supported by public funds	Other revenue sources
	Per item	Flat fee (subscription)	Per item	Flat fee		
Aims of operator	Commercial			Non-commercial	

Table 5. Scopus classification (complementary service)

Criterion	Characteristics		
Supported scholarly communication function	Certification	Awareness	Archiving
Output medium	Paper	Electronic offline	Electronic online
Review	Without peer review	With peer review	Mixed
Type of content aggregation	Discipline-specific	Institutional-specific	Spanning
Type of access	User will be charged		Free of charge for users
Revenue/funding model	Payment for usage	Directly supported by public funds	Other revenue sources
	Per item / Flat fee		
Aims of operator	Commercial		Non-commercial

Figure 8. Google Scholar classification (complementary service)

Criterion	Characteristics		
Supported scholarly communication function	*Certification*	*Awareness*	*Archiving*
Output medium	*Paper*	*Electronic offline*	*Electronic online*
Review	*Without peer review*	*With peer review*	*Mixed*
Type of content aggregation	*Discipline-specific*	*Institutional-specific*	*Spanning*
Type of access	*User will be charged*		*Free of charge for users*
Revenue/funding model	*Payment for usage* / *Per item* / *Flat fee*	*Directly supported by public funds*	*Other revenue sources*
Aims of operator	*Commercial*		*Non-commercial*

The four examples of innovative means of scholarly communication are now described using the classification scheme developed earlier (Tables 1 to 2).

The tables show very clearly the usefulness of standardized descriptions. Different cases can be compared in a structured way. This brings more rationality into the discussion about transforming the traditional system of scholarly communication, which has often been emotionally charged and politically motivated (serials crisis, open-access). The classification also allows for thinking about combinations of characteristics which do not exist up to now and which may lead to new services no one ever thought about. Examining a multitude of new services by using the classification scheme also allows to identify factors of success, and to develop hypotheses about future developments of the scholarly communication system.

FUTURE TRENDS

The classification scheme was used to describe and compare six innovative original publication media (i.e., arXiv, Public Library of Science, Biomed Central Journals, EDoc, Research papers in Economics, and Springer Open Choice), and six innovative complementary services (i.e., Google Scholar, Google Book Search, OAIster, Scopus, JSTOR, and Faculty of 1000). The following statements can be made:

- A lot of new players (e.g., software companies like Google) entered the system of scholarly communication. Established players like publishing houses and libraries express strong reservations about those activities in unusual unanimity.

- Comparing original publishing media with complementary services, it has to be assumed that the latter will have more potential for innovation. While in the case of publishing media innovations concerning business models arise (an author pays instead of subscription fees), innovative complementary services afford possibilities the established system did not have. Awareness services like Scopus or Faculty of 1000 are examples.

- The previous aspect may be sharpened into a hypothesis: It is thinkable that the traditional responsibilities for different functions in the system of scholarly communication will be inverted in the long run. Traditionally, publishing houses are responsible for the original publication media and for distributing content. The task of the libraries is to give access to the publications and to support the awareness function by providing metadata and online catalogues for free.

Nowadays, the information technology affords the possibility for the libraries to run their own noncommercial publishing houses, and to assume the responsibility for the original publishing and distributing process. For example, in Germany, many university libraries are starting publishing activities in response to the serials crisis. On the other hand, publishing houses and other players are starting activities beside their original publishing field by providing tools supporting the awareness function (e.g., Scopus and Google book search).

CONCLUSION

In the relevant literature, changes in scholarly communication are mostly analyzed as single cases (for an overview see Bailey, 2005a, 2005b) and therefore lack a broader perspective. The main catalysts for change in this field are the serials crisis, electronic publishing, open-access, and the further internationalization of scholarly communication.

This contribution aims to draw a sketch of recent developments in scholarly communication and to build a classification scheme that allows a systematic description of developments and changes. The scheme theoretically allows distinguishing 288 types of publication means and 1,296 types of complementary services.

During the development of the scheme it became obvious that a basic distinction between publication means and complementary services can be made, and be differentiated even further by using more criteria. In the case of publication means we used the criteria aggregation of content, type of access, revenue model, and aim of the service provider. For complementary services, the awareness, certification, and archiving functions were used as discriminating criteria. We showed for four examples that the classification scheme can be used for systematic description and differentia-

tion of means of scholarly communication. When the classification scheme is applied to a broader variety of existing services, the standardized description spans a multidimensional portfolio of communication forms that allows the bundling of certain communication forms into clusters. Furthermore, this depiction could act as a means for market analyses since the structured depiction of services shows which segments are still uncovered in the continuum of thinkable scholarly communication means. Thus, our approach pursues explanation as well as design aims: While, on the one hand, the multidimensional portfolio facilitates the identification (and explanation) of future developments in scholarly communication, the identification of uncovered segments, on the other hand, represents the design dimension of the approach.

Moreover, the classification may contribute to other fields of media research; it could, for example, be used to systematically describe a publishers' product portfolio, thus offering hints for product development.

REFERENCES

ARL. (2006). *Monograph and serial expenditures in research libraries*. Retrieved November 21, 2007, from http://www.arl.org/bm~doc/monser06.pdf

Bailey, C. W. (2005a). *Open-access bibliography: Liberating scholarly literature with e-prints and open-access journals*. Washington, D. C: Association of Research Libraries.

Bailey, C. W. (2005b). *Scholarly electronic publishing bibliography* (Version 58). Retrieved November 14, 2006, from http://epress.lib.uh.edu/sepb/archive/sepa.htm

BOAI. (2001). *Budapest open access initiative*. Retrieved November 21, 2007, from http://www.soros.org/openaccess/

Crow, R. (2002). *The case for institutional repositories: A SPARC position paper.* Washington, D. C.: Association of Research Libraries.

De Groot, S. P., & Knapp, A. E. (2004). *Applying the user-centered design (UCD) process to the development of a large bibliographic navigation tool: A partnership between librarian, researcher and developer.* Retrieved January 30, 2007, from http://www.info.scopus.com/news/white papers/wpl_usability_testing.pdf

De Solla Price, S. (1986). *Little science, big Science and beyond.* New York: Columbia University Press.

Geurts, P., & Roosendaal, H. (2001). Estimating the direction of innovative change based on theory and mixed methods. *Quality & Quantity, 35*(4), 407-428.

Henderson, S. (2002). The growth of printed literature in the twentieth century. In R. E. Abel & L. W. Newlin (Eds.), *Scholarly publishing: Books, journals, publishers, and libraries in the twentieth century* (pp. 1-23). Indianapolis: Wiley.

Karlsson, S. K. T. (1999). *RePEc and S-WoPEc: Internet access to electronic preprints in economics.* Retrieved November 21, 2007, from http://ideas.repec.org/p/rpc/rdfdoc/lindi.html

Kircz, J. G., & Roosendaal, H. E. (1996). Understanding and shaping scientific information transfer. In D. Shaw & H. Moore (Eds.), *Electronic publishing in science* (pp. 106-116). Paris: ICSU Press & UNESCO.

Lagoze, C., & van de Sompel, H. (2001). The open archives initiative: Building a low-barrier interoperability framework. In E. A. Fox & C. L. Borgman (Ed.), *Proceedings of the 1st ACM/IEEE-CS Joint Conference on Digital Libraries* (pp. 54-62). Roanoke, VA: ACM Press.

Machlup, F. (1977). Publishing scholarly books and journals: Is it economically viable? *The Journal of Political Economy, 85*(1), 217-225.

Morris, S. (1999): Who needs publishers? *Journal of Information Science, 1*(25), 85-88.

Poynder, R. (2005). Essential for science: Interview with Vitek Tracz. *Information Today, 1*(22), 1.

Schauder, D. (1994). Electronic publishing of professional articles: Attitudes of academics and implications for the scholarly communication industry. *Journal of the American Society for Information Science, 45*(2), 73-100.

The British Library Board. (1998). *Authors and electronic journals.* London: McKnight, C. & Price, S.

Velterop, J. (2002). *BioMed central.* Retrieved November 30, 2007, from http://www.library.yale.edu/~llicense/ListArchives/0205/msg00129.html

Willinsky, J. (2006). *The access principle: The case for open access to research and scholarship.* Cambridge, MA: The MIT Press.

Woodward, H. M., & Pilling, S. (Eds.). (1993). *The international serials industry.* Aldershot, Great Britain: Gower Publishing Ltd.

KEY TERMS

Complementary Services: Scholarly means of communication that do not fulfil the registration function. Complementary services enhance scholarly communication by support to one or more of the scholarly communication functions. Examples are the certification service Faculty of 1000 as well as the search engines Scopus and OAIster.

Electronic Publishing: Publishing process whose output is based on digital representation of the content and is therefore independent of specific media.

Functions of the Scholarly Communication: The four functions of the scholarly communication are certification, registration, awareness, and archiving.

Open Access: Scholarly communication forms that do not charge users to (legally) read, download, copy, distribute, print, search, or link to the full texts of their content.

Publication Media: Scholarly communication means which explicitly fulfil the registration function. They link a contribution to an author and thereby guarantee the authors' priority for that particular finding. Examples are journals and preprint servers.

Scholarly Communication: Authoring and publication of scholarly material in order to communicate knowledge and to foster research within the scientific community.

Serials Crisis: In the last 30 years, prices for scholarly journals increased well above the inflation rate while the budgets of the libraries' more or less stagnated. The libraries have therefore difficulties in providing scientists with the needed scientific material. This situation is known as the serial crisis.

Chapter XXII
Improving Multimedia Digital Libraries Usability Applying NLP Sentence Similarity to Multimodal Sentences

Stefano Paolozzi
Consiglio Nazionale delle Ricerche, Italy

Fernando Ferri
Consiglio Nazionale delle Ricerche, Italy

Patrizia Grifoni
Consiglio Nazionale delle Ricerche, Italy

ABSTRACT

This chapter describes multimodality as a means of augmenting information retrieval activities in multimedia digital libraries. Multimodal interaction systems combine visual information with voice, gestures, and other modalities to provide flexible and powerful dialogue approaches. The use of integrated multiple input modes enables users to benefit from the natural approach used in human communication, improving usability of the systems. However, natural interaction approaches may introduce interpretation problems as the systems' usability is directly proportional to users' satisfaction. To improve multimedia digital library usability users can express their queries by means of a multimodal sentence. The authors proposes a new approach to match a multimodal sentence with a template stored in a knowledge base to interpret the multimodal sentence and define the multimodal templates similarity.

INTRODUCTION

Multimedia digital libraries are characterized by an integrated management of typologically heterogeneous documents. The management is performed by the use of specific systems to index, search, and automatically extract data that are typical of complex contents of multimedia documents (e.g., video, audio, etc.).

Several researches and studies, over the last few years, address multimedia data analysis, computer vision and object recognition, and multimedia management in large audio and video collections. As the most complex and advanced multimedia information systems, digital libraries are emerging at an increasingly fast rate throughout the world. One of the primary difficulties in building a digital library is to support effective and efficient retrieval of the media objects, including text, image, video, and audio (Baeza-Yates & Ribeiro-Neto, 1998).

Because the information retrieval quality is widely influenced by the user's interaction with the system, it is necessary to modify the multimedia database access approach in order to take into consideration the user's actions. For this reason, the approach has to take into account the complex necessities to define queries not only with terminological data, but also with multimedia data.

Therefore, it is important to change the traditional textual interfaces, which can be used only in keywords or textual metadata searches, with more rich interfaces. These ones must allow the formulation of multidimensional queries, not only by terms but also by images, sounds, and so forth (Flickner, Sawhney, Niblack, & Ashley, 1995). In this way the retrieval can be performed according to indexes composed by text extracted from speech, main images of a sequence, simple images, shapes, colors, sounds, and so forth. Obviously we continue to maintain textual data that are related to particular aspects not specifically related with audiovisual data stored in the multimedia library.

A variety of technologies such as sketch and speech processing, video streaming, multimedia databases, and graphical user interfaces can be integrated to produce a multimodal environment.

The systems' usability is directly proportional to users' satisfaction. To improve multimedia digital library usability the users can express their queries by means of a multimodal sentence. Moreover, the system's ability to give exact or approximate answers can improve users' satisfaction.

In this chapter we analyze different approaches found in literature and propose an original one used to calculate sentence similarity. The proposed approach is based on the evaluation of users' input from the multimodal sentence analysis comparing the given sentence with a knowledge base of short sentences in order to find similarity between them. A multimodal sentence is formed by atomic elements (e.g., glyphs/graphemes, phonemes, etc.).

Because speech represents the most used modality and the prevalent one—prevalent is the modality that permits to expresses the multimodal sentence's syntax and the semantic while the use of other modalities is devoted to "support" the speech and eventually to resolve ambiguities—multimodal sentences can be described using natural language. In this way we can consider the similarity computation between multimodal sentences as the similarity computation between natural language sentences.

BACKGROUND: A BRIEF STATE-OF-THE-ART OF SENTENCE SIMILARITY ISSUES

There is a wide literature base on measuring the similarity between documents or long texts (e.g., Allen, 1995; Meadow, Boyce, & Kraft, 2000), but there are only few works relating to the measurement of similarity between very short texts (Foltz, Kintsch, & Landauer, 1998) or sentences (Li, McLean, Bandar, O'Shea, & Crockett, 2006).

According to Li et al. (2006), sentence similarity methods can be classified into three categories: methods based on the analysis of the degree of words co-occurrence, corpora analysis methods, and descriptive features-based methods.

The word cooccurrence methods are commonly used in information retrieval domains (Meadow et al., 2000). In these applications there is a precompiled word list with a relevant number of elements in order to include all meaningful words in a natural language. The similarity is measured between documents or long texts. A query is also considered as a document. Each document is represented in an n-dimensional vector using the words in the list. Relevant documents are then retrieved on the similarity between the document vector and the query vector.

Corpus-analysis methods are also widely employed. The most used method is the latent semantic analysis (LSA) (Landauer, Foltz, & Laham, 1998).

LSA uses a term-document matrix, which describes the occurrences of terms in documents; it is a sparse matrix whose rows correspond to documents and whose columns correspond to terms, that is, typically stemmed words that appear in the documents. A typical example of the weighting of the elements of the matrix is termed frequency–inverse document frequency (tf-idf): the element of the matrix is proportional to the number of times the terms appear in each document, where rare terms are upweighted to reflect their relative importance.

This matrix is common to standard semantic models as well, though it is not necessarily explicitly expressed as a matrix, since the mathematical properties of matrix are not always used. A matrix gives the relationship between terms and documents. LSA transforms this into a relationship between the terms and concepts, and a relation between the documents and the same concepts. The terms and documents are now indirectly related through the concepts.

The last category is the descriptive features-based methods. The feature vector method tries to represent a sentence using a set of predefined features (McClelland & Kawamoto, 1986). Basically, a word in a sentence is represented using semantic features; for example, nouns may have features such as HUMAN (with value of human or nonhuman) or EDIBLE (with value edible or nonedible). A variation of feature vector methods is the introduction of primary features and composite features (Hatzivassiloglou, Klavans, & Eskin, 1999). Primary features are those primitive features that compare single items from each text unit. Composite features are the combinations of pairs of primitive features. A text is then represented in a vector consisting of values of primary features and composite features. Similarity between two texts is obtained through a trained classifier.

Overall, the aforementioned methods compute similarity on the base of the cooccurring words in the texts, ignoring syntactic information. They work well for long texts because long texts have a sufficient number of cooccurring words, but are not so useful in case of short texts.

MULTIMODAL SENTENCE SIMILARITY FOR INFORMATION RETRIEVAL

As the most complex and advanced multimedia information systems, digital libraries are emerging at an increasingly fast rate throughout the world. One of the primary difficulties in building a digital library is to support effective and efficient retrieval of the media objects from the whole library, including text, image, video, and audio. The current mainstream of the retrieval technologies in most digital libraries is keyword-based retrieval. Although such technology works well with textual document, it cannot, by itself, accomplish the retrieval task in a multimedia digital library, mainly due to the limited expressive power of keyword to describe or index media objects.

A lot of applications have been developed to support information retrieval in multimedia digital libraries, showing the importance of managing heterogeneous information. A first interesting example of these applications is performing arts teaching resources online (PATRON) (Lyon, 2000). It is a framework for multimedia digital libraries to support learning and teaching in the performing arts. PATRON essentially at two levels: first as a digital library delivering resources on-demand to the user, and second as a contextual environment. A more recent project is MILOS (Amato, Bolettieri, Debole, Falchi, Rabitti, & Savino, 2006). It is a multimedia content management system specialized to support multimedia digital library applications. MILOS provides applications with functionalities for the storage of arbitrary multimedia documents and their content-based retrieval using arbitrary metadata models represented in extensible markup language (XML). These approaches show the importance of information retrieval, especially for multimedia content.

The main concept of this chapter is a multimodal sentence. In this chapter, we give the definition of multimodal language, extending the definition of visual language given by Bottoni, Costabile, Levialdi, and Mussio (1995), as a set of multimodal sentences. A multimodal sentence contains atomic elements (i.e., glyphs/graphemes, phonemes, etc.) that form the characteristic structure (CS). The CS is given by the elements which "form functional or perceptual units" for the user. A CS consists of a set of perceivable events which allow the user to evaluate the state of a virtual entity, that is, a concept that extends the virtual device concept, where events can be multimodal (i.e., visual, audio, or haptic). Virtual entities represent the elements of an interactive system that interacts with the user through the input/output devices. A multimodal sentence is defined, similarly to Celentano, Fogli, Mussio, and Pittarello's

(2004) definition, as a function of the multimodal message, the multimodal description that assign the meaning to the sentence, the interpretation function that maps the message with the description, and finally, the materialization function that maps the description with the message.

Starting from the hypothesis that speech is the most relevant modality, this work assumes that the interpretation of a multimodal sentence needs its corresponding sentence, expressed in natural language form, which matches with one template contained in the knowledge base. An approximate interpretation, which uses a semantic approach, can be provided. A template is the syntactic structure expressed using natural language that encapsulates some key concepts expressed according to the various modalities.

As discussed above, the need of interpreting sentences by characterizing the multimodal dialog has led us to propose a process devoted to obtaining the exact interpretation or its approximation, whose steps are the following:

- The user formulates his/her multimodal sentence.
- The resulting sentence is transformed in a natural language (NL) one and its template is compared with the templates sharing the same keywords (this reduces the number of the compared templates); the corresponding templates are selected.
- If there are no matches, we extract from each one of the selected templates the relative sentences that have been used to create (by example) it.
- Then the system computes the semantic similarity between each of these sentences and the user's sentence.
- The highest value of semantic similarity is used to choose the most similar template with the given sentence.

A lot of semantic knowledge bases are readily available; in this chapter we address WordNet

(Miller, 1995) for the English language. The taxonomical structure of the WordNet knowledge base is important in determining the semantic distance between words. In WordNet, words are organized into synonym sets (synsets), with semantics and relation pointers to other synsets.

One direct method for similarity computation is to find the minimum length of path connecting the two words.

However, this method may be not sufficiently accurate if it is applied to a large and general semantic net such as WordNet. For example, the minimum length from student to animal is 4 (see Figure 1), less than from student to professor; however, intuitively, student is more similar to professor than to animal.

To address this weakness, the direct path length method must be modified, as proposed by Li et al. (2006), utilizing more information from the hierarchical semantic nets. It is important to notice that concepts at upper layers of the WordNet's hierarchy have more general semantics and less similarity between them, while words that appear at lower layers have more concrete semantics and

Figure 1. A portion of WordNet semantic net

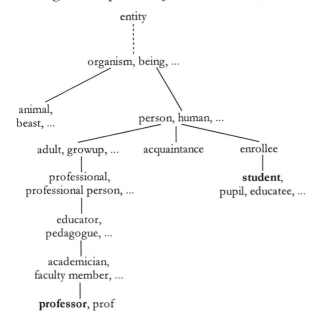

have a higher similarity. Therefore, also the depth of word in the hierarchy should be considered. In summary, we note that similarity between words is determined not only by path lengths but also by depth (level in the hierarchy). Given two words, w_1 and w_2, we need to find the semantic similarity $s(w_1, w_2)$.

More formally, given two concepts, c_1 and c_2, we need to find the semantic similarity $s(c_1, c_2)$.

Let l be the shortest path length between c_1 and c_2, and h the depth of subsumer of c_1 and c_2 (i.e., the common ancestor of both c_1 and c_2). In the hierarchical semantic nets, the semantic similarity can be written as:

$$s(c_1, c_2) = f_1(l) \cdot f_2(h)$$

The path length between two concepts, c_1 and c_2, can be computed according to one of the following cases:

- c_1 and c_2 belong to the same synset;
- c_1 and c_2 do not belong to the same synset, but their synsets contains one or more common words; or
- neither c_1 and c_2 belong to the same synset nor do their synsets contain any common word.

By the above considerations we can considered the function $f_1(l)$ as a monotonically decreasing function of l. For depth contribution, function $f_2(h)$ should be a monotonically increasing function with respect to depth h.

Using this algorithm we can compare the multimodal sentence (given by the user), that in this case represents a query to the multimedia digital library, with the stored query template. Indeed we can approximate the given sentence to one stored in the template database in order to correctly retrieve information from the digital library.

CONCLUSION

We tested our approach to verify the usability improvements. We selected 120 users to use our framework and the results (through a questionnaire) demonstrated an increase in user usability and consequently in users' satisfaction (about 32% more respect to traditional interfaces).

The use of integrated multiple input modes enables users to benefit from the natural approach used in human communication. However, natural interaction approaches introduce interpretation problems. A user can use voice, hand-writing, sketching, and gesture to retrieve information.

A user can retrieve information, such as images, video, texts, and so on, contained in a digital library by multimodal sentences in different contexts using mobile devices and/or personal computers according to the user's needs. When the user sends to the system a multimodal sentence the system has to interpret it. If the system contains the correspondent template then it provides the exact interpretation, otherwise it provides the most similar interpretation according to the similarity measure between templates. This approach improves both the usability of the digital library due to the adopted multimodal interaction and the retrieved information according to the retrieved similar templates.

The future works will regard the analysis of the proposed approach in order to improve the performance and to further increase usability and users' satisfaction.

REFERENCES

Allen, J. (1995). *Natural language understanding.* Redwood City, CA: Benjamin Cummings.

Amato, G., Bolettieri, P., Debole, F., Falchi, F., Rabitti, F., & Savino, P. (2006). Using MILOS to build a multimedia digital library application: The PhotoBook experience. In J. Gonzalo (Ed.), *Proceedings of the 10th European Conference on Digital Libraries* (*ECDL 2006*) (LNCS 4172, pp. 379-390). Alicante, Spain: Sprinter.

Amato, G., Gennaro, C., Savino, P., & Rabitti, F. (2005). MILOS: A multimedia content management system for multimedia digital library applications. In A. Agosti (Ed.), *Proceedings of the First Italian Research Conference on Digital Library Management Systems* (pp. 29-32). Padova, Italy: IEEE.

Baeza-Yates, B., & Ribeiro-Neto, B. (1999). *Modern information retrieval.* New York: Addison-Wesley Longman.

Bottoni, P., Costabile, M. F., Levialdi, S., & Mussio, P. (1995). Formalising visual languages. In *Proceedings of the 11th International IEEE Symposium on Visual Languages, VL,* (pp. 45-52). Washington, D.C.: IEEE.

Celentano, A., Fogli, D., Mussio, P., & Pittarello, F. (2004). Model-based specification of virtual interaction environments. In *Proceedings of the 2004 IEEE Symposium on Visual Languages - Human Centric Computing: Vol. 00.* (pp. 257-260). Rome: IEEE.

Flickner, M., Sawhney, H., Niblack, W., & Ashley, J. (1995). Query by image and video content: The QBIC system. *IEEE Computer, 28*(9), 23-32.

Foltz, P. W., Kintsch, W., & Landauer, T. K. (1998). The measurement of textual coherence with latent semantic analysis. *Discourse Processes, 25*(2-3), 285-307.

Hatzivassiloglou, V., Klavans, J., & Eskin, E. (1999). *Detecting text similarity over short passages: Exploring linguistic feature combinations via machine learning.* Paper presented at the SIGDAT Conference of Empirical Methods in NLP and Very Large Corpora, Maryland.

Landauer, T. K., Foltz, P. W., & Laham, D. (1998). Introduction to latent semantic analysis. *Discourse Processes, 25*(2-3), 259-284.

Li, Y., McLean, D., Bandar, Z. A., O'Shea, J. D., & Crockett, K. (2006). Sentence similarity based on semantic nets and corpus statistics. *IEEE Transactions on Knowledge and Data Engineering, 18*(8), 1138-1150.

Lyon, E. (2000). *PATRON: Using a multimedia digital library for learning and teaching in the performing arts.* Paper presented at the EDU-CAUSE 2000, Nashville.

McClelland, J. L., & Kawamoto, A. H. (1986). Mechanisms of sentence processing: Assigning roles to constituents of sentences. In D. E. Rumelhart, J. L. McClelland, & the PDP Research (Eds.), *Parallel distributed process: Vol.* 2. (pp. 272-325). MIT Press.

Meadow, C. T., Boyce, B. R., & Kraft, D. H. (2000). *Text information retrieval systems* (2nd ed.). Academic Press.

Miller, G. A. (1995). WordNet: A lexical database for English. *Communications of the ACM, 38*(11), 39-41.

KEY TERMS

Knowledge Base: A knowledge base is a special kind of database for knowledge management. It is the base for the collection of knowledge. Normally, the knowledge base consists of explicit knowledge of an organization, including trouble shooting, articles, white papers, user manuals, and others. A knowledge base should have a carefully designed classification structure, content format, and search engine.

Modality: The term is used to describe the distinct method of operation within a computer system, in which the same user input can produce different results depending of the state of the computer. It also defines the mode of communication according to human senses or type of computer input devices. In terms of human senses, the categories are sight, touch, hearing, smell, and taste. In terms of computer input devices, we have modalities that are equivalent to human senses: cameras (sight), haptic sensors (touch), microphones (hearing), olfactory (smell), and even taste. In addition, however, there are input devices that do not map directly to human senses: keyboard, mouse, writing tablet, motion input (e.g., the device itself is moved for interaction), and many others.

Multimodality: By definition, "multimodal" should refer to using more than one modality, regardless of the nature of the modalities. However, many researchers use the term "multimodal," referring specifically to modalities that are commonly used in communication between people, such as speech, gestures, handwriting, and gaze. Multimodality seamlessly combines graphics, text, and audio output with speech, text, and touch input to deliver a dramatically enhanced end-user experience. When compared to a single-mode of interface in which the user can only use either voice/ audio or visual modes, multimodal applications gives them multiple options for inputting and receiving information.

NLP: The term is the acronym of natural language processing (NLP). NLP is a range of computational techniques for analyzing and representing naturally occurring text (free text) at one or more levels of linguistic analysis (e.g., morphological, syntactic, semantic, or pragmatic) for the purpose of achieving human-like language processing for knowledge-intensive applications. NLP includes:

- **Speech synthesis:** Although this may not at first sight appear very "intelligent," the synthesis of natural-sounding speech is technically complex and almost certainly requires some understanding of what is being spoken to ensure, for example, correct intonation;

- **Speech recognition:** Basically the reduction of continuous sound waves to discrete words.
- **Natural language understanding:** Here treated as moving from isolated words to "meaning"; Natural language generation: Generating appropriate natural language responses to unpredictable inputs.
- **Machine translation:** Translating one natural language into another.

Semantic Lexicon: A lexicon is a vocabulary, containing an alphabetical arrangement of the words in a language or of a considerable number of them, with the definition of each. A semantic lexicon is a dictionary of words labelled with semantic classes so associations can be drawn between words that have not previously been encountered.

Semantic Similarity: Semantic similarity, variously also called "semantic closeness /proximity/nearness" is a concept whereby a set of documents or terms within term lists are assigned a metric based on the likeness of their meaning/ semantic content. We define two entities to be similar if: (i) both belong to the same class, (ii) both belong to classes that have a common parent class, or (iii) one entity belongs to a class that is a parent class to which the other entity belongs. Furthermore, two relationships are similar if (i) both belong to the same class, (ii) both belong to classes that have a common parent class, or (iii) one relation belongs to a class that is a parent class to which the other relation belongs.

Usability: The term identifies that quality of a system that makes it easy to learn, easy to use, and encourages the user to regard the system as a positive help in getting the job done. Usability it is defined by five quality components: Learnability, which defines how easy it is for users to accomplish basic tasks the first time they encounter the design; Efficiency, which defines users' quickness in performing tasks; Memorability, which is important when users return to the design after a period of not using it, in order to define how easily they can reestablish proficiency; Errors, which defines how many errors users make, how severe are these errors, and how easily they can recover from errors; And satisfaction, which that defines the satisfaction of the users using the systems.

User: A person, organization, or other entity that employs the services provided by an information processing system for transfer of information. A user functions as a source or final destination of user information.

WordNet: WordNet is a semantic lexicon for the English language. It groups English words into sets of synonyms called synsets, provides short, general definitions, and records the various semantic relations between these synonym sets. The purpose is twofold: to produce a combination of dictionary and thesaurus that is more intuitively usable, and to support automatic text analysis and artificial intelligence applications. WordNet was developed by the Cognitive Science Laboratory (http:// www.cogsci.princeton.edu/) at Princeton University under the direction of Professor George A. Miller (Principal Investigator). WordNet is considered to be the most important resource available to researchers in computational linguistics, text analysis, and many related areas. Its design is inspired by current psycholinguistic and computational theories of human lexical memory

Chapter XXIII
Duplicate Journal Title Detection in References

Ana Kovacevic
University of Belgrade, Serbia

Vladan Devedzic
University of Belgrade, Serbia

ABSTRACT

Our research efforts are oriented towards applying text mining techniques in order to help librarians make more informative decisions when selecting learning resources to be included in the library's offer. The proper selection of learning resources to be included in the library's offer is one of the key factors determining the overall usefulness of the library. Our task was to match abbreviated journal titles from citations with journals in existing digital libraries. The main problem is that for one journal there is often a number of different abbreviated forms in the citation report, hence the matching depends on the detection of duplicate records. We used character-based and token-based metrics together with a generated thesaurus for detecting duplicate records.

INTRODUCTION

Digital libraries need to continuously improve their collections. Knowing how a digital library and its collection are used is inextricably tied to the library's ability to sustain itself, improve its services, and meet its users' needs (McMartin, Iverson, Manduca, Wolf, & Morgan, 2006).

In Serbia, the major provider of digital learning resources is KOBSON[1] (Consortium of Serbian Libraries), which provides Serbian students, teachers, and researchers with access to foreign journals and other learning resources (Kosanović, 2002). Since the available funds are rather modest, the appropriate selection of journals to be made available through KOBSON is highly important and poses a challenge for their staff. Accordingly, our research efforts are aimed at helping librarians in general and KOBSON staff in particular to identify the journals that would be of interest to their users in order to include those journals in the library collection. In addition, we aim to help to improve the services offered to KOBSON's users so that the users can find the resources they are interested in more easily.

This chapter presents part of our current work on the realization of the illustrated research challenge. Specifically, we are working on the identification of those journals that are frequently used by domestic researchers and are therefore relevant for inclusion in KOBSON's offer. An indication that a certain journal is read and considered important by a researcher is the appearance of the journal's title in the citations of the researcher's published papers. However, manual analysis of citations is impossible due to the large volume of data that need to be processed. Likewise, automatic analysis is impeded by the fact that authors tend to use different kinds of abbreviations when writing citations. Accordingly, we are currently working on matching the journal title abbreviations found in citations with the journals (i.e., their full titles) in the KOBSON digital libraries.

In the following section we present the problem of data heterogeneity that impedes the matching process and offer solutions for resolving this problem in digital libraries.

DATA HETEROGENITY

In the real world, data are not perfectly clean and there are various reasons for that, such as data entry errors, missing check constraints, lack of standardization in recording data in different sources, and so forth. In general, data originating from different sources can vary in value, structure, semantics and the underlying assumptions (Elmagarmid et al, 2007). This is the problem of data heterogeneity. There are two basic types of data heterogeneity: structural (differently structured data in different databases) and lexical (diverse representations of the same word entity) (Elmagarmid, Ipeirotis, & Verykios, 2007). The

task of lexical heterogeneity has been explored in different research areas, such as statistics, databases, data mining, digital libraries, and natural language processing. Researchers in different areas have proposed various techniques and refer to the problem differently: record linkage (Newcomb & Kennedy, 1962), data duplication (Sarawagi & Bhamidipaty, 2002), database hardening and name matching (Bilenko, Mooney, Cohen, Ravikumar, & Fienber, 2003), data cleaning (McCallum & Wellner, 2003) or object identification (Tejada, Knoblock, & Minton, 2002), approximate matching (Guha, Koudas, Marathe, & Srivastava, 2004), fuzzy matching (Ananthakrishna, Chaudhuri, & Ganti, 2002), and entity resolution (Benjelloum, Garcia-Molina, Su, & Widom, 2005).

Data heterogeneity can have a negative impact on many common data library services. In our work we are addressing the problem of lexical heterogeneity in general and duplicate record detection in particular. The technique for matching fields depends on the particular problem, and there is no absolute solution. Basically, these techniques may be classified into the following categories:

- Character-based similarity metrics, which consider distance as the difference between characters, and is useful in the case of typographical errors (i.e., Levenshtein distance) (Levenshtein, 1966), Jaro-Winkler metrics (Winkler, 1995), and Q-Grams (Ukkonen, 1992).
- Token-based similarity metrics, which is based on statistics for common words, is useful when word order is not important (i.e., atomic strings [Monge & Elkan, 1996] and WHIRL [Cohen, 1998]).
- Phonetic similarity metrics, based on the fact that strings may be phonetically similar even if they are not similar in character or token level (i.e., double metaphone) (Philips, 2000).

The edit distance between two strings s1 and s2 is the minimum number of edit operations (i.e., insert, delete, replace) of single characters needed to transform string s1 into s2 (Levenshtein, 1966). The simple edit distance with unit cost metric is called the Leveinshtein distance. The edit distance is good for identifying typographical errors, but is typically ineffective for other types of mismatches.

William Winkler (1995) proposed improvements to Jaro's (1976) metric. Jaro's metric is based on his algorithm, which has the following steps:

1. Compute the string length of string s1 and s2 (len (s1), len (s2)).
2. Find common characters in the two strings *Nc*.
   Common characters are s1[i] and s2[j] for which s1[i]=s2[j] and
   |i-j|<0.5 min{len(s1)·len(s2)}
3. Find the number of transposition *Nt* (each nonmatching character s1[i] between s2[i]).

$$Jaro\ (s1,s2) = \frac{1}{3}\left(\frac{Nc}{len(s1)} + \frac{Nc}{len(s2)} + \frac{Nc-0.5Nt}{Nc} \right)$$

Winkler improves Jaro's metric by using the length P of the longest common prefix of s1 and s2 (Winkler, 1995). When P'=max(P,4) then

$$Jaro\text{-}Winkler(s1,s2)= (Jaro\ s1,\ s2) + \left(\frac{P'}{10}\right)\left(1 - Jaro\ (s1,s2)\right)$$

Cohen, Ravikumar, and Feinberg (2003) achieved the best results with the hybrid model of token-base similarity metrics combined with Jaro-Winkler.

Specifically for the bibliographic domain, Lawerence, Giles, and Bollacker (1999) proposed different hand-coded dedupliaction functions based on character-based and token-based similarity metrics and subfield extraction for matching citations.

INDENTIFYING JORNAL TITLES IN REFERENCES

Our goal was to match abbreviated journal titles found in part of Journal Citation Report[2] (JCR, 2005) with the journals (i.e., their full titles) in the digital libraries (KOBSON, 2005). However, manual analysis of citations is impossible due to the large volume of data that need to be processed. The matching problem stems from the fact that in JCR, titles are represented with abbreviations and not with their full names. In addition, the usage of abbreviations is not standardized, and usually there is a range of different abbreviations for one journal title. An additional source of these variations lies in errors made by authors, journal editors, or ISI data entry persons (in the case of references from the JCR). For example, there are five different abbreviated titles, for the journal *Communications of the ACM (Association for Computing Machinery)* in JCR, as shown in Table 1. Other identified problems include the change of a journal's name during time and the split of one journal into several new journals with different ISSNs. To find the correct journal we had to use

Table 1. Examples of abbreviated titles (JCR, 2005) and potential matches among journal titles in KOBSON digital library

COMMUNICATIONS OF THE ACM (Association for Computing Machinery)	COMM ACM
	COMM ACM JAN
	COMM ACM MAR
	COMMUN ACM
	COMMUNICATION ACM

some journal metadata, such as the volume, the year of publication, and external sources as well (e.g., journal Web page).

We discovered that abbreviations also depend on the part of the title where a word appears. For example, for the word LANGUAGE, the typical abbreviation is LANG; however, since only 20 characters are available for the whole string, when the title is longer, LANGUAGE might be shortened to LA (see Table 2).

In trying to identify journal titles from JCR, we perform the following steps:

- Collect data from various sources.
- Clean "dirty" data.
- Match abbreviated titles with full titles using character-based similarity metrics.
- Build a thesaurus after correct abbreviated titles.
- Match abbreviated titles with full titles using the thesaurus and token-based similarity metrics.
- Include new external data (Web resources).
- Incremental matching.

Data Collection

After collecting data from various sources (e.g., JCR, 2005; KOBSON, 2005), we have created appropriate database tables and loaded data into them.

Table 2. Examples of journal titles and their abbreviated variations in citation reports

ACM TRANSACTIONS ON PROGRAMMING LANGUAGES & SYSTEMS (Association for Computing Machinery)		
	ACM T PROGR **LANG** SYS	
	ACM T PROGRAMMING **LA**	

Cleaning

In the data cleaning process, journal titles and their abbreviations are "cleaned" from multiple delimiters (spaces), parts that bring in "noise," such as months (JAN in "COMM ACM JAN", Table 1) in abbreviated titles, and so forth. Usually, the most efficient way of cleaning after identifying the problem is to use regular expressions. For efficient cleaning, data must be "understood." In order to avoid any ambiguity we consult the domain expert when making rules for cleaning.

In addition, in the preprocessing phase after parsing, if there is no abbreviated title, we look for more information from the data source (to parse it again, e.g., when the journal is in "in press"), or delete the row when there is no additional information about the journal in the data source.

We also need to prepare the table of digital library journals for matching by cleaning extra spaces, stop words (e.g., the, at, on, etc.), and explanations of titles which are usually in parenthesis (e.g., *ACM TRANSACTIONS ON PROGRAMMING LANGUAGES & SYSTEMS [Association for Computing Machinery]*).

Matching Titles

First, we match the abbreviated titles from JCR with correctly abbreviated titles (from external source, such as http://scientific.thomson.com); 57% of the titles were matched in this way. After that we apply character-based similarity metrics and then token-based metrics. After the initial matching, in order to improve performance, we divide the reference table into three subtables of matched pairs, "candidate" matched, and unmatched pairs.

In the case of ambiguous matching, where we have several candidate titles for one abbreviated title, we must carry out further research in order to find the correct title (e.g., using metadata). In our matching we take careful note of each abbreviated title in the ambiguous matching where for one acronym title we have few candidate titles and must perform further investigation in order to find the correct title (e.g., using meta-data). In our matching we take care of the frequency of an abbreviated title in the JCR, and we first try to match the most frequent abbreviated title.

Character-Based Similarity Metrics

We used a function (further referred to as the JWS) which is based on the Jaro-Winkler algorithm (Winkler, 1995) shown before. We also tried the function based on the edit-distance algorithm, but it was not as efficient as the JWS.

We applied the JWS function on the abbreviated title found in the citations and "correct" abbreviation. We discovered that the threshold of 96 tends to be correct (Table 3).

In the JWS, the last letter(s) of a string has a negligible weight, but this is not so in our case; in the case of journal titles, that is, their abbreviations, the last letters (e.g.,, A, B, C, D, E or AM, BR) usually have a special meaning. For example, "ACTA CRYSTALLOGRAPHICA A" is a different journal than "ACTA CRYSTALLOGRAPHICA B." Therefore, we are now working on improving the process of matching, taking note of "special" last letter(s) of the abbreviation string.

The process of matching is incremental, that is, when we find a matched title for the abbreviated one, we can use that in future matching.

Sometimes for an abbreviated journal we get a few candidates (even after using metadata) and we should use some external sources (e.g., the

Table 3. The result of applying JWS in matching

MATCHED ATITLE	CORRECT ATITLE	JWS
ASTROPHYS J SUPPL SE	ASTROPHYS J SUPPL S	99
BONE JOINT SURG A	J BONE JOINT SURG AM	99
J BONE JOINT SURG B	J BONE JOINT SURG BR	99
AM J SPORTS MED	AM J SPORT MED	98
CURR OPIN GENE DEV	CURR OPIN GENET DEV	98
J NON-CRYST SOLIDS 1	J NON-CRYST SOLIDS	98

Web page of corresponding journal) or the help of domains experts.

By using the Jaro-Winkler algorithm, we managed to match 16,099 (21%) out of 76,001 unmatched records.

Thesaurus

A thesaurus can be very useful in the matching of abbreviated titles with full ones. The idea is to the find the most frequent narrow terms of the abbreviated term. The combination of narrow terms can be used in further matching in token-based similarity instead of the original abbreviated title (form JCR). A thesaurus can be generated by extracting terms from "proper" abbreviated titles and their corresponding full title from previously matched titles. First, we select those rows where the number of words in the abbreviated title is the same as their corresponding full title. Subsequently, we load the content of the terms from the abbreviated titles and terms from full titles into the thesaurus. Finally, we create relations between the loaded phrases. To improve the performance of the thesaurus usage, when creating relations between terms/phrases we take note of the frequency of each term. So frequently used abbreviations should be loaded first, for example, T- TRANSACTIONS before THROMBOSIS.

Token-Based Similarity Metrics

Matching only with Jaro-Winkler metrics was not enough, so we decided to try with token-based similarity metrics. We use token-based similarity metrics for phrases that should appear in the journal titles. Because we are trying to match abbreviated titles with full ones, we first need to find an appropriate substitution for each token in the abbreviated title and then to try to match them. We used the previously generated thesaurus with token-based similarity metrics.

The thesaurus was generated by "proper" abbreviated titles and their corresponding full title from previous matched. We created relations between the loaded terms/phrases, so that each term from an abbreviated title is related to the corresponding full term in the full title. To improve the performance of the thesaurus usage, when creating relations between terms/phrases, we take note of the frequency of each term and we can apply the JWS function (with high threshold) on phrases generated after using the thesaurus and for use in further token-based matching to improve recall.

Using External Sources

When we do not have enough information to discover the corresponding journal for an abbreviated one, we should use external sources. For example, we can find the user's published manuscripts and extract references from them, or search Web sites that provide citation reports, such as Thomson Scientific[3] or CiteSeer[4]. If this is not enough, we must consult domain experts.

Incremental Matching

As previously mentioned, once the full title for the abbreviated title has been found and it has been verify with the metadata (i.e., issue, volume, year, author, etc.), then it can be used for further matching or for thesaurus generation.

FUTUTRE TRENDS

There are a number of directions we will pursue in the immediate future. First, the presented approach for journal matching needs to be further improved. Besides the improvements already mentioned, we will also investigate the inclusion of semantics in the applied approach. To be more precise, we plan to use journal classification into thematic categories. Currently these categories (for some titles) are available in a flat form.

Second, having tackled the problem of journal matching, we intend to develop a software tool that tracks the usage of the resources (i.e., journals) provided by KOBSON's digital libraries on one hand and in accordance with KOBSON's user interests on the other, to make recommendations to the KOBSON staff regarding the exclusion of some of the existing resources as well as the inclusion of some new resources.

Additionally, we plan to develop a clustering method to group duplicate records for a given real-world entity in digital libraries, thus helping us in further matching.

Table 4. Example of using thesaurus in token-based similarity metrics

Abbreviated title in JCR	1. step Retrieved from the thesaurus: all terms related to the given narrow terms and their combinations	2. step The full journal title as result
'ACM T GRAPHIC'	({ACM} {T} {GRAPHIC}) OR ({ACM} {T} {GRAPHICS}) OR ({ACM} {TECHNOLOGIES} {GRAPHIC}) OR ({ACM} {TECHNOLOGIES} {GRAPHICS}) OR ({ACM} {TRANSACTIONS} {GRAPHIC}) OR ({ACM} {TRANSACTIONS} {GRAPHICS})	ACM TRANSACTIONS GRAPHICS

CONCLUSION

Successful data preparation has major implications for the overall data mining process. There is no universal solution, and every problem has its own characteristics. We have presented how we detect duplicate records among abbreviated journal titles and thus facilitate the matching with full title journals in digital libraries. We apply character-based and token-based similarity metrics together with the generated thesaurus. Our experience proves that the best results are achieved with the combined approach. In addition, it is often necessary to use journal metadata (e.g., the year of publication and volume) and external sources (e.g., the journal's Web site) to improve the results of the overall process.

ACKNOWLEDGMENT

We would like to express our gratitude to the KOBSON staff in general and Mrs. Biljana Kosanović in particular, for their willingness to provide us with access to the library usage tracking data, as well as for helping us make sense of that data.

REFERENCES

Ananthakrishna, R., Chaudhuri, S., & Ganti, V. (2002). Eliminating fuzzy duplicates in data warehouses. In *Proceedings of the 28th International Conference on Very Large Databases (VLDB)*, Hong Kong (pp. 586-597).

Benjelloun, O., Garcia-Molina, H., Su, Q., & Widom, J. (2005, March). *Swoosh: A generic approach to entity resolution* (Tech. Rep.). Stanford University.

Bilenko, M., Mooney, R. J., Cohen, W. W., Ravikumar, P., & Fienber, S. E. (2003). Adaptive name matching in information integration. *IEEE Intelligent Systems, 18*(5), 16-23.

Cohen, W. W. (1998). Integration of heterogeneous databases without common domains using query based on textual similarity. In *Proceedings of the 1998 ACM SIGMOD International Conference on Management of Data (SIGMOD '98)* (pp. 201-212).

Cohen, W. W., Ravikumar, P., & Feinberg, S. (2003). A comparison of string metrics for matching names and records. In *Proceedings of the KDD2003*. Retrieved August 22, 2008, from http://www.cs.cmu.edu/~pradeepr/papers/kdd03.pdf

Elmagarmid, A., Ipeirotis, P., & Verykios, V. (2007). Duplicate record detection: A survey. *IEEE Transaction on Knowledge and Data Engineering, 19*(1), 1-16

Guha, S., Koudas, N., Marathe, A., & Srivastava, D. (2004). Merging the results of approximate match operations. In *Proceedings of the 30th VLDB Conference* (pp. 636-647).

JCR. (2005). Journal citation report, Institute for Scientific Information. *Thomson*. Retrieved August 22, 2008, from http://scientific.thomson.com/products/jcr/

Jaro, M. A. (1976). *Unimatch: A record linkage system: User's manual* (Tech. Rep.). US Bureau of the Census, Washington, D.C.

KOBSON. (2005). *Internal data of the project on the evaluation of the Serbian authors publishing productivity.* Author.

Kosanović, B. (2002). Koordinirana nabavka inostranih izvora naučno-tehničkih informacija u Srbiji - stanje i perspective. *Infoteka, 3*(1-2), 55-63.

Lawrence, S., Giles, C. L., & Bollacker, K. (1999). Digital libraries and autonomous citation indexing. *IEEE Computer, 32*(6), 67-71.

Levenshtein, V. I. (1966). Binary codes capable of correcting deletitions, insertations and reversals. *Soviet Physics Doklady, 10*(8), 707-710.

McCallum, A., & Wellner, B. (2003, August). Object consolidation by graph partitioning with a conditionally trained distance metric. In *Proceedings of the ACM Workshop on Data Cleaning, Record Linkage and Object Identification*, Washington D.C.

McMartin, F., Iverson, E., Manduca, C., Wolf, A., & Morgan, G. (2006). Factors motivating use of digital libraries. In *Proceedings of the 6th ACM/IEEE-CS Joint Conference on Digital Libraries*, Chapel Hill, NC (pp. 254-255).

Monge, A. E., & Elkan, C. P. (1996). The field matching problem: Algortihms and applications. In *Proceedings of the Second International Conference Knowledge Discovery and Data Mining (KDD'96)* (pp. 267-270).

Newcomb, H. B., & Kennedy, J. M. (1962). Record linkage: Making maximum use of the discriminating power of identifying information. *Communication of the ACM, 5*(11), 563-566.

Philips, L. (2000). The double metaphone search algorithm. *C/C++ Users Journal, 18*(5).

Sarawagi, S., & Bhamidipaty, A. (2002). Interactive deduplication using active learning. In *Proceedings of the International Conference. Knowledge Discovery and Data Mining (KDD'02)* (pp. 269-278).

Tejada, S., Knoblock, C., & Minton, S. (2002, July). Learning domain-independent string transformation for high accuracy object identification. In *Proceedings of the Eight ACM SIGKDD International Conference on Knowledge Discovery and Data Mining*, Edmonton, Canada.

Ukkonen, E. (1992). Approximate string matching with q-grams and maximal matches. *Theoretical Computer Science, 92*(1), 191-211.

Winkler, W. E. (1995). Matching and record linkage. In B. G. Cox (Ed.), *Business survey methods* (pp. 355-384). Wiley.

KEY TERMS

Character-based Similarity Metrics: They consider distance as the difference between characters, and is useful in the case of typographical errors.

Data Mining: Data mining is an iterative process of searching for new, previously hidden, and usually unexpected patterns in large volumes of data.

Duplicate Record Detection: The process of identifying record replicas that refer to the same real-world entity or object in spite of the fact that they are syntactically different.

Lexical Data Heterogeneity: Refers to diverse syntax of the same word entity.

Phonetic Similarity Metrics: Based on the fact that strings may be phonetically similar if they are not similar in character or token level.

Structural Data Heterogeneity: Refers to differently structured data in different databases.

Token-based Similarity Metrics: Based on statistics of common words and are useful when word order is not important.

ENDNOTES

[1] http://nainfo.nbs.bg.ac.yu/KoBSON/page/
[2] for Serbian scientists
[3] http://scientific.thomson.com/
[4] http://citeseer.ist.psu.edu/?form=citesearch

Chapter XXIV
Word Segmentation in Indo–China Languages for Digital Libraries

Jin-Cheon Na
Nanyang Technological University, Singapore

Yin-Leng Theng
Nanyang Technological University, Singapore

Tun Thura Thet
Nanyang Technological University, Singapore

Schubert Foo
Nanyang Technological University, Singapore

Dion Hoe-Lian Goh
Nanyang Technological University, Singapore

Paul Horng-Jyh Wu
Nanyang Technological University, Singapore

ABSTRACT

This chapter introduces word segmentation methods for Indo-China languages. It describes six different word segmentation methods developed for the Thai, Vietnamese, and Myanmar languages and compare different approaches in terms of their algorithms and results achieved. The discussion and comparison of these word segmentation methods will provide underlying views about how word segmentation can be achieved and employed in Indo-China languages to support search functionality in digital libraries.

INTRODUCTION

Digital libraries are not really digitized libraries (Witten & Bainbridge, 2003). They essentially changes the way information is used in the world. A digital library is about new ways of dealing with knowledge. One of the many advantages digital libraries have over traditional libraries is the ability to search information efficiently and effectively. Users can conduct various searches, ranging from a simple title search query to a complex advanced query. It is pretty straightforward for documents written in well established western languages such as English but when it comes to languages such as Thai, Vietnamese, and Myanmar, it can be significantly challenging, mainly due to the nontrivial task of segmenting words. Word segmentation is an essential preprocess for the full-text indexing of documents written in these languages in order to support search functionality in digital libraries.

Unlike English, there are no white spaces between words in these languages. Dissimilar to Chinese, a syllable can be composed of multiple characters where a word can contain multiple syllables. It seems to be quite effortlessly easy for a native speaker to determine where word boundaries are in a sentence or a document. For the very same reason, people expect computers to determine the word boundaries automatically. Unless the issue of word segmentation is addressed properly, the indexing of terms for search functions in digital libraries will not be feasible. From the information processing perspective, it is important to index and search words in documents' contents rather than just metadata, such as titles and descriptions. In addition, for a document in one language to be translated into another language, the first step is always to segment words before doing any further processing. Therefore, word segmentation is basic yet essential in order to carry out any further information processing for documents written in these languages.

The following sections discuss word segmentation methods for the Thai language, the Vietnamese language, and the Myanmar language, and the comparison of them. The last section summarizes the current status and discusses future work.

WORD SEGMENTATION

The Thai Language

The Thai script is a member of the Indic family of scripts, descended from Brahmi. In the Thai language, a "word" is difficult to define, as it does not exhibit explicit word boundaries. Like many other Asian languages, the Thai language does not use white spaces for word boundaries. Each Thai letter is a consonant possessing an inherent vowel sound as well as inherent tones. Both the inherent vowel and tone can be modified by means of vowel signs and tone marks attached to the base consonant letter. All of the tone marks and some of the vowel signs are rendered in the script as diacritics attached above or below the base consonant. In the Unicode memory representation, these combining signs and marks are encoded after the modified consonant (Unicode Consortium, 2004). One main cause of the problems in Thai word segmentation is the lack of a clear definition of a Thai "word" (Wirot, 2002). Traditional methods of Thai word segmentation are based on unclear criteria and procedures, and have several limitations. Most of the word segmentation approaches use a dictionary for segmenting running texts.

A study conducted by Sornlertlamvanich, Potipiti, and Charoenporn (2000) used automatic corpus-based word extraction. It employed the C4.5 decision tree induction program (Quinlan, 1993) as a learning algorithm for word extraction. The induction algorithm evaluates the content of a series of attributes and interactively builds a tree. The leaves of the decision tree represent the values of the goal attributes. The method used C4.5 to prune the entire decision tree in order to reduce the effect of over fitting. It recursively traveled to each subtree to determine if the leaf or branch could reduce the expected error rate. The attributes of the learning algorithm are mutual information, entropy, frequency, and string length. Evaluation of the method was carried out with a corpus of size 1 MB, consisting of 75 articles from various fields. Thirty thousand strings were manually tagged and compared with the results produced by the method, which recorded a 84.1% accuracy for the test dataset.

Another study conducted by Wirot (2002) used a two-part approach: a syllable-based trigram model for syllable segmentation, and maximum collocation for syllable merging. Syllable segmentation was done on the basis of trigram statistics, whereas syllable merging was done on the basis of collocation between words. Many word segmentation ambiguities were resolved during the syllable segmentation process. Using a training corpus of 553,372 syllables, a newspaper was manually segmented by syllables. Witten-Bell discounting (Chen & Goodman, 1996) was used for smoothing and Viterbi algorithms were used for determining the best syllable segmentation. When tested on another corpus of 30,498 syllables, the results were 99.8% correct. After syllable segmentation, the strategy was to use collocation strength between syllables to merge syllables. The "longest matching" approach relies heavily on words listed in the dictionary and it always prefers compound words over simple words. However, the maximum collocation approach does not exhibit such preference.

The Vietnamese Language

Vietnamese, traditionally a spoken language, is a monosyllabic language that belongs to the Southeast Asian language family. Even though its alphabet is based on the Latin alphabet, the differences between it and Indo-European languages not only make it difficult for the Vietnamese to learn European languages but also to develop techniques for natural language processing. The available options are either to fit Vietnamese into a well-established European language framework or to come up with a new framework. The former had been tried but did not achieve good results, while the latter requires a great deal of human and material resources (Le, 2003). The Vietnamese language has a special linguistic unit called "tieng" which is equivalent hanzi in Chinese. One "tieng" is one sound unit and has one syllable. Unlike the hanzi of Chinese, one "tieng" has only one way of pronunciation. One or more sound units can be combined to form a word in Vietnamese. Each syllable or sound unit

in Vietnamese is composed of a (sequence of) character(s) separated by space. One of the most difficult tasks in machine translation for Vietnamese is the elimination of ambiguity in human languages (Dinh, 2002). A word in Vietnamese often has different meanings depending on its syntactical position in the sentence and the context. Another major problem is that there are few effective lexical resources available. The reliable option is to use pure statistical methods.

The study conducted by Dinh, Kiem, and Toan (2001) considered Vietnamese word segmentation as a stochastic transduction problem and it applied the weighted finite-state transducers (WFST) model. The first step was a preprocessing stage, where all the errors of sentence presentation were eliminated. Then, the sentences were introduced to the WFST model, where reduplicatives, proper nouns, date-time, and numbers were further defined. The dictionary was used in this approach, and it was arranged in the multiway tree in which each node represented a Vietnamese letter. The selection of the best word segmentation was done by the Like-Viterbi algorithm. Machine learning for ambiguous sentences through the neural network model was used instead of a rule-based model. The corpus used for calculating probability was about 2 million words from five different sources. The size of the dictionary used was about 34,000 entries. When the approach was evaluated by comparing it with a manually annotated corpus, it achieved 97% accuracy on a corpus of Vietnamese electronic textbooks.

Le (2003) employed a pure statistical model, applying the maximum probability of tri-gram in a given chunk of syllables. An unannotated corpus of 10 million words was used in this study. The aim was to maximize the probability of the chunk, using different segmentations. The probability of a chunk is the product of its n-gram probabilities, and the chunk with the maximum probability was selected as the final result. Evaluation was conducted on 100 randomly selected chunks, containing 614 words identified by the model. A native-speaking evaluator was in "agreement" with 315 (51%) of the words, and considered 402 (65%) of them "reasonable."

The study by Nguyen, Tran, Nguyen, and Nguyen (2006) also adopted a statistical model, using mutual information (MI) formulas for n-grams (Manning & Schutze, 2002). The interesting aspect in this approach is that the statistical information was retrieved directly from a commercial search engine by using a genetic algorithm to find the most reasonable segmentation. For better performance, a new way to calculate the MI of Vietnamese n-gram was represented in this study, but there was no significant difference in word segmentation results among the various MI formulas.

The Myanmar Language

Texts in the Myanmar language use the Myanmar script, which is descended from the Brahmi script of ancient South India (Unicode Consortium, 2004). The Myanmar language is more than 1,000-years-old and it is used by more than 50 million people. A Myanmar text is a string of characters without explicit word boundary markup, written in sequence from left to right. Myanmar writing does not use white spaces between words or between syllables. Thus, the computer has to determine syllable and word boundaries by means of an algorithm. Myanmar characters can be classified into three groups: consonants, medials, and vowels. Medials are subscript characters which can modify the basic consonants to form hundreds of consonants. In the Myanmar language, a word can be made up of one or more syllables which can be formed by consonants combining with vowels, although some syllables can be formed by just consonants, without any vowel. A Myanmar syllable has a base character, and may also have a prebase character, a postbase character, an above-base character, and a below-base character. Regardless of the appearance of the characters on the screen, the characters are to

be stored consistently in a sequence specified by the Unicode standard. The sequence of characters stored may not be the same as their input method from the keyboard.

The Myanmar NLP team (Myanmar NLP, 2006) has been working with the International Organization for Standardization (ISO) on the standardization of a character set for the Myanmar script. The Myanmar character set had been quite unstable in the past but its recent enhancement in the Unicode Standard Version 5.1 has resolved the key issues. Except for a proposed method by two of this chapter's authors (Thet, 2006; Thet, Na, & Ko Ko, in 2008), no published works or research have been found for Myanmar word segmentation using the Unicode standard version 5.1, which is the essential first step of any natural language processing for the Myanmar language. Most researchers have worked only on Myanmar syllable segmentation and many did not work with documents in the Unicode standards.

The proposed Myanmar word segmentation method (Thet, 2006) has two phases: syllable segmentation and syllable merging. The method uses six syllable segmentation rules: the single character rule, the special ending characters rule, the second consonant rule, the last character rule, the next starter rule, and the miscellaneous rule. Single characters such as "ဤ","ၒ", "ၑ" and "ၕ" do not need any medials or vowels to become a syllable according to the single character rule. According to the special ending character rule, characters such as ":" and "." indicate the end of a syllable. The second consonant rule prescribes that when a syllable has two consonants, the second consonant must come with either the Atha (Killer) or the Kinzi (Htutsint). The last character rule regards the last character in a sentence, a phrase, or the input file as the end of a syllable. The next starter rule provides proper segmentation of an invalid sequence of entries involving the vowel "ေ" and the miscellaneous rule covers numbers, special characters, and non-Myanmar characters.

The syllable segmentation was tested with 16 documents extracted from the Myanmar bible and literature provided by the Myanmar NLP team. The heuristic rule-based approach for syllable segmentation achieved 100% accuracy for the Myanmar language. The next step was to merge the segmented syllables to determine word boundaries. The method initially adopted the "longest matching" approach to perform syllable merging. This approach assumes that each syllable boundary is a possible word boundary, and each boundary will be discarded when a longer match is found in the dictionary. The work is later extended and improved by employing a dictionary-based statistical approach (Thet et al., 2008). The input text of segmented syllables is broken down into sentences and phrases by looking at punctuation marks and spaces. For each sentence or phrase, all possible combinations of segmented words (or merged syllables) are generated by matching segmented syllables in the sentence or phrase with word entries in the dictionary. From the resulting combinations, the one with the minimum number of segmented words is selected, and taken as the correctly segmented words of the sentence or phrase. This approach is biased to choose longer matching words in the dictionary. When there are two or more combinations with the same minimum number of segmented words, the statistical approach is used to resolve the problem. The mutual information of two syllables (i.e., bi-grams) are precalculated with the corpus, and then used to calculate the collocation strength of a sentence or phrase. The collocation strength of a sentence or phrase is the sum of the collocation strengths of all the segmented words in the sentence or phrase, whereas the collocation strength of an individual word is the sum of the positive strength minus the sum of the negative strength. As an example, for the word "BCDE" in the sentence "ABCDEF," its positive strength is the sum of the mutual information of B-C, C-D and D-E, whereas its negative strength is the sum of the mutual information of A-B and E-F. In most cases, if "BCDE" is a correctly segmented word, its positive collocation strength will be higher than its negative collocation strength. To sum up, for each sentence or phrase, the segmented syllables are merged into words with the help of a dictionary, and then the combination with the minimum number of segmented words is selected. When there are two or more such combinations, their collocation strengths are calculated, and the combination with the biggest collocation strength is selected.

For syllable merging, test results averaged 98.94% recall, 99.05% precision, and 98.99% F-measure. The errors encountered can be categorized into four groups: missing common words in the dictionary, proper nouns such as names of people and places, adopted words in Pali (or other languages), and numerical words. The dictionary used in the study, with about 30,000 entries, was provided by the Myanmar NLP team, and its coverage has been found to be relatively effective compared to dictionaries in other languages. However, this proposed method should be evaluated on a larger data set. As more Myanmar documents become available in Unicode, the use of a large corpus and statistical models could lead to interesting results. Especially it would be interesting to examine the application and effectiveness of pure statistical models without using any dictionaries.

COMPARSION OF THE METHODS

Table 1 compares six word segmentation studies for the Thai, Vietnamese, and Myanmar languages. Most methods use statistical approaches in combination with other techniques since available dictionaries do not have adequate coverage. Note that Vietnamese word segmentation does not require prior syllable segmentation because syllables in Vietnamese words are separated by white spaces. In contrast, Thai and Myanmar word segmentation do require prior syllable segmentation because syllables are not separated by white spaces. The methods proposed by Wirot (2002) and Thet et al. (2008) are similar but they employ different approaches for syllable segmentation, that is, trigram statistical approach and heuristic rule-based approach. Sornlertlamvanich et al. (2000) tried to segment words directly, without taking care of syllable segmentation first, but produced unsatisfactory results. Of the six studies, three (i.e., Dinh et al., 2001; Thet et al., 2008; Wirot, 2002) scored above 95% accuracy.

CONCLUSION

The word segmentation methods we have discussed are generally language dependant and still need improvements for better accuracy and performance. Syllable segmentation is a prior step to word segmentation in some languages like Myanmar and Thai, where a syllable can contain multiple characters without any delimiters. Since a syllable is a better defined unit than a word, and also more consistent in analysis, the methods with syllable segmentation preprocess are more effective and reliable than other methods which segment words directly without syllable segmentation. Most word segmentation approaches use a dictionary and when the coverage of the dictionary is not adequate enough, it leads to a large number of unknown or unrecognized words, adversely affecting the results. Thus, some methods use a dictionary in combination with statistical approaches or other techniques to

Table 1. Thai, Vietnamese, and Myanmar word segmentation methods

Segmentation Method	Method Used	Dictionary	Corpus	Statistics-based	Other Techniques	Results
Thai word segmentation (Sornlertlamvanich et al., 2000)	C4.5 learning algorithm using string length, frequency, mutual information and entropy		Y	Y	Y	Precision : 85% Recall: 56% F-Measure:67.5%
Thai word segmentation (Wirot, 2002)	Syllable Segmentation: Statistics based trigram model Syllable Merging: Maximum Collocation strength	Y		Y		Precision : 96.36% Recall : 97.16% F-Measure : 96.76%
Vietnamese word segmentation (Dinh et al., 2001)	Syllable Segmentation: whitespace Syllable Merging: Weighted Finite State Transducer (WFST) model and Neural Network	Y		Y	Y	97% Accuracy
Vietnamese word segmentation (Le, 2003)	Syllable Segmentation: whitespace Syllable Merging: Statistical Model and N-gram model using Maximum Probability		Y	Y		"Agreement" : 51% "Reasonable" : 65%
Vietnamese word segmentation (Nguyen et al., 2006)	Syllable Segmentation: whitespace Syllable Merging: Statistical model using online corpus approach and Genetic Algorithm		Y	Y	Y	"Acceptable" : 80%
Myanmar word segmentation (Thet et al., 2008)	Syllable Segmentation: Rule-based heuristic approach Syllable Merging: Dictionary based statistical approach	Y	Y	Y	Y	Precision : 98.94% Recall : 99.05% F-Measure : 98.99%

achieve better results. The accuracies achieved by these methods are relatively very high. However, it does not necessarily mean that they are very effective. Larger datasets and a wider scope of domains should be used for evaluations for the methods for their effectiveness. For future work, new approaches using machine learning and statistical models can be explored for word segmentation of these languages.

REFERENCES

Chen, S. F., & Goodman, J. (1996). An empirical study of smoothing techniques for language modeling. In *Proceeding of the 34th Annual Meeting on Association for Computer Linguistics*. NJ: Association for Computer Linguistics.

Dinh, D. (2002). Building a training corpus for word sense disambiguation in English-to-Vietnamese machine translation. In *Proceedings of the 19th International Conference on Computational Linguistics*. Association for Computer Linguistics.

Dinh, D., Kiem, H., & Toan, N. V. (2001). Vietnamese word segmentation. In *Proceedings of Neural Networks and Natural Language Processing* (pp. 749-756). Tokyo.

Le, A. H. (2003). A method for word segmentation in Vietnamese. Research group in computational linguistics. In *Proceedings of Corpus Linguistic 2003*. Lancaster.

Manning, C. D., & Schutze, H. (2002). *Foundations of statistical natural language processing*. London: MIT Press.

Myanmar NLP. (2006). *Myanmar Unicode reference documents and research papers*. Retrieved June 1, 2006, from http://www.myanmars.net/ unicode/doc/ index.htm

Nguyen, T. V., Tran, H. K., Nguyen, T. T. T., & Nguyen, H. (2006). Word segmentation for Vietnamese text categorization: A online corpus approach. In *Proceedings of 4th IEEE International Conference on Computer Science - Research, Innovation and Vision of the Future*, HoChiMinh City.

Quinlan, J. R. (1993). *C4.5 programs for machine learning*. CA: Morgan Kaufmann.

Sornlertlamvanich, V., Potipiti, T., & Charoenporn, T. (2000). Automatic corpus-based Thai word extraction with the c4.5 learning algorithm. In *Proceedings of the 18th Conference on Computational Linguistics* (pp. 802-807). NJ: Association for Computer Linguistics.

Thet, T. T. (2006). *Development of a word segmentation algorithm for Myanmar language*. Unpublished master's thesis, Nanyang Technological University, Singapore.

Thet, T. T., Na, J.-C., & Ko Ko, W. (2008). Word segmentation for the Myanmar language. *Journal of Information Science, 34*(5), 688-704.

Unicode Consortium. (2004). *The Unicode standard 4.0, Southeast Asian scripts*. CA: Addison Wesley.

Wirot, A. (2002). Collocation and Thai word segmentation. In *Proceeding of Joint International Conference of SNLP-Oriental COCOSDA 2002*. Thammasat University, Bangkok.

Witten, I. H., & Bainbridge, D. I. (2003). *How to build a digital library*. San Francisco: Morgan Kaufmann.

KEY TERMS

Brahmi Script: Brahmi script is the oldest member of the Brahmic family of alphabets which was related to most of the scripts of South Asia, Southeast Asia, and Tibet.

Compound Word: Compound words are words that are composed of two or more simple words. The meaning of a compound word may not be the sum of the meanings of its parts, though it can be related to the meanings of its parts.

F-Measure: F-measure, also known as balanced F-score, is the weighted harmonic mean of precision and recall.

ISO: The International Organization for Standardization (ISO) is an international standard-setting body composed of representatives from various national standards bodies.

Maximum Collocation: Syllable collocation refers to cooccurrence of syllables observed from the training corpus. If a word contains two or more syllables, those syllables will cooccur. Thus, the probability of cooccurrence will be much greater than by chance.

Precision: Precision is the ratio of the number of correctly segmented words to the number of all the segmented words.

Recall: Recall is the ratio of the number of correctly segmented words to the number of all the words in the documents.

Simple Word: Simple words are words that can have one or more syllables, but in the case of a multisyllable word, the meaning of the word is not related to the meaning of any syllable.

Syllable Segmentation: A syllable is a unit of organization for a sequence of speech sounds. Syllable segmentation is the process of determining the syllable boundaries in a sentence or a document by computer algorithms.

Unicode: The Unicode standard is the industrial standard allowing computer systems to consistently represent and manipulate text written in any languages. The Unicode Consortium, the nonprofit organization, coordinates Unicode's development.

Word Segmentation: A word is a linguistic unit made up of one or more morphemes. Word segmentation is the process of determining the word boundaries in a sentence or a document by computer algorithms.

Chapter XXV
On the Effectiveness of Social Tagging for Resource Discovery

Dion Hoe-Lian Goh
Nanyang Technological University, Singapore

Khasfariyati Razikin
Nanyang Technological University, Singapore

Alton Y. K. Chua
Nanyang Technological University, Singapore

Chei Sian Lee
Nanyang Technological University, Singapore

Schubert Foo
Nanyang Technological University, Singapore

Jin-Cheon Na
Nanyang Technological University, Singapore

Yin-Leng Theng
Nanyang Technological University, Singapore

ABSTRACT

Social tagging is the process of assigning and sharing among users freely selected terms of resources. This approach enables users to annotate/describe resources, and also allows users to locate new resources through the collective intelligence of other users. Social tagging offers a new avenue for resource discovery as compared to taxonomies and subject directories created by experts. This chapter investigates the effectiveness of tags as resource descriptors and is achieved using text categorization via support vector machines (SVM). Two text categorization experiments were done for this research, and tags and Web pages from del.icio.us were used. The first study concentrated on the use of terms as its features while the second used both terms and its tags as part of its feature set. The experiments yielded a macroaveraged precision, recall, and F-measure scores of 52.66%, 54.86%, and 52.05%, respectively. In terms of microaveraged values, the experiments obtained 64.76% for precision, 54.40% for recall, and 59.14% for F-measure. The results suggest that the tags were not always reliable indicators of the resource contents. At the same time, the results from the terms-only experiment were better compared to the experiment with both terms and tags. Implications of our work and opportunities for future work are also discussed.

INTRODUCTION

The increasing popularity of Web 2.0-based applications has empowered users to create, publish, and share resources on the Web. Such user-generated content may include text (e.g., blogs, wikis), multimedia (e.g., YouTube), and even organization/navigational structures providing personalized access to Web content. The latter includes social bookmarking/tagging systems such as del.icio.us and Connotea.

Social tagging systems allow users to annotate links to useful Web resources by assigning keywords (tags) and possibly other metadata, facilitating their future access (Macgregor & McCulloch, 2006). These tags may further be shared by other users of the social tagging system, in effect creating a community where users can create and share tags pointing to useful Web resources. Put differently, tags function both as content organizers and discoverers. Users create and assign tags to a useful resource they come across so that it would be easy for them to retrieve that resource at a later date. At the same time, other users can use one or more of these tags created to find the resource. The same tags may also be used to discover other related and relevant resources. In addition, through tags, a user can potentially locate like-minded users who hold interests in similarly-themed resources, leading to the creation of social networks (Marlow, Naaman, Boyd, & Davis, 2006).

Social tagging provides an alternative means of organizing resources when compared with conventional methods of categorization based on taxonomies, controlled vocabularies, faceted classification, and ontologies. Conventional methods require experts with domain knowledge and this often translates to a high cost of implementing such systems. They are also bound strictly by rules to ensure their classification schemes remain consistent (Morville, 2005). As the system becomes larger, the rules tend to be more complicated, leading to possible maintenance and accessibil-

ity issues. In contrast, the classification scheme in social tagging systems is deregulated. Instead of relying on (a few) experts, they are supported by a (possibly large) community of users. At the same time, tags are "flat," lacking a predefined taxonomic structure, and their use relies on shared, emergent social structures and behaviors, as well as a common conceptual and linguistic understanding within the community (Marlow et al., 2006). Tags are therefore also known as "folksonomies," short for "folk taxonomies," suggesting that they are created by lay users, as opposed to domain experts or information professionals such as librarians, and may in fact be more effective in describing the resource

While social tagging systems have become popular, it is not known if tags created by ordinary users (as opposed to experts) are useful for the discovery of information. A few studies have investigated the use of tags as resource descriptors. Examples include comparing the use of tags against author-assigned index terms in academic papers (Kipp, 2006; Lin, Beaudoin, Bui, & Desai, 2006), examining the ability of tags to classify blogs using text categorization methods (Sun, Suryanto, & Liu, 2007), and investigating the ability of del.icio.us tags to classify Web resources in a small scale study (Razikin, Goh, Cheong, & Ow, 2007). However, to be best of our knowledge, no large scale work has been conducted with del.icio.us, one of the earliest and more popular social tagging sites. The site has a diverse set of tags and Web resources, and its main function is to store, organize, and share bookmarks among a community of users.

The goal of this present chapter is to investigate if tags are useful in helping users to access relevant Web resources. Specifically, we obtain Web pages and their associated tags from del.icio.us and study whether the tags are good descriptors of these resources. Here, we adopt from techniques in text categorization (Sebastiani, 2002) and argue that an effective tag is one in which a classifier is able to assign documents to with high precision and recall. The rationale here is that if a classifier is able to accurately assign documents to their respective tags, then such tags are useful for organizing resources, implying that users would be able to utilize them for accessing information. The remainder of this chapter is organized as follows. In the next section, research related to this work is reviewed. A description of our experimental methodology and the results are then presented. We then provide a discussion of the implications of our findings and conclude with opportunities for future work in this area.

RELATED STUDIES

The use of tagging has become a popular way of organizing and accessing Web resources. Sites such as del.icio.us, Flickr, YouTube, and Last.fm offer this service for their users. Correspondingly, social tagging has also attracted much research, and work has mainly concentrated on the architecture and implementation of systems (e.g., Hammond, Hannay, Lund, & Scott, 2005; Puspitasari, Lim, Goh, Chang, Zhang, Sun, et al., 2007), usage patterns in tagging systems (e.g., Golder & Huberman, 2006; Marlow et al., 2006), user interfaces (e.g., Dubinko, Kumar, Magnani, Novak, Raghavan, & Tomkins, 2006), and the use of social tagging in search systems (e.g., Yanbe, Jatowt, Nakamura, & Tanaka, 2007) among others.

In particular, as tagging becomes an accepted practice among Web users, there is growing interest in investigating whether tags are a useful means for organizing and accessing content. For example, comparing tags with controlled vocabularies provide a basis for evaluating how tags differ from keywords assigned by experts. Lin et al. (2006) compared tags from Connotea and medical subject heading terms (MeSH terms) and found that there was only 11% similarity between MeSH terms and tags supplied by the users. The authors argued that this is because MeSH terms

serve as descriptors while tags primarily focus on areas that are of interest to users. Kipp (2006) compared tags with author supplied keywords and indexing terms to determine the overlap in terms of usage. Results indicated that about 35% of the tags were related to the terms supplied by the authors and indexing terms. However, the relationship between tags and terms were not defined formally in thesauri.

An early work on automatic text categorization in social tagging systems was done by Brooks and Montanez (2006). Their study employed articles from the blogosphere. The authors used 350 popular tags from Technorati and 250 of the most recent articles of the collected tags. Using TF-IDF to cluster documents and pairwise cosine similarity to measure the similarity of all articles in each cluster, they found that tags categorize articles in the broad sense and users in a particular domain will not likely be able to find articles with a tag relating to a specific context. Sun et al. (2007) focused on classifying whole blogs with tags, and compared the classification results based on tags alone, tags together with blog descriptions (short abstract), and blog descriptions alone. It was found that tags together with descriptions had the best classification accuracy, while tags alone were more effective than blog descriptions alone for classification. Finally, in departure from the study of tags in blogs, Razikin et al. (2007) conducted a small scale study of the effectiveness of using tags to classify Web resources in del.icio.us. Using a support vector machine (SVM) classifier, relatively high precision and recall rates of 90.22% and 99.27%, respectively, were obtained.

METHODOLOGY

Tags and Web pages from del.icio.us were mined from the site from August 2007 to October 2007. During this period, we randomly collected 100 tags and 20,210 pages that were in the English language. Pages that were primarily nontextual (e.g., images and video) were discarded. Consistent with the work of Brooks and Montanez (2006), we started mining the tags from the popular tags page. As such, our tags will be biased towards the more commonly used ones. The popularity of a tag indicates that there are a significant number of documents related to it, and therefore provide a sufficient size for the training and testing of the text classifier.

In our dataset, each tag was associated with an average of 1,331 documents, and each document was associated with an average of 6.66 tags. The minimum number of tags for a document was 1 while the largest number of tags for a single document was 65. Figure 1 shows the distribution of the tags for the number of documents. It clearly demonstrates that power law distribution applies. Interestingly, the same was observed for blogs (Sun et al., 2007). In the figure, there are 3,167 documents with one tag each while there is only a single document with the largest number of tags (65).

Two text categorization experiments were conducted in the present research. The SVM was the machine learning classifier selected for our work as it is a popular machine learning classifier used in

Web-based text categorization studies with good performance. Specifically, the SVM[light] package (Joachims, 1998) was used. Being a binary classifier, we created one classifier for each tag with the examples comprising Web pages belonging (positive examples) and not belonging (negative examples) to that tag. In total, 100 classifiers were trained with the default options of the package. The performance of the tags was evaluated based on the macroaveraged and microaveraged precision, recall, and F-measure.

The first experiment, which served as a baseline, used the terms from the Web pages as the features while the second experiment included tags, in addition to terms, as part of its feature set. The pages in our dataset were processed by removing the hypertext markup language (HTML) elements, JavaScript codes, and cascading style sheets elements. This is followed by the process of stop word removal and stemming of the remaining words. TF-IDF values of the terms were then obtained and these values were used as the feature vector for the SVM classifier. For each tag, we selected all the pages that were tagged with the keyword and these were grouped as the positive samples for the particular tag. An equal amount

Figure 1. The distribution of tags over the number of documents

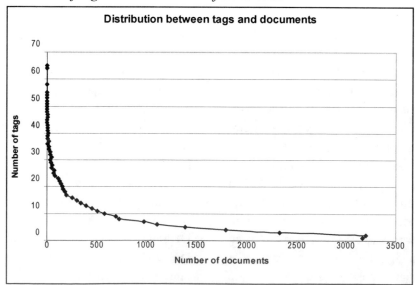

of pages, which were tagged with a different tag, were selected as negative samples. From this set of positive and negative samples, two-thirds of the pages were used as the training sample while the rest were part of the test set.

The second experiment augmented the first with additional features added with the aim of determining if these new features to the dataset would improve the results. The setup for the experiment was similar to that done for Experiment 1. The only difference is the addition of the document's tags to the feature set. The TF-IDF values for the tags were obtained and used as the feature values. Likewise in this experiment, the default parameters of the SVM package were used.

RESULTS FOR EXPERIMENT 1 – TERMS ONLY

Table 1 shows the top 15 tags which scored the highest F-measure obtained from Experiment 1. Table 2 shows the bottom 15 tags with the lowest F-measure obtained from the same experiment. In both tables, the extreme right column shows the difference in the F-measure values obtained in both. Entries in bold indicate an increase in the F-measure value for Experiment 2. The results are ranked in ascending order according to the tag's F-measure values obtained in this experiment.

As seen in Table 1, the top 15 tags that obtained the highest F-measure values had very broad meaning in that we were not able to determine a specific context with respect to the tag. Examples include "reference," "howto," and "politics." On the whole, the top 15 tags had better recall than precision values, indicating that the classifier was able to correctly assign the documents which actually belong to the tag more than 75% of the time. However, the bottom 15 tags paint a different picture (see Table 2). These tags appear to have a narrower definition in contrast to the top 15 tags. For example, the term "adobe" has a

more objective and precise meaning than "fun." The recall values for these tags were lower than its precision values, implying the classifier tended to predict more true negatives than true positives. In other words, the number of pages that did not belong to the category was higher than the pages belonging to it.

Table 3 presents the macroaveraged and microaveraged values for precision, recall, and F-measure. The macroaveraged precision and recall were 52.66% and 54.86%, respectively, while the standard deviation for precision was 4.21 and 19.05 for recall. In contrast with the standard deviation for precision, the standard deviation for recall varied greatly and a reason could be contributed by the classifier's tendency to misclassify a page which actually belongs to the tag. The macroaveraged F-measure was 52.05% and suggests that the classifier managed to predict at least half of the test data correctly with a 10.99 standard deviation across tags.

Microaveraged values show how the classifier performed based on each document. Here, the microaveraged precision was 64.76% while recall was 54.4%. From the F-measure value, the document had a 59.14% chance of being correctly classified. As shown in Table 3, both the macroaveraged and microaverage F-measure values were quite close. However, the F-measure value suggests that the users are not exactly good tag creators in the sense that other users would not be able to locate related resources using these tags. It was discussed previously that a large group of users would provide more reliable tags for resource description in contrast to expert individuals, yet this is not the case as indicated by our results. We surmise that the underlying reason is that tags can have multiple meanings and that there is no agreement on their usage in del.icio.us. As a result, the Web documents that are associated with a tag are not semantically related to each other, which in turn reduces the classifier's precision. The vocabulary problem (Furnas, Landauer, Gomez, & Dumais, 1987) is another reason that

Table 1. Top 15 tags with the highest F-measure values

Tag	Experiment 1			Experiment 2			Diff
	Precision	Recall	F-measure	Precision	Recall	F-measure	
reference	58.38	87.23	69.95	57.80	62.83	60.21	-9.74
howto	56.02	86.21	67.92	61.93	54.83	58.16	-9.76
politics	55.25	87.91	67.85	52.81	90.04	66.57	-1.28
imported	58.57	79.50	67.45	56.40	52.99	54.64	-12.81
fun	55.01	86.83	67.35	50.05	55.94	52.84	-14.51
blogs	55.07	85.74	67.06	59.14	73.92	65.71	-1.35
web	57.37	80.24	66.90	55.76	71.92	62.82	-4.08
web2.0	55.58	82.92	66.55	55.86	75.00	64.03	-2.52
inspiration	53.51	86.29	66.06	54.10	63.04	58.23	-7.83
Internet	54.90	82.18	65.83	55.17	66.22	60.19	-5.64
california	57.14	76.40	65.38	55.17	66.22	60.19	-5.64
restaurants	55.43	79.69	65.38	49.07	88.76	63.20	-2.18
osx	54.07	82.58	65.35	48.00	56.25	51.80	-13.58
recipe	56.83	73.79	64.21	54.92	69.30	61.28	-4.07
news	**54.93**	**76.52**	**63.96**	**58.19**	**88.24**	**70.13**	**6.17**

Table 2. Bottom 15 tags with the lowest F-measure values

Tag	Experiment 1			Experiment 2			Diff
	Precision	Recall	F-measure	Precision	Recall	F-measure	
templates	**49.63**	**31.60**	**38.62**	**63.27**	**43.87**	**51.81**	**13.19**
animation	46.99	31.97	38.05	52.43	22.13	31.12	-7.88
xml	47.03	31.52	37.74	51.30	28.42	36.57	-1.17
ajax	52.47	29.32	37.62	39.58	9.52	15.35	-22.27
economics	44.71	30.89	36.54	49.25	26.83	34.74	-1.80
windows	54.95	26.93	36.14	40.00	9.32	15.12	-21.02
accessories	**47.37**	**28.42**	**35.53**	**52.63**	**52.08**	**52.36**	**16.83**
cms	45.28	27.80	34.45	45.59	23.85	31.31	-3.14
journal	**51.32**	**25.83**	**34.36**	**42.74**	**35.10**	**38.55**	**4.19**
ruby	**55.56**	**24.15**	**33.67**	**55.64**	**35.75**	**43.53**	**9.86**
actionscript	43.36	26.34	32.78	49.38	21.51	29.96	-2.82
parts	**50.00**	**22.50**	**31.03**	**57.89**	**27.50**	**37.29**	**6.26**
self-improvement	43.55	23.28	30.34	44.00	18.97	26.51	-3.83
icons	**45.45**	**14.93**	**22.47**	**55.84**	**32.09**	**40.76**	**18.29**
adobe	**45.10**	**13.29**	**20.54**	**42.86**	**13.87**	**20.96**	**0.42**

Table 3. Macroaveraged and microaveraged values for Experiments 1 and 2

	Experiment 1			Experiment 2		
	Precision	Recall	F-measure	Precision	Recall	F-measure
Macroaveraged	52.66 (s = 4.21)	54.86 (s = 19.05)	52.05 (s = 10.99)	50.77 (s = 6.06)	45.24 (s = 20.75)	45.77 (s = 13.21)
Microaveraged	64.76	54.40	59.14	56.47	54.93	55.69

could contribute to our results. In other words, a tag would be associated with a diverse set of pages, and most of these pages may have been tagged only once with a particular tag.

RESULTS FOR EXPERIMENT 2 – TERMS AND TAGS

The results obtained in this Experiment 2 are shown in the right columns of Tables 1 and 2. The same tags that were selected in Experiment 1 are again shown in the table. In addition, the difference between the F-measures obtained in both experiments for the selected tags are shown, and entries in bold show an increase in values from those obtained in Experiment 1. Here, only eight of the selected tags have an increase in their F-measure values. The tag "icons" has the largest gain with 18.29. Documents belonging to this tag have an increased chance of 18.29% to be selected than before. On the other hand, the tag "ajax" suffered the largest drop in F-measure value with a decrease of 22.27%.

Table 3 shows the macroaveraged and microaveraged values for precision, recall, and F-measure obtained for this experiment. On average, all the categories had precision and recall values of 50.77% and 45.24%, respectively. The standard deviation for precision was 6.06, smaller than that for recall at 20.75. This was similar to the values obtained in the previous experiment. The F-measure score suggests that the classifier only managed to predict 45.77% of the pages correctly for each category on average, with a standard deviation of 13.21. For microaveraged values, the

classifier managed to predict the relevance of each document with a precision and recall of 56.47% and 54.93%, respectively. The microaveraged value for F-measure was 55.69%.

It can be seen from Table 3 that the macroaveraged and microaveraged values obtained in Experiment 2 were lower than those obtained in Experiment 1, implying that the addition of tags as part of the feature set did not help in improving the precision, recall, and F-measure values. This is an interesting outcome, as making use of the terms only resulted in better performance than having terms together with tags. Although tags are words themselves, they may degrade the performance of the classifier because they appear in every document associated with these tags, causing them to have smaller TF-IDF weights in the document collection.

DISCUSSION AND CONCLUSION

In contrast to taxonomies and subject directories, social tagging is an alternative means of organizing Web resources. It is growing in popularity and is being used in a number of Web sites. In this chapter, we have investigated the effectiveness of tags in assisting users to discover relevant content by employing a text categorization approach. Here, we considered tags as categories, and examined the performance of an SVM classifier in assigning a dataset of Web resources from del.icio.us to their respective tags. Two experiments were conducted. The first examined the use of document terms only as features while the second added the document's tags in addition to the previous feature set. Surprisingly, results from the first experiment were better than the second. The macroaveraged F-measure obtained from Experiment 1 was 52.05% while the F-measure from Experiment 2 was 45.77%. The microaveraged values from both experiments were 59.14% and 55.69%. Put differently, the use of terms only yielded slightly better results than using terms and tags.

The relatively low values for precision, recall, and F-measure suggest that not all tags are reliable descriptors of the document's content. Our findings are similar to Sun et al.'s (2007) work. In that study, the range of macroaveraged F-measure values obtained for the description-only experiments ranged from 32% to 41%. Perhaps the much lower values were a result of using a shorter length of text as descriptions. It was reported that the description contained an average of only 14.8 terms for each blog. While the work of Razikin et al. (2007) was similar to the present work, the results obtained in that study were better. A reason for this could be the fact that the tags chosen were not from the popular list, and thus the Web pages that were associated with these tags tended to be more specifically related to the tags themselves. As the present work used the more popular tags, the likelihood of pages being incorrectly assigned to a tag could have been much higher because of greater usage by a diversity of users, thereby contributing to the poorer performance scores.

Some implications can be drawn from our present study. First, proponents of social tagging argue that the knowledge from a group of users could be much better than those provided by an expert (Suroweicki, 2004). However, our results have shown that this may not be applicable for all the tags, as some tags were found to be good descriptors and some were not. Future research could investigate the specific characteristics that make tags good descriptors for resource discovery. For example, one could examine whether tags with objective meanings might yield better performance than those with subjective meanings.

Next, because not all tags are created equally for resource discovery, a social tagging system could assist users by suggesting tags in addition to supporting free keyword assignment. For example, after identifying characteristics of tags that serve as good resource descriptors, such tags could be used as recommendations to a tag creator for a given Web resource. In addition, a social tagging system might recommend different tags depending on whether the tag would be for public access, in which case, the recommendations would focus only on "good" tags, or for private use, in which case the recommendations could include tags that have meaning only to the creator.

In conclusion, our findings have shown different levels of effectiveness of tags as resource descriptors. There are however, some limitations to our study that provide opportunities for future work. The first concerns the use of terms and tags of the documents. These might not be the only features that could be used. Additional features like the document's title and the anchor text could prove useful for classification. Different weight schemes could be attempted for different features as well. Further, our corpus had an average of 1,331 documents per tag and future work could look into increasing the number of documents per tag, and utilize tags other than those that were popular.

ACKNOWLEDGMENT

This work is partly funded by A*STAR grant 062 130 0057.

REFERENCES

Brooks, C. H., & Montanez, N. (2006). Improved annotation of the blogosphere via autotagging and hierarchical clustering. In *Proceedings of the 15th International Conference on the World Wide Web* (pp. 625-632).

Dubinko, M., Kumar, R., Magnani, J., Novak, J., Raghavan, P., & Tomkins, A. (2006). Visualizing tags over time. In *Proceedings of the 15th International Conference on the World Wide Web* (pp. 193-202).

Furnas, G. W., Landauer, T. K., Gomez, L. M., & Dumais, S.T. (1987). The vocabulary problem in human-system communication. *Communications of the ACM, 30*(11), 964-971.

Golder, S. A., & Huberman, B. A. (2006). Usage patterns of collaborative tagging systems. *Journal of Information Science, 32*(2), 198-208.

Hammond, T., Hannay, T., Lund, B., & Scott, J. (2005). Social bookmarking tools (I). *D-Lib Magazine, 11*(4). Retrieved August 23, 2008, from http://www.dlib.org/dlib/april05/hammond/04hammond.html

Joachims, T. (1998). Text categorization with support vector machines: Learning with many relevant features. In *Proceedings of the 10th European Conference on Machine Learning* (pp. 137-142).

Kipp, M. E. (2006). *Exploring the context of user, creator and intermediate tagging.* Paper presented at the 7th Information Architecture Summit. Retrieved August 23, 2008, from http://www.iasummit.org/2006/files/109_Presentation_Desc.pdf

Lin, X., Beaudoin, J. E., Bui, Y., & Desai, K. (2006). *Exploring characteristics of social classification.* Paper presented at the 17th Workshop of the American Society for Information Science and Technology Special Interest Group in Classification Research. Retrieved August 23, 2008, from http://dlist.sir.arizona.edu/1790/

Macgregor, G., & McCulloch, E. (2006). Collaborative tagging as a knowledge organization and resource discovery tool. *Library Review, 55*(5), 291-300.

Marlow, C., Naaman, M., Boyd, D., & Davis, M. (2006). HT06, tagging paper, taxonomy, Flickr, academic article, to read. In *Proceedings of the Seventeenth Conference on Hypertext and Hypermedia* (pp. 31-40).

Morville, P. (2005). *Ambient findability.* Sebastopol, CA: O'Reilly Media.

Puspitasari, F., Lim, E. P., Goh, D. H., Chang, C. H., Zhang, J., Sun, A., et al. (2007). Social navigation in digital libraries by bookmarking. In *Proceedings of the 10th International Conference on Asian Digital Libraries, ICADL 2007* (LNCS 4822, pp. 297-306).

Razikin, K., Goh, D. H., Cheong, E. K. C., & Ow, Y. F. (2007). The efficacy of tags in social tagging systems. In *Proceedings of the 10th International Conference on Asian Digital Libraries, ICADL 2007* (LNCS 4822, pp. 506-507).

Sebastiani, F. (2002). Machine learning in automated text categorization. *ACM Computing Surveys, 34*(1), 1-47.

Sun, A., Suryanto, M. A., & Liu, Y. (2007). Blog classfication using tags: An empirical study. In *Proceedings of the 10th International Conference on Asian Digital Libraries, ICADL 2007* (LNCS 4822, pp. 307-316).

Suroweicki, J. (2004). *The wisdom of crowds: Why the many are smarter than the few and how collective wisdom shapes business, economics, societies, and nations.* New York: Doubleday.

Yanbe, Y., Jatowt, A., Nakamura, S., & Tanaka, K. (2007). Can social bookmarking enhance search in the Web? In *Proceedings of the 2007 Conference on Digital Libraries* (pp. 107-116).

KEY TERMS

Social Tagging/Social Bookmarking: The process of sharing and associating a resource, such as Web pages and multimedia, with tags.

Support Vector Machines: A vector-based machine learning technique which makes use of the maximum distance between vector classes as a decision boundary.

Text Categorization: The process of assigning documents to predefined labels using various techniques such as statistical and vector space models.

Web 2.0: Web applications that enable the sharing or creation of resources by a group of users. Some of these applications include Weblogs, wikis, and social bookmarking sites.

Chapter XXVI
Semantic Annotation and Retrieval of Images in Digital Libraries

Taha Osman
Nottingham Trent University, UK

Dhavalkumar Thakker
Nottingham Trent University, UK

Gerald Schaefer
Aston University, UK

ABSTRACT

While many digital image libraries allow access to large repositories of images, unfortunately, often the provided free-text search returns unsatisfactory retrieval results. The reason for this is that search techniques typically rely solely on statistical analysis of keyword recurrences in image annotations. In this chapter we show that through the employment of a semantic framework for image annotation, vastly improved retrieval can be accomplished. We present a semantically-enabled annotation and retrieval engine which relies on methodically structured ontologies for image annotation, and demonstrate how it provides more accurate retrieval results as well as a richer set of alternatives matchmaking the original query.

INTRODUCTION

With the ever growing amount of available multimedia information, retrieving relevant information from these repositories is an impossible task for the user without the aid of effective search tools. Most current public image retrieval engines rely on analysing the text accompanying the image to matchmake it with a user query. Various optimisations have been developed, including the use of weighting systems to emphasise those keywords that appear in closer proximity to the image location, or advanced text analysis techniques that use term weighting methods, which rely on the proximity between the anchor to an image and each word in a hypertext markup language (HTML) file (Fujii & Ishikawa, 2005). However, despite these efforts, the searches remain limited by the fact that they rely on free-text search that, while cost-effective to perform, can return irrelevant results as it is primarily based on the recurrence of exact words in the text accompanying the image.

Any significant improvement of the accuracy of matchmaking results can only be achieved if the search engine can 'comprehend' the meaning of the underlying data that describe the stored images. Semantic annotation techniques have gained wide popularity in associating plain data with 'structured' concepts that software programs can reason about (Wang, Liu, & Chia, 2006).

In this chapter we present a comprehensive semantic-based solution to image annotation and retrieval that is suitable for the commercial image provider market and acknowledges their requirements for high quality recall without sacrificing the performance of the retrieval process.

BACKGROUND

The fundamental premise of the Semantic Web is to extend the Web's current human-oriented interface to a format that is comprehensible to software programmes. For instance, in a Semantic Web scenario, intelligent agents would be able to set up an appointment between a patient and the doctor, looking at both timetables, and finding the best way to the clinic without the patient having to interfere in the process. The user would only have to specify the requirements of a task while semantic agents will complete the task on their own (Berners-Lee & Fishetti, 2000).

The concept of ontologies is fundamental to the Semantic Web. An ontology represents an area of knowledge that is used by people, databases, and applications that need to share domain information. Ontologies include computer-usable definitions of basic concepts in the domain and the relationships between them. The Web ontology language (OWL) (Parsia & Sirin, 2004) has become the de-facto standard for expressing ontologies. It adds extensive vocabulary to describe properties and classes and expresses relationships between classes (e.g., disjointness), cardinality (e.g., 'exactly one'), equality, richer typing of properties, and characteristics of properties (e.g., symmetry). OWL is designed for use by applications that need to process the content of information rather than just presenting information to humans.

Applied to image retrieval, the semantic annotation of images creates a conceptual understanding of the domains that the images represent, enabling software agents (i.e., search engines) to make more intelligent decisions about the relevance of the image to a particular user query. The use of Semantic Web concepts in image retrieval is likely to improve the computer's understanding of the image objects and their interactions. To attain such improved results, the data need a better structure, so as to make sense between different semantic concepts. Here, the Semantic Web is likely to bring such a structure that integrates concepts and interentity relations from different domains.

ONTOLOGY DEVELOPMENT

The approach that we describe in this chapter is based on a case study conducted in collaboration with a sports image provider with an image repository in excess of 4 million images (Osman, Thakker, Schaefer, Leroy, & Fournier, 2007). As the company's search engine relies on free-text search to return a set of images matching the user's requests, the returned results are often not very relevant to the user's query; in particular, if the search keywords do not recur exactly in the photo annotations. A significant improvement can therefore be gained by semantically enabling the photo search engine. A semantic-based image search will enable the search engine software to understand the 'meaning' of the user request and hence return more accurate results and a richer set of alternatives. At the same time, semantic technologies can be used to build a classification and indexing system that critically unifies the annotation infrastructure for all the sources of incoming stream of photos.

An integrative structure that combines both image attributes and domain specifications was developed, consisting of two main types of ontology classes:

- Classes to localise the event in the picture (e.g., stadium, area, etc.),
- Classes to characterise the picture itself (e.g., image size, creation date, etc.).

Since we are dealing with sports images, many other classes are also required to describe the domain, such as player, team, match, and tourna-

ment classes. In addition, we also added action and emotion classes to enable expressing relationships between objects in an image. Figure 1 shows a subset of the developed ontology tree.

Unlike database structures, ontologies represent knowledge rather than data, hence any structural problems will have a detrimental effect on their corresponding reasoning agents, especially since ontologies are open and distributed by nature, which might cause wide-spread propagation of any inconsistencies (Rector, 2003). For instance, in traditional structuring methodologies, usually the *part-of* relationship is followed to express relationships between interdependent concepts. So, for players that are *part-of* a team performing in a particular event, the approach depicted in Figure 2 is commonly taken. In this example, a player belongs to a team which takes part in a tournament. However, if a player plays for two different teams at the same time (e.g., a club and a national team) or changes clubs frequently, it is almost impossible to determine which team the player belongs to. The same problem occurs for a team which can take part in different tournaments.

A better approach to the classification is hence to start with the tournament. This solves the problems mentioned above by storing the information only within the player class as shown in Figure 3.

All semantic models use two types of properties to build relationships between classes: datatype properties and object properties. When assigning properties to a class, all its subclasses inherit their parent class's properties. Deciding

Figure 1. Subset of sport image ontology tree

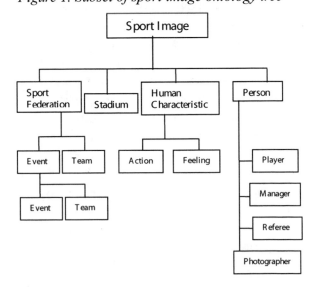

Figure 2. Example of class relationships

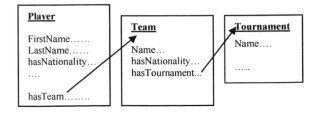

Figure 3. Reorganisation of player classification

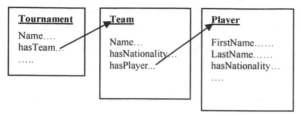

Figure 4. Resolving coverage problems in the ontology

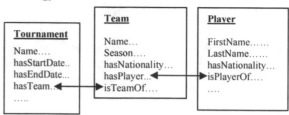

on the appropriate type of property to use is not a trivial task. While object properties link individuals of different classes together, datatype properties can just point to immediate values (e.g., text strings), which are meaningless to a reasoning software, except for performing a string-based search. For instance, allocating datatype properties to the person class in order to assign each new instance a first name and a last name is a correct use of datatype properties, because they cannot be reused by another individual. On the other hand, object properties are required to assign someone a nationality. A country is more than a mere string as it can have properties such as a currency, a capital city, many towns and villages, a language, a national flag and anthem, and so forth. A country thus needs to be an instance. Furthermore, such classes might already be defined in existing ontologies and hence can be reused.

Although consistent, the structural solution in Figure 3 is incomplete as every year a team will have a range of players leaving, either to retire or to play for another team. The same problem occurs with tournaments as from one year to another, teams taking part in the tournament change. This problem however can be easily solved by adding a start and end date for the tournament, rather than by engineering more complex object property solutions. The same reasoning can be applied to the team class, as players can change teams every season, or even sometimes twice in a season. These indications, although basic for a human reasoning, need to be defined explicitly in the ontology.

Furthermore, in order to increase the automation of available data, inverse properties are used. Consequently, there is no privileged way to reason and all properties are added in a dynamic manner. The example shown in Figure 4 represents this stage of the ontology.

Object properties such as *hasPlayer* can have an inverse property such as *isPlayerOf*. Such properties reveal the power of the Semantic Web where everything may be reused. These inverse properties automatically state that if "Team A *hasPlayer* Player B," then "Player B *isPlayerOf* Team A." A high degree of understanding is given to the computer along with automation.

Adopting the latest version of the ontology in Figure 4 will result in creating new tournaments every year, which is rather inefficient. No matter which players are playing for the team, or which tournament a team takes part into, a team is a nontemporal class and needs to remain as an abstract entity. Even though the managers change and the players come and go, the club entity that gathers players, managers, and fans stays the same. A higher degree of abstraction is required here. The underlying idea considers the fact that a player is a member of a team, which in turn is a member of a particular tournament. A new class is thus required, namely a membership class which creates the indispensable link between teams and players, as well as between teams and tournaments (as illustrated in Figure 5).

The instances from the membership class link together instances from two different classes. Owing to the properties of the membership class, all its individuals possess the following properties:

Figure 5. Membership class

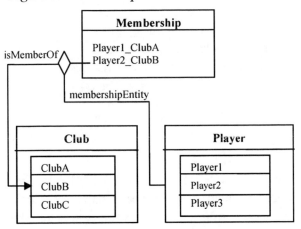

- *memberEntity,* which links to a person (i.e., player, manager, supporter, photographer, etc.)
- *isMemberOf,* which refers to the organisation (i.e., club, press association, company, etc.)
- *fromPeriod,* which depicts the day when the person was hired by the organisation
- *toPeriod,* which states the day when the person leaves the organisation

Thus, a class with the listed properties solves all the problems encountered during the building of this ontology. The club remains a static entity, as do players or managers. Moreover, this relational description allows for the retracing of the career of a person. It should also be noted that while this example is built upon the sports domain it is expandable to virtually every other domain of the society.

SEMANTIC IMAGE ANNOTATION

The Protégé ontology editor was used to construct the sport domain ontology. Protégé uses frame-based knowledge representation and adopts OWL as the ontology language (Noy, Crubézy, Ferger-son, Knublauch, Tu, Vendetti, et al., 2003). The Jena Java API (Carrol, 2004) was used to build the annotation portal to the constructed ontology.

The central component of the annotation are the images stored (as OWL descriptions) in the image library, as illustrated in Figure 6. Each image comprises an object, whose main features are stored within an independent object library. Similarly, the object characteristics, event location, and so forth are distinct from the image library. This highly modular annotation model facilitates the reuse of semantic information and reduces redundancy.

Taking into account the nature of the sports domain, we concluded that a variation of the sentence structure suggested by Hollink, Schreiber, Wielemaker, and Wielinga (2003) is best suited to design our annotation template. We opted for an 'Actor – Action – Object' structure that will allow the natural annotation of motion or emotion-type relationships without the need to involve NLP techniques (Chen, 1995). An added benefit of the structure is that it simplifies the task of the reasoner in matching actor and action annotations with entities that have similar characteristics.

SEMANTIC IMAGE RETRIEVAL

The image retrieval algorithm uses a tree comparison that traverses the ontology classes in order to find a path that represents the 'nearest neighbour'

Figure 6. Architecture of image annotation

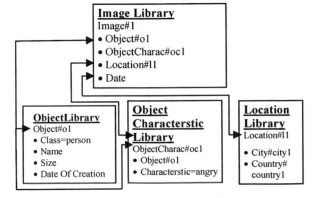

to the query. The user is also allowed to assign preferences to different segments of the query, so that, for instance, priority might be given to the player or the tournament in the specific query. In order to allow a dialog between the query and the annotated files, a semantic description generator needs to be created. Figure 7 provides a high level view of the retrieval mechanism.

User and administrator play two different roles. First, the administrator annotates the images in order to give more consistency and structure to the annotation libraries. The user can only create new requests. The semantic description generator (1) transforms the query into an OWL query, which determines a first set of images (2) on which the Semantic Web image retrieval algorithm can be applied (3). During this stage, a dialog between all the libraries is required. This algorithm uses a weighting system (4) previously set by the user in order to fine-tune the final results in accordance to the user's query (5). The last stage consists of displaying the results (6).

The nearest neighbour matchmaking algorithm continues traversing back to the upper class of the ontology and matching instances until there are no superclasses in the class hierarchy, that is, the leaf node for the tree is reached, giving a degree of match (*DoM*) of 0. The *DoM* degree is calculated according to

$$DoM = \frac{MN}{GN} \tag{1}$$

where the *MN* is the total number of matching nodes in the selected traversal path, and *GN* is the total number of nodes in the path. Then the comparison values are weighted using the user preferences according to (Osman, Thakker, & Al-Dabass, 2006):

$$m = |l_r - l_a|; \ \forall \ p \in [0,1], \ v = p \tag{2}$$

where *v* is the value assigned to the comparison, *m* is the matching level of the individuals, *p* is the user preference setting, and l_r and l_a are the levels of the request and the annotation, respectively.

Figure 7. Schematic diagram of the retrieval software

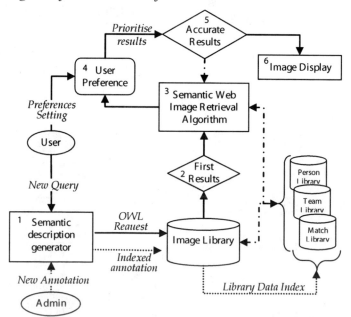

CONCLUSION

In this chapter we have presented an approach to image annotation and search that takes advantage of advances in Semantic Web technologies. The first stage of the development is to produce ontologies (domain vocabularies) that provide the search engine with a consistent view of the domain entities and possible relations between them. Annotations based on our ontology are expected to have little redundancies due to normalising the ontology structure. Our annotation process is user-focussed and takes into account the dynamics of the retrieval process. It is based on a sentence-based template suitable for modelling user queries that can involve complex relationships between the query keywords. The retrieval algorithm uses a variation of the nearest-neighbour search technique for traversing the ontology tree and can accommodate complex, relationship-driven user queries. The algorithm also allows using predefined weightings to adapt the search result in accordance to user preferences.

REFERENCES

Berners-Lee, T., & Fischetti, M. (2000). *Weaving the Web*. Harper Collins.

Carroll, J. J., Reynolds, D., Dickinson, I., Seaborne, A., Dollin, C., & Wilkinson, K. (2004). Jena: Implementing the semantic Web recommendations. In *Proceedings of the 13th International World Wide Web Conference* (pp. 74-83).

Chen, H. (1995). Machine learning for information retrieval: Neural networks, symbolic learning and genetic algorithms. *Journal of the American Society for Information Science and Technology, 46*(3), 194-216.

Fujii, A., & Ishikawa, T. (2005). Toward the automatic compilation of multimedia encyclopedias: Associating images with term descriptions on the Web. In *Proceedings of the International Conference on Web Intelligence* (pp. 536-542).

Hollink, L., Schreiber, A. T., Wielemaker, J., & Wielinga, B. (2003). *Semantic annotation of image collections.* Paper presented at the Workshop on Knowledge Markup and Semantic Annotation.

Noy, N. F., Crubézy, M., Fergerson, R. W., Knublauch, H., Tu, S. W., Vendetti, J., et al. (2003). Protege-2000: An open-source ontology-development and knowledge-acquisition environment. In *Proceedings of the AMIA Annual Symposium* (p. 953).

Osman, T., Thakker, D., & Al-Dabass, D. (2006). Semantic-driven matchmaking of Web services using case-based reasoning. In *Proceedings of the IEEE International Conference on Web Services* (pp. 29-36).

Osman, T., Thakker, D, Schaefer, G., Leroy, M., & Fournier, A. (2007). Semantic annotation and retrieval of image collections. In *Proceedings of the 21st European Conference on Modeling and Simulation* (pp. 324-329).

Parsia, B., & Sirin, E. (2004). *Pellet: An OWL DL reasoner.* Paper presented at the 3rd International Semantic Web Conference.

Rector, A. (2003). Modularisation of domain ontologies implemented in description logics and related formalisms including OWL. In *Proceedings of the 2nd International Conference on Knowledge Capture* (pp. 121-128).

Wang, H., Liu, S., & Chia, L-T. (2006). Does ontology help in image retrieval? A comparison between keyword, text ontology and multi-modality ontology approaches. In *Proceedings of the 14th Annual ACM International Conference on Multimedia*, Hawai (pp. 109-112).

KEY TERMS

Ontology: A representation of the meanings of terms in a vocabulary.

Semantic Image Retrieval: Image retrieval that takes into account the meaning of the actions and objects contained in images.

Semantics: The study of how meaning is generated in language.

Semantic Web: An extension of the Web incorporating semantic information to allow machines to understand the information contained on the Web.

Web Ontology Language (OWL): A computer-readable language in which Semantic Web ontologies can be expressed.

Section III
Users, Interactions, and Experiences

Chapter XXVII
Metadata and Metaphors in Visual Interfaces to Digital Libraries

Ali Shiri
University of Alberta, Canada

ABSTRACT

This chapter introduces a new category of digital library user interfaces called metadata-enhanced visual interfaces. Drawing on the earlier information retrieval visual interfaces that have made use of thesauri, this chapter will review and analyze metadata-enhanced visual interfaces to digital libraries based on two key variables, namely metadata elements used for visualization purposes and visual metaphors incorporated into the user interfaces. The aim of this study is to inform the design of visual interfaces for digital libraries through bringing together issues that have roots in such communities as information retrieval, digital libraries, human-computer interaction, and metadata. The findings of this study provide design ideas and implications for digital library interface design in terms of the various metadata-based information search and retrieval features for visualization purposes.

INTRODUCTION

Digital libraries are multifaceted and complex information structures that offer a wide range and variety of information-bearing objects. They vary in their content, subject matter, cultural characteristics, language, and so forth. Arms (2000) notes that "a digital library is only as good as the interface it provides to its users." The variety of digital objects and materials in a digital library poses challenges to the design of usable and easy to understand user interfaces. Visual interfaces to digital libraries have recently found widespread attention. This development is mainly due to the fact that information visualization techniques allow for rich representation of information-bearing objects found in digital libraries. There are also a number of information visualization areas related to digital libraries, namely bibliometric studies, information retrieval (query and result), scientific visualization, as well as knowledge domain visualization. This chapter will review and analyze metadata-enabled visual interfaces to digital libraries based on the richness and variety of metadata elements used and the visualization approaches adopted on the interface. The first part of this chapter will provide a brief overview of visual interfaces developed based on thesauri as one source of subject metadata. The second part of this chapter will review and analyze innovative metadata-enabled visual interfaces to digital libraries. The final section will present a general discussion of the reviewed interfaces in terms of their visualization approaches and metadata elements used within the context of digital library developments. The current study draws on the research carried out in the areas of digital libraries, interface design, human computer interaction, and metadata.

EARLIER INFORMATION RETRIEVAL VISUAL INTERFACES USING THESAURI

MeSHBrowse (Korn & Shneiderman, 1995), a prototype interface for browsing the medical subject headings (MeSH) thesaurus, employs a concept space approach and a node-link tree diagram of the concept space. Hidden interrelationships of the terms are revealed once a node is clicked. The graphical nature of the interface allows only for related categories of terms to be displayed in a two-dimensional tree structure. Cat-a-cone (Hearst & Karadi, 1997) utilizes a three-dimensional graphical interface which shows all of the top level categories initially and allows for the user to control the subsequent expansion. An alternative mode of interaction is to have the user type in a category label and see which parts of the hierarchy match or partially match that label. The interface also caters for a kind of relevance

feedback by suggesting additional categories. Users can jump easily from one category to another and can search on multiple categories simultaneously. The visual MeSH (Lin, 1999) is a graphical interface developed to interact with the MeSH thesaurus and Medline. It allows the user to look up MeSH terms in a click-and-choose environment and assists users in exploring the MeSH terms by providing several views of the concept, including tree view, neighbor view, and map view. On any of the views, the user can double-click on a term to select it. Sutcliffe, Ennis, and Hu (2000) describe a visual interface enhanced with a thesaurus called the integrated thesaurus-results browser, which provides simultaneous access to query bar, thesaurus terms and structure, as well as search results. The thesaurus is a major feature of the interface, allowing for search term selection and query specification or modification.

INNOVATIVE VISUAL INTERFACES TO DIGITAL LIBRARIES

Börner and Chen (2002) identify three usage scenarios for visual interfaces to digital libraries: (1) support the identification of the composition of a retrieval result, understand the interrelation of retrieved documents to one another, and refine a search; (2) gain an overview of the coverage of a digital library and to facilitate browsing; and (3) visualize user interaction data in relation to available documents in order to evaluate and improve digital library usage.

The present chapter aims to review and briefly analyze a specific category of digital library visual interfaces that support information seeking and retrieval based on metadata representations. I will call this category "metadata-enabled visual interfaces." The focus of these interfaces is mostly on the ways in which metadata elements and visualization approaches can be utilized to richly represent the content of digital library collections. This type of interface enables users to gain a detailed insight into the variety and vastness of digital library materials through exploring the metadata elements attached to digital objects.

Beheshti, Large, and Julian (2005) report the development of a 3-D visual interface called Virtual Reality Interface for Children's Web Portal. The interface utilizes a library metaphor as a mechanism to support browsing purposes. Metadata elements such as title and brief descriptions have been used to support users' information seeking behavior. The National Science Digital Library in the United States provides an interactive visual interface for browsing the collections held within the library using subject terms. The interface allows for browsing of the subject hierarchy. Upon clicking on a subject category, the interface shows the collections which have been assigned that subject category. The interface also offers a search option where you can search for a particular subject category within the subject structure. The Alexandria Digital Earth Prototype (ADEPT) project (Ancona & Smith, 2002) has adopted a concept-space approach to information visualization. The interface addresses a number of issues, such as access, browsing, delivery, and understanding of library items. The concept space in this project is generated from a database of concepts produced by the ADEPT knowledge organization team. Each concept record in this knowledge base includes any number of relationships to other concepts. The visual concept map depicts concepts and their relationships as well as the type of relationship between and among those concepts. The Variations2 Indiana Digital Music Project adopts an innovative approach to the visualization of a music library. The interface takes advantage of such metadata elements as composer, name of the musical instrument, date, and performer. The interface shows a three dimensional space with the metadata elements represented to support browsing and exploring of the collection.

VISUALIZATION: METAPHORS AND METADATA

In this chapter, the examination of visual metaphors and metadata focuses primarily on a select number of prototype and operational visual interfaces. A few of the interfaces reviewed were created in the late 1990s, but most of the interfaces examined here were developed after 2000. The rationale for choosing metadata and metaphors as interrelated variables in the study lies in the fact that the number of visual interfaces to digital libraries which have incorporated metadata elements is increasing. It is important to examine the variety of visual metaphors and metadata elements used in digital library interfaces to inform the future development of digital library user interfaces. Metadata are key components of well-established digital libraries and if digital libraries are to support users in their information exploration, effective visualization of already existing metadata elements will accommodate information interaction and discovery. In the following, two main themes will be discussed: visualization metaphors and metadata-enhanced visual interfaces.

VISUALIZATION METAPHORS

It seems as though interface developers agree that visualization can and should enable digital libraries to "facilitate navigation while minimizing cognitive load" (Good, Popat, Janssen, & Bier, 2005). The examination of visual interfaces demonstrates that digital library interfaces aim to visually provide users with a sense of familiarity and instinctive navigation. To this end, most visual interfaces employ real-world *spatial metaphors*. The most common metaphor is geography, or "the metaphor of exploring a geographic territory" (Constabile, Esposito, Semeraro, Fanizzi, &

Ferilli, 1998), where items or metadata represent points on a "map." For example, the paper on the intelligent digital library (IDL) interface (Constabile et al., 1998) uses this metaphor extensively; each subject is a "city" existing within a "region" of related subjects. The connections between subjects (roads), and the lines where regions begin and end (borders), are also meaningful. These mapping metaphors also employ color in recognizably geographic ways.

There are some geographical user interfaces for digital libraries which focus on real-life geographical regions, such as BALTICSEAWEB (Laitenen & Neuvonen, 1998) and Historical Directories of England and Wales. BALTICSEAWEB is a collection of environmental information about the Baltic Sea region. Historical Directories is a collection of antique trade directories. The International Children's Digital Library also encourages geographical browsing by providing a clickable rotating globe. These interfaces generally support only browsing, not searching. Where visual information (e.g., paintings, photos, and covers of books) is contained in the digital library, often metaphors such as a bookshelf or gallery are used. In these cases, rather than rely primarily on metadata for the display, the interface allows the user to view thumbnail versions of the actual visual information. Among the good operational examples of this are:

- LibraryThing, which encourages users to arrange their books on a "virtual shelf."
- The International Children's Digital Library which enables browsing through book covers by clicking graphics representing colors of books covers, categories of characters, lengths of books, age groups, and so forth.

An excellent visual interface, using "variably gridded thumbnails," is introduced by the Online Picasso Collection digital library (Chang, Leggett, Furuta, Kerne, Williams, Burns, et al., 2004). The interface makes use of a variety of metadata ele-

ments such as title, place, duration, media, size, and collection. This prototype adds a color-coded relevance ranking scheme to thumbnails harvested by a search. "Fluid Interface" is a visual interface which makes use of a large, old-fashioned desktop as its metaphor (Good et al., 2005). The aim of the interface is to provide a usable interface for personal digital libraries. The image of the desktop as a metaphor clarifies the developers' objective of providing an interface enabling users to easily view several items at once. Just as a large desktop would allow you to spread your papers out so as to refer back and forth among them, this interface relieves users of the hassles of opening and managing multiple windows and applications while examining documents. The focus of the interface is on the visualization of a document collection.

METADATA

The role and importance of metadata and their use in the development of visual interfaces to digital libraries has been emphasized in the literature (Mitchell, 1999). Metadata elements can be effectively used for providing a richer representation of digital objects and collections. In the following, we briefly review some of the visual interfaces that have incorporated metadata elements into their interface design to support users' exploration of digital libraries.

New visual interface features offer some type of interactive dynamic mapping, most commonly in the form of a Java applet. These maps, which vary greatly in appearance, rely on metadata to illustrate the relationships among search results, or among items available for browsing. Here are some examples.

- National Science Digital Library (NSDL) (Butcher, Bhushan, & Sumner, 2006)
  - o Features NSDL at a glance using color-coded interactive strand maps.

- o This map enables browsing by subject through the NSDL collections.
- o The interface provides users with a range of metadata elements such as title, URL, grade level, a short textual summary, and relevant educational standards to allow easy navigation and deeper conceptual analysis.
- Intelligent Digital Library (Constabile et al., 1998)
  - o Focuses on specific "metainformation," that is, provenance, form, functionality, and usage statistics.
  - o Employs thesauri (e.g., INSPEC's 629 terms on Artificial Intelligence) to map documents within areas of scholarly interest
  - o Bases color scheme on the "importance" of each subject (i.e., the amount of literature assigned to that subject) rather than on how subjects relate to each other. This allows users to filter out "less important" literature.
  - o Also applies the "importance" color scheme to the links between subjects (i.e., based on the amount of literature sharing that link).
- Sequence Retrieval System (SRS) Browser (Mane & Borner, 2006)
  - o Relies on the "intrinsic relationships between biological entities" to visualize both these relationships and the relationships between works of scientific literature.
  - o Draws from the metadata contained in different databases (e.g., GeneNet; PubMed) to generate strand maps of search results.
  - o Using these metadata (primarily indexing terms) enables users to search for both information about a biological entity (e.g., a gene) and information about that entity's position within the literature (e.g., which genes are commonly studied alongside one another).

- UpLib "Fluid Interface" (Good et al., 2005; Janssen, 2005a, 2005b)
  - o Aims to blur the traditional separation between searching for materials and using them.
  - o Incorporates a document-viewing function (i.e., the ReadUp widget) into the interface along with searching, browsing, and navigation visualizations.
  - o The actual metadata fields used are up to the user, though the system makes good use of certain fields, such as title, date, and file type.
- MedioVis metadata browser (Grün, Gerken, Jetter, König, & Reiterer, 2005)
  - o Focuses on the "pleasure principles" of browsing; that is, how browsing can be made as joyful and aesthetically pleasing as possible. Like the UpLib Fluid Interface, MedioVis employs "multiple coordinated views" in pursuit of a joyful browsing experience.
  - o Offers a 2-D scatterplot table visualization for search results. Here, the patron chooses which metadata are used to plot the points on the table. For example, given a set of search results, usage statistics might form the Y axis, and publication date the X axis.
  - o Can also employ shelf location metadata to create a map of the location of a specific item within a physical library space.
  - o Some of the metadata elements used by the interface are title, author, year, media type, full text, and description.
- VisAmp prototype using semantic fisheye view (SFEV) (Janecek & Pu, 2005; Janecek, Schickel, & Pu, 2005).
  - o Aims to enhance the search process for less efficient searchers, such as those searching in an unfamiliar subject area, and for users performing imprecise, exploratory browsing.

o The WordNet semantic structure is incorporated into the interface to support users' exploratory search experience. The interface allows the user to expand and modify their query using both the semantic links within WordNet and fisheye views of the image collection.

o Addresses the challenges of visualizing dense fields of information. Rather than the color-coding of other interfaces, SFEV relies on degrees of "interestingness"; more interesting results are bright and in sharp focus, while less interesting results are "faded."

CONCLUSION

An increasing number of prototype visual interfaces for digital libraries are developed and reported at various digital library conferences and in different journals. This trend points to the growing popularity and acceptance of these types of interfaces for multimedia, multimodal, and multilingual information repositories and digital libraries. An examination of a number of digital library visual interfaces showed that metadata elements, whether created manually or automatically, are capable of providing various ways in which information can be represented and visualized on the interface. As a key element in any digital library, metadata have the potential to contribute not only to information organization but also to visual interface design, human information interaction, and to a richer representation of information objects and collections. Metadata elements can be used to inform various visualization techniques and metaphors and to support users' various searching, browsing, and navigation strategies. The variety of visual metaphors used in the reviewed interfaces also provides opportunities for further research. Some interfaces have made use of spatial metaphors while other have employed such metaphors as library shelves, strand maps, and multiple views. These techniques have the potential to visualize complex information spaces. Findings of this study suggest that metadata-enhanced visual interfaces represent varying levels of focus on stages of the search process. For instance, some interfaces put more emphasis on the query formulation stage, while others focused on collection visualization. A few interfaces used metadata and visualization techniques to cater for both query formulation and result presentation. In order to maximize the benefit of metadata for interface design, future research should explore the ways in which metadata can be used to support all stages of the search process, namely query formulation, reformulation, expansion, and results presentation. For instance, subject metadata, taken from such sources as thesauri and taxonomies, can provide users with additional search terms to expand or reformulate a particular query. As was found in this study, metadata contributes to the rich representation of the collection and items in visual interfaces. One approach to this type of design would be to have metadata presented to the user along with a subset of the collection as a context. This will provide users with a better understating of the collection and enable them to formulate more specific and precise queries. With the growing number of multimedia digital collections, item-level and collection-level metadata will allow for various forms of collection surrogates to be created to support users' understanding of collections.

REFERENCES

Ancona, D., & Smith, T. R. (2002, July 18). *Visual explorations for the Alexandria digital Earth prototype.* Paper presented at the Second International Workshop on Visual Interfaces to Digital Libraries, at the ACM+IEEE Joint Conference on Digital Libraries, Portland, OR. Retrieved August 24, 2008, from http://vw.indiana.edu/visual02/Ancona.pdf

Arms, W. Y. (2000). *Digital libraries*. M.I.T. Press.

Beheshti, J., Large, A., & Julian, C. (2005, June 2-4). Designing a virtual reality interface for children's Web portals. In data, information, and knowledge in a networked world. In *Proceedings of the Canadian Association for Information Science 2005 Annual Conference*, London/Ontario.

Börner, K., & Chen, C. (Eds.). (2002). *Visual interfaces to digital libraries* (LNCS 2539, pp. 1-9). Springer-Verlag Berlin Heidelberg.

Butcher, K. R., Bhushan, S., & Sumner, T. (2006). Multimedia displays for conceptual discovery: Information seeking with strand maps. *ACM Multimedia Systems Journal, 11*(3), 236-248.

Chang, M., Leggett, J. J., Furuta, R., Kerne, A., Williams, J. P., Burns, S. A., et al. (2004, June 7-11). Collection understanding. In *Proceedings of the Joint Conference on Digital Libraries (JCDL 2004)*, Tucson, AZ (pp. 334-342).

Constabile, M. F., Esposito, F., Semeraro, G., Fanizzi, N., & Ferilli, S. (1998, September 21-23). Interacting with IDL: The adaptive visual interface. In *Proceedings of the Research and Advanced Technology for Digital Libraries, Second European Conference, ECDL '98*, Heraklion, Crete, Greece (pp. 515-534).

Good, L., Popat, A. C., Janssen, W. C., & Bier, E. A. (2005, September 18-23). A fluid interface for personal digital libraries. In *Proceedings of the 9th European Conference on Research and Advanced Technology for Digital Libraries (ECDL 2005)*, Vienna, Austria (pp. 162-173).

Grün, C., Gerken, J., Jetter, H. C., König, W., & Reiterer, H. (2005, September 18-23). Medio-Vis: A user-centred library metadata browser. In *Proceedings of the Research and Advanced Technology for Digital Libraries, 9th European Conference, ECDL 2005*, Vienna, Austria (pp. 174-185).

Hearst, M. A., & Karadi, C. (1997, July 27-31). Cat-a-cone: An interactive interface for specifying searches and viewing retrieval results using a large category hierarchy. In *Proceedings of the 20th Annual International ACM/SIGIR Conference on Research and Development in Information Retrieval (SIGIR '97)*, Philadelphia, PA. New York: ACM.

Historical Directories of England and Wales. Retrieved August 24, 2008, from http://www.historicaldirectories.org

The International Children's Digital Library. Retrieved August 24, 2008, from http://www.icdlbooks.org

Janecek, P., & Pu, P. (2005). An evaluation of semantic fisheye views for opportunistic search in an annotated image collection. *International Journal of Digital Libraries, 5*(1), 42-56.

Janecek, P., Schickel, V., & Pu, P. (2005, December 12-15). Concept expansion using semantic fisheye views. In *Proceedings of the International Conference on Asian Digital Libraries, ICADL 2005*, Bangkok, Thailand (pp. 273-282).

Janssen, W. C. (2005a, June 7-11). Demo: The UpLib personal digital library system. In *Proceedings of Joint Conference on Digital Library (JCDL'05)*, Denver, CO.

Janssen, W. (2005b, September 18-23). ReadUp: A widget for reading, research and advanced technology for digital libraries. In *Proceedings of the 9th European Conference, ECDL 2005*, Vienna, Austria (pp. 230-241).

Korn, F., & Shneiderman, B. (1995). *Navigating terminology hierarchies to access a digital library of medical images* (Tech. Rep. HCIL-TR-94-03). University of Maryland.

Laitinen, S., & Neuvonen, A. (1998, September 21-23). BALTICSEAWEB: Geographic user interface to bibliographic information. In *Proceedings of the Research and Advanced Technology for Digital Libraries, Second European Conference, ECDL '98,* Heraklion, Crete, Greece, (pp. 651-652).

LibraryThing. Retrieved August 24, 2008, from http://www.librarything.com

Lin, X. (1999, August 15-19). Visual MeSH. In M. Hearst, F. Gey, & R. Tong (Eds.), *SIGIR'99: Proceedings of 22nd Annual International ACM/SIGIR Conference on Research and Development in Information Retrieval,* Berkeley, CA. New York: ACM.

Mane, K. K., & Borner, K. (2006). SRS browser: A visual interface to the sequence retrieval system. Visualization and data analysis 2006. In R. F. Erbacher, J. C. Roberts, M. T. Gröhn, & K. Börner (Eds.), *Proceedings of the SPIE-IS&T Electronic Imaging, SPIE, 2006.*

Mitchell, S. (1999). Interface design considerations in libraries. In D. Stern (Ed.), *Digital libraries: Philosophies, technical design considerations and example scenarios* (pp. 131-182). Haworth Press.

National Science Digital Library. Retrieved August 24, 2008, from http://ndsl.org

Sutcliffe, A. G., Ennis, M., & Hu, J. (2000). Evaluating the effectiveness of visual user interfaces for information retrieval. *International Journal of Human–Computer Studies, 53*(5), 741-763.

Variations2: The Indiana University digital music library. Retrieved August 24, 2008, from http://variations2.indiana.edu/

KEY TERMS

Information Visualization: A method of presenting data or information in nontraditional, interactive graphical forms. By using 2-D or 3-D color graphics and animation, these visualizations can show the structure of information, allow one to navigate through it, and modify it with graphical interactions. (dli.grainger.uiuc.edu/glossary.htm)

Medical Subject Headings (MESH): Controlled vocabulary designed by the National Library of Medicine to search MEDLINE and other health sciences databases.

Metadata: Manually or automatically created document representations and surrogates which are used for knowledge organization and representations in digital libraries and other information retrieval applications.

Scatterplot: Scatterplot, scatter diagram, or scatter graph is a graph used in statistics to visually display and compare two or more sets of related quantitative or numerical data by displaying only finitely many points, each having a coordinate on a horizontal and a vertical axis. (Wikipedia)

Subject Metadata: Metadata associated with the subject of a document or collection usually derived from some type of controlled vocabulary.

Visual Metaphors: The visual metaphor can be defined as the representation of a new system by means of visual attributes corresponding to a different system, familiar to the user, that behaves in a similar way. An archetypical case is the desktop metaphor. In it the traditional hierarchical tree of directories and subdirectories is substituted by the graphical interface of folders and files. (http://www.infovis.net/printMag.php?num=91&lang=2)

WordNet: WordNet is a semantic lexicon for the English language. It groups English words into sets of synonyms called *synsets*, provides short, general definitions, and records the various semantic relations between these synonym sets. (Wikipedia)

Chapter XXVIII
Usability Evaluation of Digital Library

Judy Jeng
New Jersey City University, USA

ABSTRACT

This chapter introduces the concept of usability and provides examples of how usability has been used in digital library evaluations. Usability is a user-centered evaluation and has a theoretical base in human-computer interaction. The most concise definition of usability is "fit for use." The dimensions of usability may also include usefulness, usableness, ease of use, effectiveness, efficiency, satisfaction, learnability, memorability, and error tolerant. The common methods of usability evaluation are described in this chapter, including formal usability testing, usability inspection, card sort, category membership expectation, focus groups, questionnaires, think aloud, analysis of site usage logs, cognitive walkthrough, heuristic evaluation, claims analysis, concept-based analysis of surface and structural misfits (CASSM), paper prototyping, and field study. Some evaluations employed one method; some used a combination of methods. There is a need for more empirical studies in order to understand users' needs. Culturability is an interesting area to explore.

INTRODUCTION

A digital library is an information system that gives us opportunities we never had with traditional libraries or even with the Web. However, we need to have a better understanding of user's needs in order to make digital libraries more intuitive to use. Usability testing is a way of learning from users. Usability testing is a user-centered evaluation. Usability is an elusive concept that may be viewed from many perspectives. This chapter provides a brief introduction on usability and how usability has been evaluated in various digital libraries.

DIMENSIONS OF USABILITY

Usability is dynamic interplay of four components: user, task, tool, and environment (Shackel, 1991). This relationship may be illustrated as shown in Figure 1, which is a modified version from Shackel (1991, p.23), Bennett (1972, 1979), and Eason (1981). The emphasis of this modified figure is on the **interplay** relationships among user, task, and tool. All are in the context of the environment.

Usability has user focus. It has a theoretical base in human-computer interaction. Many consider usability from an interface effectiveness point of view. Kim (2002) finds that "the difference between interface effectiveness and usability is not clear" (p. 26). Interface effectiveness is one of the most important aspects of usability as it is the medium through which users communicate and interact with the system.

Perhaps the most widely cited definitions are the ones of the International Standards Organization (ISO) and Nielsen. The ISO (1994) defines usability as "the extent to which a product can be used by specified users to achieve specified goals with effectiveness, efficiency, and satisfaction in a specified context of use" (p. 10). As Dillon (2001) points out, the ISO definition is extremely useful. This ISO definition places emphasis on measurable criteria of performance (i.e., effectiveness, efficiency, and satisfaction) that are context-bound by the type of user, the type of task, and situation of use. However, Dillon also considers that the set of metrics that falls out of the effectiveness, efficiency, and satisfaction model can place undue emphasis on speed and accuracy. For many contemporary interactions, Dillon suspects user experience will prove more complicated.

Nielsen (1993) defines usability as learnability, efficiency, memorability, low error rate, and satisfaction. He treats learnability as the most fundamental criteria. The system should be easy to learn so that the user can rapidly start getting some work done with it.

The most concise definition of usability is "fit for use" (*American Heritage Dictionary of the English Language,* 2000, p. 1894). The Usability Professionals' Association (2005) defines usability as follows: "Usability is the degree to which something - software, hardware or anything else - is easy to use and a good fit for the people who use it."

Shackel (1991, p. 24) reports that the definition of usability was probably first attempted by Miller (1971) in terms of measures for "ease of use," and these were first fully discussed with an attempt at a detailed formal definition by Shackel (1981, 1984):

The capability in human functional terms to be used easily and effectively by the specified range of users, given specified training and user support, to fulfill the specified range of tasks, within the specified range of environmental scenarios. (Shackel, 1984, p. 53-54)

It is worth noting that satisfaction is the most frequently cited attribute of usability while usefulness is the attribute often overlooked (Thomas, 1998). Dillon (2001) has expressed his concern that usability measures satisfaction as if it were the only affective component worthy of consideration. He states that affect covers the host of attitudinal, emotional, and mood-related elements of experience. These exist in all human endeavors, yet have been seriously overlooked in studies of usability.

Figure 1. The four principle components in a human-machine system

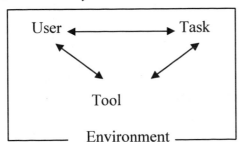

He calls for more attention to user choice, preference, perception of aesthetics, frustration, and sense of enhancement or accomplishment.

Rushinek and Rushinek (1986) found that system responsiveness (response time) is the most important variable affecting users' happiness.

METHODS OF USABILITY EVALUATION

There are a number of methods to evaluate usability. The techniques include formal usability testing, usability inspection, card sort, category membership expectation, focus groups, questionnaires, think aloud, analysis of site usage logs, cognitive walkthrough, heuristic evaluation, claims analysis, concept-based analysis of surface and structural misfits (CASSM), paper prototyping, and field study (Askin, 1998; Blandford, Keith, Connell, & Edwards, 2004; Campbell, 2001; Jeng, 2006, p. 20-24; Kantner & Rosenbaum, 1997; Keith, Blandford, Fields, & Theng, 2003; Levi & Conrad, 2002; Nielsen & Mack, 1994; Pearrow, 2000; Popp, 2001; Rosson & Carroll, 2002; Snyder, 2003).

Formal usability testing is the most productive technique in that the information gained is the most detailed and closest to the actual user. Formal usability testing has five characteristics: (a) The primary goal is to improve the usability of a product; (b) The participants represent real users; (c) The participants do real tasks; (d) The things participants do and say are observed and recorded; and (e) The data are analyzed, the real problems are diagnosed, and recommendations to fix those problems are made (Dumas & Redish, 1993).

Usability inspection has several characteristics: it applies to early designs, well-developed designs, and deployed systems; is usually less expensive than lab-based formal usability testing; does not employ real users; is expert-based (i.e., conducted by trained usability engineering practitioners); is often, but not always, guided by user tasks; and has the goal of predicting usability problems that users will encounter in real usage (Hartson, Shivakumar, & Pérez-Quiñones, 2004).

Heuristic evaluation is also sometimes called a *usability audit* or *heuristic expert review*. A small group of evaluators analyzes the interface of the site using a list of recognized usability principles, called *heuristics* (or rules of thumb). Aaccording to Blandford et al. (2004, p. 28), it is probably the most widely used usability evaluation technique because it is perceived to yield reasonable benefits for low cost. As Nielsen and Mack (1994) state, it is easy, fast, and cheap. However, it tends to focus on micro features of an interface rather than the global picture. Heuristic evaluation is often best done at the beginning of a project and then repeated at later stages of development (Hom, 2000).

Cognitive walkthrough is another method that involves expert evaluators. The evaluators design specific task scenarios. The user's goals and purpose for each task are defined and tasks are broken down into relatively small pieces. The evaluator's role is to play the part of the user working with the site, noting problems, paths, and barriers, and essentially reviewing the ease of learning of the site (Wharton, Rieman, Lewis, & Polson, 1994). Cognitive walkthrough is a relatively cheap method of cleaning up a Web site or a digital library. Since it does not involve actual users, it can be conducted any time and as frequently as desired. Cognitive walkthrough is more limited in scope than heuristic evaluation because of its rigid structure, but, at the same time, it provides a clear structure for conducting the analysis once user profiles and tasks have been defined.

Claims analysis is less structured than cognitive walkthrough. It is more difficult to learn than heuristic evaluation and cognitive walkthrough (Blandford et al., 2004, p. 32), but it supports the analyst in thinking about usability issues more deeply. Claims analysis provokes thinking about why things are the way they are, and how they could be different. In this method, the usability engineer identifies significant features in a design and generates hypotheses about the consequences these features might have for users engaged in activities.

Some usability evaluations use one primary method while some use a combination of methods.

PRIOR USABILITY STUDIES

This section briefly describes select digital library evaluations which use usability as the evaluation criteria.

The study conducted by Theng, Mohd-Nasir, and Thimbleby (2000) utilized questionnaires and heuristic evaluation to measure usability of the ACM Digital Library (http://www.acm.org), the Networked Computer Science Technical Reference Library (http://www.ncstrl.org), and the New Zealand Digital Library (http://www.nzdl.org). Their study helps to explicate the purpose of digital libraries.

Sumner and Dawe (2001) studied usability of the Digital Library for Earth System Education (DLESE, www.DLESE.org), focusing on its role in the process of educational resource reuse. The study found that the design of the search result page plays a critical role in supporting users' comprehension. The study also found that metadata play a central role to support comprehension and modification processes.

Sumner, Khoo, Recker, and Marlino (2003) conducted focus groups to study DLESE and the National Science Digital Library (NSDL, www.NSDL.org). The purpose of this study was to identify educators' expectations and requirements for the design of educational digital collections for classroom use.

Hartson et al. (2004) applied usability inspection method to evaluate the design and functionality of the Networked Computer Science Technical Reference Library (NCSTRL, http://www.ncstrol.

org). They found that the digital library's design was function-oriented and not user-oriented. The terminology used in the digital library was also a problem; there was jargon and the use of terms was designer-centered rather than user-centered.

The evaluation of DeLIver applied a mixture of methods, including transaction log analysis, surveys, interviews, focus groups, and formal usability testing to measure accessibility (Bishop, 2001; Neumann & Bishop, 1998). This evaluation demonstrated the value of data triangulation. The evaluators found the evaluation process enabled them to pursue social issues surrounding digital libraries while dealing with specific usability problems.

The evaluation of eLibraryHub also applied the approach of triangulation of data (Theng, Chan, Khoo, & Buddharaju, 2005). The study employed both quantitative and qualitative methods, including questionnaires and claims analysis, to study effectiveness, usefulness, and satisfaction.

Dorward, Reinke, and Recker (2002) evaluated Instructional Architect, which aims to increase the utility of NSDL resources for classroom teachers. The methods they employed included formal usability testing and focus groups. The evaluation centered on interface design and contents. Participants of the evaluation recommended additions of an introductory tutorial, better graphics, and a preview screen.

The usability study of the Belgian-American Research Collection at the University of Wisconsin Digital Collections Center also used both focus group and formal usability testing methods (Clark, 2004). The evaluation helped to bring in more logical and intuitive interface design.

Minnesota's Foundations Project is a multiagency collaboration to improve access to environmental and natural resources information (Quam, 2001). The researchers conducted two usability studies: one to study ease of use of the interface and one to study usefulness of controlled vocabulary. The formal usability testing was the primary evaluation method, supplemented by pretest and post-test questionnaires. The study found that controlled vocabulary is helpful to facilitate access. The digital library's interface has also been improved to lessen confusion.

The Documenting the American South (DocSouth) Digital Library, sponsored by the University Library of the University of North Carolina at Chapel Hill, employed a formal usability testing technique followed by focus groups to study interface design (Norberg, Vassiliadis, Ferguson, & Smith, 2005). The findings helped to redesign the digital library to have a flexible structure that will sustain future growth.

The usability study on the Indiana University-Purdue University Indianapolis (IUPUI) image collection employed a formal usability testing technique and focused on the evaluation of functionality, content satisfaction with, and awareness of the online resource (Kramer, 2005).

The evaluation of InfoHab (the Center of Reference and Information in Habitation) digital library employed formal usability testing, interview, and think-aloud techniques (Ferreira & Pithan, 2005). The evaluation criteria included Nielsen's five variables of learnability, efficiency, memorability, errors, and satisfaction, and focused on the digital library's interface.

Jeng (2006), in her doctoral dissertation, reports that formal usability testing is the most frequently used method in the academic library setting while for other types of digital libraries, questionnaire, focus group, and formal usability testing are three most used methods. Many digital library evaluations made use of more than one method for the benefit of data triangulation. Jeng's study also reports that satisfaction is the most frequently studied factor, followed by efficiency, ease of use, effectiveness, and usefulness (Jeng, 2006, p. 33). In addition to her doctoral study which was a cross-institutional study of two academic libraries (Jeng, 2007a, 2005a, 2005b), Jeng has been involved in the evaluations of the Moving Image Collections (http://mic.imtc.gatech.edu/) and the New Jersey Digital Highway (http://www.

njdigitalhighway.org/index.php). The evaluation of the Moving Image Collections has thus far been conducted in two parts: 1) the usefulness of the metadata (Jeng, 2007b, 2007c) and 2) usability of the Web site. The evaluation of the New Jersey Digital Highway focused primarily on usefulness of its contents. Jeng is currently evaluating a video digital library, NJVid, which received an IMLS grant ($971,512) from 2007 till 2010.

CONCLUSION AND FUTURE RESEARCH

Usability evaluation of digital libraries has received more attention in the past few years. However, there are still more papers talking about usability than those reporting with data, and perhaps it will be always that way. We need more empirical studies analyzing usability, including the provision of benchmarks for comparison, and an understanding of how to balance rigor, appropriateness of techniques, and practical limitations. Other criteria of evaluation, in addition to usability, also need to be discussed.

Digital libraries are a new form of information institution on a global scale. It will be interesting to study how people with different cultural backgrounds interpret usability, a field named "cross-cultural usability" or culturability. The term "culturability" was coined by Barber and Badre (1998), indicating the merging of culture and usability. The basic premise is simple: No longer can issues of culture and usability remain separate in designing for the World Wide Web. What is user-friendly for one culture can be vastly different for another culture. The same premise is applicable in digital libraries which serve users with different ethnic backgrounds and cultures.

REFERENCES

American Heritage dictionary of the English Language (4th ed.). (2000). Houghton Mifflin Co.

Askin, A. Y. (1998). *Effectiveness of usability evaluation methods at a function of users' learning stages.* Unpublished master's thesis, Purdue University.

Barber, W., & Badre, A. (1998, June 5). *Culturability: The merging of culture and usability.* Paper presented at the Fourth Conference on Human Factors & the Web, Basking Ridge, NJ. Retrieved November 6, 2007, from http://www.research.microsoft.com/users/marycz/hfWeb98/barber/index.htm

Bennett, J. L. (1972). The user interface in interactive systems. *Annual Review of Information Science and Technology, 7,* 159-196.

Bennett, J. L. (1979). The commercial impact of usability in interactive systems. In B. Shackel (Ed.), *Man-computer communication, infotech state-of-the-art* (Vol. 2, pp. 1-17). Maidenhead: Infotech International.

Bishop, A. P. (2001). Logins and bailouts: Measuring access, use, and success in digital libraries. *The Journal of Electronic Publishing, 4*(2). Retrieved November 6, 2007, from http://www.press.umich.edu/jep/04-02/bishop.html

Blandford, A., Keith, S., Connell, I., & Edwards, H. (2004). Analytical usability evaluation for digital libraries: A case study. In *Proceedings of the Fourth ACM/IEEE Joint Conference on Digital Libraries* (pp. 27-36). Retrieved November 6, 2007, from the ACM Digital Library database.

Campbell, N. (2001). *Usability assessment of library-related Web sites: Methods and case studies.* Chicago: LITA, American Library Association.

Clark, J. A. (2004). A usability study of the Belgian-American research collection: Measuring the functionality of a digital library. *OCLC Systems & Services: International Digital Library Perspectives, 20*(3), 115-127.

Dillon, A. (2001). Beyond usability: Process, outcome, and affect in human computer interactions. *The Canadian Journal of Information and Library Science, 26*(4), 57-69.

Dorward, J., Reinke, D., & Recker, M. (2002). An evaluation model for a digital library services tool. In *Proceedings of the Second ACM/IEEE-CS Joint Conference on Digital Libraries,* Portland, OR (pp. 322-323). Retrieved November 6, 2007, from the ACM Digital Library database.

Dumas, J. S., & Redish, J. C. (1993). *A practical guide to usability testing.* Norwood, NJ: Ablex Publishing Co.

Eason, K. D. (1981). A task-tool analysis of manager-computer interaction. In B. Shackel (Ed.), *Man-computer interaction: Human factors aspects of computers & people* (pp. 289-307). Rockville, MD: Sijthoff and Noordhoff.

Ferreira, S. M., & Pithan, D. N. (2005). Usability of digital libraries: A study based on the areas of information science and human-computer interaction. *OCLC Systems & Services, 21*(4), 311-323.

Hartson, H. R., Shivakumar, P., & Pérez-Quiñones, M. A. (2004). Usability inspection of digital libraries: A case study. *International Journal on Digital Libraries, 4*(2), 108-123.

Hom, J. (2000). *The usability methods toolbox: Heuristic evaluation.* Retrieved November 6, 2007, from http://jthom.best.vwh.net/usability/

International Standards Organization. (1994). *Ergonomic requirements for office work with visual display terminals. Part 11: Guidance on usability* (ISO DIS 9241-11). London: Author.

Jeng, J. (2005a). What is usability in the context of the digital library and how can it be measured? *Information Technology and Libraries, 24*(2), 47-56.

Jeng, J. (2005b). Usability assessment of academic digital libraries: Effectiveness, efficiency, satisfaction, and learnability. *Libri: International Journal of Libraries and Information Services, 55*(2/3), 96-121.

Jeng, J. (2006). *Usability of the digital library: An evaluation model.* Unpublished doctoral dissertation, Rutgers University.

Jeng, J. (2007a, September 25-27). Usability assessment of academic digital libraries. In *Proceedings of the Library Assessment Conference: Building Effective, Sustainable, Practical Assessment,* Charlottesville, VA (pp. 393-407).

Jeng, J. (2007b, April). *Metadata usefulness evaluation of the Moving Image Collections.* Paper presented at the 2007 Research Forum of the New Jersey Library Association Annual Conference, Long Branch, NJ. Retrieved November 6, 2007, from http://www.njla.org/conference/2007/presentations/Metadata.pdf

Jeng, J. (2007c). *Using FRBR tasks as a framework to evaluate metadata usefulness of the Moving Image Collections.* Manuscript submitted for publication.

Kantner, L., & Rosenbaum, S. (1997). Usability studies of www sites: Heuristic evaluation vs. laboratory testing. In *Proceedings of the 15ᵗʰ Annual International Conference on Computer Documentation* (pp. 153-160). Retrieved November 6, 2007, from the ACM Digital Library database.

Keith, S., Blandford, A., Fields, B., & Theng, Y. L. (2003). *An investigation into the application of claims analysis to evaluate usability of a digital library interface.* Paper presented at the Usability Workshop of JCDL 2002. Retrieved November 6, 2007, from http://www.uclic.ucl.ac.uk/annb/docs/Keith15.pdf

Kim, K. (2002). *A model of digital library information seeking process (DLISP model) as a frame for classifying usability problems.* Unpublished doctoral dissertation, Rutgers University.

Kramer, E. F. (2005). IUPUI image collection: A usability survey. *OCLC Systems & Services, 21*(4), 346-359.

Levi, M. D., & Conrad, F. G. (2002). Usability testing of world wide Web sites. *BLS research papers.* U.S. Department of Labor, Bureau of Labor Statistics. Retrieved November 6, 2007, from http://stats.bls.gov/ore/htm_papers/st960150.htm

Miller, R. B. (1971, April 12). *Human ease of use criteria and their tradeoffs* (IBM Rep. TR 00.2185). Poughkeepsie, NY: IBM Corporation.

Neumann, L. J., & Bishop, A. P. (1998, March 22-24). *From usability to use: Measuring success of testbeds in the real world.* Paper presented at the 35ᵗʰ Annual Clinic on Library Applications of Data Processing. Graduate School of Library and Information Science, University of Illinois at Urbana-Champaign. Retrieved November 6, 2007, from http://forseti.grainger.uiuc.edu/dlisoc/socsci_site/dpc-paper-98.html

Nielsen, J. (1993). *Usability engineering.* Cambridge, MA: Academic Press.

Nielsen, J., & Mack, R. L. (Eds.). (1994). *Usability inspection methods.* New York: Wiley.

Norberg, L. R., Vassiliadis, K., Ferguson, J., & Smith, N. (2005). Sustainable design for multiple audiences: The usability study and iterative redesign of the documenting the American South digital library. *OCLC Systems & Services, 21*(4), 285-299.

Pearrow, M. (2000). *Web site usability handbook.* Rockland, MA: Charles River Media.

Popp, M. P. (2001, March 15-18). *Testing library Web sites: ARL libraries weigh in.* Paper presented at the Association of College and Research Libraries, 10ᵗʰ National Conference, Denver. Retrieved November 6, 2007, from http://www.ala.org/ala/acrl/acrlevents/popp.pdf

Quam, E. (2001). Informing and evaluating a metadata initiative: Usability and metadata studies in Minnesota's Foundations Project. *Government Information Quarterly, 18*(3), 181-194.

Rosson, M. B., & Carroll, J. M. (2002). *Usability engineering: Scenario-based development of human-computer interaction.* San Francisco: Morgan Kaufmann.

Rushinek, A., & Rushinek, S. F. (1986). What makes users happy? *Communications of the ACM, 29*(7), 594-598. Retrieved November 6, 2007, from the ACM Digital Library database.

Shackel, B. (1981, September 15-18). The concept of usability. In *Proceedings of IBM Software and Information Usability Symposium,* Poughkeepsie, NY (pp. 1-30).

Shackel, B. (1984). The concept of usability. In J. L. Bennett, D. Case, J. Sandelin, & M. Smith (Eds.), *Visual display terminals: Usability issues and health concerns* (pp. 45-88). Englewood Cliffs, NJ: Prentice-Hall.

Shackel, B. (1991). Usability: Context, framework, definition, design and evaluation. In B. Shackel & S. J. Richardson (Eds.), *Human factors for informatics usability* (pp. 21-37). New York: Cambridge University Press.

Snyder, C. (2003). *Paper prototyping: The fast and easy way to design and refine user interfaces.* Boston: Morgan Kaufmann.

Sumner, T., & Dawe, M. (2001). Looking at digital library usability from a reuse perspective. In *Proceedings of the First ACM/IEEE-CS Joint Conference on Digital Libraries* (pp. 416-425). Retrieved November 6, 2007, from the ACM Digital Library database.

Sumner, T., Khoo, M., Recker, M., & Marlino, M. (2003). Understanding educator perceptions of "quality" in digital libraries. In *Proceedings of the 3rd ACM/IEEE-CS Joint Conference on Digital Libraries* (pp. 269-279). Retrieved November 6, 2007, from the ACM Digital Library database.

Theng, Y. L., Chan, M. Y., Khoo, A. L., & Buddharaju, R. (2005). Quantitative and qualitative evaluations of the Singapore National Library Board's digital library. In Y. L. Theng & S. Foo (Eds.), *Design and usability of digital libraries: Case studies in the Asia Pacific* (pp. 334-349). Hershey, PA: Information Science Publishing.

Theng, Y. L., Mohd-Nasir, N., & Thimbleby, H. (2000). Purpose and usability of digital libraries. In *Proceedings of the Fifth ACM Conference on Digital Libraries* (pp. 238-239). Retrieved November 6, 2007, from the ACM Digital Library database.

Thomas, R. L. (1998). *Elements of performance and satisfaction as indicators of the usability of digital spatial interfaces for information-seeking: Implications for ISLA.* Unpublished doctoral dissertation, University of Southern California.

Usability Professionals' Association. (2005). *What is usability?* Retrieved November 6, 2007, from http://www.upassoc.org/usability_resources/about_usability/

Wharton, C., Rieman, J., Lewis, C., & Polson, P. (1994). The cognitive walkthrough method: A practitioners guide. In J. Nielsen & R. L. Mack (Eds.), *Usability inspection methods* (pp. 105-140). New York: Wiley.

KEY TERMS

Effectiveness: Effectiveness is measured by the accuracy of tasks performed by the users, for example, the number of correct answers.

Efficiency: Efficiency is measured by speed (time and number of steps) of completing tasks.

Learnability: Learnability is measured by the learning effort of using a new system.

Memorability: Memorability is measured by the ease of reestablishing proficiency after a period of not using the system.

Satisfaction: Satisfaction is measured by the degree of pleasure of using the system. The Likert scales have been widely accepted as an economic way of measuring satisfaction.

Usableness: Usableness is about "does it work?" It refers to functions such as "Can I turn it on?" and "Can I invoke that function?"

Usefulness: Usefulness is about "does it help me?" Perceived usefulness is the extent to which an information system will enhance a user's performance.

Chapter XXIX
Digital Library Requirements:
A Questionnaire–Based Study

Stephen Kimani
Institute of Computer Science and Information Technology, JKUAT, Kenya

Emanuele Panizzi
University of Rome "La Sapienza," Italy

Tiziana Catarci
University of Rome "La Sapienza," Italy

Margerita Antona
FORTH-ICS, Greece

ABSTRACT

The gathering of user requirements is key to the gaining of a deeper understanding of the needs evolving from the user's operational context and from the use of the system. User requirements are pivotal in guiding the development process of any system. This is no less true in the arena of digital libraries (DLs). The gathering of DL requirements should be conducted with the understanding that the anticipated DL user interface should accord support to the user throughout the entire DL usage/interaction process. This chapter describes a questionnaire-based study of DL requirements based on the foregoing understanding. The study covered a wide range of issues pertinent to the design of user interfaces for DLs, including: user characteristics/profiles, current experience in DL usage, functional requirements, nonfunctional requirements, and contextual requirements. To the authors' knowledge, this is the first systematic empirical investigation of DL requirements that covers such a wide range.

INTRODUCTION

It has been said that "the digital library in a broader context is nothing but a database ...the objective of any digitization process should be the empowerment of the people" (TERI, 2004). It is worth noting that there exist many definitions of the term digital library (e.g., Borgman, 1999; Digital Library Federation, 1999); however some of the common points across different definitions are: digital libraries (DLs) can be comprised of digital as well as nondigital entities; the realm of libraries is constituted not only of library objects but also of associated processes, actors, and communities; and the content of DLs can be extremely heterogeneous. It appears that the bottom-line DL issue in this matter is to provide a coherent view of the (possibly) large collection of the available materials (Lynch & Garcia-Molina, 1995). With the foregoing statement in mind we may, to a large extent, regard a DL as an information environment. In this environment, there are producers and consumers of information and knowledge (including collaborators and stakeholders), and they may change their role or play more than one role at the same time.

The gathering of user requirements is instrumental to the gaining of a deeper understanding of the needs evolving from the user's operational environment and from the use of the system. User requirements are of key importance for guiding the development (and evaluation) process of any system. This is no less true in the arena of digital libraries. WP4 user interface and visualization is a cluster within the DELOS network of excellence on digital libraries[2]. The cluster's ultimate goal is to develop methodologies, techniques, and tools to establish a theoretically motivated and empirically supported frame of reference for designers and researchers in the field of user interfaces and visualization techniques for digital libraries, so as to enable future DL designers and developers to meet not only the technological, but also the user-oriented requirements in a balanced way.

During the first year, one of its specific objectives was to investigate the requirements for a DL user interface design. To that end, the cluster embarked on the gathering/identification of the functional requirements and nonfunctional requirements of DL users and stakeholders based on a questionnaire-based study.

The investigation involved a wide variety of issues pertinent to the design of user interfaces for DLs, ranging from user characteristics and profiles to current experience in the use of DLs, through functional and nonfunctional requirements, to requirements specifically related to the context of use. While there exist lots of related efforts (e.g., Marcum, 2003; Pasquinelli, 2002; Schilit, Price, & Golvchinsky, 1998), our study is, to the authors' knowledge, the first systematic empirical investigation of DLs user requirements that covers such a wide range of aspects. In this chapter, we describe the overall requirements emanating from the study[3].

In the rest of the chapter, we describe the questionnaires that were used in the DL requirements study; we then give some background information pertaining to the questionnaire participants. The DL requirements are then described and we then highlight future trends and conclude the chapter.

USER AND STAKEHOLDER QUESTIONNAIRES

Potential or real DL users (i.e., stakeholders and end users) have a key role toward the successful design of DLs, and the questionnaires can encourage them to word their recommendations on possible support offered by a DL. The questionnaires also enable DL users to contribute to the definition of the scope of DLs' functional and nonfunctional requirements. Apart from their use in the context of the data collection performed by the cluster, the questionnaires can also be reused in the process of designing digital libraries for the purposes of the user requirements collection phase. The questionnaires[3] consist of four parts: user background and demographics; user's current experience; DL functional requirements; and DL nonfunctional requirements.

DEMOGRAPHICS AND USER BACKGROUND

There were 45 library users (14 female, 25 male, 6 not specified) who responded to the online questionnaire. Most of the respondents range from 20 to 55 years old and they all come from Europe. Although many of them are in the field of computer science, the samples contain very divergent backgrounds (from computer scientists to humanities studies and librarians). Only a few participants reported a considerable degree of disability in one or more of the following categories: cognitive, intellectual, and visual. The sample of these 45 DL users is also characterized by multilingualism, high level of education, high experience with computing and the Internet, as well as relatively high experience with DLs. Questionnaire results indicate that the users frequently access a DL and thus they are aware of the weakness, advantages, and drawbacks of the current digital systems. In addition, as far as the type of access used for data retrieval is concerned, the vast majority of concerns are public or free access, indicating that the users are not willing to pay a lot for retrieving data and knowledge from a digital archive. Moreover, Web access is by far the most popular medium. Two thirds of the DLs gathered through the questionnaires support English as the only language of interaction. Slightly less than a quarter of all the DLs support both English and some other local language. Very few DLs offer multilingual support or only the local language.

DIGITAL LIBRARY REQUIREMENTS

This section describes the key needs and requirements concerning both the functionality of digital libraries and other nonfunctional characteristics related to interaction and importance of user interface design. The requirements are analyzed and then organized into high and low importance requirements for both DL stakeholders and end users. The realization constitutes a handy resource for guiding the development and evaluation of future DLs.

Functional Requirements

It is important for the developers and providers of DL services and systems to be well informed about the prevalent DL stakeholder and user functionalities. It is also important to know how important those functionalities are to the stakeholders and users. This subsection gives an analysis of various DL functional requirements in terms of prevalence and importance. The study analyzed the following functionalities: functions for locating information, functions for presenting resources, functions for personalization of content and services, facilities for communicating and collaborating with other DL users, and other common DL functions (e.g., social navigation support, multilingual support, personal annotation, notification/alerting services, glossaries, thesauri and dictionaries, printing/print preview facilities, and downloading/uploading facilities). In addition, some participants expressed their interest in, and attached importance to, the need for help and guidance.

- **Integration of knowledge:** Integration of knowledge is a stakeholder-oriented task. In fact, in the stakeholder's questionnaire we listed the content management functionalities of the DL. Among all the content management related functionalities listed within the questionnaire, deleting resources was rated as of low importance to stakeholders, whereas moderate importance ratings were allocated to: editing existing resources; creating new classification schemes; index facilities; creating new resources; retrieving content; and glossaries, thesauri, and dictionaries. The DL functions at the provider site that appear to be of high importance to stakeholders are: organizing resources; archiving resources; and storing metadata about resources (e.g., creator, content, technical requirements, etc.). Stakeholders rated locating resources, creating cross-reference links among similar resources,

Figure 1. Common DL functions at the provider site and their importance to DL stakeholders[1]

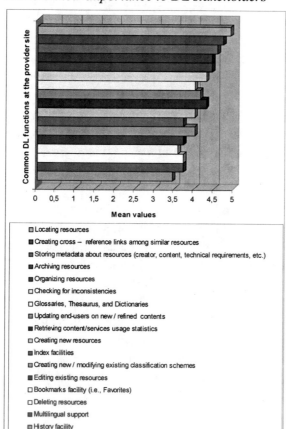

and storing metadata about resources as of highest importance. Figure 1 provides an overview of common DL functions (content management) at the stakeholder site and their importance to the stakeholders. The DL stakeholder functional requirements center around two main functional areas: content management and membership management.

- **Access to knowledge:** Among the functions for locating information, higher importance ratings were allocated to search (e.g., keywords search, parametric search), moderate importance ratings were allocated to index facilities and to navigation related functions (e.g., browsing predefined catalogues), and lower importance ratings were allocated to "See also" items (e.g., similar to the one at hand) and to functions for filtering search/browsing results (e.g., according to personal profile[s]).

- **Administration of content:** This is typically a stakeholder's task. Among all the content management-related functionalities listed in the questionnaire, history facility, multilingual support, and bookmarks facility were of low importance to stakeholders. Moderate importance ratings were allocated to modifying existing classification schemes, retrieving services usage statistics, and updating end users on new/refined contents. Checking for inconsistencies appears to be of high importance to stakeholders. Stakeholders also expressed their interest/need for "access to control policies" and for retrieval of DL usage statistical data. The reader may refer to Figure 1 above.

- **Tool creation and management:** Among the functions for the personalization of content and services, higher importance ratings were allocated to functions for the presentation of contents according to profile, and to bookmarks facility (i.e., Favorites), moderate importance ratings were allocated to the provision of suggestions for contents based on profile, and to services offered for profile definition (e.g., professional interests, personal interests, etc.), and lower importance ratings were allocated to the provision of suggestions for discussion with other library members with similar interest profiles, and to history facility. An overview of the ratings given by DL users is presented in Figure 2.

- **Membership management:** Among all the membership management-related functionalities listed in the stakeholder's questionnaire, multilingual support, monitoring usage and identifying common patterns of use, and initiating special interest discussions were rated as of low importance to stakeholders. Moderate importance was allocated to updating end users on new/refined services and in maintaining a virtual help-desk for end users (e.g., FAQs facility). DL functions related to membership management that appear to be of high importance

to stakeholders are services for subscribing and unsubscribing DL users.

- **Services – Interfaces for access to integrated knowledge:** Higher importance ratings were allocated to short description/previews, author(s)/editor(s), and title, moderate importance ratings were allocated to popularity (e.g., number of visits), to insertion/modification date, and to related items, and lower importance ratings were allocated to users' ratings and to users' discussions and reviews. An overview of the ratings is presented in Figure 3. As can be seen, the most important fields are "Title" and "Author."

- **Services – Interfaces for sharing/integration of knowledge:** Among the functions for communicating and collaborating with other DL users, higher importance ratings were allocated to shared annotation facilities (e.g., peer reviews) and to e-mail services, moderate importance ratings were allocated

Figure 2. Common functions for personalization of DL content and services, and their importance to DL users

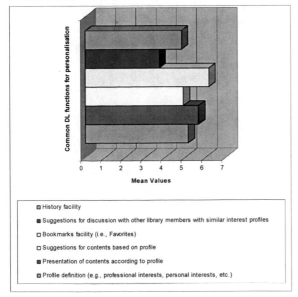

Figure 3. Common fields for presenting DL resources, and their importance to DL users

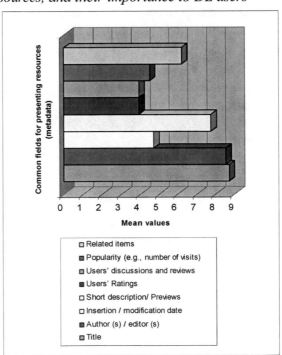

to message boards services, and lower importance ratings were allocated to video conferencing and chat. Regarding communication, e-mail is the most frequent way required for communicating, while video conferencing appears not to be strongly desired. Furthermore, among all facilities for collaboration, "track changes" facilities received the lowest scores.

- **Other DL functionalities:** Higher importance ratings were allocated to printing/print preview facilities, and to downloading/uploading facilities, while moderate importance ratings were allocated to personal annotation, and notification (alerting) services, and lower importance ratings were allocated to social navigation support (e.g., through users' rating of content) and to multilingual support.

Nonfunctional Requirements

This subsection gives an analysis of the importance of the following nonfunctional requirements: common usability requirements, common accessibility requirements, and other common nonfunctional requirements (e.g., ethics, safety, privacy, security, and system performance).

- General nonfunctional requirements at the user site and their importance according to DL users

In this part, the analysis of the importance of nonfunctional requirements according to the DL users is discussed.

Usability Requirements

Higher importance ratings were allocated to support for error prevention and handling, and ease of use of the DL, while moderate importance ratings were allocated to memorability and learnability, and lower importance ratings were allocated to

subjective satisfaction users (i.e., expert, moderate, and novel users). An overview of the ratings is presented in Figure 4. The ease of use of a DL is the most important feature. On the other hand, the satisfactory performance for the experts is the least important one. This means that the users give high importance to the simple way of communicating, accessing, retrieving, and searching content of their interest. Furthermore, in terms of usability, some participants highly rated the importance of speed and flexibility to reach the information, and mentioned that the DL should "remember" the usability and accessibility preferences and requirements of the users.

Accessibility Requirements

Higher importance ratings were allocated to support for users with dexterity and mobility impairments, moderate importance ratings were allocated to support for users with speech, hearing, and learning impairments, and lower importance ratings were allocated to support for users with reading and visual impairments.

Figure 4. Usability-related requirements and their importance to DL users

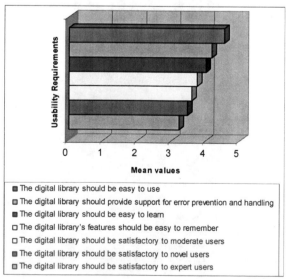

■ The digital library should be easy to use
☐ The digital library should provide support for error prevention and handling
■ The digital library should be easy to learn
☐ The digital library's features should be easy to remember
☐ The digital library should be satisfactory to moderate users
■ The digital library should be satisfactory to novel users
☐ The digital library should be satisfactory to expert users

Other Nonfunctional Requirements

Higher importance ratings were allocated to system performance, moderate importance ratings were allocated to security, privacy, and safety, and lower importance ratings were allocated to ethical requirements.

- General nonfunctional requirements at the provider site and their importance according to stakeholders

In this part of the chapter, the analysis of the importance of nonfunctional requirements is detailed according to the DL stakeholders.

Usability Requirements

Stakeholders expressed low interest in the memorability of the DL satisfaction to novel users, moderate interest in error prevention and handling and satisfaction to expert users, and high interest in the ease of use and of learning of the DL. Figure 5 provides an overview of the stakeholders' preferences over specific usability attributes for DLs.

Accessibility Requirements

Stakeholders showed relatively high interest in special services and support for users with visual impairments, reading impairments, and mobility impairments, in comparison to special features for users with learning impairments, dexterity, speech impairments, and hearing impairments.

Other nonfunctional requirements

The stakeholders rated the other nonfunctional requirements as follows: high importance to safety, system's performance (e.g., response time), privacy, scalability, and reliability (e.g., back-up facilities); moderate importance to interoperability (i.e., platform independence), extendibility

Figure 5. Usability-related requirements and their importance to DL stakeholders

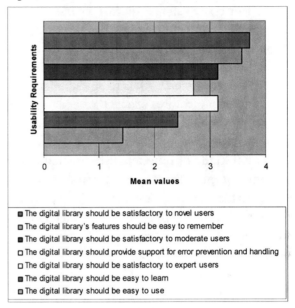

Legend:
- The digital library should be satisfactory to novel users
- The digital library's features should be easy to remember
- The digital library should be satisfactory to moderate users
- The digital library should provide support for error prevention and handling
- The digital library should be satisfactory to expert users
- The digital library should be easy to learn
- The digital library should be easy to use

(e.g., evolution of functionality and content-related requirements), adaptability (e.g., to different levels of user expertise), and compliance with national/international standards (e.g., ISO); and low importance to cost, interoperability (i.e., platform independence), portability, and ethics.

High and Low Importance Requirements

The foregoing specific functional and nonfunctional requirements were analyzed in order to identify high and low importance digital library requirements. In the sequel, the identified requirements are described, starting with the high and low importance requirements for stakeholders and then for end users.

Stakeholder Requirements

Stakeholders appear to pay particular attention to functions for locating and organizing resources, including functions for creating cross-reference links among similar resources, and functions for storing metadata about resources and checking for inconsistencies among the DL resources. Another interesting observation is that all accessibility requirements (i.e., for all kinds of disabilities) obtain a significant position in the list of requirements of high importance to DL stakeholders, whereas usability requirements fall in the group of moderately important features except the need for "ease of use" of the DL. In the group of requirements of high importance, DL stakeholders have also placed all kinds of functionalities related to the administration and management of registered DL users. On the other hand, the group of requirements that appear to be of lower value to DL stakeholders includes most of the miscellaneous functional and nonfunctional requirements, as well as usability requirements related to novel users. Furthermore, history facilities and multilingual support are of relatively low value to DL stakeholders.

End-User Requirements

DL end users, just like stakeholders, pay a lot of attention to all types of DL facilities for locating (subjectively) useful information. End users, in contrast to stakeholders, appear to pay particular attention to certain miscellaneous nonfunctional requirements such as system performance, security, privacy, safety, and other ethical requirements. Printing and up/downloading facilities are also of significant importance to DL users, followed by general usability requirements and accessibility for people with motor impairments (i.e., mobility and dexterity impairments). On the other hand, personalization is not really an important issue among DL end users, and facilities for user-to-user communication and collaboration are almost not an issue at all.

Main Lessons

The results of this initial work have led to the recognition and realization of some significant dimensions of diversity in users issues for DLs.

Concerning demographics and user characteristics, the performed investigation has established that users from a number of European countries exhibit a variety of characteristics concerning age, educational level and professional background, and purpose of DL use. Nevertheless, most users have a recurrent DL usage pattern, that is, twice a week for a duration of 1 to 5 hours. Additionally, users clearly show a tendency to use free access DLs through the World Wide Web. Functional requirements and nonfunctional requirements vary according to the users' role in DLs usage. In particular, it has emerged that end users and stakeholders of DLs tend to have different views and conceptualizations of DL systems and of their use. Overall, it appears that DL stakeholders strive for enriched functionality, whereas DL users pay more attention to the perceived behavior and reliability of a DL. At the present stage, a strong need for communication or collaboration in the DL end-user community does not seem to have emerged yet. End users view DLs as personalized environments where privacy is protected. On the other hand, stakeholders appear to view DLs as more collaborative environments. From the acquired data, it also emerges that the traditional "paper document" metaphor is still felt as prevailing in DL environments, based on the high degrees of importance placed on retrieval, printing, uploading, and so forth of documents, and with respect to the low importance placed, for example, on more digitally-oriented functions such as personal annotation of digital data. A requirement common to both end users and stakeholders concerns help and guidance. On the providers' side, appropriate information about all the functionalities and the facilities of a DL are necessary in order to be able to provide the users with satisfactory results. While it is somewhat natural that end users and stakeholders focus on different functions of a DL, it appears that they also view nonfunctional requirements differently due to their different roles. In particular, it appears that they have different views on accessibility and usability issues. The end users appear to have specific expectations concerning the reliability and usability of the DL, whereas stakeholders appear to be more aware of accessibility issues, and to pay attention to the provision of DL access to diverse target user groups. Stakeholders, as professional and expert users, also consider as more important the effectiveness of a DL user interface with respect to its ease of use, whereas end users, who may use a DL on a more occasional basis, appear to be more interested in issues such as usability, reliability, and safety. Diversity also appears when analyzing users' information needs when searching DLs. In searching behavior, users develop different individual styles, or employ combinations of methods to establish relevance judgments. Additionally, users, as opposed to stakeholders, do not appear to have a clear understanding of other possible purposes of DLs use than searching for information or document.

The above differences may find an explanation in the different levels of awareness, among end users and stakeholders, concerning the technological aspects of DLs that can differentiate them from paper-based libraries, by providing access, for example, to nontextual material, as well as support for information exchange, annotation, and cooperation.

The above shed light on some important aspects of the users' access to DLs. Such aspects need to be carefully considered in order to further investigate the implications on the design of DLs user interfaces. For example, given the differences in the priorities between end users and stakeholders, it is unlikely that a single user interface can satisfy the requirements of both target groups. This needs to be reflected also in appropriate (possibly different) metaphors, carefully elaborated in order to go beyond the physical library and paper-based model towards a more novel concept of a digital library as a collection of diverse (possibly multimodal) digital resources (e.g., software, services, etc.) in desktop and mobile environments.

FUTURE TRENDS AND CONCLUSIONS

We are living in a day when people are increasingly using a variety of computing devices in their daily lives which are not all continuously connected to a network. Such devices present an interesting opportunity for the creation of personalized information spaces, such as, DLs with collections and services that correspond to targeted needs and situations. It is also worth stressing that DL users are changing their way of using DLs. DL users are nowadays often playing more and more different roles at different times and places, for example, as consumers of information and producers of information at the same time (Bertini, Catarci, Di Bello, & Kimani, 2005).

The prioritization of requirements elaborated in this chapter has the potential to lead to the elaboration of a framework for DL user interface design. A future research consideration would be to increase the sample size of both the end user and stakeholder questionnaires. This would facilitate a richer understanding of the causal nature that exists between the respondent, functional requirements, as well as the nonfunctional requirements. It would also make it possible to use the results to formulate population inferences. Another important issue to be addressed in the context outlined above concerns the DL lifecycle. The investigation of the DL lifecycle will be targeted to provide an insight into how a DL is expected to evolve regarding users and stakeholders interaction, and how the different phases of the lifecycle are interrelated with functional or nonfunctional requirements.

This chapter has described the overall requirements emanating from the questionnaire-based study. It has in particular described the functional and nonfunctional requirements that were obtained from the study. Moreover, the chapter has identified and reported the high and low importance DL requirements based on an analysis of the foregoing specific functional and nonfunctional requirements. The chapter has also discussed the main lessons that were learned from the study.

REFERENCES

Bertini, E., Catarci, T., Di Bello, L., & Kimani, S. (2005). Visualization in digital libraries. In M. Hemmje, C. Niederee, & T. Risse (Eds.), *Integrated publication and information systems to virtual information and knowledge environments*. Springer-Verlag Berlin.

Borgman, C. L. (1999). What are digital libraries? Competing visions. *Information Processing and Management, 35*(3), 227-243.

Digital Library Federation. (1999). *A working definition of digital library*. Author.

Lynch, C., & Garcia-Molina, H. (1995). *Interoperability, scaling, and the digital libraries research agenda*. Paper presented at the IITA Digital Libraries Workshop.

Marcum, D. (2003). Requirements for the future digital library. *The Journal of Academic Librarianship, 29*(5), 276-279.

Pasquinelli, A. (2002). *Digital library technology trends* (white paper). Sun Microsystems, Inc.

Schilit, B. N., Price, M. N., & Golvchinsky, G. (1998). Digital library information appliances. In *Proceedings of the Third ACM Conference on Digital Libraries*, Pittsburgh. ACM Press.

TERI. (2004). *Report on the International Conference on Digital Libraries*. New Delhi, India: Author.

KEY TERMS

Demographics: Demographics refer to the characteristics of human populations and population segments. Demographics include aspects such as age, gender, nationality, occupation, language, and so forth.

Digital Library: Borgman (1999) defines digital libraries as:

A set of electronic resources and associated technical capabilities for creating, searching and using information. In this sense they are an extension and enhancement of information storage and retrieval systems that manipulate digital data in any medium (text, images, sounds; static or dynamic images) and exist in distributed networks. The content of digital libraries includes data, metadata that describe various aspects of the data (e.g., representation, creator, owner, reproduction rights), and metadata that consist of links or relationships to other data or metadata, whether internal or external to the digital library.

According to the Digital Library Federation (Digital Library Federation, 1999):

Digital libraries are organizations that provide the resources, including the specialized staff, to select, structure, offer intellectual access to, interpret, distribute, preserve the integrity of, and ensure the persistence over time of collections of digital works so that they are readily and economically available for use by a defined community or set of communities.

Functional Requirements: They describe system services or functions.

Nonfunctional Requirements: They define a constraint on the system or on the development process.

Questionnaire: A questionnaire is a written list of questions that is distributed to subjects/participants to gather information.

Stakeholders: Stakeholders are people who do not use the system directly but they may be affected by the system.

Users: Users are people who use/interact with the system directly.

ENDNOTES

[1]   http://www.delos.info

[2]   The reader may refer to the cluster Web site http://delos.dis.uniroma1.it for the full and more detailed report from the study.

[3]   The questionnaires have been made available to the public in a Web-based form, and can be accessed from the cluster Web site http://delos.dis.uniroma1.it.

[4]   Please note that in all figures with charts, the items in the legend are ordered such that they have a direct correspondence with the bar items in the graph itself, for example, the top-most item in the legend corresponds to the top-most bar item in the graph.

Chapter XXX
Handhelds for Digital Libraries

Spyros Veronikis
Ionian University, Greece

Giannis Tsakonas
Ionian University, Greece

Christos Papatheodorou
Ionian University, Greece

ABSTRACT

The present chapter introduces digital library services' utilization through handheld devices, such as personal digital assistants (PDAs) and smartphones. It argues that handheld devices proliferation justifies the term digital library in terms of anywhere-anytime access, and retrieval and management of information. Furthermore, these devices constitute powerful information harvesting tools that help users enhance their interaction with information spaces, both of physical and digital form. The chapter presents the services that can be accessed by means of portable devices and analyzes the main sociotechnical issues that arise and influence user interaction. Factors that affect acceptance of these devices are discussed, and future trends are presented to outline the research landscape for the forthcoming years.

INTRODUCTION

During the last years, computer technology has been evolving from the mainframe and personal computing eras to the third one, that of ubiquitous computing. Wireless communication networks and mobile computing were similarly affected by the evolution in computing devices. As a result,

people can choose among dozens of portable devices, capable of establishing radio connections, to join a computing network, such as the Internet, and realizing the vision of ubiquitous information access and delivery services. On the other hand, the Web lacks authority and quality control, is inadequately indexed, and the search interfaces are ineffective and simplistic. These reasons, along with the need for anytime access to information and the need to retrieve relevant and accurate information from anyplace, lead to the creation of digital libraries (DLs).

In this chapter we present the reasons why handhelds, like personal digital assistants (PDAs), smartphones, TabletPCs, and the most recent ultra mobile PCs (UMPCs) can be used as tools to access DL content. The approach of this chapter is user-centered and focuses on the services that can be supported by these handhelds, the interaction for use in DLs, and the acceptance of such devices.

BACKGROUND

The term PDA was coined in 1992 by John Sculley for a handheld device that offered work organizing tools, like a calendar, scheduler, address book, memos, clock, and a calculator. The potential they introduced in information delivery was quickly recognized and soon these devices were utilized, mainly, by health sciences libraries (Jones, Rieger, Treadwell, & Gay, 2000; Rios, 2004; Smith, 2002). Meanwhile, bigger screens were made available and were able to depict colorful graphics. Computing power, memory, and storage capabilities increased, and data input methods, like handwriting and virtual keyboards, were implemented. Audio playback was made available and both size and weight reached the ideal measures. Wireless networks also evolved, making anywhere information delivery a reality. Moreover, smartphones appeared, providing telephony and other communication services like e-mail, three-way communications (conferencing), and Internet access.

Apart from the physical libraries, DL organizations also found the wireless connectivity features quite attractive. Handhelds could be used to access multimedia content on a 24/7 basis. They could also keep notes and other information for reference, or even be used as communication tools.

During the last years many researchers have been studying issues that arise by the usage of such devices for information retrieval tasks. In early years of the current decade, several prototypes were implemented in various settings, such as James Madison University (McCabe, 2004), Oulu University, Finland (Aittola, Ryhänen, & Ojala, 2003), and Cornell University (Jones et al., 2000). Students from an informatics class in J.M. University used a PDA to view and edit patient records whereas students in the Oulu and Cornell universities used the PDAs to help them navigate in the university's library, access the OPAC, locate books of their interest, communicate with other persons on the network (including library personnel), take notes, scan or photograph topics from the books retrieved, and transfer data on a personal storage area. Participants in the studies expressed enthusiasm for the ability to combine mobile information access with other activities such as writing or organizing materials. Map guidance to locate a book was preferred over traditional shelf classification. Even though the service was considered easier to use from a desktop terminal, the usage of a portable device in larger libraries was appreciated. However, as Jones et al. note (2000), "their enthusiasm declined significantly when either technology purchase or student fees where suggested" (p. 98).

SERVICES ACCESSED WITH HANDHELDS

Among the advantages of DLs over physical libraries, two are of great importance: anytime and anywhere access to the library's content. Even though the existence of DLs goes back at the late 80s, the term *"anywhere"* was strongly associated with indoor places, like a home or company office where a wireline connection to the Internet or some other database system was available. Only recently, with the rapid growth of wireless communications and mobile computing, the term *"anywhere"* really reflects outdoor connections. Handhelds are used to fill this spatial gap among access points, by enabling connections to remote information providers from any point, giving a new perspective and potential to fields, like education and life-long learning, business, logistics, e-commerce, health, and entertainment.

There are three well-known and established information retrieval methods, namely searching, browsing, and asking (Rosenfeld & Morville, 2002). Nowadays, handhelds can support their users in information seeking tasks by delivering valuable services. Powerful searching tools like search engines, online catalogs, bibliographic databases, citation tools, search zones, lexicons, thesauri, and controlled vocabularies are accessible via the Web, properly formed for the small screen devices (Mobile Google, mOPACs, i-mode) and can be delivered to a user, whether the user is in an airport lobby, in a train, or sitting in a park.

In cases where the user's information needs are vague, the browsing method can help the user to start research. Handhelds can provide access to categorized content, that is, taxonomies and hierarchies, where the user can progressively narrow down the seeking procedure to find information of interest. Navigation aid is also considered a valuable service. Navigation can be site-wide to help users understand where they are and where they can go from there, or it can be local to let them know where they are and what resources are available nearby. Also, additional navigation aids like site-map trees and tables of contents offer to the user a condensed overview of the information landscape and links to major content areas let the user choose the level of abstraction the user desires, with a single tap on the screen. Map guidance can also be used when looking for a physical object (e.g., a book) in the physical library (Aittola et al., 2003) or the nearest open gas station in town. Nowadays, many handhelds integrate global positioning system (GPS) modules and geographic information systems (GIS) software to support

their users in navigating in the physical space. Since the handheld user is no longer restricted in a small area, location depended services (LDS) are now becoming available, aiming at delivering the information or service that best fits the user's location. Apart from navigation aids, other valuable tools like metadata indexes, guides, wizards, and contextual linking systems can be delivered right to the user's palm, whenever and wherever the user needs them.

In more complex information seeking tasks, searching and browsing methods are often integrated and used in an iterative fashion. When the information needs are not well defined, the user starts browsing the content and eventually performs a fine search within a subcategory. However, when this technique does not yield the desired information, asking an expert might be the solution. Thanks to their communicating features, handhelds can support live referencing by means of e-mail, Web-forms, instant messaging or chatting, and even phone calls. The lack of nearby resources for advice, like books and encyclopedias while being outdoors, makes stronger the need for remote assistance and especially when the need arises beyond office hours. Live referencing services are suitable for 24/7 access and therefore strongly match the DL profile. Many academic institutions worldwide expand their referencing services, like the Library of Congress, the Pennsylvania State University, and the National State Libraries of Australasia. However, most of the referencing services currently available are oriented to users sitting in front of a desktop terminal. One of the few pioneers in supporting mobile users is the Library of Curtin University of Technology, where users can ask the library's experts by submitting an SMS query. The lack of a keyboard makes the procedure of text input somewhat cumbersome and therefore it becomes difficult for the mobile user to describe to an expert the kind of information the user needs. On the other hand, the capabilities of the new handheld devices enable the user to contact an expert via telephony, and allow the expert to send all the necessary information, for example, short texts, summaries, and URLs, to the user's terminal. A similar example is the situation where a police officer asks from the operations center detailed information for a car by submitting the plate's number via police radio and gets the detailed data on a mobile data terminal (MDT) placed in the car.

Apart from live referencing, handhelds are also very popular in applications of static referencing, that is, the user can download information content into the device while being at home or office and look up to it whenever a need arises. Address books, dictionaries, and tables are some well known examples, but as the screens of handhelds become bigger and capable of depicting high resolution graphics, it is expected that diagrams, images, and e-books will be widely used. Marshall and Ruotolo (2002) made a study for reading on handhelds and found that reading on screen is strongly preferred when the user wants to locate and focus on short segments of a longer text (e.g., abstracts, summaries, definitions, etc.) and navigate through an extensive set of familiar materials. For example, an engineer can always carry a handbook or manual, a software developer can carry a reference guide, and a medical doctor can always have along the medical records of patients.

Besides publishers, other sources of electronic information can be digitization projects of textbooks and manuscripts that go back at the early 70s with Project Gutenberg[1] and the Perseus[2] project at Tufts University, and continue today with large-scale digitization projects, like the ones funded by Google[3] and libraries in the US and UK (e.g., the libraries of Harvard, Stanford, the University of Michigan, and Oxford University, as well as the New York Public Library [NYPL]), aiming for the online accessibility of more than 30 million full-text volumes. During the early 90s, with the evolution of electronic publishing, many textbooks were originally created in electronic

form and soon the first e-books appeared. Many e-book vendors now provide rich collections that can be accessed, displayed and read with the appropriate software on the handheld, while specialized loaning software permits libraries to apply policies on electronic content. Also, the storage capacity of the handhelds allows the user to carry hundreds or thousands of e-books on a single device.

Content management tools for annotation, storage, organization, transfer, and sharing can also help the mobile user to exploit the retrieved information in the most efficient way. For example, a student may use a device during a lecture to keep some notes, to record the lecture, to classify it as "course notes," to e-mail the notes to a friend, and finally to migrate the whole session to the student's desktop computer for post-processing.

Since handhelds are designed to extend our workplace outdoors and not completely substitute our desktop computers, we need to have most of our information in both places, indoors and outdoors. For example, a new e-mail downloaded on the handheld may also be transferred to the PC, if the user wishes so, and vice versa. The handheld and the PC can be connected by means of a cable or a cradle, or even by establishing a wireless link, for example, Bluetooth, Infrared (Heisey & Paolillo, n.d.), or WiFi. Upon connection, the synchronization software compares the files and information between the two devices and copies the most current versions of the files to both devices. That way, the user always has a backup copy of the user's data, which can be a lifesaver if the handheld is broken or stolen. When synchronization is finished, the user can continue working on the desktop computer (e.g., extending research based on the results or URLs returned from some OPAC queries) where a keyboard and a bigger display are available. User requirements studies have shown that the idea of beaming stations where one can exchange information between the devices is highly appreciated (Carney, Koufogiannakis, & Ryan, 2004).

INTERACTION ISSUES

Many challenging questions arise when one attempts to combine the two evolving technologies of DLs and mobile computing. Current broadband wireless connectivity is available for short-range coverage, forming hot-spots and dead-zones. As an alternative, mobile telephony networks offer almost everywhere-coverage except for low-speed and expensive connections, as in the case of the services provided by mobile phone operators in North America, Europe, and Japan.

Apart from wireless connectivity, another issue emerging when providing DL services to mobile users involves modifying the nature of the services to accommodate the constraints placed by the mobile context. Specifically, mobile users need services specially designed for a constantly changing context of use. Users might be changing location, carrying objects, there might be some device destruction, and so forth.

What is more, many handheld devices have small screen size, small or even no keyboard, and they are usually used in noisy environments with poor lighting conditions and many interruptions. Therefore, instead of extending the desktop paradigm, these services must meet the users' needs for brief, targeted sessions (Roussos, Marsh, & Maglavera, 2005). Today, handhelds support graphical user interfaces (GUIs) and windows, icons, menus, and a pointing device (WIMP) systems. Due to the small screen size of handhelds, usually only one application window appears at a time and therefore the devices are not considered to be multitasking. However, as Peterson (2004) notes, "Bedside is not the place to conduct a literature search on a database or to read full-text journal articles" (p. 53). Due to context constraints, mobile users' information search and delivery must be short, focused, and quick, which is sometimes called "information snacking," that is, short online visits to get specific answers.

Upon full-text presentation on demand, as in the case of e-books, information must be presented progressively in a successive disclosure fashion. A popular way is to use a text-based representation (Buyukkokten, Garcia-Molina, & Paepcke, 2001), where a tree hierarchy scheme is used to represent the information-layout structure. The first branches (nodes) of the tree represent the information headers, the second-order nodes represent the subheaders, and so on, revealing more information bits as the user moves on to deeper levels (Buchanan, Jones, & Marsden, 2003). A similar approach is scatter/gather, which proposes that similar documents are automatically clustered and key term summaries can be displayed for each cluster (Jones, Buchanan, & Thimbleby, 2002).

Besides deciding upon the content to present to the handheld user, the issue of information presentation and management is of critical value. Crestani, Landoni, and Melucci (2006) suggest that fonts must be customizable to the user's needs, especially for those with poor vision. Moreover, the user must be provided with full-text search tools, annotation modules, and screen capturing for saving image files. Furthermore, navigation tools, like subject trees, headers, bookmarks, and indicators have proved useful, that is, informing the user of how much of the text has been read. Another issue regarding content presentation in small screens concerns images. When a user is looking for textual information, the user should be given the option of not downloading accompanying images.

Regarding the layout presentation, the small screen-size is almost always inadequate to display the document retrieved in its original form. Therefore, in many cases, the user is given the option to have the document reformed. This procedure can be prompted by the user at the time the user stores some files in the handheld (e.g., when moving pdf files from a desktop PC to the handheld), or the procedure can start in real-time, from mediators that provide the information content, such as AvantGo and OpenWave, when pushing Web content to their subscribers. For example, the

Web page of a newspaper that has a multicolumn front page is reformed so that columns are placed beneath each other, instead of next to each other, and pictures are presented as thumbnails.

While the latter case makes the text easier to read by changing the font size and properly rearranging the structure of the text, it lacks the insight offered by the layout context, that is, topics arrangement, font size and face, and so forth. As an alternative, the image-based approach delivers to the user a scaled-down version of the pages of the document retrieved (Microsoft's Live Lab, 2006). This approach is very common when the information to be delivered is not generated upon request but it is usually retrieved in the form it had when published, like a digitized manuscript. However, the topic retrieved does not necessarily have to include static information; it can contain dynamic information and hyperlinks to other topics of information, much like the World Wide Web documents.

Lately, text-to-speech software is used to automatically convert e-books to spoken books. MATCH is a prototype supporting multimodal interaction with a handheld device, used as a city guide (Johnston, Bangalore, Vasireddy, Stentm Ehlen, Walker, et al., 2002). Vadas, Patel, Lyons, Starner, and Jacko (2006) made a study to assess performance of comprehending text while mobile, that is, in situations where the user is walking or sitting. They compared a head-down visual display to a speech audio display. They found that users' comprehension scores for the audio-walking condition were comparable to the scores for the visual-walking condition. Furthermore, they recorded improvements in the users' ability to navigate the environment when using the audio display.

Apart from the content presentation to a handheld user, there is also the reverse problem of giving an input to a handheld device. Predefined input, like commands, must be quickly recognized and in many cases they can be issued by code detectors or other peripheral devices connected to the handhelds through expansion slots, such as barcode and RFID readers or cameras that scan QR-codes. As an alternative, a touch screen and a pointing device such as a pen allow for easy selection of graphical objects among menu commands, icons, buttons, or drop-down lists. For free form text input, the user can use the small keyboard available or a virtual keyboard if provided. External keyboards can also be used, ranging from laptop size to laser pocket-keyboards. In addition, some sophisticated devices can recognize the user's handwriting and use lexicons that predict the word written to increase writing speed.

ASSESSING ACCEPTANCE OF HANDHELDS FOR DIGITAL LIBRARIES

Device acceptance strongly depends on several issues, such as usefulness, usability, cost, social interactions, compatibility, reliability, and security. Meta-analysis studies (Lu, Xiao, Sears, & Jacko, 2005) based on the technology acceptance model (TAM) have identified motives and barriers of PDA usage. TAM (Davis, 1989) is an approach to modeling people's intentions to use a new technology tool, taking into account two latent variables: perceived usefulness (PU) and perceived ease of use (PEoU). Their values cannot be directly measured and therefore are inferred from other sets of variables, which are visible and measurable. For instance, a big number of errors recorded when the user tries to enter a query would indicate a strong usability issue which reflects upon PEoU. The most common motives include mobility, time saving, and accuracy of information, which all affect PU. On the other hand, technical features (i.e., size, weight), small screen design, energy consumption, reliability, and input methods are shown to affect PEoU (**Dearnley**, McKnight, & Morris, 2004; Shipman & Morton, 2001). In addition, personal factors like age, subjective technical confidence, training, and so forth are expected to affect both PU and PEoU. In the specific domain of DLs it is of outmost importance that handhelds should be integrated in user's workflow and should satisfy user's work and information tasks in an integrated way.

In order to assess acceptance, formative evaluation methods are encouraged during the implementation of DL services in order to trace user requirements and needs, adjusted to specific IT skills profile. Pilot installations have used triangulation of methods to collect data. This multiple research strategy includes interviews, focus groups, user observation, think-aloud protocols, and questionnaire surveys. Since the context of mobile users differentiates strongly, the user interaction evaluation should be conducted in realistic conditions, where environmental factors affecting users' behavior (e.g., frequent interruptions) can be identified, recorded, and studied (Ryan & Gonsalves, 2005). However, as subjects are moving it is not easy to observe their interaction with the device by having an operator with a camera to look over their shoulder. In most cases, this method is rather obtrusive to the procedure, alters the behavior of the subjects, and biases the study results. As an alternative, a software program installed on the mobile device can record the whole interaction session and transfer it in real-time to the computer of a remote observer. This strategy is well-known and widely used for the evaluation of usability tests regarding human-computer interaction with desktop computers. Once data are collected from diverse sources (e.g., voice and video recordings, field notes, and interview transcripts) qualitative research software helps the researchers to manage the data, shape them, and make sense of the unstructured information so that they can explore issues, understand phenomena, validate their assumptions, and answer questions.

FUTURE TRENDS

Broadband wireless technologies, such as WiMax networks, are evolving, providing connectivity within the ranges of a city and thus making information exchange available almost anywhere. As a result, handhelds will integrate connectivity capabilities, providing multimedia access and advanced modes of information delivery.

Interfaces should adapt to the new requirements of the mobile users. Sound or voice features will enable multimodal dialectics, thus enhancing user interaction. Speech synthesis could be used to have the retrieved textual information read to the user and therefore the user will not need to look at the display. The small display problem might be solved thanks to virtual retinal display (VRD) technology (Kleweno, Seibel, Viirre, Kelly, & Furness, 2001), which projects information right into the user's eye (retina), resulting in an image similar to that of a conventional monitor. Semantic processing is expected to strongly enhance information retrieval and content presentation. Instead of presenting to the user the full retrieved information, for example, long texts, the user will be given extracted summaries or descriptions. However, the user will still have access to the full content retrieved if the user wishes so.

Services are expected to be personalized and deliver the right information, at the right time, in the right place, in the right way, and to the right person. DLs will be providing location-dependent information and services, like nearby points of interest, activities, or exhibitions, and navigation assistance to help users find their way either in physical or in digital domains.

Nowadays, many of the conventional libraries keep digital or digitized collections. We believe that in the near future we will see physical libraries merging with digital ones, to form a hybrid library, where electronic and paper-based information sources are used alongside each other, delivering valuable information either inside or outside the building. The goal is to encourage end-user resource discovery and information use in a variety of formats and from a number of local and remote sources in a seamlessly integrated way. We expect that mobile computing and distributed wireless networks will play a major role towards the vision of hybrid libraries.

REFERENCES

Aittola, M., Ryhänen, T., & Ojala, T. (2003). SmartLibrary: Location-aware mobile library service. In *Proceedings of the Mobile HCI 2003* (LNCS 2795, pp. 411-416). Berlin: Springer-Verlag.

Buchanan, G., Jones, M., & Marsden, G. (2003). Exploring small screen digital library access with the Greenstone Digital Library. In *Proceedings of the 6th European Conference on Research and Advanced Technology for Digital Libraries* (LNCS 2458, pp. 583-596). Berlin: Springer-Verlag.

Buyukkokten, O., Garcia-Molina, H., & Paepcke, A. (2001). Seeing the whole in parts: text summarization for Web browsing on handheld devices. In *Proceedings of the Tenth International World-Wide Web Conference* (pp. 652-662). New York: ACM Press

Carney, S., Koufogiannakis, D., & Ryan, P. (2004). Library services for users of personal digital assistants: A needs assessment and program evaluation. *Portal: Libraries and the Academy, 4*(3), 393-406.

Crestani, F., Landoni, M., & Melucci, M. (2006). Appearance and functionality of electronic books. *International Journal on Digital Libraries, 6*(2), 192-209.

Davis, F. D. (1989). Perceived usefulness, perceived ease of use, and user acceptance of information technology. *MIS Quarterly, (13)*, 319-340.

Dearnley, J., McKnight, C., & Morris, A. (2004). Electronic book usage in public libraries: a study of user and staff reactions to a PDA-based collection. *Journal of Librarianship and Information Science, 36*(4), 175-282.

Heisey, L., & Paolillo, M. (n.d.). *Final report: Beam-using possibilities. Infrared beaming of citations from the kiosks to patrons 'portable devices.'* Retrieved September 11, 2007, from http://www.library.cornell.edu/EMPSL/PDA-pilot-report.pdf

Johnston, M., Bangalore, S., Vasireddy, G., Stent, A., Ehlen, P., Walker, M., et al. (2002). Match: An architecture for multimodal dialogue systems. In *Proceedings of the 40th Annual Meeting on Association for Computational Linguistics* (pp. 376-383). Philadelphia, PA: Association for Computational Linguistics.

Jones, M., Buchanan, G., & Thimbleby, H. W. (2002). Sorting out searching on small screen devices. In *Proceedings of the Mobile HCI 2002* (LNCS 2411, pp. 81-94). Berlin: Springer-Verlag.

Jones, M. L. W., Rieger, R. H., Treadwell, P., & Gay, G. K. (2000). Live from the stacks: user feedback on mobile computers and wireless tools for library patrons. In *Proceedings of the Fifth ACM Conference on Digital Libraries* (pp. 95-102). New York: ACM Press.

Kleweno, C. P., Seibel, E. J., Viirre, E. S., Kelly, J. P., & Furness, T. A., III (2001). The virtual retinal display as an alternative low vision computer interface: Pilot study. *Journal of Rehabilitation Research and Development, 38*(4), 431-442.

Lu, Y., Xiao, Y., Sears, A., & Jacko, J. A. (2005). A review and a framework of handheld computer adoption in healthcare. *International Journal of Medical Informatics, (74)*, 409-422.

Marshall, C. C., & Ruotolo, C. (2002, July 14-18). Reading-in-the-small: A study of reading on small form factor devices. In *Proceedings of the 2nd ACM/IEEE-CS Joint Conference on Digital Libraries*. Portland, OR: ACM Press.

McCabe, J. (2004). Getting started with PDAs: A library-driven project at James Madison University. *Library Hi Tech News, 21*(1), 30-32.

Microsoft Live Labs. (2006). Microsoft live labs Deepfish. *Microsoft Corporation.* Retrieved September 11, 2007, from http://http://labs.live.com/deepfish/

Peterson, M. (2004). Library service delivery via hand-held computers-the right information at the point of care. *Health Information and Libraries Journal, 21*(1), 52-56.

Rios, G. R. (2004). PDA librarian. *Reference Services Review, 32*(1), 16-20.

Rosenfeld, L., & Morville, P. (2002). *Information architecture for the World Wide Web: Designing large scale Web sites.* CA: O' Reilly & Associates, Inc.

Roussos, G., Marsh, A. J., & Maglavera, S. (2005). Enabling pervasive computing with smart phones. *IEEE Pervasive Computing, 4*(2), 20-27.

Ryan, C., & Gonsalves, A. (2005). The effect of context and application type on mobile usability: An empirical study. In *Proceedings of the Twenty-Eighth Australasian Conference on Computer Science* (ACM International Conference Proceeding Series 102, pp. 115-124). Darlinghurst: Australian Computer Society, Inc.

Shipman, J. P., & Morton, A. C. (2001). The new black bag: PDAs, health care and library services. *Reference Services Review, 29*(3), 229-237.

Smith, R. (2002). Adapting a new technology to the academic medical library: Personal digital assistants. *Journal of the Medical Library Association, 90*(1), 93-94.

Vadas, K., Patel, N., Lyons, K., Starner, T., & Jacko, J. (2006). Reading on-the-go: A comparison of audio and hand-held displays. In *Proceedings of the 8th Conference on Human-Computer Interaction with Mobile Devices and Services* (ACM International Conference Proceeding Series 159, pp. 219-226). Helsinki, Finland. ACM Press.

KEY TERMS

Human Computer Interaction: The study of the interaction between computers and their users. This interaction occurs at the user interface, which includes both software and hardware, for example, general purpose computer peripherals (i.e., disk drives, CD players, etc.) and large-scale mechanical systems, such as aircraft and power plants.

Mobile Computing: A term to describe a user's ability to use technology from a nonfixed location, using battery powered, portable computing, and communication devices such as laptops, notebooks, palmtops, smartphones, and PDAs. Computing activity can take place locally, that is, the user can use a device to retrieve some information stored in it, or it can be connected wirelessly to another information/computing system with wireless LAN or wireless WAN technologies.

Personal Digital Assistants (PDAs): Handhelds that facilitate tools like a calendar, clock, calculator, address book, memos, and alarms. Newer models support multimedia playback, voice recording, e-book readers, e-mail, and Web access. There are also models that integrate global positioning system (GPS) and global system for mobile communications (GSM) modules for navigation and telephony, respectively.

Smartphone: Also known as hybrid, is any electronic handheld device that integrates the functionality of a mobile phone, personal digital assistant (PDA), or other information appliance. This is often achieved by putting "smart" capabilities, such as PDA functions, into a mobile phone. "Smart" functionality includes any additional interface, including a QWERTY board, a touch screen, or even just secure access to company mail.

Ubiquitous Computing: The idea of embedding computation into the environment by using everyday objects that enable people to interact with information-processing devices more naturally and casually than they currently do. The term was coined by Mark Weiser, chief scientist of Xerox PARC. Other terms include pervasive computing and calm technology.

Usability: ISO 9241-11 defines usability as "the extent to which a product can be used by specified users to achieve specified goals with effectiveness, efficiency, and satisfaction in a specified context of use." Usability of hypertext/Web is commonly measured using established usability dimensions covering these categories of usability defects, such as screen design, terminology and system information, system capabilities and user control, navigation, and completing tasks. Perceived usability expresses people's belief to the extent that a system is not too hard to use, and the performance benefits are not outweighed by the effort of using it.

Usefulness: This is debatable. Some make the distinction between usability and usefulness.

Although it is impossible to quantify the usefulness of a system, attempts have been made to measure its attainment in reference to system specifications and the extent of coverage of end users' tasks supported by the system, but not on end user performance testing. Perceived usefulness expresses people's intention to use (or not) a new technology to the extent that they believe it will help them perform their job better.

Wireless Networks: The term refers to communication networks, whose interconnections between nodes are implemented without the use of wires, such as a computer network. Wireless communication networks are generally implemented with some type of remote information transmission system, consisting of base stations and client terminals that use radio waves.

ENDNOTES

[1] http://www.gutenberg.org/wiki/

[2] http://www.perseus.tufts.edu/

[3] http://www.google.com/press/pressrel/print_library.html

Chapter XXXI
The CGIAR Virtual Library Bridging the Gap Between Agricultural Research and Worldwide Users

Mila M. Ramos
International Rice Research Institute (IRRI), Philippines

Luz Marina Alvaré
International Food Policy Research Institute (IFPRI), USA

Cecilia Ferreyra
International Potato Center (CIP), Peru

Peter Shelton
International Food Policy Research Institute (IFPRI), USA

ABSTRACT

This chapter introduces the Consultative Group on International Agricultural Research (CGIAR) Virtual Library as a tool for linking researchers and agricultural research results. The CGIAR is a strategic alliance of countries, international and regional organizations, and private foundations supporting 15 international agricultural centers that work in partnership with national agricultural research institutions and societies. The research results generated are numerous and cover a wide range of subject fields. While these are properly documented, locating relevant and timely information across the system's 15 centers is a long and tedious process as individual databases have to be searched. The CGIAR virtual library (CGVLibrary) project of the CGIAR Libraries and Information Services Consortium (CGIAR-LISC) was created in 2005 to address the difficulty of information retrieval across the various centers. It is now available via the WWW (http://vlibrary.cgiar.org/) and knowledge generated by the CGIAR can now be retrieved with a few mouse clicks.

INTRODUCTION: THE NEED FOR VIRTUAL LIBRARIES IN AGRICULTURAL RESEARCH

The application of information technology has made it possible to share knowledge more quickly and effectively than ever before. Access to global networks, electronic publishing, and the ensuing deluge of digital information are major trends impacting the world of information and knowledge management. New applications of the Internet have forever altered the way information providers respond to the needs of clients. Likewise, the latest brand of information technology and its diverse applications have spurred a new breed of information seekers, equipped with sophisticated computer skills and displaying a strong preference for electronic delivery of information and waning levels of patience for query response times.

Advanced capabilities of the Internet coupled with the vast expanse of digital information it carries bring significant challenges as well as opportunities. Information overload normally takes place when results returned from using Internet search engines become unmanageable, keeping the researcher distant from the desired information the user seeks. The ensuing frustration is compounded by the fact that a growing body of research information is available exclusively through commercial databases that remain closed to most public search engines, and require vast financial resources for purchasing access rights. Where databases are accessible, they may require search methods and interfaces that are unfamiliar to casual users, thereby hindering search and retrieval operations. In such a context, the need for systematic information management fully emerges (Krill, 2000), a task that becomes increasingly difficult with each advance in information technology and corresponding demand from end users.

Access to Agricultural Knowledge: Current Scenario

In agriculture, as in other professional disciplines, having access to the latest, high quality research information is more important than ever. New Web sites and Internet-accessible databases on specialized subjects, including agriculture, are launched each day, thereby making vast amounts of information available to a rapidly growing community of online users. Moreover, an increasing proportion of research information is now available in computer-readable format, either as original electronic documents or as digitized versions of hard copy publications. Meanwhile, much of the academic journal literature is also available electronically via the Internet, albeit usually through paid licenses.

Publicly available agricultural information resources are stored and managed by multiple and diverse systems. These include agricultural references in Agricola[1] that will not be found in AGRIS, as well as references in CAB International databases may not be found in either; hence, multiple searches may be required for each topic of interest, often through disjointed user interfaces. Moreover, many publications—particularly informal publications (i.e., gray literature, etc.) and those produced in developing countries—are unavailable on the Internet in any format whatsoever.

Researchers have often expressed frustration with the current process of locating and retrieving relevant research information. They demand quick and easy access to the latest, high quality research information to support their own research as well as disseminate research results as soon as they become available. Therefore, the task facing information managers (IMs) is to organize and make available targeted sets of information resources to both professional and nonprofessional audiences alike. In the day-to-day context of agricultural research, this can yield significant savings in terms of the time and energy they expend in conducting lengthy searches for relevant research information while vastly improving the overall quality and impact of their research.

The problems and opportunities described above are not unique to the world of high-speed Internet connections and state-of-the-art research facilities. An agricultural information workshop funded by the U.K. Dept. of International Development (DFID) and the International Institute for Communication and Development (IICD) recently concluded that the absence of a common reference point to information resources was a serious problem for many users in developing countries (Besemer, Addison, & Ferguson, 2003). In sum, having access to high quality, relevant research information can often spell the difference between gaining ground and falling behind in the rapidly changing context of international development.

VIRTUAL LIBRARIES: BRIDGING THE AGRICULTURAL KNOWLEDGE GAP

In order to keep pace in such an environment, librarians and information specialists have developed new tools and avenues for providing integrated access to a wide variety of information resources. Their efforts have been supported by a vast body of associated software and services developed over the past decade, along with fledging communities of practice that have offered significant amounts of user feedback. These developments form the foundation for a new model of library services, which represents a quantum leap in terms of their ability to provide comprehensive, effective, and easily accessible electronic information. Digital information on the Web is now increasingly stored, organized, and made available through *virtual libraries* (or portals), which are able to provide these services

(plus much more) regardless of document format, time, or the geographic location of the end user.

The concept of a virtual library emerged shortly after the inception of the Internet itself, though it took some time before its applications and benefits were fully appreciated. This is in part a reflection of complex, dynamic nature of the virtual library concept as well as the thinking of those seeking to manage and use information resources in new and exciting ways. Unlike traditional libraries, which are subject to the physical limitations associated with space and material holdings, the virtual library is conceived as existing everywhere, having no barriers and inviting the participation of a limitless audience of users as envisioned by Chad in his Library 2.0 paradigm (Chad & Miller, 2005) and discussed in various forums (Casey & Savastinuk, 2006). In sum, virtual libraries must fulfill the mission of traditional libraries plus much more, utilizing dynamic information sharing practices and communications infrastructure to keep pace with a rapidly changing global information environment. The digital or virtual library is not a single entity operating independently, but rather a product of committed collaboration (ARL, 1995).

THE CONSULTATIVE GROUP ON INTERNATIONAL AGRICULTURAL RESEARCH (CGIAR)

The CGIAR is a widely-dispersed organization, with 15 research centers conducting independent research on various agriculture-related subjects. Established in 1971, the mission of the CGIAR is "to achieve sustainable food security and reduce poverty in developing countries through scientific research and research-related activities in the fields of agriculture, forestry, fisheries, policy, and environment" (CGIAR, 2006). The CGIAR centers, 13 of which are located in developing countries, generate an enormous volume of research outputs on diverse agricultural topics. At present, scholarly research is being conducted by more than 8,500 CGIAR scientists in over 100 countries, on "agroforestry, biodiversity, food, forage and tree crops, pro-environment farming techniques, fisheries, forestry, livestock, food policies and agricultural research services" (CGIAR, 2006). The collective research outputs of the CGIAR centers support the advancement of knowledge, a prospect that would be significantly hampered in the absence of collaboration across the CGIAR ("CGVLibrary," 2006).

With public investment in agricultural research declining on a global scale, the CGIAR and other international organizations have been pushed to produce optimum returns on the resources they continue to receive; effectively, they are faced with the challenge of doing "more with less." In spite of declining levels of investment, such research continues to show positive effects on the economies of developing countries (Fuglie et al., 1996), an accomplishment largely aided by

the implementation of innovative approaches for sharing institutional resources, including knowledge, among much wider audiences of potential users. In the case of the CGIAR, this entails researchers working with information technology and knowledge management professionals more closely than ever before, and adopting new tools and strategies for ensuring that CGIAR research outputs reach citizens of the developing world.

THE CGIAR VIRTUAL LIBRARY: FROM IDEA TO REALITY

Having access to the latest, high quality scientific literature has always been a necessary component of the CGIAR's research. Yet the task of locating and retrieving such information from across the system's 15 centers has often been a long and tedious process. Until recently, this process entailed conducting as many as 15 separate searches,

Figure 1. The CGIAR Centers and their location

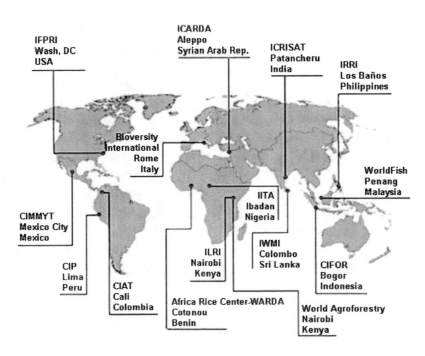

Source: http://www.cgiar.org/centers/index.html

often through disjointed interfaces. This was the basis of the InfoFinder (2006) project, which featured a tool allowing users to search across the Web sites of both the CGIAR and the Food and Agriculture Organization (FAO). The project benefited greatly from the fact that much of the information and materials being accessed already existed in digital format.

In 2003, some CGIAR IMs and the members of the CGIAR's Information and Communications Technology-Knowledge Management (ICT-KM) Program first proposed the idea of creating a virtual library. Together with the ICT-KM Program's e-publishing project,[2] the virtual library would take the InfoFinder tool to the next level, allowing for searches both inside and out of the CGIAR through the use of FAO-developed international standards for metadata. Moreover, the integration of CGXchange software would allow CGIAR staff to log on once, and have seamless access to all of the materials their centers are licensed to use.

The decision to create a virtual library marked a significant step forward in collaboration across the CGIAR, but was based largely on prior collaborative efforts among information from the 15 centers. These included a joint subscription to 93 electronic journals as well as the decision to make each center's library catalogs available online. Moreover, their collaboration was strongly supported by the fact that all but three of the centers were already using common software for managing their library holdings, thereby greatly enhancing the prospects for creating a single, integrated system.

Once the decision to move forward with the project was made, a virtual library service (VLS) was formed under the auspices of the ICT-KM Program's content for development initiative. Similar to the product they would be developing, members of the VLS team quickly demonstrated their ability to work effectively in a virtual environment. During the first year, Luz Marina Alvaré and Nancy Walczak (the Project Coordinator and Technical Advisor, respectively) from the Inter-

national Food Policy Research Institute (IFPRI) worked closely with Ron Davies, an information management consultant from Belgium, though it took nearly a year for the three to meet in person. Throughout the entire process, a team of highly skilled professionals continued working from diverse locations, mostly in an advisory capacity. They included the following teams of IMs, CGIAR researchers, and outside collaborators:

- CGIAR Information Managers: Thomas Adigun (WARDA), Cecilia Ferreyra (CIP), Nick Maliha (ICARDA), and Mila Ramos (IRRI)
- CGIAR Researchers: François Molle (IWMI), John Miles (CIAT), and Hugh Turral (IWMI)
- External Collaborators: Johannes Keizer (FAO) and Koda Traore (CTA)

As previously mentioned, the basis for the CGVLibrary was the integration of all of the information materials (including training manuals) contained in the online library catalogs of each CGIAR center. Additionally, it was decided to grant users access to the following resources via the CGVLibrary:

- Multiple CG library catalogs
- Restricted information resources, such as the full text articles of a core collection of agricultural and social science journals
- Several commercial abstracting and indexing resources
- Several free information resources such as Agricola and AGRIS
- Major university or research catalogs such as the Dutch agricultural union catalog hosted at Wageningen University

OBJECTIVES

The main objective of the CGVLibrary is "to facilitate access to library and research information within and outside the CGIAR through integrated searches of reference-related databases using a common user interface, standard protocols, and easy linking to electronic full text." It is expected to provide a one-stop shop for agricultural information, not by creating a new site, but by creating links to relevant services and reducing the turnaround time between initiating a search and generating results. Specifically, the objectives are:

1. To develop and maintain an efficient, state-of-the-art, electronic platform, wherein agricultural researchers, using a single search engine, can access information available in the libraries of the diverse CGIAR centers and other relevant free and commercial sources of information. The facility uses highly advanced software for linking users to print and digital information sources and full text documents regardless of location and time frame.

2. To establish the core of the virtual library by providing selected links to a limited number of high quality information resources available on the Internet, including academic library catalogs, free Internet databases, commercial abstracting/indexing databases, university or institutional document repositories, and commercial or licensed data sources.

3. To raise the profile of the CGIAR as a leading knowledge broker of international agricultural research. Since the time of the CGVLibrary's public launch in June 2006, user activity has grown steadily to the point that users now conduct nearly 1,000 searches per day. The vast majority of these searches are geared toward the research outputs of the CGIAR, and current usage statistics indicate that many of the users are located in developing countries. Collectively, this information underscores the overall impact of the CGVLibrary in supporting the CGIAR's

goal of providing research to professionals in the developing world.

4. To help realize ICT-KM's vision of a more unified, effective, and borderless CGIAR. The collaborative efforts of the VLS team have forged a new precedent for information sharing and effective communication across the CGIAR.

DESIGN ARCHITECTURE AND FUNCTIONALITY

From the beginning, the architects of the CGVLibrary emphasized the importance of having a simple and user-friendly interface. This emphasis stemmed not only from the diverse backgrounds of the architects themselves, who represented more than a dozen nationalities and included several nonnative English speakers, but also was intended to optimally serve the target audience of agricultural researchers from around the world. Moreover, functionality considerations for the CGVlibrary centered on the goal of allowing researchers to access the information they are looking for with as few mouse clicks as possible.

Selecting the proper software platform on which to build the virtual library quickly emerged as the team's first priority. Members of the VLS advisory team evaluated many existing models of networked digital libraries, and later advised the core team of their findings. Specifically, they were looking for established standards and software suites that had been successfully implemented for a large number of information suppliers and library systems. Dynamic linking and open URL resolution were identified as key features for enabling users to more quickly and effectively access digital information through such systems. Thus, after prolonged deliberation and consultation, members of the VLS team selected SFX® software, an award-winning link server from Ex Libris™, for the CGVLibrary. This decision was based largely on the software's strong track record among libraries and major information networks in Europe, the Americas, and the Middle East (SFX, 2007). Coupled with Ex Libris' Metalib platform, SFX supports federated searching of the various CGIAR library catalogs and databases, which utilize diverse metadata standards and integrated library systems. Thus, there was no need to merge catalogs into a centralized repository, as metasearching can be done across disparate databases.

In fact, there was another important advantage in selecting Ex Libris' Metalib and SFX software to manage the resources contained in the CGV-Library: the input of 1,500 member institutions, which collectively help manage and maintain in working order approximately 600 leading research databases and more than 800,000 items, including e-journals, books, and other online research materials (Ex Libris, 2007). Member institutions suggest new resources for inclusion in the respective central knowledge bases (CKBs) for Ex Libris' two sister products[3], and report any problems to a highly skilled technical support team that often is able to resolve matters in timely fashion. Ex Libris support staff also works independently to ensure that all resources contained in their CKBs are kept up-to-date and working properly by releasing monthly service updates for each of its members. This service is especially valuable since the amount of time and labor required to maintain such volume and diversity of resources is unavailable to many member institutions and consortia, including the CGIAR.

Following more than 2 years of discussions, research, and evaluation, a prototype was developed for beta-testing in December 2005. In June 2006, the site was publicly launched, thus offering a unique service to the agricultural information world. For the first time, users can access high quality agricultural research, including the online libraries of all 15 CGIAR centers, through a single portal. The service also helps CGIAR researchers locate and retrieve full text articles from a core of electronic journals and database systems from anywhere in the world 24/7. The CGV Library supplements existing agricultural databases, which provide partial linkage to CGIAR research results (e.g., Agricola, CABDirect, AGRIS, etc.).

Content development, meanwhile, was largely carried out by a team of CGIAR information managers while working in various parts of the world, thus showing that collaboration can transcend physical barriers. Databases and knowledge banks from the CGIAR centers were compiled and linked to the virtual library. Currently, the CGVLibrary provides access to more than 160 online databases and nearly 4,000 electronic journal titles. These resources were selected by a team of CGIAR researchers, information specialists, and outside consultants working in close collaboration with the core VLS team. Experience working with federated search tools illustrates that there is a limit to the number of resources that can be effectively cross-searched at any given time. In order to overcome this limitation, specific categories of the most important and relevant resources in a given area have been developed and organized into topic-specific QuickSets (e.g., rice, water, food policy, etc.). Users can further limit their searches to specific resources within a given QuickSet via either the metasearch function or an additional feature allowing them to search external databases from within the CGVLibrary user interface.

As evident in the above screenshot, users can now search many of these databases through a single search interface, avoiding the need to navigate between different screen displays and commands for each data source. Through the use of dynamic context-sensitive linking protocols (i.e., the OpenURL standard), users are directed to the full text of journal articles wherever they are available electronically, even when they are located in institutional repositories or external Web sites. The CGVLibrary also offers CGIAR staff several additional features, including a personalized workspace environment called "My Virtual Library." Logged-in users are able

Figure 2. The CGVLibrary main page

Source: http://vlibrary.cgiar.org

to access all of the resources, including online databases and electronic journal articles, that their particular centers are licensed to use. Moreover, users can custom-create their own QuickSets, save selected resources in personalized folders (with an option of exporting individual records in multiple bibliographic programs), and guard search results for future reference.

Information technology and management experts from across the CGIAR continue to work on improving the overall "look and feel" of the CGVLibrary while ensuring that new and existing resources are properly maintained. At present, the facility offers 18 topic-specific QuickSets (see Figure 2), which were assembled with the collaboration of researchers from all 15 centers as well as several CGIAR system-wide programs and challenge programs. Partner outreach and promotion of the CGVLibrary are carried out by several members of the team via presentations at international meetings and conferences as well as real-time online seminars ("Webinars"). Following the public launch of the CGVlibrary, such efforts primarily have focused on reaching new audiences in Latin America, where more than

800 persons from 19 different countries have participated in events showcasing the CGVLibrary. Several participants subsequently have included links to the CGVLibrary on their institutional Web sites, and future plans to promote the CGVLibrary also will include several partner institutions in Asia and Africa.

NEW DEMANDS AND WORK IMPACT

The CGVLibrary is making its presence felt across the CGIAR as well as among much wider audiences seeking access to up-to-date, relevant agricultural research information of the highest quality. A month after its launch, in July 2006, the virtual library had been searched 507 times. In the months that followed, however, there were almost 1,000 daily searches of the CGVLibrary, and these numbers are expected to continue to grow. It is worth noting that the majority of users in recent months have been from the developing world, reflecting widespread use by both CGIAR researchers (13 of the 15 centers' headquarters are located in developing countries) and their intended beneficiaries in the developing world.

The accomplishments of the VLS team, meanwhile, have not gone unnoticed. The CGVLibrary has been cited in 44 confirmed postings on the Internet, including online Weblogs ("blogs"), listservs, and online newsletters. In December 2006, the VLS team received the 2006 Science Award for Outstanding Scientific Support in recognition of the CGVLibrary's contribution to CGIAR research. Perhaps most impressive, however, the VLS team continues to receive widespread acknowledgement from scores of users both within and outside of the CGIAR. Among the most commonly cited benefits of using the CGVLibrary include access to CGIAR "gray literature," well-focused search results, an easy-to-use interface, and improved access to agricultural research for all.

Yet while many of the information technology advances behind the CGVLibrary have made the life of researchers measurably easier, the task of managing the growing body of digital information and making it available to partners throughout the world becomes increasingly complicated. Unlimited desktop access is now expected by researchers in many parts of the world, effectively requiring the integration of services and digital information systems that, until recently, have remained entirely separate. These include everything from ensuring a reliable connection to the Internet (particularly for users in the developing countries) to working with licensing agreements and data-delivery services among multiple information providers. Byrne (2003) cites many of these same issues as potential barriers to the effective provision of digital knowledge, also including infrastructure, content development, education and skills, and systemic issues, such as intellectual property concerns, in the list.

The CGVLibrary continues to face many of these same challenges, particularly in the case of providing full-text article access to non-CGIAR researchers in the developing world. To overcome this particular obstacle, the VLS team proposes to explore new tools, for example, Web 2.0, and for integrating the CGVLibrary with AGORA, HINARI, OARE, and PERI/INASP, which collectively represent a significant body of digital information available to citizens of developing countries at reduced or no cost. Furthermore, Phase II of the CGVLibrary will include a number of additional open access databases, including the online publication databases of the CGIAR (a subset of the CGIAR libraries) as well as the implementation of extensible markup language (XML) institutional repositories for additional CGIAR centers, universities, and research institutions.

Another significant challenge facing the CGVLibrary will be to deepen the integration in the search facility. Currently, all of the resources included in the CGVLibrary support federated, cross-database searching. Many of the resources that have implemented standards-based interfaces also support the ability to retrieve, view, sort, and print results as a single set. Such integration, however, is currently unavailable for those databases lacking a standards-compliant search facility. Phase II of the CGVLibrary proposes to work with database systems such as CAB International and FAO/AGRIS to develop, test, and implement XML interfaces that support standards-compliant searching. The results will have immediate benefits for the CGVLibrary (i.e., all resources included in the CGVLibrary will be integrated to the same extent) as well as spillover benefits for other digital information providers and virtual libraries as a whole; namely, the development of standard interfaces and connector technologies would greatly facilitate the sharing of information across the Web.

As these new 2.0 tools and services are implemented, the CGVLibrary will continue to require strong support in the following areas: targeting information resources, marketing and training, technical support for infrastructure development, and project coordination and management. Fortunately, the project already boasts a robust community of practice of CGIAR staff and outside consultants that is based on effective communication and intense collaboration over the course of more than 2 years.

CONCLUSION: THE WAY FORWARD

The CGVLibrary has quickly emerged as a model of excellence among agricultural information portals. Yet the work of the VLS team is far from finished, as the CGVLibrary is envisioned as a dynamic tool that must be adapted to suit the diverse needs of users. Ultimately, the CGVLibrary must strive to attain many of the characteristics of a digital library of the future, as mentioned by Marcum (cited in Martin, 2003). Specifically, it must contain a comprehensive collection of electronic resources vital to agricultural research; it must be readily accessible to all types of users, both experts and novices, and it must be well managed by a dedicated team of information professionals. Experience has demonstrated that accomplishing such goals in the rapidly changing age of digital information is infinitely more complex than in prior information ages, but they remain as important as ever for ensuring global impact.

Besemer et al. (2003) points to minimal gains in agricultural production and poverty alleviation as evidence of the limited impact of agricultural information services in the developing world. Several of the issues he mentions as hindering access to agricultural information by end-users in the developing countries derive from the decentralized nature of this information on multiple Web sites and database systems. The corresponding solution to the information gap is the creation of a "central one-stop centre," an idea on which the CGVLibrary was modeled. Thus far, the project has achieved much success in terms of enhancing access to agricultural research information worldwide, though it is perhaps still too early to

measure its impact on long term goals such as increasing agricultural productivity and poverty alleviation in the developing world.

Sustainability is one major area to be addressed by the IMs and the technical advisers behind the CGVLibrary. This requires the continuous updating and monitoring of content as well the application of new technical capacities, all of which require sufficient financial and human resources. Moreover, those charged with managing the technical aspects of the portal as well as those contributing to its content must have up-to-date knowledge of new tools and resources as they become available. Feedback from end users also will form the basis of future efforts to improve the CGVLibrary.

Phase 2 of the CGVLibrary project is now in full swing and it is guided by the following objectives:

- To increase the number of information resources available, that is, to add center catalogues not currently accessible, high value bibliographic databases maintained by programs, open access archives, and partners' information resources.
- To ensure that centers' e-publishing efforts and center publications databases are integrated and thus accessible through the CGVlibrary.
- To integrate and to make accessible the centers' image library databases.
- To enable access to information resources for NARES partners.
- To further enhance access to full text material.
- To improve access to material by helping partners to implement standards that permit deeper levels of searching.
- To develop mechanisms for optimizing searching by targeting categories of information resources.

Future improvements to the CGVLibrary will require a fortified online community that is strongly committed to sharing knowledge and skills among its members. Construction of the CGVLibrary required researchers, information managers, and technology specialists from across the CGIAR to work closely together, sharing knowledge and information every step of the way. Future efforts must mobilize even greater resources, Web 2.0 tools, and more solid cooperation from the CGIAR and beyond. The technologies and approaches behind the CGVLibrary have transformed how CGIAR works are produced, preserved, and made available to a wider global audience while solidifying the CGIAR's position as a leading knowledge broker for international agricultural research. The lessons learned must be extended to partner organizations throughout the world in order to have an even broader and deeper impact toward ensuring that research information reaches those who need it most.

REFERENCES

Association of Research Libraries (ARL). (1995). *Definition and purposes of a digital library.* Retrieved November 13, 2007, from http://www.ifla.org/documents/libraries/net/arl-dlib.txt

Besemer, H, Addison, C., & Ferguson, J. (2003). Fertile ground: Opportunities fro greater coherence in agricultural information systems (Research Rep. No. 19). *IICD.* Retrieved November 13, 2007, from http://www.ftpiicd.org/files/research/reports/report19.pdf

Byrne, A. (2003). Digital libraries: Barriers or gateways to scholarly information? *The Electronic Library, 21*(5), 414-421

Casey, M. E., & Savastinuk, L. C. (2006, September 1). Library 2.0. *Library Journal.* Retrieved November 13, 2007, from http://www.library-journal.com/article/CA6365200.html

CGIAR Content for Development Project. (2004). *"Virtual library service" proposal.* Washington, D.C.: CGIAR.

CGIAR. (2006a). *CGVLibrary* (p. 1) [Brochure]. Washington, D.C.: CGIAR. Retrieved November 13, 2007, from http://vlibrary.cgiar.org/CGVLibraryflyer.pdf

CGIAR. (2006b). *Consultative group on international agricultural research.* Retrieved November 13, 2007, from http://www.cgiar.org/who/index.html

CGVLibrary updated proposal for Phase II. (2006). Washington, D.C.: CGIAR. Retrieved November 13, 2007, from http://CGVLibrary.pbwiki.com/Activities+++TOR

Chad, K., & Miller, P. (2005). *Do libraries matter? The rise of Library2.0: A white paper.* Retrieved November 13, 2007, from http://www.talis.com/applications/downloads/white_papers/DoLibrariesMatter.pdf

Ex Libris. (2007) Retrieved November 14, 2007, from http://www.exlibrisgroup.com/newsdetails.htm?nid=543

Fuglie, K., et al. (1996). *Agricultural research and development: Public and private investments under alternative markets and institutions* (Agricultural Economics Rep. No. AER735) (p. 88). Retrieved November 13, 2007, from ttp://www.ers.usda.gov/publications/aer735/

Gladney, H. M., et al. (1994, May). *Digital library: Gross structure and requirements* (IBM Research Rep. RJ 9840). Paper presented at the Workshop on On-line Access to Digital Libraries. World Wide IEEE Computer Society Press. Retrieved November 13, 2007, from http://www.ifla.org/documents/libraries/net/rj9840.pdf

Infofinder. (2006). Retrieved February 5, 2007, from http://infofinder.cgiar.org/

Krill, P. (2000, January 7). Overcoming information overload. *InfoWorld.* Retrieved November 13, 2007, from http://www.infoworld.com/articles/ca/xml/00/01/10/000110caoverload.html

Martin, R. S. (2003). Reaching across library boundaries. In *Proceedings of the Conference on Emerging Visions for Access in the Twenty-First Century Library* (pp. 3-16). Washington, D.C.: Council on Library and Information Resources. Retrieved November 13, 2007, from http://www.clir.org/pubs/reports/pub119/martin.html

SFX. (2007) Retrieved November 13, 2007, from http://www.exlibrisgroup.com/sfx.htm

KEY TERMS

Agroforestry: Intentional growing of trees on the same site as agricultural crops and/or livestock in order to increase the total yield of products, generate short-term income, and improve environmental benefits (e.g., erosion control).

Biodiversity: The variety of life on our planet, measurable as the variety within species, between species, and the variety of ecosystems

Federated Database (or **Virtual Database**): A database system wherein constituent databases, that are geographically decentralized and using various computer systems, are interconnected via a computer network or software that allows metasearching via a single platform. Since the constituent database systems remain autonomous, a federated database system is a contrastable alternative to the task of merging together several disparate databases.

Fisheries: The science of producing fish and other aquatic resources for the purpose of providing human food, although other aims are possible (such as sport or recreational fishing), or obtaining ornamental fish or fish products such as fish oil.

Forage: Feed for livestock (e.g., cattle, sheep, goats, horses, etc.).

Forestry: The science, art, and practice of managing and using trees, forests, and their associated resources for human benefit

Interoperability: Ability of a system or a product to work with other systems or products without special effort on the part of the customer. Interoperability is made possible by the implementation of standards

Library 2.0: A new model of library service utilizing the latest in IT and is available anytime and anywhere, visible on a broad spectrum of devices, inviting collaboration by users, and integrated with services outside the walls of the physical library such as portals, virtual learning environments, and e-commerce applications.

OpenURL: A protocol for interoperability between an information resource and a service component

NARES: National Agricultural Research and Extension Services.

Virtual Federated Library: Several geographically diverse collections of machine-readable documents made available through a number of online catalogs or databases, which can be searched via a single platform or search interface.

Webinar: Online seminar that may contain audio and video, utilizing computers and telephones.

Weblogs: Personal sites consisting of regularly updated entries displayed in reverse chronological order. They read like a diary or journal, but with the most recent entry at the top.

Web 2.0: Term introduced in 2004 to characterize the new generation of applications, which may provide an infrastructure for more dynamic user participation, social interaction, and collaboration. Examples of these include blogs, wikis, social networking sites, and so forth.

ENDNOTES

[1] *Agricola, AGRIS*, and *CABDirec*t are 3 independent agricultural databases developed by the US National Agricultural Library, the Food and Agriculture Organization of the United Nations, and CAB International. The first 2 are freely available on the Web while, the third is available via paid licenses.

[2] E-publishing, an ICT-KM activity, will generate an entry point for document templates and workflow guidelines to enable a single system through which staff and partners can create standard documents throughout the CGIAR.

[3] Ex Libris' Metalib CKB contains core information on research databases and portals while the SFX CKB maintains this information for electronic journals, articles, and book titles.

Chapter XXXII
Map–Based User Interfaces for Music Information Retrieval

Robert Neumayer
Vienna University of Technology, Austria

Andreas Rauber
Vienna University of Technology, Austria

ABSTRACT

In this chapter, we introduce alternative ways to access digital audio collections. We give an overview of existing applications based on tow-dimensional, map-like representations of music collections. Further, we explain two applications for accessing audio files that are based on the Self-Organising Map, an unsupervised neural network model. These two applications—PlaySOM and PocketSOM—will be explained in greater detail, paying special attention to their unique properties and implementations for several mobile devices. These examples are supposed to gain the readers' interest for alternative interfaces to large audio collections. Besides, we hope to show that alternative interfaces are feasible for both desktop computers and mobile devices and offer a practical approach to pressing issues in accessing digital collections.

DIGITAL LIBRARIES OF AUDIO COLLECTIONS

An increasing number of users adapts new technologies like MP3 players and manages their audio collection digitally. Not only the wide availability of personal audio devices such as the Apple iPod™ drives the increasing private use of digital media files (i.e., audio and, more recently, video files); also, the music industry starts adapting new distribution channels, and at the same time, an increasingly large user base is buying their music online. This makes the need for advanced methods to browse and search for music a more pressing matter than ever. The tremendous demand for feasible means of navigating through ever-growing numbers of digital entities by a rising number of users and providers clearly shows the great potential new and more sophisticated approaches could hold.

While text-based searches for artist and track names, as well as browsing through collections that are hierarchically structured according to artist, album and track categories constitute the de-facto standard for accessing music collections on PCs and mobile devices. New means for visualising and exploring large audio collections are being developed based on automatic analysis of the acoustic content of the audio files. Different visualisations have been proposed, many using some two-dimensional landscape to map music files on. Most of them incorporate some kind of clustering (i.e., mapping from a high-dimensional feature space to a usually two-dimensional output space). A particularly interesting effect of using such unsupervised learning techniques is the potential to overcome problems stemming from manually assigned genre tags, since they may not suit every user or may simply be wrong (Pachet & Cazaly, 2000). Approaches offer varying interaction possibilities like drawing trajectories on the map, selecting the music underneath, or marking regions on a map, which are discussed in detail in this chapter.

A disc and rectangle visualisation used to display and manipulate playlists was proposed in (Torrens, Hertzog, & Arcos, 2004). The disc visualisation gives a better visual idea about the proportions within the collection, whereas zooming was more useable with the rectangle visualisation.

Several teams have been working on user interfaces based on the Self-Organising Map (SOM). The SOM is an unsupervised neural network that provides a topology-preserving mapping from a high-dimensional feature space onto a two-dimensional map in such a way that data points close to each other in input space are mapped onto adjacent areas of the output space. The SOM has been extensively used to provide visualisations of and interfaces to a wide range of data, including control interfaces to industrial

processing plants (Kohonen, Oja, Simula, Visa, & Kangas, 1996) to access interfaces for digital libraries of text documents (Rauber & Merkl, 2003).

Creating a SOM-based interface for Digital Libraries of Music (i.e., the SOM-enhanced JukeBox (SOMeJB)) was first proposed in Rauber and Frühwirth (2001) with more advanced visualizations, as well as improved feature sets being presented in Pampalk, Rauber, and Merkl (2002) and Rauber, Pampalk, and Merkl (2003). Since then, several other systems have been created based on these principles, such as the MusicMiner (Mörchen, Ultsch, Nöcker, & Stamm, 2005), which uses an emergent SOM. A very appealing three-dimensional user interface is presented in Knees, Schedl, Pohle, and Widmer (2006), automatically creating a three-dimensional musical landscape via a SOM for small private music collections. Navigation through the map is done via a video game pad, and additional information like labelling is provided using Web data and album covers.

A mnemonic SOM (i.e., a Self-Organising Map of a certain shape other than a rectangle) is used to cluster the complete works of the composer Wolfgang Amadeus Mozart to create the Map of Mozart (Mayer, Lidy, & Rauber, 2006). The shape of the SOM is a silhouette of its composer, leading to interesting clusterings (like, for example, the accumulation of string ensembles in the region of Mozart's right ear). An online demo is available at http://www.ifs.tuwien.ac.at/mir/mozart.

Another interface based on SOMs, which takes into account a user's focus of perception, is presented in Lübbers (2005), using prototypes as recommendations for adjacent clusters.

The *PlaySOM* application presented in this work is based on the original SOMeJB system, implementing a desktop interface suitable also for larger collections of several tens of thousands of music tracks.

In addition to systems designed for desktop applications handling large audio collections, the design of interfaces for mobile devices constitutes interesting and important challenges. Novel interfaces particulary developed for small-screen devices were presented in Vignoli, Gulik, and van de Wetering (2004), clustering pieces of audio based on content features as well as metadata attributes using a spring model algorithm. The main section of this chapter presents interfaces based on the *PocketSOM* in greater detail (Neumayer, Dittenbach, & Rauber, 2005), an implementation of the *PlaySOM* application specifically designed for mobile devices.

A more experimental interface, refraining from the use of a display, using motion detectors to respond to the listener's movements is presented in Hamanaka and Lee (2006). Another innovative user interface providing various ways of interaction—like similarity-based searches over sticking behaviour of tracks visualised as discs—is introduced in Goto and Goto (2005).

A good overview of various MIR systems is given in http://www.mirsystems.info/.

FEATURES FOR MUSIC INFORMATION RETRIEVAL

In order to create a map-based visualisation of a music digital library grouping similar pieces of music in neighbouring regions of the map, features need to be computed from the music that capture sound characteristics, and that allow the computation of perceived sound similarity. While a range of different sets of audio features is in use within the MIR community, we rely on *Statistical Spectrum Descriptors* (SSDs) (Lidy & Rauber, 2005). The computation of SSD features is based on the algorithm for computing Rhythm Pattern features (Rauber, Pampalk, & Merkl, 2002), using the computation of a psycho-acoustically transformed spectrogram (i.e., a Bark scale Sonogram). The SSD audio features are computed from audio tracks in standard PCM format with 44.1 kHz sampling frequency (e.g., decoded MP3 files).

Statistical Spectrum Descriptors are composed of statistical descriptors computed from several critical frequency bands of a psycho-acoustically transformed spectrogram. They describe fluctuations on the critical frequency bands in a more compact representation than Rhythm Pattern features. In a preprocessing step, the audio signal is converted to a mono signal and segmented into chunks of approximately six seconds. Usually, not every segment is used for audio feature extraction. For pieces of music with a typical duration of about four minutes, frequently, the first and last 1–4 segments are skipped, and from the remaining segments, every third one is processed.

For each segment, the spectrogram of the audio is computed using the short time Fast Fourier Transform (STFT). The window size is set to 23 ms (1024 samples) and a Hanning window is applied using 50 % overlap between the windows. The Bark scale—a perceptual scale which groups frequencies to critical bands according to perceptive pitch regions (Zwicker & Fastl, 1999)—is applied to the spectrogram, aggregating it to 24 frequency bands.

The Bark scale spectrogram is then transformed into the decibel scale. Additional psycho-acoustic transformations are applied: Computation of the Phon scale incorporates equal loudness curves, which account for the different perception of loudness at different frequencies (Zwicker & Fastl, 1999). Subsequently, the values are transformed to Sone. The Sone scale relates to the Phon scale in the way that a doubling on the Sone scale sounds to the human ear like a doubling of the loudness. This results in a representation that reflects the specific loudness sensation of the human auditory system, the Bark scale Sonogram.

On top of this representation of perceived loudness, a number of statistical descriptors is computed per critical band, in order to describe fluctuations within the critical bands extensively. Mean, median, variance, skewness, kurtosis, min- and max-value are computed for each of the 24 bands, resulting in a 168-dimensional descriptor for each selected segment. The SSD feature vector for a piece of audio is then calculated as the median of the descriptors of its segments.

INTUITIVE/ALTERNATIVE USER INTERFACES

In this section, map-based interfaces will be described in more detail. The *PlaySOM* is a Java-based implementation of the SOMeJB system featuring a wide range of visualisations and interaction possibilities. SOMs are being trained to represent music collections based on a chosen feature space representation. In the resulting map, similar music is clustered, forming, for example, clusters of classical music, pop, or hardrock, each of which is structured into more consistent subclusters. It implements an Islands of Music interface (Pampalk et al., 2002), depicting clusters of music as an island archipelago.

It allows users to draw a trajectory or rectangle on the map, subsequently offering to play the selected tracks along the path either in the chosen sequence or randomly, covering different musical styles according to the SOM's audio similarity measurements (Dittenbach, Neumayer, & Rauber, 2005). While it also supports a 3D-visualisation similar to (Knees et al., 2006), its main interaction principles are based on a variety of 2D map displays showing weather charts, labels, or class diagrams for different genres of music, which can be zoomed or panned.

Drawing trajectories on a desktop PC or touch screen enabled device offers a simple, intuitive, and novel way of music exploration. A user can choose, for example, to select a cluster in the upper right corner of the map containing classical guitar concerts. Alternatively, he or she may decide to draw a trajectory starting at an island with guitar concerts, move on to some symphonic pieces, first adagio, then presto before returning to the guitar music again. This allows to quickly create a playlist containing music of different,

yet consistent styles, offering some variability, as opposed to limiting playlist generation to music from a specific artist.

It supports different modes for selecting songs:

- Region selection: Provides a square-shaped selection tool enabling users to select the songs belonging to units inside that rectangle without preserving any order of the selected tracks.
- Line selection: Allows users to draw trajectories and select all songs belonging to units beneath, taking into account transitions between different types of music along the trajectory.

Figure 1. Visualisations of and ways of interaction with digital music collections

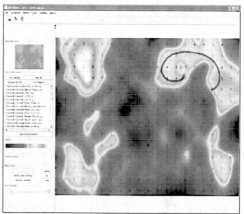

[1a][Playlist generation by drawing a trajectory visiting several Islands of Music]

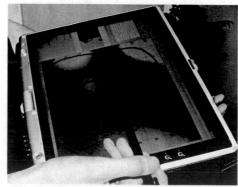

[1b][PlaySOM running on a Tablet PC.]

The resulting playlist is shown on the left-hand side of the user interface. Thereby, users can further edit the list before sending it to a music player.

Once a user has selected songs on the map, the playlist element in the interface displays the list of selected titles. It is possible to play the music in the list directly or to refine the list by manually dropping single songs from the selection. The playlist may either be played completely, or the system iterates through the trajectory, with one loop taking a specified amount of time, playing random songs that are located on the path. Other platforms like PDAs or Multimedia Jukeboxes could easily use the exported playlists, which would make *PlaySOM* a perfect, centralised music management application. The music can be either played locally or, if the music collection is stored on a server, in a streaming environment. Figure 1(a) shows the *PlaySOM*'s main window and a trajectory being drawn on an island-like map of music. The playlist window on the left shows the according selection of a smooth transition from "electronic" music over songs mostly belonging to the genre "world" back to "electronic." It also shows a visualisation control element on the lower left of the screenshot and settings to change the current visualisation and export/import functions in the menu bar of the application. To gain a more detailed view, the user can use the semantic zooming feature providing different amounts of contextual information according to the zoom level to more closely inspect the songs linked to a certain unit.

Due to its portable Java implementation, the *PlaySOM* application can easily be used on other devices like tablet PCs. Figure 1(b) presents the *PlaySOM* running on a Tablet PC being used as a touch screen application.

Map Interfaces for Mobile Devices

Another important aspect about music interfaces in general is their mobility. Both the design re-quirements and change in processing power, including limitations on human computer interaction when moving from a desktop PC to a mobile device, heavily influence the requirements. When the user input is limited to a small joystick, which many mobile phones are equipped with, an application providing access to a music collection faces severe limitations in interaction possibilities. Ease of use becomes an even more striking design goal. As mentioned, interfaces are even more important for users who do not want to do without music when they are not at home. The boom in personal audio devices has impressively shown the demand in this area. Many other applications seem possible when thinking about a streaming environment. The area of mobile music delivery and exploration will continue to grow, especially once the involved technologies reach certain levels of maturity.

Unfortunately, only few applications have been ported to mobile applications like PDAs and mobile phones. The *PocketSOM* application is the *PlaySOM's* counterpart for portable devices. *PocketSOM* runs on Java-enabled PDAs and mobile phones and allows users to navigate through their collections on a map-like display (Neumayer et al., 2005). However, due to interaction restrictions of mobile devices, the *PocketSOM* application only provides the basic functionality of selecting by drawing trajectories and a simplified refinement section, omitting means to zoom or pan the map.

The most difficult problem, however, is how to adequately display or gain access to a very large-scale dataset using these minimal interface capabilities. *PocketSOM* is a reduced version of *PlaySOM* application, which provides a simple—but intuitive—interface. Its functionality focuses on creating playlists using music maps generated by the *PlaySOM* application.

We provide three different and independent implementations, each based on a different platform, offering a common set of main features:

- After loading the datafile, the music map is displayed.
- Using the touchscreen, the user can now draw a path on the map which will result in a playlist. The songs on this playlist are selected along the path.
- Afterwards the user can manually edit the playlist, by deleting and reordering items. Finally the playlist is further processed by one of the output modes. The main interactions with *PocketSOM* such as drawing a path on the music map or editing the playlist are done via the touchscreen. Textual input which would require the use of keyboard is either kept to a minimum (e.g., a server address) or assistance will be provided (e.g., through a file open dialog) and is saved for as long as the application is running so that these settings have to be set only once.

So far, three different types of output are available:

- **Local Playback:** The playlist generated by the PocketSOM can be directly played with a local audio player. Depending on the player, the songs must be available locally or can be streamed via an Internet connection from a remote server.

i-PocketSOM Figure 2(a) shows *i-PocketSOM* running on an iPAQ Pocket PC displaying a music map, showing manually assigned labels describing the prevalent music genres within clusters. This is the first implementation of *PocketSOM,* and it is based on Java and SWT (Standard Widget Toolkit). It was developed and tested on an iPAQ Pocket PC.

e-PocketSOM is an implementation of *PocketSOM* based on ewe4, a Java-like virtual machine for Windows CE devices. *e-PocketSOM* was developed and tested on a BenQ P50 smart phone, which is shown in Figure 2(b), but is designed to run an any device supported by the

Figure 2. Various PocketSOM implementations running on a range of mobile devices

[2a][The I-PocketSOM application running on an iPaq PDA, showing a 'genre annotated' map of music]

[2b][The e-PocketSOM application running on a BenQ P50 smartphone]

continued on following page

ewe VM (e.g., PocketPC, MS SmartPhone, Casio BE-300, HandHeldPC Pro, or the Sharp Zaurus). *e-PocketSOM* offers settings for, as an examply, the target output (M3U file or VLC server) or the selection mode (random or sequential selection). *e-PocketSOM* supports the creation of multiple

Figure 2. continued

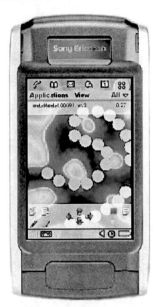

[2c][The m-PocketSOM application running on a Sony Ericsson P910 emulator and showing the map interface]

paths which are afterwards concatenated to a single playlist.

Figure 2(c) shows the third implementation of the *PocketSOM*. *m-PocketSOM* is based on JavaME5, the Java Micro Edition. Therefore, it will run on any mobile device that provides a touch screen, CLDC1.1 (Connected Limited Device Configuration 1.16), MIDP2.0 (Mobile Information Device Profile 2.07), and an implementation of the MMAPI (Mobile Media API8) that supports MP3 playback. The application was tested on different mobile phones, including Nokia 7710 and Sony-Ericsson M600.

CONCLUSION

The growing availability of music in digital formats poses a challenge both in terms of access and delivery. The co-incidental demand by an ever-growing user base further motivates research conducted in the area of audio user interfaces. The interfaces presented in this chapter are meant to give an overview of alternative ways to organise and access digital music libraries.

Future challenges in audio interface design will be scalability which will be an important issue throughout the MIR community, as well as new technologies in the area of mobile devices. The use of mobile interfaces will be of particular importance in streaming environments and corresponding business models for digital audio distribution. Besides, the music industry will play an important part by further adapting their market strategies towards persistent and flexible music delivery (anywhere, anytime).

REFERENCES

Dittenbach, M., & Neumayer, R., & Rauber, A. (2005). PlaySOM: An alternative approach to track selection and playlist generation in large music collections. In *Proceedings of the First International Workshop of the EU Network of Excellence DELOS on Audio-Visual Content and Information Visualization in Digital Libraries (AVIVDiLi'05)* (pp. 226–235). Cortona, Italy.

Goto, M., & Goto, T. (2005). Musicream: New music playback interface for streaming, sticking, sorting, and recalling musical pieces. In *Proceedings of the Sixth International Conference on Music Information Retrieval (ISMIR'05)* (pp. 404–411). London, UK.

Hamanaka, M., & Lee, S. (2006). Music scope headphones: Natural user interface for selection of music. In *Proceedings of the International Conference on Music Information Retrieval (ISMIR'06)* (pp. 302–307). Victoria, BC, Canada.

Knees, P., Schedl, M., Pohle, T., & Widmer, G. (2006). An innovative three-dimensional user interface for exploring music collections enriched with metainformation from the Web. In *Proceedings of the ACM Multimedia 2006 (MM'06)* (pp. 17–24). Santa Barbara, CA.

Kohonen, T., Oja, E., Simula, O., Visa, A., & Kangas, J. (1996). Engineering applications of the self-organizing map. In *Proceedings of the IEEE, 84*(10), 1358.

Lidy, T., & Rauber, A. (2005). Evaluation of feature extractors and psycho-acoustic transformations for music genre classification. In *Proceedings of the Sixth International Conference on Music Information Retrieval (ISMIR'05)* (pp. 34–41). London, UK.

Lübbers, D. (2005). SONIXPLORER: Combining visualization and auralization for content-based exploration of music collections. In *Proceedings of the Sixth International Conference on Music Information Retrieval (ISMIR'05)* (pp. 590–593). London, UK.

Mayer, R., Lidy, T., & Rauber, A. (2006). The map of Mozart. In *Proceedings of the International Conference on Music Information Retrieval (ISMIR'06)* (pp. 351–352). Victoria, BC, Canada.

Mörchen, F., Ultsch, A., Nöcker, M., & Stamm, C. (2005). Databionic visualization of music collections according to perceptual distance. In *Proceedings of the Sixth International Conference on Music Information Retrieval (ISMIR'05)* (pp. 396–403). London, UK.

Neumayer, R., Dittenbach, M., & Rauber, A. (2005). PlaySOM and PocketSOMPlayer: Alternative interfaces to large music collections. In *Proceedings of the Sixth International Conference on Music Information Retrieval (ISMIR'05)* (pp. 618–623). London, UK.

Pachet, F., & Cazaly, D. (2000). A taxonomy of musical genres. In *Proceedings of Content-Based Multimedia Information Access (RIAO) Conference* (pp. 827–830). Paris, France.

Pampalk, E., Rauber, A., & Merkl, D. (2002). Content-based organization and visualization of music archives. In *Proceedings of the ACM Multimedia (MM'02)* (pp. 570–579). Juan les Pins, France: ACM.

Rauber, A., & Frühwirth, M. (2001). Automatically analyzing and organizing music archives. In *Proceedings of the 5th European Conference on Research and Advanced Technology for Digital Libraries (ECDL 2001)*, LNCS (pp. 402–414). Darmstadt, Germany: Springer.

Rauber, A., & Merkl, D. (2003). Text mining in the SOMLib digital library system: The representation of topics and genres. *Applied Intelligence, 18*(3), 271.

Rauber, A., Pampalk, E., & Merkl, D. (2002). Using psycho-acoustic models and self-organizing maps to create a hierarchical structuring of music by musical styles. In *Proceedings of the 3rd International Symposium on Music Information Retrieval* (pp. 71–80). Paris, France.

Rauber, A., Pampalk, E., & Merkl, D. (2003). The SOM-enhanced JukeBox: Organization and visualization of music collections based on perceptual models. *Journal of New Music Research, 32*(2), 193.

Torrens, M., Hertzog, P., Arcos, J.L. (2004). Visualizing and exploring personal music libraries. In *Proceedings of the Fifth International Conference on Music Information Retrieval (ISMIR'04)* (pp 421–424). Barcelona, Spain.

Vignoli, F., van Gulik, R., & van de Wetering, H. (2004). Mapping music in the palm of your hand, explore and discover your collection. In *Proceedings of the Fifth International Conference on Music Information Retrieval (ISMIR'04)* (pp. 409–414). Barcelona, Spain.

Zwicker, E., & Fastl, H. (1999). Psycho-acoustics, facts, and models. *Series of Information Sciences* (Vol. 22, Ed. 2). Berlin: Springer.

KEY TERMS

Audio Features: An abstract representation of pieces of digital music. Audio features are computed from the raw audio signal. Simple features are the number of zero crossings of the audio signal or its centroid (as, for example, defined in the MPEG7 standard). More sophisticated approaches, such as MP3-based features, rhythm Patterns, Rhythm Histograms, or statistical Spectrum Descriptors take into account, for instance, findings from psycho-acoustics.

Audio Streaming: Music cannot only be played from a local hard disk, but can also be "streamed" over networks (i.e., the playback of a file can start even when its download has not completely finished). This technique is also highly relevant for live streams (e.g., Internet radio).

Digital Audio: Music files available in digital form. "Lossy" compression—like MP3 or Ogg Vorbis—are the most widely available formats, since they require less disk space than "lossless" formats, such as the Wave format.

Human-Computer Interaction (HCI): Studies the interaction between computers and human users. HCI deals with both software and hardware interfaces to computer systems.

Information Visualisation: Is concerned with the visualisation of complex or very high-dimensional data. Its main goal is to provide an intuitive and/or simplified view on more complex issues.

Mobile Device: Computer or multimedia devices other than desktop machines. In the context of portable audio devices, PDAs, MP3 players, but also mobile phones with playback capabilities, can be used to play music.

Music Information Retrieval (MIR): An area of Information Retrieval concerned with objects from the audio domain. Contrary to classic Information Retrieval, which deals with (text) documents in general, MIR deals with the analysis and retrieval of files from the music domain in audio (e.g., WAV, MP3) or symbolic (e.g., MIDI, scores) form.

Self-Organising Map: An unsupervised neural network model. Its main application is clustering of high-dimensional data onto two-dimensional maps for explorative data analysis and visualisation.

Chapter XXXIII
Patent and Trade Secret in Digital Libraries

Hideyasu Sasaki
Ritsumeikan University, Japan

ABSTRACT

In this chapter, we discuss the issues on patent and trade secret issues on digital libraries, especially patentable parameter-setting components which are implemented as computer-related inventions in digital libraries. In addition, we discuss the directions for embedding and protecting numerical parametric information as a trade secret in the patentable parameter-setting components performing retrieval operations of digital libraries with the future of intellectual property protection in the multimedia digital libraries. The scope of this chapter is restricted within the current standard of the U.S. laws and cases in transnational transaction and licensing of intellectual properties regarding the digital library.

INTRODUCTION

In this chapter, we discuss the issues on patent and trade secret issues on digital libraries, especially patentable parameter-setting components which are implemented as computer-related inventions in digital libraries. Since the U.S. Supreme Court in State Street affirmed that processes or methods are patentable, subject matter such as computer-related programs and data-processing processes for retrieval operations in digital libraries are patentable in the forms of parameter-setting components. In addition, the current techniques in parameter-setting components enclose a variety of numerical parametric information for proper retrieval operations which inventors recognize as precious know-how, and would like to cover as a trade secret.

The parameter information is often implemented in visual data processing for digital library operations. The parameter-setting components enclose a variety of numerical parametric information which inventors would like to cover as a trade secret. We discuss the directions for embedding and protecting numerical parametric information as a trade secret in the patentable parameter-setting components performing retrieval operations of digital libraries with the future of intellectual property protection in the multimedia digital libraries.

The scope of this chapter is restricted within the current standard of the U.S. laws and cases in transnational transaction and licensing of intellectual properties regarding the digital library.

BACKGROUND

In this section, we discuss two issues on the intellectual property protection regarding digital libraries. The first issue is the patent protection of the retrieval mechanisms of digital library systems. The second issue is the trade secret on the numerical parametric values for retrieval operations in the parameter-setting components.

Patentable Parameter-Setting Components

The U.S. Patent Act (2005) defines that a data-processing process or method is patentable subject matter in the form of a computer-related invention (i.e., a computer program). The computer program is patentable as far as the "specific machine [...] produce[s] a useful, concrete, and tangible result [...] for transforming [...] physical data ["physical transformation"] (In re Alappat, 1994).

The computer-related inventions often combine means for data-processing, some of which are prior disclosed inventions. Computer-related invention consists of a number of "processes" (i.e., methods or means for data processing in the form of combination of computer programs). In visual digital libraries, for example, a certain set of programs focuses on image processing, while another set of programs operates text mining. Meanwhile, in the same example, the processes in a data-processing mechanism comprise means or components for parameter-setting which is adjusted to process specific kinds of image retrieval operations (e.g., sorting proper images in certain object domains).

The problem of which process is to realize technical advancement (nonobviousness) on its combination of the prior arts, and is to be specific/enabling on its parameter-setting. These two issues are emerging problems in the advent of sophisticated data analysis technique, especially in the area of visual information retrieval in digital libraries. Uniform frameworks for protecting patentable inventions on the novel combination, and the specific parameter-setting must be formulated in engineering manner, respectively.

Trade Secret in Parameter-Settings

In the field of parameter-setting components, the DL community faces an issue that is how to protect the specific ranges of important numerical values regarding parameter-settings for performing proper and powerful retrieval operations in the form of a trade secret. Patent application on the parameter-setting components demands applicants as developers to make public the detailed know-how on the best range of parametric values in practice.

Meanwhile, the discovery of those parametric values needs considerable pecuniary investment in research and development. That kind of knowledge should be kept covered in the form of a trade secret, but not be open in public via patent application. It is necessary to prepare a scheme that determines how and which part of parameter-setting components should take the form of a trade secret, even in patentable parameter-setting components.

The problem is how to interpret the "working examples" of initial values or weights on parameter-setting and the ranges of parametric values in the DL engineering manner.

FRAMEWORKS

In this section, we outline the frameworks for intellectual property protection regarding digital library systems: patentable retrieval mechanism, and embedded trade secret on numerical parametric values for retrieval.

Framework for Patent Protection

Our already-proposed framework for patenting the data-processing mechanisms as computer-related inventions determines which type of process should be patentable in the form of a component of novel combination of prior disclosed processes and/or a component of specific parameter-setting (Sasaki & Kiyoki, 2002a, 2002b, 2005a, 2005b). The framework focuses on the following three requirements for patentability:

1. "Patentable subject matter" (entrance to patent protection),
2. "Nonobviousness" (technical advancement), and
3. "Enablement" (specification) (Merges & Duffy, 2002). The requirement for nonobviousness on the combination of the processes for data operations is listed as below:

1-a. The processes for performing certain data operations like image retrieval must comprise the combination of prior disclosed means to perform certain retrieval mechanism which is not predicated from any combination of the prior arts; in addition,

1-b. The processes for performing certain retrieval operations must realize quantitative and/or qualitative advancement.

2. Otherwise, the discussed processes are obvious, so that they are not patentable as the processes for performing certain retrieval operations.

First, a combination of prior disclosed means should not be "suggested" from any disclosed means "with the reasonable expectation of success" (In re Dow Chemical Co., 1988).

Second, its asserted function on the discussed retrieval operations must be superior to the conventional functions which are realized in the prior disclosed or patented means in the field of the object inventions (e.g., image retrieval in digital libraries). On the latter issue, several solutions for performance evaluation are proposed and applicable.

Another general strategy is restriction of the scope of problem claims into a certain narrow field to which no prior arts have been applied. This claiming strategy is known as the local optimization of application scope.

A component for parameter-setting realizes thresholding operations in the form of a computer program with a set of ranges of parametric values. In typical retrieval operations of digital libraries, parametric values determine, as thresholds for image retrieval. That parameter-setting component is to be a computer-related invention in the form of computer program, as far as that parameter-setting is sufficiently specified to enable a claimed invention or retrieval operation (U.S. Patent and Trademark Office, 1996a). The requirement for enablement on the parameter-setting component is listed as below:

1-a. The descriptions of the processes for performing a certain retrieval operation must specify the formulas for parameter-setting; otherwise,

1-b. the disclosed invention of the processes should have its copending application that describes the formulas in detail; in addition,

2-a. the processes must perform a new retrieval operation by a combination of the prior disclosed means; otherwise,

2-b. the processes should have improved formulas for parameter-setting which is based on the prior disclosed means for performing a certain retrieval operation, and also should give examples of parametric values on parameter-setting in descriptions.

For 2-b, the processes must specify the means for parameter-setting by "giving a specific example of preparing an" application to enable those skilled in the arts to implement their best mode of the processes without undue experiment (Autogiro Co. of America v. United States, 1967; Unique Concepts, Inc. v. Brown, 1991). The U.S. Patent and Trademark Office (1996b) suggested that the processes comprising the means—in other words, the components for parameter-setting must disclose at least one of the following examples of parametric values on parameter-setting:

1. Working or prophetic examples of initial values or weights on parameter-setting;
2. Working examples of the ranges of parametric values on parameter-setting.

The "working examples" are parametric values that are confirmed to work at an actual laboratory or as prototype testing results. The "prophetic examples" are given without actual work by one skilled in the art.

Simulation Example

The proposed formulation should be clear with its application to an exemplary digital library system. We apply it to "Virage Image Retrieval" (VIR), which was developed in the early 1990s as a typical content-based retrieval of visual objects stored in digital image database systems. VIR is an indexing method for an image search engine with "primitives," which compute similarity of visual features extracted out of typical visual objects (e.g., color, shape, and texture of images). VIR evaluates similarity of images with ad hoc weights (i.e., parametric values), which are given to the parameter-setting components for correlation-computation by user-preference. Its claims consist of "function containers" as means-plus-functions for feature extraction and similarity computation.

Its first claim, as described below, constitutes the primitives as the means-plus-functions. Those primitives realize a domain-general approach of CBIR by the formulas on parameter-setting.

VIR Claim # 1

A search engine, comprising: a function container capable of storing primitive functions; … a primitive supplying primitive functions … …, wherein the primitive functions include an analysis function … … of extracting features from an object … .

First, its retrieval processes consisting of the formula for parameter-setting are to be determined as patentable subject matter in the form of computer programs. Those data-processing processes generate physical transformation on a specific machine (i.e., a computer memory with certain classification results).

Second, on its nonobviousness, those data-processing processes are inventive steps that consist of combinations of the prior arts on thresholding functions as implemented in the integration of classification based on similarity computation, visual feature extraction, and automatic indexing techniques. Those combinations are not predicated from any conventional keyword-based retrieval technique. Third, on its enablement, VIR's description of preferred embodiments gives its clear specification on the formulas for parameter-setting that realizes a domain-general approach of CBIR that was a brand new technology at the time.

VIR Description

For primitives having multiple dimensions, … …, an equation for an exemplary Euclidean metric is as follows:

Primitive design. A primitive encompasses a given feature's representation, extraction, and comparison function. … … .

The constraints are as follows: Primitives, in general, map to cognitively relevant image properties of the given domain.

The formulation should take advantage of a threshold parameter (when available), … …. The retrieval mechanisms of digital library systems are patentable in the form of components of novel combinations of prior disclosed processes and/or components of specific parameter-settings while they are to satisfy the aforementioned conditions.

Embedding Trade Secret of Parametric Values

The requirement for patenting parameter-setting components as computer-related inventions demands inventors to make public their discovered "working examples" on those parameter values: initial values or ranges. The practice in patent application, nonetheless, does not always force applicants to disclose to examiners complete evidences on those initial values or ranges of parametric values, but those values as would work in their best mode at the present art. In the reality of application practice, inventors have two choices for embedding trade secrets on their know-how of parametric values in the forms of patentable parameter components:

1. On the initial values, their prophetic examples should be disclosed in patent application, instead of working examples; or,
2. On the ranges of parametric values, those ranges should be widened as possible;
3. Otherwise, the ranges of parametric values should be replaced with several initial values of prophetic examples.

The issue is when those patentable parameter-setting components should be allowed to embed trade secrets on their parametric values. The framework or set of conditions to realize that

problem depends on application cases of digital libraries.

CONCLUSIONS AND FUTURE OF DL PROTECTION

In this chapter, we have discussed issues on intellectual property protection regarding patentable parameter-setting components implemented in digital libraries. First, we have discussed our already-proposed framework for patenting the data processing or retrieval operation in the form of a combination of processes and/or a component of parameter settings. Second, we have pointed out an emerging problem on the trade secret of parameter-settings, and the possible directions for its solution.

The current status of intellectual property protection has been limited in the scope of digital copyright protection, and its technical execution and security protection, even in the multimedia digital libraries. The adoption of our proposed frameworks for digital rights protection allows the community to expand the frontiers of digital rights management and protection. The future of IP protection in the multimedia DLs should be broader by exploiting the technical analyses and implementations of patent and trade secret protections.

ACKNOWLEDGMENT

The study of this chapter is supported financially in part by the Grant-in-Aid for Scientific Research (Kakenhi) of the Japanese Government: #18700250, FY 06-09.

REFERENCES

Autogiro Co. of America v. United States. (1967). 384 F.2d 391, 155 U.S.P.Q. 697 (Ct. Cl. 1967).

In re Alappat. (1994). 33 F.3d 1526, 31 U.S.P.Q.2d 1545 (Fed. Cir. 1994) (en banc)

In re Dow Chemical Co. (1988). 837 F.2d 469, 473, 5 U.S.P.Q.2d 1529, 1531 (Fed. Cir. 1988).

Merges, R.P., & Duffy, J.F. (2002). *Patent law and policy: Cases and materials (3rd edn.)*. LexisNexis: Dayton, OH.

Sasaki, H., & Kiyoki, Y. (2002a). Patenting advanced search engines of multimedia databases. In *Proceedings of the 3rd International Conference on Law and Technology* (pp. 34–39).

Sasaki, H., & Kiyoki, Y. (2002b, December 11–14). Patenting the processes for content-based retrieval in digital libraries. In Proceedings of the 5th International Conference on Asian Digital Libraries (ICADL), Lecture Notes in Computer Science, 2555, (pp. 471–482). Singapore.

Sasaki, H., & Kiyoki, Y. (2005a). A formulation for patenting content-based retrieval processes in digital libraries. *Journal of Information Processing and Management, 41*(1), 57–74.

Sasaki, H., & Kiyoki, Y. (2005b). Multimedia digital library as intellectual property, design and usability of digital libraries. In Y.L. Theng & S. Foo (Eds.), *Case Studies in the Asia Pacific* (pp. 238–253). Hershey, PA: Idea Group Publishing.

U.S. Patent Act. (2005). 35 U.S.C. Sec. 101, 103, & 112.

U.S. Patent and Trademark Office. (1996a, February 28). *Examination guidelines for computer-related inventions*. 61 Fed. Reg. 7478.

U.S. Patent and Trademark Office. (1996b). *Examination guidelines for computer-related inventions training materials directed to business, artificial intelligence, and mathematical processing applications.*

Unique Concepts, Inc. v. Brown. (1991). 939 F.2d 1558, 19 U.S.P.Q.2d 1500 (Fed. Cir. 1991).

KEY TERMS

Combination of Processes: A patentable computer program or programs as a number of "processes"; in other words, methods or means for data processing, some of which are prior disclosed inventions.

Digital Library: A system as an infrastructure for global information, which consists of digital contents in databases and retrieval mechanisms.

Multimedia Digital Contents: Data entities which are stored in multimedia digital libraries in a variety of forms of text, images, photos or video streams, which often commingle therein.

Multimedia Digital Library: A system which consists of multimedia digital contents indexed and stored in databases for appropriate retrieval operations and the retrieval mechanisms which are optimized and applied to object domains of those databases.

Parameter-Setting: A patentable computer program or programs which realize thresholding operations with a set of ranges of parametric values.

Patentable Computer Program: A computer-related invention in the form of a data-processing process or method to produce a useful, concrete, and tangible result for transforming physical data.

Trade Secret on Parameter-Setting: A legal framework to keep secret the range of parametric values in practice, rather than just patenting parameter-setting components.

Chapter XXXIV
User–Adapted Information Services

Thomas Mandl
University of Hildesheim, Germany

ABSTRACT

This chapter describes personalization strategies adopted in digital libraries. Personalization and individualization are introduced as means to improve the usability of digital library services. The goal of personalization for digital libraries is mainly the presentation of individual results to the user. This can be modelled based on a user interest model which is applied during the search process. Two users with the same query can receive different results based on their interest profile maintained by the system. Typical approaches and systems for individualizing the results of information retrieval systems are presented. The retrieval process is described. Knowledge sources and common knowledge representation for personalization are elaborated. Most common, the search history and documents accessed in the past are exploited for modelling the user interest. Finally, the chapter mentions drawbacks and success factors for personalization and individualization systems.

INTRODUCTION

For a long time, information systems like digital libraries followed a "one size fits all" approach. However, people who use these systems are different. Consequently, systems should adapt to the individual needs and preferences of the users in order to best accommodate them. The main focus of this chapter will be the adaptation in information retrieval for digital library services.

BACKGROUND

Adaptivity can be achieved by either an active user or an active system. In the first case, the user himself has means to modify the system in some way that it better fits to her individual desires. The user himself takes the initiative for the process. More challenging is the development of systems which adapt by themselves to the needs and preferences of the users. In order to do that, the system needs to identify the user, collect knowledge about him, and draw consequences from this knowledge.

In the early days of user adaptation, user modeling in the context of artificial intelligence applications was in the focus. User modeling began with stereotyping users (Rich, 1979) and has evolved into more refined knowledge-based strategies (Kobsa, 2001). Currently, there is a trend to rely on machine learning algorithms which associate similar users or objects in order to serve personal interests.

PERSONALIZATION AND INDIVIDUALIZATION

Users are Different

Users can differ in many ways like age or culture. Most important for knowledge work which is supported by information system are cognitive differences. Users may differ in their knowledge about the interaction with the system and the domain. The differences between beginners and advanced users are an issue which is often exploited for personalization. At the same time, users may be different according to their knowledge (e.g., in a e-learning system, they may have reached different levels of knowledge). Resistance to change, intelligence, intro-/extroversion, fear of failure, and creativity are further personal features. For some interfaces, the spatial orientation capabilities may be of importance. Users can have different preferences in interaction styles. Some may prefer the keyboard, others the mouse, and again others, spoken language. Obviously, adaptation does contradict the human-computer interaction principle of consistency for interfaces. As a consequence, adaptation needs to improve the system up to an extent which exceeds these potential shortcomings. Certainly, adaptation is of specific value for beginners who start to use a system. However, for this group, it is hard to acquire knowledge.

ACQUIRING KNOWLEDGE ABOUT USERS

Systems can collect the knowledge explicitly or implicitly. Explicit knowledge gathering means that the user is asked to provide information about himself. Implicit knowledge gathering does not require time and effort from the user. The system collects this knowledge from the behavior (click data, log files) or the context (who, where, when, what, how) (Abowd & Mynatt, 2000).

In addition to collect the knowledge, the system needs to assign it to one specific user. A login is very reliable but puts a high effort on the user. Technological means like RFID chips, IP addresses, and unique mobile telephone numbers can also be used for the identification. If no means are available, the adaptation can be effective only for one session.

MODIFYING A SYSTEM

The modification of the system can affect the user interface (functions, appearance, way of interaction), the content (different knowledge objects), or the presentation (sequence, level of detail). For a digital library all of these three aspects can be of interest, however, content adaptation has been attracted most research in the digital library community. Content adaptation will be thoroughly discussed in the following section. Typical content adaptation is implemented by recommender systems which suggest new content items to users in e-commerce applications.

User interface adaptation has been the focus of much research. The adaptation initiated by users has been integrated in many systems for many years. Menus, tool bars, and other aspects of graphical user interfaces can be changed by users. Some aspects like desktop background pictures or ring tones for mobile phones are heavily used to express individuality through aesthetic elements.

Some areas for system driven improving every-day information systems have been identified. The menus in Microsoft-Windows have been implemented as an adaptive interface which displays only the most often and most recently used items, while hiding other options until the user requests the full list.

INFORMATION RETRIEVAL

The use of Internet search engines is widespread and has become part of daily life for many people. The basic technology behind search engines is information retrieval. Information retrieval deals with the storage and representation of knowledge and the retrieval of information relevant for a special user problem. The information seeker formulates a query trying to describe his information need. The query is compared to document representations which were extracted during the indexing phase. The representations of documents and queries are typically matched by a similarity coefficient such as Cosine or Dice. The most similar documents are presented to the user (Manning, Raghavan, & Schütze, 2008).

Usually, documents and queries traditionally contain natural language or more and more multimedia objects like graphics, pictures or music pieces. The content of these objects must be analysed, which is a hard task for artificial systems. Robust semantic analysis of large text collections has not yet been successfully developed. As a consequence, text documents are represented by natural language terms mostly without syntactic or semantic context. This is often called the bag-of-words approach. A few keywords or terms can only imperfectly represent an object because context and relations are lost. As information retrieval needs to deal with vague knowledge, exact processing methods are not appropriate. Vague retrieval models like the probabilistic model are more suitable (Belew, 2001).

Indexing is a process during which words describing the content of a document are chosen as content representation of this document. During automatic indexing, algorithms assign key words to documents. The indexing process for natural language documents typically consists of the following steps:

- Word segmentation
- Elimination of stopwords
- Stemming
- Compound analysis (for some languages)

Segmentation is defining the boundaries between the individual words. In European languages, most boundaries can be found by considering blanks. However, other characters need to be considered additionally. Subsequently, many words which occur frequently are eliminated. These are called stopwords and comprise usually articles, prepositions and pronouns. The most important operation during linguistic pre-processing is stemming. It maps conjugated word forms to their basic form or their stem (e.g., runs > run, walking > walk). Morphological variations of words fulfill their function only within their grammatical context. In a "bag of words" approach, all variations can be reduced to their basic form. Stemming improves efficiency also. Three main methods are used for stemming: rule-based, lexicon based and similarity based approaches. The most important algorithms are rule based. The rules describe which steps are necessary in order to obtain the stem of a word form. The number of rules necessary is still under debate (Savoy, 2006).

Weighting determines the importance of a term for a document. A term weight measures how well the term represents a document. These weights mirror different levels of relevance. First, the frequency of each term is counted. Weighting assumes that words occurring more often are better representatives for a document. Currently, advanced weighing schemes take the average and maximum length of all documents into account. Other formulas like OKAPI consider even the query terms. OKAPI has led to excellent results (Robertson et al., 1995).

The Boolean Model allows only the similarity values 1 and 0. A document either belongs to the relevant set or not. The ranking or partial match systems allow different degrees of similarity and order the result documents according to the similarity or relevance. An example for a partial match model is the vector space model which interprets the retrieval process using a spatial metaphor. All documents and the query are points in a high dimensional space. Closeness is seen as similarity. The Retrieval Status Value can be calculated as a measure of the distance between the documents which can be determined, for example, by the Euclidian distance. Information retrieval systems can be implemented in many ways by selecting a model and specific language processing tools. They interact in a complex system and their performance for a specific data collection cannot be predicted. As a consequence, the empirical evaluation of the performance is a central concern in information retrieval research (Manning et al., 2008).

INDIVIDUAL INTEREST IN DIGITAL LIBRARIES

The most popular representation scheme relies on the representation scheme used in information retrieval where a document-term-matrix stores the importance or weight of each term for each document. When a term appears in a document, this weight should be different from zero. User interest can also be stored like a document. Then the interest is a vector of terms. These terms can be ones that a user has entered or selected in a user interface or which the system has extracted from documents for which the user has shown interest by viewing or downloading them.

A typical approach exploits so called click through data and assumes that pages which a user has visited are interesting for the user. An optimized version of such a method based on much previous work is suggested by Ng, Deng, and Lun Lee (2007). Their algorithm learns user preferences and subsequently optimizes the ranking of the result documents. This method uses only positive feedback and relies on a vector support machine to learn the preferred ranking for the individual user.

An example for such a system is UCAIR which can be installed as a browser plugin. UCAIR relies on a standard Web search engine to obtain a search result and a primary ranking. This ranking is now being modified by re-ranking the documents based on implicit feedback and a stored user interest profile (Shen, Tan, & Zhai, 2005). In UCAIR, two users can receive a different result (e.g., for a query on JAVA). One user might get pages on the programming language based on his profile and another user might see results on the island.

A similar approach is taken by the system SearchGuide which focuses on collaborative search. The individualized results are based on the membership in groups and the searching and visiting behavior and preferences of the group (Coyle & Smyth, 2007).

Most systems use this method of storing the user interest in a term vector. However, this method has several drawbacks. The interest profile may not be stable and the user may have a variety of diverging interests for work and leisure which are mixed in one profile.

Advanced individualization techniques personalize the underlying system functions. The results of empirical studies have shown that relevance feedback is an effective technique to improve retrieval quality (Spink, 1995). Learning methods for information retrieval need to extend the range of relevance feedback effects beyond the modification of the query in order to achieve long-term adaptation to the subjective point of view of the user. The mere change of the query often results in improved quality; however, the information is lost after the current session.

Some systems change the document representation according to the relevance feedback information. In a vector space metaphor, the relevant documents are moved toward the query representation. This approach also comprises some problems. As only a fraction of the document is affected by the modifications, the basic data derived during the indexing process is changed to a somewhat heterogeneous state. The original indexing result is not available anymore.

Certainly, this technique is inadequate for fusion approaches where several retrieval methods are combined. In this case, several basic representations would need to be changed according to the influence of the corresponding methods on the relevant documents. The indexes are usually heterogeneous, which is often considered an advantage of fusion approaches. A high computational overload would be the consequence.

Individualize the matching function by adopting its way to calculate the similarity between document and system. The COSIMIR system uses a neural network where the relevance decision is used as training input in order to get to acquire the best match given a document and a system representation (Mandl, 2000).

The MIMOR (Multiple Indexing and Method-Object Relations) approach does not rely on changes to the document or the query representation when processing relevance feedback information for personalization. Instead, it focuses on the central aspect of a retrieval function, the calculation of the similarity between document and query. Like other fusion methods, MIMOR accepts the result of individual retrieval systems like from a black box. These results are fused by a linear combination which is stored during many sessions. The weights for the systems experience a change through learning. They adapt according to relevance feedback information provided by users and create a long-term model for future use.

That way, MIMOR learns which systems were successful in the past, and therefore in the training data. In MIMOR, the following formula gives the retrieval status value (RSV) for a document. Arguments are the RSV of the fused systems and their weights (Mandl & Womser-Hacker, 2004).

Again, another approach to adapt the knowledge objects presented to a user is reasoning based on the similarity between users. The user interest can be modeled as the interest of similar users. Such an approach does not require knowledge about the content of the knowledge objects. Book recommendations are an example for this method. Such systems are currently gaining more importance in the filed of social computing.

PERSONALIZED QUALITY METRICS

Quality evaluation is an important issue in search systems for large collections. Systems for quality metrics assessment have been developed for Web search engines and can be adopted by digital libraries or social software applications. Web pages are rated according to their quality by search engines and higher quality pages have a higher probability of appearing on top ranks in the result sets. The quality analysis takes the number of other Web pages into account which contain a link to the page under consideration. The search engine Google reported that it uses the PageRank algorithm which heuristically evaluates the quality of Web pages by assessing the links pointing to that page (Arasu, Cho, Garcia-Molina, Paepcke, & Raghavan, 2001). The algorithm relies on two assumptions:

- Pages with many in-coming links have a high PageRank value
- Links coming from pages with high PageRank values contribute more to the PageRank value

These assumptions require an iterative calculation. After reaching a satisfying level of convergence, each page has a PageRank value assigned to it. During retrieval, this PageRank is combined with the content similarity calculated as presented in section two. Both values contribute to the final raking position (Arasu et al., 2001).

Quality is a subjective and individual notion. Consequently, personalized versions of PageRank have been suggested (Jeh & Widow, 2003). A personalized PageRank does usually not calculate a real individual ranking but determines an individual combination of several different PageRank calculation. The interest of the user measured as a set of relevant pages which may be the bookmarks of the user.

SUCCESS FACTORS OF PERSONALIZATION

Users may not be willing to provide data about themselves, and may be worried about data which is stored for privacy reasons. Privacy maintaining personalization is an important research direction (Canny 2002).

Adaptation should be transparent which is difficult to implement. Modifications of a system violate the need for consistency and can be a potential problem for the usability. Adaptivity is especially important for beginners who are the group who might have the most problems reversing unwanted effects. A person does not always remain the same, interests, levels of knowledge, and preferences are bound to change.

FUTURE TRENDS

One major trend in future information systems will be context adaptation. Systems will be enabled to determine the context of a user and draw conclusions on how to modify the behavior of a system. Context recognition requires answers to the following questions:

- Who is using the system? Users need to be identified in order to access the knowledge about them which is available or which the system has previously gathered. Access restrictions and individual preferences can be effective once the identity has been determined.
- Where is the user? Location dependent services have been an advantage often mentioned in favor of further investments for mobile technology.
- When is the user interacting with the system? Obvious examples are the adaptation of a system to the daily routine of a user. Work and spare time services need to differ. Also the same service like a restaurant finder needs to consider the time of the day.
- What is the user doing?
- How is the user interacting? The user may desire different styles or modes of interaction (e.g., natural language interaction may signal that the user cannot use his hands for the interaction at the moment).

In order to acquire as much context knowledge as possible more sensor data needs to be available. Newly developed smart home environments are one path into that direction. In such environments which are highly aware of users their actions, new interaction paradigms will appear. Natural interaction means that normal activities can become input for an information system (Abowd & Mynatt, 2000). For example, walking toward a door can be interpreted as a command to open it or leaving the desk in a multi-worker office can provoke a logout. The computer is hidden from the users and is becoming more and more invisible (Norman, 1999).

CONCLUSION

Personalization is an active research area with a huge potential for improving services especially on the Web (Brusilovsky, Kobsa, & Nejdl, in press; de Bra, Smits, & Stash, 2006) and entertainment services (Ardissono, Kobsa, & Maybury, 2004). New sensor technology may lead to better individualization in physical spaces. The adaptation of content for digital library users needs to consider the specific feature of search and browsing information behavior. Users often expect new content items which they have not encountered before. Individualization services are faced with the challenge to serve individual interests without leading them to the same knowledge over and over again.

REFERENCES

Abowd, G., & Mynatt, E. (2000). Charting past, present, and future research in ubiquitous computing. *ACM Transactions on Computer-Human Interaction (TOCHI)*, *7*(1) ,29–58.

Arasu, A., Cho, J., Garcia-Molina, H., Paepcke, A., & Raghavan, S. (2001). Searching the Web. *ACM Transactions on Internet Technology, 1*(1), 2–43.

Ardissono, L., Kobsa, A., & Maybury, M. (Eds.). (2004). *Personalized digital television: Targeting programs to individual viewers.* Dordrecht, Netherlands: Kluwer Academic Publishers.

Belew, R. (2001). *Finding out about: A cognitive perspective on search engine technology and the WWW.* Cambridge University Press.

Brusilovsky, P., Kobsa, A., & Nejdl, W. (Eds.). (in press). The adaptive Web: Methods and strategies of Web personalization. Heidelberg, Germany: Springer Verlag.

Canny, J. (2002). Collaborative filtering with privacy. In *Proceedings of the IEEE Security and Privacy Conference* (pp. 45–57).

Coyle, M., & Smyth, B. (2007). Supporting intelligent Web search. *ACM Transactions on Internet Technology (TOIT), 7*(4).

De Bra, P., Smits, D., & Stash, N. (2006, August 22–25). The design of AHA! In *Proceedings of the 17th ACM Conference on Hypertext and Hypermedia (HT '06)* (pp. 171–195). Odense, Denmark: ACM Press.

Jeh, G., & Widom, J. (2003, May 20–24). Scaling personalized Web search. In *Proceedings of the Twelfth International World Wide Web Conference (WWW 2003)* (pp. 271–279). Budapest.

Kobsa, A. (2001). Generic user modeling systems. *Journal User Modeling and User-Adapted Interaction, 11*(1–2), 49–63.

Mandl, T. (2000). Tolerant information retrieval with back propagation networks. *Neural Computing & Applications, 9*(4), 280–289.

Mandl, T., & Womser-Hacker, C. (2004). A framework for long-term learning of topical user preferences in information retrieval. *New Library World, 105*(5/6), 184–195.

Manning, C., Raghavan, P., & Schütze, H. (2008). *Introduction to information retrieval.* Cambridge University Press.

Ng, W., Deng, L., & Lun Lee, D. (2007). Mining user preference using spy voting for search engine personalization. *ACM Transactions on Internet Technology (TOIT), 7*(4).

Norman, D. (1999). *Invisible computer: Why good products can fail, the personal computer is so complex and information appliances are the solution.* London: MIT.

Rich, E. (1979). User modeling via stereotypes. *Cognitive Science: A Multidisciplinary Journal, 4*, 329–354.

Robertson, S., & Spark Jones, K. (1976). Relevance weighting for search terms. *Journal of the American Society of Information Science*, 129–146.

Savoy, J. (2006). Light stemming approaches for the French, Portuguese, German and Hungarian languages. In *Proceedings of the 2006 ACM symposium on Applied computing SAC '06* (pp. 1031–1035).

Shen, X., Tan, B., & Zhai, C. (2005). Context-sensitive information retrieval using implicit feedback. In *Annual Intl ACM SIGIR Conf on Research and Development in Information Retrieval* (pp. 43–50). ACM Press.

Spink, A. (1995). Term relevance feedback and mediated database searching: Implications for information retrieval practice and systems design. *Information Processing and Management, 31*(2), 161–171.

KEY TERMS

Adaptation: Adaptation can be seen as a process of modification based on input or observation. An information system should adapt itself to the specific needs of individual users.

Association Rules: Association rules describe relationships and correlations between attributes or objects in large data sets. Several algorithms have been developed to extract such rules from large data sets.

Human-Computer Interaction (HCI): Deals with the optimization of interfaces between human users and computing systems. Technology needs to be adapted to the properties and the needs of users. The knowledge sources available for this endeavor are guidelines, rules, standards, and results from psychological research on the human perception and cognitive capabilities. Evaluation is necessary to validate the success of interfaces.

Information Retrieval: Information retrieval is concerned with the representation and knowledge and subsequent search for relevant information within these knowledge sources. Information retrieval provides the technology behind search engines.

Machine Learning: Machine learning is a subfield of Artificial Intelligence which provides algorithms for the discovery of relations or rules in large data sets. Machine learning leads to functions which can automatically classify or categorize objects based on their features. Inductive learning from labeled examples is the most well known application.

Smart Home: Enriching houses with ubiquitous technology can lead to a smart home which better supports its inhabitants by automatically regulating its functions.

User Model: The user model is the collection of knowledge and assumption of the system about one user.

Chapter XXXV
An Empirical Analysis of the Utilization of University Digital Library Resources

Hepu Deng
RMIT University, Australia

ABSTRACT

Digital resources are readily available and easily accessible with the rapid development of information and communication technologies nowadays. These digital resources, however, have not been fully utilized as demonstrated in the literature. This chapter presents a study based on an online survey in a university environment aiming to investigate the extent to which digital resources are utilized, and to identify the critical factors for the effective use of digital resources. The study reveals that the usage of digital resources is significant in higher education, and the utilization of digital resources is very much dependent on the users and purposes. The awareness and the quality of information are critical for the use of digital resources. The findings of this study shed light on the use of digital resources and help libraries better understand users' perceptions and experiences of using digital resources services in university libraries.

INTRODUCTION

Digital resources are usually referred to databases, books, journals, newspapers, magazines, archives, theses, conference papers, government papers, research reports, scripts, and monographs in a digital form (Fox & Logan, 2005; Lesk, 2005). The rapid advancement of information and communication technologies has made digital resources readily available and easily accessible (Adams & Bonk, 1995; Agnew, Gray, Blocker, Ryan, & Smith, 2006; Koh & Kim, 2004; Liew & Foo, 1999; Moyo, 2004). This is, in particular, the case in tertiary education in which digital library resources have become a critical part of an integrated learning environment (Armstrong,

Fenton, Lonsdale, Stoker, Thomas, & Urquhart, 2001; Nicholas, Huntington, & Jamali, 2007; Pancheshnikov, 2007).

The popularity of digital resources is due to the tremendous benefits that digital resources can bring to individual organizations, as well as to the potential users of the digital resources. These benefits of accessing and using digital resources include (a) accessibility in a timely and multi-user manner; (b) availability free of time, stock, and space constraints; (c) richness and variety of resources available; and (d) easiness of search through latest search engines (Adams & Bonk, 1995; Armstrong et al., 2001; Moyo, 2004). As a consequence, tremendous efforts have been made for the acquisition, management and effective use of digital resources, resulting in a rapid increase in volume and variety of collections of digital library resources (Brenner, 2005; Fox & Logan, 2005; Moyo, 2004; Roberts, 1995; Zhang, *Shen, & Ghjenniwa*, 2004; Zhang & Haslam, 2005).

There is, however, a widely held view that digital resources are not fully utilized in organizations nowadays (Fox & Logan, 2005; Jain & Babbar, 2006; Rehman & Ramzy, 2004). The inability to effectively exploit the potential of digital resources is generally attributed to the lack of awareness, the lack of competence in using digital resources, the lack of training, and the insufficient time to use the service (Adams & Bonk, 1995; Rehman & Ramzy, 2004; Roberts, 1995; Shuler, 2007). Existing research focuses more on examining and exploiting the potential of providing users with an enhanced integrating access to value-added information (Liew & Foo, 1999; Pancheshnikov, 2007; Xie, 2006). There is, however, little research into the effective use of digital resources from a user's perspective (Armstrong et al., 2001; Tsakonas & Papatheodorou, 2007). Although it is important for information professionals to provide better services, it is not sufficient to meet the needs of the users if the perception, expectation, experience, and behaviour of the users are not understood well.

This chapter presents an empirical study for investigating the extent to which digital resources are utilized, and identifying the critical factors for effectively using digital resources in a university environment. By conducting an online survey in a university environment, this study aims to understand the perception, expectation, experience and behaviors of users in their use of digital resources. The survey has revealed a number of interesting observations related to (a) the access and use of digital resources, and (b) the critical factors for effectively using digital resources. These findings contribute to a better understanding of the use of digital resources in a tertiary education environment and help libraries better understand the perceptions, experiences and behavior of users, with respect to the use of digital library service.

RESEARCH METHODOLOGY

Questionnaires are structured instruments that provide an effective means for gathering data from a potentially large number of respondents (Chauvel & Desprs, 2002; Yin, 2003). A well-designed questionnaire can gather both overall and specific opinions, experiences, and attitudes of its targeted population on a specific research topic. To understand the extent to which digital resources are utilized and to identify the critical factors for using digital resources, this study employs a questionnaire method based on a comprehensive literature on the domain of digital library and information services.

The questionnaire is developed to find out the answers to following questions:

- Who uses digital resources?
- How often do the users use digital resources?
- Where do the users use digital resources?
- What range of digital resources do the users use?

- For what purpose do the users use digital resources?
- Why do the users choose to use digital resources?
- To what degree do the users think digital resources useful?
- What are the critical factors for using digital resources?

These questions are organized in the survey along the lines of user profile, use frequency, use purpose, reasons for using digital resources, and the critical factors for effectively using digital resources (Lesk, 2005; Nicholas, Huntington, Jamali, & Watkinson, 2006; Rehman & Ramzy, 2004; Tsakonas & Papatheodorou, 2007; Xie, 2006). The selection of these dimensions in designing and developing the questionnaire is based on the review of relevant literature that shows that these issues such as the usefulness, usability, and use purpose are the most critical issues to be explored for the effective utilization of digital resources.

A university library is selected for conducting the survey. The targeted library offers diverse information services to a population of 75,000 students and staff. The library collection of digital resources has been greatly expanded since 2000 with more than 330 databases and 15,000 digital products.

The survey is conducted online in a university environment. The target participants are academic staff, administrative staff, undergraduate students, and postgraduate students in a university. The questionnaire is pilot tested, and the revised questionnaire is created on a Web page. The hyperlink is included in an invitation, which is sent to students and staff in the university via e-mail in the form of news update and student bulletin. The invitation is also sent out through some e-mailing lists, and included in the library news and student learning hub news.

AN EMPIRICAL ANALYSIS

A total of 317 responses are received from the survey. After identifying and removing some invalid submissions, 305 valid responses are obtained. SPSS v12 is used to analyze the data with respect to the objectives of the investigation in relation to the research questions as discussed above.

The profile of users directly affects the pattern of accessing and using digital resources. It is usually reflected in their positions, years in the current position, education, gender, and age. An analysis of the surveys shows that most of the 305 respondents are females (55.7%) and in the age group of 20 to 29 years (36.7%). A majority of the respondents has a university degree (72.4%), with the rest having TAFE and high school education. These respondents consist of postgraduate students (39%), undergraduate students (38%), academic staff (13.1%), administrative staff (8.5%), and TAFE students (1.3%).

The importance of digital resources to study, teaching, and research in the university is clearly shown in the survey. Among 305 respondents, only 12 respondents have not used digital resources. Figure 1 shows the frequency of use of digital resources. 180 out of 305 respondents (59%) use digital resources more than once a week. This shows the significant role that digital resources play in today's higher education environment. Such an important role has also been demonstrated in the existing research, including Armstrong et al. (2001), Fox and Logan (2005), and Kahl and Williams (2006).

The availability of digital resources without the physical and time constrains is clearly demonstrated in the survey. The study reveals that 19% respondents access and use digital resources in places including library, outside the library and outside the campus. Some use them at home, overseas, and in distant learning mode. 14.4% respondents use them outside the library and

Figure 1. An overview of frequency of use of digital resources

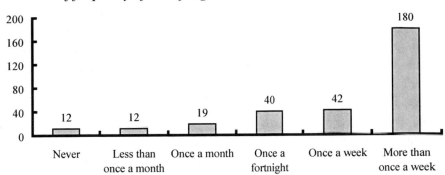

outside the campus. 14.1% respondents use them only outside the campus. 12.5% respondents use them only outside the library, and 11.8% respondents use them both at the library and outside the campus. Compared with the respondents not using them at the same group of location, 66.9% respondents use onshore outside the campus; 59.3% respondents use them outside the library on the campus; 49.2 % use them in the library; 12.5% respondents use them overseas.

An interesting pattern is emerging from the survey on the utilization of different kinds of digital resources in the library. Table 1 shows the pattern of the utilization of various kinds of digital resources. From amongst the different categories of digital resources, compared with the respondents not using the same category of resource, it is found that 82% respondents use library catalogue; 77% respondents use online journals; 68.2% respondents use Web site information;

49.5% respondents use online newspapers; 30.5% respondents use digital books; 30.2% respondents use online magazines; 22.3% respondents use online archives; 20.7% respondents use online theses; 19% respondents use digital exam papers.

Users access and use digital resources for different purposes (Nicholas et al., 2006; Pancheshnikov, 2007; Shuler, 2007; Zhang et al., 2004). These purposes include (a) gathering information on a specific topic; (b) gaining general information; (c) getting answers to specific questions; (d) completing assignments; (e) reviewing literature; (f) writing essays; and (g) helping making decisions. The survey shows that 82.3% respondents are to gather information on a specific topic and 70.2% respondents are to gain general information. 69.5% respondents are to get answers to specific questions, and 55.4% respondents are to complete assignments. It is obvious that an understanding of this situation would help library administrators and management better organize their digital resources with respect to their specific circumstances and the characteristics of their digital resources users.

The reasons for using digital resources are very much in alignment with the potential benefit that digital resources offer (Armstrong et al., 2001; Fox & Logan, 2005; Jacobs, Jacobs, & Yeo, 2005; Moyo, 2004; Tsakonas & Papatheodorou, 2007). There are 86.2% respondents who think

Table 1. An overview of utilization of digital library resources

Library catalogue	82.0%
Online journals	77.0%
Web site information	68.2%
Online newspapers	49.5%
Electronic books	30.5%
Online magazines	30.2%
Online archives	22.3%
Digital theses	20.7%
Digital exam papers	19.0%

the easiness to access is their reason to use digital resources, 73.1% respondents who think time saving is the reason. As expected, 72.5% respondents think that the wide variety of resources attract them to use digital resources, and 54.1% respondents attribute the availability of digital resources and the effective search tools for the use of digital resources. Other widely cited reasons include the freedom of physical space limitation and the quality of information.

A lack of training in how to effectively use digital resources is still a major issue that library faces today (Adams & Bonk, 1995; Moyo, 2004) even this is well recognized in the library professionals (Pancheshnikov, 2007; Raza & Nath, 2007; Roberts, 1995). Nearly half of respondents (49.5%) including 3.9% nonusers have not undertaken any training at all. As a result it is not surprising to find out that only 55.1% respondents believe digital resources are extremely useful, 31.8% respondents believe quite useful, and 6.6% respondents think useful.

The critical factors for effectively accessing and using digital resources (Hollmann, Ardö, & Stenström, 2007; Tsakonas & Papatheodorou, 2007) are investigated in the survey. Ten critical factors are identified based on an analysis of the survey results. Table 2 shows a description of these ten factors.

DISCUSSION

The survey shows that the use of digital resources in the university library is very common which is consistent with existing research findings (Fox & Logan, 2005; Jain & Babbar, 2006; Moyo, 2004; Rehman & Ramzy, 2004; Tsakonas & Papatheodorou, 2007). Reasons for using them are credited to the accessibility, time saving, availability and variety of digital resources, availability of search tools, and no physical space limitation. A majority of users believes that digital resources are useful to help them gain new ideas or insights, compare different views, undertake research project, and write theses or papers.

Further analysis based on the user's groups shows that the different users have different experiences from the use of digital resources (Moyo, 2004; Xie, 2006). Among the academic staff, administrative students, postgraduate students by course, postgraduate students by research, undergraduate students, TAFE students, a majority of academic staff (77.5%), and postgraduate students (72.5%), by research, believe that digital resources are extremely useful. This may be because the nature of their work and study is highly knowledge-intensive (Chauvel & Desprs, 2002; Lesk, 2005; Nicholas et al., 2007; Roberts, 1995). This observation is further reinforced by the fact that the relatively low percentage of undergraduate students (36.2%) and TAFE students (25%) think that digital resources are extremely useful.

The user group classified by the years in current position does not show significant difference in their experience of using digital resources. This implies that there is not a strong relationship between the seniority and using digital resources. Users in different age group show that more than half of the respondents think that digital resources are extremely useful in the users over 30 years old. This observation, in fact, conforms to the aforementioned finding, given that most of undergraduate students and TAFE students are

Table 2. Critical factors affecting the effective use of digital resources

Rarely find what I need	Information overload
Lack of supporting equipments	Out-of-date Information
Time consuming	Inaccessible
Need of guidelines	Need of examples
Inadequacy of training/help	Push of digital resources

in the age group of younger than 30. Those users with postgraduate (73.4%) and PhD qualification (72%) think that digital resources are extremely useful, with less than half of the rest of users thinking so.

The female and male users do not show any significant difference in their experiences, perceptions, and behaviors in using digital resources (Kahl & Williams, 2006; Xie, 2006). According to the purpose, users who gather information on a specific topic and get answers to specific questions significantly believe that digital resources are extremely useful comparing with those who do not have the same purpose, the percentage being almost double. This really shows that the utilization of digital resources very much depends on the users and the purposes of using digital resources.

The awareness of digital resources is an important factor to the use of digital resources (Jain & Babbar, 2006; Nicholas et al., 2007). There are 77.7% respondents who agree or strongly agree that promoting the use of digital resources from the perspective of library should be better implemented and improved which is consistent with what Rehman and Ramzy (2004) have identified. Other significant issues for improving the use of digital resources are the quality of the information available, training, help, examples and guidelines. It seems that skills and supporting equipments do not significantly affect the use of digital resources, given that Web technology, search tools, and supporting equipments are common and easy to use nowadays. On the other hand, finding relevant, up-to-date, accessible information in a time-saving manner satisfies users the most, and it is still a challenge to both the user, as well as the library on the effective and efficient utilization of digital resources in libraries.

CONCLUSION

This chapter aims to explore the utilization of digital resources from the user's perspective and to identify the critical factors for effectively using the digital resources available in a library environment. By conducting an online survey in a university environment, the chapter aims to understand the perception, expectation, experience, and behavior of users in their use of digital resources. The chapter shows that the use of digital resources is significant in the university investigated. A majority of users believes that digital resources are useful. It is also found the different users with different purposes are significant different in the process of using digital resources. The awareness and the quality of information are the two most important factors for using digital resources.

REFERENCES

Adams, J.A., & Bonk, S.C. (1995). Digital information technologies and resources: Use by university faculty and faculty preferences for related library services. *College and Research Libraries, 56,* 119–131.

Agnew, S., Gray, L., Blocker, L., Ryan, C.E., & Smith, K.L. (2006). Experiencing the electronic resources and libraries conference. *Serials Review, 32*(3), 195–203.

Armstrong, C., Fenton, R., Lonsdale, R., Stoker, D., Thomas, R., & Urquhart, C. (2001). A study of the use of digital information systems by higher education students in the UK. *Program, 35*(3), 241–262.

Brenner, A.L. (2005). Digital library use: Social practice in design and evaluation. *Library and Information Science Research, 27*(1), 131–133.

Chauvel, D., & Desprs, C. (2002). A review of survey research in knowledge management: 1997–2001. Journal of Knowledge Management, 6(3), 207–223.

Fox, E.A., & Logan, E. (2005). An Asian digital libraries perspective. *Information Processing and Management, 41*(1), 1–4.

Gonçalves, M.A., Moreira, B.L., Fox, E.A., & Watson, L.T. (2007). What is a good digital library? A quality model for digital libraries. *Information Processing and Management, 43*(5), 1416–1437.

Hollmann, J., Ardö, A., & Stenström, P. (2007). Effectiveness of caching in a distributed digital library system. *Journal of Systems Architecture, 53*(7), 403–416.

Jacobs, J.A., Jacobs, J.R., & Yeo, S. (2005). Government information in the digital age: The once and future federal depository library program. *The Journal of Academic Librarianship, 31*(3), 198–208.

Jain, P.K., & Babbar, P. (2006). Digital libraries initiatives in India. *The International Information and Library Review, 38*(3), 161–169.

Kahl, C.M., & Williams, S.C. (2006). Accessing digital libraries: A study of ARL members' digital projects. *The Journal of Academic Librarianship, 32*(4), 364–369.

Koh, J., & Kim, Y.G. (2004). Knowledge sharing in virtual communities: An e-business perspective. *Expert Systems with Applications, 26*, 155–166.

Lesk, M. (2005). Scope of digital libraries. *Understanding Digital Libraries, 2*, 361–373.

Liew, C.L., & Foo, S. (1999). Derivation of interaction environment and information object properties for enhanced integrated access and value-adding to digital documents. *Aslib Proceedings, 256–268.*

Moyo, L.M. (2004). Digital libraries and the emergence of new service paradigms. *The Digital Library, 22(3), 220–230.*

Nicholas, D., Huntington, P., & Jamali, H.R. (2007). The use, users, and role of abstracts in the digital scholarly environment. *The Journal of Academic Librarianship, 33*(4), 446–453.

Nicholas, D., Huntington, P., Jamali, H.R., & Watkinson, A. (2006). The information seeking behaviour of the users of digital scholarly journals. *Information Processing and Management, 42*(5), 1345–1365.

Pancheshnikov, Y. (2007). Integrating print and digital resources in library collections. *Library Collections, Acquisitions, and Technical Services, 31*(2), 111–112.

Raza, M.M., & Nath, A. (2007). Use of IT in university libraries of Punjab, Chandigarh and Himachal Pradesh: A comparative study. *The International Information and Library Review, 39*(3–4), 11–227.

Rehman, S., & Ramzy, V. (2004). Awareness and use of digital information resources. *Library Review, 53(3), 150–156.*

Roberts, J. (1995). Faculty knowledge about library services at the university of the West Indies. *New Library World, 96, 14–22.*

Santos, R.L.T., Roberto, P.A., Gonçalves, M.A., & Laender, A.H.F. (2007, August). A Web services-based framework for building componentized digital libraries. *Journal of Systems and Software, Available online 8 August 2007.*

Shuler, J.A. (2007). Public policies and academic libraries—the shape of the next digital divide. *The Journal of Academic Librarianship, 33*(1), 141–143.

Tsakonas, G., & Papatheodorou, C. (2007). Exploring usefulness and usability in the evaluation of open access digital libraries. *Information Processing and Management,*

Xie, H. (2006). Evaluation of digital libraries: Criteria and problems from users' perspectives. *Library and Information Science Research, 28*(3), 433–452.

Yin, R.K. (2003). *Case study research: Design and methods* (3 ed.). California: Sage.

Zhang, S., Shen, W., & Ghjenniwa, H. (2004). A review of Internet-based product information sharing and visualization. *Computers in Industry, 54,* 1–15.

Zhang, X., & Haslam, M. (2005). Movement toward a predominantly electronic journal collection. *Library Hi Tech, 23*(1), 82–89.

KEY TERMS

Digital Library: A collection of digital resources in an organized manner.

Digital Resources: Databases, books, journals, newspapers, magazines, archives, theses, conference papers, government papers, research reports, scripts, and monographs in a digital form.

Chapter XXXVI
Visualisation of Large Image Databases

Gerald Schaefer
Aston University, UK

Simon Ruszala
Teleca, UK

ABSTRACT

Following the ever-growing sizes of image databases, effective methods for visualising such databases and navigating through them are much sought after. These methods should provide an "overview" of a complete database together with the possibility to zoom into certain areas during a specific search. It is crucial that the user interacts in an intuitive way with such a system in order to effectively arrive at images of interest. In this chapter, we look at several techniques that have been presented in the literature and allow for browsing and navigation of large image databases.

INTRODUCTION

Content-Based Image Retrieval (CBIR) is increasingly playing a major role in image retrieval systems, such as those provided by stock photo companies. Initially, concept-based methods were adopted where each image is individually annotated and categorised before keyword or free text searches can be performed. This approach is still extensively used in many image database systems but the need for more automated index-ing techniques has led to the adoption of CBIR, which is based on features computed directly from images and a defined similarity between these features resulting in a computed resemblance between images that ideally corresponds to the visual similarity humans would assign. Both paradigms are useful for different reasons and are combined in some cases to increase the effectiveness of a retrieval system.

While content-based retrieval systems typically allow the formulation of query-by-example searches where a query image is provided by the user and the system retrieves the closest matches from the database, this type of search is often not very useful. Rather, a possibility to effectively and efficiently browse the whole database is sought. Often, images are displayed in a one-dimensional linear fashion, either in rank order after a query or in the order they were read in from the database. Clearly, this gives no indication to the user of where a certain image can be found unless queried. When visualising larger datasets, the number of images is simply too large to be realistically viewable on a single screen. Drawbacks like this have, therefore, led to the research and development of how to arrange the images in such a way that they are positioned on the screen in relation to all other images. While this may cause significantly more images to be displayed at once the advantage is that all images are visualised at once and clusters of related images will appear which can then be investigated further. With the images positioned relative to their similarity with other images, the display gives structure, as zooming into an area will mean that all neighbouring images will be alike.

Displaying an entire dataset on a single screen and allowing the user to localise specific areas to explore further, creates the option of browsing the database whilst also giving an indication of the size of the collection. Navigation can be accomplished through a top-down hierarchical approach by zooming into an area of interest, and thus gives more visual information on the entire range of the database to the user. Using this approach to visualisation is a widely desired feature by both users with personal image albums and businesses that manage larger image compilations.

In this chapter, we review six methods that have been used to visualise image datasets and introduce their ability to browse through them. Besides explaining the underlying techniques, advantages, and disadvantages of each method will be highlighted and a recommendation for a useful visualisation system provided.

PRINCIPAL COMPONENT ANALYSIS (PCA)

Principal component analysis transforms a number of high dimensional correlated variables into a smaller number of uncorrelated variables called principal components and allows to reduce the dimensionality whilst preserving the "essence" of the data. High dimensional data is normally vast in size and ungraspable by the human mind, making some form of representation necessary.

In order to calculate the principal components, the mean vector of the data (which also defines the first principal component) is calculated and subtracted from the samples (hence, resulting in a distribution centred around the origin). Using singular value decomposition (SVD), the remaining components are obtained by producing a diagonal matrix with eigenvalues in descending order. Each singular value is proportional to the square root of the variances and the corresponding eigenvectors are the principal components. Once these have been calculated, all samples (i.e., images) in the database can be projected onto the principal components and the projection weights be used for assigning coordinates for the display of each image thumbnail (i.e., for the display in a two-dimensional space, such as a monitor the first two principal components would be used).

Using this linear strategy is more limited than their nonlinear counterparts, but has advantages. Results shown are reliable, with genuine properties of the original data if image similarity is based on an L_2 norm (Euclidean distance). If distances between images are based on another norm (e.g., L_1 norm—"Manhattan" distance) or indeed any other distance function, the results will not be as reliable which follows from the fact that PCA maximises the captured variance in a least-squares Euclidean way. Hence, if accuracy of thumbnail positions is of primary interest, further configuration re-arrangements should be considered as any nonlinear correlation between variables is not captured. On the plus side, the mapping of images to display coordinates is straightforward. The way to compute these positions is efficient as PCA calculates them using a linear approach, so that the overall computational complexity is relatively low.

MULTIDIMENSIONAL SCALING (MDS)

Multidimensional scaling (Kruskal & Wish, 1978) expresses the similarities between different objects in a small number of dimensions, allowing for a complex set of interrelationships to be summarised in a single figure. MDS can be used to analyse any kind of distance or similarity/dissimilarity matrix created from a particular dataset.

There exist two types of multidimensional scaling methods: metric and nonmetric MDS. In metric MDS, the distances between the data items are given and a configuration of points that would give rise to the distances is sought. This perfect reproduction of distances is not always possible, and in such cases nonmetric MDS can be used. In nonmetric MDS, rank orders of similarity Euclidean distances and rank orders in the original space are compared to produce a set of metric coordinates which most closely approximate their nonmetric distances.

The application of MDS for image database display and navigation was first proposed by Rubner, Guibas, and Tomasi (1997), which presented a way of not only visualising the retrieved images in terms of decreasing similarities, but also according to their common similarities. By employing nonmetric MDS to implant all images by their similarities in a two or three dimensional Euclidean space, these calculated distances could be preserved.

For nonmetric calculations, a similarity matrix needs to be obtained from the CBIR features. Euclidean distances are calculated and compared according to Kruskal's stress equation (Kruskal

& Wish, 1978), which expresses the difference between the similarity values and the projected Euclidean values between all images. The aim of nonmetric MDS is to assign locations to the input data so that the overall stress is minimal. Typically, an initial configuration is found through PCA as described earlier. While the degree of goodness-of-fit after this is, in general, fairly high, it still can be optimised. To do so, the locations of the points are updated in such a way as to reduce the overall stress. If, for instance, the distance between two specific samples has been overestimated it will be reduced to correct this deviation. It is clear that this modification will have implications for all other distances calculated. Therefore, the updating of the coordinates and the recalculation of the stress is performed in an iterative way where during each iteration the positions are slightly changed until the whole configuration is stable and the algorithm has converged to a minimum where the distances between the projected samples correspond accurately to the original distances. Several termination conditions can be applied such as an acceptable degree of goodness-of-fit, a predefined maximal number of iterations or a threshold for the overall changes in the configuration. Once the calculation is terminated, the points can then be mapped onto the screen.

Image database navigation starts initially with a global display of the entire database with images positioned in relation to how similar they are to each others. The user then has the ability to zoom into certain regions of interest to enlarge and allow for further querying. The images selected in the area have their similarity distances recalculated and projected back into two-dimensional format. This accommodates for the enlargement so as to occupy the entire screen when displayed. While this allows for a better spreading of the images on the available visualisation space it also has the disadvantage of requiring further calculations due to the reapplication of MDS on the zoomed-in area. Clearly, this is not a desirable attribute of the system, as ideally it would respond in real time.

All other querying methods are still achievable as long as the appropriate CBIR techniques have been implemented. Retrieval of images from either a sketch or an example, results in the appropriate images being displayed around the selected image in accordance to their similarity.

The main disadvantages of this accurate positioning system is the computational time needed to re-calculate the stress value to obtain the best available configuration of points. As it is based on a quadratic approach its computational complexity is of order $O(N^2)$, where N is the number of images in the database, making it unsuitable for interactive visualisation of a large number of images.

FASTMAP

Another approach which proposes mapping points such that the dissimilarity distances have little discrepancies, is the FastMap algorithm introduced in (Faloutsos & Lin, 1995). In general, this can be considered as a computational simplification of the MDS procedure based on geometrical reflection. Vector projections and distances are updated to a degree of accuracy to discover the best configuration of points by iteratively discovering the direction of the strongest component vector.

FastMap aims to display images in a global manner, similar to that of MDS and PCA, where the positioning of images depends on the dissimilarities between all pairs of images. In addition, it attempts to improve on existing methods by computing the results and then displaying them in a more realistic time scale. The FastMap algorithm automatically extracts suitable distance features from each object, and approximations are made between the interpoint distance and the results being estimated. This approach can be calculated in a fast manner, especially in comparison to that of completing a full multipoint matrix.

Linear mapping is used to produce the results; the idea behind this is to calculate the properties of two pivot objects that parse through a carefully selected line in n-d space using the cosine law. Pivot objects are ideally two objects that are as far apart as possible and are chosen using a linear heuristic algorithm. This process chooses one object at random and another by finding the point furthest from it, this found object is then set as the furthest from the arbitrary one and both are returned as the pivot objects. This heuristic algorithm is completed until all objects have been mapped onto lines.

When a query by example is performed the pivot objects values are required for knowing the lines of appropriate points so the query can be mapped into a point in k-d space. For this reason storage of each pair of pivot objects is required after each recursive call. Querying methods are performed at a faster rate than other systems, due to its integration with fine-tuned access methods such as R-trees and R*-trees. The results can be extended causing the mapping of two objects on a line in two-dimensional space, whilst still preserving some of the distance information. For mapping to occur in k-d space, projections of all other calculated distances need to be estimated. These can then be placed onto several lines in n-d space by construction; recursively repeating this procedure results in the ability to project these points into k-d space.

Since all steps of the algorithm can be performed in a linear fashion the overall computational complexity is only $O(N)$, which compares favourably to the $O(N^2)$ that is required by MDS while this is achieved without a significant loss of accuracy.

PICSOM

The picSOM system introduced in (Laaksonen, Koskela, Laakkso, & Oja, 2000) employs self organising maps (SOMs) (Kohonen, 1990) for retrieval and browsing of large image database. In particular, tree structured self organising maps (TS-SOMs) are applied as image similarity ranking method and are used for creating a hierarchical representation of the images in a particular database. For each statistical feature vector used to retrieve images, a two-dimensional TS-SOM is created, resulting in numerous TS-SOMs grouped in parallel for calculating the best similarity results. If necessary, additional feature vectors can be introduced and integrated with ease. The main advantage is that the user can specify different queries for different features with the system automatically computing the input data and retrieving the results dependent on the queries selected.

TS-SOMs are essentially a vector quantisation algorithm which uses a hierarchical structure as its indexing method where each level in the structure contains its self-organising map. Using TS-SOMs instead of SOMs reduces the computational complexity dramatically.

The picSOM engine also tries to learn progressively what the user wants from the interaction of previous searches thus performing relevance feedback. Training the system this way means that it can predict, to a certain extent, what type of images a particular user is after. Over a number of searches some image weights are increased to an extent that images retrieved on the forthcoming queries should contain these neighbouring images with increased weights from the training scheme. Applying a weighting system that helps the user track down images of significance before they have been viewed is a great feature and not available in many other retrieval systems.

3D MARS

An interesting interactive visualisation approach to displaying image databases is presented in (Nakazato & Huang, 2001). The 3D MARS system displays the images in a projection-based immersive virtual reality environment. The user navigates through the database in a large three-di-

mensional VR CAVE, using a wand which allows the control of image selection and retrieval from the database. This concept enables the viewer to see a stereoscopic view of the space by displaying the images on four walls (top, bottom, left, and right) encompassing the user. Having large screens surrounding the user on four different sides means that many more images can be displayed at one time and in all three of the x, y, and z axes. This approach can also be expanded to accommodate six sides completely immersing the user as if inside a room and all walls of the room showing the images. Using a CAVE virtual reality system like this is very unique but expensive with hardware equipment not feasibly available to the general user; instead it would be used by specific companies with a real need for image database navigation interaction.

As in other methods, a similarity matrix for each of the CBIR techniques adopted is calculated. Biased Discriminant Analysis (Zhou & Huang, 2000) is used to calculate the CBIR feature weights. These weights are combined and an overall weight assigned to each image.

Browsing can be performed in two ways: the user either initiates a manual search through the image database in hope they will come across a similar image (this occurs when no querying has taken place, and as the images are randomly positioned, there is no structure to where images will initially be placed); or alternatively, browsing can be accomplished after a query has taken place. The system retrieves all images similar to the query and displays them according to their similarity using colour axes stating the directions of the most similar colours. The number of results retrieved can either be predefined, or the entire re-arranged database can be returned. Browsing then becomes a lot easier, due to the colour axes as the three primary colours are used. If the user browses in one of these directions then images relating to that colour can be viewed, the further away they venture from the axis means the images decrease in that particular colour. An advantage of this system is that it allows numerous selections of images for querying performed for one particular search. Selecting several images for querying causes the rearrangement of the entire database, typically yielding a more accurate representation of the database for viewing. A better structure needs to be established to achieve the initial display for browsing as the likelihood of coming across an image sought after in a database of, for example, 500,000 is rather low.

HIERARCHICAL CLUSTERING

Based on a hierarchical clustering scheme the approach presented in (Krishnamachari & Abdel-Mottaleb, 1999) stores groups of similar images at different levels of a hierarchical tree. Top level images of this tree are fairly dissimilar allowing the user to choose from a diverse range of images, hence narrowing down the types of images sought after. Descending down the tree allows refining the search as the images displayed become more alike. This eliminates the linear browsing method so abundant in other existing systems.

Images are initially arranged by assigning similarities between all pairs of images through automatically calculated local histograms consisting of 16 rectangular regions. Then, by using a histogram intersection algorithm, computation of a single weight for all interrelationships is conducted. Clustering is performed so that at the beginning each image from the database is allocated its individual cluster. The two most similar clusters are then selected and merged into one. Re-calculation of the similarities between merged and unmerged clusters is performed and the procedure is repeated until a complete tree structure is established where each node along the tree corresponds to a cluster. For each cluster a representative image, selected by choosing the most diverse images from the subgroups representing as many clusters as possible so as not to eliminate any further paths down the tree, is used for navigation around the tree.

Browsing is performed by the user selecting a representative image which in turn returns the lower level cluster of images. If the retrieved images are not relevant, navigation back up the tree is possible. Query-by-example still exists in this system with the query histogram being compared against each cluster's combined histogram hence identifying the most suitable group of images, while certain images with similar weights from that cluster can then be compared individually to further refine the search. This technique of querying is considerably quicker than previous methods, due to only a subset of the images being compared for similarity instead of the entire database. Results using databases with more than 3,500 images have shown that the retrieval accuracy based on this approach is high while the computational time is relatively low. Although browsing of the database is possible, the images returned are displayed in a one-dimensional manner causing problems when it comes to large databases as the number of levels in the hierarchical tree becomes so large that searching through it is cumbersome. Also, it is inevitable that some images will be grouped incorrectly, which results in the image becoming "lost," unless accidentally stumbled upon while searching in other clusters for different images.

CONCLUSION

The Mars 3D CAVE system represents an interesting interactive approach to display image databases which can make the user feel as if they were immersed in the database. However, unfortunately, systems like this are less available and researched, due to the cost of specialist hardware and the impracticality of their size. Searching using this method, after training, would be easier, quicker, and more productive as the images are displayed like pictures in an art gallery, but the problems of global browsing are still apparent as there is no spatial arrangement. Querying results from this system is similar in the layout used by PCA/MDS and FastMap making it very easy to use and understand but the global view of the database is not extremely informative. PicSOM is let down somewhat by the way the results are displayed, although the time required to compute a query, even in large datasets, is very low and the accuracy is increased with each search due to the integrated relevance feedback mechanism. Hierarchical clustering allows for browsing in a linear display approach but does not allow an appropriate global visualisation of the total database. It is quick to compute and retrieves images accurately but becomes increasingly complex with larger databases. This results in a more time consuming search procedure for the user as navigation through numerous clusters has to be performed.

PCA, MDS, and FastMap all use the same display technique with the difference between them being the time taken to compute and the accuracy at which they do this. PCA is the most inaccurate of the three, but with a linear approach the time taken to complete the algorithm is also the shortest. MDS goes one step further by re-calculating the configuration of points until optimal degree of fit to the original data is achieved. This process is computationally significantly more demanding as it uses a quadratic iterative algorithm approach, but the level of accuracy is optimal. FastMap eliminates some of the complexity by reverting to a linear time algorithm to calculate distances between images. The accuracy reached by this algorithm is very good and its time requirements reasonable.

REFERENCES

Faloutsos, C., & Lin, K. (1995). FastMap : A fast algorithm for indexing, datamining and visualization of traditional and multimedia datasets. In *Proceedings of SIGMOD95* (pp. 163–174).

Kohonen, T. (1990) The self-organizing map. In *Proceedings of the IEEE* (Vol. 78, pp. 1464–1480).

Krishnamachari, S., & Abdel-Mottaleb, M. (1999). Image browsing using hierarchical clustering. In *Proceedings of IEEE Int. Symposium Computers and Communication* (pp. 301–307).

Kruskal, J.B., & Wish, M. (1978). Multidimensional scaling. *SAGE University Paper Series on Quantitive Applications in the Social Sciences.* Newbury Park: Sage Publications.

Laaksonen, T., Koskela, J., Laakkso, P., & Oja, E. (2000). PicSOM—content-based image retrieval with self organising maps. *Pattern Recognition Letters, 21*, 1199–1207.

Nakazato, M., & Huang, T.S. (2001). 3D MARS: Immersive virtual reality for content-based image retrieval. In *Proceedings of IEEE Int. Conference Multimedia and Expo* (pp. 44–47).

Rubner, Y., Guibas, L., & Tomasi, C. (1997). The earth mover's distance, multi-dimensional scaling, and color-based image retrieval. In *Proceedings of ARPA Image Understanding Workshop* (pp. 661–668).

Zhou, X., & Huang, T.S. (2000). A generalized relevance feedback scheme for image retrieval. In *Proceedings of Internet Multimedia Management Systems* (pp. 348–355).

KEY TERMS

Content-Based Image Retrieval (CBIR): Retrieval of images based not on keywords or annotations, but based on features extracted directly from the image data.

Image Database Navigation: The browsing of a complete image collection based, for example, on CBIR concepts.

Multidimensional Scaling (MDS): A dimensionality reduction technique used for projecting high-dimensional data into a low-dimensional space in an optimal way that introduces as little distortion to the original data as possible.

Principal Component Analysis (PCA): An orthogonal linear transform used to transform data into a new coordinate system which maximises the variance captured by the first few base vectors (the principal components).

Query-By-Example Retrieval: Retrieval paradigm in which a query is provided by the user and the system retrieves instances similar to the query.

Section IV
Case Studies and Applications

Chapter XXXVII
Towards Multimedia Digital Libraries

Cláudio de Souza Baptista
University of Campina Grande, Brazil

Ulrich Schiel
University of Campina Grande, Brazil

ABSTRACT

A multimedia digital library copes with the storage and retrieval of resources of different media such as video, audio, maps, images, and text documents. The main improvement with regard to textual digital libraries is the possibility of retrieving documents in different media combining metadata and content analysis. Content-based Indexing and Retrieval is a complex and ongoing research field with specific problem statements for each media. A prototype of a multimedia digital library is presented.

INTRODUCTION

Digital libraries are a combination of available resources, coupled with services which provide access to them. Although most of the resources are in digital form, and can therefore be retrieved from a client machine, there are those which may be available only in hard-copy. In such cases, indexing and searching services are provided, enabling end-users to discover which resources are available and where they can be located. However, recent advances in multimedia technology have radically changed information systems.

Multimedia involves not only the manipulation of alpha-numerical data, but also new data types such as audio, video, images, maps, and text. These new data types are known as multimedia data and the development of information systems that cope with them has become a highly attractive research area. One of such information systems are multimedia digital libraries.

A multimedia digital library copes with the storage and retrieval of resources of different media such as video, audio, maps, images, and text documents. Previously, searching and indexing procedures were restricted to alpha-numeric data types. In the context of textual resources, this is acceptable and efficient, but is not true for multimedia data types where interpretation of their semantics is required for effective indexing and searching. Furthermore, there are specific domains, such as spatial and temporal applications, which require tailored searching, browsing, and indexing mechanisms.

Multimedia digital libraries have some characteristics that make them different from other digital libraries. Some of these main characteristics are presented below:

- **Data model:** Due to the high complexity of multimedia data, it is imperative to provide a model with high level of abstraction that can use a hierarchical approach in order to represent content, relationships, structure, behavior, and dynamics of objects. Furthemore, each media needs a specific data model.
- **Large objects:** Multimedia digital libraries need to cope with sometimes very large objects of data. Instead of some kilobytes to store a record in a conventional system, mega- or even gigabytes of storage are required for multimedia objects.
- **Indexing:** Multimedia digital libraries must provide new index techniques such as content-based information retrieval that enables not only exact match queries, but also similarity queries. In these, fuzzy operators may be needed, and a ranking list of approximate matches is given as a result. Due to the large size of objects and some special features such as continuous playing, new techniques of indexing and buffering, which require real-time constraints, and synchronization, are necessary.
- **Interface:** Multimodal interfaces are required with some facilities such as visual query, browsing, audio-visual interface, and virtual reality.

- **Preprocessing:** Some treatment must be given to multimedia data before using them; such procedures include compression techniques, data quality enhancement, and addition of metadata in order to deliver more semantic information to raw data.

This paper describes the main issues on designing a multimedia digital library. We discuss backgorund issues on digital libraies, and highlight the relevance of multimedia metadata.

Next section focuses on a new query paradigm based on content-based retrieval for images, video, and audio. Finally, future trends and a conclusion are addressed.

BACKGROUND

Digital Libraries Evolution

Digital libraries have evolved from the concepts associated with traditional paper-based libraries. These libraries include mechanisms that support electronic documents in different formats and media involving new issues and challenges.

The first generation is characterized by defining the role of a library, and the services provided, without making use computerized information systems. The collections and resources are indexed and searched via manual indexing cards. Users are allocated cards with their personal details, plus loan and reservation information. A library can be viewed as a collection of resources and services. Resources include books, journals, magazines, games, maps, videos, and audio material. Services include loan, reservation, searching, and facilities to physically access the collections. There is specific copyright legislation, in which ownership and authorship are clearly defined. Rules for accessing the collection are previously specified and there is a community of users who obtain authorization in order to use the library services and resources. As a rule, a resource does not change its content; for instance, an individual book will never change its contents and authorship, although new editions of the same book might appear. Various people, including staff members and users, interact with the library. Users are the consumers of the library resources and they utilize its services. It is also important to mention that, as the resources are physical, the notions of loan and reservation services are very important. When users borrow a copy of a specific resource, they are allowed to retain the resource for a prespecified period of time which is established according to the library policies. Furthermore, when users need resources that have already been lent to other users, the reservation service is used. Lastly, it is important to note that libraries need a physical location to store the collections, and there is also a timetable of the library open hours.

The second generation involves the computerization of the library system, which results in transforming the manual card system into an electronic one. In this case, collections and resources are indexed and searched via special purpose software, and other services, such as loan and reservation, are also computerized. Firstly, each library developed an individual system which could be accessed locally. The Online Public Access Catalogues software, commonly known as OPAC, was widely adopted as the library system. Although it is still used in libraries, OPAC demonstrates several limitations, such as poor user interface, and it often provides a centralized solution implemented on expensive mainframes. Apart from these features, OPAC provides information about user borrowing details; searches based on different attributes such as title, author, subject, ISBN, and classmark; a boolean search including stop-lists (words that should not appear in the search); searches based on the type of resource, such as book or periodical; and browsing, based on attributes mentioned previously.

Another major problem that was not encompassed by OPAC was the ability to interconnect and interoperate across a network of library cata-

logue servers. With the advent and acceptability of the Internet as the infrastructure upon which interconnectivity and interoperability can be built, it was then realized how important and feasible it was to provide interlibrary communication. A user could, therefore, pose a query that could traverse and retrieve information from different library catalogues which are distributed across different locations. The adoption of standards which enabled interoperability between libraries distributed geographically was required. In order to fulfill that requirement, the ANSI/ISO Z39.50 (1995) standard was adopted. This standard defines an application protocol which enables access to heterogeneous and distributed resources using a unique interface. Z39.50 is based on client-server architecture which functions as a seamless gateway to remote database systems. The Z39.50 facilities include connection, searching, retrieving, manipulation of error messages, and access to information about content, such as, for example, a schema in a database.

The main advance in the third generation is the fact that library information systems now provide not only index and search services, but also retrieval, as resources move from a hard copy paper-based format to a mainly digital one. Such as traditional libraries, digital libraries are a combination of available resources, coupled with services which provide access to them. Although most of the resources are in digital form, and can therefore be retrieved from a client machine, there are those which may be available only in hard-copy. In such cases, searching services are provided, enabling end-users to discover which resources are available and where they can be located. For digital documents, the indexing service can be completely automatic, which is not the case for hard-copy ones.

Some researchers argue that digital libraries will deal with both digital and traditional resources for many years to come. Digital libraries involve actors, who interact with the system, and components, which execute the different services provided. These actors can be categorized according to the role they play in the system; they include data-providers, data-consumers, and librarians (or data managers). Data-providers are responsible for creation and collection of the data set in a way that makes it interesting for the class of users. This is accomplished by providing a rich semantic description of the data sets, usually using metadata. Data-consumers are the digital library end-users who utilize its services in order to discover a particular data set that meets their requirements in a particular application domain. Finally, librarians are responsible for the administration of the digital library services and resources. Their role includes organizing the classification of the collections, inclusion of new documents, defining the policies and rules of utilization, maintaining a catalogue of users and data-providers, and deciding with which other digital library they would like to intercommunicate.

The fourth generation introduces the retrieval of resources of different media such as video, audio, maps, images, and text documents. Previously, searching and indexing procedures were restricted to alphanumeric data types. In the context of textual resources, this is acceptable and efficient, but is not true for multimedia data types, where interpretation of their content is required for effective indexing and searching. Furthermore, documents with spatial and temporal information require tailored searching, browsing and indexing mechanisms. This generation is still evolving; while it is feasible to think in terms of a general digital library that may deal with all the complexities of those different data types, it is likely that specific type-dependent data repositories—such as video, image, geo-referenced, and textual digital libraries—will emerge. It is imperative that these libraries interoperate so that queries across different digital libraries supporting different data types can be accomplished.

Important Issues on Digital Libraries

The main innovation in the field of digital libraries is evident in the fact that most of resources are in electronic format. In this format, there is no need for physical resources linked to loan, access, and reservation. Resources are ideally held in a distributed database which should be accessed over the Internet. The user, instead of taking a hard copy of the document in the library, downloads a new copy. The quality of the data can become more difficult to assess if the Internet is used not only as a client access to the library but also as a repository of information. Following some researchers' definitions of the term digital library, which advocate that the Internet can be viewed as a huge digital library, the problem of data quality erupts (Arms, 2001). As a consequence of this, there should be concerns about data accuracy, originator, and integrity, once they are not easily measured (as they are in traditional libraries). There are difficulties in determining how to charge for the library services, and especially, how to guarantee copyrights on the data which are downloaded by users. Moreover, security is a great issue with the increasing influx of new viruses and hacker attacks. This issue will be addressed later in this chapter. Social and psychological aspects must be taken into consideration in the move to a digital format, given that everything is now accessible via a computer system, and less human interaction is therefore required. This can result in difficulties on making effective use of the library, as usability issues must be thoroughly addressed. Further, multilanguage interfaces and facilities, such as thesauri and translators, should also be provided. One the other hand, a reservation service becomes useless, since indefinite soft copies are allowed from a document.

Security is a major problem in digital libraries, particularly with reference to unauthorized use of library resources. The usual security approach that has been adopted is to establish an access control to the library resources. Under this arrangement, data consumers should have a registration record with their contact information, and should be given a login name for authorization and a password for authentication. A security log recording all access made should exist in order to enable effective auditing. Ethical policies should be explained to all users in order to make sure they use the library appropriately.

Copyright is another important issue in digital libraries, as governments have not yet agreed a method by which to effectively establish copyright laws for digital data (Onsrud & Lopez, 1998). The problem of copyright legislation is more evident now that data can be downloaded, and each country may have its own specific legislation. Guaranteeing that the user will not alter data and resell them is a high priority. Spatial data is usually very expensive to capture and generate, so it is highly important that intellectual property rights be imposed and obeyed. Moreover, users are usually interested in a specific part of the spatial data set. Copyright is related to the use, replication and update of data and usually lasts for a certain period of time. Aslesen (1998) has classified the former as usage rights, and the latter two as marketing rights (which include selling and distribution processes).

MULTIMEDIA METADATA

Metadata have been defined in the computing literature as data about data, information needed to make data useful, or information that describes the content, quality, condition, along with other characteristics of data (Sheth & Klas, 1998). Metadata aid the search, semantic interpretation, and retrieval of data. The metadata concept is not new, and has been used in several applications, in a transparent way, for many years.

However, the wide dissemination of information on the Internet, and the large data sets available demand that metadata play a crucial role by allowing more accurate searches, data

quality and interoperability of these huge data sets. Sometimes it is very difficult to draw a line between data and metadata representing a clear boundary. For instance, one can ask whether a thumbnail of an image would be considered data or metadata. The same applies to an abstract of a document, a video or audio clip. One solution may be to consider metadata as data themselves, integrating metadata into the data model. This approach provides transparency and simplicity to the way in which metadata are handled (Bohm & Rakow, 1994).

Textual metadata for multimedia documents have been investigated for many years and, as a result, some standards like SGML and Dublin Core have been proposed. Bohm presents a classification of metadata for multimedia resources in which SGML is emphasized (Bohm & Rakow, 1994). Some examples of multimedia metadata are:

- **Audio:** Number of samples per second, number of channels, audio class, the coding in which it has been recorded, and a speaker identification;
- **Video:** Duration time, number of frames per second, compression technique, color, texture, lighting, video class, and keyframes;
- **Image:** Resolution (dpi), format, compression technique, colour histogram, image brightness, and object name, location, and composition;
- **Text:** Indices on word tokens, author name, date, publication, keywords, and publisher.

Dublin Core is a proposal of a metadata element set used for the discovery and cataloguing of resources stored on the Web. The Dublin Core metadata set was initially proposed in a Metadata Workshop in 1995 (Weibel, Godby, Miller, & Daniel, 1995). Dublin Core was designed to be extensible (it permits the addition of new metadata elements); interoperable (it can be used by several resource discovery tools); and simple to use (it could be used by novice authors without much background in structuring documents for library cataloguing). The Dublin Core element set has fifteen elements: title, creator, subject, description, publisher, contributor, date, type, format, identifier, source, language, relation, coverage, and rights. Furthermore, Dublin Core is syntax independent, which means that it can be encoded in languages such as HTML and XML. Also, all elements are repeatable, modifiable and optional. The elements can be refined using qualifiers.

QUERYING DIGITAL LIBRARIES USING CONTENT-BASED RETRIEVAL

A classic manner of querying a digital library is by object attributes. For example, a user may discover the book authors by accessing the author attribute of a table Books. Exact match is used for retrieving objects which satisfy the query constraints. Nonetheless, this paradigm is not applicable to multimedia data and a new one has been developed for querying multimedia database. This new paradigm is known as content-based retrieval (Chu & Taira, 1997; Gupta & Jain, 1997; Hsu, Smolier, & Zhang, 1994). While in content-based retrieval, the query is textual, some isolated efforts has been done to stay the query itself in the media to be retrieved. For instance, a system for music retrieval by humming has been developed by Ghias, Loghan, Chamberlin, & Smith (1995).

In content-based retrieval, users may place a query for something that is similar to the information provided. Basically, the user submits a query to the database by object content. This concept is in fact not new; it is derived from domain-oriented relational calculus (Garcia-Molina, Ullman, & Widom, 2001). One of the best known implementations of this calculus is the query language QBE (Query by Example) proposed by IBM (Zloof, 1977). The novelty in the content-based retrieval concept is that the queries are submitted to a multimedia database, so it not only compares strings but also tries to discover the degrees of similarity among images, sounds and videos. Therefore, the system must provide a large collection of image, video and audio processing tools such as analysis, classification, and pattern recognition of these data types.

The concept of similarity is fundamental in content-based retrieval. In conventional database systems, data are stored and retrieved by keywords or numbers, which enables the system to manipulate data efficiently. Usually, when a query is submitted to the system, an exact match response appears as a result, as, for example, with the query "retrieve all employees whose salaries are 1,500.00 pounds."

Concerning image databases, the exact match is substituted by the similar match. For instance, in a facial database in a police station, the policeman could ask the database for pictures similar to a suspect's picture. In this case, if there is more than one picture that approximates that of the suspect, the system creates an ordered list. In this ordered list, a rank is used to express to what extent each picture in the database is similar to the suspect's picture. Usually, query by content is done within the following features:

Color: The user asks for images similar to a particular one, concerning the color distribution. The system uses a color histogram to match the images that satisfy the user's query. The user can provide more details such as the foreground and background colors, as, for example, with the query *"retrieve the images that have green in foreground and blue in the background."* Some special words such as "mostly," "some," can be used to give more semantics to the users query, as, for example, with the query *"retrieve images that are mostly pink"* or *"show me the images that have some yellow."*

Texture: Using mathematical representation, images can be classified according to scale of texture. An example of query using texture is *"retrieve images that have a texture similar to this sample."*

Shape: Information about area, circularity, can be used to retrieve objects by their shapes, as, for example, with the query *"retrieve images that have circle inside square shapes."*

Sound: Using algorithms for audio recognition, the system reads samples provided by the user and looks for similar samples sequence in an audio database. For example, *"retrieve all songs that have a similar tune to this one."*

Spatial: Using spatial operators like right-of, left-of, in-front-of, behind, beside, inside, and far-from, the system can run spatial queries such as *"retrieve images that have a house with the neighbor on the right being a hospital."*

Temporal: Using temporal topological operators, queries such as *"retrieve video that shows this image after that one"* are possible.

Video: In this case, the system must provide algorithms for indexing and retrieval of video segments. The user can ask about a given scene in a movie, or about some objects that are contained in a movie, by using a high level language. For example, as with the query *"retrieve clips that contain a flying bird."*

Text: Using text pattern recognition algorithms and image similarity retrieval, the system is able to match some text with a sample. For instance, in a text database, users would like to know all books that mention a given quotation. Another example is a bank system that implements automatic signature recognition.

Several content-based retrieval products have been proposed so far including IBM QBIC

(Flickner, Sawhney, Ashley, Huang, Dom, Gorkani, et al., 1995), VIRAGE (Bach, Fuller, Gupta, Hampapur, Horowitz, Humphrey, et al., 1999), Excalibur (Informix, 1998), Blobworld (Carson, Thomas, Belongie, Hellerstein, & Malik, 1996), and Visualseek (Smith & Chang, 1996).

A MULTIMEDIA DIGITAL LIBRARY PROTOTYPE

We have developed a multimedia digital library prototype, called Freebie (Jamesson, Baptista, Schiel, Silva, Menezes, & Fernandes, 2006), an opensource multimedia digital library, which copes with image, video, audio, and text. Freebie was designed in a four-tier architecture, using the Model-View-Controller design pattern. These tiers are described in the following. The Viewer tier is responsible for the user interface. It was developed using HTML, JSP, JavaScript and Struts technologies. It is composed of the following pages: data insertion, data maintainance, searching, metadata result presentation, document details, and error page.

The Controller tier is responsible for receiving the requests from the users, through the viewer, and transforming them into actions which will call the Freebie functions in the Model tier. These functions, which compose the Freebie business logic, are: object inclusion; metadata exhibition; metadata update; object deletion; and object searching.

The persistence tier is implemented in the Postgresql object-relational database system. The communication between the Java classes and the data stored in the database server is done via the JDBC protocol.

When a multimedia object is entered into the system, depending on its type, metadata are extracted automatically and inserted in the database using the Dublin Core metadata set.

For text documents, we are using the Jakarta POI Java API for dealing with files in the Microsoft

OLE2. We are also extracting text from PDF files using the PDFBox Java API. Text indexing is done using Tsearch V2–Full Text Search, which is an Postgresql package which enables to parse a text, extract the stopwords and index the remaining text using GiST-Generalized Index Search Trees and store these terms in the database server. After that, user may query the indexed document using any word of the text besides the traditional query on metadata.

Concerning images, Freebie extracts metadata from JPEG images, through EXIF (Exchangeable Image File Format), which is a format used by many digital cameras. Also, when an image in any format is inserted into the digital library, a thumbnail of it is automatically generated and stored as a metadata for that image, so that in the metadata result set, users may visualize this thumbnail before downloading the full image. EXIF may contain data about camera manufacturer and model, date and time, resolution, exposure, flash, geographic coordinates, title, comments (description), authos, copyrights, and so on. Freebie uses the Metadata Extraction Java API to extract EXIF metadata.

Video and audio are stored in a URL and their Dublin Core metadata should be entered manually into the digital library. We are working on the integration of Freebie with VideoLib, so that the query capabilities of the latter may be used in the former (Rego, Baptista, Silva, Schiel, Figueirêdo, 2006).

Users may query the multimedia objects in Freebie by using any of the Dublin Core elements. Moreover, three kinds of spatial coordinates are associated to the documents: concerning the content, the authors and the place of publication. This information can also be used in the query.

Queries on documents are posed in a different page so that users may input the terms they would like to search. After submitting the query, a result set metadata page is displayed as shown in Figure 1. Users may select one of the returned objects to retrieve their full metadata description and their full content.

FUTURE TRENDS AND CONCLUSION

Multimedia digital libraries are definitively in the research agenda of digital libraries. Therefore, there are many issues which could be explored in order to improve the service provided by such libraries. The first issue, is to address multi-modal user interfaces so that users may not only

Figure 1. Freebie result set metadata

effectively query the underlying multimedia documents using an appropriate search tool, but also they might have an appropriate environment for the ingestion process and the management activities.

The second issue is to explore new indexing techniques for audio and video, and to extend the content-based query processing to these media. Furthermore, several multimedia data have spatio-temporal characteristics. These may also be adequately indexed and retrieved .

The third issue is the integration of mobile computing with digital libraries, so that users may access multimedia content from mobile devices from anywhere and anytime. There are many concerns such as device limitation, context awareness, low bandwidth, and so on.

The fourth issue is related to the extension of the well know digital library standards, such as Z39.50 and OAI, to cope with multimedia content.

Lastly, the use of service oriented architecture enhanced with multimedia capabilities is a new trend on distributed multimedia digital libraries.

REFERENCES

ANSI/NISO Z39.50. (1995). *Information retrieval (Z39.50): Application service definition and protocol specification.* Technical report, Z39.50 Maintenance Agency.

Arms, W. (2001). *Digital libraries* (2nd ed.). MIT Press.

Aslesen, L. (1998). Intellectual property and mapping: A European perspective. In P. Burrough, & I. Masser (Eds.), *European Geographic Infrastructures: Opportunities and Pitfalls, GISDATA 5* (pp. 127–135). Taylor & Francis.

Bach, J., Fuller, C., Gupta, A., Hampapur, A., Horowitz, B., Humphrey, R., et al. (1996). The vi-rage image search engine: An open framework for image management. *SPIE Storage and Retrieval for Image and Video Databases.*

Baldonado, Chang, M. Gravano, C.L., & Paepcke, A. (1997). The Stanford digital library metadata architecture. *International Journal of Digital Libraries, 1,* 108–121.

Bohm, K., & Rakow, T. (1994). Metadata for multimedia documents. *ACM SIGMOD Record, 23*(4), 21–26.

Carson, C., Thomas, M., Belongie, S., Hellerstein, J.M., & Malik, J. (1999). Blobworld: A system for region-based image indexing and retrieval. In *Third International Conference on Visual Information Systems.* SpringerVerlag.

Flickner, M., Sawhney, H., Ashley, J., Huang, Q., Dom, B., Gorkani, M., et al. (1995). Query by image and video content: the QBIC system. *IEEE Computer, 28*(9), 23–32.

Garcia-Molina, H., Ullman, J.D., & Widom, J.D. (2001). *Database systems: The complete book* (1st ed.). Prentice Hall.

Ghias, A., Loghan, J., Chamberlin, D., & Smith, B. (1995). Query by humming—musical information retrieval in an audio database. *Proceedings of the third ACM International Conference on Multimedia* (pp. 231--236), San Francisco, CA

Gupta, A., & Jain, R. (1997). Visual information retrieval. *Communications of the ACM, 40*(5), 71–79.

Hsu, C-C., Chu, W., & Taira, R.A. (1996). Knowledge-based approach for retrieving images by content. *IEEE Transactions on Knowledge and Data Engineering, 8*(6), 522–532.

Informix Inc. (1998). *Informix answers online* (Version 1.91). CD-ROM.

Jain, R., & Hampapur, A. (1994). Metadata in video databases. *ACM SIGMOD Record, 23*(4) 27–33.

Jamesson, W., Baptista, C.S., Schiel, U., Silva, E.R., Menezes, L.C., & Fernandes, R.M. (2006). Freebie: Uma biblioteca digital baseada em software livre com suporte a buscas textual e espacial. In *Proceedings of the 12th Brazilian Symposium on Multimedia and the Web WebMedia* (pp. 155–164).

Onsrud, H., & Lopez, X. (1998). Intellectual property rights in disseminating digital geographic data, products and services: Conflicts and commonalities among EU and U.S. approaches. In P. Burrough, & I. Masser (Eds.), *European Geographic Infrastructures: Opportunities and Pitfalls, GISDATA 5* (pp. 127–135). Taylor & Francis.

Rego, A.S., Baptista, *C.S.*, Silva, E.R., Schiel, U., Figueirêdo, H.F. (2007). VideoLib: A video digital library with support to spatial and temporal dimensions. In *Proceedings of the 22nd Annual ACM Symposium on Applied Computing* (pp. 1074-1078). Seoul, Korea.

Sheth, A., & Klas, W. (Editors). (1998). *Multimedia data management—using metadata to integrate and apply digital media.* McGraw-Hill.

Smith, J., & Chang, S. (1996). VisualSEEk: A fully automated content-based image query system. In *Proceedings of the Fourth ACM Multimedia Conference (MULTIMEDIA'96)* (pp. 87–98). New York: ACM Press.

Smolier, S., & Zhang, H. (1994). Content-based indexing and retrieval. *IEEE Multimedia, 1*(2), 62–72.

Weibel, S., Godby, J., Miller, E., & Daniel, R. (1995). *OCLC/NCSA metadata workshop report.* Technical report, Office of Research, OCLC Online Computer Library Center, Inc.

Zloof, M. (1977). Query-by-example: A database language. *IBM Systems Journal, 16*(4), 324–343.

KEY TERMS

Content-Based Extraction: Process of extracting information from nontext multimedia data.

Document Indexing: The process of extracting the information contained in a document, creating an index. While the index is always a set of terms, the source document may be in form of text or other media, as video, images, sound.

Digital Library: An environment for retrieval of digital documents. In contrast to a conventional library, documents if interest are not taken away from the library, but can be downloaded or prompted at the host of the user.

Information Retrieval: The process of finding information in a set of documents by use of a computer.

Multimedia Data: Sources in form of text, video, image, maps, or sound.

Multimedia Document: A document which contains more than one media. Whereas, in hardcopy documents only text, image and maps can be combined, electronic documents can contain any combination of multimedia data.

Chapter XXXVIII
BIVALDI the Digital Library of the Valencian Bibliographic Inheritance

Nuria Lloret Romero
Polytechnic University of Valencia, Spain

Margarita Cabrera Méndez
Polytechnic University of Valencia, Spain

Alicia Sellés Carot
Masmedios Ltd., Spain

Lilia Fernandez Aquino
Masmedios Ltd., Spain

ABSTRACT

The Biblioteca Valenciana was created by the decree 5/1985 of the 8th of January and is presented primarily as "upper library centre of the Generalitat Valenciana and basic bibliographic deposit" which depends on the Conselleria for Culture, Education, and Sport. For this reason, it is the head of the library system of the Comunidad Valenciana, Conselleria, and as such, it has established objectives in the eighth article of the Law 10/1986 of 30th of December of Organización Bibliotecaria de la Comunidad Valenciana between which are emphasised "to meet, to conserve and divulge the Valencian bibliographic inheritance and all the printed, sound and visual production, about the Comunidad Valenciana." It is also made up as "receiver of one of the examples proceeding from the offices of the Depósito Legal "and it is attributed the obligation of fulfilling the collective catalogue of the Valencian bibliographic and cultural inheritance. Furthermore, the Valancian library must insert itself into the denominated National Libraries, and for this reason, in the Comunidad Valenciana, it is in charge of uniting history, tradition, and in the future of the obtaining of political libraries, because it is defined as "central expert of the carefully worked political library in the Valencian library system" and, for this reason, must be in charge of "elaborating and divulging the bibliographic information about the Valencian editorial production and of maintaining the cooperation with the library services of different scopes." In fulfilment of its responsibilities and with the intention of obtaining the maximum spread of the bibliographic and cultural inheritance, the Biblioteca Valenciana, in the setting of its Digitization policy, has dedicated and dedicates many resources in four lines or different solutions. In the first place, it coedits with different publishers, monographs, or titles of magazines which permit the recuperation and spreading of the Valencian inheritance. Some examples are Ruedo Ibérico, L'Espill, or La República de les Lletres. In the second place, it digitalizes different resources which can be consulted from the catalogue. This solution is especially oriented to the preservation and conservation of the collections, and enables the users to be able to see from their computers the supplies to which the descriptions belong, and can decide if they are useful or not for their consultation, instead of indiscriminately asking for them, thus reducing the moving and manipulation of the original copies. The library is also working on the digitalization of material, especially all personal files, which do not belong to them, but which are of great importance. Finally, the Biblioteca Valenciana has begun the Biblioteca Valenciana Digital, (BIVALDI), which is the object of the present project, and which we are going to describe in detail in the following sections.

BIVALDI: Biblioteca Valenciana Digital

In the month of May in 2002, the Biblioteca Valenciana starts a project of digitalization denominated Biblioteca Valenciana Digital (BIVALDI). It refers to a digital library in which it is able to consult relevant and significant Valencian scientific and literary works, apart from works which are considered to be of interest for the development and improvement of scientific investigation about the historic, bibliographic, and cultural inheritance.

This deals with an ambitious project which is not created as a repository of any determined theme or as a reflection of the resources which are taken care of in the Biblioteca Valenciana. The Biblioteca Valenciana Digital intends to recuperate the Valencian bibliographic inheritance, which means it intends to be the meeting place of works that form part of said inheritance irrespective of its location. For this reason, we find in BIVALDI works which are not property of the Biblioteca Valenciana and which cannot be acquired, or because they are unique examples or because they are not on the market. But this is not the only objective of BIVALDI; it is also created for the necessity to offer more information, which means it is intended to incorporate, together with the work, informative elements of added value about the authors, the works, the printers, and so on.

All investigators and the general public who consult BIVALDI will be able to enjoy the works thanks to an easily manageable informatics platform which permits simple surfing. One of the outstanding attractions of this library platform is that the user can surf, not only in an individual way through the original digitalized text or through its transcription and/or translation when they are necessary, but also in a simultaneous way on the same screen, with the original work together with its transcription and translation. Also the user, as has already been mentioned, counts on wide information about the author and his work. This deals with bibliographies and specialised studies about the works, the printers, biographies of the writers, and so on.

Logically, to be able to begin this project, the Biblioteca Valenciana needs the collaboration with other institutions for the obtaining and later digitalization, or for obtaining the digital reproduction.

Between others, the University of Valencia has provided the digitalization of the incunables of *Les obres o trobes en laors de la Verge Maria*—which is the first literary work printed in Spain in the year 1474; from *Tirant lo Blanch* by Joanot Martorell; from *Regiment de la cosa pública*—work of Francesc Eisimenis; *de l'Omelia sobre lo psalm "De profundis"* by Jeroni Fuster; from *l'Omelia sobre lo psalm "Miserere mei Deus"* by Narcís Vinoles; from *Lo somni* by Joan Joan; from *Lo procés de les olives;* and from the incunable of 1493 which contains the *Historia de la Pació* by Bemat Fenollar and Pere Martínez, *la Contemplació a Jesús Crucificat* by Joan Escrivá and Bemat Fenollar and *l'Oració a la Sacratíssima Verge Maria* by Joan Rois de Corella, the last of the great Valencian medieval writers. Because of this, the Valencian City Council has authorised the digitalization of two incunables. On one hand, the translation of *Imitació de Jesucris*—better known as the Kempis—related under the name of *Menyspreu del món* by Miguel Pérez, a Barcelona edition which is the oldest translation of printed work in the world in the Romance language; on the other hand, the translation of *Les Meditationes vitae Christi* by Ludolf de Saxonia, a version of the "Cartoxá," requested to the Valencian authorities by King Fernando el Católico from Castille.

On the other hand, the Hispanic Society has provided the digital reproduction of the two unique pages of the *Biblia valenciana*, printed in 1478 and attributed to Bonifacio Ferrer. Also included in BIVALDI is the digitization of the copy of *Tirant lo Blanch* kept in the American Institute, which has permitted the changing of the pages in bad condition or lost of the first edition of "Tirant," the first novel of the Valencian literature kept, as we have aforementioned in the University of Valencia.

L'Abadia de Montserrat has given permission for the digitalization of the copy of *Antidotarium clarificatum*, by Nicolau Spíndeler and printed in 1495, and of the work of the Valencian Amau de Vilanova, doctor to popes and kings, which is kept in the Catalan Institute.

Also, BIVALDI has been able to count on the collaboration of the Biblioteca Nacional de España, which has given permission for the digitalization of the *Obra a llaors de Sent Cristófol* and *Vita Christi* by sor Isabel de Villena—a work by one of the most important writers of the medieval Europe—an incomplete copy of which is kept in the Biblioteca Valenciana.

Collections

We can talk about two large phases in the development and implantation of the BIVALDI Project. In its first phase, BIVALDI was thought of and began to work as a Library of Manuscripts and Incunabulum in which would be included three large collections: Incunabulum manuscripts and the book of the statutory times and important prolific Valencian writers.

In the second phase, and with the intention of widening the access to the works which form part of the Valencian bibliographic and cultural inheritance, not only manuscripts and incunables, changes were carried out in the design and structure of the informatic platform of the Biblioteca Valenciana Digital.

Principal and Functioning Characteristics

To be able to enter to the works, it is necessary to be registered as a user. The registration process entails the user filling in a series of details and information, and will then receive a user's name and password for electronic mail.

Finding the Works

Finding the works can be carried out in two different manners:

Figure 1. First development of BIVALDI

Figure 2. BIVALDI at the present time

- By means of a browser. In BIVALDI, the user counts on two options for searching. On one hand, a general search, introducing key words about the author, title, printer, and so on; and on the other hand, an advanced search in which the search can be marked or defined.
- Surfing in the collections and subcollections (Browsing) which can be accessed from the chosen catalogue page. This means that the user will be able to see available works or works that are going to be available in the near future, surfing in theme libraries, collections, or subcollections which have been previously mentioned.

Record Card of the Work

Once the title or work is chosen, the user is shown the record-card of the work. This is about the bib-

Figure 3. Images of the catalogue and of the available works in one of the subcollections

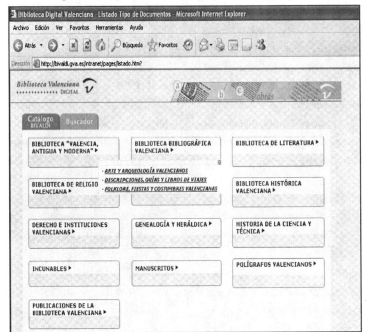

liographic information of the original digitalized work, not of the digital facsimile. The information is formed by the title of the work, the name or names of the author, the details of the physical description of the work, the information of edition (place, date, and publisher or printer), access to a general bibliography, and notes of lesser importance or related to the digital reproduction of the work.

As can be seen in the image, the name of the author is a link which takes us to a pdf with an up to date biography of the author and the name of the printer. When this deals with a printer studied by Serrano Morales in his work *Reseña histórica de las imprentas que han existido en Valencia desde la introducción del arte tipográfico hasta 1868, con noticias bio-biográficas de los principales impresores* (Valencia: Imp. F. Doménech, 1898–1899), another link which opens the text the author dedicates to him in said work to which has been passed an OCR and which is offered in BIVALDI in pdf form.

Bibliography and notes are two other links which also open record cards in pdf form in which can be found, in the first place, a bibliographic selection which refers to the author, his works, and his period, and the notes which have been considered interesting about the process of the digitilazation of the original (for example, mistakes of pagination in the original, XXX).

Furthermore, the user will also find in the record card a connection to the catalographic card of the work in the catalogue of the Biblioteca Valenciana, when the work is to be found there and another to the record card of the Catálogo Colectivo del Patrimonio Bibliográfico Español.

At the bottom of the card, by means of icons, the user is able to accede to the properly said work (original document, transcription, translation, thumbnails or miniatures, and complementary studies)

Surfing and Visualization of the Works

The simple surfing consists in the lineal visualization of the images which form part of the work or of the documents pdf which make up the transcription or translation of the work. From the visualization screen of the document, in the upper part, we find an icon which permits the image to be seen in detail and in which the percentage of zoom can be chosen and applied in the visualization.

It is important to emphasise that the images offered are in form JPEG at a medium resolution. The selection of this form was taking into account two factors:

- **Size of file:** After several tests of optimization of the image, a high-quality visualization of the image was obtained, with a low level of file size.
- **Speed:** The high speed of the discharge of the file is a very important factor in the design of the system; for this, once the size of the file was optimised, the progressive codification of the same was undertaken.

In this way, the user visualises the file in a progressive manner, thus reducing the waiting time.

Also, for reasons of intellectual property, a watermark has been inserted on the images, and a function has been created which impedes the storage of the image. The user will only be able to print the image, not store it.

But the translations, transcriptions, and the studies are offered in pdf form, as it is not dealing with images of the works, but with the texts. These works have been digitalised in black and white for their conversion into text by means of OCR.

The multiple surfing consists in the visualisation of the images of the work and of the equivalents in text form of the transcription and/or translation. As in the simple surfing, we have the possibility of seeing the images in detailed mode.

System Design

For the planning of the system of the project of the Biblioteca Valenciana, the characteristics of

Figure 4. Simple surfing on the original document

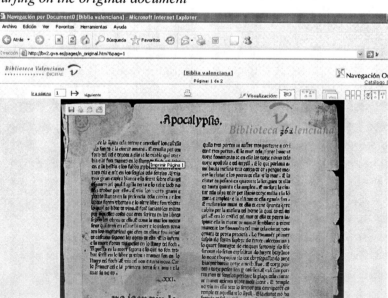

Figure 5. Multiple surfing transcription

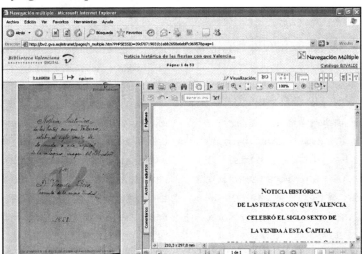

some of the existing digital libraries were reviewed at the moment of the design and, taking into account that it had to contemplate the most positive of the best libraries, adapting it to our necessities and offering added value services, the most important points on which the development was based were:

- Taking into account the possible enlargements and/or changes that could occur in the future design of the system ought to offer a wide and simple structure.
- The access to the digital library from Internet must be clear and well defined, avoiding intermediate pages which confuse the users.
- Access ought to be given from as many points as possible, like this entrance to the documents is permitted from all possible fields: title, author, publisher, and so on, as much in the facsimile edition as in the studies, translations, and transcriptions, if they exist.
- Upon entering the documents, a bibliographic outline or a card with all the facts will be available, as well as a connection to the catalographic card of the example.

- Inside the catalogue of the Biblioteca Valenciana, there will also be a link on the card to be able to accede to the digitalised document. It has been connected with the catalographic content of the Web of the Biblioteca Valenciana (http://bv.gva.es/), trying not to repeat information already existing on the Web.
- Surfing between documents must be as active as possible, allowing the connection between the same page of the document in all its versions (studies, transcriptions, translations).
- An image of the digitalised documents is offered to the user, allowing him to enlarge or reduce as he/she likes. Also offered is the opportunity for the user to be able to make mini-images or thumbnails of all the pages of the works to then be able to accede to the desired page.

Development and Structure of the System

BIVALDI is an "ad hoc" tool for the Biblioteca Valencina, although it is communicated with the opac ABSYS of the library, which was developed under the following parameters:

- Operative System: Windows 2000 Server
- Web Service: Apache 1.3
- Datum Service Base: Sql Server 2000

The previous graph shows the structure and diagram of the flow of the system in which, as can be observed, exist two different parts. On one hand, the public part which takes the user to visualise the record card of the work, and on the other hand, the private part or Intranet, in which is carried out all the maintenance and insertion of facts in the data base which can then be visualised in the public part.

Metadata

A very important question in the development of the system was the recuperation of the information from outside the same tool, which means the capacity of the searchers to find the internal information of the database. Logically, as a consequence of the established structure, in the BIVALDI Web, most of the pages are dynamic and show the information from the database. These dynamic pages count on URL of the type:

http://bv2.gva.es/pages/listado.htm?PHPSESSID =ec4673de6dee9f6b116746de2716d2ee

For this reason, the only information of the digitalized works in the pages which can be visualised are the title of the work in the title of the page htm, but not in the metatags. For example:

```
<html>
<head>
<title>Navegaci&oacute;n por Document0 Ex-
positio in cantica ...</title>
</head>
```

Given the importance of the metadata for the description of the works which BIVALDI contains, the database has some stored procedures and some triggers which generate static pages when the content of the cards of the works is changed, so that they can be indexed by the Web searchers.

The function is the following: in the HOME exists a hidden connection (which the searchers can see but is invisible to the user) which opens a connection to the collection index, which at the same time, is tied with a list of the contained cards. Each connection of each card is an htm page with Meta tags, in which are inserted the fields from the database, author, work, title, and describers. Each card "fictional" redirects the searcher to the page which we denominate card of the work (http://bv2.gva.es/pages/ficha.htm?id=65).

BIIVALDI in the Present: Conclusions

After four years of activity, BIVALDI is a consolidated project which has been constituted as a Digital reference library. This affirmation is supported among other reasons because BIVALDI counts on more than 10,000 users (mostly Spanish, but also from many other provenances), and is mentioned and analysed in a large number of jobs related to digital libraries .

We can affirm that BIVALDI is carrying out the two objectives with which it began. On one hand, the work which BIVALDI is doing in the matter of divulging the inheritance of the Valencian culture. The Biblioteca Valenciana Digital, has taken part as a cultural institution in the digital publication of works related to the different cultural and historical events like the Viciana year, declared by the Cortes Valencianas in commemoration of the fifth century of the birth of the reporter and historian Rafael Martí de Viciana, the first century of the birth of the Valencian writer Lluís Guarner, the commemoration of the seventieth anniversary of

"Les Normes de Castelló o Normes del 32" or the fourth century of Quijote. At the same time, it is still a digital library with an element of added value and information, which makes it different from the rest of digital libraries.

But it is also certain that technologies have evolved, the users have become much more demanding in the matter, and BIVALDI, despite being prepared for the evolution, has not managed it. At the present, if we surf in the different digital libraries, Spanish or not, we can find solutions or functions which BIVALDI lacks—for example, forms of works different to the images or texts, or the participation of the users with opinions, assessments, and so on.

The object of this is not to make an exhaustive analysis of potential or new paths for BIVALDI, but we would like to emphasise certain aspects or questions which we consider relevant.

In the first place, one of the principle questions to comment on is the updating of the contents and the increase of the works. The majority of similar projects have grown much faster in regards to the quantity of available works. The fact that BIVALDI has not grown as much as digital libraries which were opened at about the same time can be justified, as we have been able to see during the making of the study, by the availability of the works and the necessity to collaborate with other institutions to be able to increase the collections, but also for the work of digitalisation and process of treating and preparing the works, such as the maintenance of the database. We must remember that the Biblioteca Valenciana is a young institution which must dedicate extra efforts to the technical treatment of the resources in custody to be able to comply with its other functions, such as diffusion.

Another question which we consider very important is the necessity for the registration of the users, for two reasons. In the first place, the process of registration is inconvenient to the users and provokes situations such as not registering. They do not remember their password, and

because of a mistake in the datum, they do not receive the mail that gives them their code. In the second place, and for questions of visibility and recuperation of the works, it is impossible to accede directly to a work if you are not identified as a user. The elimination of this process favours the usage and the appeal of the tool, and it would suppose too many conflicts in the matter of the protection of the rights of intellectual properties because, as we have already seen, in BIVALDI, other mechanisms exist for the protection of the texts, like the watermarks and the impossibility of storing the images.

Related to the above question is the visibility by the searchers of the contents of the database and the mechanisms of insertion of metadata in the record cards of the works. The solution which was chosen is not the most efficient and does not give the required results. Other possibilities exist such as *mod rewrite*, which would allow not only the insertion of metadata (Dublin core) in the dynamic pages, but also the change of the URL in which could be included the code words of the work which would logically increase its visibility in the searchers.

The relation with the OPAC of the Biblioteca Valenciana is also another interesting question. We believe that the bonds between the two platforms ought to be strengthened in such a way that the relation between the two portals is increased. It is true that BIVALDI does not intend to be the reflection of the Library catalogue, but as a project of the Valencian library mechanisms of uniting both further, then the linking of its initial page and the URL of the card in the registration of the work ought to begin. This is not evident until the complete register is visible.

The last point we would like to emphasise is a question of accessibility. In the present, the accessibility is a key question for any Web service. It is true that at the moment of introduction, the accessibility was not an aspect to take into account in almost any Web project, but it would be interesting to establish the possibility of adapting little by little all the resources and elements of BIVALDI to all members of the public.

REFERENCES

Alía Miranda, F. (coord.). (2004). *Del texto al hipertexto, las bibliotecas Universitarias ante el reto de la digitalización.* Cuenca: Ediciones de la Universidad de Castilla la Mancha.

Alvite Díez, M.L., & Rodríguez Bravo, B. (2006). *Colecciones de libros electrónicos en las bibliotecas universitarias españolas.* In *Actas de las VIII Jornadas de Gestión de la Información* (pp. 147–159). Madrid.

Bas Martín, N. (2004). *La Biblioteca Valenciana, una biblioteca nacional valenciana. BiD: Textos universitaris de biblioteconomia i documentació,* ISSN 1575–5886, N°. 13.

Chiner Gimeno, J.J. (2003). *Vells llibres i noves tecnologies al volant dels lletraferits valencians: la Biblioteca Valenciana Digital (BIVALDI). Llengua i literatura: Revista anual de la Societat Catalana de Llengua i literatura,* ISSN 0213–6554, N°. 14, 563–572.

Ferrer Sapena, A., et al. (2005). Guía metodológica para la implantación de una biblioteca digital universitaria. Gijón: Trea.

García Gómez, F.J. (2004). *La formación de usuarios en la biblioteca Anales de Documentación,* 7. pp. 97–122. pública virtual. *Recursos y procedimientos en las bibliotecas públicas españolas.*

Herrera Morillas, J.L. (2001). *El fondo antiguo de las bibliotecas universitarias de Andalucía, Extremadura y Murcia: colecciones, textos normativos y recursos virtuales.* Boletín de la Asociación Andaluza de Bibliotecarios, *64*, 53–73.

Herrera Morillas, J.L. (2004). *Tratamiento y difusión digital del libro antiguo: directrices metodológicas y guías de recursos.* Gijón: Trea.

Lloret Romero, N., & Cabrera Méndez, M. (2001a). *Análisis del sistema para el desarrollo de la Biblioteca Valenciana Digital de Incunables.* II Jornadas de Bibliotecas Digitales, Almagro. Retrieved August 23, 2008, from http://imhotep.unizar.es/jbidi/jbidi2001/25_2001.pdf

Lloret Romero, N., & Cabrera Méndez, M. (2001b). *Análisis del sistema para el desarrollo de la Biblioteca Valenciana Digital de Incunables".* II Jornadas de Bibliotecas Digitales, Almagro. Retrieved August 23, 2008, from http://imhotep.unizar.es/jbidi/jbidi2001/25_2001.pdf

Llueca Fonollosa, C. (2005). *Webs sempre accessibles: les biblioteques nacionals i els dipòsits digitals nacionals = Webs siempre accesibles: las bibliotecas nacionales y los depósitos digitales nacionales.* BiD: textos universitaris de biblioteconomia i documentació, 15. Retrieved August 23, 2008, from http://eprints.rclis.org/archive/00005456/02/15lluec2.pdf

Méndez Rodríguez, E.M. (2002). *Metadatos y recuperación de información: estándares, problemas y aplicabilidad en bibliotecas digitales.* Gijón: Trea.

Ocón Pérez de Obanos, Á., & Gómez Martín, M. (2004). *Hacia una biblioteca digital del fondo antiguo de la Universidad de Granada. El proyecto Ilíberis. Boletín de la Asociación Andaluza de Bibliotecarios,* n ° 77, pp. 49–60. Retrieved August 23, 2008, from http://www.aab.es/pdfs/baab77/77a2.pdf

Peset Mancebo, F. (2003). *Bibliotecas digitales en Internet de libro raro, antiguo e incunables.* Anales de Documentación, 6, pp. 241–260.

Saorín Pérez, T. (2004). *Los portales bibliotecarios.* Madrid: Arco libros.

Seguí i Francés, R. (2005). *La biblioteca Valenciana: un breu balanç.* In: *Jornadas sobre Bibliotecas Nacionales (València). Las bibliotecas nacionales del siglo XXI.* Valencia Biblioteca Valenciana.

CONSULTED PROJECTS

General File of the Indias, http://www.mcu.es/archivos/jsp/plantillaAncho.jsp?id=61

Dioscórides (Complutense University), http://www.ucm.es/BUCM/diosc/00.htm

Gabriel, (National Libraries of Europe), http://portico.bl.uk./gabriel/treasures/entree.html

Gallica, (National French Library), http://gallica.bnf.fr/

Miguel de Cervantes Virtual Library, http://www.cervantesvirtual.com

Nacional Library of Spain, http://www.bne.es/esp/bidigital.htm

National Digital Library (Biblioteca del Congreso de Estados), http://www.memory.loc.gov/ammem/dli2/html/lcndlp.html

National Digital Library (Biblioteca del Congreso de Estados), http://www.memory.loc.gov/ammem/dli2/html/lcndlp.html

Sancho el Sabio Foundation Library, http://www.fsancho-sabio.es/

Universales Library, http://www.culture.gouv.fr/culture/bibliuni/engbu1.htm

Vatican Apostolic Library, http://bav.vatican.va/it/v_home_bav/home_bav.shtm

KEY TERMS

Biblioteca Valenciana: Valencian bibliographic collections library.

BIVALDI: Valencian digital inheritance library collection.

Digitization: Digitization means acquiring, converting, storing, and providing information in a computer format that is standardized, organized, and available on demand from common system. With specialized scanners, manuscripts are converted into compressed digital signals and stored systematically for future reference.

Incunabulum: A book single sheet, or image that was printed, before the year 1501 in Europe.

Manuscripts: The word *manuscript* is derived from the Latin *manu scriptus*, literally "written by hand."

Chapter XXXIX
Digital Libraries as a Foundation of Spatial Data Infrastructures

Rubén Béjar
University of Zaragoza, Spain

J. Nogueras-Iso
University of Zaragoza, Spain

Miguel Ángel Latre
University of Zaragoza, Spain

Pedro Rafael Muro-Medrano
University of Zaragoza, Spain

F. J. Zarazaga-Soria
University of Zaragoza, Spain

ABSTRACT

This chapter introduces Spatial Data Infrastructures (SDI) and establishes their strong conceptual and technical relationships with geographic digital libraries (geolibraries). The authors describe the origin of SDIs and highlight their role as geographic resources providers. Then, they give several examples of the use of techniques and tools taken from the digital libraries world in the development of SDIs. The purpose of this chapter is establishing a solid foundation for those aspects of SDIs that can make profit from the knowledge and tools provided by the digital library community. It will also point the key differences between SDIs and geolibraries in order to provide a broader view of these infrastructures.

INTRODUCTION

According to the Global Spatial Data Infrastructure (GSDI) Association (http://www.gsdi.org), "The term 'Spatial Data Infrastructure' (SDI) is often used to denote the relevant base collection of technologies, policies, and institutional arrangements that facilitate the availability of and access to spatial data." These data are those related to positions on the Earth's surface, and are the central component of any Geographic Information System (GIS). GISs, as defined by the United Kingdom Association for Geographic Information (AGI) (http://www.agi.org.uk), allow to capture, store, check, integrate, manipulate, analyse, and display spatial data.

On the one hand, the fact that most data, including spatial data, is nowadays digital, and the growth of the telecommunication networks, specially the Internet, and the existence of GIS have provided the technical foundations to develop this kind of infrastructures. On the other hand, this dependency on digital data and networks, the emphasis on discovery, evaluation and access to data, and the fact that metadata and catalogs are needed, show that a conceptual foundation on the field of digital libraries (DL) is required.

In the next sections, the evolution and current state of SDIs is described, emphasizing the fact that DLs provide several of the conceptual pillars that support them. As SDIs also include components that go beyond those in the field of DLs, they are presented and discussed before the conclusions.

BACKGROUND

The concept of National Spatial Data Infrastructure (NSDI) was first defined, for the United States, by the Mapping Science Committee of the National Research Council (1993). In April 1994, Bill Clinton signed an Executive Order (nr. 12906, April 11, 1994) for the establishment of the NSDI, forcing the cooperation among federal and local agencies in collecting, spreading, and using geographic information.

In 1996, the GSDI was created to promote global access to geographic information. Also in 1996, the Australian and New Zealand Information Council (ANZLIC) (http://www.anzlic.org.au) defined the Australian Spatial Data Infrastructure (ASDI). In 1999, the Government of Canada sponsored a national partnership initiative, Geo-Connections, to improve access to geospatial information and to accelerate the development of a Canadian Geospatial Data Infrastructure (CGDI) (http://cgdi.gc.ca).

In November 2001, the European Commission launched INSPIRE (INfrastructure for SPatial InfoRmation in Europe) (http://inspire.jrc.it), an initiative to create a European directive to guide national and regional SDI development. The directive entered into force on May 15th, 2007 (European Parliament and The European Council, 2007).

Nowadays, the GSDI Web site lists several dozens of SDI initiatives, local, regional, and national. Generally speaking, most of these initiatives have common views and objectives for SDI, as first defined by the USA NSDI, though of course they are adapted to the different realities (economical, political) of the geographic areas for what they have been established.

In parallel to the birth of the NSDI concept in the USA in 1994, the Alexandria Digital Library (ADL) Project began. This project intended to address some of the problems detected in map libraries. ADL project created the term geolibrary, defining it as "[…] a library containing georeferenced objects and with a search mechanism based on geographic location as the primary search key" (Goodchild, 2004, pp. 2–3). In 1998, a panel under the aegis of the USA Mapping Science Committee conducted a workshop on distributed geolibraries, which conclusions were published as a report by a panel on Distributed Geolibraries of the National Research Council (National

Academy Press,1999). This report intended to update the concept of NSDI in the Internet era, with an emphasis on its foundation on distributed geolibraries. This report includes several findings related to NSDI which point that DLs can include any kind of information with an association to a geographic place, besides the maps and images of the Earth covered by the NSDI, and that the NSDI underemphasized the importance of the geoinformation dissemination issues, which could—and should—be sustained by distributed geolibraries concepts and techniques.

GEOLIBRARIES AS A FOUNDATION OF SDIS

As stated in the previous section, over a typical definition of a DL, geolibraries add georeferenced resources and a search mechanism based in geographic location. But these apparently simple, added elements are distinctive enough to give geolibraries several research matters of their own: based on their experience in the ADL project, Janée, Frew, and Hill (2004) identify up to seven mayor issues that arise in geolibraries simply because of the special kind of content they hold: discovery of georeferenced resources, gazetteer integration, specialized ranking of search results, strong data typing and scalability, spatial context for user interfaces and the need for sophisticated geospatial resource access mechanisms.

Even with their own distinctive issues, geolibraries are still DLs, and SDIs share so many important elements with them both, that basing SDI development on the field of geolibraries, and thus on the field of DLs, provides a solid conceptual and technical foundation to build.

If digital libraries hold collections of digital resources then geolibraries must hold collections of digital spatial resources. But as explained before, SDIs were born with the objective to promote the creation, maintenance and *distribution* of geographic information. Taking into considera-

tion the fact that most of this information is now in digital form, it is easy to recognize that one of the first roles for SDIs is very close to being a geolibrary.

Other important characteristic of digital libraries is that their resources are described by means of *metadata*. As geographic information resources have some unique properties (for example, location based in coordinates), there are different standards specifically designed for their metadata. Some of these standards are the evolution of library metadata adapted to the characteristics of geographic resources, like the Z39.50 application profile for geospatial metadata (Nebert, 2000). There are also other geographic metadata standards. One of the most important ones is the Content Standard for Digital Geospatial Metadata (CSDGM) developed for the USA by the Federal Geographic Data Committee (FGDC) (1998), which is a national standard but it has been adopted in many other countries (South Africa, Canada, and so on). More recently, in May 2003, the International Organization for Standardization (ISO) released the international standard 19115 (International Organization for Standardization, 2003), which includes a complex metadata schema to describe geographic information and services. These geographic metadata standards appeared in a very specific scope, but they have been later mapped to other, more general metadata standards (e.g., the Dublin Core Metadata Initiative (DCMI) proposal) via crosswalks or other technological solutions (Nogueras-Iso, Zarazaga-Soria, Lacasta, Béjar, & Muro-Medrano, 2004), in order to support interoperability.

Metadata are also of the uppermost importance in most SDI initiatives. All these initiatives show a strong emphasis in the necessity to create metadata for all pieces of geographic information, in order to leverage them to their maximum potential. Nogueras-Iso, Zarazaga-Soria, and Muro-Medrano (2004) give a thorough view of geographic metadata in SDIs, including collections, metadata standards interoperability and heterogeneity of geographic metadata content. Applications for the creation of metadata are important to facilitate the management of any digital library. Special tools exist for geographic metadata standards like CatMDEdit (Zarazaga-Soria, Lacasta, Nogueras-Iso, Torres, Muro-Medrano, 2003). CatMDEdit is an open source Java application that can be downloaded from http://catmdedit.sourceforge.net/. It supports the creation of metadata records that follow the ISO 19915 or the FGDC CSDGM metadata standards. It also supports the creation of DCMI records, emphasizing thus the relationship between different metadata standards that appeared in different scopes.

Digital libraries offer *search services* for the resources they hold. These services are typically based on the existence of metadata for those resources. As pointed in the previous section, a search mechanism based on geographic location as the primary search key is required in geolibraries. This is also true for SDIs, which should include catalog services that allow for this spatial search. Some of the catalog specifications for geographic data are evolutions of the search and retrieval protocols created for digital libraries. For instance, the Z39.50 protocol is included as one possible implementation for the Open Geospatial Consortium (OGC) catalog interface specification (Nebert, Whiteside, & Vretanos, 2007). This catalog interface was designed with the geospatial community in mind, but it is a generic system, that supports metadata for generic resources. It includes, for example, Dublin Core Metadata support, and makes it the reference for the "core queryable and returnable properties." It is currently referenced as the standard catalog interface for all relevant SDI initiatives.

Another important issue with SDI catalogs is that they are designed to facilitate distributed searches. Even with the existence of a common standard for catalog interface and another one for the structure of geographic information metadata, there are still several interoperability challenges to solve. One of these challenges is the selection of

appropriate vocabularies for key metadata terms, which is a problem in general digital libraries too (Heath, McArthur, & Vetter, 2005). A common approach to harmonize metadata in digital libraries is the use of controlled vocabularies, like controlled lists or thesauri. These controlled terms are typically used by catalogs to improve searches. Some existing thesauri that are useful to describe thematic geographic information are the General Multilingual Environmental Thesaurus (GEMET) (http://www.eionet.eu.int/GEMET), developed by the European Environment Information and Observation Network, or the Agriculture vocabulary (AGROVOC) (http://www.fao.org/agrovoc/), by the Food and Agriculture Organization of the United Nations. To facilitate the management of thesauri in the geographic context the CatMDEdit application, described before, has been integrated with a thesaurus management tool called ThManager (Lacasta, Nogueras-Iso, López-Pellicer, Muro-Medrano, Zarazaga-Soria, 2007).

As highlighted by Janée et al. (2004), searching in geolibraries requires the use of gazetteers. A gazetteer is a geographic dictionary of place names associated to their location on Earth. A natural approach to build gazetteers would be the use of thesauri, because in many cases, place names have a hierarchical organization (e.g., names of administrative units) that is naturally represented in a thesaurus. The SDIGER project, a pilot to create an SDI for water management between France and Spain, successfully followed this strategy. In this project, a thesaurus for Spain and France place names was built. The place names were taken from the Spanish National Statistics Institute (Instituto Nacional de Estadística), Spanish Public Administration, and the French National Institute for Statistics and Economic Studies (Institut National de la Statistique et des Études Économiques) and organized into a place names thesaurus (Zarazaga-Soria et al., 2007).

In order to integrate properly ontologies and thesauri in SDIs, and following their distributed, Web-services-based architecture, recent research proposes specialized Web services to manage lexical ontologies and thesauri. These services also would provide ontology-based support to other SDI components. The Web Ontology Service (Lacasta, Nogueras-Iso, Béjar, Muro-Medrano, & Zarazaga-Soria, 2007) is a component designed to support the management and use of ontologies in SDIs.

The final goal of a digital library is to provide access to the managed digital resources it contains. Likewise, SDIs must provide visualization and *access to geographic information*, usually through specialized standard geographic Web services, like the Web Map Service (WMS), Web Feature Service (WFS) and Web Coverage Service (WFS) defined by the Open Geospatial Consortium (http://www.opengeospatial.org), and the ISO TC/211 committee (http://www.isotc211.org). These services provide access to geographic resources of different types, with different levels of granularity and with more or less processing. The WMS provides the capability to take geographic information and produce graphic maps. This capability can be used to provide a preview of geographic information resources when searching for them in an SDI catalog. WFS and WCS are Web services designed to give access to geographic information with little or no processing. An important issue with these services is that they can extract parts from geographic information resources, allowing thus a fine-grained access to them.

SDIS BEYOND GEOLIBRARIES

As mentioned before, some of the foundations of SDIs can be traced to DLs by means of geolibraries; but they also have fundamental components that do not fall in the DL domain. Indeed SDIs are also supported by advances in the fields of distributed interoperable GIS and Information Infrastructures (II).

Although the original views of SDIs include—directly or indirectly—the necessity to provide at least search, visualization, and data download services (Nebert, 2004), the current trends in the evolution of distributed interoperable GIS, based in standard geographic Web services, have made some authors (Bernard & Craglia, 2005) argue that these services, and their architecture, chaining, and orchestration, have become the fundamental component of SDIs. This trend would eventually give SDIs full distributed GIS capabilities, a goal that involves not only the setup of an infrastructure to search for, and access to, geographic Web services and data, but also new design and architectural patterns, semantically aware interoperation mechanisms, and the applications that would allow final users to exploit them. This is obviously an enormous challenge for GIS research.

SDIs also share characteristics with other kind of *Information Infrastructures*. Hanseth and Monteiro (in press) give the basic characteristics of IIs, which can be recognized also in the more specialized SDIs: enabling function, shared by a community, of sociotechnical nature, open, heterogeneous and as an evolution of an installed base. As Georgiadou (2006) points, under this perspective, the social and technical components of SDIs are not separable and to understand them completely, it is necessary to explore the sociotechnical processes and practices that can lead to a cultivated approach, in opposition to a construction approach, to SDIs. This point is also sustained by Nedovic and Budhathoki (2006), who believe that SDIs are not built, but cultivated from a social and technical installed base, and enabled by IIs and information and communication technologies. These perspectives show a different, less technical approach to SDIs, and they need to be taken into consideration for a comprehensive understanding of these infrastructures.

Finally, SDIs have some other non-technical, infrastructural, elements that can be considered characteristic for them. First of all, SDI efforts are mainly *sustained by public administrations*. There are laws and regulations (the INSPIRE directive in Europe (European Parliament and the European Council, 2007) or the USA NSDI executive order (nr. 12906, April 11, 1994)), public funding for SDI (Annoni, Craglia, & Smit, 2002), issues related to the access to public information and e-government (Zarazaga-Soria, Nogueras-Iso, Béjar, & Muro-Medrano, 2005), and the recommendation of political sustainability and a legal framework for the success of NSDIs (Annoni et al., 2002). In this subject, they are nearer to the traditional public infrastructures (i.e., transport networks) than to IIs.

The other main characteristic of SDIs is that they are markedly *hierarchical* (on Chan, Feeney, Rajabifard, & Williamson, 2001), mainly because of two factors: on the one hand, using geographic data of the appropriate scale is basic to achieve fast and precise results in analysis or visualization, depending on the area of interest: from large scale data for small areas to small scale data for the whole Earth. On the other hand, public administrations, key stakeholders, developers, and maintainers in most SDI initiatives, are typically hierarchical because government duties are shared according to their areas of responsibility, local, regional/state, national or supranational, which determine the scale of the spatial data they need.

CONCLUSION

This chapter has given an introduction to the field of SDIs emphasizing its roots in components taken from geolibraries, which are DLs specialized in dealing with georeferenced resources.

It has been also sustained that SDIs have a separate identity, mainly because of their foundations in at least other two important fields: distributed interoperable GIS and IIs. Advances in geographic Web services interoperability from the former, and a sociotechnical perspective from the latter are the main contributions of these two

areas to SDIs. There are also two issues that are characteristic for SDIs but not, in general, for geolibraries, GIS, or IIs: the necessity to count on firm public sector support and a markedly hierarchical structure.

It is also worth to mention a new emerging paradigm named collaborative GIS (Balramand & Dragievi, 2006). Collaborative GIS integrates theories, tools and technologies oriented towards the participation of people in group spatial decisions. It would be desirable that collaborative GIS are built on top of the support that SDIs provide, in order to leverage these infrastructures. Indeed SDIs seem a perfect support for collaboration, because of their open and distributed nature.

Geolibraries have already provided conceptual support for the development of SDIs, but it is not over yet: further advance in geographic Web services interoperability will require structured descriptions, i.e. metadata, service catalogs and geographic ontologies to facilitate the interoperation of services that work on spatial data. Also improved search and ranking mechanisms and specialized thesauri will have to be developed for SDI catalogs, in order to deal with geographic data but also with the foreseeable increasing number of geographic Web services. Finally the fact that IIs in general, an SDIs in particular, are heterogeneous, shared and open, establish also new challenges because SDIs will have to be well organized and managed, as any other geolibrary or DL, but also integrated in this new, less controlled and structured environment.

REFERENCES

Annoni, A., Craglia, M., & Smit, P. (2002). Comparative Analysis of NSDI. In *Proceedings of the 8th EC-GI&GIS Workshop*. Dublin, Ireland.

Balramand, S., & Dragievi, S. (Eds.). (2006). *Collaborative Geographic Information Systems*. Idea Group Publishing.

Bernard, L., & Craglia, M. (2005). SDI—from spatial data infrastructure to service driven infrastructure. In *Proceedings of the First Research Workshop on Cross-learning on Spatial Data Infrastructures and Information Infrastructures, Enschede, the Netherlands.* Retrieved August 27, 2008, from http://gi-gis.jrc.it/ws/crosslearning/papers/PP Lars Bernard - Max Craglia.pdf

Chan, T., Feeney, M., Rajabifard, A., & Williamson, I. (2001). The dynamic nature of spatial data infrastructures: A method of descriptive classification. *Geomatica, 55*(1), 65–72.

European Parliament and the European Council. (2007). *Directive of the European Parliament and of the Council establishing an infrastructure for spatial information in the European community (INSPIRE).* Join text approved by the Conciliation Committee, provided for in Article 251(4) of the EC Treaty. 2004/0175(COD), PE-CONS 3685/06. Retrieved August 27, 2008, from http://register. consilium.europa.eu/pdf/en/06/st03/st03685. en06.pdf

Federal Geographic Data Committee. (1998). *Content standard for digital geospatial metadata, version 2.0.* Document FGDC-STD-001-1998, Metadata Ad Hoc Working Group.

Georgiadou, Y. (2006). SDI ontology and implications for research in the developing world. *International Journal of Spatial Data Infrastructures Research, 1,* 51–64. Retrieved August 27, 2008, from http://ijsdir.jrc.it/editorials/georgiadou.pdf

Goodchild, M.F. (2004). The Alexandria digital library project: Review, assesment, and prospects. *D-Lib Magazine, 10*(5). Retrieved August 27, 2008, from http://www.dlib.org/dlib/may04/goodchild/05goodchild.html

Hanseth, O., & Monteiro, E. (in press). *Understanding information infrastructure.* Retrieved August 27, 2008, from http://heim.ifi.uio. no/~oleha/Publications/bok.html

Heath, B., McArthur, D., & Vetter, R. (2005). Metadata lessons from the iLumina digital library. *Communications of the ACM, 48*(5), 68–74.

International Organization for Standardization. (2003). *Geographic information—metadata.* International standard 19115.

Janée, G., Frew, J., & Hill, L.L. (2004). Issues in georeferenced digital libraries. *D-Lib Magazine, 10*(5). Retrieved August 27, 2008, from http://www.dlib.org/dlib/may04/janee/05janee.html

Lacasta, J., Nogueras-Iso, J., Béjar, R., Muro-Medrano, P.R., & Zarazaga-Soria, F.J. (2007). A Web ontology service to facilitate interoperability within a spatial data infrastructure: Applicability to discovery. *Data & Knowledge Engineering, 63*(3), 947–971.

Lacasta, J., Nogueras-Iso, J., López-Pellicer, F.J., Muro-Medrano, P.R., & Zarazaga-Soria, F.J. (2007). ThManager: An open source tool for creating and visualizing SKOS. *Information Technology and Libraries, 26*(3), 39–51.

National Academy Press. (1999). *Distributed geolibraries: Spatial information resources, summary of a workshop.* Panel on Distributed Geolibraries, National Research Council.

Nebert, D.D. (2000). Z39.50 *Application profile for geospatial metadata or*

"GEO". Tech. Rep. Version 2.2, U.S. Federal Geographic Data Committee, U.S. Geological Survey.

Nebert, D.D. (Ed.). (2004). *Developing spatial data infrastructures: The SDI cookbook v.2.0.* Global Spatial Data Infrastructure.

Nebert, D., Whiteside, A., & Vretanos, P. (Eds.). (2007). *OpenGIS catalogue services specification.* Version 2.0.2. Reference Number OGC 07-006r1. Open Geospatial Consortium Incorporated.

Nedovic, Z., & Budhathoki, N.R. (2006). Technological and institutional interdependences and SDI—the Bermuda square?. *International Journal of Spatial Data Infrastructures Research, 1*, 36–50. Retrieved August 27, 2008, from http://ijsdir.jrc.it/editorials/budic_nama.pdf

Nogueras-Iso, J., Zarazaga-Soria, F.J., Lacasta, J., Béjar, R., & Muro-Medrano, P.R. (2004). Metadata standard interoperability: Application in the geographic information domain. *Computers, Environment and Urban Systems, 28*(6), 611–634.

Nogueras-Iso, J., Zarazaga-Soria, F.J., & Muro-Medrano, P.R. (2005). *Geographic information metadata for spatial data infrastructures—resources, interoperability and information retrieval*. Springer-Verlag.

Zarazaga-Soria, F.J., Lacasta, J., Nogueras-Iso, J., Torres, M.P., & Muro-Medrano, P.R. (2003). A Java tool for creating ISO/FGDC geographic metadata. *Geodaten- und Geodienste-Infrastrukturen - von der Forschung zur praktischen Anwendung. Beiträge zu den Münsteraner GI-Tagen. IfGI prints, 18*, 17–30.

Zarazaga-Soria, F.J., Nogueras-Iso, J., Béjar, R., & Muro-Medrano, P.R. (2004). Political aspects of spatial data infrastructures. Electronic government. In R. Traunmüller (Ed.), *Lecture Notes in Computer Science*, (Vol. 3183, pp. 392–395). Springer.

Zarazaga-Soria, F.J., Nogueras-Iso, J., Latre, M.Á., Rodríguez, A., López, E., Vivas, P., & Muro-Medrano, P.R. (2007). Providing spatial data infrastructure services in a cross-border scenario: SDIGER project. *Research and Theory in Advancing Spatial Data Infrastructure Concepts* (pp. 107–119). California: ESRI Press.

KEY TERMS

Gazetteer: A geographical dictionary that associates georeferences to place names.

Geolibrary: A library containing georeferenced objects and with a search mechanism based on geographic location as the primary search key.

Georeference: Information that relates data to a position on the Earth's surface, typically by means of coordinates.

GIS: A system for capturing, storing, analyzing, managing, and viewing data spatially referenced to the Earth.

Spatial Data: Data related to positions on the Earth's surface.

Spatial Data Infrastructure: The relevant base collection of technologies, policies, and institutional arrangements that facilitate the availability of and access to spatial data.

Chapter XL
DL and GIS:
Path to a New Collaboration Paradigm

O. Cantán Casbas
San Jorge University, Spain

J. Nogueras-Iso
University of Zaragoza, Spain

F. J. Zarazaga-Soria
University of Zaragoza, Spain

ABSTRACT

A new collaboration paradigm is in order between Digital Libraries (DL) and Geographic Information Systems (GIS). These important Information Technology (IT) fields have witnessed great progress in the last few years, only to be surpassed by even greater expectations. Nonetheless, this extraordinary advance has come at a cost: the very proliferation of different representation formats, proprietary standards, protocols and platforms in which information is published or served is hindering the further development of these fields. One discouraging and generally ignored aspect of this situation is that both DL and GIS practitioners have been trying to deal with these problems in an isolated fashion, blind to each others' achievements and approximations. The result is a lack of synergy and duplication of efforts. In this chapter, the authors share their experience in the GIS field to propose a collaborative approximation to solve some of the most recurrent problems both in DL and GIS.

INTRODUCTION

In 1938, H.G. Wells—the English novelist famous for his works in science fiction—envisioned a world encyclopedia in which all human knowledge would be available for everyone, a "complete planetary memory for all mankind." Pretentious as it was at the time, nowadays, that exciting dream is within the reach of our hands. Nonetheless a lot of arduous work remains to be done as it is indicated by the recurring frustration of many users of DL and Geographic Information (GI) services. The proliferation of different representation formats, proprietary standards, protocols, and platforms in which information is published or served pose a multiplicity of barriers both to end users and information professionals.

The response to these obstacles should be organization and collaboration. We could be much further along the road to success if only a more constructive and collaborative interrelation among the different IT fields were achieved. If we consider, for example, the case of Spatial Data Infrastructures (SDI), we observe that the research and development of these systems have been performed mostly by researchers outside the DL community, circumstance that in many occasions has led to the oversimplification of library issues. Besides, many advances in the GI domain could be of great help for the DL practitioners. In this contribution, the authors—active practitioners in the SDI field—share some of the lessons learned during architectural design and standardization activities carried out in the GI domain.

BACKGROUND

Digital libraries hold great expectations. Their projected role is to serve as an access point to a vast set of information sources and services: they should offer new opportunities to assemble, organize, and access large volumes of information from multiple repositories. Nonetheless, and according to the Digital Library Federation (DLF) Service Framework Working Group, "the research library community has not yet transitioned to a shared understanding of how a library and its services are organized in an increasingly networked environment" (Dempsey & Lavoie, 2005, p. 1). The primary reason adduced is the weak and inconsistent adoption of interoperability standards.

The DL field is a far embracing one. For example, it is possible to define a digital library that specializes in GI resources. Usually, this kind of digital library is called a geolibrary (Goodchild, 1998). In conjunction with Geographic Information Systems (GIS), geolibraries constitute the technology base for the development of Spatial Data Infrastructures (SDI). The concept of SDI originated in 1994 as the framework for the optimization of the creation, maintenance and distribution of geographic information. The main components of a SDI include data providers, end-users, data networks, technologies, databases and metadata, institutional arrangements, policies, and standards (Coleman & Nebert, 1998).

SDIs, with their integrated geolibraries, could have bridged the gaps between the GI and DL communities. Unfortunately this has not been the case. As was noted by Boxall (2002), "even the recently released Cookbook for Global Spatial Data Infrastructures (GSDI) makes almost no mention of libraries, and those few instances tend to be quaint" (p. 4). Even the activities of ISO TC 211 and other standards development organizations (SDO) tend to involve more nonlibrarians than DL practitioners. This lack of collaboration represents another obstacle on the development of these two fields. A more collaborative relationship could bring about mutual benefits: for example, the transition of SDI to GSDI is a continuous source of valuable know-how which could help DL along the road to a more networked and interoperable environment.

A new collaborative paradigm is called for between the DL and the GI domains, a paradigm whose goal must be to engage research beyond the boundaries of specialized core areas in order to find solutions and strategies that can yield greater knowledge integration and synthesis (Balramand & Dragievi, 2006). There is no need to duplicate effort: librarians can contribute to geography and geographers to librarianship, for we have common goals and similar backgrounds.

THE PROGRESSIVE CONVERGENCE OF GIS AND DL

The first geographic information systems consisted mainly of proprietary and monolithic applications working in isolation to satisfy highly specialized user needs. This usually had the adverse side effect of data duplication and low return of investment (ROI) due to the mass proliferation of *data islands* unable to work together. By emphasizing the problems of production of digital geoinformation, the importance of effective processes of dissemination to users and other systems was underemphasized. Even the vision of the USA National Spatial Data Infrastructure (NSDI), as was expressed by the Mapping Science Committee (MSC) in 1993 (NRC, 1993) and later refined in a 1997 MSC workshop that assembled a group of experts to focus on the future of spatial data in society (NRC, 1997), could not anticipate the enormous impact and potential of the distributed computing environment that was about to emerge from the commoditation of Internet.

By contrast, one of the central concerns of DL since their inception in the mid-1990s has been to develop an organized and structured global infrastructure with accurate and effective searching and retrieval capabilities beyond those of traditional search engines. Besides, DL also represent a form of information technology in which social impact matters as much as technological advancement. These two important aspects of DL, distributed operation and social concern, have been progressively adopted by GIS as this field expanded into wider audiences and broader operational environments. This approximation of GIS towards DL contributes to reduce the gap between these two content management fields.

Conversely, the complexity and heterogeneity of geospatial information has typically exceeded that of DL. The volume of information necessary to describe the ever complex geospatial resources, what is collectively known as metadata, has been increasing steadily. As a matter of fact, a typi-cal GI metadata standard can easily have more than three hundred elements. In the case of DL, this tendency has also been reinforced and as a consequence recent standards can consist of more than two hundred elements –as an example, the MARC 21 Format for Authority Data Update No. 7 (October 2006) has reached two hundred fields. The standardization efforts carried out by the GI community aimed at facilitating data and operational interoperability among metadata islands have been intense, especially since 1994 when the Open Geospatial Consortium was founded. The current situation is still a troublesome one but a lot of lessons have been learned. The DL community should take note of them and act accordingly.

The best example of convergence between DL and GI is materialized in geolibraries. The inherent complexity of geospatial information management is closely aligned with one of the most urgent tasks faced by DL. As was noted by Theng and Foo (2005), one of the main challenges for the next generation digital libraries is to cope with the discovery, manipulation, and exploitation of new types of digital content in a context of metadata and services interoperability. In order to be able to support these new demands, the DL functionality has to be appropriately extended far beyond that required to manipulate simple digital content. This work has been under way in geolibraries for several years so it can be valuable for DL to take advantage of this research background.

ARCHITECTURAL EVOLUTION OF A GEOLIBRARY CATALOG

Both DL and GI systems have evolved in response to increasingly complex requirements to manage the vast quantities of electronic information that are being produced, collected and consumed. Originally, these systems were conceived as isolated, standalone and proprietary applications. Through private Application Programming Interfaces (API) these legacy systems communicated with some sort of content management infrastructure in order to gain access to geographic data. Although nowadays this scheme of operation is outclassed, local and corporate levels are still relying significantly on this type of infrastructures in which customized functionality and easy of development, but not interoperability, are the main concerns.

A common paradigm of operation is shared among all geolibraries, but each application domain and organization has its own particularities, ranging from different information models to specific network services. Figure 1 shows three modifications to the basic architecture which adapt to different contexts.

On the left, the basic system serves requests from SRW clients making use of the metadata managed by a proprietary Geospatial Catalog Server (Tolosana, Portolés-Rodríquez, Nogueras-Iso, Muro-Medrano, & Zarazaga-Soria, 2005). On the right the source of metadata is a CSW-compliant server instead of a proprietary catalog server. Finally, in the middle of the illustration a source is being harvested using OAI. CSW –Catalogue Search for the Web (OGC 04-006r1, 2007), SRW –Search Retrieve Webservice (Sanderson, 2004) and OAI—Open Archives Initiative (Lagoze & Van de Sompel, 2004)—are well-known infor-

mation retrieval protocols widely accepted in the GI and DL fields. The focal point here is that the same architectural pattern recurs in every specific operational environment.

In order for those isolated systems to integrate effectively into an interoperable environment, a greater emphasis have to be laid on open metadata standards and protocols as the key enablers to resource discovery, evaluation and exploitation. Besides, a more effective and systematic enterprise solution for metadata management is required. There is an urgent need for a metadata infrastructure capable of supporting complex requirements of specialized users and subsystems but also being able to accommodate less sophisticated users without needless complication. Generally called a Managed Metadata Environment (MME), this new infrastructure is defined as the architectural components, people, processes and policies that are required to properly and systematically gather, retain and disseminate metadata to different users and systems in a practical and effective manner. The principal conceptual elements of a MME, according to Marco and Jennings (2004), are depicted in Figure 2.

The metadata integration layer takes the various sources of metadata, integrates them, and loads the harmonized metadata into the metadata repository. This repository is responsible for the

Figure 1. Architectural variations of geolibraries

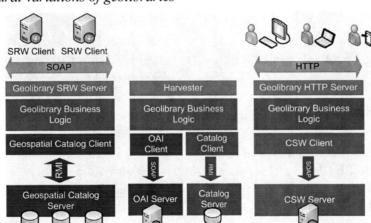

Figure 2. Managed metadata environment

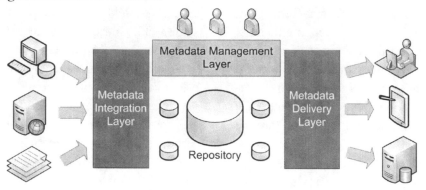

cataloging and persistent storage of the metadata and pointers to the metadata in a distributed metadata environment. The metadata management layer provides systematic management of the metadata repository and the other MME components. Finally, the metadata delivery layer delivers the metadata from the repository to the end users and any applications or tools that require metadata. This delivery process adapts to user needs by using crosswalks to translate between metadata standards and by using the adequate communication protocols.

In the section *Lessons Learned,* we present our specific implementation of a MME to exemplify the importance of a flexible architecture to facilitate the management of diverse metadata standards and protocols.

GI STANDARDIZATION EFFORTS

In the recent years, the performance of two key publicly traded GIS companies, namely Intergraph and Leica GeoSystems, has outperformed NASDAQ indexes many times over (Rana & Sharma, 2006). The existing 5 billion USD global geospatial technology industry was predicted to rise to 30 billion USD by 2005 compared to the predicted 2 billion USD for 2004. These spectacular results

give an idea of the importance and relevance of GI Technology worldwide. However, the situation of accessibility and utility of geodata is still not satisfactory. To achieve the goals of coordination across the different GI actors related to acquisition, use, sharing, and interoperability of data, the continuing challenge of the development of content and interoperability standards must be addressed.

Simplified Timeline of GI standards

In the GI domain, information has usually been collected and described in different proprietary ways and systems have been designed for only one specific mission. This has resulted in wasteful redundancies and a reduced ability to perform critical shared operations. As a consequence, and since 1990, voluntary, consensus-based, interoperability standards are increasingly being developed by industry consortia. Figure 3 shows a simplified timeline of some of the most relevant GI standards initiatives.

In 1987, even before metadata became a ubiquitous buzzword, a standardized format for exchanging information about scientific data sets was conceived. This was the Directory Interchange Format (DIF), a product of an Earth Science and Applications Data Systems Workshop (ESADS)

Figure 3. Important GI standards initiatives

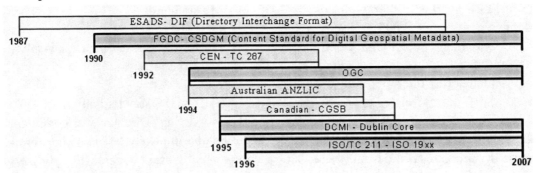

on catalogue interoperability. A few years later, in the United States, the Federal Geographic Data Committee (FGDC) started working on the Content Standard for Digital Geospatial Metadata (CSDGM).

In 1992, this time in Europe, a specific Technical Committee at the European level within the European Committee for Standardization (CEN) was set up: CEN/TC 287—Geographic Information. The technical committee finished its work in 1999 resulting in a set of ENV (European experimental standards) in the field of GI. With the beginning of the work by ISO/TC 211, and due to the Vienna Agreement between CEN and ISO, CEN/TC 287 left new items to be developed to ISO/TC211. Since then ISO/TC211 has issued more than 20 standards for GI transfer and management, in particular the ISO 19100-series standards.

Additionally, in 1994, the Open Geospatial Consortium (OGC) began working on another kind of interoperability standards: those that govern the software interfaces used to access, manage, and communicate geospatial data within operational IT systems. Nowadays, the OGC/FGCD/ISO standards have reached a threshold level of maturity which can bolster a new era in interoperable GI data and services.

LESSONS LEARNED

For almost a decade, the authors have been working as part of a multidisciplinary team on different GI projects, ranging from the development of local SDI to the active involvement and development of the Spanish SDI. As one of our policies has been adopting and implementing interoperability standards as soon as possible, during these years, we have gathered a series of lessons learned that could be helpful for the DL practitioners.

- **Lesson 1: Interoperability is the problem, standardization (part of) the solution.**

The rapid growth of information resources has multiplied the interoperability problems. Even today most existing internet map and data servers are not interoperable. It is well acknowledged that GI interoperability is dependent on voluntary, consensus-based standards, but many actors, for a number of reasons ranging from the use of third party middleware to internal cultural resistance and lack of management support, continue to be reluctant to their adoption. Hopefully this situation is starting to change thanks to the consolidation of the ISO/OGC/FGDC standards.

In the DL community, the interoperability problem has also sparked vigorous discussions (Feng, Manfred, & Hoppe, 2005). Besides, technical interoperability is not enough, for it is also necessary an infrastructure for semantic agreement, and implementing interoperability must be considered at different levels of operation (e.g., schema, record, and repository levels). By adopting well supported and flexible standards these interoperability problems could be alleviated but not completely eliminated.

Regarding data content standards, whereas a typical DL metadata standard like Dublin Core has only 15 elements, the typical GI metadata standard ISO19115 has more than 350 elements. This gap in complexity is likely to shorten in the coming years as librarians are already making increasing use of more complex formats such as Metadata Object Description Schema (MODS) and Metadata Encoding and Transmission Standard (METS). Concerning publishers, there is a tendency towards supplying more metadata about the publications they put out, for instance cover art, quotes from reviews, descriptive texts, author biographies and other useful material. These new demands on metadata do not cope well with the representational capacities provided by MARC, so DLs will have to migrate to more convenient and complex standards, both in terms of semantic richness and cross interoperability.

- **Lesson 2: Standards leverage existing technology investments.**

One of the promises of interoperable standards has been the possibility of reducing both the need of new data acquisition and new software development. According to a study performed by NASA (2005), the projects that adopted and implemented geospatial interoperability standards saved 26.2% compared to the projects that relied upon a proprietary standard. One way to interpret this result is that for every USD $4 spent on projects based on proprietary platforms, the same value could be

achieved with USD $3 if the projects were based on open standards.

- **Lesson 3: Standardization is much easier said than done.**

OGC and ISO standards already form the basis of most existing SDIs. However, compliant and interoperable implementations of these broad-ranging standards are still scarce (Figure 4). A solution for this problem is the definition of profiles, which are used to select between alternatives left open by a standard, to make certain options mandatory, to add new features and to combine the interface specification with a specific information model (Senkle, Voges, & Remke, 2004). In this manner, those organizations which reject the adoption of global standards because they are perceived as not meeting their business needs could realize the benefits of standardization while at the same time satisfying their specific goals.

- **Lesson 4: Standards require the support of political and public administrations at different levels.**

At least three stakeholder groups have an active role in geospatial standards setting: political and public administrations, industry, and SDO/Standards-Setting Organizations (SSO). Suc-

Figure 4. Adoption of some OGC specifications

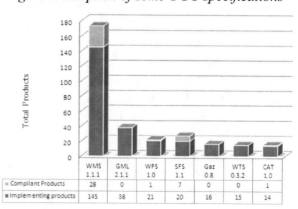

cessful standardization depends on these three parties coming together to make common cause to advance goals beneficial to all parties.

The role of political and public administrations with regard to geospatial standards is indispensable. They need to partner with SDOs and SSOs to develop local profiles of minimal standards, which are more likely to be adopted and accepted by users and vendors. Two relevant examples are the Executive Order (nr. 12906, April 11, 1994) signed by Bill Clinton for the establishment of the "National Spatial Data Infrastructure" in the United States, and the European Directive INSPIRE to create the INfrastructure for SPatial InfoRmation in Europe.

- **Lesson 5: Adopt standards but devise a flexible and extensible architecture.**

It is recommended to adopt interoperability standards early in the project life cycle, even if they are not universally agreed upon. As was pointed by Hillman and Westbrooks (2004),

Figure 5. Simplified architectural approximation

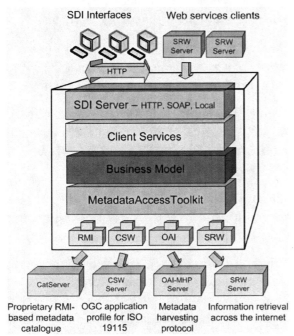

"waiting for emerging standards to settle down is a futile exercise; it will probably not happen in our lifetimes" (p. 16). The system architecture devised by the authors for their geospatial catalog-geolibrary is based on the principles of flexibility and extensibility (Figure 5).

The core of this layered architecture is the Business Model layer (BML), which is responsible of implementing a general resource access paradigm with a universal metadata model. The layers below the BML are in charge of accessing the different sources using the appropriate standards and protocols. Some of this standards are open/ interoperable (e.g., ISO 19115, SRW) but others are proprietary. The use of translation crosswalks among the resource representations enable the BML to operate in its universal representation.

The layers above the BML are responsible for receiving the service requests from external clients, both in proprietary or standard protocols, and translating them to the universal representation used by the BML. When the requests have been satisfied, the responses are returned upwards for adequate translation according to the requesting clients.

Using this architecture, the core processing layers remain stable no matter the subsequent protocols and data standards needed. Only new source connectors, crosswalks and servers are required. This simplifies and speeds up the support of new sources and clients and thus the development and adaptability of the SDI.

CONCLUSION

The 21st-century library will be handling increasing amounts of digital materials. In an online world, where there are many heterogeneous resources, DL practitioners must get better at selecting and providing the adequate infrastructures, services and resources. There is a generalized sense that DLs are faced with apparently insurmountable problems, so the pressures to find new approaches and to take advantage of new technologies are high. New content and interoperability standards, along with new practices and technological approximations, must be devised to cope with all this new universe of information and services. However, this situation is not new for the GI community: geolibraries have been part of SDI for several years and have undergone important standardization and development efforts. And in this respect the experiences and lessons learned by the GI community could be very valuable. Thus the authors believe that a new collaboration paradigm is required between the DL and GI communities to leverage our efforts in the pursuit of H.G. Well's dream.

REFERENCES

Balramand, S., & Dragievi, S. (2006). *Collaborative geographic information systems*. Idea Group Publishing.

Boxall, J. (2002). Geolibraries, the global spatial data infrastructure and digital earth: A time for map libraries to reflect upon the moonshot. *INSPEL*, 1–21.

Coleman, D.J., & Nebert, D.D. (1998). Building a North American spatial data infrastructure. *Cartography and Geographic Information Systems, 25*(3), 151–160.

Dempsey, L., & Lavoie, B. (2005). *DLF service framework for digital libraries*. Progress Report.

Feng, L., Manfred, A.J., & Hoppe, J. (2005). Beyond information searching and browsing: Acquiring knowledge from digital libraries. *Information Processing and Management*, 97–120.

Goodchild, M.F. (1998). The geolibrary. In S. Carver (Ed.), *Innovations in GIS 5* (pp. 59–68). London: Taylor and Francis.

Hillman, D.I., & Westbrooks, E.L. (2004). *Metadata in practice*. American Library Association.

Lagoze, C., & Van de Sompel, H. (Eds.) (2004). *The open archives initiative protocol for metadata harvesting (PROTOCOL VERSION 2.0)*. Retrieved August 27, 2008, from http://www.openarchives.org/OAI/2.0/openarchivesprotocol.htm

Marco, D., & Jennings, M. (2004). *Universal meta data models*. Wiley Publishing, Inc.

NASA. (2005). *Geospatial interoperability return on investment study*. Booz Allen Hamilton.

NRC (National Research Council). (1993). *Toward a coordinated spatial data infrastructure for the nation*. Washington, D.C.: National Academy Press.

NRC. (1997). *The future of spatial data and society: Summary of a workshop*. Washington, D.C.: National Academy Press.

OGC 04-006rl. (2005). *OpenGIS® catalogue services specification*. Open Geospatial Consortium Inc.

Rana, S., & Sharma, J. (2006). *Frontiers of geographic information technology*. Springer.

Sanderson, R. (2004). *SRW: Search/Retrieve Webservice, (version 1.1)*. Retrieved August 27, 2008, from http://srw.cheshire3.org/SRW-1.1.pdf

Senkle, K., Voges, U., & Remke, A. (2004). An ISO 19115/19119 profile for OGC catalogue services CSW 2.0. *10th EC GI & GIS Workshop, ESDI State of the Art*. Warsaw, Poland.

Theng, Y.L., & Foo, S. (Eds.) (2005). *Design and usability of digital libraries*. Idea Group Inc.

Tolosana-Calasanz, R., Portolés-Rodríquez, D., Nogueras-Iso, J., Muro-Medrano, P.R., & Zarazaga-Soria, F.J. (2005). CatServer: A server of GATOS. In *Proceedings of the 8th AGILE*

Conference on Geographic Information Science (pp. 359–366).

KEY TERMS

Digital Library: The collection of services and the collection of information objects that support users in dealing with information objects, and the organization and presentation of those objects via electronic/digital means.

Geographic Information System (GIS): A collection of computer tools and approaches to capture, manage and transform spatially referenced data for planning and decision taking.

Geolibrary: A library filled with georeferenced information which is based upon the notion that information can have a geographic footprint.

Interoperability: A condition that exists when the distinctions between information systems are not a barrier to accomplishing a task that spans multiple systems.

Profile: Technique of referencing technical specifications (e.g., standards and specifications). A standards profile permits the creation of a bundle of standards, each one tailored, extended, or constrained to meet the needs of the committee developing a standards profile

Spatial Data Infrastructure: A federated system that accesses multiple, distributed spatial services and data repositories.

Standard: A set of criteria (some of which may be mandatory), voluntary guidelines, and best practices.

Chapter XLI
Digital Libraries Beyond Cultural Heritage Information

Piedad Garrido Picazo
University of Zaragoza, Spain

Jesús Tramullas Saz
University of Zaragoza, Spain

Manuel Coll Villalta
University of Zaragoza, Spain

ABSTRACT

This chapter introduces digital libraries as a means of cultural heritage access and diffusion. It argues that digital libraries, combined with superimposed information techniques, offers a potentially more substantive approach to understanding the historical documentation analysis problem. Furthermore, the authors hope that understanding the documental and technological assumptions constructs through the use of programming and automatic interpreter will not only inform researches of a better scheme for labelling cultural heritage information but also assist in the need of involved other areas such as multiagent systems, pattern matching, information management and information visualization based on content association, to solve the vast majority of problems set out in the work context, and the result is a versatile digital library prototype which covers the cultural heritage information that the users need.

INTRODUCTION

Thanks to a research project granted by the Regional Ministry of Science, Technology and University, the research work team has detected problems in the limitations of the classical models of representation and information retrieval which are insufficient due to the large amount of information at the potential users' disposal. These problems were seen as serious in the second half of this decade, and they were the origin of Berners-Lee and Fischetti's (1997) new proposal known as the semantic Web.

The experiences and the projects undertaken to date have been gradually revealing that the approaches based on the mere digitalization of the information and documentation on cultural heritage are not sufficient to face the information needs of the different types of users. The immense amount of multimedia information about cultural heritage does not come with the complementary referential information that the users need (Crane, 2002).

The chapter is organized as follows: a background about the more relevant cultural heritage digital library contributions using labelling languages. The second section describes the problem of managing historical documentation in digital format, the methodology followed to develop an automatic interpreter, which analyzes and manages historical texts, the role of a built-in multiagent system to improve the information retrieval process combined with pattern matching techniques and the information management and visualization. Finally, the last section presents some concluding remarks.

BACKGROUND

By and large, cultural heritage digital libraries are characterized by the diversity of their collection contents (Crane, 2002). The bibliography available on these digital library types shows that in situations of heterogeneity, the metadata schemes used to describe the different contents become extremely important since they are used to deal with problems related to information retrieval and interoperability. Baldonado, Chang, Gravano, and Paepcke (1997) proposed a metadata-based interoperability model which used the Dublin Core (Tolosana-Calasanz, Nogueras-Iso, Béjar, Muro-Medrano, & Zarazaga-Soria, 2006) and MARC schemes (Chandler, Foley, & Hafez, 2000).

Given its simplicity, the use of the nonqualified Dublin Core Metadata Scheme in cultural heritage digital libraries predominates.

Nevertheless, the use of Dublin Core presents problems which have been pointed out by some researchers. Foulonneau, Cole, Habing, and Shreeves (2005) posed the problem, which assumes the lack of consistency of the Dublin Core metadata in OAI repositories. The comparative study on repositories with cultural heritage metadata undertaken by Hutt and Riley (2005) pointed out it and Halbert, Haczmarek, and Hagedorn (2003) had already warned about the problems detected in the use of Dublin Core in these contexts.

In the field on which our work centers, the use of Dublin Core has had to be gradually completed by integrating tools which offer the semantic relations that the metadata scheme does not offer (De Gendt, Isaac, Van Der Meijt, & Schlobach, 2006). So, we can present two starting points from the works reviewed:

1. Dublin Core is excessively simple for its use in cultural heritage digital libraries without other complementary schemes.
2. A more complete model must be proposed which incorporates a descriptive metadata scheme of both an element and collection type, and the description tool scheme (thesaurus, ontology).

HISTORICAL INFORMATION ANALYSIS

The Web information service, under consideration, is the Digital Aragon Encyclopedia (http://www.enciclopedia-aragonesa.com).

Since the cultural heritage information preservation is a very wide and diverse field; the current chapter shows how to manage a portion of this information: historical texts.

Currently, there are two aspects to deal with the task of historical text analysis in digital libraries. It is obvious that by means of human effort it is possible the whole analysis of all the existing information in this kind of documents, but a complete coordinated reader group is needed, and the analysis time will be proportional both the reading speed analysis and the number of readers. The second aspect consists of, in some way, performing an automatic analysis via a computer which can be able to extract the relevant information and to structure in a way legible by the human being and the external automatic system.

The most interesting feature to face with the historical documentation automatic analysis is based on the fact that their texts accomplish these two properties:

1. A group of events is exposed (they have been taken place in a concrete place and moment) associated with a group of entities.
2. Besides, a huge amount of entity intrinsic information is carried out in the form of associations among other entities. Semantic association falls in the role of them.

From these properties, it is inferred that the extracted information after the analysis process must have a network structure, where each node is an entity related to other nodes and the human being effective semantic information is stored in the arch labels, which would contain the association role among nodes and the date and place in case if it is a dated event.

Among other aspects over digital libraries services, the digital information product developed attempts to improve the voice search engine so that it is not only limited to information access through subject matter categories or/and alphabetical indexes as currently (Brocks, Thiel, Stein, & Dirsch-Weigand, 2001). For this reason, a set of voices has been selected to work with, los Reyes de Aragón (the king and queen of Aragon):

Once the set of voices was analyzed, it was observed that this label did not offer any improvement to the management, storage and retrieval of this cultural heritage information portion, only it contributes to a documental structure to organize. Therefore, we decided to build an ad-hoc ontology since certain initiatives have been taken regarding this matter, which is directed to the exchange and integration of heterogeneous scientific documentation related only to museum collections (ISO 21127, 2006).

Unlike the COLLATE Project (http://www.collate.de/), the use of an ontology in this project is not due to the lack of semantic relations between the collection elements since this aspect is completely covered with the topic maps paradigm, described in the (ISO 13250, 2003). Its use is to provide a clear idea of how to organize this information and how to detect patterns of relations which not only allow the automatic interpreter not to make mistakes when the set of voices on this subject matter increases (Giunchiglia, Yatskevich, & Shvaiko 2007), but also allows it to be reused in other encyclopaedic information sectors such as heraldry, lineage, and so on.

Then, we propose a hybrid XTM/DITA scheme[1] to storage information. On the one hand, XTM defines how to store and interpret all the associations among entities (external structure)

Figure 1. An XML-labelled example voice

```
<voz subcategoriaId="38">
  <vozId>
    98
  </vozId>
  <nombre>
    Abd al-Malik ibn Hudayl ibn Razin
  </nombre>
  <descripcion>
    Segundo soberano de la taifa de Albarracín, entre 1045 y 1103, con el titulo de Husam al-Dawla (Sable del Estado).
  </descripcion>
</voz>
```

Figure 2. Topic Map structure

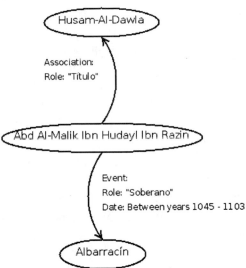

with this subset of metadata: "topic," "baseName," "baseNameString," "instanceOf," "topicRef," "member," "association," "occurrence," and a new label (<date>) to describe an event. On the other hand, the description of each entity (internal structure) with basic DITA labels: "topic id," "shortdesc" and "conbody." Afterwards, we developed an interpreter which automatically labels this set of voices by working with it (Maier & Delcambre, 2000).

The differences between both formats of information representation, are clear, and the benefits of a combined DITA and XTM metadata scheme (Gelb, 2007) solves part of the problems set out in the project contribution section, as well as being utterly innovative in this application field. DITA (2007) as a metadata scheme for cultural heritage technical documentation and XTM (Park & Hunting, 2002) to facilitate the creation of labelled information resource systems, specially designed for being used with links to other resources making possible to link information by using semantic criteria and informative contents.

The Automatic Interpreter

The aim of the historical information analysis is to extract a group of associations among entities, which on the whole they describe all the relevant information about the document covered entities. So, the interpreter algorithm must be able to read the text and, in some way, to detect associations among entities or related event to an entity and to store them in one or several manners.

Then, the core of the problem lies in the detection method that has to be used to determine if a concrete information section can be turned into an association or an event, just as the method to infer both the metadata, indicating the role or the data and the place, and the participating entities. For this, it has been used two approximations. The former was a first level algorithm, where the analysis was carried out directly over the text. First, a phrase extraction from the text, and second a division in words. Each word was analyzed to determine if the role was an association (consulting a database about lineage, heraldry, inherited titles, and so on) or if it mentioned an entity (detecting if it was a proper noun). When an entity was detected, the presence of a role was investigated in the rest of the phrase, if the process was successful; an association among topics was generated. To detect events, a basic exploration based on finding the presence of a bracket (the general pattern used to recognize the date of an event).

This exploring algorithm has been catalogued as first level because the detection is directly based on text words, and a generation of associations and events is carried out from the keywords previously found, they give us clues about the presence of relevant information. The analogy between this exploration method and daily life is when we wish to find some information in a large amount of text, and a sequential reading is carried out finding concrete keywords which give us clues to the text information position.

The results of this type of analysis were positive, since it was a functional approximation to the historical text automatic analysis. For instance, for two hundred voices, hundred of associations were generated and tens of events, with an accuracy of roughly a seventy per cent, (if the algorithm is compared with human interpretation).

Nevertheless, it could be done better. The analysis was fundamentally dependent on the dictionary, and it failed in proportional relation to the description expression complexity. It was necessary to go the analysis ahead to an upper level, dictionary independent. This new approach could reduce complex expressions to simpler ones and later, they could be analyzed by a simple interpreter.

So, a second level algorithm has been developed. This algorithm gathers an entity descriptive text, and a morphological analysis, throughout a Freeling package adaptation, is performed. Now on, the algorithm won't analyze the word textual forms but it will analyse the sentence morphological structure to strip redundant information and generating events and associations.

The first step, once we have the morphological structure organized, is to build a filter to delete Spanish stop words. After we make little analysis word by word to correct certain mistakes Freeling system makes (for instance, to catalogue common nouns like proper nouns, to appoint verbs as common nouns and to resolve known certain acronyms such as Z or id.). The double type system has been included and a word could be catalogued in several manners simultaneously (that is: "era" as verb [was] or common noun [epoch] in Spanish language), in order to prevent mistakes in the following analysis phases.

The second analysis phase consists of, sentence by sentence, contrasting its syntax with a series of predefined patterns. These predefined patterns define linguistic forms of expression which give us relevant information, of which extraction is the algorithm desired aim. In depth, the algorithm uses a rule engine to compare the preprogrammed patterns against the syntax of each sentence of the entity descriptive text. This verification is carried out in each sentence position, with the objective of doing a thorough verification and sentence preambles or conclusions do not dull the analysis abilities, just as to simplify the patterns in many ways. It would be a hard work to elaborate all the possible syntax patterns for the majority of Spanish sentences, taking into account sentence beginning and ending expression formulas, although it will be commented later. So, the necessary predefined patterns will be those morphological combinations which describe the more common expression formulas that enunciate the relevant information, in a way of association among entities or related events to the interpreted entity. This means that analysis problem is moving from an own level to a morphological level.

Next it is described an operation algorithm example down to this analysis phase. We have the following sentence of a fictitious entity: "A comienzos de su reinado, se casó con Magdalena de Folcaquier (At the beginning of his reign, he married to Magdalena Folcaquier)." In the first phase, those nonrelevant information words will be leaked. The second step will do a morphological analysis, describing the sentence with the following structure: "A (At; SP, preposition) comienzos (beginning; NC, common noun) de (of; SP, preposition) su (his; DP, possessive determiner) reinado (reign; NC, common noun) se casó[2] (he married; VM, main casar verb conjugation) con (to; SP, preposition) Magdalena de Folcaquier (Magdalena Folcaqier; NP, proper noun)." This morphological structure will be matched with the series of algorithm predefined patterns, with the aim of finding relevant information. If one of the predefined patterns is "VM SP NP" then from the word "casó" that sentence matches this pattern. To observe carefully that this pattern covers a wide range of sentences which describe an action over other entity.

So, if an enough number of patterns are developed, it is possible to monopolize a great amount of the linguistic formulas of the voice description field.

However, redundant information presents some problems, that is, the text provides too much information and sometimes, the redundant or inaccurate information is incorrectly extracted. To avoid it, the algorithm has summary patterns. These summary patterns define syntax rules to redundant sentences and then, they are removed (just in part, the redundant information treatment is described ahead) in a way that subsequent patterns do not take out erroneous information.

To come into the pattern rule operation, an example of a fictitious sentence again: "Hijo (NC) de (SP) Pedro II (NP), rey (NC) de (SP) Aragón (NP) y (CC) Juana (NP), condesa (NC) de (SP) Urdiel (NP) (Son of Peter II, king of Aragón and Juana, countess of Urdiel)." As we can observe, to the treated entity, the fact that "Pedro I" (Peter II) was "rey de Aragón" (King of Aragón) and "Juana" was "condesa de Urdiel" (countess of Urdiel) is irrelevant and so this redundant information is removed. If a summary pattern (which finds this sort of redundant information and it is able to eliminate them) was programmed, the task for the later analysis patterns will be easier.

An interesting summary pattern is, for example: "NP NC SP NP," of which activation produces the elimination of the three last words. The example sentence will trigger this rule from the "Pedro II" word. The resulting sentence looks as follows: "Hijo de Pedro II y Juana, condesa de Urdiel" (Son of Peter II and Joan, countess of Urdiel). Following the check, this rule would trigger again from the "Juana" word, and the summarized final sentence would be: "Hijo (NC) de (SP) Pedro II (NP) y (CC) Juana (NP)" (Son of Peter II and Joan). If predefined patterns based on this kind of expressions were programmed, it would be able to extract relevant information, which in this case is the fact that this entity is "hijo" (son) of the entities "Pedro II" (Peter II) and "Juana" (Joan). Nevertheless, the risk of the summary patterns is that they are equally able to remove relevant information in concrete cases.

For the event detection, there are three types of patterns: the beginning-ending detection patterns, bracket analysis and the event common patterns. The first ones are based on a common feature in historic documentation. For a historical entity, the beginning and ending dates and places are always between brackets in the first line. To extract such important information, a series of patterns, able to find combinations of expressions of these types, are developed. The second, bracket analysis, includes a very common bibliographic formula, the introduction of dates between brackets in the sentences, showing the moment of the described event. The bracket analysis patterns are capable of finding this expressive figure and turning into a series of words that the third type patterns detect.

For example, the "batalla de Roma (315-340)" (battle of Rome) sentence would be detected and it would be converted in the following analysed sentence "batalla de Roma entre 315 y 340" (battle of Rome between 315 and 340). The last kind is the event detection patterns, which are the most common, and they include expressions which describe events such as the previous sentence, and once detected extract the relevant information. Finally, when this entire pattern group has been checked, the whole sentences which are between brackets are removed in order to make easier the later analysis.

When a rule is triggered because of the fact that a sentence has found some pattern, its associated rule is activated, and it executes an associated procedure. The procedure could modify the sentence (if we are before synthesis, summary or bracket patterns) or it could generate associations or events. In the last case, the triggered rule points out to the procedure the word positions that it denotes: the rule of the association and the data and place if they are in the presence of an event and entity at which refers.

With those data, the procedure extracts the sentence words and it generates associations and/or events.

Once the second phase of the analysis has ended, we will have obtained a list of associations and events. Subsequently, the third phase at stake consists of the verification lists, of which objective is removing those associations with null or invalid dates. Also in this phase a "reference solving" is done.

The purpose of this search is to solve the following problem: referenced entities appeared in the lists can exist as a topic in the analyzed historical document. Even it is possible that the entity refers to a document topic, but it has been named with an alternative form. In this case, the algorithm must replace the part of the association which cites the entity by its real name (an example: the "Alfonso X El Sabio" [Alfonso X the Wise]) topic would find called inside the text like "Alfonso X" (Alfonso X) or "Alfonso El Sabio" (Alfonso X the Wise), being in both cases a valid reference but it shall be replaced by the right name.

The algorithm behaviour to check the references is to extract those reference words which start by capital letter. Later, topic by topic carry out the same operation with its title and compares them.

It gives us as a valid reference which has the great number of fitting words and always with a number >= 2. Indeed, it substitutes the association text by the right topic name which has been referenced. Once the dependencies are generated, the "unidirectionality" or "bidirectionality" is calculated inside the association lists by means of a crossing-search.

Finally, the relevance roles of associations and events are computated. To solve this computation there are two approaches. The first one consists of prefixed relevancies associated to prefixed roles, letting the rest of roles with null relevance. By this way, the algorithm would assign relevancies in function of a predefined table. Nevertheless, this method is not flexible. The second approach, which is used in the final algorithm, consists of the count of roles. It is assigned more relevance to the more frequent roles and less relevance to the uncommon ones. This method is more flexible, independent of the predefined tables and the information domain. Once the relevance has been assigned, a filter is executed to eliminate the irrelevant dates (that is, uncommon roles).

As an additional comment, information is not removed during the summary process seen before instead a second analysis is realized to extract topic redundant information but it could be valid for document context. An example based on the previous ones: "Hijo (NC) de (SP) Pedro II (NP), rey (NC) de (SP) Aragón (NP) y (CC) Juana (NP), condesa (NC) de (SP) Urdiel (NP)" (Son of Peter II, king of Aragón and Joan, countess of Urdiel), we saw that "rey (NC) de (SP) Aragón (NP)" (king of Aragón) and "condesa (NC) de (SP) Urdiel (NP)" (countess of Urdiel) were removed. To the analyzed topic context, this information is strange, but from a global point of view, it isn't. So, it would be interesting to store it temporarily since it is relevant information inside the document in general. To achieve it, the algorithm calls a rescue method, generating associations in the possible situations.

These associations are orphans, as they don't know beforehand the topic at which they refer.

The algorithm then finds (in a similar way to the reference analysis) what topic each association is referred, and if it is found, the algorithm links this association with the referred topic. To the previous example, it would search the topic named "Pedro II" (Peter II) and it would assign it the association "rey (role) de Aragón (referred entity)" (king of Aragón) and it would find topic "Juana" (Joan) and it would assign the association "condesa (role) de Urdiel (referred entity)" (countess of Urdiel). In case it did not find the referred topic, the algorithm could create a new topic with these associations, but it was ruled out for being outside of the strictly necessary. Results show that the second level algorithm produces around three thousand associations and one thousand events from two hundred voices. It implies the increase of the order of magnitude in the results. Additionally, the accuracy of the generated dates is approximately of a ninety per cent. Around 20% more than with the first level.

Information Management

Once we have the event and association lists, their storage is done via three different ways.

1. To generate an XML document with a XTM/DITA hybrid format with all the available topic information including the related events and associations with each topic. The relations will be navigable as long as the referred entities has been found and they were other topics from the own document. Also, it has the possibility to examine references to entities in other documents and merge to them, although the current algorithm only works with the original document.

2. The JDO storage using the JPOX technology. Obtaining an object-oriented database with the peculiarity that below there is a relational database management system,

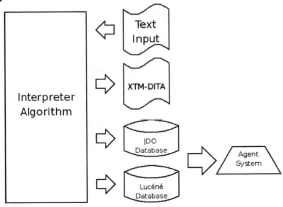

Figure 3. Interpreter algorithm inputs and outputs

so it is useful for the programmer which loves the object-oriented database features and the programmer or user who needs a relational database. All the original information is stored in a database that later could be queried through agents, Web system, applications, and so on.

3. The third and last method consists of the topic indexation by means of an adapted Lucene analyzer. This indexation will let us to find whatever desired topic.

Search Agents System

Finally, it has been developed a multiagent system via JADE platform. There is a specific agent in charge of receiving the external agent requests and answering with the topic results from a search. This agent validates a connection against the object-oriented database created and used Lucene to identify, from a search string, what topic must be extracted from the database. The agent accepts several possibilities to make advanced searches, a lot of search agents could operate simultaneously, but there are not agents which modify data.

Additionally, to check the flexibility system, another search agent has been developed, capable of the following process: from a character string the agent is able to look up Google and send the results from this service to the original agent. In other words, the search agent prototype developed let us to build versions to make searches in any environment.

Furthermore, to the GUI (Graphical User Interface), two different types of agents from a unified interface agent prototype, have been developed. Each version solves a different interface problem. The former is a console user interface agent and the latter a graphical user interface agent. Both have the same detection and communication system with any search agent.

Finally, an agent allows showing a 3D topic tree from a query made by using the multiagent system built.

Information Visualization

Once all the interpreted historical information is prepared, processed, and stored in different storage devices, a graphical visualization of it is possible.

The XTM/DITA format offers us the feature to represent the information like mesh nodes, in which each node represents an information topic, and the links among nodes are labelled with a role which plays an association among them.

The distance among nodes is inversely proportional to the relevance of roles that plays associations among topics. (An example: two related topics by family will be nearer among them than a territorial association). The algorithm is based on multiply a scalar distance by 100% minus a percentage obtained to compare the relevance of each role against the obtained maximum relevance in the analysis.

By this way, with a quick outlook, the mesh density can be observed in those zones of which topics and their associations were really relevant between them.

The 2D representation is based on an extended interrelated topic mesh both lengthwise and crosswise (see Figure 4).

Figure 4. 2D representation example

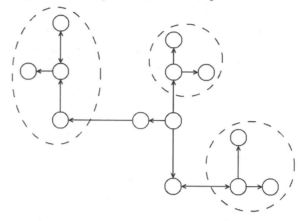

Figure 5. 3D representation example

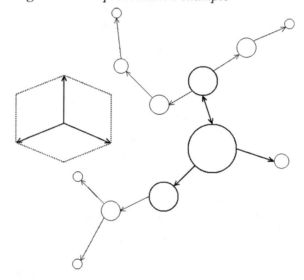

The 3D representation follows similarly; each mesh topic is surrounded by the associated topics, but it extends to the high, wide, and long. All the distance calculations would be similar or equal, and the only condition is the 3D positioning of the mesh nodes.

CONCLUSION

Both the development of a methodology and a digital information processing model which covers the requirements established in the semantic Web and which adapt to the peculiarities of cultural heritage-related information and documents, and the use of superimposed information for the description and subsequent information handling within the scope of digital libraries (Crane & Wulfman, 2003) are factors of a completely new work proposal which also offers the potential required to solve the vast majority of problems set out in the research context, such as searches that are limited to subject matter categories or alphabetical indexes, and flexibility.

On the one hand, the historical document analysis problem has been solved at the beginning by means of a limited first level system, and later by a second level system, utterly flexible but dependent on a pattern system.

The analysis problem has been displaced from a computing approach to a linguistic approach, consisting of setting those ways of expression used to cultural heritage information description. The elaborated patterns in the current algorithm only carry out correctly with Spanish language, which unfortunately, is very flexible and varied. There are other languages more structured which facilitate the expression pattern development, but as a conclusion we can say that the language is not a feature which hinders the automatic document analysis.

There are other technologies which do textual analysis but there is little technology capable of synthesizing, extracting relevant information, cataloguing and generating it in a topic network from an opaque historical text. Previously all the tasks have to be done by hand via text understanding reading. Nowadays, using this technology the computer will not be able to understand but it will be able to at least evaluate the information and infer the substantial.

It is very interesting to see it from another point of view, too. A suitable document writing based on discrete linguistic expressive figures would let a versatile analysis from a preprogrammed analysis algorithm with adjusted patterns to detect this set of figures. However, currently, the algorithm has several complex stands-up to solve: writing, orthographical, grammatical mistakes and the morphological variety. All of them cause the algorithm effectiveness will be reduced always.

On the other hand, an effective XTM-based labelling of information has been achieved and combined with other metadata languages that are appropriate both element and collection levels at digital libraries: DITA, FOAF, SKOS, MODS, RDF (Park & Hunting, 2002). An improvement of the information retrieval process will be automatically accomplished and this will assist the digital information preservation process (Premis & Rlg/Oclc, 2005) as XTM is based on XML. Furthermore, the developed prototype also incorporates an information retrieval system based on personal agents and soft-computing (Crestani & Passi, 2000) that not only enables the information requested by the user in GEA, but also outside GEA online (Herrera & Passi 2006). This helps to contribute OAI functionality or a "harvesting" approach (Halbert et al., 2003), which is currently in great demand and necessary, and which has been incorporated into other projects such as zOAC.

Finally, we have fulfilled an important objective creating 2D and 3D information visualization and trying to make the best of digital information despite constant changes in technological devices.

REFERENCES

Baldonado, M., Chang, C-C.K., Gravano, L., & Paepcke, A. (1997). Metadata for digital libraries: Architecture and design rationale. In *Proceedings of the second ACM international conference on Digital libraries* (pp. 47–56). Philadelphia. New York: ACM.

Berners-Lee, T., & Fischetti, M. (1997). *Weaving the Web*. San Francisco: Physica-Verlag.

Brocks, H., Thiel, U., Stein, A., & Dirsch-Weigand, A. (2001). Customizable retrieval functions based on user tasks in the cultural heritage domain. In *Proceedings of the 5th European Conference on Digital libraries*, LNCS 2163 (pp. 37–48). Heidelberg: Springer.

Chandler, A., Foley, D., & Hafez, A.M. (2000). Mapping and converting essential federal geographic data committee (FGDC) metadata into MARC21 and Dublin Core. Towards an alternative to the FGDC clearinghouse. *D-Lib Magazine, 6*(1).

Crane, G. (2002). Cultural heritage digital libraries: Needs and components. In *Proceedings of the 6th European Conference on Digital libraries*. LNCS 2458 (pp. 626637). Heidelberg: Springer.

Crane, G., & Wulfman, C. (2003). Towards a cultural heritage digital library. In *Proceedings of the 3rd ACM/IEEE-CS joint conference on Digital libraries* (pp. 75–86). Houston. New York: ACM.

Crestani, F., & Passi, G. (2000). *Soft computing in information retrieval: Techniques and applications*. Heidelberg: Physica-Verlag.

Foulonneau, M., Cole, T.W., Habing, T.G., & Shreeves, S.L. (2005). Using collection descriptions to enhance an aggregation of harvested item-level metadata. In *Proceedings of the 5th ACM/IEEE-CS joint conference on Digital libraries* (pp. 32–41). Denver. New York: ACM.

De Gendt, V., Isaac, A., Van Der Meijt, L., & Schlobach, S. (2006). Semantic Web techniques for multiple views on heterogeneous collections: A case study. In *Proceedings of the 10th European Conference on Digital libraries*, LNCS 4172 (pp. 426–437). Heidelberg: Springer.

DITA. (2007). *Darwin information typing architecture OASIS standard*. Retrieved August 28, 2008, from http://dita.xml.org

Gelb, J. (2007) Optimizing your content development using topic maps. In *Proceedings of DITA North American Conferences*. San José, CA.

Giunchiglia, F., Yatskevich, M., & Shvaiko, P. (in press). Semantic matching: Algorithms and implementation. *Journal on Data Semantics*.

Halbert, M., Kaczmarek, J., & Hagedorn, K. (2003). Findings from the Mellon metadata harvesting initiative. In *Proceedings of the 7th European Conference on Digital libraries*, LNCS 2769 (pp. 58–69). Heidelberg: Springer.

Herrera, E., & Passi, G. (2006). Special issue on soft approaches to information retrieval and information access on the Web. *Journal of the American Society for Information Science and Technology*, ACM Digital library, *57*, 511–514.

Hutt, A., & Riley, J. (2005). Semantics and syntax of Dublin Core usage in open archives initiative data providers of cultural heritage materials. In *Proceedings of the 5th ACM/IEEE-CS joint conference on Digital libraries* (pp. 262–270). Denver. New York: ACM.

ISO 13250. (2003). *Information technology—SGML applications—Topic maps*.

ISO 21127. (2006). *A reference ontology for the interchange of cultural heritage information*.

Maier, D., Delcambre, L. (1999). Superimposed information for the Internet. *ACM SIGMOD Workshop on The Web and Databases*. Philadelphia.

Park, J., Hunting, S. (2002). *XML topic maps: Creating and using topic maps for the Web*. Addisson-Wesley.

Premis, W.G., & Rlg/Oclc, W.G. (2005). *Preservation metadata: implementation strategies*.

Tolosana-Calasanz, R., Nogueras-Iso, J., Béjar, R., Muro-Medrano, P.R., &Zarazaga-Soria, F.J. (2006). Semantic interoperability based on Dublin Core hierarchical one-to-one mappings.

International Journal of Metadata, Semantics and Ontologies, 1(3), 183.

KEY TERMS

Dublin Core (DC): A set of metadata descriptors about resources on the Internet. It contains fifteen element descriptions for the use in resource description endorsed in the ISO Standard 15836-2003.

Freeling: An Open Source Suite of Language Analyzers (http://www.lsi.upc.es/~nlp/freeling/).

JADE: Java Agents Development Framework (http://jade.tilab.com/).

JDO, JPOX: Java Persistent Objects (JPOX) is a free and fully compliant implementation of the JDO specifications, and Java Data Objects (Java Data Objects). API is a standard interface-based Java model abstraction of persistence.

Lucene: Lucene is a free/open source information retrieval library (http://lucene.apache.org/).

Machine Readable Cataloging Record (MARC): The former normalized format of automatized bibliographic register.

Open Archive Cataloguer (zOAC): Applies the OAI-PMH protocol for automatic metadata harvesting and aggregation of bibliographic records and has been developed over the Web application server Zope.

Open Archives Initiative (OAI): An initiative to develop and promote interoperability standards to facilitate the efficient dissemination of content (http://www.openarchives.org/).

ENDNOTES

[1]   The use of the topic maps paradigm specification understanding by a computer, known as XTM (XML for Topic Maps) combined with DITA (Darwin Information Typing Architecture OASIS standard)

[2]   It is a pronominal verb.

Chapter XLII
Reference Services in Digital Environment

Wan Ab. Kadir Wan Dollah
MARA University of Technology, Malaysia

Diljit Singh
University of Malaya, Malaysia

ABSTRACT

Information and communication technologies have been used to assist in various functions of library and information units. Digital reference services that is becoming widely available especially in academic libraries and public libraries around the world provide assistance to remote users especially through e-mail format. This chapter clarifies the concept, format and background of digital reference services. It also focuses on issues, trends and challenges in digital reference services, besides discussing on technological developments in digital reference services. The benefits and limitations of the services are also highlighted in this chapter.

INTRODUCTION

Reference service plays a vital role in terms of providing personalized assistance to library users in accessing and using suitable information resources to meet their information needs. Rapid development in information and communication technologies (ICTs) in the past three decades have significantly influenced both the way libraries provide information services to their users and the way they choose to access information. Digital reference service is gaining popularity especially in academic and public libraries.

THE CONCEPT OF DIGITAL REFERENCE SERVICES

The term digital reference service is also known as virtual reference service, online reference, Web-based reference service, and electronic reference service.

Lankes (1998) defines digital reference as Internet-based question and answer services that connect users with individuals who possess specialized subject or skill expertise. Janes, Carter, and Memmott (1999) define digital reference as a mechanism by which people can submit their questions and have them answered by a library staff member through some electronic means (e-mail, Web forms, chat, and so on) not in person or over the phone.

In general, a digital reference service has four elements as follows:

1. The user of the service,
2. The interface (e-mail, Web form, chat, videoconference, and so on),
3. The information professional, and
4. Electronic resources (including electronic or CD-based resources, Web resources, local digitized material, and so on), as well as print resources (Berube, 2003, p. 1)

BACKGROUND OF REFERENCE SERVICES

Reference services have been constantly developing from the traditional, to automated, to hybrid, and now to digital.

Technological innovation has played a key role in reference librarianship in the second half of the twentieth century. Telephone service began to appear alongside traditional face-to-face and postal reference services early in the twentieth century (Bopp, 1995). In the 1960s, libraries began to explore new technologies such as microfilm and microfiche, tapes and sound recordings. The 1970s and 1980s brought about significant changes with the emergence of full-text databases and electronic card catalogs in many academic, public, and special libraries (Grohs, Reed, & Allan, 2003).

Eventually the electronic catalogue databases became the online public access catalogues (OPACs) providing local as well as remote access.

With OPACs, the users can specify their queries as asset of keywords linked by logical operators AND, OR and NOT. Another major change in the process of storage, retrieval and dissemination of information was brought by the invention of CD-ROMs. By the late 1990s, many libraries moved from CD-ROM to providing databases through the Internet. The Internet introduced new possibilities and interactive technologies such as e-mail, chat, and instant messaging to the reference desk (Penka, 2003).

According to Kasowitz (2001), many libraries and organizations have responded to an increased need for formal methods of remote communication between information seekers and information professionals by providing reference service via the Internet, or digital reference service, to their users. Wasik (2003) traced the origins of digital reference services to the library field, where libraries sought to augment traditional services by providing reference assistance in an electronic environment. Lankes (2000) gives five reasons for moving to electronic reference services:

1. Increasing access to resources beyond the library
2. Lack of geographic constrains for users
3. The need to differentiate services to different populations of users in the face of shrinking budgets
4. Increases in complexity of information resources and the need for specialized knowledge
5. New options for answering reference questions (Lankes, p. 187)

Academic libraries were the first to provide digital reference services in the early 1980s (Gross, McClure, & Lankes, 2001). One of the first services to go online was the Electronic Access to Reference Services (EARS) launched by the University of Maryland Health Services Library in Baltimore in 1984 (Wasik, 2003; quoted from Weise and Bergendale, 1986). EARS allowed patrons to make reference queries or request to various library services via e-mail, using terminals either on or outside campus (Braxton & Brunsdale, 2004).

The number of academic and public libraries offering e-mail reference service continues to grow making e-mail the most common vehicle for providing digital reference services. Kawakami (2003) noted that with the advent of the World Wide Web, libraries created online forms that asked the user to input specific information such as format type or time period and thus give the librarian guidance as to what the user needed. Libraries also posted FAQs on their Web pages in the hopes that the user would find his question answered therein. FAQs however, do not have an interactive component and may not address a user's particular question.

Throughout the 1990s e-mail reference became increasingly important. By the early 1990s, Ask-A-Librarian e-mail reference services were common. By the mid 1990s, at least 75 % of 122 ARL (Association Research Libraries) member libraries and 45 % of academic libraries offered digital reference service via electronic mail or a Web form (Goetsch, Sowers, & Todd, 1999; Janes et al., 1999). Digital reference services become important and effective resources for meeting information needs of thousands of users, and the number of the user requests to these services has continued to increase. By the end of the 1990s, 99 % of 70 academic libraries offered e-mail reference and 29 % offered real time reference service (Tenopir, 2001).

The new millennium brought the advent of live reference in academic libraries with the use of chat or commercial call centre software to communicate with users in real time. Kawakimi (2003) wrote that technologies that have been adapted from the commercial sector allow the librarian to conduct a synchronous or real time dialogue with a user to clarify an information need and use application sharing to deliver information online.

Collaboration has been initiated by various libraries with the implementation of national, regional and international reference services. For instance, the Library of Congress began its Collaborative Digital Reference Service projects to test the provision of professional library-quality reference service to users anytime anywhere (24 hours per day, 7 days per week), through an international digital network of libraries.

FORMATS OF DIGITAL REFERENCE

Before the existence of Internet in the early 1990s, librarians relied on the correspondence, the telephone, and the fax machine to help users who were unable to come in to the library for reference service. With the advent of Internet-based tools, librarians now have a greatly expanded set of options (Francoeur, 2002).

The terms *asynchronous* and *synchronous* have been used by researchers to describe the service delivery of digital reference (Berube, 2003; Francoeur, 2002; Han & Goulding, 2003; McClennen, 2002; Wells & Hanson, 2003).

The two broad categories of digital reference service models are as follows:

1. *Asynchronous transactions*, which involves time delay between the question and answer.
   a. E-mail reference
   b. Web Forms
   c. Ask-A-Librarian Service
2. *Synchronous transaction* which takes place in "real-time" with an immediate response to the query.
   a. Text-based chat/online chat reference
   b. Video-conferencing or Web-cam services
   c. Digital Reference Robots
3. *Collaborative digital reference services (CDRS).*

ISSUES, TRENDS AND CHALLENGES IN DIGITAL REFERENCE

There are many digital reference services available at present. LiveRef at *http://www.public. iastate.edu/~CYBERSTACKS/LiveRef.htm* keeps a registry of real-time digital reference services. Francoeur (2001) reports that as of April 2001, 272 libraries had a chat reference services in place. Libraries in United States have spearheaded DRS and those in other countries are following suit (Chowdhury & Margariti, 2004, p. 50).

In the Summer 2000 issue of *Reference and User Services Quarterly*, David Lankes discussed on the overwhelming demand of AskA services and other digital reference services. This demand has led to the emergence of several concerns, including:

1. How to manage the overwhelming use of digital reference services;
2. How digital reference changes library practice, such as the reference interview; and
3. Software and customer service operations that provide real-time service. (p. 352)

It is important to recognize that as the Internet issues constrain the need to re-evaluate reference service and it is important for reference librarians to continue to evolve along with it.

Gross et al. (2001) noted that despite e-mail remains the main vehicle for digital reference services in libraries, libraries are currently experimenting with various applications that provide synchronous interaction between the user and the librarian. Several libraries, including the University of Michigan, University of California, Irvine, and a joint project with the University of California, Berkerley and North Carolina State University, report undertaking synchronous digital reference using video conferencing, but these experiments have not been largely successful.

In the same vein, McClure et al. (2002) claim that many libraries are now providing digital reference services, either as an integrated component of their regular reference service, as a separate service, or as part of a collaborative consortium. Many other libraries are thinking about or are about to implement such services. Additionally, an increasing number of AskA services have been developed in the commercial, educational and non-profit sectors that are not directly affiliated with any specific library (e.g., AskJeeves, Internet Public Library, Ask Dr. Math, Ask Joan of Art, AskERIC).

Many libraries are experimenting with live reference service. However, it has been noted that most libraries in the USA are still in the first phase even after several years' experimentation (Tunender, 2002). Janes (2002) argued that libraries have been providing digital reference services for a few years and they should move on from experimenting to defining new services.

TECHNOLOGICAL DEVELOPMENT IN DRS

Technological development is creating new ways for librarians to provide reference services to remote users. Computer-based reference has significantly improved library service to contemporary users, from the introduction of online and cataloguing databases to local and wide area networks to electronic reference sources. The widespread of the Internet in the 1990s has shown a new era for libraries in terms of networking opportunities. More specifically, virtual reference or Web-based reference has had a major impact on the referral function. *Library Trends* (vol. 50, no. 2, 2001) examines the extent to which and how technological advances have changed basic reference practice.

Technologies that can support synchronous digital reference can be divided into three categories:

1. Chat software;
2. Remote control software (RCS); and
3. Web contact centre software.

The different technologies can offer different benefits such as low cost (chat software), ability to control the patron's browser and authentication (RCS), and features designed especially for digital reference such as question queuing, scripted messages and session transcripts, as in the case with Web contact software, such as MCLS's (Metropolitan Cooperative Library System), and 24/7 Reference (http://www.247ref.org/) (Chowdhury & Margariti, 2004, p. 51)

BENEFITS AND LIMITATIONS OF DRS

Digital reference services have a number of benefits and limitations. As a new powerful method of delivering a reference service, DRS provides more alternatives and flexibility to users. According to Johnson, Newton, and Reid (2004), using digital reference services could be a time saver for users, and using the Internet is generally cheaper than using a telephone. Digital reference services provide an extra choice for users, and may take some of the load of a busy reference desk, although it does not lessen the overall workload for the library.

Lam (2003) wrote that e-mail reference offer users the convenience of asking for information or reference assistance whenever and wherever they are as long as the Internet is accessible. Users can make requests from remote sites, notably from their home or office computer workstations. Accessible 24 hours a day and unrestricted by geography, DRS are a powerful means for the free exchange of information and the promotion of interactive learning where the learning or teaching situation is characterized by participation on the part of the learner.

E-mail reference also has the advantage of providing more clear and complete answers than what could possibly be given at a busy reference desk. When answering a question through e-mail, the reference librarian usually has more time to think about the question, the user's information need, and if necessarily, consult with other librarians who have more related expertise or knowledge.

Smith (2001) noted that written responses may be preferable to the "on the spot" oral response received when questionnaire are asked in-person, over the telephone or using videoconferencing or voice chat. In fact, written response are less likely to be misunderstood or forgotten. Since the reference interview is conducted in writing, librarians easily can electronically file e-mail and Web form requests and their responses so that the response can be retrieved later when similar questions are asked or the same user returns. Although user asking questions using text-chat also receive written answers, chat is synchronous, so librarians must reply immediately, which often will not provide the opportunity to give a well-written response.

However, there are several limitations or weaknesses of reference queries by E-mail or Web forms. According to Bopp and Smith (2001), the major disadvantage of accepting reference queries by e-mail or Web page is the asynchronous nature of the interaction: library staff cannot interview the user in real time. As Abels (1996) has pointed out when e-mail is used to communicate, an interchange of questions and answers to clarify the question can result in substantial delays in providing the answer. A question that arrives during office hours, for example may be answered shortly, but late-night queries are not answered until the next morning. Additionally, questions cannot be answered immediately if the library staff is not available.

Synchronous or real time digital reference can be implemented to overcome those problems.

With chat technologies and video conferencing, users can access information and receive real time guidance from librarian.

Online chat reference is a real time conversation or interviews between the reference librarians and the remote users or researchers using a computer and the Internet.   Instant messaging software products such as AOL allow librarian to communicate synchronously in the shared environment. Through text-based chat, the user can type words on a keyboard and these words directly appear on the librarian's computer monitor. With voice chat, user can communicate by speaking or by typing and either their voice or their typed words are transmitted to the librarian's computer. Examples of how a library could use online chat are to have a link stated *Chat with a Librarian* or *Click for life help* on the library home pages with text around the link informing users the hours online chat reference service is available.

The main benefit of using online chat reference is that it happens in real time whereby as soon as a user types a query, the question appears on the librarian's monitor. The librarian can respond promptly simply by typing. The librarian can ask for clarification and receive a quick response for the vague question. Once the request is clear, the librarian can immediately answer the question or indicate that research is needed.

However, online chat services can be available only when a reference librarian is on duty, so remote researchers would not be able to send reference requests anytime throughout the day as they could with e-mail or Web form reference services. There should be a mechanism alerting librarians that someone has initiated a chat session, such as beep, librarians would have to monitor their computer screens constantly, which would be inconvenient.

Videoconferencing or Web-cam for reference services is where video and audio are delivered in real time to and from the library over the Internet. Desktop videoconferencing requires that both locations have a computer, Internet connection, digital camera and microphone. Videoconferencing provides benefit where both librarians and users are able to speak as well as seeing each other during the remote reference interviews. However, videoconferencing will not be an option for the average person with a reference question. Although videoconferencing software can be downloaded at no cost, remote users also must have a digital camera and microphone as well as someone who knows how to use them (Smith, 2001).

By implementing collaborative digital reference services, the institutions can get many benefits, such as sharing of expertise and resources, expanding hours of service and providing access to a larger collection of knowledge resulting from digital reference services (e.g., question-answer archives).

CONCLUSION

Reference and information services have always been the main element of library services. They provide personalized assistance to library users in accessing suitable information resources to meet their needs. Over time, various technological developments have affected the provision of reference services especially after the introduction of online library services. Librarians should take full advantage of e-mail, Web, and other means of digital reference services in this digital library environment.

REFERENCES

Abels, E.G. (1996). The e-mail reference interview. *RQ, 35*(Spring), 348.

Berube, L. (2003). *Digital reference overview: An issue paper from the networked services policy task group.* Retrieved August 29, 2008, from http://www.ukoln.ac.uk/public/nsptg/virtual/

Bopp, R.E., & Smith, L.C. (Eds.). (2001). *Reference and information services: An introduction* (3rd ed.). Colorado: Libraries Unlimited, Inc.

Braxton, S.M., & Brunsdale, M. (2004). E-mail reference as a substitute for library receptionist. *The Reference Librarian, 85*, 19–31.

Bunge, C.A. (1999). Reference services. *Reference Librarian, 66*, 185–199.

Bunge, C.A., & Bopp, R.E. (2001). History and varieties of reference services. In

Chowdhury, G.G. (2002). Digital libraries and reference services: Present and future. *Journal of Documentation, 58*(3), 258–283.

Chowdhury, G.G., & Chowdhury, S. (2003). *Introduction to digital libraries.* London: Facet Publishing.

Chowdhury, G., & Margariti, S. (2004). Digital reference services: A snapshot of the current practices in Scottish libraries. *Library Review, 53*(1), 50–60.

Connor, E. (Ed.). (2006). *An introduction to reference services in academic libraries.* New York: The Haworth Information Press.

Francoeur, S. (2002). Digital Reference. In *The Teaching Librarian.* Retrieved August 29, 2008, from http://www.teachinglibrarian.org/digref.htm

Goetsch, L., Sowers, L., & Todd, C. (1999). SPEC kit 251: Electronic reference service: Executive summary. Retrieved August 29, 2008, from *http://www.arl.org/spec/251sum.html*

Gorman, G.E. (Ed.). (2002). *The digital factor in library and information services.* London: Facet Publishing.

Grohs, K., Reed, C., & Allen, N. (2003). Marketing the virtual library. In A. Hanson, & B.L. Levin (Eds.), *Building a virtual library* (pp. 133–147). London: Information Science Publishing.

Gross, M., McClure, C.R., & Lankes, R.D. (2001). *Assessing quality in digital reference services*: *Overview of key literature on digital reference.* Florida: Information Institute.

Han, L., & Goulding, A. (2003). Information and reference services in the digital library. *Information Services and Use, 23*, 251–262.

Huling, N. (2002). Reference services and information access. In J.R. Schement (Ed.), *Encyclopedia of Communication and Information* (pp. 867–874). New York: Gale Group.

Janes, J. (2002). *What is reference for?* Retrieved August 29, 2008, from http://www.ala.org/ala/rusa/rusaprotools/futureofref/whatreference.htm

Janes, J., Carter, D., & Memmott, P. (1999). Digital reference services in academic libraries. *Reference and User Services Quarterly, 39*(2), 145–150.

Kasowitz, A.S. (2001). Trends and issues in digital reference services. *ERIC Digest, November.*

Kawakami, A.K. (2003). Real-time digital reference. In M.A. Drake (Ed.), *Encyclopedia of Library and Information Science* (2nd ed., pp. 2463–2474). New York: Marcel Dekker.

Lam, K. (2003). Exploring virtual reference: What it is and what it may be. In R.D. Lankes et al. (Eds.), *Implementing digital reference services: Setting standards and making it real* (pp. 31–40). London: Facet Publishing.

Lankes, R.D. (1998). *AskA starter kit: How to build and maintain digital reference services.* Syracuse: ERIC Clearinghouse on Information and Technology.

Lankes, R.D. (2000a). The foundations of digital reference. In R.D. Lankes, J.W. Collins, & A.S. Kasowitz (Eds.), *Digital Reference Services in the New Millennium: Planning, Management and Evaluation* (pp. 1–10). New York: Neal-Schuman Publications.

Lankes, R.D. (2000b). The birth cries of digital reference: An introduction to this special issue. *Reference and User Services Quarterly, 39*(4), 352–354.

Lankes, R.D. et al. (Eds.). (2003). *Implementing digital reference services: Setting standards and make it real*. London: Facet Publishing.

Lankes, R.D., Collins, J.W., & Kasowitz, A.S. (Eds.). (2000). *Digital reference service in the new millennium: Planning, management and evolution*. New York: Neal Schuman.

McClennen, M. (2002). *Software, systems and standards in digital reference: A research agenda*. Retrieved August 29, 2008, from http://www.ipl.org/div/papers/symposium-2002/systems.html

Penka, J.T. (2003). The technological challenges of digital reference: An overview. *D-Lib Magazine, 9*(2). Retrieved August 29, 2008, from http://www.dlib.org/dlib//february03/penka/02penka.html

Pomerantz, J., Nicholson, S., & Lankes, R.D. (2003, April) Digital reference triage: Factors influencing question routing and assignment. *The Library Quarterly, 73*(2), 103–120.

Pomerantz, J. et al. (2004). The current state of digital reference: Validation of a general digital reference model through a survey of digital reference services. *Information Processing and Management, 40*, 347–363.

Smith, B. (2001). Enhancing reference services through technology. In J.D. Edwards (Ed.), *Emerging Solutions in Reference Services: Implications for Libraries in the New Millennium*. New York: The Haworth Information Press. Su, S.S. (2002). Web-based reference services: The user intermediary interaction perspective. In G.E. Gorman (Ed.), *The Digital Factor in Library and Information Services* (pp. 185–207). London: Facet Publishing.

Tenopir, C. (2001). Virtual reference services in a real world. *Library Journal, 126*(11), 38–40.

Tenopir, C., & Ennis, L. (2002, Spring). A decade of digital reference 1991–2001. *Reference and User Service Quarterly, 41*(3), 264–273.

Tunender, H. (2002). Digital reference: Trends, techniques, and changes. *Library Hi Tech News, 19*(4), 5–6.

VandeCreek, L.M. (2006). E-mail reference evaluation: Using the results of a Satisfaction survey. *The Reference Librarian, 93*, 99–108.

Wasik, J.M. (2003a). *Building and maintaining digital reference services*. Retrieved August 29, 2008, from http://www.michaellorenzen.com/eric/ref-serv.html

Wasik, J.M. (2003b). *Digital reference evaluation*. Retrieved August 29, 2008, from http://www.vrd.org/AskA/digref-assess.shtml

Wells, A.T., & Hanson, A. (2002). E-reference. In A. Hanson, & B.L. Levin (Eds.), *Building a Virtual Library* (pp. 95–120). London: Information Science Pub.

Wikipedia. (2006). *Digital reference services*. Retrieved August 29, 2008, from http://en.wikipedia.org/wiki/Digital-reference-services

KEY TERMS

Ask-A-Librarian Service: Usually provides a free, quick reference service and the basic answers to brief, factual questions.

Collaborative Digital Reference Service: Where two or more libraries team up to offer reference services using any of the digital reference services format.

Digital Reference Robots: Use of artificial intelligence to response to questions—for instance, the Ask Jeeves service that is available on the Internet.

Digital Reference Services: A concept that shows reference services delivered electronically, often in real-time, where the users employ computers or other Internet technology to communicate with reference staff, without being physically present in the library.

E-Mail Reference: A main format of digital reference services where user sends the library an e-mail with a reference query and the library may reply by e-mail, telephone, correspondence, and so on.

Online Chat Reference: or instant messaging is where librarians and users can "talk" to each other in real-time in the Internet using special text-based software.

Reference Services: Refer to the provision of information to people entering a library and requesting assistance from the library staff or in short personal assistance provided to library users seeking for information.

Video Conferencing: This form of digital reference is where librarians and users are able to see each other in the monitor through a camera.

Web Forms: The forms which pops up when user clicks on a button on the library's Web sites. The question can be typed in with other specific information and then sent to the library by clicking on a *send* button.

Chapter XLIII
USGS Digital Libraries for Coastal and Marine Science

Frances L. Lightsom
U.S. Geological Survey, USGS Woods Hole Science Center, USA

Alan O. Allwardt
ETI Professionals, USGS Pacific Science Center, USA

ABSTRACT

The U.S. Geological Survey (USGS) has developed three related digital libraries providing access to topical and georeferenced information for coastal and marine science: the Marine Realms Information Bank (MRIB) and its two offshoots, the Monterey Bay Science Digital Library and Coastal Change Hazards Digital Library. These three members of the MRIB family run on the same software and share a common database, but they employ different user interfaces targeting different audiences. This chapter reviews (1) distributed geolibraries, the conceptual foundation for MRIB, (2) the modular software of MRIB, permitting the rapid development of customized user interfaces, and (3) the Electronic Index Card (EIC) Creation Utility, encouraging users to contribute new metadata records to the MRIB database. The accompanying discussion addresses several challenges facing digital library developers: providing for scalability in the system; ensuring interoperability with other systems; and meeting the demands of characterizing information while facilitating its search and retrieval.

INTRODUCTION

The Coastal and Marine Geology Program (CMGP) of the U.S. Geological Survey (USGS) has developed a family of distributed digital libraries providing access to topical and georeferenced information for coastal and marine science. This digital library system includes three user interfaces targeting different audiences:

1. The Marine Realms Information Bank (MRIB; http://mrib.usgs.gov/), developed in 2001, is a general-purpose user interface providing access to free online scientific in-

formation about oceans, coasts, and coastal watersheds. MRIB encourages its users to discover these information resources by browsing a faceted classification with twelve main categories, including author, agency, discipline, feature type, named location, and "hot topics" (Figure 1). MRIB was also one of the first digital libraries to utilize interactive maps for searching and retrieving georeferenced information.

2. The geographic search capabilities of MRIB were ideally suited for creating the Monterey Bay Science (MBS) Digital Library (http://mrib.usgs.gov/mbs/), a regional pilot project providing access to scientific information about the Monterey Bay National Marine Sanctuary and coastal watersheds of central California (Figure 2). The MBS user interface, released in 2004, serves as a model for any regionally focused digital library based on the MRIB software architecture.

3. The newest addition to the CMGP digital library system is the Coastal Change Hazards (CCH) Digital Library (http://mrib.usgs.gov/cch/), released in 2006. The specialized CCH user interface (Figure 3) focuses on natural hazards and human impacts in the coastal zone and replaces the MRIB hot topics with a more specific topical classification. Crosswalks between the MRIB and CCH topical classifications ensure that online resources originally cataloged for one interface can be searched and retrieved using the other interface. The Coastal Change

Figure 1. The Marine Realms Information Bank (MRIB), featuring three search options: by category, location, and keyword. The "Submit a Document" link at the bottom of the page connects the user to the Electronic Index Card (EIC) Creation Utility

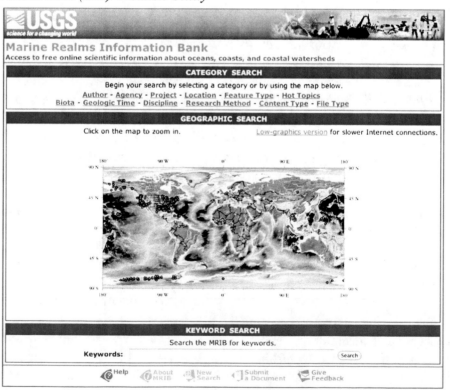

Figure 2. The Monterey Bay Science (MBS) Digital Library, a regionally focused member of the Marine Realms Information Bank (MRIB) family. The customized MBS user interface provides access to about one-fourth of the MRIB database

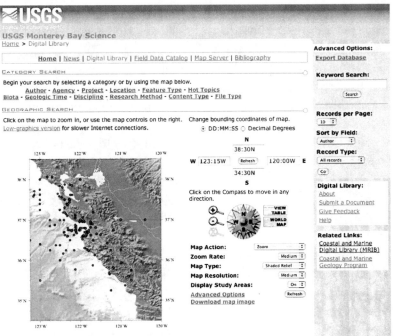

Figure 3. The Coastal Change Hazards (CCH) Digital Library, a topically focused member of the Marine Realms Information Bank (MRIB) family. The customized CCH user interface provides access to about one-third of the MRIB database

Hazards Digital Library serves as a model for any topically focused digital library based on the MRIB software architecture.

These three closely related digital libraries, which run on the same software and share a common database, constitute the MRIB family of digital libraries. In the discussion that follows, the term "MRIB" will be used in a generic sense for all three members of the family, whereas "Marine Realms Information Bank" will refer specifically to the parent interface.

BACKGROUND

The rationale for MRIB can be found in two National Research Council (NRC) studies released in 1999. One study, *Science for Decisionmaking*, was an external review of the USGS Coastal and Marine Geology Program (CMGP) conducted by NRC at the request of the USGS. The final report posed three "grand challenges" for CMGP over the next few decades, including development of a "national knowledge bank on the geologic framework of the country's coastal and marine regions" (Committee to Review, 1999, p. 48–49). In response to this NRC recommendation, CMGP has designed a knowledge bank prototype including three complementary components: a digital library (Marine Realms Information Bank), a field data catalog (InfoBank), and an Internet map server/GIS data catalog (see http://marine.usgs.gov/kb/).

The other NRC study, titled *Distributed Geolibraries*, was characterized by its authors as a "vision for the future" of information retrieval: providing access to online resources in response to geographic queries (Panel on Distributed Geolibraries, 1999). The Alexandria Digital Library, a collaborative project coordinated by the University of California, Santa Barbara, was an early test bed for this concept, addressing fundamental issues in the search and retrieval of georeferenced information resources (see Janée, Frew, & Hill, 2004). Another successful Web-based system for organizing and accessing georeferenced information is the 4DGeoBrowser, developed at the Woods Hole Oceanographic Institution (Lerner & Maffei, 2001). The flexible 4DGeoBrowser software has been used to create more than a dozen separate Web applications serving the oceanographic community, including the initial version of the Marine Realms Information Bank (see http://4dgeo.whoi.edu/ for links to these individual applications). Related research on the design of coastal Web atlases is summarized in O'Dea, Cummins, Wright, Dwyer, and Ameztoy (2007), with links to several examples.

MRIB DESIGN

MRIB is a distributed geolibrary providing access to selected online information resources for coastal and marine science, including Web sites, full-text reports, digital maps, and downloadable data. MRIB does not store original data or information on its server but rather the metadata records and hyperlinks for online resources maintained on other servers. The MRIB user interface facilitates searching by topical category, location, or keyword, and the metadata records can be downloaded in several formats (including plain text, comma-separated values, XML, and KML).

MRIB employs a faceted classification for topical searching. Each of the twelve main categories includes a controlled vocabulary representing a hierarchy of associations or concepts. This knowledge organization system (KOS) is designed to accommodate a wide range of users, including scientists, public servants, advocacy groups, educators, students, and the general public (for additional details on the KOS employed in MRIB, see Marincioni, Lightsom, Riall, Linck, Aldrich, & Caruso, 2004; for a general discussion of KOS applications in digital libraries, see Hodge, 2000).

Most of the online resources cataloged in MRIB are georeferenced and thus searchable by map coordinates or place name. The MRIB gazetteer currently lists more than 1,700 place names along with their rectangular bounding boxes (see http://mrib.usgs.gov/meta/location.txt). Subcategories in the gazetteer include oceans, continents, geopolitical units, administrative units (exclusive economic zones, marine sanctuaries, and hydrologic regions), and marine cadastres.

The three basic search operations—topical, geographic, and keyword—can be applied repeatedly, in any combination, until the search parameters are appropriately focused. At each stage of this process MRIB displays the search results in browsable tables or interactive maps (at the user's discretion) and provides links to the original online resources. The map view allows users to display search results in a variety of spatial contexts by selecting the desired background map layers: latitude and longitude grid lines, political units, exclusive economic zones, marine cadastres, and coastal hydrologic regions. Experience has suggested that a "lightweight" GIS functionality of this type is ideal for georeferenced digital libraries with a varied clientele (see Janée et al., 2004).

The modular software architecture of MRIB (Figure 4) has permitted rapid development of two customized user interfaces (in addition to the original interface): the regionally focused Monterey Bay Science (MBS) Digital Library and the topically focused Coastal Change Hazards (CCH) Digital Library. Crosswalks between the generalized topical classification employed by the Marine Realms Information Bank (MRIB hot topics) and the specialized topical classification employed by the Coastal Change Hazards Digital Library (CCH topics) ensure full interoperability between these interfaces. In the MRIB topical hierarchy there are four top-level terms: Environment; Hazards and Disasters; Resources; and Science and Scientists. In contrast, the CCH topical hierarchy has three, very different top-level terms: Agents of Coastal Change; Effects of Coastal Change; and Human Responses to Coastal Change. Nevertheless, many *specific* topics can be found at the lower levels of both hierarchies: Hurricanes and Typhoons; Tsunamis; Climate Change; Saltwater Intrusion; and so on. Constructing the crosswalks, therefore, was simply a matter of mapping semantically equivalent "pigeonholes" from one topical hierarchy to the other. In operation, this process is

Figure 4. MRIB software architecture, illustrating the modular design that permits the rapid development of customized user interfaces like the Monterey Bay Science Digital Library and the Coastal Change Hazards Digital Library (see figures 2 and 3)

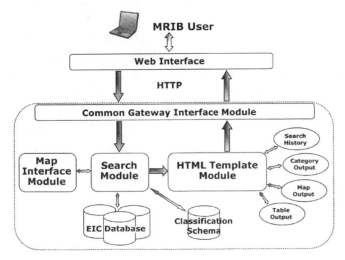

transparent to the user and allows a single MRIB database to be searched from two different topical perspectives.

All digital libraries that provide access to information on other servers will be plagued, sooner or later, by dead links: much of the information found online is, by nature, ephemeral (Nelson & Allen, 2002). To combat this problem MRIB has incorporated software to detect standard 404 error messages ("Not Found"), but this measure solves only part of the problem. Many Webmasters employ "soft 404" messages, whereby invalid Web addresses redirect to a valid Web page offering a customized error message ("We're sorry, but the page you requested cannot be found …"). Alternatively, invalid addresses for lower-level Web pages might simply redirect to the home page; Webmasters often resort to this tactic when they overhaul the URL syntax for their Web sites, in order to help long-time users adjust to the sudden change. While "soft 404" messages may have merits (tips for re-navigating are usually offered), they do complicate the task of writing programs to detect dead links automatically. For this reason, the MRIB cataloger still relies upon labor-intensive inspection (and blind luck) to find and remove many dead links. Occasionally a dead link can even be resurrected (in a sense) by finding a cached version of the Web page in the Internet Archive (http://www.archive.org/). The MRIB cataloger has employed this strategy to re-establish access to a few online documents with enduring value.

Although the MRIB Team compiled the initial catalog and will continue adding entries, the creators of scientific information can be uniquely qualified to catalog their own online resources (especially in complex or newly emerging fields of research). Consequently, MRIB encourages its users to submit new metadata records with the Electronic Index Card (EIC) Creation Utility, a series of online forms and menus for the numerous controlled-vocabulary and free-text metadata fields. Users can open personal MRIB accounts, with password-protected files and directories for arranging the provisional EICs they have submitted. These accounts allow user-contributors to preview, rearrange, edit, or delete their own cards prior to final approval by the MRIB Team (as well as update cards *after* approval). The MRIB Team reviews all user contributions for suitability and accuracy before incorporating them into the public database. As this database grows, user participation will become even more important for updating old metadata records and weeding out dead links that the MRIB software is unable to detect.

Software Specifications

MRIB has been created with open-source software and open standards in the public domain. The code base of MRIB is written in Perl, version 5.8.8 (http://www.perl.com/). Generic Mapping Tools (GMT), version 4.1.1 (http://gmt.soest.hawaii. edu/), with modifications by the MRIB programmer, Guthrie Linck, is used to generate the base maps and data plots. Elevation data from several sources are used in conjunction with GMT: the ETOPO1 one-minute global relief database (http://www.ngdc.noaa.gov/mgg/global/global.html); the SRTM 1- and 3-arc-second land data (http://srtm.usgs.gov/); and the NGDC 3-arc-second coastal relief model for the conterminous United States, Hawaii, and Puerto Rico (http://www.ngdc.noaa.gov/mgg/coastal/coastal.html). Map images are available in JPEG (the default), GIF, and PNG formats. The MRIB public Webserver is a dual 2.4 GHz processor running the Apache HyperText Transfer Protocol (HTTP) server, version 2.2.3 (http://www.apache.org/), along with the Apache perl module (mod_perl, version 2.0.2). The operating system is Ubuntu Linux 8.04 (http://www.ubuntu.com/).

FUTURE DIRECTIONS

Bates (1998, 2002) discusses digital library design in the context of fundamental research by information scientists over a period of several decades. One important design consideration is the *scalability* of the system, an issue that can manifest itself in subtle ways. For instance, will a controlled vocabulary initially designed for a small digital library function as intended in a much larger system? Will a particular search strategy remain effective when the digital library grows? Along these lines, Bates argues that domain size, both current and projected, should be taken into consideration when designing search services for a digital library: browsing is feasible only in a small domain; directed searching becomes necessary as the domain increases in size; and linking is especially effective in a very large domain (e.g., the Internet).

MRIB allows its users to employ browsing, directed searching, and linking at different stages of the search process. The MRIB database is large enough to require directed searching (topical, geographic, or keyword) of its metadata records in order to retrieve a manageable subset that can be easily browsed. One form of linking is obvious, of course—when the user visits an external information resource for which MRIB provides a metadata record. Viewed as a *search mechanism*, however, linking is indirect (and serendipitous) in a distributed digital library like MRIB: the external resources themselves may provide links to additional online information that has not been indexed in the library.

Browsing serves another function in MRIB, and here the need for additional fine-tuning has become apparent. The faceted classification includes twelve categories, each with a detailed controlled vocabulary designed for precise, domain-specific resource description. By browsing these vocabulary lists the user selects as many topical subcategories as are needed to narrow the search. The underlying principle is simple, as

noted by Bates (1998): most users can recognize the information they need more readily than they can recall it. As the MRIB database has grown, however, the original goal of creating precise, domain-specific resource descriptions has had an unintended consequence: the controlled vocabularies for most of the twelve facets have become so long and complex that *browsing* them raises serious usability issues for both the indexer and the user. Thus, the decision has been made to simplify these controlled vocabularies (with some obvious exceptions, such as the author list).

These changes in the MRIB metadata scheme will also (1) improve interoperability with the more generalized topical categories of the USGS Thesaurus (http://www.usgs.gov/science/) and (2) facilitate harvesting through a federated service such as the Open Archives Initiative (see Lagoze & Van de Sompel, 2001). Achieving these goals will require striking the proper balance between the finely granular metadata required for domain-specific resource description and the coarsely granular metadata appropriate for cross-domain search and retrieval (Lagoze, 2001).

To improve geographic searching, the rectangular latitude-longitude bounding boxes in the MRIB gazetteer will be soon replaced with polygonal footprints in order to eliminate many of the false drops inherent in the current system. Most of North America, for example, falls within the bounding box for the Pacific Ocean. Consequently, a gazetteer search for the Pacific Ocean yields more than 50% false drops because of the numerous hits for the Atlantic and Gulf coasts of North America. This example may be extreme because of the peculiar shape of the Pacific basin, but it serves to illustrate a general problem for any georeferencing system relying upon bounding boxes that are *necessary but not sufficient* to define irregular geographic areas.

With appropriate modifications, MRIB software could accommodate geospatial information from a wide range of natural and social sciences. The MRIB content metadata standard and software protocols will be documented in a forthcoming USGS publication to facilitate adapting the MRIB system for other disciplines.

CONCLUSION

Lagoze, Krafft, Payette, and Jesuroga (2005) suggest that digital libraries differ from Internet search engines by *adding value* to online resources. A well-designed digital library offers a carefully selected, manageable collection of resources, organized to provide context and to highlight interrelationships that might otherwise be overlooked. Lagoze and his colleagues also argue that a digital library should encourage user collaboration in order to benefit from the "wisdom of crowds." The MRIB family of distributed digital libraries illustrates these points. MRIB adds value to online resources for coastal and marine science by providing selectivity, topical context, and spatial context. The Electronic Index Card (EIC) Creation Utility allows users to contribute new metadata records and help the MRIB Team keep the old ones current. This "grassroots" collaboration by users will also ensure that MRIB remains abreast of emerging research.

As a public science agency, the USGS is responsible for delivering timely, reliable data and information essential to meeting national needs and international obligations (Committee on Future Roles, 2001; Hutchinson, Sanders, & Faust, 2003). In the marine realm, the role of the USGS as an information agency has taken on added importance as the United States moves toward an integrated ocean policy (see U.S. Commission on Ocean Policy, 2004). The USGS Coastal and Marine Geology Program (CMGP) fulfills this responsibility in part by creating digital libraries like MRIB for a wide range of users wishing to learn about coastal and marine science, gather data for research, and make informed decisions.

DISCLAIMER

Any use of trade, product, or firm names is for descriptive purposes only and does not imply endorsement by the U.S. Government.

REFERENCES

Bates, M.J. (1998). Indexing and access for digital libraries and the Internet: Human, database, and domain factors. *Journal of the American Society for Information Science, 49,* (13), 1185–1205.

Bates, M.J. (2002). Speculations on browsing, directed searching, and linking in relation to the Bradford Distribution. In H. Bruce, R. Fidel, P. Ingwersen, & P. Vakkari (Eds.), *Emerging frameworks and methods: Proceedings of the Fourth International Conference on Conceptions of Library and Information Science (CoLIS 4)* (pp. 137–150). Greenwood Village, CO: Libraries Unlimited.

Committee on Future Roles, Challenges, and Opportunities for the U.S. Geological Survey, National Research Council. (2001). *Future roles and opportunities for the U.S. Geological Survey.* Washington, DC: National Academy Press.

Committee to Review the USGS Coastal and Marine Geology Program, National Research Council. (1999). *Science for decisionmaking: Coastal and marine geology at the U.S. Geological Survey.* Washington, DC: National Academy Press.

Hodge, G. (2000). *Systems of knowledge organization for digital libraries: Beyond traditional authority files.* Washington, DC: Digital Library Federation, Council on Library and Information Resources.

Hutchinson, D.R., Sanders, R., & Faust, T. (2003). *Making USGS information effective in the electronic age* (U.S. Geological Survey Open-File

Report 03-240). Retrieved August 29, 2008, from http://pubs.usgs.gov/of/2003/of03-240/

Janée, G., Frew, J., & Hill, L.L. (2004, May). Issues in georeferenced digital libraries. *D-Lib Magazine, 10*(5). Retrieved August 29, 2008, from http://www.dlib.org/dlib/may04/janee/05janee.html

Lagoze, C. (2001, January). Keeping Dublin Core simple: Cross-domain discovery or resource description? *D-Lib Magazine, 7*(1). Retrieved August 29, 2008, from http://www.dlib.org/dlib/january01/lagoze/01lagoze.html

Lagoze, C., Krafft, D.B., Payette, S., & Jesuroga, S. (2005, November). What is a digital library anymore, anyway? *D-Lib Magazine, 11*(1). Retrieved August 29, 2008, from http://www.dlib.org/dlib/november05/lagoze/11lagoze.html

Lagoze, C., & Van de Sompel, H. (2001). The Open Archives Initiative: Building a low-barrier interoperability framework. In *Proceedings of the 1st ACM/IEEE-CS Joint Conference on Digital Libraries (JCDL 2001)* (pp. 54–62). New York: ACM Press.

Lerner, S., & Maffei, A. (2001). *4D GeoBrowser: A Web-based data browser and server for accessing and analyzing multi-disciplinary data* (Technical Report WHOI-2001-13). Woods Hole, MA: Woods Hole Oceanographic Institution.

Marincioni, F., Lightsom, F.L., Riall, R.L., Linck, G.A., Aldrich, T.C., & Caruso, M.J. (2004). Integrating digital information for coastal and marine sciences. *Journal of Digital Information Management, 2*(3), 132–141.

Nelson, M.L., & Allen, B.D. (2002, January). Object persistence and availability in digital libraries. *D-Lib Magazine, 8*(1). Retrieved August 29, 2008, from http://www.dlib.org/dlib/january02/nelson/01nelson.html

O'Dea, L., Cummins, V., Wright, D., Dwyer, N., & Ameztoy, I. (2007). *Report on coastal mapping and informatics, Trans-Atlantic Workshop 1: Potentials and limitations of coastal Web atlases.* Cork, Ireland: University College Cork. Retrieved August 29, 2008, from http://workshop1.science.oregonstate.edu/final_rpt

Panel on Distributed Geolibraries, National Research Council. (1999). *Distributed geolibraries: Spatial information resources, summary of a workshop.* Washington, DC: National Academy Press.

U.S. Commission on Ocean Policy. (2004). *An ocean blueprint for the 21st century: Final report.* Washington, DC: U.S. Commission on Ocean Policy.

KEY TERMS

Controlled Vocabulary: A list of preferred terms for indexing information resources, ideally with precise definitions and guidelines for application.

Crosswalk: A semantic mapping between the elements of two metadata standards, facilitating interoperability.

Distributed Geolibrary: In the online environment, a distributed geolibrary allows patrons to search centralized metadata records for information about specific places and then retrieve the original online resources from servers distributed across the Internet.

Faceted Classification: An indexing system that employs several mutually exclusive metadata fields to characterize information resources.

False Drop: An instance of retrieving information that is not relevant to a given search.

Gazetteer: In the traditional sense, a gazetteer is a dictionary of place names. Digital gazetteers, in contrast, link place names to specific bounding boxes or polygonal footprints for the purposes of map display or information retrieval.

Georeferencing: The practice of indexing information resources by geospatial coordinates, place names, or geographic codes.

Granularity: The level of descriptive detail in a metadata record, usually representing a balance between the competing demands of fully characterizing information resources and facilitating the process of search and retrieval.

Interoperability: The ability of different information systems to exchange resources through shared standards.

Knowledge Organization System (KOS): Any formalized scheme for managing information resources, including authority files, subject headings, taxonomies, thesauri, semantic networks, and ontologies.

Chapter XLIV
Digital Preservation

Stephan Strodl
Vienna University of Technology, Austria

Christoph Becker
Vienna University of Technology, Austria

Andreas Rauber
Vienna University of Technology, Austria

ABSTRACT

The rapid ongoing changes in software and hardware put digital information at risk. The challenge is to keep electronic data accessible, viewable, and usable for the future when the original software to interpret them has become unavailable. Digital preservation has thus turned into on of the most pressing challenges not only within the digital library community, but also in other areas such as archives and data centres. This chapter introduces the concepts and challenges in the field of digital preservation including the OAIS reference model. We give an overview about the projects and initiatives worldwide dealing with this challenge. We furthermore present preservation planning as a key concept at the heart of preservation endeavours in detail.

INTRODUCTION

Digital objects have become the dominant way that we create, shape, and exchange information. They increasingly contain essential parts of our cultural, intellectual and scientific heritage; they form a central part of our economy, and increasingly shape our private lives. The ever-growing heterogeneity and complexity of digital file formats together with rapid technological changes turn the preservation of digital information into a pressing challenge. The challenge is to keep electronic data accessible, viewable, and usable for the future, to ensure the survival of our digital artifacts when the original software or hardware to interpret them correctly becomes unavailable (UNESCO, 2003b).

Digital preservation deals with the long-term storage and access to digital objects. The Digital Preservation Coalition defines it as "the series of managed activities necessary to ensure continued access to digital materials" and adds that it "refers to all of the actions required to maintain access to digital materials beyond the limits of media failure or technological change" (Jones & Beagrie, 2002). The focus lies on "born digital" objects, not digitisation, which is a challenging field in itself (Digicult, 2004).

Rosenthal (Rosenthal, Robertson, Lipkis, Reich, & Morabito, 2005) describes requirements for digital preservation systems. A range of tools exists today to support the variety of preservation strategies such as migration or emulation. Yet, different preservation requirements across institutions and settings make the decision on which solution to implement very difficult.

In this chapter, we give an overview about the current state of the art, the major challenges as well as proposed solutions in digital preservation. We will further highlight current research activities in this field, with a specific focus on planning and evaluating preservation strategies.

THE CURRENT STATE OF RESEARCH

The companion document to the UNESCO charter for the preservation of the digital heritage (UNESCO, 2003a) provides a good overview of preservation strategies. Research on technical preservation issues is focused on two dominant strategies—migration and emulation. Migration requires the repeated copy or conversion of digital objects from one technology to a more stable or current, be it hardware or software. Each migration incurs certain risks and preserves only a certain fraction of the characteristics of a digital object. The Council of Library and Information Resources (CLIR) published different kinds of risks for a migration project (Lawrence, Kehoe, Rieger, & Walters, 2000).

Emulation as the second important strategy is a means of overcoming technological obsolescence of hardware and software by developing techniques for imitating obsolete systems on future generations of computers (Jones & Beagrie, 2002). Jeff Rothenberg (Rothenberg, 1999) envisions a framework of an ideal preservation surrounding. The Universal Virtual Computer (UVC) concept (Van der Hoeven, Van der Diessen, & Van En Meer, 2005) uses elements of both migration and emulation, allowing digital objects to be reconstructed in their original appearance. The UVC is independent of any existing hardware or software, it simulates a basic architecture including memory, register and rules. An emerging approach of emulation is modular emulation. Jeffrey van der Hoeven presented the modular emulator called Dioscuri in (Van der Hoeven & Wijngaarden, 2005). It imitates the hardware environment by emulating the components of the hardware architecture. Each hardware components is run as individual emulators and the components are assembled in order to create a full emulation process.

Several other preservation strategies have been proposed. The Computer Museum is based on preserving the technical environment that runs the system, including the hardware, the operating system, original application software, media drives, etc. Another approach is Normalisation, a technique for the collection of different file formats, which are converted to a single chosen file format (CLIR & LoC, 2002).

Several common file formats are being adapted to achieve more stable long-term archiving. The most relevant is probably PDF/A, which defines a subset of PDF optimized for long-term preservation (ISO, 2004). Other examples are the Open Document Format for Office Applications (ISO, 2006) and MPEG-7 (ISO, 2002).

Metadata became a heavily debated issue in the field of digital preservation. Initiatives in the field of metadata are Dublin Core[1], METS[2] and Premis[3].

For stable long-term management of digital collections persistent identifiers are required. An overview about persistent identifier activities are provided in (Hilse & Kothe, 2006).

A number of tools and services have been developed that perform content characterization specifically for digital preservation. The National Library of New Zealand Metadata Extraction Tool (National Library of New Zealand, 2007) extracts preservation metadata for various input file formats. Harvard University Library's tool JHove (Harvard University Library, 2007) enables the identification and characterisation of digital objects. An emerging approach for characterisation is the family of eXtensible Characterisation Languages (XCL) (Becker, Rauber, Heydegger, Schnasse, & Thaller, 2008). It supports the automatic validation of document conversions and the evaluation of migration quality by hierarchically decomposing a document and representing documents from different sources in an abstract XML language.

The Reference Model for an Open Archival Information System (OAIS) ((CCSDS), 2002) was published 2002 by the Consultative Committee for Space Data Systems (CCSDS) and adopted as ISO standard ISO 14721:2003 (ISO, 2003). It has proven to be a very useful high-level reference model, describing participants, roles and responsibilities as well as the exchange of information. Because of its growing acceptance in the community, the OAIS model is the most common framework for digital preservation systems. The model is described in detail in the next section.

Many projects and initiatives worldwide deal with the challenge of digital preservation and providing services and information. Because of the enormous increase in interest, the number of projects is growing rapidly. The following section can thus only present an incomplete overview, which is not meant to be an assessment.

The National Digital Information Infrastructure and Preservation Program (NDIIPP) collects, archives and preserves the burgeoning amounts of digital content for current and future generations.[4]

The Arts and Humanities Data Service (AHDS) and the University of London Computer Centre started the DAAT Project (Digital Asset Assessment Tool) (ULCC, 2006) to develop a tool to identify the preservation needs of various digital holdings.

PREMIS (Preservation Metadata Implementation Strategies) is a joint effort of the Research Libraries Group (RLG) and the library consortium OCLC (Online Computer Library Center). Aim of the project is the development and recommendation of best practices for implementing preservation metadata.[5]

PRONOM is a file format repository which provides technical information about electronic records. Currently the fourth version of PRONOM is available. This initiative also develops automatic file format identification tool named DROID (Digital Record Object Identification).[6]

PANIC (Preservation Webservices Architecture for Newmedia and Interactive Collections) addresses the challenges of integrating and leveraging services and tools into a Preservation Services Architecture. Also the comparison of different preservation strategies for multimedia data and the development of recommendations and guidelines for multimedia content are part of PANIC (Hunter & Choudhury, 2006).[7]

CAMiLEON is developing and evaluating a range of technical strategies for the long term preservation of digital materials. One of the projects is the comparison between Emulation and Migration. The project is a joint undertaking between the Universities of Michigan (USA) and Leeds (UK) and is funded by JISC and NSF.[8]

PADI (Preserving Access to Digital Information) is an initiative started by The National Library of Australia that aims to provide mechanisms to ensure that information in digital form is managed with appropriate consideration for preservation and future access.[9]

The LOCKSS[10] program (Lots of Copies Keep Stuff Safe) has developed a peer-to-peer system using the world wide Web for preserving archival information. The first version was launched in 1999. LOCKSS is an open source software that deploys a large number of independent, low-cost, persistent and accessible Web caches. It allows the peers to cooperatively detect and repair damaged content. For obsolete file formats LOCKSS supports a format migration(Rosenthal, Lipkis, Robertson, & Morabito, 2005).

The Portico project[11] was launched in 2002 by JSTOR[12] to archive electronic publications. Portico receives the source files from the publishers and systematically normalises the source to an archival format based upon the NLM Archive and Interchange DTD (National Center for Biotechnology Information, 2007).

The Digital Curation Centre (DCC) supports UK institutions in storing, managing and preserving data. The aim of the project is to establish community relationships and develop services for digital preservation.[13]

The Digital Preservation Coalition (DPC) aims to secure the preservation of digital resources in the UK. DPC hosts the Digital Preservation Award to bestow leading and advanced digital preservation projects. DPC, in cooperation with PADI, publish a quarterly current awareness digest.[14]

The Electronic Resource Preservation and Access Network (ERPANET) established a European Consortium bringing together memory organisations (museums, libraries and archives), ICT and software industry, research institutions, and government organizations to provide a knowledge-base of developments in the area of preservation of cultural heritage and scientific digital objects.[15]

Several projects in this domain have been initiated under the 6th framework program of the European Union. One of the main objectives of the DELOS Digital Preservation Cluster, which is part of the EU-funded DELOS Network of Excellence on Digital Libraries[16], was the establishment of testbeds and validation metrics. The DELOS Digital Preservation Testbed (Strodl, Rauber, Rauch, Hofman, Debole, & Amato, 2006) allows the selection of the most suitable preservation strategy for individual requirements by combining a structured workflow for requirements specification and evaluation by means of a standardised testbed laboratory infrastructure.[17]

PLANETS (Permanent Long-term Access through Networked Services) develops systems and tools which support the accessibility and use of digital cultural and scientific resources. More specifically, the project is developing methods and tools based on a distributed service infrastructure on which services for preservation action, preservation characterization and preservation planning can be coordinated and combined with each other. The PLANETS Testbed will use this framework to provide a stable foundation for testing different preservation actions in a well-defined setting.[18] The decision support software Plato uses this stable foundation to evaluate the suitability for a given purpose of preservation actions according to institution-specific criteria in a controlled and automated way and thus build the basis for specifying well-defined and accountable preservation plans.

Digital Preservation Europe (DPE) is a coordinated Action of the EU 6th framework program bringing together leading institutions and researchers to provide a coherent platform for research and collaboration. Aspects covered by DPE include audit and certification, and the establishment of a research roadmap. DPE is conducting a yearly Digital Preservation Challenge with the aim to raise the profile of digital preservation among researchers and foster awareness of the issues the community is facing. DPE also initiated the Digital Preservation Europe Exchange Program (DPEX), which supports the exchange of researchers in the field of digital preservation.[19]

CASPAR (Cultural, Artistic and Scientific knowledge for Preservation, Access and Retrieval) is targeted at implementing, extending, and validating the OAIS reference model.[20]

THE OAIS REFERENCE MODEL

The Reference Model for an Open Archival Information System (OAIS) was published in 2002 by the Consultative Committee for Space Data Systems (CCSDS). ISO 14721:2003 defines an OAIS as:

an archive, consisting of an organization of people and systems, that has accepted
the responsibility to preserve information and make it available for a Designated
Community.((CCSDS), 2002)

The OAIS model:

provides a framework for describing and comparing different long term preservation
strategies and techniques.((CCSDS), 2002)

Figure 1 shows the main functional components of the model. When a producer submits a digital object into the system, it has to be packaged together with required metadata as a Submission Information Package (SIP). The Ingest module provides the services and functions to accept SIPs from Producers. It further performs quality assurance and generates an Archival Information Package (AIP) complying to the archive's standards. Ingest also extracts descriptive information from the AIPs and coordinates updates to Archival Storage and Data Management.

Archival Storage stores, maintains and retrieves AIPs, while Data Management populates, maintains and accesses descriptive information about archived objects as well as administrative data. Every action inside the archive that affects the object is added to the metadata of the AIP.

The Access component is responsible for supporting consumers in finding, requesting and receiving information stored in the system. Access functions include access control, coordinating requests, generating responses as Dissemination Information Packages (DIPs) and delivering the responses to Consumers.

The Preservation Planning entity monitors the environment and provides recommendations to ensure the long-term accessibility of the stored information. This includes monitoring and evaluation of the archive and periodical recommendations on archival updates for migration. A central component is the development of preservation strategies and standards as well as packaging designs and plans.

Figure 1. Functional entities of the OAIS reference model ((CCSDS), 2002)

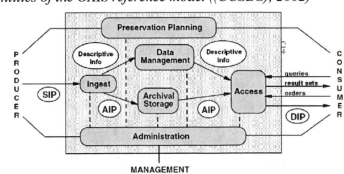

PRESERVATION PLANNING

A range of tools exists today to support the variety of preservation strategies such as migration or emulation. Yet, different preservation requirements across institutions and settings make the decision on which solution to implement very difficult.

Preservation Planning, i.e. evaluating preservation strategies and choosing the most appropriate strategy, has turned into a crucial decision process, depending on both object characteristics as well as institutional requirements. The selection of the preservation strategy and tools is often the most difficult part in digital preservation endeavours; technical as well as process and financial aspects of a preservation strategy form the basis for the decision on which preservation strategy to adopt.

The Planets Preservation Planning approach allows the assessment of all kinds of preservation actions against individual requirements and the selection of the most suitable solution. It enforces the explicit definition of preservation requirements and supports the appropriate documentation and evaluation by assisting in the process of running preservation experiments. In the PLANETS project, the DELOS Preservation Testbed forms the basis for the Preservation Planning approach, which is described in (Rauch & Rauber, 2004) and in detail in (Strodl et al., 2006).

Figure 2 provides an overview of the workflow of the Planets Preservation Planning approach, which was described in (Strodl, Becker, Neumayer, & Rauber, 2007). The process consists of three phases, which are described in the following:

1. Define requirements describes the scenario, the collection that is being considered as well as institutional policies and obligations. Then the requirements and goals for a preservation solution in a given application domain are defined. In the so-called objective tree, high-

Figure 2. Planets preservation planning approach

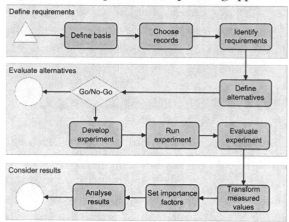

level goals and detailed requirements are collected and organised in a tree structure. While the resulting trees usually differ through changing preservation settings, some general principles can be observed. At the top level, the objectives can usually be organized into four main categories:

*   *File characteristics* describe the visual and contextual experience a user has by dealing with a digital record. Subdivisions may be "Content", "Context", "Structure", "Appearance", and "Behaviour" (Rothenberg & Bikson, 1999), with lowest level objectives being e.g. color depth, image resolution, forms of interactivity, macro support, or embedded metadata.

*   *Record characteristics* describe the technical foundations of a digital record, the context, the storage medium, interrelationships and metadata.

*   *Process characteristics* describe the preservation process. These include usability, complexity or scalability.

*   *Costs* have a significant influence on the choice of a preservation solution. Usually, they may be divided in technical and personnel costs.

The objective tree is usually created in a workshop setting with experts from different domains contributing to the requirements gathering process. The tree documents the individual preservation requirements of an institution for a given partially homogeneous collection of objects. Examples include scientific papers and dissertations in PDF format, historic audio recordings, or video holdings from ethnographic studies. Typical trees may contain between 50 to several hundred objectives, usually organised in 4–6 hierarchy levels.

Measurable effects are assigned to the objectives that have been defined in the previous step. Wherever possible, these effects should be objectively measurable (e.g., e per year, frames per second). In some cases, (semi-) subjective scales will need to be employed (e.g., degrees of openness and stability, support of a standard, degree of file format adoption, and so on).

2. Evaluate alternatives identifies and evaluates potential alternatives. The alternatives' characteristics and technical details are specified; then the resources for the experiments are selected, the required tools set up, and a set of experiments is performed. Based on the requirements defined in the beginning, the results of the experiments are evaluated to determine the degree to which the requirements defined in the objective tree were met.

3. Consider results aggregates the results of the experiments to make them comparable. The measurements taken in the experiments might all have different scales. In order to make these comparable, they are transformed to a uniform scale using transformation tables. The resulting scale might, for example, range from 0 to 5. A value of 0 would in this case denote an unacceptable result and thus serve as a drop-out criterion for the whole preservation alternative.

4. Then the importance factors are set, as not all of the objectives of the tree are equally important, and the alternatives are ranked. The stability of the final ranking is analysed with respect to minor changes in the weighting and performance of the individual objectives using Sensitivity Analysis. The results are finally evaluated by taking non-measurable influences on the decision into account. After this analysis, a clear and well argued accountable recommendation for one of the alternatives can be made.

In order to simplify the process, to guide users and to automate the process of conducting experiments, a software tool called Plato is being developed. This tool implements the above described workflow, while validating user input and improving automation through the integration of automated services such as object format identification and risk assessment. Thus it supports the documentation and improves the automation of the preservation planning workflow.

CONCLUSION AND FUTURE TRENDS

While the last decade showed significant advances in research and practice, there a still many challenges left to overcome. Among them is the application of existing approaches to large-scale repositories, cross-institutional and interdisciplinary collaboration, and the concretisation of the OAIS model. An overview of a research agenda in the digital preservation landscape is given in the DPE Research Roadmap (DigitalPreservationEurope, 2006).

REFERENCES

Becker, C., Rauber, A., Heydegger, V., Schnasse, J., & Thaller, M. (2008). A generic xml language for characterising objects to support digital preservation. In *Proceedings of the 23rd annual*

ACM symposium on applied computing. New York: ACM.

(CCSDS), C. (2002, January). *Reference model for an open archival information system (OAIS) - blue book.* Retrieved August 29, 2008, from http://public.ccsds.org/publications/archive/650x0b1.pdf

CLIR & LoC. (2002). *Building a national strategy for digital preservation: Issues in digital media archiving.* Washington, D.C.: Council on Library and Information Resources Washington, D.C. and Library of Congress. Retrieved August 29, 2008, from http://www.clir.org/pubs/reports/pub106/pub106.pdf

Digicult. (2004, February). *Digital collections and the management of knowledge.* Retrieved August 29, 2008, from http://www.digicult.info/downloads/html/8/8.html

DigitalPreservationEurope. (2006, June). *Research roadmap.* Retrieved August 29, 2008, from http://www.digitalpreservationeurope.eu/publications/dpe_research_roadmap_D72.pdf

Harvard University Library. (2007). *Jhove - jstor/harvard object validation environment.* Retrieved August 29, 2008, from http://hul.harvard.edu/jhove

Hilse, H.-W., & Kothe, J. (2006, November). *Implementing persistent identifiers* (Tech. Rep.).London and Amsterdam: Consortium of European Research Libraries.

Hoeven, J., Van Der Diessen, R., & Van En Meer, K. (2005). Development of a universal virtual computer (UVC) for long-term preservation of digital objects. *Journal of Information Science, 31*(3), 196–208.

Van der Hoeven, J., & Van Wijngaarden, H. (2005, September). *Modular emulation as a long term preservation strategy for digital objects.* Retrieved August 29, 2008, from http://www.iwaw.net/05/papers/iwaw05-hoeven.pdf

Hunter, J., & Choudhury, S. (2006, April). PANIC—an integrated approach to the preservation of complex digital objects using semantic Web services. In *International journal on digital libraries: Special issue on complex digital objects* (Vol. 6, No. 2, pp. 174–183). Berlin, Heidelberg: Springer.

ISO. (2002). *Information technology—multimedia content description interface—part 1: Systems ISO/IEC 15938-1:2002.*

ISO. (2003). *Space data and information transfer systems—open archival information system—reference model (ISO 14721:2003).*

ISO. (2004). *Document management—electronic document file format for long-term preservation—part 1: Use of PDF 1.4 (PDF/A) ISO/CD 19005-1.*

ISO. (2006). *Information technology—open document format for office applications ISO/IEC 26300:2006.*

Jones, M., & Beagrie, N. (2002). *Preservation management of digital materials: A handbook.* London, UK: Digital Preservation Coalition. Retrieved August 29, 2008, from http://www.dpconline.org/graphics/handbook

Lawrence, G., Kehoe, W., Rieger, O., & Walters, A., W.H., & Kenney. (2000). *Risk management of digital information: A file format investigation,.* CLIR.

National Center for Biotechnology Information of the National Library of Medicine. (2007). *NLN journal archiving and interchange tag suite.* Retrieved August 29, 2008, from http://dtd.nlm.nih.gov

National Library of New Zealand. (2007). *Metadata extraction tool.* Retrieved August 29, 2008, from http://meta-extractor.sourceforge.net

Rauch, C., & Rauber, A. (2004, December). Preserving digital media: Towards a preservation solution evaluation metric. In *Proceedings of the 7th International Conference on Asian Digital Libraries (ICADL 2004)* (pp. 203–212). Berlin, Heidelberg: Springer.

Rosenthal, D.S.H., Lipkis, T., Robertson, T.S., & Morabito, S. (2005, January). Transparent format migration of preserved Web content. *D-Lib Magazine, 11*. Retrieved August 29, 2008, from http://www.dlib.org/dlib/january05/rosenthal/01rosenthal.html

Rosenthal, D.S.H., Robertson, T., Lipkis, T., Reich, V., & Morabito, S. (2005, November). Requirements for digital preservation systems. *D-Lib Magazine, 11*. Retrieved August 29, 2008, from http://www.dlib.org/dlib/november05/rosenthal/11rosenthal.html

Rothenberg, J. (1999). *Avoiding technological quicksand: Finding a viable technical foundation for digital preservation*. Council on Library and Information Resources Washington D.C. Retrieved August 29, 2008, from http://www.clir.org/pubs/reports/rothen-berg/contents.html

Rothenberg, J., & Bikson, T. (1999). *Carrying authentic, understandable and usable digital records through time* (Tech. Rep.). The Hague, Netherlands: Report to the Dutch National Archives and Ministry of the Interior.

Strodl, S., Becker, C., Neumayer, R., & Rauber, A. (2007). How to choose a digital preservation strategy: Evaluating a preservation planning procedure. In *Proceedings of the 7th ACM IEEE Joint Conference on Digital Libraries (JCDL'07)* (pp. 29–38). New York: ACM.

Strodl, S., Rauber, A., Rauch, C., Hofman, H., Debole, F., & Amato, G. (2006, November 27–30). The DELOS test bed for choosing a digital preservation strategy. In *Proceedings of the 9th International Conference on Asian Digital Libraries (ICADL 2006)* (pp. 323–332). Berlin, Heidelberg: Springer.

ULCC. (2006). *DAAT: Digital asset assessment tool*. Retrieved August 29, 2008, from http://ahds.ac.uk/about/projects/daat

UNESCO. (2003a, March). *Guidelines for the preservation of digital heritage* (No. CI-2003/WS/3.). Retrieved August 29, 2008, from unesdoc.unesco.org/images/0013/001300/130071e.pdf

UNESCO. (2003b, October 17). *UNESCO charter on the preservation of digital heritage*. (Adopted at the 32nd session of the General Conference of UNESCO).

KEY TERMS

Archive or Repository: An organization that intends to preserve information for access and use by a designated community ((CCSDS), 2002).

Digital Object: An object composed of a set of bit sequences ((CCSDS), 2002).

Digital Preservation: The series of managed activities necessary to ensure continued access to digital materials for as long as necessary. It refers to all of the actions required to maintain access to digital materials, both digitised and born digitally, beyond the limits of media failure or technological change (Jones & Beagrie, 2002).

Emulation: A means of overcoming technological obsolescence of hardware and software by developing techniques for imitating obsolete systems on future generations of computers (Jones & Beagrie, 2002).

Migration: A means of overcoming technological obsolescence by transferring digital resources from one hardware/software generation to the next (Jones & Beagrie, 2002).

OAIS: Model Reference Model for an Open Archival Information System ((CCSDS), 2002).

Preservation Planning: The process of defining a procedure for preserving a given collection of digital objects. The plan treats organisational, technical and financial aspects of the specific preservation problem at hand.

ENDNOTES

[1]   http://dublincore.org

[2]   http://www.loc.gov/standards/mets

[3]   www.oclc.org/research/pmwg

[4]   http://www.digitalpreservation.gov

[5]   http://www.loc.gov/standards/premis

[6]   http://www.nationalarchives.gov.uk/pronom

[7]   http://www.metadata.net/panic

[8]   http://www.si.umich.edu/CAMILEON

[9]   http://www.nla.gov.au/padi

[10] http://www.lockss.org

[11] http://www.portico.org

[12] http://www.jstor.org

[13] http://www.dcc.ac.uk

[14] http://www.dpconline.org

[15] http://www.erpanet.org

[16] http://www.delos.info

[17] http://www.dpc.delos.info

[18] http://www.planets-project.eu

[19] http://www.digitalpreservationeurope.org

[20] http://www.casparpreserves.eu

Chapter XLV
Visual Pattern Based Compressed Domain Image Retrieval

Gerald Schaefer
Aston University, UK

ABSTRACT

While image retrieval and image compression have been pursued separately in the past, compressed domain techniques, which allow processing or retrieval of images without prior decompression, are becoming increasingly important. In this chapter we show that such midstream content access is possible and present a compressed domain retrieval method based on a visual pattern based compression algorithm. Experiments conducted on a medium sized image database demonstrate the effectiveness and efficiency of the presented approach.

INTRODUCTION

With the rise of the Internet and the availability of affordable digital imaging devices, the need for content-based image retrieval (CBIR) is ever increasing. While many methods have been suggested in the literature only few take into account the fact that—due to limited resources such as disk space and bandwidth—virtually all images are stored in compressed form. In order to process them for CBIR they first need to be uncompressed and the features calculated in the pixel domain.

Often these features are stored alongside the images which seems counterintuitive to the original need for compression. The desire for techniques that operate directly in the compressed domain providing, so-called midstream content access, is therefore evident (Picard, 1994). Colour Visual Pattern Image Coding (CVPIC) is one of the first so-called 4th criterion image compression algorithms (Schaefer & Qiu, 2000; Schaefer, Qiu, & Luo, 1999). A 4th criterion algorithm allows—in addition to the classic three image coding criteria of image quality, efficiency, and bitrate—the image data to be queried and processed directly in its compressed form; in other words the image data is directly meaningful without the requirement of a decoding step. The data that is readily available in CVPIC compressed images is the colour information of each of the 4 × 4 blocks the image has been divided into, and information on the spatial characteristics of each block, in particular on whether a given block is identified as a uniform block (a block with no or little variation) or a pattern block (a block where an edge or gradient has been detected).

In this chapter we show how to make direct use of this information and present an image retrieval algorithm that allows for efficient and effective retrieval directly in the compressed domain of CVPIC. We utilise the fact that colour and edge information is readily available in CVPIC and extract these features with suitable methods. Integrating the two scores achieves image retrieval based on both (spatial) colour and shape aspects. Experimental results obtained from querying the UCID dataset (Schaefer & Stich, 2004) show that this approach not only allows retrieval directly in the compressed domain but also outperforms techniques such as colour histograms, colour coherence vectors and color correlograms.

COLOUR VISUAL PATTERN IMAGE CODING (CVPIC)

The Colour Visual Pattern Image Coding (CVPIC) image compression algorithm introduced in (Schaefer et al., 1999) is an extension of the work in (Chen & Bovic, 1990). The underlying idea is that within a 4 × 4 image block only one discontinuity is visually perceptible.

CVPIC first performs a conversion to the CIEL*a*b* colour space (CIE, 1986) as a more appropriate image representation. As many other colour spaces, CIEL*a*b* comprises one luminance and two chrominance channels. CIEL*a*b* however, was designed to be a uniform representation, meaning that equal differences in the colour space correspond to equal perceptual differences. A quantitative measurement of these colour differences was defined using the Euclidean distance in the L*a*b* space and is given in ΔE units.

A set of 14 patterns of 4 × 4 pixels has been defined in (Chen & Bovic, 1990). All these patterns contain one edge at various orientations (vertical, horizontal, plus and minus 45°) as can be seen in Figure 1 where + and − represent different intensities. In addition a uniform pattern where all intensities are equal is being used.

The image is divided into 4 × 4 pixel blocks. Determining which visual pattern represents each block most accurately then follows. For each of the visual patterns the average L*a*b* values for the regions marked by + and − respectively (i.e., the mean values for the regions on each side of the pattern) are calculated.

The colour difference of each actual pixel and the corresponding mean value is then obtained and averaged over the block. The visual pattern that leads to the lowest difference value (given in CIEL*a*b* ΔE units) is chosen.

In order to allow for the encoding of uniform blocks the average colour difference to the mean colour of the block is also determined. A block is coded as uniform if either its variance in colour is

Figure 1. The 14 edge patterns used in CVPIC

++++	++++	++++		---+	--++	-+++	
----	++++	++++		---+	--++	-+++	
----	----	++++		---+	--++	-+++	
----	----	----		---+	--++	-+++	
--++	-+++	++++	++++	----	----	---+	--++
---+	--++	-+++	++++	----	---+	--++	-+++
----	---+	--++	-+++	---+	--++	-+++	++++
----	----	---+	--++	--++	-+++	++++	++++

very low, or if the resulting image quality will not suffer severely when coded as a uniform rather than as an edge block. To meet this requirement two thresholds are defined. The first threshold describes the upper bound for variations within a block (i.e., the average colour difference to the mean colour of the block). Every block with a variance below this value will be encoded as uniform. The second threshold is related to the difference between the average colour variation within a block and the average colour difference that would result if the block were coded as a pattern block (i.e., the lowest variance possible for an edge block). If this difference is very low (or if the variance for a uniform pattern is below those of all edge patterns) coding the block as uniform will not introduce distortions much more perceptible than if the block is coded as a pattern block

For each block, one bit is stored which states whether the block is uniform or a pattern block. In addition, for edge blocks an index identifying the visual pattern needs to be stored. Following this procedure results in a representation of each block as 5 bits (1 + 4 as we use 14 patterns) for an edge block and 1 bit for a uniform block describing the spatial component, and the full colour information for one or two colours (for uniform and pattern blocks respectively). The colour components are quantised to 64 universally predefined colours adopted from (Qiu, 2003). Each colour can hence be encoded using 6 bits. Therefore, in total a uniform block takes 7 (=1+6) bits, whereas a pattern block is stored in 17 (=5+2*6) bits. We found that this yielded an average compression ratio of about 1:30. We note, that the information could be further encoded to achieve lower bitrates. Both the pattern and the colour information could be entropy coded (Schaefer et al., 1999). In here however, we refrain from this step as we are primarily interested in a synthesis of coding and retrieval.

CVPIC IMAGE RETRIEVAL

We note from above that for each image block in CVPIC both colour and edge information is readily available in the compressed form: each block is coded either as a uniform block or as a pattern block. While for a uniform block only its colour needs to be stored, each pattern block contains two colours and belongs to one of 14 edge classes. We make direct use of this information for the purpose of image retrieval (Schaefer & Lieutaud, 2004).

It is well known that colour is an important cue for image retrieval. In fact, simple descriptors such as histograms of the colour contents of images (Swain & Ballard, 1991) have been shown to work well and have hence been used in many CBIR systems. Further improvements can be gained by incorporating spatial information as techniques such as colour coherence vectors (Pass & Zabih, 1996) and border/interior pixel histograms (Stehling, Nascimento, & Falcao, 2002) have shown. Here the colour information is not summarised in one histogram but is represented in two separate histograms: one histogram of coherent pixels (i.e., pixels in uniform areas) and one histogram of scattered pixels for the colour coherence vector approach respectively one histogram of border pixels (i.e., those part of an edge) and one histogram of interior pixels in the border/interior pixel histogram technique. Our approach is fairly similar to these techniques but requires no explicit computation that provides the classification into the two categories. Rather we utilise the (precalculated) division into uniform and pattern blocks. Pixels that are part of a uniform area (i.e., "coherent" or "interior" pixels) will more likely be contained within a uniform block. On the other hand pixels that form part of an edge (i.e., "border" pixels) will fall into pattern blocks. We can therefore immediately distinguish between these two types of pixels without any further calculation (as would need to be done for colour coherence vector or border/interior pixel calculation). We hence create two colour histograms: a uniform histogram H^u by considering only uniform blocks and a nonuniform histogram H^n calculated solely from edge blocks. While exact histograms could be calculated by simply adding the appropriate number of pixels to the relevant colour bins while scanning through the image we suggest a simpler, computationally less intensive, method. Instead of weighing the histogram increments by the relative pixel proportions we simply increment the affected colour bins (two for an edge block, one for a uniform block) by 1 (we note that this puts more emphasis on the nonuniform histogram than on the uniform one). We also wish to point out that the resulting histograms are *not* normalised as is often the case with histogram based descriptors. The reason for this is that by not normalising we preserve the original ratio between uniform and pattern blocks—an image feature that should prove important for distinguishing between images with similar colour content.

Having calculated H^u and H^n two CVPIC images can be compared by calculating a weighted sum of the L_1 norm between their histograms

$$d_{colour}(I_1, I_2) = \alpha \sum_{k=1}^{N} \left| H_1^u(k) - H_2^u(k) \right| + (1-\alpha) \sum_{k=1}^{N} \left| H_1^n(k) - H_2^n(k) \right|$$

(1)

where α can be set so as to put more or less emphasis on either of the two histograms. We set $\alpha=0.5$, i.e. weigh the two histograms equally.

While image retrieval based on colour usually produces useful results, integration of this information with another paradigm such as texture or shape will result in an improved retrieval performance. Shape descriptors are often calculated as statistical summaries of local edge information such as in (Jain & Vailaya, 1996) where the edge orientation and magnitude is determined at each pixel location and an edge histogram calculated. Exploiting the CVPIC image structure an effective shape descriptor can be determined very efficiently. Since each (pattern) block contains

exactly one (precalculated) edge and there are 14 different patterns, we simply build 1×14 histogram of the edge indices. Again, no normalisation is applied. The edge histogram hence adds up to half the nonuniform colour histogram. We decided not to include a bin for uniform blocks, since these give little indication of shape (rather they describe the absence of it). Edge histograms H_1^S and H_2^S are compared by

$$d_{shape}(I_1, I_2) = \sum_{k=1}^{N} \left| H_1^s(k) - H_2^s(k) \right|$$

(2)

Having calculated d_{colour} and d_{shape} for two images these two scores can now be combined in order to allow for image retrieval based on both colour and shape features which results in

$$d(I_1, I_2) = \alpha \sum_{k=1}^{N} \left| H_1^u(k) - H_2^u(k) \right|$$
$$+ \beta \sum_{k=1}^{N} \left| H_1^n(k) - H_2^n(k) \right| + (1-\alpha-\beta) \sum_{k=1}^{N} \left| H_1^s(k) - H_2^s(k) \right|$$

(3)

Again, the weights α and β can be adjusted so as to make either of the two colour features or the shape descriptor more dominant. In our experiment we opted for equal weights between colour and shape features and equal weights between uniform and nonuniform colour histograms (i.e., $\alpha=\beta=0.25$).

EXPERIMENTS

We evaluated the presented algorithm using the UCID dataset (Schaefer & Stich, 2004). UCID (available from http://vision.cs.aston.ac.uk), an Uncompressed Colour Image Database, consists of 1338 colour images all preserved in their uncompressed form which makes it ideal for the testing of compressed domain techniques. UCID also provides a ground truth of 262 assigned query images each with a number of predefined corresponding matches that an ideal image retrieval system would return.

We compressed the database using the CVPIC coding technique and performed compressed domain image retrieval as detailed above, based on the queries defined in the UCID set. As performance measure we used the modified average match percentile (AMP) from (Schaefer & Stich, 2004) which is defined as

$$MP_Q = \frac{100}{S_Q} \sum_{i=1}^{S_Q} \frac{N - R_i}{N - i} \qquad (4)$$

with $R_i < R_{i+1}$ and

$$AMP = \frac{1}{N_Q} \sum MP_Q \qquad (5)$$

where R_i is the rank the ith match to query image Q was returned, S_Q is the number of corresponding matches for Q, N_Q is the number of defined query images and N the total number of images in the database. A perfect retrieval system would achieve an AMP of 100 whereas an AMP of 50 would mean the system performs as well as one that returns images in random order.

In order to relate the results obtained we also implemented colour histogram based image retrieval (8 × 8 × 8 RGB histograms) according to (Swain & Ballard, 1991), colour coherence vectors (Pass & Zabih, 1996), border/interior pixel histograms (Stehling et al., 2002) and colour auto correlograms (Huang, Kumar, Mitra, Zhu,

& Zabih, 1997). Results for all methods can be found in Table 1.

From there, we can see that our compressed-domain approach is not only capable of achieving good retrieval performance, but that it actually clearly outperforms all other methods. While the border/interior pixel approach achieves an AMP of 91.27 and all other methods perform worse, CVPIC colour/shape histograms provide an average match percentile of 94.24, that is almost 3.0 higher than the next best methods. This is indeed a significant difference as a drop in match percentile of 3 will mean that 3% more of the whole image database need to be returned in order to find the images that are relevant; as typical image database nowadays can contain tens of thousands to hundreds of thousands images this would literally mean additionally thousands of images. The superiority of the CVPIC approach is especially remarkable so as it is based on images compressed to a medium compression ratio, i.e. images with a significantly lower image quality that uncompressed images whereas for all other methods the original uncompressed versions of the images were used. Furthermore, methods such as colour histograms, colour coherence vectors and colour correlograms are known to work fairly well for image retrieval and are hence among those techniques that are widely used in this field. This is further illustrated in Figure 2 which shows a sample query images of the UCID database together with the five top ranked images returned by all methods. Only the CVPIC technique manages to retrieve four correct model images in the top five (with the next correct model coming up in sixth place) while colour correlograms retrieve three and all other methods only two.

CONCLUSION

In this chapter, we presented an image retrieval technique that operates directly in the compressed domain of CVPIC compressed images. By exploit-

Table 1. Retrieval results based on the UCID database

	AMP
Colour histograms	90.47
Colour coherence vectors	91.03
Border/interior pixel histograms	91.27
Colour correlograms	89.96
CVPIC retrieval (α=β=0.25)	**94.24**

Figure 2. Sample retrieval from the UCID database

Query image

Colour histograms

Colour coherence vectors

Border/interior pixel histograms

Colour correlograms

CVPIC retrieval

ing the fact that CVPIC encodes both colour and edge information these features can be directly used for image retrieval. Two types of histograms are built: two colour histograms (one of uniform areas and one of edge areas) and one shape histogram. Histograms are compared using histogram intersection and the resulting scores weighted to provide an overall similarity between two images. Experimental results on a medium-sized colour image database show that the suggested method performs well, outperforming techniques such as colour histograms, colour coherence vectors, and colour correlograms.

REFERENCES

Chen, D., & Bovik, A. (1990). Visual pattern image coding. *IEEE Trans. Communications, 38*, 2137–2146.

CIE. (1986). Colorimetry. *CIE Publications 15.2*. Commission International de L'Eclairage, 2nd edition.

Huang, J., Kumar, S.R., Mitra, M., Zhu, W.-J., & Zabih, R. (1997). Image indexing using color correlograms. In *IEEE Int. Conference Computer Vision and Pattern Recognition* (pp. 762–768).

Jain, A.K., & Vailaya, A. (1996). Image retrieval using color and shape. *Pattern Recognition, 29*(8), 1233–1244.

Pass, G., & Zabih, R. (1996). Histogram refinement for content-based image retrieval. In *3rd IEEE Workshop on Applications of Computer Vision* (pp. 96–102).

Picard, R.W. (1994). Content access for image/video coding: The fourth criterion. *Technical Report 195*. MIT Media Lab.

Qiu, G. (2003). Colour image indexing using BTC. *IEEE Trans. Image Processing, 12*(1), 93–101.

Schaefer, G., & Lieutaud, S. (2004). CVPIC compressed domain image retrieval by colour and shape. In *Int. Conference on Image Analysis and Recognition* (Vol. 3211, pp. 778–786). Springer Lecture Notes on Computer Science.

Schaefer, G., & Qiu, G. (2000). Midstream content access based on colour visual pattern coding. In *Proceedings of SPIE—Storage and Retrieval for Image and Video Databases VIII* (Vol. 3972, pp. 284–292).

Schaefer, G., Qiu, G., & Luo, M.R. (1999). Visual pattern based colour image compression. In *Proceedings of SPIE—Visual Communication and Image Processing 1999*, (Vol. 3653, pp. 989–997).

Schaefer, G., & Stich, M. (2004). UCID—an uncompressed colour image database. In *Proceedings of SPIE—Storage and Retrieval Methods and Applications for Multimedia 2004* (Vol. 5307, pp. 472–480).

Stehling, R.O., Nascimento, M.A., & Falcao, A.X. (2002). A compact and efficient image retrieval approach based on border/interior pixel classification. In *11ʰ Int. Conf. on Information and Knowledge Management* (pp. 102–109).

Swain, M.J., & Ballard, D.H. (1991). Color indexing. *Int. Journal Computer Vision, 7*(11), 11–32.

KEY TERMS

Colour Histogram: A feature often used for CBIR where colour space is quantised and the numbers of pixels that fall within each quantisation bin are stored.

Compressed-Domain Image Retrieval: CBIR performed directly in the compressed domain of images (i.e., without a need to uncompress the images first).

Content-Based Image Retrieval (CBIR): Retrieval of images based not on keywords or annotations but based on features extracted directly from the image data.

Image Compression: The process of storing images in a more compact form by removing redundant data and/or discarding visually less important information.

Image Similarity Metric: Quantitative measure whereby the features of two images are compared in order to provide a judgement related to the visual similarity of the images.

Query-By-Example Retrieval: Retrieval paradigm in which a query is provided by the user and the system retrieves instances similar to the query.

Chapter XLVI
Music Information Retrieval

Thomas Lidy
Vienna University of Technology, Austria

Andreas Rauber
Vienna University of Technology, Austria

ABSTRACT

This chapter provides an overview of the relatively young but increasingly important domain of Music Information Retrieval, an Information Retrieval subdomain, which investigates efficient and intelligent methods to analyze, recognize, retrieve and organize music. After describing the background and the problems that are addressed by research in this domain the chapter gives a brief introduction to methods for the extraction of semantic descriptors from music, which are fundamental to a great number of tasks in Music Information Retrieval. In the subsequent sections, music retrieval, music classification and music library visualization systems are described. All of these systems are developed for the purpose of enhancing organization, access and retrieval in potentially large digital music libraries.

INTRODUCTION

The increasing popularity and size of digital music libraries, both professional repositories and personal audio collections, calls for advanced methods for efficient organization and retrieval. Traditional search based on file name, song title, or artist does not meet the advanced requirements of people working with large music libraries because it either presumes exact knowledge of these meta-data or involves browsing of long lists in the archive.

Modern Music Information Retrieval (MIR) systems rely on content-based music similarity and offer a multitude of new technologies to organize, access and explore digital music libraries. A range of different feature extraction techniques has been developed, which analyze music and extract descriptors that allow computing similarity between pieces of music. On top of the features extracted from music, standard information retrieval techniques are applied in order to enable to search for specific pieces of music, or for tracks from a certain musical genre.

Queries may be formulated by providing audio examples: example songs, excerpts of recorded audio or even hummed melodies. MIR systems then retrieve music by computed similarity.

The application of machine learning algorithms enables classification of music by artist, by genre or other categories, using the extracted music descriptors. These methods allow a MIR system to detect music from a particular artist, to recognize the genre of a piece of music or even its mood, or to organize an entire music library into a pre-defined genre taxonomy. By contrast, the use of unsupervised learning techniques overcomes genre boundaries and considers audio similarity independently from genre labels. These approaches facilitate the organization of a digital music library by an automatic clustering of the pieces of music. Clusters containing similar music are exhibited by a variety of visualizations. One particular approach that has been chosen is the use of Self-Organizing Maps (SOMs) to create maps of music libraries. A range of different visualization methods developed for SOMs enhance the view of the cluster structures in the music library. Applications have been developed that facilitate interaction with the digital music library, retrieval of music and discovery of yet unknown music. Together with ad-hoc creation of style- and situation-based playlists, these systems allow for novel methods of access to digital music libraries.

BACKGROUND

The term *Music Information Retrieval* has been first mentioned by Kassler (1966). For a long period, however, there was little research on this topic. First beat detection systems were published in the late 1970s and 1980s. The domain of content-based music retrieval experienced a major boost in the late 1990s when mature techniques for the automated description of the content of music became available. In the 1990s, also first systems for classification and clustering of sound events (Feiten & Günzel, 1994) and discrimination of speech and music (Scheirer & Slaney, 1997) were presented. The first works on music style recognition were using MIDI or other symbolic music as input (Dannenberg, Thom, & Watson, 1997). Then, research on audio-based approaches for music classification became increasingly important (Foote, 1997). Since around 2000, the problem of clustering and visualizing large music libraries and supporting better access to them has been addressed.

The International Conference on Music Information Retrieval (ISMIR) is the most important forum for researchers and people interested in Music IR. In the annual MIREX (Music Information Retrieval Evaluation eXchange) benchmarking event, state-of-the-art approaches for music description, classification and other tasks are evaluated and compared.

Downie (2003) provides a review of nearly all aspects of Music Information Retrieval, including contributions from the pre-digital era. The review covers different classes of music descriptors, describes a range of MIR systems and discusses also the challenges in MIR. Orio (2006) explains and reviews different aspects of music and music processing, discusses the role of the users, and gives an introduction to scientific MIR evaluation campaigns. He also describes several systems for MIR.

MUSIC DESCRIPTORS

An essential part of most Music Information Retrieval tasks is the automatic description of music. As computers are not capable to grasp semantics in music directly, algorithms have been devised that extract (numerical) features from music which capture aspects such as loudness, tempo, beat, rhythm, timbre, pitch, harmonics, melody, and so on. These features are also called music descriptors.

In music feature extraction, there are two main directions, according to the representation of music: Extraction from symbolic music (e.g., MIDI format), where music is stored as notations, which has the advantage that statistics about notes, onsets and pitch (and consequently the melody) can be extracted directly (Ghias, Logan, Chamberlin, & Smith, 1995; Neve & Orio, 2004). However, the actual sound of the music is not available, which makes "computer audition" difficult, particularly when information about the instruments is missing. Contrarily, music stored as digital audio wave forms (e.g., in WAV or MP3 format) contains the sound as a mixed signal, but the extraction of individual voices or instruments and their structure is difficult. Most of the audio-based approaches perform a signal analysis in the frequency domain in order to derive music descriptors.

In the time domain (i.e., from the wave form itself), simple features such as Zero Crossing Rate, RMS energy and others, can be computed. The Zero Crossing Rate (ZCR) is the number of times the signal crosses the 0-line (i.e., changes from a positive to a negative amplitude value) within one second. It can determine the noisiness of a signal and thus be used e.g. to distinguish between speech and music, or as a simple a measure of the dominant frequency of a signal. Root Mean Square (RMS) energy is determined by computing the mean of the square of all sample values in a time frame and taking the square root. It provides a good indication of loudness in a time frame and may also serve for higher-level tasks such as audio event detection, segmentation or tempo/beat estimation.

The spectrum of a signal is commonly obtained by a Fourier analysis, which transforms the signal into the frequency domain. For functions sampled at discrete time intervals, such as digital audio wave forms, a Discrete Fourier Transform (DFT) is used, usually in form of the computationally faster Fast Fourier Transform (FFT) algorithm. In order to obtain a Spectrogram, the chang-

ing spectrum over time, a Short-Time Fourier Transform (STFT) has to be performed, i.e. many Fourier Transforms for multiple short-time windows of the length of a few audio samples. From the spectral representation of the signal, features such as the Spectral Centroid, Rolloff and Flux, etc. can be calculated. Spectral Flux measures the amount of change in the spectrum between two frames (computed as the squared differences in frequency distribution). Spectral Centroid is a measure of brightness of the sound. It is the "center of gravity" (i.e., the frequency where the energy of all frequencies below that point is equal to the energy of all frequencies above it). Spectral Rolloff indicates the "skewness" of the spectral shape.

Most of the more sophisticated feature extractors also perform a spectrum analysis as their first step. Frequently, also psycho-acoustic transformations are included in feature calculation, in order to simulate the human auditory system. For Mel Frequency Cepstral Coefficients (MFCCs), a feature set which originated from the speech recognition domain, the Mel scale is applied on the frequency range, which was defined empirically through human listening tests. It models perceived pitch distances and is approximately a logarithmic scale, which corresponds more closely to the human auditory system than the linearly spaced frequency bands of a spectrum. For MFCC calculation usually the Discrete Cosine Transform (DCT) is used instead of the Fourier Transform.

Many Music IR software frameworks such as MARSYAS (Tzanetakis, 2002), M2K (Downie, Ehmann, & Hu, 2005) or CLAM (Amatriain, Arumí, & Garcia, 2006) incorporate these common descriptors and a number of further developed feature sets. MARSYAS, for instance, also includes Beat Histograms, Pitch Histograms and Wavelet Transform features. The Wavelet Transform is another alternative to the Fourier Transform, which overcomes the issue of the trade-off between time and frequency resolution. For high frequency ranges, it provides low frequency resolution but high time resolution, whereas in low frequency ranges, it provides high frequency and lower time resolution. This is a closer representation of what the human ear perceives from sound. MARSYAS is, moreover, able to compute descriptors directly from MPEG (MP3) compressed audio, without decoding the audio to a wave form. The MPEG-7 standard (ISO, 2002) also contains a number of audio descriptors, however without giving details about a concrete implementation.

Further feature sets for Music IR are Rhythm Patterns (Rauber, Pampalk, & Merkl, 2002), Statistical Spectrum Descriptors and Rhythm Histograms (Lidy & Rauber, 2005). They have in common that they compute a Bark-scale Sonogram (c.f., Figure 1). The Bark scale is a perceptual scale, similar to the Mel scale, which groups frequencies in the auditory range into 24 critical bands (Zwicker & Fastl, 1999). After aggregating frequencies according to the Bark scale the spectrogram is transformed into the Decibel scale, followed by application of another psycho-acoustic model: By considering equal loudness curves, which equalize the different human perception of loudness at different frequencies (Zwicker &

Fastl, 1999), the values are transformed into the unit Phon and subsequently into the unit Sone, reflecting the specific loudness sensation of the human auditory system. The Sone scale relates to the Phon scale in the way that a doubling on the Sone scale sounds to the human ear like a doubling of the loudness. From this Sonogram representation a Statistical Spectrum Descriptor (SSD) is derived by computing seven statistical measures on each of the 24 critical bands. Applying a Fourier Transform on the Sonogram the magnitudes of modulation for different modulation frequencies are derived. A Rhythm Pattern (c.f., Figure 2) exhibits this modulation strength per modulation frequency (in a range of 0 to 10 Hz) for all critical bands. High values for a particular modulation frequency in a number of adjacent (often lower) bands indicate rhythm in a piece of music. A Rhythm Histogram aggregates this information for all bands and indicates fluctuations (or rhythm) in a more general and more compact way.

In the annual Music Information Retrieval Evaluation eXchange (MIREX, 2008) state-of-the-art methods for music description are evaluated and compared.

MUSIC RETRIEVAL SYSTEMS

On top of the features computed from music, standard information retrieval techniques can be applied to search for specific pieces of music, or for tracks from a certain musical genre. The techniques are comparing the feature vectors from each piece of music and calculating a distance between them. This allows computing the similarity between all pieces of music in a music collection or digital libary. Distance metrics play an important role for retrieval of the most similar pieces of music. Depending on the feature space the Euclidean distance may not be appropriate and other metrics (cosine distance, different Minkowski metrics, Kullback-Leibler divergence,

Figure 1. Sonogram (Bark scale)

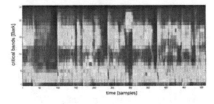

Figure 2. Rhythm pattern

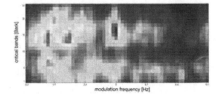

and so on) might be a better choice. Advanced approaches analyze distribution and evolution of features computed at several temporal positions in the music and apply Gaussian Mixture Models or Hidden Markov Models.

For search and retrieval, queries may be formulated by providing audio or notation-based examples: example songs, excerpts of recorded audio, hummed melodies, melody excerpts entered on a piano roll on the screen, and so on. The MIR systems then retrieve music by computed similarity. A survey on MIR systems has been done by Typke, Wiering, & Veltkamp (2005), an overview of current MIR systems and a description of them is provided on http://www.mirsystems.info.

MUSIC CLASSIFICATION

With the use of music descriptors and the application of machine learning algorithms, it is possible to classify music into a pre-determined list of categories, e.g. musical genres. It is necessary that a number of pieces of music is annotated with meta-data labels, i.e. if yet no genre assignment exists, a part of the music collection has to be labeled manually. From the labeled data, a classifier can then learn and induce models for unclassified data. With the use of the model and a descriptor extracted from the music, the classifier is then—depending on the desired application—able to detect music from a particular artist, to recognize the genre of a piece of music, to recognize moods in music or to categorize an entire music library into a pre-defined class hierarchy (e.g., a genre taxonomy). This is extremely helpful for the categorization and/or labeling of large digital music libraries.

Potentially, every supervised classification algorithm from the machine learning domain can be applied. The adequacy of a particular algorithm depends in most cases on the features used for music description. Classifiers which are frequently used for music genre classification are k-Nearest

Neighbor and Support Vector Machines. A survey on automatic music genre classification is available in Scaringella, Zoia, & Mlynek (2006).

Classification approaches are also used for evaluating and benchmarking music descriptors (Lidy & Rauber, 2005). Disposing of a music collection which is entirely labeled the result of classification can be measured in terms of accuracy, precision and recall, among other measures. Thus, the performance of a particular algorithm for music feature extraction can be evaluated and compared to other approaches. Frequently, a cross-validation approach is used for evaluation: To reduce the effect of the choice of a particular training and test set (and thus avoid a potential bias due to a well-chosen set and/or overfitting), the music collection is split randomly into n (e.g. 10) equally sized subsets. In n runs, each subset is selected once as the test set, while the remaining subsets are used for training. Measures are then calculated as the average of the results of each of the n tests.

In order to facilitate benchmarking in the Music Information Retrieval domain, the annual MIREX campaign has been established, in which the state-of-the-art music description and retrieval approaches are evaluated within a series of different tasks, reflecting current problems in Music IR (MIREX, 2008). This benchmarking campaign enables the comparison of the most effective music feature extractors and MIR systems.

CLUSTERING AND VISUALIZATION IN MUSIC INFORMATION RETRIEVAL

Facing the growing number and size of music collections or archives, new methods for visualization of these music collections are developed. These approaches enable both a concise overview and efficient access to music collections.

In 2000, a set of 3D tools for working with sound collections has been presented, including *Timbregram, TimbreSpace* and *GenreGram* (Tzanetakis & Cook, 2000). Audio similarity is visualized by Cano, Kaltenbrunner, Gouyon, & Battle (2002) using the FastMap algorithm, enabling also to browse music archives. Disc- and tree-map-based visualizations using meta-data information have been presented by Torrens, Hertzog, & Arcos (2004). An artist map interface particularly suited for hand-held devices has been developed by Van Gulik, Vignoli, & van de Wetering (2004). It clusters pieces of audio based on content features as well as meta-data attributes using a spring model algorithm. *Musicream* (Goto & Goto, 2005) is an interface, in which pieces of music are represented by discs that stream down on the screen enabling unexpected encounters with music pieces. Disc colors reflect similarity in musical pieces, indicating the mood of a piece. With a sticking function similar pieces are attracted like using a magnet and the meta-playlist function enables visual playlist arrangement with a high degree of freedom.

Self-Organizing Maps have become very popular for the visualization of music collections. A Self-Organizing Map (SOM) is an unsupervised neural network providing a topology-preserving mapping from the high-dimensional feature space onto a two-dimensional output space (Kohonen, 2001). First, SOMs have been applied to organize sounds based on pitch, duration and loudness (Cosi, De Poli, & Lauzzana 1994; Feiten & Günzel, 1994) or using MFCC features (Spevak & Polfreman, 2001). Automatic organization of music collections on SOMs has been demonstrated by Rauber and Frühwirth (2001). Related to this work, Rauber, Pampalk, & Merkl (2003) presented an Islands of Music visualization using Self-Organizing Maps and Rhythm Pattern features. An interactive implementation of Islands of Music on both personal computers as well as portable devices has been shown by Neumayer, Dittenbach, & Rauber (2005) in form of the PlaySOM software.

Another work on exploring music collections by Pampalk, Dixon, & Widmer (2004) uses Aligned-SOMs, which allow changing interactively the focus of organization among different aspects, like e.g. timbre or rhythm. Knees, Pampalk, & Widmer (2004) apply SOMs to organize music at the artist level using artist information mined from the Web. Mörchen, Ultsch, Nöcker, and Stamm (2005) employ Emergent SOMs for visualization of music collections, which are particularly suitable for the creation of large maps. Mayer, Merkl, and Rauber (2005) present the Mnemonic SOM which allows a map to take any arbitrary shape, for better memorization of locations on a SOM. The approach has been demonstrated also in conjunction with the *Map of Mozart*, clustering all works composed by Mozart (Mayer, Lidy, & Rauber, 2006). SOMs are also utilized to enable live clustering of radio stations and thus the recognition of radio stations' program content of (Lidy & Rauber, 2006).

A review of visualization approaches in Music Information Retrieval is provided in Cooper, Foote, Pampalk, and Tzanetakis (2006).

CONCLUSION

Music Information Retrieval addresses research issues for categorizing, organizing, searching in and accessing digital music libraries. The core of most MIR systems consists of an approach for extracting features (descriptors) from digital music. With these features, a range of tasks such as semi-automatic classification of music into categories, recognition and identification of pieces of music and/or their genre and/or artist, retrieval of music and clustering of digital music libraries are enabled. The MPEG-7 standard also contains a definition of audio descriptors. However, the methods for efficient audio description are constantly improved, and compared and evaluated in the annual MIREX campaign. Additionally, an increasing number of applications for intuitive visualization and interaction with music collections is developed, many of them based on unsupervised clustering methods relying on computed music similarity.

REFERENCES

Amatriain, X., Arumí, P., & Garcia, D. (2006). CLAM: A framework for efficient and rapid development of cross-platform audio applications. In *Proceedings of ACM Multimedia 2006*. Santa Barbara, CA.

Cano, P., Kaltenbrunner, M., Gouyon, F., & Battle, E. (2002). On the use of fastmap for audio retrieval and browsing. In *Proceedings of the International Conference on Music Information Retrieval (ISMIR)*. Paris, France.

Cooper, M., Foote, J., Pampalk, E., & Tzanetakis, G. (2006). Visualization in audio-based music information retrieval. *Computer Music Journal, 30*(2), 42–62.

Cosi, P., De Poli, G., & Lauzzana, G. (1994). Auditory modelling and self-organizing neural networks for timbre classification. *Journal of New Music Research, 23*(1), 71–98.

Dannenberg, R.B., Thom, B., & Watson, D. (1997). A machine learning approach to musical style recognition. In *Proceedings of the International Computer Music Conference (ICMC)* (pp. 344–347). Thessaloniki, Greece.

Downie, J.S. (2003). *Annual review of information science and technology* (Vol. 37, pp. 295–340). Medford, NJ: Information Today.

Downie, J.S., Ehmann, A.F., & Hu, X. (2005). Music-to-knowledge (M2K): a prototyping and evaluation environment for music digital library research. In *Proceedings of the Joint Conference on Digital Libraries (JCDL)* (p. 376). Denver, CO.

Feiten, B., & Günzel, S. (1994). Automatic indexing of a sound database using self-organizing neural nets. *Computer Music Journal, 18*(3), 53–65.

Foote, J.T. (1997). Content-based retrieval of music and audio. In C. Kuo (Ed.), *Proceedings of SPIE Multimedia Storage and Archiving Systems II* (Vol. 3229, pp. 138–147).

Ghias, A., Logan, J., Chamberlin, D., & Smith, B.C. (1995). Query by humming: Musical information retrieval in an audio database. In *Proceedings of the Third ACM International Conference on Multimedia* (pp. 231–236). San Francisco, CA: ACM.

Goto, M., & Goto, T. (2005). Musicream: New music playback interface for streaming, sticking, sorting, and recalling musical pieces. In *Proceedings of the International Conference on Music Information Retrieval (ISMIR)*. London, UK.

ISO. (2002). Information technology—multimedia content description interface—part 4: audio. ISO/IEC 15938-4:2002. *International Organisation for Standardisation. Mpeg-7*. Retrieved August 30, 2008, from http://www.chiariglione.org/mpeg/standards/mpeg-7/mpeg-7.htm

Kassler, M. (1966). Toward musical information retrieval. *Perspectives of New Music, 4*(2), 59–67.

Knees, P., Pampalk, E., & Widmer, G. (2004). Artist classifiction with Web-based data. In *Proceedings of the International Conference on Music Information Retrieval (ISMIR)*. Barcelona, Spain.

Kohonen, T. (2001). Self-organizing maps (3rd ed.). *Springer Series in Information Sciences* (Vol. 30). Springer, Berlin.

Lidy, T., & Rauber, A. (2005). Evaluation of feature extractors and psycho-acoustic transformations for music genre classification. In *Proceedings of the International Conference on Music Information Retrieval* (pp. 34–41). London, UK.

Lidy, T., & Rauber, A. (2006). Visually profiling radio stations. In *Proceedings of the International Conference on Music Information Retrieval*. Victoria, Canada.

Mayer, R., Lidy, T., & Rauber, A. (2006). The map of Mozart. In *Proceedings of the International Symposium on Music Information Retrieval (IS-MIR)*. Victoria, Canada.

Mayer, R., Merkl, D., & Rauber, A. (2005). Mnemonic SOMs: Recognizable shapes for self-organizing maps. In *Proceedings of the Workshop On Self-Organizing Maps (WSOM)* (pp. 131–138). Paris, France.

MIREX. (2008). *Music Information Retrieval Evaluation eXchange (MIREX)*. Retrieved August 30, 2008, from http://www.music-ir.org/mirexwiki/index.php/Main_Page

Mörchen, F., Ultsch, A., Nöcker, M., & Stamm, C. (2005). Databionic visualization of music collections according to perceptual distance. In *Proceedings of the International Conference on Music Information Retrieval (ISMIR)*. London, UK.

Neumayer, R., Dittenbach, M., & Rauber, A. (2005). PlaySOM and PocketSOMPlayer—alternative interfaces to large music collections. In *Proceedings of the International Conference on Music Information Retrieval (ISMIR)* (pp. 618–623). London, UK.

Neve, G., & Orio, N. (2004). Indexing and retrieval of music documents through pattern analysis and data fusion techniques. In *Proceedings of the International Conference on Music Information Retrieval (ISMIR)*. Barcelona, Spain.

Orio, N. (2006). Music retrieval: A tutorial and review. *Foundations and Trends in Information Retrieval, 1*(1), 1–90.

Pampalk, E., Dixon, S., & Widmer, G. (2004). Exploring music collections by browsing different views. *Computer Music Journal, 28*(2), 49–62.

Rauber, A., & Frühwirth, M. (2001). Automatically analyzing and organizing music archives. In *Proceedings of the European Conference on Research and Advanced Technology for Digital Libraries (ECDL)*. Darmstadt, Germany: Springer.

Rauber, A., Pampalk, E., & Merkl, D. (2002). Using psycho-acoustic models and self-organizing maps to create a hierarchical structuring of music by musical styles. In *Proceedings of the International Conference on Music Information Retrieval (ISMIR)* (pp. 71–80). Paris, France.

Rauber, A., Pampalk, E., & Merkl, D. (2003). The SOM-enhanced JukeBox: Organization and visualization of music collections based on perceptual models. *Journal of New Music Research, 32*(2), 193–210.

Scaringella, N., Zoia, G., & Mlynek, D. (2006). Automatic genre classification of music content: A survey. *Signal Processing Magazine, IEEE, 23*(2), 133–141.

Scheirer, E., & Slaney, M. (1997). Construction and evaluation of a robust multifeature speech/music discriminator. In *Proceedings of the International Conference on Acoustics, Speech and Signal Processing (ICASSP '97)* (pp. 1331–1334). Munich, Germany.

Spevak, C., & Polfreman, R. (2001). Sound spotting—a frame-based approach. In *Proceedings of the Second International Symposium on Music Information Retrieval: ISMIR 2001* (pp. 35–36). Bloomington, IN.

Torrens, M., Hertzog, P., & Arcos, J.L. (2004). Visualizing and exploring personal music libraries. In *Proceedings of the International Conference on Music Information Retrieval (ISMIR)*. Barcelona, Spain.

Typke, R., Wiering, F., & Veltkamp, R. C. (2005). A survey of music information retrieval systems. In *Proceedings of the International Conference on Music Information Retrieval (ISMIR)*. London, UK.

Tzanetakis, G. (2002). *Manipulation, analysis and retrieval systems for audio signals*. Doctoral thesis, Computer Science Department, Princeton University.

Tzanetakis, G., & Cook, P. (2000). 3D graphic tools for isolated sound collections. In *Proceedings of the Conference on Digital Audio Effects (DAFx)*. Verona, Italy.

Van Gulik, R., Vignoli, F., & van de Wetering, H. (2004). Mapping music in the palm of your hand, explore and discover your collection. In *Proceedings of the International Conference on Music Information Retrieval (ISMIR)*. Barcelona, Spain.

Zwicker, E., & Fastl, H. (1999). Psychoacoustics—facts and models. *Springer Series of Information Sciences* (Vol. 22). Springer, Berlin.

KEY TERMS

Descriptor: Numerical measure intended to describe semantic aspects of music, such as timbre or rhythm. Sometimes, a set of multiple measures is refered to as descriptor.

Digital Audio: Representation of a music recording in digitally sampled wave form in the form of a mixed signal. Information of individual sources of the signal is not explicitly available and can be derived partly by extensive analysis of the signal.

Feature: Numerical measure describing an aspect of music which is useful for Music IR tasks. Multiple features together are also refered to as feature set. The term descriptor is frequently used as synonym for the terms feature or feature set.

Feature Extraction: Method or algorithm which analyses music and computes (extracts) features from it.

Feature Vector: A feature set, when used as input for classification or clustering methods, is refered to as feature vector. An individual scalar value in this feature vector is also refered to as an attribute or feature.

Music Information Retrieval Evaluation Exchange (MIREX): Annual benchmarking event for comparison of state-of-the-art Music IR approaches.

Music Information Retrieval (MIR): Research domain that covers automatic extraction of music descriptors for similarity-based search, retrieval, classification and organization of music in (potentially large) music collections.

Self-Organizing Map (SOM): An unsupervised neural network providing a topology-preserving mapping from a high-dimensional input space onto a two-dimensional output space. Used as algorithm for clustering and organizing music collections, enabling intuitive views of and/or interaction with music collections.

Symbolic Music: Music stored in a notation-based format (e.g., MIDI), which contains excplicit information about note onsets and pitch on individual tracks (for different instruments), but in contrast to Digital Audio no sound.

Chapter XLVII
The Strategic Plan of Digital Libraries

Juha Kettunen
Turku University of Applied Sciences, Finland

ABSTRACT

This abstract describes the networked cooperation of the academic libraries and the consortium of the digital libraries of the Finnish universities of applied sciences and their strategic plan for the Web service. It argues that it is reasonable to plan the strategies for the network, because no single library has complete control over all the aspects that are necessary to develop the cooperation between the libraries. The strategy is the basis for a cooperation enabling electronic services for the libraries. The findings of this study are useful to the administrators of educational institutions aiming to plan a networked strategy and improve the cost-efficient cooperation of otherwise independent organisations.

INTRODUCTION

Strategic management builds bridges between the perceived present situation and the desired future position described by the vision (Bush & Coleman, 2000; Fidler, 2002; Johnson & Scholes, 2002). Higher education institutions adapt their strategies to the education policy and changing environment. Strategic planning has an important role in academic libraries (Adeyoyin, 2005; Huotari & Iivonen, 2005; Decker & Höppner, 2006).

The networked cooperation of the academic libraries has been playing an increasingly im-portant role in the universities. The planning of a networked strategy is different from the planning of a single library strategy, because there is no single organisational unit who owns the strategy or is responsible for its implementation. The network strategy aims to gain commitment to a systematic cooperation and achieve strategic objectives that cannot be achieved by any single library alone.

The purpose of this article is to describe the consortium of the digital libraries of 29 Finnish universities of applied sciences and their strategic plan for the Web service. The strategic plan was made in 2006 jointly for the network of libraries to promote their electronic services. The strategy is the basis for a cost-efficient cooperation enabling electronic services for the libraries. The strategy of digital libraries is also an example of the fruitful cooperation of the Finnish universities of applied sciences.

This article is organised as follows: The background section introduces first the main characteristics of the consortium of the libraries of the Finnish universities of applied sciences and their shared strategic outlines. The main attention of the article is focused on the strategy for the Web service of digital libraries. Thereafter some future trends are presented. Finally, the results of the article are summarized in the concluding section.

BACKGROUND

The Consortium of Libraries

The consortium of the libraries of the Finnish universities of applied sciences (Amkit Consortium) was founded in 2001. The purpose of the consortium is to coordinate cooperation between the respective libraries of the institutions. In Finland there are 29 universities of applied sciences, which are professionally-oriented higher education institutions. The libraries cooperate actively with the libraries of the 20 traditional universities, the libraries of vocational institutions and other libraries. The result of the Google search engine indicates that there are many other consortia of digital libraries, but they take different forms.

The number of personnel is nearly 500 in the libraries of the universities of applied sciences. They are located in 80 towns and at 200 locations. This reflects the remotely located branches of the institutions. The development of the libraries was rapid during the 1990s when the Finnish Polytechnics were established in higher education. At the beginning of 2006 the polytechnics adopted the new English translation "university of applied

sciences," which reflects the English names of the professionally-oriented higher education institutions in the European Higher Education Area. The European area has defined in the Bologna Process by the European Ministers responsible for higher education (Berlin Communiqué, 2003; Kettunen & Kantola, 2006b, 2007).

The consortium of libraries is a typical network to exchange information and cooperate. It is also a network to gain commitment to a joint strategy of the libraries. The presence of network suggests that much of the success of libraries lies outside a given library residing in the cooperative network.

The networks, work groups and informal communities of practice have an essential role in the exchange of information and knowledge (Kettunen, 2004a; Kettunen & Kantola, 2006a).

Academic libraries seek efficient ways to produce high quality output given the limited financial resources (Brooks, Revill, & Shelton, 1997). Cost-efficiency is a natural choice for strategy in the public sector, where primary management emphasise desired outputs and cost reduction. Typically, taxpayers provide the financial resources for libraries, which have limited annual budgets for activities and investments. Cost-efficiency can be achieved by increasing cooperation between the libraries and taking advantage of the economy of scale across the physical and intellectual assets of the libraries.

Strategic Plan of the Consortium

The network strategy of libraries defines the outlines for the activities required by the network. The network strategy provides the insight and direction to guide the libraries and their cooperation. Each library is then able to define its own strategic themes and implement them. Each library has a responsibility to develop its own action plan describing how development work and processes will deliver the output to implement the network strategy. The additional funding provided by the

Ministry of Education has maintained sufficient coherence and ensured that the main objectives have been achieved. The network strategy is a sub-strategy of an overall network strategy, which has been planned for the Finnish universities of applied sciences (Kettunen, 2004b, 2007).

The strategic themes of the network strategy of the libraries are as follows:

- Systematic and nationwide cooperation of the libraries
- Cooperation within the library network and with the learning process

The vision of the libraries is as follows:

- Library is the dynamic interface of learning and research.
- Library is an efficient and high-quality service-point, a partner and developer in the library network, and a notable regional, national and international trend-setter for its subject areas.

The mission of the libraries is as follows:

- The library produces information skills to enhance learning and critical thinking and to support applied research and professional competence.
- The main tools include transforming collections, expert services and content production into networks.

The consortium of libraries has numerous cooperative projects including library system acquisition and implementation (Endeavor's Voyager), a library portal implementation project, electronic acquisitions (consortium licences), quality management, public relations and communications and information skills studies and virtual learning environments. The Voyager Library Automation System is used by the Finnish university libraries. Voyager, developed by

Endeavor Information Systems, is widely used in many countries (Breeding, 2006; Guy, 2000; Pace, 2004).

MAIN FOCUS OF THE ARTICLE

Strategic Plan of the Web Service of Digital Libraries

The joint strategic plan of the digital libraries of the universities of applied sciences was prepared to promote the Web service of the libraries. The strategic plan was completed in 2006 and it updates the earlier strategy for virtual libraries planned in 2003. Both of these strategies were planned to support the more general strategic plan of the consortium of libraries prepared for the planning period 2004–2007.

The cornerstones of the strategic plan include four perspectives:

- Content
- Facilities
- Knowledge
- Cooperation

The desired strategic objective of the libraries is to achieve a high-quality Web service which supports the core processes of the institutions. The core processes include the learning process and professionally-oriented research. Modern facilities, wide-ranging knowledge and widespread cooperation are the means to put together the Web service.

Cornerstones of the Strategic Plan

The contents of the Web service of libraries include high-quality collections, which can be utilised using the Web. A study by Nitecki and Hernon (2000) examines the service quality of libraries. The libraries supplement their collections from the Finnish Electronic Library (FinELib) or other acquisition consortia. In addition, the purpose is to provide the publications of the universities of applied sciences using the Web.

The facilities, software and other tools are necessary to support the efficient Web service. The libraries provide portals to acquire information and software of digital libraries. The tools of the libraries must have links to the institution's other information systems such as the virtual learning environments and student and study registers. The lightweight directory access protocol (LDAP) is a great advantage for the flexible and safe use, especially in distant use of the information systems. The Web service also uses interactive tools, especially the real-time network information service.

The knowledge of the personnel plays an important role. The employees are aware of the electronic collections and they have a good knowledge of the use, administration and quality evaluation of the collections. In addition, the libraries provide guidance and counselling to their customers, also in the Web. The libraries develop their own pedagogical knowledge and content production and follow the new opportunities in their field of expertise. Customer's information seeking and management skills promote the aims of information literacy (ALA, 2006).

Cooperation is essential for libraries to put together and maintain the Web services. Cooperation enables the effective use of the scarce resources of libraries. The libraries of universities of applied sciences also cooperate with partners from outside the libraries, including the teachers and experts of the information services.

Action Plan

Table 1 describes the action plan of the consortium of libraries including the responsibilities and actions taken. The consortium of digital libraries includes the pedagogical, e-material and facility groups. The libraries clearly have the largest responsibilities. The Web service of libraries is

a valuable actor in providing high-quality collections using the Web and developing electronic tools of the libraries.

The consortium of libraries annually negotiates about the licences for e-resources, which are purchased jointly from FinELib or other sources for the libraries. The joint principles of the libraries are described in the portal of the consortium. The consortium starts the planning and creation of the publication archives. The libraries also provide customers with the contents of other producers including, for example, electronic learning objectives produced by other universities of applied sciences. The consortium negotiates with the publisher and content producers about the development of e-material appropriate for the universities of applied sciences.

The facilities are purchased with the help of the information technology consortium of the universities of applied sciences. The libraries provide the Web service through the portals including the portal of universities, regional portals and portal of the Finnish Virtual University of Applied Sciences. The libraries keep up to date on the development of new facilities and are ready to implement them.

The training of the Web service and information literacy is planned and implemented by the pedagogical group of the consortium. The e-material group of the consortium arranges seminars and workshops concerning the e-collections. The topics include content, licences, copyrights, and e-collections in library education. Training is also arranged on metadata for the information specialist and the teachers of the Web service. The libraries provide training for information literacy in their own institutions for the students, teachers and other members of the personnel. The directors of the libraries encourage their personnel to participate especially in pedagogical training and the training in content production.

The cooperation of libraries is necessary. The consortium of libraries and the libraries participate in the national and international networks. The consortium participates and, if necessary, establishes multidisciplinary and cooperative projects to develop Web services. The consortium makes sure that the results of the cooperative projects are utilised after the project is over. The facility group of the consortium promotes Voyager cooperation, for example, by solving problems to establish a joint catalogue. The technology group of the consortium monitors the development of the metadata banks. The libraries seek ways of multidisciplinary cooperation in their institutions. The virtual information specialists develop the cooperation between the library and e-learning in their institutions.

Every library must be active both in its institution and in the national and international cooperation to achieve the strategic objectives. The transparency of the activities of the consortium must be increased by efficient communication. Successful cooperation requires sufficient human resources to achieve the objectives defined in the strategic plan.

FUTURE TRENDS

The libraries of the universities of applied sciences hone and adapt their strategies to the changing

Table 1. Action plan of the consortium of libraries

Responsibility	Action
The consortium of libraries	• The consortium annually negotiates about the licences for e-resources, which are jointly purchased from FinELib or other sources for the libraries • The consortium negotiates with the content producers and publishers about the development of e-material appropriate for their respective institutions • The Voyager cooperation will continue • The purchase of information technology tools • Training on metadata provided for the teachers of the Web service and information specialists
The pedagogical group	• Planning and provision of training for information literacy
The e-material group	• Arrangement of workshops and seminars concerning the e-collections
The facility group	• Solves problems and establishes a joint catalogue
The technology group	• Supports and supervises the development of metadata banks
Libraries	• The supplement to collections from FinELib or other acquisition consortia with the help of the consortium • Provide the publications of the universities of applied sciences using the Web • Provide portals for the students and personnel to acquire information and software of digital libraries • Participate and establish multidisciplinary and cooperative projects to develop Web services • Make sure that the results of cooperative projects are implemented and utilised after the project is over • Training in information literacy for students, teachers and personnel in their own institutions • The library personnel participates in content production and pedagogical training • The virtual information specialists seek ways how the library can support the e-learning of the degree programmes • The provision of the Web service through various portals including the portal of universities, regional portals and the portal of the Finnish Virtual University of Applied Sciences • Provide the customers with the contents of electronic learning objectives produced by the other universities of applied sciences
Web service of libraries	• Provision of high-quality collections which can be utilised using the Web • The electronic tools of the library are connected with the institution's other information systems such as the student and study registers and virtual learning environment • Provision of interactive tools such as the real-time network information service

environment. The environment includes education policy, changes in the local environment, and the institution itself in which the libraries operate. The environmental changes force the libraries to plan new strategies, which will be tested in real time with students, members of the personnel and other customers. The purpose of strategic management is to build a bridge from the perceived situation of the libraries to their desired future situation described in the vision of the strategic plan.

Increase in open access is an obvious future trend. Open access provides free online access to digital content. It is most suitable and best-known for peer-reviewed scholarly and journal articles, which are published without expectation of payment. In open access, publishing journals make their articles openly accessible immediately on publication. In open access, self-archiving authors make copies of their own published articles openly accessible.

CONCLUSION

The strategic plan of digital libraries has been planned for the network, because no single library has complete control over all the aspects that are necessary to develop the cooperation between the libraries. The proper strategy process across the different libraries, financial resources and knowledge about the development of digital libraries are essential elements for a successful network strategy. The approach presented in this article can also be used for other networks and other regions.

A general pattern of the network strategy is that the strategic themes and objectives and outlines of action plans are formulated for networks. Then strategic themes and objectives are defined for each library of the institution. The institutional strategic plans can then be implemented using detailed action plans and other management tools. Typically the individual organisations align their financial and human resources with their internal

processes to achieve the strategic objectives.

The strategic planning of networks is very similar with the autonomous strategic planning. The strategic planning and management of networks is typically less developed than the planning of proper organisations, which prepare detailed budgets and human resource plans. They also define indicators and set target values for the planning period. The autonomous organisations must also emphasise the organisational culture and define values to give meaning to the workplace and form the basis for the characteristic spirit of an organisation.

REFERENCES

Adeyoyin, S.O. (2005). Strategic planning for marketing library services. *Library Management, 26*(8/9), 494–507.

American Library Association (ALA). (2006). *Standards and guidelines*. Retrieved August 30, 2008, from http://www.ala.org/ala/acrl/acrlstandards/standardsguidelines.htm

Berlin Communiqué. (2003). *Bologna process Berlin 2003, realising the European higher education area*. Communiqué of the conference of Ministers responsible for higher education in Berlin on September 19, 2003.

Breeding, M. (2006). Reshuffling the deck. *Library Journal*. Retrieved August 30, 2008, from http://www.libraryjournal.com/article/CA6319048.html

Brooks, P., Revill, D., & Shelton, T. (1997). The development of scale to measure the quality of an academic library from the perspective of its users. In J. Brockman (Ed.), *Quality Management and Benchmarking in the Information Sector, Results of Recent Research*. British Library Research and Innovation Report 47. London: British Library.

Bush, T., & Coleman, M. (2000). *Leadership and strategic management in education.* London: Paul Chapman Publishing.

Decker, R., & Höppner, M. (2006). Strategic planning and customer intelligence in academic libraries. *Library Hi Tech, 24*(4), 504–514.

Fidler, B. (2002). *Strategic management for school development.* London: Paul Chapman Publishing.

Guy, F. (2000). Progress towards the development of digital libraries: The experiences of some national libraries in North America, Australasia and Europe. *Russian Digital Libraries Journal, 3*(3). Retrieved August 30, 2008, from http://www.elbib.ru/index.phtml?page=elbib/eng/journal/2000/part3/guy

Huotari, M.-L., & Iivonen, M. (2005). Knowledge processes: A strategic foundation for the partnership between the university and its library. *Library Management, 26*(6/7), 324–335.

Johnson, G., & Scholes, K. (2002). *Exploring corporate strategy: Text and cases.* Cambridge: Prentice Hall.

Kettunen, J. (2004a). The strategic evaluation of regional development in higher education. *Assessment & Evaluation in Higher Education, 29*(3), 357–368.

Kettunen, J. (2004b). Bridge building to the future of Finnish polytechnics. *Journal of Higher Education Outreach and Engagement, 9*(2), 43–57.

Kettunen, J. (2007). The strategic evaluation of academic libraries. *Library Hi-Tech, 25*(3), 409–421.

Kettunen, J., & Kantola, M. (2006a). Strategies for virtual learning and e-entrepreneurship. In F. Zhao (Ed.), *Entrepreneurship and Innovations in E-Business: An Integrative Perspective* (pp. 107–123). Hershey: Idea Group Publishing.

Kettunen, J., & Kantola, M. (2006b). The implementation of the Bologna Process. *Tertiary Education and Management, 12*(3), 257–267.

Kettunen, J., & Kantola, M. (2007). Strategic planning and quality management in the Bologna Process. *Perspectives, Policy and Practice in Higher education, 11*(3), 67–73.

Nitecki, D.A., & Hernon, P. (2000). Measuring service quality at Yale University's libraries. *Journal of Academic Librarianship, 26*(4), 259–273.

Pace, A.K. (2004). Dismantling integrated library systems. *Library Journal*, Retrieved August 30, 2008, from http://libraryjournal.com/article/CA374953.html

KEY TERMS

Finnish National Electronic Library (FinELib): Acquires Finnish and international resources to support teaching, learning, and research. The library negotiates agreements for electronic resources on a centralised basis for its member organisations and cooperates with universities, research institutes, and public libraries.

Information Literacy: Information literacy includes competencies that an informed citizen of an information society should possess to participate intelligently and actively in society.

Lightweight Directory Access Protocol (LDAP): In computer networking, LDAP is a networking protocol for querying and modifying directory services running over TCP/IP.

Open Access: The free online availability of digital content, typically scientific, or scholarly journal articles which are published electronically without expectation of payment.

Strategic Themes: Describe the strategy of an organisation in a concise way. They describe what management believes must be done to succeed and achieve the desired outcomes.

Voyager Library System: An integrated library system used by many academic and other libraries. It provides users with keyword searching, parallel searching across other libraries, databases and access to electronic journals and URL links straight from the catalogue screen. Voyager is broken down into different modules that are focused on helping with certain tasks commonly done in libraries. For example, Web Voyage lets people search the library catalog using a normal web browser. The system is produced by Endeavor Information Systems.

Web Service: A software system designed to support interoperable machine-to-machine interaction over a network.

Chapter XLVIII
Software Process Asset Libraries Using Knowledge Repositories

Leonardo Bermón-Angarita
Carlos III University of Madrid, Spain

Antonio Amescua-Seco
Carlos III University of Madrid, Spain

Maria Isabel Sánchez-Segura
Carlos III University of Madrid, Spain

Javier García-Guzmán
Carlos III University of Madrid, Spain

ABSTRACT

This paper establishes the incorporation of knowledge management techniques as a means to improve actual software process asset libraries. It presents how knowledge management contributes to the creation of a new generation of process libraries as repositories of knowledge as well as the mechanisms to allow the acquisition, storage, collaborating, sharing and distribution of knowledge related to the software development processes. It exposes aspects about organization and structure of this kind of digital libraries oriented to software process engineering, defining a lifecycle of the software process assets and a set of services and functions for its effective use in small and medium software development enterprises.

INTRODUCTION

An underlying aspect of the software development is the process. There is a direct relation between processes quality and developed software products (Fuggetta, 2000). During the development of software projects, the organizations need people, technology and processes for creating, acquiring and sharing knowledge about how build software. The process-oriented approach is dedicated to study and understand the sequence of steps and activities necessary for developing the software product, establishing a technical and organizational framework for applying methods, tools and people to software development.

The personnel involved in software development accumulate knowledge. The main disadvantage is that this knowledge is not gathered, hence the knowledge is lost, past errors are repeated again, and the knowledge transference is not easy. The software process knowledge can be stored in a Software Processes Asset Library (PAL) so that in future projects the results could be reached easily and helping to achieve the Software Process Improvement (SPI). But there is little information about what kinds of processes must be captured in the PAL, what processes to ignore, and the need to consider different process representations, materials for different roles and purposes. Moreover, a PAL that achieves to standardize and reuse a software process must describe the process, store it in a suitable format, identify the desired process in a database and retrieve it and adapt it to organizational needs. There are many works about the process description and few researches about the rest of functions (storage, search, recovery, and adaptation).

The goal of this work is to define a set of functionalities of a new generation of PAL, using Knowledge Management (KM) techniques and reusing mechanisms like key elements in order to obtain an institutionalized process to gather and use the know-how in Small and Medium Software Enterprises (SME).

The remainder of this work is structured as follows. Section 2 illustrates the background and definitions. Section 3 presents a review of the literature. Section 4 shows the structure of the PAL proposed, a set of functionalities for creating a new generation of PAL, and it highlights the contributions to the Software Engineering field. Section 5 describes conclusions remarks, and finally, future trends are presented.

BACKGROUND AND DEFINITIONS

This section presents concepts related to the application of knowledge repositories in software process asset libraries for helping to implement SPI strategies using KM.

Software Process Improvement

The objective of SPI is to implement and institutionalize improvement practices to develop software in the organization (i.e., to create new knowledge at an organizational level, creating processes that help the organization to acquire experience of existing sources that will be applied to new projects).

For an effective deployment of SPI it is necessary to facilitate the means for the organization continually gathering pieces of information valuable to attaining improvement and to package and infuse the synthesized experience into future projects. In such a way that it can assemble sub-processes in constructive fashion (Aaen et al., 2002).

The successful SPI models like CMMI in large companies offer incentives for their adoption in new environments but they must be adapted appropriately for its effective fulfillment.

SMEs have a great interest in how to introduce and sustain a SPI initiative, minimizing the limitations of its size and maximizing the benefits inherent in its culture. For the use of SPI models, these companies need to tailor the models to address the problems related to the size and key aspects like documentation, management, reviews, resources, and training.

Process Asset Library

The SPI actions are oriented to create processes that help the organization to acquire experience of existing sources that will be able to be applied to software engineering projects. Therefore, it is necessary to store the knowledge, to package it and provide the mechanisms to reuse it into others projects.

The processes assets must be stored in an organized, well-indexed library with search capacities and easily accessible by anyone who needs process guidance information or other process support materials (Garcia, 2004). PAL facilitates standardization and process improvement in organizations and is a key enabler for achieving higher capability maturity.

Some purposes of a PAL include provide a central knowledge base for acquiring, defining, and disseminating guidance about processes related to the organization's tasks, provide mechanisms for sharing knowledge about the organization's process assets and how they are used, and assemble and reuse sub processes to obtain modified and adapted processes to specific projects.

PAL offers the typical services of a digital library as collection (management of collections of digital resources, locals or distributed, without restriction of format), value-added services (products created according to needs and requirement of the users), personalization (interaction spaces defined by the users) and lifecycle of the information (with different stages and tracking of each resource).

For a small organization, a PAL is a key element that reduces training time to introduce improvements in the software process, and helps lead to a process-focused culture that provides a backbone of discipline for the organization. In addition, an effective PAL is a key element in supporting time reduction needed for planning new projects, a typical area where small projects are challenged (Garcia, 2004).

For a large organization, a PAL provides one of the infrastructure elements required to support movement from one set of behaviors to another, by making public the "new rules" that the organization intends to live by. A well-designed and deployed PAL also reduces planning, implementation, and training time in the large organization, especially for processes that are only intermittently performed. In these processes in particular, having access to relevant guidance to "refresh" even competent practitioners can prove a potent accelerator of confidence, and as a follow on, speed of execution (Garcia, 2004).

Knowledge Management and Knowledge Repositories

The term knowledge can be defined as "a justified belief that increases an entity's capacity for effective action" (Nonaka & Takeuchi, 1995). This knowledge is the main asset that has the organizations and can be managed to guarantee their generation, appropriation and transference between different users.

Rus, Lindvall, & Sinha (2002) define three refinement levels of knowledge:

- **Data:** Sets of discrete and objective data.
- **Information:** Data with added value for a determined context.
- **Knowledge:** Information with added value (information about relationships between elements and their implications in the decisions making process).

Knowledge is generally classified as tacit or explicit (Nonaka & Takeuchi, 1995). The tacit knowledge is highly personal, not verbalized, intuitive and not articulated, and derived from experience and beliefs. The explicit knowledge is formal and systematic, can be expressed without ambiguities by writing, drawings, databases, and so on.

KM can be defined like the discipline that studies creation, preservation, application and reuse of knowledge that is available in an organization; its objective is to create knowledge shared between all users. The basic KM activities include: knowledge identification, capture, integration, retrieve, dissemination, use, and maintenance. At the core of a KM system, there is a knowledge repository, supporting reuse and sharing organizational knowledge.

The repository of knowledge stores two types of knowledge (Handzic, 2005): (a) structured concrete information and knowledge in databases, documents and artifacts. (b) The representation of unstructured abstract information and knowledge of human actors. The repositories can have the following functions: codification (structuring knowledge content) and customization (providing guidance to organizing, linking and navigating knowledge).

Knowledge Management in Software Process Improvement

Managing knowledge in software engineering is a human and knowledge intensive activity. Knowledge has to be collected, organized, stored and retrieved to establish a stable process that is independent of individual software engineers.

Two types of knowledge can be identified in software development (Rus et al., 2002): knowledge embedded in the products and meta-knowledge (knowledge about the products and processes).

An important problem is that just a fraction of all knowledge related to software process is captured and made explicit (Rus et al., 2002). Therefore, it is need building repositories for sharing and retaining of knowledge about software processes. A knowledge-based PAL will be an approach and tool for turning tacit knowledge into explicit knowledge, and can benefit it from the ideas of KM.

RELATED WORKS

Related work comes mainly from knowledge management and software process improvement areas.

One major challenge for SPI efforts is to create strategies for managing knowledge about software development. Baskerville and Pries-Heje (1999) used knowledge management as underlying theory to develop a set of key process areas for a supplement to the CMM in small or medium sized enterprises that develop software. Mathiassen and Pourkomeylian (2001) argued that SPI efforts depend on the implicit and individual knowledge of practitioners in an organization. To change software development practices, the organization should improve the practitioners' existing knowledge (both theoretical and practical) of its software practices. Knowledge about the new processes should thus be made available on different organizational levels. Kautz and Nielsen (2001) studied how knowledge, learning and IT support occur in small software organizations. They used a framework that distinguishes different models of knowledge and learning, different types of knowledge and different knowledge and learning processes. Kautz and Thaysen (2001) introduced the knowledge management process model as a means of properly integrating knowledge management with business processes. A coordinating process includes an ongoing improvement cycle (analyze, define, plan, and effect) and the operational processes of creating, collecting, storing, updating, and sharing knowledge.

There are several proposals of experience-based repositories as tools that promote SPI in organizations. Scott et al. (2002) developed EPG/ER, a process-centered experience repository in a small organization. This repository uses software process to structure experience and make it available for reuse. It includes examples of documents, checklists or unstructured experiences such anecdotes and lessons learnt. Basili et al. (1994) developed the Experience Factory intending to institutionalize the collective learning of an organization by developing, updating, and delivering to the project organization experience packages. The project organization offers the experience factory their products, the plans used in their development, and the data gathered during development and operation. Borges and Falbo (2002) proposed Pro-Know-How as tool that allows sharing knowledge by an experience repository should be built containing the organizational standard process as well as the artifacts and informal knowledge obtained throughout the projects.

Software process models represent knowledge about software development. They describe activities to be carried out in software development as well as the products to be created and the resources and tools used. MILOS (Maurer & Holz, 2002) is a process-centered knowledge management and coordination support approach. This approach distinguishes between three kinds of knowledge: generic (reusable knowledge), knowledge on specific projects and project data, creating a feedback loop for continuous learning. Dingsøyr and Conradi (2003) developed WoX, a knowledge repository that allow solving a specific technical problem, getting an overview of problem areas, avoiding redundancy in having to explain the same solution to several people, improving individual work situation by adjusting technical tools and finding who has a specific competence in the company.

However, none of these works offers support for managing of the lifecycle of the process asset providing reuse capabilities to different projects and to built effective organizational knowledge repositories making stored process knowledge more accessible and visible.

KM is a relatively recent discipline and their techniques and deployment tools have not yet defined and require validation. Some issues for solving are (King et al., 2002): how to identify the organizational knowledge that should be captured in KM systems; how to design and develop a KM system, including its tools and applications; and what methodologies and processes must be adapted or created for KM.

Alavi and Leidner (2001) propose five research questions concerning the application of IT in KM initiatives: consequences of increasing the breadth and depth of knowledge via IT for organizational performance, ways of ensuring that knowledge captured via technology is effectively modified where necessary prior application, ways of ensuring that IT captures modifications to knowledge along with the original knowledge, development of trust in knowledge captured via technology, and factors related to the quality and usefulness of IT systems applied to KM initiatives.

PAL USING KNOWLEDGE MANAGEMENT

A full service digital library must accomplish all essential services of traditional libraries and also exploit the well-known advantages of digital storage, searching, and communication (Gladney, Belkin, Ahmed, Fox, Ashany, & Zemankova, 1994). Building digital libraries involves the integration of complex systems, including collections of documents with varied structure, media, and content.

PAL being a collection of digital assets with information related to software process covers some aspects and interesting points for design and development of digital libraries. As start point of our research in repositories of knowledge applied to software process we defined an organization and structure of the PAL elements, we studied the nature of the items stored, and we defined the interactions with the users and a set of minimum services offered based on knowledge management.

Organization and Structure

PAL is a requirement for software process definition. The PAL conformed for formal and informal knowledge will require of an integrated approach for its construction including information contained in its own database, documents and distributed capabilities.

The PAL content can be modeled by a layers-based approach. Figure 1 shows the repository architecture proposed. The layers are:

- **Organizational infrastructure:** The main roles of the assets repository are: Repository Manager (manages asset storage and configuration and ensure assets are accessible to developers), Asset Producer (creates assets), Asset Editor (abstracts, indexes and refines assets), Asset Consumer (localizes, reads, use and extends with annotations the assets), Asset Evaluator (reviews and approves assets) and Experts/novices (users with different level of expertise).
- **Presentation layer:** Queries to the repository must be derived when a user recognizes an information need within his activities.
- **Security layer:** Mechanisms for authorization, authentication, and accounting of the users.
- **KM layer:** Support for KM activities.
- **SPI layer:** Support for application of SPI guidelines tailored to SME.
- **Conceptual layer:** Using ontologies for modeling the PAL knowledge, structuring its components and providing information

searching and dissemination mechanisms. There are three kinds of ontologies: enterprise ontology considers features of the software development company, context ontology models software projects and assets ontology formalizes the repository content.

Nature of the Process Assets

Each software process asset has the next stages in the lifecycle: planning (a general definition of an asset is obtained), specification (a set of metadata for setting the scope of an asset is obtained), development (the content of an asset is developed), classification (allocation of a developed asset to knowledge areas in the organization), publication (the catalog of assets is published and ready for using by users), instantiation (as the contents of an asset can be null, instances of the assets can be generated with content related to a specific context), query (the users can search particular assets by different methods), reuse (the use of an

Figure 1. PAL structure

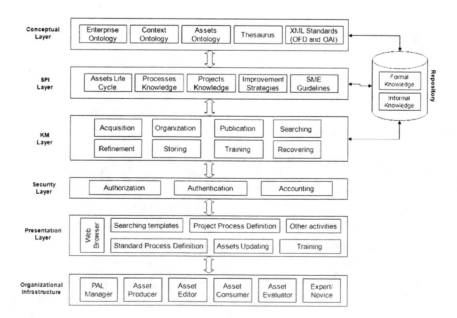

470

asset in a specific project), evaluation (periodical review of assets metadata and content), maintenance (collaborative process of improvement of the catalog), and retire (the assets are unsubscribed of the catalog).

The roles assigned to the stages of the lifecycle are:

- **Asset producer:** Planning, development and specification.
- **Asset editor:** Classification, publication, maintenance and retire.
- **Asset consumer:** Instantiation, query and evaluation.
- **Asset evaluator:** Evaluation.

The PAL has associated a database with the metadata of the assets and a file system where the contents of the assets are stored. Each asset in the catalog has an URL associated to the localization of the content.

Services of the Assets Library

Maier (2002) classifies the functions of KM systems as integrative functions, interactive functions and bridging functions:

- **Integrative functions:** support the handling of knowledge elements in the sense of an asynchronous transfer of explicit knowledge.
- **Interactive functions:** focus on joint knowledge development between knowledge producers and knowledge consumers.
- **Bridging functions:** these are aimed at linking knowledge elements to knowledge networks and to also enrich the context for searching and presenting knowledge.

The PAL proposed integrate these functions and define two general kinds of services: SPI functions and KM functions.

SPI Services

SPI services are oriented to integrative functions managing software process and projects using the knowledge repository, helping to establish SPI strategies oriented for SMEs. The SPI services identified for the PAL include:

- Management of process assets lifecycle.
- Management of enterprise knowledge (including people, resources and projects).
- Assets with different kind of knowledge: formal (standard process, life cycle models, and tailoring guides) and informal (lessons learned and better practices). The assets can be reused packing and using them in other projects.
- Support for SME incorporating application guides and examples for this kind of organizations.
- SPI statistics with historical tracking of the lifecycle of the assets.

KM Services

KM services are oriented to interactive functions managing the repository from KM point of view, offering facilities for the main KM processes. The KM services identified for the PAL include:

- **Searching:** Visual navigation of categories using hyperbolic trees, showing relationships between the assets.
- **Recovering:** Using search assistants, search by attributes, user-initiated filters, ranking of assets.
- **Acquisition:** Importing of external assets and creating of internal assets.
- **Refinement:** Labeling, indexing, ordering, abstraction, standardization and categorization of assets.
- **Publication:** Publication of structured and non-structured contents, personalized

distribution, comments and annotation of assets.

- **Training and learning:** Support for experts and novices users.

Benefits of the Proposed PAL

In the PAL, each resource is a software process asset that contains non-structured and structured elements in different formats. The PAL proposed is Knowledge-based, with relevant information that helps in interpretation of the context of small and medium enterprises. For an effective application in SME, the PAL involves the organizational structure, includes examples of assets adapted to this kind of enterprises and supports assets with resumed and detailed content.

The PAL proposed has search mechanisms (with relevant criteria, multiple attributes, user-initiated filters and meta-searches) to obtain results that help do the activities affectively.

One essential feature is the personalization (i.e., the collaborative construction of knowledge in the PAL). The PAL is not a static repository; it is above all a dynamic library built by the active participation and collaboration of the all users in

a basic workflow that implements the lifecycle of the assets.

At the domain of software engineering, the PAL projected will help to minimize development efforts by the assets reuse (packing elements with tailoring guides according to the context). The PAL will offer support for CMMI including formal and informal knowledge about the software process.

The new PAL functions integrate KM and SPI capabilities allowing that assets are organized, structured and classified using ontologies, thesaurus and XML standards (*Open Document Format* for documents and *Open Archives Initiative* for the digital library).

The PAL proposed can be used in SMEs. The software developers needs process guidance information like examples, data, templates, or other process support materials. The PAL will be an organized, well-indexed, searchable repository of process assets and by the knowledge management techniques will be easily accessible by the users.

For example, to elaborate a project plan, the developers need query the standard process, lifecycle strategies and templates available in

Figure 2. Example of use of a PAL

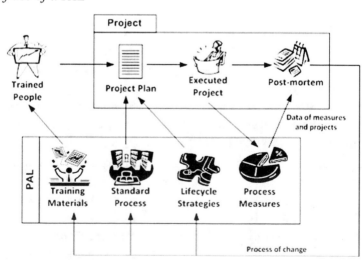

the library (Figure 2). The people will apply the process and measures of all projects are collected in the PAL. In this way, the organization will provide data about the application of techniques and methods in conjunction with projects data. When the project is finished, a post-mortem analysis is realized and proposals for improving the process are made (Cuevas, 2002).

CONCLUSION

One of the main challenges with respect to the construction of knowledge repositories of an organization is to find technologies that store process knowledge in a more effective way. KM techniques will allow the PAL to become a knowledge repository. The application of KM to SPI is not only a technological issue; it must study individual and organizational aspects, standards application for an effective accomplishment of the PAL that supports the organizational software process definition.

The planning, design and construction of PAL can use concepts of digital libraries and knowledge repositories in SPI that allow to create, to transfer and mainly to use and to reuse the information concerning the software process.

The development of a PAL involves research about how storage information in different formats and multiple purposes and that can reused in other contexts. It is a priority to know how package and transfer processes knowledge as corporate assets.

Future efforts are to develop technological support to implement a PAL and to resolve the key questions presented and to enhance knowledge management at the organizational level in SMEs.

FUTURE TRENDS

This work is in an initial phase that requires empirical validation to demonstrate the influence of new techniques in software process to build software products with quality.

There is no commonly accepted methodology for developing knowledge repositories. Moreover, the concept of PAL is independent of technology. Therefore, a methodology for building KM-based PAL must be developed.

Other future works are to build the ontologies and thesaurus that allow modeling and implementing the functions of the knowledge repository. Using ontologies, the users can share and filter the knowledge about the software assets by a common terminology.

Finally, a technological and organizational infrastructure will be obtained and validated considering the functionalities defined and the real use of this kind of digital libraries in small and medium software enterprises.

ACKNOWLEDGMENT

This work has been partially funded by the Spanish Ministry of Science and Technology through the TIC2004-7083 project.

REFERENCES

Aaen, I. et al. (2001). A conceptual MAP of software process improvement. *Scandinavian Journal of Information Systems, Special Issue on Trends in the Research on Software Process Improvement in Scandinavia, 13*, 123–146.

Alavi, M., & Leidner, D. (2001). Knowledge management and knowledge management systems:

Conceptual foundations and research issues. *MIS Quaterly, 25*(1), 107–136.

Basili, V. et al. (1994). Experience factory. *Encyclopedia of Software Engineering, 1,* 476–496. John Wiley & Sons.

Baskerville, R., & Pries-Heje, J. (1999). *Managing knowledge capability and maturity. Information systems: Current issues and future change.* Norwell, MA: IFIP/Kluwer Academic Publisher.

Borges, L., & Falbo, R. (2002). Managing software process knowledge. In *Proceedings of the International Conference on Computer Science, Software Engineering, Information Technology, e-Business, and Applications* (CSITeA'2002) (pp. 227–232).

Cuevas, G. (2002). *Gestión del Proceso Software* (pp. 132–136). Centro de Estudios Ramón Areces S.A.

Dingsøyr, T., & Conradi, R. (2003). Usage of Intranet tools for knowledge management in a medium-sized software consulting company. *Book chapter in Managing Software Engineering Knowledge* (pp. 49–67). Springer Verlag.

Fuggetta, A. (2000). Software process: A roadmap. In *Proceedings of The Future of Software Engineering.* Limerick, Ireland.

Garcia, S. (2004). *Improving process improvement with process asset libraries.* Software Engineering Institute.

Gladney, H., Belkin, N., Ahmed, Z., Fox, E., Ashany, R., & Zemankova, M. (1994). Digital library: Gross structure and requirements. In *Proceedings of the First Annual Conference on the Theory and Practice of Digital Libraries.* San Antonio, Texas, EEUU.

Handzic, M. (2005). *Knowledge management: Through the technology glass.* World Scientific Publishing Company.

Kautz, K., & Nielsen, P. (2001). Knowing and implementing SPI. *Improving Software Organisations—From Principles to Practice.* Addison-Wesley.

Kautz, K., & Thaysen, K. (2001). Knowledge, learning and IT support in a small software company. In *Proceedings of the European Conference on Information Systems.* Bled, Slovenia.

King, W. et al. (2002). The most important issues in knowledge management. *Communications of the ACM, 45*(9), 93–97.

Maier, R. (2002). State-of-practice of knowledge management systems: Results of an empirical study. *Upgrade, 3*(1), 15–23.

Mathiassen, L., & Pourkomeylian, P. (2001). Knowledge management in a software process improvement unit. *International Conference on Managing Knowledge: Conversations and Critiques.* University of Leicester, England.

Maurer F., & Holz, H. (2002). Integrating process support and knowledge management for virtual software development teams. *Annals of Software Engineering, 4*(1–4), 145–168.

Nonaka, I., & Takeuchi, H. (1995). *The knowledge creating company: How Japanese companies create the dynamics of innovation.* New York: Oxford University Press.

Rus, I., Lindvall, M., & Sinha, S. (2002). Knowledge management in software engineering. *IEEE Software, 19*(3), 26–38.

Scott, L. et al. (2002). A process-centred experience repository for a small software organisation. In *Proceedings of the 2002 Asia-Pacific Software Engineering Conference* (pp. 603–609).

KEY TERMS

Codification: to systematize and store information that represents the knowledge of the company, and makes this available for the people in the company.

Customization: to support the flow of information in a company by storing information about knowledge sources, like a "yellow pages" of in-house expertise.

Knowledge Management: It is the systematic, explicit, and deliberate building, renewal, and application of knowledge to maximize an enterprise's knowledge related effectiveness and returns from its knowledge and intellectual capital assets.

PAL: It an organized, well-indexed, searchable repository of process assets that is easily accessible by anyone who needs process guidance information like examples, data, templates, or other process support materials.

Process Software Improvement: It is a systematic procedure to improve the performance of an existing process system by changing the current processes or adding new processes for correction or avoidance of the problems identified in the old system by process assessment.

Ontology: A formal and explicit specification of a shared conceptualization.

SME: Small companies (size less than 100 persons), small organizations (belongs a more large organization, size less than 50 persons) and small projects (executed in organizations; size less than 20 persons).

Chapter XLIX
The Role and Integration of Digital Libraries in E-Learning

Han Lee Yen
Nanyang Technological University, Singapore

ABSTRACT

In recent years, the development of information technologies and network distributions has brought about the creation of useful learning resources, one of which is the e-learning environment. With its promise of ease and ready accessibility, e-learning, a term generally used to refer to computer-aided learning, is fast becoming ubiquitous in educational institutes. In terms of enhancing the online learning experience, digital libraries have tremendous potential in offering resources that can support e-learning. In this chapter, the concepts of "e-learning" and "digital library" are examined. In addition, the role of digital libraries and their integration into the e-learning environment are also discussed.

INTRODUCTION

Educators and learners have long relied on libraries as their main sources of learning resources and libraries have in turn played a supporting role to education by providing the infrastructure that promotes the creation, assimilation and leverage of knowledge (Wang & Hwang, 2004). This relationship has been described as symbiotic where "one cannot be separated from the other, and the existence of one is an impossibility without the other" (Islam, 1968, paragraph 1).

However, with the proliferation and development of the Internet and network distributions and the growth of e-learning in recent years, libraries are facing new challenges to the way they develop, manage and deliver their services and resources to their users (Sharifabadi, 2006). With personal computers becoming affordable and remote access to information through the Internet becoming ubiquitous, educators and learners can now choose the most appropriate information services that would best meet their needs. In so doing, they may bypass the library altogether (Joint, 2006; Kibirige & DePalo, 2001), in favour of more readily accessible online information services. To address this problem, as well as to harness the potentialities of the burgeoning information technology, many libraries have gone electronic or partially electronic so as to position themselves to meet the new challenges (Wang & Hwang, 2004).

BACKGROUND: E-LEARNING AND DIGITAL LIBRARY DEFINED

The term e-learning, a term used widely in different educational contexts, can mean different things to different people. In fact, it has many manifestations, such as online learning, virtual education, computer-assisted learning, distance learning, etc. These different terminologies make developing a general definition for e-learning difficult. One underlying common point is the idea of the distance between the instructor and the learner, and the use of technology to access or deliver learning materials (Catherall, 2005; Sharifabadi, 2006).

However, our quest to develop a general definition for e-learning should not be confined to just looking at it in terms of delivering resources and materials via an electronic means. Due consideration to the learners and the learning process are also important. As such, Sharifabadi (2006) presents a definition that encompasses these aspects, defining e-learning as "the use of the internet to access materials to interact with the content, instructor, and other learners; and to obtain the support during the learning process in order to acquire knowledge, to construct personal meaning and to grow from the learning experience" (p. 390).

Just as the term "e-learning" has many manifestations, the term "digital library" has different variants, including electronic library, referring to a library with electronic records; virtual library, a library not bound by a physical location; hybrid library, a library that contains both hard copy and electronic formats. Often, these refer to the same thing (Kibirige & DePalo, 2001).

The Digital Library Federation (1998) defines digital libraries as:

organizations that provide the resources, including the specialized staff, to select, structure, offer intellectual access to, interpret, distribute, preserve the integrity of, and ensure the persistence over time of collections of digital works so that they are readily and economically available for use by a defined community or set of communities. (paragraph 1)

This "middle-man" view of the digital library is echoed by Fuchs, Muscogiuri, Niederée, and Hemmje (2004) who see it as supporting the information seeking needs of the users by mediating between the available content that has been preselected and structured, and the users.

THE ROLE OF DIGITAL LIBRARIES IN E-LEARNING

The digital library brings together its vast collection of printed resources, through library catalogues, electronic resources, such as electronic book collections and licensed journal databases, selected internet resources and electronic course reserves and tutorials, and makes it available to the user at the click of the mouse (Sharifabadi, 2006). With a personal computer and an Internet connection, the user can gain access to these resources anytime anywhere.

However, as Sharifabadi (2006) points out, it is not enough to see the digital library as simply a digitized collection of resources, but also as "an environment bringing together collections, services and people to support the full cycle of creation, dissemination, use and preservation of data, information and knowledge" (p. 392).

This suggests that instead being passive consumers of information, the content residing in the digital library, the user community is also actively involved in creating new knowledge that is preserved in the digital library which is disseminated and used by other members of the community. This is especially true in terms of the course materials and scholarly research that faculty members produce.

Thus, the digital library plays the role of a facilitator in classifying and providing knowledge and resources to the community of users and encouraging the interaction and exchange of knowledge and information among users. This sharing of knowledge and information within the community encourages collaborations which in turn support teaching and learning objectives. The key here is the active role played by the library and librarians as part of the community (Sharifabadi, 2006).

THE ROLE OF THE LIBRARIAN IN E-LEARNING

The days of the library as the only source of information for research and scholarly activity by the faculty and students are over. With basic infrastructure laid out and a high penetration rate of personal computers, faculty members and students are being drawn to the Internet and the World Wide Web to search for and retrieve the information they require. The accessibility and ease of use of the Internet and Internet search engines may be a reason for their popularity, especially among students.

While it is true that researchers and students conducting research now have an alternative source of information to aid their research, at present, the Internet and Internet search engines are not considered reliable enough for serious research. With a myriad of information on different topics available on the Internet, it is not an easy task trying to verify the truth and authenticity

of something posted on the Web. This is not a problem with the digital library where these issues would already have been addressed by the librarians. What this means is that libraries are still essential and integral to the scholarly research and activity of the faculty and students.

Moreover, there is, at present, a shift in thinking of the librarian as the custodian of the vast resources in the library to that of an educator. This is especially true when faced with the growing popularity of the Internet. This is because librarians must now educate the users in information literacy, and train them in effective information retrieval, be it from the library collection itself, or from the Internet (Wang & Hwang, 2004).

INTEGRATING A DIGITAL LIBRARY INTO AN E-LEARNING ENVIRONMENT

Integrating a digital library into an e-learning environment is not an easy undertaking and for it to be successful, it is suggested that the digital library should

- Include all the relevant learning resources;
- Organize these resources into logical categories;
- Build a knowledge vocabulary, including a thesaurus;
- Generate indexes and search mechanisms; and
- Continually refine the organizational categories. (Wang, 2003)

Besides the above considerations, the issues of content and technology should also be addressed. As Frumkin (2004) points out, "A digital library, at its core, is really a very simple thing; it is content, provided through digital services" (p. 155). Therefore, digital libraries are responsible for the acquisition of resources as well as rights of access to electronic resources which might be held at third parties. They are also responsible for making the tools that allow the effective access and use of these resources available to their users (Johnston, 2001). Thus the content, whether print or digital, is the essence of the library, and the development of the collection should take into account the suitability of the content to its target users.

In addition, the technical infrastructure must be in place for integration to be successful. This would include making access to the digital library materials and resources available outside the physical confines of the library. However, because technology can be unstable and are restricted by limitations, the focus should not be just on technology, but also on people (Wang, 2003).

One area of consideration involving technology and people is the user interface, which is the first point of contact and interaction between the digital library and the user. Since the many services that a digital library can offer its users are provided through the user interface, it is important that consideration is given to the way it is designed. Kibirige and DePalo (2001) suggest having two kinds of design interfaces available, one for the novice and the other for the advanced user.

Four possible options for the provision of service by the digital library in e-learning are suggested:

- **The *laissez-faire* model:** As its name suggests, the learners in this model are given the freedom of choice to choose the type of resources and services that are able to meet their needs. The drawback is the lack of quality control and limited coverage (Johnston, 2001).
- **The intermediary model:** Where the digital library identifies and classifies the resources in its collection, whether owned by the library or by a third party but accessible via the library, and provides access to these resources (Johnston, 2001). Like

most academic libraries, The University of Western Australia Library provides such services under its Course Materials Online service, which is a consolidation of reading lists for the different courses offered by the university.

- **The advanced model:** On top of the resources in its collection, the digital library preserves in its collection the course materials that have been created by the instructors in e-learning. (Wang & Hwang, 2004). This is perhaps the most attractive model because it integrates both the collection of the digital library and the course materials generated by the instructors and allows users ready access to both. The Wageningen University and Research Centre Digital Library adopts this model by making the textbooks and lecture notes used in the university's courses available to its users. Another university library with such services is The Stanford University Libraries.
- **The quasi-all-inclusive model:** Where the information needs of the whole community of instructors and learners are met. This can be achieved by reproducing everything that is used in relation to the e-learning curricula, such as textbooks, newspapers, multimedia resources, and so on, everything that may be relevant to the existing curricula. (Wang & Hwang, 2004). The University of Pennsylvania Libraries is one such library that has adopted such a model, making the course content of its courses available to its users.

CONCLUSION

Libraries play an important role in education and learning, where the survival of one is questionable with the demise of the other. With education moving away from the tradition classroom and going online, the growth of network technologies and learners becoming more net-savvy, the role of the libraries in supporting teaching, learning and research has in fact been strengthen, not diminished. This is because with digital libraries, librarians can now provide users with ready access to their collection 24/7, anytime, anywhere, which is one of the reasons for the popularity of the Internet. This has also meant that librarians have had to shift from being mere custodians of library collections to educators, teaching users such skills like information retrieval and literacy. Finally, issues of content, technology and user interface are some considerations when integrating the digital library in e-learning.

REFERENCES

Catherall, P. (2005). *Delivering e-learning or information services in higher education.* Oxford, UK: Chandos Publishing (Oxford) Limited.

Digital Library Federation. (1998). *A working definition of digital library [1998].* Retrieved August 30, 2008, from http://www.diglib.org/about/dldefinition.htm

Frumkin, J. (2004). Defining digital libraries. *OCLC Systems & Services International Digital Library Perspectives, 20*(4), 155–156.

Fuchs, M., Muscogiuri, C., Niederée, C., & Hemmje, M. (2004). Digital libraries in knowledge management: An e-learning case study. *International Journal on Digital Libraries, 4,* 31–35.

Islam, K.M.S. (1968). The role of libraries in education. *The Eastern Librarian, 3*(1).

Johnston, P. (2001). After the big bang: Forces of change and e-learning. *Ariadne, 27.*

Joint, N. (2006). Common principles in managing digital libraries and managing VLEs. *Library Review, 55*(4), 232–236.

Kibirige, H., & DePalo, L. (2001). The education function in a digital library environment: A challenge for college and research libraries. *The Electronic Library, 19*(5), 283–295.

Sharifabadi, S.R. (2006). How digital libraries can support e-learning. *The Electronic Library, 24*(3), 389–401.

Wang, M.-Y. (2003) The strategic role of digital libraries: Issues in e-learning environments. *Library Review, 52*(3), 111–115.

Wang, M.-Y., & Hwang, M.-J. (2004). The e-learning library: only a warehouse of learning resources? *The Electronic Library, 22*(5), 408–415.

KEY TERMS

Content: A term used generally to refer to the elements on a Web page, such as text and graphics. In education, content refers to the curriculum.

Digital: A method of encoding, storing, processing, and transmitting information in binary language.

Information: Data, facts, concepts or instructions which can be communicated and added to the knowledge of the person receiving it.

Infrastructure: In Information Technology, it refers to the underlying foundation or framework of a computer system, including but not limited to the hardware, software, and network.

Internet: A collection of interconnected networks of computers which operates worldwide using a set of compatible communications protocols.

Knowledge: Information, relationships, facts, assumptions, heuristics, and models that have been derived through the formal and informal analysis or interpretation of data.

World Wide Web: Also known as the Web, it refers to a collection of hypermedia pages that are accessible via the Internet using a Web browser.

Chapter L
Development of Digital Libraries in Pakistan

Kanwal Ameen
University of the Punjab, Lahore, Pakistan

Muhammad Rafiq
Government College University Lahore, Pakistan

ABSTRACT

This chapter aims to discuss the development of digital libraries in Pakistan. It gives an account of the digital transformation taking place in the country and reviews a few digital library initiatives. It discusses a number of issues associated with the development of digital libraries with specific reference to Pakistan. The major issues appear are as follows: misconception about digital libraries; lack of technological applications; lack of human resources with needed skills; copyright and publishing; cultural divide; digital divide, and insufficient financial support. The authors believe that understanding the underlying issues will not only accelerate the development of DL in Pakistan, but also in other developing countries with more or less common environment.

THE CONTEXT

Extensive discussions on the definition and scope of digital libraries (DL) have appeared in the literature since 1990s. Both computer scientists and library professionals emphasize different aspects of DL while defining this term or concept. Chowdhury and Chowdhury (2003) conclude, after giving a brief evolution of the DL concept, that two different schools of thought, one emphasizing the enabling technologies [computer scientists or engineers] and the other the service aspect of digital libraries [library professional], may be noted in the literature. The third dimension of DL is social which reflects users' perceptions and expectations regarding service aspects and it surely is important to consider those. Chen and Zhou (2005) state that DL is a technology in which social impact matters as much as technological advancement. It is hard to evaluate a new technology in the absence of real users ... (p. 2).

In Pakistan, the phrases electronic library (EL), virtual library (VL) and DL have been in use interchangeably. However, the term DL is getting common, though with different meanings for different people. For this paper, it is considered that digital library (DL) is "a managed collection of information, with associated services, where the information is stored in the digital formats and accessible over a network" (Arms, 2000, p.2). As a matter of fact, DL culture is just at beginning level in Pakistan. The creation of DL involves a number of technological, social, usability, financial, and legal issues. Accordingly, library professionals, academicians, higher authorities and users in Pakistan are in confusion regarding their perception, creation, ownership, content management, collection management, usability, access, copyright issues, needed skills, infrastructure and so forth. Furthermore, there are only a few local studies available on the development of IT and digital library scenario in the country—for example, Ramzan (2004) reported the extent of hardware, software, their utilisation levels, and degree of changes that have occurred in the use of IT in Pakistani libraries. He reveals that hardware and software were available in majority of libraries and majority of librarians used computers in their daily works. However, lack of computer literacy among librarians; improper planning; nonavailability of standard library software; lack of standardization and quality control; librarians' absence in decision making, and bureaucratic attitude of the management are major problems preventing the wider use of computers in libraries. This chapter makes a brief review of the current status of the digital culture. Before discussing these issues, it seems appropriate to have a brief look at the present scenario of IT developments and library setup in the country.

DIGITAL TRANSFORMATION

Several indicators reveal that Pakistan is witnessing digital transformation. A most recent study by Shafique and Mahmood (2008) reveals that "An information society is emerging at a very fast pace in Pakistan" (p. 76). It states that the information society applications such as e- learning, computer supported political participation, e-government initiatives, telemedicine, information and communication technologies (ICTs), cellular phones, satellite dishes, the Internet, and so on indicate a prominent growth.

Pakistan's ICT infrastructure seen a significant expansion in recent years (Digital Review of Asia Pacific, http://www.digital-review.org/05_Pakistan.htm). Internet has become an essential tool for scholarly and business communication in Pakistan. The use of broadband services has started to grow in homes and offices located in major cities. This trend is expected to accelerate. Efforts to network the country continue, and so far, over 1,898 towns and cities have been plugged into the Internet backbone (Shafique & Mahmood, 2008). The demand for digitized contents is ever increasing worldwide and the same phenomenon is emerging in Pakistan.

LIBRARIES AND INFORMATION RESOURCE CENTERS IN PAKISTAN

Unfortunately, there is no comprehensive and current directory available to quote the latest number of libraries/information resource centers in Pakistan. However, an overview is given in the following:

National Library of Pakistan (NLP)

NLP is responsible for publishing the National Bibliography, to serve as depository library for

Pakistani and Asian Development Bank publications, and to work as an ISBN issuing agency. It also exchanges government documents with USA, SAARC, and works with other national libraries around the world (National Library of Pakistan, 2008). Currently, NLP maintains a bibliographic database of English and Urdu collections. There are no plans for developing a digital library so far. The library Website, however, has been maintained which offer Web OPAC (http://www.nlp.gov.pk/).

Academic Libraries

The academic sector constitutes the major group of libraries in the country. These may be divided into three groups:

i. *School libraries*: None of the published directories included information about school libraries. It is assumed that almost 80% schools are without any library facility, specifically government schools. Haider (2002) mentioned, "School library is yet to be recognized as a component of the school curriculum" and a vast majority of schools "do not possess any sort of book collection." Under the given circumstances, one can hardly think of the development of digital libraries in schools, specifically in public sector.

ii. *College libraries*: There are 700 college libraries in the country (Zaheer, 2002), and this makes them the largest group of academic libraries. These libraries face enormous problems such as poor services, out-dated collections, financial constraints, and inadequate and demotivated professional staff.

iii. *University libraries*: According to the Higher Education Commission (2008a), there are 122 Universities and Degree Awarding Institutions in the country. University libraries comparatively are in a better position regarding collections and staff. However, the top professional positions in these libraries are either vacant or filled on a temporary basis. University libraries also face a number of problems such as procurement of latest information sources, equipment, viable financial resources, unequal access to information technology, electronic media (Ameen & Haider, 2007; Haider, 2004). Nonethless the establishment of HEC-National Digital Library (HEC-NDL), a Higher Education Commission (HEC) project, in 2004 is a milestone in the development of digital libraries in the country. It is providing access to thousands of digital resources while bringing new challenges and opportunities for library professionals.

Following the definition of DL adopted for this study, we may classify such initiatives in following two types of digital library models practiced in university libraries of the country:

i. Libraries digitize their own resources and make them available online through their Web pages.
ii. Libraries offer access to subscribed/free digital information resources of other e-publishers by providing links through libraries' Web pages.

Most of the university libraries follow 2nd model and major accessible resources are from HEC–National Digital Library (e.g., Government College University, 2008; Lahore University of Management Sciences, 2008). Besides facilitating access to HEC digital libraries, university libraries have also developed their own Websites with links to free Web resources and use VL/DL phrase for them. However university libraries are also preparing to follow the first model. A number of digitization initiatives have been taking place in university libraries. Arif, Rehman, and Rafiq (2006) report,

"Multimedia and Microfilming Section of the central Library of the University of the Punjab is currently involved in digitization activities and offers scanning services of rare reading material as well as providing scanned images on CD-ROMs to researchers. The service is available on demand basis. Digitization is the major activity of the section but, online access is not still available to these indigenous digitized resources."

The coauthor also is personally involved in International Islamic University (IIU) Library's Electronic Theses & Dissertation (ETD) Project. The ultimate objective of the ETD project is to digitize and provide online access to theses and dissertations submitted by IIU students.

Public Libraries

There are 500 public libraries in Pakistan (Zaheer, 2002). The big cities do possess the library facilities, but the 80% people living in rural areas have no access to this facility (Mahmood, 1998). Public libraries are maintained by local bodies and face different problems e.g. inadequate financial, human, and information resources; poor service structure; ill-kept library buildings, and so on (Haider, 1998; 2001). Digital Library is still a dream for public libraries of Pakistan.

DL INITIATIVES IN PAKISTAN

United Nations Digital Library (UNDL) (http://library.un.org.pk/gsdl/cgi-bin/library.exe, 2002)

UNDL in Pakistan is the first of its kind. This is an online repository of the full-text digital documents of the various United Nations Agencies, Programmes and Funds active in Pakistan. The collection comprises the general documents, reports, publications, newsletters, press releases and other public information items. This repository is a centralized information resource of the United Nations information on or about Pakistan (UNO, 2008). It offers efficient browsing and searching facility and easy, equal access to the required information with an online full-text display of the document. For the United Nations System and Agencies in Pakistan, this facility provides a centralized opportunity to showcase, share and preserve their digital documents as well as disseminate them in much faster, easier, more varied ways, to a wider range of audience. United Nations Digital Library is using Greenstone Digital Library Software to manage its resources (http://www.un.org.pk/library/).

HEC-National Digital Library (HEC-NDL) (http://www.digitallibrary.edu.pk)

There is visible and commendable development of DLs in the field of higher education. HEC-National Digital Library, a project of Higher Education Commission (HEC) Pakistan, is a unique project providing *access* to full-text digital databases to users of public and private universities and nonprofit research and development organizations throughout Pakistan. It was initially introduced as a collaborative project of the UK based International Network for the Availability of Scientific Publications (INASP), in connection with the implementation of their Programme for the Enhancement of Research Information (PERI). Implementation of the PERI programme in Pakistan allowed the HEC to provide a vast quantity of scholarly publications to the researchers. Inclusion in the programme enables the participating institution to access over 23,000 high quality, peer-reviewed journals, databases and articles across a wide range of disciplines based on electronic (online) delivery. A recent addition is the inclusion of 45000 ebooks in the resources (i.e., Ebrary, McGraw Hill Collections, Oxford University Press eBooks) (HEC-National Digital Library, 2008). Said (2006, p.7) states that the budget allocation for the HEC-NDL programme has doubled each financial year and the total amount for 2005/6 is Pak Rs. 200,000,000 (approximately USD$ 3,278,688).

The HEC has also explored the provision of free online books. In order to assess the performance of educational institutions participating in the programme, usage statistics in term of the number of articles downloaded have been collected for the year 2005. There has been a significant and definitive increase in the total number of full-text articles downloaded over the previous year. Overall usage has been exemplary, whereby a total of 666,986 full-texts downloads from public sector universities have been recorded, with about 350,000 downloads from the participating private universities and local research institutions. The usage statistics compiled for the year 2005 signify that the cost per article for our Digital Library calculates to less than USD$2.30 per article, which is borne by the HEC (Said, 2006, p. 20).

Pakistan Research Repository (http://www.eprints.hec.gov.pk/, 2006)

The Higher Education Commission (HEC) of Pakistan initiated a project *Pakistan Research Repository* (PRR*)* in 2006. The project can be designated a showcase of intellectual output of Pakistani higher education institutions. The initial drive for development of content in the repository has been an initiative to digitize and make freely available online every PhD and M.Phil thesis published in Pakistani universities. The basic objective of the project is to promote the international visibility of research originating out of institutes of higher education in Pakistan.

The repository has already made 1600 Ph.D. theses available in full text, whilst 300 theses have been digitized and are in the process of being uploaded. An additional 500 Ph.D. theses are in the process of digitization. HEC has introduced a systematic mechanism for the collection and digitization of the remaining theses. Once completed, the repository will include all Ph.D. theses published by institutions in Pakistan which

are estimated to be approximately 3200 PhD in number (Higher Education Commission, 2008).

PRR offers various methods of searching and browsing by institution, department, subject area, author and full-text of documents. Arrangements in this manner ultimately allow users of the repository to view the aggregated research output of whole institutions, departments within institutions, or of individual scientists themselves. This repository is running on GNU EPrints 2.3.13.1 open source software to manage and make accessible its digital information resources on the Web.

PRR is an excellent research aid for researchers as well as libraries. This project opened up new academic avenues by providing electronic access to indigenous academic research. PRR is one of a few sources that can provide access to indigenous research of Pakistan. Academic Libraries may consider PRR a benchmark to initiate institutional repositories in their parent organizations.

Allama Iqbal Urdu Cyber Library (http://www.iqbalcyberlibrary.net/)

Allama Iqbal Urdu Cyber Library, a project of Iqbal Academy, Pakistan, is the first digital library of books in the Urdu language. The Academy is a statutory body of the Government of Pakistan and a center of excellence for Iqbal Studies. The aims and objectives of the Academy are to promote and disseminate the study and understanding of the works and teachings of Allama Iqbal (the late National poet). The library has books on Iqbal studies, Urdu classics, literature, poetry and prose (Allama Iqbal Urdu Cyber Library Network, http://www.iqbalcyberlibrary.net/). It has the goal of publishing 500 electronic books by 2008. A quarterly CD-ROM of electronic books is also published by the Academy. The library contents are available on http://www.iqbalcyberlibrary.net/.

CHALLENGES AND ISSUES ASSOCIATED WITH BUILDING DLS IN PAKISTAN

The issues associated with the building of DLs are intermingled, interdependent and overlapping and include the following:

Concept/ Perception

All concerned quarters, from parent organizations or funding bodies to end users to academicians to library professionals, lack certainty regarding the concept, construction prerequisites and potentials of DLs. A recent study, (Hussain, 2006), reports that library professionals are confused about the basic concept of digital libraries. Moreover, their advantages are over-glorified as compared to the efforts and cost associated with their construction, be it digitization project of the owned collection or subscription model. Moreover, the copyright issues are complex to tackle in absence of proper and effective laws.

Technological

Efforts to connect the country through wires are on their way and remarkable expansion in ICT infrastructure has made. Despite that existing library infrastructures are unable to support digitization projects. Ramzan (2004) reported that, in Pakistan, only 21% libraries have digital scanners and 5% respondents had OCR software for digitization in their libraries. Due to the limited, unequal access to ICT facilities, nonavailability of digitization hardware and software and meager financial resources, only a few university libraries have been able to digitize a limited number of selected documents. College libraries are still far way from building digital collections or providing users with access to digital resources as mostly they do not posses computers and internet access. The situation for public libraries is similar.

Human Resources with Needed Skills

Digitizing documents needs library staff with certain knowledge and set of technological, managerial skills. However, a vast majority of working professionals in Pakistani libraries lack sufficient digital competency to make use of ICT applications (Ameen, 2005). This holds true especially for the older generation (Rehman & Ahmad, 2007). As a matter of fact, librarians are still struggling to automate their library catalogs, which is only possible where they, themselves, possess sufficient IT literacy. The library schools also suffer from an incapacity to impart the needed skills because of the shortage of the faculty members with this specialization (Mahmood, 2003). By and large, the academic enrichment lacks in this regard among both faculty and working professionals.

Copyright and Publishing Issues

There is no agreement on publishing policy for digitized documents (Hussain, 2006). The copyright issues of foreign publications in this regard are hard to handle for librarians. The annual low production ratio of local publications adds to the issue of digital collection and content management.

Cultural Divide

Digital information paradigm is still in its infancy in the country, therefore, users are not conversant with seeking, accessing and retrieving needed information. Users consider online digital resources unreliable due to the peculiar circumstances of the country, particularly the low bandwidth and power supply. Senior users prefer to have print version rather than browsing databases. Librarians also exhibit a fear of change and are not responsive to it at the desired level. The usability of the existing services is low and rising gradually. Said (2006) states,

"The provision of access to databases is, however, not enough. As mentioned above, a major challenge has been spreading awareness of the resources acquired because they have been introduced into an environment that is historically very limited in its understanding of digital libraries. Librarians are traditional in their approach towards library management, given their experience of operating out of hybrid libraries, and find the electronic world slightly overwhelming" (p. 13).

Digital Divide

Despite the ICT friendly policies of the present government and generous funding for viable projects contributing towards the growth of digital transformation, there still exists wide digital divide within Pakistan—between the big and the small cities, between the rich and the poor and between the ICT literate and IT stressed users. Therefore, the existing digital free resources are not fully used by various segments of the community. For example, still a number of faculty members of Library and Information Science (LIS) schools either do not have their own personal e-mail accounts or they do not use them regularly. HEC is working on promoting digital culture through training workshops for faculty members and librarians.

Financial Support

Developing a digital library project needs substantial financial resourcing and few libraries are able to make a convincing and realistic plan to obtain such money besides getting funds for traditional collection development. Librarians and higher administration have misconceptions regarding the costs involved in the DL projects. B. Jaswal (Personal Communication, January 2007), the pioneer of both introducing library automation and developing DL in Pakistan using Greenstone, stated in an interview with the principal author that

"people (neither librarians nor administration) do not understand the prerequisites of creating a real DL, hence the project, if any, more likely would suffer due to lack of needed staff and money."

FUTURE OF DL IN PAKISTAN

The scarcity of needed human, financial and material resources is the major hindrance in the development of digital libraries in Pakistan. The meager opportunities for continuing education and professional development are available to learn the sophisticated skills needed to develop DL. However, a few developments that have taken place in recent years are worth mentioning. Department of Library and Information Science, University of the Punjab has incorporated an optional course on "Digital Libraries" in PhD course work that was opted by the coauthor in 2007. A few workshops on the use of Greenstone Digital Library Software have also been conducted in last couple of years by Pakistan Library Automation Group (a private group of professionals). The information professionals widely participated in these workshops. Department of Library & Information Science, University of the Punjab, Lahore has also arranged a workshop on Greenstone Digital Library Software for M.Phil/PhD students in 2007. However, the participant opined that these kinds of workshops were just of introductory nature and they need extensive learning to be able to develop DL (M. Rafiq, Personal Communication, January 2008).

The attitude of Government of Pakistan to digital culture is encouraging as a significant number of e-government initiatives have been taken place with supportive IT policies (Shafique & Mahmood, 2008). Government is providing infrastructure and financial support for digital initiatives in public sector organizations. Nevertheless, specific funding for developing digital libraries is hardly granted. HEC also offers grants for the development of university libraries. In recent years these grants were mainly used for physical facilities and infrastructural development instead of digital library developments.

It appears that digital era is on rise in Pakistan in all kinds of institutions including libraries. Therefore, libraries need to plan to serve the users' information needs through digital content delivery. Despite the issues discussed above, the scope of taking initiatives to develop digital libraries is encouraging in Pakistan. Libraries can meet the users' ever growing information needs by developing DL and providing remote access to communities with access to ICT. Digital libraries can also enhance the status of LIS profession and library services. However the sustainability of the DLs needs to be ensured with appropriate governmental and institutional support and professional commitment.

CONCLUSION

The development of digital libraries in Pakistan is in the beginning and the use of available online databases is still low. The digital culture needs to be developed in order to make the utmost use of the emerging digital developments. The number of libraries working on building a digital library is very limited, and is dominated by university libraries mainly.

It appears that a vast majority of libraries in Pakistan will be dealing with paper-based collections in the foreseeable future. Mostly large university and public libraries will head towards a hybrid culture gradually, and there are remote chances of turning into *only* digital libraries. The building of digital libraries and digital culture are big challenges ahead for library and information professionals: how will the implementation and usage of digital libraries develop? What might their future be and how much will they cost? Would it be cost effective spending hundreds of million rupees on building DLs? These are questions whose answers are still hazy.

REFERENCES

Ameen, K. (2005). *Philosophy and framework of collection management and its application in university libraries of Pakistan: An appraisal.* Unpublished doctoral dissertation, University of the Punjab, Lahore, Pakistan.

Ameen, K., & Haider, S.J. (2007). Evolving paradigm and challenges of collection management in university libraries of Pakistan. *Collection Building, 26*(2), 54–58.

Arif, M., Shafiq-ur-Rehman, & Rafiq, M. (2006). *Microfilming and multimedia section of Punjab university library: A case study* (unpublished report). Deptartment of Library and Information Science, University of the Punjab, Lahore.

Arms, W. (2000). *Digital libraries.* Cambridge, MA: MIT Press.

Chen, H., & Zhou, Y (2005). Survey and history of digital library development in the Asia Pacific. In Y.-L. Theng, & S. Foo (Eds.), *Design and Usability of Digital Libraries: Case Studies in the Asia Pacific.* Hershey: Information Science Publishing.

Chowdhury, G.G., & Chowdhury, S. (2003). *Introduction to digital libraries.* London: Facet Publishing.

Government College University. (2008). *GC university library.* Retrieved August 30, 2008, from http://gcu.edu.pk/library/S_FullJour.htm

Haider, S. J. (1998). Public libraries and development planning in Pakistan: A review of past efforts and future needs. *Asian Libraries, 7*(2), 47–57.

Haider, S.J. (2001). Public library facilities in Pakistan. *Public Libraries Quarterly, 19*(4), 27–42.

Haider, S.J. (2002). School libraries in Pakistan. *Information Development, 18*(1), 27–33.

Haider, S.J. (2004). Coping with change: Issues facing university libraries in Pakistan. *The Journal of Academic Librarianship, 30*(3), 229–236.

Higher Education Commission. (2008a). *Our institutes*. Retrieved August 30, 2008, from http://app.hec.gov.pk/universityfinal2/Region-University.aspx

Higher Education Commission. (2008b). *Pakistan research repository*. Retrieved August 30, 2008, from http://eprints.hec.gov.pk/

Hussain, A. (2006). *Perceptions of LIS professionals regarding digital library*. Unpublished master thesis, University of the Punjab, Lahore.

IMLS. (2002). *Status of technology and digitization in the nation's museums and libraries*. Washington, D.C.: Institute of Museum and Library Services.

Lahore University of Management Sciences. (2008). *Virtual library*. Retrieved August 30, 2008, from http://library.lums.edu.pk/vl/vl.htm

Mahmood, K. (1998). Pakistani librarianship during the 1990s: A literature review. In *Information Technology in Libraries: A Pakistani Perspective*. Lahore: Pak Book Corporation.

Mahmood, K. (2003). A comparison between needed competencies of academic librarians and LIS curricula in Pakistan. *The Electronic Library, 21*(2), 99–109.

National Library of Pakistan. (2008). *About national library of Pakistan*. Retrieved August 30, 2008, from http://www.nlp.gov.pk/html/Aboutus.htm

Ramzan, M. (2004). Levels of information technology (IT) applications in Muslim world libraries. *The Electronic Library, 22*(3), 274–280.

Rehman, S., & Ahmad, P. (2007). Challenges and opportunities for libraries in Pakistan. *Pakistan Library and Information Science Journal, 38*(3), 6–11.

Reitz, J.M. (2004). Dictionary for library and information science. Westport, CT: Libraries Unlimited.

Said, A (2006). *Accessing electronic information: A study of Pakistan's digital library*. Oxford: INSAP.

Shafique, F., & Mahmood, K. (2008). Indicators of the emerging information society in Pakistan. *Information Development, 24*(1), 66–78.

UNO. (2008). *United Nations digital library*. Retrieved August 30, 2008, from http://library.un.org.pk/gsdl/cgi-bin/library.exe

Zaheer, M.A. (2002). *National library of Pakistan: Annual report to CDNL 2001-2002*. Edinburgh.

KEY TERMS

Digital Divide: A term coined by former Assistant Secretary of Commerce for Telecommunication and Communication Larry Irving, Jr., to focus public awareness on the gap in access to information resources and services between those with the means to purchase the computer hardware and software necessary to connect to the Internet and low-income families and communities that cannot afford network access. Public libraries are helping to bridge the gap between information "haves" and "have-nots" with the assistance of substantial grants from industry leaders such as Bill Gates of Microsoft. The E-rate established by the *Telecommunications Act of 1996 (TCA)* has helped schools, public libraries, and rural health care institutions bridge the gap. *Digital Divide Network* is a Web site devoted to the issue. Synonymous with *information gap*. (Reitz, 2004, p. 216).

Digital Library (DL): "A managed collection of information, with associated services, where the information is stored in the digital formats and accessible over a network" (Arms, 2000, p. 2).

Digitization: Defined as "the process of converting, creating, and maintaining books, art works, historical documents, photos, journals, etc. in electronic representations so they can be viewed via computer and other devices" (IMLS, 2002, p. 22). Digitization of valued information resources opens up new avenues of access, use, and research and is an important aspect in the development of digital libraries.

Information and Communication Technologies (ICT): The computing and communications facilities and features that variously support teaching, learning, and a range of activities in education.

Section V
Digital Library Education and Future Trends

Chapter LI
Core Topics in Digital Library Education*

Seungwon Yang
Digital Library Research Laboratory, Virginia Tech, USA

Barbara M. Wildemuth
University of North Carolina at Chapel Hill, USA

Jeffrey P. Pomerantz
University of North Carolina at Chapel Hill, USA

Sanghee Oh
University of North Carolina at Chapel Hill, USA

Edward A. Fox
Digital Library Research Laboratory, Virginia Tech, USA

ABSTRACT

This chapter introduces the effort of developing a digital library (DL) curriculum by an interdisciplinary team from Virginia Tech and the University of North Carolina at Chapel Hill. It presents the foundations of the curriculum building, the DL curriculum framework, the DL educational module template, a list of draft modules that are currently developed and evaluated by multiple experts in the area, and more details about the resources used in the draft modules and DL-related workshop topics mapped to the DL curriculum framework. The use of information systems such as DLs is increasing in education and businesses. To better-support their users, DLs must include both a well-organized underlying architecture and a set of services designed to address their potential users' information needs. For this vision of the future to come to fruition, information professionals need to be educated to establish and manage digital libraries. The proposed curriculum framework provides a firm foundation for these important educational activities.

FOUNDATIONS FOR A DIGITAL LIBRARY CURRICULUM PROPOSAL

Modern societies are producing and consuming an enormous amount of information every day. The need for quality organized information has been growing rapidly. Various digital libraries (DLs) (Arms, 2000; Fox & Urs, 2002; Lesk, 1997; Lesk, 2005; Witten & Bainbridge, 2003) have been developed to address this need. However, additional focus on education for people who design and administer digital libraries is needed. We can begin to solve this problem through development of curricular recommendations for digital library education.

Several disciplines have an interest in the development of a graduate-level curriculum for digital library education; hence it can be argued that this effort must be interdisciplinary in order to be successful (Kajberg & Lørring, 2005). In particular, computer science and information and library science have been actively developing courses and programs in this area (Ma, Clegg, & O'Brien, 2006). Efforts to date have been locally-based and dependent upon specific institutional needs. The current effort takes a broader view, in order to develop a curriculum framework that will be useful across institutions and across disciplines. This framework is based on analyses of the ACM/IEEE-CS Computing Curriculum 2001 (Joint Task Force, 2001), the 5S framework for digital libraries (Gonçalves, Fox, Watson, & Kipp, 2004), papers presented at recent DL conferences and published in *D-Lib Magazine* (Pomerantz, Wildemuth, Yang, & Fox, 2006c), the readings assigned in DL-related courses (Pomerantz, Oh, Yang, Fox, & Wildemuth, 2006a), and a survey of digital librarians about their job responsibilities (Choi & Rasmussen, 2006a, 2006b).

Computing Curriculum 2001 as a Starting Point

The ACM/IEEE-CS Computing Curriculum 2001 (CC2001) (Joint Task Force, 2001) covers a variety of areas in computer science, including information management. In turn, the area of information management includes digital libraries as one of its 14 components (including such areas as information models and systems, database systems, data modeling, transaction processing, information storage and retrieval, and hypertext and hypermedia).

The CC2001 goes on to identify a number of topics that should be included in a course on digital libraries. These topics include: "Digitization, storage and interchange; Digital objects, composites, and packages; Metadata (Daniel & Lagoze, 1997; DCMI 2006, http://www.dublincore.org), cataloging, author submission; Naming, repositories (Kahn & Wilensky, 1995), archives; Spaces (conceptual, graphical, 2/3D, VR); Architectures (agents, buses, wrappers/mediators, interoperability); Services (searching, linking, browsing, and so forth); Intellectual property rights management, privacy, protection (watermarking); [and] Archiving and presentation, integrity" (Joint Task Force, 2001, p. 140). This specification of a digital library course served us as an early starting point; these topics were incorporated into our initial curriculum framework, which had 19 topic groups (Pomerantz, Wildemuth, Oh, Yang, & Fox, 2006b).

The 5S Theoretical Framework

The name of the 5S framework (Gonçalves, 2004; Gonçalves et al., 2004; Gonçalves & Fox, 2002; Gorton, 2007; Shen, 2006; Zhu, 2002) comes from the fact that all five elements of this framework—"stream," "structure," "space," "scenario," and "society"—start with "s." Informally, these five elements are described as:

1. **Streams:** All types of content, as well as communications and flows over networks or into sensors, or sense perceptions. Examples include: text, video, audio, image. These can be formalized as a sequence (list).

2. **Structures:** Organizational schemes, including data structures, databases, and knowledge representations. Examples include: collection, catalog, hypertext, document metadata. These can be formalized as a graph, with labels and a labeling function.

3. **Spaces:** 2D and 3D interfaces, GIS data, representations of documents and queries. Examples include: spaces used in indexing, browsing, and searching services, as well as interfaces. These can be formalized as a set (vector, topological, measurable, measure, probability spaces).

4. **Scenarios:** System states and events, or situations of use by human users or machine processes, yielding services or transformations of data. Examples include: searching, browsing, recommending. These can be formalized as a sequence of related transition events on a state set.

5. **Societies:** Both software "service managers" and fairly generic "actors" who could be (collaborating) human (users). Examples include: service managers (software), actors (learners, teachers, and so on). These can be formalized as a pair (i.e., a set of communities and a set of relationships).

Analyzing our initial curriculum framework through the lens provided by the 5S framework resulted in a streamlined framework of nine basic components: collection development; digital objects/composites/packages; metadata, cataloging, and author submission; architecture and interoperability; data visualization; services; intellectual property rights management, privacy, and protection; social issues and the future of DLS; and archiving and preservation.

Analysis of DL Publications

Based on the draft framework, a content analysis was conducted of papers published in the past decade on the broad topic of DLs (Pomerantz et al., 2006c). The corpus of papers included those presented at the ACM International Conference on Digital Libraries (1996–2000) and the ACM/IEEE-CS Joint Conference on Digital Libraries (2001–2005), as well as the papers published in *D-Lib Magazine* (July 1995–February 2006). The full corpus included 1,064 papers. The purpose of this analysis was to identify those topics related to DLs that were the most prominent in these publication venues, and thus would be important to include in DL courses.

In both subsets of the corpus, the topic most frequently written about was Services (searching, links, browsing, and so on), followed closely by Architecture and Interoperability. All topics in the draft framework were included among the topics of the publications, and the topics of all of the publications fit into the draft framework, providing support for its validity.

Analysis of Readings Assigned in DL Courses

While the analysis of conference papers and *D-Lib Magazine* articles provides a broad overview of current research in DLs and can validate the draft curriculum framework from the perspective of DL research, it did not provide a check for the correspondence between the framework and current educational practices. A second analysis was therefore undertaken (Pomerantz et al., 2006a). Syllabi from 40 DL courses offered in schools of library and information science were collected and analyzed, and the readings assigned and the topics of these readings were identified. A total of 1,738 readings were included in this analysis. While many of the assigned readings were on topics already included in the curriculum framework (and allowed us to decompose some core topics into subtopics), other assigned readings suggested that the framework should be expanded. In particular, the topics of project management and an overview component were added to the framework, based on this analysis. project management was the area in which the most readings were assigned; other frequently-occurring topics included architecture, collection development, and information/knowledge organization.

Survey of Digital Librarians about their Job Responsibilities

During 2005, Choi and Rasmussen (2006a, 2006b) conducted a survey of "current practitioners in charge of digitization projects or digital library projects" (2006a, p. 187). They received 48 responses from librarians in 39 different libraries. Of interest for curriculum development are their results concerning the skills and knowledge needed by digital librarians. These included technology-related skills and knowledge (e.g., DL architecture and software, technical and quality standards, and Web markup languages), library-related skills and knowledge (e.g., digital archiving and preservation, the needs of users, and cataloging and metadata), and other skills and knowledge (e.g., communication and interpersonal skills, and project management and leadership skills).

The specific skills and knowledge identified were mapped onto the draft curriculum framework. A few of those identified by Choi and Rasmussen were not included in the draft framework. Specifically, two technology-related skills (database development and database management systems, and Web design skills) and three other skills (communication and interpersonal skills, grant/proposal writing skills, and teaching and group presentation skills) were not included in the curriculum framework proposed here because they are more general skills needed by information professionals practicing in most contexts, and not specific to DL.

Core Topics in DL Workshops

Since the development of the curriculum framework, we have completed an analysis of DL work-

shops, to further ensure the framework's validity. DL practitioners and researchers often gather in workshops to share knowledge and to collaborate with the others. Therefore, by investigating the topics appearing in workshops worldwide, we might be able to spot the currently popular topics. A list of conference series' that are relevant to digital libraries was obtained from the DELOS Web site[2]. Then, each conference Web site was visited and its workshop titles were retrieved if available. The result is shown below[3]. The conference titles are represented in italics and the workshops of the corresponding conferences are in the bulleted list:

European Conference on Research and Advanced Technology for Digital Libraries (ECDL)

- CLEF 2007: Cross Language Evaluation Forum
- Workshop on "Foundations of Digital Libraries"
- LADL 2007 Cross-Media and Personalized Learning Applications on top of Digital Libraries
- Towards an European Repository Ecology: Conceptualizing Interactions between Networks of Repositories and Services
- Networked Knowledge Organization Systems and Services
- Libraries in the Digital Age: What If ...?

Joint Conference on Digital Libraries (JCDL)

- Developing a Digital Libraries Education Program
- 1st Workshop on Digital Library Foundations
- 7th International Workshop on Web Archiving and Digital Preservation (IWAW'07)
- Contextualized Attention Metadata: Personalized Access To Digital Resources (CAMA2007)

Libraries in Digital Age (LIDA)

- DIALOG and ISI Web of Knowledge
- Methods and Techniques for Web Usability
- Demonstration of MORAE, an Integrated Tool for Web Usability Evaluation
- Scopus—the New Generation Database
- Linking Teaching and Learning: Assessment of Information Competence in Higher Education
- The Millennial Generation: Its Use of Academic Library Services and Expectations from the Digital Library

American Society for Information Science & Technology (ASIS&T)

- Research into Practice: Studying Producers and Consumers in Social Computing Environments
- Making DSpace Your Own
- Taxonomies in Search
- 3rd Annual Social Informatics Research Symposium: The Social Web, Social Computing and the Social Analysis of Computing
- 18th Annual SIG CR Classification Research Workshop
- Social Information Architecture
- 7th SIG USE Symposium: Mobility and Social Networks in Information Behavior
- RSS 2.0 for Current Awareness and Alerts: A Hands-On "Getting Started" Experience
- Information Architecture 3.0

Cross Language Evaluation Forum (CLEF)

- Multilingual Textual Document Retrieaval (Ad Hoc)
- Cross Language Image Retrieval
- Cross Language Speech Retrieval
- Query Classification Task

- Search Tasks
- Monolingual

Dublin Core and Metadata Initiative (DC)

- Introduction to the Semantic Web
- Metadata That Works

Each workshop title was mapped to the closest core topic in the DL module framework shown in Figure 2. The result is shown in Figure 1. From 33 workshops, the most frequent workshop topics were Information/knowledge organization" (approx. 24%), Services (approx. 27 %) and Management and evaluation (approx. 21%). One of the possible reasons that the Digital objects and Collection development topics were not frequently discussed in the workshops might be because they are basic components of DLs and are taken for granted by workshop attendees. They might have preferred to know more about the big three topics listed above, where new technologies and approaches are continuously introduced. Regarding the User behavior" topic, one observation is that it might be more of interest in meetings labeled as concerning library and information science more generally, rather than during the smaller number of events in the DL area.

It is expected that the popularity of the three topics—Information/knowledge organization, services, and management/evaluation—will continue, considering that the new collaborations among the researchers from the workshop might solve many problems and at the same time introduce many new questions. Thus, to answer those questions, more workshops on related topics could appear.

THE CURRICULUM FRAMEWORK

Based on the prior curricular work, theoretical work, and empirical studies described above, a curriculum framework is proposed (see Figure 2).

Figure 1. Mapping of workshop titles to DL curriculum framework core topics

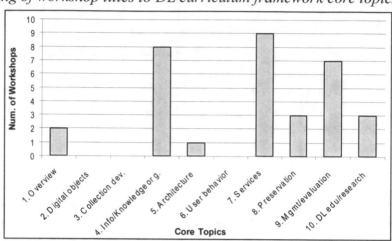

It consists of ten core DL topics, which are further decomposed into subtopics. Each core topic and its subtopics are described in detail here.

Topic 1: *Overview.* This component of the curriculum is intended to provide a brief overview of DLs and their operations through various foundational topics such as definitions, conceptual frameworks, models, theories, and history. Its purpose is to support student learning of the more specific topics introduced in later components of the curriculum.

Topic 2: *Digital Objects.* The Digital Objects (Kahn & Wilensky, 1995) component starts from the discussion of the question, "What is a document?" It then progresses to a discussion of how the definition is expanded in DL settings. The various digital object file types—such as texts, images, pictures, maps, or audio or video files—are to be addressed. The original characteristics of these resources, their uses and applications in DLs, and the related standards, technologies, and issues associated with making them readily usable and accessible in DLs are topics that will be included in the Text resources, Multimedia, and File formats/Transformations subcomponents of the curriculum.

Topic 3: *Collection Development.* The Collection Development component covers issues concerning how to build and maintain the collection of online resources in a particular DL. Like other libraries, DLs need policies related to their resource selection and de-selection criteria, focusing on issues like the following: What is the scope of a particular DL collection? What resources should the DL collect, taking into consideration its scope, mission, goals, and other criteria? What particular types of resources should a DL collect: should it collect only online or born digital resources, or should it also collect analog resources and then digitize them? How should budgeting and personnel management proceed if the DL is a division of a large-scale institution? Should DLs have their own budgets or facilities to proceed with digitization? The subtopics included in this component are the process of developing resource collections, resource selection policies, digitization, markup for e-publishing, and harvesting of materials from extant Web sites.

Topic 4: *Information/Knowledge Organization.* Valuable collections cannot be efficiently utilized unless they are organized systematically. This component of the curriculum covers important concepts in representing and organizing digital objects into collections through several subcomponents. The Information architecture component will cover topics such as hypertext, which makes a dynamic organization of information possible through its hyperlinks, or its extended term, hypermedia, which provides linked information of plain text, audio, video, and images. The Metadata (Daniel & Lagoze, 1997; DCMI, 2006), cataloging, metadata markup, and metadata harvesting component will cover intellectual, structural, administrative, and technical approaches to creating,

maintaining, and updating metadata. The Ontologies, classification, and categorization component will cover various approaches to developing ontology/classification/categorization schema. The Subject description, vocabulary control, thesauri, and terminologies component will discuss various approaches to controlling terminology. The Object description and organization for a specific domain component will cover topics such as Metadata Object Description Schema (MODS), which is a schema for bibliographic elements, and

Figure 2. Proposed DL curriculum framework

CORE TOPICS			
1	Overview	1-a (10-c): Conceptual frameworks, models, theories, definitions	1-b: History of digital libraries and library automation
2	Digital Objects	2-a: Text resources 2-b: Multimedia	2-c (8-c): File formats, transformation, migration
3	Collection Development	3-a: Collection development / selection policies 3-b: Digitization	3-c: Harvesting 3-d: Document and e-publishing / presentation markup
4	Info/ Knowledge Organization	4-a: Information architecture (e.g., hypertext, hypermedia) 4-b: Metadata 4-c: Ontologies, classification, categorization	4-d: Subject description, vocabulary control, thesauri, terminologies 4-c: Object description and organization for a specific domain
5	Architecture (agents, mediators)	5-a: Architecture overviews 5-b: Application software 5-c: Identifiers, handles, DOI, PURL	5-d: Protocols 5-e: Interoperability 5-f: Security
6	User Behavior/ Interactions	6-a: Info needs, relevance 6-b: Online information seeking behavior and search strategy	6-c: Sharing, networking, interchange (e.g., social) 6-d: Interaction design, info summarization and visualization, usability assessment
7	Services	7-a: Search engines, IR, indexing methods 7-b: Reference services 7-c: Recommender systems	7-d: Routing, community filtering 7-e: Web publishing (e.g., wiki, rss, Moodle, etc.)
8	Preservation	8-a: Approaches to archiving and repository development	8-b: Sustainability 8-c (2-c): File formats, transformation, migration
9	Management and Evaluation	9-a: Project management 9-b: DL case studies 9-c: DL evaluation, user studies 9-d: Bibliometrics, Webometrics	9-e: Intellectual property 9-f: Cost/economic issues 9-g: Social issues
10	DL education and research	10-a: Future of DLs 10-b: Education for digital librarians	10-c (1-a): Conceptual framework, theories, definitions 10-d: DL research initiatives

might be used in library applications. Together, these subcomponents can introduce students to the range of issues associated with organizing materials in a DL.

Topic 5: *Architecture.* This component of the curriculum is critical, since it encompasses so many important conceptual and technical topics associated with the successful management of DLs. The common terminology of DLs and related online databases will be reviewed and naming strategies for making DL functions and services easily recognizable to users will be discussed, as well as the long-term and short-term access and security of DL architectures. The specific subcomponents to be included are: Architecture overviews; Application software; Identifiers, handles, DOI, PURL (Kahn & Wilensky, 1995); Protocols; Interoperability; and Security.

Topic 6: *User Behavior/Interactions.* This component encompasses various issues regarding the interactions between DLs and their users. Understanding the detail of user interactions and behavioral patterns is one of the important design considerations in developing successful DLs. Subcomponents are: Information needs, relevance; Online information seeking behaviors and search strategy; Sharing, networking, interchange (e.g., social); and Interaction design, info summarization and visualization; Usability assessment.

Topic 7: *Services.* DLs provide various services for people, including at least the following four types: (1) searching, browsing, discovery, and exploration; (2) alerting, recommending, and routing; (3) other types of user need or information satisfaction services; and (4) infrastructure services (creation, adding value). These services are developed and updated based on the continuous investigation and analysis of user needs and information seeking behaviors, which are covered in *Topic 6: User Behavior/Interactions.* Both au-

tomated and human-intermediated services will be covered in this component, including topics related to integration or separation of these two approaches. In addition, services will be illustrated by the interactions between systems (computers) and humans (users or DL staff), depending on how users obtain assistance within the context of a particular DL. For example, when users search or browse resources in DLs, the human-computer interaction is an iterative cycle as users continuously ask systems to gather results, and the systems keep searching and displaying results based on the updated queries. Human-intermediated reference services in DLs, which enable users to ask questions of librarians or other experts, are examples of computer-mediated human-to-human interaction. Automated filtering and routing functions are good examples of computer-to-computer interaction, because pre-set algorithms run the systems without any human intervention. The variety of subtopics included in this component are: Search engines, information retrieval (IR), indexing methods; Reference services; Recommender systems; Routing, community filtering; Web publishing (e.g., Wiki, RSS, Moodle, and so on).

Topic 8: *Preservation.* This module covers the long-term plans of a DL for digital resource preservation (Gladney, 2004), migration, emulation, and so on, including the creation of preservation and administrative metadata. The fundamental strategies for preserving digital resources and examples of preservation models for DLs will be covered. One of the subtopics—File formats, transformation, migration—also appears in *Topic 2: Digital Objects* because understanding the different types and formats of digital objects is an essential part of developing preservation strategies.

Topic 9: *Management and evaluation.* As was identified via the analysis of existing courses on DLs, project management skills are critical to the success of a DL. This component will cover basic project management skills involved in project planning (e.g., defining work requirements, defining the quantity and quality of the work to be completed, and defining the resources needed) and monitoring a project to its successful completion (e.g., tracking progress, comparing the actual outcome to the predicted outcome, analyzing the project's impacts, and making any adjustments needed along the way). In addition to these fundamental project management skills, this component will address several related issues through subcomponents on Project management; DL case studies; DL evaluation (Gonçalves, Moreira, Fox, & Watson, 2007), user studies; Bibliometrics, Webometrics; Legal issues (e.g., copyright); Cost/economic issues; and Social issues.

Topic 10: *DL Education and Research.* The curriculum framework provides closure in a component addressing DL education and future research topics. This component will explicitly examine the possible futures of digital libraries.

Because the field of digital librarianship will continue to evolve as creative ideas and new technologies emerge, it is expected that the curriculum framework also will continue to evolve. However, we believe that it provides a strong basis for current curriculum development—in specific DL courses, certificate programs focusing on DLs, and degree programs in digital librarianship.

MODULE DEVELOPMENT

It is expected that, over time, an educational module will be developed for each subtopic in the curriculum framework. The modules being developed can be implemented within the context of a DL course or series of courses, or in other related courses having a DL component. The process for developing these modules is described in this section.

After receiving feedback from the project's advisory board and going through a few revisions, the project team developed the module template as shown in Figure 3. Its structure resembles that

Figure 3. A template of DL lesson modules

```
                          Module Template
  1. Module name
  2. Scope
  3. Learning objectives
  4. 5S characteristics of the module
  5. Level of effort required (in-class and out-of-class time required for students)
  6. Relationships with other modules (flow between modules)
  7. Prerequisite knowledge/skills required (completion optional)
  8. Introductory remedial instruction (completion optional;
     the body of knowledge for the prerequisite knowledge/skills required)
  9. Body of knowledge (topics might be skipped or studied in different orders)
     Topic 1
     (Theories and background knowledge of the topic)
     Topic 2 ...
     Topic 3 ...
  10. Resources (textbooks, required and optional readings for instructors and students)
  11. Concept map (created by students)
  12. Exercises / Learning activities
  13. Evaluation of learning objective achievement
  14. Glossary
  15. Additional useful links
  16. Contributors
```

of a course syllabus with additional sections (e.g., 5S characteristics of the module, concept map).

The scope description and the learning objectives will define what is to be included in each module, as well as what will not be covered. In addition, a module's relationships to other modules within the framework will be specified. The other sections such as Learning objectives, Level of effort required, Body of knowledge, Resources, Exercises/Learning activities might be decided depending on the module scope description. Most modules can be taught and studied using 1.5 to 2.5 in-class hours with additional out-of-class hours, which span from 1–7 hours depending on the amount of exercises assigned and the level of difficulty of the learning activities. The 5S characteristics description makes sure that the module is on a solid foundation, connecting the module directly to the 5S theoretical framework. The Body of knowledge section is where the actual content of the lesson will be provided, in the form of lecture notes. These notes can be easily modified for a particular implementation of the module. Creating concept maps is one of several possible effective learning methods. Concept maps will be created by the students for each module (and for some resources assigned for the module). There should be a clear logical connection among Learning objectives, Body of knowledge, Exercises/learning activities, and Evaluation of learning objective achievements. This will insure that the students have focused learning experiences aimed toward the learning objectives.

There are seven draft modules currently developed out of 41 modules in the DL module framework that is shown in Figure 2. To see the actual modules, please visit http://curric.dlib.vt.edu. They include:

- 1-b: History of digital libraries and library automation
- 3-b: Digitization
- 5-b: Application software
- 6-a: Information needs, relevance
- 6-b: Online information seeking behaviors and search strategy
- 7-b: Reference services
- 9-c: DL evaluation, user studies

Those modules were selected for early development based on the literature analysis of DL topics and the teaching experiences of the project team members. After formative evaluation through expert review, they will be field-tested in actual university classrooms.

CONCLUSION

As digital libraries become commonplace (i.e., as people come to assume that they will access a digital library when they need information), DLs must become reliable and trustworthy resources. They must include both a well-organized underlying architecture and a set of services designed to address their potential users' information needs. For this vision of the future to come to fruition, information professionals need to be educated to establish and manage digital libraries. The proposed curriculum framework provides a firm foundation for these important educational activities.

REFERENCES

Arms, W. Y. (2000). *Digital libraries.* Cambridge, MA: MIT Press.

Choi, Y., & Rasmussen, E. (2006a). What do digital librarians do? In *Proceedings of the Joint Conference on Digital Libraries* (pp. 187–188). Retrieved August 30, 2008, from http://doi.acm.org/10.1145/1141753.1141789

Choi, Y., & Rasmussen, E. (2006b). What is needed to educate future digital librarians: A study of current practice and staffing patterns in academic and research libraries. *D-Lib Magazine, 12*(9). Retrieved August 30, 2008, from http://doi:10.1045/september2006-choi

Daniel, R., & Lagoze, C. (1997, November). Extending the Warwick framework: From metadata containers to active digital objects. *D-Lib Magazine, 3*(11). Retrieved August 30, 2008, from http://www.dlib.org/dlib/november97/daniel/11daniel.html

Dublin Core Metadata Initiative (DCMI). (2006). Web site: http://www.dublincore.org/

Fox, E.A., & Urs, S. (2002). Digital libraries. In B. Cronin (Ed.), *Annual Review of Information Science and Technology (ARIST), Ch. 12* (pp. 503–589). Information Today, for the American Society for Information Science & Technology.

Gladney, H.M. (2004). Trustworthy 100-year digital objects: Evidence after every witness is dead. *ACM Transactions on Information Systems, 22*(3), 406–436. Retrieved August 30, 2008, from http://doi.acm.org/10.1145/1010614.1010617

Gonçalves, M.A. (2004). *Streams, structures, spaces, scenarios, and societies (5S): A Formal digital library framework and its applications.* Doctoral dissertation, Virginia Tech. Retrieved August 30, 2008 from http://scholar.lib.vt.edu/theses/available/etd-12052004-135923/

Gonçalves, M.A., & Fox, E.A. (2002). 5SL—a language for declarative specification and generation of digital libraries. In *Proceedings of the Joint Conference on Digital Libraries* (pp. 263–272). Retrieved August 30, 2008, from http://doi.acm.org/10.1145/544220.544276

Gonçalves, M.A., Moreira, B.L., Fox, E.A., & Watson, L.T. (2007). "What is a good digital library?"—A quality model for digital libraries. In *Information Processing & Management, 43*(5), 1416–1437. Retrieved August 30, 2008, from http://dx.doi.org/10.1016/j.ipm.2006.11.010

Gonçalves, M.A., Fox, E.A., Watson, L.T., & Kipp, N.A. (2004). Streams, structures, spaces, scenarios, societies (5S): A formal model for digital libraries. *ACM Transactions on Information Systems, 22*(2), 270–312. Retrieved August 30, 2008, from http://doi.acm.org/10.1145/984321.984325

Gorton, D.C. (2007). *Practical digital library generation into DSpace with the 5S Framework.* Master's thesis, Virginia Tech. Retrieved August 30, 2008, from http://scholar.lib.vt.edu/theses/available/etd-04252007-161736/

Joint Task Force on Computing Curricula. (2001). *Computing Curricula 2001: Computer Science.* Association for Computing Machinery, and IEEE Computer Society. Retrieved August 30, 2008, from http://www.sigcse.org/cc2001/

Kahn, R., & Wilensky, R. (1995). *A framework for distributed digital object services.* Reston, VA: CNRI. Retrieved August 30, 2008, from http://www.cnri.reston.va.us/k-w.html

Kajberg, L., & Lørring, L. (Eds.) (2005). *European curriculum reflections on library and information science education.* Copenhagen: Royal School of Library and Information Science. Retrieved August 30, 2008, from http://biblis.db.dk/uhtbin/hyperion.exe/db.leikaj05

Lesk, M. (1997). *Practical digital libraries: Books, bytes and bucks.* San Francisco, CA: Morgan Kaufmann Publishers.

Lesk, M. (2005). *Understanding digital libraries* (2nd ed.). San Francisco, CA: Morgan Kaufmann Publishers.

Ma, Y., Clegg, W., & O'Brien, A. (2006). Digital library education: The current status. In *Proceedings of the Joint Conference on Digital Libraries* (pp. 165–174). Retrieved August 30, 2008, from http://doi.acm.org/10.1145/1141753.1141786

Novak, J.D., & Gowin, D.B. (1984). *Learning how to learn.* Cambridge, UK: Cambridge University Press.

Pomerantz, J., Oh, S., Yang, S., Fox, E.A., & Wildemuth, B.M. (2006a). The core: Digital library education in library and information science programs. *D-Lib Magazine, 12*(11). Retrieved August 30, 2008, from http://doi:10.1045/november2006-pomerantz

Pomerantz, J., Wildemuth, B.M., Oh, S., Yang, S., & Fox, E.A. (2006b). Digital libraries curriculum development. *D-Lib Magazine, 12*(7/8). Retrieved August 30, 2008, from http://doi:10.1045/july2006-inbrief

Pomerantz, J., Wildemuth, B.M., Yang, S., & Fox, E.A. (2006c). Curriculum development for digital libraries. In *Proceedings of the Joint Conference on Digital Libraries* (pp. 175–184). Retrieved August 30, 2008, from http://doi.acm.org/10.1145/1141753.1141787

Shen, R. (2006). *Applying the 5S framework to integrating digital libraries.* Doctoral dissertation, Virginia Tech. Retrieved August 30, 2008, from http://scholar.lib.vt.edu/theses/available/etd-04212006-135018/

Witten, I.H., & Bainbridge, D. (2003). *How to build a digital library.* San Francisco, CA: Morgan Kaufmann Publishers.

Zhu, Q. (2002). *5SGraph: A modeling tool for digital libraries.* Master's thesis, Virginia Tech. Retrieved August 30, 2008, from http://scholar.lib.vt.edu/theses/available/etd-11272002-210531/

KEY TERMS

5S Framework: A formal model and theory developed to describe digital libraries in particular, but more generally able to aid description of information systems; the basic elements, describable using well understood mathematical constructs, are: societies, scenarios, spaces, structures, and streams.

Architecture: How a digital library system, system component, or federation of systems is constituted or organized to operate.

Curriculum: A set of courses constituting a particular area of specialization.

Digital Library (DL): A complex information system that can be described using the 5S framework, with parts: digital object, metadata object, catalog, repository, index, user, user interface, and services (including search and browse).

Digital Librarian: An information professional responsible for the design, development, and/or maintenance of a digital library, including both its collections and the services it offers to its users.

Digital Object: An electronic document, multimedia content item, or representation of information in computer form (i.e., made of 0s and 1s)—the basic unit of what is stored in or taken out of a digital library.

Interdisciplinary Curriculum Development: The development of a curriculum or curriculum framework jointly undertaken by collaborators from two or more academic disciplines. For example, in this case, this effort is undertaken by collaborators from computer science and from library and information science.

Metadata: A set of information about a digital object, serving needs such as content description and administration.

Module: A unit of educational content and content description that can be worked with, relative free from dependency on other similar units of content—typically a part of a course.

ENDNOTES

[1] Support for this work was received from the US National Science Foundation, Grants IIS-

0535057 to Virginia Tech and IIS-0535060 to the University of North Carolina at Chapel Hill.

3   http://www.delos.info/index. php?option=com_content&task=view&id =465&Itemid=254

2   No online proceedings of workshops were available for the International Conference on Asian Digital Libraries (ICADL) and the Russian Conference on Digital Libraries (RCDL).

Chapter LII
Digital Libraries as Centres of Knowledge:
Historical Perspectives from European Ancient Libraries

Natalie Pang
Monash University, Australia

ABSTRACT

Using historical perspectives from ancient libraries in Europe, this chapter is focused on the core role of libraries as centres of knowledge. Though not intended to be a comprehensive historical account, these perspectives are seen as a starting point in the discussion in looking at digital libraries as similar centres or repositories of knowledge. The ways technological and social contexts have been adapted in ancient libraries are discussed, which helped to shed light on the next part of the discussion on digital libraries. Digital libraries are not only considered in terms of their technological aspirations, but also in their social constructions. It is hoped that the discussion will contribute to a collective understanding of immediate and future directions of libraries, their challenges and promises, and how they have evolved as places for local communities.

INTRODUCTION

Since its inception the study and practice of digital libraries have called on research and work dealing with the social construction, and the role of digital libraries in traditional libraries. Digital libraries have provided what people now refer to as hybrid libraries, typically referring to the implementa-

tion and use of digital technologies and resources within the walls of what used to be "traditional" libraries. Chowdhury and Chowdhury (2003) defined such libraries as "where digital and printed information resources co-exist and are brought together in an integrated information service accessible locally as well as remotely" (Chowdhury & Chowdhury, 2003, p. 6). The presence of digital libraries within traditional libraries has provided a complex infusion of physical and digital spaces, which can become a powerful ally to small but growing libraries faced with space issues.

Given the increasing complexity of digital libraries, researchers have attempted to define their meaning and scope. Borgman (2003, p. 652) defined digital libraries as "sets of electronic resources and associated technical capabilities for creating, searching, and using information." Within this definition lies the closely knitted relationship between digital contents and the technological functions and services concerning the creation, search, and usage of these digital resources. Waters (1998, p. 1) comprehended a broad definition, which stated that digital libraries

are organisations that provide the resources, including the specialised staff, to select, structure, offer intellectual access to, interpret, distribute, preserve the integrity of, and ensure the persistence over time of collections of digital works so that they are readily and economically available for use by a defined community or set of communities.

In a sense, going by this definition, any library that has allocated any resource (including staffing) to making digital works available for use by one or more target communities would already have a digital library.

Though an instrument that has widened the possibilities of design and deliveries of services; the presence of digital libraries can also be a rather perplexing one. Are they substitutes or perfect complements of traditional libraries? What is the future of libraries, given the changing circumstances and conditions of the larger societies? For the purpose of this article it is necessary to return to the historical beginnings of libraries; though this is not intended to be an exhaustive historical account.

Due to space limitations the discussion is focused on libraries in the European ancient world. The discussion begins with an account of the first

mega library of the ancient world: the Library of Alexandria. From there the discussion leads on, from the decline of knowledge and libraries during the dark ages till the renaissance period, a time of great revelations in knowledge when many geniuses and inventors also emerged. The renaissance period also reflected the rise of a new order for libraries—with the growth of university libraries and a society that were largely pursuing literacy and knowledge.

After drawing insights from the European accounts of technological use and transformations in libraries, the article will then focus on a more recent piece of library history: digital libraries. Are they replacements of libraries as new centres of knowledge or are they essential complements to libraries?

A VERY SHORT HISTORY

There has always been an innate knowing that knowledge is absolutely critical to status and survival. In the ancient world, the ability to know things about the seasons, farming, river tides, time, calendars, would often create the difference between the rich and the poor (Finley, 1965). While this is nothing new, it is imperative to highlight that libraries, in the role of knowledge cultivation and construction, have always involved technologies.

One of the greatest accomplishment in library history (Hessel, 1955), the Library of Alexandria, was founded around 300 B.C. A mega library and a centre of knowledge that was public, it was the first of its kind (Casson, 2001). The Greeks knew the importance of having a repository of records, archives, literature and scholarly works that was of quality and trustworthy—to a heightened intellectual life. Scholars attribute this growth to the emphasis on the centres of learning (other smaller private and public libraries) and the Library of Alexandria found there—creating a city of literacy based on knowledge production

(Boren, 1977; Krasner-Khait, 2001; Sitwell, 1984). Unfortunately, this great library was mysteriously destroyed later, with many citing fires during Roman occupation of Alexandria in 48BC-50BC by Julius Caesar as the cause (Arnott, 1970; Casson, 2001; Lipsius, 1907).

Other royal libraries were rising to existence by the beginning of second century B.C. (Casson, 2001) in Rhodes, Athens, through to the development of libraries in the Roman Empire. Such growth reflected significant influences in literacy and learning.

Like many other successful civilisations of their times, Rome had libraries functioning as centres of knowledge and learning, and formed a large part of the Roman society. The accumulation of knowledge and acquisition was one significant aspect of the Roman lifestyle. The engineering feats of the Romans were attributed to the knowledge and records of scrolls and manuscripts found in these centres of knowledge (Arnott, 1970; Boren, 1977). In the beginning, the libraries were only accessible to scholars, scientists, and teachers—but by the third century libraries were added to the baths, where the public masses would go to socialise and read (Krasner-Khait, 2001; Sitwell, 1984). Such transfers of knowledge were crucial to libraries' growth, and at the same time reflected the penetration of libraries in the social spaces of public communities of people.

Several events in ancient history looked to propel the libraries towards extinction, such as the dark ages with the decline of literacy and libraries being open only to a privileged few. Stark (2005), in his book, shed a different light to the Dark Ages and the common perception of Christianity as an enemy of progress. In the monasteries and churches, knowledge was being stored which brought about the beginning of some great technological innovations, and the reestablishment of literacy. There was continuity in the effort to store critical information—turning them into pastoral houses of knowledge. The monasteries and churches were instrumental in making this happen (Stark, 2005).

Because of the religious communities that emerged which were also institutionalised, small libraries were formed—forming the groundwork for what became known as a time of great learning: the renaissance and a new age for libraries. The monastic communities that were formed in Egypt created theological libraries that formed an emphasis for learning in the eastern half of the Roman Empire (Johnson, 1970; Krasner-Kahit, 2001; Parsons, 1952).

This was manifested in 529 AD through a decree of Benedict to govern the lifestyles of monks. This rule mandated that

Between Easter and the calends of October let them apply themselves to reading from the fourth hour until the sixth hour [...] and in these days of Lent, let them receive a book apiece from the library and read it straight through. These books are to be given out at the beginning of Lent. (Krasner-Khait, 2001)

It also became common for monasteries to lend to other monasteries—a familiar form of the interlibrary loan as we know today.

As Europe emerged out of darkness, people began looking to the Greek and Roman literature for inspiration (Johnson, 1970; Krasner-Kahit, 2001). Not only was this period marked with the appearance of great scientists, inventors, and other; it was also marked with institutional revelations, such as the establishment of the Vatican Library in Italy in the 1400s, the forming of the Laurentian Library by the famous Florentine family. Universities were growing, and accompany this growth was the development of university libraries (Johnson, 1970). Bookmaking was revolutionalised by Gutenberg, replacing printed books with handwritten ones. A historical milestone, this technological revolution brought about dramatic changes to making the written word accessible to the masses (Krasner-Khait, 2001).

This period marked a golden age of literacy, where the absorption of knowledge in arts, literature, science, architecture, and technology was equally matched by their dissemination, another key growth factor for libraries. Also marking this period was the rise of commerce and exploration, and the knowledge amassed by the people and institutions of this period translated into the rich and diverse collections found in various libraries.

It is important at this point to clarify what may be misunderstood as technological determinisms from these historical accounts. While it may be that technological revolutions had propelled libraries towards certain heights (such as the printing of books), it may also be suggested that these revolutions had come about as an outcome of the core nature of libraries. As Pang, Schauder, Quartly, and Dale-Hallett (2006) had argued with structuration theory, the duality of technology makes clear the distinctions between technology as a form of structure and agent yet recognises them as iteratively dependent on each other. The application of this theory recognises that the structural properties of social systems impose themselves as influencing mediums and at the same time, outcomes of the social practices they "recursively organise" (Giddens, 1986, p. 25). This is also known as the duality of structure (Giddens, 1986). Ferguson and Bunge (2007, p. 53) pointed out that "personalised service and equity of access" is within the nature of libraries and librarians—so much so that they make technologies easier and more available to their users.

Using this assumption, it could be perceived in hindsight that: technological revolutions had also been driven by demand and the evolutionary use of literary materials in libraries, the role of libraries as centres of knowledge had led to the adoption of processes to facilitate certain functions such as the interlibrary loans and the integration of the library into social lifestyles (such as the addition of libraries to the baths in the Roman empire). In such technological breakthroughs and transformations of processes, the design, development, and use of technology plays a critical role.

From this short history the library as a place is also manifested: they begin usually as access points to resources, but as people came together the library also opened itself for other opportunities such as social interactions that were necessary to accompany communities' pursuits of knowledge. Regardless of the societies and cultures they were in, the libraries were important as institutions providing sources of literacy, knowledge, and innovations. Technological developments were keys to creating and disseminating them—and also form a core character of libraries.

DIGITAL LIBRARIES: PRACTICE OR ASPIRATION?

It may seem recent; but the ideology and aspiration driving digital libraries is not. H.G. Wells, a famous early science fiction writer, wrote in 1937:

The whole human memory can be, and probably in a short time will be, made accessible to every individual...this new all-human cerebrum need not be concentrated in any one single place. It can be reproduced exactly and fully, in Peru, China, Iceland, Central Africa, or wherever else seems to afford an insurance against danger and interruption. It can have at once, the concentration of a craniate animal and the diffused vitality of an amoeba. (Wells, 1937, p. 87)

Wells saw the potential distributed intelligence can offer, given the availability of access around the clock, sophisticated searching, organisation of information, and the availability of interoperable file formats and languages. This potential which he foresaw is fulfilled with the advent of the Internet and World Wide Web, and more importantly, the digital libraries of today.

Ferguson and Bunge (1997) recognised that the presence of digital libraries implies a social construction of librarians, library services, user communities, and the way they interact with one another and with the library. Freeman (2007) expresses this explicitly, in his discussion of libraries as places where technologies are integrated within physical spaces, and recognised such redesigned spaces to imply social constructions of communities.

It must be realised that digital libraries have been created by people who work within conventional libraries, but also by people who do not consider themselves as practitioners of libraries (Arms, 2000). As we learn from history, libraries have always adopted technology within their walls—so the appearance of digital libraries is far from strange. Yet digital libraries are not simply technologies—they have the capacity to provide access to collections of resources, anywhere and anytime, and make a single copy available to multiple people. They are rich repositories of knowledge that have no physical boundaries and in addition, possess the ability to link to other digital libraries; expanding their capacity as digital centres of knowledge. It is undeniable that there are distinct advantages that digital libraries have that traditional libraries do not have. So a paradigm shift has now appeared: digital libraries can exist as part of a larger library, or on their own. The question is this: if digital libraries are better left to exist on their own, does it imply the decline of physical libraries? At this point, it is hard not to wonder if the library is being replaced by this digital centre of knowledge.

After all, the justification for libraries has changed with time, from the use of libraries as an instrument to preserve democracy to the contemporary idea of gaining competitive advantages with efficient information transfer (Lesk, 2005). The emphasis on history has been deliberate in order to derive relevant lessons from them. Other than natural disasters, the decline of libraries in history has been characterised by libraries closing themselves to the communities, reserving technological developments to only a privileged few. By the same token, a key success

factor attributed to the growth of libraries is the dissemination and use amongst the communities they serve. It may be clear then, that digital libraries with its distributed intelligence and the potential to reach a wider audience may prove to be a powerful asset to libraries than ever before; even though some of them may not have been developed by librarians themselves.

As seen from history, the library had been important as spaces for interactions: whether as points of access to information resources, preservation of collections, for social interactions, as institutions of collaborations or presenting opportunities for training and development. In his research with academic libraries, Freeman (2007, p. 372) found that students want their libraries to "feel bigger than they are," and interestingly, prefer the traditional spaces of their libraries although the presence of new technologies is acknowledged as essential. This is clear in highlighting the social role that libraries have in inspiring learning and facilitating knowledge exchange within their communities. Although with the World Wide Web, the library finds itself having to reposition itself as a place, and more importantly, for the communities it serves. Digital libraries bring the library to the user without the user leaving the comforts of his own home, office, or internet café; and yet can still be a powerful ally for the traditional library with integrated searching abilities and digital materials to complement existing physical collections.

However, a number of issues remain, posing challenges to both the library and the digital library. Unlike the libraries of the past the collections contained in digital libraries are distributed—instead of one place the points of access can be numerous. With access rather than ownership being a key success factor of libraries, there are considerable challenges in the licensing and usage frameworks of digital libraries. There are significant issues with the economic models for libraries and publishers. Publishers and content providers have traditionally relied on selling copies of an item—while in the digital library the definition of a copy and the number of people who can have access to one copy has changed. This is an important issue especially for hybrid libraries with shrinking library budgets, and who provides both printed and digital resources. While the cost of physical space may not be as relevant for digital libraries, there are significant costs associated with the research and development of digital libraries. Other social issues remain, such as the lack of financial support for independent digital library developments, lack of available infrastructure, poor information literacy rates amongst users, lack of trained staff (Chowdhury & Chowdhury, 2003).

Perspectives on the library as a place are changing with the digital library, especially with the presence of community interaction in history. Yet this needs not be displaced, only changed. With the digital library there are new opportunities for community engagement, such as cooperative cataloguing (Lerner, 1999), interactive reference services, or even collaborative creation of metadata with users using participative technologies such as tagging.

Although digital libraries can function as centres of knowledge providing access to resources globally around the clock, the discussion has so far argued for a social and cultural role for libraries. Jeanneney (2007) agreed, further clarifying that libraries have been misunderstood and simply reduced to places where books and other resources are provided. As shown from the historical account of libraries from Europe in the first part of the chapter, while they function as centres of knowledge, they are also the understated organisers of potentially chaotic knowledge resources and exchanges, and the patient information therapists who guide users to the resources they want. So there remains an essential need for physical libraries; as much as digital libraries are needed within libraries.

Within the library, technological issues are also more prevalent than before, with the diverse structures and implementations of digital libraries. Yet a solution presents itself, with the possibility of digital libraries being used as archives and preserve potentially-obsolete materials (Arms, 2000; Lerner, 1999).

CONCLUSION

History has proven that since the beginning of libraries, they have been part of what civilisation stood for. They are centres and repositories of knowledge that were started because people realised the importance of sharing and accumulation of knowledge—which can only become more valuable the more they are being used. More importantly, libraries stand as institutions that are also representative of a type of cooperation: in the sharing of resources and spaces they foster literate communities and institutions that are empowered and inspired to collaborate. Regardless of their instruments, the core reason of their being and existence has not changed—only evolved with the digital library. Perspectives from the short historical account reveal that digital libraries can act as a powerful facility for libraries to augment their roles as houses of knowledge.

REFERENCES

Arms, W. (2000). *Digital libraries*. Cambridge: The MIT Press.

Arnott, P.D. (1970). *Romans and their world: An introduction to the Roman world*. London: Macmillan.

Boren, H.C. (1977). *Roman society: A social, economic, and cultural history*. Lexington: Mass.

Borgman, C. (2003). The invisible library: Paradox of the global information infrastructure. *Library Trends, 51*(Spring), 652–675.

Casson, L. (2001). *Libraries in the ancient world.* London: Yale University Press.

Chowdhury, G.G., & Chowdhury, S. (2003). *Introduction to digital libraries.* London: Facet Publishing.

Ferguson, C.D., & Bunge, C.A. (2007). Value propositions. In D. Kresh (Ed.), *The whole digital library handbook* (pp. 51–56). Chicago: American Library Association.

Finley, M.I. (1965). Technical innovation and economic progress in the ancient world. *Economic History Review, 2*(8), 37.

Freeman, G. (2007). Reinventing the library. In D. Kresh (Ed.), *The Whole Digital Library Handbook* (pp. 370–373). Chicago: American Library Association.

Giddens, A. (1986). *The constitution of society: Outline of the theory of structuration.* Berkeley: University of California Press.

Hessel, A. (1955). *A history of libraries* (R. Peiss, Trans.). New Jersey: The Scarecrow Press.

Jeanneney, J.-N. (2007). *Google and the myth of universal knowledge.* Chicago: The University of Chicago Press.

Johnson, E.D. (1970). *History of libraries in the western world.* Metuchen: Scarecrow Press Inc.

Krasner-Khait, B. (2001). Survivor: The history of the library. *History Magazine* (October/November).

Lerner, F. (1999). *Libraries through the ages.* New York: The Continuum Publishing Company.

Lesk, M. (2005). *Understanding digital libraries.* San Francisco: Elsevier Inc.

Lipsius, J. (1907). *Brief outline of the history of libraries.* Antwerp: The Platin Press.

Pang, N., Schauder, D., Quartly, M., & Dale-Hallett, L. (2006). User-centred design, e-research, and adaptive capacity in cultural institutions: The case of the women on farms gathering collection. In C. Khoo, D. Singh, & A. Chaudhry (Eds.), *Proceedings of the Asia-Pacific Conference on Library & Information Education & Practice (A-LIEP 2006)* (pp. 526–535). Singapore.

Parsons, E.A. (1952). *The Alexandrian library: Glory of the Hellenic world.* New York: Elsevier Press.

Sitwell, N.H. (1984). *The world the Romans knew.* London: Hamilton.

Stark, R. (2005). *The victory of reason.* New York: Random House.

Waters, D.J. (1998). What are digital libraries? *Council on library and information resources issues July/August*(1), 5–6.

Wells, H.G. (1937). *World brain: The idea of a permanent world encyclopaedia.* Retrieved August 30, 2008, from http://art-bin.com/art/obrain.html

KEY TERMS

Digital Libraries: Conceived narrowly as sets or repositories of electronic resources and associated technical capabilities for creating, searching and using information (Borgman, 2003); or broadly as organisations providing resources to ensure the availability and sustainability of digital works (Waters 1998).

Duality of Structure: Structure as the medium and outcome of the conduct it recursively organizes; the structural properties of social systems do not exist outside of action but are chronically implicated in its production and reproduction.

Hybrid Libraries: Typically refers to libraries with both digital and printed information resources which are made available via an integrated information service.

Structuration: The cumulative effect of people's living and working within social frameworks (through a dynamics that Giddens calls structuration) is the production and reproduction of culture. The cultural context is continuously generated and regenerated through the interplay of action and structure (the "duality of structure"). Social structure both supports and constrains the endeavours of individuals, communities, and societies (Giddens, 1984, pp. 1–40). Structuration theory holds that "man actively shapes the world he lives in at the same time as it shapes him" (Giddens, 1982, p. 21). The structuring of social relations across time and space is viewed in virtue of the duality of structure (Giddens, 1984, p. 377).

Chapter LIII
The European Approach Towards Digital Library Education:
Dead End or Recipe for Success?

Wolfgang Ratzek
Stuttgart Media University, Germany

ABSTRACT

Triggered by a rapid diffusion of ICT within the last two decades, libraries have undergone a (r)evolutionary change in both mission and services. Step by step, libraries diversified their mission from a media holding institution towards a multimedia content provider in a physical and digital environment. To run a library in this way, highly qualified staff with LIS background is brought into focus. The article deals with the situation in European LIS institutions and its programs, particularly with regard to digital library. The crucial question will be: what kind of paradigm, if at all, exists with regard to the digital library phenomenon? Furthermore, some trends in libraries services and conceptions are presented.

A NEW QUANTUM LEAP?

During the last two decades, we can make out two vital reasons why libraries changed from a mere media holding institution towards a multimedia access and content provider in a physical and a digital environment: The rapid development of effective and efficient information and communication technology (ICT) and the vital change of patron behavior. Both tendencies are captured in terms like hybrid library, virtual library, digital library, or simply: the Information and Knowledge Society. As a library cannot offer its services without more or less visible and qualified staff, we will now have a look at the LIS educational and training programs in Europe, especially in Germany, Great Britain and the Nordic Countries.

THE BURDEN OF BEING TRENDY

An excellently managed and organized library is an innovative library, or better: a learning library. Learning from our patrons by listening is a very helpful method. Another one: Learning how to use ICT to improve access to both analog and digital information resources, which can be found in my library or in the depth of the Internet (keyword: deep or semantic Web). These skills have something to do with research, qualified and motivated staff, and the readiness for experiments. But how far shall we go? In what trend shall we invest our scarce resources? How can we make out a "Mayfly" in advance? Against the background, we will now describe the status of digital libraries in European LIS programs. A good orientation is given by Saracevic and Dalbello (2001). They simply ask:

- "Why teach digital libraries?" (→ Actual library practice)
- "What to teach about digital libraries?" (→ Selection problem)
- "How to teach digital libraries?" (→ Curricula, course offering)

Having scanned LIS programs on B.A. and M.A. level, especially in Germany, in the Nordic Countries and the United Kingdom, we, in general recognized that all centers of education and training offer courses in electronic data processing (EDP), digital document handling, information retrieval, library software, and sometimes also JAVA, XML, PHP and so on. At first sight most of the LIS institutions of higher education in Europe seem to be prepared to meet the digital challenge.

The key question in this context is: What kind of "philosophy," or better: paradigm do these centers cultivate? Do they handle the subject "digital library (DL)" as a phenomenon, which is to be found in the world of libraries, that means: outside of the LIS institutions, or do they regard the DL as a challenge for own research and development? Depending on the perspective, one can concentrate on analyzing the phenomenon and offering relevant tools (in the sense of knowledge acquisition), on the other hand, one can educate and train specialists to take part in research projects (in the sense of a institution of *applied* science). To become engrossed in DL, we should not turn a blind eye to other library concepts and trends.

FUTURE TRENDS

Trying to be a fortune-teller in a complex or chaotic world is a very unpleasant venture. In the wake of the last two decades there are at least four scenarios for the nature of a library. Scenario one describes the library as a physical meeting place with library near services and various non-library services for leisure activities (e.g., Kindergarten, fitness center, Internet workspaces). The Idea Store concept in the United Kingdom is a successful example for this strategy. Another scenario can be found nearly everywhere in public and scientific libraries all over the world (in Idea Stores too): The hybrid library, a synthesis of a physical library with its holding and digital based services like a (Web-)OPAC or access to the Internet in general and to the deep Web (e.g., with costs content in particular). A third scenario focuses on the DL per se.

Actually, we have no generally accepted definition of DL (Saracevic & Dalbello, 2001). In a broader sense, DL may be subdivided into the virtual or Internet-based library like the German "Virtual Special Libraries" (ViFA: Virtuelle Fachbibliotheken) or "The European Library" hosted at the National Library of the Netherlands and the fully automated library like the Jurong City Library in Singapore or the Swedish Bokomaten: a "complete" library of the size of an ATM for train stations, gas stations or department stores. Last but not least, the Cybrary—the library in cyberspace—which is up to now science fiction, as one may marvel at films like Disclosure or Time Machine (by Simon Wells [2002], the great-grandson of H.G. Wells). The idea is, of course, a consequent technological evolution. In this context a librarian turns into a Cybrarian (i.e., an avatar "who" offers virtual [digital] services for real patrons). An example is the avatar-based search engine Ms. Dewey (http://www.msdewey. com/). Another variant: patrons surf themselves through the depth of cyberspace, like Michael Douglas in Disclosure did, and take over the job of a librarian. No matter what perspective we favor, LIS professionals must ensure that no-one will get lost in hyperspace. And here education and training of LIS students come into play. Davis and Moran (2005) identify the following weak point in LIS education:

Students have traditionally taken courses such as collection development where they learned how to acquire and evaluate books, journals, and other vehicles of scholarly communication. This type of preparation is still essential, but in an era when the process of scholarly communication is being transformed, it is not sufficient.

In addition Sommerville, Huston, and Miriamdotter (2006) emphasize:

Moving from an inward focus on acquiring books and other printed materials to an outward orientation that emphasizes seamless user access to systems, services, and sources requires questioning fundamental beliefs and values, communication patterns, structures and core working assumptions, as we better align our organization with the priorities of the emerging eUniversity.

FIT FOR THE FUTURE?

As the IT-evolution in general and the DL phenomenon in particular is—at the moment—unstop-pable, we have to look at how LIS newcomers in Europe are prepared for the digital future (in the sense of Davis & Moran, 2005).

In all European countries like Germany, Norway or the United Kingdom data handling, retrieval tools, database systems are part of the programs, but DL libraries" seem to be mostly just a subject matter in both B.A. and M.A. programs. The findings of Saracevic and Dalbello (2001) back up the thesis that DL in most countries is a phenomenon of the practice community, in other words: a library immanent development and not a part of LIS curricula.

Only Humboldt University Berlin/Germany (for winter term 2006/07) and Universita Degli Studi Di Parma (Parma University/Italy) appointed a professor with main focus on DL. At Department of Information Science at Loughborough University (United Kingdom) courses in "Advanced Internet and DL" are offered. Being prepared for the future includes more than a profound IT knowledge, or better: Information and media competencies. This is just one side of the medal, the other side shows that an adequate LIS program design has to take into account the problems arising from management of DL such as Digital Right Management, copyright, marketing, financing, controlling and so on.

These and other relevant subjects are part of the newly established (first enrollment for winter term 2007/08) "International Master in Digital Library Learning" (DILL). DILL stands for a joint two-year Master's program (120 ECTS credits) set up by the Oslo University College (Norway), Tallinn University (Estonia), and Parma University (Italy). Semesters will be spent in all three partner countries. Only 30 Students, 10 from Europe (EU members or members of the European Free Trade Association/EFTA) and 20 from so-called third countries, will pass the selection process. Students will acquire a joint Master's degree (120 ECTS), recognised by the Consortium partners. The tuition fees vary from 1,750 to 2,500 Euros per year, depending on nationality.

THE MENTAL GAP

LIS students are indeed prepared for the future. In general, offer all LIS programs that are needed to meet the expectations of potential employers in the field of IT. Courses in information and knowledge management, information retrieval methods, library software as well as programming are integral part of almost all European LIS curricula. On closer examination we will make out a "mental gap." Many LIS programs ignore the information science aspect and concentrate on pure practical librarianship and, in addition, an aversion to science (in the sense of applied science).

Ontology based information extraction, automatic indexing or semantic based peer-to-peer systems are rather exceptional in European LIS programs, especially in those programs with main focus on library (e.g., Germany).

To put it in a nutshell, Web-services in the sense of a Web-OPAC and library networks have hardly to do with Web-services in the sense of Web 2.0. Of course, efforts have been made towards Blogs, Wikis, RSS feed (Clyde, 2004), ontology and taxonomy, but all these efforts are based on prefabricated structures and made available as owner controlled services. The Web 2.0 philosophy represents the "join in Web" rules the evolution, that is to say folksonomy instead of taxonomy. Web services, a standardized way of integrating Web-based applications by using XML, WSDL, SOAP and UDDI, is rather a matter of computer science and business intelligence than of librarians/LIS students. Two excellent examples for Web 2.0 applications within LIS education come, surprisingly, from Germany. The E-Journal "Libreas—Library Ideas" (http://www.ib.hu-berlin.de/~libreas/libreas_neu/index.html) is both a DL (in a broader sense) and a Web 2.0 application (Weblogs, RSS 2.0 feed, Atom 1.0 feed). Libreas is hosted at the Institute of Library and Information Science at Humboldt University Berlin (Germany) and made by both students and old stagers. At summer term 2007, students at the Faculty of Information and Communication at Stuttgart Media University will carry out a project called "Corporate Wiki," a cooperation between a publishing house and the author (as project leader).

CONCLUSION

There is a silent (r)evolution going on in the LIS education and training towards a computer science variant. All centers of LIS education and training offer courses in EDP in general and courses in digital document handling, programming or library software in particular. Consequently, the DL phenomenon reached LIS education and training. The main question is: In what way? The answer is: A lot of LIS centers only teach DL (in the sense of informing), some practice DL (in workshops), and very few take part in projects with libraries (in the sense of applied science).

There is a certain danger—especially in the field of "libraries"—that librarians become job creators for computer scientist whereas the need for librarian is shrinking at the same time (e.g., in Germany). At present, there is no danger that the library profession will die out, or less provocative: will be replaced by pure IT specialists without LIS background, few examples come from Germany and Norway.

Librarians, of course, are IT specialist too, but we are more than pipeline managers. The key question must therefore be: Are we pure developer of services or are we service providers, or better: content providers? There is only a slight but far-reaching difference. Librarians are well advised if they keep in mind what they are inn for: Tried and tested services for scientists, researchers, students, and other target groups in order to cover their information needs. Librarians will profit from the digital (r)evolution, if they are able to combine ICT with new services and intelligent way of delivering.

In doing so, a DL as a simple database is acceptable in the first run, the WWW-based (digital) library is a must and belongs to Web 1.0, the future is the next generation Internet, represented by the Semantic Web (keyword: Ontology) and the Web 2.0.

If librarians want to survive as librarians, we have to keep in close touch with our patrons (customers) and their needs. Taylor made services for individuals who are seeking orientation in more and more chaotic structures will be the right strategy against the Google hype. We need, therefore, librarians with various competencies like empathy, special and general knowledge as well as an obvious interest in helping people to cover their needs for information. In that case, librarians become accepted intermediaries between the virtual and physical world of information, like librarians in Singapore, in the USA or in the Nordic Countries. As the library of the future will be a global library, LIS educations and training should also take place within a global learning infrastructure. And here LIS institutions come into play.

REFERENCES

Clyde, L.A. (2004). *Weblogs for libraries*. Oxford, Hampshire.

Davis, C.L., & Moran, B.B. (2005). Scholarly communication: Preparing tomorrow's professionals: LIS schools and scholarly communication. *Association of College and Research Libraries, C&RL News, 66*(1). Retrieved August 30, 2008, from http://www.ala.org/ala/acrl/acrlpubs/crl-news/backissues2005/january05/preparingprofessionals.htm

Saracevic, T., & Dalbello, M. (2001). A survey of digital library education. In *Proceedings of the American Society for Information Science and Technology* (Vol. 38, pp. 209–223).

Sommerville, M.M., Huston, M.E., Miriamdotter, A. (2005). Building on what we know: Staff development in the digital age. *The Electronic Library, 23*(3), 480–491.

KEY TERMS

Cyberspace: A neologism composed of Cybernetics and Space. Often used as a synonym for the Internet. A term coined in science fiction literature (especially by William Gibson). Since the 1980's a subject of computer scientists dealing with Virtual Realities (VR)—an ICT based system for seamless man-machine interaction represented (e.g., by a flight simulator or computer generated building where investors may walk around).

Cybrarian: A virtual librarian in Cyberspace. An Avatar represents a human being in a virtual environment. In this context, a Cybrarian substitutes a physical librarian in a Cyberlib (a library in Cyberspace).

Deep Web: Also called the hidden or invisible Web. Search engines like Google scan the surface only (keywords: visible or surface Web) (i.e., harvesting indexed pages). The Deep Web, in general, consists of special (online) databases, where the surfer needs a password or registration, or dynamic pages, where the result is generated after a query (e.g., stock market prices or flight schedules).

Semantic Web: A project of the WWW consortium lead by Tim Berners Lee. The traditional WWW is characterized by documents coded in HTML (Hypertext Markup Language) (i.e., carrying pure metadata for Web search engines). The Semantic Web is designed for exchange of documents carrying machine-readable semantic information generated through XML (eXentsible Markup Language) or RDF (Resource Description Framework). This does not mean that the computer comprehends the content, it just means that the computer is able to process well-defined problems by pattern matching.

Social Software: User-friendly, easy to use software tools for user generated Web content (also called collaborative software) (e.g., Internet Relay Chat [IRC], Instant Messaging [Skype], Web logs [Technorati], Wikis [Wikipedia], Social networking [OpenBC, now XING or MySpace]).

Virtual Library: The entire content of a (digital) library made accessible via the Internet. The content may come from different providers (e.g., the "German Virtual Libraries").

WEB 2.0: The traditional WWW is mostly characterized by prefabricated content, the WEB 2.0, the join in Internet is characterized by user generated Web content (see Social software).

Web Service: A standardized network for machine-to-machine data exchange. The communication procedure between a service requester and a service provider is based on three standards: Universal Description, Discovery and Integration (UDDI), Web Services Description Language (WSDL), and Simple Object Access Protocol (SOAP).

Chapter LIV
New Roles of Digital Libraries

Faisal Ahmad
University of Colorado at Boulder, USA

Tamara Sumner
University of Colorado at Boulder, USA

Holly Devaul
Digital Learning Sciences, USA

ABSTRACT

The limited scope of digital libraries can be attributed to the brick and mortar vision of the library metaphor. In order to extend scope of digital libraries, in this chapter we examine the current supports and future possibilities afforded by digital libraries to support conventional consumers (i.e., information-users and information-curators), as well as emerging new types of consumers such as distributed computer applications. A functional analysis of conventional libraries is coupled with metaphor design methodology to explore new promising applications and usage scenarios for digital libraries.

INTRODUCTION

Since their conception, digital libraries have made significant contributions in organizing and structuring information, exploring innovative user interface designs, establishing workflow practices, and providing a venue for obtaining empirical data on user behaviors. Patrons have benefited from the sophisticated services for locating and using information, while librarians have been provided with new services for curation: (e.g., preserving, reviewing, sharing, and administering collections). Although these services come close to fulfilling the goals of conventional libraries, the potential of computational technologies to support digital library operations has not been fully realized.

The limited scope of digital library (DL) services can be attributed to the brick and mortar vision of the library metaphor, which initially guided a multidisciplinary research community in gathering around and working on a common set of problems. However, DLs have arrived at a juncture (Lynch, 2005) at which they are now capable of either redefining the library metaphor or breaking away from it in order to investigate promising new research directions. Along either path future DL research will focus primarily on consumers; improving support for conventional consumers (i.e., information-users and information-curators) (Levy & Marshal, 1995), as well as emerging new types of consumers. From the information-user perspective, DLs need to improve support for sense making activities by providing cognitive tools, offering gateways to knowledge networks and providing support for personalization of content and interaction. From the information-curator perspective, DLs need to improve support for automation of administrative operations, such as automatic detection of resource quality and metadata creation. The new types of consumers—unique to DLs—are distributed computer applications. These applications use DLs as rich topic specific semistructured information repositories. In this scenario, the role of DLs is as ubiquitous information rich platforms that can be used as a springboard by a wide array of applications.

In this chapter, we investigate the future of DLs in terms of the support provided for the end users and distributed computer applications. This consumer focus facilitates contextually grounded research and development which targets real world issues and acts as a mirror for reflecting on research.

We will briefly present our methodology for systematically exploring the future of DLs and then highlight some of the roles a DL can play to support its diverse set of users. A new breed of consumer will be introduced with discussion on how DLs can provide support to this consumer group. Discussion focuses on providing ways to judge the relevance and importance of various DL roles with respect to the contextual requirements.

FUNCTIONAL ROLES OF LIBRARIES

A close inspection of ways in which conventional libraries are used provides insight into their functional roles (e.g., conventional libraries serve as a repository of books, as a group meeting place, and a place to conduct research). In this chapter, we extend these functional roles in order to support changing practices and needs of emerging consumers. Metaphors are used to draw analogies and explore new DL roles for servicing its consumers. Use of metaphor is a well established technique in human computer interaction design (Madsen, 1994), and is particularly used for generating future application designs.

ROLES OF DIGITAL LIBRARIES TO SUPPORT END USERS

In order for a DL to be useful and usable, its users should be able to complete their tasks with relative ease and should feel satisfied with the experience. The complexity and the diversity of user[1] populations and tasks demand interfaces, tools and services that are tailored to specific user needs. Hence a wide variety of DL interfaces, tools, and services will be required to meet these needs and improve user experiences. It is impossible to exhaustively list future DL roles hence we focus here on succinctly describing a few promising DL roles resulting from our research experience.

DIGITAL LIBRARIES AS A SIEVE

The growth in Internet usage[2] (200% between the years 2000–2006[3]) is resulting in an intensifying problem of information overload; consequently people face an ever increasing level of difficulty in filtering desired information from irrelevant information. DLs—as a gateway to the WWW—are addressing some of the information overload is-sues by rigorously cataloging topic-specific high quality online resources and exposing them via sophisticated search and browse interfaces. This approach has been hampered by current practices that rely on manual cataloging processes, per-ceived as necessary for quality assurance, that are not scaleable to the growing needs of information repositories and their users.

Recent research has focused on automating the process of metadata generation (Han Giles, Manavoglu, Zha, Zhang, & Fox, 2003; Liddy, Allen, & Finneran, 2003). Han et al. have used support vector machines (SVM) a supervised machine learning method, to extract 15 metadata fields from headers of computer science research papers. Four of the 15 extracted fields directly correspond to Dublin Core metadata fields (i.e., title, creator, description, and subject), hence mak-ing them useful for a wide variety of cataloging practices. They used word level and sentence level features to train SVM classifiers to extract these metadata fields with an overall accuracy of 93%. In addition to this generic automated metadata creation effort a number of concentrated efforts are targeted towards automating the generation of specific metadata fields with high precision. For example, Newman, Hagedorn, Chemudugunta, and Smyth (2007) have used statistical topic mod-eling techniques coupled with specialized natural language processing techniques to extract subjects from loosely structured documents. Their evalua-tion shows that in 83% of cases the automatically generated topic labels were meaningful and these labels always enhanced the subject metadata field. In another effort researchers have attempted to automatically assign science education content standards to DL resources (Diekema, Yilma-zel, Bailey, Harwell, & Liddy, 2007; Yilmazel, Balasubramanian, Harwell, Bailey, Diekema, & Liddy, 2007).

In the United States, science education stan-dards are statements of learning goals that specify what a student should know, understand or be able to do at different grade levels. Therefore in order to make DL resources more relevant to educa-tional practice, DL resources must be aligned to state and national science educational standards. To automate this alignment process Diekema et al. use hierarchal text classification techniques with a moderate level of success. Although not perfect, automatic alignments between resources and standards can be a great support to human cataloging processes when a large number of potentially relevant standards can be provided as candidates for assignment (Devaul, Diekema, & Ostwald, 2007). In other work researchers have used text summarization techniques to dynamically generate concise descriptions of Web resources to supplement DL search results (McKeown, Elhadad, & Hatzivassiloglou, 2003). In the same vein, work on automated assessment of DL resource quality has been undertaken (Custard & Sumner, 2005) in which quality indicators are identified and used to train a SVM classifier to make binary judgments about resource quality. Evaluation of this classifier shows that it was able to correctly identify the quality of 75 out of 80 resources, producing an accuracy of 94%.

Although automated metadata extraction al-gorithms are in their infancy, promising results of early efforts indicate that as the computational techniques mature, an increasing number of traditional functions performed by information-curators will be automated. This transition will change the responsibilities of information-cura-tors from manually cataloging and organizing collections to managing, tuning and supervising computational applications.

DL cataloging processes generate rich meta-data that underlies sophisticated filtering strate-gies. But an information filter is meaningful only with respect to a particular user information need. Thus relevance and quality of information can have different meanings depending on the user perspective; for example, accuracy of information might be most critical to one user while currency of information most important to another. The problem of multiplicity of the quality and relevance criteria becomes more severe as the diversity of the online user population increases. State of the art DLs have made some progress in this direction by enriching their interfaces with flexible searching and filtering mechanisms. For example, the Digital Library for the Earth System Education (DLESE[4]) provides a keyword-based search interface coupled with options for restricting the search to resource types such as lesson plans or audio-visual materials (Figure 1). The filtering options available in the DLESE interface were designed to support the needs of a particular set of users (i.e., teachers, educators, and students). The National Science Digital Library (NSDL[5]) also provides filtering mechanisms similar to DLESE suitable for education-focused audiences. MathDL[6] provides another interesting example. It uses a standard keyword search interface, but the search results are laid out in a two-column table

Figure 1. Search and filtering options (digital library for earth system education)

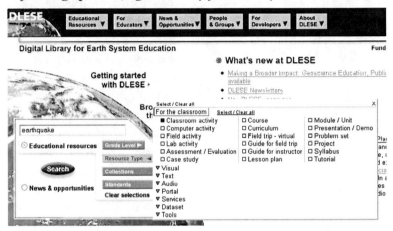

Figure 2. Search result interface for MathDL

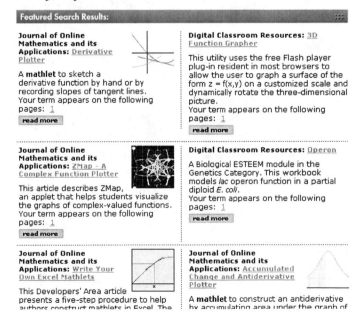

format to support quick assessment of resource relevance. Each cell of the table contains the title, a link, a brief description of the resource, the number of pages in the resources, and a picture depicting the resource. This concise representation helps users to quickly skim and assess the value of resource for the task at hand. A search result set for the keyword function is shown in Figure 2. We anticipate this trend to continue and DLs will provide specialized information filtering interfaces for a diverse set of tasks and user populations.

DIGITAL LIBRARIES AS INFORMATION NETWORKS

The primary information structuring mechanism used by state of the art DLs are topical document collections. Users can either browse or search for information within collections or across collections. Once a relevant document is found users can inspect the document collection to find related documents. This mechanism offers a low level of connectivity between documents and thus has limited navigational and exploratory affordances. Moreover, the hierarchical nature of collections is not readily amenable to modeling complex connectivity patterns implicit in the information e.g. document co-citation patterns, and document co-use patterns extracted for user logs. Recent research have addressed these issues by offering richer information modeling paradigms and visualization interfaces. The NSDL digital repository project (Lagoze, Krafft, Payette, & Jesuroga, 2005) provides a set of rich metadata modeling constructs that allows modeling complex relationships between diverse information types. These metadata primitives enable direct representation of complex connectivity patterns among documents in addition to hierarchal collection structure. Among other uses, this rich hyper-representation of information can be used to search relevant information within and across

DLs and generate novel visualizations of the content.

The Strand Map Service (SMS) (Ahmad, Gu, & Sumner, 2006a, 2006b; Sumner et al., 2005) provides a conceptual browsing interface while ignoring collection and library boundaries. The SMS conceptual browsing interface can be used in two ways: (1) users can find information relevant to particular concept by using it as an index to DLs, and (2) users can browse the DL content by directly interacting with a concept map. Figure 3 shows a conceptual browsing interface for DLESE. In this interface users can directly interact with the concepts, explore interdependencies of concepts, and retrieve materials useful for teaching and learning about a particular concept. An example of a conceptual browsing interface which transcends DL boundaries and uses concepts as common index to different DLs is shown in Figure 4. Here, the small icons at the bottom of each concept provide additional information and supporting educational resources available in digital libraries as well as in a commercial Web site. A user can click on the *exclamation icon* (⊕) to see detailed description of the concept drawn from the Strand Map Service, the *beaker icon* (⚗) to see general science resources drawn from NSDL, the *Earth icon* (🜨) to see Earth science resources drawn from DLESE, the *camera icon* (📷) to see visual & interactive resources drawn from NSDL, the book icon (📕) to see books relevant to teaching the concept drawn from Amazon, and the *do-not-enter icon* (⊘) to see search results from the World Wide Web drawn from Yahoo. The resource listings for each are displayed as pop-ups that can be bookmarked for future access. Additionally, if the user is not satisfied with the quality or suitability of the resources returned clicking on the *search-in-context icon* (🔍) opens a search popup window for further querying. Typing a new keyword and clicking the search button updates the resources that appear in each of the icons for this concept accordingly. The search popup window also facilitates the search process

Figure 3. Concept browsing interface for DLESE

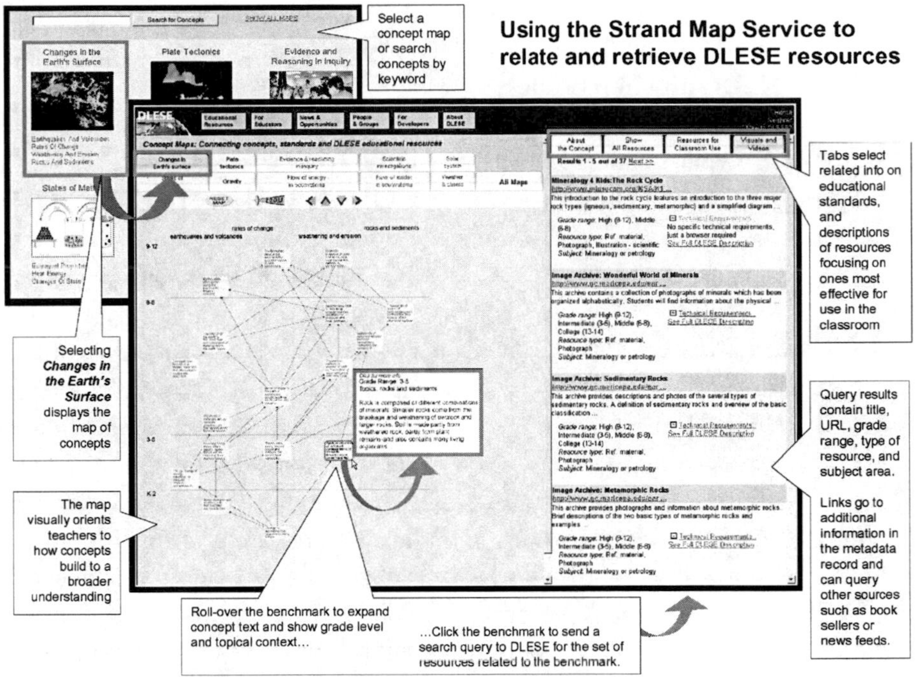

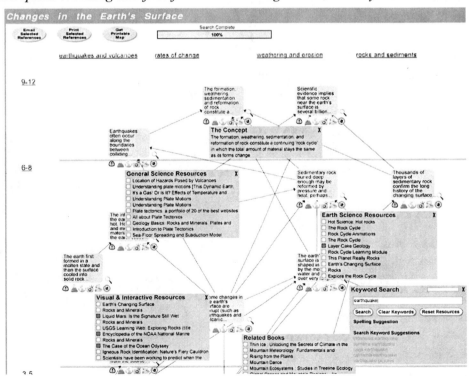

Figure 4. Conceptual browsing interface for Nederland High School library web-site

by providing support for spelling corrections and keyword suggestions.

The rich information modeling and visualization capabilities in the NSDL digital repository and in conceptual browsing interfaces is indicative of the trend towards rich hypermedia information modeling and navigational structures in DL development.

DIGITAL LIBRARIES AS GLUE BETWEEN DIGITAL AND NON-DIGITAL CONTENT

Users often need different or multiple representations of content to understand a particular concept. Emergence of specialized and hybrid DLs that focus on particular content types are addressing this need, in that some DLs focus only on providing single content type[7] while others accumulate and make available a multiplicity of content types[5]. A commonality between these two types of DLs is the digital nature of the content. Although digital content is sufficient for most purposes, it is insufficient for some important content types that are available in conventional libraries. For example, special collections that contain sculptures or artifacts other than documents are of great value to researchers (Levy & Marshal, 1995). One example of such an attempt is the Science Museum of Minnesota[8], (Figure 5) which offers a textual description of an artifact along with an image. In order to highlight salient features of this artifact the translation of inscriptions engraved in the artifact are dynamically superimposed on the image when the mouse rolls over a particular section.

Other than few ad hoc attempts at integrating physical artifacts with digital medium, there has not been a comprehensive attempt to take DLs beyond the boundaries of digital medium. As a consequence not a single model exists that aims to integrate non-digital content into DLs. In the future, DLs will have to take a proactive stance to develop new models that bridge the gap between digital and non-digital content to enable richer forms of content types and interactions.

DIGITAL LIBRARIES AS CONTEXTUAL ENCYCLOPEDIAS

The global information economy is highly dependent on the availability of right information in the right format at the right time and at the right location. In the previous sections, we have touched upon the issue of the right information in the right format. The issues of location and time are a challenge for conventional libraries however the DL paradigm brings the information to the users when and where it is needed. Web-accessible DLs that can be accessed anywhere, anytime using a desktop computer increase user access significantly. The next logical step is to further expand the meaning of anywhere and anytime, such that DLs become ubiquitous. Two promising directions to accomplish this are: (1) making DL interfaces available through multiplicity of devices (e.g., mobile phones and handheld PDAs), and (2)

Figure 5. An artifact displayed at the online site of Science Museum of Minnesota

Cuneiform Collection

Over five thousand years ago, the people dwelling in southern Iraq invented one of the world's earliest systems of writing. They did not do so in order to write stories or letters, nor yet to publicize the deeds of gods and kings, though soon enough writing came to be used for those purposes. They invented writing because they needed a means of accounting for the receipt and distribution of resources. For their numbers had grown and their society had become complex in the alluvial plains of the lower Tigris and Euphrates rivers, an environment which required attentive management in order to sustain a large, agriculture-based civilization. Hence the need for organizing labor and resources; hence the need for accounting and accountability. The accounting system the people of ancient Iraq developed comprised both a method of recording language in writing, and a method of authenticating and authorizing records and transactions, through sealing them with personal or official seals.

SMM 7: Roll cursor over lines to see translation.

making the DL interfaces context aware, e.g. if a user needs information about the Eiffel Tower while standing at the base of it, he might need information about the average wait time in the ticket line, but if a user needs information about the Eiffel Tower while talking to a friend in Japan he might need historical information. A number of digital library and related research initiatives are attempting to address the demands for context and location-aware information by exploiting the increasing power of mobile computational devices. For example some of the recent research work on DLs have looked at hand held device interfaces to DLs (Naaman, Song, Paepcke, & Garcia-Molina, 2004; Sharples, Corlett, & Westmancott, 2002). Other lines of research are investigating the social and context aware dimensions of computer and information use (Reid, Hull, Melamed, & Speakman, 2003; Sharples, Taylor, & Vavoula, 2007; Tamminen, Oulasvirta, & Toiskallio, 2004; Theng, Tan, Lim, Zhang, Goh, Chatterjea, et al., 2007). We anticipate this trend to continue to the extent that handheld mobile devices will become major consumers of DL information. This conviction is also supported by the increasing number of mobile devices sold in the U.S. (sale of Web-enabled mobile phones grew by 75% in 2005).

DIGITAL LIBRARIES AS A PERSONAL WORK ORGANIZER

People like to collect information as they perform knowledge tasks over a period of time. An example of this phenomenon is bookmarks saved by users in their Web-browsers. Hundreds of bookmarks are collected, updated, and revisited. Recent developments in DLs have focused on personal digital collections. A variety of generic tools and information organization abstractions are provided by personal DLs, which mostly fall short of supporting task specific performances. On the other hand little research has been carried out in supporting task specific performances given the wide variety of

tasks people are engaged in (Cousins, Paepcke, Wingord, Bier, & Pier, 1997; Meyyappan, Al-Hawamdeh, & Foo, 2002; Vakkari, 2001). For example, the work by Vakkari (2001) investigated the information needs associated with each stage in writing a master's research proposal. He found that during the three task stages different types of information were used by the students. In the pre-focus phase general background information was most relevant, in the focus formation phase faceted background information was most relevant, and in the post-focus phase more specific information was sought after. Similarly, work by Meyyappan et al. (2002) investigated the task of writing a master's dissertation by conducting interviews and focus groups with faculty and students. By analyzing these data they were able to do comprehensive task decomposition and articulate subtasks and the information needs for each of the subtasks within the dissertation writing process. Using this hierarchal subtask model they created an interface to contextualize and align information to the needs of specific tasks. These studies and systems represent a growing interest in contextualizing DL information in a more task-oriented manner. We therefore envision that task-specific support by DLs in the realm of personal DLs will be the next development in the evolving DL world.

ROLES OF DIGITAL LIBRARIES TO SUPPORT DISTRIBUTED COMPUTATIONAL APPLICATIONS

Distributed computational applications are the most exciting types of consumers brought into the library world because of the advent of network technology. Presently most DLs are focused on creating portals for human interaction; hence little attention has been paid to making the same information available for consumption by distributed computational applications. This trend is likely to change as applications start to mediate and contextualize information for use in every day activities. Here we briefly mention two promising roles of DLs for supporting a variety of online applications.

DIGITAL LIBRARIES AS AN INFORMATION WAREHOUSE FOR CYBER-INFRASTRUCTURE

Cyber-infrastructure is an evolving concept with no clear definition; but most definitions of cyber-infrastructure share the common aspects of e-science, e-research, e-learning, grid computing and networked environment (Sumner, Marlino, & Wright, 2004). An immense knowledge base is a prerequisite to supporting this rich set of distributed computational applications. DLs have the potential to fuel the components of cyber-infrastructure by exposing collections of structured information. The textual information contained in DL collections can form the substrate for artificial intelligence techniques such as statistical natural language processing and machine learning for a variety of purposes such as data mining, information extraction, question answering, and construction of broad knowledge bases. These new kinds of computational uses of DL collections will challenge the collection curation practices that are currently geared towards serving human consumers. Although it is hard to predict the exact nature of the changes that will be required of the DL collection curation and cataloging processes, we anticipate that some of the knowledge engineering practices prevalent in the artificial intelligence community will be infused in the collection curation processes. Access to such a diverse set of primary information in the DL collections and the information derived from them will present a challenge to disseminate and share this information. Due to the diversity of cyber-infrastructure components, we anticipate an initial proliferation of structured information formats and information exchange protocols.

Through maturation, the DL community will come to consensus on supporting a standardized core set of services that will become the cornerstone of cyber-infrastructure.

DIGITAL LIBRARIES AS A SEMIFORMAL KNOWLEDGE MODEL FOR INTELLIGENT ONLINE APPLICATIONS

To a large extent, intelligent applications depend on formal knowledge models. Primarily the semantic Web community has undertaken the task of representing the WWW in a computation-friendly format with the help of formal ontologies. However, this approach appears not very scalable and is already challenged by folksonomies (Friedman, 2005). In comparison, DLs provide a middle ground for intelligent applications. These applications can use the semiformal and informal knowledge representations from DLs to inform their intelligent behavior. For instance, the knowledge organization service offered by the Strand Map Service (Sumner, Ahmad, Bhushan, Gu, Molina, Willard, et al., 2005) can be used to generate an intelligent concept-based recommender system. Summary Street is a another example where DL resources can be used effectively (Wade-Stein & Kintsch, 2004). Summary Street is an intelligent tutoring environment built to provide assistance in summary writing tasks. It uses latent semantic analysis to provide high level content-related feedback to students during the summarization process. In order to build appropriate latent semantic space, it requires a large corpus of relevant textual information. DL collections are well suited to provide the required textual content for systems like Summary Street. In more recent work researchers have used DL resources to generate knowledge maps for representing concepts in scientific domains (Ahmad, Chica, Butcher, Sumner, & Martin, 2007; Chica, Ahmad, Sumner, Martin, & Butcher, in press).

In this research, a multidocument summarization technique was used to extract educationally relevant domain science concepts from a set of DL resources. These concepts were then connected to form a knowledge map using lexical chains and machine learning techniques. This automatically generated domain knowledge map was then used successfully to diagnose misconceptions in student knowledge maps. In addition to diagnosing student misconceptions this application dynamically selected DL resources to provide instruction for each of the misconceptions. Considering this and related work, we anticipate an ever increasing use of DL resources by intelligent applications.

DISCUSSION

Metaphor analysis of DL roles indicates that DLs can play a much larger role in the knowledge economy than at present. The key to unlocking this potential is to understand the theoretical and pragmatic limitations of current DLs and systematically extend them in new directions. The metaphorical analysis technique and the consumer focus adopted in this chapter grounds the future research agenda of DLs in the context of their use. Our methodology has highlighted two types of equally important DL consumers that have very specific needs. We see the interaction between these consumers to be complementary and mutually reinforcing, where the input and output of one consumer type can be used and reused by the other consumer types. For instance, DL resource access logs can be used to train algorithms that can predict successful user interaction patterns and hence provide guidance to new users when performing a similar task. In addition to the synergistic interaction between the human consumers and computational consumers of DLs, different roles of DLs are not necessarily mutually exclusive but interact in complex ways. Even with this complex interaction between DL functional roles we can assess the importance of

certain roles by judging its core value or consumer demand. Core value of a DL role can be estimated by enumerating how many other roles depend on the proper functioning of this role. It is our view that DLs as information sieves are a critical role because almost all other roles rely on the proper functioning of this role. From a human consumer perspective DLs as a contextual encyclopedia and DLs as personal work organizers are key roles that should be supported by virtue of their use in a wide variety of situations.

In order to fully realize the DL functional roles outlined in this chapter, as well as others, we believe that the real challenge lies in the development of research programs that can explore the intricate details of enacting these roles. Human centered research is needed to understand the information and interaction needs of human consumers for different activities, tasks and contexts. A parallel research agenda is also needed to leverage existing artificial intelligence techniques to make effective use of DL resources in distributed computational applications. In all cases this research must prove its value in the knowledge economy by rigorous multifaceted evaluation in real world situations.

CONCLUSION

In this chapter, we have presented an overview of the state of the art of digital libraries. Our analysis shows that contemporary digital libraries hold great potential for further research and development if we recognize and extend the limitations posed by the conventional library metaphor. Additionally, we propose a systematic way to extend the digital library research agenda through consumer focused functional role analysis.

REFERENCES

Ahmad, F., Chica, S.D.L., Butcher, K., Sumner, T., & Martin, J.H. (2007). Towards automatic conceptual personalization tools. In *Proceedings of the ACM/IEEE-CS joint conference on Digital libraries (JCDL)*. Vancouver, Canada.

Ahmad, F., Gu, Q., & Sumner, T. (2006a). Concept space interchange protocol: A protocol for concept map based resource discovery in educational digital libraries. In *Proceedings of the European Conference on Digital Libraries (ECDL)*. Alicante, Spain.

Ahmad, F., Gu, Q., & Sumner, T. (2006b). A technological infrastructure for developing curriculum based on learning progressions. In *Proceedings of World Conference on Educational Multimedia, Hypermedia & Telecommunications (Ed-Media)*. Orlando, FL.

Chica, S.D.L., Ahmad, F., Sumner, T., Martin, J.H., & Butcher, K. (in press). Computational foundations for personalizing instruction with digital libraries. *International Journal of Digital Libraries, Special Issue on Digital Libraries and Education*.

Cousins, S.B., Paepcke, A., Wingord, T., Bier, E.A., & Pier, K. (1997). The digital library integrate task environment (DLITE). In *Proceedings of the ACM Digital Library Conference*. Philadelphia, PA, USA.

Custard, M., & Sumner, T. (2005). Using machine learning to support quality judgments. *D-Lib Magazine, 11*.

Devaul, H., Diekema, A., & Ostwald, J. (2007). *Computer-assisted assignment of educational standards using natural language processing.* Unpublished technical report.

Diekema, A.R., Yilmazel, O., Bailey, J., Harwell, S.C., & Liddy, E.D. (2007). Standards alignment for metadata assignment. In *Proceedings of the ACM/IEEE-CS joint conference on Digital libraries (JCDL)*. Vancouver, Canada.

Friedman, P.K. (2005). Folksonomy. *Anthropology News, 46*, 38–38.

Han, H., Giles, C.L., Manavoglu, E., Zha, H., Zhang, Z., & Fox, E.A. (2003). Automatic document metadata extraction using support vector machines. In *Proceedings of the ACM/IEEE-CS joint conference on Digital libraries (JCDL)*. Houston, TX.

Lagoze, C., Krafft, D.B., Payette, S., & Jesuroga, S. (2005). What is a digital library anymore, anyway? *D-Lib Magazine, 11*.

Levy, D.M., & Marshal, C.C. (1995). Going digital: A look at assumptions underlying digital libraries. *Communications of the ACM, 38*, 77–84.

Liddy, E.D., Allen, E.E., & Finneran, C.M. (2003). MetaTest: Evaluation of metadata from generation to use. In *Proceedings of the ACM/IEEE-CS joint conference on Digital libraries (JCDL)*. Houston, TX.

Lynch, C. (2005). Where do we go from here? *D-Lib Magazine, 11*.

Madsen, K.H. (1994). A guide to metaphorical design. *Communications of the ACM, 37*, 57–62.

McKeown, K.R., Elhadad, N., & Hatzivassiloglou, V. (2003). Leveraging a common representation for personalized search and summarization in a medical digital library. In *Proceedings of the ACM/IEEE-CS joint conference on Digital libraries (JCDL)*. Houston, TX.

Meyyappan, N., Al-Hawamdeh, S., & Foo, S. (2002). Task based design of a digital work environment (DWE) for an academic community. *Information Research, 7*(2).

Naaman, M., Song, Y.J., Paepcke, A., & Garcia-Molina, H. (2004). Automatic organization for digital photographs with geographic coordinates. In *Proceedings of the ACM/IEEE-CS joint conference on Digital libraries (JCDL)*. Tuson, AZ.

Newman, D., Hagedorn, K., Chemudugunta, C., & Smyth, P. (2007). Subject metadata enrichment using statistical topic models. In *Proceedings of* the *ACM/IEEE-CS joint conference on Digital libraries (JCDL)*. Vancouver, Canada.

Reid, J., Hull, R., Melamed, T., & Speakman, D. (2003). Schminky: The design of a cafe based digital experience. *Personal and Ubiquitous Computing, 7*(3–4), 197–202.

Sharples, M., Corlett, D., & Westmancott, O. (2002). The design and Implementation of a mobile learning resource. In *Personal and Ubiquitous Computing, 6*, 220–234.

Sharples, M., Taylor, J., & Vavoula, G. (2007). A theory of learning for the mobile age. In R. Andrews, & C. Haythornthwaite (Eds.), *Handbook of Elearning Research* (pp. 221–247). Sage Publications.

Sumner, T., Ahmad, F., Bhushan, S., Gu, Q., Molina, F., Willard, S., et al. (2005). Linking learning goals and educational resources through interactive concept map visualizations. *International Journal on Digital Libraries, 5*, 18–24.

Sumner, T., Marlino, M., & Wright, M. (2004). *Geoscience education and cyberinfrastructure workshop report*. Boudler: UCAR.

Tamminen, S., Oulasvirta, A., & Toiskallio, K. (2004). Understanding the mobile context. In *Personal and Ubiquitous Computing, 8*(2), 135–143.

Theng, Y.-L., Tan, K.-L., Lim, E.-P., Zhang, J., Goh, D.H.-L., Chatterjea, K., et al. (2007). Mobile g-portal supporting collaborative sharing and learning in geography fieldwork: An empirical study. In *Proceedings of the ACM/IEEE-CS joint conference on Digital libraries (JCDL)*. Vancouver, Canada.

Vakkari, P. (2001). A theory of the task based information retrieval process: A summary and generalization of a longitudinal study. *Journal of Documentation, 57*(1), 44–60.

Wade-Stein, D., & Kintsch, E. (2004). Summary street: Interactive computer support for writing. *Cognition and Instruction, 22*(3), 333–362.

Yilmazel, O., Balasubramanian, N., Harwell, S.C., Bailey, J., Diekema, A. R., & Liddy, E.D. (2007). Text categorization for aligning educational standards. In *Proceedings of the 40th Hawaii International Conference on System Sciences*. Big Island, HI.

KEY TERMS

Cataloging: The process of creating and assembling metadata about a document.

Concept Map: Concept maps are graphical knowledge representations that are composed to two components: (1) Nodes: represent the concepts, and (2) Links: connect concepts using a relationship.

Cyber-Infrastructure: Cyber-infrastructure describes new research environments in which the capabilities of advanced computing tools are readily available to researchers and learners in an interoperable network.

Hypermedia: An extension to hypertext that links multimedia elements in addition to text elements.

Information-Curators: An individual who organizes and manages information and services in order to fulfill information-user needs.

Information-Users: An individual who makes use of information in any way to complete a task.

Metadata: Metadata is structured or descriptive information about a document. Metadata can be created by the document creator or by a cataloger.

Metaphorical Design: A software design methodology that utilize metaphors for eliciting user requirements and representing system functionality in the user interface.

ENDNOTES

1   Here, the user encompass information-users as well as information-curators
2   Here, Internet usage is used in broader term of publishing and consuming information
3   Internet world statistics (http://www.Internetworldstats.com/stats.htm)
4   Digital Library for Earth System Education (http://www.dlese.org)
5   National Science Digital Library (http://nsdl.org)
6   The MAA Mathematical Sciences Digital Library (http://mathdl.maa.org/mathDL/)
7   Harvard Smithsonian Digital Video Library (http://hsdvl.org)
8   Science Museum of Minnesota (http://www.smm.org/anthropology/cuneiform/)

Chapter LV
A Review of Progress in Digital Library Education

Yongqing Ma
Victoria University of Wellington, New Zealand

Warwick Clegg
Victoria University of Wellington, New Zealand

Ann O'Brien
Loughborough University, UK

ABSTRACT

In this entry, we review the history, development and current status of digital library (DL) courses and programmes now being offered, mainly by universities/institutions with accredited programmes or courses by CILIP (the Chartered Institute of Library and Information Professionals) and ALA (American Library Association), and review the latest thinking and potential curriculum developments on the topic of how best to educate and train digital librarians. Trends in digital library education (DLE) are presented including:

- *Data from four major and earlier studies relating to DLE,*
- *Main survey date: institutions offering DL programmes /courses as at the end of October 2006.*
- *Recent developments of DL curriculum (potential standard models) as at the end of June 2007.*

BACKGROUND: BRIEF HISTORY OF DIGITAL LIBRARY EDUCATION (DLE)

The history of digital libraries (DLs) themselves can be characterized as short and volatile, and DLE history is even shorter. The DL is a new form of managing the knowledge record and cultural heritage on both small and large scales. Thousands of digital collections continue to be created around the world. Large amounts of research effort and money have been devoted to

DL research throughout the world over the past decade, but very little on research regarding how Librarians may best be educated and equipped to work in the digital domain.

DL education can be defined as the programmes or courses specific to the training and educating of students who will be able to build and manage DLs after graduation. It is evident that there is already a shortage of supply, a lack of information professionals with the right combination of skills, and a particularly serious shortage in specialist areas such as digital librarians and digital recording managers (Fisher, 2002; Wilder, 2002). DLE started sometime in the middle of the 1990s as a consequence of the fast development of DLs. Spink and Cool (1999) thought that DLE programmes were "choices for rationale," and that DLE "reacts with a time lag to both research and practical developments in DL." Our latest studies (Ma, O'Brien, & Clegg, 2006, 2007) on DLE show there is a progression from a stage where educators are exploring basic questions such as "why and what to teach about digital libraries?" to more focused academic questions like "how and what is best practice in DLE?"

It is well known that the term "digital library (DL)" means different things to different people (Arms 2005; Borgman, 1999). Many academics in DLE have been, and are still, struggling to construct a suitable or standard curriculum for their students (Borgman, 2001; IU & UIUC, 2004; Jacso, 2000). DLE is faced with many questions and it is clear that there is a pressing need to develop suitable education programmes to train and equip new librarians and information professionals who will be capable and comfortable in working in a digital environment. The combination of social trends and technology is here the push for educational developments.

Most DL courses have been taught either in Library and Information Science (LIS) or Computer Science (CS) programmes. It is noted that DL programmes or courses offered by CS are now based on the Computing Curriculum (CC) 2001 Information Management (IM) Areas (defining curricula by ACM & IEEE-CS for CS). In contrast, the DL curriculum offered by LIS has varied more widely from time-to-time and place-to-place. There has been little agreement as to the contents and scope of these programmes or courses offered by LIS (Rose, 2001; Saracevic & Dalbello, 2001), and a lack of cooperation between institutions, or between LIS and CS disciplines until late 2005.

There was little or no funding for education in DL (Spink & Cool, 1999) in the last century. However, there are some encouraging changes in the past few years. For example, the Institute of Museum and Library Services (IMLS) in the USA has funded several projects in digital library education as part of their "Librarians for the 21st Century Programme" in late 2004.

There has been significant progress in the development of DL curricula from the LIS perspective. For example, Indiana University and the University of Illinois at Urbana—Champaign (IU & UIUC, 2004) were awarded a grant from IMLS on a collaborative DLE project. This grant is aimed at "building up an effective digital library curriculum through library school and academic library partnership." Progress in this three-year project was presented, in at least three workshops held with the Joint Conference on Digital Libraries (JCDL) in June 2005, 2006 and 2007 (Brancolini & Mostafa, 2006; Dolan, 2005; IU & UIUC, 2007). At the same time, other library schools with grants from IMLS from the Laura Bush 21st Century Librarians Programme, such as Pittsburgh and Drexel, are also exploring aspects of the development of DL curricula.

The National Science Foundation (NSF) in the USA awarded a three-year grant of over half a million dollars in 2006 to Virginia Tech (VT) and the University of North Carolina (UNC) to develop a digital library curriculum. The project (VT, 2006) is titled "Collaborative Research: Curriculum Development: Digital Libraries," and is led by academics from CS at VT and LIS at UNC. It is perhaps the first formal cooperation in this field between CS and LIS and between institutions, and is a most welcome and necessary development.

THE CURRENT STATUS IN DLE

It is clear that the topic of DL education is a new and fast moving one and could involve several subject domains. The evidence and data collected here is mainly based on a literature review and online information posted by educational institutions in the DL sector. From the LIS perspective, the Web sites searched here were mainly those maintained by institutions with ALA accredited programmes in the USA and Canada and those universities with library study programmes ac-

credited by CILIP in the UK. All URLs were valid at the end of October 2006. The detailed data collected in our study can be found in Ma (2006), and the majority of the data has also been checked and updated at the end of October 2006. Tables 1 and 2 summarise the position at that date, incorporating data from Spink and Cool (1999), Saracevic and Dalbello (2001), Liu (2004), Ma (2006) and Ma, O'Brien, and Clegg, (2006).

Our recent study (Ma, O'Brien, & Clegg, 2006) and updated data indicate that the number of institutions offering DL programmes or courses is still growing. It is notable that there have been some changes in the institutions offering courses in DL. In some cases, the content of an earlier DL course has been fully integrated to a current standard Master's programme, in recognition that DL material is moving into mainstream library education.

Table 1. Summary of the number of institutions offering DLE from 1999 to 2006

Year of the Survey	1999	2001	2004	2006#	2006*
LIS-CILIP***	1	1	2	4	4
LIS-ALA****	10	15(+32)**	21	32	34
CS & Some LIS (not CILIP or ALA)	4(CS) & 4LIS	2(CS) & 2(LIS)	8(CS) & 9(LIS)	7(CS) & 8(LIS)	6(CS) 8(LIS)
In Total	19	20 (+32)**	40	51	52

Data based on the reference of Ma (2006) as at the end of January 2006.

* Data based on the reference of Ma, O'Brien & Clegg (2006) as at the end of October 2006.

**DL contents integrated in other courses.

*** CILIP – the Chartered Institute of Library and Information Professionals.

**** ALA – American Library Association.

Table 2. Types of offerings at the beginning of 2006

No of Institutions	LIS-CILIP	LIS-ALA	CS	LIS-Others	Total No
Independent DL Programmes	2	3	1	3	8
CAS* & other Concentration or Specialization	0	11	0	3	14
Integrated DL courses in standard LIS or CS programmes	2	18	6	3	29
Number of DL (in total)	4	32	7	8	51

* CAS is Certificate of Advanced Study

KEY RESEARCH QUESTIONS IN DL EDUCATION

Why Teach about DL?

The major reasons for teaching DL are recognised as follows:

- There is a clear demand for the hiring of digital librarians in digital information management, and this is a worldwide trend;
- There is increasing demand for the development of educational DLs and other types of managed digital collections such as Institutional Repositories.

The increasing funds available for DL education show progressive recognition of the points above. Hence there is a situation of growing demand for information professionals specializing in digital information management and increasing provision of courses and programmes (e.g., Borgman, 2001). There is consequently a pressing need for educators to develop a clear understanding of the essential components of a programme in DLE.

What to Teach about DL?

Many educators from LIS believe that "defining digital librarianship is a complex area and the knowledge and skills needed to perform DL jobs are difficult to acquire in the graduate library school curriculum" (e.g., IU & UIUC, 2004). It is also clear that there are significant differences in entry-level knowledge, disciplinary values and vocabularies, and potential employer expectations between CS and LIS.

It is noted that the DL curriculum areas from LIS and CS are still rather different. That offered by LIS provides a wide range of modules covering many aspects of DL, such as creating, maintaining, evaluating and developing DLs. Curricula from the CS side appear more specialized

in computer-concentrated topics related to DL. But the contents of DL education programmes provided from both professional sides do have a degree of commonality. For example, courses such as information storage and retrieval, computer-human interaction and user interface are included in both curricula (Ma, 2006).

Other studies have also pointed out that there is a strong focus on systems, structures and processes in CS, but LIS is perhaps a "meta-discipline concerned with documentary products and activities of other disciplines" (Wildemuth, 2006). Detailed analysis of these differences in DL curriculum have also been summarised in previous surveys and in the literature (Coleman, 2002; Liu, 2004; Pomerantz, et al., 2006b, 2007; Rose, 2001). It remains the case, however, that there is currently no widely-accepted formal curriculum framework for digital librarianship. Hence academics in library and information science (LIS) are in a position to "re-invent the wheel" as they consider how to incorporate all of the DL technologies to their DLE, and no formal widely accepted framework of DLE in LIS side has yet been established. This is a particular difficulty in the traditionally one-year UK Masters programmes in LIS. Note that comparisons here are difficult to make with complete accuracy as some qualifications are based around full-scale independent programmes, whereas other programmes are of a more traditional structure but have modules on DLs incorporated.

In the past decade, individual educators from LIS have developed significant anecdotal knowledge of what topics are critical to DLE and what topics are not (Coleman, 2002; Liu, 2004; Rose, 2001; Saracevic & Dalbello, 2001; Spink & Cool,1999). For example, Liu (2004) suggested that a curriculum designed for digital libraries should include these areas: history and definitions of digital library, building and organizing digital libraries, integrating and interoperating digital information, policy and legal issues in digital libraries, interface design and services, digital library evaluation, collaboration and global perspectives on digital libraries, and the future of digital libraries in society. However, little formal effort has been expended on understanding the knowledge requirements in DL curriculum design or structure until very recently, say from 2005 (Dolan, 2005).

Some academics from CS such as Fox and colleagues (Fox & Urs, 2002; Goncalves et al., 2004) have developed a formal model that they referred to as 5S (structures, scenarios, spaces, societies and streams) for teaching DL based on CC 2001IM, a joint effect of ACM and IEEE-CS defining curricula for CS programs which includes DLs as one of 14 knowledge modules under Information Management.

With a new grant from NSF this curriculum model is now being developed further together with academics from a LIS background (Pomerantz, et al., 2006a; VT, 2006). In this very first codiscipline and coinstitutional study in DLE, UNC-VT (Pomerantz et al., 2006b) identified and suggested a set of 10 core DL topics (Overview; Collection Development; Digital Objects; Information/Knowledge Organization; Architecture [agents, mediators]; Space; Services [searching, linking, browsing, annotating, and so on]; Archiving, Preservation, Integrity; DLE & Research) and 34 related topics, which are central to the curriculum in LIS programs. They studied the most frequently-assigned books, journals, journal articles, and authors in DL courses and found that varied from the place-to-place. In one of their latest studies, (Pomerantz et al., 2007) reading assignments across CS courses on DL and DLs related topics have been analyzed, and even less consistency found compared with those of LIS programs. It was also not surprising to find that LIS and CS programs view some DL-related topics differently; in particular, the approaches to Architecture and Service differ. They suggested that an interdisciplinary curriculum development should make clear these trends and help academics decide how best to structure and shape DL courses and curricula.

Table 3. DL -related modules in some LIS programmes outside North America

No	University	Type #	Taught Credits ♦	DL Credits
1	City (UK)	2C	120	30 (25%)
2	Leeds Metropolitan (UK)**	2C	120	40 (33%)
3	London Metropolitan (UK)*	1C + 1E	120 ***	60 (50%)
4	Strathclyde (UK)*	4 C	120***	85 (63%)
5	UCL (UK)	1E	120	20 (17%)
6	Hong Kong (China)	1E	60	12 (20%)
7	NTU (Singapore)	1E	20***	4 (20%)
8	University of Malaya (Malaysia)	1E	24	3 (13%)
9	QUT (Australia)**	2 E	144***	24 (17%)
10	VUW (NZ)	1C + 1E	150***	30 (20%)

* Independent programmes for students specialising in DL.
**Certificate courses for students specialising in DL.
***Detailed course syllabus is on line.
 # Type of Module: C—Core; E—Elective;
♦ Taught Credits – Credits points (in total) required for the taught part of the studies (excludes project and dissertation);
UCL - University of Central London; NTU – Nanyang Technological University;
QUT – Queensland University of Technology; VUW – Victoria University of Wellington

In one of our latest studies (Ma, O'Brien, & Clegg, 2007), we used this suggested standard (UNC-VT) set of categories as a starting point and normalised our data to investigate the commonality/diversity of programme structure between ten institutions outside North America which offer DL education in their library schools. This study indicated that the DL module-based credit weighting for the sample set of library schools considered here varied from 13% to 63%

Table 4. DL topics percentage coverage (Core topics and related topics adapted from reference [Pomerantz et al., 2006a])

No	Core Topics	Related Topics	LM	ST	VUW	QUT	LB
1	Overview		10	10	10	10	
2	Collection Development	a-Digitization b-Doc. & E-Publishing-mark-up	10	10	10	10	10
3	Digital Objects	a-Text resources b-Multimedia c-File documents transformation	10	10	6.7	6.7	6.7
4	Information/ Knowledge Organisation	a-Metadata, harvesting cataloguing b-Ontology, classification, categorization; c-Vocabulary control d-Bibliographic, bibliometrics, Webmetrics	10	10	10	7.5	10
5	Architecture	a-Interoperability b-Sustainability c-Interface design, usability assessment d-Search engines & IR e-Identifiers, handles, DOI, PURL f-Info summarisation, visualization g-Recommender system h-Applications i -Web-publishing j-Security	10	10	5	4	2
6	Spaces	a-Storage b-Repositories, archives		5	5		
7	Services	a-Info. needs, relevance, evaluation b-Search strategy, info seeking behaviour, user modelling c-Reference services d-Routing, community, filtering e-Sharing, networking, Interfacing	10	10	8	8	6
8	Archiving, preservation, integrity			10	10	10	10
9	Project Management	a-DL development for specific domain b-DL project examples c-DL evaluation d-Legal issues e-Cost; economic issues f-Social Issues g-Future DLs	10	10	8.5	7	5.8
10	DLE & Research		10	10	10	10	
	Total coverage (%)	% of core & related topics (if 10% per core model)	~80	~85	~83	~73	~50

LM – London Metropolitan University (UK); LB—Loughborough University (UK) ST— Strathclyde University (UK); QUT – Queensland University of Technology (Australia); VUW – Victoria University of Wellington (New Zealand) (excluding project or dissertation work). This is summarised in Table 3 below. Considering (where online information permits comparison) the coverage of a proposed standard set of DL topics and sub-topics, we find that this is at 80% or above for three of the five schools studied (see Table 4), Loughborough University (LB) is no lower than 50% for a programme that does not have a specific focus on DL topics.

How to teach about DL?

It is critical for every successful education programme in DL to have a complete and up-to-date understanding of the skills and knowledge needed to create and manage DLs, and to teach students in a systematic and comprehensive way. However, the level of faculty, the background of students, and the type of DL programmes and courses can vary considerably from institution to institution.

With the recent grants from IMLS, NSF, and other professional organisations, there has been significant progress in exploring best practice in DL education at individual institutions, and this aspect is continuing to develop rapidly. For example, our latest researches indicate that most educational institutions have recognized the need for a combination of theoretical knowledge and practical experience in digital library education. Almost every DL course now includes some degree of hands-on research work in its grading and assignments, and welcome cross-disciplinary and cross-institutional cooperation has emerged in DLE. Further research programmes on DLE are progressing (Brancolini & Mostafa, 2006) and likely to lead to a consensus view of an optimum pedagogical framework.

FUTURE TRENDS

- The number of institutions offering DLE is still growing. Many of these are currently programmes or courses accredited by CILIP (22%, 4/18) in the UK and ALA (61%, 34/56) in the USA and Canada.

- About 44% of institutions in the LIS sector (16/36) with ALA and CILIP accreditation are offering fully independent DL programmes, across a range of levels – and especially at Certificate level. The levels here are expected to broaden, from undergraduate to Ph.D.

- There are increasing opportunities for funding to develop new initiatives in DLE, especially in the USA.

- There will be more opportunities for students from different backgrounds to enter postgraduate programmes specialising in Digital Libraries, driven by shortages of professionals in this area.

- There will be increased in-service training (short or modular courses) for existing librarians to facilitate their career development in digital competence.

- The DLE curriculum design and focused teaching areas are progressively more systematic and comprehensive. Most DL programmes are now based on a combination of theory and practice, and a standard, optimized model of best practice in DLE is likely to emerge eventually.

- Educators in the DL area are working increasingly closely with practitioners in DL developments. Cross-disciplinary and cross-institutional collaboration on DL curriculum developments will continue to increase, and both a framework and much common core material will be agreed for DL education within the next few years.

- Professional bodies will have a continuing, and likely growing, role in accrediting the structure and content of DL programmes, and this quality control will give future employers confidence in the capabilities of students who graduate from these programmes.

CONCLUSION

The latest evidence on DLE indicates that it is increasingly seen to be highly beneficial for educators worldwide to work more closely with DL practitioners, and for there to be more opportunities to share curriculum development to arrive at a common understanding of core and elective educational needs in this important new area. A "standard" DL educational model is likely to be based on a combination of theoretical knowledge and real working experience in DLs, together with some integrated core modules from LIS and CS programmes.

REFERENCES

Arms, W.Y. (2005) A Viewpoint Analysis of the Digital Library. *D-Lib Magazine, 11*(7/8). Retrieved October, 8, from http://www.dlib.org/dlib/july05/arms/07arms.html

Borgman, C. (1999). What are Digital Libraries? Competing vision. *Information Processing and Management 35*(3), 227-243.

Borgman. C. (2001). Where is the Librarian in the Digital Library? *Communication of the ACM. 44*(5). 66-68.

Brancolini, K.R. and Mostafa, J (2006). JCDL 2006 Workshop Report. *D-Lib Magazine, 12*(7/8). Retrieved October 25, 2006, from: http://www.dlib.org/dlib/july06/brancolini/07brancolini.html

Coleman, A. (2002). The Road Ahead for Education in Digital libraries. *D-Lib Magazine, 8*(7/8). Retrieved August 6, from http://www.dlib.org/dlib/july02/coleman/07coleman.html

Dolan, M. (2005). JCDL Workshop Summary. *D-Lib Magazine, 11*(7/8). Retrieved October 10, 2005, from http://www.dlib.org/dlib/july05/07inbrief.html#DOLAN

Fisher, W. (2002). The Electronic Resources Librarian Position: a Public Services Phenomenon. *Library Collections, Acquisitions, & Technical Services, 27*(1), 3-17.

Fox, E.A. & Urs, S.R. (2002). Digital Libraries. *Annual Review of Information Science and Technology Volume.* 36, 503-589.

Goncalves, M. et al., (2004). Streams, Structures, Spaces, Scenarios, Societies (5S): A Formal Model for Digital Libraries. *ACM Transactions on Information Systems.* 22. 270-312.

IU & UIUC, (2004) Indiana University and University of Illinois at Urbana-Champaign, Proposal for Project on 'Building an Effective Digital Library Curriculum through Library School and Academic Library Partnership'. Retrieved October 5, 2005 from http://lair.indiana.edu/research/dlib/proposal.pdf

IU & UIUC, (2007). Indiana University and University of Illinois at Urbana-Champaign. JCDL 2007 Workshop, Retrieved July 8, from http://lair.indiana.edu/research/dlib/jcdl07/index.php

Jacso, P. (2000). What is Digital Librarianship? *Computers in Libraries.* 20(1), 54-55.

Liu, Y.Q. (2004). Is the Education on Digital Libraries Adequate? *New Library World.* 105(1196/1198), 60-68. Retrieved October, 5 2005 from http://www.emeraldinsight.com/Insight/ViewContentServlet?Filename=Published/EmeraldFullTextArticle/Articles/0721050105.html

Ma, Y. (2006). Education for Library Information Specialist (LIS): Is There the Case for Digital Library? Loughborough: MA dissertation, University of Loughborough.

Ma, Y., O'Brien, A. & Clegg, W. (2006). Digital Library Education: the Current Status. *Proceeding of the 6th ACM/IEEE-CS Joint Conference on Digital Libraries (JCDL'06)* (pp.165-174). ACM Press. Retrieved July, 10, 2006 from http://delivery. acm.org/10.1145/1150000/1141786/p165-ma.pdf?key1=1141786&key2=8184620021&coll=portal&dl=ACM&CFID=798309&CFTOKEN=77332738

Ma, Y., O'Brien, A. & Clegg, W. (2007). Digital Library Education: Some International Course Structure Comparisons. *Proceeding of the 7th ACM/IEEE-CS Joint Conference on Digital Libraries (JCDL'07)* (pp.490). ACM Press. Retrieved July, 10, 2007 from http://delivery.acm.org/10.1145/1260000/1255289/p490-ma.pdf?key1=1255289&key2=8046720021&coll=portal&dl=ACM&CFID=36056742&CFTOKEN=34866767

Pomerantz, J., Wildemuth, B. Yang, S. & Fox, E. (2006a). Curriculum Development for Digital Libraries. *Proceeding of the 6th ACM/IEEE-CS Joint Conference on Digital Libraries (JCDL'06)* (pp.175-184). ACM Press. Retrieved July, 10, 2006 from http://delivery.acm.org/10.1145/1150000/1141787/p175-pomerantz.pdf?key1=1141787&key2=5994620021&coll=portal&dl=ACM&CFID=798309&CFTOKEN=77332738

Pomerantz, J., Wildemuth, B. Yang, S. & Fox, E. (2006b). The Core: Digital Library Education in Library and Information Science Programs. *D-Lib Magazine.* 12(11). Retrieved December, 5, 2006 from http://www.dlib.org/dlib/november06/pomerantz/11pomerantz.html

Pomerantz, J., Oh, S., Wildemuth, B. Yang, S.. & Fox, E. (2007). Digital Library Education in Computer Science Programs *Proceeding of the 6th ACM/IEEE-CS Joint Conference on Digital Libraries (JCDL'07)* (pp.177-178). ACM Press.

Retrieved August, 5 2007 from http://delivery. acm.org/10.1145/1260000/1255208/p177-pomerantz.pdf?key1=1255208&key2=5515620021&coll=portal&dl=ACM&CFID=36056742&CFTOKEN=34866767

Rose, H. 2001. Digital Libraries and Education Trends and Opportunities. *D-Lib Magazine 7*(7/8). Retrieved October, 5, 2005 from http://www.dlib.org/dlib/july01/roes/07roes.html

Saracevic, T. and Dalbello, M.A. (2001). A Survey of Digital Library Education. *Proceeding of American Society for Information Science, 38,* 209-223.

Spink, A. and Cool, C. (1999). Education for Digital Libraries. *D-Lib Magazine 5*(5).

VT, (2006). Virginia Tech, *UNC Create DL Curriculum.* Retrieved November, 21, 2007. from http://www.cs.vt.edu/whatsnews/virginia_tech, unc_create_digital_library_curriculum.html

Wildemuth, B. (2006). *CS and ILS as Disciplinary Homes for DLE.* Presentation at DLE workshop on JCDL06. Retrieved October 5, 2006, from http://lair.indiana.edu/research/dlib/jcdl06/unc.pdf

Wilder, S.J. (2002) New Hires in Research Libraries, Demographic Trends and Hiring Priories. *ARI,* 221.

KEY TERMS

Computer Science (CS): The study of the theoretical foundations of information and computation, and their implementation and application in computer systems.

Digital Library (DL): A library in which collections are stored in digital formats (as opposed to print, microform, or other media) and accessible by computers. The digital content may be stored locally, or accessed remotely via computer networks. A digital library is a type of information storage and retrieval system.

Digital Library Education (DLE): The study of issues relating to appropriate professional preparation staff in digital libraries.

Library and Information Science (LIS): The study of issues related to the library and information field.

Chapter LVI
The Future of Learning with Digital Libraries

Chang Chew-Hung
Nanyang Technological University, Singapore

John G. Hedberg
Macquarie University, Australia

ABSTRACT

While the prospect of using digital libraries for learning becomes more appealing with growing repositories of resources, it is not clear what factors other than the use of technology, determine the learning outcome for an individual. The focus of research on using digital libraries for learning has been on the richness of information that digital libraries afford and on the ability of digital libraries to organize information for information query and research. Any meaningful learning activity using digital libraries must therefore utilize their features for exploration and information gathering around a well designed task or inquiry, to result in effective higher order learning outcomes. The design of the inquiry task is provided by a teacher or even devised by the student, but it is not necessarily inherent within the digital library. However, digital libraries have the capabilities to be more supportive of student learning by providing tools that support processes such as investigation, analysis, transduction of information and scaffolding of inquiry process. Often, students use the digital library for information gathering but turn to other software applications for organizing information and constructing the arguments and learning artifacts for the learning task. While it requires the teachers'—and maybe students'—resourcefulness to choose the right type of tool for the activity, the future of learning with digital libraries rests on integrating supportive tools into a seamless learning environment.

INTRODUCTION

As educators explore the application of new technologies, often they grope towards an effective understanding of how they might be best employed in learning contexts. Researchers have compared one medium with or against other media for decades. Such media comparisons have regularly come under criticism. Indeed, a typical study of the influence of one medium on learning has focused on comparing the "relative achievement of groups who have received similar subject matter from different media presentations" (Clark, 1983, p. 445). Consequently, "media selection" or the establishment of the best medium or a best mix of media becomes the main objective of such studies. However, learning involves a complicated process of interaction between specific tasks, particular learner traits, various components of representation and pedagogical strategy (Clark & Salomon, 1986). In fact, Clark (1983) argued that most summaries and meta-analyses of media comparison studies "clearly suggest that media do not influence learning under any conditions" (Clark, 1983, p. 445).

Indeed Clark (1983) used the analogy of a truck delivering groceries to illustrate that the role of media in learning was less impactful than the content being delivered. Thus it is not just the vehicle of delivering content that is consequential for learning outcomes. To quote:

... media are mere vehicles that deliver instruction but do not influence student achievement any more than the truck that delivers our groceries causes changes in our nutrition. Basically, the choice of vehicle might influence the cost and extent of distributing instruction, but only the content of the vehicle can influence achievement. (Clark, 1983, p. 445)

Nowadays we have a range of delivery options that can be more responsive to the consumer needs. With electronic delivery we can be more responsive to the consumers' needs and at the same time cost only what the consumer would like to pay. Suppose the consumer only wants one packet of milk. Delivery with a truck may be fast but certainly not cost effective. Some types of learning outcomes might be better achieved with delivery through alternative media. Indeed, the focus should be on affordances rather than conveyances and the inherent abilities of the consumer to "drive" effective use of what is being accessed. It is not what the technology can do but what the user can use technology for that should drive the issue of how learning can be enhanced by technology. To take this proposition one step further, it is important to consider how technology use should be responsive to effective learning.

OUR PROPOSITION

Marchionini and Maurer (1995) propose that digital libraries play crucial roles in learning in that they provide a platform for sharing, serve as a reservoir of information sources and "serve a social and intellectual role by bringing people and ideas together" (Jayawardana, Hewagamage, & Hirakawa, 2001). While existing digital libraries such as the Digital Library for Earth System Education (DLESE), Artemis digital library and the Alexandria digital library have developed with education as their aim, these libraries replicate traditional library roles and consequently support traditional modes of learning. Scholars such as Kuhlthau (1997) examined relationships of information-seeking behaviour in school students using digital libraries. Kuhlthau's work focuses on an information search process model related to the cognitive, affective states and search activities of the users, including task initiation, topic selection, prefocus exploration, focus formulation, information collection and search closure. Indeed, she posits that information seeking is a holistic process over time, of seeking meaning rather than simply answering questions. Thus effective use of digital libraries focuses on the learning process rather than on the capabilities of the digital libraries. However, information seeking behavior is only one aspect of how digital libraries can be used for learning. Marchionini and Maurer (1995) have suggested that a meaningful use of the digital library for learning requires active interaction on the part of the user (learner) and their skill with task conceptualization and technological understanding on what they are using. We argue that these facets will be highly influential on the learning outcome. In previous work (Jayawardana, Hewagamage, & Hirakawa, 2001; Kuhlthau, 1997; Marchionini & Maurer, 1995), the integrative support tools that enable students to make meaning out of the information gathered are absent from digital libraries.

AN EXAMPLE OF A PROTOTYPE

Contemporary learning management systems (LMS) allow the teacher to organize resources in a predetermined order which then prescribes a structured learning strategy. A digital library has the possibility of being more open-ended and user driven becoming, in effect, a potentially disruptive pedagogy (Hedberg, 2006). Christensen's (1997) idea of disruptive innovations suggests that the use of digital libraries as an alternative strategy to the LMS might ensure that learning outcomes might be achieved more effectively. The digital library requires more from the user but it can also be designed to support the retrieval and manipulation of information. In Christensen's conception, a disruptive technology or disruptive innovation is a new technological innovation, product, or service that ultimately takes over the existing dominant technology or product, often the innovation might initially be a poorer quality but eventually it offers a new functionality and improved quality superseding an older technology. Digital libraries such as in our instance, the G-portal (Chang & Hedberg, 2006), provide users

(both teachers and learners) with the opportunity to take control of their choice of resources (Stewart, 2003), ways of representing their ideas, using existing resources, creating new resources, reviewing and commenting on the quality of the resources and even developing their own learning strategies as they seek to answer authentic tasks posed about a real-world problem.

The G-portal development project was initiated as an attempt to extend the existing capabilities of digital repositories and to explore the importance of a move into multimodal representations of ideas and concepts (Goh, Theng, Lim, Zhang, Chang, & Chatterjea, 2006; Lim, Zhang, Li, Wang, Chang, Chatterjea, et al., 2006; Chang, Hedberg, Theng, Lim, Teh, & Goh, 2005). The experimental digital repository hosts digital assets that are used by students to solve authentic problems based on real world data and resources. G-Portal serves an active role in collaborative learning activities in which students conduct a virtual field study of an environmental problem, within a geospatial context—in particular, beach erosion and sea level rise. G-Portal not only functions as a digital library of information resources, it also provides manipulation and analytical tools that can operate on the information provided. Thus the digital library not only serves as a repository but it also provides the tools with which students can retrieve information, collaborate on a group project and work with multimodal data representations.

CAPABILITIES OF THE G-PORTAL

The G-portal extends the range of capabilities that support learners in their construction of geographical knowledge. For example, a personal workspace is provided to each user (or group of users) to build his/her (or their) own collections of resources and annotations in form of personalized projects. The unique attribute of a personalized project is the accessibility, which can be private or public. A private project is visible and accessible to the creator only and a public project is accessible to all the users, but the major outcome is a reworking of resources and ideas into a form that the user wishes to describe a geographical phenomenon. The personalized project management module enables the users to create, manipulate, export and delete their own projects. As part of this project tools several capabilities are provided, some of these are also provided in the growing public resource collections in tools such as Google Earth (see http://earth.google.com/). The growing future options that exist in digital libraries that extend the user support function include:

1. *Personal Resource structuring and Project management.* Users specify the basic attributes of the project collections and can decide whether the project is public or private, this attribute is common on popular blogs and ensures that the creator of the display/resources can chose what is shared. The concept of personal project space allows individuals to work in their personalized environment with a mix of private and public data and at the same time share part of the data with their team members. (This attribute is typical of Google video, YouTube and other shared video resources). In G-portal this allows users to explore the information, process the information, solve the problem posed and ultimately construct a geographical understanding of it. Transduction of text into images or other modes of representation may also be possible within these personal projects.

2. *Built-in tools.* Some built-in tools such as zoom and measurement tools allow the students to query the data spatially. Essentially this allows users to select data by non-linear methods and encourage inquiry based on some analogy of the real world spatial context—the map. A certain degree of manipulation and consequent analysis of the data using these tools may support

the learner in constructing meaning of the information.

3. *Layer management of complex data sets related to the same spatial landscape.* Within a project, data layers can be defined to maintain resources in different logical groupings. Properties including name, description and type (resource layer or annotation layer) are specified for each layer. Within a personal project, appropriate layers can be defined to group resources logically. However, the layers and the assignment of resources to layers can only updated by the original data owners. Indeed, the data layers emulate what a Geographic Information System does; it represents real world objects in layers. The information on each layer can then be used for comparison and analysis. For example, patterns may be described when objects across various layers are toggled "on" or "off" (See Figure 1 for an example).

4. *Schema and resource management.* Every resource in the digital library is created using a resource schema that serves as a template. In a personal projects, schemas can be user-defined to meet the needs of a learning activity for a single user (or team of users). In a collaborative learning setting, it is also quite likely to have multiple users exchanging resources among their personal projects. Essentially the schema and resource management allows users to reuse objects that have been created by others. While recognising the degree of reliability may differ for objects created by other users with different expertise, the reusability option may support student learning. The link back to the original data points or sources reduces the current problems of attribution of source. Thus the schema and resource management of the digital library can reduce the tedious assessment task for students who copy and reproduce without adding their own thought and value. It also ensures that the teacher as

Figure 1. G-portal Interface with an example of an object represented in space and multiple sources of data can be attached to a simple illustration

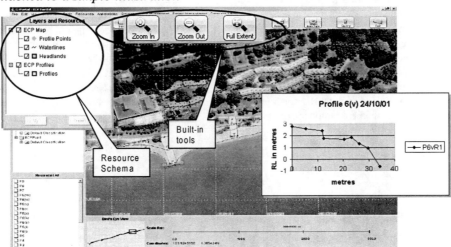

marker can determine the correct attribution of the resource data.

5. *Personalized Project Export.* By providing each user with a personalized workspace in the digital library, the management of the resources (information) becomes much easier for each learning activity. This allows users to create the object of their learning activity and to share for assessment a documented artefact.

6. *Review and commenting.* The users are able to input comments and rank the usefulness of the resources. The system then generates an average rating, together with comments about each resource. While the idea of review and commenting is fairly ubiquitous in many content management systems, the G-portal project uses this function to allow users to assess the relative usefulness of resources at a glance.

The example of the G-portal prototype illustrates one way in which digital libraries can be made more integrative and support student learning through including capabilities such as resource and schema management and layering to help students organize the information. The

prototype also presents opportunities for spatial and non-spatial query of information. Finally the personalized project management module and the review and commenting module allow learners to manipulate and assess the quality of the information resources for solving their particular learning activity. In summary, the capabilities of the system thus allow for, information storage, organization, retrieval, query, manipulation, evaluation and further creation of new information. While these functions can be achieved by combining different application software and traditional digital libraries, the strength of the G-portal example is that the tools are integrated.

USING THE G-PORTAL DIGITAL LIBRARY FOR LEARNING

While the G-Portal has been used in several applications in education, the authors have chosen to show an early implementation of the G-Portal as an example of how it supports learning. The reason for this choice is that the opportunities presented at that early stage provide excellent examples of our argument for a disruptive pedagogy.

Figure 2. Task given to the students to use G-portal to solve a real life geographic problem

> As part of your familiarization with using the G-portal, please complete the following task:
>
> You have been asked to examine Profiles 6IV, 6V, & 6VI by a resort development to assess the state of this stretch of beach at ECP. In particular, why do you think the beach profiles looks different at different times of the year? Investigate this question using the G-portal and other online resources. Present your report (using MS Word or MS Power Point or any other supporting software) to explain your findings. You should include visuals where necessary to illustrate your point. Visuals can be gathered form the G-Portal and from the internet. Remember that your target audience is the developer of the resort.
>
> You will have 40 minutes to complete the report.

An inquiry task was designed for a group of university undergraduate students who were studying a course on Coastal and Ocean Systems, which required the use of the G-Portal digital library. The students were given a task of using available geographic data to solve an authentic problem for a resort development consultancy. The detailed task is given in Figure 2 below.

The activity emphasises the students' knowledge construction process but require, in addition, a fuller description of the learning activity. Note that the undergraduate students were from the second year Coastal and Ocean Systems module at the National Institute of Education. This module traditionally requires the students to investigate a stretch of the local coast and solve some geographical problems resulting from the investigation. An introduction to the G-portal was given at the beginning of the module. The students then accessed the information via the G-portal throughout the semester.

The investigation by the students took place along a stretch of the east coast parkway coast. The main foci of the task was to identify and suggest possible coastline changes and the resulting impacts on the environment and land use of the study area. As the students were performing this task, the way they use the G-portal on the computer, together with a headshot of their faces was recorded into a single video clip. The footage was then analysed to answer these questions:

1. How did students find information?
2. How did students form arguments in their discussion/artefacts?
3. Were the students aware of the modality of the information sources and artefacts?
4. How did the students construct artefacts?

The observation included how the student spent time performing each of the sub tasks described in the list above. This allowed a detailed description of how each group used the G-portal in the task, while also providing the basis for analysing the relationship between each segment of the activity.

In terms of finding information, the students used only the built-in tools and the resource and schema management tool of the G-portal. While one group showed that they did use the Web to find additional information, it was primarily to find an image they could use to decorate their introductory slide. This presents the development team some challenges. For example, the non-use of other G-portal capabilities such as personal project management and layer management may indicate that these capabilities are not easily accessible to the user. These are areas that the user interface could be improved on. The issue might also have arisen from the lack of visibility in the design elements, however, digital libraries must consider issues of user-interface design as it scaffolds learning.

The choice of software application the students used to construct their artefacts influenced the way they approach the task. For example, one group chose to use Microsoft Word which lead to more discussion on the procedure followed by analysis and finally a theoretical and causal explanation for their solution. Another group chose Microsoft PowerPoint and this led to theoretical and causal explanations after each beach profile was analysed. Perhaps digital libraries in the future need to provide some handy tools at the user's disposal which enable them to manipulate the contents for their learning task. Certainly, a counter-argument could be that the antecedent learning styles of the two groups of students predetermines how they will carry out the task, regardless of software tools, but this needs further exploration.

While one group used three modes of representation, namely text, numbers and images, another group only created one piece of text artefact with three diagrams to which no references were made. Again this can be attributed to the application chosen and its affordances for information representation. This becomes clearer upon examining the way the students created their artifacts. One group mostly "wrote" their final artefact while the other group copied and pasted images, calculated rates of erosion and added textual explanations. While the G-Portal facilitates the transduction of various modes of information representation, the process is not implicit and requires the use of third-party applications.

The analyses of the artefacts suggested that the G-portal was useful to some extent in providing resources to support students finding information. There is evidence that at least one group was able employ multimodality in the construction of their learning artefacts and that the way students approached the task was determined to some degree by their chosen software application. Thus using digital libraries for education requires the development of an environment that supports the creation of new information, new conclusions and the compilations of supportive evidence.

G-Portal has been used for various education applications (Lim, Sun, Liu, Hedberg, Chang, Teh, et al., 2004; Chang & Hedberg, 2006; Chatterjea, Chang, Theng, Lim, Goh, & Zhang, 2006). New features have been added for each iteration. The limitations found in this early study reinforce the proposition that for digital libraries to be used meaningfully in learning, they must provide both teachers and learners an opportunity to take control of their choice of resources and the ways of representing their ideas. This goes beyond simple information storage and retrieval. It should be a tool that supports students in all facets of the inquiry process and creating meaningful artifacts which illustrate their process and products.

DISCUSSION AND CONCLUSION

The future of information repositories is being explored in large scale digitization projects at Google, the Million Book Project, MSN, and Yahoo! (Albanese, 2005). Improvements in book handling, presentation technologies, and development of alternative depositories and business models, should result in digital libraries rapidly growing in popularity. In addition, projects such as the Digital Library Integrated Task Environment (DLITE) uses a work centre metaphor (Cousins, Paepcke, Winograd, Bier, & Pier, 2004) to organize information to be stored, processed and retrieved, allowing greater ease of use. While digital libraries such as Digital Work Environment (DWE) extend the functions of DLs to provide functionality based on work tasks (Meyyappan, Al-Hawamdeh, & Foo, 2002). The DLs are structured for a predetermined workflow, albeit derived from a detailed survey on the needs of that work task. However, these information repositories will remain simply repositories unless we develop pedagogies and distributed cognitive tools that ensure users are able to access and manipulate the information they contain. While the G-portal example is just one way in which digital libraries can evolve to support learning, given that many recent instances are providing multimodal representations of ideas and concepts, more users will become engaged and excited by the options. It should be expected that they will grow in their ability to explain their ideas, not as semantic facts but as dynamic illustrations that can be created to demonstrate their understanding. The movement beyond the very limited LMS into a world of digital libraries can also support students' learning processes in ways that are largely unavailable to them at the present.

By taking the idea of a disruptive pedagogy further, we propose that the way digital libraries are developed for learning might be radically changed. A digital library by itself is unlikely to be a very useful learning tool unless the learning is situated within an appropriate context, as the coastal erosion learning task has illustrated. Usually, the design of the learning task is as important, if not more important, than what the digital library can potentially offer as simple resources. On this premise it seems that the responsibility of creating a useful learning task with the digital library should not rest solely on digital library developers. A good learning task can only be designed when the tool provides support and affordances to ensure meaningful learning tasks are designed in the first place. In other words, digital library developers have to engage in dialogue with teachers, students, and education researchers in order to create a learning future for digital libraries. While digital libraries draw on the teachers'—and maybe students'—resourcefulness to use the right type of tool for the activity, their future in learning rests on integrating supportive tools seamlessly.

REFERENCES

Albanese, A. (2005). Google to digitize 15 million books. *LibraryJournal.com*. Retrieved August 30, 2008, from http://libraryjournal.com/article/CA491156.html

Chang, C.H., & Hedberg, J.G. (2006). The role of digital libraries in teaching and learning geography. In K.C. Goh, & S. Yongvanit (Eds.), *Change and Development in Southeast Asia in an Era of Globalisation*. Singapore: Pearson Prentice Hall.

Chang, C.H., Hedberg, J., Theng, Y.L., Lim, E.P., Teh, T.S., & Goh, D. (2005, June 7–11). Evaluating g-portal for geography learning and teaching. Accepted to JCDL2005, *Digital Libraries Cyberinfrastructure for Research and Education* (pp. 21– 22). Denver, CO.

Chatterjea, K., Chang, C.H., Theng, Y.L., Lim, E.P, Goh, D.H.L., & Zhang, J. (2006, June). *Supporting holistic understanding of geographical problems: Field work and g-portal.* Presented at International Geographic Union, Commission for Geographic Education Conference. Brisbane.

Christensen, C.M. (1997). *The innovator's dilemma.* Cambridge, MA: Harvard Business School Press.

Clark, R.E. (1983). Reconsidering research on learning from media. *Review of Educational Research, 53*(4), 445–459.

Cousins, S.B., Paepcke, A., Winograd, T., Bier, E.A., & Pier, K. (2004). The effectiveness of automatically structured queries in digital libraries. In *Proceedings of the 4th ACM/IEEE-CS Joint Conference on Digital Libraries* (pp. 98–107). Tuscon, AZ.

Goh, D.L.H., Theng, Y.L., Lim, E.P., Zhang, J., Chang, C.H., & Chatterjea, K. (2006). G-Portal: A platform for learning geography. In A. Tatnall (Ed.), *Encyclopaedia of Portal Technology and Applications.* Hershey, PA: Idea Group Publishing.

Hedberg, J.G. (2006). E-learning futures? Speculations for a time yet to come. *Studies in Continuing Education, 28*(2), 173–185.

Jayawardana, C., Hewagamage, K.P., & Hirakawa,M. (2001). Personalization tools for active learning in digital libraries. *The Journal of Academic Media Librarianship, 8*(1). Retrieved August 30, 2008, from http://wings.buffalo.edu/publications/mcjrnl/v8n1/active.html

Kuhlthau C.C. (1997). Learning in digital libraries: An information search process approach. *Library Trends, 45*(4), 708–724.

Lim, E.P., Goh, D.H.L, Liu, Z., Ng, W.K., Khoo, C.S.G., & Higgins, S.E. (2002). G-Portal: A map-based digital library for distributed geospatial and georeferenced resources. In *International Conference on Digital Libraries, Proceedings of the Second ACM/IEEE-CS Joint Conference on Digital Libraries* (pp. 351–358).

Lim, E.P., Sun, A.X., Liu, Z.H., Hedberg, J., Chang, C.H., Teh, T.S., et al. (2004). Supporting field study with personalized project space in a geographical digital library. *7th International Conference of Asian Digital Libraries, ICADL2004, LNCS 3334* (pp. 553–562). Springer-Verlag.

Lim, E.P., Zhang, J., Li, Y., Wang, Z., Chang, C.H., Chatterjea, K., et al. (2006) G-Portal—a cross disciplinary digital library research program from Singapore. In E.P. Lim (Ed.), *IEEE Technical Committee on Digital Libraries Bulletin—Special Issue on Asian Digital Libraries*, Lim (Vol. 3, No. 1). Retrieved August 30, 2008, from http://www.ieee-tcdl.org/Bulletin/v3n1/lim/lim.html

Marchionini, G., & Maurer, H. (1995). The roles of digital libraries in teaching and learning. *Communications of the ACM Archive, 38*(4), 67–75.

Meyyappan, N., Al-Hawamdeh, S., & Foo, S. (2002). Task based design of a digital work environment (DWE) for an academic community. *Information Research, 7*(2). Retrieved August 30, 2008, from http://informationr.net/ir/7-2/paper125.html

Stewart, R. (2003). Using digital libraries to teach oceanography. In *Proceedings of the 19th International Conference on Interactive Information Processing Systems (IIPS) for Meteorology, Oceanography, and Hydrology.*

Chapter LVII
Computational Sense for Digital Librarians

Michael B. Twidale
University of Illinois, USA

David M. Nichols
University of Waikato, New Zealand

ABSTRACT

This chapter discusses the role of technology in digital library education. It explores how elements of computer science and library science can be blended to produce an appropriate "computational sense" for future digital librarians. Elements of this approach include: metacognitive skills in learning about new computational resources, fluency in tailoring applications and a view of computing applications as codesigned artifacts that can evolve in response to the changing needs of users. The development of spreadsheets is used as an example of technological development that was well-designed to support both ease of use and incremental skill acquisition. The discussion in this chapter aims to inform the development of digital library software tools—particularly those used in educational contexts.

INTRODUCTION

The rapid progress of digital library technology from research to implementation has created a force for change in the curricula of library schools. The education of future librarians has always had to adapt to new technologies but the pace, complexity and implications of digital libraries (DL) pose considerable challenges. In this chapter we explore how we might successfully blend elements of computer science and library science to produce effective educational experiences for the digital librarians of tomorrow. We first outline the background to current digital librarian education and then propose the concept of *computational sense* as an appropriate meeting point for these two disciplines.

BACKGROUND

There is an ongoing debate on what it means to be a digital librarian (Coleman, 2005; Marion, 2001; Mostafa, Brancolini, Smith, & Mischo 2005; Pomerantz, Oh, Yang, Fox, & Wildemuth, 2006a; Pomerantz, Wildemuth, Yang, & Fox, 2006b). It is similar to being a traditional librarian in terms of ethos and applicability of core guiding theories, including access, cataloguing, collection development and teaching people both search skills and general information literacy. It can be viewed as simply integrating a set of digital information resources into access services provided around preexisting paper-based resources. However, it also requires additional technical skills, extending the librarian's role into new areas. For example, DL creation can be more akin to publishing than collection development, involving aspects of editing, revision and aligning to data and metadata standards.

The topic of digital librarianship is subject to rapid change (Pomerantz et al., 2006b), as it is partially defined by the availability and functionality of appropriate software. The ease of building a digital library or an institutional repository has been radically changed over the past decade by the emergence of software such as Greenstone (Witten & Bainbridge, 2003) and DSpace (Tansley, Smith, & Walker, 2005). For example, courses presented in library schools are often based around similar material presented in tutorials at digital library conferences. Education based around digital library software inevitably brings with it techniques and concepts from computer science; especially as most of these courses combine theory and practice (Ma, Clegg, & O'Brien, 2006). The practically-oriented *How to Build a Digital Library* (Witten & Bainbridge, 2003), is the most-assigned book on DL syllabi (Pomerantz et al., 2006a). The interdisciplinary nature of the topic is also highlighted by the appearance of digital library courses in computer science curricula (Pomerantz, Oh, Wildemuth, Yang, & Fox, 2007; Yang, Fox, Wildemuth, Pomerantz, & Oh, 2006).

Issues that can cause problems for library students vary from the basic (such as selecting the appropriate software version, downloading and installing) to advanced topics involving customization and extensibility (Nichols, Bainbridge, Downie, & Twidale, 2006). A recent survey on the issue of interface customization in Greenstone 2 included these responses: "I spent far more time trying to customize our interface than I did adding content to our library," "interface design is currently geared very much toward programmers," and "format statements are overly complex for most librarians" (Nichols, Bainbridge, & Twidale, 2007).

Within library and information science, the discussion of the integration of digital libraries into existing curricula can also be considered a part of a larger ongoing exploration of how to integrate librarianship and information science. This is particularly challenging as the latter may or may not be viewed as incorporating diverse topics such as the design of novel information retrieval systems, knowledge management, medical informatics, cultural informatics and the preservation of different kinds of media. The integration of these topics as well as the integration of systems centric, information-centric and user-centric approaches to analysis and design ensure that there is often considerable diversity in the approaches to what is taught and how, and a near-constant debate about LIS curriculum development (Kajberg & Lørring, 2005).

This background suggests that careful consideration is needed to understand the interactions between digital library education, software and computer science.

COMPUTATIONAL SENSE

As libraries have become more computerised, librarians have had to learn more and more about computer systems, file formats and Web servers. Over time, commodity software can hide away certain levels of complexity as a basic infrastructure is developed. But innovative computer applications will always require a degree of explicit support and tinkering. For example, the Greenstone software development team has, over several years, developed a variety of tools to abstract away from technical details to simplify the tasks of creating and maintaining digital collections. Despite this work, the experiences of using digital library software can still be disconcerting for some students (Nichols et al., 2006). This state of affairs is more a reflection on the state-of-the-art in content management systems than a criticism of any particular software applications.

From the perspective of software developers the power of digital library software derives from the flexibility of computer programming languages. Indeed, the Greenstone digital library suite embeds programming language constructs into its customization features; providing considerable flexibility for collection design but at the expense of learnability (Nichols, Bainbridge, Marsden, Patel, Cunningham, Thompson, et al., 2005). A practical example is the nature of conditional statements ("if," "then," "else") in Greenstone macros, which:

- Have a unique syntax (rather than reusing an existing language such as JavaScript or PHP)
- Have a different syntax to conditional statements in Greenstone formatting statements
- Have no error checking at design time (such as the red underlining of spell checkers or Visual Studio)
- Have no integrated documentation (such as found in modern programming development environments)

At one level it is simple to say that these can be corrected through more software development.

The larger question is whether this is the right direction for systems that are to be used in digital librarian education. The resulting system could be very similar to an IDE (Integrated Development Environment) of the sort regularly used by computer science students and programmers.

This raises the question: should future librarians be forced to become programmers in order to graduate? We believe that digital librarians should not have to become programmers but that they *do* need to acquire a fluency with information technology beyond a traditional MLS degree. We coin the term *computational sense* to describe this level of fluency. It covers a range of issues that remain in flux and are clearly open for debate; we outline a few of them below for illustration. Computational sense differs from the notion of "computational thinking" (Wing, 2006) in that it is concerned with embedded socio-technical systems rather than the fundamental concepts of the nature of computation. In rather simplistic terms, computational sense is about thinking about *what* we might reasonably try to build an application to do for us, while computational thinking is about *how* the application might do it.

Comfort and Fluency with Computational Systems

Of course a digital librarian should be comfortable in using the latest technologies available. However, although necessary we do not believe this is sufficient for librarians to be able to take active roles in exploiting the potential of a rapidly changing set of technologies.

That is, our claim extends substantially beyond the desirability of learning basic Information Technology skills. As we outline below, digital librarians need to be able not merely to use a rapidly changing set of computer applications, but to play an active role in selecting them, combining them, integrating them into workflows and use scenarios, appropriating, tailoring, customising and innovating with them. It can also mean designing new applications or being involved in their radical redesign.

Meta-Cognitive Skills in Learning about new Computational Resources

Simply providing training in a particular technology is insufficient because technologies change so rapidly. New versions of applications contain new functionalities, new interfaces and hence new possibilities for how they might be used. New applications become available to complement or replace existing applications. Online resources and computational services can enhance or disrupt what users expect or want to be able to do with existing resources. For example, consider patrons' changing reactions to library catalogues in the light of their experiences with Amazon and Google. Once a patron has encountered a very flexible application that allows rather messy searching, and that can cope elegantly with misspellings and typing errors, this experience radically changes their tolerance for older systems that require an interaction that closely resembles the traditional careful composition of a precise database query. The existence proof of a simpler, faster way of searching based on rapid iterations of initially rather vague searches suddenly makes unacceptable activities required of the user that are clearly more for the benefit of the application and its programmer than the user. A classic example is the requirement that title queries omit leading articles—now this constraint provokes consternation and irritation amongst patrons that they should have to interact in this manner. In the past, patrons might have put up with such requirements as part of the arcana of access to a mystical fount of knowledge. Nowadays, they are more likely to complain, "But you don't have to do that on Amazon, why should I have to do it here?"

Of course for a library it can seem unfair that their systems, functionalities and interfaces are being compared with those developed by multi-billion dollar corporations, but people's expectations continually rise once the implicit belief that "it has to be that way because that is the way that computers are" is irrevocably destroyed.

With multiple alternate options online, libraries are no longer necessarily regarded by potential patrons as the monopoly supplier of access to information. Instead they may just use Google (often poorly) and grab the first plausible-looking source. Libraries now have many competitors and need to compete to remain relevant, to serve their patrons with the superior products and services they usually possess, but that are in danger of being ignored.

Consequently, practising librarians need to be able to learn about the latest versions of applications and new ways of combining existing applications quickly—maybe without formal training. This can be done, but probably requires the teaching of the metacognitive skills that can facilitate more efficient and effective learning both by individuals and communities within and across organisations. That is, how can we teach our students so that in their professional careers they will be able to rapidly familiarise themselves with new technologies and develop innovative and appropriate uses for those technologies in their libraries, given that those technologies currently do not even exist?

Fluency in Incremental Tailoring and Combining of Applications for Evolving Needs

Even if they do not directly program new digital library applications, librarians are likely to be involved directly or indirectly in the installation and use of those applications, which invariably involves tailoring work. Modern applications typically come with a host of options, and the defaults are often less than ideal. Making a resource useful and usable in a particular context typically involves a range of tailoring activities ranging from selecting between options, choosing modules to install, including or linking the application to the resources it will use or provide, integrating the software with other applications or provisions and "skinning" the interface to create an integrated, consistent and coherent look-and-feel for end users as part of a focus on usability. All these require varying levels of technical expertise. They also require the ability to interact productively with others, both stakeholders with far less technical skill, and also technical experts, but lacking local knowledge of use-in-context. Although somewhat daunting-sounding, this information intermediary role is one firmly within the bounds of the ethos of traditional librarianship (Erlich & Cash, 1994).

A Sense of Applications as Ongoing Co-Designed Artefacts rather than Technological Givens

Computational sense should include an understanding and an expectation that digital librarians be involved not just in the selection, analysis, and facilitation of learning and use of computational artefacts, but that they should also be involved in the *design* of those artefacts. At the very least it should empower digital librarians to take a more direct role in larger-scale design processes. Applications should not be taken as technological givens, to be coped with by librarians in their information intermediary role of helping end-users. Rather these applications need to be regarded as *provisional*, changing and amenable to change by librarians. In many existing cases this still might not actually be feasible, but we believe that it is worth considering what it would take to give more librarians the skills necessary to not merely critique inadequate systems but to get involved in actually improving them. Design does not necessarily require programming. As noted above, tailoring is one aspect of design, but there are others. As well as in-house design, there are various approaches to wider involvement in larger codesign processes, including participatory design (Kyng & Mathiassen, 1997) and the involvement

of lead users (Von Hippel, 2005) as well as open source software development. Modern systems are frequently in a process of near-continual redesign as new versions and modules are released, which at least raises the possibility of greater involvement by people with appropriate skills.

A Sense of the Feasibility of Potential Design Options

To be fully involved in ongoing codesign, it is very helpful to have a good sense of what is feasible in current systems development and what is not. A qualitative sense of the relative costs of different design options is also helpful as the design space is collectively explored. Typically, computer science students are expected to acquire these rich qualitative skills by repeated practice: they are rarely explicitly taught. We speculate that it might be possible to teach these skills of design judgement without requiring considerable practical programming experience. If so, it would allow digital librarians to engage in far more productive interactions both with vendors and systems development teams, as advocates for stakeholders and use-in-context as different functionalities and possibilities are uncovered. If you don't have a sense of what it is reasonable to ask for, you are inclined to select just from the options on offer. All design involves trade-offs and compromises, but when these are done in ignorance of whole categories of costs, benefits, and opportunities, truly innovative design possibilities are overlooked.

Spreadsheets as a Guiding Metaphor

To illustrate our vision, we use an example from an earlier round of technological innovation coinciding with the advent of the personal computer in the 1980s. Prior to that time, people who wanted to do mathematical calculations on computers (including scientists and financial experts) would have had to write a program in a programming language (such as FORTRAN). This was, for many, daunting or prohibitively expensive in terms of money, opportunity cost or effort-risk-reward calculations. With the advent of the early spreadsheet programs, many people started using them because they were far easier to both learn and use. Although intended for accounting calculations, the ease of learning and use encouraged innovation and appropriation by many others with needs to manipulate numbers. Nevertheless, spreadsheets were not completely trivial to use. One needed basic numeracy to be able to use them productively and not generate nonsense—what we might call a numerical sense. One just did not need to know how to program. Ability to program certainly helped in avoiding certain classic errors, and was essential for more complex calculations that either the spreadsheet software of the day could not manage or where the programming of macros was needed. But programming ceased to be a prerequisite and the skills of sophisticated spreadsheet use, planning, design and debugging could be taught to people who had not first learned to program.

FUTURE TRENDS

We believe that it is possible to extract some of the skills traditionally acquired (explicitly but more often implicitly) from long experience of programming, and teach these to librarians under the label of computational sense. In so doing we can widen the number of people able to productively engage with information technologies, just as spreadsheets widened the use of computers by numerate people far beyond the range of those willing to invest time in learning FORTRAN.

This approach challenges the developers of digital library software to produce tools as useful and useable as the spreadsheet. We expect software to improve in its representations of library science concepts but rapid progress will only be made by partnerships between software developers and educators. One practical step would be for digital library courses to require their students to submit experience reports back to the software developers; thus encouraging the students to focus on the relationship between their technical skills and the software environment. Additionally this allows students to see themselves as codesigners of digital library software, a role closer to that which they will encounter in their professional lives.

The topics listed earlier are orthogonal to those in discussions of digital library curricula (Pomerantz et al., 2006b) as computational sense relates to the practical coordination of the curricula topics in building a functioning system. It is this *combination* of theory and practice that makes digital libraries a challenging discipline.

Effects of Falling Costs of Hardware and Sensors

The need for computational sense is caused not just by the growing development and use of digital libraries, important though that may be. Falling costs of interconnectivity of computers have already had profound effects, justifying the resources devoted to digital libraries when their content can easily and cheaply shared worldwide. This will continue, creating not just more of current use of resources but also new kinds of use, as computer connectivity becomes nearly ubiquitous and new kinds of mobile connectivity such as via cellphones becomes feasible. It is likely that the information needs of patrons while on a city street interacting with their cellphone will be very different from when they are sat at a computer at work or at home or when in a physical library space. These needs will likely coevolve with the available functionalities, interface and suitably organised and indexed information. Design of appropriate information services will need librarians with understanding of information, indexing, information needs and the potential of computational technologies.

Falling hardware costs, especially for storage are having another significant impact on what can feasibly be done with information. As affordable personal information storage devices move in capacity from gigabytes to terabytes and collective resources from terabytes to petabytes, it becomes feasible and economic to store what in the past we would have regarded as ephemeral and only potentially valuable data. This can include the ever-growing amount of text of varying degrees of formality, from conventional books and articles to memos, working documents, drafts and e-mails. It can also include more memory intensive resources such as images, video and sensor data. For example, it is possible to imagine videotaping and storing every single meeting. This may well be socially or organizationally undesirable, but it is no longer economically infeasible.

There is likely to be an increasing demand for help not just with accessing information created by others, but with storing and organizing information created locally. The challenges of archiving an organization's e-mail and Web pages are just an early indicator of this issue. The growth of ubiquitous computing, low cost sensors and increasing networking means that the quantity of data that can be collected and might be shared is exploding. Currently there is a lot of interest in digitization and scholarly repositories. When coupled with new kinds of media and huge amounts of sensor data, this creation and use of information begins to have a substantial impact in e-science, e-social science and humanities computing.

Librarians are ideally positioned to advise on the storage, accessing and indexing of this information, creating many new opportunities, but ones that are in constant flux as new data sources become available and older data needs to be converted or merged into new formats. A database (or a federation of many databases) of sensor data may not normally be considered as a digital library, but it has many critical similarities, and those creating and maintaining them are effectively librarians even if they do not realize their role or indeed their lack of experience and need for advice on librarianship.

Social Software

The current flurry of interest in Web 2.0 applications serves to remind us of how incremental changes to software can have qualitatively dramatic impacts on how applications are perceived and used. Blogs, wikis, podcasts, tagging, mashups, and other social software have many precursors in earlier applications, but when made sufficiently easy to adopt, use, appropriate, combine and innovate with, they can lead to dramatic rates of creativity. With Web 2.0 applications, much of this comes from combining data and applications, challenging our views of, say, carefully optimized monolithic digital libraries. The challenge comes to design information structures that can cope with frequent change and unexpected use. Optimization of anticipated use may be less important that robustness and flexibility under unexpected use.

This means that in teaching computational sense we need to provide not just a comfort and fluency with computer applications, and a sense of how to go about refining them or designing new ones. Additionally, we need to provide a sense of the nature of information in use and how metadata can help as well as a sense of programmability.

The history of computing applications developed for use in library contexts is one of significant innovations from small numbers of very talented, enthusiastic self-taught individuals branching out from a home in computer science or librarianship to embrace the other discipline. Can we actually teach people to take on this kind of multidisciplinary role? We doubt there are many who are willing to become both expert computer scientists and expert librarians, but we do think that it is possible to have large numbers who are at least confident in conversing about design across disciplinary boundaries.

There is already a professional group of systems librarians, who by virtue of their work have inevitably acquired computational sense. However, we believe that there needs to be a set of basic understandings of the processes of using and designing computer applications, a sense of what might be possible and what is reasonable to expect or even demand that ought to pervade the whole profession, not just a particular specialism.

By analogy, within traditional librarianship there is a widespread belief that all librarians should at least understand the basic concepts of cataloguing and classification, not just those who are intending to be full time cataloguers. This is because the underlying principles of cataloguing and classification pervade all kinds of activities throughout the profession. We are claiming that in an increasingly computerised profession, there is a similar need for a certain basic level of understanding of what computers do, how they do it and what is likely to be possible in the future—a set of issues that extends beyond basic IT literacy and confidence in using current computer applications.

Supporting New Kinds of Help-giving

Librarianship has always been about being an information intermediary. Sometimes this is done behind the scenes both by careful traditional cataloguing and by the design of information access interfaces such as online catalogues so that patrons can find their way to the information they want, seemingly on their own. But there remains the role of more explicit intermediation, via reference interviews and education and training interactions, helping patrons learn how to use new applications, and more advanced features of existing ones, as well as various information literacy skills to make sense of what they find and how to make informed choices when faced with incredible riches of modern resources.

Just as librarians need to acquire metacognitive skills to maintain their own ongoing professional development in the light of more applications, new versions, new interfaces, and new uses, so they need to acquire the technical and pedagogical skills to help their patrons to do likewise. Thus, the computational sense skills needed to be constantly learning new things also need to support the constant sharing of this knowledge in the teaching of new things. Traditionalist models of fixed training will not work for either librarians or patrons—there is just too much and it changes too quickly. What are the longer lasting skills that remain when the particular applications learned at library school become obsolete, say 18 months after graduation?

Computational sense is clearly closely related to information literacy, and shares many components, but we believe the distinctions to be important and worth noting. Information literacy involves a fluency with existing available computational tools and treats their use as a contextualized activity where attention is paid not just to how the tools are used to find information, but what that information is, and how it should be assessed and used in inform further tool use. It focuses on intelligent use of tools to hand to achieve current goals. By contrast computational sense is more concerned with the future than the present—the consideration of which new tools and features might be built, how and why, and how they might be integrated with current and future forms of working. Information literacy and computational sense are consequently not in competition or contradictory analyses of computer use. Rather they are highly complementary, but serve different goals.

Research Issues

Although advocating for computational sense as a way to allow people to exploit the potential of new technologies and applications to meet the traditional concerns of helping people access information, we do not believe that this is a solved problem that just requires implementation. Considerable research is needed to help us understand these issues and how to address them pedagogically, organizationally and technically.

As with any other issues in the use of libraries, and in computer systems in general, much can be learned from a user-centred approach. Ethnographic studies of existing practice would be highly informative. These could highlight both best practice (people acquiring and applying what we would call computational sense, the adoption and application of new technologies or new uses of technologies in library contexts) as well as current pathologies (such as computer applications that visibly frustrate people's attempts to learn, share, appropriate or innovate, or organizational mechanisms that hinder formal and informal applications of computational sense).

An analysis of existing practice can then inform design interventions to try and address challenges of how best to teach, or perhaps nurture the acquisition of computational sense through exploration and innovation with new technologies. All these issues are mirrored for the *developers* of digital library software, who have the design challenge to make their systems understandable, tailorable, and extensible.

CONCLUSION

Computational sense extends beyond the notion of programming to encompass an ability to understand the broader notions of the capabilities of software and the sociotechnical issues of usability, system deployment and maintenance. In this chapter, we have proposed some characteristics of computational sense and how they might influence the design of the curriculum for digital librarians. Current software used in courses on digital libraries has to balance (in an ad hoc manner) elements of computer science with traditional library science. We have provided several computational sense

topics that should help clarify the design of both courses and software involved in the education of digital librarians.

REFERENCES

Coleman, A. (2005). Interdisciplinarity, interactivity, and interoperability for educating the digerati. *Education for Information, 23*(4), 233–243.

Erlich, K., & Cash, D. (1994). Turning information into knowledge: Information finding as a collaborative activity. In *Proceedings of Digital Libraries '94* (DL'94) (pp. 119–125). College Station, TX.

Kajberg, L., & Lørring, L. (Eds.). (2005). *European curriculum reflections on library and information science education.* The Royal School of Library and Information Science, Copenhagen, Denmark. Retrieved August 30, 2008, from http://www.asis.org/Bulletin/Dec-06/EuropeanLIS.pdf

Kyng, M., & Mathiassen, L. (Eds.). (1997). *Computers and design in context.* Cambridge, MA: MIT Press.

Ma, Y., Clegg, W., & O'Brien, A. (2006). Digital library education: The current status. In *Proceedings of the 6th ACM/IEEE-CS Joint Conference on Digital Libraries (JCDL'06)* (pp. 165–174). New York: ACM Press.

Marion, L. (2001). Digital librarian, cybrarian, or librarian with specialized skills: Who will staff digital libraries? In H. Thompson (Ed.), *Crossing the Divide: Proceedings of the Tenth National Conference of the Association of College and Research Libraries* (pp. 143–149). Chicago, IL: American Library Association.

Mostafa, J., Brancolini, K., Smith, L.C., & Mischo, W. (2005). Developing a digital library education program. In *Proceedings of the 5th ACM/IEEE-CS Joint Conference on Digital Libraries (JCDL'05)* (p. 427). New York: ACM Press.

Nichols, D.M., Bainbridge, D., Downie, J.S., & Twidale, M.B. (2006). Learning by building digital libraries. In *Proceedings of the 6th ACM/IEEE-CS Joint Conference on Digital Libraries (JCDL'06)* (pp. 185–186). New York: ACM Press.

Nichols, D.M., Bainbridge, D., Marsden, G., Patel, D., Cunningham, S.J., Thompson, J., et al. (2005). Evolving tool support for digital librarians. In Y.-L. Theng, & S. Foo (Eds.), *Design and Usability of Digital Libraries: Case Studies in the Asia Pacific* (pp. 171–189). Information Science Publishing, London.

Nichols, D.M., Bainbridge, D., & Twidale, M.B. (2007). Constructing digital library interfaces. In *Proceedings of the 7th ACM/IEEE Joint Conference on Digital Libraries (JCDL '07)* (pp. 331–332). New York: ACM Press.

Pomerantz, J., Oh, S., Wildemuth, B.M., Yang, S., & Fox, E.A. (2007). Digital library education in computer science programs. In *Proceedings of the 7th ACM/IEEE Joint Conference on Digital Libraries (JCDL '07)* (pp. 177–178). New York: ACM Press.

Pomerantz, J., Oh, S., Yang, S., Fox, E.A., & Wildemuth, B. (2006a). The core: Digital library education in library and information science programs. *D-Lib Magazine, 12*(11). Retrieved August 30, 2008, from http://www.dlib.org/dlib/november06/pomerantz/11pomerantz.html

Pomerantz, J., Wildemuth, B.M., Yang, S., & Fox, E.A. (2006b). Curriculum development for digital libraries. In *Proceedings of the 6th ACM/IEEE-CS Joint Conference on Digital Libraries (JCDL'06)* (pp. 175–184). New York: ACM Press.

Tansley, R., Smith, M., & Walker, J.H. (2005). The DSpace open source digital asset management system: Challenges and opportunities. In *Proceedings of the 9th European Conference on Research and Advanced Technology for Digital Libraries (ECDL 2005)* (pp. 242–253). LNCS 3652. Springer.

Von Hippel, E. (2005). *Democratizing innovation.* Cambridge, MA: MIT Press.

Yang, S., Fox, E.A., Wildemuth, B., Pomerantz, J., & Oh, S. (2006). Interdisciplinary curriculum development for digital library education. In *Proceedings of the 9th International Conference on Asian Digital Libraries (ICADL 2006)* (pp. 61–70). LNCS 4312. New York: Springer.

Wing, J.M. (2006). Computational thinking. *Communications of the ACM, 49*(3), 33–35.

Witten, I.H., & Bainbridge, D. (2003). *How to build a digital library.* San Francisco, CA: Morgan Kaufmann.

KEY TERMS

Computational Sense: A familiarity with the capabilities of computer applications and the ability to easily grasp the difficulty in implementing a computer-based solution. Typically acquired by learning a programming language.

Digital Librarianship: The knowledge and skills needed to design and implement digital information services.

Incremental Tailoring: The process of making small changes to a computer application to achieve a final effect; typically, this involves changes to the interface for the end user.

Programmers: People with skills in writing and maintaining computer programs. Typically programmers will have been through several computer science courses.

Programming Language: A high-level set of instructions to control the behaviour of a computer. Although high-level compared with the electronics of computers programming languages are still difficult to learn and most people cannot write a computer program.

Chapter LVIII
Digital Libraries Overview and Globalization

Soh Whee Kheng Grace
Nanyang Technological University, Singapore

ABSTRACT

Library digitization on a global basis is essential in the twenty-first century. The digital library development initiatives in most countries depend substantially on their national libraries. This chapter focuses on an overview of how national libraries of 14 countries in the Asia-Pacific region are involved in digital library initiatives. Most libraries participate in the collaborative efforts to build digital libraries with support from their government. Some focus on digitization and preservation activities, while others concentrate on digitization standards. Requirements for digital library implementation from a global perspective are essential. With the understanding of the current situation in Asia Pacific, we can understand the readiness of national libraries aiming for globalization in this part of the world, and action can be taken to achieve the aim. The globalization of digital libraries is what the world should be heading towards as we enter the next century.

INTRODUCTION

There are many definitions of digital libraries, and the concept of digital libraries is invoked in various contexts. It might refer to the system in which a collection is located, or it could refer to the organization underlying a collection. Therefore, the digital library is a system that stores mass digital information resources in different formats and allows their access by end users through net-

work transmission. It is also an organization that provides the resources to select, structure, access, interpret, distribute, and preserve the integrity and usability of collections of digital works so that they are available for use by a specific community or set of communities (Digital Library Federation, 2004; Zhou, 2005).

It is essential for libraries worldwide to aim for globalization in the twenty-first century. When countries around the world exchange digital information, it increases worldwide relations (Ani & Biao, 2005). An interconnected global digital library can contain the unique cultural treasures of various countries, and by offering free access, it would help people understand one another better (Billington, 2005). The term "globalization" implies that it is a worldwide phenomenon. Therefore it plays a great role contributing economically, socially, culturally, and politically in the world society. It also increases the cooperation among many nations (Iwe, 2005).

The Internet is commonly used today; therefore, libraries should overcome the limitations of physical distance to deliver information through online means. Bultmann, Hardy, Muir, and Wictor (2006) state that digitization improves access to material, saves storage space and minimizes the handling of originals, which helps in the preservation of material. Undertaking digitization initiatives will attract new users and support distance learning (Baba, 2005). Tedd and Large (2005) added that digitization processes are becoming more affordable and effective, therefore digital libraries are being established worldwide, and many countries are digitizing their collections (Bultmann et al., 2006). It is, therefore, the right time for libraries to aim for globalization. In the next section, an overview of how the national libraries of countries in the Asia-Pacific region are involved in digital library development initiatives is discussed.

OVERVIEW OF ACTIONS

There are 58 countries in the Asia-Pacific region (Foo & Theng, 2005), and these include countries in East Asia, South Asia, Southeast Asia and Oceania. This section focuses on 14 countries, mainly four in East Asia—China, Japan, Korea, Taiwan; two in South Asia—India and Sri Lanka; six in Southeast Asia—Indonesia, Malaysia, Philippines, Singapore, Thailand, Vietnam; and two in Oceania—Australia and New Zealand.

East Asia

China, Japan, Korea and Taiwan are advancing in their digital library initiatives and digitization efforts. They have collaborated or cooperated with their partners internally. More work in the international arena should be encouraged.

National Library of China (http://www.nlc.gov.cn)

China has been undertaking a number of digital library projects since 1996. The China National Digital Library (CNDL) project (http://www.nlc. gov.cn/ndlc/index.htm) is one of the collaborative projects that the National Library of China (NLC) is leading. Its partners include libraries, universities, research institutions, and Internet-based companies (Liu & Zhang, 2001). The NLC aims to construct the largest collection of Chinese resources of excellent quality to provide efficient services to both China and the world through the nation's backbone networks and international principle technologies (Zhou, 2005). The China Academic Library and Information System (CALIS) is a nationwide academic library consortium (http://www.calis.edu.cn). Its resource and information service network involves the cooperation of libraries and organizations, such as NLC, Online Computer Library Center (OCLC, USA), the British Library and National Institute of Informatics, Japan (Yao, Chen, & Dai, 2004).

To develop the Chinese Pilot Digital Library (CPDL) project, the NLC aims to cooperate with nine public libraries in China. The objective is to unify distributed resources and construct standardized digital libraries. There is ongoing research and they have made good progress on metadata standards (Liu, 2004; Zhou, 2005). The CNDL, CALIS and CPDL are funded by national investment, which is under the Chinese government (Zhou, 2005). The NLC adopts modern technology, leads the standardization of the digitization of libraries, and works to provide online services (Library Society of China, 2006). There is ongoing research work on various standards and specifications for digital libraries. The next focus is to plan to retrain librarians to become digital librarians (Zhou, 2005).

National Diet Library, Japan (http://www.ndl.go.jp/en/index.html)

The only national library in Japan is the National Diet Library (NDL). It has been cooperating with libraries in various projects, and is supportive of the United Nations Educational, Scientific and Cultural Organization (UNESCO) "Virtual Memory of the World" project. The NDL's digital library contains approximately 55,000 digitized volumes of books published during the Meiji period (1867–1912), of which the copyright has expired. Its collection includes rare books and information on Diet session proceedings. This digital library has a search function but it offers only a Japanese interface and there is no distinction between government and nongovernment publications in its database. An online exhibition of its digitized collection (http://www.ndl.go.jp/constitution/e/) contains the digital images and texts of government documents, diplomacy records, and political figures' diaries. It is displayed in both English and Japanese but no search function is available (Koga, 2005).

The Web Archiving Project (WARP) is the NDL's main project since it started in 2002. It is supposed to collect selective Japanese Web content but several government agencies have not allow their Web sites to be included in WARP (http://warp.ndl.go.jp). At present, it provides snapshots of archived content and lacks a search function for its government Web contents (Koga, 2005). Currently, the NDL is working on principles for legislation for acquiring and providing the networked electronic publications. The issue on how to develop standards for metadata creation is also one of the priorities of NDL (Yokoyama, 2006).

National Library of Korea (http://www.nl.go.kr)

National Library of Korea (NLK) aims to become a world library by 2010. One of its goals is to be the global portal and gateway for library and information centers (Hee, Duk, & Young, 2006). The NLK is publicizing the establishment of the National Digital Library (NDL), which is funded by the government (Hee et al., 2006; Lee, 2006a). The NDL (http://www.dlibrary.go.kr) contains digital publications and online information resources that would meet the user demand for service and improve efficiency in searching for information (Lee, 2006a). In addition, the NLK has become the key organization to develop an integrated national digital library system that connects seven major domestic institutes, including the NLK, the National Assembly Library, Korea Research and Development Information Center, Korea Education and Research Information Service, Science Library of Korea Advanced Institute of Science Technology, Korea Institute of Industry and Technology Information, and Library of Court. The NLK has also proposed a basic model of a digital library that provides one-stop information service for users, and builds databases for article indexes and abstracts, which includes complete bibliographies and full-texts for the visually impaired (Bae, Jeong, Shim, & Kwak, 2007).

As for standards, the NLK is using a standardized tool, Korean Machine Readable Cataloguing (KORMARC) Rules, as a Korean standard for processing publication information. The Dublin Core Metadata Initiative (DCMI) Metadata description (ISO 15836) as a descriptive format is used by the NLK for digital resources to build the Online Archiving and Searching Internet Sources (OASIS). It has agreed to set up a metadata center to maintain the metadata registry and provide guidance for reusing various metadata. Recognizing the need to promote the cooperation of libraries and other institutions, the NLK joins the DCMI affiliate program to aid in the active utilization of metadata (Lee, 2006b).

National Central Library, Taiwan (http://www.ncl.edu.tw/english/index.asp)

In Taiwan, many digital library initiatives have become full-fledged projects (Urs, 2005). The National Central Library (NCL) is the only national library in Taiwan. Its "Remote Electronic Access/Delivery of Document Services" (READncl: http://readopac.ncl.edu.tw/eindex. htm) allows users to retrieve, copy, fax and e-mail the indexes and full-text information of its rich collection since 1998. Its collection has about five million pages of text images. Furthermore, the NCL cooperates with professional groups and academic organizations to digitize content in specific disciplines (Ke & Hwang, 2000). Currently, the NCL collaborates with the National Archives in the National Digital Archives Project (Baba, 2005). This project involves the digitization of its unique cultural heritage collections (Chen, Chen, Chen, & Hsiang, 2002). It also involves the digitization of public access resources, including Chinese periodicals, newspapers and government reports.

South Asia

The national libraries of India and Sri Lanka in South Asia have also been undertaking digitization work, and they see the importance of collaboration both nationally and internationally. Though there is still much work to be done, they have had a good start.

National Library of India (http://www.nlindia.org/modernisation.html)

In India, many reputable funded activities on digitization initiatives are undertaken mainly by academic and research-oriented institutions both nationally and internationally. The National Library of India (NLI) has been digitizing frequently-used rare books and documents published before 1900, as well as Indian publications on compact discs. Currently, a total of 25 million pages of selected books in Indian and English languages have been recorded. Moreover, there are also East India Company records, diaries and materials on paper and palm leaves, but the digitization activities are currently fragmented and diversified. The government of India and major research organizations are supportive of collaborating with national and international agencies on large projects, therefore several libraries are taking part in digitization activities (Dasgupta, 2005). Few works are being headed by NLI.

The libraries undertaking digitization activities face many problems and barriers. Most projects are independent and involve one-time effort. They lack well-conceived and carefully-planned objectives. Besides, there is no policy framework at the national level, and there is a lack of well-trained personnel for digital works. Technological problems include the lack of non-standard technical activities and multiple Indian language optical character recognition (OCR) facilities. Furthermore, it is difficult to sustain digitization efforts and digital libraries, due to the lack of proper preservation policies (Dasgupta, 2005). The plan for India in the near future is to extend the digitization efforts from books to other sources. Research on Indian language technology is ongoing. The aim is to create a central portal for all the digital library efforts in India, and to have new technologies for digitalizing sources (Balakrishnan, 2006).

National Library of Sri Lanka (http://www.natlib.lk)

The National Library of Sri Lanka (NLSL) is playing a major role in the collection and preservation of the nation's intellectual heritage (Gangabadadarachchi & Amarasiri, 2006). It is collaborating with the Department of National Archives for the compilation of the National Bibliography, and this is sponsored by the President's fund. The NLSL is also restoring the museum library collection by working with the Department of National Museums. This project is funded by the Japanese government (Baba, 2005). Its current work is to digitize the national library's collection, and it has started a project on the development of a digital library (Gangabadadarachchi & Amarasiri, 2006).

Southeast Asia

The national libraries of developed countries in Southeast Asia are collaborating with their partners to provide easy access to information. As for developing countries in Southeast Asia, the development of digital libraries and the sustainability of digitization efforts would require both the support from their government as well as international collaboration.

Bandung Institute of Technology Central Library, Indonesia (www.itb.ac.id)

Urs (2005) stated that Indonesia has its first Indonesian Digital Library Network (IDLN: http://as.lib.itb.ac.id) when it collaborated with the government and diverse sectors, together with grant support from the International Development Research Center (IDRC) of Canada, and the Indonesian Foundation for Telecommunication and Information Network (YLTI). This digital library initiative began after the development of a Web site for the Bandung Institute of Technology (ITB) Central Library (Sulistyo-Basuki, 2004).

National Library of Malaysia (http://www.pnm.my)

With support from the government, Malaysia has started a national program on digital library development with a well-defined national framework (Urs, 2005). The National Digital Library System (http://www.mylib.com.my) is developed by the National Library of Malaysia (NLM) to create a knowledge-rich society. This system could facilitate the networking and sharing of digital resources among all libraries (Shaifol & Nasir, 2005). The NLM has also developed the International Islamic Digital Library (http://www.iidl.net) (Baba, 2005). With the collaboration of the Department of Museums and Antiquity, and the National Archives, the NLM has a portal on Malaysia's monarchy, which is the institution of the King of Malaysia (http://www.yangdipertuanagong.com). The National IT Council under the Demonstrator Application Grants Scheme (DAGS) funded this project (Baba, 2005).

Furthermore, the NLM and 22 academic libraries have joint digitization efforts. During the process of digitization, most libraries face problems. They need manpower and training to carry out the digitization work, as well as guidelines and standards for digitization and the handling of copyright issues (Shaifol & Nasir, 2005). As a member of the steering committee, the NLM was involved in formulating the guidelines for the preservation of electronic records, which is coordinated by the National Archives of Malaysia. The next digital initiative for the NLM would be to discuss collaboration efforts with the National Archives, National Museum and the National Art Gallery (Baba, 2005).

National Library of the Philippines (http://www.nlp.gov.ph)

Philippine eLib (http://www.elib.gov.ph) is the first public digital library in Philippines. This collaborative project involving the National Library of the Philippines (NLP), University of the Philippines and government departments provides 25 million pages of digitized Filipino rare books, serials, government publications, maps, photos, bibliographic records and online databases of full-text journals (Phillippine eLibrary Project, http://www.ndl.go.jp/en/publication/cdnlao/054/544.html).

The NLP and its partners—the National Museum, Cultural Centre of the Philippines, Records Management and Archives Office, National Historical Institute and Commission of the Filipino language—are involved in the Association of Southeast Asian Nations–Committee on Culture and Information (ASEAN-COCI) project, which handles the preservation of cultural heritage and the dissemination of cultural materials among ASEAN countries (Baba, 2005).

National Library Board (NLB), Singapore (http://www.nlb.gov.sg)

To support the digital library infrastructure, the National Library Board (NLB) of Singapore has embraced e-learning through the delivery of content and programmes. Currently, the NLB's digital library offers access to two e-learning courses. It hopes to increase its e-learning course repository (Tan & Munoo, 2006). The NLB is collaborating with the National Archives of Singapore (NAS) and the Singapore National Museum, which comprises the Singapore History Museum, Singapore Art Museum and Asian Civilization Museum, on a number of cultural heritage projects, including content digitization and cataloguing of the NAS posters database (Baba, 2005). The NLB aims to provide the world's knowledge to Singapore and creating real-time knowledge access. Therefore, it would create the collaborative space and environment, playing a leading role in the building of Singapore's collection of knowledge assets and a supporting role to collaborators and partners ("Library 2010," http://www.nlb.gov.sg/CPMS. portal?_nfpb=true&_pageLabel=Library2010).

National Library of Thailand (http://www.nlt.go.th)

The National Library of Thailand (NLT) has reported its involvement in the National Cultural Heritage preservation and conservation under the Department of Fine Arts Policy. Participants of this project include the National Archives and Museum as well as private archives, museums, and art galleries (Baba, 2005). Tedd and Large (2005) gave an example of a digital library in Thailand, belonging to the Child Institute Foundation (http://www.childthai.org). The NLT offers a bibliographic database of books and periodicals. It plans to provide the digitized form of rare books and manuscripts for users to view online in the future. At present, the NLT's resources are difficult to access. The local government should play an important role in digital initiatives (Salaladyanant, 2006).

National Library of Vietnam (http://www.nlv.gov.vn)

The National Library of Vietnam (NLV), located in Hanoi, has started a project on digital libraries. This project targets to provide published materials in various formats to about five million overseas Vietnamese. The NLV is working with the Vietnamese Nom Preservation Foundation to digitize old Chinese and Vietnamese manuscripts, and they aim to put the digital copies of the collection on an online database (National Library of Vietnam, http://www.nla.gov.au/lap/Viet07_000.rtf). The NLV has also started digitizing 50,000 pages of doctoral thesis synopses (Nguyen, 2004)

The NLV has many projects in collaboration with foreign partners. A project on bridging the digital divide in 64 provincial/city libraries and nearly 700 district libraries in Vietnam is being carried out together with the NLV, General Sciences Library of Ho Chi Minh City and the government. This project is funded by the Bill and Melinda Gates Foundation, and is expected to lay the foundations for the funding from Global Libraries Program of the Bill and Melinda Gates Foundation. The NLV, the National Library of Laos, the National Library of Cambodia and other libraries have been digitizing old French materials and this project is funded by the Government of France. It aims to offer easy access for users through digital media and to provide preservation of the originals (National Library of Vietnam, 2007).

Oceania

In the Oceania region, national libraries of Australia and New Zealand have developed a number of digital libraries and there are ongoing projects to enhance their online services. Both countries are looking into metadata activities and areas that will enhance their services.

National Library of Australia (http://www.nla.gov.au)

The National Library of Australia (NLA), through its digital library programs and initiation, coordination and promotion, has developed an important digital library capability in the form of digital collection sites and services (Gatenby, 2007; Urs, 2005). The NLA, the National Film and Sound Archive and other cultural institutions have produced three portals. Picture Australia (http://www.pictureaustralia.org) is the NLA's image service, which provides more than a million Australia-related images from cultural institutions and agencies, including libraries, museums, galleries and archives (Baba, 2005; Gatenby, 2007). Music Australia (http://www.musicaustralia.org) offers online access to Australian music resources, including digitized music, music scores, musicians, composers, and a wide range of other music-related materials (Baba, 2005). The Australia Dancing portal (http://www.australiadancing.org) grants users access to current and historical information about dance in Australia. The NLA plans to release People Australia in 2008—a database containing biographical records of people and organizations (Gatenby, 2007).

The NLA and National Archives are cooperating in metadata activities (Baba, 2005). It also collaborates with new partners, for instance, Flickr to harvest metadata for Australia-related

pictures, and Google to make Libraries Australia records accessible through its services. The NLA has started a project to use open search protocol for an integrated search of the collections of Australian libraries and other cultural institutions. To make the NLA collections visible in the global context, its relationship with Google and OCLC plays a major role. The current work includes digitizing a greater range of sources and providing access to full-text content, starting with searchable Australian old newspapers. The NLA has identified some enhancements in services for the near future, for instance, improving the accessibility of online full-text resources and search functionality, especially for extending integrated searching (Gatenby, 2007).

National Library of New Zealand (http://www.natlib.govt.nz)

The National Library of New Zealand (NLNZ) is the leading agency for handling collaborative projects. EPIC (http://www.epic.org.nz) is a self-funded consortium of 179 libraries and all schools in New Zealand for the purchase of e-content (Rigby, O'Donovan, & Searle, 2006). The Matapihi (http://www.matapihi.org.nz) is a Web-based metadata gateway service to the online digital collections. It provides a window to people, places and events of New Zealand. It enables cross-searching and selection of 75,000 records of pictures, sounds and objects. This project is made available through the collaboration of eight organizations: the NLNZ, archives, libraries, museums and galleries in New Zealand (Baba, 2005; Rigby, et al., 2006). Through the collaboration with other libraries, archives and museums, the NLNZ and its partners have increased confidence and skills, and they have better collections, which could attract more users (Rigby et al., 2006).

The NLNZ is currently working with the DCMI Date Working Group to provide for the interoperable representation of commonly recorded dates

(Rigby et al., 2006). It has also been working on the preservation metadata. The problems that the NLNZ is facing include the lack of international consensus on the preservation metadata, which restricts the full implementation of a preservation metadata strategy at the library, and the lack of a common standard, which gives rise to the difficulty of moving resources from conceptual development to practical implementation. Furthermore, the project on preservation metadata also requires funding (Knight, 2005).

RECOMMENDATIONS

From a global perspective, one must look into the language and technology for digital libraries. The requirements of users and services should also be considered (Tedd & Large, 2005). It is essential for countries to seek collaboration both domestically and internationally in digital library initiatives. This section briefly discusses these areas of consideration.

Language is closely connected to the different aspects of heritage, including culture, literature, history, philosophy and education (Woldering, 2006). A global digital library that manages cross-cultural communication requires the support of a multilingual catalogue and search interfaces (Gao, 2006). The global network of digital libraries must be a network that appreciates and values the multiple perspectives of distinct cultures, and to achieve the vision of worldwide access to information, knowledge must be created and stored in formats and architectures accessible to everyone (Mason, 2005). English could be used in the globalization effort, as it is the language most commonly used. Therefore, multilingual services that can interface English with other languages are essential (Xia, 2006). Most national libraries in Asia-Pacific region see the need to have English interfaces for their digital libraries; for instance, the national libraries of Korea, Taiwan, Malaysia and New Zealand have English interfaces. The

national libraries of China and Japan are working to create an English interface.

The technology for digital libraries covers a wide aspect. Tedd and Large (2005) classify it into three areas. In term of standards and interoperability, metadata, presentation standards, digital object locators and protocols should be considered. Another area on digital information sources includes full-text materials, metadata sources, multimedia materials, Web sites and quality issues, suppliers of some digital information sources and the creation of digitized sources. The subject disciplines, curation and preservation are to be considered too. For organizing access to digital information sources, the software and architecture, interface design, searching and browsing functions should be taken into account. Young, Horwood, and Sullivan (2006) included technical infrastructure, middleware, and access to resources between institutions as requirements for consideration.

It is important to consider security, access rights, liability, privacy issues, and intellectual property rights when there is sharing of data and transmission across national boundaries. For successful distribution of information on either the national or international level, the rights and responsibilities of those who provide and use the data should be clearly spelt out (Young et al., 2006). Due to copyright laws, only books that are noncopyrighted or those books that are permitted by authors are digitized. Professor Raj Reddy proposed a "Consortium for Compensating for Creating Contents" scheme for authors (Balakrishnan, 2006). User and community needs are areas of consideration too (Young et al., 2006). Librarians have to meet the challenges of the changing environment, in term of its cultural, technical and professional relativities (Omekwu & Eteng, 2006). Gorman (2006) encourages librarians to play a major role in educating people, preparing library users for productive global information use.

Collaborating with partners both domestically and internationally in digital libraries-related projects would yield bigger and better collections. It is more cost-effective with the shared infrastructure, facilities, hardware and software, and attracts more funding opportunities. Collaborative projects also promote the use of cross-domain standards, benchmarking and professional development and are good for raising profiles and marketing. However, collaboration requires common terminology to be used between partners, prevention of tensions between organizational cultures, and the reconciliation of different standards. It demands flexibility between parties, innovation and commitment to reach a common goal. It is crucial to manage collaborative projects with effective communication and people skills as well as an understanding of technology and management practices (Rigby et al., 2006).

CONCLUSION

National libraries of developed countries in the Asia-Pacific region are progressing well in their digital library initiatives, and their governments are supportive in funding the projects and in collaboration with other partners, both domestically and internationally. Some national libraries of developing countries have realized the importance of reaching out to their people with digital information, and are moving ahead in digital library initiatives with international collaborative efforts and funding.

In the Asia-Pacific region, almost 70% of the populations have little or no connectivity to the digital world (Foo & Theng, 2005). Though national libraries might be involved in digital library initiatives, they might not have the capability to serve their people with digital content, and the people might not be able to afford the Internet connection to access digital information. Foo and Theng (2005) discussed the importance of eliminating or closing the digital gap to improve the current situation.

Globalization has drawn the world closer together. Rich nations enjoy the benefit of digital technologies but poor nations will be lagging behind in this knowledge age. Researchers at Harvard University and MIT have created a Web site to help close the digital divide (Digital Divide. org, 2007; Tedd & Large, 2005). But there are many factors and issues to look into for closing the digital gap. Governments and organizations play an important role in promoting globalization by promulgating beneficial policies and providing financial sponsorship (Xia, 2006) for the construction of digital libraries. Therefore, the aim for globalization of digital libraries depends a great deal on collaborative work. With the support of governments, international agencies and business entities, developing countries will have funding and staffing to undertake digital library initiatives (Byrne, 2005).

There are great challenges for countries in the Asia-Pacific region to work towards globalization. Currently, most national libraries are working towards providing their people's needs and have yet to set goals and objectives to reach out to the world with their information. However, current efforts put into digitization by most Asia-Pacific countries would reap their rewards in time to come. It is not impossible for these libraries to aim for globalization.

REFERENCES

Ani, O.E., & Biao, E.P. (2005). Globalization: Its impact on scientific research in Nigeria. *Journal of librarianship and information science, 37*(3), 153–160.

Baba, D.Z. (2005). Networking cultural heritage: An overview of initiatives for collaboration among national libraries, museums and archives in Asia and Oceania. *World Library and Information Congress: 71st IFLA general conference and council.*

Retrieved August 30, 2008, from http://www.ifla. org/IV/ifla71/Programme.htm

Bae, K.J., Jeong, Y.S., Shim, W.S., & Kwak, S.J. (2007). The ubiquitous library for the blind and physically handicapped—a case study of the LG Sangnam library, Korea. *IFLA Journal, 33*(3), 210–219.

Balakrishnan, N. (2006). Universal digital library connecting users to digital contents. *13th Biennial Conference and Exhibition*. Retrieved August 30, 2008, from http://www.vala.org.au/conf2006. htm

Billington, J. (2005). A digital library that all nations can learn from James Billington. *London: The Financial Times Limited*.

Bultmann, B., Hardy, R., Muir, A., & Wictor, C. (2006). Digitised content in the UK research library and archives sector. *Journal of librarianship and information science, 38*(2), 105–122.

Byrne, A. (2005). Promoting the global information commons. *International Federation of Library Associations and Institutions*. Retrieved August 30, 2008, from http://www.ifla.org/III/ wsis/wsis-24Feb05.html

Chen, C.C., Chen, H.H., Chen, K.H., & Hsiang, F. (2002). The design of metadata for the digital museum initiative in Taiwan. *Online Information Review, 26*(5), 295–306.

Dasgupta, K. (2005). National policy for library and information systems and services in India: The new scenario. *Alexandria, 17*(2), 97–103.

Digital Divide.org. (2007). *Ushering in the second digital revolution*. Retrieved August 30, 2008, from http://www.digitaldivide.org

Digital Library Federation. (2004). *A working definition of digital library [1998]*. Retrieved August 30, 2008, from http://www.diglib.org/ about/dldefinition.htm

Foo, S., & Theng, Y.L. (2005). Digital library trends in the Asia Pacific. *Digital Library Asia*.

Gangabadadarachchi, V., & Amarasiri, M.S.U. (2006). Digital collection building initiatives of National Library and Document Centre. *Sri Lankan Journal of Librarianship and Information Management, 2*(1), 38–43.

Gao, L.X.L. (2006). Accessing and using Australian university libraries' online resources and services – an offshore experience. *13th Biennial Conference and Exhibition*. Retrieved August 30, 2008, from http:// www.vala.org.au/conf2006. htm

Gatenby, P. (2007). Rapid and easy access: Finding and getting resources in Australian libraries and cultural institutions. *World Library and Information Congress: 73rd IFLA General Conference and Council*. Retrieved August 30, 2008, from http://www.ifla.org/IV/ifla73/index.htm

Gorman, G.E. (2006). For whom is the new information millennium? *Online Information Review, 30*(1), 5–7.

Hee, Y.Y., Duk, H.C., & Young, S.K. (2006). Libraries in Korea: A general overview. *IFLA Journal, 32*(2), 93–103.

Iwe, J.I. (2005). Globalization of information and the Nigerian librarian. *IFLA Journal, 31*(4), 44–51.

Ke, H.R., & Hwang, M.J. (2000). The development of digital libraries in Taiwan. *The Electronic Library, 18*(5), 336–346.

Knight, S. (2005). Preservation metadata: National Library of New Zealand experience. *Library Trends, 54*(1), 91–110.

Koga, T. (2005). Innovation beyond institutions: New projects and challenges for government information service institutions in Japan. *World Library and Information Congress: 71st IFLA general conference and council.* Retrieved August 30, 2008, from http://www.ifla.org/IV/ifla71/Programme.htm

Lee, C.J. (2006a). The role of the National Library of Korea in the competitiveness enhancement of libraries. *World Library and Information Congress: 72nd IFLA general conference and council.* Retrieved August 30, 2008, from http://www.ifla.org/IV/ifla72/papers/117-Lee-en.pdf

Lee, J.S. (2006b). Bibliographic control in Korea: Focus on the National Library of Korea. *World Library and Information Congress: 72nd IFLA general conference and council.* Retrieved August 30, 2008, from http://www.ifla.org/IV/ifla72/papers/084-Lee-en.pdf

Library Society of China. (2006). The vigorous advancement of libraries in China. *IFLA Journal, 32*(2), 113–118.

Liu, J. (2004). Metadata development in China. *D-Lib Magazine, 10*(12). Retrieved August 30, 2008, from http://www.dlib.org/dlib/december04/liu/12liu.html

Liu, Y.Q., & Zhang, J. (2001). Digital library infrastructure: A case study on sharing information resources in China. *International Information & Library Review, 33*, 205–220.

Mason, R.M. (2005). The critical role of librarian/information officer as boundary spanner across cultures—humans as essential components in global digital libraries. *World Library and Information Congress: 71st IFLA general conference and council.* Retrieved August 30, 2008, from http://www.ifla.org/IV/ifla71/Programme.htm

Nguyen, T.T.V. (2004). Country report Vietnam. *Conference of Directors of National Libraries.* Retrieved August 30, 2008, from http://consorcio.bn.br/cdnl/2005/HTML/CR%20Vietnam.htm

Omekwu, C.O., & Eteng, U. (2006). Roadmap to change: Emerging roles for information professionals. *Library Review, 55*(4), 267–277.

Rigby, F., O'Donovan, M., & Searle, S. (2006). National, cross-sector, collaborative projects that worked at the National Library of New Zealand Te Puna Matauranga o Aotearoa. *13th Biennial Conference and Exhibition.* Retrieved August 30, 2008, from http://www.vala.org.au/conf2006.htm

Salaladyanant, T. (2006). Digital libraries in Thailand. In C. Khoo, D. Singh, & A.S. Chaudhry (Eds.), *Proceedings A-LIEP 2006: Asia-Pacific Conference on Library & Information Education & Practice 2006 (A-LIEP 2006)* (pp. 148–155). Singapore.

Shaifol, Y.M., & Nasir, K. (2005). Digitization and sustainability of local collection: An observation of digitization activities among Malaysian universities libraries. *World Library and Information Congress: 71st IFLA general conference and council.* Retrieved August 30, 2008, from http://www.ifla.org/IV/ifla71/Programme.htm

Sulistyo-Basuki, L. (2004). Digitization of collections in Indonesian academic libraries. *Electronic library and information systems, 38*(3), 194–200.

Tan, D., & Munoo, R. (2006). Thinking about capacity building and sustainability of information literacy programmes: Re-engineering experiences by the National Library Board, Singapore. *World Library and Information Congress: 72nd IFLA general conference and council.* Retrieved August 30, 2008, from http://www.ifla.org/IV/ifla72/Programme2006.htm

Tedd, L.A., & Large, A. (2005). Digital libraries in context. In *Digital libraries principles and practice in a global environment* (pp.6-23). K.G. Munchen: Saur Verlag GmbH.

Urs, S.R. (2005). Digital libraries in the Asia-Pacific region: An overview. *Digital library Asia.*

Woldering, B. (2006). Connecting with users: Europe and multilinguality. *13th Biennial Confer-*

ence and Exhibition. Retrieved August 30, 2998, from http://www.vala.org.au/conf2006.htm

Xia, J.F. (2006). Scholarly communication in East and Southeast Asia: traditions and challenges. *IFLA Journal, 32*(2), 104–112.

Yao, X.X., Chen, L., & Dai, L.F. (2004). Current situation and future development of CALIS. *Library Management, 25*(6–7), 277–282.

Yokoyama, Y. (2006). Japanese national bibliography in the digital environment. *World Library and Information Congress: 72nd IFLA general conference and council.* Retrieved August 30, 2008, from http://www.ifla.org/IV/ifla72/Programme2006.htm

Young, E., Horwood, L., & Sullivan, S. (2006). Supporting E-research at the University of Melbourne. *13ᵗʰ Biennial Conference and Exhibition.* Retrieved August 30, 2008, from http://www.vala.org.au/conf2006.htm

Zhou, Q. (2005). The development of digital libraries in China and the shaping of digital librarians. *The Electronic Library, 23*(4), 433–441.

KEY TERMS

Consortium: A cooperative arrangement among groups or institutions for a common purpose.

Curation: The process of examining, testing, and selecting digital information to be included in a database collection.

Digital Divide/Gap: The imbalance in resources and skills that create a gap between those people with effective access to information technology, and those without access to it.

Dublin Core Metadata Initiative (DCMI): An open organization engaged in the development of interoperable online metadata standards that support a wide range of purposes and business models.

Infrastructure: The basic structure or features of a system.

Interoperability: The ability of different vendor devices to transmit data and exchange information, while having the total capability to process and act upon such information independently. This relies heavily on international standards.

Korean Machine Readable Cataloguing (KORMARC): A Korean standard for the representation and communication of bibliographic information in machine-readable form.

Metadata: The structured data that describes the characteristics of a resource. It is data about data; a library catalog in digitized format.

Middleware: The connectivity software that consists of a set of services that enables multiple processes interacting with one or more machines across a network.

Optical Character Recognition (OCR): The digital translation of images of handwritten, typewritten or printed text that is captured by a scanner into machine-editable text.

Protocol: A set of rules or standards that controls the connection, communication, and data transfer between two electronic devices or two computing endpoints.

Compilation of References

(CCSDS), C. (2002, January). Reference model for an open archival information system (OAIS) - blue book. Retrieved August 29, 2008, from http://public.ccsds.org/publications/archive/650x0b1.pdf

"GEO". Tech. Rep. Version 2.2, U.S. Federal Geographic Data Committee, U.S. Geological Survey.

Aaen, I. et al. (2001). A conceptual MAP of software process improvement. Scandinavian Journal of Information Systems, Special Issue on Trends in the Research on Software Process Improvement in Scandinavia, 13, 123–146.

Abberley, D., Kirby, D., Renals, S., & Robinson, T. (1999). The THISL broadcast new retrieval system. In Proceedings of the ESCA ETRW Workshop Accessing Information in Spoken Audio (pp.14-19).

Abels, E.G. (1996). The e-mail reference interview. RQ, 35(Spring), 348.

Abney, S. (1991). Parsing by chunks. In R. Berwick, S. Abney, & C. Tenny (Eds.), Principle-based parsing. Dordrecht: Kluwer Academic Publishers.

Abowd, G., & Mynatt, E. (2000). Charting past, present, and future research in ubiquitous computing. ACM Transactions on Computer-Human Interaction (TOCHI), 7(1) ,29–58.

Adam, N. R, Holowczak, R., Halem, R., & Yesha, Y. (1996). Digital library task force. IEEE Computer, 29(8).

Adami, A., Kajarekar, S., & Hermansky, H. (2002). A new speaker change detection method for two-speaker segmentation. Paper presented at ICASSP-02.

Adams, J.A., & Bonk, S.C. (1995). Digital information technologies and resources: Use by university faculty and faculty preferences for related library services. College and Research Libraries, 56, 119–131.

Adeyoyin, S.O. (2005). Strategic planning for marketing library services. Library Management, 26(8/9), 494–507.

ADL. (2001). Sharable content object reference model (SCORM) version 1.2.

Advanced distributed learning. (2007). SCORM® version 1.2. Retrieved November 15, 2007, from http://www.adlnet.gov/scorm/history/Scorm12/index.aspx

Afantenos, S., Doura, I., Kapellou, E., & Karkaletsis, V. (2004). Exploiting cross-document relations for multi-document evolving summarization. In G. A. Vouros & T. Panayiotopoulos (Eds.), Proceedings of the 3rd Helenic Conference on Artificial Intelligence (LNCS 3025, pp. 410-419). Berlin: Springer-Verlag.

Agnew, S., Gray, L., Blocker, L., Ryan, C.E., & Smith, K.L. (2006). Experiencing the electronic resources and libraries conference. Serials Review, 32(3), 195–203.

Ahadi, S. M., & Woodland, P. C. (1997). Combined Bayesian and predictive techniques for rapid speaker adaptation of continuous density hidden Markov models. Computer Speech and Language, 11, 187-206.

Ahmad, F., Chica, S.D.L., Butcher, K., Sumner, T., & Martin, J.H. (2007). Towards automatic conceptual personalization tools. In Proceedings of the ACM/IEEE-CS joint conference on Digital libraries (JCDL). Vancouver, Canada.

Ahmad, F., Gu, Q., & Sumner, T. (2006b). A technological infrastructure for developing curriculum based on learning progressions. In Proceedings of World Conference on Educational Multimedia, Hypermedia & Telecommunications (Ed-Media). Orlando, FL.

Ahmad, F., Gu, Q., & Sumner, T. (2006a). Concept space interchange protocol: A protocol for concept map based resource discovery in educational digital libraries. In Proceedings of the European Conference on Digital Libraries (ECDL). Alicante, Spain.

Aittola, M., Ryhänen, T., & Ojala, T. (2003). SmartLibrary: Location-aware mobile library service. In Proceedings of the Mobile HCI 2003 (LNCS 2795, pp. 411-416). Berlin: Springer-Verlag.

Akbacak, M., & Hansen, J. H. L. (2003). Environmental sniffing: Noise knowledge estimation for robust speech systems. In Proceedings of the IEEE ICASSP-2003: Inter. Conf. Acoust. Speech & Signal, Hong Kong (Vol. 2, pp. 113-116).

Akbacak, M., & Hansen, J. H. L. (2006). A robust fusion method for multilingual spoken document retrieval systems employing tiered resources. In Proceedings of the ISCA INTERSPEECH-2006/ICSLP-2006, Pittsburgh (pp. 1177-1180).

Akbacak, M., & Hansen, J. H. L. (2007). Environmental sniffing: Noise knowledge estimation for robust speech systems. IEEE Transactions on Audio, Speech and Language Processing, 15(2), 465-477.

Aktas, M., Nacar, N., & Menczer, F. (2004). Personalizing PageRank based on domain profiles. In Proceedings of the KDD Workshop on Web Mining and Web Usage (pp. 83-90).

Alavi, M., & Leidner, D. (2001). Knowledge management and knowledge management systems: Conceptual foundations and research issues. MIS Quaterly, 25(1), 107–136.

Albanese, A. (2005). Google to digitize 15 million books. LibraryJournal.com. Retrieved August 30, 2008, from http://libraryjournal.com/article/CA491156.html

Aleman-Meza, B., Halaschek, C., Arpinar, I. B., & Sheth, A. (2003). Context-aware semantic association ranking (Tech. Rep. 03-010). University of Georgia, LSDIS Lab, Computer Science.

Aleman-Meza, B., Halaschek, C., Sheth, A., Arpinar, I. B., & Sannapareddy, G. (2004). SWETO: Large-scale Semantic Web test-bed. In Proceedings of the 16th International Conference on Software Engineering & Knowledge Engineering Workshop on Ontology in Action, Knowledge Systems Inst. (pp. 490-493).

Aleman-Meza, B., Halaschek-Wiener, C., Sahoo, S. S., Sheth, A., & Arpinar, I. B. (2005). Template based semantic similarity for security applications (Tech. Rep.). University of Georgia, LSDIS Lab, Computer Science Department.

Alía Miranda, F. (coord.). (2004). Del texto al hipertexto, las bibliotecas Universitarias ante el reto de la digitalización. Cuenca: Ediciones de la Universidad de Castilla la Mancha.

Allan, J., Gupta, R., & Khandelwal, V. (2001). Temporal summaries of new topics. In Proceedings of the 24th Annual International ACM SIGIR Conference on Research and Development in Information Retrieval (pp.10-18). New York: ACM.

Allen, J. (1995). Natural language understanding. Redwood City, CA: Benjamin Cummings.

Ally, M., Clevelend-Innes, M., Boskic, N., & Larwill, S. (2006). Learners' use of learning objects. Journal of Distance Education, 21(2), 44-57. Retrieved November 16, 2007, from Academic Research Library database (Document ID: 1255253871).

Alvarez, F., Garza-Salazar, D., Lavariega, J., & Gómez-Martínez, L. (2005, July). PDLib: Personal digital libraries with universal access. Paper presented at the Joint International Conference on Digital Libraries, Denver, CO.

Alvite Díez, M.L., & Rodríguez Bravo, B. (2006). Colecciones de libros electrónicos en las bibliotecas universitarias españolas. In Actas de las VIII Jornadas de Gestión de la Información (pp. 147–159). Madrid.

Amato, G., Bolettieri, P., Debole, F., Falchi, F., Rabitti, F., & Savino, P. (2006). Using MILOS to build a multimedia digital library application: The PhotoBook experience. In J. Gonzalo (Ed.), Proceedings of the 10th European Conference on Digital Libraries (ECDL 2006) (LNCS 4172, pp. 379-390). Alicante, Spain: Sprinter.

Amato, G., Gennaro, C., Savino, P., & Rabitti, F. (2005). MILOS: A multimedia content management system for multimedia digital library applications. In A. Agosti (Ed.), Proceedings of the First Italian Research Conference on Digital Library Management Systems (pp. 29-32). Padova, Italy: IEEE.

Amatriain, X., Arumí, P., & Garcia, D. (2006). CLAM: A framework for efficient and rapid development of cross-platform audio applications. In Proceedings of ACM Multimedia 2006. Santa Barbara, CA.

Ameen, K. (2005). Philosophy and framework of collection management and its application in university libraries of Pakistan: An appraisal. Unpublished doctoral dissertation, University of the Punjab, Lahore, Pakistan.

Ameen, K., & Haider, S.J. (2007). Evolving paradigm and challenges of collection management in university libraries of Pakistan. Collection Building, 26(2), 54–58.

American Heritage dictionary of the English Language (4th ed.). (2000). Houghton Mifflin Co.

American Library Association (ALA). (1995). Code of ethics of the American Library

American Library Association (ALA). (2006). Standards and guidelines. Retrieved August 30, 2008, from http://www.ala.org/ala/acrl/acrlstandards/standardsguidelines.htm

Amina Said. (2006). Accessing electronic information: A study of Pakistan's digital library. Oxford: INSAP.

Aminin, M., & Gallinari, P. (2002). The use of unlabeled data to improve supervised learning for text summarization. In Proceedings of the 25th Annual International ACM SIGIR Conference (pp. 105-112). ACM.

Ananthakrishna, R., Chaudhuri, S., & Ganti, V. (2002). Eliminating fuzzy duplicates in data warehouses. In Proceedings of the 28th International Conference on Very Large Databases (VLDB), Hong Kong (pp. 586-597).

Ancona, D., & Smith, T. R. (2002, July 18). Visual explorations for the Alexandria digital Earth prototype. Paper presented at the Second International Workshop on Visual Interfaces to Digital Libraries, at the ACM+IEEE Joint Conference on Digital Libraries, Portland, OR. Retrieved August 24, 2008, from http://vw.indiana.edu/visual02/Ancona.pdf

Anderson, B., & Hawkins, L. (1996). Development of CONSER cataloging policies for remote access computer file serials. The Public-Access Computer Systems Review, 7(1), 6-25.

Ando, R., Boguraev, B., Byrd, R., & Neff, M. (2000). Multi-document summarization by visualizing topic content. In Proceedings of ANLP/NAACL 2000 Workshop on Automatic Summarization (pp.79-98). Morristown, NJ: ACL.

Angheluta, R., Mitra, R., Jing, X., & Moens, M. (2004). K.U.Leuven summarization system at DUC 2004. In Proceedings of the Document Understanding Conference 2004. Retrieved April 4, 2007, from http://www-nlpir.nist.gov/projects/duc/pubs.html.

Angkititrakul, P., & Hansen, J. H. L. (2006). Advances in phone-based modeling for automatic accent classification. IEEE Trans. Audio, Speech & Language Proc., 14(2), 634-646.

Angkititrakul, P., & Hansen, J. H. L. (2007). Discriminative in-set/out-of-set speaker recognition. IEEE Transactions on Audio, Speech and Language Processing, 15(2), 498-508.

Ani, O.E., & Biao, E.P. (2005). Globalization: Its impact on scientific research in Nigeria. Journal of librarianship and information science, 37(3), 153–160.

Annoni, A., Craglia, M., & Smit, P. (2002). Comparative Analysis of NSDI. In Proceedings of the 8th EC-GI&GIS Workshop. Dublin, Ireland.

ANSI/NISO Z39.50. (1995). Information retrieval (Z39.50): Application service definition and protocol specification. Technical report, Z39.50 Maintenance Agency.

Anyanwu, K., Maduko, A., & Sheth, A. (2005). SemRank: Ranking complex relationship search results on the Semantic Web. In Proceedings of the WWW 2005 Conference.

Anyanwu, K., & Sheth, A. P. (2003). ρ-Queries: Enabling querying for semantic associations on the Semantic Web. In Proceedings of the 12th International World Wide Web Conference.

Aone, C., Okurowski, M. E., & Gorlinsky, J. (1998). Trainable, scalable summarization using robust NLP and machine learning. In Proceedings of the 17th International Conference on Computational Linguistics and 36th Annual Meeting of Association for Computational Linguistics (Vol. 1, pp. 62-66). Morristown, NJ: ACL.

Apache Lucene. Retrieved August 14, 2008, from http://lucene.apache.org/

Apperley, M., Keegan, T. T., Cunningham, S. J., & Witten, I. H. (2002). Delivering the Maori-language newspapers on the Internet. In J. Curnow, N. Hopa, & J. McRae (Eds.), Rere atu, taku manu! Discovering history, language and politics in the Maori-language newspapers (pp. 211-232). Auckland University Press.

Arampatzis, A. T., Tsoris, T., Koster, C. H. A., & Van der Weide, P. (1998). Phrase-based information retrieval. Information Processing & Management, 34(6), 693-707.

Arasu, A., Cho, J., Garcia-Molina, H., Paepcke, A., & Raghavan, S. (2001). Searching the Web. ACM Transactions on Internet Technology, 1(1), 2–43.

Ardissono, L., Kobsa, A., & Maybury, M. (Eds.). (2004). Personalized digital television: Targeting programs to individual viewers. Dordrecht, Netherlands: Kluwer Academic Publishers.

Arif, M., Shafiq-ur-Rehman, & Rafiq, M. (2006). Microfilming and multimedia section of Punjab university library: A case study (unpublished report). Deptartment of Library and Information Science, University of the Punjab, Lahore.

ARL. (2006). Monograph and serial expenditures in research libraries. Retrieved November 21, 2007, from http://www.arl.org/bm~doc/monser06.pdf

Arms, W. Y. (2000). Digital libraries. Cambridge, MA: MIT Press.

Arms, W.Y. (2005). A viewpoint analysis of the digital library. D-Lib Magazine, 11(7/8). Retrieved August 30, 2008, from http://www.dlib.org/dlib/july05/arms/07arms.html

Armstrong, C., Fenton, R., Lonsdale, R., Stoker, D., Thomas, R., & Urquhart, C. (2001). A study of the use of digital information systems by higher education students in the UK. Program, 35(3), 241–262.

Arnott, P.D. (1970). Romans and their world: An introduction to the Roman world. London: Macmillan.

Arslan, L. M., & Hansen, J. H. L. (1997). A study of temporal features and frequency characteristics in American English foreign accent. The Journal of the Acoustical Society of America, 102(1), 28-40.

Ashling, J. (2008). Preserving 19th century British Library newspaper. Information Today, 25(1), 28.

Askin, A. Y. (1998). Effectiveness of usability evaluation methods at a function of users' learning stages. Unpublished master's thesis, Purdue University.

Aslesen, L. (1998). Intellectual property and mapping: A European perspective. In P. Burrough, & I. Masser (Eds.), European Geographic Infrastructures: Opportunities and Pitfalls, GISDATA 5 (pp. 127–135). Taylor & Francis.

Association of Research Libraries (ARL). (1995). Definition and purposes of a digital library. Retrieved November 13, 2007, from http://www.ifla.org/documents/libraries/net/arl-dlib.txt

Australian flexible learning framework. (2007). Metadata (for Vetadata profile and guides). Retrieved November 15, 2007, from http://e-standards.flexiblelearning.net.au/vetadata/index.htm

Autogiro Co. of America v. United States. (1967). 384 F.2d 391, 155 U.S.P.Q. 697 (Ct. Cl. 1967).

Azzam, S., Humphreys, K., & Gaizauskas, R. (1999). Using coreference chains for text summarization. In Proceedings of the ACL-99 Workshop on Conference and its Applications (pp. 77-84). Morristown, NJ: ACL.

Baba, D.Z. (2005). Networking cultural heritage: An overview of initiatives for collaboration among national libraries, museums and archives in Asia and Oceania. World Library and Information Congress: 71st IFLA general conference and council. Retrieved August 30, 2008, from http://www.ifla.org/IV/ifla71/Programme.htm

Bach, J., Fuller, C., Gupta, A., Hampapur, A., Horowitz, B., Humphrey, R., et al. (1996). The virage image search engine: An open framework for image management. SPIRE Conference. Storage and Retrieval for Still Image and Video Databases IV.

Baclawski, K., & Niu, T. (2005). Ontologies for bioinformatics. MIT Press.

Bae, K.J., Jeong, Y.S., Shim, W.S., & Kwak, S.J. (2007).

Baeza-Yates, B., & Ribeiro-Neto, B. (1999). Modern information retrieval. New York: Addison-Wesley Longman.

Bailey, C. W. (2005). Open-access bibliography: Liberating scholarly literature with e-prints and open-access journals. Washington, D. C: Association of Research Libraries.

Bailey, C. W. (2005). Scholarly electronic publishing bibliography (Version 58). Retrieved November 14, 2006, from http://epress.lib.uh.edu/sepb/archive/sepa.htm

Bainbridge, D., Edgar, K. D., McPherson, J. R., & Witten, I. H. (2003). Managing change in a digital library system with many interface languages. In Proceedings of the European Conference on Digital Libraries ECDL2003, Trondheim, Norway.

Bainbridge, D., Ke, K.-Y. J., & Witten, I. H. (2006). Document level interoperability for collection creators. In Proceedings of the Joint Conference on Digital Libraries, Chapel Hill, NC (pp. 105-106).

Bainbridge, D., McKay, D., & Witten, I. H. (2004). Greenstone developer's guide. Retrieved May 24, 2007, from http://www.greenstone.org/manuals/gsdl2/en/html/Develop_en_index.html

Bainbridge, D., Thompson, J., & Witten, I. H. (2003). Assembling and enriching digital library collections. In Proceedings of the Joint Conference on Digital Libraries, Houston.

Baker, K. D. (2006). Learning objects and process interoperability. International Journal on ELearning, 5(1), 167-172. Retrieved November 16, 2007, from Academic Research Library database (Document ID: 986673161).

Balakrishnan, N. (2006). Universal digital library connecting users to digital contents. 13th Biennial Conference and Exhibition. Retrieved August 30, 2008, from http://www.vala.org.au/conf2006.htm

Baldonado, Chang, M. Gravano, C.L., & Paepcke, A. (1997). The Stanford digital library metadata architecture. International Journal of Digital Libraries, 1, 108–121.

Baldonado, M., Chang, C-C.K., Gravano, L., & Paepcke, A. (1997). Metadata for digital libraries: Architecture and design rationale. In Proceedings of the second ACM international conference on Digital libraries (pp. 47–56). Philadelphia. New York: ACM.

Balramand, S., & Dragievi, S. (2006). Collaborative geographic information systems. Idea Group Publishing.

Barbara, D. (1999). Mobile computing and databases: A survey. Knowledge and Data Engineering, 11(1), 108-117.

Barber, W., & Badre, A. (1998, June 5). Culturability: The merging of culture and usability. Paper presented at the Fourth Conference on Human Factors & the Web, Basking Ridge, NJ. Retrieved November 6, 2007, from http://www.research.microsoft.com/users/marycz/hf-Web98/barber/index.htm

Barnaghi, P. M., & Kareem, S. A. (2006). A flexible architecture for semantic annotation and automated multimedia presentation generation, In Proceedings of the 1st International Workshop on Semantic-enhanced Multimedia Presentation Systems.

Barnaghi, P. M., & Kareem, S. A. (2007). Relation robustness evaluation for the Semantic associations. The Electronic Journal of Knowledge Management, 5(3), 265-272.

Barzilay, R., & Elhadad, M. (1998). Using lexical chains for text summarization. In Proceedings of the ACL-97/EACL-97 Workshop on Intelligent Scalable Text Summarization (pp. 10-17). Morristown, NJ: ACL.

Bas Martín, N. (2004). La Biblioteca Valenciana, una biblioteca nacional valenciana. BiD: Textos universitaris de biblioteconomia i documentació, ISSN 1575–5886, Nº. 13.

Basili, V. et al. (1994). Experience factory. Encyclopedia of Software Engineering, 1, 476–496. John Wiley & Sons.

Baskerville, R., & Pries-Heje, J. (1999). Managing knowledge capability and maturity. Information systems: Current issues and future change. Norwell, MA: IFIP/Kluwer Academic Publisher.

Bates, M.J. (1998). Indexing and access for digital libraries and the Internet: Human, database, and domain factors. Journal of the American Society for Information Science, 49, 1(3), 1185–1205.

Bates, M.J. (2002). Speculations on browsing, directed searching, and linking in relation to the Bradford Distribution. In H. Bruce, R. Fidel, P. Ingwersen, & P. Vakkari (Eds.), Emerging frameworks and methods: Proceedings of the Fourth International Conference on Conceptions of Library and Information Science (CoLIS 4) (pp. 137–150). Greenwood Village, CO: Libraries Unlimited.

Baxendale, P. B. (1958). Machine-made index for technical literature: An experiment. IBM Journal of Research and Development, 2(4), 354-361.

Baziz, M., Boughanem, M., Pasi, P., & Prade, H. (2006). A fuzzy logic approach to information retrieval using an ontology-based representation of documents. Fuzzy logic and the Semantic Web. Elsevier.

Becker, C., Rauber, A., Heydegger, V., Schnasse, J., & Thaller, M. (2008). A generic xml language for characterising objects to support digital preservation. In Proceedings of the 23rd annual ACM symposium on applied computing. New York: ACM.

Beheshti, J., Large, A., & Julian, C. (2005, June 2-4). Designing a virtual reality interface for children's Web portals. In data, information, and knowledge in a networked world. In Proceedings of the Canadian Association for Information Science 2005 Annual Conference, London/Ontario.

Belew, R. (2001). Finding out about: A cognitive perspective on search engine technology and the WWW. Cambridge University Press.

Bell, T. C., Cleary, J. G., & Witten, I. H. (1990). Text compression. Englewood Cliffs, NJ: Prentice Hall.

Bell, T.C., Moffat, A., & Witten, I. H. (1994, June). Compressing the digital library. In Proceedings of the Digital Libraries '94, College Station, TX (pp. 41-46).

Benjelloun, O., Garcia-Molina, H., Su, Q., & Widom, J. (2005, March). Swoosh: A generic approach to entity resolution (Tech. Rep.). Stanford University.

Bennett, J. L. (1972). The user interface in interactive systems. Annual Review of Information Science and Technology, 7, 159-196.

Bennett, J. L. (1979). The commercial impact of usability in interactive systems. In B. Shackel (Ed.), Man-computer communication, infotech state-of-the-art (Vol. 2, pp. 1-17). Maidenhead: Infotech International.

Berlin Communiqué. (2003). Bologna process Berlin 2003, realising the European higher education area. Communiqué of the conference of Ministers responsible for higher education in Berlin on September 19, 2003.

Bernard, L., & Craglia, M. (2005). SDI—from spatial data infrastructure to service driven infrastructure. In Proceedings of the First Research Workshop on Cross-learning on Spatial Data Infrastructures and Information Infrastructures, Enschede, the Netherlands. Retrieved August 27, 2008, from http://gi-gis.jrc.it/ws/crosslearning/papers/PP Lars Bernard - Max Craglia.pdf

Berners-Lee, T., & Fischetti, M. (1997). Weaving the Web. San Francisco: Physica-Verlag.

Berners-Lee, T., Handler, J., & Lassila, O. (2001, May). The Semantic Web. Scientific American, 35-43.

Berners-Lee., T., Hendler, J., & Lassila, O. (2001). The Semantic Web. Scientific American, 284(5), 35-35.

Bertini, E., Catarci, T., Di Bello, L., & Kimani, S. (2005). Visualization in digital libraries. In M. Hemmje, C. Niederee, & T. Risse (Eds.), Integrated publication and information systems to virtual information and knowledge environments. Springer-Verlag Berlin.

Berube, L. (2003). Digital reference overview: An issue paper from the networked services policy task group. Retrieved August 29, 2008, from http://www.ukoln. ac.uk/public/nsptg/virtual/

Besemer, H, Addison, C., & Ferguson, J. (2003). Fertile ground: Opportunities fro greater coherence in agricultural information systems (Research Rep. No. 19). IICD. Retrieved November 13, 2007, from http://www.ftpiicd. org/files/research/reports/report19.pdf

Bhargava, B. K., & Annamalai, M. (1995). Communication costs in digital library databases. Database and Expert Systems Applications, 1-13.

BibTeX. Retrieved August 14, 2008, from http://www. bibtex.org/

Bilenko, M., Mooney, R. J., Cohen, W. W., Ravikumar, P., & Fienber, S. E. (2003). Adaptive name matching in information integration. IEEE Intelligent Systems, 18(5), 16-23.

Billington, J. (2005). A digital library that all nations can learn from James Billington. London: The Financial Times Limited.

Bishop, A. P. (2001). Logins and bailouts: Measuring access, use, and success in digital libraries. The Journal of Electronic Publishing, 4(2). Retrieved November 6, 2007, from http://www.press.umich.edu/jep/04-02/ bishop.html

Blandford, A., Keith, S., Connell, I., & Edwards, H. (2004). Analytical usability evaluation for digital libraries: A case study. In Proceedings of the Fourth ACM/IEEE Joint Conference on Digital Libraries (pp. 27-36). Retrieved November 6, 2007, from the ACM Digital Library database.

Boag, S. et al (2003). XQuery 1.0: An XML query language (working draft). Retrieved August 12, 2008, from http://www.w3.org/TR/2003/WD-xquery-20030822/

BOAI. (2001). Budapest open access initiative. Retrieved November 21, 2007, from http://www.soros.org/openaccess/

Bohm, K., & Rakow, T. (1994). Metadata for multimedia documents. ACM SIGMOD Record, 23(4), 21–26.

Bopp, R.E., & Smith, L.C. (Eds.). (2001). Reference and information services: An introduction (3rd ed.). Colorado: Libraries Unlimited, Inc.

Boren, H.C. (1977). Roman society: A social, economic, and cultural history. Lexington: Mass.

Borgamon, C. L. (2000). From Gutenberg to the global infrastructure: Access to information in the networked world. Cambridge: MIT Press.

Borges, L., & Falbo, R. (2002). Managing software process knowledge. In Proceedings of the International Conference on Computer Science, Software Engineering, Information Technology, e-Business, and Applications (CSITeA'2002) (pp. 227–232).

Borgman, C. L. (2000). From Gutenberg to the global information infrastructure: Access to information in the networked world. Cambridge, MA: MIT Press.

Borgman, C. (2003). The invisible library: Paradox of the global information infrastructure. Library Trends, 51(Spring), 652–675.

Borgman, C. L. (1999). What are digital libraries? Competing visions. Information Processing and Management, 35(3), 227-243.

Borgman. C. (2001). Where is the librarian in the digital library? Communication of the ACM, 44(5), 66–68.

Borko, H., & Bernier, L. (1975). Abstracting concepts and methods. San Diego: Academic Press.

Bormans, J., & Hill, K. (2002). MPEG-21 overview v.5. Retrieved August 14, 2008, from http://www.chiariglione. org/mpeg/standards/mpeg-21/mpeg-21.htm

Börner, K., & Chen, C. (Eds.). (2002). Visual interfaces to digital libraries (LNCS 2539, pp. 1-9). Springer-Verlag Berlin Heidelberg.

Bottoni, P., Costabile, M. F., Levialdi, S., & Mussio, P. (1995). Formalising visual languages. In Proceedings of the 11th International IEEE Symposium on Visual Languages, VL, (pp. 45-52). Washington, D.C.: IEEE.

Bou-Ghazale, S. E., & Hansen, J. H. L. (2000). A comparative study of traditional and newly proposed features for recognition of speech under stress. IEEE Transactions on Speech & Audio Processing, 8(4), 429-442.

Boxall, J. (2002). Geolibraries, the global spatial data infrastructure and digital earth: A time for map libraries to reflect upon the moonshot. INSPEL, 1–21.

Brainstorming report. (2001, June, 13-15). Digital libraries: Future directions for a European research program. San Cassiano, Venice, Italy: Alta Badia-Italy.

Brancolini, K.R., & Mostafa, J. (2006). JCDL 2006 workshop report. D-Lib Magazine, 12(7/8). Retrieved August 30, 2008, from http://www.dlib.org/dlib/july06/brancolini/07brancolini.html

Brandow, R., Mitze, K., & Rau, L. F. (1995). Automatic condensation of electronic publications by sentence selection. Information Processing and Management, 31(5), 675-685.

Braxton, S.M., & Brunsdale, M. (2004). E-mail reference as a substitute for library receptionist. The Reference Librarian, 85, 19–31.

Breeding, M. (2006). Reshuffling the deck. Library Journal. Retrieved August 30, 2008, from http://www.libraryjournal.com/article/CA6319048.html

Brenner, A.L. (2005). Digital library use: Social practice in design and evaluation. Library and Information Science Research, 27(1), 131–133.

Brill, E. (1992). A simple rule based part-of-speech tagger. Paper presented at the Third Conference on Applied Natural Language Proceedings (pp. 152-155). ACM Press.

Brin, S., & Page, L. (1998). The anatomy of a large-scale hypertextual Web search engine. In Proceedings of the WWW 1998 Conference (pp 107-117).

Brocks, H., Thiel, U., Stein, A., & Dirsch-Weigand, A. (2001). Customizable retrieval functions based on user tasks in the cultural heritage domain. In Proceedings of the 5th European Conference on Digital libraries, LNCS 2163 (pp. 37–48). Heidelberg: Springer.

Broekstra, J., Kampman, A., & Harmelen, F. V. (2002). Sesame: An architecture for storing and querying RDF and RDF schema. In Proceedings of the 1st International Semantic Web Conference (LNCS 2342, pp. 54-68). Springer-Verlag.

Brooks, C. H., & Montancz, N. (2006). Improved annotation of the blogosphere via autotagging and hierarchical clustering. In Proceedings of the 15th International Conference on the World Wide Web (pp. 625-632).

Brooks, P., Revill, D., & Shelton, T. (1997). The development of scale to measure the quality of an academic library from the perspective of its users. In J. Brockman (Ed.), Quality Management and Benchmarking in the

Information Sector, Results of Recent Research. British Library Research and Innovation Report 47. London: British Library.

Bruns, C. W. (2007). 19th century U.S. newspaper archive. Choice: Current Reviews for Academic Libraries, 45(2), 256-258.

Brusilovsky, P., Kobsa, A., & Nejdl, W. (Eds.). (in press). The adaptive Web: Methods and strategies of Web personalization. Heidelberg, Germany: Springer Verlag.

Buchanan, G. (2006). FRBR: Enriching and integrating digital libraries. In Proceedings of the Joint Conference on Digital Libraries, Chapel Hill (pp. 260-269).

Buchanan, G., & Hinze, A. (2005). A generic alerting service for digital libraries. In Proceedings of the Joint Conference on Digital Libraries, Denver (pp. 131-140).

Buchanan, G., Bainbridge, D., Don, K. J., & Witten, I. H. (2005). A new framework for building digital library collections. In Proceedings of the Joint Conference on Digital Libraries, Denver (pp. 23-31).

Buchanan, G., Jones, M., & Marsden, G. (2003). Exploring small screen digital library access with the Greenstone Digital Library. In Proceedings of the 6th European Conference on Research and Advanced Technology for Digital Libraries (LNCS 2458, pp. 583-596). Berlin: Springer-Verlag.

Bultmann, B., Hardy, R., Muir, A., & Wictor, C. (2006). Digitised content in the UK research library and archives sector. Journal of librarianship and information science, 38(2), 105–122.

Bunge, C.A. (1999). Reference services. Reference Librarian, 66, 185–199.

Bunge, C.A., & Bopp, R.E. (2001). History and varieties of reference services. In

Busetti, E., Dettori, G., Forcheri, P., & Ierardi, M. G. (2007). A pedagogical approach to the design of learning objects for complex domains. International Journal of Distance Education Technologies, 5(2), 1-10, 13-17. Retrieved November 16, 2007, from ABI/Inform Global database (Document ID: 1205735741).

Bush, T., & Coleman, M. (2000). Leadership and strategic management in education. London: Paul Chapman Publishing.

Butcher, K. R., Bhushan, S., & Sumner, T. (2006). Multimedia displays for conceptual discovery: Information seeking with strand maps. ACM Multimedia Systems Journal, 11(3), 236-248.

Buyukkokten, O., Garcia-Molina, H., & Paepcke, A. (2001). Seeing the whole in parts: text summarization for Web browsing on handheld devices. In Proceedings of the Tenth International World-Wide Web Conference (pp. 652-662). New York: ACM Press

Buyukkokten, O., Kaljuvee, O., Garcia-Molina, H., Paepcke, A., & Winograd, T. (2002). Efficient Web browsing on handheld devices using page and form summarization. ACM Transactions on Information Systems, 20(1), 82-115.

Byrne, A. (2003). Digital libraries: Barriers or gateways to scholarly information? The Electronic Library, 21(5), 414-421

Byrne, A. (2005). Promoting the global information commons. International Federation of Library Associations and Institutions. Retrieved August 30, 2008, from http://www.ifla.org/III/wsis/wsis-24Feb05.html

Callan, J., & Smeaton, A. (2003). Personalization and recommender systems in digital libraries (Tech. Rep.). NSF-EU DELOS Working Group.

Campbell, N. (2001). Usability assessment of library-related Web sites: Methods and case studies. Chicago: LITA, American Library Association.

CANARIE, & Industry Canada. (2002). A report on learning object repositories: Review and recommendations for a Pan-Canadian approach to repository implementation in Canada. Ottawa: Author. Retrieved November 19, 2007, from http://www.canarie.ca/funding/elearning/lor.pdf

CanCore Learning Resource Metadata Initiative. (2007). CanCore guidelines for the "access for all" digital resource description metadata elements. Retrieved November 15, 2007, from http://www.cancore.ca/guidelines/drd/

Candela, L., Castelli, D., Pagano, P., & Simi, M. (2005). From heterogeneous information spaces to virtual documents. In E. A. Fox, E. J. Neuhold, P. Premsmit, & V. Wuwongse (Eds.), Digital Libraries. Implementing Strategies and Sharing Experiences: 8th International Conference on Asian Digital Libraries, ICADL 2005 (LNCS, pp. 11-22). Berlin: Springer-Verlag.

Candela, L., Castelli, D., Pagano, P., & Simi, M. (2006). OpenDLibG: Extending OpenDLib by exploiting a gLite grid infrastructure. In Proceeding of the 10th European Conference on Research and Advanced Technology for Digital Libraries, ECDL 2006 (LNCS, pp.) Berlin: Springer-Verlag.

Canny, J. (2002). Collaborative filtering with privacy. In Proceedings of the IEEE Security and Privacy Conference (pp. 45–57).

Cano, P., Kaltenbrunner, M., Gouyon, F., & Battle, E. (2002). On the use of fastmap for audio retrieval and browsing. In Proceedings of the International Conference on Music Information Retrieval (ISMIR). Paris, France.

Carbonell, J. G., & Goldstein, J. (1998). The use of MMR, diversity-based reranking for reordering documents and producing summaries. In Proceedings of the 21st Annual International ACM SIGIR Conference on Research and Development in Information Retrieval (pp. 335-336). New York: ACM.

Carl, L., & Herbert, V. S. (2001). The open archives initiative: Building a low-barrier interoperability framework. In Proceedings of the 1st ACM/IEEE-CS Joint Conference on Digital Libraries, Virginia.

Carney, S., Koufogiannakis, D., & Ryan, P. (2004). Library services for users of personal digital assistants: A needs assessment and program evaluation. Portal: Libraries and the Academy, 4(3), 393-406.

Carr, L., & Harnad, S. (2005). Keystroke economy: A study of the time and effort involved in self-archiving. Retrieved March 14, 2006, from http://eprints.ecs.soton.ac.uk/10688/01/KeystrokeCosting-publicdraft1.pdf

Carroll, J. J., Reynolds, D., Dickinson, I., Seaborne, A., Dollin, C., & Wilkinson, K. (2004). Jena: Implementing the semantic Web recommendations. In Proceedings of the 13th International World Wide Web Conference (pp. 74-83).

Carson, C., Thomas, M., Belongie, S., Hellerstein, J.M., & Malik, J. (1999). Blobworld: A system for region-based image indexing and retrieval. In Third International Conference on Visual Information Systems. SpringerVerlag.

Casey, M. E., & Savastinuk, L. C. (2006, September 1). Library 2.0. Library Journal. Retrieved November 13, 2007, from http://www.libraryjournal.com/article/CA6365200.html

Casson, L. (2001). Libraries in the ancient world. London: Yale University Press.

Catherall, P. (2005). Delivering e-learning or information services in higher education. Oxford, UK: Chandos Publishing (Oxford) Limited.

Castelli, D., & Pagano, P. (2003). A system for building expandable digital libraries. Paper presented at the ACM/IEEE 2003 Joint Conference on Digital Libraries JCDL 2003 (pp. 335-345). Berlin: Springer-Verlag.

Castelli, D., & Pagano, P. (2002). OpenDLib: A digital library service system. In M. Agosti & C. Thanos (Eds.),

Research and Advanced Technology for Digital Libraries: Sixth European Conference ECDL 2002 (LNCS, pp. 292-308). Berlin: Springer-Verlag.

Categories for the Description of Works of Art (CDWA). Retrieved August 20, 2008, from http://www.getty.edu/research/institute/standards/cdwa/

Celentano, A., Fogli, D., Mussio, P., & Pittarello, F. (2004). Model-based specification of virtual interaction environments. In Proceedings of the 2004 IEEE Symposium on Visual Languages - Human Centric Computing: Vol. 00. (pp. 257-260). Rome: IEEE.

Celino, I., Valle, E. D., Cerzza, D., & Turati, A. (2006). Squiggle: A semantic search engine for indexing and retrieval of multimedia content. In Proceedings of the 1st International Workshop on Semantic-Enhanced Multimedia Presentation Systems.

CGIAR. (2006). CGVLibrary (p. 1) [Brochure]. Washington, D.C.: CGIAR. Retrieved November 13, 2007, from http://vlibrary.cgiar.org/CGVLibraryflyer.pdf

CGIAR. (2006). Consultative group on international agricultural research. Retrieved November 13, 2007, from http://www.cgiar.org/who/index.html

CGIAR Content for Development Project. (2004). "Virtual library service" proposal. Washington, D.C.: CGIAR.

CGVLibrary updated proposal for Phase II. (2006). Washington, D.C.: CGIAR. Retrieved November 13, 2007, from http://CGVLibrary.pbwiki.com/Activities+++TOR

Chad, K., & Miller, P. (2005). Do libraries matter? The rise of Library2.0: A white paper. Retrieved November 13, 2007, from http://www.talis.com/applications/downloads/white_papers/DoLibrariesMatter.pdf

Chan, T., Feeney, M., Rajabifard, A., & Williamson, I. (2001). The dynamic nature of spatial data infrastructures: A method of descriptive classification. Geomatica, 55(1), 65–72.

Chandler, A., Foley, D., & Hafez, A.M. (2000). Mapping and converting essential federal geographic data committee (FGDC) metadata into MARC21 and Dublin Core. Towards an alternative to the FGDC clearinghouse. D-Lib Magazine, 6(1).

Chandrasekaran, B., Josephson, J. R., & Benjamins, V. R. (1999). What are ontologies, and why do we need them? IEEE Intelligent Systems, 20-26.

Chang, C.H., & Hedberg, J.G. (2006). The role of digital libraries in teaching and learning geography. In K.C. Goh, & S. Yongvanit (Eds.), Change and Development in Southeast Asia in an Era of Globalisation. Singapore: Pearson Prentice Hall.

Chang, C.H., Hedberg, J., Theng, Y.L., Lim, E.P., Teh, T.S., & Goh, D. (2005, June 7–11). Evaluating g-portal for geography learning and teaching. Accepted to JCDL2005, Digital Libraries Cyberinfrastructure for Research and Education (pp. 21– 22). Denver, CO.

Chang, M., Leggett, J. J., Furuta, R., Kerne, A., Williams, J. P., Burns, S. A., et al. (2004, June 7-11). Collection understanding. In Proceedings of the Joint Conference on Digital Libraries1 (JCDL 2004), Tucson, AZ (pp. 334-342).

Chatterjea, K., Chang, C.H., Theng, Y.L., Lim, E.P, Goh, D.H.L., & Zhang, J. (2006, June). Supporting holistic understanding of geographical problems: Field work and g-portal. Presented at International Geographic Union, Commission for Geographic Education Conference. Brisbane.

Chauvel, D., & Desprs, C. (2002). A review of survey research in knowledge management: 1997–2001. Journal of Knowledge Management, 6(3), 207–223.

Chen, C. C, Chen, H. H., & Chen, K. H. (2001). The design of metadata interchange for Chinese information and implementation of metadata management system. Bulletin of the American Society for Information Science and Technology, 27(5), 21-27.

Chen, C. C., Chen, H. H., Chen, K. H., & Hsiang, J. (2002). The design of metadata for the digital museum initiative in Taiwan. Online Information Review, 26(5), 295-306.

Chen, C. C., Yeh, J. H., & Sie, S. H. (2006). A research project to convert traditional Chinese calligraphic paintings to SCORM-compatible e-learning materials. In Proceedings of the 9th International Conference of Asian Digital Libraries (ICADL2006), Kyoto, Japan.

Chen, C. C., Yeh, J. H., & Sie, S. H. (2005). Government ontology and thesaurus construction: A Taiwan experience. In Proceedings of the 8th International Conference of Asian Digital Libraries (ICADL2005), Bankok, Tailand.

Chen, C.C., Chen, H.H., Chen, K.H., & Hsiang, F. (2002). The design of metadata for the digital museum initiative in Taiwan. Online Information Review, 26(5), 295–306.

Chen, D., & Bovik, A. (1990). Visual pattern image coding. IEEE Trans. Communications, 38, 2137–2146.

Chen, H. (1995). Machine learning for information retrieval: Neural networks, symbolic learning and genetic algorithms. Journal of the American Society for Information Science and Technology, 46(3), 194-216.

Chen, H., & Zhou, Y (2005). Survey and history of digital library development in the Asia Pacific. In Y.-L. Theng, & S. Foo (Eds.), Design and Usability of Digital Libraries: Case Studies in the Asia Pacific. Hershey: Information Science Publishing.

Chen, L., & Sycara, K. (2004). Webmate: A personal agent for browsing and searching. In Proceedings of the 2nd International Conference on Autonomous Agents & Multiagent Systems (pp. 132-139).

Chen, S. F., & Goodman, J. (1996). An empirical study of smoothing techniques for language modeling. In Proceeding of the 34th Annual Meeting on Association for Computer Linguistics. NJ: Association for Computer Linguistics.

Chen, S., & Gopalakrishnan, P. (1998). Speaker, environment and channel change detection and clustering via the Bayesian information criterion. In Proceedings of the Broadcast News Trans. & Under. Workshop.

Chennupati, K. R. (2007, December) Case for virtual Salar Jung Museum. Deccan Chronicle, 5, 9. Retrieved February 20, 2008, from http://deccan.com/cultureplus/cultureplus.asp

Chesta, C., Siohan, O., & Lee, C. H. (1999). Maximum a posterior linear regression for hidden Markov model adaptation. In Proceedings of Eurospeech-99, Budapest (pp. 203-206).

Chica, S.D.L., Ahmad, F., Sumner, T., Martin, J.H., & Butcher, K. (in press). Computational foundations for personalizing instruction with digital libraries. International Journal of Digital Libraries, Special Issue on Digital Libraries and Education.

Chiner Gimeno, J.J. (2003). Vells llibres i noves tecnologies al volant dels lletraferits valencians: la Biblioteca Valenciana Digital (BIVALDI). Llengua i literatura: Revista anual de la Societat Catalana de Llengua i literatura, ISSN 0213–6554, Nº. 14, 563–572.

Choi, Y., & Rasmussen, E. (2006). What do digital librarians do? In Proceedings of the Joint Conference on Digital Libraries (pp. 187–188). Retrieved August 30, 2008, from http://doi.acm.org/10.1145/1141753.1141789

Choi, Y., & Rasmussen, E. (2006). What is needed to educate future digital librarians: A study of current practice and staffing patterns in academic and research libraries. D-Lib Magazine, 12(9). Retrieved August 30, 2008, from http://doi:10.1045/september2006-choi

Chomsky, N. (1957). Syntactic structures. The Hague: Mouton.

Chou, W. (1999). Maximum a posterior linear regression with elliptically symmetric matrix priors. In Proceedings of Eurospeech (pp. 1-4).

Chowdhury, G., & Margariti, S. (2004). Digital reference services: A snapshot of the current practices in Scottish libraries. Library Review, 53(1), 50–60.

Chowdhury, G.G. (2002). Digital libraries and reference services: Present and future. Journal of Documentation, 58(3), 258–283.

Chowdhury, G.G., & Chowdhury, S. (2003). Introduction to digital libraries. London: Facet Publishing.

Christensen, C.M. (1997). The innovator's dilemma. Cambridge, MA: Harvard Business School Press.

Chudamani, K. S. (2005). Metadata and content management. Srels Journal of Information Management, 2, 205-209.

Chudamani, K. S., & Nagarathna, H. C. (2006). Interoperability between Dublin Core, UNIMARC, MARC21, with AACR2R as the standards frameworks for cataloging in the digital environment. Paper presented at Planner INFLIBNET, Silchar, India.

Church, K. (1988). A stochastic parts program and noun phrase parser for unrestricted text. In Proceedings of the Second Conference on Applied Natural Language Processing (pp. 136-143). Austin, TX: ACL.

Churchill, D. (2007). Towards a useful classification of learning objects. Educational Technology, Research and Development, 55(5), 479-497. Retrieved November 16, 2007, from Academic Library database (Document ID: 1361006251).

CIE. (1986). Colorimetry. CIE Publications 15.2. Commission International de L'Eclairage, 2nd edition.

Clark, J. A. (2004). A usability study of the Belgian-American research collection: Measuring the functionality of a digital library. OCLC Systems & Services: International Digital Library Perspectives, 20(3), 115-127.

Clark, J., & DeRose, S. (1999). XPath: XML path language (Version 1.0). Retrieved August 12, 2008, from http://www.w3.org/TR/1999/REC-xpath-19991116

Clark, R.E. (1983). Reconsidering research on learning from media. Review of Educational Research, 53(4), 445–459.

Clayton, J. F. (2006). Learning objects: Seeking simple solutions. In J. Clayton & B. Gower (Eds.), Final report: E-learning collaborative development find: Open source learning object repository (pp. 121-126). Hamilton: Tertiary Education Commission.

Cleveland, G. (1998). Digital libraries: Definitions, issues and challenges. Retrieved August 21, 2008, from http://www.ifla.org/VI/5/op/udtop8/udtop8.htm

CLIR & LoC. (2002). Building a national strategy for digital preservation: Issues in digitalmedia archiving. Washington, D.C.: Council on Library and Information Resources Washington, D.C. and Libraryof Congress. Retrieved August 29, 2008, from http://www.clir.org/pubs/reports/pub106/pub106.pdf

Clyde, L.A. (2004). Weblogs for libraries. Oxford, Hampshire.

Cohen, S. (1994, November). Feature-oriented domain analysis: Domain modeling (tutorial notes). Paper presented at the 3rd International Conference on Software Reuse, Rio de Janeiro.

Cohen, W. W. (1998). Integration of heterogeneous databases without common domains using query based on textual similarity. In Proceedings of the 1998 ACM SIGMOD International Conference on Management of Data (SIGMOD '98) (pp. 201-212).

Cohen, W. W., Ravikumar, P., & Feinberg, S. (2003). A comparison of string metrics for matching names and records. In Proceedings of the KDD2003. Retrieved August 22, 2008, from http://www.cs.cmu.edu/~pradeepr/papers/kdd03.pdf

Cole, B. (2005, March). Search engines tackle the desktop. IEEE Computer, 38(3), 14-17.

Coleman, A. (2002). The road ahead for education in digital libraries. D-Lib Magazine, 8(7/8). Retrieved August 30, 2008, from http://www.dlib.org/dlib/july02/coleman/07coleman.html

Coleman, A. (2005). Interdisciplinarity, interactivity, and interoperability for educating the digerati. Education for Information, 23(4), 233–243.

Coleman, D.J., & Nebert, D.D. (1998). Building a North American spatial data infrastructure. Cartography and Geographic Information Systems, 25(3), 151–160.

Committee on Future Roles, Challenges, and Opportunities for the U.S. Geological Survey, National Research Council. (2001). Future roles and opportunities for the U.S. geological survey. Washington, DC: National Academy Press.

Committee to Review the USGS Coastal and Marine Geology Program, National Research Council. (1999). Science for decisionmaking: Coastal and marine geology at the U.S. geological survey. Washington, DC: National Academy Press.

Connor, E. (Ed.). (2006). An introduction to reference services in academic libraries. New York: The Haworth Information Press.

Constabile, M. F., Esposito, F., Semeraro, G., Fanizzi, N., & Ferilli, S. (1998, September 21-23). Interacting with IDL: The adaptive visual interface. In Proceedings of the Research and Advanced Technology for Digital Libraries, Second European Conference, ECDL '98, Heraklion, Crete, Greece (pp. 515-534).

Cooper, M., Foote, J., Pampalk, E., & Tzanetakis, G. (2006). Visualization in audio-based music information retrieval. Computer Music Journal, 30(2), 42–62.

Cornell University. (2001). Mixing and mapping metadata to provide integrated access to digital Library collections. In Proceedings of the International Conference on Dublin Core and Metadata Applications (DC-2001), Japan. Retrieved August 20, 2008, from http://www.nii.ac.jp/dc2001/proceedings/product/paper-23.pdf

Corporation of National Research Initiative - Reston USA. Retrieved August 14, 2008, from http://www.cnri.reston.va.us/k-w.html

Cosi, P., De Poli, G., & Lauzzana, G. (1994). Auditory modelling and self-organizing neural networks for timbre classification. Journal of New Music Research, 23(1), 71–98.

Cousins, S.B., Paepcke, A., Wingord, T., Bier, E.A., & Pier, K. (1997). The digital library integrate task environment (DLITE). In Proceedings of the ACM Digital Library Conference. Philadelphia, PA, USA.

Cousins, S.B., Paepcke, A., Winograd, T., Bier, E.A., & Pier, K. (2004). The effectiveness of automatically structured queries in digital libraries. In Proceedings of the 4th ACM/IEEE-CS Joint Conference on Digital Libraries (pp. 98–107). Tuscon, AZ.

Coyle, M., & Smyth, B. (2007). Supporting intelligent Web search. ACM Transactions on Internet Technology (TOIT), 7(4).

Crane, G. (2002). Cultural heritage digital libraries: Needs and components. In Proceedings of the 6th European Conference on Digital libraries. LNCS 2458 (pp. 626637). Heidelberg: Springer.

Crane, G., & Wulfman, C. (2003). Towards a cultural heritage digital library. In Proceedings of the 3rd ACM/IEEE-CS joint conference on Digital libraries (pp. 75–86). Houston. New York: ACM.

Craven, M., DiPasquo, D., Freitag, D., McCallum, A., Mitchell, T., Nigam, K., et al. (2000). Learning to construct knowledge bases from the World Wide Web. Artificial Intelligence, 69-113.

Crestani, F., & Passi, G. (2000). Soft computing in information retrieval: Techniques and applications. Heidelberg: Physica-Verlag.

Crestani, F., Landoni, M., & Melucci, M. (2006). Appearance and functionality of electronic books. International Journal on Digital Libraries, 6(2), 192-209.

Croft, W. B., Turtle, H. R., & Lewis, D. D. (1991). The use of phrases and structured queries in information retrieval. In Proceedings of the SIGIR 1991.

Crow, R. (2002). The case for institutional repositories: A SPARC position paper. Washington, D. C.: Association of Research Libraries.

Cruz-Lara, S., Chen, B. H., & Hong, J. S. (2002, November 14-15). Distributed content management framework for digital museum exhibitions. In Proceedings of EUROPIX Scholars Network Conference, Tampere, Finland. Retrieved February 20, 2008, from http://www.acten.org/cgi-bin/WebGUI/www/index.pl/sc_announcements

Cuevas, G. (2002). Gestión del Proceso Software (pp. 132–136). Centro de Estudios Ramón Areces S.A.

Custard, M., & Sumner, T. (2005). Using machine learning to support quality judgments. D-Lib Magazine, 11.

Cutting, D., Kupiec, J., Pedersen, J., & Sibun, P. (1992). A practical part-of-speech tagger. Paper presented at the Third Conference on Applied Natural Language Processing (pp. 133-140). ACM Press.

Dahn, I. (2006). A metadata profile to establish the context of small learning objects: The slicing book approach. International Journal on ELearning, 5(1), 59-66. Retrieved November 16, 2007, from Academic Research library database (Document ID: 986673111).

Dai, H., & Mobasher, B. (2002). Using ontologies to discover domain-level Web usage profiles. In Proceedings of the 2nd Workshop on Semantic Web Mining, Finland.

Daniel, R., & Lagoze, C. (1997, November). Extending the Warwick framework: From metadata containers to active digital objects. D-Lib Magazine, 3(11). Retrieved August 30, 2008, from http://www.dlib.org/dlib/november97/daniel/11daniel.html

Dannenberg, R.B., Thom, B., & Watson, D. (1997). A machine learning approach to musical style recognition. In Proceedings of the International Computer Music Conference (ICMC) (pp. 344–347). Thessaloniki, Greece.

Dasgupta, K. (2005). National policy for library and information systems and services in India: The new scenario. Alexandria, 17(2), 97–103.

Davis, C.L., & Moran, B.B. (2005). Scholarly communication: Preparing tomorrow's professionals: LIS schools and scholarly communication. Association of College and Research Libraries, C&RL News, 66(1). Retrieved August 30, 2008, from http://www.ala.org/ala/acrl/acrlpubs/crlnews/backissues2005/january05/preparingprofessionals.htm

Davis, F. D. (1989). Perceived usefulness, perceived ease of use, and user acceptance of information technology. MIS Quarterly, (13), 319-340.

Dayal, U., Kuno, H., & Wilkinson, K. (2003). Making the Semantic Web real. IEEE Data Engineering Bulletin, 26(4), 4.

DCMI metadata terms. Dublin Core metadata initiative. Retrieved August 14, 2008, from http://www.dublincore.org/documents/dcmi-terms/

De Bra, P., Smits, D., & Stash, N. (2006, August 22–25). The design of AHA! In Proceedings of the 17th ACM Conference on Hypertext and Hypermedia (HT '06) (pp. 171–195). Odense, Denmark: ACM Press.

De Gendt, V., Isaac, A., Van Der Meijt, L., & Schlobach, S. (2006). Semantic Web techniques for multiple views on heterogeneous collections: A case study. In Proceedings of the 10th European Conference on Digital libraries, LNCS 4172 (pp. 426–437). Heidelberg: Springer.

De Groot, S. P., & Knapp, A. E. (2004). Applying the user-centered design (UCD) process to the development of a large bibliographic navigation tool: A partnership between librarian, researcher and developer. Retrieved January 30, 2007, from http://www.info.scopus.com/news/white papers/wp1_usability_testing.pdf

De Solla Price, S. (1986). Little science, big Science and beyond. New York: Columbia University Press.

Dearnley, J., McKnight, C., & Morris, A. (2004). Electronic book usage in public libraries: a study of user and staff reactions to a PDA-based collection. Journal of Librarianship and Information Science, 36(4), 175-282.

Decker, R., & Höppner, M. (2006). Strategic planning and customer intelligence in academic libraries. Library Hi Tech, 24(4), 504–514.

Degemmis, M., Lops, P., & Basile, P. (2006). An intelligent personalized service for conference prticipants. In F. Esposito, Z. W. Ras, D. Malerba, & G. Semeraro (Eds.), Foundations of Intelligent Systems: Proceedings of ISMIS 2006, 16th International. Symposium on

Methodologies for Intelligent Systems (LNAI 4203, pp. 707-712). Berlin: Springer.

Degemmis, M., Lops, P., & Semeraro, G. (2007). A content-collaborative recommender that exploits Word-Net-based user profiles for neighborhood formation. User Modeling and User-Adapted Interaction: The Journal of Personalization Research, 17(3), 217-255.

DeJong, G. (1982). An overview of the FRUMP system. In W. G. Lehnert & M. H. Ringle (Eds.), Strategies for natural language processing (pp. 149-176). Hillsdale, NJ: Lawrence Erlbaum Associates.

Deligiannidis, L., Sheth, A. P., & Aleman-Meza, B. (2006). Semantic analytics visualization. In Proceedings of the Intelligence and Security Informatics, ISI-2006 (pp. 48-59).

Dempsey, L. (1999). Scientific, industrial, and cultural heritage: A shared approach. Ariadne, 22. Retrieved August 20, 2008, from http://www.ariadne.ac.uk/issue22/

Dempsey, L., & Heery, R. (1997). Metadata: An overview of current resource description practice. Peer review draft of deliverable for Work Package 3 of Telematics for research project DESIRE. Retrieved August 12, 2008, from http://www.ukoln.ac.uk/metadata/DESIRE/overview/

Dempsey, L., & Lavoie, B. (2005). DLF service framework for digital libraries. Progress Report.

Devaul, H., Diekema, A., & Ostwald, J. (2007). Computer-assisted assignment of educational standards using natural language processing. Unpublished technical report.

Dharanipragada, S., & Rao, B. (2001). MVDR-based feature extraction for robust speech recognition. Paper presented at ICASSP-01, Utah.

Diekema, A.R., Yilmazel, O., Bailey, J., Harwell, S.C., & Liddy, E.D. (2007). Standards alignment for metadata assignment. In Proceedings of the ACM/IEEE-CS joint conference on Digital libraries (JCDL). Vancouver, Canada.

Digicult. (2004, February). Digital collections and the management of knowledge. Retrieved August 29, 2008, from http://www.digicult.info/downloads/html/8/8.html

Digital Divide.org. (2007). Ushering in the second digital revolution. Retrieved August 30, 2008, from http://www.digitaldivide.org

Digital Library Federation. (1998). A working definition of digital library [1998]. Retrieved August 30, 2008, from http://www.diglib.org/about/dldefinition.htm

Digital Library Federation. What is digital library? Retrieved April 12, 2007, from www.clir.org/diglib

DigitalPreservationEurope. (2006, June). Research roadmap. Retrieved August 29, 2008, from http://www.digitalpreservationeurope.eu/publications/dpe_research_roadmap_D72.pdf

Dillon, A. (2001). Beyond usability: Process, outcome, and affect in human computer interactions. The Canadian Journal of Information and Library Science, 26(4), 57-69.

Ding, L., Finin, T., & Joshi, A. (2004). Analyzing social networks on the Semantic Web. IEEE Intelligent Systems, 8(6).

Ding, L., Finin, T., Joshi, A., Pan, R., Cost, R. S., Peng, Y., et al. (2004). Swoogle: A search and metadata engine for the Semantic Web. In Proceedings the 13th ACM international Conference on Information and Knowledge Management (pp. 652-659).

Ding, L., Zhou, L., Finin, T., & Joshi, A. (2005). How the Semantic Web is being used: An analysis of FOAF documents. In Proceedings of the 38th International Conference on System Sciences (pp. 113.3).

Dingsøyr, T., & Conradi, R. (2003). Usage of Intranet tools for knowledge management in a medium-sized software consulting company. Book chapter in Managing Software Engineering Knowledge (pp. 49–67). Springer Verlag.

Dinh, D. (2002). Building a training corpus for word sense disambiguation in English-to-Vietnamese machine translation. In Proceedings of the 19th International Conference on Computational Linguistics. Association for Computer Linguistics.

Dinh, D., Kiem, H., & Toan, N. V. (2001). Vietnamese word segmentation. In Proceedings of Neural Networks and Natural Language Processing (pp. 749-756). Tokyo.

DITA. (2007). Darwin information typing architecture OASIS standard. Retrieved August 28, 2008, from http://dita.xml.org

Dittenbach, M., & Neumayer, R., & Rauber, A. (2005). PlaySOM: An alternative approach to track selection and playlist generation in large music collections. In Proceedings of the First International Workshop of the EU Network of Excellence DELOS on Audio-Visual Content and Information Visualization in Digital Libraries (AVIVDiLi'05) (pp. 226–235). Cortona, Italy.

Dolan, M. (2005). JCDL workshop summary. D-Lib Magazine, 11(7/8). Retrieved August 30, 2008, from http://www.dlib.org/dlib/july05/07inbrief.html#DOLAN

Dorward, J., Reinke, D., & Recker, M. (2002). An evaluation model for a digital library services tool. In Proceedings of the Second ACM/IEEE-CS Joint Conference on Digital Libraries, Portland, OR (pp. 322-323). Retrieved November 6, 2007, from the ACM Digital Library database.

Downes, S. (2001). Learning objects: Resources for distance education worldwide. The International Review of Research in Open and Distance Learning, 2(1). Retrieved November 21, 2007, from http://www.irrodl.org/index.php/irrodl/article/view/32/378

Downie, J.S. (2003). Annual review of information science and technology (Vol. 37, pp. 295–340). Medford, NJ: Information Today.

Downie, J.S., Ehmann, A.F., & Hu, X. (2005). Music-to-knowledge (M2K): a prototyping and evaluation environment for music digital library research. In Proceedings of the Joint Conference on Digital Libraries (JCDL) (p. 376). Denver, CO.

DSpace Federation. Retrieved August 14, 2008, from http://www.dspace.org/

Dubinko, M., Kumar, R., Magnani, J., Novak, J., Raghavan, P., & Tomkins, A. (2006). Visualizing tags over time. In Proceedings of the 15th International Conference on the World Wide Web (pp. 193-202).

Dublin Core collection description application profile. Retrieved August 20, 2008, from http://www.ukoln.ac.uk/metadata/dcmi/collection-application-profile/2003-08-25/

Dublin Core Metadata Initiative (DCMI). (2006). Web site: http://www.dublincore.org/

Dublin core metadata initiative. (2007). Dublin core education application profile (working draft of v0.4). Retrieved November 18, 2007, from http://docs.google.com/View?docid=dn8z3gs_38cgwkvv

Dublin core metadata initiative. (2007). Dublin core metadata element set, version 1.1. Retrieved November 15, 2007, from http://dublincore.org/documents/dces/

Dublin core metadata initiative. Education working group. (2006). Education application profile. Retrieved November 15, 2007, from http://projects.ischool.washington.edu/sasutton/dcmi/DC-EdAP-7-18-06.html

Dumas, J. S., & Redish, J. C. (1993). A practical guide to usability testing. Norwood, NJ: Ablex Publishing Co.

Duval, E., Hodgins, W., Sutton, S. A., & Weibel, S. L. (2002). Metadata principles and practicalities. D-Lib Magazine, 8(4). Retrieved November 21, 2007, from http://www.dlib.org/dlib/april02/weibel/04weibel.html

Eason, K. D. (1981). A task-tool analysis of manager-computer interaction. In B. Shackel (Ed.), Man-computer interaction: Human factors aspects of computers & people (pp. 289-307). Rockville, MD: Sijthoff and Noordhoff.

Edmundson, H. P. (1969). New methods in automatic extracting. Journal of the ACM, 16(2), 264-285.

Education network Australia. (2007). EdNA metadata standard v1.1. Retrieved November 15, 2007, from http://www.edna.edu.au/edna/go/resources/metadata/edna_metadata_profile

Elmagarmid, A., Ipeirotis, P., & Verykios, V. (2007). Duplicate record detection: A survey. IEEE Transaction on Knowledge and Data Engineering, 19(1), 1-16

Embley, D. W., Campbell, D. M., Smith, R. D., & Liddle, S. W. (1998). Ontology-based extraction and structuring of information from data-rich unstructured documents. In Proceedings of the CIKM'98: Conference on Information and Knowledge Management, Bethesda (pp. 52-59). New York: ACM Press.

Encoded archival description (EAD). Retrieved August 20, 2008, from http://www.loc.gov/ead/

EndNote. Retrieved August 14, 2008, from http://www.endnote.com/

Endres-Niggemeyer, B. (2002). SimSum: An empirically founded simulation of summarizing. Information Processing & Management, 36(4), 659-682.

Endres-Niggemeyer, B., Maier, E., & Sigel, A. (1995). How to implement a naturalistic model of abstracting: Four core working steps of an expert abstractor. Information Processing & Management, 31(5), 631-674.

EPrints for digital repositories. Retrieved December 2007, from http://www.eprints.org

Eprints. (2007). EPrints for digital repositories. Retrieved November 15, 2007, from http://www.eprints.org/

Erlich, K., & Cash, D. (1994). Turning information into knowledge: Information finding as a collaborative activity. In Proceedings of Digital Libraries '94 (DL'94) (pp. 119–125). College Station, TX.

Ershova, T. V., & Hohlov, Y. E. (2001). Integration of Russian electronic information resources of social value on the basis of DL concept. Russian Digital Libraries Journal, 4(1), 32-41.

European Parliament and the European Council. (2007). Directive of the European Parliament and of the Council establishing an infrastructure for spatial information in the European community (INSPIRE). Join text approved by the Conciliation Committee, provided for in Article 251(4) of the EC Treaty. 2004/0175(COD), PE-CONS 3685/06. Retrieved August 27, 2008, from http://register.consilium.europa.eu/pdf/en/06/st03/st03685.en06.pdf

Ex Libris. (2007) Retrieved November 14, 2007, from http://www.exlibrisgroup.com/newsdetails.htm?nid=543

Fagan, J. L. (1989). The effectiveness of a nonsyntactic approach to automatic phrase indexing for document retrieval. Journal of the American Society for Information Science, 40(2), 115-132.

Falkovych, K., Werner, & Nack, F. (2004). Semantic-based support for the semi-automatic construction of multimedia presentations. In Proceedings of the Interaction Design and the Semantic Web Workshop, the 13th World Wide Web Conference.

Faloutsos, C., & Lin, K. (1995). FastMap: A fast algorithm for indexing, data mining and visualization of traditional and multimedia datasets. In Proceedings of SIGMOD95 (pp. 163–174).

Farmer, L. (2007). Digital library of information science and technology. Reference Reviews, 21(2), 11.

Farzindar, A., & Lapalme, G. (2004). LetSum, an automatic legal text summarizing system. In T. F. Gordon (Ed.), Volume 120 of Frontiers in Artificial Intelligence and Applications: Proceedings of the 17th Annual Conference on Legal Knowledge and Information Systems (pp. 11-18). Amsterdam: IOS Press.

Federal Geographic Data Committee. (1998). Content standard for digital geospatial metadata, version 2.0. Document FGDC-STD-001-1998, Metadata Ad Hoc Working Group.

Fedora Project. Retrieved August 14, 2008, from http://www.fedora.info/

Feiten, B., & Günzel, S. (1994). Automatic indexing of a sound database using self-organizing neural nets. Computer Music Journal, 18(3), 53–65.

Fellbaum, C. (1998). WordNet: An electronic lexical database. MIT Press.

Feng, L., Manfred, A.J., & Hoppe, J. (2005). Beyond information searching and browsing: Acquiring knowledge from digital libraries. Information Processing and Management, 97–120.

Ferguson, C.D., & Bunge, C.A. (2007). Value propositions. In D. Kresh (Ed.), The whole digital library handbook (pp. 51–56). Chicago: American Library Association.

Ferreira, S. M., & Pithan, D. N. (2005). Usability of digital libraries: A study based on the areas of information science and human-computer interaction. OCLC Systems & Services, 21(4), 311-323.

Ferrer Sapena, A., et al. (2005). Guía metodológica para la implantación de una biblioteca digital universitaria. Gijón: Trea.

Fidler, B. (2002). Strategic management for school development. London: Paul Chapman Publishing.

Finley, M.I. (1965). Technical innovation and economic progress in the ancient world. Economic History Review, 2(8), 37.

Fisher, W. (2002). The electronic resources librarian position: A public services phenomenon. Library Collections, Acquisitions, & Technical Services, 27(1), 3–17.

Flickner, M., Sawhney, H., Ashley, J., Huang, Q., Dom, B., Gorkani, M., et al. (1995). Query by image and video content: the QBIC system. IEEE Computer, 28(9), 23–32.

Flickner, M., Sawhney, H., Niblack, W., & Ashley, J. (1995). Query by image and video content: The QBIC system. IEEE Computer, 28(9), 23-32.

Foltz, P. W., Kintsch, W., & Landauer, T. K. (1998). The measurement of textual coherence with latent semantic analysis. Discourse Processes, 25(2-3), 285-307.

Foltz, P., Kintsch W., & Landauer, K. (1998). Textual coherence using latent semantic analysis. Discourse Processes, 25(2&3), 285-307.

Foo, S. (in press). Online virtual exhibitions: Concepts and design considerations. DESIDOC (Defence Scientific Information & Documentation Centre) Bulletin of Information Technology.

Foo, S., & Theng, Y.L. (2005). Digital library trends in the Asia Pacific. Digital Library Asia.

Foote, J.T. (1997). Content-based retrieval of music and audio. In C. Kuo (Ed.), Proceedings of SPIE Multimedia Storage and Archiving Systems II (Vol. 3229, pp. 138–147).

Foulonneau, M., Cole, T.W., Habing, T.G., & Shreeves, S.L. (2005). Using collection descriptions to enhance an aggregation of harvested item-level metadata. In Proceedings of the 5th ACM/IEEE-CS joint conference on Digital libraries (pp. 32–41). Denver. New York: ACM.

Fox, E.A., & Logan, E. (2005). An Asian digital libraries perspective. Information Processing and Management, 41(1), 1–4.

Fox, E.A., & Urs, S. (2002). Digital libraries. In B. Cronin (Ed.), Annual Review of Information Science and Technology (ARIST), Ch. 12 (pp. 503–589). American Society for Information Science.

Fox, E.A., & Urs, S.R. (2002). Digital libraries. Annual Review of Information Science and Technology Volume, 36, 503–589.

Frakes, W. B. (1992), Stemming algorithms. In W. B. Frakes & R. Baeza-Yates (Eds.), Information retrieval: Data structures and algorithms (pp.131-161). Englewood Cliffs, NJ: Prentice-Hall.

Francoeur, S. (2002). Digital Reference. In The Teaching Librarian. Retrieved August 29, 2008, from http://www.teachinglibrarian.org/digref.htm

Freed, N. (1996). RFC 2046, MIME part two: Media types. IETF. Retrieved August 12, 2008, from http://www.ietf.org/rfc/rfc2046.txt

Freeman, G. (2007). Reinventing the library. In D. Kresh (Ed.), The Whole Digital Library Handbook (pp. 370–373). Chicago: American Library Association.

Friedman, P.K. (2005). Folksonomy. Anthropology News, 46, 38–38.

Frumkin, J. (2004). Defining digital libraries. OCLC Systems & Services International Digital Library Perspectives, 20(4), 155–156.

Fuchs, M., Muscogiuri, C., Niederée, C., & Hemmje, M. (2004). Digital libraries in knowledge management: An e-learning case study. International Journal on Digital Libraries, 4, 31–35.

Fuggetta, A. (2000). Software process: A roadmap. In Proceedings of The Future of Software Engineering. Limerick, Ireland.

Fuglie, K., et al. (1996). Agricultural research and development: Public and private investments under alternative markets and institutions (Agricultural Economics Rep. No. AER735) (p. 88). Retrieved November 13, 2007, from ttp://www.ers.usda.gov/publications/aer735/

Fujii, A., & Ishikawa, T. (2005). Toward the automatic compilation of multimedia encyclopedias: Associating images with term descriptions on the Web. In Proceedings of the International Conference on Web Intelligence (pp. 536-542).

Fujii, A., & Itou, K. (2003). Building a test collection for speech-driven Web retrieval. In Proceedings of Eurospeech-2003, Geneva (pp. 1153-1156).

Furnas, G. W., Landauer, T. K., Gomez, L. M., & Dumais, S.T. (1987). The vocabulary problem in human-system communication. Communications of the ACM, 30(11), 964-971.

Futrelle, R. (1999). Summarization of diagram in document. In I. Mani & M. Maybury (Eds.), Advance in automatic summarization (pp. 403-421). Cambridge, MA: MIT Press.

Galvez, C., Moya-Anegón, F., & Solana, V. H. (2005). Term conflation methods in information retrieval: Non-linguistic and linguistic approaches. Journal of Documentation, 61(4), 520-547.

Gangabadadarachchi, V., & Amarasiri, M.S.U. (2006). Digital collection building initiatives of National Library and Document Centre. Sri Lankan Journal of Librarianship and Information Management, 2(1), 38–43.

García Gómez, F.J. (2004). La formación de usuarios en la biblioteca Anales de Documentación, 7. pp. 97–122. pública virtual. Recursos y procedimientos en las bibliotecas públicas españolas.

Garcia, S. (2004). Improving process improvement with process asset libraries. Software Engineering Institute.

Garcia-Molina, H., Ullman, J.D., & Widom, J.D. (2001). Database systems: The complete book (1st ed.). Prentice Hall.

Garfinkel, S. L. (2003). Understanding privacy-email-based identification and authentication: An alternative to PKI. IEEE Security & Privacy, 1(6), 20-26.

Garza-Salazar, D., & Lavariega, J. (2003). Information retrieval and administration of distributed documents in Internet: The Phronesis digital library project. Knowledge based information retrieval and filtering from Internet (pp. 53-73). Kluwer Academic Publishers.

Gatenby, P. (2007). Rapid and easy access: Finding and getting resources in Australian libraries and cultural institutions. World Library and Information Congress: 73rd IFLA General Conference and Council. Retrieved August 30, 2008, from http://www.ifla.org/iv/ifla73/index.htm

Gauvain, J.-L., & Lee, C.-H. (1994). Maximum a posteriori estimation for multivariate Gaussian mixture observations of Markov chains. IEEE Trans. on Speech and Audio Proc., 2, 291-298.

Gelb, J. (2007) Optimizing your content development using topic maps. In Proceedings of DITA North American Conferences. San José, CA.

Georgiadou, Y. (2006). SDI ontology and implications for research in the developing world. International

Journal of Spatial Data Infrastructures Research, 1, 51–64. Retrieved August 27, 2008, from http://ijsdir.jrc.it/editorials/georgiadou.pdf

Geurts, P., & Roosendaal, H. (2001). Estimating the direction of innovative change based on theory and mixed methods. Quality & Quantity, 35(4), 407-428.

Ghias, A., Logan, J., Chamberlin, D., & Smith, B.C. (1995). Query by humming: Musical information retrieval in an audio database. In Proceedings of the Third ACM International Conference on Multimedia (pp. 231–236). San Francisco, CA: ACM.

Giddens, A. (1986). The constitution of society: Outline of the theory of structuration. Berkeley: University of California Press.

Gill, T. (2004, May 3). Building semantic bridges between museums, libraries and archives: The CIDOC conceptual reference model. First Monday, 9(5). Retrieved August 20, 2008, from http://www.firstmonday.org/

Gill, T. et al. (2002, January). Re-inventing the wheel? Standards, interoperability and digital cultural content. D-Lib Magazine, 8(1). Retrieved August 20, 2008, from http://www.dlib.org/dlib/january02/01contents.html

Giunchiglia, F., Yatskevich, M., & Shvaiko, P. (in press). Semantic matching: Algorithms and implementation. Journal on Data Semantics.

Gladney, H. M., et al. (1994, May). Digital library: Gross structure and requirements (IBM Research Rep. RJ 9840). Paper presented at the Workshop on On-line Access to Digital Libraries. World Wide IEEE Computer Society Press. Retrieved November 13, 2007, from http://www.ifla.org/documents/libraries/net/rj9840.pdf

Gladney, H., Belkin, N., Ahmed, Z., Fox, E., Ashany, R., & Zemankova, M. (1994). Digital library: Gross structure and requirements. In Proceedings of the First Annual Conference on the Theory and Practice of Digital Libraries. San Antonio, Texas, EEUU.

Gladney, H.M. (2004). Trustworthy 100-year digital objects: Evidence after every witness is dead. ACM Transactions on Information Systems, 22(3), 406–436. Retrieved August 30, 2008, from http://doi.acm.org/10.1145/1010614.1010617

Goetsch, L., Sowers, L., & Todd, C. (1999). SPEC kit 251: Electronic reference service: Executive summary. Retrieved August 29, 2008, from http://www.arl.org/spec/251sum.html

Goh, D. H.-L., Chua, A., Khoo, D. A., Khoo, E. B.-H., Mak, E. B.-T., & Ng, M. W.-M (2006). A checklist for evaluating open source digital library software. Online Information Review, 30(4), 360-379.

Goh, D.L.H., Theng, Y.L., Lim, E.P., Zhang, J., Chang, C.H., & Chatterjea, K. (2006). G-Portal: A platform for learning geography. In A. Tatnall (Ed.), Encyclopaedia of Portal Technology and Applications. Hershey, PA: Idea Group Publishing.

Golbeck, J., Fragoso, G., Hartel, F., Hendler, J., Oberthaler, J., & Parsia, B. (2003). The National Cancer Institute's thésaurus and ontology. Journal of Web Semantics, 1(1).

Golder, S. A., & Huberman, B. A. (2006). Usage patterns of collaborative tagging systems. Journal of Information Science, 32(2), 198-208.

Goldstein, J., Kantrowitz, M., Mittal, V., & Carbonell J. (1999). Summarizing text documents: Sentence selection and evaluation metrics. In Proceedings of the 22nd Annual International ACM SIGIR Conference (pp.121-128). ACM.

Goldstein, J., Mittal, V., Carbonell, J., & Kantrowitz, M. (2000). Multi-document summarization by sentence extraction. In Proceedings of ANLP/NAACL 2000 Workshop on Automatic Summarization (Vol. 4, pp. 40-48). Morristown, NJ: ACL.

Goncalves, M. et al. (2004). Streams, structures, spaces, scenarios, societies (5S): A formal model for digital libraries. ACM Transactions on Information Systems, 22, 270–312.

Goncalves, M.A. (2004). Streams, structures, spaces, scenarios, and societies (5S): A Formal digital library framework and its applications. Doctoral dissertation, Virginia Tech. Retrieved August 30, 2008 from http://scholar.lib.vt.edu/theses/available/etd-12052004-135923/

Goncalves, M.A., & Fox, E.A. (2002). 5SL—a language for declarative specification and generation of digital libraries. In Proceedings of the Joint Conference on Digital Libraries (pp. 263–272). Retrieved August 30, 2008, from http://doi.acm.org/10.1145/544220.544276

Gonçalves, M.A., Fox, E.A., Watson, L.T., & Kipp, N.A. (2004). Streams, structures, spaces, scenarios, societies (5S): A formal model for digital libraries. ACM Transactions on Information Systems, 22(2), 270–312. Retrieved August 30, 2008, from http://doi.acm.org/10.1145/984321.984325

Goncalves, M.A., Moreira, B.L., Fox, E.A., & Watson, L.T. (2007). "What is a good digital library?"—A quality model for digital libraries. In Information Processing &

Management, 43(5), 1416–1437. Retrieved August 30, 2008, from http://dx.doi.org/10.1016/j.ipm.2006.11.010

Gonçalves, M.A., Moreira, B.L., Fox, E.A., & Watson, L.T. (2007). What is a good digital library? A quality model for digital libraries. Information Processing and Management, 43(5), 1416–1437.

Gong, Y., & Liu, X. (2001). Generic text summarization using relevance measure and latent semantic analysis. In Proceedings of the 24th Annual International ACM SIGIR Conference (pp. 19-25). ACM.

Good, L., Popat, A. C., Janssen, W. C., & Bier, E. A. (2005, September 18-23). A fluid interface for personal digital libraries. In Proceedings of the 9th European Conference on Research and Advanced Technology for Digital Libraries (ECDL 2005), Vienna, Austria (pp. 162-173).

Goodchild, M.F. (1998). The geolibrary. In S. Carver (Ed.), Innovations in GIS 5 (pp. 59–68). London: Taylor and Francis.

Goodchild, M.F. (2004). The Alexandria digital library project: Review, assesment, and prospects. D-Lib Magazine, 10(5). Retrieved August 27, 2008, from http://www.dlib.org/dlib/may04/goodchild/05goodchild.html

Gorman, G.E. (Ed.). (2002). The digital factor in library and information services. London: Facet Publishing.

Gorman, G.E. (2006). For whom is the new information millennium? Online Information Review, 30(1), 5–7.

Gorton, D.C. (2007). Practical digital library generation into DSpace with the 5S Framework. Master's thesis, Virginia Tech. Retrieved August 30, 2008, from http://scholar.lib.vt.edu/theses/available/etd-04252007-161736/

Goto, M., & Goto, T. (2005). Musicream: New music playback interface for streaming, sticking, sorting, and recalling musical pieces. In Proceedings of the Sixth International Conference on Music Information Retrieval (ISMIR'05) (pp. 404–411). London, UK.

Gotz, D., & Mayer-Patel, K. (2005). A framework for scalable delivery of digitized spaces. International Journal on Digital Libraries, 5(3), 205-218.

Government College University. (2008). GC university library. Retrieved August 30, 2008, from http://gcu.edu.pk/library/S_FullJour.htm

Greenberg, J., Pattuelli, C., Parsia, B., & Davenport Robertson, W. (2002). Author-generated Dublin Core metadata for web resources: A baseline study in an organization. Journal of Digital Information, 2(2), Article 78. Retrieved March 28, 2006, from http://jodi.ecs.soton.ac.uk/Articles/v02/i02/Greenberg/

Greenstein, D. (2002). Next-generation digital libraries. Retrieved September 26, 2006, from http://www.vala.org.au/vala2002/2002pdf/01Grnstn.pdf

Greenstone digital library software. Retrieved August 14, 2008, from http://www.greenstone.org/

Greenstone. (2007). Retrieved May 11, 2007, from http://www.greenstone.org/

Griffin, D. (2007). National archives takes charge of securing Whitehall's digital legacy. Information World Review, 238, 6.

Grohs, K., Reed, C., & Allen, N. (2003). Marketing the virtual library. In A. Hanson, & B.L. Levin (Eds.), Building a virtual library (pp. 133–147). London: Information Science Publishing.

Gross, M., McClure, C.R., & Lankes, R.D. (2001). Assessing quality in digital reference services: Overview of key literature on digital reference. Florida: Information Institute.

Gruber, T. R. (1993). A translation approach to portable ontology specifications. Knowledge Acquisition, 5(2), 199-220.

Grün, C., Gerken, J., Jetter, H. C., König, W., & Reiterer, H. (2005, September 18-23). MedioVis: A user-centred library metadata browser. In Proceedings of the Research and Advanced Technology for Digital Libraries, 9th European Conference, ECDL 2005, Vienna, Austria (pp. 174-185).

Guarino, N. (1998, June). Formal ontology in information systems. In Proceedings of FOIS'98, Trento, Italy (pp. 3-15). Amsterdam: IOS Press.

Guarino, N., Masolo, C., & Vetere, G. (1999). OntoSeek: Content-based access to the Web. IEEE Intelligent Systems, 14(3), 70-80.

Guha, R., & McCool, R., (2003). TAP: A Semantic Web test-bed. Journal of Web Semantics, 1(1), 81-88.

Guha, R., McCool, R., & Miller, E. (2003). Semantic search. In Proceedings of the WWW 2003 Conference.

Guha, S., Koudas, N., Marathe, A., & Srivastava, D. (2004). Merging the results of approximate match operations. In Proceedings of the 30th VLDB Conference (pp. 636-647).

Gupta, A., & Jain, R. (1997). Visual information retrieval. Communications of the ACM, 40(5), 71–79.

Guy, F. (2000). Progress towards the development of digital libraries: The experiences of some national libraries in North America, Australasia and Europe. Russian Digital Libraries Journal, 3(3). Retrieved August 30, 2008, from http://www.elbib.ru/index.phtml?page=elbib/eng/journal/2000/part3/guy

Hahn, U., & Mani, I. (2000). The challenges of automatic summarization. IEEE Computer, 33(11), 29-36.

Haider, S. J. (1998). Public libraries and development planning in Pakistan: A review of past efforts and future needs. Asian Libraries, 7(2), 47–57.

Haider, S.J. (2004). Coping with change: Issues facing university libraries in Pakistan. The Journal of Academic Librarianship, 30(3), 229–236.

Haider, S.J. (2001). Public library facilities in Pakistan. Public Libraries Quarterly, 19(4), 27–42.

Haider, S.J. (2002). School libraries in Pakistan. Information Development, 18(1), 27–33.

Halbert, M., Kaczmarek, J., & Hagedorn, K. (2003). Findings from the Mellon metadata harvesting initiative. In Proceedings of the 7th European Conference on Digital libraries, LNCS 2769 (pp. 58–69). Heidelberg: Springer.

Hamanaka, M., & Lee, S. (2006). Music scope headphones: Natural user interface for selection of music. In Proceedings of the International Conference on Music Information Retrieval (ISMIR'06) (pp. 302–307). Victoria, BC, Canada.

Hamilton, S., & Pors, N. O. (2003). Freedom of access to information and freedom of expression: The Internet as a tool for global social inclusion. Library Management, 24(8/9), 407-416.

Hammond, T., Hannay, T., Lund, B., & Scott, J. (2005). Social bookmarking tools (I). D-Lib Magazine, 11(4). Retrieved August 23, 2008, from http://www.dlib.org/dlib/april05/hammond/04hammond.html

Han, H., Giles, C.L., Manavoglu, E., Zha, H., Zhang, Z., & Fox, E.A. (2003). Automatic document metadata extraction using support vector machines. In Proceedings of the ACM/IEEE-CS joint conference on Digital libraries (JCDL). Houston, TX.

Han, L., & Goulding, A. (2003). Information and reference services in the digital library. Information Services and Use, 23, 251–262.

Handzic, M. (2005). Knowledge management: Through the technology glass. World Scientific Publishing Company.

Hansen, J. H. L. (1996). Analysis and compensation of speech under stress and noise for environmental robustness in speech recognition. Speech Communications, Special Issue on Speech Under Stress, 20(2), 151-170.

Hansen, J. H. L., Huang, R., Zhou, B., Seadle, M., Deller, J. R., Jr., Gurijala, A. R., et al. (2005). SpeechFind: Advances in spoken document retrieval for a national gallery of the spoken word. IEEE Trans. on Speech and Audio Proc., 13(5), 712-730.

Hansen, J. H. L., Zhou, B., Akbacak, M., Sarikaya, R., & Pellom, B. (2000). Audio stream phrase recognition for a national gallery of the spoken word: 'One small step'. In Proceedings of the ICSLP-2000: Inter. Conf. Spoken Lang. Proc., Beijing (Vol. 3, pp. 1089-1092).

Hanseth, O., & Monteiro, E. (in press). Understanding information infrastructure. Retrieved August 27, 2008, from http://heim.ifi.uio.no/~oleha/Publications/bok.html

Hardy, H., Shimizu, N., Strzalkowski, T., Ting, L., Wise, G., & Zhang, X. (2002). Cross-document summarization by concept classification. In Proceedings of the 25th Annual International ACM SIGIR Conference on Research and Development in Information Retrieval (pp. 121-128). New York: ACM.

Harris, Z. S. (1951). Methods in structural linguistics. Chicago: University of Chicago Press.

Hartson, H. R., Shivakumar, P., & Pérez-Quiñones, M. A. (2004). Usability inspection of digital libraries: A case study. International Journal on Digital Libraries, 4(2), 108-123.

Harvard University Library. (2007). Jhove-jstor/harvard object validation environment. Retrieved August 29, 2008, from http://hul.harvard.edu/jhove

Hatzivassiloglou, V., Klavans, J., & Eskin, E. (1999). Detecting text similarity over short passages: Exploring linguistic feature combinations via machine learning. Paper presented at the SIGDAT Conference of Empirical Methods in NLP and Very Large Corpora, Maryland.

Haveliwala, T. (2002). Topic sensitive PageRank. In Proceedings of the 11th International World Wide Web Conference (pp. 517-526).

Haynes, D. (2004). Metadata for information management and retrieval. London: Facet Publishing.

Hearst, M. A. (1993). Subtopic structuring for full-length document access. In Proceedings of the 16th Annual International ACM SIGIR Conference (pp. 56-68). ACM.

Hearst, M. A., & Karadi, C. (1997, July 27-31). Cat-a-cone: An interactive interface for specifying searches and viewing retrieval results using a large category hierarchy. In Proceedings of the 20th Annual International ACM/SIGIR Conference on Research and Development in Information Retrieval (SIGIR '97), Philadelphia, PA. New York: ACM.

Heath, B., McArthur, D., & Vetter, R. (2005). Metadata lessons from the iLumina digital library. Communications of the ACM, 48(5), 68–74.

Hedberg, J.G. (2006). E-learning futures? Speculations for a time yet to come. Studies in Continuing Education, 28(2), 173–185.

Hee, Y.Y., Duk, H.C., & Young, S.K. (2006). Libraries in Korea: A general overview. IFLA Journal, 32(2), 93–103.

Heery, R., & Patel, M. (2000). Application profiles: Mixing and matching metadata schemas. Ariadne, 25. Retrieved November 21, 2007, from http://www.ariadne.ac.uk/issue25/app-profiles/

Heisey, L., & Paolillo, M. (n.d.). Final report: Beam-using possibilities. Infrared beaming of citations from the kiosks to patrons 'portable devices.' Retrieved September 11, 2007, from http://www.library.cornell.edu/EMPSL/PDA-pilot-report.pdf

Henderson, S. (2002). The growth of printed literature in the twentieth century. In R. E. Abel & L. W. Newlin (Eds.), Scholarly publishing: Books, journals, publishers, and libraries in the twentieth century (pp. 1-23). Indianapolis: Wiley.

Herrera Morillas, J.L. (2001). El fondo antiguo de las bibliotecas universitarias de Andalucía, Extremadura y Murcia: colecciones, textos normativos y recursos virtuales. Boletín de la Asociación Andaluza de Bibliotecarios, 64, 53–73.

Herrera Morillas, J.L. (2004). Tratamiento y difusión digital del libro antiguo: directrices metodológicas y guías de recursos. Gijón: Trea.

Herrera, E., & Passi, G. (2006). Special issue on soft approaches to information retrieval and information access on the Web. Journal of the American Society for Information Science and Technology, ACM Digital library, 57, 511–514.

Hessel, A. (1955). A history of libraries (R. Peiss, Trans.). New Jersey: The Scarecrow Press.

Higgs, P. E., Meredith, S., & Hand, T. (2003). Technology for sharing: Researching learning objects and digital rights management. Final report. Flexible learning leader 2002 report. Retrieved November 23, 2007, from http://leaders.flexiblelearning.net.au/fl_leaders/fll02/finalreport/final_hand_higgs_meredith.pdf

Higher Education Commission. (2008). Our institutes. Retrieved August 30, 2008, from http://app.hec.gov.pk/universityfinal2/RegionUniversity.aspx

Higher Education Commission. (2008). Pakistan research repository. Retrieved August 30, 2008, from http://eprints.hec.gov.pk/

Hillman, D.I., & Westbrooks, E.L. (2004). Metadata in practice. American Library Association.

Hillmann, D. I., & Phipps, J. (2007). Application profiles: Exposing and enforcing metadata quality. In Proceedings of the International Conference on Dublin Core and Metadata Applications 2007. Retrieved November 24, 2007, from http://www.dcmipubs.org/ojs/index.php/pubs/article/viewFile/41/20

Hilse, H.-W., & Kothe, J. (2006, November). Implementing persistent identifiers (Tech. Rep.).London and Amsterdam: Consortium of European Research Libraries.

Hirao, T., Isozaki, H., Maeda, E., & Matsumoto, Y. (2002). Extracting important sentences with support vector machines. In Proceedings of the 19th International Conference on Computational Linguistics (pp. 1-7). Morristown, NJ: ACL.

Historical Directories of England and Wales. Retrieved August 24, 2008, from http://www.historicaldirectories.org

Hodge, G. (2000). Systems of knowledge organization for digital libraries: Beyond traditional authority files. Washington, DC: Digital Library Federation, Council on Library and Information Resources.

Hoeven, J., Van Der Diessen, R., & Van En Meer, K. (2005). Development of a universal virtual computer (UVC) for long-term preservation of digital objects. Journal of Information Science, 31(3), 196–208.

Hollink, L., Schreiber, A. T., Wielemaker, J., & Wielinga, B. (2003). Semantic annotation of image collections. Paper presented at the Workshop on Knowledge Markup and Semantic Annotation.

Hollmann, J., Ardö, A., & Stenström, P. (2007). Effectiveness of caching in a distributed digital library system. Journal of Systems Architecture, 53(7), 403–416.

Hom, J. (2000). The usability methods toolbox: Heuristic evaluation. Retrieved November 6, 2007, from http://jthom.best.vwh.net/usability/

Hong, J. S., Chen, B. H., & Hung, S. H. (2004). Toward intelligent styling for digital museum exhibitions: Modularization framework for aesthetic hypermedia presentations. International Journal on Digital Libraries, 4, 64-68.

Hong, J. S., Chen, B. H., Hung, S. H., & Hsiang, J. (2005). Toward an integrated digital museum system: The Chi Nan experiences. International Journal on Digital Libraries, 5(3), 231-251.

Hori, C., & Furui, S. (2000). Automatic speech summarization based on word significance and linguistic likelihood. In Proceedings of the IEEE ICASSP-00: Inter. Conf. Acoust. Speech, Sig. Proc. (Vol. 3, pp. 1579-1582).

Hovy, E. H., & Lin, C. (1999). Automated text summarization in SUMMARIST. In I. Mani & M. T. Maybury (Eds.), Advances in automatic text summarization (pp. 81-94). Cambridge, MA: MIT Press.

Hsu, C-C., Chu, W., & Taira, R.A. (1996). Knowledge-based approach for retrieving images by content. IEEE Transactions on Knowledge and Data Engineering, 8(6), 522–532.

Huang, J., Kumar, S.R., Mitra, M., Zhu, W.-J., & Zabih, R. (1997). Image indexing using color correlograms. In IEEE Int. Conference Computer Vision and Pattern Recognition (pp. 762–768).

Huang, R., & Hansen, J. H. L. (2006). Advances in unsupervised audio classification and segmentation for the broadcast news and NGSW corpora. IEEE Trans. Audio, Speech and Language Processing, 14(3), 907-919.

Huang, R., & Hansen, J. H. L. (2007). Dialect/accent classification using unrestricted audio. IEEE Trans. on Audio, Speech and Language Processing, 15(2), 453-464.

Huling, N. (2002). Reference services and information access. In J.R. Schement (Ed.), Encyclopedia of Communication and Information (pp. 867–874). New York: Gale Group.

Hull, D. A. (1996). Stemming algorithms: A case study for detailed evaluation. Journal of the American Society for Information Science, 47(1), 70-84.

Hunt, L., Lundberg, M., & Zuckerman, B. (2005). InscriptiFact: A virtual archive of ancient inscriptions from the Near East. International Journal of Digital Libraries, 5, 153-166.

Hunter, J., & Choudhury, S. (2006, April). PANIC—an integrated approach to the preservation of complex digital objects using semantic Web services. In International journal on digital libraries: Special issue on complex digital objects (Vol. 6, No. 2, pp. 174–183). Berlin, Heidelberg: Springer.

Huotari, M.-L., & Iivonen, M. (2005). Knowledge processes: A strategic foundation for the partnership between the university and its library. Library Management, 26(6/7), 324–335.

Hussain, A. (2006). Perceptions of LIS professionals regarding digital library. Unpublished master thesis, University of the Punjab, Lahore.

Hutchinson, D.R., Sanders, R., & Faust, T. (2003). Making USGS information effective in the electronic age (U.S. Geological Survey Open-File Report 03-240). Retrieved August 29, 2008, from http://pubs.usgs.gov/of/2003/of03-240/

Hutt, A., & Riley, J. (2005). Semantics and syntax of Dublin Core usage in open archives initiative data providers of cultural heritage materials. In Proceedings of the 5th ACM/IEEE-CS joint conference on Digital libraries (pp. 262–270). Denver. New York: ACM.

Ibekwe-SanJuan, F., & SanJuan, E. (2004). Mining for knowledge chunks in a terminology network. In I. C. McIlwaine (Ed.), Volume 9 of Advances in Knowledge Organization: Proceedings of the 8th International Society for Knowledge Organization Conference (pp. 41-46). Verkehrs-Nr: Ergon-Verlag.

IEEE. (2002). Draft standard for learning object metadata. IEEE 1484.12.1-2002. Retrieved August 12, 2008, from http://ltsc.ieee.org/doc/wg12/LOM_1484_12_1_v1_Final_Draft.pdf

IEEE. (1990). Glossary. Retrieved August 17, 2008, from http://www.sei.cmu.edu/str/indexes/glossary/interoperability.html

IEEE Learning Technology Standards Committee. (1999). IEEE 1484 learning objects metadata (IEEE LOM) mappings to Dublin Core. Learning object metadata: Draft document v3.6. Retrieved November 15, 2007, from http://www.ischool.washington.edu/sasutton/IEEE1484.html

IFLA study group on the functional requirements for bibliographic records. (1998). Functional requirements for bibliographic records: Final report. Muenche: Saur, K.G. Retrieved August 11, 2008, from http://www.ifla.org/VII/s13/frbr/frbr.htm

IMLS. (2002). Status of technology and digitization in the nation's museums and libraries. Washington, D.C.: Institute of Museum and Library Services.

IMS Global Learning Consortium, Inc. (2001). IMS digital repositories white paper version 1.6. Retrieved August 12, 2008, from http://www.imsproject.org/imsdr_whitepaper_v1p6.pdf

IMS Global Learning Consortium, Inc. (2003). IMS digital repositories interoperability: Core functions information model version 1.0 final specification. Retrieved August 12, 2008, from http://www.imsglobal.org/digitalrepositories/index.cfm

In re Alappat. (1994). 33 F.3d 1526, 31 U.S.P.Q.2d 1545 (Fed. Cir. 1994) (en banc)

In re Dow Chemical Co. (1988). 837 F.2d 469, 473, 5 U.S.P.Q.2d 1529, 1531 (Fed. Cir. 1988).

Infofinder. (2006). Retrieved February 5, 2007, from http://infofinder.cgiar.org/

Informix Inc. (1998). Informix answers online (Version 1.91). CD-ROM.

International Organization for Standardization. (2003). Geographic information—metadata. International standard 19115.

International Organization for Standardization/International Electrotechnical Commission Joint Technical Committee. (2007). Metadata standards. Retrieved November 15, 2007, from http://metadata-stds.org/

International Standards Organization. (1994). Ergonomic requirements for office work with visual display terminals. Part 11: Guidance on usability (ISO DIS 9241-11). London: Author.

Islam, K.M.S. (1968). The role of libraries in education. The Eastern Librarian, 3(1).

ISO. (2004). Document management—electronic document file format for long-term preservation—part 1: Use of PDF 1.4 (PDF/A) ISO/CD 19005-1.

ISO. (2002). Information technology—multimedia content description interface—part 1: Systems ISO/IEC 15938-1:2002.

ISO. (2002). Information technology—multimedia content description interface—part 4: audio. ISO/IEC 15938-4:2002. International Organisation for Standardisation. Mpeg-7. Retrieved August 30, 2008, from http://www.chiariglione.org/mpeg/standards/mpeg-7/mpeg-7.htm

ISO. (2006). Information technology—open document format for office applications ISO/IEC 26300:2006.

ISO. (2003). Space data and information transfer systems—open archival information system—reference model (ISO 14721:2003).

ISO 13250. (2003). Information technology—SGML applications—Topic maps.

ISO 21127. (2006). A reference ontology for the interchange of cultural heritage information.

ISO TC 46/SC 4 N515. (2003). Information and documentation – the Dublin Core metadata element set. Retrieved November 18, 2007, from http://www.niso.org/international/SC4/n515.pdf

IU and UIUC. (2004). Indiana University and University of Illinois at Urbana-Champaign, proposal for project on building an effective digital library curriculum through library school and academic library partnership. Retrieved August 30, 2008, from http://lair.indiana.edu/research/dlib/proposal.pdf

IU and UIUC. (2007). Indiana University and University of Illinois at Urbana-Champaign. JCDL 2007 workshop. Retrieved August 30, 2008, from http://lair.indiana.edu/research/dlib/jcdl07/index.php

Iwe, J.I. (2005). Globalization of information and the Nigerian librarian. IFLA Journal, 31(4), 44–51.

Jacobs, J.A., Jacobs, J.R., & Yeo, S. (2005). Government information in the digital age: The once and future federal depository library program. The Journal of Academic Librarianship, 31(3), 198–208.

Jacobs, P., & Rau, L. (1990). SCISOR: Extracting information from on-line news source. Communications of the ACM, 33(11), 88-97.

Jacso, P. (2000). What is digital librarianship? Computers in Libraries, 20(1), 54–55.

Jain, A.K., & Vailaya, A. (1996). Image retrieval using color and shape. Pattern Recognition, 29(8), 1233–1244.

Jain, P.K., & Babbar, P. (2006). Digital libraries initiatives in India. The International Information and Library Review, 38(3), 161–169.

Jain, R. (1996). Infoscopes: Multimedia information systems. In B. Furht (Ed.), Multimedia systems and techniques (pp. 217-253). Kluwer.

Jain, R., & Hampapur, A. (1994). Metadata in video databases. ACM SIGMOD Record, 23(4) 27–33.

Jamesson, W., Baptista, C.S., Schiel, U., Silva, E.R., Menezes, L.C., & Fernandes, R.M. (2006). Freebie: Uma biblioteca digital baseada em software livre com suporte a buscas textual e espacial. In Proceedings of the 12th Brazilian Symposium on Multimedia and the Web (pp. 155–164). WebMedia.

Janecek, P., & Pu, P. (2005). An evaluation of semantic fisheye views for opportunistic search in an annotated image collection. International Journal of Digital Libraries, 5(1), 42-56.

Janecek, P., Schickel, V., & Pu, P. (2005, December 12-15). Concept expansion using semantic fisheye views. In Proceedings of the International Conference on Asian Digital Libraries, ICADL 2005, Bangkok, Thailand (pp. 273-282).

Janée, G., Frew, J., & Hill, L.L. (2004). Issues in georeferenced digital libraries. D-Lib Magazine, 10(5). Retrieved August 27, 2008, from http://www.dlib.org/dlib/may04/janee/05janee.html

Janée, G., Frew, J., & Hill, L.L. (2004, May). Issues in georeferenced digital libraries. D-Lib Magazine, 10,(5). Retrieved August 29, 2008, from http://www.dlib.org/dlib/may04/janee/05janee.html

Janes, J. (2002). What is reference for? Retrieved August 29, 2008, from http://www.ala.org/ala/rusa/rusaprotools/futureofref/whatreference.htm

Janes, J., Carter, D., & Memmott, P. (1999). Digital reference services in academic libraries. Reference and User Services Quarterly, 39(2), 145–150.

Jansen, B., Spink, A., & Saracevic, T. (2000). Real life, real users and real needs: A study and analysis of user queries on the Web. Information Processing and Management, 36(2), 207-227.

Janssen, W. (2005b, September 18-23). ReadUp: A widget for reading, research and advanced technology for digital libraries. In Proceedings of the 9th European Conference, ECDL 2005, Vienna, Austria (pp. 230-241).

Janssen, W. C. (2004). Collaborative extensions for the uplib system. In Proceedings of the 4th Joint Conference on Digital Libraries (pp. 239-240). ACM Press.

Janssen, W. C. (2005a, June 7-11). Demo: The UpLib personal digital library system. In Proceedings of Joint Conference on Digital Library (JCDL'05), Denver, CO.

Jaro, M. A. (1976). Unimatch: A record linkage system: User's manual (Tech. Rep.). US Bureau of the Census, Washington, D.C.

Jatowt, A., & Ishizuka, M. (2004). Change summarization in Web collections. In Proceedings of the 5th International Conference on Web Information Systems Engineering (pp. 303-312). Berlin: Springer-Verlag.

Jayawardana, C., Hewagamage, K.P., & Hirakawa,M. (2001). Personalization tools for active learning in digital libraries. The Journal of Academic Media Librarianship, 8(1). Retrieved August 30, 2008, from http://wings.buffalo.edu/publications/mcjrnl/v8n1/active.html

JCR. (2005). Journal citation report, Institute for Scientific Information. Thomson. Retrieved August 22, 2008, from http://scientific.thomson.com/products/jcr/

Jeanneney, J.-N. (2007). Google and the myth of universal knowledge. Chicago: The University of Chicago Press.

Jeh, G., & Widom, J. (2003). Scaling personalized Web search. In Proceedings of the 12th International World Wide Web Conference (pp. 271-279).

Jeh, G., & Widom, J. (2003, May 20–24). Scaling personalized Web search. In Proceedings of the Twelfth International World Wide Web Conference (WWW 2003) (pp. 271–279). Budapest.

Jeng, J. (2007, April). Metadata usefulness evaluation of the Moving Image Collections. Paper presented at the 2007 Research Forum of the New Jersey Library Association Annual Conference, Long Branch, NJ. Retrieved November 6, 2007, from http://www.njla.org/conference/2007/presentations/Metadata.pdf

Jeng, J. (2005). Usability assessment of academic digital libraries: Effectiveness, efficiency, satisfaction, and learnability. Libri: International Journal of Libraries and Information Services, 55(2/3), 96-121.

Jeng, J. (2006). Usability of the digital library: An evaluation model. Unpublished doctoral dissertation, Rutgers University.

Jeng, J. (2007, September 25-27). Usability assessment of academic digital libraries. In Proceedings of the Library Assessment Conference: Building Effective, Sustainable, Practical Assessment, Charlottesville, VA (pp. 393-407).

Jeng, J. (2007). Using FRBR tasks as a framework to evaluate metadata usefulness of the Moving Image Collections. Manuscript submitted for publication.

Jeng, J. (2005). What is usability in the context of the digital library and how can it be measured? Information Technology and Libraries, 24(2), 47-56.

Joachims, T. (1998). Text categorization with support vector machines: Learning with many relevant features. In Proceedings of the 10th European Conference on Machine Learning (pp. 137-142).

Johnson, E.D. (1970). History of libraries in the western world. Metuchen: Scarecrow Press Inc.

Johnson, G., & Scholes, K. (2002). Exploring corporate strategy: Text and cases. Cambridge: Prentice Hall.

Johnston, M., Bangalore, S., Vasireddy, G., Stent, A., Ehlen, P., Walker, M., et al. (2002). Match: An architecture for multimodal dialogue systems. In Proceedings of the 40th Annual Meeting on Association for Computational Linguistics (pp. 376-383). Philadelphia, PA: Association for Computational Linguistics.

Johnston, P. (2001). After the big bang: Forces of change and e-learning. Ariadne, 27.

Joint Information Systems Committee (JISC). Cedars project. Retrieved August 20, 2008, from http://www.leeds.ac.uk/cedars/indexold.htm

Joint Task Force on Computing Curricula (IEEE-CS and ACM). (2001). Computing Curricula 2001: Computer Science. Retrieved August 30, 2008, from http://www.sigcse.org/cc2001/

Joint, N. (2006). Common principles in managing digital libraries and managing VLEs. Library Review, 55(4), 232–236.

Jones, K. S., & Galliers, J. R. (1996). Evaluating natural language processing systems: An analysis and review. In J. G. Carbonell & J. Siekmann (Eds.), Volume 1083 of lecturer notes in artificial intelligence. Berlin: Springer-Verlag.

Jones, M. L. W., Rieger, R. H., Treadwell, P., & Gay, G. K. (2000). Live from the stacks: user feedback on mobile computers and wireless tools for library patrons. In Proceedings of the Fifth ACM Conference on Digital Libraries (pp. 95-102). New York: ACM Press.

Jones, M., & Beagrie, N. (2002). Preservation management of digital materials: A handbook. London, UK: Digital Preservation Coalition. Retrieved August 29, 2008, from http://www.dpconline.org/graphics/handbook

Jones, M., Buchanan, G., & Thimbleby, H. W. (2002). Sorting out searching on small screen devices. In Proceedings of the Mobile HCI 2002 (LNCS 2411, pp. 81-94). Berlin: Springer-Verlag.

Jones, S., Jones, M., Barr, M., & Keegan, T. K. (2004). Searching and browsing in a digital library of historical maps and newspapers. Journal of Digital Information, 6(2), 12-19.

Kahl, C.M., & Williams, S.C. (2006). Accessing digital libraries: A study of ARL members' digital projects. The Journal of Academic Librarianship, 32(4), 364–369.

Kahn, R., & Wilensky, R. (1995). A framework for distributed digital object services. Reston, VA: CNRI. Retrieved August 30, 2008, from http://www.cnri.reston.va.us/k-w.html

Kajberg, L., & Lørring, L. (Eds.) (2005). European curriculum reflections on library and information science education. Copenhagen: Royal School of Library and Information Science. Retrieved August 30, 2008, from http://biblis.db.dk/uhtbin/hyperion.exe/db.leikaj05

Kajberg, L., & Lørring, L. (Eds.). (2005). European curriculum reflections on library and information science education. The Royal School of Library and Information Science, Copenhagen, Denmark. Retrieved August 30, 2008, from http://www.asis.org/Bulletin/Dec-06/EuropeanLIS.pdf

Kantner, L., & Rosenbaum, S. (1997). Usability studies of www sites: Heuristic evaluation vs. laboratory testing. In Proceedings of the 15th Annual International Conference on Computer Documentation (pp. 153-160). Retrieved November 6, 2007, from the ACM Digital Library database.

Karlsson, S. K. T. (1999). RePEc and S-WoPEc: Internet access to electronic preprints in economics. Retrieved November 21, 2007, from http://ideas.repec.org/p/rpc/rdfdoc/lindi.html

Karttunen, L. (1983). KIMMO: A general morphological processor. Texas Linguistics Forum, 22, 217-228.

Karttunen, L., Kaplan, R. M., & Zaenen, A. (1992). Two-level morphology with composition. In Proceedings of the 15th International Conference on Computational Linguistics (COLING'92) (pp. 141-148). ACM Press.

Karvounarakis, G., Alexaki, S., Christophides, V., Plexousakis, D., & Scholl, M. (2002). RQL: A declarative query language for RDF. In Proceedings of the 11th World Wide Web Conference (pp. 592-603).

Kasowitz, A.S. (2001). Trends and issues in digital reference services. ERIC Digest, November.

Kassler, M. (1966). Toward musical information retrieval. Perspectives of New Music, 4(2), 59–67.

Kautz, K., & Nielsen, P. (2001). Knowing and implementing SPI. Improving Software Organisations—From Principles to Practice. Addison-Wesley.

Kautz, K., & Thaysen, K. (2001). Knowledge, learning and IT support in a small software company. In Proceedings of the European Conference on Information Systems. Bled, Slovenia.

Kawakami, A.K. (2003). Real-time digital reference. In M.A. Drake (Ed.), Encyclopedia of Library and Information Science (2nd ed., pp. 2463–2474). New York: Marcel Dekker.

Ke, H.R., & Hwang, M.J. (2000). The development of digital libraries in Taiwan. The Electronic Library, 18(5), 336–346.

Kearney, P., & Anand, S.S. (2005). Employing a domain ontology to gain insight into user behavior. In Proceedings of the 3rd Workshop on Intelligent Techniques for Web Personalization, Scotland.

Keith, S., Blandford, A., Fields, B., & Theng, Y. L. (2003). An investigation into the application of claims analysis to evaluate usability of a digital library interface. Paper presented at the Usability Workshop of JCDL 2002. Retrieved November 6, 2007, from http://www.uclic.ucl.ac.uk/annb/docs/Keith15.pdf

Kelly, D., & Teevan, J. (2003). Implicit feedback for inferring user preference: A bibliography. SIGIR Forum, 32(2), 18-28.

Kettunen, J. (2004). Bridge building to the future of Finnish polytechnics. Journal of Higher Education Outreach and Engagement, 9(2), 43–57.

Kettunen, J. (2007). The strategic evaluation of academic libraries. Library Hi-Tech, 25(3), 409–421.

Kettunen, J. (2004). The strategic evaluation of regional development in higher education. Assessment & Evaluation in Higher Education, 29(3), 357–368.

Kettunen, J., & Kantola, M. (2006). The implementation of the Bologna Process. Tertiary Education and Management, 12(3), 257–267.

Kettunen, J., & Kantola, M. (2006). Strategies for virtual learning and e-entrepreneurship. In F. Zhao (Ed.), Entrepreneurship and Innovations in E-Business: An Integrative Perspective (pp. 107–123). Hershey: Idea Group Publishing.

Kettunen, J., & Kantola, M. (2007). Strategic planning and quality management in the Bologna Process. Perspectives, Policy and Practice in Higher education, 11(3), 67–73.

Keystone DLS. Retrieved August 14, 2008, from http://www.indexdata.dk/keystone/

Kibirige, H., & DePalo, L. (2001). The education function in a digital library environment: A challenge for college and research libraries. The Electronic Library, 19(5), 283–295.

Kim, K. (2002). A model of digital library information seeking process (DLISP model) as a frame for classifying usability problems. Unpublished doctoral dissertation, Rutgers University.

King, W. et al. (2002). The most important issues in knowledge management. Communications of the ACM, 45(9), 93–97.

Kintsch, W., & van Dijk, T. A. (1983). Strategies of discourse comprehension. New York: Academic Press.

Kipp, M. E. (2006). Exploring the context of user, creator and intermediate tagging. Paper presented at the 7th Information Architecture Summit. Retrieved August 23, 2008, from http://www.iasummit.org/2006/files/109_Presentation_Desc.pdf

Kircz, J. G., & Roosendaal, H. E. (1996). Understanding and shaping scientific information transfer. In D. Shaw & H. Moore (Eds.), Electronic publishing in science (pp. 106-116). Paris: ICSU Press & UNESCO.

Kiryakov, A., Popov, B., Terziev, I., Manov, D., & Ognyanoff, D. (2005). Semantic annotation, indexing, and retrieval. Elsevier's Journal of Web Semantics, 2(1).

Kleweno, C. P., Seibel, E. J., Viirre, E. S., Kelly, J. P., & Furness, T. A., III (2001). The virtual retinal display as an alternative low vision computer interface: Pilot study. Journal of Rehabilitation Research and Development, 38(4), 431-442.

Knees, P., Pampalk, E., & Widmer, G. (2004). Artist classifiction with Web-based data. In Proceedings of the International Conference on Music Information Retrieval (ISMIR). Barcelona, Spain.

Knees, P., Schedl, M., Pohle, T., & Widmer, G. (2006). An innovative three-dimensional user interface for exploring music collections enriched with metainformation from the Web. In Proceedings of the ACM Multimedia 2006 (MM'06) (pp. 17–24). Santa Barbara, CA.

Knight, S. (2005). Preservation metadata: National Library of New Zealand experience. Library Trends, 54(1), 91–110.

Kobsa, A. (2001). Generic user modeling systems. Journal User Modeling and User-Adapted Interaction, 11(1–2), 49–63.

KOBSON. (2005). Internal data of the project on the evaluation of the Serbian authors publishing productivity. Author.

Koga, T. (2005). Innovation beyond institutions: New projects and challenges for government information service institutions in Japan. World Library and Information Congress: 72nd IFLA general conference and council. Retrieved August 30, 2008, from http://www.ifla71/Programme.htm

Koh, J., & Kim, Y.G. (2004). Knowledge sharing in virtual communities: An e-business perspective. Expert Systems with Applications, 26, 155–166.

Kohonen, T. (2001). Self-organizing maps (3rd ed.). Springer Series in Information Sciences (Vol. 30). Springer, Berlin.

Kohonen, T. (1990) The self-organizing map. In Proceedings of the IEEE (Vol. 78, pp. 1464–1480).

Kohonen, T., Oja, E., Simula, O., Visa, A., & Kangas, J. (1996). Engineering applications of the self-organizing map. In Proceedings of the IEEE, 84(10), 1358.

Koike, H. (1995). Fractal views: A fractal-based method for controlling information display. ACM Transaction on Information Systems, 13(3), 305-323.

Korn, F., & Shneiderman, B. (1995). Navigating terminology hierarchies to access a digital library of medical images (Tech. Rep. HCIL-TR-94- 03). University of Maryland.

Kosanović, B. (2002). Koordinirana nabavka inostranih izvora naučno-tehničkih informacija u Srbiji - stanje i perspective. Infoteka, 3(1-2), 55-63.

Koskenniemi, K. (1983). Two-level morphology: A general computational model for word-form recognition and production. Helsinki: Department of General Linguistics, University of Helsinki.

Kramer, E. F. (2005). IUPUI image collection: A usability survey. OCLC Systems & Services, 21(4), 346-359.

Krasner-Khait, B. (2001). Survivor: The history of the library. History Magazine (October/November).

Krill, P. (2000, January 7). Overcoming information overload. InfoWorld. Retrieved November 13, 2007, from http://www.infoworld.com/articles/ca/xml/00/01/10/000110caoverload.html

Krishnamachari, S., & Abdel-Mottaleb, M. (1999). Image browsing using hierarchical clustering. In Proceedings of IEEE Int. Symposium Computers and Communication (pp. 301–307).

Kruskal, J.B., & Wish, M. (1978). Multidimensional scaling. SAGE University Paper Series on Quantitive Applications in the Social Sciences (pp. 07–011). Newbury Park: Sage Publications.

Kuhlthau C.C. (1997). Learning in digital libraries: An information search process approach. Library Trends, 45(4), 708–724.

Kupiec, J. (1993). Murax: A robust linguistic approach for question answer using an on-line encyclopedia. In R.

Korfhage, E. Rasmussen, & P. Willett (Eds.), Proceedings of the 16th Annual International ACM SIGIR Conference on Research and Development in Information Retrieval (pp. 160-169). ACM Press.

Kupiec, J. (1992). Robust part-of-speech tagging using a Hidden Markov model. Computer Speech and Language, 6, 225-242.

Kupiec, J., Pedersen, J., & Chen, F. (1995). A trainable document summarizer. In Proceedings of the 18th Annual International ACM SIGIR Conference on Research and Development in Information Retrieval (pp. 68-73). New York: ACM.

Kurimo, M., Zhou, B., Huang, R., & Hansen, J. H. L. (2004). Language modeling structures in audio transcription for retrieval of historical speeches. Paper presented at the EUSIPCO-2004, 12th European Signal Processing Conference, Vienna, Austria (Paper 1530).

Kyng, M., & Mathiassen, L. (Eds.). (1997). Computers and design in context. Cambridge, MA: MIT Press.

Laaksonen, J., Koskela, M., Laakkso, P., & Oja, E. (2000). PicSOM: Content-based image retrieval with self organising maps. Pattern Recognition Letters, 21, 1197-1207.

Lacasta, J., Nogueras-Iso, J., Béjar, R., Muro-Medrano, P.R., & Zarazaga-Soria, F.J. (2007). A Web ontology service to facilitate interoperability within a spatial data infrastructure: Applicability to discovery. Data & Knowledge Engineering, 63(3), 947–971.

Lacasta, J., Nogueras-Iso, J., López-Pellicer, F.J., Muro-Medrano, P.R., & Zarazaga-Soria, F.J. (2007). ThManager: An open source tool for creating and visualizing SKOS. Information Technology and Libraries, 26(3), 39–51.

Lagoze, C. (2001, January). Keeping Dublin Core simple: Cross-domain discovery or resource description? D-Lib Magazine, 7(1). Retrieved August 29, 2008, from http://www.dlib.org/dlib/january01/lagoze/01lagoze.html

Lagoze, C., Krafft, D.B., Payette, S., & Jesuroga, S. (2005). What is a digital library anymore, anyway? D-Lib Magazine, 11.

Lagoze, C., & Van de Sompel, H. (2001). The open archives initiative: Building a low-barrier interoperability framework. In Proceedings of the 1st ACM/IEEE-CS Joint Conference on Digital Libraries (JCDL '01), Roanoke, VA. New York: ACM.

Lagoze, C., & Van de Sompel, H. (2001). The open archives initiative: Building a low-barrier interoperability framework. In Proceedings of the 1st ACM/IEEE-CS

Joint Conference on Digital Libraries (JCDL 2001) (pp. 54–62). New York: ACM Press.

Lagoze, C., & Van de Sompel, H. (Eds.) (2004). The open archives initiative protocol for metadata harvesting (PROTOCOL VERSION 2.0). Retrieved August 27, 2008, from http://www.openarchives.org/OAI/2.0/openarchivesprotocol.htm

Lagoze, C., Krafft, D.B., Payette, S., & Jesuroga, S. (2005, November). What is a digital library anymore, anyway? D-Lib Magazine, 11(1). Retrieved August 29, 2008, from http://www.dlib.org/dlib/november05/lagoze/11lagoze.html

Lagoze, C., Payette, S., Shin, E., & Wilper, C. (2005). Fedora: An architecture for complex objects and their relationships. International Journal on Digital Libraries, 6, 124-138.

Lahore University of Management Sciences. (2008). Virtual library. Retrieved August 30, 2008, from http://library.lums.edu.pk/vl/vl.htm

Laitinen, S., & Neuvonen, A. (1998, September 21-23). BALTICSEAWEB: Geographic user interface to bibliographic information. In Proceedings of the Research and Advanced Technology for Digital Libraries, Second European Conference, ECDL '98, Heraklion, Crete, Greece, (pp. 651-652).

Lam, K. (2003). Exploring virtual reference: What it is and what it may be. In R.D. Lankes et al. (Eds.), Implementing digital reference services: Setting standards and making it real (pp. 31–40). London: Facet Publishing.

Lam-Adesina, M., & Jones, G. J. F. (2001). Applying summarization techniques for term selection in relevance feedback. In Proceeding of the 24th Annual International ACM SIGIR Conference (pp. 1-9). ACM.

Lamping, J., Rao, R., & Pirolli, P. (1995). A focus+context technique based on hyperbolic geometry for visualizing large hierarchies. In Proceedings of the ACM Conference on Human Factors in Computing Systems, New York (pp. 401-408).

Landauer, T. K., Foltz, P. W., & Laham, D. (1998). Introduction to latent semantic analysis. Discourse Processes, 25(2-3), 259-284.

Langzhou, C., Gauvain, J.-L., Lamel, L., & Adda, G. (2003). Unsupervised language model adaptation for broadcast news. In Proceedings of the IEEE ICASSP-03: Inter. Conf. Acoust. Speech, Sig. Proc. (Vol. 1, pp. 220-223).

Lankes, R.D. (1998). Ask A starter kit: How to build and maintain digital reference services. Syracuse: ERIC Clearinghouse on Information and Technology.

Lankes, R.D. (2000). The birth cries of digital reference: An introduction to this special issue. Reference and User Services Quarterly, 39(4), 352–354.

Lankes, R.D. (2000). The foundations of digital reference. In R.D. Lankes, J.W. Collins, & A.S. Kasowitz (Eds.), Digital Reference Services in the New Millennium: Planning, Management and Evaluation (pp. 1–10). New York: Neal-Schuman Publications.

Lankes, R.D. et al. (Eds.). (2003). Implementing digital reference services: Setting standards and make it real. London: Facet Publishing.

Lankes, R.D., Collins, J.W., & Kasowitz, A.S. (Eds.). (2000). Digital reference service in the new millennium: Planning, management and evolution. New York: Neal Schuman.

Lapata, M., & Barzilay, R. (2005). Automatic evaluation of text coherence: Models and representations. In L. P. Kaelbling & A. Saffiotti (Eds.), Proceedings of the 19th International Joint Conference on Artificial Intelligence (pp. 1085-1090). San Francisco: Morgan Kaufmann Publishers Inc.

Laux, A., & Martin, L. (2000). XUpdate - XML update language, XML:DB initiative. Retrieved August 12, 2008, from http://www.xmldb.org/xupdate/xupdate-wd.html

Lawrence, G., Kehoe, W., Rieger, O., & Walters, A., W.H., & Kenney. (2000). Risk management of digital information: A file format investigation,. CLIR.

Lawrence, S., Giles, C. L., & Bollacker, K. (1999). Digital libraries and autonomous citation indexing. IEEE Computer, 32(6), 67-71.

Le, A. H. (2003). A method for word segmentation in Vietnamese. Research group in computational linguistics. In Proceedings of Corpus Linguistic 2003. Lancaster.

Lee, C.J. (2006a). The role of the National Library of Korea in the competitiveness enhancement of libraries. World Library and Information Congress: 72nd IFLA general conference and council. Retrieved August 30, 2008, from http://www.ifla71/Programme.htm

Lee, J.S. (2006b). Bibliographic control in Korea: Focus on the National Library of Korea. World Library and Information Congress: 72nd IFLA general conference and council. Retrieved August 30, 2008, from http://www.ifla71/Programme.htm

Leggetter, C., & Woodland, P. (1995). Maximum likelihood linear regression for speaker adaptation of continuous density hidden Markov models. Computer Speech and Language, 9, 171-185.

Lerner, F. (2000). Libraries through the ages. New York: The Continuum Publishing Company.

Lerner, S., & Maffei, A. (2001). 4DGeoBrowser: A Web-based data browser and server for accessing and analyzing multi-disciplinary data (Technical Report WHOI-2001-13). Woods Hole, MA: Woods Hole Oceanographic Institution.

Lesk, M. (1997). Practical digital libraries: Books, bytes and bucks. San Francisco, CA: Morgan Kaufmann Publishers.

Lesk, M. (2005). Scope of digital libraries. Understanding Digital Libraries, 2, 361–373.

Lesk, M. (2005). Understanding digital libraries. San Francisco: Elsevier Inc.

Lester, P. (2006). Is the virtual exhibition the natural successor to the physical? Journal of the Society of Archivists, 27(1), 5-101.

Levenshtein, V. I. (1966). Binary codes capable of correcting deletitions, insertations and reversals. Soviet Physics Doklady, 10(8), 707-710.

Levi, M. D., & Conrad, F. G. (2002). Usability testing of world wide Web sites. BLS research papers. U.S. Department of Labor, Bureau of Labor Statistics. Retrieved November 6, 2007, from http://stats.bls.gov/ore/htm_papers/st960150.htm

Levy, D.M., & Marshal, C.C. (1995). Going digital: A look at assumptions underlying digital libraries. Communications of the ACM, 38, 77–84.

Li, Y., McLean, D., Bandar, Z. A., O'Shea, J. D., & Crockett, K. (2006). Sentence similarity based on semantic nets and corpus statistics. IEEE Transactions on Knowledge and Data Engineering, 18(8), 1138-1150.

Library of Congress. (2005). Machine readable cataloging 21 (MARC 21). Retrieved August 20, 2008, from http://www.loc.gov/marc/

Library of Congress. (2007). MARC standards. Retrieved November 18, 2007, from http://www.loc.gov/marc/

Library of Congress. (2004). Metadata encoding and transmission standard (METS). Retrieved August 20, 2008, from http://www.loc.gov/standards/mets/

Library of Congress 2. Metadata object description schema (MODS). Retrieved August 14, 2008, from http://www.loc.gov/standards/mods/

Library of Congress. METS: An overview & tutorial. Retrieved August 14, 2008, from http://www.loc.gov/standards/mets/METSOverview.v2.html

Library Society of China. (2006). The vigorous advancement of libraries in China. IFLA Journal, 32(2), 113–118.

LibraryThing. Retrieved August 24, 2008, from http://www.librarything.com

Liddy, E.D., Allen, E.E., & Finneran, C.M. (2003). MetaTest: Evaluation of metadata from generation to use. In Proceedings of the ACM/IEEE-CS joint conference on Digital libraries (JCDL). Houston, TX.

Lidy, T., & Rauber, A. (2005). Evaluation of feature extractors and psycho-acoustic transformations for music genre classification. In Proceedings of the Sixth International Conference on Music Information Retrieval (ISMIR'05) (pp. 34–41). London, UK.

Lidy, T., & Rauber, A. (2005). Evaluation of feature extractors and psycho-acoustic transformations for music genre classification. In Proceedings of the International Conference on Music Information Retrieval (pp. 34–41). London, UK.

Lidy, T., & Rauber, A. (2006). Visually profiling radio stations. In Proceedings of the International Conference on Music Information Retrieval. Victoria, Canada.

Liesaputra, V., Witten, I. H., & Bainbridg, D. (in press). Creating and reading realistic books. IEEE Computer Magazine.

Liew, C.L., & Foo, S. (1999). Derivation of interaction environment and information object properties for enhanced integrated access and value-adding to digital documents. Aslib Proceedings, 256–268.

Lim, E.P., Goh, D.H.L, Liu, Z., Ng, W.K., Khoo, C.S.G., & Higgins, S.E. (2002). G-Portal: A map-based digital library for distributed geospatial and georeferenced resources. In International Conference on Digital Libraries, Proceedings of the Second ACM/IEEE-CS Joint Conference on Digital Libraries (pp. 351–358).

Lim, E.P., Sun, A.X., Liu, Z.H., Hedberg, J., Chang, C.H., Teh, T.S., et al. (2004). Supporting field study with personalized project space in a geographical digital library. 7th International Conference of Asian Digital Libraries, ICADL2004, LNCS 3334 (pp. 553–562). Springer-Verlag.

Lim, E.P., Zhang, J., Li, Y., Wang, Z., Chang, C.H., Chatterjea, K., et al. (2006) G-Portal—a cross disciplinary digital library research program from Singapore. In E.P.

Lim (Ed.), IEEE Technical Committee on Digital Libraries Bulletin—Special Issue on Asian Digital Libraries, Lim (Vol. 3, No. 1). Retrieved August 30, 2008, from http://www.ieee-tcdl.org/Bulletin/v3n1/lim/lim.html

Lim, J. C., & Foo, S. (2003). Creating virtual exhibitions from an XML-based digital archive. Journal of Information Science, 29(3), 143-158.

Lin, C. (1995). Topic identification by concept generalization. In Proceedings of the 33rd Annual Meeting of the Association for Computation Linguistics (pp. 308-310). Morristown, NJ: ACL.

Lin, C. (1999). Training a selection function for extraction. In Proceedings of the 8th International Conference on Information and Knowledge Management (pp. 55-62). New York: ACM.

Lin, C. Y., & Hovy, E. H. (1997). Identifying topics by position. In Proceedings of the Applied Natural Language Processing Conference (pp. 283-290). San Francisco: Morgan Kaufmann.

Lin, X. (1999, August 15-19). Visual MeSH. In M. Hearst, F. Gey, & R. Tong (Eds.), SIGIR'99: Proceedings of 22nd Annual International ACM/SIGIR Conference on Research and Development in Information Retrieval, Berkeley, CA. New York: ACM.

Lin, X., Beaudoin, J. E., Bui, Y., & Desai, K. (2006). Exploring characteristics of social classification. Paper presented at the 17th Workshop of the American Society for Information Science and Technology Special Interest Group in Classification Research. Retrieved August 23, 2008, from http://dlist.sir.arizona.edu/1790/

Lipsius, J. (1907). Brief outline of the history of libraries. Antwerp: The Platin Press.

Liu, J. (2004). Metadata development in China. D-Lib Magazine, 10(12). Retrieved August 30, 2008, from http://www.dlib.org/dlib/december04/liu/12liu.html

Liu, Y.Q. (2004). Is the education on digital libraries adequate? New Library World, 105(1196/1198), 60–68. Retrieved August 30, 2008, from http://www.emeraldinsight.com/Insight/ViewContentServlet?Filename=Published/EmeraldFullTextArticle/Articles/0721050105.html

Liu, Y.Q., & Zhang, J. (2001). Digital library infrastructure: A case study on sharing information resources in China. International Information & Library Review, 33, 205–220.

Lloret Romero, N., & Cabrera Méndez, M. (2001a). Análisis del sistema para el desarrollo de la Biblioteca Valenciana Digital de Incunables. II Jornadas de Bibliote-

cas Digitales, Almagro. Retrieved August 23, 2008, from http://imhotep.unizar.es/jbidi/jbidi2001/25_2001.pdf

Llueca Fonollosa, C. (2005). Webs sempre accessibles: les biblioteques nacionals i els dipòsits digitals nacionals = Webs siempre accesibles: las bibliotecas nacionales y los depósitos digitales nacionales. BiD: textos universitaris de biblioteconomia i documentació, 15. Retrieved August 23, 2008, from http://eprints.rclis.org/archive/00005456/02/15lluec2.pdf

Lourdi, E., Nikolaidou, M., & Papatheodorou, C. (2004, December 27-29). Implementing digital folklore collections. In Proceedings of ISCA Third International Conference on Computer Science, Software Engineering, Information Technology, e-Business, and Applications (CSITeA-04), Cairo, Egypt.

Lovins, J. B. (1968). Development of a stemming algorithm. Mechanical Translation and Computational Linguistics, 11, 22-31.

Lu, L., & Zhang, H. (2002). Speaker change detection and tracking in real-time news broadcasting analysis. France: ACM Multimedia.

Lu, L., Zhang, H., & Jiang, H. (2002). Content analysis for audio classification and segmentation. IEEE Trans. Speech & Audio Proc., 10(7), 504-516.

Lu, Y., Xiao, Y., Sears, A., & Jacko, J. A. (2005). A review and a framework of handheld computer adoption in healthcare. International Journal of Medical Informatics, (74), 409-422.

Lübbers, D. (2005). SONIXPLORER: Combining visualization and auralization for content-based exploration of music collections. In Proceedings of the Sixth International Conference on Music Information Retrieval (ISMIR'05) (pp. 590–593). London, UK.

Luhn, H. (1958). The automatic creation of literature abstracts. IBM Journal of Research and Development, 2(2), 159-165.

Luhn, H. P. (1958). The automatic creation of literature abstracts. IBM Journal of Research and Development, 2(2), 159-165.

Lynch, C. (2005). Where do we go from here? D-Lib Magazine, 11.

Lynch, C. A. (1991). The Z39.50 information retrieval protocol: An overview and status report. ACM SIGCOMM Computer Communication Review, 21(1), 58-70.

Lynch, C. A. (1997, April). The Z39.50 information retrieval standard. Part I: A strategic view of its past, present and future. D-Lib Magazine. Retrieved November

21, 2007, from http://www.dlib.org/dlib/april97/04lynch.html

Lynch, C. A. (2003). Institutional repositories: Essential infrastructure for scholarship in the digital age. ARL, 226, 1-7.

Lynch, C., & Garcia-Molina, H. (1995). Interoperability, scaling, and the digital libraries research agenda. Paper presented at the IITA Digital Libraries Workshop.

Lyon, E. (2000). PATRON: Using a multimedia digital library for learning and teaching in the performing arts. Paper presented at the EDUCAUSE 2000, Nashville.

Ma, Y. (2006). Education for library information specialist (LIS): Is there the case for digital library? Master's dissertation, University of Loughborough.

Ma, Y., Clegg, W., & O'Brien, A. (2006). Digital library education: The current status. In Proceedings of the Joint Conference on Digital Libraries (pp. 165–174). Retrieved August 30, 2008, from http://doi.acm.org/10.1145/1141753.1141786

Ma, Y., O'Brien, A., & Clegg, W. (2006). Digital library education: The current status. In Proceeding of the 6th ACM/IEEE-CS Joint Conference on Digital Libraries (JCDL'06) (pp. 165–174). ACM Press. Retrieved August 30, 2008, from http://delivery.acm.org/10.1145/1150000/1141786/p165-ma.pdf?key1=1141786&key2=8184620021&coll=portal&dl=ACM&CFID=798309&CFTOKEN=77332738

Ma, Y., O'Brien, A., & Clegg, W. (2007). Digital library education: Some international course structure comparisons. In Proceeding of the 7th ACM/IEEE-CS Joint Conference on Digital Libraries (JCDL'07) (pp. 490). ACM Press. Retrieved August 30, 2008, from http://delivery.acm.org/10.1145/1260000/1255289/p490-ma.pdf?key1=1255289&key2=8046720021&coll=portal&dl=ACM&CFID=36056742&CFTOKEN=34866767

Macgregor, G., & McCulloch, E. (2006). Collaborative tagging as a knowledge organization and resource discovery tool. Library Review, 55(5), 291-300.

Machlup, F. (1977). Publishing scholarly books and journals: Is it economically viable? The Journal of Political Economy, 85(1), 217-225.

Macromedia, Inc. (2001). Getting started with eLearning standards. Retrieved August 12, 2008, form http://download.macromedia.com/pub/solutions/downloads/elearning/standards.pdf

Madria, S., Mohania, M., Bhowmick, S., & Bhargava, B. (2002). Mobile data and transaction management. Information Sciences—Informatics and Computer Science: An International Journal, 141(3-4), 279-309.

Madsen, K.H. (1994). A guide to metaphorical design. Communications of the ACM, 37, 57–62.

Magnini, B., & Strapparava C. (2001). Improving user modelling with content-based techniques. In M. Bauer, P. J. Gmytrasiewicz, & J. Vassileva (Eds.), Proceedings of 8th International Conference on User Modeling 2001 (LNCS 2109, pp. 74-83). Berlin: Springer.

Mahmood, K. (1998). Pakistani librarianship during the 1990s: A literature review. In Information Technology in Libraries: A Pakistani Perspective. Lahore: Pak Book Corporation.

Mahmood, K. (2003). A comparison between needed competencies of academic librarians and LIS curricula in Pakistan. The Electronic Library, 21(2), 99–109.

Maier, D., Delcambre, L. (1999). Superimposed information for the Internet. ACM SIGMOD Workshop on The Web and Databases. Philadelphia.

Maier, R. (2002). State-of-practice of knowledge management systems: Results of an empirical study. Upgrade, 3(1), 15–23.

Managing gigabytes (MG). New Zealand Digital Library. Retrieved August 14, 2008, from http://www.nzdl.org/html/mg.html

Mandl, T. (2000). Tolerant information retrieval with backpropagation networks. Neural Computing & Applications, 9(4), 280–289.

Mandl, T., & Womser-Hacker, C. (2004). A framework for long-term learning of topical user preferences in information retrieval. New Library World, 105(5/6), 184–195.

Mane, K. K., & Borner, K. (2006). SRS browser: A visual interface to the sequence retrieval system. Visualization and data analysis 2006. In R. F. Erbacher, J. C. Roberts, M. T. Gröhn, & K. Börner (Eds.), Proceedings of the SPIE-IS&T Electronic Imaging, SPIE, 2006.

Mani, I. (2001a). Automatic summarization. Amsterdam: John Benjamins Publishing Company.

Mani, I. (2001b). Summarization evaluation: An overview. In Proceedings of the 2nd NTCIR Workshop on Research in Chinese and Japanese Text Retrieval and Text Summarization. Tokyo: National Institute of Informatics.

Mani, I., & Bloedorn, E. (1999). Summarizing similarities and differences among related documents. Information Retrieval, 1(1-2), 35-67.

Mani, I., & Maybury, M. (1999). Advances in automatic text summarization. Cambridge, MA: MIT Press.

Mani, I., & Maybury, M. T. (1999). Introduction. In I. Mani & M. T. Maybury (Eds.), Advances in automatic text summarization (p. ix). Cambridge, MA: MIT Press.

Mani, I., Firmin, T., House, D., Chrzanowski, M., Klein, G., Hirschman, L., et al. (1998). The TIPSTER SUMMAC text summarization evaluation: Final report (MITRE Tech. Rep. MTR 98W0000138). McLean, VA: MITRE Corporation.

Mann, W., & Thompson, S. (1988). Rhetorical structure theory: Toward a functional theory of text organization. Text, 8(3), 243-281.

Manning, C. D., & Schutze, H. (2002). Foundations of statistical natural language processing. London: MIT Press.

Manning, C., & Schütze, H. (1999). Word sense disambiguation. Foundations of statistical natural language processing (pp. 229-264). Cambridge: The MIT Press.

Manning, C., Raghavan, P., & Schütze, H. (2008). Introduction to information retrieval. Cambridge University Press.

Marchionini, G., & Maurer, H. (1995). The roles of digital libraries in teaching and learning. Communications of the ACM Archive, 38(4), 67–75.

Marco, D., & Jennings, M. (2004). Universal meta data models. Wiley Publishing, Inc.

Marcum, D. (2003). Requirements for the future digital library. The Journal of Academic Librarianship, 29(5), 276-279.

Marincioni, F., Lightsom, F.L., Riall, R.L., Linck, G.A., Aldrich, T.C., & Caruso, M.J. (2004). Integrating digital information for coastal and marine sciences. Journal of Digital Information Management, 2(3), 132–141.

Marion, L. (2001). Digital librarian, cybrarian, or librarian with specialized skills: Who will staff digital libraries? In H. Thompson (Ed.), Crossing the Divide: Proceedings of the Tenth National Conference of the Association of College and Research Libraries (pp. 143–149). Chicago, IL: American Library Association.

Marlow, C., Naaman, M., Boyd, D., & Davis, M. (2006). HT06, tagging paper, taxonomy, Flickr, academic article, to read. In Proceedings of the Seventeenth Conference on Hypertext and Hypermedia (pp. 31-40).

Marshall, C. C., & Ruotolo, C. (2002, July 14-18). Reading-in-the-small: A study of reading on small form factor devices. In Proceedings of the 2nd ACM/IEEE-CS Joint Conference on Digital Libraries. Portland, OR: ACM Press.

Martin, R. S. (2003). Reaching across library boundaries. In Proceedings of the Conference on Emerging Visions for Access in the Twenty-First Century Library (pp. 3-16). Washington, D.C.: Council on Library and Information Resources. Retrieved November 13, 2007, from http://www.clir.org/pubs/reports/pub119/martin.html

Maskey, S. R., & Hirschberg, J. (2003). Automatic summarization of broadcast news using structural features. In Proceedings of Eurospeech-2003, Geneva (pp. 1173-1176).

Mason, R.M. (2005). The critical role of librarian/information officer as boundary spanner across cultures—humans as essential components in global digital libraries. World Library and Information Congress: 71st IFLA general conference and council. Retrieved August 30, 2008, from http://www.ifla.org/IV/ifla71/Programme.htm

Massih-Reza, A., & Gallinari, P. (2001). Learning for text summarization using labeled and unlabeled sentences. In Proceedings of the 2001 International Conference on Artificial Neural Networks (pp. 1177-1184). Berlin: Springer-Verlag.

Mathiassen, L., & Pourkomeylian, P. (2001). Knowledge management in a software process improvement unit. International Conference on Managing Knowledge: Conversations and Critiques. University of Leicester, England.

Matsuo, Y., Hamasaki, M., Nakamura, Y., Nishimura, T., Hasida, K., Takeda, H., et al. (2006). Spinning multiple social networks for Semantic Web. American Association for Artificial Intelligence.

Maurer F., & Holz, H. (2002). Integrating process support and knowledge management for virtual software development teams. Annals of Software Engineering, 4(1–4), 145–168.

Mayer, R., Lidy, T., & Rauber, A. (2006). The map of Mozart. In Proceedings of the International Conference on Music Information Retrieval (ISMIR'06) (pp. 351–352). Victoria, BC, Canada.

Mayer, R., Merkl, D., & Rauber, A. (2005). Mnemonic SOMs: Recognizable shapes for self-organizing maps. In Proceedings of the Workshop On Self-Organizing Maps (WSOM) (pp. 131–138). Paris, France.

McCabe, J. (2004). Getting started with PDAs: A library-driven project at James Madison University. Library Hi Tech News, 21(1), 30-32.

McCallum, A., & Wellner, B. (2003, August). Object consolidation by graph partitioning with a conditionally trained distance metric. In Proceedings of the ACM

Workshop on Data Cleaning, Record Linkage and Object Identification, Washington D.C.

McClelland, J. L., & Kawamoto, A. H. (1986). Mechanisms of sentence processing: Assigning roles to constituents of sentences. In D. E. Rumelhart, J. L. McClelland, & the PDP Research (Eds.), Parallel distributed process: Vol. 2. (pp. 272-325). MIT Press.

McClennen, M. (2002). Software, systems and standards in digital reference: A research agenda. Retrieved August 29, 2008, from http://www.ipl.org/div/papers/symposium-2002/systems.html

McKay, D., Shukla, P., Hunt, R., & Cunningham, S. J. (2004). Enhanced browsing in digital libraries: Three new approaches to browsing in Greenstone. International Journal on Digital Libraries, 4(4), 283-297.

McKeown, K., & Radev, D. (1995). Generating summaries of multiple news articles. In Proceedings of the 18th Annual International ACM SIGIR Conference on Research and Development in Information Retrieval (pp. 74-82). New York: ACM.

McKeown, K.R., Elhadad, N., & Hatzivassiloglou, V. (2003). Leveraging a common representation for personalized search and summarization in a medical digital library. In Proceedings of the ACM/IEEE-CS joint conference on Digital libraries (JCDL). Houston, TX.

McKeown, R., Chang, S., Cimino, J., Feiner, K., Friedman, C., Gravano, L., et al. (2001). PERSIVAL, a system for personalized search and summarization over multimedia healthcare information. In Proceedings of the 1st ACM/IEEE-CS Joint Conference on Digital Libraries (pp. 331-340). New York: ACM.

McLean, N. (2001). Collaborative online learning and information services (COLIS) consortium. Retrieved August 12, 2008, from http://www.colis.mq.edu. au/goals/synopsis.htm

McLean, N. (2002). Libraries and e-learning: Organizational and technical interoperability. Retrieved August 12, 2008, from http://www.colis.mq.edu.au/ news_archives/demo/docs/lib_e_learning.pdf

McMartin, F., Iverson, E., Manduca, C., Wolf, A., & Morgan, G. (2006). Factors motivating use of digital libraries. In Proceedings of the 6th ACM/IEEE-CS Joint Conference on Digital Libraries, Chapel Hill, NC (pp. 254-255).

MDA. SPECTRUM units of information. Retrieved August 20, 2008, from http://www.mda.org.uk/spectrum.htm/

Meadow, C. T., Boyce, B. R., & Kraft, D. H. (2000). Text information retrieval systems (2nd ed.). Academic Press.

Méndez Rodríguez, E.M. (2002). Metadatos y recuperación de información: estándares, problemas y aplicabilidad en bibliotecas digitales. Gijón: Trea.

Merges, R.P., & Duffy, J.F. (2002). Patent law and policy: Cases and materials (3rd edn.). LexisNexis: Dayton, OH.

Metadata for education group. (2004). UK learning object metadata core (draft 0.2). Retrieved November 15, 2007, from http://www.cetis.ac.uk/profiles/uklomcore/uklomcore_v0p2_may04.doc

Metros, S. E. (2005). Learning objects: A rose by any other name... EDUCAUSE Review, 40(4), 12-13. Retrieved November 15, 2007, from http://www.educause.edu/apps/er/erm05/erm05410.asp?bhcp=1

Metros, S. E., & Bennett, K. (2002). Learning objects in higher education. EDUCAUSE Research Bulletin, 2002(19), 1-10. Retrieved November 15, 2007, from http://www.educause.edu/ir/library/pdf/ERB0219.pdf

Meyyappan, N., Al-Hawamdeh, S., & Foo, S. (2002). Task based design of a digital work environment (DWE) for an academic community. Information Research, 7(2). Retrieved August 30, 2008, from http://informationr.net/ir/7-2/paper125.html

Microsoft Live Labs. (2006). Microsoft live labs Deepfish. Microsoft Corporation. Retrieved September 11, 2007, from http://http://labs.live.com/deepfish/

Mihalcea, R. (2004). Graph-based ranking algorithms for sentence extraction, applied to text summarization. In Proceedings of the 42nd Annual Meeting of Association for Computational Linguistics. Morristown, NJ: ACL.

Mika, P. (2005). Flink: Semantic Web technology for the extraction and analysis of social networks. Journal of Web Semantics Science, 3(2-3), 211-223.

Miller, G. A. (1995). WordNet: A lexical database for English. Communications of the ACM, 38(11), 39-41.

Miller, R. B. (1971, April 12). Human ease of use criteria and their tradeoffs (IBM Rep. TR 00.2185). Poughkeepsie, NY: IBM Corporation.

Millington, P., & Nixon, W. J. (2007). EPrints 3 pre-launch briefing. Ariadne, 50.

Milne, D. N., Witten, I. H., & Nichols, D. N. (2007). A knowledge-based search engine powered by Wikipedia. In Proceedings of the ACM Conference on Information and Knowledge Management, Lisbon, Portugal (pp. 445-454).

MIREX. (2007). Music Information Retrieval Evaluation eXchange (MIREX). Retrieved August 30, 2008, from http://www.music-ir.org/mirexwiki/index.php/Main_Page

Mitchell, S. (1999). Interface design considerations in libraries. In D. Stern (Ed.), Digital libraries: Philosophies, technical design considerations and example scenarios (pp. 131-182). Haworth Press.

Mitchell, T. (1997). Machine learning. New York: McGraw-Hill.

Mladenic, D. (1999). Text-learning and related intelligent agents: A survey. IEEE Intelligent Systems, 14(4), 44-54.

Moghaddam, B., Tian, Q., Lesh, N., Shen, C., & Huang, T. S. (2004). Visualization and user-modeling for browsing personal photo libraries. International Journal of Computer Vision, 56(1-2), 109-130.

Moh, Y., Nguyen, P., & Junqua, J.-C. (2003). Towards domain independent speaker clustering. In Proceedings of the IEEE ICASSP-03: Inter. Conf. Acoust. Speech, Sig. Proc. (Vol. 2, pp. 85-88).

Monge, A. E., & Elkan, C. P. (1996). The field matching problem: Algortihms and applications. In Proceedings of the Second International Conference Knowledge Discovery and Data Mining (KDD'96) (pp. 267-270).

Moodle. (2007). Moodle: A free, open source course management system for online learning. Retrieved November 15, 2007, from http://moodle.org/

Mooney, R. J., & Roy, L. (2000). Content-based book recommending using learning for text categorization. In P. J. Nürnberg, D. L. Hicks, & R. Furuta (Eds.), Proceedings of the 5th ACM Conference on Digital Libraries (pp. 195-204). New York: ACM.

Mörchen, F., Ultsch, A., Nöcker, M., & Stamm, C. (2005). Databionic visualization of music collections according to perceptual distance. In Proceedings of the Sixth International Conference on Music Information Retrieval (ISMIR'05) (pp. 396–403). London, UK.

Mori, K., & Nakagawa, S. (2001). Speaker change detection and speaker clustering using VQ distortion for broadcast news speech recognition. In Proceedings of the IEEE ICASSP-01: Inter. Conf. Acoust. Speech, Sig. Proc. (Vol. 1, pp. 413-416).

Mori, T., Nozawa, M., & Asada, Y. (2005). Multi-answer-focused multi-document summarization using a question-answering engine. ACM Transactions on Asian Language, 4(3), 305-320.

Morris, A., Kasper, G., & Adams, D. (1992). The effects and limitations of automatic text condensing on reading comprehension performance. Information Systems Research, 3(1), 17-35.

Morris, G., Kasper, G. M., & Adams, D. A. (1992). The effect and limitation of automated text condensing on reading comprehension performance. Information System Research, 3(1), 17-35.

Morris, S. (1999): Who needs publishers? Journal of Information Science, 1(25), 85-88.

Morville, P. (2005). Ambient findability. Sebastopol, CA: O'Reilly Media.

Mostafa, J., Brancolini, K., Smith, L.C., & Mischo, W. (2005). Developing a digital library education program. In Proceedings of the 5th ACM/IEEE-CS Joint Conference on Digital Libraries (JCDL'05) (p. 427). New York: ACM Press.

Moving Picture Experts Group. (1999). Description of core experiments for MPEG-7 color/texture descriptors (Tech. Rep. ISO/IEC JTC1/SC29/WG11/ N2929). Author.

Moyo, L.M. (2004). Digital libraries and the emergence of new service paradigms. The Digital Library, 22(3), 220–230.

Mullins, J. L., Allen, F. R., & Hufford, J. R. (2007). Top ten assumptions for the future of academic libraries and librarians: A report from the ACRL research committee. C&RL News, 68(4). Retrieved February 20, 2008, from http://www.ala.org/ala/acrl/acrlpubs/crlnews/backissues2007/april07/tenassumptions.cfm.

MuseiCapitolini.Net (MC). Retrieved August 12, 2008, from http://museicapitolini.net/hyperrecord/index.xml

Myaeng, S., & Jang, D. (1999). Development and evaluation of statistically based document summarization system. In I. Mani & M. T. Maybury (Eds.), Advances in automatic text summarization (pp. 61-70). Cambridge, MA: MIT Press.

Myanmar NLP. (2006). Myanmar Unicode reference documents and research papers. Retrieved June 1, 2006, from http://www.myanmars.net/unicode/doc/index.htm

MyCoRe open source project (MyCoRe). Retrieved August 12, 2008, from http://www.mycore.de/

MySQL database. Retrieved August 14, 2008, from http://www.mysql.com/

Naaman, M., Song, Y.J., Paepcke, A., & Garcia-Molina, H. (2004). Automatic organization for digital photographs with geographic coordinates. In Proceedings of the ACM/IEEE-CS joint conference on Digital libraries (JCDL). Tuson, AZ.

Nakazato, M., & Huang, T. S. (2001). 3D MARS: Immersive virtual reality for content-based image retrieval. Paper presented at the IEEE International Conference on Multimedia and Expo.

Nakazato, M., & Huang, T.S. (2001). 3D MARS: Immersive virtual reality for content-based image retrieval. In Proceedings of IEEE Int. Conference Multimedia and Expo (pp. 44–47).

NASA. (2005). Geospatial interoperability return on investment study. Booz Allen Hamilton.

Nash, S. S. (2005). Learning objects, learning object repositories and learning theory: Preliminary best practices for online courses. Interdisciplinary Journal of Knowledge and Learning Objects, 2005(1), 217-228. Retrieved November 22, 2007, from http://ijklo.org/Volume1/v1p217-228Nash.pdf

National Academy Press. (1999). Distributed geolibraries: Spatial information resources, summary of a workshop. Panel on Distributed Geolibraries, National Research Council.

National Center for Biotechnology Information of the National Library of Medicine. (2007). NLN journal archiving and interchange tag suite. Retrieved August 29, 2008, from http://dtd.nlm.nih.gov

National Library of New Zealand. (2007). Metadata extraction tool. Retrieved August 29, 2008, from http://meta-extractor.sourceforge.net

National Library of Pakistan. (2008). About national library of Pakistan. Retrieved August 30, 2008, from http://www.nlp.gov.pk/html/Aboutus.htm

National Science Digital Library. Retrieved August 24, 2008, from http://ndsl.org

Navratil, J. (2001). Spoken language recognition-a step toward multilinguality in speech processing. IEEE Transactions on Speech & Audio Processing, 9, 678-685.

Nebert, D., Whiteside, A., & Vretanos, P. (Eds.). (2007). OpenGIS catalogue services specification. Version 2.0.2. Reference Number OGC 07-006r1. Open Geospatial Consortium Incorporated.

Nebert, D.D. (Ed.). (2004). Developing spatial data infrastructures: The SDI cookbook v.2.0. Global Spatial Data Infrastructure.

Nedovic, Z., & Budhathoki, N.R. (2006). Technological and institutional interdependences and SDI—the Bermuda square?. International Journal of Spatial Data Infrastructures Research, 1, 36–50. Retrieved August 27, 2008, from http://ijsdir.jrc.it/editorials/budic_nama.pdf

Nelson, M.L., & Allen, B.D. (2002, January). Object persistence and availability in digital libraries. D-Lib Magazine, 8(1). Retrieved August 29, 2008, from http://www.dlib.org/dlib/january02/nelson/01nelson.html

Neukirchen, C., Willett, D., & Rigoll, G. (1999). Experiments in topic indexing of broadcast news using neural networks. In Proceedings of the IEEE ICASSP-99: Inter. Conf. Acoust. Speech, Sig. Proc. (Vol. 2, pp. 1093-1096).

Neumann, L. J., & Bishop, A. P. (1998, March 22-24). From usability to use: Measuring success of testbeds in the real world. Paper presented at the 35th Annual Clinic on Library Applications of Data Processing. Graduate School of Library and Information Science, University of Illinois at Urbana-Champaign. Retrieved November 6, 2007, from http://forseti.grainger.uiuc.edu/dlisoc/soc-sci_site/dpc-paper-98.html

Neumayer, R., Dittenbach, M., & Rauber, A. (2005). PlaySOM and PocketSOMPlayer: Alternative interfaces to large music collections. In Proceedings of the Sixth International Conference on Music Information Retrieval (ISMIR'05) (pp. 618–623). London, UK.

Neumeyer, L. R., Sankar, A., & Digalakis, V. V. (1995). A comparative study of speaker adaptation techniques. In Proceedings of Eurospeech-95 (pp. 1127-1130).

Neve, G., & Orio, N. (2004). Indexing and retrieval of music documents through pattern analysis and data fusion techniques. In Proceedings of the International Conference on Music Information Retrieval (ISMIR). Barcelona, Spain.

New Zealand. Ministry of Education. Te Kete Ipurangi. (2007). The metadata record. Retrieved November 15, 2007, from http://www.tki.org.nz/e/tki/help/metadata.php

Newcomb, H. B., & Kennedy, J. M. (1962). Record linkage: Making maximum use of the discriminating power of identifying information. Communication of the ACM, 5(11), 563-566.

Newman, D., Hagedorn, K., Chemudugunta, C., & Smyth, P. (2007). Subject metadata enrichment using statistical topic models. In Proceedings of the ACM/IEEE-CS joint conference on Digital libraries (JCDL). Vancouver, Canada.

Ng, W., Deng, L., & Lun Lee, D. (2007). Mining user preference using spy voting for search engine personalization. ACM Transactions on Internet Technology (TOIT), 7(4).

Nguyen, T. V., Tran, H. K., Nguyen, T. T. T., & Nguyen, H. (2006). Word segmentation for Vietnamese text categorization: A online corpus approach. In Proceedings of 4th IEEE International Conference on Computer Science - Research, Innovation and Vision of the Future, HoChiMinh City.

Nguyen, T.T.V. (2004).Country report Vietnam. Conference of Directors of National Libraries. Retrieved August 30, 2008, from http://consorcio.bn.br/cdnl/2005/HTML/CR%20Vietnam.htm

Nicholas, D., Huntington, P., & Jamali, H.R. (2007). The use, users, and role of abstracts in the digital scholarly environment. The Journal of Academic Librarianship, 33(4), 446–453.

Nicholas, D., Huntington, P., Jamali, H.R., & Watkinson, A. (2006). The information seeking behaviour of the users of digital scholarly journals. Information Processing and Management, 42(5), 1345–1365.

Nichols, D.M., Bainbridge, D., & Twidale, M.B. (2007). Constructing digital library interfaces. In Proceedings of the 7th ACM/IEEE Joint Conference on Digital Libraries (JCDL '07) (pp. 331–332). New York: ACM Press.

Nichols, D.M., Bainbridge, D., Downie, J.S., & Twidale, M.B. (2006). Learning by building digital libraries. In Proceedings of the 6th ACM/IEEE-CS Joint Conference on Digital Libraries (JCDL'06) (pp. 185–186). New York: ACM Press.

Nichols, D.M., Bainbridge, D., Marsden, G., Patel, D., Cunningham, S.J., Thompson, J., et al. (2005). Evolving tool support for digital librarians. In Y.-L. Theng, & S. Foo (Eds.), Design and Usability of Digital Libraries: Case Studies in the Asia Pacific (pp. 171–189). Information Science Publishing, London.

Nielsen, J. (1993). Usability engineering. Cambridge, MA: Academic Press.

Nielsen, J., & Mack, R. L. (Eds.). (1994). Usability inspection methods. New York: Wiley.

NISO. The OpenURL framework for context-sensitive services standard. Retrieved August 14, 2008, from http://www.niso.org/standards/standard_detail.cfm?std_id=783

Nitecki, D.A., & Hernon, P. (2000). Measuring service quality at Yale University's libraries. Journal of Academic Librarianship, 26(4), 259–273.

Nobata, C., Sekine, S., Uchimoto, K., & Isahara, H. (2003). A summarization system with categorization of document sets. Paper presented at the Third NTCIR Workshop.

Nogueras-Iso, J., Zarazaga-Soria, F.J., & Muro-Medrano, P.R. (2005). Geographic information metadata for spatial data infrastructures—resources, interoperability and information retrieval. Springer-Verlag.

Nogueras-Iso, J., Zarazaga-Soria, F.J., Lacasta, J., Béjar, R., & Muro-Medrano, P.R. (2004). Metadata standard interoperability: Application in the geographic information domain. Computers, Environment and Urban Systems, 28(6), 611–634.

Nonaka, I., & Takeuchi, H. (1995). The knowledge creating company: How Japanese companies create the dynamics of innovation. New York: Oxford University Press.

Norberg, L. R., Vassiliadis, K., Ferguson, J., & Smith, N. (2005). Sustainable design for multiple audiences: The usability study and iterative redesign of the documenting the American South digital library. OCLC Systems & Services, 21(4), 285-299.

Norman, D. (1999). Invisible computer: Why good products can fail, the personal computer is so complex and information appliances are the solution. London: MIT.

Novak, J.D., & Gowin, D.B. (1984). Learning how to learn. Cambridge, UK: Cambridge University Press.

Noy, N. F., Crubézy, M., Fergerson, R. W., Knublauch, H., Tu, S. W., Vendetti, J., et al. (2003). Protege-2000: An open-source ontology-development and knowledge-acquisition environment. In Proceedings of the AMIA Annual Symposium (p. 953).

Noy, N., & McGuinness, D. (2001). Ontology development 101: A guide to creating your first ontology. Retrieved August 21, 2008, from http://protege.stanford.edu/publications/ ontology_ development/ontology101-noy-mcguinness.html

NRC (National Research Council). (1993). Toward a coordinated spatial data infrastructure for the nation. Washington, D.C.: National Academy Press.

NRC. (1997). The future of spatial data and society: Summary of a workshop. Washington, D.C.: National Academy Press.

NSO. (2004). Understanding metadata. NISO Press.

O'Dea, L., Cummins, V., Wright, D., Dwyer, N., & Ameztoy, I. (2007). Report on coastal mapping and informatics, Trans-Atlantic Workshop 1: Potentials and limitations of coastal Web atlases. Cork, Ireland: University College Cork. Retrieved August 29, 2008, from http://workshop1. science.oregonstate.edu/final_rpt

OAI. (2006). The open archive initiative. Retrieved December 2006, from www.openarchives.org

Oberle, D., Berendt, B., Hotho, A., & Gonzalez, J. (2003). Conceptual user tracking. In Proceedings of the 1st Atlantic Web Intelligence Conference.

Ocón Pérez de Obanos, Á., & Gómez Martín, M. (2004). Hacia una biblioteca digital del fondo antiguo de la Universidad de Granada. El proyecto Ilíberis. Boletín de la Asociación Andaluza de Bibliotecarios, n° 77, pp. 49–60. Retrieved August 23, 2008, from http://www. aab.es/pdfs/baab77/77a2.pdf

OGC 04-006r1. (2005). OpenGIS® catalogue services specification. Open Geospatial Consortium Inc.

Omekwu, C.O., & Eteng, U. (2006). Roadmap to change: Emerging roles for information professionals. Library Review, 55(4), 267–277.

Onsrud, H., & Lopez, X. (1998). Intellectual property rights in disseminating digital geographic data, products and services: Conflicts and commonalities among EU and U.S. approaches. In P. Burrough, & I. Masser (Eds.), European Geographic Infrastructures: Opportunities and Pitfalls, GISDATA 5 (pp. 127–135). Taylor & Francis.

OpenDLib. A digital library service system. Retrieved December 2007, from http://www.opendlib.com

Oracle database. Retrieved August 14, 2008, from http://www.oracle.com/database/index.html

Orio, N. (2006). Music retrieval: A tutorial and review. Foundations and Trends in Information Retrieval, 1(1), 1–90.

Osman, T., Thakker, D, Schaefer, G., Leroy, M., & Fournier, A. (2007). Semantic annotation and retrieval of image collections. In Proceedings of the 21st European Conference on Modeling and Simulation (pp. 324-329).

Osman, T., Thakker, D., & Al-Dabass, D. (2006). Semantic-driven matchmaking of Web services using case-based reasoning. In Proceedings of the IEEE International Conference on Web Services (pp. 29-36).

Ou, S., Khoo, S., & Goh, D. (2005). Constructing a taxonomy to support multi-document summarization of dissertation abstracts. Journal of Zhejiang University SCIENCE, 6A(11), 1258-1267.

Ou, S., Khoo, S., & Goh, D. (2007). Automatic multi-document summarization of research abstracts: Design and user evaluation. Journal of the American Society for Information Science and Technology, 58(10), 1-17.

Ou, S., Khoo, S., & Goh, D. (in press). Design and development of a concept-based multi-document summarization systems for research abstracts. Journal of Information Science.

Pace, A.K. (2004). Dismantling integrated library systems. Library Journal, Retrieved August 30, 2008, from http://libraryjournal.com/article/CA374953.html

Pachet, F., & Cazaly, D. (2000). A taxonomy of musical genres. In Proceedings of Content-Based Multimedia Information Access (RIAO) Conference (pp. 827–830). Paris, France.

Page, L., Brin, S., Motwani, R., & Winograd, T. (1998). The PageRank citation ranking: Bringing order to the Web (Tech. Rep.). Stanford University Database Group. Retrieved August 26, 2008, from http://dbpubs.stanford. edu:8090/pub/1999-66.

Paice, C. (1990). Constructing literature abstracts by computer: Techniques and prospects. Information Processing and Management, 26(1), 171-186.

Paice, C. D. (1996). A method for evaluation of stemming algorithms based on error counting. Journal of the American Society for Information Science, 47(8), 632-649.

Pampalk, E., Dixon, S., & Widmer, G. (2004). Exploring music collections by browsing different views. Computer Music Journal, 28(2), 49–62.

Pampalk, E., Rauber, A., & Merkl, D. (2002). Content-based organization and visualization of music archives. In Proceedings of the ACM Multimedia (MM'02) (pp. 570–579). Juan les Pins, France: ACM.

Pancheshnikov, Y. (2007). Integrating print and digital resources in library collections. Library Collections, Acquisitions, and Technical Services, 31(2), 111–112.

Panel on Distributed Geolibraries, National Research Council. (1999). Distributed geolibraries: Spatial information resources, summary of a workshop. Washington, DC: National Academy Press.

Pang, N., Schauder, D., Quartly, M., & Dale-Hallett, L. (2006). User-centred design, e-research, and adaptive capacity in cultural institutions: The case of the women on farms gathering collection. In C. Khoo, D. Singh, & A. Chaudhry (Eds.), Proceedings of the Asia-Pacific Conference on Library & Information Education & Practice (A-LIEP 2006) (pp. 526–535). Singapore.

Park, J., Hunting, S. (2002). XML topic maps: Creating and using topic maps for the Web. Addisson-Wesley.

Parsia, B., & Sirin, E. (2004). Pellet: An OWL DL reasoner. Paper presented at the 3rd International Semantic Web Conference.

Parsons, E.A. (1952). The Alexandrian library: Glory of the Hellenic Hellenic world. New York: Elsevier Press.

Pasquinelli, A. (2002). Digital library technology trends (white paper). Sun Microsystems, Inc.

Pass, G., & Zabih, R. (1996). Histogram refinement for content-based image retrieval. In 3rd IEEE Workshop on Applications of Computer Vision (pp. 96–102).

Patel, M., et al. (2005, May). Metadata requirements for digital museum environments. International Journal on Digital Libraries, 5(3), 179-192. Retrieved August 20, 2008, from http://www.springerlink.com

Patel, M., White, M., Mourkoussis, N., Walczak, K., Wojciechowski, R., & Chmielewski, J. (2005). Metadata requirements for digital museums environment. International Journal of Digital Libraries, 5, 179-192.

Paulsen, M. F. (2002, July). Online education systems: Discussion and definition of terms. Retrieved August 21, 2008, from http://home.nettskolen.com/~mortenantos

Payette, S., & Thornton, S. (2002). The Mellon Fedora project: Digital library architecture meets XML and Web services. In M. Agosti & C. Thanos (Eds.), Research and Advanced Technology for Digital Libraries: Sixth European Conference ECDL 2002 (LNCS, pp. 406-421). Berlin: Springer-Verlag.

Pazzani, M., & Billsus, D. (1997). Learning and revising user profiles: The identification of interesting Web sites. Machine Learning, 27(3), 313-331.

Pazzani, M., Muramatsu, J., & Billsus, D. (1996). Syskill & Webert: Identifying interesting Web sites. In Proceedings of the 13th National Conference on Artificial Intelligence, Portland (pp. 54-61).

Pearrow, M. (2000). Web site usability handbook. Rockland, MA: Charles River Media.

Penka, J.T. (2003). The technological challenges of digital reference: An overview. D-Lib Magazine, 9(2). Retrieved August 29, 2008, from http://www.dlib.org/dlib//february03/penka/02penka.html

Peset Mancebo, F. (2003). Bibliotecas digitales en Internet de libro raro, antiguo e incunables. Anales de Documentación, 6, pp. 241–260.

Peterson, M. (2004). Library service delivery via hand-held computers-the right information at the point of care. Health Information and Libraries Journal, 21(1), 52-56.

Philips, L. (2000). The double metaphone search algorithm. C/C++ Users Journal, 18(5).

Picard, R.W. (1994). Content access for image/video coding: The fourth criterion. Technical Report 195. MIT Media Lab.

Pirkola, A. (2001). Morphological typology of languages for IR. Journal of Documentation, 57(3), 330-348.

Pitoura, E., & Samaras, G. (1998). Data management for mobile computing. Kluwer Academic Publishers.

Pomerantz, J. et al. (2004). The current state of digital reference: Validation of a general digital reference model through a survey of digital reference services. Information Processing and Management, 40, 347–363.

Pomerantz, J., Nicholson, S., & Lankes, R.D. (2003, April) Digital reference triage: Factors influencing question routing and assignment. The Library Quarterly, 73(2), 103–120.

Pomerantz, J., Oh, S., Wildemuth, B., Yang, S., & Fox, E. (2007). Digital library education in computer science programs. In Proceedings of the 6th ACM/IEEE-CS Joint Conference on Digital Libraries (JCDL'07) (pp. 177–178). ACM Press. Retrieved August 30, 2008, from http://delivery.acm.org/10.1145/1260000/1255208/p177-pomerantz.pdf?key1=1255208&key2=5515620021&coll=portal&dl=ACM&CFID=36056742&CFTOKEN=34866767

Pomerantz, J., Oh, S., Wildemuth, B.M., Yang, S., & Fox, E.A. (2007). Digital library education in computer science programs. In Proceedings of the 7th ACM/IEEE Joint Conference on Digital Libraries (JCDL '07) (pp. 177–178). New York: ACM Press.

Pomerantz, J., Oh, S., Yang, S., Fox, E.A., & Wildemuth, B. (2006a). The core: Digital library education in library and information science programs. D-Lib Magazine, 12(11). Retrieved August 30, 2008, from http://www.dlib.org/dlib/november06/pomerantz/11pomerantz.html

Pomerantz, J., Oh, S., Yang, S., Fox, E.A., & Wildemuth, B.M. (2006a). The core: Digital library education in library and information science programs. D-Lib Magazine, 12(11). Retrieved August 30, 2008, from http://doi:10.1045/november2006-pomerantz

Pomerantz, J., Wildemuth, B., Yang, S., & Fox, E. (2006a). Curriculum development for digital libraries. In Proceedings of the 6th ACM/IEEE-CS Joint Conference on Digital Libraries (JCDL'06) (pp. 175–184). ACM Press. Retrieved August 30, 2008, from http://delivery.

acm.org/10.1145/1150000/1141787/p175-pomerantz. pdf?key1=1141787&key2=5994620021&coll=portal&dl=ACM&CFID=798309&CFTOKEN=77332738

Pomerantz, J., Wildemuth, B., Yang, S., & Fox, E. (2006b). The core: Digital library education in library and information science programs. D-Lib Magazine, 12(11). Retrieved August 30, 2008, from http://www.dlib.org/dlib/november06/pomerantz/11pomerantz.html

Pomerantz, J., Wildemuth, B.M., Oh, S., Yang, S., & Fox, E.A. (2006b). Digital libraries curriculum development. D-Lib Magazine, 12(7/8). Retrieved August 30, 2008, from http://doi:10.1045/july2006-inbrief

Pomerantz, J., Wildemuth, B.M., Yang, S., & Fox, E.A. (2006b). Curriculum development for digital libraries. In Proceedings of the 6th ACM/IEEE-CS Joint Conference on Digital Libraries (JCDL'06) (pp. 175–184). New York: ACM Press.

Pomerantz, J., Wildemuth, B.M., Yang, S., & Fox, E.A. (2006c). Curriculum development for digital libraries. In Proceedings of the Joint Conference on Digital Libraries (pp. 175–184). Retrieved August 30, 2008, from http://doi.acm.org/10.1145/1141753.1141787

Pope, N. L. (1998). Digital libraries: Future potentials and challenges. Digital Libraries, 63-16(3/4), 147-155.

Popp, M. P. (2001, March 15-18). Testing library Web sites: ARL libraries weigh in. Paper presented at the Association of College and Research Libraries, 10th National Conference, Denver. Retrieved November 6, 2007, from http://www.ala.org/ala/acrl/acrlevents/popp.pdf

Porter, M. F. (1980). An algorithm for suffix stripping. Program, 14, 130-137.

PostgreSQL. Retrieved August 14, 2008, from http://www.postgresql.org/

Powel, A. L., French, J. C., Callan, J. P., & Connell, M. (2002). The impact of database selection on distributed searching. In Proceedings of the SIGIR Conference.

Poynder, R. (2005). Essential for science: Interview with Vitek Tracz. Information Today, 1(22), 1.

Premis, W.G., & Rlg/Oclc, W.G. (2005). Preservation metadata: implementation strategies.

Pretschner, A., & Gauch, S. (1999). Ontology-based personalized search. In Proceedings of the 11th IEEE International Conference on Tools with Artificial Intelligence (pp. 391-398).

Pushpagiri, V. P., & Rahman, S. (2002). DLNET: A digital library architecture for lifelong learning. In P.

Kommers, V. Petrushin, Kinshuk, & I. Galeev (Eds.), Proceedings of the 2nd IEEE International Conference on Advanced Learning Technologies, Kazan, Russia (pp. 155-160).

Puspitasari, F., Lim, E. P., Goh, D. H., Chang, C. H., Zhang, J., Sun, A., et al. (2007). Social navigation in digital libraries by bookmarking. In Proceedings of the 10th International Conference on Asian Digital Libraries, ICADL 2007 (LNCS 4822, pp. 297-306).

Qiu, G. (2003). Colour image indexing using BTC. IEEE Trans. Image Processing, 12(1), 93–101.

Quam, E. (2001). Informing and evaluating a metadata initiative: Usability and metadata studies in Minnesota's Foundations Project. Government Information Quarterly, 18(3), 181-194.

Qui, F., & Cho, J. (2006). Automatic identification of user interest for personalized search. In Proceedings of the 15th International World Wide Web Conference (pp. 727-236).

Quinlan, J. R. (1993). C4.5 programs for machine learning. CA: Morgan Kaufmann.

Radev, D., Fan, W., & Zhang, Z. (2001). WebInEssence: A personalized Web-based multi-document summarization and recommendation system. In Proceedings of the Automatic Summarization Workshop of the 2nd Meeting of the North American Chapter of the Association for Computational Linguistics. Morristown, NJ: ACL.

Radev, D., Jing, H., & Budzikowska, M. (2000). Centroid-based summarization of multiple documents: Sentence extraction, utility-based evaluation and user studies. In Proceedings of the ANLP/NAACL 2000 Workshop on Automatic Summarization (pp. 21-30). Morristown, NJ: ACL.

Ramzan, M. (2004). Levels of information technology (IT) applications in Muslim world libraries. The Electronic Library, 22(3), 274–280.

Rana, S., & Sharma, J. (2006). Frontiers of geographic information technology. Springer.

Rauber, A., & Frühwirth, M. (2001). Automatically analyzing and organizing music archives. In Proceedings of the 5th European Conference on Research and Advanced Technology for Digital Libraries (ECDL 2001), LNCS (pp. 402–414). Darmstadt, Germany: Springer.

Rauber, A., & Merkl, D. (2003). Text mining in the SOMLib digital library system: The representation of topics and genres. Applied Intelligence, 18(3), 271.

Rauber, A., Pampalk, E., & Merkl, D. (2002). Using psycho-acoustic models and self-organizing maps to create a hierarchical structuring of music by musical styles. In Proceedings of the 3rd International Symposium on Music Information Retrieval (pp. 71–80). Paris, France.

Rauber, A., Pampalk, E., & Merkl, D. (2002). Using psycho-acoustic models and self-organizing maps to create a hierarchical structuring of music by musical styles. In Proceedings of the International Conference on Music Information Retrieval (ISMIR) (pp. 71–80). Paris, France.

Rauber, A., Pampalk, E., & Merkl, D. (2003). The SOM-enhanced JukeBox: Organization and visualization of music collections based on perceptual models. Journal of New Music Research, 32(2), 193.

Rauber, A., Pampalk, E., & Merkl, D. (2003). The SOM-enhanced JukeBox: Organization and visualization of music collections based on perceptual models. Journal of New Music Research, 32(2), 193–210.

Rauch, C., & Rauber, A. (2004, December). Preserving digital media: Towards a preservation solution evaluation metric. In Proceedings of the 7th International Conference on Asian Digital Libraries (ICADL 2004) (pp. 203–212). Berlin, Heidelberg: Springer.

Raza, M.M., & Nath, A. (2007). Use of IT in university libraries of Punjab, Chandigarh and Himachal Pradesh: A comparative study. The International Information and Library Review, 39(3–4), 11–227.

Razikin, K., Goh, D. H., Cheong, E. K. C., & Ow, Y. F. (2007). The efficacy of tags in social tagging systems. In Proceedings of the 10th International Conference on Asian Digital Libraries, ICADL 2007 (LNCS 4822, pp. 506-507).

Rector, A. (2003). Modularisation of domain ontologies implemented in description logics and related formalisms including OWL. In Proceedings of the 2nd International Conference on Knowledge Capture (pp. 121-128).

Rego, A.S., Baptista, C.S., Silva, E.R., Schiel, U., Figueirêdo, H.F. (2007). VideoLib: A video digital library with support to spatial and temporal dimensions. In Proceedings of rhe 22nd Annual ACM Symposium on Applied Computing. Seoul, Korea.

Rehman, S., & Ahmad, P. (2007). Challenges and opportunities for libraries in Pakistan. Pakistan Library and Information Science Journal, 38(3), 6–11.

Rehman, S., & Ramzy, V. (2004). Awareness and use of digital information resources. Library Review, 53(3), 150–156.

Reid, J., Hull, R., Melamed, T., & Speakman, D. (2003). Schminky: The design of a cafe based digital experience. Personal and Ubiquitous Computing, 7(3–4), 197–202.

Reitz, J.M. (2004). Dictionary for library and information science. Westport, CT: Libraries Unlimited.

Research Libraries Group. (2005). Descriptive metadata guidelines for RLG cultural materials. RLG. Retrieved August 20, 2008, from http://www.rlg.org/en/pdfs/RLG_desc_metadata.pdf

Research Support Libraries Program (RSLP). Collection description schema. Retrieved August 20, 2008, from http://www.ukoln.ac.uk/metadata/rslp/

Resnik, P. (1995). Disambiguating noun groupings with respect to WordNet senses. In Proceedings of the 3rd Workshop on Very Large Corpora. MIT Press.

Reuters. (2007, November 29). KODAK digital archive services preserves 75 years of Pittsburgh Steelers history. Retrieved February 20, 2008, from http://www.reuters.com/article/pressRelease/idUS46928+29-Nov-2007+BW20071129

Rich, E. (1979). User modeling via stereotypes. Cognitive Science: A Multidisciplinary Journal, 4, 329–354.

Richardson, M., & Domingos, R. (2002). The intelligent surfer: Probabilistic combination of link and content information in PageRank. Advances in Neural Information Processing Systems, 14. MIT Press.

Rigby, F., O'Donovan, M., & Searle, S. (2006). National, cross-sector, collaborative projects that worked at the National Library of New Zealand Te Puna Matauranga o Aotearoa. 13th Biennial Conference and Exhibition. Retrieved August 30, 2008, from http://www.vala.org.au/conf2006.htm

Rios, G. R. (2004). PDA librarian. Reference Services Review, 32(1), 16-20.

RLG and the library consortium OCLC. (2005). Preservation metadata maintenance activity. Retrieved August 20, 2008, from http://www.loc.gov/standards/premis/

Roberts, J. (1995). Faculty knowledge about library services at the university of the West Indies. New Library World, 96, 14–22.

Robertson, S. E., & Sparck Jones, K. (1997). Simple, proven approaches to text retrieval (Tech. Rep.). Cambridge University.

Robertson, S. E., & Walker, S. (1999). Okapi/Keenbow at TREC-8). In Proceedings of TREC-8.

Robertson, S., & Spark Jones, K. (1976). Relevance weighting for search terms. Journal of the American Society of Information Science, 129–146.

Roche, E. (1996). Finite-state transducers: Parsing free and frozen sentences. In Proceedings of the ECAI 96 Workshop Extended Finite State Models of Language (pp. 52-57). Budapest, Hungary: ECAI.

Roche, E., & Schabes, Y. (1995). Deterministic part-of-speech tagging with finite state transducers. Computational Linguistics, 21(2), 227-253.

Roche, E., & Schabes, Y. (1997). Finite state language processing. Cambridge, MA: MIT Press.

Rodden, K., Basalaj, D., Sinclair, W., & Wood, K. (1999). Evaluating a visualisation of image similarity as a tool for image browsing. In Proceedings of the IEEE Symposium on Information Visualization (pp. 36-43).

Rose, H. (2001). Digital libraries and education trends and opportunities. D-Lib Magazine, 7(7/8). Retrieved August 30, 2008, from http://www.dlib.org/dlib/july01/roes/07roes.html

Rosenfeld, L., & Morville, P. (2002). Information architecture for the World Wide Web: Designing large scale Web sites. CA: O' Reilly & Associates, Inc.

Rosenthal, D.S.H., Lipkis, T., Robertson, T.S., & Morabito, S. (2005, January). Transparent format migration of preserved Web content. D-Lib Magazine, 11. Retrieved August 29, 2008, from http://www.dlib.org/dlib/january05/rosenthal/01rosenthal.html

Rosenthal, D.S.H., Robertson, T., Lipkis, T., Reich, V., & Morabito, S. (2005, November). Requirements for digital preservation systems. D-Lib Magazine, 11. Retrieved August 29, 2008, from http://www.dlib.org/dlib/november05/rosenthal/11rosenthal.html

Rosson, M.B., & Carroll, J.M. (2002). Usability engineering: Scenario-based development of human-computer interaction. San Francisco: Morgan Kaufmann.

Rothenberg, J. (1999). Avoiding technological quicksand: Finding a viable technical foundation for digital preservation. Council on Library and Information Resources Washington D.C. Retrieved August 29, 2008, from http://www.clir.org/pubs/reports/rothen-berg/contents.html

Rothenberg, J., & Bikson, T. (1999). Carrying authentic, understandable and usable digital records through time (Tech. Rep.). The Hague, Netherlands: Report to the Dutch National Archives and Ministry of the Interior.

Roussos, G., Marsh, A. J., & Maglavera, S. (2005). Enabling pervasive computing with smart phones. IEEE Pervasive Computing, 4(2), 20-27.

RSS. (2006). RSS 2.0 specification. RSS advisory board. Retrieved December 2006, from www.rssboard.org/rss-specification

Rubner, Y., Guibas, L., & Tomasi, C. (1997). The earth mover's distance, multi-dimensional scaling, and color-based image retrieval. In Proceedings of ARPA Image Understanding Workshop (pp. 661–668).

Rubner, Y., Guibas, L., & Tomasi, C. (1997). The earth mover's distance, multi-dimensional scaling, and color-based image retrieval. In Proceedings of the Image Understanding Workshop (pp. 661-668).

Rüger, S. (2006). Putting the user in the loop: Visual resource discovery. Paper presented at the Workshop on Adaptive Multimedia Retrieval (AMR, Glasgow, July 2005) (LNCS 3877, pp. 1-18).

Rumelhart, D. E. (1975). Notes on a schema for stories. In D. G. Bobrown & A. M. Collins (Eds.), Representation and understanding: Studies in cognitive science (pp. 211-236). New York: Academic Press.

Rus, I., Lindvall, M., & Sinha, S. (2002). Knowledge management in software engineering. IEEE Software, 19(3), 26–38.

Rushinek, A., & Rushinek, S. F. (1986). What makes users happy? Communications of the ACM, 29(7), 594-598. Retrieved November 6, 2007, from the ACM Digital Library database.

Ruszala, S. D., & Schaefer, G. (2004). Visualisation models for image databases: A comparison of six approaches. In Proceedings of the Irish Machine Vision and Image Processing Conference (pp. 186-191).

Rutledge, L., Alberink, M., Brussee, R., Pokraev, S., van Dieten, W., & Veenstra, M. (2003). Finding the story: Broader applicability of semantics and discourse for hypermedia generation. In Proceedings of the 14th ACM Conference on Hypertext and Hypermedia (pp. 67-76).

Ryan, C., & Gonsalves, A. (2005). The effect of context and application type on mobile usability: An empirical study. In Proceedings of the Twenty-Eighth Australasian Conference on Computer Science (ACM International Conference Proceeding Series 102, pp. 115-124). Darlinghurst: Australian Computer Society, Inc.

Saavedra, A. (2007). Context based search in personal digital libraries. Unpublished mater's thesis, Tecnologico de Monterrey.

Salaladyanant, T. (2006). Digital libraries in Thailand. In C. Khoo, D. Singh, & A.S. Chaudhry (Eds.), Proceedings A-LIEP 2006: Asia-Pacific Conference on Library & Information Education & Practice 2006 (A-LIEP 2006) (pp. 148—155). Singapore.

Salton, G. (1989). Automatic text processing: The transformation, analysis and retrieval of information by computer. Reading, MA: Addison-Wesley.

Salton, G., & Buckley, C. (1988). Term-weighting approaches in automatic text retrieval. Information Processing and Management, 24(5), 513-523.

Salton, G., & McGill, M. J. (1983). Introduction to modern information retrieval. New York: McGraw-Hill.

Salton, G., Singhal, A., Mitra, M., & Buckley, C. (1997). Automatic text structuring and summarization. Information Processing and Management, 33(2), 193-207.

Sanderson, M. (1998). Accurate user directed summarization from existing tools. In Proceedings of the 7th International Conference on Information and Knowledge Management (CIKM 98) (pp. 45-51).

Sanderson, R. (2004). SRW: Search/Retrieve Webservice, (version 1.1). Retrieved August 27, 2008, from http://srw.cheshire3.org/SRW-1.1.pdf

Santos, N, Campos, F. C. A, & Braga-Villela, R. M. (2005, October). A digital library for lifelong education on e-learning domain. In Proceedings of the World Conference on E-learning in Corporate, Government, Healthcare, & Higher Education (E-Learn 2005), Vancouver (Vol. 4, pp. 3121-3128).

Santos, R.L.T., Roberto, P.A., Gonçalves, M.A., & Laender, A.H.F. (2007, August). A Web services-based framework for building componentized digital libraries. Journal of Systems and Software, Available online 8 August 2007.

Saorín Pérez, T. (2004). Los portales bibliotecarios. Madrid: Arco libros.

Saracevic, T., & Dalbello, M. (2001). A survey of digital library education. In Proceedings of the American Society for Information Science and Technology (Vol. 38, pp. 209–223).

Saracevic, T., & Dalbello, M.A. (2001). A survey of digital library education. In Proceeding of American Society for Information Science, 38, 209–223.

Saraclar, M., & Sproat, R. (2004). Lattice-based search for spoken utterance retrieval. In Proceedings of the HLT-NAACL 2004, Boston (pp. 129-136).

Saraclar, M., Riley, M., Bocchieri, E., & Goffin, V. (2002). Towards automatic closed captioning: Low latency real time broadcast news transcription. In Proceedings of the ICSLP-2002: Inter. Conf. Spoken Lang., Denver (pp. 1741-1744).

Sarawagi, S., & Bhamidipaty, A. (2002). Interactive deduplication using active learning. In Proceedings of the International Conference. Knowledge Discovery and Data Mining (KDD'02) (pp. 269-278).

Sarikaya, R., & Hansen, J. H. L. (2000). High resolution speech feature parameterization for monophone based stressed speech recognition. IEEE Signal Processing Letters, 7(7), 182-185.

Sasaki, H., & Kiyoki, Y. (2002a). Patenting advanced search engines of multimedia databases. In Proceedings of the 3rd International Conference on Law and Technology (pp. 34–39).

Sasaki, H., & Kiyoki, Y. (2002b, December 11–14). Patenting the processes for content-based retrieval in digital libraries. In Proceedings of the 5th International Conference on Asian Digital Libraries (ICADL), Lecture Notes in Computer Science, 2555, (pp. 471–482). Singapore.

Sasaki, H., & Kiyoki, Y. (2005a). A formulation for patenting content-based retrieval processes in digital libraries. Journal of Information Processing and Management, 41(1), 57–74.

Sasaki, H., & Kiyoki, Y. (2005b). Multimedia digital library as intellectual property, design and usability of digital libraries. In Y.L. Theng & S. Foo (Eds.), Case Studies in the Asia Pacific (pp. 238–253). Hershey, PA: Idea Group Publishing.

Savoy, J. (2006). Light stemming approaches for the French, Portuguese, German and Hungarian languages. In Proceedings of the 2006 ACM symposium on Applied computing SAC '06 (pp. 1031–1035).

Scaringella, N., Zoia, G., & Mlynek, D. (2006). Automatic genre classification of music content: A survey. Signal Processing Magazine, IEEE, 23(2), 133–141.

Schaefer, G., & Lieutaud, S. (2004). CVPIC compressed domain image retrieval by colour and shape. In Int. Conference on Image Analysis and Recognition (Vol. 3211, pp. 778–786). Springer Lecture Notes on Computer Science.

Schaefer, G., & Qiu, G. (2000). Midstream content access based on colour visual pattern coding. In Proceedings of SPIE—Storage and Retrieval for Image and Video Databases VIII (Vol. 3972, pp. 284–292).

Schaefer, G., & Stich, M. (2004). UCID—an uncompressed colour image database. In Proceedings of SPIE—Storage and Retrieval Methods and Applications for Multimedia 2004 (Vol. 5307, pp. 472–480).

Schaefer, G., & Ruszala, S. (2005). Image database navigation: A globe-al approach. In Proceedings of the International Symposium on Visual Computing (LNCS 3804, pp. 279-286). Springer.

Schaefer, G., & Ruszala, S. (2006). Hierarchical image database navigation on a hue sphere. In Proceedings of the International Symposium on Visual Computing (LNCS 4292, pp. 814-823). Springer.

Schaefer, G., Qiu, G., & Luo, M.R. (1999). Visual pattern based colour image compression. In Proceedings of SPIE—Visual Communication and Image Processing 1999, (Vol. 3653, pp. 989–997).

Schauder, D. (1994). Electronic publishing of professional articles: Attitudes of academics and implications for the scholarly communication industry. Journal of the American Society for Information Science, 45(2), 73-100.

Scheirer, E., & Slaney, M. (1997). Construction and evaluation of a robust multifeature speech/music discriminator. In Proceedings of the International Conference on Acoustics, Speech and Signal Processing (ICASSP'97) (pp. 1331–1334). Munich, Germany.

Schilit, B. N., Price, M. N., & Golvchinsky, G. (1998). Digital library information appliances. In Proceedings of the Third ACM Conference on Digital Libraries, Pittsburgh. ACM Press.

Schlesinger, J., Conroy, J., Okurowski, M., & O'Leary, D. (2003). Machine and human performance for single and multidocument summarization. IEEE Intelligent Systems, 18(1), 46-54.

Schuler, D. (1994). Social computing. Communications of the ACM, 37(1), 28-29.

Schwarz, C. (1990). Automatic syntactic analysis of free text. Journal of the American Society for Information Science, 41(6), 408-417.

Scott, L. et al. (2002). A process-centred experience repository for a small software organisation. In Proceedings of the 2002 Asia-Pacific Software Engineering Conference (pp. 603–609).

Seadle, M. (2004). Copyright in a networked world: Ethics and infringement. Library HiTech, 22(1), 106-110.

Sebastiani, F. (2002). Machine learning in automated text categorization. ACM Computing Surveys, 34(1), 1-47.

Seguí i Francés, R. (2005). La biblioteca Valenciana: un breu balanç. In: Jornadas sobre Bibliotecas Nacionales (València). Las bibliotecas nacionales del siglo XXI. Valencia Biblioteca Valenciana.

Semeraro, G., Degemmis, M., Lops, P., & Basile P. (2007). Combining learning and word sense disambiguation for intelligent user profiling. In M. Veloso (Ed.), Proceedings of the Twentieth International Joint Conference on Artificial Intelligence IJCAI-07 (pp. 2856-2861). San Francisco: Morgan Kaufmann.

Senkle, K., Voges, U., & Remke, A. (2004). An ISO 19115/19119 profile for OGC catalogue services CSW 2.0. 10th EC GI & GIS Workshop, ESDI State of the Art. Warsaw, Poland.

Severson, W. (1997). The principles of information ethics. Amonk, N.Y: M.E. Sharpe.

SFX. (2007) Retrieved November 13, 2007, from http://www.exlibrisgroup.com/sfx.htm

Shackel, B. (1981, September 15-18). The concept of usability. In Proceedings of IBM Software and Information Usability Symposium, Poughkeepsie, NY (pp. 1-30).

Shackel, B. (1984). The concept of usability. In J. L. Bennett, D. Case, J. Sandelin, & M. Smith (Eds.), Visual display terminals: Usability issues and health concerns (pp. 45-88). Englewood Cliffs, NJ: Prentice-Hall.

Shackel, B. (1991). Usability: Context, framework, definition, design and evaluation. In B. Shackel & S. J. Richardson (Eds.), Human factors for informatics usability (pp. 21-37). New York: Cambridge University Press.

Shadbolt, N., Hall, W., & Berners-Lee, T. (2006). The Semantic Web revisited. IEEE Intelligent Systems.

Shafique, F., & Mahmood, K. (2008). Indicators of the emerging information society in Pakistan. Information Development, 24(1), 66–78.

Shaifol, Y.M., & Nasir, K. (2005). Digitization and sustainability of local collection: An observation of digitization activities among Malaysian universities libraries. World Library and Information Congress: 71st IFLA general conference and council. Retrieved August 30, 2008, from http://www.ifla.org/IV/ifla71/Programme.htm

Sharifabadi, S.R. (2006). How digital libraries can support e-learning. The Electronic Library, 24(3), 389–401.

Sharples, M., Corlett, D., & Westmancott, O. (2002). The design and Implementation of a mobile learning resource. In Personal and Ubiquitous Computing, 6, 220–234.

Sharples, M., Taylor, J., & Vavoula, G. (2007). A theory of learning for the mobile age. In R. Andrews, & C. Haythornthwaite (Eds.), Handbook of Elearning Research (pp. 221–247). Sage Publications.

Shen, R. (2006). Applying the 5S framework to integrating digital libraries. Doctoral dissertation, Virginia Tech. Retrieved August 30, 2008, from http://scholar.lib. vt.edu/theses/available/etd-04212006-135018/

Shen, X., & Zhai, C. X. (2003). Exploiting query history for document ranking in interactive information retrieval. In Proceedings of the SIGIR Conference (pp. 377-378).

Shen, X., Tan, B., & Zhai, C. (2005). Context-sensitive information retrieval using implicit feedback. In Annual Intl ACM SIGIR Conf on Research and Development in Information Retrieval (pp. 43–50). ACM Press.

Sheridan, P., & Smeaton, A. F. (1992). The application of morpho-syntactic language processing to effective phrase matching. Information Processing & Management, 28(3), 349-369.

Sheth, A., & Klas, W. (Editors). (1998). Multimedia data management—using metadata to integrate and apply digital media. McGraw-Hill.

Sheth, A., Aleman-Meza, B., Arpinar, I. B., Bertram, C., Warke, Y., Ramakrishnan, C., et al. (2005). Semantic association identification and knowledge discovery for national security applications. Journal of Database Management on Database Technology, 16(1), 33-53.

Shinoda, K., & Lee, C. H. (1997). Structural MAP speaker adaptation using hierarchical priors. In Proceedings of the IEEE Workshop on Automatic Speech Recognition and Understanding, Santa Barbara, CA (pp. 381-388).

Shipman, J. P., & Morton, A. C. (2001). The new black bag: PDAs, health care and library services. Reference Services Review, 29(3), 229-237.

Shiri, A. (2003). Digital library research: Current developments and trends. Library Review, 52(5), 198-202.

Shuler, J.A. (2007). Public policies and academic libraries—the shape of the next digital divide. The Journal of Academic Librarianship, 33(1), 141–143.

Shum, S. B., Motta, E., & Domingue, J. (2000, August/September). ScholOnto: An ontology-based digital library server for research documents and discourse. International Journal on Digital Libraries, 3(3), 237-248.

Silberztein, M. (1993). Dictionnaires électroniques et analyse automatique de textes: Le systéme INTEX. Paris: Masson.

Silberztein, M. (2000). INTEX: An FST toolbox. Theoretical Computer Science, 231(1), 33-46.

Silver, D. (1997). Interfacing American culture: The perils and potentials of virtual exhibitions. American Quarterly, 49(4), 825-850.

Singhal, A., & Pereira, F. (1999). Document expansion for speech retrieval. Paper presented at the 22nd ACM SIGIR Conference, Berkeley, CA.

Siohan, O., Myrvoll, T. A., & Lee, C. H. (2002). Structural maximum a posteriori linear regression for fast HMM adaptation. Computer Speech and Language, 16(1), 5-24.

Sitwell, N.H. (1984). The world the Romans knew. London: Hamilton.

Smadja, F. (1993). Retrieving collocations from text: XTRACT. Computational Linguistics, 19(1), 143-177.

Smeulders, A. W. M., Worring, M., Santini, S., Gupta, G., & Jain, R. (2000). Content-based image retrieval at the end of the early years. IEEE Transactions on Pattern Analysis and Machine Intelligence, 22(12), 1249-1380.

Smith, B. (2001). Enhancing reference services through technology. In J.D. Edwards (Ed.), Emerging Solutions in Reference Services: Implications for Libraries in the New Millennium. New York: The Haworth Information Press. Su, S.S. (2002). Web-based reference services: The user intermediary interaction perspective. In G.E. Gorman (Ed.), The Digital Factor in Library and Information Services (pp. 185–207). London: Facet Publishing.

Smith, J., & Chang, S. (1996). VisualSEEk: A fully automated content-based image query system. In Proceedings of the Fourth ACM Multimedia Conference (MULTIMEDIA'96) (pp. 87–98). New York: ACM Press.

Smith, M., Barton, M., Bass, M., Branschofsky, M., McClellan, D., Tansley, R., et al. (2003). Dspace: An open source dynamic digital repository. D-Lib Magazine, 9(1).

Smith, R. (2002). Adapting a new technology to the academic medical library: Personal digital assistants. Journal of the Medical Library Association, 90(1), 93-94.

Smolier, S., & Zhang, H. (1994). Content-based indexing and retrieval. IEEE Multimedia, 1(2), 62–72.

Snyder, C. (2003). Paper prototyping: The fast and easy way to design and refine user interfaces. Boston: Morgan Kaufmann.

Sommerville, M.M., Huston, M.E., Miriamdotter, A. (2005). Building on what we know: Staff development in the digital age. The Electronic Library, 23(3), 480–491.

Sornlertlamvanich, V., Potipiti, T., & Charoenporn, T. (2000). Automatic corpus-based Thai word extraction with the c4.5 learning algorithm. In Proceedings of the 18th Conference on Computational Linguistics (pp. 802-807). NJ: Association for Computer Linguistics.

Sparck Jones, K., & Tait, J. I. (1984). Automatic search term variant generation. *Journal of Documentation, 40*(1), 50-66.

Sparck-Jones, K. (1999). Automatic summarising: Factors and directions. In I. Mani & M. Maybury (Eds.), Advances in automatic text summarization. Cambridge, MA: MIT Press.

Sparck-Jones, K., & Galliers, J. (1996). Evaluating natural language processing systems: An analysis and review. Springer-Verlag.

SPARQL Query Language for RDF (2007, November 12). W3C proposed recommendation. Retrieved August 17, 2008, from http://www.w3.org/TR/rdf-sparql-query/

Specht, M., & Kravcik, M. (2006). Authoring of learning objects in context. *International Journal of ELearning, 5*(1), 25-33. Retrieved November 16, 2007, from Academic Research Library database (Document ID: 986665391).

Speretta, M., & Gauch, S. (2004). Personalizing search based in user search history. In Proceedings of the CIKM Conference.

Spevak, C., & Polfreman, R. (2001). Sound spotting—a frame-based approach. In Proceedings of the Second International Symposium on Music Information Retrieval: ISMIR 2001 (pp. 35–36). Bloomington, IN.

Spinella, M. P. (2007). JSTOR: Past, present, and future. *Journal of Library Administration, 46*(2), 55-78.

Spink, A. (1995). Term relevance feedback and mediated database searching: Implications for information retrieval practice and systems design. *Information Processing and Management, 31*(2), 161–171.

Spink, A., & Cool, C. (1999). Education for digital libraries. *D-Lib Magazine, 5*(5).

Staken, K. (2001). XMLDB: Application programming interface for XML databases, XML:DB initiative. Retrieved August 12, 2008, from http://www.xmldb.org/xapi /xapi-draft.html

Stamou, S., Ntoulas, A., & Christodoulakis, D. (2007). TODE: An ontology based model for the dynamic population of Web directories. Data management with ontologies: Implementations, findings and frameworks. Hershey, PA: IGI Global, Inc.

Stark, R. (2005). *The victory of reason*. New York: Random House.

Stehling, R.O., Nascimento, M.A., & Falcao, A.X. (2002). A compact and efficient image retrieval approach based on border/interior pixel classification. In 11th Int.

Conf. on Information and Knowledge Management (pp. 102–109).

Stein, G., Strzalkowski, T., & Wise, G. (2000). Interactive, text-based summarization of multiple documents. *Computational Intelligence, 16*(4), 606-613.

Stewart, R. (2003). Using digital libraries to teach oceanography. In Proceedings of the 19th International Conference on Interactive Information Processing Systems (IIPS) for Meteorology, Oceanography, and Hydrology.

Strodl, S., Becker, C., Neumayer, R., & Rauber, A. (2007). How to choose a digital preservation strategy: Evaluating a preservation planning procedure. In Proceedings of the 7th ACM IEEE Joint Conference on Digital Libraries (JCDL'07) (pp. 29–38). New York: ACM.

Strodl, S., Rauber, A., Rauch, C., Hofman, H., Debole, F., & Amato, G. (2006, November 27–30). The DELOS test bed for choosing a digital preservation strategy. In Proceedings of the 9th International Conference on Asian Digital Libraries (ICADL 2006) (pp. 323–332). Berlin, Heidelberg: Springer.

Strzalkowski, T. (1996). Natural language information retrieval. *Information Processing & Management, 31*(3), 397-417.

Strzalkowski, T., Lin, F., Wang, J., & Pérez-Carballo, J. (1999). Evaluating natural language processing techniques in information retrieval: A TREC perspective. In T. Strzalkowski (Ed.), Natural language information retrieval (pp. 113-145). Dordrecht: Kluwer Academic Publishers.

Sturges, P. (2001). The library and freedom of information: Agent or icon? *Alexandria, 13*(1), 3-16.

Sturges, P., Davies, E., Dearnley, J., Iliffe, U., Oppenheim, C., & Hardy, R. (2003).

Sugiyama, K., Hatano, K., & Yoshikawa, M. (2004). Adaptive Web search based on user profile constructed without any effort from users. In Proceedings of the 13th International World Wide Web Conference (pp. 675-684).

Sulistyo-Basuki, L. (2004). Digitization of collections in Indonesian academic libraries. *Electronic library and information systems, 38*(3), 194–200.

Sumner, T., & Dawe, M. (2001). Looking at digital library usability from a reuse perspective. In Proceedings of the First ACM/IEEE-CS Joint Conference on Digital Libraries (pp. 416-425). Retrieved November 6, 2007, from the ACM Digital Library database.

Sumner, T., Ahmad, F., Bhushan, S., Gu, Q., Molina, F., Willard, S., et al. (2005). Linking learning goals and educational resources through interactive concept map visualizations. International Journal on Digital Libraries, 5, 18–24.

Sumner, T., Khoo, M., Recker, M., & Marlino, M. (2003). Understanding educator perceptions of "quality" in digital libraries. In Proceedings of the 3rd ACM/IEEE-CS Joint Conference on Digital Libraries (pp. 269-279). Retrieved November 6, 2007, from the ACM Digital Library database.

Sumner, T., Marlino, M., & Wright, M. (2004). Geoscience education and cyberinfrastructure workshop report. Boudler: UCAR.

Sun, A., Suryanto, M. A., & Liu, Y. (2007). Blog classification using tags: An empirical study. In Proceedings of the 10th International Conference on Asian Digital Libraries, ICADL 2007 (LNCS 4822, pp. 307-316).

Sun, J., Zeng, H., Liu, H., Lu, Y., & Chen, Z. (2005). CubeSVD: A novel approach to personalized Web search. In Proceedings of the 14th International World Wide Web Conference (pp. 382-390).

Sun, S. (1998). Internationalization of the handle system: A persistent global name service. In Proceeding of the 12th International Unicode Conference. Retrieved August 12, 2008, from http://www.cnri.reston.va.us/unicode-paper.ps

Suroweicki, J. (2004). The wisdom of crowds: Why the many are smarter than the few and how collective wisdom shapes business, economics, societies, and nations. New York: Doubleday.

Sutcliffe, A. G., Ennis, M., & Hu, J. (2000). Evaluating the effectiveness of visual user interfaces for information retrieval. International Journal of Human–Computer Studies, 53(5), 741-763.

Swain, M.J., & Ballard, D.H. (1991). Color indexing. Int. Journal Computer Vision, 7(11), 11–32.

Tamminen, S., Oulasvirta, A., & Toiskallio, K. (2004). Understanding the mobile context. In Personal and Ubiquitous Computing, 8(2), 135–143.

Tan, D., & Munoo, R.(2006). Thinking about capacity building and sustainability of information literacy programmes: Re-engineering experiences by the National Library Board, Singapore. World Library and Information Congress: 72nd IFLA general conference and council. Retrieved August 30, 2008, from http://www.ifla.org/IV/ifla72/Programme.htm

Tansley, R., Bass, M., & Smith, M. (2003, August 17-22). DSpace as an open archival information system: Current status and future directions. In Proceedings of the 7th European Conference Research and Advanced Technology for Digital Libraries, ECDL 2003, Trondheim, Norway (pp. 446-460). Springer-Verlag.

Tansley, R., Bass, M., Stuve, D., Branschofsky, M., Chudnov, D., McClellan, G., et al. (2003). The DSpace institutional digital repository system: Current functionality. In Proceedings of the Third ACM/IEEE-CS Joint Conference on Digital Libraries (pp. 87-97). IEEE Computer Society.

Tansley, R., Smith, M., & Walker, J.H. (2005). The DSpace open source digital asset management system: Challenges and opportunities. In Proceedings of the 9th European Conference on Research and Advanced Technology for Digital Libraries (ECDL 2005) (pp. 242–253). LNCS 3652. Springer.

Tedd, L.A., & Large, A. (2005). Digital libraries in context. In Digital libraries principles and practice in a global environment (pp.6-23). K.G. Munchen: Saur Verlag GmbH.

Teevan, J., Dumais, S., & Horvitz, E. (2005). Personalizing search via automated analysis of interests and activities. In Proceedings of the 28th International Conference on Research and Development in Information Retrieval (pp. 449-456).

Tejada, S., Knoblock, C., & Minton, S. (2002, July). Learning domain-independent string transformation for high accuracy object identification. In Proceedings of the Eight ACM SIGKDD International Conference on Knowledge Discovery and Data Mining, Edmonton, Canada.

Tenopir, C. (2001). Virtual reference services in a real world. Library Journal, 126(11), 38–40.

Tenopir, C., & Ennis, L. (2002, Spring). A decade of digital reference 1991–2001. Reference and User Service Quarterly, 41(3), 264–273.

TERI. (2004). Report on the International Conference on Digital Libraries. New Delhi, India: Author.

Teufel, S., & Moens, M. (1998). Sentence extraction and rhetorical classification for flexible abstracts. In Proceedings of the AAAI Spring Symposium on Intelligent Text Summarization (pp. 89-97), Menlo Park, CA: AAAI.

Teufel, S., & Moens, M. (2002). Summarizing scientific articles: Experiments with relevance and rhetorical status. Computational Linguistics, 28(4), 409-445.

The British Library Board. (1998). Authors and electronic journals. London: McKnight, C. & Price, S.

The handle system. Corporation for National Research Initiatives. Retrieved August 14, 2008, from http://www.handle.net/

The International Children's Digital Library. Retrieved August 24, 2008, from http://www.icdlbooks.org

The International DOI Foundation (IDF). (2002). DOI introductory overview. Retrieved August 12, 2008, from http://www.doi.org/overview/sys_overview_021601.html

The Learning Technology Standards Committee of the IEEE Computer Society. (2001). Retrieved August 21, 2008, from http://jtc1sc36.org/doc/36N0175.pdf at July 4th 2005)

The MASIE Center e-Learning Consortium. (2002). Making sense of learning specifications & standards: A decision maker's guide to their adoption. Retrieved August 12, 2008, from http://www.masie.com/standards/S3_Guide.pdf

The open archives initiative protocol for metadata harvesting. Retrieved August 20, 2008, from http://www.openarchives.org/

The ubiquitous library for the blind and physically handicapped—a case study of the LG Sangnam library, Korea. *IFLA Journal, 33*(3), 210–219.

Theng, Y. L., Chan, M. Y., Khoo, A. L., & Buddharaju, R. (2005). Quantitative and qualitative evaluations of the Singapore National Library Board's digital library. In Y. L. Theng & S. Foo (Eds.), Design and usability of digital libraries: Case studies in the Asia Pacific (pp. 334-349). Hershey, PA: Information Science Publishing.

Theng, Y. L., Mohd-Nasir, N., & Thimbleby, H. (2000). Purpose and usability of digital libraries. In Proceedings of the Fifth ACM Conference on Digital Libraries (pp. 238-239). Retrieved November 6, 2007, from the ACM Digital Library database.

Theng, Y.L., & Foo, S. (Eds.) (2005). Design and usability of digital libraries. Idea Group Inc.

Theng, Y.-L., Tan, K.-L., Lim, E.-P., Zhang, J., Goh, D.H.-L., Chatterjea, K., et al. (2007). Mobile g-portal supporting collaborative sharing and learning in geography fieldwork: An empirical study. In Proceedings of the ACM/IEEE-CS joint conference on Digital libraries (JCDL). Vancouver, Canada.

Thet, T. T. (2006). Development of a word segmentation algorithm for Myanmar language. Unpublished master's thesis, Nanyang Technological University, Singapore.

Thet, T. T., Na, J.-C., & Ko Ko, W. (in press). Word segmentation for the Myanmar language. Journal of Information Science.

Thomas, R. L. (1998). Elements of performance and satisfaction as indicators of the usability of digital spatial interfaces for information-seeking: Implications for ISLA. Unpublished doctoral dissertation, University of Southern California.

Tolle, K. M. & Chen, H. (2000). Comparing noun phrasing techniques for use with medical digital library tools. Journal of the American Society for Information Science, 51(4), 352-370.

Tolosana-Calasanz, R., Nogueras-Iso, J., Béjar, R., Muro-Medrano, P.R., & Zarazaga-Soria, F.J. (2006). Semantic interoperability based on Dublin Core hierarchical one-to-one mappings. International Journal of Metadata, Semantics and Ontologies, 1(3), 183.

Tolosana-Calasanz, R., Portolés-Rodríquez, D., Nogueras-Iso, J., Muro-Medrano, P.R., & Zarazaga-Soria, F.J. (2005). CatServer: A server of GATOS. In Proceedings of the 8th AGILE Conference on Geographic Information Science (pp. 359–366).

Tombros, A., & Sanderson, M. (1998). Advantage of query biased summaries in information retrieval. In Proceedings of the 21st ACM SIGIR Conference on Research and Development in Information Retrieval (pp. 2-10). New York: ACM.

Torrens, M., Hertzog, P., & Arcos, J.L. (2004). Visualizing and exploring personal music libraries. In Proceedings of the International Conference on Music Information Retrieval (ISMIR). Barcelona, Spain.

Torrens, M., Hertzog, P., Arcos, J.L. (2004). Visualizing and exploring personal music libraries. In Proceedings of the Fifth International Conference on Music Information Retrieval (ISMIR'04) (pp 421–424). Barcelona, Spain.

Tsakonas, G., & Papatheodorou, C. (2007). Exploring usefulness and usability in the evaluation of open access digital libraries. Information Processing and Management,

Tunender, H. (2002). Digital reference: Trends, techniques, and changes. Library Hi Tech News, 19(4), 5–6.

Typke, R., Wiering, F., & Veltkamp, R. C. (2005). A survey of music information retrieval systems. In Proceedings of the International Conference on Music Information Retrieval (ISMIR). London, UK.

Tzanetakis, G. (2002). Manipulation, analysis and retrieval systems for audio signals. Doctoral thesis, Computer Science Department, Princeton University.

Tzanetakis, G., & Cook, P. (2000). 3D graphic tools for isolated sound collections. In Proceedings of the Conference on Digital Audio Effects (DAFx). Verona, Italy.

Tzekou, P., Stamou, S., Kozanidis, L., & Zotos, N. (2007, December 16-19). Effective site customization based on Web semantics and usage mining. In Proceedings of the 3rd International IEEE SITIS Conference: Information Management and Retrieval Technologies Track, Shanghai, China.

Tzoukermann, E., Klavans, J. L., & Jacquemin, C. (1997). Effective use of natural language processing techniques for automatic conflation of multi-word terms: The role of derivational morphology, part of speech tagging, and shallow parsing. In Proceedings 20th Annual International ACM SIGIR Conference on Research and Development in Information Retrieval (SIGIR'97), Philadelphia (pp. 148-155).

U.S. Commission on Ocean Policy. (2004). An ocean blueprint for the 21st century: Final report. Washington, DC: U.S. Commission on Ocean Policy.

U.S. Patent Act. (2005). 35 U.S.C. Sec. 101, 103, & 112.

U.S. Patent and Trademark Office. (1996a, February 28). Examination guidelines for computer-related inventions. 61 Fed. Reg. 7478.

U.S. Patent and Trademark Office. (1996b). Examination guidelines for computer-related inventions training materials directed to business, artificial intelligence, and mathematical processing applications.

Ukkonen, E. (1992). Approximate string matching with q-grams and maximal matches. Theoretical Computer Science, 92(1), 191-211.

ULCC. (2006). DAAT: Digital asset assessment tool. Retrieved August 29, 2008, from http://ahds.ac.uk/about/projects/daat

UNESCO. (2003a, March). Guidelines for the preservation of digital heritage (No. CI-2003/WS/3.). Retrieved August 29, 2008, from unesdoc.unesco.org/images/0013/001300/130071e.pdf

UNESCO. (2003b, October 17). UNESCO charter on the preservation of digital heritage. (Adopted at the 32nd session of the General Conference of UNESCO).

Unicode Consortium. (2004). The Unicode standard 4.0, Southeast Asian scripts. CA: Addison Wesley.

Unique Concepts, Inc. v. Brown. (1991). 939 F.2d 1558, 19 U.S.P.Q.2d 1500 (Fed. Cir. 1991).

University of Milwaukee, Center for International Education. (2007). What are learning objects? Retrieved November 15, 2007, from http://www.uwm.edu/Dept/CIE/AOP/LO_what.html

UNO. (2008). United Nations digital library. Retrieved August 30, 2008, from http://library.un.org.pk/gsdl/cgi-bin/library.exe

Urs, S. R. (2004). Copyright, academic research libraries: Balancing the rights of stakeholders in the digital age. Program: Electronic Library and Information Systems, 38(3), 201-207.

Urs, S.R. (2005). Digital libraries in the Asia-Pacific region: An overview. Digital library Asia.

Usability Professionals' Association. (2005). What is usability? Retrieved November 6, 2007, from http://www.upassoc.org/usability_resources/about_usability/

User privacy in the digital library environment: An investigation of policies and preparedness. Library Management, 24(1/2), 44-50.

Vadas, K., Patel, N., Lyons, K., Starner, T., & Jacko, J. (2006). Reading on-the-go: A comparison of audio and hand-held displays. In Proceedings of the 8th Conference on Human-Computer Interaction with Mobile Devices and Services (ACM International Conference Proceeding Series 159, pp. 219-226). Helsinki, Finland. ACM Press.

Vakkari, P. (2001). A theory of the task based information retrieval process: A summary and generalization of a longitudinal study. Journal of Documentation, 57(1), 44–60.

Van der Hoeven, J., & Van Wijngaarden, H. (2005, September). Modular emulation as a long term preservation strategy for digital objects. Retrieved August 29, 2008, from http://www.iwaw.net/05/papers/iwaw05-hoeven.pdf

Van Gulik, R., Vignoli, F., & van de Wetering, H. (2004). Mapping music in the palm of your hand, explore and discover your collection. In Proceedings of the International Conference on Music Information Retrieval (ISMIR). Barcelona, Spain.

VandeCreek, L.M. (2006). E-mail reference evaluation: Using the results of a Satisfaction survey. The Reference Librarian, 93, 99–108.

Varadarajan, V. S., & Hansen, J. H. L. (2006). Analysis of Lombard effect under different types and levels of background noise with application to in-set speaker ID systems. In Proceedings of the ISCA INTERSPEECH-2006/ICSLP-2006, Pittsburgh (pp. 937-940).

Variations2: The Indiana University digital music library. Retrieved August 24, 2008, from http://variations2.indiana.edu/

Vasconcelos, N., & Lippman, A. (1998, October). Bayesian modeling of video editing and structure: Semantic features for video summarization and browsing. Paper presented at the IEEE ICIP (Vol. 3, pp.153-157).

Velterop, J. (2002). BioMed central. Retrieved November 30, 2007, from http://www.library.yale.edu/~llicense/ListArchives/0205/msg00129.html

Vignoli, F., van Gulik, R., & van de Wetering, H. (2004). Mapping music in the palm of your hand, explore and discover your collection. In Proceedings of the Fifth International Conference on Music Information Retrieval (ISMIR'04) (pp. 409–414). Barcelona, Spain.

Villanova University Digital Library (VUDL). Retrieved August 12, 2008, from http://digital.library.villanova.edu/

Virginia Tech (VT). (2006). UNC create DL curriculum. Retrieved August 30, 2008, from http://www.cs.vt.edu/whatsnews/virginia_tech,_unc_create_digital_library_curriculum.html

Von Hippel, E. (2005). Democratizing innovation. Cambridge, MA: MIT Press.

Voutilainen, A. (1997). A short introduction to NPtool. Retrieved August 16, 2008, from http://www.lingsoft.fi/doc/nptool/intro/

VRA core categories (2002, February 20). Retrieved August 20, 2008, from http://www.vraweb.org/vracore3.htm

W3C. Resource description framework (RDF). Retrieved August 14, 2008, from http://www.w3.org/RDF/

W3C. Resource description framework (RDF). Retrieved August 20, 2008, from http://www.w3.org/RDF/

Wade-Stein, D., & Kintsch, E. (2004). Summary street: Interactive computer support for writing. Cognition and Instruction, 22(3), 333–362.

Walls, F., Jin, H., Sista, S., & Schwartz, R. (1999). Probabilistic models for topic detection and tracking. In Proceedings of the IEEE ICASSP-99: Inter. Conf. Acoust. Speech, Sig. Proc. (Vol. 1, pp. 521-524).

Wang, F. L., & Yang, C. C. (2006). Impact of document structure on hierarchical summarization. In Proceedings of 9th International Conference on Asian Digital Libraries (pp. 459-469). Springer.

Wang, H., Liu, S., & Chia, L-T. (2006). Does ontology help in image retrieval? A comparison between keyword, text ontology and multi-modality ontology approaches. In Proceedings of the 14th Annual ACM International Conference on Multimedia, Hawai (pp. 109-112).

Wang, H.-M., Meng, H., Schone, P., Chen, B., & Lo, W.-K. (2001). Multi-scale-audio indexing for translingual spoken document retrieval. In Proceedings of the IEEE ICASSP-01: Inter. Conf. Acoust. Speech, Sig. Proc. (Vol. 1, pp. 605-608).

Wang, J. Z., Li, J., & Wiederhold, G. (1997). TID - Trusted image dissemination: Image filtering for secure distribution of medical information. Retrieved October, 12, 2007, from http://infolab.stanford.edu/pub/gio/TIHI/TID.html

Wang, J. Z., Li, J., & Wiederhold, G. (2001). SIMPLIcity: Semantics-sensitive integrated matching for picture libraries. IEEE Transactions on Pattern Analysis and Machine Intelligence, 23(9), 947-963.

Wang, M.-Y. (2003) The strategic role of digital libraries: Issues in e-learning environments. Library Review, 52(3), 111–115.

Wang, M.-Y., & Hwang, M.-J. (2004). The e-learning library: only a warehouse of learning resources? The Electronic Library, 22(5), 408–415.

Wasik, J.M. (2003). Building and maintaining digital reference services. Retrieved August 29, 2008, from http://www.michaellorenzen.com/eric/ref-serv.html

Wasik, J.M. (2003). Digital reference evaluation. Retrieved August 29, 2008, from http://www.vrd.org/AskA/digref-assess.shtml

Waters, D.J. (1998). What are digital libraries? Council on library and information resources issues July/August(1), 5–6.

Weibel, S., Godby, J., Miller, E., & Daniel, R. (1995). OCLC/NCSA metadata workshop report. Technical report, Office of Research, OCLC Online Computer Library Center, Inc.

Weinstein, P., & Alloway, G. (1997, July). Seed ontologies: Growing digital libraries as distributed, intelligent systems. In Proceedings of the Second ACM Digital Library Conference, Philadelphia (pp. 83-91). ACM Press.www.1. e-Learning Cybrary: http://www.co-i-l.com/elearning/about/

Wells, A.T., & Hanson, A. (2002). E-reference. In A. Hanson, & B.L. Levin (Eds.), Building a Virtual Library (pp. 95–120). London: Information Science Pub.

Wells, H.G. (1937). World brain: The idea of a permanent world encyclopaedia. Retrieved August 30, 2008, from http://art-bin.com/art/obrain.html

Wharton, C., Rieman, J., Lewis, C., & Polson, P. (1994). The cognitive walkthrough method: A practitioners guide. In J. Nielsen & R. L. Mack (Eds.), Usability inspection methods (pp. 105-140). New York: Wiley.

White, R., Jose, J. M., & Ruthven, I. (2001). Query-based Web page summarization: A task-oriented evaluation. In Proceedings of the 24th Annual International ACM SIGIR Conference on Research and Development in Information Retrieval (SIGIR'2001), New Orleans (pp. 412-413).

Wikipedia. (2006). Digital reference services. Retrieved August 29, 2008, from http:// en.wikipedia.org/wiki/ Digital-reference-services

Wildemuth, B. (2006). CS and ILS as disciplinary homes for DLE. Presentation at DLE workshop on JCDL06. Retrieved August 30, 2008, from http://lair.indiana. edu/research/dlib/jcdl06/unc.pdf

Wilder, S.J. (2002) New hires in research libraries, demographic trends and hiring priories. ARI, 221.

Wiley, D. A. (2000). Connecting learning objects to instructional design theory: A definition, a metaphor, and a taxonomy. The instructional use of learning objects (section 1). Retrieved November 15, 2007, from http://reusability.org/read/chapters/wiley.doc

Willinsky, J. (2006). The access principle: The case for open access to research and scholarship. Cambridge, MA: The MIT Press.

Wing, J.M. (2006). Computational thinking. Communications of the ACM, 49(3), 33–35.

Wirot, A. (2002). Collocation and Thai word segmentation. In Proceeding of Joint International Conference of SNLP-Oriental COCOSDA 2002. Thammasat University, Bangkok.

Witten, I. H. (2003). How to build a digital library. Morgan Kaufmann.

Witten, I. H., & Bainbridge, D. (2003). How to build a digital library. San Francisco: Morgan Kaufmann.

Witten, I. H., & Bainbridge, D. (2005). Creating digital library collections with Greenstone. Library Hi Tech., 23(4), 541-560.

Witten, I. H., & Bainbridge, D. I. (2003). How to build a digital library. San Francisco: Morgan Kaufmann.

Witten, I. H., Bainbridge, D., & Boddie, S. J. (2001). Power to the people: End-user building of digital library collections. In Proceedings of the Joint Conference on Digital Libraries, Roanoke, VA.

Witten, I. H., Boddie, S. J., Bainbridge, D., & McNab, R. J. (2000). Greenstone: A comprehensive open-source digital library software system. In Proceedings of the 5th Conference on Digital Libraries (pp. 113-121). ACM Press.

Witten, I. H., Cunningham, S. J., Vallabh, M., & Bell, T. C. (1995, June). A New Zealand digital library for computer science research. In Proceedings of the Digital Libraries '95, Austin (pp. 25-30).

Witten, I. H., Don, K. J., Dewsnip, M., & Tablan, V. (2004). Text mining in a digital library. International Journal of Digital Libraries, 4(1), 56-59.

Witten, I. H., McNab, R. J., Boddie, S. J., & Bainbridge, D. (2000). Greenstone: A comprehensive open-source digital library software system. In Proceedings of the Fifth ACM Conference on Digital Libraries DL '00. ACM Press.

Witten, I. H., Moffat, A., & Bell, T. C. (1999). Managing gigabytes: Compressing and indexing documents and images. Morgan Kaufmann.

Witten, I., & Bell, T. (1991). The zero-frequency problem: Estimating the probabilities of novel events in adaptive text compression. IEEE Transactions on Information Theory, 37(4), 1085-1094.

Witten, I.H., & Bainbridge, D. (2003). How to build a digital library. San Francisco, CA: Morgan Kaufmann Publishers.

Witten, I.H., & Bainbridge, D. (2003). How to build a digital library. San Francisco, CA: Morgan Kaufmann.

Woldering, B. (2006). Connecting with users: Europe and multilinguality. 13th Biennial Conference and Exhibition. Retrieved August 30, 2998, from http://www.vala. org.au/conf2006.htm

Woodland, P. C. (1999). Speaker adaptation: Techniques and challenges. In Proceedings of the IEEE Workshop on Automatic Speech Recognition & Understanding, Keystone, CO (pp. 85-90).

Woodward, H. M., & Pilling, S. (Eds.). (1993). The international serials industry. Aldershot, Great Britain: Gower Publishing Ltd.

Wu, H., Radev, D., & Fan, W. (2004). Towards answer-focused summarization using search engines. In M. T. Maybury (Ed.), New directions in question answering (pp. 227-236). Menlo Park: AAAI.

Wu, S., & Witten, I. H. (2006). Towards a digital library for language learning. In Proceedings of the European Conference on Digital Libraries, Alicante, Spain.

www.libsys.co.in/home.html

Xia, J.F. (2006). Scholarly communication in East and Southeast Asia: traditions and challenges. IFLA Journal, 32(2), 104–112.

Xie, H. (2006). Evaluation of digital libraries: Criteria and problems from users' perspectives. Library and Information Science Research, 28(3), 433–452.

Xie, Z., Li, X., Di Eugenio, B., Nelson, P., Xiao, W., & Tirpak, T. (2004). Using gene expression programming to construct sentence ranking functions for text summarization. In Proceedings of the 20th International Conference on Computational Linguistics (pp. 1381-1384).Morristown, NJ: ACL.

Yan, H. (2004). Digital content management: The search for a content management system. Library Hi Tech., 22(4), 355-365.

Yanbe, Y., Jatowt, A., Nakamura, S., & Tanaka, K. (2007). Can social bookmarking enhance search in the Web? In Proceedings of the 2007 Conference on Digital Libraries (pp. 107-116).

Yang, C. C., & Wang, F. L. (2003). Fractal summarization: Summarization based on fractal theory. In Proceedings of the 26th Annual International ACM SIGIR Conference (pp. 392-392). ACM.

Yang, C. C., & Wang, F. L. (2003). Fractal summarization for mobile devices to access large documents on the Web. In Proceedings of the 12th International World Wide Web Conference (p. 215-224). ACM.

Yang, C. C., & Wang, F. L. (in press). Hierarchical summarization of large documents. Journal of the American Society for Information Science and Technology.

Yang, R., Chennupati, K. R., & Foo, S. (2007, August 27-31,). Virtual archival exhibition system: An authoring tool for developing web-based virtual exhibitions. In Proceedings of the International Conference on Dublin Core and Metadata Applications (DC-2007), Singapore (pp. 96-105).

Yang, S., Fox, E.A., Wildemuth, B., Pomerantz, J., & Oh, S. (2006). Interdisciplinary curriculum development for digital library education. In Proceedings of the 9th International Conference on Asian Digital Libraries (ICADL 2006) (pp. 61–70). LNCS 4312. New York: Springer.

Yao, X.X., Chen, L., & Dai, L.F. (2004). Current situation and future development of CALIS. Library Management, 25(6–7), 277–282.

Yapanel, U., & Hansen, J. H. L. (2003). A new perspective on feature extraction for robust in-vehicle speech recognition. In Proceedings of Eurospeech-03, Geneva (pp. 1281-1284).

Yeh, J. H., & Chen, C. C. (2003). The x-system: Design and implementation of a digital archive system (Tech. Rep.) Retrieved August 12, 2008, from http://mars.csie.ntu.edu.tw/~jhyeh/xsys.pdf

Yilmazel, O., Balasubramanian, N., Harwell, S.C., Bailey, J., Diekema, A. R., & Liddy, E.D. (2007). Text categorization for aligning educational standards. In Proceedings of the 40th Hawaii International Conference on System Sciences. Big Island, HI.

Yin, R.K. (2003). Case study research: Design and methods (3 ed.). California: Sage.

Yokoyama, Y. (2006). Japanese national bibliography in the digital environment. World Library and Information Congress: 71th IFLA general conference and council. Retrieved August 30, 2008, from http://www.ifla71/Programme.htm

Young, E., Horwood, L., & Sullivan, S. (2006). Supporting E-research at the University of Melbourne. 13th Biennial Conference and Exhibition. Retrieved August 30, 2008, from http://www.vala.org.au/conf2006.htm

Yu, C., Meng, W., Wu, W., & Liu, K. (2001). Efficient and effective metasearch for text databases incorporating linkages among documents. In Proceedings of the ACM SIGMOD Conference.

Z39.50 maintenance agency page. Retrieved August 14, 2008, from http://www.loc.gov/z3950/agency/

Zaheer, M.A. (2002). National library of Pakistan: Annual report to CDNL 2001-2002. Edinburgh.

Zarazaga-Soria, F.J., Lacasta, J., Nogueras-Iso, J., Torres, M.P., & Muro-Medrano, P.R. (2003). A Java tool for creating ISO/FGDC geographic metadata. Geodaten- und Geodienste-Infrastrukturen - von der Forschung zur praktischen Anwendung. Beiträge zu den Münsteraner GI-Tagen. IfGI prints, 18, 17–30.

Zarazaga-Soria, F.J., Nogueras-Iso, J., Béjar, R., & Muro-Medrano, P.R. (2004). Political aspects of spatial data infrastructures. Electronic government. In R. Traunmüller (Ed.), Lecture Notes in Computer Science, (Vol. 3183, pp. 392–395). Springer.

Zarazaga-Soria, F.J., Nogueras-Iso, J., Latre, M.Á., Rodríguez, A., López, E., Vivas, P., & Muro-Medrano, P.R. (2007). Providing spatial data infrastructure services in a cross-border scenario: SDIGER project. Research and Theory in Advancing Spatial Data Infrastructure Concepts (pp. 107–119). California: ESRI Press.

Zebra index data. Retrieved August 14, 2008, from http://www.indexdata.dk/zebra/

Zechner, K., & Waibel, A. (2000, May). Minimizing word error rate in textual summaries of spoken language. In Proceedings of NAACL-ANLP-2000, Seattle (pp. 186-193).

Zeng, M. L. (2005). Construction of controlled vocabularies: A primer. Retrieved May 25, 2007, from http://www.slis.kent.edu/~mzeng/Z3919/index.htm

Zeng, M. L., & Chan, L. M. (2004). Trends and issues in establishing interoperability among knowledge organization systems. Journal of the American Society for Information Science and Technology, 55(5), 377-95.

Zhang, S., Shen, W., & Ghjenniwa, H. (2004). A review of Internet-based product information sharing and visualization. Computers in Industry, 54, 1–15.

Zhang, X., & Haslam, M. (2005). Movement toward a predominantly electronic journal collection. Library Hi Tech, 23(1), 82–89.

Zhang, Z., Blair-Goldensohn, S., & Radev, D. (2002). Towards CST-enhanced summarization. In Proceedings of the 18th National Conference on Artificial Intelligence (pp. 439-445). Menlo Park, CA: AAAI.

Zhou, B., & Hansen, J. H. L. (2002). SPEECHFIND: An experimental on-line spoken document retrieval system for historical audio archives. In Proceedings of the ICSLP-2002: International Conferference on Spoken Language Processing, Denver (Vol. 3, pp. 1969-1972).

Zhou, B., & Hansen, J. H. L. (2005a). Efficient audio stream segmentation via the T2 statistic based Bayesian information criterion. IEEE Trans. Speech & Audio Proc., 13(4), 467-474.

Zhou, B., & Hansen, J. H. L. (2005b). Rapid discriminative acoustic modeling based on Eigenspace mapping for fast speaker adaptation. IEEE Trans. Speech & Audio Proc., 13(4), 554-564.

Zhou, Q. (2005). The development of digital libraries in China and the shaping of digital librarians. The Electronic Library, 23(4), 433–441.

Zhou, X., & Huang, T.S. (2000). A generalized relevance feedback scheme for image retrieval. In Proceedings of Internet Multimedia Management Systems (pp. 348–355).

Zhu, Q. (2002). 5SGraph: A modeling tool for digital libraries. Master's thesis, Virginia Tech. Retrieved August 30, 2008, from http://scholar.lib.vt.edu/theses/available/etd-11272002-210531/

Zloof, M. (1977). Query-by-example: A database language. IBM Systems Journal, 16(4), 324–343.

Zotos, N., Tzekou, P., Tsatsaronis G., Kozanidis, L., Stamou, S., & Varlamis, I. (2007). To click or not to click? The role of contextualized and user-centric Web snippets. In Proceedings of the SIGIR 2007 Workshop on Focused Retrieval (pp. 57-64). Dunedin: University of Otago.

Zwicker, E., & Fastl, H. (1999). Psycho-acoustics, facts, and models. Series of Information Sciences (Vol. 22, Ed. 2). Berlin: Springer.

Zwicker, E., & Fastl, H. (1999). Psychoacoustics—facts and models. Springer Series of Information Sciences (Vol. 22). Springer, Berlin.

About the Contributors

Schubert Foo is Professor and Associate Dean, College of Humanities, Arts and Social Sciences, Nanyang Technological University, Singapore. He received his BSc (Hons), MBA and PhD from the University of Strathclyde, UK. He is a Chartered Engineer, Chartered IT Professional, Fellow of the Institution of Mechanical Engineers, and Fellow of the British Computer Society. He is a Board Member of the National Library Board, and an Advisor of the National Archives of Singapore Board. He has published in excess of 170 publications in the areas of multimedia technology, Internet technology, multilingual information retrieval, digital libraries and knowledge management. He coauthored a book *Knowledge Management: Tools and Techniques* with Ravi Sharma and Alton Chua, and coedited a book *Social Information Retrieval Systems: Emerging Technologies and Applications for Searching the Web Effectively* with Dion Goh in 2007.

Dion Hoe-Lian Goh has a PhD in computer science and is an Associate Professor at the Division of Information Studies, Wee Kim Wee School of Communication and Information. He is also Director of the school's Master of Science in Information Systems program. His research areas are in the areas of information retrieval, digital libraries, text mining, the use of information technology in education, and the evaluation of information systems and services.

Jin-Cheon Na is an Assistant Professor in the Division of Information Studies in the Wee Kim Wee School of Communication and Information at Nanyang Technological University. His research interests are digital library, text mining, information retrieval, hypermedia system, and human-computer interaction.

Yin-Leng Theng's (PI) research in digital libraries and user interface design has won her two research grants from the Engineering and Physical Sciences Research Council (EPSRC, UK) during her four years of teaching at Middlesex University (London). She has participated in varying capacities as principal investigator, coinvestigator, and collaborator in numerous research projects in the United Kingdom and Singapore since 1998. These projects involve usable and useful interfaces for hypertext systems, the Web and mobile environments; e-learning building tools and learning objects; usability evaluation techniques; and geospatial digital libraries. She is particularly interested and involved in research into technology acceptance and users' attitudes.

* * *

Faisal Ahmad is a full-time PhD student at the University of Colorado at Boulder, Department of Computer Science. He obtained his Master's degree from the same university. His Master's thesis investigated the core architectural components enabling concept space-based resource discovery for educational digital libraries. Faisal's current research is concerned with personalization of digital library interactions using concept maps.

Esther Olajope Akomolafe-Fatuyi received BSc Education (1976); MA Library Science (1979), University of Wisconsin, Madison; diploma in Computer Studies, Beijing, China, 1994; and PhD in Library and Information Management, Emporia State University (2006). She taught university students in Nigeria and America. She was Head of the Department of Library and Information Services at the National Research Institute for Chemical Technology (NARICT) Zaria, Nigeria (1981–1998). Her research interests are Corporate Information Resource Management, and the Affect of Culture on the Diffusion of Innovative Libraries. She is married with three children. She is currently a consultant on information management at an accounting firm.

Mohammed Nasser Al-Suqri is assistant professor at the Department of Library and Information Science, College of Arts and Social Science, Sultan Qaboos University. He received his PhD in Library and Information Management from Emporia State University, School of Library and Information Management; a Master's degree in Library and Information Science from Pratt Institute, School of Information and Library Science; and a Bachelor's degree in Library and Information Science from Sultan Qaboos University, Department of Library and Information Science. Mohammed Nasser Al-Suqri conducts research in the area of information needs and information-seeking behavior of academic scholars in developing countries; information needs and seeking behavior of students, Digital Divide, and digital libraries.

Alan O. Allwardt (aallwardt@usgs.gov) has a varied academic background, with advanced degrees in geology, library and information science, and history of science. He is currently employed by ETI Professionals as an information specialist contracted to the Coastal and Marine Geology Program (CMGP) of the U.S. Geological Survey (USGS). As cataloger for the Marine Realms Information Bank (MRIB), Alan contributes to the CMGP Knowledge Management Project. He lives and works in Santa Cruz, California, USA.

Luz Marina Alvaré is Head of IFPRI's Library and Knowledge Management Unit. Her work focuses on ways to connect information and knowledge with research for development. She is very innovative in her approach of implementing new technological services for IFPRI staff, as well as policymakers and key stakeholders to be able to preserve, organize and disseminate research information. Luz Marina joined IFPRI in 2000 after working for10 years at the Centro Internacional de Agricultura Tropical (CIAT) in Cali, Colombia.

Kanwal Ameen is Assistant Professor at the Department of LIS, University of the Punjab (Uop), Lahore, Pakistan. She has 23 years' professional and teaching experience at the UoP. On her credit are more than 20 research papers in national and international journals besides book chapters. Her research interests are user-focused services, impact of IT on library services, collection management, marketing of LIS services, Information seeking behaviors, application of qualitative research in LIS and professional development. She is the chief-editor of *Pakistan Journal of LIS,* published by the UoP. She has widely traveled to attend and contribute in international conferences. Dr. Kanwal got international scholarships including Fulbright (2000–2001). She is personal member of ALA, IFLA, CILIP, Secretary, IFLA Discussion Group on LIS Education in Developing Countries and Chair, Continuing Education Committee, PLA (Pb). She can be reached at kanwal@dlis.pu.edu.pk and kanwal.ameen@gmail.com.

Antonio de Amescua has been a full professor of the Computer Science Department at the Carlos III Technical University of Madrid since 1991. He holds a BS in Computer Science and a PhD in Computer Science from the Polytechnic University of Madrid. Also, he has done software engineering work in public and private companies as a software engineering consultant. He has been researching new software engineering methods and participated in other projects sponsored by the European Union. He was the research project leader for the development of the Information System Development Methodology for the Spanish Administration.

Margherita Antona holds a PhD from the Department of Electronic Engineering of the University of Kent, UK, in the area of Human-Computer Interaction. She is a member of the Human-Computer Interaction Laboratory and Centre for Universal Access and Assistive Technologies (CUA&AT) of FORTH-ICS since 1993. Currently, she is the Coordinator of CUA&AT. Her current research interests include universal access, design for all, computer-supported user interface design, adaptive and Intelligent Interfaces, and assistive technologies. She has participated in several European and national research and development projects. She is member of the Editorial Board of the international journal "Universal Access in the Information Society," published by Springer, as well as of the Program Committee and Paper Review Committee in various international conferences and workshops.

Lilia Fernandez Aquino graduated from the University of la Havana in Information and Communication Systems. Director of Masmedios Ltd. Assistant Professor in the Polytechnic University of Valencia, and Member of the Research group CALSI.

David Bainbridge is a Senior Lecturer in Computer Science at the University of Waikato, New Zealand. He holds a PhD in computer science from the University of Canterbury, New Zealand, where he studied as a Commonwealth Scholar. Since moving to Waikato, he has developed his interest in digital media, with an emphasis on digital libraries. He coauthored with Witten of the book *How to Build a Digital Library*, and has published in the areas of image processing, music information retrieval, digital libraries, data compression, and text mining. David has also worked as a research engineer for Thorn EMI in the area of photorealistic imaging, and graduated from the University of Edinburgh in 1991 as the class medalist in Computer Science.

Cláudio de Souza Baptista is an associate professor in the Computer Science Department and Director of the Information Systems Laboratory at the University of Campina Grande, Brazil. He received a PhD degree in Computer Science from the University of Kent at Canterbury, United Kingdom in 2000. His research interests include database, digital libraries, geographical information systems, multimedia systems, and decision support systems.

Payam M. Barnaghi is an Assistant Professor at the School of Computer Science and Information Technology, University of Nottingham, Malaysia Campus. His research areas include knowledge-driven presentation generation, information search and retrieval, multimedia on the Semantic Web, and Ontologies

Pierpaolo Basile is a PhD student in Informatics at the University of Bari (Italy) since November 2005. His research is devoted to the application of machine learning techniques for natural language processing. The topic of his studies concerns semantic text analysis obtained by integrating lexical resources, ontologies and statistical methods in the learning process in order to extract concepts from unstructured text.

Christoph Becker is currently a PhD researcher at the Department of Software Technology and Interactive Systems at the Vienna University of Technology. He received his BSc and MSc in Computer Science and an MSc in Business Informatics from the Vienna University of Technology. Since 1998, he has been working as an independent IT consultant and software architect in a wide range of IT projects in different domains. He is involved in European research projects in the field of Digital Preservation (PLANETS, DELOS, DPE).

Leonardo Bermon is a PhD Computer Science student in the Software Engineering Lab group at Carlos III University. He has worked in universities in Colombia during ten years. He is a professor at National University of Colombia. He has both a bachelor of computer science degree and the grade of Magister in Computer Science from Industrial University of Santander, Colombia. His research interests include Software Process Engineering and Knowledge Management.

Rubén Béjar holds an MS degree in Computer Science from the University of Zaragoza (Spain) since 1999. He is currently a tenured Assistant Professor at the Department of Computer Science and Systems Engineering at the same university. He is working with the Advanced Information Systems Lab (IAAA) and the Aragón Institute for Engineering Research (I3A), where he has been involved in several R&D projects related with the software engineering aspects of Geographic Information Systems and Spatial Data Infrastructures, and has coauthored several publications in that area.

Regina Braga is professor of Computer Science Department at Federal University of Juiz de Fora, Brazil. She is a member of Brazilian Computer Society. Dr. Braga received her PhD degree (2000) from Federal University of Rio de Janeiro. Her main researche areas are: Web information integration, software components, and semantic Web services.

Fernanda Campos is a professor at the Computer Science Department, Federal University of Juiz de Fora, Brazil. She is a member of the Brazilian Computer Society. Dr. Campos received her PhD degree (1999) from Federal University of Rio de Janeiro, in Software Engineering. Her main research areas are: ontology, software components, semantic Web services, and software quality.

Leonardo Candela is a researcher at Networked Multimedia Information Systems (NMIS) Laboratory of the Institute of Information Science and Technologies—Italian National Research Council (ISTI—CNR). He graduated in Computer Science in 2001 at University of Pisa and completed a PhD in Information Engineering in 2006 at University of Pisa. In 2001, he joined the NMIS Laboratory and was involved in the CYCLADES (http://www.ercim.org/cyclades) and Open Archives Forum (www.oaforum.org) projects. He is currently involved in the DILIGENT (http://www.diligentproject.org) and DRIVER (http://www.driver-repository.eu) projects, and he is an active member of the DELOS (http://www.delos.info) working group on the Digital Library Reference Model (http://www.delos.info/ReferenceModel). He is member of the OAI-ORE (http://www.openarchives.org/ore/) Liaison Group. His research interests include Digital Library (Management) Systems and Architectures, Digital Libraries Models, Distributed Information Retrieval, and Grid Computing.

Alicia Selles Carot graduated from the Salamanca University in Information and Library Systems. She is head of the Contents Department in Masmedios Ltd., Master in Legal Issues in the Information Society, and Member of AEDOC (Digital Rights Management Association).

Óscar Cantán Casbas holds an MS degree in Computer Science from the University of Zaragoza (Spain). In 1998, he joined the Advanced Information Systems Laboratory where he worked as an R&D Engineer in the GIS field for more than seven years. He also worked as an assistant professor at the University of Zaragoza for three years before joining the University of San Jorge, where he has been working since 2006 in the Computer Engineering School. He is coauthor of more than 20 publications and has participated in diverse R&D projects. His research interests range from spatial data infrastructures to enterprise resource planning systems.

Donatella Castelli is a Senior Researcher working at the Information Science and Technologies—Italian National Research Council (ISTI—CNR) since 1988. She graduated in Computer Science at the Department of Computer Science of the University of Pisa, and there, she was employed as researcher for two years before joining ISTI-CNR Networked Multimedia Information Systems. Since 1996, she has scientifically coordinated several European and National funded projects on digital libraries, acquiring considerable experience in this domain. She is currently leading the activity of the DELOS Network of Excellence on Digital Libraries dedicated to the definition of a Reference Model for digital libraries. Her current research interests include digital library architectures and infrastructures, information object modeling, and interoperability.

Tiziana Catarci received her PhD in Computer Science from the University of Rome, where she is currently a Full Professor. She has published over 100 papers and 10 books in a variety of subjects, comprising User Interfaces for Databases, 2D and 3D Data Visualization, Adaptive Interfaces, Visual Metaphors, Usability Testing, Data Quality, Cooperative Database Systems, Database Integration, Web Access. Professor Catarci is regularly in the programming committees of the main database and human-computer interaction conferences and is associate editor of ACM SIGMOD Digital Symposium Collection (DiSC), VLDB Journal, World Wide Web Journal, and Journal of data Semantics.

Chao-Chen Chen received the BS degree in library science from Catholic Fu-Jen University, Taipei, Taiwan, in 1980, and the MS and PhD degree in library and information science from National Taiwan University, Taipei, Taiwan, in 1984 and 1994, respectively. Her current research interests include digital libraries and digital archives, library automation, information organization and metadata, electronic publishing, and electronic learning.

Alton Y.K. Chua is Assistant Professor at Nanyang Technological University. He teaches in the M.Sc (KM) program. His research interests lie primarily in knowledge management and communities of practice. Alton has authored numerous papers in publications, such as the Journal of the American Society of Information Science and Technology, International Journal of Information Management, and the Journal of Intellectual Capital.

Warwick Clegg earned Honours Degree in Physics at Liverpool University, then moved to the Electrical Engineering Department at the University of Manchester. Warwick's MSc and PhD work at Manchester developed a life-long interest in advanced methods for data storage technologies. He is the author of over 200 journal and conference papers and has supervised 23 PhD students. Following a period at the University of Plymouth, in 2003 he moved to take up his present post as Pro Vice-Chancellor for Information Technology, and later, also the inaugural Dean of a new Faculty of Engineering at Victoria University of Wellington in New Zealand.

Hepu Deng is an Associate Professor at the School of Business Information Technology, RMIT University, Australia. He holds a Bachelor degree in Mathematics, a Postgraduate Diploma in Management Engineering, and a Master's degree and a PhD in Business Systems. His research interests include multicriteria analysis, neural networks, approximate reasoning, fuzzy logic, preference modeling, knowledge management and their applications in business. He has published more than ninety refereed articles in various international journals and conferences, including IEEE Transaction on Systems, Man and Cybertices, European Journal of Operational research, Computers and Operational Research, International Journal of Approximate Reasoning, International Journal of Computer and Information Sciences, and International Journal of the Operational Research Society.

Holly Devaul holds a BA in Human Ecology and an MS in Wildlife Biology. Holly coordinates and conducts workshops on tool use for digital library collection builders, user focus groups to inform service and interface design, and teacher workshops on integrating technology and digital libraries into teaching and learning. A special focus of her work involves investigating how to embed educational standards within digital libraries. She is a collaborator in the Center for Natural Language Processing's work developing tools to support standards assignment and alignment and is cochair of the NSDL Educational Standards Working Group.

Vladan Devedžić is a professor in and the Head of the Department of Software Engineering at FON—School of Business Administration, University of Belgrade. His research interests focus on practical engineering aspects of developing intelligent software systems, while his long-term goal is to merge ideas from intelligent systems and software engineering. He has authored/coauthored more than 270 research papers, published in international and national journals or presented at international and national conferences, as well as six books on intelligent systems and software engineering.

Wan Ab. Kadir Wan Dollah received an MLib (Wales), Postgraduate Diploma in Library Science (UiTM), and BAHons (Malaya). He is a Lecturer at the Faculty of Information Management, MARA University of Technology, Malaysia. Prior to teaching he worked for more than 10 years in academic library. His areas of interest are reference and information sources and services, world of knowledge and information sources and services in social science. He also teaches in the areas of digital libraries and multimedia applications.

Cecilia Ferreyra is Head of the Library Unit of the International Potato Center (CIP). Her work focuses on planning, setting goals and objectives for the future of CIP's Library services, while focusing on determining the needed services, the most effective way to deliver them, and the resources needed to support them.

Fernando Ferri received the degrees in Electronics Engineering and the PhD in Medical Informatics. He is actually senior researcher at the National Research Council of Italy. From 1993 to 2000, he was professor of "Sistemi di Elaborazione" at the University of Macerata. He is the author of more than 100 papers in international journals, books, and conferences. His main methodological areas of interest are: Human-Computer Interaction Visual Languages, Visual Interfaces, Sketch-based Interfaces, Multimodal Interfaces, Data and knowledge bases, Geographic Information Systems, and Virtual Communities. He has been responsible for several national and international research projects.

Edward A. Fox holds a PhD and MS in Computer Science from Cornell University, and a BS from M.I.T. Since 1983, he has been at Virginia Polytechnic Institute and State University (Virginia Tech), where he serves as Professor of Computer Science. He directs the Digital Library Research Laboratory, the Networked Digital Library of Theses and Dissertations, the Digital Library Curriculum Development project, and a number of other R&D projects. In addition to his courses at Virginia Tech, Dr. Fox has taught over 70 tutorials in more than 25 countries. His research interests include digital libraries, (multimedia) information storage and retrieval, and educational technologies.

Carmen Galvez is a PhD in Documentation from the University of Granada in 2003. She is an associate professor at Department of Information Science, University of Granada. She is a member of the Associated Unit to Spanish National Research Council (CSIC) and the Scimago Research Group. She has published different articles in international journals on subjects relating to term unification through Finite-State Transducers (FST) and submitted numerous papers to international congresses. Her research interests include Natural Language Processing (NLP) and Information Extraction (IE). At present, she has interest in Biomedical Natural Language Processing (BioNLP), Biomedical Text-Mining, and Bio-Bibliometrics.

Javier García-Guzmán received an engineering degree and PhD in Computer Science from the Carlos III University of Madrid. He has seven years of experience as a software engineer and consultant in public and private companies. He has participated in numerous research projects financed with public (European and national) and private funds. His current research interest is formal measurement of processes improvement, ISO 15504 assessments, software capacity rapid audits, evaluations for pre-diagnosis according to ISO 15504 and CMMI, and management of knowledge related to software engineering.

David A. Garza-Salazar received the BSc in Computer Sciences from Tecnologico de Monterrey (ITESM) in 1985. Dr. Garza-Salazar received the PhD degree in Computer Science from Colorado State University in 1995. Currently, he is chairman of the College in Engineering at Tecnologico de Monterrey. His research areas include high performance computing, parallel computing, and digital libraries. He is member of the ACM, the IEEE-Computer Society, Sigma-Xi, American Association for Engineering Education, and the Microsoft Research Committee for Latin America.

Lorena G. Gomez received the BSc in Computer Science and the MSC in Computer Science; both degrees from Tecnologico de Monterrey (ITESM), in 1986 and 1990 respectively. Dr. Gomez received the PhD degree in Computer Science from Arizona State University, in 2002. Currently, she is an Assistant Professor at ITESM. Dr. Gomez research interests include databases systems, OO databases, computer education, and digital libraries. She has been member of the National System of Researchers (SNI-candidate) in Mexico, and she is member of the Upsilon Pi Epsilon Honor Society in Computer Science and the Phi Kappa Phi Honor Society.

Gary Gorman is professor of information management at Victoria University of Wellington, New Zealand. He received his library science postgraduate degrees at the University of London, and since the early 1980s, has taught in the fields of library science and information management in Australia and New Zealand. He is a Fellow of the Chartered Institute of Library and Information Professionals (UK) and the Royal Society for the Arts (RSA), and has written more than a dozen books and more than 100 peer-reviewed papers in international scholarly journals. Among his forthcoming books are titles on information needs analysis, on quantitative research for information managers, on resource evaluation, and on personal knowledge management. He is editor/associate, editor/reviews editor of several scholarly and professional journals such as *Online Information Review and Library Collections, Acquisitions, and Technical Services*. His special interest is developing countries in Asia, where he is actively engaged in a number of research endeavours related to professional education, information services, and information networks (including consortia). Gary is also interested in a range of topics related to management and use of information in organisations, and information quality.

Soh Whee Kheng Grace is currently a MSc (Information Studies) student at the Division of Information Studies, School of Communication and Information, Nanyang Technological University (Singapore). She completed her Bachelor of Computing at Monash University (Australia). Her research interests include digital libraries, information technology in education, and E-learning.

Patrizia Grifoni received the degrees in Electronics Engineering. She is actually a researcher at the National Research Council of Italy. From 1994 to 2000, she was professor of "Elaborazione digitale delle immagini" at the University of Macerata. She is the author of more than 80 papers in international journals, books, and conferences. Her scientific interests have evolved from Query Languages for statistical and Geographic Databases to the focal topics related to Human-Computer Interaction, Multimodal Interaction, Visual Languages, Visual Interfaces, Sketch-based Interfaces, Accessing Web Information and Virtual Communities. She was responsible of several research projects.

Svenja Hagenhoff has been an assistant professor at the Institute of Information Systems, University of Goettingen, since 2002. She finished her doctoral thesis in information systems in 2001. In 2008, she finished her state doctorate (Habilitation) and passed the postdoctoral lecture qualification in management and information systems. She was visiting researcher at the University of California Los Angeles, and interim professor at the University of Hildesheim, Germany. She was also a guest lecturer at the University of Luebeck, Germany. She holds a Master's in Management from the University of Goettingen, Germany. Svenja

Hagenhoff has research experience in the field of internet economics and information markets, e-learning, knowledge management and innovation management, and service oriented architectures.

John H. L. Hansen received the BSEE degree from the College of Engineering, Rutgers University, New Brunswick, NJ, in 1982, and the MS and PhD degrees in electrical engineering from the Georgia Institute of Technology, Atlanta, in 1983 and 1988, respectively. He joined the Erik Jonsson School of Engineering and Computer Science, University of Texas at Dallas (UTD), Richardson, in the fall of 2005, where he is Professor and a Department Chairman of Electrical Engineering and holds the Distinguished University Chair in Telecommunications Engineering. He is a director of the Center for Robust Speech Systems (CRSS) at UTD. Previously, he served as Department Chairman and Professor in the Department of Speech, Language, and Hearing Sciences, and Professor in the Department of Electrical and Computer Engineering, at the University of Colorado at Boulder, Boulder, (1998–2005). His research interests span the areas of digital speech processing, analysis and modeling of speech and speaker traits, speech enhancement, feature estimation in noise, robust speech recognition with emphasis on spoken document retrieval, and in-vehicle interactive systems. He is an IEEE Fellow, served as an IEEE Signal Processing Distinguished Lecturer for 2005/2006.

Judy Jeng received a PhD from Rutgers University, School of Communication, Information, and Library Studies. She has served as the evaluation consultant for three digital libraries—the Moving Image Collections (http://mic.imtc.gatech.edu/), the New Jersey Digital Highway (http://www.njdigitalhighway.org/index.php), and the NJVid. Judy has published and presented widely in *Libri, Information Technology and Libraries*, Library Assessment Conference, ALA, ASIS&T, and JCDL. Judy received the LITA Student Writing Award for her paper published in *ITAL,* and honorable mention for her paper published in *Libri: International Journal of Libraries and Information Services*. Judy is currently the Head of Collection Services at the New Jersey City University Library.

Juha Kettunen is the Rector of the Turku University of Applied Sciences, Finland. He was previously the Director of the Vantaa Institute for Continuing Education, University of Helsinki and Director of the Advanced Management Education Centre, University of Jyväskylä. He holds a PhD from the University of Bristol, UK, and a DSc from the University of Jyväskylä, Finland.

Christopher S. G. Khoo is an associated professor at Nanyang Technology University, Singapore. His main research interests are related to natural language processing, information extraction and knowledge discovery, text and data mining, intelligent interfaces, and information retrieval. He was the editor of the Singapore Journal of Library and Information Management from 1997 to 2002.

Wooil Kim received the BS, MS, and PhD degrees in Electronics Engineering from Korea University, Seoul, Korea, in 1996, 1998, and 2003, respectively. He is currently Research Assistant Professor in the Erik Jonsson School of Engineering and Computer Science, University of Texas at Dallas (UTD), Richardson, U.S.A. since Sept., 2007. He is also a member of the Center for Robust Speech Systems (CRSS) at UTD. Previously, he was a Research Associate in UTD (August 2005–August 2007) and a Post-Doctoral Researcher in the Electrical and Computer Engineering, Carnegie Mellon University, Pittsburgh, U.S.A. (August 2004–August 2005) and Korea University (September 2003–August 2004) respectively. His research interests are robust speech recognition in adverse environment, acoustic modeling for large vocabulary continuous speech recognition, and spoken document retrieval.

Stephen Kimani is currently an academic and research member of Jomo Kenyatta University of Agriculture and Technology (Kenya) and is affiliated with the University of Rome "La Sapienza" (Italy). He has been a postdoctoral researcher with the University of Rome "La Sapienza" (2004–2006). Dr. Stephen

Kimani holds PhD in Computer Engineering (University of Rome "La Sapienza", Italy, 2004) and MSc in Advanced Computing (University of Bristol, UK, 1998). His main research interest is in Human-Computer Interaction (HCI). In particular, as HCI relates to areas/aspects such as: User Interfaces, Usability, Accessibility, Visualization, Visual Information Access, Visual Data Mining, Digital Libraries, and Ubiquitous Computing.

Ana Kovačević is a PhD candidate at the University of Belgrade. She is currently working on her thesis: *Web Mining Visualization of Learning Objects*, supervised by Professor Vladan Devedžić. She has graduated from the School of Electrical Engineering, the University of Belgrade, Serbia, in 1993. She completed her Master's at School of Electrical Engineering, University of Belgrade in 2003, on the subject of *Multimedia DBMS,* supervised by Professor Miroslav Bojović. Her research interests are: databases, Web mining, text mining, digital libraries, visualization, and multimedia. She is a member of GOOD-OLD-AI, the society for object-oriented design and artificial intelligence.

Jayan C Kurian is an Mphil candidate at the Faculty of Computer Science and Engineering. His research interest includes Semantic Web, Hypermedia Presentation Generation, and User Adaptation.

Miguel Ángel Latre holds an MS degree in Computer Science from the University of Zaragoza (Spain) since 1999. He is currently a tenured Assistant Professor at the Department of Computer Science and Systems Engineering at the same university. He is working with the Advanced Information Systems Lab (IAAA) and the Aragón Institute for Engineering Research (I3A), where he has been involved in several R&D projects related with the application of Geographic Information Systems and Spatial Data Infrastructures to the Hydrologic domain, and has coauthored several publications in that area.

Juan C. Lavariega received the BSc in Computer Science and the MSC in Computer Science, both degrees from Tecnologico de Monterrey (ITESM), in 1987 and 1990, respectively. Dr. Lavariega received the PhD degree in Computer Science from Arizona State University, in 1999. Currently, he is an Associate Professor at ITESM. His research interests include specification methods in software engineering, databases systems, digital libraries, and mobile computing. He is member of the National System of Researchers (SNI-level 1) in Mexico, and he is a member of the ΛCM, the IEEE Computer Society, and the Upsilon Pi Epsilon Honor Society in Computer Science.

Chei Sian Lee has a PhD in Management Information Systems and is an Assistant Professor at Nanyang Technological University at the Division of Information Studies, Wee Kim Wee School of Communication and Information. Her research areas are in computer-mediated communication, distributed work environments, and organizational impacts of information systems.

Thomas Lidy is Research Assistant at the Department of Software Technology and Interactive Systems of the Vienna University of Technology (TU Vienna). He received his MSc in Computer Science from the Vienna University of Technology in 2007. His research focus is on music information retrieval, in particular feature extraction methods for digital audio, music classification, and clustering and visualization of digital music libraries. He participates actively in the annual MIREX benchmarking campaign and was coorganizer of the ISMIR 2007 conference. He is the author of numerous papers in refereed international conferences and workshops and served as coreviewer for several major international conferences.

Frances L. Lightsom (flightsom@usgs.gov) is a supervisory oceanographer at the Woods Hole Science Center of the U.S. Geological Survey (USGS), where her responsibilities include; 1) development of online systems for organizing and providing access to scientific information, 2) preservation of scientific records, and 3) management of information science and information technology systems for support of scientific research. Fran graduated from Oberlin College and has a PhD in physical oceanography from the Joint Program in Oceanography at Massachusetts Institute of Technology (MIT) and Woods Hole Oceanographic Institution (WHOI).

Pasquale Lops is Assistant Professor at the Department of Informatics, University of Bari. He completed his PhD in 2005 at the University of Bari, under the supervision of Professor Giovanni Semeraro. His primary interests lie in the areas of machine learning, recommender systems, digital libraries, user modelling, and universal access. He has published over 50 papers, and he is involved in several research projects.

Irene Lourdi is an archivist-librarian working in Libraries Computer Centre of University of Athens. She is a PhD student in the Department of Archival and Library Sciences at Ionian University in Corfu. She is a member of Laboratory on Digital Libraries and Electronic Publishing at Ionian University and her research interests include digital libraries, metadata schemas administration and integration policies.

Nyein Chan Lwin Lwin is a recent graduate of the MSc (Information Systems) programme from Nanyang Technological University. She is currently an analyst programmer in an Application Consultant in National Computer Systems.

Yongqing Ma obtained her BEng study at Zhejiang University (P.R.China) in 1982, and subsequently worked as a Certified Engineer and professional editor in China. At the beginning of 1995, she was awarded a PhD studentship from Plymouth University (UK), and, so developed her knowledge and skills in advanced information storage technologies. She worked at Cardiff, and then Oxford Universities, enjoying advanced research there following her PhD degree in 1999. She decided to develop a career in Information and Library Management (ILM) and completed her MA study with Loughborough University in 2006. Yongqing is working on developing a future career in the ILM sector.

Thomas Mandl is Assistant Professor for Information Science at the University of Hildesheim, Germany where he is teaching in the programme *International Information Management*. He studied information and computer science at the University of Regensburg, Germany and at the University of Illinois at Champaign/Urbana. He worked as a research assistant at the Social Science Information Centre in Bonn, Germany. His research interests include information retrieval, human-computer interaction, applications of machine learning, and international information systems.

Margarita Cabrera Mendez graduated from the Polytechnic University of Valencia in Audiovisual and Fine Arts. Multimedia systems Master, from the Polytechnic University of Valencia. Professor in the Polytechnic University of Valencia in Audiovisual contents distribution, and Member of the Research group CALSI.

Pedro Rafael Muro-Medrano holds MS and PhD degrees in industrial engineering from the University of Zaragoza (Zaragoza, Spain). He has worked in the private industry for two years and has hold different visiting research positions at the Carnegie Mellon University's Robotics Institute (Pittsburgh, PA), the University of Maryland (College Park, MD) and the U.S. National Institutes of Health (Bethesda, MD). Currently, he is the head of the Advanced Information Systems Laboratory (IAAA) at the Computer Science and Systems Engineering Department and the Engineering Research Institute of Aragón (I3A) from the University of Zaragoza.

Robert Neumayer received his Business Informatics from the University of Vienna in 2005. After that he spent a year at Trinity College Dublin as. Since July 2006, he has been employed as research assistant at the Institute for Interactive Systems and Software Technology of the Vienna University of Technology. He also received a degree in Computer Science (intelligent systems) from the Vienna University of Technology in October 2007. His main research interests include: Information Retrieval and Data Mining, as well as Digital Preservation.

David Nichols is a Senior Lecturer in the Department of Computer Science at the University of Waikato, Hamilton, New Zealand. He has a BSc (Hons) and a PhD in Computing, both from Lancaster University (UK). His interests include digital libraries (as part of the Greenstone project), human-computer interaction, and open source software.

Mara Nikolaidou is an Associate Professor in the Department of Informatics and Telematics at Harokopio University of Athens. She holds a PhD and Bachelor degree on Computer Science from the Department of Informatics and Telecommunication at the University of Athens. She is a member of IEEE and ISCA. Her research interests include software and information system engineering, e-government, and digital libraries.

Javier Nogueras-Iso holds MS and PhD degrees in Computer Science from the University of Zaragoza (Spain). After working for the Economic and Social Committee of the European Communities (Brussels) in 1998, he started his research at the Computer Science and Systems Engineering Department of the University of Zaragoza, where he is currently a tenured Assistant Professor. Additionally, he is a member of the Aragón Institute for Engineering Research and has completed a postdoctoral stay at the Institute of Environment and Sustainability of the Joint Research Centre (Ispra, Italy). His research interests are focused on Spatial Data Infrastructures, and Geographic Information Retrieval.

Ann O'Brien worked for ten years as an academic librarian before moving to the Department of Information Science, Loughborough University where she is a lecturer in information organization. Her teaching and research interests lie in various aspects of digital information organization, such as metadata, cataloguing, classification, and all kinds of subject indexing. As Director of the Postgraduate Programme in Information and Library Management, she takes a great interest in current and future developments in LIS education.

Sanghee Oh is a PhD student in the School of Information and Library Science at University of North Carolina at Chapel Hill. She earned her MLIS degree in library and information science from University of California at Los Angeles. She is currently involved in the Digital Library Curriculum Development project (http://curric.dlib.vt.edu), a joint project between Virginia Tech and University of North Carolina at Chapel Hill, funded by NSF. Her areas of research include information seeking behaviors, user-centered system design and development, human computer interaction, and digital libraries.

Björn Ortelbach works at Henkel as an IT controller. He finished his doctoral thesis in 2007 at the Institute of Information Systems, University of Goettingen. He holds a Master's in Business Information Systems from the University of Goettingen. Björn Ortelbach has experience in the fields of information markets, publishing industry, and controlling.

Taha Osman obtained his PhD in the Fault-Tolerance of Distributed Computing Systems in 1998. He is currently a Senior Lecturer at Nottingham Trent University, where he leads the Semantic Web services research network. His research interests are in the areas of intelligent agents, the semantic Web, and information retrieval systems.

Shiyan Ou is a postdoctoral research fellow in Research Institute in Information and Language Processing, University of Wolverhampton, UK. She obtained her PhD degree from Nanyang Technological University, Singapore. Her research interests include automatic text summarization, information extraction, text mining, opinion mining, and question answering. She has published three journal papers and nine conference papers in the area of automatic text summarization.

Pasquale Pagano is a Senior Research Associate of the Networked Multimedia Information Systems Laboratory of the Institute of Information Science and Technologies—Italian National Research Council (ISTI—CNR). He received his MSc in Information Systems Technologies from the Department of Computer Science of the University of Pisa (1998), and his PhD degree in Information Engineering from the Department of Information Engineering: Electronics, Information Theory, Telecommunications of the same university (2006). He has a strong background in digital library distributed architectures. He has participated in the design of the most relevant DL systems developed by ISTI—CNR. Currently, Pasquale is the technical support manager of the "DILIGENT: A testbed DIgital Library Infrastructure on Grid ENabled Technology" project. He is also leading the development and deployment of the OpenDLib (http://www.opendlib.com) digital library service system in different application areas (libraries, archives, commercial publishing organizations). His current research interests include digital libraries services and architectures.

Natalie Pang is a PhD student in Monash University's Faculty of Information Technology. Her PhD research investigates the concept of the knowledge commons using an interdisciplinary investigation of the literature and case studies of cultural institutions from Australia and Singapore. Prior to embarking on her PhD, she has been working in Monash University in Malaysia as a researcher in areas of telecommunications, digital libraries, and social computing. She has worked in various cross-disciplinary areas of information technology and has taught in Singapore, Malaysia, and Australia. Natalie is a key member of several research projects in Australia, Singapore, and China. Other than a part-time staff member of the Centre for Community Networking Research group and full-time PhD student of the Faculty, she is also a contributing member of several international research networks such as the Peer to Peer Foundation and the Institute for the Future. She has also served as Research Associate for Museum Victoria and a visiting scholar to the Singapore Internet Research Centre at Nanyang Technological University.

Emanuele Panizzi received the Dr. Eng. Laurea degree in Electronic Engineering in 1992. From 1994, he was a researcher in the APE parallel computer project at INFN, Italy. In 1997, he became Assistant Professor in Computer Engineering at University of L'Aquila, Italy. Since 2001, he was Assistant Professor in Computer Science at University of Rome "La Sapienza" until December 2004 when he qualified as Associate Professor in Computer Science. His current interests are in the Human-Computer Interaction area and include usability, computer-supported collaborative work, user interfaces for digital libraries, for Web applications and mobile devices.

Stefano Paolozzi received his degree in Informatics Engineering at the University of "ROMA TRE." He is a PhD student in Computer Science at the "ROMA TRE" University under supervision of Professor Paolo Atzeni. His research activity with Multi Media and Modal Laboratory (M3L) of the IRPPS-CNR of Italy is sponsored by a fellowship (assegno di ricerca). He is mainly interested in Model Management, Multimodal Interaction, Multimedia Database, Temporal Database, Ontology Alignment, Ontology Versioning, NLP, Context-Aware Systems.

Christos Papatheodorou holds a BSc and a PhD in Computer Science from the Department of Informatics, Athens University of Economics and Business, Greece. Currently, he is an Assistant Professor at the Department of Archive and Library Sciences, Ionian University, Corfu, Greece, where he teaches Information Systems, Information Retrieval, and Metadata. His research interests include Digital Libraries Evaluation, Metadata Interoperability, User Modeling, Personalization, and Web Mining. He has been involved as researcher or coordinator in several national and international R&D projects, such as DELOS Network of excellence, funded by the European Union. He has participated to the programme committee of various international conferences and workshops (such as the European Conference on Digital Libraries, 2005).

Piedad Garrido Picazo is a Computer Science and System Engineering Department assistant professor at Teruel College of Engineering (University of Zaragoza). Her research areas are focused on digital libraries, database management systems, information retrieval semantic engines, and topic maps. She develops several research projects about free software documental information management tools and she has coordinated the "Free Software to Digital Information Services" book edited by Prentice Hall.

Jeffrey P. Pomerantz is an Assistant Professor in the School of Information and Library Science at the University of North Carolina—Chapel Hill. He earned his PhD from the School of Information Studies at Syracuse University, and his MS(LIS) from Simmons College. Much of Pomerantz's work has been on digital reference services, and the integration of physical library-style services into digital libraries. Pomerantz's recent work has involved evaluations of collaborative online library services. Additional information about Pomerantz is available at: http://ils.unc.edu/~jpom.

George Pyrounakis is a software developer in the Libraries Computer Center at the University of Athens. He also works as a researcher in the Department of Informatics and Telecommunications at the University of Athens. He holds a MSc and Bachelor degree on Computer Science from the same department. Currently, he is studying for his PhD on digital library architectures. His research interests include digital libraries and distributed systems.

Muhammad Rafiq is a PhD Scholar at the Deptartment of Library and Information Science, University of the Punjab, Lahore (Pakistan). He is also serving in International Islamic University, Islamabad (Pakistan) as Manager Information Resource Center. He is an active library trainer and has 10 years experience of managing prominent academic libraries of Pakistan. He is also IFLA/OCLC Early Career Development Fellow 2004 and Associate to Mortenson Center for International Library Programs. His research interest areas are: Digital Libraries, Human-Computer Interaction, and Information Technology in Libraries. He can be reached at rafiqlibrarian@yahoo.com and rafiqlibrarian@gmail.com.

Mila Medina Ramos is a Filipina Librarian, who holds a Bachelor's and Master's degree in Library Science obtained from the University of the Philippines. She underwent on-the-job training at the U.S. National Agricultural Library in Maryland and the Deakin University, Australia. She also took up distance education courses from the University of Cincinnati. Mrs. Ramos is currently the Chief Librarian of the International Rice Research Institute (IRRI), based in Los Baños, Laguna, Philippines. The IRRI Library has the world's most comprehensive collection of technical rice literature, and serves the information needs of worldwide clients.

Wolfgang Ratzek a graduate of the Free University of Berlin (FU Berlin) in 1986, received an MA in Information Science and Scandinavistics in 1986, and a PhD in Information Science in 1991 from FU Berlin. He is a Professor at the faculty of Information and Communication, Stuttgart Media University. His research interests include Marketing, LIS policy, Information and Knowledge Society. His professional experience includes leading positions in the field of consulting and marketing. He is also a member of the editorial board of Communication Booknotes Quarterly (USA), B.I.T. online and Information—Wissenschaft und Praxis (Germany).

Andreas Rauber is Associate Professor at the Department of Software Technology and Interactive Systems of the Vienna University of Technology (TU Vienna). He received his MSc and PhD in Computer Science from the Vienna University of Technology in 1997 and 2000, respectively. He is actively involved in several research projects in the field of digital libraries, focusing on text and music information retrieval, the organization and exploration of large information spaces, as well as Web archiving and digital preservation. He has published numerous papers in refereed journals and international conferences, and served as PC member and reviewer for several major journals, conferences, and workshops. He also coorganized the ECDL 2005 and ISMIR 2007 conferences.

Khasfariyati Razikin is a project officer at the Division of Information Studies, Wee Kim Wee School of Communication and Information, Nanyang Technological University, Singapore. Her research interests lies in information retrieval, natural language processing, and machine learning.

Nuria Lloret Romero is the Head of the Deptartment DCADHA (Polytechnic University of Valencia). Graduated from the University of Valencia, Master of Development of online I.T. systems supports CD ROM (MASDOC) distributed by the University of Barcelona. Ph. "Methodology for the development of self-training multimedia tools for Digital libraries." Head of Research Group CALSI. She is professor in the UPV in Computer Science Faculty teaching on Planning of IST and Quality of Information services. Project Expert Evaluator of the European Community for the IST Program..FESABID, President 1999. She was President of the Hispano-American Caucus of IFLA, and from August of 1998 to 2005, Member Executive Committee of EBLIDA from 1999–2002.

Simon Ruszala obtained his BSc and MSc degrees from Nottingham Trent University. He is currently working for Teleca.

Maria-Isabel Sanchez-Segura has been a faculty member in the Computer Science Department at Carlos III University of Madrid since 1998. She is an associate professor at this department. Her research interests include: Software Engineering, interactive systems, and usability in interactive systems. She holds a BS in Computer Science (1997), an MS in Software Engineering (1999), and a PhD in Computer Science (2001) from the Universidad Politecnica of Madrid.

Neide Santos earned a Master's of Education degree from the Federal University of Rio de Janeiro in 1989 and a DSc degree in Engineering of Production at the same university in 1994. She is an associate professor in the Department of Computer Science at the State University of Rio de Janeiro. Her main areas of interest are Computers in Education, CSCL, Educational Hypermedia, Artificial Intelligence and Education, and Web-based Education.

Sarah-Jane Saravani is Library Manager at the Waikato Institute of Technology, Hamilton, New Zealand. She has worked in libraries since the early 1990s, beginning her career in the National Library of New Zealand. She has an MA in History from Otago University, Dunedin, plus the Diploma in Librarianship from Victoria University, Wellington (1991). She is a member of the IT-019-01 Australia/New Zealand Standards subcommittee on Information Technology for Learning, Education, and Training, metadata subgroup. She has a particular interest in the contribution of metadata to the preservation and sharing of digital resources, and has a strong focus on the flexible delivery of educational resources.

Hideyasu Sasaki graduated from the University of Tokyo in 1994, received an LLM from the University of Chicago Law School in 1999, an MS and a PhD in Cybernetic Knowledge Engineering (Media and Governance) with honors from Keio University in 2001 and 2003, respectively. He is an associate professor at

Department of Information Science and Engineering, Ritsumeikan University. He was an assistant professor at Keio University from 2003 to 2005. His research interests include content-based metadata indexing and image retrieval, digital libraries, multimedia databases, and intellectual property law and management. He has been admitted to practice as an Attorney-and-Counselor at Law in the New York State Bar, since 2000.

Jesús Tramullas Saz is a Document Management Systems full professor Department at University of Zaragoza. His research areas are centered on digital libraries and document repositories, of which he has run several of them. He cooperates in free software tools development and evaluation to the digital libraries development and management information. He is a member of the 50 AENOR's Technical Committee (Information and Documentation), "Internet Information Retrieval" author book and "Free Software to Digital Information Services" coordinator book.

Gerald Schaefer gained his PhD in computer vision from the University of East Anglia. He worked at the Colour and Imaging Institute, University of Derby as a Research Associate (1997–1999), as Senior Research Fellow at the School of Information Systems, University of East Anglia (2000–2001), and as Senior Lecturer in Computing at the School of Computing and Informatics at Nottingham Trent University (2001–2006). In September 2006, he joined the School of Engineering and Applied Science at Aston University. His research interests include colour image analysis, physics-based vision, image retrieval, and image coding. He is the author of more than 120 scientific publications in these areas.

Ulrich Schiel has graduated in Mathematics with Master's in Computer Science at PUC-Rio de Janeiro, Brazil and Dr.rcr.nat. in Computer Science at University of Stuttgart, Germany. Full professor of Federal University of Campina Grande, Brazil since 1978. Research interests are Temporal Databases, Digital Libraries, Ontologies and Semantic Web Services, Information Systems on the Web, and Decision Support Systems.

Lutz Seidenfaden is Assistant to a Member of the Board of Festo Corporation. He finished his doctoral thesis in 2007 at the Institute of Information Systems, University of Goettingen. He holds a Master's in Business Information Systems from the University of Goettingen. Lutz Seidenfaden has experience in the fields of P2P services and architectures, information markets, and publishing industry.

Giovanni Semeraro is Associate Professor at the Department of Informatics, University of Bari. His research activity mainly concerns machine learning, semantic Web, and personalization. He was head of the research units of the University of Bari for the EC 6th Framework Programme Integrated Project VIKEF (2004–07) and DELOS, a Network of Excellence on Digital Libraries (2004–07). He has published over 150 papers.

Peter Shelton joined IFPRI in 2006, assuming his present role as Information and Knowledge Management Specialist in May of this year. His work focuses on researching and implementing Web-based technologies and training staff in their applications for supporting research. Prior to joining IFPRI, Peter worked with the Cornell International Institute for Food, Agriculture, and Development (CIIFAD) in the management of online databases.

Ali Shiri is an Assistant Professor at the School of Library and Information Studies in the University of Alberta, teaching courses on digital libraries and knowledge organization. Ali's research interests lie in the areas of digital libraries, visual user interfaces, information search behavior, application of knowledge organization systems in digital libraries, and social tagging. Ali is the Electronic Discussions Communications officer for the American Society for Information Science and Technology Special Interest Group on Digital Libraries (ASIS&T SIG-DL), and is currently serving as the Journal of Digital Information Theme editor.

Shun-Hong Sie received the MS degree in library science from Catholic Fu-Jen University, Taipei, Taiwan, in 2006. His current research interests include digital libraries and digital archives, library automation, and internet service architecture.

Manuele Simi is a Software Engineer and Developer. He received his BSc in Computer Science from the University of Pisa in 2001. He has been employed for several IT companies as Software Engineer and Developer and coordinator of small teams. In 2002, he joined the Information Science and Technologies—Italian National Research Council (ISTI—CNR). His professional experience covers the design and implementation of reusable components, libraries, Web services, GUIs, and Web applications for different target platforms. He has worked extensively with Perl, C/C++ and Java, and he is experienced in UML modelling. He has been involved in small projects as well as in very large projects with a significant experience in designing and implementing Service Oriented Architectures. At ISTI-CNR, he has worked for the Scholnet and DILIGENT projects, and he was one of the main implementers of the OpenDLib (http://www.opendlib.com) digital library service system. He has published a number of articles in some Italian magazines dedicated to the software development field.

Diljit Singh PhD, MSc (Florida State), BSc, DipEd (Malaya) is an Associate Professor and currently the Deputy Dean at the Faculty of Computer Science and Information Technology, University of Malaya.

Martha Sordia-Salinas received the BSc in Computer Science and the MSC in Computer Science, both degrees from Tecnologico de Monterrey in 1984 and 1989, respectively. Currently, Miss Sordia-Salinas is an Assistant Professor at ITESM, and her research interests are digital libraries, and mobile computing applied in digital libraries.

Sofia Stamou is an Adjunct Lecturer at the Computer Engineering and Informatics Department of Patras University, Greece. Her area of expertise is natural language processing, semantics, Web information management and retrieval with emphasis on linguistic analysis of textual data. Her research interests include text processing, Web mining, data classification, lexical ontologies, and semantic networks. She received both her PhD (2006) and MSc (2002) degrees in Computer Science from the Computer Engineering and Informatics Department of Patras University and a Diploma in Linguistics from the University of Ioannina, Greece in 1999. She has coordinated several EU-funded projects in the area of semantic text processing, and she has served as a reviewer to many international journals and conferences.

Stephan Strodl is currently research assistant at the Department of Software Technology and Interactive Systems at the Vienna University of Technology. His research interest is digital preservation, and he is involved several European research projects in the field of Digital Preservation.

Tamara Sumner is Executive Director of DLS. She is responsible for leadership of the institute, strategy development, and the conduct of our research program. Sumner is also an Associate Professor at the University of Colorado, with a joint appointment between the Institute of Cognitive Science and the Department of Computer Science. She has significant experience in the theory, design, and evaluation of interactive learning environments, human-centered systems, digital libraries, and intelligent information systems. Since 2000, she has published over 50 articles on these topics.

Dhavalkumar Thakker obtained his Master's degree in Data Communication Systems from Brunel University and his PhD from the School of Science and Technology at Nottingham Trent University. His research interests are distributed computing technologies, Web services composition, the semantic Web, and ontologies.

Tun Thura Thet is a PhD student in the Division of Information Studies in the Wee Kim Wee School of Communication and Information at Nanyang Technological University. He is working on sentiment-based classification and searching for digital libraries for his PhD dissertation work.

Giannis Tsakonas is a PhD candidate student in Department of Archives and Library Sciences, Ionian University, Corfu, Greece. He also is librarian in the Library and Information Service, University of Patras, Greece. His research interests include user-centred digital library evaluation, information behavior, and visual communication.

Michael Twidale is an Associate Professor in the Graduate School of Library and Information Science at University of Illinois. He has a BA (Hons) from Cambridge University and a PhD in Computing from Lancaster University (UK). His interests include computer-supported cooperative working and learning; collaborative technologies in digital libraries and museums; user interface design and evaluation; user error analysis; visualization of information; and the development of interfaces to support the articulation of plans, goals, and beliefs.

Spyros Veronikis holds a Diploma and an MSE in Electronic and Computer Engineering from Democritus University of Thrace, Greece. Currently, he is a PhD candidate at the Department of Archives and Library Sciences, Ionian University, Corfu, Greece. His research interests include wireless communications, mobile computing, and integration of diverse information sources.

Manuel Coll Villalta studied Technical Engineer Management Computing at Teruel Collage of Engineering (University of Zaragoza). Now, he is finishing the Computer Science Engineering at the Faculty of Engineering in the same university. He is very interested in free software development tools. He is in charge of the DEREditor project, available at http://sourceforge.net/projects/dereditor. He collaborates with the rest of the authors, in some research projects, like a research grant holder in digital information services analysis, development, and management tools.

Fu Lee Wang is a Lecturer in the Department of Computer Science at the City University of Hong Kong. He received BEng in Computer Engineering and MPhil in Computer Science from the University of Hong Kong, and PhD in Information System from the Chinese University of Hong Kong. His research interests include automatic summarization, information retrieval, and information systems. He is a member of ACM and IEEE. He has published about 50 articles in journals and proceedings of international conferences—for instance, Journal of the American Society for Information Science and Technology (JASIST), Decision Support Systems (DSS), Information Processing Letters, IW3C, SIGIR, and more.

Wei Wang is a PhD candidate at the Faculty of Computer Science and Engineering. His research interest includes Semantic Web, Information Search and Retrieval, Machine Learning, and Social Network Analysis.

Barbara M. Wildemuth is a professor in the School of Information and Library Science at the University of North Carolina at Chapel Hill. Her research interests are focused on the ways in which people retrieve and use information retrieved from computer-mediated information systems. In particular, much of her work has investigated people's interactions with digital video (as part of the Open Video project, http://www.open-video.org/) and with health information (including studies of medical students' use of databases, health information provision by public libraries, a computer-based adaptive multimedia system for patients to provide information to their doctors, and the design of personal health records). She teaches courses in systems analysis, user interface design, human information interactions, information ethics, and research methods.

Ian H. Witten is Professor of Computer Science at the University of Waikato in New Zealand where he codirects (in conjunction with Bainbridge) the New Zealand Digital Library research project. His research interests include information retrieval, machine learning, text compression, and programming by demonstration. He has published widely in these areas, including several books, the most recent being *Managing Gigabytes* (1999), *How to Build a Digital Library* (2003), *Data Mining* (2005), and *Web Dragons* (2007), all from Morgan Kaufmann. He received an MA in mathematics from Cambridge University, England; an MSc in computer science from the University of Calgary, Canada; and a PhD in electrical engineering from Essex University, England.

Paul Horng-Jyh Wu is a Senior Fellow in the Division of Information Studies in the Wee Kim Wee School of Communication and Information at Nanyang Technological University. His research interests are electronic records, document and business process management, digital archiving and heritage informatics, and Web annotation and intelligence.

Christopher C. Yang is an associate professor in the Department of Systems Engineering and Engineering Management and the director of the Digital Library Laboratory at the Chinese University of Hong Kong. He received his BS, MS, and PhD in Electrical and Computer Engineering from the University of Arizona. He has also been an assistant professor in the Department of Computer Science and Information Systems at the University of Hong Kong and a research scientist in the Department of Management Information Systems at the University of Arizona. His recent research interests include cross-lingual information retrieval and knowledge management, Web search and mining, security informatics, text summarization, multimedia retrieval, information visualization, digital library, and electronic commerce. He has published over 150 referred journal and conference papers.

Seungwon Yang is a PhD student in the department of Computer Science at Virginia Tech. He received his BS degree in CS from the same university. He is a member of the Digital Library Research Laboratory at Virginia Tech. His current research project is the Digital Library Curriculum Development project (http://curric.dlib.vt.edu), which is a collaborative interdisciplinary project with the University of North Carolina at Chapel Hill. His research interests are DL theory, educational technology, computer-supported collaborative learning and human-computer interaction. In his free time, he practices Zen and Ba Gua Zhang.

Jian-hua Yeh received the BS, MS, and PhD degree in computer science and information engineering from National Taiwan University, Taipei, Taiwan, in 1992, 1995, and 2000, respectively. After finishing postdoctoral research in the same institute in 2004, he joined the Department of Computer and Information Science at Aletheia University as an assistant professor. His research interests include clustering and classification, data mining and knowledge discovery, semantic Web and ontology processing, knowledge management, and information retrieval.

Han Lee Yen began her teaching career as a Speech and Drama Teacher, working with youths and children in various schools in Singapore. She has been teaching English Language and Literature and Communication for more than ten years, two of which were spent in the countryside of Niigata, Japan. She is currently pursuing her MSc in Information Studies at Nanyang Technological University.

F. Javier Zarazaga-Soria holds an MS degree in Computer Science from the University of Valencia and a PhD degree from the University of Zaragoza. He did his Master's thesis at Road Safety Engineering Laboratory (University of London). In September 1994, he started collaborating with the Advanced Information Systems Laboratory and as assistant professor at the University of Zaragoza. He obtained a tenured position as Associated Professor there in 2003. He is coauthor of more than 50 publications, and has participated in many R&D projects. His research interests include metadata management, information retrieval, and ontologies in the context of spatial data infrastructures.

644

Index

Symbols